Sir George Biddell Airy, Thomas Maclear

Verification and Extension of La Caille's Arc of Meridian at the Cape

of Good Hope

Sir George Biddell Airy, Thomas Maclear

Verification and Extension of La Caille's Arc of Meridian at the Cape of Good Hope

ISBN/EAN: 9783337813291

Printed in Europe, USA, Canada, Australia, Japan

Cover: Foto ©Thomas Meinert / pixelio.de

More available books at **www.hansebooks.com**

UNREDUCED OBSERVATIONS

MADE WITH

BRADLEY'S ZENITH SECTOR

ON

HEERELOGEMENTS BERG, CLANWILLIAM DISTRICT;

IN

MAY AND JUNE, 1843.

ARC OF THE MERIDIAN.—CAPE OF GOOD HOPE.

MAY 12, 1843.—FACE OF SECTOR EAST.

Number of B.A.C.	Time by Chronometer.	Micr. for Plumb-line on Dot.	Micr. for Observation of Star.	Micr. for Plumb-line on Dot.	Mean of Micr. for Plumb-line on Dot.	Star's Apparent Zenith Distance.	Barom.	Thermometers.		
								Attd.	Upper.	Lower.
	h m s	rev. pts.	rev. pts.	rev. pts.	rev. pts.	° ′ rev. pts.	in.			
7992	22 49 12·0	10 21·8	13 19·8	10 21·7	10 21·75	N. 1 30+2 32·05	27·798			46·4
2293	6 52 45·0	3 21·2	8 3·7	3 20 5	3 20·85	N. 3 10+4 16·85	27·756			65·5
	9 16 46·0	12 26·3	9 15·5	12 27·0	12 26 65	N 3 50+3 11·15				
3521	10 11 18·5	12 17·5	13 13·6	12 17·5	12 17·5	N. 3 45+0 30·10				
3596	10 22 33·5	8 29·3	11 5·6	8 28·7	8 29·0	N. 3 5+2 10·6	27·722			52·2
	11 25 26·0	8 10·4	5 28·5	8 9·5	8 9·95	N. 1 5−2 15·45				
4015	11 44 56·4	9 28·0	11 18·8	9 27·8	9 27·9	S. 1 5−1 24·9	27·680			51·6
4278	12 36 6·0	10 18·6	11 8·0	10 18·6	10 18·6	N. 4 30+0 23·4	27·663			52·2
4458	13 11 29·0	9 31·6	10 11·2	9 31·4	9 31·5	S. 3 55−0 13·7				
4548	13 30 14·5	10 26·3	15 22·8	10 26·6	10 26 45	N. 3 10+4 30·35				
4579	13 36 49·8	11 25·5	8 24·5	11 23·3	11 24 4	S. 0 15+2 33·9				
4623	13 42 50·0	11 22·3	12 11·5	11 21·7	11 22·0	S. 0 15−0 23·5				
4686	13 57 11·5	12 1·5	7 21·2	12 2·0	12 1·75	S. 3 35+4 14·55				
4784	14 19 20·4	12 12·7	14 20·2	12 13·0	12 12 85	N. 3 10+2 7·35	27·650			51·0
4852	14 33 54·0	13 14·7	10 32·8	13 14 3	13 14·5	S. 2 30+2 15·7				
4891	14 41 33·5	15 13·7	15 16·0	15 13·7	15 13·7	N. 4 40−0 2·3				
5032	15 8 35·0	13 28·8	12 18·1	13 29·1	13 28·95	N. 2 25−1 10·85				
5151	15 29 20·5	12 25·3	9 0·3	12 24·8	12 25·05	N. 2 45−3 24·75				
5227	15 40 57·8	11 13·8	10 31·1	11 13·4	11 13·6	S. 1 10+0 16·5	27·640			50·5
5272	15 47 33·5	13 4·4	10 1·7	13 4·0	13 4 2	N. 3 15−3 2·5				
5374	16 1 38·0	12 20·5	10 1·0	12 20·3	12 20·4	N. 3 0−2 19·4				
5435	16 9 50·0	11 25·4	6 23·2	11 25·4	11 25·4	N. 1 30−5 2·2				
5632	16 39 53 0	10 16·8	7 15·7	10 16·8	10 16·8	S. 2 0+3 1·1				
5735	16 54 24·0	9 28·4	9 10·8	9 28·5	9 28·45	S. 1 55+0 17·65				

MAY 15, 1843.—FACE OF SECTOR WEST.

3926	11 25 48·5	13 29·3	28 2·0	13 29·8	13 29·55	N. 0 55+14 6·45				
4015	11 45 7·0	13 28·5	22 18·3	13 29·3	13 28·9	S. 1 0−8 23·4				
4278	12 35 40·5	15 18·5	16 12·8	15 18·9	15 18·65	N. 4 30+0 28·15				
4458	13 11 59·5	12 24·5	13 27·0	12 24 55	12 24·55	S. 3 55+1 2·45				
4517	13 23 52·5	11 11·5	7 31·0	11 11·7	11 11·6	N. 3 10+3 14·6	27·885			46·6
4548	13 29 57·5	11 11·7	7 33·4	11 11·5	11 11·6	N. 3 10+3 12·2				
4579	13 36 54·5	11 24·7	16 8·3	11 25·3	11 25·0	S. 0 15+4 17·3				
4623	13 42 54·0	11 25·6	12 18·5	11 25·6	11 25·55	S. 0 15+0 26·95				
4686	13 57 39·0	12 22·5	18 16·4	12 22·1	12 22·3	S. 3 35+5 28·1				
4784	14 19 3·5	12 5·1	11 17·6	12 5·0	12 5·05	N. 3 10+0 21·45	27·880	46·04	46·6
5032*	15 8 48·5	12 4·8	23 31·5	12 4·7	12 4·75	N. 2 30−11 26·75	27·900			46·3
5227	15 41 9·0	12 22·4	14 21·8	12 22·5	12 22·45	S. 1 10+1 33·35				
5272	15 47 17·0	12 5·5	16 24·0	12 3·5	12 4·5	N. 3 15−4 20·1				
5374	16 1 22·5	12 12·3	16 18·1	12 12·1	12 12·2	N. 3 0−4 5·9				
5435	16 9 44·4		10 17·7	12 28·5	12 28·5	N. 1 25+2 10·8				
5632	16 40 11·3	12 3·4	16 20·3	12 2·1	12 2·75	S. 2 0+4 17·55	27·900		45·1	45·6
5735	16 54 41·0	12 15·7	14 14·8	12 15·7	12 15·7	S. 1 55+1 33·1				
5817	17 7 7·0	12 1·8	14 0·3	12 2·0	12 1·9	S. 0 30+1 32·4	27·900		44·6	45·4

MAY 16, 1843.—FACE OF SECTOR EAST.

1602	5 34 10·5	14 13·0	12 6·5	14 12·8	14 12·9	S. 2 10+2 6·4			47·8	48·0
2293	6 52 36·0	13 33·8	18 15·5	13 33·8	13 33·8	N. 3 10+4 15·7				
4458	13 12 3·0	12 7·0	12 22·1	12 8·0	12 7·5	S. 3 55−0 14·6	27·902			
4517	13 24 2·2	15 18·5	20 15·1	15 18·6	15 18·55	N. 3 10+4 30·55				
4548	13 30 7·0	15 18·6	20 10·8	15 18·4	15 18·5	N. 3 10+4 26·3				

* Bisecting Wire adjusted between the transits of 4784 and 5032. Again, after the transit of 5817.

MAY 16, 1843.—FACE OF SECTOR EAST—(continued).

Number of B.A.C.	Time by Chronometer	Micr. for Plumb-line on Dot.	Micr. for Observation of Star.	Micr. for Plumb-line on Dot.	Mean of Micr. for Plumb-line on Dot.	Star's Apparent Zenith Distance.	Barom.	Thermometers. Attd.	Upper.	Lower.
	h m s	rev. pts.	rev. pts.	rev. pts.	rev. pts.	° ' rev. pts.	in.			
4579	13 37 2·0	11 24·5	8 22·4	11 23·8	11 24·15	S. 0 15+3 1·75				
4623	13 43 1·7	11 24·0	12 12·4	11 24·5	11 24·25	S. 0 15—0 22·15				
4686	13 57 43·8	11 25·3	7 12·7	11 23·0	11 24·15	S. 3 35+4 11·45	27·902		47·5	47·4
4784	14 19 13·5	10 2·0	12 6·0	10 1·9	10 1·95	N. 3 10+2 4·05	27·900		47·3	47·4
4852	14 34 20·5	10 3·2	7 22 0	10 2·0	10 2·6	S. 2 30+2 14·6				
4891	14 41 18·5	9 14·5	9 11·7	9 14·4	9 14·45	N. 4 40—0 2·75				
5032	15 8 32·5	9 23·6	8 9·2	9 24·1	9 23·85	N. 2 25—1 14·65				
5054	15 12 13·5	9 33·6	4 29·8	9 32·6	9 33·10	S. 3 40+5 3·3				
5151	15 29 16·0	12 12·0	8 17·5	12 12·5	12 12·25	N. 2 45—3 28·75				
5227	15 41 16·0	9 24·7	9 7·4	9 25·3	9 25·0	S. 1 10+0 17·6				
5272	15 47 26·5	10 12·5	7 7·0	10 12·7	10 12·6	N. 3 15—3 5·6				
5374	16 1 31·8	9 32·7	7 9·8	9 32·4	9 32·55	N. 3 0—2 22·75				
5435	16 9 52·0	11 5·8	14 32·0	11 5·6	11 5·7	N. 1 25+3 26·3				
5632	16 40 17·0	10 27·5	7 26·8	10 27·0	10 27·25	S. 2 0+3 0·45	27·882		47·12	47·0
5735	16 54 46·3	10 20·7	10 3·1	10 21·0	10 20·85	S. 1 55+0 17·75				
5881	17 17 34·5	10 30·8	11 14·5	10 30·5	10 30·65	N. 2 15+0 17·85				
5915	17 23 14·8	10 32·7	10 11·5	10 32·6	10 32·65	S. 5 0+0 21·15				
6016	17 39 14·3	11 14·5	11 9·6	11 14·4	11 14·45	N. 0 20—0 4·85				
6074	17 49 15·4	11 32·8	11 11·7	11 32·8	11 32·8	N. 1 45—0 21·1				
6115	17 55 58·4	11 6·8	8 8·2	11 6·7	11 6·75	N. 1 35—2 32·55				
6145	18 0 14·0	10 32·6	8 20·4	10 32·5	10 32·55	N. 1 15—2 12·15				
6186	18 7 18·0	10 26·7	11 24 8	10 26·1	10 26·4	S. 4 50—0 32·4				
6233	18 14 1·5	10 30·5	13 19·4	10 30·5	10 30·5	S. 2 30—2 22·9				
6285	18 21 2·8	11 6·9	17 9·5	11 7·0	11 6·95	S. 1 10—6 2·55	27·880		46·58	46·6
6305	18 23 55·5	11 7·0	13 1·5	11 7·0	11 7·0	S. 1 10—1 28·5				
6489	18 52 51·0	12 21·6	17 14·3	12 21·6	12 21·6	N. 1 50+4 26·7				
6525	18 57 51·0	11 22·0	13 26·2	11 21·5	11 21·75	N. 3 5+2 4·45				
6639	19 17 15·5	11 10·0.	12 21·0	11 9·8	11 9·9	N. 1 55+1 11·1				

MAY 17, 1843.—FACE OF SECTOR WEST.

Number of B.A.C.	Time by Chronometer	Micr. for Plumb-line on Dot.	Micr. for Observation of Star.	Micr. for Plumb-line on Dot.	Mean of Micr. for Plumb-line on Dot.	Star's Apparent Zenith Distance.	Barom.	Thermometers. Attd.	Upper.	Lower.
1802	5 34 4·5	13 27·7	17 15·3	13 27·6	13 27·65	S. 2 10+3 21·65	27·866		71·24	64·0
2293	6 52 37·5	13 32·4	11 0·4	13 32·3	13 32·35	N. 3 10+2 31·95				
4458	13 11 57·2	9 17·3	10 21·0	9 17·4	9 17·35	S. 3 55+1 3·65	27·868		48·7	48·4
4517	13 24 3 4	8 17·0	5 3·6	8 16·5	8 16·75	N. 3 10+3 13·15				
4548	13 30 8·0	8 16·3	5 6·3	8 15·5	8 15·90	N. 3 10+3 9·6				
4579	13 37 0·0	10 10·0	14 28·0	10 10·5	10 10·25	S. 0 15+4 17·75				
4623	13 42 59·5	10 10·3	11 4·2	10 10·4	10 10·35	S. 0 15+0 27·85				
4686	13 57 38·5	11 16·7	17 12·7	11 16·8	11 16·75	S. 3 35+5 29·95	27·855		48·56	48·6
4719*	14 6 48·0	10 1·8	10 26·4	10 1·0	10 1·4	N. 3 25—0 25·0				
4784	14 19 14·2	9 30·7	9 11·0	9 30·0	9 30·35	N. 3 10+0 19·35				
Anon.	14 24 15·5	9 31·5	9 21·0	9 30·8	9 31·15	S. 0 40—0 10·15				
4852	14 34 16·0	9 27·8	13 27·4	9 28·0	9 27·9	S. 2 30+3 33·5				
4891	14 41 20·5	10 7·4	11 25·3	10 7·4	10 7·4	N. 4 40—1 17·9				
4916	14 46 20·0		11 7·6	10 16·3	10 16·3	S. 1 15+0 25·3				
Anon.	14 53 37·0	9 32·3	16 25·1	9 32·6	9 32·45	0 0+6 26·65				
Anon†	14 58 11·0	11 0·0	11 28·3	10 33·7	10 33·85	S. 0 20+0 28·45				
5032	15 8 32·3	10 10·7	13 7·8	10 10·6	10 10·65	N. 2 25—2 31·15				
5054	15 12 3·0	11 16·2	18 4·8	20 14·1		S. { 3 40+6 22·6 / 3 45—2 9·3 }				
5151	15 29 16·5	11 17·8	16 29·4	11 17·7	11 17·75	N. 2 45—5 11·65				
Anon.	15 34 31·5	12 3·5	18 0·3	12 3·3	12 3·4	N. 0 55—5 30·9				
5227	15 41 12·5	10 19·7	22 19·3	10 19·8	10 19·75	S. 1 10+1 33·55				
5272	15 47 27·5	11 29·1	16 14·6	11 28·2	11 28·65	N. 3 15—4 19·95				

Nos. 4623, 5435, and 6074, double.—The larger stars observed.—5054 shade touching telescope.
* Leaving the field.   † Past meridian.

MAY 17, 1843.—FACE OF SECTOR WEST—(continued).

Number of B.A.C.	Time by Chronometer.	Micr. for Plumb-line on Dot.	Micr. for Observation of Star.	Micr. for Plumb-line on Dot.	Mean of Micr. for Plumb-line on Dot.	Star's Apparent Zenith Distance.	Barom.	Thermometers.		
								Attd.	Upper.	Lower.
	h m s	rev. pts.	rev. pts.	rev. pts.	rev. pts.	° ′ rev. pts.	in.			
5374	16 1 33·0	11 8·0	15 13·9	11 7·6	11 7·8	N. 3 0-4 6·1				
5435	16 9 52·0	10 13·3	8 2·7	10 13·2	10 13·25	N. 1 2+2 10·55				
Anon*	16 14 4·3	11 0·5	14 22·2	11 1·0	11 0·75	S. 0 50+3 21·45				
Anon.	16 31 48·5	10 21·3	16 1·3	10 21·6	10 21·45	S. 0 30+5 13·85				
5632	16 40 13·2	11 29·6	16 13·2	11 29·8	11 29·70	S. 2 0+4 17·50	27·885		47·84	48·0
5735	16 54 42·7	9 22·2	11 22·5	9 22·2	9 22·2	S. 1 55+2 0·3				
5817	17 7 5·2	8 28·9	10 28·9	8 28·8	8 28·85	S. 0 30+2 0·05				
5881	17 17 35·3	9 7·6	10 4·4	9 6·8	9 7·2	N. 2 15-0 31·2				
5915	17 23 8·0	9 21·3	11 26·4	9 21·5	9 21·4	S. 5 0+2 5·0				
5960	17 30 1·0	9 26·0	7 15·0	9 25·4	9 25·7	S. 0 10-2 10·7				
6016	17 39 12·7	9 23·7	11 9·5	9 23·4	9 23·55	N. 0 20-1 19·05				
6074†	17 49 15·0	9 11·4	11 14·3	9 10·5	9 10·95	N. 1 45-2 3·35				
6115‡	17	9 11·7	13 27·0	9 11·7	9 11·7	N. 1 30+4 15·3				
6145‡		9 29·5	13 23·0	9 20·2	9 29·35	N. 1 15-3 27·65				
6186	18 7 11·0	11 20·2	12 3·8	11 20·0	11 20·1	S. 4 50+0 17·7				
6233	18 13 57·0	11 2·5	9 32·0	11 3·3	11 2·9	S. 2 30-1 4·9				
6285	18 20 59·5	10 24·0	6 2·8	10 23·8	11 23·9	S. 1 10-4 21·1				
6489	18 52 52·2	11 25·7	8 14·5	11 24·4	11 25·05	N. 1 50+3 10·55				
6525	18 57 53·0	12 2·8	11 14·3	12 2·8	12 2·8	N. 3 5+0 22·5	27·815		47·3	47·4

MAY 18, 1843.—FACE OF SECTOR EAST.

Number of B.A.C.	Time by Chronometer.	Micr. for Plumb-line on Dot.	Micr. for Observation of Star.	Micr. for Plumb-line on Dot.	Mean of Micr. for Plumb-line on Dot.	Star's Apparent Zenith Distance.	Barom.	Thermometers.		
								Attd.	Upper.	Lower.
1802	5 34 10·3	11 0 6	8 25·5	10 32·4	10 33·5	S. 2 10+2 8·0	27·805		65·7	62·5
2293	6 52 44·1	11 25·1	16 6·4	11 25·1	11 25·1	N. 3 10+4 15·3				
4458	13 12 14·5	11 2·0	11 17·0	11 2·0	11 2·0	S. 3 55-0 15·0	27·800	48·9	48·9	48·6
Anon.	13 14 40·2		13 33·5	12 1·4		S. 0 25 1 32·1				
4517	13 24 11·3	12 1·1	16 31·6	12 1·3	12 1·2	N. 3 10+4 30·4				
4548	13 30 15·8	12 1·3	16 27·7	12 1·4	12 1·35	N. 3 10+4 26·35				
4579	13 37 7·0	9 18·5	6 17·0	9 18·6	9 18·55	S. 0 15+3 1·55				
4623	13 43 7·2	9 18·6	10· 7·6	9 18·7	9 18·65	S. 0 15-0 22·95				
4686	13 57	9 22·5	14 7·2	9 21·2	9 21·85	S. 3 40-4 19·35				
Anon.	14 24 22·3	9 32·8	11 24·4	9 31·3	9 32·05	S. 0 40-1 26·35				
4852	14 34 22·8	8 26·5	6 11·8	8 25·8	8 26·15	S. 2 30+2 14·35				
4891	14 41 28·2	11 20·3	11 17·3	11 20·3	11 20·3	N. 4 40-0 3·0				
4916	14 46 27·5	9 21·8	10 11·5	9 20·9	9 21·35	S. 1 15-0 24·15				
Anon.	14 53 43·5	10 0·0	13 23·9	10 0·0	10 0·0	S. 0 5-3 23·9				
Anon§	14 58 6·5	11 15·0	10 33·2	10 14·5	10 14·75	S. 0 20-0 18·45				
5032	15 8 39·3	10 26·8	9 11·3	10 27·1	10 26·95	N. 2 25-1 15·65				
5064	15 12 9·5	11 27·7	15 19·0	11 24·8	11 26·25	S. 3 45-3 26·75				
5151	15 29 23·5	12 1·7	8 8·0	12 2·1	12 1·9	N. 2 45-3 27·9	27·800	48·6	48·9	48·5
Anon.	15 34 38·0	9 26·2	5 8·8	9 25·2	9 25·7	N. 0 55-4 16·9				
5227	15 41 19·4	9 13·3	8 30·5	9 13·0	9 13·15	S. 1 10+0 16·05				
5272	15 47 34·5	9 15·0	6 9·3	9 15·1	9 15·05	N. 3 15-3 5·75				
5374	16 1 40·0	9 11·0	6 21·8	9 11·3	9 11·15	N. 3 0-2 23·35				
Anon.	16 31 55·31	8 26·3	4 27·0	8 26·9	8 26·6	S. 0 30+3 33·6				
5588	16 33 54	8 15·3	8 32·8	8 15·4	8 15·35	N. 0 10+0 17·45				
5632	16 40 19·2	8 7·6	5 7·5	8 6·5	8 7·05	S. 1 55+0 16·4				
5735	16 54 49·5	9 3·4	8 21·1	9 3·6	9 3·5	S. 1 55+0 16·4				
5817	17 7 12·0	9 19·6	9 1·5	9 20·0	9 19·8	S. 0 30+0 18·3	27·800	48·2	48·0	48·0
5861	17 17 42	10 18·7	11 1·3	10 18·7	10 18·7	N. 2 15+0 16·6				
5915	17 23 14·5	12 2·5	11 15·0	12 2·0	12 2·25	S. 5 0+0 21·25				
5960	17 30 8·5	12 8·3	16 2·7	12 8·5	12 8·4	S. 0 10-3 28·3				
6016	17 39 19·5	9 27·1	9 22·5	9 27·1	9 27·1	N. 0 20-0 4·6				
6074	17 40 22	10 10·2	9 22·8	10 10·5	10 10·35	N. 1 45-0 21·55				

* Double; Space bisected.   † Double.   ‡ Time not noted.   § Time doubtful.

♃ MAY 18, 1843.—FACE OF SECTOR EAST—(continued).

Number of B.A.C.	Time by Chronometer.	Micr. for Plumb-line on Dot.	Micr. for Observation of Star.	Micr. for Plumb-line on Dot.	Mean of Micr. for Plumb-line on Dot.	Star's Apparent Zenith Distance.	Barom.	Attd.	Upper.	Lower.
	h m s	rev. pts.	rev. pts.	rev. pts.	rev. pts.	° ' rev. pts.	in.			
6115	17 56 5·5	10 26·1	16 24·4	10 26·0	10 26·05	N. 1 30+5 32·35				
6145	18 0 19·8	10 30·8	8 18·5	10 31·0	10 30·9	N. 1 15—2 12·4				
6186	18 7 17·0	10 17·6	11 16·4	10 17·3	10 17·45	S. 4 50—0 32·95				
6233	18 14 3·5	11 13·6	14 2·2	11 13·5	11 13·55	S. 2 30—2 22·65				
6285	18 21 6·5	11 2·1	17 5·3	11 1·8	11 1·95	S. 1 10—6 3·35				
6305	18 23 50·5	11 1·8	12 30·5	11 2·2	11 2·0	S. 1 10—1 28·5				
6489	18 52 58·2	11 3·0	15 30·4	11 3·3	11 3·15	N. 1 50+4 27·25				
6639	19 17 22·3	10 11·7	11 23·9	10 12·2	10 11·95	N. 1 55+1 11·95				
7992		7 1·7	10 0·0	7 1·6	7 1·65	N. 1 30+2 32·35	27·800	46·8	46·8	46·3

♀ MAY 19, 1843.—FACE OF SECTOR WEST.

Number of B.A.C.	Time by Chronometer.	Micr. for Plumb-line on Dot.	Micr. for Observation of Star.	Micr. for Plumb-line on Dot.	Mean of Micr. for Plumb-line on Dot.	Star's Apparent Zenith Distance.	Barom.	Attd.	Upper.	Lower.
1802	5 34 9·2	0 23·8	13 10·3	9 23·5	9 23·65	S. 2 10+3 20·65	27·770	65·9	75·5	66·0
2293	6 52 40·0	8 31·3	5 30·8	8 31·4	8 31·35	N. 3 10+3 0·55				
4458	13 12 2·0	9 25·3	10 28·6	9 25·5	9 25·4	S. 3 55+1 3·2				
4517	13 24 6·5	9 0·0	5 20·6	8 33·7	8 33·85	N. 3 10+3 13·25				
4548*	13 30 11·2	8 33·6	5 23·8	8 33·8	8 33·7	N. 3 10+3 9·9				
4579	13 37 2·0		14 16·8	9 32·9		S. 0 15+4 17·9	27·770	53·3	53·6	53·3
4023	13 43 3·3	9 32·9	10 26·5	9 32·9	9 32·9	S. 0 15+0 27·6				
4686	13 57 42·5	9 28·8	6 26·8	9 30·6	9 29·7	S. 3 40—3 2·9				
4719†	14 6 14·5	9 26·4	10 10·9	9 25·7	9 20·05	N. 3 25—0 27·85				
4784	14 19		8 30·3	9 17·6		N. 3 10+0 21·3				
4852	14 24 19·2	8 21·0	8 11·0	8 21·2	8 21·1	S. 0 40—0 10·1				
4852	14 34 19·5	8 24·4	12 23·2	8 24·8	8 24·6	S. 2 30+3 32·6				
4891	14 41 22·5	6 12·6	7 31·3	6 11·8	6 12·2	N. 4 40—1 10·1				
4916	14 46 23·5	9 10·7	10 0·9	9 10·4	9 10·55	S. 1 15+0 24·35				
Anon.	14 53 39·8	8 13·6	6 6·7	8 13·6	8 13·6	S. 0 5—2 6·9				
Anon.	14 57 51·5	8 23·6	9 18·5	8 23·4	8 23·5	S. 0 20+0 29·0				
5032	15 8 34·3	9 10·1	12 7·5	9 9·6	9 9·85	N. 2 25—2 31·65				
5054‡	15 12 33·0	10 23·5	8 12·3	10 23·4	10 23·45	S. 3 45—2 11·15				
5151	15 29 18·5	8 4·3	13 13·9	8 1·6	8 2·05	N. 2 45—5 10·95				
Anon.	15 34 33·5	8 20·7	14 18·1	8 20·6	8 20·65	N. 0 55—5 31·45				
5227	15 41 14·5	8 4·0	10 3·5	8 4·5	8 4·25	S. 1 10+1 33·25				
5272	15 47 28·5	9 2·0	13 24·1	9 0·8	9 1·4	N. 3 15—4 22·7				
5374	16 1 33·8	9 18·8	13 26·0	9 18·8	9 18·8	N. 3 0—4 7·2				
Anon.	16 31 52·0	10 7·6	15 20·5	10 7·6	10 7·6	S. 0 30+5 12·9				
5598‖	16 33 47·5	10 10·4	11 7·0	10 9·8	10 10·1	N. 0 10—0 30·9	27·780	52·9	53·3	52·9
5632	16 40 14·0	11 4·0	15 20·3	11 4·0	11 4·0	S. 2 0+4 16·3				
5735	16 54 43·7	8 28·2	10 27·9	8 28·2	8 28·2	S. 1 55+1 33·7				
5817	17 7 5·5	8 18·0	10 17·6	8 18·0	8 18·0	S. 0 30+1 33·6				
5881	17 17 35·2	8 14·1	9 11·4	8 13·6	8 13·85	N. 2 15—0 31·55				
5915	17 23 39·3	10 16·8	12 20·5	10 17·0	10 16·9	S. 5 0+2 9·6				
6016	17 39 13·0	7 22·0	9 8·7	7 21·7	7 21·85	N. 0 20—1 20·85				
6074	17 49 15·2	12 10·3	14 14·0	12 9·7	12 10·0	N. 1 45—2 4·0				
6115	17 55 58·5	10 29·3	6 13·7	10 29·0	10 29·15	N. 1 30+4 15·45				
6145	18 0 12·8	11 10·4	5 5·4	11 10·4	11 10·4	N. 1 15—3 29·0				
6186	18 7 12·0	9 10·1	9 27·4	9 10·3	9 10·2	S. 4 50+0 17·2				
6233	18 13 47·5	9 23·2	8 18·6	9 22·8	9 23·0	S. 2 30—1 4·4				
6275	18 20 56·2	9 6·6	10 22·7	9 6·7	9 6·7	S. 1 10—1 16·0				
6285	18 21 3·5	9 0·8	4 18·8	9 6·8	9 6·8	S. 1 10—4 22·0				
6305	18 23 52·3	9 6·8	8 27·9	9 6·8	9 6·8	S. 1 10—0 12·9				
6414	18 42 50·2	8 26·2	12 19·2	8 27·0	8 26·6	N. 1 5—3 26·6				
6489	18 52 51·2	8 27·0	8 26·4	8 26·7	8 26·7	N. 1 50+3 8·9				
6525	18 57 51·5	5 31·8	5 9·5	5 30·6	5 31·2	N. 3 5+0 21·7				
6639	19 17 14·5	8 7·5	8 13·1	8 7·6	8 7·55	N. 1 55—0 5·55	27·780	51·8	51·7	51·8

* 4ˢ past middle wire.   † 5ˢ past middle wire.—Plumb-line in motion.   ‡ 20ˢ past middle wire.   7992 Leaving the field.

♄ MAY 20, 1843.—FACE OF SECTOR EAST.

Number of B.A.C.	Time by Chronometer	Micr. for Plumb-line on Dot.	Micr. for Observation of Star.	Micr. for Plumb-line on Dot.	Mean of Micr. for Plumb-line on Dot.	Star's Apparent Zenith Distance.	Barom.	Thermometers.		
								Attd.	Upper.	Lower.
	h m s	rev. pts.	rev. pts.	rev. pts.	rev. pts.	° ′ rev. pts.	In.			
1802	5 34 12·5	10 19·9	8 13·75	10 20·2	10 20·05	S. 2 10+2 6·30		64·0	68·4	65·9
2293	6 52 41·2	11 8·1	15 17·2	11 7·8	11 7·95	N. 3 10+4 9·25	27·736			
						S. 3 55−0 14·4				
4458	13 12 7·2	11 0·6	11 24·0							
4517	13 24 4·5	11 21·1	16 16·9	11 21·5	11 21·3	N. 3 10+4 29·6				
4548	13 30 9·5	11 21·6	16 13·6	11 21·7	11 21·05	N. 3 10+4 25·95				
4579*	13 37 31·5		6 30·4	9 30·5		S. 0 15+3 0·1				
4623	13 43 5·5	9 30·4	10 19·0	9 30·5	9 30·45	S. 0 15−0 22·55				
4686	13 57 48·5	10 3·4	14 21·5	10 2·6	10 3·0	S. 3 40−4 18·5	27·760	54·1	54·3	53·9
4719	14 6 13·3	11 4·4	11 27·3	11 4·8	11 4·6	N. 3 25+0 22·7				
4784	14 19 16·5	10 19·8	12 23·0	10 20·2	10 20·0	N. 3 10+2 3·0				
Anon.	14 24 22·5	10 11 2	12 1·3	10 9·5	10 10·35	S. 0 40−1 24·95				
4852	14 34 24·8	8 30·3	6 16·0	8 30·5	8 30·4	S. 2 30+2 14·4				
4891	14 41 21·3	9 9·6	9 7·1	9 9·3	9 9·45	N. 4 40−0 2·35				
4916	14 46 26·5	8 20·7	9 11·2	8 20·8	8 20·75	S. 1 15−0 24·45				
Anon.	14 53 42·5	8 18·5	12 6 3	8 18·8	8 18·65	S. 0 5−3 21·65				
Anon.	14 57 54·5	8 17·9	9 2·5	8 18·0	8 17·95	S. 0 20−0 18·55				
5032	15 8 34 8	9 23·1	8 7·8	9 23·0	9 23·0	N. 2 25−1 15·25				
5054	15 12 13·5	9 14·8	13 8·3	9 14·2	9 14·5	S. 3 45−3 27·8				
5151	15 29 19·5	9 30·8	6 2·4	9 31·0	9 30·9	N. 2 45−3 28·5				
Anon.	15 34 35·5	8 2·3	3 19·0	8 2·0	8 2·15	N. 0 55−4 16·25				
5227	15 41 19·6		8 23·5	9 6·45		S. 1 10+0 16·95				
5272	15 47 29·5	9 20·0	6 15·3	9 20·0	9 20·0	N. 3 15−3 4·7				
5374	16 1 35·0	9 12·4	6 24·4	9 12·4	9 12·4	N. 0 −2 22·0				
5435	16 9 55·7	8 33·2	12 25 8	8 33·1	8 33·15	N. 1 25+3 26·65				
Anon†	16 14 44·5	9 27·6	7 22·2	9 27·5	9 27·55	S. 0 50+2 5·35				
5588	16 33 52·2	9 10·7	0 29·6	9 10·7	9 10·7	N. 0 10+0 18·9	27·780	53·0	53·1	53·2
5632	16 40 21·0	9 13·0	6 13·2	9 12·4	9 12·7	S. 2 0+2 33·5				
5735	16 54 50·0	9 14·0	8 31·5	9 13·9	9 13·95	S. 1 55+0 16·45				
5817	17 7 11·0	8 9·4	7 25·8	8 10·4	8 9·9	S. 0 30+0 18·1				
5881	17 17 38·0	7 33·8	8 17·0	7 33·8	7 33·8	N. 2 15+0 17·2				
5915‡	17 23 19·5	9 27·5	9 7·0	9 27·8	9 27·65	S. 5 0+0 20·65				
6016	17 39 17·8	7 2·2	6 32·0	7 2·4	7 2·3	N. 0 20−0 4·3				
6074	17 49 18·8	9 6·8	8 19 7	9 7·3	9 7·05	N. 1 45−0 21·35				
6115	17 56 1·7	9 31·5	15 30·0	9 31·4	9 31·45	N. 1 30+5 32·55				
6145	18 0 17·2	8 23·1	6 10·2	8 23·0	8 23·05	N. 1 15−2 12·85				
6186	18 7 22·8	10 25·5	11 26·5	10 25·5	10 25·5	S. 4 50−1 1·0				
6233	18 14 6·0	11 27·0	14 17·8	11 27·0	11 27·0	S. 2 30−2 24·8				
6275	18 20 3·0	11 3·1	11 5·4	11 3·2	11 3·15	S. 1 10−0 2·25				
6285	18 21 6·8	11 3·1	17 6·7	11 3·15	11 3·15	S. 1 10−6 3·55				
6305	18 24 59·5	11 3·2	12 32·7	11 3·2	11 3·2	S. 1 10−1 29·5				
6414	18 42 55·0	9 11·4	7 1·4	9 11·35	9 11·35	N. 1 5−2 9·95	27 800	52·3	52·3	52·0
6489	18 52 55·2	8 24·7	13 18·7	8 24·2	8 24·45	N. 1 50+4 28·25				
6639	19 17 19·2	10 7·5	11 20·7	10 7·6	10 7·55	N. 1 55+1 13·15	27·800	51·6	51·4	51·5

☉ MAY 21, 1843.—FACE OF SECTOR WEST.

Number of B.A.C.	Time by Chronometer	Micr. for Plumb-line on Dot.	Micr. for Observation of Star.	Micr. for Plumb-line on Dot.	Mean of Micr. for Plumb-line on Dot.	Star's Apparent Zenith Distance.	Barom.	Attd.	Upper.	Lower.
2293	6 52 39·0	10 12·3	7 13·3	10 12·7	10 12·5	N. 3 10+2 33 2	27·820	63·3	69·1	63·3
4458	13 12 5·2	11 14·8	12 18·2	11 14·8	11 14·8	S. 3 55+1 3·4				
4517	13 24 4·5	11 2·0	7 22·9	11 2·25	11 2·25	N. 3 10+3 13·35				
4548	13 30 9·2	11 2·6	7 26·5	11 2·5	11 2·55	N. 3 10+3 10·05				
4579	13 37 4·0	10 23·4	15 7·4	10 23·4	10 23·45	S. 0 15+4 17·95				
4 23	13 43 4·0	10 23·5	11 18·1	10 23·4	10 23·45	S. 0 15+0 28·65				
4686	13 57 45·4	11 5·3	8 3·8	11 5·7	11 5·5	S. 3 40−3 1·7				
4784	14 19 16·0	8 1·3	7 15·5	8 1·3	8 1·3	N. 3 10+0 19·8				

* Past the middle wire.   † Open double.—The space bisected.   ‡ The second uncertain —After the observations of the 20th, a piece of twine was found twisting the plumb-line.

☉ MAY 21, 1843.—FACE OF SECTOR WEST—(continued).

Number of B.A.C.	Time by Chronometer.	Micr. for Plumb-line on Dot.	Micr. for Observation of Star.	Micr. for Plumb-line on Dot.	Mean of Micr. for Plumb-line on Dot.	Star's Apparent Zenith Distance.	Barom.	Thermometers.		
								Attd.	Upper.	Lower.
	h m s	rev. pts.	rev. pts.	rev. pts.	rev. pts.	° ′ rev. pts.	in.			
Anon.	14 24 20·5	8 15·8	8 6·7	8 15·7	8 15·75	S. 0 40—0 9·05				
4852	14 34 23·5	8 18·5	12 18·2	8 18·8	8 18·65	S. 2 30+3 33·55	27·815	50·4	50·4	50·2
4891	14 41 20·8	9 19·9	11 3·4	9 18·8	9 19·35	N. 4 40—1 18·05				
4916	14 46 25·4	11 2·2	11 27·0	11 2·2	11 2·2	S. 1 15+0 25·7				
Anon.	14 53 42·2	10 9·1	8 3·6	10 8·3	10 8·7	S. 0 5—2 5·1				
Anon.	14 57 54·0	10 16·0	11 12·1	10 16·5	10 16·25	S. 0 20+0 29·85				
5032	15 8 34·3	9 26·4	12 23·6	9 25·5	9 25·95	N. 2 25—2 31·65				
5151	15 29 18·5	9 30·4	15 6·9	9 29·0	9 29·7	N. 2 45—5 11·2				
Anon.	15 34 35·5	9 19·3	15 18·1	9 19·2	9 19·25	N. 0 55—5 32·85				
5227	15 41 17·0	9 0·8	11 1·3	9 0·9	9 0·85	S. 1 10+2 0·45				
5272	15 47 29·0	9 8·5	13 30·3	9 7·3	9 7·9	N. 3 15—4 22·4				
5374	16 1 34·5	8 20·8	12 27·8	8 20·9	8 20·85	N. 3 0—4 6·05				
5435	16 9 54·2	8 10·4	8 10·7	8 10·7	8 10·55	N. 1 25+2 10·85				
Anon.	16 14 10·5	7 32·4	11 20·0	7 32·6	7 32·5	S. 0 50+3 21·5				
5588	16 33 50·8	9 19·1	9 18·2	9 18·2	9 18·65	N. 0 10—0 31·65				
5632	16 40 18·7	9 21·2	14 4·3	9 21·5	9 21·35	S. 2 0+4 16·05				
5735	16 54 48·5	9 21·8	11 21·6	9 21·8	9 21·8	S. 1 55+1 33·8				
5817	17 7 7·6	9 12·3	11 12·2	9 12·3	9 12·3	S. 0 30+1 33·9	27·825	50·5	50·0	50·3
5881	17 17 37·0	8 33·3	9 30·5	8 32·6	8 32·95	N. 2 15—0 31·55				
5915*	17 23 43·5	10 19·5	12 22·6	10 19·5	10 19·5	S. 5 0+2 3·1	27·815	50·0	50·0	50·0
5900	17 30 5·5	9 27·4	7 17·0	9 26·5	9 26·95	S. 0 10—2 9·95				
6016	17 39 16·2	10 5·8	11 27·1	10 5·5	10 5·65	N. 0 20—1 21·45				
6074	17 49 17·5	10 24·5	12 28·0	10 23·7	10 24·1	N. 1 45—2 3·9				
6115	17 56	10 6·7	5 24·7	10 6·8	10 6·75	N. 1 30+4 16·05	27·815	50·0	50·0	50·0
6145	18 0 15·7	10 18·0	14 13·1	10 17·8	10 17·9	N. 1 15—3 29·2				
6186	18 7 20·0	11 32·3	12 16·0	11 32·0	11 32·15	S. 4 50+0 17·85				
6233	18 14 3·2	10 10·5	9 6·7	10 10·8	10 10·65	S. 2 30—1 3·95	27·815	49·8	49·6	49·8
6275	18 19 59·5	10 11·0	11 25·9	10 10·8	10 10·9	S. 1 10+1 50·0				
6285†	18 21	10 10·8	5 23·8	10 10·8	10 10·8	S. 1 10—4 21·0				
6305	18 23 57·6	10 10·8	9 32·1	10 10·7	10 10·75	S. 1 10—0 12·65				
6414	18 42 53·5	10 1·7	13 27·3	10 7·0	10 1·2	N. I 5—3 26·1				
6489	18 52 53·0	10 11·8	7 2·7	10 11·8	10 11·8	N. 1 50+3 9·1				
6525	18 57 54·0	10 22·3	9 32·8	10 21·8	10 22·05	N. 3 5+0 23·25				
6639	19 17 17·4	10 23·3	10 27·5	10 22·8	10 23·05	N. 1 55—0 4·45	27·814	49·3	49·1	49·4

☽ MAY 22, 1843.—FACE OF SECTOR EAST.

Number of B.A.C.	Time by Chronometer.	Micr. for Plumb-line on Dot.	Micr. for Observation of Star.	Micr. for Plumb-line on Dot.	Mean of Micr. for Plumb-line on Dot.	Star's Apparent Zenith Distance.	Barom.	Thermometers.		
								Attd.	Upper.	Lower.
1802	5 34 20·5	12 23·7	10 20·8	12 24·0	12 23·85	S. 2 10+2 3·05				
2293	6 52 45·5	11 9·9	15 27·2	11 10·1	11 10·0	N. 3 10+4 17·2	27·740	52·2	52·2	52·0
4458	13 12 13·7	15 28·5	16 9·5	15 28·5	15 28·5	S. 3 55—0 15·0				
4517	13 24 10·5	10 29·0	15 25·7	10 29·4	10 29·2	N. 3 10+4 30·5				
4548	13 30 15·0	10 29·2	15 22·1	10 29·2	10 29·2	N. 3 10+4 26·9				
4579	13 37 11·4	9 30·5	6 29·1	9 30·4	9 30·45	S. 0 15+3 1·35				
4623	13 43 11·4	9 30·2	10 18·5	9 30·0	9 30·1	S. 0 15—0 22·4				
4686	13 57 55·0	9 29·9	14 13·7	9 28·8	9 29·35	S. 3 40—4 18·35				
4719	14 6 17·4	11 11·1	12 1·1	11 11·3	11 11·2	N. 3 25+0 23·9				
4784‡	14 19 47·0	8 30·2	10 33·4	8 30·2	8 30·2	N. 3 10+2 3·2				
Anon.	14 24 36·6	9 13·7	11 1·6	9 13·3	9 13·5	S. 0 40—1 26·6				
4852	14 34 30·5	11 24·0	9 9·0	11 23·5	11 23·75	S. 2 30+2 14·75				
4891	14 41 25·5	12 32·2	12 29·7	12 32·0	12 32·1	N. 4 40—0 2·4				
4916	14 46 33·2	10 10·7	11 1·6	10 10·3	10 10·5	S. 1 15—0 25·1				
Anon.	14 53 48·0	10 1·0	13 25·0	10 1·0	10 1·0	S. 0 5—3 24·0				
Anon.	14 58 0·0	10 18·2	11 6·3	10 18·0	10 18·1	S. 0 20—0 22·2				
5054	15 12 20·0	10 30·6	14 21·6	10 29·8	10 30·2	S. 3 45—3 25·4				

☾ MAY 22, 1843.—FACE OF SECTOR EAST—(continued).

Number of B.A.C.	Time by Chronometer.	Micr. for Plumb-line on Dot.	Micr. for Observation of Star.	Micr. for Plumb-line on Dot.	Mean of Micr. for Plumb-line on Dot.	Star's Apparent Zenith Distance.	Barom.	Thermometers.		
								Attd.	Lower.	Upper.
	b m s	rev. pts.	rev. pts.	rev. pts.	rev. pts.	° ′ rev. pts.	in.			
5151	15 20 23·8	10 23·2	6 29·1	10 23·7	10 23·45	N. 2 45—3 28·35				
Anon.	15 34 40·7	10 22·8	6 7·3	10 22·5	10 22·65	N. 0 55—4 15·35				
5227	15 41 26·2	9 29·1	9 12·3	9 29·0	9 29·05	S. 1 10+0 16·75				
5272	15 47 34·6	11 11·2	8 6·0	11 11·5	11 11·35	N. 3 15—3 5·35	27·740	50·4	50·4	50·3
5374	16 1 40·2	11 0·0	8 12·3	11 0·3	11 0·15	N. 3 0—2 21·85				
5435	16 10 1·6	9 9·0	13 1·8	9 9·0	9 9·0	N. 1 25+3 26·8				
Anon*	16 14 17·5	10 22·2	8 16·6	10 22·0	10 22·1	S. 0 50+2 5·5				
5588	16 33 58·8	10 25·6	11 11·4	10 25·8	10 25·7	N. 0 10+0 19·7				
5632	16 40 27·7	10 7·1	7 7·2	10 7·0	10 7·05	S. 2 0+2 33·85				
5735	16 54 57·5	10 2·25	9 20·25	10 2·3	10 2·28	S. 1 55+0 16·03		49·8	49·8	49·8
5817	17 7 17·2	9 18·5	9 0·8	9 18·4	9 18·45	S. 0 30+0 17·65				
5881	17 17 43·3	10 18·4	11 2·5	10 18·7	10 18·55	N. 2 15+0 17·95				
5915†	17 23	10 31·0	10 9·8	10 30·8	10 30·9	S. 5 0+0 21·1				
5960	17 30 9·2	10 15·5	14 9·6	10 15·4	10 15·45	S. 0 10—3 28·15				
6016	17 39 23·5	9 29·6	9 26·3	9 30·0	9 29·8	N. 0 20—0 3·5				
6074‡	17 49 23·3	10 10·0	9 23·0	10 10·1	10 10·05	N. 1 45—0 21·05				
6115	17 56 7·2	10 16·2	16 14·8	10 16·4	10 16·3	N. 1 30+5 32·5				
6145	18 0 22·4	10 24·6	8 12·0	10 24·5	10 24·55	N. 1 15—2 12·55				
6186	18 7 29·0	10 13·2	11 11·8	10 12·0	10 12·6	S. 4 50—0 33·2				
6233	18 14 13·3	9 4·1	11 29·5	9 4·1	9 4·1	S. 2 30—2 24·4				
6275	18 20 10·0	8 28·2	8 30·4	8 28·3	8 28·25	S. 1 10—0 2·15				
6285	18 21 13·0	8 28·3	14 32·1	8 28·5	8 28·4	S. 1 10—6 3·7				
6305	18 24 6·3	8 28·5	10 23·6	8 28·4	8 28·45	S. 1 10—1 29·15				
6414	18 43 1·5	8 22·3	6 12·4	8 23·0	8 22·65	N. 1 5—2 10·25				
6489	18 53 1·2	9 16·8	14 10·6	9 16·9	9 16·85	N. 1 50+4 27·75				
6525	18 58 0·3	9 4·5	11 8·8	9 4·0	9 4·25	N. 3 5+2 4·55				
6639	19 17 24·8	8 20·1	9 33·0	8 20·0	8 20·05	N. 1 55+1 12·95	27·742	50·0	50·2	50·0

☽ MAY 23, 1843.—FACE OF SECTOR WEST.

Number of B.A.C.	Time by Chronometer.	Micr. for Plumb-line on Dot.	Micr. for Observation of Star.	Micr. for Plumb-line on Dot.	Mean of Micr. for Plumb-line on Dot.	Star's Apparent Zenith Distance.	Barom.	Thermometers.		
								Attd.	Lower.	Upper.
1802§	5 34 15·4	10 13·7	13 33·0	10 13·4	10 13·55	S. 2 10+3 19·45	27·735	63·2	71·1	63·2
2293	6 52 44·5	10 12·9	7 12·7	10 12·9	10 12·9	N. 3 10+3 0·2				
4458	13 12 12·8	10 27·4	11 31·2	10 27·1	10 27·25	S. 3 55+1 3·95	27·774	52·2	52·2	51·9
4517	13 24 10·5	9 3·6	5 24·6	9 3·5	9 3·55	N. 3 10+3 12·95				
4548	13 30 14·8	9 3·7	5 28·6	9 3·7	9 3·7	N. 3 10+3 9·1				
4579	13 37 9·7	8 27·4	13 12·3	8 27·5	8 27·45	S. 0 15+4 18·85				
4623	13 43 9·6	8 27·7	9 22·7	8 27·7	8 27·7	S. 0 15+0 29·0				
4686	13 57 52·5	10 12·3	7 12·1	10 12·2	10 12·25	S. 3 40—3 0·15				
4719‖	14 6	10 3·0	10 30·7			N. 3 25—0 27·7				
4784	14 19 21·4	10 28·7	10 10·0	10 28·7	10 28·7	S. 3 10+0 18·7				
Anon‖	14 24	11 13·0	11 4·4	11 12·7	11 12·85	S. 0 40—0 8·45				
4852	14 34 28·8	11 14·2	16 15·2	11 14·5	11 14·35	S. 2 30+4 0·85				
4891	14 41 25·0	9 15·4	11 1·3	9 15·4	9 15·4	N. 4 40—1 19·9				
4916	14 46 31·6	9 22·1	10 15·5	9 22·8	9 22·45	S. 1 15+0 27·05				
Anon.	14 53 46·6	9 26·9	7 22·6	9 26·8	9 26·85	S. 0 5—2 4·25				
Anon.	14 58 0·0	9 9·5	10 6·7	9 9·3	9 9·4	S. 0 20+0 31·3				
5092	15 8 30·6	9 20·7	12 17·5	9 19·4	9 20·05	N. 2 25—2 31·45				
5151	15 29 23·6	8 1·5	13 11·5	8 0·8	8 1·15	N. 2 45—5 10·35				
Anon.	15 34 41·0	7 13·0	13 12·1	7 13·3	7 13·15	N. 0 55—5 32·95				
5227	15 41 23·8	7 14·3	9 15·5	7 14·5	7 14·4	S. 1 10+2 1·1				
5272	15 47 34·2	8 26·8	13 14·4	8 25·4	8 26·1	N. 3 15—4 22·3				
5435	16 10 0·5	9 2·2	6 28·8	9 3·4	9 2·8	N. 1 25+2 8·0				
Anon.	16 14 15·0	8 16·6	12 4·5	8 16·6	8 16·6	S. 0 50+3 21·9				
5632	16 40 25·5	9 29·1	14 13·0	9 29·3	9 29·2	S. 2 0+4 17·8	27·750	52·5	52·7	52·4

* As hitherto the space between the stars bisected.　　　　† 15 seconds past meridian.
‡ Double.—Declinations nearly equal.—The preceding observed.—Good definition on the 22nd.
§ Very strong sun glare through the tent canvas above.　　　　‖ ‖ 10 seconds past the middle wire when bisected.

♪ MAY 23, 1843.—FACE OF SECTOR WEST—(continued.)

Number of B.A.C.	Time by Chronometer.	Micr. for Plumb-line on Dot.	Micr. for Observation of Star.	Micr. for Plumb-line on Dot.	Mean of Micr. for Plumb-line on Dot.	Star's Apparent Zenith Distance.	Barom.	Thermometers. Attd.	Upper.	Lower.
	h m s	rev. pts.	rev. pts.	rev. pts.	rev. pts.	o ' rev. pts.	in.			
6115*	17 56 6·0	10 15·5	5 33·0	10 15·7	10 15·6	N. 1 30+4 16·6				
6145	18 0 21·5	10 21·1	14 14·8	10 20·8	10 20·95	N. 1 15—3 27·85				
6186	18 7 26·4	11 30·0	12 15·0	11 29·8	11 29·9	S. 4 50+0 19·1				
6233	18 14 9·8	10 31·6	9 30·2	10 31·5	10 31·55	S. 2 30—1 1·35				
6275	18 20 7·5	10 7·6	11 23·7	10 7·6	10 7·6	S. 1 10+1 16·1				
6285	18 21 9·0	10 7·6	5 21·6	10 7·5	10 7·55	S. 1 10—4 19·95				
6305	18 24 3·3	10 7·5	9 29·8	10 7·3	10 7·4	S. 1 10—0 11·6	27·760	52·7	52·7	52·6

♀ MAY 24, 1843.—FACE OF SECTOR EAST.

Number of B.A.C.	Time by Chronometer.	Micr. for Plumb-line on Dot.	Micr. for Observation of Star.	Micr. for Plumb-line on Dot.	Mean of Micr. for Plumb-line on Dot.	Star's Apparent Zenith Distance.	Barom.	Attd.	Upper.	Lower.
1802	5 34 26·5	10 23·2	8 20·2	10 22·8	10 23·0	S. 2 10+2 2·8				
2293	6 52 49·5	11 7·2	15 25·6	11 7·2	11 7·2	N. 3 10+4 18·4				
4458†	13 12 15·2	11 5·0	11 18·8	11 5·0	11 5·0	S. 3 55—0 13·8				
Anon.	13 14 49·5	10 12·7	12 14·0	10 13·0	10 12·85	S. 0 25 2 1·15				
4517	13 24 19·6	10 21·8	15 21·0	10 21·7	10 21·75	N. 3 10+4 33·25				
4548	13 30 23·8	10 21·8	15 15·8	10 21·8	10 21·8	N. 3 10+4 28·0				
4579	13 37 16·8	9 32·6	6 32·8	9 32·3	9 32·45	S. 0 15+2 33·65				
4623‡	13 43 16·0	9 32·4	10 20·7	9 32·5	9 32·45	S. 0 15—0 22·25				
4686	13 57 56·2	9 15·5	13 32·3	9 14·5	9 15·0	S. 3 40—4 17·3				
4719	14 6 26·7	8 28·7	9 19·45	8 28·7	8 28·7	N. 3 25+0 24·75				
Anon.	14 24 32·3	10 20·8	12 12·4	10 20·4	10 20·6	S. 0 40—1 25·8	27·842	52·5	53·4	52·4
4852	14 34 33·4	10 12·1	7 29·8	10 11·5	10 11·8	S. 2 30+2 16·0				
4891	14 41 35·3	10 16·9	10 15·7	10 17·3	10 17·1	N. 4 40—0 1·4				
Anon.	14 46 37·0	9 18·0	10 7·8	9 17·8	9 17·9	S. 1 15—0 23·9				
Anon.	14 53 53·2	9 8·2	12 31·0	9 8·0	9 8·1	S. 0 5—3 22·9				
Anon.	14 58 5·2	10 1·2	10 21·6	10 1·0	10 1·1	S. 0 20—0 20·5				
5032	15 8 48·2	10 18·3	9 3·8	10 18·4	10 18·35	N. 2 25—1 14·55				
5054	15 12 20·0	10 3·1	13 26·7	10 3·0	10 3·05	S. 3 45—3 23·65				
5151	15 29 32·5	10 0·55	6 8·0	10 1·2	10 0·88	N. 2 45—3 26·88	27·845	52·5	54·0	52·8
Anon.	15 34 48·0	9 10·5	4 28·3	9 10·7	9 10·6	N. 0 55—4 16·3				
5227	15 41 30·6	9 27·9	9 9·2	9 27·4	9 27·65	S. 1 10+0 18·45				
5272	15 47 44·0	10 6·6	7 1·4	10 6·9	10 6·75	N. 3 15—3 5·35				
5374	16 1 49·4	9 27·3	7 5·2	9 27·8	9 27·55	N. 3 0—2 22·35				
5435	16 10 9·0	9 21·4	13 14·1	9 21·2	9 21·2	N. 1 25+3 26·9				
Anon.	16 14 22·0	9 13·4	7 6·6	9 12·6	9 13·0	S. 0 50+2 6·4				
5588	16 34 4·4	9 2·3	9 16·6	9 2·5	9 2·4	N. 0 10+0 14·2				
5632§	16 40 28·0	9 21·5	6 21·4	9 20·5	9 21·0	S. 2 0+2 33·6				
5735	16 55 0·2	8 32·1	8 14·7	8 32·1	8 32·1	S. 1 55+0 17·4				
5817	17 7 21·8	9 6·6	8 22·0	9 6·3	9 6·45	S. 0 30+0 18·45				
5881	17 17 51·5	10 17·9	11 2·7	10 17·8	10 17·85	N. 2 15+0 18·85				
5915	17 23 25·4	10 18·2	9 30·7	10 18·3	10 18·25	S. 5 0+0 21·55				
5960	17 29 53·5	9 31·1	1 0·7	9 31·7	9 31·4	S. 0 10—8 30·7				
6016	17 39 29·5	9 32·0	9 29·5	9 32·2	9 32·1	N. 0 20—0 2·6				
6074	17 49 31·5	10 15·7	9 30·9	10 16·0	10 15·85	N. 1 45—0 18·95				
6115	17 56 14·5	9 27·5	15 28·7	9 27·6	9 27·55	N. 1 30+6 1·15				
6145	18 0 29·6	9 32·4	7 22·3	9 32·7	9 32·55	N. 1 15—2 10·25				
6186§	18 7 26·5	9 10·2	10 9·4	9 10·0	9 10·1	S. 4 50—0 33·3				
6233	18 13 56·8	8 31·9	11 23·1	8 31·8	8 31·85	S. 2 30—2 25·25				
6275	18 20 14·2	11 17·2	11 19·0	11 17·4	11 17·3	S. 1 10—0 1·7				
6285	18 21 18·5	11 17·4	17 22·4	11 17·5	11 17·45	S. 1 10—6 4·95				
6305	18 24 11·0	11 17 6	13 12·4	11 17·6	11 17·6	S. 1 10—1 28·8				
6489	18 53 9·2	10 12·0	15 6·6	10 12·0	10 12·0	N. 1 50+4 28·6	27·840	51·1	51·6	50·9
6525	18 58 9·3	10 13·2	12 21·1	10 13·2	10 13·2	N. 3 5+2 7·9				
6639	19 17 32·2	10 22·5	12 3·8	10 22·5	10 22·5	N. 1 55+1 15·3				

* Dense fog coming up.
‡ Bad definition.
† Adjusted the instrument for Azimuth.
§ The seconds of transit doubtful of Nos. 5632 and 6186.

♃ MAY 25, 1843.—FACE OF SECTOR WEST.

Number of B.A.C	Time by Chronometer.	Micr. for Plumb-line on Dot.	Micr. for Observation of Star.	Micr. for Plumb-line on Dot.	Mean of Micr. for Plumb-line on Dot.	Star's Apparent Zenith Distance.	Barom.	Thermometers.		
								Attd.	Upper.	Lower.
	h m s	rev. pts.	rev. pts	rev. pts.	rev. pts.	° ′ rev. pts.	in.			
2203	6 52 48·0	9 15·0	6 13·8	9 15·0	9 15·0	N. 3 10+3 1·2				
7992	22 49 23·0	12 33·2	11 18·5	12 33·4	12 33·3	N. 1 30+1 14·8				

♀ MAY 26, 1843.—FACE OF SECTOR WEST.

Number of B.A.C	Time by Chronometer.	Micr. for Plumb-line on Dot.	Micr. for Observation of Star.	Micr. for Plumb-line on Dot.	Mean of Micr. for Plumb-line on Dot.	Star's Apparent Zenith Distance.	Barom.	Thermometers.		
								Attd.	Upper.	Lower.
1802	5 34 24·0	13 19·0	17 5·4	13 19·0	13 19·0	S. 2 10+3 20·4				
2293	6 52 51·5	9 24·5	6 22·5	9 24·8	9 24·65	N. 3 10+3 2·15				
4458	13 12 17·8	10 18·2	11 21·3	10 17·6	10 17·9	S. 3 55+1 3·4	27·920	59·7	60·4	60·2
4517	13 24 18 2	9 4·6	5 25·8	9 4·4	9 4·5	N. 3 10+3 12·7				
4548	13 30 22·3	9 4·8	5 29·4	9 4·5	9 4·65	N. 3 10+3 9·25				
4579	13 37 0·0	9 21·8	14 4·9	9 22·4	9 22·1	S. 0 15+4 16 8				
4623	13 43 21·7	9 21·0	10 16·2	9 22·5	9 22·2	S. 0 15+0 28·0				
4686	13 57 58·6	10 13·8	7 11·3	10 13·7	10 13·75	S. 3 40—3 2·45				
4719	14 6 25·5	9 5·3	9 32·2	9 5·3	9 5·3	N. 3 25—0 26·9				
4784	14 19 28·5	8 30·1	8 9·5	8 30·3	8 30·2	N. 3 10+0 20·7				
Anon.	14·24 33·5	9 30·0	9 18·0	9 29 5	9 29·75	S. 0 40—0 10·85				
4852	14 34 35·5	10 9·5	14 8·2	10 9·5	10 9·5	S. 2 30+3 32·7				
4891	14 41 33·5	8 33·0	10 17·9	8 33·3	8 33·15	N. 4 40—1 18·75				
4916*	14 46		12 16 2	11 25·2		S. 1 15—0 25·0				
Anon.	14 53 54·0	11 32·5	9 26·6	11 32·4	11 32·45	S. 0 5—2 5·85				
Anon.	14 58 6·0	11 9·3	12 4·3	11 9·0	11 9·15	S. 0 20+0 29·15				
5032	15 8 47·0	10 16·3	13 13·3	10 16·4	10 16·35	N. 2 25—2 30·95				
5054	15 12 23·5	11 9·4	8 32·0	11 9·5	11 9·45	S. 3 45—2 11·45				
5151	15 29 30·8	9 19·5	14 30·6	9 19·8	9 19·65	N. 2 45—5 10·95				
Anon.	15 34 47·2	10 30·1	16 27·4	10 30·9	10 30·5	N. 0 55—5 30·9				
5227	15 41 31·0	11 9·5	13 9·3	11 9·6	11 9·55	S. 1 10+1 33·75				
5272	15 47 41·5	9 31·3	14 19·1	9 31·2	9 31·25	N. 3 15—4 21·85				
5374	16 1 46·5	9 16·2	13 23·3	9 16·5	9 16·35	N. 3 0—4 6·95				
5435	16 10 7·6	9 2·0	6 26·1	9 1·8	9 1·9	N. 1 25+2 9·8				
Anon.	16 14 22·3	10 10·1	13 31·0	10 10·5	10 10·3	S. 0 50+3 20·7				
5588	16 34 3·7	10 1·0	10 18·4	9 20·4	9 20·7	N. 0 10—0 31·7				
5632	16 40 31·7	8 27·7	13 10·4	8 27·8	8 27·75	S. 2 0+4 10·05				
5735	16 55 1·5	9 11·5	11 10·7	9 11·3	9 11·4	S. 1 55+1 33·3	27·920	57·9	57·7	57·5
5817	17 7 22·2	10 1·8	11 33·5	10* 1·5	10 1·65	S. 0 30+1 31·85				
5881	17 17 49·5	10 26·0	11 22·45	10 26·2	10 26·1	N. 2 15—0 30·35				
5915	17 23 30·2	11 33·4	14 2·6	11 33·7	11 33·55	S. 5 0+2 3·05				
5960	17 30 18·5	10 23·6	8 11·3	10 23·8	10 23·7	S. 0 10—2 12·4				
6016	17 39 26·0	10 14·7	12 0·1	10 15·4	10 15·05	N. 0 20—1 19·05				
6074	17 49 30·6	11 1·1	13 4·4	11 1·7	11 1·4	N. 1 45—2 3·0				
6115	17 56 13·6	10 25·7*	6 8·5	10 24·6	10 25 15	N. 1 30+4 16·65				
6145	18 0 28·8	10 29 8	14 24·4	10 29·6	10 29·7	N. 1 15—3 28·7				
6186	18 7 33·4	11 21·4	12 4·2	11 21·6	11 21·5	S. 4 50+0 10·7				
6233	18 14 17·7	10 33·3	9 28·3	10 33 4	10 33·35	S. 2 30—1 5·05				
6275†	18 20	10 12·0	11 25·4	10 13·0	10 12·5	S. 1 10+1 12·9				
6285†	18 21	10 12·5	5 25·7	10 13·2	10 12·85	S. 1 10—4 21·15				
6305†	18 24	10 13·4	9 33·5	10 13·0	10 13·2	S. 1 10—0 13·7				
6414	18 43 6·5	9 15·5	13 6·7	9 15·6	9 15·55	N. 1 5—3 25·15				
6480	18 53 6·6	8 31 6	5 20·1	8 31·9	8 31·75	N. 1 50+3 11·65				
6525	18 59 6·6	10 26 2	10 1·5	10 24·4	10 25·3	N. 3 5 4·0 23·8				
6639	19 17 30·2	11 12 8	11 16·4	11 13·0	11 12 0	N. 1 55—0 3·5	27·900	57·4	57·1	57·6

May 26.—As the Arch, when free, did not swing from end to end at a constant distance from the plumb-line, all the screws of the tripod above were relaxed, and the pivots brought to bear equally.

* Bisected 10 seconds after passing the middle wire.   † Time of transit not noted.

♄ MAY 27, 1843.—FACE OF SECTOR EAST.

Number of B.A.C.	Time by Chronometer.	Micr. for Plumb-line on Dot.	Micr. for Observation of Star.	Micr. for Plumb-line on Dot.	Mean of Micr. for Plumb-line on Dot.	Star's Apparent Zenith Distance.	Barom.	Attd.	Upper.	Lower.
	h m s	rev. pts.	rev. pts.	rev. pts.	rev. pts.	o ' rev. pts.	in.			
2209*	6 53 5·0	11 18·6	16 2·3	11 19·3	11 18·05	N. 3 10+4 17·35	27·845	60·1	60·8	60·0
4458	13 12 20·5	10 3·6	10 17·8	10 4·0	10 3·8	S. 3 55—0 14·0				
4517	13 24 32·4	11 13·4	16 7·3	11 12·8	11 13·1	N. 3 10+4 28·2				
4548	13 30 37·0	11 13·0	16 3·2	11 12·5	11 12·75	N. 3 10+4 24 45				
4852†	14 34 40·5	8 8·7	5 26·5	8 7·6	8 8·15	S. 2 30+2 15·65				
4916	14 46 45·5	9 20·4	10 8·4	9 19·7	9 20·05	S. 1 15+0 22·35				
Anon.	14 54 3·4	10 29·6	14 16·2	10 29·0	10 29·3	S. 0 5—3 20·9				
Anon.	14 58 12·5	10 31·4	11 15·4	10 30 4	10 30·9	S. 0 20—0 18·5				
5032	15 9 1·2	11 26·4	10 10 5	11 26·5	11 26·45	N. 2 25—1 15·95				
5151	15 29 45·5	11 15·4	7 19·6	11 15·0	11 15·2	N. 2 45—3 29·6				
Anon.	15 34 58·3	11 7·3	6 23·6	11 7·2	11 7·25	N. 0 55—4 17·65				
5227	15 41 37·6	11 5·6	10 20·7	11 5·0	11 5·3	S. 1 10+0 18·6				
5272	15 47 57·0	11 27·3	8 21·3	11 27·5	11 27·4	N. 3 15—3 6·1				
5374	16 2 2·0	11 25·4	9 1·4	11 25·2	11 25·3	N. 3 0—2 23·9				
5435	16 10 19·5	12 12·4	16 2·6	12 12·2	12 12·3	N. 1 25+3 24·3				
Anon.	16 14 30·0	12 14·4	10 9·3	12 14·6	12 14·5	S. 0 50+2 5·2				
5588	16 34 14 2	11 27·6	12 11·2	11 28·5	11 28·05	N. 0 10+0 17·15	27·846	58·5	58·8	58·3
5632	16 40 37·2	11 8·3	8 7 6	11 8·4	11 8·35	S. 2 0+3 0·75				
5817	17 7 30·5	11 32·8	11 14·3	11 32·7	11 32·75	S. 0 30+0 18·45				
5881	17 18 3·5	12 20·0	13 3·4	12 19·7	12 19·85	N. 2 15+0 17·55				
5915	17 23 29·2	13 2·3	12 15·7	13 1·9	13 2·1	S. 5 0+0 20·4				
5960	17 30 24·2	10 26·4	12 25·0	10 26·0	10 26·0	S. 0 10—1 32·8				
6016	17 39 30·3	11 11·2	11 5·7	11 10·8	11 11·0	N. 0 20—0 5·3				
6074	17 49 43·2	9 8·3	8 20·4	9 8·0	9 8·15	N. 1 45—0 21·75				
6115	17 56 25·8	10 17·3	16 14·9	10 16·8	10 17·05	N. 1 30+5 31·85				
6145	18 0 40·3	10 5·8	7 26·5	10 5·2	10 5·5	N. 1 15—2 13·0				
6186	18 7 32·4	9 30·8	10 30·2	9 30·7	9 30·75	S. 4 50—0 33·45				
6233	18 14 21·2	10 13·1	13 2·4	10 13·4	10 13·25	S. 2 30—2 23·15				
6275	18 20 21·1	10 9·0	10 9·0	10 9·0	10 9·0	S. 1 10—0 0·0				
6285	18 21 25·0	10 9·0	16 13·2	10 8·8	10 8·9	S. 1 10—6 4·3				
6305	18 24 18·2	10 9·0	12 3·7	10 8·5	10 8·75	S. 1 10—1 28·95				
6414	18 43 18·4	10 22·7	8 12·3	10 22·5	10 22 6	N. 1 5—2 10·3				
6489	18 53 20·2	10 14·1	15 7·0	10 14·4	10 14·25	N. 1 50+4 26·75				
6525	18 58 22·5	11 26·2	13 31·2	11 26·4	11 26·3	N. 3 5+2 4·9				
6639	19 17 43·8	10 16·5	11 28·3	10 16·0	10 16·25	N. 1 55+1 12·05	27·840	57·1	57·4	57·2

⊙ MAY 28, 1843.—FACE OF SECTOR WEST.

Number of B.A.C.	Time by Chronometer.	Micr. for Plumb-line on Dot.	Micr. for Observation of Star.	Micr. for Plumb-line on Dot.	Mean of Micr. for Plumb-line on Dot.	Star's Apparent Zenith Distance.	Barom.	Attd.	Upper.	Lower.
1802	5 34 27·2	10 10·0	13 28·5	10 9·6	10 9·8	S. 2 10+3 18·7	27·800	61·3	62·2	61·2
2293	6 52 54·2	10 12·3	7 10·6	10 12 4	10 12·35	N. 3 10+3 1·75				
4458	13 12 24·5	12 20 6	13 23·3	12 20·8	12 20·7	S. 3 55+1 2 6				
4517	13 24 21·5	9 31·6	6 18·6	9 31·4	9 31·5	N. 3 10+3 12·9				
4548	13 30 26 6	9 31·5	6 22·0	9 31·55	9 31·55	N. 3 10+3 9·55				
4579	13 37 22·0	9 24·8	14 8 0	9 25·0	9 24·9	S. 0 15+4 17·1				
4623	13 43	9 24·9	10 19·1	9 24·7	9 24·8	S. 0 15+0 28·3				
4686	13 58 5·0	11 14·4	8 12·7	11 14·3	11 14·35	S. 3 40—3 1·65				
4719	14 6 29·5	10 21·0	11 13·6	10 20·7	10 20·85	N. 3 25—0 26·75				
4784	14 19 33·0	10 18·7	9 32·1	10 17·7	10 18·2	N. 3 10+0 20 1				
Anon.	14 24 38·0	11 33·4	11 24·6	11 33·4	11 33·4	S. 0 40—0 8·8	27·785	61·5	62·2	61·4
4852‡	14 34 40·8	13 4·0	17 3·3	13 4·0	13 4·0	S. 2 30+3 33·3				
4891	14 41 37·2	9 22·3	11 6·7	9 22·0	9 22·15	N. 4 40—1 18·55				
4916	14 46 44·0	9 30·3	10 22·1	9 30·0	9 30·15	S. 1 15+0 25·95				
Anon.	14 53 59·2	10 2·1	7 31·3	10 1·8	10 1·95	S. 0 5—2 4·65				
Anon.	14 58	10 25·4	11 22·9	10 26·0	10 25·7	S. 0 20+0 31·2				

* Immediately after the transit of this star, the instrument was shifted a small quantity in Azimuth.
† At 14ʰ sidereal time, the Plumb-line appearing to be curved near the arch, it was replaced by a new one.
‡ Plumb-line oscillating owing to wind.—Excellent definition this evening.

☉ MAY 28, 1843.—FACE OF SECTOR WEST—(continued).

Number of B.A.C.	Time by Chronometer.	Micr. for Plumb-line on Dot.	Micr. for Observation of Star.	Micr. for Plumb-line on Dot.	Mean of Micr. for Plumb-line on Dot.	Star's Apparent Zenith Distance.	Barom.	Thermometers.		
								Attd.	Upper.	Lower.
	h m s	rev. pts.	rev. pts.	rev. pts.	rev. pts.	o ' rev. pts.	in.			
5032	15 8 57·5	10 16·0	13 12·7	10 15·4	10 15·7	N. 2 25—2 31·0				
5151	15 29 29·5	6 22·4	11 33·7	6 21·7	6 22·05	N. 2 45—5 11·65				
Anon.	15 34 52·5	10 14·0	16 11·6	10 13·3	10 13·65	N. 0 55—5 31·95				
5227	15 41 36·3	10 8·0	12 8·3	10 7·5	10 7·75	S. 1 10+2 0·55				
5272	15 47 45·5	11 2·7	15 25·1	11 2·6	11 2·65	N. 3 15—4 22·45				
5374	16 1 50·5	9 23·2	13 29·0	9 23·8	9 23·5	N. 3 0—4 5·5				
5435	16 10 11·2	10 13·3	8 2·3	10 13·3	10 13·3	N. 1 25+2 11·0				
Anon.	16 14 26·5	10 3·8	13 24·3	10 4·0	10 3·9	S. 0 50+3 20·4				
5588	16 34 9·0	10 18·1	11 15·3	10 18·2	10 18·15	N. 0 10—0 31·15				
5632	16 40 37·8	10 18·7	15 0·4	10 17·5	10 18·1	S. 2 0+4 16·3				
5735	16 55 7·8	10 3·2	12 2·7	10 3·1	10 3·15	S. 1 55+1 33·55				
5817	17 7 27·5	9 32·2	11 31·7	9 32·2	9 32·2	S. 0 30+1 33·5				
5881	17 17 54·6	9 10·6	10 6·6	9 10·4	9 10·5	N. 2 15—0 30·1				
5915	17 23 37·5	10 17·6	12 20·8	10 17·4	10 17·5	S. 5 0+2 3·3				
5960	17 30 20·5	9 9·1	6 33·3	9 8·6	9 8·85	S. 0 10—2 9·55				
6016	17 39 34·5	9 28·6	11 14·4	9 28·5	9 28·55	N. 0 20—1 19·85				
6074	17 49 34·5	9 12·0	11 14·5	9 12·3	9 12·15	N. 1 45—2 2·35				
6115	17 56 17·5	8 19·3	4 2·7	8 19·5	8 19·4	N. 1 30+4 16·7				
6145	18 0 33·2	10 15·6	14 8·9	10 15·6	10 15·6	N. 1 15—3 27·3				
6186	18 7 39·6	11 4·3	11 21·2	11 4·3	11 4·3	S. 4 50+0 16·9				
6233	18 14 22·5	10 8·1	9 2·0	10 8·1	10 8·1	S. 2 30—1 6·1				
6275	18 20 19·7	11 2·6	12 16·7	11 2·6	11 2·6	S. 1 10+1 14·1				
6285	18 21 23·0	11 2·6	6 14·5	11 2·7	11 2·65	S. 1 10—4 22·15				
6305	18 24 16·2	11 2·7	10 23·3	11 2·7	11 2·7	S. 1 10—0 13·4				
6414	18 43 11·0	11 21·1	15 11·1	11 21·0	11 21·05	N. 1 5—3 24·05				
6489	18 53 11·0	11 4·8	7 28·6	11 4·4	11 4·6	N. 3 45+3 10·0				
6525	18 58 10·4	11 7·6	10 18·0	11 7·4	11 7·5	N. 3 5+0 23·5				
6699	19 17 34·4	11 11·8	11 14·2	11 11·5	11 11·65	N. 1 55—0 2·55	27·800	60·1	60·1	60·2
7992	22 49 30·4	11 14·7	9 32·0	11 14·5	11 14·6	N. 1 30+1 16·6				

☾ MAY 29, 1843.—FACE OF SECTOR EAST.

Number of B.A.C.	Time by Chronometer.	Micr. for Plumb-line on Dot.	Micr. for Observation of Star.	Micr. for Plumb-line on Dot.	Mean of Micr. for Plumb-line on Dot.	Star's Apparent Zenith Distance.	Barom.	Thermometers.		
								Attd.	Upper.	Lower.
2293*	6 52	10 22·7	15 8·7	10 22·6	10 22·65	N. 3 10+4 20·05	27·800	72·3	78·1	72·5
4458	13 12 24·3	11 5·2	11 19·0	11 5·2	11 5·2	S. 3 55—0 13·8				
4517	13 24 35·3	11 7·0	16 3·6	11 7·0	11 7·0	N. 3 10+4 30·6				
4548	13 30 40·2	11 7·0	15 33·0	11 7·0	11 7·0	N. 3 10+4 26·0				
4579	13 37 28·6	8 6·1	5 3·0	8 6·2	8 6·15	S. 0 15+3 3·15				
4623	13 43 28·8	8 6·2	8 27·6	8 6·2	8 6·2	S. 0 15—0 21·4				
4686	13 58 5·6	9 8·7	13 25·9	9 8·8	9 8·75	S. 3 40—4 17·15				
4719	14 6 42·5		11 18·7	10 29·6	10 29·6	N. 3 25+0 23·1				
4784	14 19 46·8	10 28·0	12 31·1	10 28·1	10 28·05	N. 3 10+2 3·05				
Anon.	14 24 44·4	10 31·8	12 25·0	10 32·1	10 31·95	S. 0 40—1 27·05				
4852	14 34 44·3	11 12·4	8 29·8	11 12·7	11 12·55	S. 2 30+2 10·75				
4891	14 41 53·4	12 8·8	12 5·6	12 8·9	12 8·85	N. 4 40—0 3·25				
4916	14 46 49·8		10 3·5	9 13·0		S. 1 15—0 24·5				
Anon.	14 54 7·5	9 32·4	13 19·6	9 32·4	9 32·4	S. 0 5—3 21·2				
Anon.	14 58 18·5	9 22·8	10 8·5	9 22·6	9 22·7	S. 0 20—0 19·8				
5032	15 9 3·5	10 13·8	8 32·6	10 13·5	10 13·65	N. 2 25—1 15·05				
5151	15 29 48·6	10 30·9	7 2·1	10 30·85	10 30·85	N. 2 45—3 28·75				
Anon.	15 35 1·4	10 24·4	6 7·8	10 24·6	10 24·5	N. 0 55—4 16·7				
5227	15 41 42·2	10 20·5	10 2·1	10 20·6	10 20·55	N. 1 10+0 18·45				
5272	15 48 0·5	11 25·4	8 19·7	11 25·0	11 25·2	N. 3 15—3 5·5				
5374	16 2 5·5	10 29·7	8 5·8	10 29·4	10 29·55	N. 3 0—2 23·75	27·870	60·4	60·4	59·9
5435	16 10 23·5	11 15·9	15 7·8	11 15·0	11 15·45	N. 1 25+3 26·35				

* 15 seconds past the middle wire.—Observation hurried—the "stop" not clamped.   ☾ 29.—Remarkably good definition this night.

☾ MAY 29, 1843.—FACE OF SECTOR EAST—(continued).

Number of B.A.C.	Time by Chronometer.	Micr. for Plumb-line on Dot.	Micr. for Observation of Star.	Micr. for Plumb-line on Dot.	Mean of Micr. for Plumb-line on Dot.	Star's Apparent Zenith Distance.	Barom.	Thermometers. Attd.	Upper.	Lower.
	h m s	rev. pts.	rev. pts.	rev. pts.	rev. pts.	° ′ rev. pts.	in.			
Anon.	16 14 33·2	12 11·1	10 4·0	12 10·6	12 10·85	S. 0 50+2 6·85				
Anon.	16 34 17·8	10 10·8	10 28·6	10 10·6	10 10·7	N. 0 10+0 17·9				
5632	16 40 42·0	10 6·7	7 6·4	10 6·5	10 6·6	S. 2 0+3 0·2				
5817	17 7 35·4	11 4·0	10 19·9	11 4·6	11 4·3	S. 0 30+0 18·4				
5881	17 18 6·18	12 2·0	12 20·8	12 2·2	12 2·1	N. 2 15+0 18·7				
5915	17 23 34·4	11 25·6	11 3·4	11 25·0	11 25·3	S. 5 0+0 21·9				
5960	17 30 30·8	11 7·8	15 1·4	11 7·6	11 7·7	S. 0 10—3 27·7				
6016	17 39 43·6	10 12·5	10 8·3	10 12·3	10 12·4	N. 0 20—0 4·1				
6074	17 49 46·0	11 15·8	10 29·7	11 16·0	11 15·9	N. 1 45—0 20·2				
6115	17 56 29·5	12 3·5	18 2·7	12 3·5	12 3 5	N. 1 30+5 33·2				
6145	18 0 45·0	11 27·3	9 15·0	11 27·0	11 27·15	N. 1 15—2 12·15				
6186	18 7 38·6	12 14·7	13 13·4	12 14·4	12 14·55	S. 4 50—0 32·85				
6233	18 14 25·7	12 3·6	14 27·8	12 3·8	12 3·7	S. 2 30—2 24·1				
6275	18 20 25·6	11 4·1	11 5·9	11 3·9	11 4·0	S. 1 10—0 1·9				
6285	18 21 19·5	11 3·9	17 8·2	11 4·1	11 4·0	S. 1 10—6 4·2				
6305	18 24 22·5	11 4·1	12 33·7	11 4·0	11 4·05	S. 1 10—1 29·65				
6414	18 43 21·7	9 11·2	7 2·1	9 11·6	9 11·4	N. 1 5—2 9·3				
6489	18 53 23·0	9 27·0	14 21·0	9 27·0	9 27·0	N. 1 50+4 28·0	27·880	56·5	56·8	56·5
6639	19 17 40·7	11 21·9	13 0·3	11 21·6	11 21·75	N. 1 55+1 12·55				

♂ MAY 30, 1843.—FACE OF SECTOR WEST.

Number of B.A.C.	Time by Chronometer.	Micr. for Plumb-line on Dot.	Micr. for Observation of Star.	Micr. for Plumb-line on Dot.	Mean of Micr. for Plumb-line on Dot.	Star's Apparent Zenith Distance.	Barom.	Attd.	Upper.	Lower.
2293	6 53 22·5	11 25·5	8 24·2	11 25·4	11 25·45	N. 3 10+3 1·25	27·958	83·3	74·8	73·1
4458	13 12 27·2	12 5·2	13 8·4	12 4 6	12 4·9	S. 3 55+1 3·5	27·960	59·7	59·5	59·2
4517	13 24 30·2	9 32·0	6 18·3	9 31·9	9 31·9	N. 3 10+3 13·6				
4548	13 30 35·5	9 31·8	6 22·3	9 31·9	9 31·85	N. 3 10+3 9·55				
4579	13 37 27·2	10 14·6	14 32·5	10 14·5	10 14·55	S. 0 15+4 17·95				
4623	13 44 27·2	10 14·6	11 8·8	10 14·8	10 14·7	S. 0 15+0 28·1				
4686	13 58 8·5	11 11·5	8 10·7	11 11·8	11 11·65	S. 3 40—3 0·95				
4719	14 6 38·2	8 15·5	9 7·8	8 15·6	8 15·55	N. 3 25—0 26·25				
4764	14 19 41·5	8 5·7	7 19·2	8 5·0	8 5·35	N. 3 10+0 20·15				
Anon.	14 24 43·2	9 29·7	9 20·3	9 29·6	9 29·65	S. 0 40—0 9·35				
4852	14 34 44·2	10 19·7	14 19·7	10 19·7	10 19·7	S. 2 30+4 0·0				
4891	14 41 46·2	6 22·2	8 5·7	6 21·8	6 22·0	N. 4 40—1 17·7				
4916	14 46 48·2	8 32·1	9 24·1	8 32·2	8 32·15	S. 1 15—0 25·95				
Anon.	14 54 5·8	9 22·4	7 16·8	9 22·7	9 22·55	S. 0 5—2 5·75				
Anon.	14 58	10 4·3	10 33·4	10 4·7	10 4·5	S. 0 20+0 28·9				
5032	15 8 59·2	10 17·7	13 13·7	10 18·0	10 17·85	N. 2 25—2 29·85				
5054	15 12 32·5	11 7·6	8 32·2	11 7·9	11 7·75	S. 3 45—2 9·55				
5151	15 29 43·3	9 10·8	14 21·3	9 11·0	9 10·9	N. 2 45—5 10·4				
Anon.	15 34 58·6	10 18·9	16 15·8	10 19·0	10 18·95	N. 0 55—5 30·85				
5227	15 41 40·8	10 4·4	12 6·3	10 5·0	10 4·7	S. 1 10+2 1·6				
5272	15 47 53·5	7 15·5	12 2·3	7 15·4	7 15·45	N. 3 0—4 6·0				
5374	16 1 59·4	9 7·0	13 13·2	9 7·4	9 7·2	N. 3 0—4 6·0				
5435	16 10 18·0	10 20·8	10 7·0	10 20·9	10 20·85	N. 1 25+2 10·15				
Anon.	16 14 33·0	10 15·6	14 2·2	10 15·4	10 15·5	S. 0 50+3 20·7				
5588	16 34 15·5	10 32·8	11 30·7	10 32·7	10 32·75	N. 0 10—0 31·95				
5632	16 40 41·7	10 33·4	15 18·3	10 33·0	10 33·2	S. 2 0+4 19·1	27·975	59·5	59·0	59·0
5735	16 55 11·4	10 22·7	12 22·5	10 22·4	10 22·55	S. 1 55+1 33·95				
5817	17 7 32·8	9 27·4	11 27·0	9 27·3	9 27·35	S. 0 30+1 33·65				
5881	17 18 2·4	10 7·2	11 3·8	10 7·4	10 7·3	N. 2 15—0 30·5				
5915	17 23 38·0	11 14·5	13 20·7	11 15·0	11 14·75	S. 5 0+2 5·95				
5960	17 30 29·2	8 10·1	5 32·6	8 9·8	8 9·95	S. 0 10—2 11·35				
6016	17 39 40·4	8 19·3	10 5·5	8 19·7	8 19·5	N. 0 20—1 20·0				

May 29.—The definition remarkably good.
30.—Excellent definition.

♂ MAY 30, 1843.—FACE OF SECTOR WEST—(continued).

Number of B.A.C.	Time by Chronometer.	Mier. for Plumb-line on Dot.	Mier. for Observation of Star.	Mier. for Plumb-line on Dot.	Mean of Mier. for Plumb-line on Dot.	Star's Apparent Zenith Distance	Barom.	Thermometers. Attd.	Upper.	Lower.
	h m s	rev. pts.	rev. pts.	rev. pts.	rev. pts.	° ′ rev. pts.	in.			
6074	17 49 42·4	9 27·3	11 29·6	9 27·3	9 27·3	N. 1 45—2 2·3				
6115	17 56 25·4	8 25·5	4 8·7	8 25·3	8 25·4	N. 1 30+4 16·7				
6145	18 0 40·2	8 24·8	12 18·5	8 24·6	8 24·7	N. 1 15—3 27·8				
6186	18 7 41·2	9 32·2	10 16·9	9 32·1	9 32·15	S. 4 50+0 18·75				
6233	18 14 26·5	9 16·0	8 10·3	9 16·3	9 16·15	S. 2 30—1 5·85				
6275	18 20 23·5	9 14·5	10 27·6	9 13·8	9 14·15	S. 1 10+1 13·45				
6285	18 21 28·0	9 13 8	4 26·3	9 13·9	9 13·85	S. 1 10—4 21·55				
6305	18 24 20·8	9 14·3	8 33·9	9 14·0	9 14·15	S. 1 10—0 14·25				
6414	18 43 18·2	9 28·4	13 19·2	9 28·7	9 28·55	N. 1 5—3 24·65				
6489	18 53 19·0	9 32·1	6 21·1	9 31·9	9 32·0	N. 1 50+3 10·9				
6525	18 58 19·5	10 28·9	10 5·3	10 28·9	10 28·9	N. 3 5+0 23·6				
6639	19 17 42·8	10 11·4	10 15·5	10 11·2	10 11·3	N. 1 55—0 4·2	27·975	59·0	59·0	59·0

☿ MAY 31, 1843.—FACE OF SECTOR EAST.

Number of B.A.C.	Time by Chronometer.	Mier. for Plumb-line on Dot.	Mier. for Observation of Star.	Mier. for Plumb-line on Dot.	Mean of Mier. for Plumb-line on Dot.	Star's Apparent Zenith Distance	Barom.	Attd.	Upper.	Lower.
1802	5 34	11 13·3	9 12·5	11 13·4	11 13·35	S. 2 10+2 0·85	28·000	72·9	78·8	72·9
2293	6 53 15·5	7 26·9	12 11·5	7 26·7	7 26·8	N. 3 10+4 18·7	28·000	71·4	76·6	71·6
4458	13 12 29·2	6 14·4	6 27·4	6 14·5	6 14·45	S. 3 55—0 12·95	27·984	61·9	63·0	61·5
4517	13 24 39·4	9 13·4	14 8·2	9 13·4	9 13·4	N. 3 10+4 28·8				
4548	13 30 43·8	9 13·5	14 5·1	9 13·4	9 13·45	N. 3 10+4 25·65				
4579	13 37 33·8	8 3·3	5 0·2	8 3·4	8 3·35	S. 0 15+3 3·15				
4623	13 43 34·5	8 3·5	8 25·2	8 3·6	8 3·55	S. 0 15—0 21·65				
4686	13 58 11·5	8 13·4	12 29·5	8 13·2	8 13·3	S. 3 40—4 16·2				
4719	14 6 48·0	10 17·2	11 4·9	10 16·8	10 17·0	N. 3 25+0 21·9				
4784	14 19 50·8	10 15·8	12 18·7	10 15·8	10 15·8	N. 3 10+2 2·9				
Anon.	14 24 39·4	9 19·5	11 10·7	9 19·6	9 19·55	S. 0 40—1 25·15				
4852	14 34 49·7	9 26·7	7 10·2	9 26·8	9 26·75	S. 2 30+2 16·55				
4891	14 41 58·5	10 20·0	10 16·5	10 20·3	10 20·15	N. 4 40—0 3·65				
4916	14 46 54·7	11 1·9	11 25·3	11 2·0	11 1·95	S. 1 15+0 23·35				
Anon.	14 54 12·3	10 16·9	14 3·4	10 16·8	10 16·85	S. 0 5—3 20·55				
Anon.	14 58 23·8	10 30·4	11 15·8	10 30·3	10 30·35	S. 0 20—0 19·45				
5032	15 9 9·0	11 0·0	9 18·5	10 33·9	10 33·95	N. 2 25—1 15·45				
5151	15 29 53·5	11 7·2	7 11·4	11 7·0	11 7·1	N. 2 45—3 29·7				
Anon.	15 35 6·8	11 0·3	6 16·9	11 0·1	11 0·2	N. 0 55—4 17·3				
Anon.	16 14 38·5	12 6·0	10 1·1	12 6·0	12 6·0	S. 0 50+2 4·9				
5735	16 55 16·4	9 28·2	9 10·2	9 28·1	9 28·15	S. 1 5+0 17·95				
5817	17 7 39·2	10 4·0	9 19·6	10 3·8	10 3·9	S. 0 30+0 18·3	27·976	61·9	62·6	61·7
6414	18 43 26·0	9 27·6	7 19·4	9 27·7	9 27·65	N. 1 5—2 9·25				
6489	18 53 27·7	10 1·0	14 28·4	10 0·8	10 0·9	N. 1 50+4 27·5				
6525	18 58 29·5	10 18·5	12 24·2	10 18·8	10 18·65	N. 3 5+2 5·55	27·940	60·8	61·2	60·6

FACE OF SECTOR WEST.

Number of B.A.C.	Time by Chronometer.	Mier. for Plumb-line on Dot.	Mier. for Observation of Star.	Mier. for Plumb-line on Dot.	Mean of Mier. for Plumb-line on Dot.	Star's Apparent Zenith Distance	Barom.	Attd.	Upper.	Lower.
5374	16 2 1·5	11 5·6	15 11·5	11 5·4	11 5·5	N. 3 0—4 6·0				
5588	16 34 18·0	11 7·3	12 5·4	11 7·4	11 7·35	N. 0 10—0 32·05				
5881	17 18 4·4	11 0·0	11 31·8	11 0·0	11 0·0	N. 2 15—0 31·8				
5915	17 23 41·0	12 5·4	14 9·7	12 5·2	12 5·3	S. 5 0+2 4·4				
6016	17 39 44·0	9 0·3	10 20·8	9 0·4	9 0·35	N. 0 20—1 20·45				
6074	17 49 45·0	9 30·4	11 33·3	9 30·5	9 30·45	N. 1 45—2 2·85				
6115	17 56 27·8	9 21·1	5 5·0	9 21·3	9 21·2	N. 1 30+4 16·2				
6145	18 0 42·4	9 19·8	13 13·7	9 20·0	9 19·9	N. 1 15—3 27·8				
6186	18 7 44·2	10 30·1	11 13·8	10 30·3	10 30·2	S. 4 50+0 17·6				
6233	18 14 29·4	9 24·5	8 19·5	9 24·6	9 24·55	S. 2 30—1 5·05				
6725	18 20 26·8	9 25·8	11 4·8	9 26·0	9 25·9	S. 1 10+1 12·9				
6285	18 21 30·5	9 26·0	5 3·7	9 25·6	9 25·8	S. 1 10—4 22·1				

MAY 31.—No. 1802, 15 seconds past the middle wire when bisected.—Owing to the difference in temperature between the upper and lower thermometers, the micrometer run from 2° 10′ to 2° 15′ was taken, and found to be 8ʳ 30ᵈ, 53.

☿ MAY 31, 1843.—FACE OF SECTOR WEST—(continued).

Number of B.A.C.	Time by Chronometer.	Micr. for Plumb-line on Dot.	Micr. for Observation of Star.	Micr. for Plumb-line on Dot.	Mean of Micr. for Plumb-line on Dot.	Star's Apparent Zenith Distance.	Barom.	Thermometers. Attd.	Upper.	Lower.
	h m s	rev. pts.	rev. pts.	rev. pts.	rev. pts.	° ' rev. pts.	in.			
6305	18 24 23·5	9 25·6	9 12·2	9 25·5	9 25·55	S. 1 10—0 13·35				
6639	19 17 45·8	10 1·8	10 5·6	10 1·8	10 1·8	N. 1 55—0 3·8				

♃ JUNE 1, 1843.

Number of B.A.C.	Time by Chronometer.	Micr. for Plumb-line on Dot.	Micr. for Observation of Star.	Micr. for Plumb-line on Dot.	Mean of Micr. for Plumb-line on Dot.	Star's Apparent Zenith Distance.	Barom.	Thermometers. Attd.	Upper.	Lower.
1802	5 34 38·4	10 32·0	14 16·8	10 31·7	10 31·85	S. 2 10+3 18·95	27·900	81·9	75·7	75·4
4458	13 12 31·2	12 13·7	13 17·4	12 13·5	12 13·6	S. 3 55+1 3·8	27·898	62·4	62·4	62·6
4517	13 24 35·0	10 14·8	7 1·5	10 14·4	10 14·6	N. 3 10+3 13·1				
4548	13 30	10 14·5	7 5·4	10 14·5	10 14·5	N. 3 10+3 9·1				
5054	15 12 37·5	12 22·0	10 13·5	12 22·0	12 22·0	S. 3 45—2 8·5				
5817	17 7 38·0	10 10·5	12 10·5	10 10·2	10 10·35	S. 0 30+2 0·15				
6489	18 53 24·0	13 18·0	10 7·2	13 17·6	13 17·8	N. 1 50+3 10·6				
6639	19 17 47·0	12 13·3	12 17·4	12 13·5	12 13·4	N. 1 55—0 4·0	27·875	58·5	58·6	58·5

FACE OF SECTOR EAST.

Number of B.A.C.	Time by Chronometer.	Micr. for Plumb-line on Dot.	Micr. for Observation of Star.	Micr. for Plumb-line on Dot.	Mean of Micr. for Plumb-line on Dot.	Star's Apparent Zenith Distance.	Barom.	Thermometers. Attd.	Upper.	Lower.
2293	6 53 17·5	11 0·55	15 19·95	11 0·60	11 0·58	N. 3 10+4 19·37				
4784	14 19 54·0	10 0·4	12 3·3	10 0·4	10 0·4	N. 3 10+2 2·9				
Anon.	14 24 52·2	9 22·4	11 14·2	9 22·5	9 22·45	S. 0 40—1 25·75				
Anon.	14 58 25·5	10 13·6	10 32·3	10 13·4	10 13·5	S. 0 20—0 18·8				
6145	18 0 51·5	12 19·7	10 6·1	12 19·9	12 19·8	N. 1 15—2 13·7				
6186	18 7 46·4	11 8·9	12 7·2	11 8·7	11 8·8	S. 4 50—0 32·4				
6233	18 14 34·5	15 9·9	17 33·2	15 10·2	15 10·05	S. 2 30—2 23·15				
6275	18 20 33·5	10 29·9	10 31·3	10 29·7	10 29·8	S. 1 10—0 1·5				

♄ JUNE 3, 1843.

Number of B.A.C.	Time by Chronometer.	Micr. for Plumb-line on Dot.	Micr. for Observation of Star.	Micr. for Plumb-line on Dot.	Mean of Micr. for Plumb-line on Dot.	Star's Apparent Zenith Distance.	Barom.	Thermometers. Attd.	Upper.	Lower.
4458	13 12 41·0	10 16·9	10 29·7	10 16·9	10 16·9	S. 3 55—0 12·8	27·978	54·3	55·2	54·3
4517	13 24 47·0	10 29·0	15 24·3	10 29·2	10 29·1	N. 3 10+4 29·2				
4548	13 30 51·5	10 29·1	15 20·4	10 29·3	10 29·2	N. 3 10+4 25·2				
4579	13 37 41·5	10 9·5	7 6·1	10 9·5	10 9·5	S. 0 15+3 3·4				
4623	13 43 41·7	10 9·5	10 30·0	10 8·8	10 9·15	S. 0 15—0 20·85				
4719	14 6 53·5	10 6·6	10 28·6	10 6·5	10 6·55	N. 3 25+0 22·05				
4784	14 19 56·5	10 20·7	12 22·8	10 20·5	10 20·6	N. 3 10+2 2·2				
4891	14 42 2·5	10 16·5	10 12·7	10 16·7	10 16·6	N. 4 40—0 3·9				
4916	14 47 1·0	9 8·3	9 31·4	9 8·6	9 8·45	S. 1 15—0 22·95				
Anon.	14 54 19·6	9 0·1	12 20·7	9 0·2	9 0·15	S. 0 5—3 20·55				
5054	15 12 46·5	8 29·8	12 20·1	8 29·8	8 29·8	S. 3 45—3 24·3				
5151	15 29 59·5	11 2·8	7 6·7	11 2·6	11 2·7	N. 2 45—3 30·0	27·975	55·6	53·7	55·4
Anon.	15 35 14·5	11 1·7	6 18·0	11 1·3	11 1·5	N. 0 55—4 17·5				
5227	15 41 56·0	10 12·3	9 26·8	10 12·4	10 12·35	S. 1 10+0 19·55				
5272	15 48 10·0	11 18·7	8 11·6	11 19·4	11 19·05	N. 3 15—3 7·45				
5374	16 2 15·2	11 24·4	8 33·7	11 24·4	11 24·4	N. 3 0—2 24·7				
5435	16 9 35·5	10 14·6	14 4·0	10 14·3	10 14·45	N. 1 25+3 23·55				
5588	16 34 31·0	9 33·8	10 16·2	9 33·8	9 33·8	N. 0 10+0 16·4				
5632	16 40 56·0	10 7·7	7 5·3	10 7·4	10 7·55	S. 2 0+3 2·25				
5735	16 55 26·5	10 18·3	9 33·7	10 18·4	10 18·35	S. 1 15+0 18·05				
5817	17 7 48·5	10 17·5	9 31·5	10 17·4	10 17·45	S. 0 30+0 19·95				
5881	17 18 18·0	10 13·9	10 30·3	10 14·0	10 13·95	N. 2 15+0 16·35				
6016	17 39 55·5	11 9·7	11 4·1	11 10·0	11 9·85	N. 0 20—0 5·75				
6115	17 56 41·0	10 1·4	15 33·6	10 1·5	10 1·45	N. 1 30+5 32·15				
6145	18 0 55·5	10 0·6	7 22·4	10 0·6	10 0·6	N. 1 15—2 12·2				
6186	18 7 54·5	9 24·3	10 22·0	9 23·7	9 24·0	S. 4 50—0 32·0				
6233	18 14 41·0	9 22·4	12 11·0	9 22·5	9 22·45	S. 2 30—2 22·55				

June 1.—4548, bisected 4 seconds before passing the middle wire.
  3.—At 17ʰ 49ᵐ found a cob-web extending from the plumb-line shade to the plumb-line.—Beautiful definition.

♄ June 3, 1843 —Face of Sector East—(continued).

Number of B.A.C.	Time by Chronometer	Micr. for Plumb-line on Dot.	Micr. for Observation of Star.	Micr. for Plumb-line on Dot.	Mean of Micr. for Plumb-line on Dot.	Star's Apparent Zenith Distance.	Barom.	Thermometers.		
								Attd.	Lower.	Upper.
	h m s	rev. pts.	rev. pts.	rev. pts.	rev. pts.	° ′ rev. pts.	in.			
0285	18 21 43·5	9 24·7	15 27·6	9 24·7	9 24·7	S. 1 10—6 2·9				
6305	18 24 36·0	9 24·8	11 19·1	9 24·8	9 24·8	S. 1 10—1 28·3				
6414	18 43 34·5	10 1·4	7 25·4	10 1·5	10 1·45	N. 1 5—2 10·05				
6525	18 58 35·5	11 17·9	13 23·7	11 18·1	11 18·0	N. 3 5+2 5·7				
6639	19 17 58·0	9 20·4	11 8·0	9 29·4	9 29·4	N. 1 55+1 12·6	27·932	54·1	54 9	54·4

☉ June 4, 1843.— Face of Sector West.

Number of B.A.C.	Time by Chronometer	Micr. for Plumb-line on Dot.	Micr. for Observation of Star.	Micr. for Plumb-line on Dot.	Mean of Micr. for Plumb-line on Dot.	Star's Apparent Zenith Distance.	Barom.	Thermometers.		
								Attd.	Lower.	Upper.
4458	13 12 40·5	11 10·6	12 14·7	11 11·0	11 10·8	S. 3 55+1 3·9				
4517	13 24 43·0	8 23·5	5 10·5	8 23·6	8 23·55	N. 3 10+3 13·05				
4548	13 30 47·5	8 23·5	5 13·6	8 23·5	8 23·5	N. 3 10+3 9·9				
4579	13 37 40·5	10 26·8	15 11·6	10 26·8	10 26·8	S. 0 15+4 18·8				
4623	13 43 40·5	10 26·8	11 21·8	10 27·0	10 26·9	S. 0 15+0 28·9				
4852	14 34 57·8	10 11·5	14 12·7	10 11·6	10 11·55	S. 2 30+4 1·15	27·842	59·9	60·8	59·8
4891	14 42 0·0	8 30·7	10 14·8	8 30·4	8 30·55	N. 4 40—1 18·25				
4916	14 46	10 21·9	11 14·9	10 21·7	10 21·8	S. 1 15+0 27·1				
Anon.	14 54 18·0	10 20·2	8 14·2	10 19·2	10 19·7	S. 0 5—2 5·5				
5054	15 12 45·3	12 8·3	10 0·5	12 8·7	12 8·5	S. 3 45—2 8·0				
5151	15 29 56·0	9 30·1	15 17·5	9 30·1	9 30·1	N. 2 45—5 11·4				
Anon.	15 35 10·7	10 5·9	16 3·4	10 5·7	10 5·8	N. 0 55—5 31·6				
5227	15 41 53·0	10 24·7	12 24·8	10 24·3	10 24·5	S. 1 10+2 0·3				
5272	15 48 6·5	11 2·7	15 24·7	11 2·3	11 2·5	N. 3 15—4 22·2				
5374	16 2 12·5	10 12·5	14 19·8	10 12·5	10 12·5	N. 3 0—4 7·3				
5435	16 10 32·0	10 15·5	8 5·3	10 14·6	10 15·05	N. 1 25+2 9·75				
5632	16 40 53·5	10 26·4	15 9·4	10 26·4	10 26·4	S. 2 0+4 17·0				
5735	16 55 24·5	10 23·6	12 23·7	10 23·6	10 23·6	S. 1 55+2 0·1				
5817	17 7 46·0	11 2·3	13 1·4	11 2·4	11 2·35	S. 0 30+1 33·05	27·830	57·7	58·3	57·7
5881	17 18 14·7	10 29·7	11 26·2	10 29·8	10 29·75	N. 2 15—0 30·45				
6016	17 39 53·5	10 23·8	12 9·4	10 23·6	10 23·7	N. 0 20—1 19·7				
6145	18 0 53·0	12 3·1	15 30·2	12 3·2	12 3·15	N. 1 15—3 27·05				
6186	18 7 54·5	11 33·3	12 16·7	11 32·8	11 33·05	S. 4 50+0 17·65				
6233	18 14 38·5	10 12·0	9 5·0	10 12·5	10 12·25	S. 2 30—1 7·25				
6275	18 20	10 0·9	11 13·8	10 0·9	10 0·9	S. 1 10+1 12·9				
6305	18 24 33·5	10 0·9	9 21·6	10 0·8	10 0·85	S. 1 10—0 13·25				
6414	18 43 30·7	11 16·8	15 6·8	11 16·8	11 16·8	N. 1 5—3 24·0				
6489	18 53 31·5	11 19·8	8 7·8	11 19·8	11 19·8	N. 1 50+3 12·0				
6639	19 17 55·2	12 1·0	12 3·0	12 1·2	12 1·1	N. 1 55—0 1·9	27·820	57·7	58·5	57·8

June 4.—No. 6275.—Bisected 10 seconds past the middle wire.

 5.—Took down the Sector.

UNREDUCED OBSERVATIONS

MADE WITH

BRADLEY'S ZENITH SECTOR

ON

THE KAMIES BERG, CLANWILLIAM DISTRICT;

IN

JULY AND AUGUST, 1843.

♂ JULY 25, 1843.—FACE OF SECTOR EAST.

Number of B.A.C.	Time by Chronometer.	Micr. for Plumb-line on Dot.	Micr. for Observation of Star.	Micr. for Plumb-line on Dot.	Mean of Micr. for Plumb-line on Dot.	Star's Apparent Zenith Distance	Barom.	Attd.	Upper.	Lower.
	h m s	rev. pts.	rev. pts.	rev. pts.	rev. pts.	° ' rev. pts.	in.			
4852	14 33 5·2	8 3·8	11 24·5	8 3·7	8 3·75	S. 4 10—3 20·75				42·2
4891	14 40 11·0	11 6·0	8 11·2	11 5·7	11 5·85	N. 3 5—2 28·65				
4916	14	9 10·4	7 7·3	9 10·6	9 10·5	S. 2 50+2 3·2				
Anon.	14 52 27·5	10 31·3	11 26·3	10 31·5	10 31·4	S. 1 40—0 28·9				
Anon.	14 56 42·0	10 27·6	8 21·9	10 27·6	10 27·6	S. 1 55+2 5·7				
5032	15 7 22·2	11 6·7	15 30·2	11 7·0	11 6·85	N. 0 45+4 23·35				
5151	15 28 6·5	10 8·9	12 19·0	10 9·2	10 9·05	N. 1 5+2 9·95				
Anon.	15 33 21·2	9 30·7	11 18·6	9 30·8	9 30·75	S. 0 45—1 21·85				
5227	15 40 2·4	9 12·4	5 32·4	9 12·8	9 12·6	S. 2 45+3 14·2				
5272	15 46 17·8	11 13·7	14 12·2	11 13·5	11 13·6	N. 1 35+2 32·6				
5374	16 0 23·5	11 8·5	14 23·3	11 8·7	11 8·6	N. 1 20+3 14·7				
5435	16 8 42·4	11 1·4	12 0·5	11 1·7	11 1·55	S. 0 10—0 32·95				
5498	16 18 54·8	11 24·7	15 10·8	11 24·5	11 24·6	N. 4 15+3 20·2				
5588	16 32 37·0	9 2·0	6 26·4	9 1·8	9 1·9	S. 1 25+2 9·5				
5632	16 39 3·0	9 14·7	12 17·7	9 14·5	9 14·6	S. 3 40—3 3·1				
5735	16 53 33·2	9 10·5	5 32·1	9 10·7	9 10·6	S. 3 30+3 12·5				
5817	17 5 55·3	9 14·7	6 4·0	9 14·9	9 14·8	S. 2 5+3 10·8				
5881	17 16 25·5	9 27·5	7 17·7	9 28·2	9 27·85	N. 0 40—2 10·15				
5960	17 28 51·5	9 21·5	10 20·9	9 21·2	9 21·35	S. 1 45—0 33·55				
5964	17 29 49·5		8 27·3	9 21·2		S. 1 45+0 27·9				
6016	17 38 3·5	9 19·6	6 21·5	9 19·6	9 19·6	S. 1 15+2 32·1				39·8
6074	17 48 6·5	9 25·4	15 8·8	9 26·2	9 25·8	N. 0 5+5 17·0				
6115	17 54 49·0	9 22·4	12 27·9	9 22·7	9 22·55	S. 0 5—3 5·35				
6145	17 59 29·5	9 0·9	12 30·5	9 0·9	9 0·9	S. 0 25—3 29·6				
6285	18 19 51·0		12 10·2	9 1·8	9 1·73	S. 2 45—3 8·47				
6305	18 22 43·0	9 1·8	8 1·0	9 1·6	9 1·73	S. 2 45+1 0·73				39·5
6414	18 41 42·3	9 10·8	13 5·4	9 10·8	9 10·8	S. 0 35—3 28·6				
6489	18 51 43·0	9 16·4	11 17·1	9 16·2	9 16·2	N. 0 15+2 0·8				
6525	18 56 44·5	9 24·4	9 3·0	9 24·3	9 24·35	N. 1 30—0 21·35				
6639	19 16 7·0	10 22·0	9 7·6	10 21·6	10 21·8	N. 0 20—1 14·2				
Anon.	19 20 19·5		11 23·3	14 29·7		N. 0 35—3 6·4				
6753	19 34 32·6	12 10·7	13 19·4	12 10·5	12 10·6	S. 0 55—1 8·8				
6877	19 53 26·5	9 12·5	14 6·8	9 12·3	9 12 4	S. 2 10—4 28·4				
6948	20 5 10·5		8 8·6	11 2·1		S. 0 5+2 27·5				
7026	20 16 1·5		11 30·1	16 17·0		N 0 50—4 20·9				
7057	20 20 26·0		13 16·4	15 0·3		N. 0 45—1 17·9				
Anon.	20 32 48·5		11 21·0	13 26·0		N. 0 25—2 5·0				
7207	20 39 12·2	9 26·9	11 17·2	9 27·0	9 26·95	S. 4 0—1 24·25				
7557		9 27·7	15 11·4	9 28·0	9 27·85	S. 3 25—5 17·55				
7657	21 50 55·3	9 3·1	9 6·9	9 3·6	9 3·35	N. 1 10+0 3·55				
Anon.	21 54 49·0		10 1·9	8 26·0		N. 1 10+1 9·9				41·0
7842	22 21 38·5	9 3·8	6 14·7	9 3·8	9 3·8	S. 2 45+2 23·1				
7966	22 42 51·0	9 2·3	9 5·5	9 2·3	9 2·3	S. 3 20—0 3·2				
7992	22 48 3·5	10 28·4	11 7·2	10 28 3	10 28·35	S. 0 5—0 12·85				
1802	5 32 58·8	10 0·5	14 17·4	10 0·4	10 0·45	S. 3 50—4 16·95				
2293	6 51 31·8	9 30·5	12 2·3	9 31·3	9 30 9	N. 1 35+2 5·4				

♀ JULY 26, 1843.—FACE OF SECTOR WEST.

Number of B.A.C.	Time by Chronometer.	Micr. for Plumb-line on Dot.	Micr. for Observation of Star.	Micr. for Plumb-line on Dot.	Mean of Micr. for Plumb-line on Dot.	Star's Apparent Zenith Distance	Barom.	Attd.	Upper.	Lower.
4458	13 11 6·2	8 11·1	12 13·2	8 11·8	8 11·45	S. 5 30+4 1·75				
4546	13 28 55·0	6 28·2	6 17·4	6 28·5	6 28·5	N. 1 35+0 11·1				
4579	13 35 56·5	8 28·3	7 14·0	8 28·3	8 28·3	S. 1 55—1 14·3				
4623	13 41 56·5	9 25·8	13 19·7	9 25·7	9 25·75	S. 1 50+3 27·95				
4686	13 56 46·5	10 22·1	10 21·2	10 22·5	10 22·3	S. 5 15—0 1·1	25·210	51·8	54·3	51·8

July 25.—No. 4916.—Time not noted.
    No. 5498.—Chronometer not audible on account of the wind.
    No. 6145.—Nearly leaving the field.
    No. 7557.—30 seconds past the middle wire when bisected.
July 26 —No. 4546.—Very faint.

No. 5435.—Double. The preceding observed.
No. 6074.—Double. The following observed.
Nos. 6285 & 6305.—Clamp not moved while observing these stars.
No. 4623.—Double. The preceding observed.

☿ JULY 26, 1843.—FACE OF SECTOR WEST—(*continued*).

Number of B.A.C.	Time by Chronometer.	Micr. for Plumb-line on Dot.	Micr. for Observation of Star.	Micr. for Plumb-line on Dot.	Mean of Micr. for Plumb-line on Dot.	Star's Apparent Zenith Distance.	Barom.	Thermometers.		
								Attd.	Upper.	Lower.
	h m s	rev. pts.	rev. pts.	rev. pts.	rev. pts.	o ′ rev. pts.	in.			
4719	14 4 58·0	10 17·6	14 8·9	10 17·3	10 17·45	N. 1 50—3 25·45				
4784	14 18 1·5	10 6·3	12 18·7	10 6·3	10 6·3	N. 1 35—2 12·4				
Anon.	14 23	10 32·3	13 23·5	10 32·1	10 32·2	S. 2 15+2 25·3				
4852	14 33 21·0	10 5·5	8 6·9	10 5·6	10 5·55	S. 4 10—1 32·65				
4891	14 40 4·5	9 23·2	14 5·3	9 23·2	9 23·2	N. 3 5—4 16·1				
4916	14 45 21·0	9 21·3	13 15·6	9 21·4	9 21·35	S. 2 50+3 28·25				
Anon.	14 52 4·0	9 23·4	10 19·0	9 23·4	9 23·4	S. 1 40+0 29·6				
Anon.	14 56 46·0	9 13·7	13 10·9	9 13·8	9 13·75	S. 1 55+3 31·15				
5032	15 7 21·5	9 25·4	6 24·5	9 25·6	9 25·5	N. 0 45+3 1·0				
5054	15 16 12·2	10 29·1	11 21·3	10 29·3	10 29·2	S. 5 20+0 26·1				
5151	15 28 5·5	9 32·9	9 12·3	9 32·7	9 32·8	N. 1 5+0 20·5				
Anon.	15 33 6·0	10 14·4	10 14·5	10 14·4	10 14·4	S. 0 45+0 0·1				
5227	15 40 13·7	11 9·6	16 12·6	11 9·3	11 9·45	S. 2 45+5 3·15				
5272	15 46 15·5	10 2·7	8 27·1	10 2·8	10 2·75	N. 1 35+1 9·65				
5374	16 0 21·5	8 23·7	6 31·8	8 23·6	8 23·65	N. 1 20+1 25·85	25·300	48·7	48·9	48·6
5435	16 8 45·2	9 19·7	10 10·4	9 19·6	9 19·65	S. 0 10+0 24·75				
Anon.	16 13 5·0	9 31·4	16 19·5	9 31·6	9 31·5	S. 2 25+6 22·0				
5498	16 18 44·2	8 19·2	6 19·2			N. 4 15+2 0·0				
5588	16 32 44·5	8 11·4	12 9·7	8 11·0	8 11·2	S. 1 25+3 32·5				
5632	16 39 17·0	9 12·2	7 33·0	9 12·2	9 12·2	S. 3 40—1 13·2				
5735	16 53 47·0	9 27·3	14 29·5	9 27·6	9 27·45	S. 3 30+5 2·05				
5817	17 6 4·5	8 31·2	13 31·8	8 31·5	8 31·35	S. 2 5+5 0·45	25·300	47·5	48·2	47·2
5881	17 16 26·5	8 8·6	12 6·6	8 9·2	8 8·9	N. 0 40—3 31·7				
5960	17 29 0·0	8 10·5	8 33·5			S. 1 45+0 23·0				
5964	17 29 57·5		10 28·1	8 10·8		S. 1 45+2 17·3				
6016	17 38 10·0	9 5·0	13 26·3	9 5·5	9 5·25	S. 1 15+4 21·05				
6074	17 48 8·5	9 11·4	5 16·8	9 11·2	9 11·3	N. 0 5+3 28·5				
6115	17 54 52·0	9 23·3	8 7·2	9 22·9	9 23·1	S. 0 5—1 15·9				
6145	17 59 7·8	9 28·7	7 24·0	9 28·2	9. 28·45	S. 0 25—2 4·45				
6233	18 13 3·5	10 20·7	12 16·4	10 20·6	10 20·65	S. 4 5+1′29·75				
6275	18 16 58·5	10 11·3	14 26·1		10 11·2	S. 2 45+4 14·9				
6285	18 20 2·5		8 26·0		10 11·2	S. 2 45—1 19·2				
6305	18 22 55·0	10 11·0	12 33·6	10 11·3	10 11·2	S. 2 45+2 22·4				
6414	18 41 46·5	10 18·8	8 12·0	10 19·3	10 19·05	S. 0 35—2 7·05				
6489	18 51 45·2	11 26·4	11 14·8	11 26·0	11 26·2	N. 0 15+0 11·4				
6525	18 56 42·5	10 31·7	13 7·7	10 31·4	10 31·55	N. 1 30—2 10·15				
6639	19 16 8·2	8 29·1	11 30·8	8 29·2	8 29·15	N. 0 20—3 1·65				
Anon.	19 20 20·5	8 27·6	13 21·2	8 26·8	8 27·2	N. 0 35—4 28·0				
6753	19 34 38·2	9 31·2	10 12·3	9 33·8	9 32·5	S. 0 55+0 13·8				
6877	19 53 35·5	10 18·3	7 11·9	10 18·5	10 18·4	S. 2 10—3 0·5				
6948	20 5 14·5	10 0·5	14 16·3	10 0·3	10 0·4	S. 0 5+4 15·9				
7026	20 16 32·5	9 17·4	15 27·8	9 17·6	9 17·5	N. 0 50—6 10·3	25·310	46·4	46·4	46·4
7057	20 20 26·4	9 1·3	12 4·8	9 2·1	9 1·7	N. 0 45—3 3·1				
Anon.	20 32 49·5	8 12·5	12 3·4	8 12·6	8 12·55	N. 0 25—3 24·85				
7207	20 39 27·0	8 1·1	8 0·8	8 2·4	8 1·75	S. 4 0—0 0·95				
Anon.	20 52 36·0	7 15·3	11 8·9	7 15·1	7 15·2	N. 0 40—3 27·7	25·310	45·1	44·6	45·1
7557	21 34 52·0	9 8·0	5 16·4	9 9·0	9 8·5	S. 3 25—3 26·1				
7657	21 50 54·0	8 22·9	10 7·4	8 23·0	8 22·95	N. 1 10—1 18·45				
Anon.	21 54 45·5	8 23·0	9 3·3	8 23·0	8 23·0	N. 1 10—0 14·3				
7842	22 21 49·0	9 32·8	14 11·8	9 32·7	9 32·75	S. 2 45+4 13·05				
7966	22 42	10 5·2	11 26·2	10 5·3	10 5·25	S. 3 20+1 20·95		43·2	43·0	43·2
7992	22 48 7·0	9 9·8	10 19·5	9 10·2	9 10·0	S. 0 5+1 9·5				
2293	6 51 30·5	11 4·9	10 22·5	11 4·3	11 4·6	N. 1 35+0 16·1				

Anon. 16ʰ. 13ᵐ.—Double. The interval bisected.
No. 5964.—Plumb-line vibrating from wind.
No. 7026.—Bisected when 22 seconds past the middle wire.
No. 7966.—Time not noted.

Good definition this night.

♃ July 27, 1843.—Face of Sector East.

Number of B.A.C.	Time by Chronometer.	Micr. for Plumb-line on Dot.	Micr. for Observation of Star.	Micr. for Plumb-line on Dot.	Mean of Micr. for Plumb-line on Dot.	Star's Apparent Zenith Distance.	Barom.	Attd.	Upper.	Lower.
	h m s	rev. pts	rev. pts	rev. pts	rev. pts	° ʹ rev. pts	in.			
4891	14 40 15·7	11 19·1	8 24·9	11 19·0	11 19·05	N. 3 5—2 28·15				
4916	14 45 18·2	8 4·9	6 0·7	8 4·8	8 4·85	S. 2 50+2 4·15				
Anon.	14 52 34·7	9 16·0	10 10·4	9 16·3	9 16·15	S. 1 40—0 28·25	25·200	45·0		45·1
Anon.	14 56 46·0	10 13·0	8 5·8	10 13·0	10 13·0	S. 1 55+2 7·2				
5032	15 7 28·3	10 9·0	14 31·5	10 8·8	10 8·9	N. 0 45+4 22·6				
5054	15 11		11 15·1	10 18·2		S. 5 20—0 30·9				
5151	15 28 12·5	11 12·0	13 21·2	11 12 3	11 12·15	N. 1 5+2 9·05	25·200	44·2	47·1	44·3
Anon.	15 33 27·8	10 29·4	12 17·2	10 29·2	10 29·3	S. 0 45—1 21·9				
5227	15 40 10·7	8 31·4	5 18·8	8 31·3	8 31·35	S. 2 45+3 12·55				
5272	15 46 23·3	10 12·0	13 12·8	10 14·0	10 13·0	N. 1 35+2 33·8				
5374	16 0 28·7	10 16·7	13 31·0	10 16·6	10 16·65	N. 1 20+3 14·35				
5435	16 8 48·7	10 23·8	11 22·3	10 23·9	10 23·85	S. 0 10—0 32·45				
Anon.	16 13 2·5	10 27·7	5 27·3	10 27·8	10 27·75	S. 2 25+5 0·45				
5498	16 18 59·8	11 3·0	14 24·0	11 3·2	11 3·1	N. 4 15+3 20·9				
5588	16 32 45·2	10 10·2	7 33·3	10 10·2	10 10·2	S. 1 25+2 10·9				
5632	16 39 12·0	10 11·3	13 13·4	10 11·0	10 11·15	S. 3 40—3 2·25				
5735	16 53 41·5	9 26·7	6 14·0	9 26·6	9 26·65	S. 3 30+3 12·65				
5817	17 6 3·0	9 23·5	6 11·8	9 23·3	9 23·4	S. 2 5+3 11·6				
5881	17 16 31·5	9 19·8	7 9·1	9 19·3		N. 0 40—2 9·95				
5960	17 28 59·2	8 27·8	0 27·5		8 27·65	S. 1 45—0 33·85				
5964	17 29 56·2		7 33·0	8 27·5	8 27·65	S. 1 45+0 28·65				
6016	17 38 10·2	8 25·3	5 26·8	8 25·3	8 25·3	S. 1 15+2 32·5				
6074	17 48 12·5	8 23·8	14 6·8	8 24·4	8 24·1	N. 0 5+6 16·7				
6115	17 54 55·5	8 21·6	11 26·3	8 21·7	8 21·65	S. 0 5—3 4·65				
6145	17 59 10·5	9 15·0	13 7·2	9 15·2	9 15·1	S. 0 25—3 26·1				
6233	18 13	8 3·5	7 31·7	8 3·8	8 3·65	S. 4 5+0 5·95				
6275	18 18 55·5	7 18·3	4 24·2		7 18·2	S. 2 45+2 28·0				
6285	18 19 59·2		10 26·0	7 18·3	7 18·2	S. 2 45—3 7·8				
6305	18 22 52·0		6 17·4	7 18·0	7 18·2	S. 2 45+1 0·8				
6414	18 41 49·0	8 15·7	12 10·2	8 15·7	8 15·7	S. 0 35—3 28·5				
6489	18 51 49·5	9 8·0	11 8·7	9 8·1	9 8·05	N. 0 15+1 34·65				
6525	18 56 50·0	10 11·2	9 24·1	10 11·7	10 11·45	N. 1 30—0 21·35				
6639	19 16 13·4	10 5·0	8 24·9	10 4·8	10 4·9	N. 0 20—1 14·0	25·196	41·5	41·7	41·4
Anon.	19 20 25·3	11 11·3	8 4·8	11 11·1	11 11·2	N. 0 35—3 6·4				
6753	19 34 39·5	10 0·5	11 8·7	10 0·5	10 0·5	S. 0 55—1 8·2				
6877	19 53 34·0	9 22·5	14 17·0	9 22·3	9 22·4	S. 2 10—4 28·6				
6948	20 5 17·2	10 0·0	7 6·3	9 33·7	9 33·85	S. 0 5+2 27·55				
7026	20 16 6·5	10 10·3	5 23·5	10 11·1	10 10·7	N. 0 50—4 21·2				
7057	20 20 31·5	11 6·7	9 24·7	11 6·7	11 6·7	N. 0 45—1 16·0				
Anon.	20 32 54·5	13 7·5	11 3·8	13 7·5	13 7·5	N. 0 25—2 3·7				
7207	20 39 21·5	10 16·5	12 6·8	10 16·3	10 16·3	S. 4 0—1 24·4				
Anon.	21 0 16·0		8 33·7	7 1·3		0 0+1 32·4				
7386	21 7 35·5	8 21·8	13 26·2	8 22·0	8 21·9	S. 2 30—5 4·3				
Anon.	21 24 51·5	12 1·3	9 33·6	12 1·4	12 1·35	0 0+2 1·75	25·200	41·4	41·5	41·4
7557	21 34 40·0	9 23·3	15 5·8	9 23·4	9 23·35	S. 3 25—5 16·45				
7842	22 21 46·0	10 12·6	7 22·4	10 12·4	10 12·5	S. 2 45+2 24·1				
7992	22 48 9·4	11 25·2	12 5·5	11 26·2	11 25·7	S. 0 5—0 13·8	25·190	40·1	40·6	40·0
2293	6 51	12 6·0	14 11·7	12 5·8	12 5·9	N. 1 35+2 5·8	25·250	40·5	43·3	40·6

♀ July 28, 1843.—Face of Sector West.

Number of B.A.C.	Time by Chronometer.	Micr. for Plumb-line on Dot.	Micr. for Observation of Star.	Micr. for Plumb-line on Dot.	Mean of Micr. for Plumb-line on Dot.	Star's Apparent Zenith Distance.	Barom.	Attd.	Upper.	Lower.
4686	13 56 52·2	9 20·9	9 19·8	9 20·5	9 20·7	S. 5 15—0 0·9				
Anon.	14 5 4·6	8 20·7	12 12·0	8 20·7	8 20·7	N. 1 50—3 25·3				
4784	14 18 8·2	8 27·7	11 6·1	8 27·7	8 27·7	N. 1 35—2 12·4				

July 27.—No. 5054.—Bisected when 10 seconds past the middle wire.
No. 6233.—Hurried. Lamp going out. Time not noted.
Nos. 6275, 6285, & 6305.—Clamp not touched while observing these stars.
Anon. 21ʰ. 0ᵐ.—Bisected when 15 seconds past the middle wire.
Several stars lost this night owing to fog.

♀ JULY 28, 1843.—FACE OF SECTOR WEST—(continued).

Number of B.A.C.	Time by Chronometer.	Micr. for Plumb-line on Dot.	Micr. for Observation of Star.	Micr. for Plumb-line on Dot.	Mean of Micr. for Plumb-line on Dot.	Star's Apparent Zenith Distance.	Barom.	Thermometers.		
								Attd.	Upper.	Lower.
	h m s	rev. pts.	rev. pts.	rev. pts.	rev. pts.	o ' rev. pts.	in.			
Anon.	14 23 23·0	9 26·0	12 15·6	9 26·0	9 26·0	S. 2 15+2 23·6				
4852	14 33 27·0	10 0·5	8 2·0	10 0·5	10 0·5	S. 4 10−1 32·5				
4891	14 40 10·5	10 19·2	15 2·6	10 19·0	10 19·1	N. 3 5−4 17·5				
Anon.	14 45	11 18·9	15 12·6	11 18·8	11 18·85	S. 2 50+3 27·75				
Anon.	14 52	10 31·8	11 26·7	10 31·4	10 31·6	S. 1 40+0 29·1				
5032	15 7	9 27·1	6 25·2	9 26·7	9 26·9	N. 0 45+3 1·7				
5054	15 11 17·7	10 15·1	11 7·8	10 14·6	10 14·85	S. 5 20+0 26·95				
5151	15 28	9 13·1	8 25·8	9 12·5	9 12·8	N. 1 5+0 21·0	25·2 0	47·3	47·7	47·3
Anon	15 33	9 23·6	9 23·6	9 23·5	9 23·55	S. 0 45+0 0·05				
5227	15 40	10 8·6	15 11·8	10 8·9	10 8·75	S. 2 45+5 3·05				
5272	15 46	9 24·0	8 13·8	9 24·5	9 24·25	N. 1 35+1 10·45				
5374	16 0	9 24·8	7 33·2	9 24·9	9 24·85	N. 1 20+1 25·65				
5435	16 8	10 0·3	10 25·6	10 0·4	10 0·35	S. 0 10+0 25·25				
Anon.	16 13	10 3·5	16 28·3	10 3·5	10 3·5	S. 2 25+6 24·8				
5498	16 18 51·5	10 24·5	8 25·2	10 24·0	10 24·25	N. 4 15+1 33·05				
Anon.	16 32	10 27·6	14 27·0	10 28·2	10 27·9	S. 1 25+3 33·1				
5632	16 39 23·1	10 32·5	9 20·2	10 33·0	10 32·75	S. 3 40−1 12·55				
5735	16 53 52·8	11 2·8	16 4·8	11 2·5	11 2·65	S. 3 30+5 2·15				
5817	17 6	8 19·0	13 19·6	8 19·0	8 19·0	S. 2 5+5 0·6				
5881	17 16	8 20·2	12 18·2	8 19·8	8 20·0	N. 0 40−3 32·2	25·210	46·0	46·4	46·1
5960	17 29	9 8·5	9 32·5		0 8·45	S. 1 45+0 24·05				
Anon.	17 29		5 13·0	9 8·4	0 8·45	S. 1 45+3 29·45				
6016	17 38	8 30·0	13 17·0	8 30·0	8 30·0	S. 1 15+4 21·0				
6074	17 48 15·5	9 1·7	5 8·8	9 1·8	9 1·75	N. 0 5+3 26·95				
6115	17 54 58·0	8 33·7	7 18·4	8 33·5	8 33·6	S. 0 5−1 15·2				
6145	17 59	9 8·0	7 4·0	9 7·8	9 7·9	S. 0 25−2 3·9				
6233	18 13 10·0	9 16·9	11 13·0	9 16·8	9 16·85	S. 4 5+1 30·15				
Anon.	18 18	9 6·3	13 23·4		9 6·4	S. 2 45+4 17·0				
6285	18 20		7 22·7	9 6·4	9 6·4	S. 2 45−1 17·7				
6305	18 22		11 30·1	9 6·5	9 6·4	S. 2 45+2 23·7				
Anon	18 41	9 3·1	6 30·3	9 3·1	9 3·1	S. 0 35−2 6·8				
6489	18 51	7 30·3	7 21·8	7 30·5	7 30·4	N. 0 15+0 8·6				
6525	18 56	9 31·8	12 8·4	9 31·6	9 31·7	N. 1 30−2 10·7				
6639	19 16	9 30·5	12 33·0	9 30·5	9 30·5	N. 0 20−3 2·5	25·200	45·0	44·8	45·0
Anon.	19 20	9 16·4	14 10·1	9 16·4	9 16·4	N. 0 35−4 27·7				
6753	19 34	9 0·0	9 13·4	8 33·8	8 33·9	S. 0 55+0 13·5				
6877	19 53	9 30·2	6 24·4	9 30·3	9 30·25	S. 2 10−3 5·85				
Anon.	20 5	8 25·4	13 8·7	8 25·3	8 25·35	S. 0 5+4 17·35				
Anon	20 16	8 26·5	15 2·6	8 26·7	8 26·6	N. 0 50−6 10·0				
Anon.	20 20	9 22·5	12 27·2	9 22·7	9 22·6	N. 0 45−3 4·6				
Anon.	20 32	10 25·8	14 17·6	10 26·5	10 26·15	N. 0 25−3 25·45				
7207	20 39 34·0	11 13·3	11 11·8	11 13·3	11 13·3	S. 4 0−0 1·5				
Anon.	20 52	7 6·5	11 0·3	7 6·5	7 6·5	N. 0 40−3 27·8				
Anon.	20 50 54·5	6 32·8	6 27·7	6 32·8	6 32·8	0 0+0 5·1				
7386	21 7	7 29·8	4 16·6	7 29·6	7 29·7	S. 2 30−3 13·1				
Anon.	21 11 42·0	7 32·1	4 33·9	7 31·4	7 31·75	N. 0 30+2 31·85	25·200	43·7	43·7	43·6
Anon.	21 24	7 30·0	11 18·8	7 30·0	7 30·0	0 0+3 22·8				
7557	21 34 58·2	9 11·7	5 19·2	9 12·2	9 11·95	S. 3 25−3 26·75				
7657	21 50	8 27·8	10 12·9	8 27·5	8 27·65	N. 1 10−1 19·25				
Anon.	21 54	8 27·7	9 9·1	8 27·8	8 27·75	N. 1 10−0 15·35				
7842	22 21	9 29·0	14 7·5	9 29·2	9 29·1	S. 2 45+4 12·4				
Anon.	22 32 30·0		10 4·3	10 11·3		N. 0 10+1 6·0				
7966	22 43 9·5	10 26·3	12 9·7	10 26·1	10 26·2	S. 3 20+1 17·5				
7992	22 48 12·2	9 33·0	11 7·8	9 32·6	9 32·8	S. 0 5+1 9·0	25·200	44·1	44·2	44·2
2293	6 51 34·8	10 16·8	9 31·6	10 16·4	10 16·6	N. 1 35+0 19·0	25·265	51·8	57·6	51·8

Anon. 17ʰ. 29ᵐ.—A group of five stars.
No. 6489.—Bisected when 10 seconds past the middle wire.
No. 6525.—No time to examine the upper dot.
Strong N. wind. Chronometer seldom heard, consequently the times of transit, generally, could not be noted.

♄ JULY 29, 1843.—FACE OF SECTOR EAST.

Number of B.A.C.	Time by Chronometer.	Micr. for Plumb-line on Dot.	Micr. for Observation of Star.	Micr. for Plumb-line on Dot.	Mean of Micr. for Plumb-line on Dot.	Star's Apparent Zenith Distance.	Barom.	Thermometers.		
	h m s	rev. pts.	rev. pts.	rev. pts.	rev. pts.	° ' rev. pts.	in.	Attd.	Upper.	Lower.
4458	13 11 0·5	10 25·7	8 12·6	10 26·0	10 25·85	S. 5 30+2 13·25	25·205	56·1	61·3	56·3
4579	13 36 3·5	11 0·7	14 5·9	11 0·6	11 0·65	N. 1 55−3 5·25				
4623	13 42 3·0	10 14·5	8 11·8	10 14·5	10 14·5	S. 1 50+2 2·7				
4686	13 56 43·0	11 19·4	13 8·3	11 18·8	11 19·1	S. 5 15−1 23·2				
Anon.	14 5 13·6	13 12·2	11 10·5	13 11·8	13 12·0	N. 1 50−2 1·5				
4784	14 18 17·0	10 5·6	9 18·8	10 7·2	10 6·5	N. 1 35−0 21·7				
4852	14 33 20·5	10 0·0	13 22·7	9 33·7	9 33·85	S. 4 10−3 22·85				
4891	14 40 24·0	11 17·5	8 25 0	11 17·5	11 17·5	N. 3 5−2 26·5				
Anon.	14 45 24·0	11 5·0	9 1·1	11 5·3	11 5·15	S. 2 50+2 4·05				
Anon.	14 52 40·2	12 9·6	13 4·4	12 9·5	12 9·55	N. 1 40−0 28·85				
Anon.	14 56 52·2	10 3·3	7 29·8	10 3·0	10 3·15	S. 1 55+2 7·35				
5032	15 7 35·4	10 4·4	14 27·8	10 4·5	10 4·45	N. 0 45+4 23·35				
5054	15 11	10 2·9	11 0·8	10 2·9	10 2·9	S. 5 20−0 31·9				
5151	15 28 19·6	11 17·4	13 27·2	11 17·8	11 17·6	N. 1 5+2 9·6				
Anon.	15 33 34·8	12 8·7	13 30·3	12 8·8	12 8·75	S. 0 45−1 21·55				
5227	15 40 17·0	10 0·1	6 20·3	10 0·0	10 0·05	S. 2 45+3 13·75				
5272	15 46 30·5	10 4·4	13 4·1	10 4·5	10 4·45	N. 1 35+2 33·65				
5374	16 0		13 13·4	9 31·7		N. 1 20+3 15·7				
5435	16 8 55·5	10 3·5	11 1·6	10 3·4	10 3·45	S. 0 10−0 32·15				
Anon.	16 13 8·8	9 12·4	13 11·3	9 12·0	9 12·2	S. 2 30−3 33·1				
5498	16 19 6·8	11 12·2	14 33·4	11 12·5	11 12·35	N. 4 15+3 21·05				
Anon.	16 32 51·6	8 26·0	6 15·7	8 25·7	8 25·85	S. 1 25+2 10·15				
5632	16 39 17·5	8 26·6	11 29·6	8 26·6	8 26·6	S. 3 40−3 3·0				
5735	16 53 48·0	8 5·2	4 27·6	8 5·2	8 5·2	S. 3 30+3 11·6				
5881	17 16 49·0	9 9·5	7 1·0	9 9·3	9 9·4	N. 0 40−2 8·4				
5960	17 29 6·0	9 5·2	10 5·3	9 5·3	9 5·3	S. 1 45−1 0·0				
Anon.	17 30 3·3		8 11·3	9 5·4	9 5·3	S. 1 45+0 28·0				
6016	17 38 17·5	9 25·4	6 27·7	9 24·8	9 25·1	S. 1 15+2 31·4				
6074	17 48 19·5	9 33·6	15 18·2	9 33·9	9 33·75	N. 0 5+5 18·45				
6115	17 55 2·3	9 30·5	13 2·9	9 30·5	9 30·5	~. 0 5−3 6·4				
6145	17 59 17·2	9 31·1	13 23·9	9 30·8	9 30·95	S. 0 25−3 26·95				
6233	18 13 3·4	9 29·7	9 24·5	9 29·6	9 29·65	N. 4 5+0 5·15				
Anon.	18 19 1·7	8 26·6	6 0·2		8 26·73	S. 2 45+2 26·53	25·250	48·6	50·0	48·4
6285	18 20 5·2		12 1·7	8 26·7	8 26 73	S. 2 45−3 8·97				
6305	18 22 55·2		7 27·5	8 26·9	8 26·73	~. 2 45+0 33·23				
Anon.	18 41 55·8	8 30·6	12 27·1	8 30·6	8 30·6	S. 0 35−3 30·5				
6489	18 51 56·4	8 19·4	10 21·2	8 19·6	8 19·5	N. 0 15+2 1·7				
6525	18 56 57·2	8 23·9	8 4·0	8 24·3	8 24·1	N. 1 30−0 20·1				
6639	19 16 20·2	8 25·6	7 12·5	8 25·7	8 25·65	N. 0 20−1 13·15				
Anon.	19 20 32·5	8 22·5	5 17·6	8 22·6	8 22·55	N. 0 35−3 4·95				
6753	19 34 46·5	9 2·3	10 12·0	9 2·3	9 2·3	S. 0 55−1 9·7				
6877	19 53 40·7	8 31·7	13 27·6	8 31·5	8 31·6	S. 2 10−4 30·0				
Anon.	20 5 24·2	9 8·0	6 16·1	9 8·3	9 8·15	S. 0 5+2 26·05				
Anon.	20 16 14·0	8 25·2	13 2·5	8 25·3	8 25·25	N. 0 45+4 11·25				
Anon.	20 20 39·6	8 25·3	7 9·3	8 25·3	8 25·3	N. 0 45−1 16·0				
Anon.	20 33 1·5	8 25·8	6 24·0	8 26·1	8 25·95	N. 0 25−2 1·95				
7207	20 39 27·5	8 14·6	10 5·5	8 14·6	8 14·6	S. 4 0−1 24·9				
Anon.	20 52 49·3	9 1·8	6 31·8	9 1·8	9 1·8	N. 0 40−2 4·0				
Anon.	20 59 59·5	8 23·6	10 21·1	8 23·5	8 23·55	0 0+1 31·55				
7386	21 7 45·0	8 17·1	13 21·8	8 17·3	8 17·2	S. 2 30−5 4·6				
Anon.	21 11 48·8	9 29·2	14 16·5	9 20·4	9 29·3	N. 0 30+4 21·2				
Anon	21 24 56·2	9 30·8	7 33·4	9 30·7	9 30·7	0 0+1 31·3				
7557	21 34 53·8	10 8·3	15 25·5	10 8·4	10 8 35	S. 3 25−5 17·15				
7657	21 51 8·2	10 24·3	10 28·1	10 24·4	10 24 35	N. 1 10+0 3·75	25·215		49·3	49·8
Anon.	21 54 59·2	10 24·3	11 32·8	10 24·4	10 24 35	N. 1 10+1 8·45				

No. 5054.—10 seconds past the middle wire when bisected.
No. 5374.—20 seconds past the middle wire when bisected.
No. 6525.—The second reading for plumb-line on dot repeated three times.
Good definition throughout the night.

♄ JULY 29, 1843.—FACE OF SECTOR EAST—(continued).

Number of B.A.C.	Time by Chronometer.	Micr. for Plumb-line on Dot.	Micr. for Observation of Star.	Micr. for Plumb-line on Dot.	Mean of Micr. for Plumb-line on Dot.	Star's Apparent Zenith Distance.	Barom.	Attd.	Upper.	Lower.
	h m s	rev. pts.	rev. pts.	rev. pts.	rev. pts.	° ' rev. pts.	In.			
7842	22 21 52·5	11 0·4	8 10·3	11 0·4	11 0·4	S. 2 45+2 24·1				
Anon.	22 32 56·5	10 25·3	13 22·5	10 25·2	10 25·25	N. 0 10+2 31·25				
7966	22 43 5·7	10 18·3	10 22·4	10 18·4	10 18·35	S. 3 20—0 4·05				
7992	22 48 17·0	10 31·4	11 12·0	10 31·6	10 31·5	S. 0 5—0 14·5				
2293	6 51 54·5	6 28·6	9 3·8	6 28·4	6 28·5	N. 1 35+2 9·3	25·250	53·2	60·4	52·2

☉ JULY 30, 1843.—FACE OF SECTOR WEST.

Number of B.A.C.	Time by Chronometer.	Micr. for Plumb-line on Dot.	Micr. for Observation of Star.	Micr. for Plumb-line on Dot.	Mean of Micr. for Plumb-line on Dot.	Star's Apparent Zenith Distance.	Barom.	Attd.	Upper.	Lower.
4579	13 36 5·7	7 31·4	6 15·1	7 31·6	7 31·5	S. 1 55—1 16·4				
4623	13 41	7 20·0	11 10·8	7 19·9	7 19·95	~. 1 50+3 24·85				
4686	13 56 49·2	8 19·8	8 17·6	8 19·8	8 19·8	S. 5 15—0 2·2				
Anon.	14 5 15·0	8 12·2	12 1·8	8 12·5	8 12·35	N. 1 50—3 23·45				
4784	14 18 16·8	8 11·0	10 21·0	8 11·1	8 11·05	N. 1 35—2 10·85				
Anon.	14 23 22·6	8 11·4	11 0·9	8 11·3	8 11·35	S. 2 15+2 23·55				
4852	14 33 25·0	9 1·0	7 2·7	9 1·6	9 1·3	S. 4 10—1 32·6	25·200	55·0	58·8	55·0
4891	14 40 21·0	8 26·8	13 7·5	8 26·9	8 26·85	N. 3 5—4 14·65				
Anon.	14 45 28·3	9 30·8	13 24·1	9 31·0	9 30·9	S. 2 50+3 27·2				
Anon.	14 52 45·0	9 28·7	13 23·8	9 29·0	9 28·85	S. 1 40+0 28·95				
Anon.	14 56 55·5	8 30·4	12 27·6	8 30·6	8 30·5	S. 1 55+3 31·1				
5032	15 7 35·8	8 1·2	4 33·6	8 1·0	8 1·1	N. 0 45+3 1·5				
5054	15 11 15·2		9 28·5	9 3·9		S. 5 20+0 24·6				
5151	15 28 20·0	8 22·6	8 1·3	8 22·2	8 22·4	N. 1 5+0 21·1				
Anon.	15 33 37·0	8 19·6	8 19·4	8 19·5	8 19·55	S. 0 45—0 0·15				
5227	15 40 21·5	9 23·3	14 26·8	9 23·4	9 23·35	S. 2 45+5 3·45				
5272	15 46 30·5	8 25·1	7 13·7	8 24·5	8 24·8	N. 1 35+1 11·1		52·0	54·1	51·9
5374	16 0 36·0	8 28·5	7 2·4	8 28·0	8 28·25	N. 1 20+1 25·85				
5435	16 8 57·5	8 22·8	9 14·0	8 22·8	8 22·8	S. 0 10+0 23·2				
Anon.	16 13 13·0	10 20·4	8 11·3	10 20·2	10 20·3	S. 2 30—2 9·0				
5498	16 19 3·6	8 26·6	6 26·6	8 26·1	8 26·1	N. 4 15+1 33·5				
Anon.	16 32 55·0	9 13·2	13 12·1	9 13·4	9 13·3	~. 1 25+3 32·8				
5632	16 39 23·6	9 33·4	8 22·0	9 33·7	9 33·55	S. 3 40—1 10·65				
5735	16 53 53·4	10 15·6	15 19·7	10 15·3	10 15·45	S. 3 30+5 4·25				
5817	17 6 13·5	10 19·4	15 21·5	10 19·6	10 19·5	S. 2 5+5 2·0				
5881	17 16 40·0	9 30·7	13 28·4	9 30·0	9 30·35	N. 0 40—3 32·05				
5900	17 29 9·5	9 11·3	10 0·6		9 11·3	S. 1 45+0 23·3				
Anon.	17 30 7·5		11 28·7	9 11·3	9 11·3	~. 1 45+2 17·4				
6016	17 38 20·5	9 12·8	13 33·0	9 12·7	9 12·75	S. 1 15+4 20·25				
6074	17 48 21·5	10 10·6	6 15·7	10 10·6	10 10·6	N. 0 5+3 28·9	25·200	50·4	52·0	50·2
6115	17 55 4·5	10 20·0	9 4·4	10 19·8	10 19·9	S. 0 5—1 15·5				
6145	17 59 19·7	10 23·7	8 19·8	10 23·6	10 23·65	S. 0 25—2 3·85				
6233	18 13 9·5	10 22·6	12 19·7	10 22·7	10 22·65	S. 4 5+1 30·05				
Anon.	18 19 6·5	10 11·8	14 28·7		10 11·75	S. 2 45+4 16·95				
6285	18 20 10·5		8 27·0	10 11·8	10 11·75	S. 2 45—1 18·75				
6305	18 23 3·4	10 11·6	13 1·1	10 11·8	10 11·75	S. 2 45+2 23·35				
Anon.	18 41 58·5	10 29·5	8 22·5	10 29·7	10 29·6	S. 0 35—2 7·1				
6489	18 51 58·0	10 17·2	10 6·0	10 17·0	10 17·1	N. 0 15+0 11·1				
6325	18 56 57·5	10 19·8	12 29·5	10 19·7	10 19·7	N. 1 30—2 9·8				
6639	19 16 22·0	10 6·5	13 8·4	10 6·2	10 6·35	N. 0 20—3 2·05				
Anon.	19 20 34·0	10 16·2	15 8·7	10 16·4	10 16·3	N. 0 35—4 6·4				
6753	19 34 49·3	10 24·8	11 3·0	10 24·8	10 24·8	S. 0 55+0 12·2	25·185		60·9	49·2
6877	19 53 45·0	10 20·0	7 13·3	10 19·8	10 19·9	S. 2 10—3 6·6				
Anon.	20 5 26·2	10 10·0	14 26·4	10 10·0	10 10·0	S. 0 5+4 16·4				
Anon.	20 16 15·0	10 20·0	7 31·9	10 19·8	10 19·9	N. 0 45+2 22·0				
Anon.	20 20 40·2	10 19·8	13 23·9	10 20·2	10 20·0	N. 0 45—3 3·9				

No. 2293.—Exceedingly bad definition.

July 30.—The top cone having too much play, it was firmly screwed down before the commencement of the observations. Calm night, and excellent definition.

⊙ July 30, 1843.—Face of Sector West—(continued).

Number of B.A.C.	Time by Chronometer.	Micr. for Plumb-line on Dot.	Micr. for Observation of Star.	Micr. for Plumb-line on Dot.	Mean of Micr. for Plumb-line on Dot.	Star's Apparent Zenith Distance.	B atom.	Thermometers.		
								Attd.	Upper.	Lower.
	h m s	rev. pts.	rev. pts.	rev. pts.	rev. pts.	° ' rev. pts.	in.			
Anon	20 23 33·5		10 30·3	14 11·7		N. 0 30+3 15·4				
Anon.	20 33 3·0	13 27·7	17 19·0	13 27·7	13 27·7	N. 0 25−3 25·3				
7207	20 39 33·7	11 15·2	11 14·5	11 15·1	11 15·15	S. 4 0−0 0·65				
Anon	20 52 50·2	8 20·3	12 12·8	8 20·4	8 20·35	N. 0 40−3 26·45				
Auon	21 0 0·5	8 9·8	8 3·3	8 9·5	8 9·65	0 0+0 6·35				
7386	21 7 47·2	9 29·9	6 15·4	9 29·7	9 29·8	S. 2 30−3 14·4				
Anon.	21 24 57·7	9 26·8	13 14·7	9 26·7	9 26·75	0 0+3 21·95				
7557	21 34 59·0	10 26·6	7 0·3	10 27·2	10 26·9	S. 3 25−3 26·6				
7657	21 51 8·5	8 26·9	10 11·5	8 27·5	8 27·2	N. 1 10−1 18·3				
Anon.	21 54 59·5	8 27·3	9 6·7	8 27·4	8 27·35	N. 1 10−0 13·35				
7842	22 21 57·5	9 33·8	14 11·8	9 33·5	9 33·65	S. 2 45+4 12·15	25·180	47·8	49·3	47·5
Anon.	22 32 58·7	9 22·4	8 13·4	9 22·5	9 22·45	N. 0 10+1 9·05				
7966	22 43 11·0	10 5·3	11 22·6	10 4·8	10 5·05	S. 3 20+1 17·55				
7992	22 48 19·2	9 15·6	10 24·0	9 15·5	9 15·55	S. 0 5+1 9·35				
1802	5 33 19·7	11 9·5	8 11·3	11 9·4	11 9·45	S. 3 50−2 32·15				
2293	6 51 45·2	8 32·4	8 11·4	8 32·4	8 32·4	N. 1 35+0 21·0				

☾ July 31, 1843.—Face of Sector East.

Number of B.A.C.	Time by Chronometer.	Micr. for Plumb-line on Dot.	Micr. for Observation of Star.	Micr. for Plumb-line on Dot.	Mean of Micr. for Plumb-line on Dot.	Star's Apparent Zenith Distance.	B atom.	Attd.	Upper.	Lower.
4458	13 11 9·8	7 17·3	5 3·5	7 17·5	7 17·4	S. 5 30+2 13·9				
4579	13 36 11·2	9 11·3	12 14·0	9 11·5	9 11·4	S. 1 55−3 2·6	25·170	54·9	59·4	55·0
4623	13 42 11·6	9 5·8	7 0·5	9 5·6	9 5·7	S. 1 50+2 5·2				
4686	13 56 51·4	10 3 4	11 26·6	10 3·0	10 3·2	S. 5 15−1 23·4				
Anon.	14 5 23·0	10 32·3	8 28·6	10 32·2	10 32·25	N. 1 50−2 3·65				
4784	14 18 26·5	10 31·1	10 7·8	10 31·0	10 31·05	N. 1 35−0 23·25				
Anon	14 23 28·0	12 0·0	10 30·7	11 33·0	11 33·5	S. 2 15+1 2·8				
4852	14 33 28·0	9 31·4	13 18·7	9 31·1	9 31·1	S. 4 10−3 21·45				
4891	14 40 32·4	11 20·3	8 26·6	11 20·0	11 20·15	N. 3 5−2 27·55				
Anon.	14 45 33·5	7 14·5	5 10·9	7 14·5	7 14·5	S. 2 50+2 4·2				
Anon.	14 52 49·5	7 22·3	8 17·0	7 22 1	7 22·2	S. 1 40−0 28·8				
Anon.	14 57 1·2	8 3·0	5 29·8	8 3·4	8 3·2	S. 1 55+2 7·4				
5032	15 7 44·0	8 30·7	13 19·4	8 30·3	8 30·5	N. 0 45+4 22·9				
5054	15 11 15·5	10 3·4	11 0·0	10 3·0	10 3·2	S. 5 20−0 30·8				
5151	15 28 28·2	10 27·3	13 1·3	10 27·0	10 27·15	N 1 5+2 8·15				
Anon.	15 33 43·3	10 17·7	12 4·5	10 17·5	10 17·6	S. 0 45−1 20·9				
5227	15 40 25·4	9 29·0	6 15·0	9 28·8	9 28·9	S. 2 45+3 13·9				
5272	15 46 39·2	10 13·0	13 12·1	10 13·2	10 13·1	N. 1 35+2 33·0				
5374	16 0 45·2	10 4·5	13 18·7	10 4·4	10 4·45	N. 1 20+3 14·25				
5435	16 9 4·2	9 32·0	10 30·0	9 32·2	9 32 1	S. 0 10−0 31·9				
Anon.	16 13 17·0	9 9·2	13 7·6	9 9·4	9 9·3	S. 2 30−3 32·3				
5498	16 19 15·5	14 20·0	18 5·3	14 20·3	14 20·15	N. 4 15+9 19·15				
Anon.	16 33 0·0	8 3·6	5 27·3	8 3·3	8 3·45	S. 1 25+2 10·15				
5632	16 39 25·5	7 33·0	11 0·9	7 33·3	7 33·15	S. 3 40−3 1·75				
5735	16 53 55·7	7 2·5	3 22·8	7 1·8	7 2·15	S. 3 30+3 13·35				
5817	17 6 17·3	7 32·9	4 20·5	7 32·3	7 32·6	S. 2 5+3 12·1	25·180	46·2	49·3	46·2
5881	17 16 47·5	9 25·0	7 14·5	9 25·0	9 25·0	N. 0 40−2 10·5				
5960	17 29 14·0	10 3·0	11 1·9		10 3·0	S. 1 45−0 32·9				
Anon.	17 30 11·3		9 8·5	10 3 0	10 3·0	S. 1 45+0 28·5				
6016	17 38 25·5	10 6·4	7 7·5	10 6·4	10 6·4	S. 1 15+2 32·9				
6074	17 48 37·5	10 13·8	15 30·4	10 13·8	10 13·8	N. 0 5+5 16·6				
6115	17 55 10·8	10 15·6	13 20·0	10 15·5	10 15·55	S. 0 3−3 4·45				
6145	17 59 25·5	10 14·0	14 5·5	10 14·4	10 14·2	S. 0 25−3 25·3				
6233	18 13 11·0	10 32·4	10 26·7	10 32·4	10 32 4	S. 4 5+0 5·7				
Anon.	18 19 9 5	10 29·4	8 1·6		10 29 37	S. 2 45+2 27·77				

No. 4891.—The lamp-tray touched the tube.
July 31.—Calm night, and good definition.
Great care taken in making the observations; yet they vary *inter se* more than could have been expected.

☾ JULY 31, 1843.—FACE OF SECTOR EAST—(continued).

Number of B.A.C.	Time by Chronometer.	Micr. for Plumb-line on Dot.	Micr. for Observation of Star.	Micr. for Plumb-line on Dot.	Mean of Micr. for Plumb-line on Dot.	Star's Apparent Zenith Distance.	Barom.	Thermometers.		
								Attd.	Upper.	Lower.
	h. m. s.	rev. pts.	rev. pts.	rev. pts.	rev. pts.	° ′ rev. pts.	in.			
6285	18 20 13·5		14 2·8	10 29·4	10 29·37	S. 2 45−3 7·43				
6305	18 23 6·2		9 28·4	10 29·3	10 29·37	S. 2 45+1 0·97				
Anon.	18 42 4·0	10 24·1	14 17·8	10 24·2	10 24·15	S. 0 35−3 27·65				
6489	18 52 4·8	11 3·2	13 3·0	11 3·2	11 3·2	N. 0 15+1 33·8	25·175	45·1	46·9	45·2
6525	18 57 5·5	10 9·6	9 22·5	10 9·8	10 9·7	N. 1 30−0 21·2				
6639	19 16 28·6	9 33·5	8 10·3	9 33·5	9 33·5	N. 0 20−1 14·2				
Anon.	19 20 41·0	10 0·1	6 27·6	10 0·4	10 0·25	N. 0 35−3 6·65				
6753	19 34 54·5	9 31·8	11 5·3	9 32·2	9 32·0	S. 0 55−1 7·3				
6877	19 53 49·0	9 20·5	14 14·8	9 20·5	9 20·5	S. 2 10−4 28·3		44.8	46·0	44·8
Anon.	20 16 22·5	10 4·3	14 13·8	10 4·0	10 4·15	N. 0 45+4 9·65				
Anon.	20 20 47·5	10 4·1	8 21·0	10 3·9	10 4·0	N. 0 45−1 17·0				
Anon.	20 23 40·0	9 33·5	15 1·8	9 33·6	9 33·55	N. 0 30+5 2·25				
Anon	20 32 10·3	9 9·2	7 4·4	9 10·3	9 9·75	N. 0 25−2 5·35				
7207	20 39 35·5	9 15·5	11 5·6	9 15·8	9 15·65	S. 4 0−1 23·95				
Anon.	20 52 57·5	9 22·6	7 16·4	9 22·4	9 22·5	N. 0 40−2 6·1				
Anon.	21 0 7·5	9 20·3	11 15·5	9 20·3	9 20·3	0 0+1 29·2				
7386	21 7 51·2	9 1·3	14 5·0	9 1·5	9 1·4	S. 2 30−5 3·6	25·165	44·2	45·3	44·3
Anon.	21 11 57·7	9 23·3	14 8·8	9 22·8	9 23·05	N. 0 30+4 19·75				
Anon.	21 25 4·5	9 8·8	7 10·5	9 8·4	9 8·6	0 0+1 32·1				
7557	21 35 16·0	9 4·5	14 20·5	9 4·7	9 4·6	S. 3 25−5 15·9				
7657	21 51 16·7	9 19·8	9 23·3	9 19·8	9 19·8	N. 1 10+0 3·5				
Anon.	21 55 7·6	9 19·8	10 27·4	9 19·9	9 19·85	N. 1 10+1 7·55				
7842	22 22 0·5	9 0·5	6 10·5	9 0·2	9 0·35	S. 2 45+2 23·85				
Anon.	22 33 5·2	9 8·0	12 4·5	9 8·3	9 8·15	N. 0 10+2 30·35				
7066	22 43 13·5	9 15·4	9 19·3	9 15·3	9 15·35	S. 3 20−0 3·95	25·148	44·2	45·5	44·4
7992	22 48 25·8	10 10·8	10 25·3	10 10·8	10 10·8	S. 0 5−0 14·8				
1802	5 33 21·5	10 14·0	14 32·8	10 14·2	10 14·1	S. 3 50−4 18·7	25·150	54·3	54·0	54·2
2293	6 51 53·4	10 15·9	12 23·2	10 16·0	10 15·95	N. 1 35+2 7·25				

♂ AUGUST 1, 1843.—FACE OF SECTOR WEST.

Number of B.A.C.	Time by Chronometer.	Micr. for Plumb-line on Dot.	Micr. for Observation of Star.	Micr. for Plumb-line on Dot.	Mean of Micr. for Plumb-line on Dot.	Star's Apparent Zenith Distance.	Barom.	Attd.	Upper.	Lower.
4623	13 42 12·6	11 10·8	15 3·4	11 11·2	11 11·0	S. 1 50+3 26·4				
4686	13 56 55·2	10 30·4	10 28·0	10 31·0	10 30·7	S. 5 15−0 2·7				
Anon.	14 5 21·0	9 13·6	13 5·1	9 13·8	9 13·7	N. 1 50−3 25·4				
4784	14 18 23·0	10 26·8	13 3·2	10 27·0	10 26·9	N. 1 35−2 10·3				
Anon.	14	11 10·5	13 32·1	11 10·5	11 10·5	S. 2 15+2 21·6				
4852	14 33 36·0	9 3·9	7 4·2	9 4·0	9 3·95	S. 4 10−1 33 75				
4891	14 40 28·5	8 21·0	13 2·5	8 21·2	8 21·1	N. 3 5−4 15·4				
Anon.	14 45 34·0	9 21·3	13 13·5	9 21·3	9 21·3	S. 2 50+3 26·2				
Anon.	14 52 50·5	9 15·6	10 10·3	9 15·6	9 15·6	S. 1 40+0 28·7				
Anon.	14 57 2·4	9 8·5	13 5·4	9 9·0	9 8·75	S. 1 55+3 30·65	25·120	51·1	53·1	51·0
5032	15 7 43·2	9 6·4	6 4·4	9 6·4	9 6·4	N. 0 45+3 2·0				
5054	15 11 21·0	9 12·8	10 3·7	9 13·0	9 12·9	S. 5 20+0 24·8				
5151	15 28 27·0	8 27·8	8 7·2	8 27·8	8 27·8	N. 1 5+0 20·6				
Anon.	15 33 44·2	9 1·0	9 1·0	9 1·3	9 1·15	S. 0 10−0 0·15				
5227	15 40 28·0	9 17·7	14 20·4	9 17·7	9 17·7	S. 2 45+5 2·7				
5272	15 46 37·5	8 23·8	7 13·2	8 23·6	8 23·7	N. 1 35+1 10·5				
5374	16 0 43·3	8 18·1	6 26·0	8 17·6	8 17·85	N. 1 20+1 25·85	25·120	49·3	50·4	49·2
5435	16 9 4·5	8 15·5	9 6·8	8 15·5	8 15·5	S. 0 10+0 25·3				
Anon.	16 13 19·2	9 17·0	7 7·9	9 16·6	9 16·8	S. 2 30−2 8·9				
5498	16 19 11·8	9 6·6	7 8·5	9 6·4	9 6·5	N. 4 15+1 32·0				
Anon.	16 33 1·3	9 28·8	13 27·3	9 29·0	9 28·9	S. 1 25+3 32·4				
5632	16 30 28·5	9 24·8	8 12·4	9 24·8	9 24·8	S. 3 40−1 12·4				
5735	16 53 59·5	9 13·3	14 15·4	9 13·2	9 13·25	S. 3 30+5 2·15				

August 1.—Calm night and good definition.
Anon. 14[b].—Bisected when 20 seconds past the middle wire.

♂ August 1, 1843.—Face of Sector West—(continued).

Number of B.A.C.	Time by Chronometer.	Micr. for Plumb-line on Dot.	Micr. for Observation of Star.	Micr. for Plumb-line on Dot.	Mean of Micr. for Plumb-line on Dot.	Star's Apparent Zenith Distance.	Barom.	Attd.	Upper.	Lower.
	h m s	rev. pts.	rev. pts.	rev. pts.	rev. pts.	o ' rev. pts.	in.			
5817	17 6 18·7	9 20·8	14 21·6	9 20·8	9 20·8	S. 2 5+5 0·8				
5881	17 16 47·5	8 30·4	12 28·7	8 30·3	8 30·35	N. 0 40−3 32·35				
6016	17 38 25·5	10 28·9	15 15·0	10 28·8	10 28·85	S. 1 15+4 20·15				
6074	17 48 28·5	10 16·0	6 21·7	10 15·8	10 15·9	N. 0 5+3 28·2				
6115	17 55 11·5	10 3·8	8 22·5	10 3·6	10 3·7	S. 0 5−1 15·2				
6145	17 59 26·5	10 17·5	8 13·3	10 17·5	10 17·5	S. 0 25−2 4·2				
6233	18 13 15·0	10 12·7	12 7·3	10 12·6	10 12·65	S. 4 5+1 28·65		48·6	49·3	48·4
Anon.}	18 19 12·5	10 27·1			10 27·1	S. 2 45+4 16·4				
6285			9 8·9	10 27·0	10 27·1	S. 2 45−1 18·2				
6305}	18 23 9·5	10 27·1	13 16·0	10 27·2	10 27·1	S. 2 45+2 23·5				
Anon.	18 42 5·5	10 22·1	8 14·8	10 22·0	10 22·05	S. 0 35−2 7·25				
6489	18 52 5·5	11 3·6	10 26·0	11 3·5	11 3·55	N. 0 15+0 11·55				
6525	18 57 5·0	11 17·5	13 28·0	11 17·1	11 17·3	N. 1 30−2 10·7				
6639	19 16 29·0	11 26·0	14 28·2	11 26·1	11 26·05	N. 0 20−3 2·15				
Anon.	19 20 41·0	12 16·4	17 9·8	12 16·9	12 16·65	N. 0 35−4 27·15				
6877	19 53 51·0	11 22·3	8 15·9	11 22·6	11 22·45	S. 2 10−3 6·55	25·110	48·2	48·9	48·2
Anon.	20 5 33·5	9 12·3	13 28·0	9 12·5	9 12·4	N. 0 45+4 15·6				
Anon.	20 16 22·3	9 20·4	6 31·4	9 20·4	9 20·4	N. 0 45+2 23·0				
Anon	20 20 47·2	9 20·3	12 24·1	9 20·4	9 20·35	N. 0 45−3 3·75				
Anon.	20 23 40·0	9 2·4	5 21·0	9 2·0	9 2 2	N. 0 30+3 15·2				
Anon	20 33 10·0	8 28·4	12 21·0	8 28·6	8 28·5	N. 0 25−3 26·5				
7207	20 39 39·5	9 29·5	9 27·8	9 29·6	9 29·55	S. 4 0−0 1·75				
Anon.	20 52 58·2	9 22·2	4 18·1	9 22·2	9 22·2	N. 0 35+5 4·1				
Anon.	21 0 8·0	9 26·8	9 21·3	9 26·6	9 26·7	0 0+0 5·4				
7386	21 7 54·0	10 4·5	6 25·2	10 4·4	10 4·45	S. 2 30−3 13·25				
Anon.	21 11 57·0	10 3·0	7 4·4	10 3·0	10 3·0	S. 2 30+0 32·6				
Anon.	21 25 5·0	9 28·6	13 16·4	9 28·7	9 28·65	0 0+3 21·75				
7557	21 35 5·0	9 25·9	5 32·3	9 25·6	9 25·75	S. 3 25−3 27·45	25·115	49·3	48·2	47·4
7657	21 51 16·0	8 24·6	10 9·7	8 24·7	8 24·65	N. 1 10−1 19·05				
Anon.	21 55 7·2	8 24·8	9 5·3	8 24·8	8 24·8	N. 1 10−0 14·5				
7842	22 22 3·5	9 29·5	14 8·2	9 29·8	9 29·65	S. 2 45+4 12·55				
Anon.	22 33 5·5	9 10·5	8 1·8	9 10·5	9 10·5	N. 0 10+1 8·7				
7966	22 43 17·0	9 2·2	10 20·0	9 2·0	9 2·1	S. 3 20+1 17·9				
7992	22 48 26·0	9 31·7	11 6·3	9 31·4	9 31·55	S. 0 5+1 8·75	25·115	46·9	47·8	46·9
1802	5 33 26·4	7 5·5	4 8·3	7 5·2	7 5·35	S. 3 50−2 31·05	25·225	50·4	54·5	50·3
2293	6 51 52·7	8 31·2	8 11·5	8 30·7	8 30·95	N. 1 35+0 19·45				

☿ August 2, 1843.—Face of Sector East.

Number of B.A.C.	Time by Chronometer.	Micr. for Plumb-line on Dot.	Micr. for Observation of Star.	Micr. for Plumb-line on Dot.	Mean of Micr. for Plumb-line on Dot.	Star's Apparent Zenith Distance.	Barom.	Attd.	Upper.	Lower.
4458	13 11 16·2	9 1·3	6 22·4	9 0·8	9 1·05	S. 5 30+2 12·65	25·125	53·2	55·2	53·7
4686	13 56 57·5	10 9·7	11 33·6	10 9·4	10 9·55	S. 5 15−1 24·05				
4784	14 18 36·3	12 13·2	11 24·5	12 13·1	12 13·15	N. 5 10−0 22·65				
Anon.	14 23 34·3	12 14·8	11 12·3	12 14·6	12 14·7	S. 2 15+1 2·4				
4852	14 33 35·2	12 23·4	16 11·3	12 23·3	12 23·35	S. 4 10−3 21·95				
4891	14 40 39·3	13 20·4	10 27·7	13 20·6	13 20·5	N. 3 5−2 26·8				
Anon.	14 45 39·0	10 20·2	8 16·5	10 20·3	10 20·25	S. 2 50+2 3·75				
Anon.	14 52 55·8	10 9·8	11 4·4	10 9·8	10 9·8	S. 1 40−0 28·6				
5032	15 7 55 0	9 32·4	14 21·3	9 32·2	9 32·3	N. 0 45+4 23·0				
5054	15 11	10 17·0	11 14·3	10 16·7	10 16·85	S. 5 20−0 31·45				
5151	15 28 35·2	10 21·8	12 30·7	10 21·8	10 21·8	N. 1 5+2 8·9				
5227	15 40 35·0	9 3·4	5.23·9	9 3·6	9 3·5	S. 2 45+3 13·6				
5272	15 46 46·0	8 30·8	11 29·0	8 30·6	8 30·7	N. 1 35+2 32·9				
5374	16 0 51·5	8 31·3	12 11·4	8 31·3	8 31·3	N. 1 20+3 14·1				
5435	16 9 11·2	9 1 5	9 33·3	9 1·6	9 1·55	S. 0 10−0 31·75				

August 1.—No. 6285.—Bisected when 25 seconds past the middle wire.
No. 5054.—12 seconds past the middle wire when bisected.
The small stars in the early part of the evening could not be seen owing to thin cloud. A halo round the moon. Towards midnight the heavens became perfectly clear. Light N E. air. Good definition, but plumb-line generally vibrating.

♉ August 2, 1843.—Face of Sector East—(continued).

Number of B.A.C.	Time by Chronometer	Micr. for Plumb-line on Dot.	Micr. for Observation of Star.	Micr. for Plumb-line on Dot.	Mean of Micr. for Plumb-line on Dot.	Star's Apparent Zenith Distance.	Barom.	Thermometers.		
								Attd.	Upper.	Lower.
	h m s	rev. pts.	rev. pts.	rev. pts.	rev. pts.	° ′ rev. pts.	in.			
Anon.	16 13 24·0	9 14·3	13 12·2	9 14·0	9 14·15	S. 2 30−3 32·05				
5498	16 19 22·0	10 9·3	13 29·2	10 9·3	10 9·3	N. 4 15+3 19·9				
Anon.	16 33 6·7	9 15·3	7 5·7	9 15·3	9 15·3	S. 1 25+2 9·6	25·140	50.4	51·3	50·2
5632	16 39 32·6	9 17·4	12 19·1	9 17·6	9 17·5	S. 3 40−3 1·6				
5735	16 54 2·3	9 1·7	5 22·6	9 1·7	9 1·7	S. 3 30+3 13·1				
5817	17 6 24·6	8 31·5	5 18·6	8 31·4	8 31·45	S. 2 5+3 12·85				
5881	17 16 54·5	9 4·2	6 27·5	9 4·2	9 4·2	N. 0 40−2 10·7				
5960	17 29 20·0	9 16·3	10 15·3		9 16·15	S. 1 45−0 33·15				
Anon.	17 30 20·0		8 21·4	9 16·0	9 16·15	S. 1 45+0 28·75				
6016	17 38 33·0	9 12·0	6 13·8	9 12·2	9 12·1	S. 1 15+2 32·3				
6074	17·48 35·2	9 25·6	15 8·1	9 25·5	9 25·55	N. 0 5+5 16·55				
6115	17 55 17·5	10 4·5	13 9·4	10 4·8	10 4·65	S. 0 5−3 4·75				
6145	17 59 33·5	7 30·8	11 23·3	7 30·8	7 30·8	S. 0 25−3 26·5				
6233	18 13 17·8	8 23·1	8 16·4	8 23·0	8 23·05	S. 4 5+0 6·65				
Anon.	18 19 16·5	9 15·8	6 21·4		9 15·88	S. 2 45+2 28·48				
6285	18 20 19·5		12 23·1	9 16·0	9 15·88	S. 2 45−3 7·22				
6305	18 23 13·5	9 15·9	8 14·5	9 15·8	9 15·88	S. 2 45+1 1 38				
Anon.	18 42 9·2	9 13·6	13 7·0	9 13·5	9 13·55	S. 0 35−3 28·05				
6489	18 52 14·0	9 12·3	11 12·4	9 12·6	9 12·45	N. 0 15+1 33·95				
6525	18 57 13·5	9 10·0	8 22·7	9 10·0	9 10·0	N. 1 30−0 21·3				
6639	19 16 37·0	8 33·1	7 18·4	8 33·3	8 33·2	N. 0 20−1 14·8				
Anon.	19 20 48·5	9 4·5	5 30·6	9 4·3	9 4·4	N. 0 35−3 7·8				
6753	19 35 1·0	8 17·8	9 25·7	8 17·8	8 17·8	S. 0 55−1 7·9	25·130	48·9	50·0	49·4
6877	19 53 56·0	9 8·5	14 3·0	9 8·6	9 8·55	S. 2 10−4 28·45				
Anon.	20 5 39·5	9 13·7	6 20·3	9 13·7	9 13·7	S. 0 5+2 27·4				
Anon.	20 16 30·2	10 12·3	14 21·8	10 11·8	10 12·05	N. 0 45+4 9·75				
Anon.	20 20 54·7	10 11·8	8 28·4	10 11·8	10 11·8	N. 0 45−1 17·4				
Anon.	20 23 47·0	9 23·0	14 25·0	9 23·3	9 23·15	N. 0 30+5 1·85				
Anon.	20 33 17·0	9 18·0	7 13·4	9 18·0	9 18·0	N. 0 25−2 4·6				
7207	20 39 42·5	9 9·8	10 33·2	9 9·9	9 9·85	S. 4 0−1 23·35				
Anon.	20 53 5·5	10 14·5	8 7·9	10 14·0	10 14·25	N. 0 40−2 6·35				
Anon.	21 0 15·0	9 30·6	11 26·0	9 31·0	9 30·8	0 0+1 29·2				
7386	21 7 58·5	10 4·8	15 8·0	10 5·0	10 4·9	S. 2 30−5 3·1				
Anon.	21 12 5·0	10 26·0	15 10·8	10 25·8	10 25·9	N. 0 30+4 18·9				
Anon.	21 25 12·2	10 24·2	8 25·1	10 23·8	10 24·0	0 0+1 32·9				
7557	21 35 8·6	10 5·5	15 21·0	10 5·4	10 5·45	S. 3 25−5 15·55				
7657	21 51 24·0	10 15·7	15 18·3	10 15·8	10 15·75	N. 1 10+0 2·55				
Anon.	21 55 15·2	10 15·7	11 23·4	10 16·0	10 15·85	N. 1 10+1 7·55				
7842	22 22 8·0	9 20·0	9 20·0	9 20·0	9 20·0	S. 2 45+2 24·4				
Anon.	22 33 13·0	9 20·1	12 16·8	9 20·0	9 20·05	N. 0 10+2 30·75	25·110	48·6	49·1	48·6
7966	22 43 20·2	9 23·1	9 26·9	9 23·1	9 23·1	S. 3 20−0 3·8				
7902	22 48 33·0	9 30·9	10 11·6	9 31·2	9 31·05	S. 0 5−0 14·55				
1802	5 33 29 0	9 26·2	14 10·4	9 26·9	9 26·55	S. 3 50−4 17·85	25·120	55·8	60·8	55·9
2293	6 52 1·2	9 27·8	12 1·4	9 28·1	9 27·95	N. 1 35+2 7·45				

♃ August 3, 1843.—Face of Sector West.

4458	13 11 15·5	9 28·0	13 28·0	9 27·5	9 27·75	S. 5 30+4 0·25	25·320	61·5	64·8	61·4
4579	13 36 18·7	9 10·1	7 28·6	9 10·0	9 10·05	S. 1 55−1 15·45				
4623	13 42 17·0	8 26·8	12 19·4	8 27·0	8 26·9	S. 1 50+3 26·5				
4686	13 56 57·0	9 6·4	9 4·0	9 6·6	9 6·5	S. 5 15−0 2·5				
4784	14 18 34·2	9 0·4	11 12·2	9 0·3	9 0·35	N. 1 35−2 11·85				
4852	14 33 35·2	10 30·2	8 31·5	10 30·0	10 30·1	S. 4 10−1 32·6				
4891	14 40 40·5	8 7·2	12 24·8	8 7·6	8 7·4	N. 3 5−4 17·4				

August 3.—No. 4623.—The second of transit uncertain.

♃ August 3, 1843.—Face of Sector West—(continued).

Number of B.A.C.	Time by Chronometer.	Micr. for Plumb-line on Dot.	Micr. for Observation of Star.	Micr. for Plumb-line on Dot.	Mean of Micr. for Plumb-line on Dot.	Star's Apparent Zenith Distance.	Barom.	Attd.	Upper.	Lower.
	h m s	rev. pts.	rev. pts.	rev. pts.	rev. pts.	° ' rev. pts.	in.			
Anon.	14 45 39·0		12 15·2	8 22·0		S. 2 50+3 27·2				
Anon.	14 52 56·0	8 25·5	9 20·2	8 25·4	8 25·45	S. 1 40−0 28·75				
Anon.	14 57 8·0	8 31·3	12 28·4	8 31·5	8 31·4	S. 1 55+3 31·0				
5032	15 7 51·5	9 7·3	6 5·9	9 7·4	9 7·35	N. 0 45+3 1·45				
5054	15 11 21.2	10 5 5	10 31·0	10 5·6	10 5·55	S. 5 20+0 25·45				
5151	15 28 36·0	9 19·7	8 33·4	9 19·6	9 19·65	N. 1 5+0 20·25				
Anon.	15 33 50·5	10 16·3	10 16·7	10 16·5	10 16·4	S. 0 45+0 0·3				
5227	15 40 35·0	11 8·0	16 10·5	11 8·4	11 8·2	S. 2 45+5 2·3				
5272	15 46 47·0	10 18·4	9 9·0	10 18·4	10 18·4	N. 1 35+1 9·4				
5374	16 0 52·0	10 16·0	8 24·6	10 16·0	10 16·0	N. 1 20+1 25·4	25·110	56·8	58·1	56·9
5435	16 9 11·5	10 9·7	11 0·8	10 9·6	10 9·65	S. 0 10+0 25·15				
Anon.	16 13 23·0	10 30·8	8 21·8	10 30·6	10 30·7	S. 2 30−2 8·9				
5498	16 19 24·5	10 27·5	8 29·7	10 27·4	10 27·45	N. 4 16+1 31·75				
5632	16	11 27·9	10 13·7	11 27·3	11 27·6	S. 3 40−1 13·9				
5735	16 54 1·0	10 10·5	15 13·0	10 10·8	10 10·65	S. 3 30+5 2·35				
5817	17 6 24·5	9 22·7	14 24·0	9 23·0	9 22·85	S. 2 5+5 1·15				
Anon.	17 30 18·5	10 24·5	13 7·8	10 24·5	10 24·5	S. 1 45+2 17·3	25·100	56·5	57·6	56·4
6145	17 59 33·0	9 0·4	6 31·7	9 0·3	9 0·35	S. 0 25−2 2·65				
6233	18 13 17·2	8 33·7	10 29·8	8 33·6	8 33·65	S. 4 5+1 30·15				
Anon.	18 19 16·0	9 23·7	14 5·7		9 23·53	S. 2 45+4 16·17				
0285	18 20 19·6		8 4·3	9 23·3	9 23·53	S. 2 45−1 19·23				
6305	18 23 14·4	9 23·4	12 12·5	9 23·7	9 23·53	S. 2 45+2 22·97				
Anon.	18 42	9 20·0	7 12·7	9 20·0	9 20·0	S. 0 35−2 7·3				
6489	18 52	9 10·4	9 0·2	9 10·4	9 10·4	N. 0 15+0 10·2				
6525	18 57	8 26·8	11 3·0	8 27·2	8 27·0	N. 1 30−2 10·0				
6639	19 16	9 8·4	12 10·8	9 8·5	9 8·45	N. 0 20−3 2·35				
6753	19 35	9 21·0	9 33·8	9 20·8	9 20·9	S. 0 55+0 12·9				
6877	19 53	10 14·6	7 9·0	10 14·9	10 14·7	S. 2 10−3 5·7				
Anon.	20 5	9 25·3	14 7·4	9 25·4	9 25·35	S. 0 5+4 16·05				
Anon.	20 16	9 9·4	6 21·4	9 9·5	9 9·45	N. 0 45+2 22·05				
Anon.	20 20	9 9·5	12 13·9	9 9·5	9 9·5	N. 0 45−3 4·4				
Anon.	20 23	9 32·6	6 17·8	9 32·7	9 32·65	N. 0 30+3 14 85				
Anon.	20 33	9 28·6	13 21·2	9 28·7	9 28·65	N. 0 25−3 26·55				
7207	20 39	10 32·7	10 31·7	10 32·7	10*32·7	S. 4 0−0 1·00				
Anon.	20 53	10 20·4	14 14·0	10 20·5	10 20·45	N. 0 40−3 27·55				
7386	21 7	10 12·8	6 33·7	10 12·6	10 12·7	S. 2 30−3 13·0				
Anon.	21 11	8 14·4	5 15·9	8 14·0	8 14·2	N. 0 30+2 32·3				
Anon.	21 25	8 8·4	11 30·7	8 8·4	8 8·4	0 0+3 22 3				
7557	21 35	9 2·6	5 10·4	9 2·5	9 2·55	S. 3 25−3 26·15				
7657	21 51	8 33 7	10 19·3	8 33·7	8 33·7	N. 1 10−1 19·6	25·100	55·0	55·4	55·1
Anon.	21 55	8 33·7	9 14·7	8 33·6	8 33·65	N. 1 10−0 15·05				
7842	22 22		13 25·0	9 12·0		S. 2 45+4 13·0				
Anon.	22 33	9 11·8	8 3·8	9 11·6	9 11·7	N. 0 10+1 7·9				
7966	22 43	10 2·7	11 21·0	10 2·3	10 2·5	S. 3 20+1 18·5				
7992	22 48 33·3	8 19·6	9 29·0	8 20·0	8 19·8	S. 0 5+1 9·2				

♄ August 5, 1843.

4458	13 11 25·2	10 3·5	14 3·4	10 3·0	10 3·25	S. 5 30+4 0·15				

Face of Sector East.

4579	13 36 30·5	10 7·3	13 10·7	10 7·3	10 7·3	S. 1 55−3 3·4				
4623	13 42 30·4	9 14·7	7 11·3	9 14·7	9 14·7	S. 1 50+2 3·4				
4686	13 57 11·8	9 24·2	11 14·0	9 24·3	9 24·25	S. 5 15−1 23·75				
4784	14 18 43·5	10 15·0	9 25·9	10 15·3	10 15·45	N. 1 35−0 23·55				

August 3.—No. 5632.—25 seconds past the middle wire when bisected.
The instants of transit for the stars between Nos. 6305 and 7992 were not noted; they were bisected when transiting the wire. Warm north wind.

♄ August 5, 1843.—Face of Sector East—(continued).

Number of B. A. C.	Time by Chronometer.	Micr. for Plumb-line on Dot.	Micr. for Observation of Star.	Micr. for Plumb-line on Dot.	Mean of Micr. for Plumb-line on Dot.	Star's Apparent Zenith Distance.	Barom.	Attd.	Upper.	Lower.
	h m s	rev. pts.	rev. pts.	rev. pts.	rev. pts.	° ′ rev. pts.	in.			
4852	14 33 48·5	9 20·7	13 8·6	9 20·7	9 20·7	S. 4 10−3 21·9				
4891	14 40 49·0	10 3·9	7 10·0	10 3·5	10 3·7	N. 3 5−2 27·7				
Anon.	14 45 52·2	9 14·5	7 10·7	9 14·3	9 14·4	S. 2 50+2 3·7				
Anon.	14 53 8·4	9 23·5	10 18·0	9 23·4	9 23·45	S. 1 40−0 28·55				
Anon.	14 57 16·7	9 23·6	7 16·4	9 23·6	9 23·6	S. 1 55+2 7·2				
5032	15 8 2·0	11 3·9	15 28·8	11 4·4	11 4·15	N. 0 45+4 24·65				
5054	15 11 36·8	9 30·5	10 27·8	9 30·3	9 30·4	S. 5 20−0 31·4				
5151	15 28 46·5	10 1·5	12 12·1	10 1·6	10 1·55	N. 1 5+2 10·55				
Anon.	15 34 1·0	10 1·3	11 23·8	10 1·4	10 1·35	S. 0 45−1 22·45				
5227	15 40 48·0	9 5·4	5 26·2	9 5·3	9 5·35	S. 2 45+3 13·15				
5272	15 46 56·5	9 27·0	12 26·3	9 26·9	9 26·95	N. 1 35+2 33·35				
5374	16 1 2·6	10 8·8	13 23·4	10 8·8	10 8·8	N. 1 20+3 14·6				
5435	16 9 23·0	9 22·3	10 19·9	9 22·0	9 22·15	S. 0 10−0 31·75				
Anon.	16 13 36·8	9 27·0	13 24·5	9 27·5	9 27·25	S. 2 30−3 31·25				
5498	16 19 32·2	9 33·8	13 20·4	9 33·8	9 33·8	N. 4 15+3 20·6	25·110	54·3	55·0	54·4
Anon.	16 33 18·6	9 18·3	7 7·0	9 18·0	9 18·15	S. 1 25+2 11·15				
5632	16 39 46·2	9 18·4	12 20·3	9 18·6	9 18·5	S. 3 40−3 1·8				
5735	16 54 16·2	9 11·3	5 31·3	9 10·8	9 11·05	×. 3 30+3 13·75				
5817	17 6 37·3	9 17·0	6 4·3	9 17·3	9 17·15	S. 2 5+3 12·85				
5960	17 29 33·5	11 2·3	12 1·4		11 2·15	S. 1 45−0 33·25				
Anon.	17 30 31·4		10 7·3	11 2·0	11 2·15	S. 1 45+0 28·85				
6016	17 38 45·2	11 24·7	8 24·7	11 24·0	11 24·65	S. 1 15+2 33·95				
6074	17 48 47·0	9 18·9	15 1·5	9 18·9	9 18·9	N. 0 5+5 16·6				
6115	17 55 29·8	9 30·4	13 1·0	9 30·6	9 30·5	S. 0 5−3 4·5				
6145	17 59 45·2	10 13·2	14 4·5	10 13·4	10 13·3	S. 0 25−3 25·2				
6233	18 13 32·8	10 17·5	10 11·6	10 17·5	10 17·5	S. 4 5+0 5·9				
Anon.	18 19 30·5	10 15·6	7 22·1		10 15·7	S. 2 45+2 27·6				
6285	18 20 33·8		13 23·8	10 15·8	10 15·7	S. 2 45−3 8·1				
6305	18 23 27·2		9 15·0	10 15·7	10 15·7	S. 2 45+1 0·7	25·110	53·2	53·4	53·3
Anon.	18 41	10 22·6	14 18·3	10 22·5	10 22·55	N. 0 15+2 0·85				
6489	18 52 23·2	10 23·0	12 24·0	10 23·3	10 23·15	N. 1 30−0 20·9				
6525	18 57 24·0	11 14·5	10 27·4	11 14·1	11 14·3	N. 0 20−1 13·7				
6639	19 16 47·5	11 2·5	9 22·8	11 2·5	11 2·5	N. 0 20−1 13·7				
Anon.	19 20 59·5	10 0·6	6 27·9	10 0·0	10 0·3	N. 0 35−3 6·4				
6753	19 35 14·2	8 23·8	9 31·8	8 24·2	8 24·0	S. 0 55−1 7·8				
6877	19 54 8·7	8 23·9	13 18·8	8 24·3	8 24·1	S. 2 10−4 28·7				
Anon.	20 5 51·6	9 4·7	6 11·4	9 4·9	9 4·75	S. 0 5+2 27·35				
Anon.	20 16 41·2	10 5·7	14 15·4	10 5·4	10 5·55	N. 0 45+4 9·85				
Anon.	20 21 6·2	10 5·4	8 22·9	10 5·4	10 5·4	N. 0 45−1 16·5				
Anon.	20 23 58·2	10 11·2	15 14·4	10 11·4	10 11·3	N. 0 30+5 3·1				
Anon.	20 33 28·6	10 32·4	8 28·5	10 32·3	10 32·35	N. 0 25−2 8·85				
7207	20 39 56·0	11 11·2	13 0·4	11 11·3	11 11·25	S. 4 0−1 23·15				
Anon.	20 53 17·3	10 24·1	8 18·3	10 23·8	10 23·95	N. 0 40−2 5·65				
Anon.	21 0 26·4	9 18·1	11 13·7	9 18·3	9 18·2	0 0+1 29·5				
7386	21 8 11·7	9 24·7	14 27·5	9 24·8	9 24·75	S. 2 30−5 2·75				
Anon.	21 12 16·2	11 4·0	15 24·5	11 4·0	11 4·0	N 0 30+4 20·5				
Anon.	21 25 23·5	12 9·3	10 11·8	12 9·4	12 9·35	0 0+1 31·55				
7557	21	10 25·4	16 6·7	10 25·3	10 25·35	N. 1 10+0 3·9				
7657	21· 51 35·5	10 27·3	10 31·2	10 27·3	10 27·3	N. 1 10+0 3·9				
Anon.	21 55 26·3	10 27·2	12 1·1	10 27·2	10 27·2	N. 1 10+1 7·0				
7842	22 21 2·0	8 24·3	5 30·6	8 24·2	8 24·25	S. 2 45+2 27·65				
7966	22 33 24·0	9 6·3	12 3·5	9 6·3	9 6·3	N. 0 10+2 31·2	25·105	52·5	53·4	52·8
7992	22 43 34·0	9 6·5	9 10·5	9 6·5	9 6·5	S. 3 20−0 4·0				
	22 48 44·4	9 29·0	10 9·8	9 29·2	9 29·1	S. 0 5−0 14·7	25·140	56·7	61·9	56·6
2293	6 52 11·6	10 2·6	12 10·4	10 2·4	10 2·5	N. 1 35+2 7·9				

August 5.—No. 5227.—The seconds of transit uncertain.

Anon. 18ʰ. 41ᵐ.—The illuminating lamp went out when bisecting this star. The time of transit not noted, nor of No. 7557.

No. 5960 and Anon. 17ʰ. 30ᵐ.—Clamp not touched between these observations.

H

ARC OF THE MERIDIAN.—CAPE OF GOOD HOPE.

☉ AUGUST 6, 1843.—FACE OF SECTOR EAST.

Number of B.A.C.	Time by Chronometer.	Micr. for Plumb-line on Dot.	Micr. for Observation of Star.	Micr. for Plumb-line on Dot.	Mean of Micr. for Plumb-line on Dot.	Star's Apparent Zenith Distance.	Barom.	Attd.	Upper.	Lower.
	h m s	rev. pts.	rev. pts.	rev. pts.	rev. pts.	° ′ rev. pts.	in.			
4458	13 11 34·2	10 14·4	8 2·2	10 14·4	10 14·4	S. 5 30+2 12·2				
4579	13 36 33·3	8 32·0	12 1·9	8 31·4	8 31·7	S. 1 55−3 4·2	25·245	63·3	68·0	63·5
4623	13 42 34·0	9 9·0	7 6·4	9 8·8	9 8·9	S. 1 50+2 2·5				
4686	13 57 15·8	11 2·0	12 26·3	11 1·9	11 1·95	S. 5 15−1 24·35				
4784	14 18 48·2	9 28·7	9 4·8	9 28·4	9 28·55	N. 1 35−0 23·75				
FACE OF SECTOR WEST.										
4852	14 33 48·5	8 19·5	6 19·5	8 19·2	8 19·35	S. 4 10−1 33·85				
4801	14 40 50·5	6 30·3	11 11·9	6 30·0	6 30·15	N. 3 5−4 15·75				
Anon.	14 53 7·8	11 27·3	12 21·6	11 27·6	11 27·45	S. 1 40+0 28·15				
Anon.	14 57 19·2	12 0·6	15 30·3	12 0·7	12 0·65	S. 1 55+3 29 65				
5032	15 8 2·5	9 19·6	6 17·1	9 19·3	9 19·45	N. 0 45+3 2·35				
5054	15 11 34·3	11 2·8	11 28·2	11 2·9	11 2·85	S. 5 20+0 25·35				
5151	15 28 46·5	8 32·1	8 10 6	8 31·9	8 32·0	N. 1 5+0 21·4				
Anon.	15 34 1·5	9 14·8	9 13·8	9 14·8	9 14·8	S. 0 45−0 1·0				
5227	15 40 43·5	9 31·0	14 33·4	9 31·0	9 31·0	S. 2 45+5 2·4				
5272	15 46 57·5	9 11·8	8 1·3	9 11·7	9 11·75	N. 1 35+1 10·45				
5374	16 1 3·3	9 11·4	7 19·0	9 11·2	9 11·3	N. 1 20+1 26·3				
5435	16 9 22·5	9 31·7	10 22·8	9 31·8	9 31·75	S. 0 10+0 25·05				
Anon.	16 13 35·5	10 8·4	8 0·0	10 8·4	10 8·4	S. 2 30−2 8·4				
5498	16 19 34·2	10 15·0	8 16·8	10 14·8	10 14·9	N. 4 15+1 32·1				
Anon.	16 33 18·4	10 29·5	14 28·5	10 29·7	10 29·6	S. 1 25+3 32·9				
5632	16 39 44·2	10 27·6	9 14·5	10 27·7	10 27·65	S. 3 40−1 13·15				
5735	16 54 14·5	10 27·8	15 30·0	10 27·8	10 27·8	S. 3 30+5 2·2				
5817	17 6 36·2	10 23·3	15 23·8	10 23·4	10 23·35	S. 2 5+5 0·45				
5881	17 17 6·3	10 21·5	14 19·5	10 21·3	10 21·4	N. 0 40−3 32·1				
5960	17 29 33·3	11 1·1	11 24·4		11 1·15	S. 1 45+0 23·25				
Anon.	17 30 30·5		13 18·7	11 1·2	11 1·15	N. 0 45−3 17·55				
6016	17 36 44·0	11 13·6	16 0·3	11 13·7	11 13·65	S. 1 15+4 20·65	25·125	56·8	58·1	57·0
6074	17 48 47·0	11 28·4	8 0·4	11 28·2	11 28·3	N. 0 5+3 27·9				
6115	17 55 29·8	11 24·6	10 9·2	11 24·6	11 24·6	S. 0 5−1 15·4				
6145	17 59 44·4	12 23·7	10 19·8	12 23·7	12 23·7	S. 0 25−2 3·9				
6233	18 13 20·5	12 33·4	14 29·5	12 33·7	12 33·55	S. 4 5+1 29·95				
Anon.	18 19 28·5	11 29·7	16 11·8		11 29·53	S. 4 45+1 16·27				
6285	18 20 32·4		10 10·6		11 29 3	N. 2 45−1 18·93				
6305	18 23 25·3	11 29·5	14 19·1	11 29·6	11 29·53	S. 2 45+2 23·57				
Anon.	18 42 23·0	9 29·3	7 21·8	9 29·0	9 29·15	S. 0 35−2 7·33				
6480	18 52 24·0	9 25·4	9 13·4	9 25·3	9 25·35	N. 0 15+0 11·95				
6525	18 57 24·5	10 7·4	12 17·8	10 7·4	10 7·4	N. 0 30−2 10·3				
6639	19 16 47·5	10 21·5	13 23·9	10 21·5	10 21·5	N. 0 20−3 2·4				
Anon.	19 21 1·0	10 27·5	15 21·6	10 27·5	10 27·5	S. 0 35−4 28·05				
6753	19 35 13·7	9 28·4	10 7·0	9 28·4	9 28·4	S. 0 55+0 12 6	25·150	55·0	57·0	56·1
6877	19 54 7·5	9 18·2	6 12·1	9 18·3	9 18·25	S. 2 10−3 6·15				
Anon.	20 5 52·0	9 5·8	13 22·0	9 5·7	9 5·75	N. 0 5+4 16·25				
Anon.	20 15 50·5	9 5·5	6 9·5		9 5·7	N. 0 45+2 30·2				
Anon.	20 16 41·5		6 17·0	9 5·9	9 5·7	N. 0 45+2 22·7				
Anon.	20 21 6 0	9 5·9	12 9·8	9 5·8	9 5·85	N. 0 45−3 3·95				
Anon.	20 23 59·0	10 18·2	7 2·2	10 18·1	10 18·15	N. 0 30+3 15·05				
Anon.	20 33 29·4	10 0·6	13 26·4	10 0·4	10 0·5	N. 0 25−3 25·9				
7207	20 39 54·0	11 26·0	11 25·0	11 26·2	11 26·1	S. 4 0−0 1·1				
Anon.	20 53 17·0	9 9·1	13 3·1	9 8·9	9 9·0	N. 0 40−3 28·1				
Anon.	21 0 26·7	9 16·4	9 11·3	9 16·3	9 16·35	S. 0 0+0 5·05				
7386	21 8 10·0	9 16·0	6 1·6	9 16·0	9 16·0	S. 2 30−3 14·4				
Anon.	21 12 16·3	8 33·3	6 0·5	8 33·2	8 33·25	N. 0 30+2 32·75				
Anon.	21 25 23·5	10 3·5	13 25·8	10 3·6	10 3·55	0 0+3 22·25	25·110	55·4	55·9	55·4

August 6.—Anon. 20h. 15m.—This star was observed by accident; it is of the 6th or 6½th magnitude.
Calm until 20h. S. T. Afterwards light north air. Hazy horizon. Excellent definition.
No. 5960 and Anon. 17h. 30m.—Clamp not touched between these observations.
Anon. 18h. 19m., Nos. 6285 and 6305.—Clamp not touched between these observations.
Anon. 20h. 15m. and Anon. 20h. 16m.—Clamp not touched between these observations.

☉ AUGUST 6, 1843.—FACE OF SECTOR WEST—(continued).

Number of B.A.C.	Time by Chronometer.	Micr. for Plumb-line on Dot.	Micr. for Observation of Star.	Micr. for Plumb-line on Dot.	Mean of Micr. for Plumb-line on Dot.	Star's Apparent Zenith Distance.	Barom.	Attd.	Upper.	Lower.
	h m s	rev. pts.	rev. pts.	rev. pts.	rev. pts.	o ' rev. pts.	in.			
7557	21 35 20·5	11 10·4	7 17·4	11 10·2	11 10·3	S. 3 25-3 26·9				
7657	21 51 35·5	9 30·8	11 15·7	9 31·0	9 30·9	N. 1 10-1 18·8				
Anon.	21 55 26·5	9 31·0	10 11·7	9 31·2	9 31·1	N. 1 10-0 14·6				
7842	22 22 19·3	10 4·5	14 16·8	10 4·6	10 4·55	S. 2 45+4 12·25				
Anon.	22 33 24·4	9 19·1	8 10·4	9 18·8	9 18·95	N. 0 10+1 8·55				
7966	22 43 33·0	10 4·4	11 23·0	10 4·4	9 4·4	S. 3 20+1 18·6				
7992	22 48 43·0	9 24·5	11 0·2	9 24·8	9 24·65	S. 0 5+1 9·55				
1802	5 33 41·2	10 15·8	7 17·4	10 15·7	10 15·75	S. 3 50-2 32·35				
2293	6 52 13·0	9 15·2	8 29·7	9 15·0	9 15·1	N. 1 35+0 19·4	25·130	57·2	61·2	57·3

☾ AUGUST 7, 1843.—FACE OF SECTOR WEST

Number of B.A.C.	Time by Chronometer.	Micr. for Plumb-line on Dot.	Micr. for Observation of Star.	Micr. for Plumb-line on Dot.	Mean of Micr. for Plumb-line on Dot.	Star's Apparent Zenith Distance.	Barom.	Attd.	Upper.	Lower.
4458	13 11 33·7	9 30·8	13 30·0	9 30·8	9 30·8	S. 5 30+3 33·2				
4579	13 36 34·5	9 2·8	7 20·7	9 3·0	9 2·9	S. 1 55-1 16·2				
4623	13 42 34·0	9 9·0	13 0·4	9 9·0	9 9·0	S. 1 50+3 25·4				
Anon.	14 45 54·0	11 5·3	14 32·4	11 5·5	11 5·4	S. 2 50+3 27·0				
5960	17 29 37·5	8 31·0	9 21·8		8 31·15	S. 1 45+0 24·65				
Anon.	17 30 35·0		11 15·2	8 31·3	8 31·15	S. .1 45+2 18·05				
6016	17 38 49·0	9 2·8	13 24·9	9 3·0	9 2·9	S. 1 15+4 22·0				
6074	17 48 50·7	9 6·0	5 12·0	9 6·0	9 6·0	N. 0 5+3 28·0				
6115	17 55 33·7	9 5·5	7 24·3	9 5·5	9 5·5	S. 0 5-1 15·2				
Anon	19 21 2·0	9 14·5	14 7·5	9 14·5	9 14·5	N. 0 35-4 27·0				
6753	19 35 18·2	9 25·0	10 3·8	9 25·2	9 25·1	S. 0 55+0 12·7				
Anon.	21 0 30·0	13 11·5	13 5·8	13 11·4	13 11·45	0 0+0 5·65				
2293	6 52 16·2	8 7·3	7 21·4	8 7·4	8 7·35	N. 1 85+0 19·95				

FACE OF SECTOR EAST.

Number of B.A.C.	Time by Chronometer.	Micr. for Plumb-line on Dot.	Micr. for Observation of Star.	Micr. for Plumb-line on Dot.	Mean of Micr. for Plumb-line on Dot.	Star's Apparent Zenith Distance.	Barom.	Attd.	Upper.	Lower.
4686	13 57 20·8	8 27·4	10 17·4	8 27·3	8 27·35	S. 5 15-1 24·05				
4784	14 18 51·5	11 29·8	11 6·0	11 30·0	11 29·9	N. 1 35-0 23·9				
5054	15 11 46·5	10 0·0	10 30·5	9 33·9	9 33·95	S. 5 20-0 30·55				
Anon.	15 34 10·5	10 1·7	11 23·5	10 1·4	10 1·55	S. 0 45-1 21·95		59·7	60·6	59·8
Anon.	16 13 45·5	10 1·6	14 0·0	10 1·6	10 1·6	S. 2 30-3 32·4				
Anon.	16 33 27·7	10 20·7	8 9·45	10 20·6	10 20·65	S. 1 45+2 14·0	25·150	58·9	59·4	58·9
5817	17 6 46·5	11 17·1	8 4·5	11 17·0	11 17·05	S. 2 5+3 12·55				
6233	18 13 40·7	8 24·3	8 18·2	8 24·8	8 24·55	S. 4 5+0 6·35	25·150	57·4	57·9	57·3
Anon.	20 6 0·0	10 14·8	7 21·8	10 14·7	10 14·75	S. 0 5+2 26·95				
Anon.	20 15 58·5	10 25·0	15 8·3	10 25·0	10 25·0	N. 0 45+4 17·3				
Anon.	20 16 49·5	10 25·0	15 0·6	10 25·0	10 25·0	N. 0 45+4 9·6				
Anon.	20 24 6·4	10 22·6	15 26·3	10 23·0	10 22·8	N. 0 30+5 3·5				
7657	21 51 42·8	8 6·8	8 10·4	8 6·9	8 6·85	N. 1 10+0 3·55		55·2	55·4	53·4
Anon.	21 55 34·2	8 7·0	9 15·0	8 7·0	8 7·0	N. 1 10+1 8·0				
Anon.	22 33 31·8	9 19·3	12 16·7	9 19·4	9 19·35	N. 0 10+2 8·90				
7966	22 43 42·8	9 22·5	9 26·4	9 22·6	9 22·55	S. 3 20-0 3·85				
1802	5 33 51·2	8 8·5	12 27·8	8 8·5	8 8·5	S. 3 50-4 19·3	25·125	52·3	54 3	52·4

♂ AUGUST 8, 1843.—FACE OF SECTOR WEST.

Number of B.A.C.	Time by Chronometer.	Micr. for Plumb-line on Dot.	Micr. for Observation of Star.	Micr. for Plumb-line on Dot.	Mean of Micr. for Plumb-line on Dot.	Star's Apparent Zenith Distance.	Barom.	Attd.	Upper.	Lower.
4458	13 11 36·5	7 27·4	11 26·8	7 27·0	7 27·2	S. 5 20+3 33·4	25·150	62·2	66·0	62·4
4579	13 36 38·3	8 5·1	6 23·0	8 4·8	8 4·95	S. 1 55-1 15·95				
4623	13 42 37·3	8 7·7	11 32·1	8 7·4	8 7·55	S. 1 50+3 24·55				
4686	13 57 16·5	8 14·6	8 10·7	8 15·0	8 14·8	S. 5 15-0 4·1				
4784	14 18 52·0	10 3·6	12 15·1	10 3·8	10 3·7	N. 1 35-2 11·4				
4852	14 33 54·5	9 29·9	7 30·7	9 30·1	9 30·0	S. 4 10-1 33·3				

August 7.—Good definition. Light north air.
A part of the night employed in taking micrometer runs.
No. 5960 and Anon. 17ʰ. 30ᵐ.—Clamp not touched between these observations.

♂ AUGUST 8, 1843.—FACE OF SECTOR WEST—(*continued*).

Number of B.A.C.	Time by Chronometer.	Micr. for Plumb-line on Dot.	Micr. for Observation of Star.	Micr. for Plumb-line on Dot.	Mean of Micr. for Plumb-line on Dot.	Star's Apparent Zenith Distance.	Barom.	Attd.	Upper.	Lower.
	h m s	rev. pts.	rev. pts.	rev. pts.	rev. pts.	° ′ rev. pts.	in.			
4891	14 40 58·0	8 29·8	13 11·9	8 30·1	8 29·95	N. 3 5−4 15·95				
Anon.	14 45 58·2	9 14·7	4 9·4	9 14·5	9 14·6	S. 2 55−5 5·2				
Anon.	14 53 15·5	9 4·7	9 33·3	9 4·8	9 4·75	S. 1 40+0 28·55				
5032	15 8 10·4	10 33·9	7 32·4	11 0·2	11 0·05	N. 0 45+3 1·05				
5054	15 11 41·4	12 25·5	13 17·0	12 25·5	12 25·5	S. 5 20+0 25·5				
5151	15 28 54·5	10 32·5	10 12·5	10 32·7	10 32·6	N. 1 5+0 20 1				
5227	15 40 51·5	11 23·0	16 25·5	11 23·0	11 23·0	S. 2 45+5 2·5				
5272	15 47 5·5	8 27·8	7 18·5	8 27·7	8 27·75	N. 1 35+1 9·25				
5374	16 1 10·8	9 8·2	7 16·2	9 8·1	9 8·15	S. 1 20+1 25·95				
5435	16 9 27·0	9 15·8	10 7·5	9 15·8	9 15·8	S. 0 10+0 25·7				
Anon.	16 13 43·5	10 4·5	7 30·2	10 4·3	10 4·4	S. 2 30−2 8·2				
5498	16 19 42·5	9 32·6	8 1·0	9 32·6	9 32·6	N. 4 15+1 31·6	25·110	56·8	57·4	56·9
Anon.	16 33 26·4	10 26·6	14 25·6	10 26·5	10 26·55	S. 1 25+3 33·05				
5632	16 39 52·2	11 6·5	9 28·5	11 6·5	11 6·5	·. 3 40−1 12·0				
5735	16 54 22·5	9 6 3	14 9·2	9 6·4	9 6·35	S. 3 30+5 2·85				
5817	17 6 44·2	8 24·8	13 26·5	8 24·8	8 24·8	S. 2 5+5 1·7				
5881	17 17 14·2	8 25 6	12 24·5	8 25·6	8 25·6	N. 0 40−3 32·9				
5960	17 29 45·5	9 17·5	10 7·4		9 17·6	S. 1 45+0 23·8	25·110	55·8	56·3	56·0
Anon.	17 30 37·5		12 1·3	9 17·7	9 17·6	S. 1 45+2 17·7				
6016	17 38 52·2	9 17·8	14 5·1	9 18·0	9 17·9	S. 1 15+4 21·2				
6074	17 48 54·6	9 16·2	5 22·0	9 16·1	9 16·1	N. 0 5+3 28·1				
6115	17 55 37·2	9 5·2	7 25·0	9 5·4	9 5·3	S. 0 5−1 14·3				
6145	17 50 52·4	9 6·4	7 2·5	9 5·8	9 6·1	S. 0 25−2 3·6				
6233	18 13 37·8	9 28·3	11 23·5	9 28·5	9 28·4	S. 4 5+1 29·1	25·110	55·0	55·8	55·0
Anon.	18 19 36·8	8 9·6	12 26·6	8 9·8	8 9·62	S. 2 45+4 16·98				
6285	18 20 40·5		6 24·4	8 9·5	8 9·62	S. 2 45−1 19·22				
6305	18 23 36·5	8 0·6	10 33·3	8 9·6	8 9·62	S. 2 45+2 23·68				
Anon.	18 42 31·5	8 31·5	6 24·6	8 31·3	8 31·3	S. 0 35−2 6·8				
6489	18 52 32·3	8 27·0	8 16·2	8 26·8	8 26·9	N. 0 15+0 10·7				
6525	18 57 33·0	8 17·0	10 27·5	8 17·3	8 17·15	N. 1 30−2 10·35				
6639	19 16 56·0	7 33·4	11 2·3	7 33·6	7 33·5	N. 0 20−3 2·8				
Anon.	19 21 8·5	7 33·7	12 28·4	7 33·9	7 33·8	N. 0 35−4 28·6				
6753	19 35 22·0	8 15·0	8 29·5	8 16·1	8 16·0	ℛ. 0 55+0 13·5				
6877	19 54 16·2	8 7·9	5 2·0	8 7·8	8 7·85	S. 2 10−3 5·85				
Anon.	20 6 0·2	8 9·5	12 26·5	8 9·6	8 9·55	S. 0 5+4 16·95				
Anon.	20 14	9 5·3	6 8·5	9 5·0	9 5·0	N. 0 45+2 30·5				
Anon.	20 16 50·0		6 16·9	9 5·0	9 5·0	N. 0 45+2 22·1				
Anon.	20 21 15·0	9 4·9	12 9·4	9 4·8	9 5·0	N. 0 45−3 4·4				
Anon.	20 24 7·0	9 6·3	5 24·8	9 5·8	9 6·05	N. 0 30+3 15·25				
Anon.	20 33 37·0	9 15·2	13 7·3	9 15·6	9 15·4	N. 0 25−3 25·0	25·100	54·0	54·5	54 0
7207	20 40 3·0	10 7·4	10 6·7	10 7·7	7·5	S. 4 0−0 0·85				
Anon.	20 53 24·0	9 6·6	13 0·6	9 7·0	9 6·8	N. 0 40−3 27·8				
Anon.	21 0 34·2	9 13·2	9 8·2	9 12·8	9 13·0	0 0+0 4·8				
7386	21 8 17·8	9 3·8	5 24·5	9 3·6	9 3·7	S. 2 30−3 13·2				
Anon.	21 12 24·5	7 28·5	4 30·2	7 28·3	7 28·4	N. 0 30+2 32·2				
Anon	21 25 31·5	8 11·2	11 33·5	8 11·4	8 11·3	0 0+3 22·2				
7557	21 35 28·5	8 28·1	5 0·7	8 28·4	8 28·25	S. 3 25−3 27·55				
7657	21 51 43·5	8 3·5	9 22·9	8 3·7	8 3·5	N. 1 10−1 19·3				
Anon.	21 55 34·5	8 3·5	8 17·6	8 3·5	8 3·5	N. 1 10−0 14·1				
7842	22 22 27·5	9 8·6	13 21·5	9 8·5		S. 2 45+4 12·95				
Anon.	22 33 32·5	9 2·7	7 28·7	9 2·1	9 2·4	N. 0 10+1 7·7				
7966	22 43 41·8	9 24·2	11 8·6	9 24·2		S. 3 30+1 14·2				
7992	22 48 52·5	8 26·6	10 2·4	8 26·6	8 26·6	S. 0 5+1 9·8	25·105	52·0	53·2	53·0
1802	5 33 48·5	9 13·4	6 13·7	9 13·2	9 13·3	S. 3 50−2 33·6				
2293	6 52 20·5	8 12·8	7 25·8	8 12·5	8 12·05	N. 1 35+0 20·85	25·120	54·9	59·0	54·8

August 8.—Calm until 21ʰ. S. T. ; then a light northerly air. Beautiful definition.
No. 5960 and Anon. 17ʰ. 30ᵐ.—Clamp not touched between these observations.
Anon. 18ʰ. 19ᵐ., Nos. 6285 and 6305.—Clamp not touched between these observations.
Anon. 20ʰ. 14ᵐ., Anon. 20ʰ. 16ᵐ., and Anon. 20ʰ. 21ᵐ.—Clamp not touched between these observations.

☿ August 9, 1843.—Face of Sector East.

Number of B.A.C.	Time by Chronometer.	Micr. for Plumb-line on Dot.	Micr. for Observation of Star.	Micr. for Plumb-line on Dot.	Mean of Micr. for Plumb-line on Dot.	Star's Apparent Zenith Distance.	Barom.	Thermometers. Attd.	Upper.	Lower.
	h m s	rev. pts.	rev. pts.	rev. pts.	rev. pts.	° ′ rev. pts.	in.			
4458	13 11 48·7	8 17·4	6 4·3	8 17·0	8 17·2	S. 5 30+2 12·9	25·130	57·7	60·6	57·8
4686	13 57 28·7	10 8·3	11 31·5	10 8·1	10 8·2	S. 5 15—1 23·3				
4852	14 34 5·2	9 26·7	13 13·6	9 26·7	9 26·7	S. 4 10—3 20·9				
4891	14 41 2·5	10 29·3	8 0·8	10 29·3	10 29·3	N. 3 5—2 28·5				
4916	14 46 7·3	9 26·3	7 21·6	9 25·9	9 26·1	S. 2 50+2 4·5				
Anon.	14 53 23·5	9 3·7	9 31·8	9 4·2	9 3·95	S. 1 40—0 27·85				
Anon.	14 57 35·2	8 15·8	6 6·8	8 15·8	8 15·8	S. 1 55+2 9·0				
5032	15 9 17·0	8 29·9	13 19·2	8 30·5	8 30·2	N. 0 45+4 23·0				
5054	15 11 53·6	7 18·6	8 14·6	7 18·7	7 18·65	S. 5 20—0 29·95				
5151	15 29 1·5	11 7·0	13 15·7	11 6·8	11 6·9	N. 1 5+2 8·8				
Anon.	15 34 17·5	9 33·5	11 21·2	9 33·6	9 33·55	S. 0 45—1 21·65				
5227	15 41 0·5	9 21·0	6 6·9	9 21·1	9 21·05	S. 2 45+3 14·15				
5272	15 47 11·5	9 33·7	12 31·9	9 33·6	9 33·15	N. 1 35+2 32 25				
5374	16 1 17·2	10 2·0	13 15·5	10 1·8	10 1·9	N. 1 20+3 13·6				
5435	16 9 37·5	10 17·8	11 14·8	10 18·0	10 17·9	S. 0 10—0 30·9				
Anon.	16 13 52·0	10 18·0	14 14·8	10 18·0	10 18·0	S. 2 30—3 30·8				
5498	16 19 46·0	11 21·1	15 6·0	11 20·8	11 20·95	N. 4 15+3 19·05				
5588	16 33 35·0	8 22·3	6 10·0	8 22·3	8 22·3	S. 1 25+2 12·3	25·100	50·7	51·4	50·8
5632	16 40 2·5	8 24·1	11 25·4	8 24·2	8 24·15	S. 3 40—3 1·25				
5735	16 54 32·5	8 30·7	5 16·3	8 30·8	8 30·75	S. 3 30+3 14·45				
5817	17 6 53·2	9 31·0	6 17·7	9 31·2	9 31·1	S. 2 5+3 13·4				
5881	17 17 21·0	9 30·8	7 20·2	9 31·0	9 30·9	N. 0 40—2 10·7				
5960	17 29 49·5	9 33·1	10 31·2		9 33·1	S. 1 45—0 32·1				
5964	17 30 46·5		9 3·6	9 33·1	9 33·1	S. 1 45+0 29·5				
6074	17 40 2·0	9 25·1	15 7·7	9 25·2	9 25·15	N. 0 5+5 16·55	25·100	48·9	49·3	48·9
6115	17 55 45·3	10 1·9	13 5·7	10 1·8	10 1·85	S. 0 3—3 3·85				
6145	17	9 11·4	13 3·4	9 11·8	9 11·6	S. 0 25—3 25 8				
6233	18 13 48·5	9 1·0	8 28·1	9 0·8	9 0·9	S. 4 5+0 6·8				
6285	18 20 50·0	9 1·3	12 8·5	9 1·4	9 1·35	S. 2 45—3 7·15				
6305	18 23 41·0	9 1·4	7 33·8	9 1·3	9 1·35	S. 2 45+1 1·55				
6489	18 52 39·0	12 25·4	14 25·7	12 25·8	12 25·6	N. 0 15+2 0 1				
6525	18 57 38·6	12 25·8	12 3·0	12 25·8	12 25·8	N. 1 30—0 22·8				
6639	19 17 2·4	12 19·8	11 5·5	12 20·2	12 20·0	N. 0 20—1 14·5				

♃ August 10, 1843.—Face of Sector East.

2293	6 52 38·5	6 22·4	8 32·8	6 22·6	6 22·5	N. 2 35+2 10·3	25·090	32·0	32·0	32·0

♀ August 11, 1843.—Face of Sector East.

6074	17 49 8·5	9 28·8	15 11·5	9 28·6	9 28·7	N. 0 5+5 16·8	25·075	36·9	37·2	36·6
6115	17 55 51·2	9 31·9	13 2·2	9 32·2	9 32·05	S. 0 5—3 4·15				
6233	18 13 48·0	9 19·6	9 13·5	9 19·8	9 19·7	S. 4 15+0 6·2				
6275	18 19 48·2	9 8·5	6 15·7		9 8·68	S. 2 45+2 26·98				
6285	18 20 51·0		12 16·7	9 8·8	9 8·68	S. 2 45—3 8·02				
6305	18 23 43·8	9 8·7	8 8·5	9 8·7	9 8·68	S. 2 45+1 0·18				
6414	18 42 44·0	9 4·3	12 32·6	9 4·2	9 4·25	S 0 35—3 28·35				
6489	18 52 45·4	9 9·0	11 10·0	9 8·6	9 8·9	N. 0 15+2 1·1				
6525	18 57 47·5	9 3·8	8 16·3	9 3·8	9 3·8	N. 1 30—0 21·5				
6639	19 17 9·0	8 26·7	7 12·4	8 26·6	8 26·65	N. 0 20—1 14·25	25·070	36·1	36·3	36·0
Anon.	19 21 22·2	9 25·6	6 19·5	9 25·8	9 25·7	S. 0 55—1 7·45				
6753	19 35 34·3	9 25·2	10 32·8	9 25·5	9 25·35	S. 0 55—1 7·45				
6877	19 54 27·0	10 0·0	14 28·4	10 0·0	10 0·0	S. 2 10—4 28·4				

August 9.—Nos. 5960 and 5964.—Clamp not touched between these observations.
Several stars lost in the early part of this evening from fog. Bad definition when it cleared off.
August 10.—Frost. Bad definition. Examined the adjustments of the Instrument, and adjusted the Azimuth error by means of the upper Azimuth screw. The Instrument was deranged in Azimuth, when covering it with tarpauling yesterday.
August 11.—Dense fog until 17ʰ. 30ᵐ S.T. Good definition after the fog cleared away.
Nos. 6275, 6285, and 6305.—Clamp not touched between these observations.

♀ AUGUST 11, 1843.—FACE OF SECTOR EAST—(continued).

Number of B.A.C.	Time by Chronometer.	Micr. for Plumb-line on Dot.	Micr. for Observation of Star.	Micr. for Plumb-line on Dot.	Mean of Micr. for Plumb-line on Dot.	Star's Apparent Zenith Distance.	Barom.	Thermometers. Attd.	Upper.	Lower.
	h m s	rev. pts.	rev. pts.	rev. pts.	rev. pts.	o ' rev. pts.	in.			
6948	20 6 12·5	10 13·8	7 20·8	10 13·7	10 13·75	S. 0 5+2 26·95	25·070	35·4	35·6	35·1
7011	20 15 12·6	11 3·7	15 21·1	11 3·8	11 3·76	N. 0 45+4 17·34				
7026	20 17 3·7		15 13·4	11 3·8	11 3·76	N. 0 45+4 9·64				
7057	20 21 28·5	11 3·8	9 20·7	11 3·7	11 3·76	N. 0 45−1 17·06				
Anon.	20 24 21·0	11 11·7	16 15·1	11 11·8	11 11·75	N. 0 30+5 3·35				
Anon.	20 33 50·5	9 32·1	7 28·4	9 32·3	9 32·2	N. 0 25−2 3·8				
7207	20 40 11·5	9 26·1	11 10·4	9 26·0	9 26·05	S. 4 0−1 24·35				
Anon.	20 53 38·6	11 5·2	8 33·5	11 5·4	11 5·3	N. 0 40−2 5·8				
Anon.	21 0 47·6	11 9·6	13 5·3	11 9·5	11 9·55	0 0+1 29·75		34·9	35·2	34·6
7386	21 8 29·5	11 21·9	16 25·7	11 21·8	11 21·85	8. 2 30−5 3·85				
Anon.	21 12 38·5	10 7·6	14 27·2	10 7·3	10 7·45	N. 0 30+4 19·75				
Anon.	21 25 44·5	9 32·1	7 33·3	9 32·3	9 32·2	0 0+1 32·9				
7557	21 35 39·0	9 26·3	15 8·2	9 26·3	9 26·3	8. 3 25−5 15·9				
7657	21 51 58·2	9 21·5	9 25·5	9 21·5	9 21·5	N. 1 10+0 4·0				
Anon.	21 55 49·5	9 21·6	10 29·8	9 21 8	9 21·7	N. 1 10+1 8·1				
7842	22 22 38·5	10 2·0	7 12·5	10 2·0	10 2·0	S. 2 45+2 23·5	25·065	34·3	34·5	34·2
7909	22 33 46·0	9 24·9	12 23·2	9 24·8	9 24·85	N. 0 10+2 32·35				
7966	22 43 50·0	11 1·7	11 6·4	11 1·8	11 1·75	S. 3 20−0 4·65				
7992	22 49 5·5	11 6·1	11 21·2	11 6·0	11 6·05	S. 0 5−0 15·15	25·065	33·8	34·2	33·5
2293	6 52 35·2	8 10·8	10 21·3	8 11·4	8 11·10	N. 1 35+2 10·2	25·070	36·0	36·7	35·9

♄ AUGUST 12, 1843.—FACE OF SECTOR WEST.

4458	13 11 47·0	9 25·9	13 25·3	9 25·9	9 25·9	S. 5 30+3 33·4	25·100	42·4	45·3	42·3

FACE OF SECTOR EAST.

4579	13 36 53·2	9 20·6	12 26·0	9 20·2	9 20·4	S. 1 55−3 5·6				
4623	13 42 53·0	9 7·9	7 7·1	9 7·8	9 7·85	S. 1 50+2 0·75				

FACE OF SECTOR WEST.

4686	13 57 29·0	8 32·7	8 30·5	8 32·6	8 32·65	S. 5 15−0 2·15				
4852	14 34 7·0	8 33·5	7 0·6	8 33·4	8 33·45	S. 4 10−1 32·85				
4891	14 41 12·2	8 25·9	13 8·5	8 26·3	8 26·1	N. 3 5−4 16·4				
Anon.	14 53 28·6	9 23·5	10 18·8	9 23·5	9 23·5	S. 1 40+0 29·1				
5032	15 8 24·3	9 7·5	6 6·6	9 7·6	9 7·55	N. 0 45+3 0·95				
5054	15 11 54·5	9 23·7	10 15·0	9 24·2	9 23·95	S. 5 20+0 25·05				
5151	15 29 8·2	9 18·8	8 32·6	9 18·4	9 18·6	N. 1 5+0 20·0				
Anon.	15 34 22·0	10 5·0	10 5·4	10 5·1	10 5·05	S. 0 45+0 0·35				
5227	15 41 4·0	10 12·4	15 15·5	10 12·3	10 12·35	S. 2 45+5 3·15				
5272	15 47	10 1·5	8 25·3	10 1·5	10 1·5	N. 1 35+1 10·2	25·080	38·3	39·2	38·3
5374	16 1 25·5	9 26·5	8 1·4	9 26·4	9 26 45	N. 1 20+1 25·05				
5435	16 9 43·6	9 27·8	10 19·8	9 28·2	9 28·0	S. 0 10+0 25·8				
Anon.	16 13 56·0	11 2·1	8 28·1	11 2·0	11 2·05	S. 2 30−2 7·95				
5498	16 19 56·0	8 30·8	6 33·8	8 30·6	8 30·7	N. 4 15+1 30·9				
5586	16 33 39·5	9 8·8	13 8·9	9 9·0	9 8·9	S. 1 25+4 0·0				
5632	16 40 4·2	9 8·3	7 30·4	9 8·0	9 8·15	S. 3 40−1 11·75				
5735	16 54 34·5	9 27·2	14 29·9	9 27·3	9 27·25	S. 3 30+5 2·65				
5817	17 6 56·5	10 5·4	15 7·5	10 5·4	10 5·4	S. 2 5+5 2·1	25·090	36·3	37·2	36·3
5881	17 17 27·0	9 22·3	13 21·8	9 22·5	9 22·5	N. 0 40−3 33·4				
5960	17 29 53·5	10 19·4	11 9·5		10 19·45	S. 1 45+0 24·05				
5964	17 30 51·0		13 4·0	10 19·5	10 19·45	S. 1 45+2 18·55				
6016	17 39 5·5	10 23·4	15 10·9	10 23·5	10 23·45	S. 1 15+4 21·45				
6074	17 49 7·5	10 31·9	7 4·6	10 32·0	10 31·95	N. 0 5+3 27·35	25·080	35·4	36·1	35·6
6115	17 55 51·0	9 19·9	8 5·4	9 19·6	9 19·75	S. 0 5−1 14·35				

August 11.—Nos. 7011, 7026, and 7057.—Clamp not touched between these observations.
The observation, of α Columbæ lost, owing to the water in the plumb-line cistern being frozen.
August 12.—No. 5272.—The time of transit not noted.
Nos. 5960 and 5964.—Clamp not touched between these observations.

♄ August 12, 1843.—Face of Sector West—(continued).

Number of B.A.C.	Time by Chronometer.	Micr. for Plumb-line on Dot.	Micr. for Observation of Star.	Micr. for Plumb-line on Dot.	Mean of Micr. for Plumb-line on Dot.	Star's Apparent Zenith Distance.	Barom.	Thermometers.		
								Attd.	Upper.	Lower.
	h m s	rev. pts.	rev. pts.	rev. pts.	rev. pts.	° ′ rev. pts.	in.			
6145	18 0 5·5	9 11·7	7 8·3	9 11·5	9 11·6	S. 0 25—2 3·3				
6233	18 13 40·3	9 8·4	11 5·1	9 8·8	9 8·6	S. 4 5+1 30·5				
6275	18 19 49·5	9 20·6	14 3·7		9 20·58	S. 2 45+4 17·12	25·065	35·0	35·6	35·2
6285	18 20 52·5		8 2·5	9 20·3	9 20·58	S. 2 45—1 18·08				
6305	18 23 45·7	9 20·8	12 11·1	9 20·6	9 20·58	S. 2 45+2 24·52				
6414	18 42 43·4	9 32·8	7 27·7	9 33·0	9 32·9	S. 0 35—2 5·2				
6489	18 52 45·0	9 30·2	9 20·5	9 30·3	9 30·25	N. 0 15+0 9·75				
6525	18 57 46·0	10 16·0	12 28·0	10 16·2	10 16·1	N. 1 30—2 11·9				
6039	19 17 8·8	10 3·5	13 7·2	10 3·5	10 3·5	N. 0 20—3 3·7				
Anon.	19 21 21·2	10 5·4	15 1·4	10 5·6	10 5·5	N. 0 35—4 29·9				
6753	19 35 34·5	10 27·0	11 6·6	10 26·9	10 26·95	S. 0 55+0 13·65				
6877	19 54	10 13·8	7 7·7	10 13·4	10 13·6	S. 2 10—3 5·9	25·070	34·2	34·5	34·3
6948	20		14 3·3	9 20·4		S. 0 5+4 10·9				
7011	20 15 12·0	9 25·8	6 31·4		9 25·72	N. 0 45+2 28·32				
7026	20 17 2·5	9 25·5	7 4·4	9 25·7	9 25·72	N. 0 45+2 21·32				
7057	20 21 27·5	9 25·8	12 31·0	9 25·8	9 25·72	N. 0 45—3 5·28				
Anon.	20 24 20·3	10 3·5	6 24·3	10 3·6	10 3·55	N. 0 30+3 13·25				
Anon.	20 33 50·5	9 14·1	13 5·8	9 13·9	9 14·0	N. 0 25—3 25·8				
7207	20 40 14·5	10 3·7	10 3·6	10 3·6	10 3·65	S. 4 0—0 0·05				
Anon.	20 53 38·5	9 25·3	13 20·9	9 25·7	9 25·5	N. 0 40—3 29·4				
Anon.	21 0 47·5	9 28·4	9 24·4	9 28·3	9 28·35	0 0+0 3·95				
7386	21 8 30·5	10 6·5	6 28·3	10 6·8	10 6·65	S. 2 30—3 12·55				
Anon.	21 12 37·5	9 28·6	6 32·0	9 28·3	9 28·45	N. 0 30+2 30·45				
Anon.	21 25 44·5	9 27·8	13 18·0	9 28·0	9 27·9	0 0+3 24·1				
7557	21 35 40·2	10 0·5	6 8·9	10 0·8	10 0·65	S. 3 25—3 25·75				
7657	21 51 57·0	9 11·7	10 32·0	9 12·0	9 11·85	N. 1 10—1 20·15				
Anon.	21 55 48·2	9 11·6	9 27·4	9 11·9	9 11·75	N. 1 10—0 15·65				
7842	22 22 40·0	9 27·8	14 7·5	9 27·5	9 27·65	S. 2 45+4 13·85				
7909	22 33 45·5	9 27·0	8 20·5	9 27·3	9 27·15	N. 0 10+1 6·65	25·070	33·7	34·2	34·2
7966	22 43 52·5	9 24·8	11 10·3	9 24·7	9 24·75	S. 3 20+1 19·55				
7992	22 49 5·4	9 3·4	10 13·5	9 3·3	9 3·35	S. 0 5+1 10·15				
1802	5 34 0·2	10 2·0	7 3·4	10 2·1	10 2·05	S. 3 50—2 32·65	25·075	35·0	36·5	35·1
2293	6 52 33·5	10 10·8	9 24·3	10 10·6	10 10·7	N. 1 35+0 20·4	25·080	38·4	41·9	38·5

☉ August 13, 1843.—Face of Sector East.

4458	13 11 56·0	10 8·0	7 32·0	10 7·8	10 7 9	S. 5 30+2 9·9	25·105	47·8	52·5	47·9
4023	13 42 58·0	9 10·6	7 8·2	9 10·3	9 10·45	S. 1 50+2 2·25				
4686	13 57 37·3	8 26·5	10 18·7	8 26·7	8 26·6	S. 5 15—1 26·1				
4852	14 34 14·7	9 20·7	13 10·0	9 20·8	9 20·75	S. 4 10—3 23·25				
Anon.	14 53 35·2	8 1·6	8 33·0	8 2·2	8 1·9	S. 1 40—0 31·0				
5032	15 8 29·2	8 16·9	13 8·1	8 16·9	8 16·9	N. 0 45+4 25·2				
5054	15 12 2·2	8 27·6	9 26·8	8 27·6	8 27·6	S. 5 20—0 33·2				
5151	15 29 15·4	9 11·3	11 22·8	9 11·2	9 11·25	N. 1 5+2 11·55				
5227	15 41 12·0	8 7·4	4 30·7	8 7·4	8 7·4	S. 2 45+3 10·7				
5272	15 47 25·5	8 25·4	11 26·1	8 25·6	8 25·5	N. 1 35+3 0·6				
5374	16 1 31·0	9 13·8	12 30·0	9 13·8	9 13·8	N. 1 20+3 16·2				
5436	16 9 50·5	11 3·8	12 3·5	11 3·6	11 3·8	S. 0 10—0 33·7				
Anon.	16 14 3·5	11 11·4	15 11·6	11 11·3	11 11·35	S. 2 20+0 25·0				
5408	16 20 2·2	11 2·3	14 23·4	11 1·7	11 2·0	N. 4 15+3 21·4				
5588	16 33 46·5	11 3·2	8 27·4	11 3·3	11 3·25	S. 1 25+2 9·85	25·090	41·0	41·4	41·0
5632	16 40 12·6	10 13·7	13 17·1	10 13·3	10 13·5	S. 3 40—3 3·6				
5735	16 54 43·0	10 8·7	6 31·2	10 8·9	10 8·8	S. 3 30+3 11·6				
5817	17 7 4·2	9 30·4	6 19·4	9 30·4	9 30·4	S. 2 5+3 11·0				

August 12.—Nos. 6275, 6285 and 6305.—Clamp not touched between these observations.
No. 6877 and 6948.—The times of transit not noted.
Nos. 7011, 7027, and 7057.—Clamp not touched between these observations.
Good definition.

⊙ August 13, 1843.—Face of Sector East—(continued).

Number of B.A.C.	Time by Chronometer.	Micr. for Plumb-line on Dot.	Micr. for Observation of Star.	Micr. for Plumb-line on Dot.	Mean of Micr. for Plumb-line on Dot.	Star's Apparent Zenith Distance.	Barom.	Thermometers.		
								Attd.	Upper.	Lower.
	h m s	rev. pts.	rev. pts.	rev. pts.	rev. pts.	° ' rev. pts.	in.			
5881	17 17 34·2	9 28·0	7 18·0	9 27·5	9 27·75	N. 0 40−2 9·75				
6016	17 39 12·4	10 13·7	7 16·3	10 13·8	10 13·75	S. 1 15+2 31·45				
6074	17 49 14·5	11 9·0	16 27·0	11 8·9	11 8·95	N. 0 5+5 18·05				
6115	17 55 57·5	10 3·0	13 8·7	10 3·0	10 3·0	S. 0 5−3 5·7				
6145	18 0 12·5	9 27·3	13 19·3	9 27·0	9 27·15	S. 0 25−3 26·15				
6233	18 13 8·4	9 23·6	9 17·9	9 23·3	9 23·45	S. 4 5+0 5·55				
6275	18 19 56·5		6 10·0	9 3·0	9 3·08	S. 2 45+2 27·08				
6285	18 21 1·0		12 11·4	9 3·2	9 3·08	S. 2 45−3 8·32				
6305	18 23 53·5	9 3·1	8 2·1	9 3·0	9 3·08	S. 2 45+1 0·98				
6414	18 42 51·0	9 10·6	13 5·9	9 11·2	9 10·9	S. 0 35−3 20·0	25·090	38·8	39·0	38·6
Anon.	19 21 28·0	10 3·4	6 30·8	10 3·0	10 3·2	N. 0 35−3 6·4				
6753	19 35 41·8	10 17·8	11 26·5	10 17·7	10 17·75	S. 0 55−1 8·75				
6877	19 54 36·0	10 14·6	15 9·8	10 14·8	10 14·7	S. 2 10−4 29·1				
6948	20 6 19·5	10 9·0	7 17·0	10 9·1	10 9·05	S. 0 5+2 26·05	25·090	38·8	39·0	38·8
7011	20 15 18·5	10 28·6	15 13·0	10 28·5	10 28·48	N. 0 45+4 18·52				
7026	20 17 9·5		15 4·8	10 28·6	10 28·48	N. 0 45+4 10·32				
7057	20 21 34·5	10 28·4	9 12·0	10 28·3	10 28·48	N. 0 45−1 16·48				
Anon.	20 24 26·0	10 24·3	15 27·9	10 24·6	10 24·45	N. 0 30+5 3·45				
Anon.	20 33 57·0	10 23·5	8 19·6	10 23·7	10 23·6	N. 0 25−2 4·0				
7207	20 40 22·8	11 8·1	12 32·3	11 8·0	11 8·05	S. 4 0−1 24·25				
Anon.	20 53 44·5	11 9·7	9 4·0	11 9·5	11 9·6	N. 0 40−2 56·0				
Anon.	21 0 54·8	11 19·2	13 15·0	11 19·2	11 19·2	0 0+1 29·8				
7386	21 8 38·5	10 21·9	15 26·8	10 22·0	10 21·95	S. 2 30−5 4·85				
Anon.	21 12 44·3	10 28·5	15 15·3	10 28·8	10 28·65	N. 0 30+4 20·65				
Anon.	21 25 52·0	10 1·9	8 4·9	10 1·9	10 1·9	0 0+1 31·0				
7557	21 35 49·3	9 12·3	14 28·7	9 12·2	9 12·25	S. 3 25−5 16·45				
7657	21 52 3·5	9 12·0	9 16·0	9 11·8	9 11·9	N. 1 10+0 4·1				
Anon.	21 55 54·5	9 11·8	10 20·8	9 11·8	9 11·8	N. 1 10+1 9·0				
7842	22 22 48·0	8 22·4	5 32·9	8 22·0	8 22·2	S. 2 45+2 23·3				
7909	22 33 52·2	9 22·8	12 20·4	9 23·0	9 22·9	N. 0 10+2 31·5				
7966	22 43 58·5	9 30·8	10 1·5	9 31·0	9 30·9	S. 3 20−0 4·6				
7992	22 49 12·5	9 24·6	10 5·6	9 24·7	9 24·65	S. 0 5−0 14·95	25·090	40·6	40·8	40·8
1802	5 34 9·5	9 16·4	14 4·2	9 16·4	9 16·4	S. 3 50−4 21·80	25·000	41·4	42·8	41·3
2293	6 52 40·7	10 27·4	13 4·2	10 27·5	10 27·45	N. 1 35+2 10·75				

August 13.—Nos. 6275, 6285, and 6305.—Clamp not touched between these observations.
Nos. 7011, 7027, and 7057.—Clamp not touched between these observations.
Had definition.
August 14.—Began to dismount the Sector. In the evening the sky became overcast, which was followed by frost and snow. On the 15th, the thermometer sunk to 30°, and afterwards heavy snow showers. On the 17th, ice one inch thick.

UNREDUCED OBSERVATIONS

MADE WITH

BRADLEY'S ZENITH SECTOR

AT

THE ROYAL OBSERVATORY, NEAR CAPE TOWN;

FROM

OCTOBER, 1843, TO JUNE, 1844.

☉ October 29, 1843.—Face of Sector West.

Number of B.A.C.	Time by Chronometer.	Micr. for Plumb-line on Dot.	Micr. for Observation of Star.	Micr. for Plumb-line on Dot.	Mean of Micr. for Plumb-line on Dot.	Star's Apparent Zenith Distance.	Barom.	Thermometers.		
								Attd.	Lower.	Out.
	h. m. s.	rev. pts.	rev. pts.	rev. pts.	rev. pts.	° ' rev. pts.	in.			
7906	22 44	7 32·0	9 16·7	7 31·8	7 31·9	N. 0 15—1 18·8	30·160	63·0	62·0	57·0
7992	22 48	8 9·0	9 18·0	8 8·8	8 8·9	N. 3 30—1 9·1				
4686	13 57 43·5	13 25·0	13 2·0	13 24·8	13 24·9	S. 1 40—0 22·9	30·220	63·0	62·0	62·4

☾ October 30, 1843.—Face of Sector East.

Number of B.A.C.	Time by Chronometer.	Micr. for Plumb-line on Dot.	Micr. for Observation of Star.	Micr. for Plumb-line on Dot.	Mean of Micr. for Plumb-line on Dot.	Star's Apparent Zenith Distance.	Barom.	Attd.	Lower.	Out.
6115	17 56 1·0	12 23·8	18 31·5	12 23·5	12 23·65	N. 3 30+1 7·85				
6233	18 14 4·5	10 30·7	8 25·4	10 30·5	10 30 6	S. 0 30+2 5·2				
6489	18 52 55·0	11 2·5	11 3·3	11 2·45	11 2·48	N. 3 50+0 0·62	29·840	63·0	67·2	71·2
7386	21 8 44·0	11 6·3	14 5·3	11 6·0	11 6·15	N. 1 5+2 33 15	29·821	64·0		
7557	21 35 56·5	11 17·8	14 28·7	11 17·8	11 17·8	N. 0 10+3 10·9			64·5	63·2
Anon.	21 55 56·0	12 1·3	11 5·8	12 1·3	12 1·3	N. 4 45—0 29·5				
7909	22 33	12 31·3	13 23·6	12 31·5	12 31·4	N. 3 45+0 26·2				
7966	22	11 29·8	9 28·6	11 30·1	11 29·95	N. 0 15—2 1·35				
7992	22 48	12 3·7	10 14·4	12 3·5	12 3·6	N. 3 30—1 23·2				
8201	23 24 55·5	10 9·0	10 23·4	10 9·0	10 9·0	S. 4 45—0 14·4	29·830	63·0	63·2	60·4

♂ October 31, 1843.—Face of Sector West.

Number of B.A.C.	Time by Chronometer.	Micr. for Plumb-line on Dot.	Micr. for Observation of Star.	Micr. for Plumb-line on Dot.	Mean of Micr. for Plumb-line on Dot.	Star's Apparent Zenith Distance.	Barom.	Attd.	Lower.	Out.
4686	13 57 48·5	10 30·1	10 17·2	10 30·4	10 30·25	S. 1 40—0 13·05	30·056	64·8		68·0

☿ November 1, 1843.—Face of Sector West.

Number of B.A.C.	Time by Chronometer.	Micr. for Plumb-line on Dot.	Micr. for Observation of Star.	Micr. for Plumb-line on Dot.	Mean of Micr. for Plumb-line on Dot.	Star's Apparent Zenith Distance.	Barom.	Attd.	Lower.	Out.
5915	17 23 21·5	11 17·4	7 24·6	11 17·2	11 17·3	S. 3 5—3 26·7	30·053	65·6		66·3
7842	22 22 55·5	12 4·8	7 29·6	12 4·5	12 4·65	N. 0 45+4 9·05				
7909	22 33 54·0	9 18·7	8 22·0	9 18·8	9 18·75	N. 3 45+0 30·75				
7992	22 49 17·5	10 2·8	11 22·8	10 2·9	10 2·85	S. 3 30—1 19·95	30·152	63·5	64·0	59·5
8201	23 24 59·5	9 22·7	9 2·6	9 23·0	9 22·85	S. 4 45—0 20·25				
1802	5 34 20·7	8 9·8	5 14·2	8 10·0	8 9·9	S. 0 15—2 29·7				
2293	6 52	9 32·5	9 12·75	9 32·6	9 32·55	N. 5 10+0 19·80				
4686	13 57 51·7	11 5·0	10 24·0	11 4·6	11 4·8	S. 1 40—0 14·8	30·200	63·0	66·0	68·0

♃ November 2, 1843.—Face of Sector East.

Number of B.A.C.	Time by Chronometer.	Micr. for Plumb-line on Dot.	Micr. for Observation of Star.	Micr. for Plumb-line on Dot.	Mean of Micr. for Plumb-line on Dot.	Star's Apparent Zenith Distance.	Barom.	Attd.	Lower.	Out.
5915	17 23 28·2	11 13·5	15 2·1	11 14·0	11 13·75	S. 3 5—3 22·35	30·120	66·0	66·0	69·6
6489	18 53 3·8	9 14·4	9 22·5	9 14·6	9 14·5	N. 3 50+0 8·0				
4686	13 57 59·5	11 14·9	11 28·0	11 15·3	11 15·1	S. 1 40—0 12·9	30·130	65·0	65·5	75·4

♀ November 3, 1843.—Face of Sector East.

Number of B.A.C.	Time by Chronometer.	Micr. for Plumb-line on Dot.	Micr. for Observation of Star.	Micr. for Plumb-line on Dot.	Mean of Micr. for Plumb-line on Dot.	Star's Apparent Zenith Distance.	Barom.	Attd.	Lower.	Out.
5915	17 23 31·5	11 20·8	15 11·6	11 20·8	11 20·8	S. 3 5—3 24·8	30·065	69·0	68·2	72·8
6115	17 56 11·3	11 28·5	13 10·1	11 28·5	11 28·5	N. 3 30+1 15·6			67·5	69·0
6489	18 53 6·5	8 7·3	9 21·45	9 13·3	8 7·35	N. 0 10+3 8·05	30·050	67·3	67·3	71·6
7557	21 35	8 7·3	11 24·6	8 7·4	8 7·35	N. 0 10+3 17·25				
7657	21 51 17·5	9 7·2	7 15·6	9 7·2	9 7·2	N. 4 45—1 25·6				
Anon.	21 56 5·5	9 7·0	8 19·7	9 7·0	9 7·0	N. 4 45—0 21·3	30·062	66·0	66·2	65·5
7842	22 23 6·8	8 27·8	13 2·7	8 27·8	8 27·8	N. 0 45+4 8·9				
7900	22 34 8·0	11 11·2	12 9·9	11 11·2	11 11·2	N. 3 45+0 32·7				
7966	22 44 20·0	8 15·2	6 20·4	8 15·0	8 15·1	N. 0 15—1 28·7				
7992	22 49 28·2	8 27·6	7 10·6	8 27·6	8 27·6	N. 3 30—1 17·0	30·070	66·0	66·4	65·4

October 30.—Shifted the bisecting wire towards the right in order to diminish the error in collimation.
    31.—Strong S.E. wind with bad definition.
November 3.—Very bad definition. The second of transit of No. 2293 uncertain.
    No. 7909 has been hitherto printed as an anonymous star.

♀ NOVEMBER 3, 1843.—FACE OF SECTOR EAST—(*continued*).

Number of B.A.C.	Time by Chronometer.	Micr. for Plumb-line on Dot.	Micr. for Observation of Star.	Micr. for Plumb-line on Dot.	Mean of Micr. for Plumb-line on Dot.	Star's Apparent Zenith Distance.	Barom.	Thermometers.		
								Attd.	Lower.	Out.
	h m s	rev. pts.	rev. pts.	rev. pts.	rev. pts.	° ′ rev. pts.	in.			
8025	22 55 22·5	8 26·4	9 27·65	8 26·0	8 26·2	S. 1 40−1 1·45				
8201	23 25 10·3	9 4·7	9 25·7	9 4·6	9 4·65	S. 4 45−0 21·05	30·074	65·4	66·2	65·0
1802	5 34 31·5	10 4·2	13 0·4	10 4·5	10 4·35	S. 0 15−2 30·05			65·2	
2293	6 52 57·0	9 22·5	10 10·0	9 22·5	9 22·5	N. 5 10+0 21·5			65·5	
4686	13 58 2·7	9 20·4	9 32·05	9 20·8	9 20·6	S. 1 40−0 11·45	30·087	65·0	66·5	

♄ NOVEMBER 4, 1843.—FACE OF SECTOR WEST.

Number of B.A.C.	Time by Chronometer.	Micr. for Plumb-line on Dot.	Micr. for Observation of Star.	Micr. for Plumb-line on Dot.	Mean of Micr. for Plumb-line on Dot.	Star's Apparent Zenith Distance.	Barom.	Attd.	Lower.	Out.
7557	21 36 5·7	8 15·1	4 30·5	8 14·85	8 14·98	N. 0 10+3 18·48	30·056	65·8	66·2	63·0
Anon.	21 56 15·0	9 6·0	9 26·7	9 5·8	9 5·9	N. 4 45−0 20·8				
7842	22 23 4·5	9 5·7	4 29·2	9 5·3	9 5·5	N. 0 45+4 10·3				
7909	22 34 3·0	9 22·3	8 24·9	9 21·7	9 22·0	N. 3 45+0 31·1				
7966	22 44 18·0	9 24·3	11 18·9	9 24·2	9 24·25	N. 0 15−1 28·65				
7992	22 49 25·7	10 0·9	11 21·4	10 0·8	10 0·85	N. 3 30−1 20·55				
8025	22 55 20·7	11 0·0	9 33·9	11 0·2	11 0·1	S. 1 40−1 0·2				
8201		13 18·9	13 0·4	13 18·9	13 18·9	S. 4 45−0 18·5	30·076	66·0	67·0	62·4
1802	5 34 29·7	9 8·0	6 12·0	9 7·8	9 7·9	S. 0 15−2 29·9	30·020	66·0	65·6	61·0
2293	6 52 54·0	8 31·9	8 13·0	8 31·7	8 31·8	N. 5 10+0 18·8	29·983	65·0	65·4	60·5

☉ NOVEMBER 5, 1843.— FACE OF SECTOR WEST.

Number of B.A.C.	Time by Chronometer.	Micr. for Plumb-line on Dot.	Micr. for Observation of Star.	Micr. for Plumb-line on Dot.	Mean of Micr. for Plumb-line on Dot.	Star's Apparent Zenith Distance.	Barom.	Attd.	Lower.	Out.
4686	13 58 6·4	9 32·7	9 18·8	9 32·4	9 32·55	S. 1 40−0 13·75	29·985	65·0	65·0	66·0

☿ NOVEMBER 8, 1843.—FACE OF SECTOR EAST.

Number of B.A.C.	Time by Chronometer.	Micr. for Plumb-line on Dot.	Micr. for Observation of Star.	Micr. for Plumb-line on Dot.	Mean of Micr. for Plumb-line on Dot.	Star's Apparent Zenith Distance.	Barom.	Attd.	Lower.	Out.
4686	13 58 17·0	9 16·7	9 27·7	9 16·8	9 16·75	S. 1 40−0 10·95	30·140	62·5	62·8	61·2

♃ NOVEMBER 9, 1843.—FACE OF SECTOR EAST.

Number of B.A.C.	Time by Chronometer.	Micr. for Plumb-line on Dot.	Micr. for Observation of Star.	Micr. for Plumb-line on Dot.	Mean of Micr. for Plumb-line on Dot.	Star's Apparent Zenith Distance.	Barom.	Attd.	Lower.	Out.
7557	21 36 23·8	9 4·4	9 15·6	9 3·3	9 3·85	N. 0 10+0 11·75				
7613	21 45 18·5	8 21·0	9 3·5	8 20·7	8 20·85	S. 4 10−0 16 65	30·152	61·8	64·0	55·5
7992	22 49 44·5	10 3·7	8 15·45	10 3·5	10 3·6	N. 3 30−1 22·15				
8025	22 55 39·5	9 23·5	10 19·2	9 23·5	9 23·5	S. 1 40−0 29·7	30·106	61·7	63·0	54·0
8201	23 25 28·0	10 8·4	10 23·7	10 8·5	10 8·45	S. 4 45−0 15·25			63·0	54·0
2293	6 53 12·2	11 7·5	11 27·1	11 7·7	11 7·6	N. 5 10+0 19·5	30·074	61·2	61·6	47·4

♀ NOVEMBER 10, 1843.—FACE OF SECTOR WEST.

Number of B.A.C.	Time by Chronometer.	Micr. for Plumb-line on Dot.	Micr. for Observation of Star.	Micr. for Plumb-line on Dot.	Mean of Micr. for Plumb-line on Dot.	Star's Apparent Zenith Distance.	Barom.	Attd.	Lower.	Out.
5915	17 23	9 27·5	8 1·3	9 27·8	9 27·65	S. 3 5−3 26·35			63·5	
6115	17 56 26·5	9 6·7	7 24·6	9 6·5	9 6·6	N. 3 30+1 16·0	30·054	63·5	63·5	63·6
7657	21 52 31·5	9 26·3	11 19·0	9 26·3	9 26·3	N. 4 45−1 26·7	30·069	63·3	62·6	58·4
7842	22 23 22·0	9 20·0	5 10·25	9 20·0	9 20·0	N. 0 45+4 9·75				
7909	22 34 22·5	9 11·8	8 14·75	9 11·6	9 11·7	N. 3 45+0 30·95			63·4	57·5
7966	22 44 35·5	8 32·0	10 28·4	8 31·8	8 31·9	N. 0 15−1 30·5				
7992	22 49 43·2	8 24·45	10 9·95	8 24·4	8 24·4	N. 3 30−1 19·52				
8025	22 55 39·7	8 27·0	7 27·3	8 27·2	8 27·1	S. 1 40−0 33·8	30·081	62·5	63·6	55·7
1802	5 34 47·6	8 25·5	5 31·1	8 25·7	8 25·6	S. 0 15−2 28·5	30·073	61·5	62·2	52·5
2293	6 53 11·2	8 12·1	7 28·6	8 12·2	8 12·15	N. 5 10+0 17·55	30·053	61·5	62·3	52·2

November 5.—After the observation of No. 4686, the sky became cloudy.
8.—No. 4686, faint and uncertain from cloud.
9.—No. 2293.—The pulley weight increased to 22 ounces.
10.—Several stars lost in the evening from clouds.

☾ NOVEMBER 13, 1843.—FACE OF SECTOR EAST.

Number of B.A.C.	Time by Chronometer.	Micr. for Plumb-line on Dot.	Micr. for Observation of Star.	Micr. for Plumb-line on Dot.	Mean of Micr. for Plumb-line on Dot.	Star's Apparent Zenith Distance.	Barom.	Attd.	Lower.	Out.
	h m s	rev. pts.	rev. pts.	rev. pts.	rev. pts.	° ' rev. pts.	in.			
7557	21 36 30·3	8 6·0	11 22·45	8 5·8	8 5·9	N. 0 10+3 16·55	30·007	61·5	61·4	54·5
7992	22 49 56·8	12 8·4	10 24·8	12 8·0	12 8·2	N. 3 30—1 17·4	30·044	60·7	61·3	54·4
8201	23 25 41·2	7 25·3	8 11·1	7 25·5	7 25·4	S. 4 45—0 19·7	30·050	60·6	61·2	54·4
1802	5 35 1·5	8 8·3	11 1·95	8 8·1	8 8·2	S. 0 15—2 27·75			61·2	
2293	6 53 25·6	8 15·6	9 0·2	8 15·7	8 15·65	N. 5 10+0 18·55	30·109	60·2	61·2	49·3

♂ NOVEMBER 14, 1843.—FACE OF SECTOR WEST.

Number of B.A.C.	Time by Chronometer.	Micr. for Plumb-line on Dot.	Micr. for Observation of Star.	Micr. for Plumb-line on Dot.	Mean of Micr. for Plumb-line on Dot.	Star's Apparent Zenith Distance.	Barom.	Attd.	Lower.	Out.
7613	21 45 29·0	7 7·8	6 20·55	7 7·7	7 7·75	S. 4 10—0 21·2				58·3
7909	22 34 34·8	7 3·0	6 6·4	7 2·8	7 2·9	N. 3 45+0 30·5	30·181	61·8	61·6	
7966	22 44 48·5	7 24·5	9 20·7	7 24·7	7 24·6	N. 0 15—1 30·1	30·192	61·6	61·8	55·2
7992	22 49 55·5	8 15·5	10 3·0	8 15·7	8 15·6	N. 3 30—1 21·4			61·6	
8025	22 55 51·5	8 9·0	7 9·7	8 9·1	8 9·05	S. 1 40—0 33·35	30·196	61·8	61·6	54·1
8201	23 25 41·0	9 28·2	9 10·0	9 28·0	9 28·1	S. 4 45—0 18·1	30·205	60·5	61·6	54·0
1802	5 35 0·6	8 24·8	5 32·3	8 24·8	8 24·8	S. 0 15—2 26·5			60·2	
2293	6 53	8 29·0	8 12·8	8 29·0	8 29·0	N. 5 10+0 16·2			59·0	

☿ NOVEMBER 15, 1843.—FACE OF SECTOR EAST.

Number of B.A.C.	Time by Chronometer.	Micr. for Plumb-line on Dot.	Micr. for Observation of Star.	Micr. for Plumb-line on Dot.	Mean of Micr. for Plumb-line on Dot.	Star's Apparent Zenith Distance.	Barom.	Attd.	Lower.	Out.
5632	16 40 6·7	10 23·0	12 6·3	10 22·6	10 22·9	S. 0 5—1 17·4				66·2
5015	17 23	7 17·0	11 9·8	7 16·8	7 16·9	S. 3 5—3 26·9	30·118	62·0	62·5	66·2
6233	18 14 53·5	8 29·3	6 33·7	8 29·3	8 29·3	S. 0 30+1 29·6			62·8	66·2
6489	18 53	9 22·4	9 32·6	9 22·0	9 22·2	N. 3 50+0 10·4	30·108	63·5		65·6
7613	21 45 39·5	8 33·1	9 20·3	8 32·9	8 32·95	N. 0 10—0 21·3	30·060	63·6	62·8	62·6
7842	22 23 42·7	9 16·7	13 24·0	9 16·6	9 16·65	N. 0 45+4 7·35				
7909	22 34 42·8	9 2·4	10 0·3	9 2·0	9 2·2	N. 3 45+0 32·1				
Anon.	22 42 23·0	8 12·5	14 9·7	8 12·7	8 12·6	N. 0 15+5 31·1				
7966	22 44 56·5	8 12·7	6 16·5	8 12·4	8 12·55	N. 0 15—1 30·05				
7992	22 49	9 2·7	7 19·4	9 2·5	9 2·6	N. 3 30—1 17·2			62·8	
8025	22 55 59·5	8 9·6	9 10·65	8 9·6	8 9·6	S. 1 40—1 1·05	30·050	62·5		63·3
8201	23 25 47·8	8 15·0	9 0·9	8 15·2	8 15·1	S. 4 45—0 19·8			63·5	
1802	5 35 7·2	11 28·55	14 22·4	11 28·5	11 28·53	S. 0 15—2 27·87			61·8	
2293	6 53 32·5	10 14·5	10 32·75	10 14·8	10 14·65	N. 5 10+0 18·10	29·907	61·0	61·4	57·0

☾ NOVEMBER 20, 1843.—FACE OF SECTOR WEST.

Number of B.A.C.	Time by Chronometer.	Micr. for Plumb-line on Dot.	Micr. for Observation of Star.	Micr. for Plumb-line on Dot.	Mean of Micr. for Plumb-line on Dot.	Star's Apparent Zenith Distance.	Barom.	Attd.	Lower.	Out.
4686	13 58 50·5	11 8·0	10 28·0	11 7·8	11 7·9	S. 1 40—0 13·9	29·965	63·5	64·5	55·4

♀ DECEMBER 1, 1843.—FACE OF SECTOR WEST.

Number of B.A.C.	Time by Chronometer.	Micr. for Plumb-line on Dot.	Micr. for Observation of Star.	Micr. for Plumb-line on Dot.	Mean of Micr. for Plumb-line on Dot.	Star's Apparent Zenith Distance.	Barom.	Attd.	Lower.	Out.
6233	18 15 36·7	11 27·9	13 21·0	11 27·7	11 27·8	S. 0 30+1 27·2	29·980	66·7	70·2	74·0
7992	22 50 47·5	9 6·4	10 28·7	9 7·2	9 6·8	N. 3 30—1 21·9	29·968	67·5	67·6	65·8
1802	5 35 53·2	9 14·8	6 26·1	9 14·6	9 14·7	S. 0 15—2 22·6	29·987	66·0	66·4	61·0

♄ DECEMBER 2, 1843.—FACE OF SECTOR EAST.

Number of B.A.C.	Time by Chronometer.	Micr. for Plumb-line on Dot.	Micr. for Observation of Star.	Micr. for Plumb-line on Dot.	Mean of Micr. for Plumb-line on Dot.	Star's Apparent Zenith Distance.	Barom.	Attd.	Lower.	Out.
6233	18 15 45·3	3 24·1	1 30·3	3 23·9	3 24·0	S. 0 30+1 27·7	30·114	67·0	69·5	73·2
6489	18 54 32·0	8 8·8	8 20·3	8 8·6	8 8·7	N. 3 50+0 11·6				73·0
7613	21 46 29·4	7 8·2	7 29·2	7 7·8	7 8·0	S. 4 10—0 21·2			68·5	
7992	22 50 54·5	8 4·1	6 18·5	8 4·0	8 4·05	N. 3 30—1 19·55	30·144	68·5	68·2	69·3

November 13.—Cloudy after the transit of No. 2293.

15.—Nos. 5915 and 6489.—Bisected when 10 seconds past the middle wire. No. 7992.—The time of transit not noted.

20.—Almost continued unfavourable weather for observing for the last 10 days.

December 2.—" Black South Easter."—The Devil's Berg cap cloud extends to the Zenith of the Observatory to-day.

♄ DECEMBER 2, 1843.—FACE OF SECTOR EAST—(continued).

Number of B.A.C.	Time by Chronometer.	Micr. for Plumb-line on Dot.	Micr. for Observation of Star.	Micr. for Plumb-line on Dot.	Mean of Micr. for Plumb-line on Dot.	Star's Apparent Zenith Distance.	Barom.	Thermometers. Attd.	Lower.	Out.
	h m s	rev. pts.	rev. pts.	rev. pts.	rev. pts.	° ′ rev. pts.	in.			
1802	5 35	9 30·5	12 19·8	9 30·7	9 30·6	S. 0 15—2 23·2	30·130	66·4	66·6	62·6
5632	16 42 1·7	9 4·7	10 25·4	9 4·5	9 4·6	S. 0 5—1 20·8	30·078	67·0	68·8	74·9

☉ DECEMBER 3, 1843.—FACE OF SECTOR WEST.

5915		9 13·0	5 22·2	9 13·0	9 13·0	S. 3 5—3 24·8	30·072	68·0	69·5	74·0
6233	18 15 43·2	9 6·7	10 33·0	9 6·7	9 6·7	S. 0 30+1 26·3	30·063	68·0	69·5	73·2
6489	18 54 29·7	8 16·7	8 4·9	8 16·7	8 16·7	N. 3 50+0 11·8	30·051	68·0	70·0	72·2
7613	21 46 28·5	8 15·4	7 28·0	8 15·2	8 15·3	S. 4 10—0 21·3	30·024	68·0	69·0	68·2
7992	22 50 50·5	8 15·6	10 3·0	8 15·8	8 15·7	N. 3 30—1 21·3	30·036	68·0	68·6	65·0
1802	5 35 57·5	9 6·1	6 18·7	9 6·3	9 6·2	S. 0 15—2 21·5	30·062	65·5	67·0	54·8
4686	13 59 29·5	8 15·1	8 0·2	8 15·0	8 15·05	S. 1 40—0 14·85	30·141	65·8	66·0	67·2

☾ DECEMBER 4, 1843.—FACE OF SECTOR EAST.

7613	21 46 37·3	8 23·9	9 11·1	8 23·9	8 23·9	S. 4 10—0 21·2	30·084	67·7	68·0	68·0
7992	22 50 58·6	9 7·2	7 22·2	9 7·4	9 7·3	S. 3 30—1 19·1	30·087	67·3	68·0	65·0
1802	5 36 5·0	8 28·1	11 16·4	8 28·3	8 28·2	S. 0 15—2 22·2	30·036	65·6	65·6	58·2
2293	6 54 27·0	8 31·1	9 10·4	8 31·3	8 31·2	N. 5 10+0 13·2	30·022	65·5	65·6	57·8

♃ DECEMBER 7, 1843.—FACE OF SECTOR WEST.

1802	5 36 8·8	11 6·7	8 21·0	11 6·7	11 6·7	S. 0 15—2 19·7	30·004	65·6	66·2	63·3
2293	6 54 30·5	9 8·1	8 31·7	9 8·1	9 8·1	N. 5 10+0 10·4	29·989	65·6	66·2	62·6
4686		9 22·1	9 8·9	9 22·1	9 22·1	S. 1 40—0 13·2	30·011	66·4	66·3	68·9

♀ DECEMBER 8, 1843.—FACE OF SECTOR EAST.

1802	5 36 18·8	7 6·2	9 26·7	7 6·0	7 6·1	S. 0 15—2 20·6	30·090	65·5	66·2	57·0
2293	6 54 37·5	7 19·8	7 32·3	7 19·6	7 19·7	N. 5 20+0 12·6	30·081	65·5	65·6	58·5

♄ DECEMBER 9, 1843.—FACE OF SECTOR WEST.

6233		7 12·4	9 5·5	7 12·4	7 12·4	S. 0 30+1 27·1			68·0	
7992	22 51 7·5	6 3·4	8 25·5	6 3·2	6 3·3	N. 3 30—2 22·2	30·064	67·5	70·2	63·4

☾ DECEMBER 11, 1843.—FACE OF SECTOR WEST.

1802	5 36 20·8	7 12·8	4 27·4	7 13·0	7 12·9	S. 0 15—2 19·5	30·070	68·5	68·5	62·0
2293	6 54 42·0	9 29·0	8 19·6	8 28·9	8 28·95	N. 5 10+0 9·35	30·092	68·2	68·2	60·7
4458	13 14 13·5	8 23·0	12 10·9	8 23·0	8 23·0	S. 1 55+3 21·9	30·120	66·8	67·2	66·2
4686	13 59 53·5	8 14·6	7 33·8	8 14·5	8 14·55	S. 1 40—0 14·75			67·5	
5915		9 27·7	6 2·7	9 27·7	9 27·7	S. 3 5—3 25·0	30·121	68·6	68·4	72·3

♂ DECEMBER 12, 1843.—FACE OF SECTOR EAST.

7992	22 51 21·0	11 5·7	9 20·5	11 5·8	11 5·75	N. 3 30—1 19·25	30·102	69·4	71·0	69·5
1802	5 36 28·0	10 26·5	13 10·55	10 26·3	10 26·4	S. 0 15—2 18·15	30·134	68·0	69·0	58·2
2293	6 54 49·0	9 21·6	9 31·4	9 21·7	9 21·65	N. 5 10+0 9·75	30·121	67·5	69·0	57·4

Dec. 3.—No. 5915.—Bisected while leaving the field.
7.—No. 4686.—A blotch.
9.—No. 6233.—Bisected at 4 seconds past the R. A. wire.
11.—No. 5915.—The star very faint and the observation uncertain.

L

☿ DECEMBER 13, 1843.—FACE OF SECTOR EAST.

Number of B.A.C.	Time by Chronometer.	Micr. for Plumb-line on Dot.	Micr. for Observation of Star.	Micr. for Plumb-line on Dot.	Mean of Micr. for Plumb-line on Dot.	Star's Apparent Zenith Distance.	Barom.	Thermometers. Attd.	Lower.	Out.
	b m s	rev. pts.	rev. pts.	rev. pts.	rev. pts.	° ′ rev. pts.	in.			
7992	22 51 23·5	9 9·3	7 19·7	9 9·1	9 9·2	N. 3 30—1 23·5	30·066	69·5	69·5	69·8
1802	5 36 31·0	8 29·3	11 11·15	8 29·2	8 29·25	S. 0 15—2 15·9	30·095	67·6	69·2	61·3

♃ DECEMBER 14, 1843.—FACE OF SECTOR EAST.

Number of B.A.C.	Time by Chronometer.	Micr. for Plumb-line on Dot.	Micr. for Observation of Star.	Micr. for Plumb-line on Dot.	Mean of Micr. for Plumb-line on Dot.	Star's Apparent Zenith Distance.	Barom.	Attd.	Lower.	Out.
1802	5 36 34·2	8 18·6	11 3·3	8 18·6	8 18·6	S. 0 15—2 18·7	30·160	67·6	67·5	59·4
2293	6 54 54·8	9 8·5	9 20·2	9 8·5	9 8·5	N. 5 10+0 11·7	30·158	67·0	67·6	57·5
4686	14 0 41·0	8 31·9	9 12·15	8 31·8	8 31·85	S. 1 40—0 14·3	30·235	66·0	64·8	64·2

♀ DECEMBER 15, 1843.—FACE OF SECTOR WEST.

Number of B.A.C.	Time by Chronometer.	Micr. for Plumb-line on Dot.	Micr. for Observation of Star.	Micr. for Plumb-line on Dot.	Mean of Micr. for Plumb-line on Dot.	Star's Apparent Zenith Distance.	Barom.	Attd.	Lower.	Out.
1802	5 36 34·0	9 33·2	7 15·7	9 33·3	9 33·25	S. 0 15—2 27·55	30·146	65·4	65·0	58·4
2293	6 54 54·2	9 22·7	9 14·0	9 22·5	9 22·6	N. 5 10+0 8·6	30·119	65·5	65·5	57·8
4458	13 14 26·9	9 15·7	13 3·45	9 15·5	9 15·6	S. 1 55+3 21·85	30·126	65·5	65·6	65·6
4686	14 0 7·0	9 11·0	8 30·3	9 10·8	9 10·9	S. 1 40—0 14·6	30·122	66·6	65·6	67·6
5632	16 42 35·5	9 6·1	7 20·0	9 6·4	9 6·25	S. 0 5—1 20·25	30·105	67·2	66·0	72·9

♄ DECEMBER 16, 1843.—FACE OF SECTOR EAST.

Number of B.A.C.	Time by Chronometer.	Micr. for Plumb-line on Dot.	Micr. for Observation of Star.	Micr. for Plumb-line on Dot.	Mean of Micr. for Plumb-line on Dot.	Star's Apparent Zenith Distance.	Barom.	Attd.	Lower.	Out.
6233	18 16 45·0	9 15·3	7 21·0	9 15·2	9 15·25	S. 0 30+1 28·25	30·084	67·5	67·5	72·7
7992	22 51 31·5	9 31·0	8 11·4	9 31·1	9 31·05	N. 3 30—1 19·65	30·050	68·2	68·5	68·7
2293	6 54 55·0	9 8·6	9 19·1	9 8·6	9 8·6	N. 5 10—0 10·5			66·0	

☾ JANUARY 1, 1844.—FACE OF SECTOR EAST.

Number of B.A.C.	Time by Chronometer.	Micr. for Plumb-line on Dot.	Micr. for Observation of Star.	Micr. for Plumb-line on Dot.	Mean of Micr. for Plumb-line on Dot.	Star's Apparent Zenith Distance.	Barom.	Attd.	Lower.	Out.
4686	14 1 0·0	8 32·3	9 12·5	8 32·7	8 32·5	S. 1 40—0 14·0	30·118	67·8	68·2	66·2
5632	16 43 29·7	8 8·5	9 30·2	8 8·3	8 8·4	S. 0 5—1 21·8	30·116	68·4	70·2	72·7
5915	17 26 33·0	7 30·0	11 28·4	7 30·2	7 30·1	S. 3 5—3 32·3	30·120	68·0	70·5	74·4

♂ JANUARY 2, 1844.—FACE OF SECTOR EAST.

Number of B.A.C.	Time by Chronometer.	Micr. for Plumb-line on Dot.	Micr. for Observation of Star.	Micr. for Plumb-line on Dot.	Mean of Micr. for Plumb-line on Dot.	Star's Apparent Zenith Distance.	Barom.	Attd.	Lower.	Out.
1802	5 37 31·0	8 30·6	11 10·1	8 30·7	8 30·65	S. 0 15—2 13·45	30·132	69·2	69·6	65·6
2293	6 55 51·7	9 9·1	9 14·2	9 9·4	9 9·25	N. 5 10+0 4·95	30·125	69·2	69·0	65·4
4686	14 1 5·2	9 4·3	9 19·2	9 4·2	9 4·25	S. 1 40—0 14·95	30·110	68·5	68·4	68·0

FACE OF SECTOR WEST.

Number of B.A.C.	Time by Chronometer.	Micr. for Plumb-line on Dot.	Micr. for Observation of Star.	Micr. for Plumb-line on Dot.	Mean of Micr. for Plumb-line on Dot.	Star's Apparent Zenith Distance.	Barom.	Attd.	Lower.	Out.
5632	16 43 26·2	8 28·2	7 6·7	8 28·0	8 28·1	S. 0 5—1 21·4	30·112	68·6	69·6	69·4
5915	17 26 32·0	9 0·9	5 4·7	9 1·1	9 1·0	S. 3 5—3 30·3	30·120	69·7	69·9	74·4
6233	18 17 15·5	8 32·5	10 24·7	8 32·5	8 32·5	S. 0 30+1 26·2	30·126	69·7	70·0	74·4

☿ JANUARY 3, 1844.—FACE OF SECTOR WEST.

Number of B.A.C.	Time by Chronometer.	Micr. for Plumb-line on Dot.	Micr. for Observation of Star.	Micr. for Plumb-line on Dot.	Mean of Micr. for Plumb-line on Dot.	Star's Apparent Zenith Distance.	Barom.	Attd.	Lower.	Out.
2293	6 55 50·5	8 30·8	8 28·7	8 30·8	8 30·8	N. 5 10+0 2·1	30·044	68·5	69·0	66·3

FACE OF SECTOR EAST.

Number of B.A.C.	Time by Chronometer.	Micr. for Plumb-line on Dot.	Micr. for Observation of Star.	Micr. for Plumb-line on Dot.	Mean of Micr. for Plumb-line on Dot.	Star's Apparent Zenith Distance.	Barom.	Attd.	Lower.	Out.
5632	16 43 36·5	9 32·0	11 20·3	9 32·0	9 32·0	S. 0 5—1 22·3	30·020	68·8	68·9	71·4
5915	17 26 39·2	10 14·4	14 13·4	10 14·1	10 14·25	S. 3 5—3 33·15	30·008	69·6	69·4	75·8
6233	18 17 22·0	7 29·8	6 4·5	7 29·6	7 29·7	S. 0 30+1 25·2	29·988	69·8	69·6	81·5

December 14.—No. 4686.—Leaving the field.
16.—No. 6233.—Past the middle wire when bisected.
Mr. Maclear absent on duty at Piquet Berg and French Hoek from December 18 to December 31; hence no observations during this interval.

Number of B.A.C.	Time by Chronometer.	Micr. for Plumb-line on Dot.	Micr. for Observation of Star.	Micr. for Plumb-line on Dot.	Mean of Micr. for Plumb-line on Dot.	Star's Apparent Zenith Distance.	Barom.	Thermometers. Attd.	Lower.	Out.
	h m s	rev. pts.	rev. pts.	rev. pts.	rev. pts.	° ′ rev. pts.	in.			
	♃ January 4, 1844.—Face of Sector East.									
1802	5 37 36·5	8 18·3	10 30·55	8 18·2	8 18·25	S. 0 15−2 12·3	29·903	70·8	70·5	70·0
2293	6 55 58·5	8 29·9	9 0·3	8 30·2	8 30·05	N. 5 10+0 4·25	29·882	70·8	70·0	65·2
	Face of Sector West.									
5632	16 43 35·5	7 25·5	6 5·7	7 25·5	7 25·5	S. 0 5−1 19·8	29·850	68·9	69·8	67·0
5915	17 26 37·8	9 1·1	5 3·4	9 1·2	9 1·15	S. 3 5−3 31·75	29·861	69·5	70·1	69·7
	♀ January 5, 1844.—Face of Sector West.									
7992	22 52 25·8	6 27·0	8 15·1	6 27·2	6 27·1	N. 3 30−1 22·0	29·831	70·8	70·5	72·6
	♄ January 6, 1844.—Face of Sector West.									
1802	5 37 39·5	6 26·3	4 15·2	6 26·4	6 26·35	S. 0 15−2 11·15	30·280	68·2	68·0	56·7
2293	6 56 0·0	8 12·3	8 10·9	8 12·1	8 12·2	N. 5 10+0 1·3	30·285	67·8	67·8	56·5
4686	14 1 12·0	8 22·5	8 10·9	8 22·6	8 22·55	S. 1 40−0 11·65	30·277	67·0	65·5	61·2
	☉ January 7, 1844.—Face of Sector West.									
7992	22 52 33·5	9 14·0	11 1·4	9 14·0	9 14·0	N. 3 30−1 21·4	30·215	68·5	69·0	68·0
1802	5 37 42·0	9 2·0	6 25·4	9 2·0	9 2·0	S. 0 15−2 10·6	30·208	66·5	66·8	66·5
2293	6 56 3·0	9 3·2	9 2·5	9 3·1	9 3·15	N. 5 10+0 0·65	30·191	66·2	66·2	60·8
	Face of Sector East.									
4458	13 15 40·2	8 27·6	5 3·1	8 27·8	8 27·7	S. 1 55+3 24·6	30·128	66·0	66·0	61·5
4686	14 1 20·2	9 15·5	9 28·0	9 15·5	9 15·5	S. 1 40−0 12·5	30·124	66·0	66·2	63·6
	☾ January 8, 1844.—Face of Sector East.									
1802	5 37 49·5	9 23·1	12 0·5	9 23·1	9 23·1	S. 0 15−2 11·4	30·047	69·4	68·8	71·3
2293	6 56 10·2	10 6·1	10 9·4	10 6·0	10 6·05	N. 5 10+0 3·35	30·045	68·7	69·0	68·7
4686		9 16·6	9 27·2	9 16·4	9 16·5	S. 1 40−0 10·7	30·028	68·4	68·5	71·3
5632	16 43 50·2	9 16·7	11 2·7	9 16·7	9 16·7	S. 0 5−1 20·0	30·035	69·0	69·0	73·0
5915	17 26 55·3	9 16·9	13 14·5	9 16·7	9 16·8	S. 3 5−3 31·7	30·043	70·3	69·2	76·6
6233	18 17 37·5	9 6·2	7 14·5	9 6·0	9 6·1	S. 0 30+1 25·6	30·061	73·0	70·0	75·6
	♂ January 9, 1844.—Face of Sector West.									
7992	22 52 39·0	9 5·5	10 26·2	9 5·9	9 5·7	N. 3 30−1 20·5	30·025	71·6	70·0	74·8
1802	5 37 48·5	9 2·4	6 25·8	9 2·6	9 2·5	S. 0 15−2 10·7	30·046	70·2	69·8	69·5
2293	6 56 7·5	8 19·0	8 18·5	8 19·1	8 19·05	N. 5 10+0 0·55	30·038	69·6	69·5	69·0
5632	16 43 51·5	9 8·2	7 21·75	9 8·4	9 8·3	S. 0 5−1 20·55	30·045	70·0	71·5	85·0
5915	17 26 55·5	9 25·1	5 26·75	9 24·9	9 25·0	S. 3 5−3 32·25	30·045	70·8	76·0	88·1
6233	18 17 36·5	9 15·4	11 6·05	9 15·4	9 15·4	S. 0 30+1 24·65	30·050	73·7	78·5	90·0
	☿ January 10, 1843.—Face of Sector East.									
7992	22 52 45·2	9 21·8	8 2·8	9 22·2	9 22·0	N. 3 30−1 19·2	30·028	73·4	74·0	84·4
1802	5 37 55·0	9 8·6	11 19·1	9 8·5	9 8·55	S. 0 15−2 10·55	30·062	72·4	74·0	75·5
2293	6 56 15·0	9 18·7	9 21·7	9 18·6	9 18·65	N. 5 10+0 3·05	30·069	72·2	72·9	69·6

January 8.—No. 4686.—Leaving the field when bisected.

♃ January 11, 1844.—Face of Sector East.

Number of B.A.C.	Time by Chronometer.	Micr. for Plumb-line on Dot.	Micr. for Observation of Star.	Micr. for Plumb-line on Dot.	Mean of Micr. for Plumb-line on Dot.	Star's Apparent Zenith Distance.	Barom.	Thermometers. Attd.	Lower.	Out.
	h m s	rev. pts.	rev. pts.	rev. pts.	rev. pts.	° ′ rev. pts.	in.			
1802	5 37 57·5	8 26·5	11 2·75	8 26·6	8 26·55	S. 0 15—2 10·2	30·020	71·8	72·0	68·7
2293	6 56 17·5	9 32·0	10 0·5	9 31·8	9 31·9	N. 5 10+0 2·6	29·990	71·7	72·0	69·6
4686	14 1 31·5	7 17·0	7 29·05	7 17·0	7 17·0	S. 1 40—0 12·05	29·940	70·8	71·5	70·5

Face of Sector West.

5632	16 43 57·5	9 4·6	7 17·8	9 4·6	9 4·6	S. 0 5—1 20·8	29·943	72·0	73·0	78·9
5915	17 26 59·0	9 18·9	5 21·75	9 19·1	9 19·0	S. 3 5—3 31·25	29·934	72·0	74·0	81·5
6233	18 17 41·0	9 9·2	10 32·4	9 9·3	9 9·25	S. 0 30+1 23·15	29·931	72·8	73·2	83·2

♀ January 12, 1844.—Face of Sector West.

7992	22 52 45·0	9 7·0	10 29·2	9 7·2	9 7·1	N. 3 30—1 22·1	29·907	74·0	74·3	77·2
1802	5 37 55·5	9 9·8	6 33·8	9 9·4	9 9·6	S. 0 15—2 9·8	29·960	72·6	72·6	68·4
2293	6 56 14·5	8 22·0	8 21·4	8 22·1	8 22·05	N. 5 10+0 0·65	29·953	72·4	72·3	67·7

Face of Sector East.

4458	13 15 54·0	7 5·1	3 12·7	7 5·3	7 5·2	S. 1 55+3 26·5	29·976	71·5	71·2	67·5
4686	14 1 34·7	9 26·7	10 4·6	9 26·7	9 26·7	S. 1 40—0 11·9	29·992	71·8	71·4	68·2
5632	16 44 3·2	9 20·2	11 6·8	9 20·4	9 20·3	S. 0 5—1 20·5	30·018	72·6	72·3	73·4
5915	17 27 7·0	9 19·0	13 16·05	9 18·7	9 18·85	S. 3 5—3 31·2	30·013	72·6	72·5	76·3

♄ January 13, 1844.—Face of Sector East.

| 7992 | 22 52 52·5 | 10 1·6 | 8 15·9 | 10 1·2 | 10 1·4 | N. 3 30—1 19·5 | 30·027 | 73·6 | 73·4 | 74·4 |

Face of Sector West.

4458	13 15 53·7	9 17·1	13 8·05	9 17·3	9 17·2	S. 1 55+3 24·85	30·063	71·0	70·3	65·0
4686	14 1 33·2	9 13·3	9 0·3	9 13·1	9 13·2	S. 1 40—0 12·9	30·067	70·8	70·0	66·0
5632	16 44 2·2	9 3·4	7 16·3	9 3·5	9 3·45	S. 0 5—1 21·15	30·100	71·2	71·2	69·8

Face of Sector East.

| 5915 | 17 27 9·3 | 9 1·5 | 12 33·75 | 9 1·3 | 9 1·4 | S. 3 5—3 32·35 | 30·098 | 71·4 | 71·5 | 73·9 |

☉ January 14, 1844.—Face of Sector West.

7992	22 52 51·5	9 7·6	10 28·05	9 7·9	9 7·75	N. 3 30—1 20·9	30·087	72·7	72·5	72·4
1802	5 38 1·7	9 19·0	7 9·25	9 19·0	9 19·0	S. 0 15—2 9·75	30·096	70·5	69·6	64·3
2293	6 56 20·0	9 12·6	9 12·5	9 12·7	9 12·65	N. 5 10+0 0·15	30·068	70·5	69·2	63·7

Face of Sector East.

| 4458 | 13 15 59·5 | 9 15·0 | 5 23·9 | 9 15·1 | 9 15·05 | S. 1 55+3 25·15 | 30·021 | 69·5 | 68·8 | 63·2 |
| 4686 | 14 1 39·5 | 9 10·0 | 9 21·05 | 9 10·1 | 9 10·05 | S. 1 40—0 11·0 | 30·023 | 69·6 | 68·6 | 65·4 |

☾ January 15, 1844.—Face of Sector West.

| 1802 | 5 38 3·7 | 9 10·0 | 7 0·7 | 9 9·6 | 9 9·8 | S. 0 15—2 9·1 | 29·970 | 70·2 | 69·9 | 63·6 |
| 2293 | 6 56 22·3 | 9 3·5 | 9 4·0 | 9 3·8 | 9 3·65 | N. 5 10+0 0·35 | 29·957 | 69·6 | 69·5 | 64·4 |

Face of Sector East.

5632		9 14·8	11 1·55	9 14·5	9 14·65	S. 0 5—1 20·9	29·953	70·4	69·9	73·0
5915	17 27 15·0	9 18·1	13 16·5	9 18·1	9 18·1	S. 3 5—3 32·4	29·946	70·4	70·0	77·4
6233	18 17 56·2	9 32·0	8 6·1	9 31·8	9 31·9	S. 0 30+1 25·8	29·940	70·8	70·5	80·4

January 11.—Very strong wind; the Sector shutter in danger of being carried away.
No. 5915.—The line of sight parti·lly obstructed by the shutter pole.
15.—No. 5632.—Time of transit not noted.

☿ JANUARY 16, 1844.—FACE OF SECTOR EAST.

Number of B.A.C.	Time by Chronometer.	Micr. for Plumb-line on Dot.	Micr. for Observation of Star.	Micr. for Plumb-line on Dot.	Mean of Micr. for Plumb-line on Dot.	Star's Apparent Zenith Distance.	Barom.	Thermometers.		
								Attd.	Lower.	Out.
	h m s	rev. pts.	rev. pts.	rev. pts.	rev. pts.	° ' rev. pts.	in.			
7992	22 53 1·0	10 0·8	8 24·7	10 0·7	10 9·75	N. 3 30—1 19·05	29·897	72·0	71·8	73·7
1802	5 38 10·2	9 26·5	12 0·3	9 26·2	9 26·35	S. 0 15—2 7·95	29·908	70·5	70·0	66·5
2293	6 56 29·5	10 7·1	10 7·75	10 7·3	10 7·2	N. 5 10—0 0·55	29·926	70·4	69·8	66·2

FACE OF SECTOR WEST.

4686	14 1 39·5	9 31·7	9 20·2	9 31·5	9 31·6	S. 1 40—0 11·4	29·936	70·0	69·8	66·8
5632	16 44 9·8	9 29 8	8 8·8	9 30·1	9 29·95	S. 0 5—1 21·15			70·4	
6233	18 17 55·5	9 23·2	11 12·05	9 23·1	9 23·15	S. 0 30+1 22·9	30·007	71·4	71·0	75·4

♃ JANUARY 18, 1844.—FACE OF SECTOR WEST.

7992	22 53 3·0	9 5·0	10 25·5	9 4·8	9 4·9	N. 3 30—1 20·6	29·913	72·3	72·5	76·6
1802	5 38 12·3	9 3·9	6 30·0	9 4·1	9 4·0	S. 0 15—2 8·0	29·996	71·4	70·6	65·7
2293	6 56 30·2	9 19·2	9 21·1	9 19·1	9 19·15	N. 5 10—0 1·95	29·997	71·0	70·5	65·4

FACE OF SECTOR EAST.

4686	14 1 49·7	9 31·2	10 7·95	9 31·0	9 31·1	S. 1 40—0 10·85	30·034	69·8	69·2	64·1
5632	16 44 18·2	9 26·3	11 13·25	9 26·2	9 26·25	S. 0 5—1 21·0	30·056	70·4	70·2	70·2

FACE OF SECTOR WEST.

5915	17 27 18·2	10 12·2	6 13·3	10 12·4	10 12·3	S. 3 5—3 33·0	30·064	70·6	70·5	72·8

FACE OF SECTOR EAST.

6233	18 18	7 24·1	5 33·65	7 24·3	7 24·2	S. 0 30+1 24·55	30·068	71·3	70·8	73·5

♀ JANUARY 19, 1844.—FACE OF SECTOR EAST.

7992	22 53 7·0	10 13·3	8 29·25	10 13·7	10 13·5	N. 5 30—1 18·25	30·035	72·4	71·8	73·3
1802	5	9 30·7	12 4·7	9 30·8	9 30·75	S. 0 15—2 7·95	30·012	70·5	70·0	66·7
2293	6 56 35·8	10 17·8	10 17·65	10 17·8	10 17·8	N. 5 10—0 0·15	29·993	70·4	69·7	66·4

FACE OF SECTOR WEST.

4686	14 1 48·5	10 13·75	10 3 6	10 13·35	10 13·55	S. 1 40—0 9·95	29·927	70 0	69·3	67·3

FACE OF SECTOR EAST.

5915	17 27 26·2	9 14·0	13 12·05	9 13·7	9 13·85	S. 3 5—3 32·2			70·6	

♄ JANUARY 20, 1844.—FACE OF SECTOR WEST.

7992	22 53 8·2	8 1·3	9 21·15	8 1·2	8 1·25	N. 3 30—1 19·90	29·851	73·6	73·0	87·0
1802	5 32 2·5	9 6·1	6 32·5	9 6·0	9 6·05	S. 0 15—2 7·55	29·847	71·4	69·2	63·6
2293	6 51 21·8	8 30·8	9 0·1	8 30·7	8 30·75	N. 5 10—0 3·35	29·850	71·8	71·2	61·7

☉ JANUARY 21, 1844.—FACE OF SECTOR EAST.

1802	5 33 30·0	10 16·2	12 23·45	10 16·0	10 16·1	S. 0 15—2 7·35	30·080	72·2	72·0	64·4
2293	6 51 49·0	10 15·6	10 16 0	10 15·9	10 15·75	N. 5 10+0 0·25	30·089	72·0	71·6	62·8

Jan. 19.—No. 7992.—Bad observation.
No. 1802.—Time of transit not noted.
20.—Nos. 1802 and 2293.—A different chronometer employed for these two observations.

☽ JANUARY 22, 1844.—FACE OF SECTOR WEST.

Number of B.A.C.	Time by Chronometer.	Micr. for Plumb-line on Dot.	Micr. for Observation of Star.	Micr. for Plumb-line on Dot.	Mean of Micr. for Plumb-line on Dot.	Star's Apparent Zenith Distance.	Barom.	Thermometers.		
								Attd.	Lower.	Out.
	h m s	rev. pts.	rev. pts.	rev. pts.	rev. pts.	° ′ rev. pts.	in.			
1802	5 33 28·5	9 8·7	7 0·2	·9 8·5	9 8·6	S. 0 15—2 8·4			71·2	
2293	6 51 48·0	8 23·5	8 25·55	8 23·4	8 23·45	N. 5 10—0 2·1	30·103	71·4	71·0	67·6
6233	18 13 17·0	5 2·5	6 25·1	5 2·3	5 2·4	S. 0 30+1 22·7	30·052	71·8	72·0	76·7

☿ JANUARY 24, 1844.—FACE OF SECTOR EAST.

7992	22 48 26·5	9 27·3	8 9·0	9 27·5	9 27·4	N. 3 30—1 18·4			73·0	
1802	5 33 36·0	8 24·0	10 31·45	8 24·3	8 24·15	S. 0 15—2 7·3	30·037	71·6	71·0	67·7
2293	6 51 56·2	9 12·6	9 9·6	9 12·2	9 12·4	N. 5 10—0 2·8	30·040	71·4	71·2	66·8

FACE OF SECTOR WEST.

5632		8 27·7	7 7·0	8 27·8	8 27·75	S. 0 5—1 20·75	30·028	70·0	70·4	68·0
5915		9 12·7	5 15·3	9 12·5	9 12·6	S. 3 5—3 31·3	30·018	70·8	70·8	69·5

FACE OF SECTOR EAST.

6233	18 13 26·3	8 25·7	7 1·75	8 25·9	8 25·8	S. 0 30+1 24·05	30·018	71·4	71·0	72·3

♃ JANUARY 25, 1844.—FACE OF SECTOR EAST.

7992	22 48 30·5	10 0·6	8 15·45	10 0·5	10 0·55	N. 3 30—1 19·1	29·965	73·4	72·2	75·4

FACE OF SECTOR WEST.

1802	5 33 35·5	9 21·5	7 15·7	9 21·5	9 21·5	S. 0 15—2 5·8	29·941	71·6	71·5	67·3
2293	6 51 56·5	8 31·7	9 1·25	8 31·8	8 31·75	N. 5 10—0 3·5	29·948	71·1	72·0	66·4

FACE OF SECTOR EAST.

4686		8 28·4	9 2·0	8 28·5	8 28·45	S. 1 40—0 7·55	29·913	70·6	70·0	65·4
5632	16 39 43·5	9 5·8	10 26·6	9 6·0	9 5·9	S. 0 5—1 20·7	29·942	70·8	70·8	70·4
5915	17 22 47·2	8 31·4	12 29·8	8 31·7	8 31·55	S. 3 5—3 32·25	29·944	71·4	71·1	71·6

FACE OF SECTOR WEST.

6233	18 13 24·0	10 33·0	12 21·75	10 33·2	10 33·1	S. 0 30+1 22·65	29·955	71·5	71·0	72·8

♀ JANUARY 26, 1844.—FACE OF SECTOR WEST.

7992	22 48 36·0	11 10·4	12 29·4	11 10·3	11 10·35	N. 3 30—1 19·05	29·940	73·0	72·4	78·5
4686	13 57 13·5	10 12·3	10 2·1	10 12·7	10 12·5	S. 1 40—0 10·4	30·055	69·5	69·0	61·4
5632	16 39 42·0	9 12·0	7 25·5	9 12·2	9 12·1	S. 0 5—1 20·6	30·083	60·6	69·3	67·4
5915	17 22 45·0	9 16·0	5 17·25	9 16·1	9 16·05	S. 3 5—3 32·8	30·081	69·8	69·8	68·8

FACE OF SECTOR EAST.

6233	18 13 31·70	8 14·9	6 25·0	8 15·1	8 15·0	S. 0 30+1 24·0	30·074	70·4	70·0	70·8

♄ JANUARY 27, 1844.—FACE OF SECTOR EAST.

7992		9 3·5	7 17·7	9 3·5	9 3·5	N. 3 30—1 19·8			71·4	
1802	5 33 45·0	8 20·0	10 27·1	8 20·2	8 20·1	S. 0 15—2 7·0	30·026	69·8	69·2	62·5
2293	6 52 5·5	9 7·9	9 5·85	9 7·9	7·9	N. 5 10—0 2·05	30·035	69·4	68·6	62·6
4686	13 57 20·0	8 16·95	8 25·75	8 17·0	8 16·98	S. 1 40—0 8·77	30·022	69·8	68·4	63·4
5632	16 39 48·6	9 5·05	10 26·7	9 5·0	9 5·03	S. 0 5—1 21·67	30·007	69·8	69·0	67·3
5915	17 22 52·5	8 29·4	12 28·8	8 29·4	8 29·4	S. 3 5—3 33·4	30·078	69·8	70·3	69·4

Jan. 22.—No. 1802.—Faint, owing to cloud.
24.—Nos. 5632 and 5915.—The times of transit not noted.
25.—No. 4686.—Leaving the field when bisected.
27.—No. 7992.—Bisected 5 seconds after transit.

♄ JANUARY 27, 1844—(continued).—FACE OF SECTOR WEST.

Number of B.A.C.	Time by Chronometer.	Micr. for Plumb-line on Det.	Micr. for Observation of Star.	Micr. for Plumb-line on Det.	Mean of Micr. for Plumb-line on Det.	Star's Apparent Zenith Distance.	Barom.	Thermometers.		
								Attd.	Lower.	Out.
	h m s	rev. pts.	rev. pts.	rev. pts.	rev. pts.	o ′ rev. pts.	in.			
6233		10 18·8	12 8·4	10 18·9	10 18·85	S. 0 30+1 23·55	30·079	70·0	70·6	70·6

⊙ JANUARY 28, 1844.—FACE OF SECTOR WEST.

1802	5 33 44·0	11 13·0	9 6·55	11 12·8	11 12·9	S. 0 15—2 6·35	30·175	70·3	70·0	64·0
2293	6 52 3·5		10 5·45	10 1·5		N. 5 10—0 3·95	30·183	69·5	69·6	62·2
4686	13 57 18·6	10 29·8	10 20·4	10 29·8	10 29·8	S. 1 40—0 9·4	30·130	66·6	67·0	60·2
5632	16 39 47·5	8 7·3	6 19·75	8 7·5	8 7·4	S. 0 5—1 21·65	30·129	68·8	68·0	64·8
5915	17 21 50·5	9 8·0	5 6·05	9 6·1	9 6·05	S. 3 5—4 0·0	30·124	68·5	68·2	66·8
6233	18 13 32·5	9 7·8	10 29·05	9 7·6	9 7·7	6. 0 30+1 21·35			68·6	

☾ JANUARY 29, 1844.—FACE OF SECTOR EAST.

1802	5 33 50·50	8 19·75	10 26·4	8 19·7	8 19·73	S. 0 15—2 6·67	30·063	70·0	68·1	60·4
2293	6 52 10·0	9 29·95	9 27·85	9 30·05	9 30·0	N. 5 10—0 2·15	30·056	69·6	68·5	59·7
4686	13 57 25·5	8 6·4	8 15·5	8 6·2	8 6·3	S. 1 40—0 9·2	30·000	67·5	67·7	59·4
5632	16 39 54·5	8 33·5	10 20·7	8 32·9	8 33·2	S. 0 5—1 21·5	30·018	68·0	66·2	63·9
5915	17 22 58·5	9 15·2	13 13·5	9 15·1	9 15·15	S. 3 5—3 32·35	30·014	68·6	67·0	66·2
6233	18 13 40·2	9 29·5	8 5·0	9 29·5	9 29·5	S. 0 30+1 24 5	30·000	68·9	68·7	67·8

♂ JANUARY 30, 1844.—FACE OF SECTOR WEST.

7992	22 48 39·6	9 4·9	10 23·8	9 5·0	9 4·95	N. 3 30—1 18·85	29·938	71·7	72·0	79·2
1802	5 33 49·3	8 31·6	8 26·65	8 31·7	8 31·65	S. 0 15—2 5·0	29·978	70·7	69·5	65·0
2293		7 14·6	7 19·8	7 14·3	7 14·45	N. 5 10—0 5·35	29·970	70·6	68·6	64·4
4686	13 57 24·5	9 8·0	8 33·75	9 7·8	9 7·9	S. 1 40—0 8·15	29·923	69·8	69·6	58·0
5915	17 22 56·3	9 13·55	5 16·5	9 13·55	9 13·55	S. 3 5—3 31·05	29·947	69·4	66·0	67·0

☿ JANUARY 31, 1844.—FACE OF SECTOR EAST.

7992	22 48 45·2	10 19·5	9 1·15	10 19·3	10 19·4	N. 3 30—1 18·25	29·933	72·6	73·4	80·8
1802	5 33 56·5	8 13·8	10 19·4	8 13·7	8 13·75	S. 0 15—2 5·66	30·021	71·0	70·2	65·0
2293	6 52 14·3	9 21·7	9 18·0	9 21·6	9 21·65	N. 5 10—0 3·65	30·029	70·8	70·0	62·5

♃ FEBRUARY 1, 1844.—FACE OF SECTOR WEST.

1802	5 33 54·5	9 33·5	7 27·9	9 33·5	9 33·5	S. 0 15—2 5·6	30·176	69·8	69·1	69·8
2293	6 52 13·5	8 18·9	8 23·5	8 18·8	8 18·85	N. 5 10—0 4·65	30·180	69·8	68·8	60·0
4623		11 9·0	15 1·9	11 9·3	11 9·15	N. 1 45—3 26·75	30·161	67·0	67·4	59·8

FACE OF SECTOR EAST.

4686	13 57 34·5	9 13·2	9 23·3	9 13·3	9 13·25	S. 1 40—0 10·05	30·163	67·5	67·5	59·8
4852	14 34 9·2	9 11·6	11 16·0	9 11·2	9 11·4	S. 0 35—2 4·6	30·166	67·5	67·6	60·1
5915	17 22 23·8	9 17·5	13 17·5	9 17·45	9 17·48	S. 3 5—4 0·02	30·182	68·4	69·0	67·9
6233	18 13 49·0	9 15·4	7 26·6	9 15·4	9 15·4	S. 0 30+1 22·8	30·183	69·0	69·2	69·5

♀ FEBRUARY 2, 1844.—FACE OF SECTOR WEST.

7992	22 48 49 2	9 15·6	11 0·35	9 15·5	9 15·55	N. 3 30—1 18·80	30·136	70·6	70·0	74·3
1802	5 33 58·5	9 17·4	7 12·05	9 17·2	9 17·3	S. 0 15—2 5·25	30·153	69·5	69·8	63·8

Jan. 27.—No. 6233.—15 seconds past the middle wire when bisected.
29.—No. 5632.—Bad image.
30.—No. 1802.—Bad image.
No. 2293.—The time of transit not noted.
Feb. 1.—No. 4623.—The time of transit not noted.

♀ FEBRUARY 2, 1844.—FACE OF SECTOR WEST—(continued).

Number of B.A.C.	Time by Chronometer.	Micr. for Plumb-line on Dot.	Micr. for Observation of Star.	Micr. for Plumb-line on Dot.	Mean of Micr. for Plumb-line on Dot.	Star's Apparent Zenith Distance.	Barom.	Attd.	Lower.	Out.
	h m s	rev. pts.	rev. pts.	rev. pts.	rev. pts.	° ' tev. pb.	in.			
2293	6 52 18·5	9 8·0	9 13·1	9 7·9	9 7·95	N. 5 10—0 5·15	30·155	69·4	69·4	62 4
5632	16 40 2·7	8 32·7	7 12·1	8 32·5	8 32·6	S. 0 5—1 20·5	30·134	66·6	67·0	62 3
6233	18 13 48·3	5 8·75	6 31·95	5 8·8	5 8·78	S. 0 30+1 23·17	30·109	67·7	68·0	68·7

ℂ FEBRUARY 5, 1844.— FACE OF SECTOR EAST.

Number of B.A.C.	Time by Chronometer.	Micr. for Plumb-line on Dot.	Micr. for Observation of Star.	Micr. for Plumb-line on Dot.	Mean of Micr. for Plumb-line on Dot.	Star's Apparent Zenith Distance.	Barom.	Attd.	Lower.	Out.
7992		7 19·65	9 1·5			N. 3 30—1 15·85	29·917	73·5	73·2	81·3
1802	5 34 11·2	8 12·5	10 17·7	8 12·2	8 12·35	S. 0 15—2 5·35	29·927	72·5	72·3	69·0
2293	6 52 27·5	8 25·7	8 20·0	8 25·5	8 25·6	N. 5 10—0 5·6	29·935	71·0	71·0	66·5

FACE OF SECTOR WEST.

Number of B.A.C.	Time by Chronometer.	Micr. for Plumb-line on Dot.	Micr. for Observation of Star.	Micr. for Plumb-line on Dot.	Mean of Micr. for Plumb-line on Dot.	Star's Apparent Zenith Distance.	Barom.	Attd.	Lower.	Out.
4458	13 12 2·5	0 19·5	13 17·25	9 19·7	9 19·6	S. 1 55+3 31·65	29·876	69·4	69·0	61·7
4517	13 23 51·0	8 31·4	8 18·0	8 31·6	8 31·5	N. 5 10+0 13·5				
4548	13 29 54·5	8 31·55	8 21·6	8 31·5	8 31·53	N. 5 10+0 9·93	29·871	69·4	69·6	61·0
4579	13 36 55·5	9 19·5	8 3·4	9 19·5	9 19·5	N. 1 40+1 16·1			69·6	
4623	13 42 55·2	9 11·25	13 1·7	9 11·5	9 11·38	N. 1 45—3 24·32				
4686	13 57 42·3	9 20·5	9 13·7	9 20·5	9 20·5	S. 1 40—0 6·8	29·876	69·4	69·6	60·6

ℂ FEBRUARY 12, 1844.—FACE OF SECTOR EAST.

Number of B.A.C.	Time by Chronometer.	Micr. for Plumb-line on Dot.	Micr. for Observation of Star.	Micr. for Plumb-line on Dot.	Mean of Micr. for Plumb-line on Dot.	Star's Apparent Zenith Distance.	Barom.	Attd.	Lower.	Out.
4458	13 12 28·5	8 28·6	4 29·5	8 28·6	8 28·6	S. 1 55+3 33·1	29·867	65·8	65·8	60·7
4517	13 24 1·0	10 6·3	10 20·1	10 6·4	10 6·35	N. 5 10+0 13·75				
4548	13 30 18·5	10 6·4	10 17·75	10 6·35	10 6·38	N. 5 10+0 11·37	29·867	65·8	66·0	60·4
4579	13	9 14·0	10 29·95	9 14·2	9 14·1	N. 1 40+1 15·85			66·0	
4623	13 43 19·5	9 3·5	5 11·25	9 3·5	9 3·5	N. 1 45—3 26·25			66·0	
4686	13 58 8·8	8 26·0	8 32·1	8 26·0	8 26·0	S. 1 40—0 6·1	29·868	65·6	66·1	60·4
4784	14 19 25·0	9 4·3	6 25·95	9 4·0	9 4·15	N. 5 10—2 12·2			66·1	
Anon.	14 24 36·0		7 30·8			S. 1 40—0 0·1			66·1	62·2
4852	14 34 42·3	11 2·3	13 6·0	11 2·8	11 2·55	S. 0 35—2 3 45			66·1	
4916	14 46 42·5	9 20·3	5 31·6	9 20·2	9 20·65	N. 5 10—3 22·65			66·1	
Anon.	14 54 6·0	9 31·65	9 8·0	9 31·7	9 31·68	N. 1 55—0 23·68				
5032	15 8 44·5	9 33·5	13 1·9	9 33·65	9 33·65	N. 4 20+3 2·25	29·870	65·6	66·0	61·2
5632	16 40 37·0	9 19·0	11 4·5	9 18·8	9 18·9	S. 0 5—1 19·6	29·892	65·6	65·5	62·4

FACE OF SECTOR WEST.

5915	17 23 34·0	9 24·0	5 23·5	9 24·2	9 24·1	S. 3 5—4 0·6	29·896	65·8	66·0	64·7

FACE OF SECTOR EAST.

6233	18 14 22·7	9 16·4	7 26·35	9 16·3	9 16·35	S. 0 30+1 24·0	29·898	66·4	66·3	67·6

♀ FEBRUARY 14, 1844.—FACE OF SECTOR EAST.

Number of B.A.C.	Time by Chronometer.	Micr. for Plumb-line on Dot.	Micr. for Observation of Star.	Micr. for Plumb-line on Dot.	Mean of Micr. for Plumb-line on Dot.	Star's Apparent Zenith Distance.	Barom.	Attd.	Lower.	Out.
4458	13 12 35·5	9 24·8	5 25·0	9 24·9	9 24·85	S. 1 55+3 33·85	30·191	67·2	67·3	60·7
4517	13 24 20·2	9 19·0	9 31·5	9 19·0	9 19·0	N. 5 10+0 12·5			67·4	
4548	13 30 34·5	9 19·0	9 28·75	9 19·0	9 19·0	N. 5 10+0 9·75	30·191	67·2	67·4	60·8
4579	13 37 36·2	8 26·4	10 8·05	8 26·4	8 26·4	N. 1 40+1 15·65				
4623	13 43 26·2	9 12·0	5 19·0	9 12·1	9 12·05	N. 1 45—3 27·05			67·4	
4686	13 58 17·0	9 14·0	9 19·45	9 14·1	9 14·05	S. 1 40—0 5·40	30·192	67·2	67·4	60·8
4719	14 6 28·0	9 27·7	6 1·0	9 27·8	9 27·75	N. 5 25—3 26·75				
4784	14 19 31·2	9 4·5	6 25·5	9 4·5	9 4·5	N. 5 10—2 13·0				
Anon.	14 24 43·0	9 5·7	6 18·2	9 5·5	9 5·5	N. 1 20—2 21·4			67·2	
4852	14 34 49·3	8 31·9	11 0·8	8 31·8	8 31·85	S. 0 35—2 2·95	30·200	66·7	67·2	60·9
4916	14 46 49·2	9 20·5	6 2·3	9 26·5	9 26·5	N. 0 45—3 24·2			67·8	

Feb. 5.—No. 7992.—12 seconds past the middle wire when bisected.
No. 4623.—Double, the preceding observed.
No. 4916.—Has been hitherto printed as an anonymous star.

☿ FEBRUARY 14, 1844 —FACE OF SECTOR EAST—(continued).

Number of B.A.C.	Time by Chronometer.	Micr. for Plumb-line on Dot.	Micr. for Observation of Star.	Micr. for Plumb-line on Dot.	Mean of Micr. for Plumb-line on Dot.	Star's Apparent Zenith Distance.	Barom.	Thermometers.		
								Attd.	Lower.	Out.
	h m s	rev. pts.	rev. pts.	rev. pts.	rev. pts.	° ′ rev. pts.	in.			
Anon.	14 54 0·2	9 27·5	9 3·75	9 27·5	9 27·5	N. 1 55—0 23·75				
5032	15 8 50·0	9 22 6	12 25·0	9 22·6	9 22·6	N. 4 20+3 2·4	30·196	66·4	66·9	61·4
				FACE OF SECTOR WEST.						
5032	16 40 38·2	8 28·0	7 7·8	8 28·0	8 28·0	S. 0 5—1 20·2	30·218	66·7	66·8	63·4
				FACE OF SECTOR EAST.						
5915	17 23 47·5	9 12·6	13 10·4	9 12·8	9 12·7	S. 3 5—3 31·7	30·221	66·7	67·0	64·4
6233	18 14 28·5	9 7·3	7 18·0	9 7·5	9 7·4	S. 0 30+1 22·8			67·2	

♃ FEBRUARY 15, 1844.—FACE OF SECTOR WEST.

2293	6 52 56·2	10 10·4	10 18·5	10 10·2	10 10·3	N. 5 10—0 8·2	30·200	68·0	67·6	65·0
4458	13 12 38·0	9 11·0	13 11·8	9 11·3	9 11·15	S. 1 55+4 0·65	30·140	67·8	67·5	68·8
4517	13 24 19·0	8 26·6	8 14·0	8 26·5	8 26·55	N. 5 10+0 12·55				
4548	13 30 23·5	8 20·5	8 17·9	8 26·4	8 26·45	N. 5 10+0 8·55	30·136	67·8	67·8	69·2
4579	13 37 25·2	9 6·75	7 26·8	9 6·75	9 6·75	N. 1 40+1 13·95			68·0	
4623	13 43 25·2	9 2·0	12 29·75	9 3·2	9 3·05	N. 1 45—3 26·7	30·137	68·0	68·0	69·4
4686	13 58 13·0	9 16·7	9 12·5	9 16·8	9 16·75	S. 1 40—0 4·25				
4719	14 6 26·3	9 26·8	13 19·4	9 26·9	9 26·85	N. 5 25—3 26·55				
4784	14 19 29·5	10 0·7	12 13·7	10 0·9	10 0·8	N. 5 10—2 12·9				
4852	14 34 48·2	8 11·7	6 7·75	8 11·9	8 11·8	S. 0 35—2 4·05	30·140	67·6	67·8	70·1
4916	14 46 48 2	8 20·6	12 8·75	8 21·0	8 20·8	N. 0 45—3 21·95			68·2	
Anon.	14 54 0·0	8 13·6	9 5·4	8 13·5	8 13·55	N. 1 55—0 25·85	30·150	67·8	68·1	70·4
5032	15 8 49·5	9 3·5	6 0·1	9 3·3	9 3·4	N. 4 20+3 3·3	30·145	67·8	68·0	70·0
5151	15 29 32·5	9 22·9	9 0·3	9 22·8	9 22·85	N. 4 40+0 22·55	30·140	67·8	68·0	69·4
5272		10 15·8	9 4·6	10 15·8	10 15·8	N. 5 10+1 11·2	30·140	67·8	68·0	71·4
5032	16 40 41·5	9 30·4	8 10·0	9 30·0	9 30·2	S. 1 0—1 20·2	30·142	67·8	67·8	71·8
5915	17 23 45·0	9 19·3	5 19·95	9 19·2	9 19·25	S. 3 5—3 33·3	30·150	67·8	68·0	74·1
6233	18 14 26·5	9 2·0	10 25·0	9 2·2	9 2 1	S. 0 30+1 22·9	30·147	68·2	68·3	

♀ FEBRUARY 16, 1844.—FACE OF SECTOR EAST.

7992	22 49 34·4	9 17·3	8 1·9	9 17·5	9 17·4	N. 3 30—1 15·5	30·136	70·4	70·2	84·7
1802	5 34 44·0	8 32·3	11 1·05	8 32·3	8 32·3	S. 0 15—2 2·75	30·111	70·8	70·5	69·0
4686	13 58 20·5	9 17·3	9 22·4	9 17·1	9 17·2	S. 1 40—0 5·2	30·034	69·2	68·9	67·8
4719	14 6 34·0	9 29·1	6 1·95	9 29·2	9 29·15	N. 5 25—3 27·2	30·034	69·2	69·0	67·8
4784	14 19 37·0	9 1·9	6 22·4	9 2·0	9 1·95	N. 5 10—2 13·55	30·034	69·2	69·0	67·8
Anon.	14 24 48·0	8 28·6	6 6·7	8 28·5	8 28·55	N. 1 20—2 21·85			69·0	
4852	14 34 55·0	9 8·3	11 12·0	9 8·3	9 8·3	S. 0 35—2 3·7			69·0	
4916	14 46 54·8	9 12·6	5 22·4	9 13·0	9 12·8	N. 0 45—3 24·4	30·034	68·8	69·0	65·6
Anon.	14 54 8·2	9 12·0	8 21·5	9 11·8	9 11·8	N. 1 55—0 24·4	30·034	68·8	69·0	65·6
Anon.	14 58 20·5	9 6·4	5 13·6	9 6·5	9 6·45	N. 1 40—3 26·85	30·034	68·8	69·0	65·8
5032	15 8 56·6	9 4·2	12 7·5	9 4·25	9 4·23	N. 4 20+3 3·27	30·034	68·8	68·9	66·2
5151	15 29 40·0	8 31·9	9 19·4	8 31·7	8 31·8	N. 4 40+0 21·8			68·9	
5227	15 41 47·5	9 2·7	13 3·3	9 2·7	9 2·7	N. 0 45+4 0·6			68·8	
5272	15 47 49·5	9 10·2	10 21·4	9 10·0	9 10·1	N. 5 10+1 11·3	30·044	68·8	68·8	67·7
5915	17 23 53·8	8 20·8	12 19·0	8 20·6	8 20·7	S. 3 5—3 32·3	30·042	68·4	68·4	66·7
6233	18 14 34·5	9 7·5	7 18·0	9 7·6	9 7·55	S. 0 30+1 23·55	30·037	69·0	68·9	68·4

♄ FEBRUARY 17, 1844.—FACE OF SECTOR EAST.

2293	6 53 6·5	9 5·05	8 31·95	9 5·05	9 5·05	N. 5 10—0 7·1	29·963	70·8	70·5	66·3
5632	16 40 51·5	10 18·4	12 2·9	10 18·5	10 18·45	S. 0 5—1 18·45			68·5	

Feb. 15.—No. 5272 —The time of transit not noted.
No. 4719.— Has been hitherto printed as an anonymous star.

N

♄ FEBRUARY 17, 1844—(continued).—FACE OF SECTOR WEST.

Number of B.A.C.	Time by Chronometer.	Micr. for Plumb-line on Dot.	Micr. for Observation of Star.	Micr. for Plumb-line on Dot.	Mean of Micr. for Plumb-line on Dot.	Star's Apparent Zenith Distance.	Barom.	Thermometers.		
								Attd.	Lower.	Out.
	h m s	rev. pts.	rev. pts.	rev. pts.	rev. pts.	° ' rev. pts.	in.			
1802	5 34 42·0	9 16·5	7 13·6	9 16·5	9 16·5	S. 0 15—2 2·9	29·959	71·0	71·2	68·0
4458	13 12 40·0	8 24·25	12 25·05	8 24·45	8 24·35	S. 1 55+4 0 7			69·0	
4517	13 24 23·5	8 21·8	8 9·55	8 21·8	8 21·8	N. 5 10+0 12·25				
4548	13 30 27·0	8 21·9	8 13·0	8 21·8	8 21·85	N. 5 10+0 8·85	29·880	09·0	69·1	63·6
4579	13 37 30·5	8 25·5	7 11·5	8 25·7	8 25·6	N. 1 40+1 14·1				
4686	13 58 21·0	10 17·5	10 13·05	10 17·6	10 17·55	S. 1 40—0 4·5	29·881	68·6	69·1	62·6
4719	14 6 29·5	8 26·0	12 18·2	8 25·9	8 25·95	N. 5 25—3 26·25				
4784	14 39 33·3	8 27·7	11 5·8	8 27·5	8 27·6	N. 5 10—2 12·2	29·881	68·6	69·0	62·5
4852	14 34 54·0	9 6·85	7 2·5	9 6·9	9 6·88	S. 0 35—2 4 38				
4916	14 46 53·2	8 4·1	11 25·0	8 4·2	8 4·15	N. 0 45—3 20·85	29·885	68·5	09·1	62·2
Anon.	14 54 5·5	8 13·8	9 5·5	8 14·0	8 13·9	N. 1 55—0 25·6			69·2	
Anon.	14	8 22·3	12 17·6	8 22·5	8 22·4	N. 1 40—3 29·2				
5032	15 8 52·5	9 30·95	6 27·3	9 31·1	9 31·03	N. 4 20+3 3 73	29·885	08·4	69·0	01·6
5151	15 29 36·2	8 31·6	8 8·2	8 31·4	8 31·5	N. 4 40+0 23·3	29·881	08·4	69·0	61·4
5272	15 47 45·5	9 15·4	8 2·5	9 15·6	9 15·5	N. 5 10+1 13·0	29·862	08·4	69·0	61·4
5915	17 24 51·5	10 13·4	6 14·7	10 13·3	10 13·35	S. 3 5—3 32 65	29·914	68·5	68·6	65·7
6233	18 14 33·2	8 26·5	10 13·8	8 26·4	8 26·45	S. 0 30+1 21·35	29·937	09·4	69·0	68·3

☿ FEBRUARY 19, 1844.—FACE OF SECTOR EAST.

Number of B.A.C.	Time by Chronometer.	Micr. for Plumb-line on Dot.	Micr. for Observation of Star.	Micr. for Plumb-line on Dot.	Mean of Micr. for Plumb-line on Dot.	Star's Apparent Zenith Distance.	Barom.	Attd.	Lower.	Out.
1802	5 34 53·2	8 19·0	10 21·4	8 19·0	8 19·0	S. 0 15—2 2·4	30·193	09·6	70·2	63·0
2293	6 53 12·8	10 8·5	10 0·5	10 8·4	10 8·45	N. 5 10—0 7·95	30·214	70·0	69·6	62·9
4458	13 12 49·2	9 25·6	5 23·8	9 25·4	9 25·5	S. 1 55+4 1 7	30·168	07·8	67·4	61·6
4517	13 24 35·5	9 22·0	9 33·2	9 22·0	9 22·0	N. 5 10+0 11·2				61·6
4548	13 30 40·5	9 22·1	9 30·1	9 22·1	9 22·1	N. 5 10+0 8·0	30·164	67·5	67·6	61·8
4579	13 37 41·2	9 10·0	10 24·9	9 10·2	9 10·1	N. 1 40+1 14·8				
4623	13 43 41·5	9 10·9	5 17·3	9 11·1	9 11·0	N. 1 45—3 27·7			67·5	
4686	13 58 29·5	9 7·5	9 10·95	9 7·3	9 7·4	S. 1 40—0 3·55	30·186	67·5	67·6	61·4
4719	14 6 42·0	9 28·9	6 1·55	9 29·2	9 29·05	N. 5 25—3 27·5				
4784	14 19 45·5	9 7·4	6 26·7	9 7·4	9 7·4	N. 5 10—2 14·7	30·166	67·5	67·4	61·4
Anon.	14	8 19·4	5 28·5	8 19·2	8 19·3	N. 1 20—2 24 8			67·6	
4852	14 35 3·0	8 31·4	10 32·9	8 31·6	8 31·5	S. 0 35—2 1·4				
4916	14 47 4·0	9 15·7	5 24·2	9 15·8	9 15·75	N. 0 45—3 25·55	30·167	66·8	67·6	61·5
Anon.	14 54 17·8	9 10·3	8 18·8	9 10·3	9 10·3	N. 1 55—0 25·5				
Anon.	14	9 25·9	5 32·0	9 25·9	9 25·9	N. 1 40—3 27·9				
5032	15 9 6·0	9 5·0	12 6·6	9 5·0	9 5·0	N. 4 20+3 1·6	30·168	66·8	07·5	61·6
5054	15 12 53·0		8 12·0	8 33·5		S. 1 45+0 21·5			67·4	
5151	15 29 49·5	9 23·5	10 9·55	9 23·5	9 23·55	N. 4 40+0 20·0	30·168	66·8	67·4	61·6
5227	15 42 55·0	10 1·3	13 33·7	10 1·2	10 1·25	N. 0 45+3 32·45	30·175	66·6	67·4	61·6
5632	16 40 58·5	9 24·5	11 8·5	9 24·3	9 24·4	S. 0 5—1 18·1	30·193	66·5	67·3	61·8
5915	17 24 4·0	9 5·2	13 4·1	9 6·0	9 5·6	S. 3 5—3 32·5	30·196	66·7	67·5	63·4
6233	18 14 44·5	9 11·7	7 20·2	9 11·7	9 11·7	S. 0 30+1 25·5	30·200	67·4	67·4	64·9

♀ FEBRUARY 21, 1844.—FACE OF SECTOR WEST.

Number of B.A.C.	Time by Chronometer.	Micr. for Plumb-line on Dot.	Micr. for Observation of Star.	Micr. for Plumb-line on Dot.	Mean of Micr. for Plumb-line on Dot.	Star's Apparent Zenith Distance.	Barom.	Attd.	Lower.	Out.
1802	5 34 54·5	12 7·4	10 4·2	12 7·4	12 7·4	S. 0 15—2 3·2	29·936	71·0	72·3	09 3
2293	6 53 12·6	8 29·5	9 3·9	8 29·5	8 29·5	N. 5 10—0 8·4	29·938	70·8	71·3	68·0
5032	15 9 7·8	9 14·0	6 14·0	9 14·1	9 14·1	N. 4 20+3 2·9	29·905	70·2	69·0	65·6
5054	15 12 56·2	9 29·1	10 14·3	9 29·0	9 29·05	S. 1 45+0 19·25	29·905	70·2	69·3	65·6
5151	15 29 51·0	8 27·9	8 3·6	8 27·6	8 27·6	N. 4 40+0 9·0			80·6	65·6
5227	15 41 58·0	9 10·1	5 7·0	9 10·0	9 10·05	N. 0 45+4 3·05			89·5	65·4
5272	15 48 0·2	10 0·2	7 21·4	9 0·2	9 0·2	N. 5 10+1 12·8	29·928	89·8		65 3
5632	16 41 0·2	9 4·0	7 17·6	9 4·0	9 4·0	S. 0 5—1 20·4	29·946	89·5	68·6	64·4
5915	17 24 4·0	9 18·3	5 18·7	9 18·2	9 18·25	S. 5—3 33 55	29·958	69·4	68·6	66·8

Feb. 17.—Anon. 14ᵇ.—Observed at 20 seconds after passing the meridian wire. A bad observation.
19.—Between the observations of 5227 and 5632, the tube was turned a little by the upper adjusting screw; that the arch might swing true to the plumb-line.

☿ FEBRUARY 21, 1844.—FACE OF SECTOR WEST—(continued).

Number of B.A.C.	Time by Chronometer.	Micr. for Plumb-line on Dot.	Micr. for Observation of Star.	Micr. for Plumb-line on Dot.	Mean of Micr. for Plumb-line on Dot.	Star's Apparent Zenith Distance.	Barom.	Thermometers.		
								Attd.	Lower.	Out
	h m s	rev. pts.	rev. pts.	rev. pts.	rev. pts.	o ′ rev. pts.	in.			
6233	18 14 46·0	9 5·7	10 25·7	9 5·5	9 5·6 °	S. 0 30+1 20·1	29·980	69·8	69·4	68·3

♃ FEBRUARY 22, 1844.—FACE OF SECTOR WEST.

4686	13 58 35·0	8 29·4	8 25·95	8 29·5	8 29·45	S. 1 40—0 3·5	29·954	70·4	70·2	66·7
4719	14 6 47·0	8 14·9	12 8·55	8 15·1	8 15·0	N. 5 25—3 27·55		70·4	70·4	66·7
4784	14 19 50·0	8 19·0	11 0·2	8 19·4	8 19·2	N. 5 10—2 15·0	29·957	70·4		
4852	14 35 9·0	13 18·75	11 16·25	13 18·95	13 18·85	S. 0 35—2 2·6			70·4	66·4
4916	14 47 9·0	9 10·8	13 6·6	9 17·0	9 16·9	N. 0 45—3 23·7			70·4	65·8
Anon.	14 54 22·5	9 7·0	10 0·1	9 7·0	9 7·0	N. 1 55—0 27·1	29·956	70·4		65·7
5032	15 9 10·2	9 15·25	6 14·6	9 15·1	9 15·18	N. 4 20+3 0·58			70·4	
5054	15 12 50·5	9 33·8	10 20·8	9 33·8	9 33 8	S. 1 45+0 21·0			70·5	65·3
5151	15 29 53·8	9 26·3	9 4·8	9 26·1	9 26 2	N. 4 40+0 21·4				65·3
5227	15 42 0·5	10 1·7	6 0·0	10 1·6	10 1·65	N. 0 45+4 1·65	29·966	09·7		65·3
5272	15 48 2·5	8 25·0	7 13·5	8 25·0	8 25·0	N. 5 10+1 11·5			70 6	65·2
5632	16 41 3·5	9 21·8	8 2·4	9 21·8	9 21·8	S. 0 5—1 19·4	29·986	68·7	70·2	65·7
5915	17 24 7·7	9 25·75	5 26·5	9 25·5	9 25·63	S. 3 5—3 33·13	29·996	69·8	70·2	67·3
6233	18 14 49·2	8 14·55	11 10	9 14·5	9 14·53	S. 0 30+1 20·47	30·000	70·4	70·2	67·7

☉ FEBRUARY 25, 1844.—FACE OF SECTOR WEST.

7992	22 49 55·5	9 26·0	11 8·2	9 26·0	9 26·0	N. 3 30—1 16 2	30·053	78·0	78·4	84·6

☽ APRIL 8, 1844.—FACE OF SECTOR EAST.

4458	13 15 13·2	8 18·7	4 7·7	8 18·7	8 18·7	S. 1 55+4 11·0			66·0	
4517	13 26 59·5	9 9·4	9 13·4	9 9·3	9 9·3	N. 5 10+0 4·05	30·265	65·4	66·1	63·7
4548	13 33 5·0	9 9·4	9 9·7	9 9·4	9 9·4	N. 5 10+0 0·3			66·2	
4579	13 40 4·3	8 31·9	10 3·4	8 31·9	8 31·9	N. 1 40+1 5·5				
4623	13 46 4·4	9 1·2	4 32·4	9 1·4	9 1·3	N. 1 45—4 2·9	30·264	65·4	66·2	64·4
4686	14 0 53·4	9 26·0	9 22·0	9 25·8	9 25·9	S. 1 40+0 3·9				
4719	14 9 5·8	10 14·9	6 14·7	10 15·5	10 15·2	N. 5 25—4 0·5				
4784	14	9 13·9	6 26·6	9 14·1	9 14·0	N. 5 10—2 21·4	30·261	65·6	65·8	64·7
Anon.	14	8 31·5	5 33·4	8 31·5	8 31·5	N. 1 20—2 32·1				
4852	14 37 27·5	8 22·9	10 17·3	8 22·9	8 22·9	S. 0 35—1 28·4				
4916	14 49 28·1	8 21·9	4 24·5	8 21·8	8 21·85	N. 0 45—3 31·35				
Anon.	14 56 41·5	9 0·8	8 2·35	9 0·6	9 0·7	N. 1 55—0 32·35	30·263	65·6		64·6
5032	15 11 30·0	9 17·9	12 15·0	9 18·0	9 17·95	N. 4 20+2 31·05			65·8	
5054	15 15 18·0	8 28·1	8 1·9	8 28·2	8 28·15	S. 1 45+0 26·25				
5151		9 23·5	10 5·2	9 23·1	9 23·3	N 4 40+0 15·9				
5227	15 44 20·5	9 23·2	13 16·8	9 23·3	9 23·25	N. 0 45+3 29·55	30·241	65·6	65·8	65·0
5272	15 50 23·2	10 4·2	11 11·8	10 4·4	10 4·3	N. 5 10+1 7·5				
5374		10 0·7	11 25·0	10 0·7	10 0·7	N. 4 55+1 24·4				
5632	16 43 22·7	9 33·0	11 16·5	9 32·8	9 32·9	S. 0 5—1 17·6	30·231	65·6	65·8	65·0
5735	16 57 52·2	10 9·1	14 11·2	10 9·3	10 9·2	0 0+4 2·0				
5817	17 10 10·2	9 5·5	13 6·5	9 5·5	9 5·5	N. 1 25+4 1·0				
5881	17 20 33·2	9 9·2	5 14·3	9 9·1	9 9·15	N. 4 15—3 28·85				
5915	17 26 26·7	8 12·4	12 11·9	8 12·2	8 12·3	S. 3 5—3 33·6			65·8	

♂ APRIL 9, 1844.—FACE OT SECTOR WEST.

2293	6 55 31·4	8 3·7	8 15·8	8 3·6	8 3·65	N. 5 10—0 12·15	30·228	67·9	68·6	72·9

April 8.—The wind so strong as to endanger the open roof-shutter.
Left the Sector-room to observe the moon, immediately after the observation of No. 5151.
Nos. 4719 and 4916 were formerly registered as anonymous stars.

♂ APRIL 9, 1844.—FACE OF SECTOR WEST—(continued).

Number of B.A.C.	Time by Chronometer.	Micr. for Plumb-line on Dot.	Micr. for Observation of Star.	Micr. for Plumb-line on Dot.	Mean of Micr. for Plumb-line on Dot.	Star's Apparent Zenith Distance.	Barom.	Thermometers.		
								Attd.	Lower.	Out.
	h m s	rev. pts.	rev. pts.	rev. pts.	rev. pts.	° ′ rev. pts.	in.			
4852	14 37 26·0	9 26·2	7 31·5	9 26 2	9 26·2	S. 0 35—1 28·7	30·195	66·4	66·8	65·4
4916		9 9·0	13 6·2	9 9 0	9 9·0	N. 0 45—3 31·2				
Anon.		8 26·6	9 27·0	8 27·0	8 26·8	N. 1 55—1 0·2				
5032	15 11 27·7	7 9·7	4 15·2	7 9 8	7 9·75	N. 4 20+2 28·55				
5054	15 15 16·2	8 3·5	8 31·4	8 3 5	8 3·5	S. 1 45+0 27·9	30·192	66·6	67·4	66·3
5151	15 32 11·0	8 9·1	7 25·6	8 9·0	8 9·05	N. 4 40+0 17·45			67·4	
Anon.	15 37 31·0	8 13·3	8 19 6	8 13·3	8 13·3	N. 2 50—0 6·3				
5227	15 44 18·5	8 31·5	5 1·1	8 31·4	8 31·4	N. 0 45+3 30·3				
5272	15 50 20·5	8 23·4	7 19·0	8 24·8	8 24·1	N. 5 10+1 5·1				
5374	16 4 26·4	9 13·5	7 24·3	9 13·5	9 13·5	N. 4 55+1 23·2	30·185	65·8	67·4	60·7
5435	16 12 50·0	9 26·9	10 19·6	9 26·7	9 26·8	N. 3 25—0 26·8				
Anon.	16 17 9·2	10 0·3	7 22·6	10 0 3	10 0·3	N. 1 5+2 11·7			67·4	
5588	16 36 48·5	8 18·5	12 17·3	8 18·5	8 18·5	N. 2 10—3 32·8				
5632	16 43 20·6	8 15·3	6 33·8	8 15·5	8 15·4	S. 0 5—1 15·6	30·167	65·4	67·2	60·7
5735	16 57 50·2	9 15·8	5 16·2	9 15·7	9 15·75	0 0+3 33·55				
5817	17 10 8·2	9 11·8	5 11·0	9 12·0	9 11·9	N. 1 25+4 0·9				
5881	17 20 30·5	9 19·1	13 14·2	9 19·1	9 19·1	N. 4 15—3 29·1	30·163	65·0	66·9	60·3
5915	17 26 24·7	10 6·5	6 8·5	10 6·7	10 6·6	S. 3 5—3 32·1			66·9	
5960	17 33 5·8	9 14·3	10 0·0	9 14·3	9 14·3	N. 1 50—0 19·7				
6186	18 10 27·4	9 25·8	13 5·5	9 26·0	9 25 9	S. 2 50+3 13·6			66·1	
6233	18 17 6·2	9 28·8	11 15·7	9 28·7	9 28·75	S. 0 30+1 20·95				
6414		12 13·7	10 3·4	12 13·5	12 13·6	N. 3 0+2 10·2				
6489	18 55 48·2	10 23·0	10 5·5	10 23·0	10 23·0	N. 3 50+0 17·5			65·8	

♀ APRIL 10, 1844.—FACE OF SECTOR EAST.

Number of B.A.C.	Time by Chronometer.	Micr. for Plumb-line on Dot.	Micr. for Observation of Star.	Micr. for Plumb-line on Dot.	Mean of Micr. for Plumb-line on Dot.	Star's Apparent Zenith Distance.	Barom.	Thermometers.		
2293	6 55 39·2	10 17·3	10 8·0	10 17·2	10 17·25	N. 5 10—0 9·25	30·111	68·2	69·8	72·0
4623	13 46 10·2	9 25·5	5 20·1	9 25·3	9 25·4	N. 1 45—4 5·3	30·081	68·4	69·0	77·7
4686	14 0 59·5	8 25·9	8 20·6	8 25·9	9 25·3	S. 1 40+0 5·3				
4719	14 9 12·0	9 23·7	5 22·3	9 23·7	9 23·7	N. 5 25—4 1·4				
4784	14 22 15·9	9 20·0	6 32·4	9 20·0	9 20·0	N. 5 10—2 21·6	30·080	68·6	69·3	76·4
Anon.	14 27 27·5	9 16·7	6 17·8	9 16·5	9 16·6	N. 1 20—2 32·8	30·072	68·4	69·3	74·0
4852	14 37 34·0	10 13·5	12 7·0	10 13·5	10 13·5	S. 0 35—1 27·5				
4916	14 49 34·0	9 26·3	5 26·0	9 26·2	9 26·25	N. 0 45—4 0·25				
Anon.	14 56 47·2	9 10·3	8 9·6	9 10·3	9 10·3	N. 1 55—1 0·7	30·070	68·5		70·4
Anon.	15 0 59·5	9 9·8	5 6·9	9 9·6	9 9·7	N. 1 40—4 2·8				69·9
5032	15 11 35·4	9 33·8	12 27·9	9 33·6	9 33·7	N. 4 20+2 28·2				
5054	15 15 24·5	9 33·8	9 7·6	9 34·0	9 33·9	S. 1 45+0 26·3				
5227		8 16·1	12 9·8	8 16 3	8 16·2	N. 0 45+3 27·6	30·066	68·8	69·3	69·2
5272	15 50 28·5	8 16·6	9 24·3	8 16·5	8 16·55	N. 5 10+1 7·75				
5374	16 4 34·5	8 18·8	10 8·0	8 18·9	8 18·85	N. 4 55+1 23·15				
5435		8 14·4	7 23·4	8 14 2	8 14·3	N. 3 25—0 24·9	30·058	63·0	69·3	68·0
5632	16 43 28·4	7 29·5	9 12·3	7 28·3	7 28·4	N. 0 5+1 17·9			69·3	
5735	16 57 58·0	9 26 3	13 29·0	9 26·3	9 26·3	0 0+4 2·7				
5881	17 20 38·3	10 17·4	6 21·8	10 17·8	9 26·3	N. 4 15—3 29·8			69 0	
5915	17 26 33·3	9 1·3	13 1·0	9 1·3	9 1·3	S. 3 5—3 33·7				
5960	17 33 11·2	8 24·0	8 4·7	8 24·2	9 24·1	N. 1 50—0 19·4				
6074	17 52 19·7	9 26·9	13 25·3	9 26·9	9 26·9	N. 3 40+3 32·4				
6115	17 59 3·2	9 29·5	11 18·0	9 29·7	9 29·6	N. 3 30+1 22·4				
6145	18 3 18·8	8 31·2	11 7·3	8 31·2	8 31·2	N. 3 10+2 10·1				
6186	18 10 35·5	8 28·3	5 17·5	8 28·0	8 28·15	S. 2 50+3 10·65				
6233	18 17 14·2	9 11·8	7 24·7	9 12·0	9 12·0	S. 0 30+1 21·2			68·7	
6305	18 27 5·2	9 10·5	6 33·3	9 16·5	9 16·5	N. 0 50—2 17·2	30·061	67·0		62·6
6414	18 45 57·0	9 10·9	11 23·3	9 10·7	9 10·7	N. 3 0+2 12·5				
6489	18 55 55·7	8 33·2	9 19·7	8 33·4	8 33·3	N. 3 50+0 20·4	30·058	67·0	68·5	61·0

April 9.—Nos. 5588 and 6414 were formerly registered as anonymous stars.
10.—No. 5227.—Observed at 10 seconds past the meridi-n wire.
Left the Sector-room to observe the moon immediately after the transit of 6489.
Good definition: scattered cumuli.

♃ APRIL 10, 1844.—FACE OF SECTOR EAST—*(continued)*.

Number of B.A.C.	Time by Chronometer.	Micr. for Plumb-line on Dot.	Micr. for Observation of Star.	Micr. for Plumb-line on Dot.	Mean of Micr. for Plumb-line on Dot.	Star's Apparent Zenith Distance.	Barom.	Thermometers.		
								Attd.	Lower.	Out.
	h m s	rev. pts.	rev. pts.	rev. pts.	rev. pts.	° ′ rev. pts	in.			
7992	22 52 15·5	10 1·7	8 20·3	10 1·7	10 1·7	N. 3 30—1 6·4	30·064	67·0	68·0	72·8

♃ APRIL 11, 1844.—FACE OF SECTOR WEST.

2293	6 55 38·0	9 3·5	9 16·5	9 3·7	9 3·6	N. 5 10—0 12·9	29·970	69·0	70·3	70·2
4458	13 15 18·5	8 9·2	12 23·8	8 9·0	8 9·1	S. 1 55+4 14·7	29·957	68·4	68·4	62·8
4517	13 27 3·0	7 18 8	7 17·5	7 19·0	7 18·9	N. 5 10+0 1·4				
4548	13 33 7·5	7 18·9	7 21·7	7 18·9	7 18·9	N. 5 10—0 2·8				
4579	13 40 9 0	9 28·3	8 23·9	9 28·3	9 28·3	N. 1 40+1 4·4				
4623	13 46 9·5	9 15·1	13 17·0	9 14·7	9 14·9	N. 1 45—4 3·0	29·946	67·8		62·4
4686	14 0 58·5	9 20·7	10 2·5	9 30·0	9 29·85	S. 1 40+0 6·65			69·0	
4784	14 20 14·5	9 29·6	12 19·1	9 30·3	9 29·95	N. 5 10—2 23·15	29·943	88·0		62·3
Anon.	14	9 29·1	12 27·7	9 29·5	9 29·3	N. 1 20—2 32·4	29·935	67·7	69·0	62·4
5032	15 11 34·0	8 23·3	5 29·5	8 23·5	8 23·4	N. 4 20+2 27·9	29·926	68·8	69·1	63·3
Anon.	15 37 37·0	8 27·9	8 31·7	8 27·9	8 27·9	N. 2 50—0 3·8				
5227	15 44 25·2	9 28·8	5 32·3	9 28·6	9 28·7	N. 0 45+3 36·4				
5272	15 50 26·5	9 20·3	8 15·4	9 20·5	9 20·4	N. 5 10+1 5·0	29·917	68·2	60·2	64·4
5374	16 4 33·2	0 9·5	7 20·6	9 9·5	9 9·5	N. 4 55+1 22·9				63·7
5435	16 12 56·5	9 10·0	10 0·5	9 10·0	9 10·0	N. 3 25—0 24·5				
Anon.	16 17 16·5	9 22·0	7 7·3	9 22·9	9 22 9	N. 1 5+2 15·6				
5632	16 43 28·5	8 18·3	6 33·7	8 18·1	8 18·2	S. 0 5—1 18·5	29·890	68·0	69·2	63·3
5735	16 57 57·2	8 12·1	4 11·9	8 12·0	8 12·05	0 0+4 0·15				
5817	17 10 14·8	8 27·4	4 25·3	8 27·2	8 27·3	N. 1 25+4 2·0			69·2	62·8

♄ APRIL 13, 1844.—FACE OF SECTOR EAST.

4458	13 15 28·2	8 30·5	4 18·4	8 30·5	8 30·5	S. 1 55+4 12·1	30·207	67·4	68·0	61·4
4517	13 27 14·2	9 8·0	9 10·0	9 8·0	9 8·0	N. 5 10+0 2·0			68·0	
4548	13 33 19·0	9 8·0	9 6·9	9 8·0	9 8·0	N. 5 10—0 1·1				
4579	13 40 20·5	9 1·3	10 5·2	9 1·3	9 1·3	N. 1 40+1 3·9	30·196	66·8	67·8	61·4
4623	13 40 20·2	9 6·2	5 1·7	9 6·0	9 6·1	N. 1 45—4 4·4			67·8	
4686	14 1 9·2	9 2·2	8 28·4	9 2·4	9 2·3	S. 1 40+0 7·9				
4719	14 9 22·6	8 33·4	4 31·6	8 33·3	8 33·35	N. 5 25—4 1·75	30·188	66·6	67·5	61·8
4784	14 22 26·0	8 31·3	6 9·0	8 31·4	8 31·35	N. 5 10—2 22·35			67·3	
Anon.	14 27 37·2	8 20·7	5 22·0	8 20·5	8 20·6	N. 1 20—2 32·6			67·2	62·4
4852	14 37 43·8	9 0·0	10 27·2	9 0·0	9 0·0	S. 0 35—1 27·2	30·190	66·6	67·2	
4916	14 49 43·8	9 32·3	5 33·7	9 32·1	9 32·2	N. 0 45—3 32·5				
Anon.	14 56 57·2	10 9·8	9 11·4	10 9·7	10 9·75	N. 1 55—0 32·35	30·194	66·4	67·2	62·0
Anon.	15 1 10·0	9 13·5	5 12·7	9 13·7	9 13·6	N. 1 40—4 0·9			67·3	
5032	15 11 45·7	9 5·6	12 1·0	9 5·9	9 5·7	S. 1 45+0 28·15				62·0
5054	15 15 34·4	8 27·9	7 33·8	8 28·0	8 27·95	S. 1 45+0 28·15			67·2	
5151	15 32 29·3	9 32·7	10 14·8	9 32·5	9 32·6	N. 4 40+0 16·2				
Anon.	15 37 49·0	9 24·2	9 21·5	9 24·1	9 24·15	N. 2 50—0 2·05				
5227	15 44 36 2	10 0·4	13 29·0	10 0·4	10 0·4	N. 0 45+3 28·6	30·178	67·3	67·2	61·7
5272	15 50 39·2	9 7·2	10 14·5	9 7·4	9 7·3	N. 5 10+1 7·2	30·172	66·0	67·2	61·7
5374	16 4 44·4	9 10·3	11 0·8	9 10·3	9 10·3	N. 4 55+1 22·9				
5435	16 13 8·0	8 30·4	8 5·6	8 30·2	8 30·3	N. 3 25—0 24·7				
Anon.	16 17 27·2	9 8·9	11 19·5	9 9·0	9 8·95	N. 1 5+2 10·55	30·178	66·0	67·1	62·0
5588	16 37 7·0	10 4·3	6 7·0	10 4·3	10 4·3	S. 0 5—1 16·55				
5632	16 43 38·7	9 10·8	10 27·3	9 10·7	9 10·75	N. 2 10—3 31·3				
5735	16 58 8·0	9 11·9	13 12·5	9 12·1	9 12·0	0 0+4 0·5				
5817	17 10 26·2	10 1·5	14 1·7	10 1·7	10 1·6	N. 1 25+4 0·1			67·1	
5881	17 20 48·6	8 30·5	5 1·3	8 30·5	8 30·5	N. 4 15—3 29·2				

April 11.—Anon. 14ʰ.— Observed at 10 seconds past the meridian wire. Correction + 0″·025.
Good definition when the clouds permitted stars to be seen.
Totally overcast after the transit of 5817.
13.—Anon. 16ʰ 17ᵐ.—Open double: the space bisected.

o

♭ APRIL 13, 1844.—FACE OF SECTOR EAST—(continued).

Number of B.A.C.	Time by Chronometer.	Micr. for Plumb-line on Dot.	Micr. for Observation of Star.	Micr. for Plumb-line on Dot.	Mean of Micr. for Plumb-line on Dot.	Star's Apparent Zenith Distance.	Barom.	Thermometers. Attd.	Lower.	Out.
	h m s	rev. pts.	rev. pts.	rev. pts.	rev. pts.	° ' rev. pts	in.			
5915	17 26 43·2	8 11·9	12 9·05	8 11·7	8 11 8	S. 3 5—8 31·25	30·157	66·0	67·0	60·7
5960	17 33 21·5	9 1·9	8 18·0	9 1·9	9 1·9	N. 1 50—0 17·9				
6016	17 42 31·3	9 13·4	13 30·2	9 13·5	9 13·45	N. 2 15+4 16·75				
6074	17 52 30·2	9 3·6	13 2 6	9 3·7	9 3·65	N. 3 40+3 32·95				
6115	17 59 13·2	9 13·2	11 0·5	9 13·2	9 13·2	N. 3 30+1 21·3				
6145	18 3 29·0	9 14·6	11 24·2	9 14·7	9 14·65	N. 3 10+2 9·55				
6186	18 10 45·7	8 23·5	5 12·4	8 23·4	8 23·45	S. 2 50—3 11·05				
6233	18 17 24·2	9 5·0	7 18·5	9 5·3	9 5 15	S. 0 30—1 20·65				
6275	18 23 19·5	9 29·4	5 21·0		9 29·28	N. 0 50—4 8·28				
6285	18 24 22·5		11 21 6	9 29·2	9 29·28	N. 0 50+1 26·32				
6305	18 27 15·5	9 29·2	7 13·2	9 29·3	9 29·28	N. 0 50—2 16·08				
6414	18 45 57·5	10 2·6	12 17·5	10 2·6	10 2·6	N. 3 0+2 14·9				
6489	18 56 6·0	10 7·9	10 27·4	10 8·0	10 7·95	N. 3 50+0 19·45				
6525	19 1 4·3	10 9·0	8 6·5	10 9·0	10 9·0	N. 5 5—2 2·5	30·162	65·5	66·7	59·8
6639	19 20 29·5	8 26·4	5 31·7	8 26·3	8 26·35	N. 3 55—2 28·65				
7557	21 39 10·2	10 20·0	14 22·5	10 19·6	10 19·8	N. 0 10+4 2·7	30·168	66·2	66·4	63·0
7992	22 52 25·8	11 24·8	10 20·5	11 25·0	11 24·9	N. 3 30—1 4·4	30·163	66·2	67·0	67·0

⊙ APRIL 14, 1844.—FACE OF SECTOR WEST.

Number of B.A.C.	Time by Chronometer.	Micr. for Plumb-line on Dot.	Micr. for Observation of Star.	Micr. for Plumb-line on Dot.	Mean of Micr. for Plumb-line on Dot.	Star's Apparent Zenith Distance.	Barom.	Thermometers. Attd.	Lower.	Out.
4458	13 15 27·6	10 11·3	14 26·3	10 11·5	10 11·4	S. 1 55+4 14·9	29·985	67·0	68·0	61·2
4517	13 27 13·7	9 8·2	9 7·4	9 8·4	9 8·3	N. 5 10+0 0·9				
4548	13 33 18·2	9 8·4	9 11·3	9 8·3	9 8·35	N. 5 10—0 2·95				
4579	13 40 19·5	9 16·3	8 16·3	9 16·5	9 16·4	N. 1 40+1 0·1				
4623	13 46 19·5	9 4·8	13 10·2	9 5·0	9 4·9	N. 1 45—4 5·3			68·2	
4686	14 1 8·5	9 9·9	9 18·2	9 9·7	9 9·8	S. 1 40+0 8 4				
4719	14 9 21 0	8 25·3	12 28·9	8 25·1	8 25·2	N. 5 25—4 3·7				
4784	14 22 24·5	8 11·7	11 0·6	8 11·7	8 11·7	N. 5 10—2 22·9				
4852	14 37 42·5	9 10·5	7 17·4	0 10·7	9 10·6	S. 0 35—1 27·2			67·9	
4916	14 49 42·8	8 19·0	12 18·3	8 19·2	8 19·1	N. 0 45—3 33·2			68·0	
Anon.	14 56 55·7	8 33·0	10 1·0	8 32·8	8 32·9	N. 1 55—1 2·1	29·957	66·0		
Anon.		9 7·3	13 12·7	9 7·5	9 7 4	N. 1 40—4 5·3				59·2
5032	15 11 44·0	10 4·8	7 11·9	10 4·8	10 4·8	N. 4 20+2 26·9				
5054	15 15 33·0	9 30 5	10 26·2	9 30·6	9 30·5	S. 1 45+0 29·7				
5151	15 32 27·5	9 8·0	8 29·1	9 7·8	9 7·9	N. 4 40+0 12·8				
Anon.	15 37 47·5	9 16·0	9 21·0	9 15·8	9 15·9	N. 2 50—0 5·1				
5227	15 44 35 0	9 15·9	5 20·4	9 16·0	9 15·95	N. 0 45+3 29·55				
5272	15 50 36·8	9 21·0	8 17·2	9 20·8	9 20·8	N. 5 10+1 3·6	29 951	65·8	68·0	59·7
5374	16 4 42·5	10 1·6	8 16·3	10 1·2	10 1·4	N. 4 55+1 19·1			68·0	
5435	16 13 6 2	9 27·8	10 21·5	9 27·8	9 27 8	N. 3 25—0 27·7				
Anon.	16 17 27·5	10 10·3	8 0·4	10 10·3	10 10·3	N. 1 5+2 9·0				
5586	16 37 6·0	9 18·8	13 19·3	9 18·8	9 18·8	N. 2 10—4 0·5				
5632	16 43 37·4	9 26·5	8 12·9	9 26·5	9 26·5	S. 0 5—1 13·6	29·944	65 6	67·6	60·2
5735	16 58 7·2	8 21·6	4 23·3	8 21 6	8 21 6	0 0+3 32·3				60·2
5817	17 10 25·0	8 7·8	4 10·3	8 7·8	8 7·8	N. 1 25+3 31·5	29·950	65·0	67·4	60·2
5881	17 20 47·0	8 12·5	12 10·3	8 12·5	8 12 5	N. 4 15—3 31·8				
5915	17 26 42·0	9 25·0	5 26·7	9 24·9	9 24·95	S. 3 5—3 32·25	29·942	65·7	67·4	60·3
5960	17 33 20·0	8 32 5	9 19·0	8 32·5	8 32·5	N. 1 50—0 20·5				
6016	17 42 30·5	8 21·7	5 21·7	8 21·5	8 21·6	N. 2 15+4 13·6				
6074	17 52 38·7	8 19·3	4 22·4	8 19·3	8 19·3	N. 3 40+3 30·9				
6115	17 59 12·0	8 10·5	6 24·0	8 10·3	8 10·4	N. 3 30+1 20·4				
6145	18 3 27·2	8 18·5	6 10·8	8 18·4	8 18·45	N. 3 10+2 7·65				
6186	18 10 44·5	9 8·4	12 21·5	9 8·4	9 8·4	S. 2 50+3 13·1				
6233	18 17 23·2	8 27·5	10 10·7	8 27·4	8 27·45	S. 0 30+1 23·25				

April 13.—No. 6074.—Double. The preceding observed, the larger one.
Excellent definition. A few stars lost by occasional clouds.
No. 7992.—By an oversight, the 8 ounce counterpoise was on while observing this star.
April 14.—4623.—Double. The larger bisected.
The Anon. preceding 5032 was leaving the field when observed. Correction + 0″·222.
Anon. 16ʰ 17ᵐ.—The observation uncertain, owing to the star being very faint.

⊙ APRIL 14, 1844.—FACE OF SECTOR WEST—(continued).

Number of B.A.C.	Time by Chronometer.	Micr. for Plumb-line on Dot.	Micr. for Observation of Star.	Micr. for Plumb-line on Dot.	Mean of Micr. for Plumb-line. on Dot.	Star's Apparent Zenith Distance.	Barom.	Thermometers. Attd.	Lower.	Out.
	h m s	rev. pts.	rev. pts.	rev. pts.	rev. pts.	° ′ rev. pts.	in.			
6275	18 23 16·5	8 26·0	13 4·6		8 26 0	N. 0 50—4 12·6	29·900	65·5	67·4	58·7
6285	18 24 21·5		6 33·0	8 25·9	8 26·0	N. 0 50+1 27·0				
6305	18 27 14·6	8 26·0	11 6·7	8 26·1	8 26·0	N. 0 50—2 14·7				
6414	18 46 6·0	7 29·9	5 18·8	7 30·0	7 29·95	N. 3 0+2 11·15				
6489	18 56 4·5	7 29·9	7 13·8	7 29·7	7 29·8	N. 3 50+0 16·0				
6525	19 1 2·0	8 14·3	10 21·1	8 14·5	8 14·4	N. 5 5—2 6·7	29·961	65·5	67·0	57·8
6639	19 20 28·5	8 23·5	11 19·4	8 23·1	8 23·3	N. 3 55—2 30·1				
6753	19 38 57·5	8 22·0	8 29·6	8 22·0	8 22·0	N. 2 40—0 7·6				
6877	19 57 54·5	8 12·4	4 32·4	8 12·5	8 12·45	N. 1 25+3 14·05	29·961	65·0	67·0	57·4
7992	22 52 24·4	8 20·7	9 25·9	8 20·8	8 20·75	N. 3 30—1 5·15				

☿ APRIL 17, 1844.—FACE OF SECTOR EAST.

Number of B.A.C.	Time by Chronometer.	Micr. for Plumb-line on Dot.	Micr. for Observation of Star.	Micr. for Plumb-line on Dot.	Mean of Micr. for Plumb-line. on Dot.	Star's Apparent Zenith Distance.	Barom.	Attd.	Lower.	Out.
4852	14	8 13·4	10 6·3	8 13·5	8 13·45	S. 0 35—1 26·85	30·166	64·4	64·6	57·3
4916	14	8 17·0	4 16·4	8 17·2	8 17·1	N. 0 45—4 0·7				
Anon.	14	8 8·3	7 8·5	8 8·5	8 8·5	N. 1 55—0 33·9	30·170	64·2		58·2
Anon.	15 1 23·3	8 8·6	4 7·3	8 8·4	8 8·5	N. 1 40—4 1·2				
5032	15 11 58·0	8 30·0	11 25·6	8 30·0	8 30·0	N. 4 20+2 29 6			64·6	
5054	15 15 48·0	8 4·4	7 10·6	8 4·5	8 4·45	S. 1 45+0 27·85	30·166	64·3		58·6
5151	15 32 41·8	7 19·8	8 0·3	7 19·7	7 19·75	N. 4 40+0 14·55			64·7	
5227	15 44 49·3	9 0·5	12 28·3	9 0·5	9 0·5	N. 0 45+3 27·8				
5272	15 50 51·0	9 8·5	10 16·3	9 8·7	9 8·6	N. 5 10+1 7·7				
5374	16 4 56·0	8 32·8	10 23·0	8 32·8	8 32·8	N. 4 55+1 24·2			64·6	59·6
5435	16 13 20·5	8 12·5	7 22·4	8 12·7	8 12·6	N. 3 25—0 24·2	30·157	64·2	64·3	59·8
Anon.	16 17 40·0	8 26·8	11 5·5	8 28·9	8 28·85	N. 1 5+2 10·65				
5586	16 37 19·8	10 0·6	6 2·4	10 0·6	10 0·0	N. 2 10—3 32 2				
5632	16 43 52·0	9 10·2	10 27·0	9 10·3	9 10·25	S. 0 5—1 16·75				
5735	16 58 21·5	9 5·0	13 7·7	9 5·0	9 5·0	0 0+4 2·7	30·150	64·2		59·4
5817	17 10 39·0	9 32·6	13 33·6	9 32·8	9 32·7	N. 1 25+4 0 9				
5881	17 21 1·2	10 23·7	6 29·3	10 23·8	10 23·75	N. 4 15—3 28·45				
5915	17 26 56·8	9 16·0	13 15·2	9 16·1	9 16·05	S. 3 5—3 33·15	30·146	64·2	64·5	59·5
5960	17 33 34·3	9 30·2	9 12·0	9 30·3	9 30·3	N. 1 50—0 18·3				
5964	17 34 31·8		7 16·9	9 30·4	9 30·3	N. 1 50—2 13·4				
6016	17 42 44·2	9 33·8	14 16·3	9 33·8	9 33·8	N. 2 15+4 16·5				
6074	17 52 42·5	9 13·6	13 13·1	9 14·0	9 13·8	N. 3 40+3 33·3	30·145	64·0	64·6	59·5
6115	17 59 26·0	9 10·0	10 32·3	9 10·1	9 10·05	N. 3 30+1 22·25				
6145	18 3 41·7	8 8·9	10 18·9	8 8·9	8 8·9	N. 3 10+2 10·0				
6186	18 10 59·7	7 16·9	4 6·6	7 16·9	7 16·9	S. 2 50+3 10·3				
6233	18	8 24·8	7 4·3	8 24·8	8 24·8	S. 0 30+1 20·5				
6275	18 23 12·2	9 8·1	5 0·5		9 8·03	N. 0 50—4 7·53				
6285	18 24 35·3		11 1·9	9 7·9	9 8·03	N. 0 50+1 27·87				
6305	18 27 28·2	9 8·1	6 27·5	9 8·0	9 8·03	N. 0 50—2 14·53	30·143	63·6	64·2	58·4
6114	18 46 20·2	9 8·9	11 23·4	9 8·7	9 8·8	N. 3 0+2 14·6				
6489	18 56 18·7	9 29·3	10 15·0	9 29·3	9 29·3	N. 3 50+0 19·7				
6525	19 1 16·2	10 8·8	8 6·8	10 8·9	10 8·85	N. 5 5—2 2·05				
Anon.	19 24 54·2	9 18·0	13 29·8	9 18·0	9 18·0	N. 4 5+4 11·8				
6877	19 58 6·2	8 29·2	12 10·3	8 29·2	8 29·2	N. 1 25+3 15·1	30·148	63·8	64·4	56·0
7992	22 52 38·2	8 6·3	7 2·7	8 6·4	8 6·35	N. 3 30—1 3·65	30·146	64·4	64·0	60·2

♃ APRIL 18, 1844.—FACE OF SECTOR WEST.

Number of B.A.C.	Time by Chronometer.	Micr. for Plumb-line on Dot.	Micr. for Observation of Star.	Micr. for Plumb-line on Dot.	Mean of Micr. for Plumb-line. on Dot.	Star's Apparent Zenith Distance.	Barom.	Attd.	Lower.	Out.
1802	5 37 42·5	9 11·4	7 7·2	9 11·4	9 11·4	S. 0 15—2 4·2	30·024	67·0	67 2	71·6
2293	6 55 59·5	9 5·2	9 14·6	9 5·4	9 5·3	N. 5 10—0 9·3	30·020	67·0	67·2	64·8

April 17.—It is to be always understood hereafter, that when the minutes and seconds are omitted from the "chronometer" column, the stars were bisected at the meridian wire, although for some reason, the time of transit was not noted,—unless the contrary is stated.
No. 5964.—Was formerly registered as anonymous.
No. 6074.—A beautiful double star.
Good definition throughout the observations of the 17th.

♃ April 18, 1844.—Face of Sector West—(continued).

Number of B.A.C.	Time by Chronometer.	Micr. for Plumb-line on Dot.	Micr. for Observation of Star.	Micr. for Plumb-line on Dot.	Mean of Micr. for Plumb-line on Dot.	Star's Apparent Zenith Distance.	Barom.	Thermometers. Attd.	Lower.	Out.
	h m s	rev. pts.	rev. pts.	rev. pts.	rev. pts.	° ' rev. pts.	in.			
4458	13 15 42·0	10 1·2	14 16·4	10 1·4	10 1·3	S. 1 55+4 15·1			65·8	
4517	13 27 25·8	9 8·3	9 7·5	9 8·5	9 8·4	N. 5 10+0 0·9				54·4
4548	13 33 31·2	9 8·4	9 11·3	9 8·4	9 8·4	N. 5 10—0 2·9				
4579	13 40 32·2	9 7·6	8 6·9	9 7·7	9 7 65	N. 1 40+1 0·75	29 918	63·6		54·7
4623	13 46 32·3	8 32·1	13 5·0	8 32 5	8 32 3	N. 1 45—4 6·7	29 915	63·6	65·7	55·3
4686	14 1 22·0	10 10·4	10 19·7	10 10·6	10 10·5	S. 1 40+0 9·2				
4719	14 9 33·2	9 28·2	13 32·0	9 28 0	9 28·1	N. 5 25—4 3·9				
4784	14 22 37·0	9 32·1	12 22·3	9 32 3	9 32 2	N. 5 10—2 24·1				55·4
Anon.	14 27 49·5	10 9·0	13 8·2	10 8·8	10 8·9	N. 1 20—2 33·3			65·5	
4852	14	10 22·9	8 30·7	10 23·0	10 22·95	S. 0 35—1 26·25	29 917	63·8	65·3	56·0
4916	14 49 56·0	9 25·0	13 24·5	9 25·4	9 25·2	N. 0 45—3 33·3				
Anon.	14 57 9·2	9 30·0	10 32·0	9 30·2	9 30·1	N. 1 55—1 1·9				
5032	15 11 56·3	14 5·8	11 12·5	14 5·8	14 5·8	N. 4 20+2 27·3	29 913	63 8	65·4	57·3
5054	15 15 46·8	13 22·5	14 17·8	13 22 5	13 22·3	S. 1 45+0 29·3			65·5	
5151	15 32 40·0	10 5·1	9 26·3	10 5·1	10 5·1	N. 4 40+0 12 8				
Anon.	15 38 0·2	9 5·1	9 10·6	9 5·1	9 5·1	N. 2 50—0 5·5				
5227	15 44 48·0	9 2·5	5 8·6	9 2·6	9 2 55	N. 0 45+3 27·95			65·2	
5272	15 50 49·4	9 1·8	7 31·4	9 2·1	9 1·95	N. 5 10+1 4·55	29 896	63 6	65·2	57·3
5374	16 4 55·5	8 31·2	7 8·7	8 31·0	8 31·1	N. 4 55+1 22·4				
5435	16 13 19·2	9 6·2	9 32·6	9 6·0	9 6·1	N. 3 25—0 26·5			65·2	57·3
Anon.	16 17 39·5	9 30·5	7 19·9	9 30·7	9 30·6	N. 1 5+2 10·7				
5588	16 37 18·7	10 6·3	14 6·6	10 6·3	10 6·3	N. 2 10—4 0·3				
5632	16 43 51·3	9 28·9	8 14·4	9 28·9	9 28·9	S. 0 5—1 14·5	29·884	63·8		56·4
5735	16 58 20 5	9 20·8	5 22·4	9 20·9	9 20·85	0 0+3 32·45	29·887	64·0	65·4	56·9
5817	17	9 28·5	5 30·1	9 28·5	9 28·5	N. 1 25+3 32·4				
5881	17 20 59·5	9 22·3	13 18·3	9 22 5	9 22·4	N. 4 15—3 29·9	29 890	64·0	65·3	57·0
5915	17 26 55·5	10 5·1	6 8·1	10 4·7	10 4·9	S. 3 5—3 30·8				
5960	17	9 1·7	9 19·2	9 1·5	9 1·6	N. 1 50—0 17·6				
6016	17 42 43·4	8 31·0	4 15·4	8 30·8	8 30·9	N. 2 15+4 15·5				
6074	17 52 41·5	8 28·8	4 31·3	8 28·8	8 28·8	N. 3 40+3 31·5	29 895	64·0	65·4	58·0
6115	17 59 25·4	9 20·3	8 0·4	9 20·5	9 20·4	N. 3 30+1 20·0				
6145	18 3 41·2	9 14·6	7 7·0	9 14·7	9 14·65	N. 3 10+2 7·65				
6186	18 10 59·0	9 13·3	12 25·9	9 13 1	9 13·2	S. 2 50+3 12·7			65·4	
6233	18 17 37·2	9 16·6	11 4·0	9 16·7	9 16·65	S. 0 30+1 21·35				
6275	18 23 32·0	9 3·8	13 12·0		9 3·7	N. 0 50—4 8 3				
6285	18 24 35·5		7 10·1	9 3 6	9 3·7	N. 0 50+1 27·6				
6305	18 27 28·5	9 3·7	11 18·2	9 3·7	9 3·7	N. 0 50—2 14·5	29·900	63 6	65·4	58·4
6489	18 56 18·2	9 32·0	8 14·3	8 32·2	8 32·1	N. 3 50+0 17·8				
6525	19 1 15·5	8 9·9	10 15·0	8 9·9	8 9·9	N. 5 5—2 5·1	29·905	64·0	65·4	58·4
6639	19 20 41·5	8 13·9	11 10·8	8 13·9	8 13·9	N. 3 55—2 30·9			65·4	
6753	19 39 12·2	7 26·9	7 31·9	7 26·9	7 26·9	N. 2 40—0 5·0	29·914	64·2	64·4	58·0
6877	19 58 7·8	8 9·1	4 29·8	8 9·3	8 9·2	N. 1 25+3 13·4				
6948	20 9 46·0	8 6·5	3 16·0	8 6·5	8 6·5	N. 3 25+4 24·5	29·920	64·2	64·4	58·0

☉ April 21, 1844.—Face of Sector East.

4458	13 15 56·2	8 2·5	3 24·7	8 2·5	8 2·5	S. 1 55+4 11·8	30·355	62·4	62·3	56·9
4517	13 27 39·5	8 16·5	8 19·4	8 16·6	8 16·55	N. 5 10+0 2·85				
4548	13 33 44·5	8 16·7	8 16·7	8 16·7	8 16·7	N. 5 10—0 0·0				
4579	13 40 46·8	7 31·8	9 1·9	7 31·8	7 31·8	N. 1 40+1 4 1				
4623	13 46 46·7	9 13·8	5 9·7	9 13 9	9 13·85	N. 1 45—4 4·15	30·358	62·4	62·4	56·8
4686	14 1 37·2	9 14·3	9 8·3	9 14·5	9 14·4	S. 1 40+0 6·1				
4719	14 9 48·2	9 11·4	5 9·1	9 11·4	9 11·4	N. 5 25—4 2·3	30·354	62·4	62·5	56 0
4784	14 22 51·5	9 17·8	6 29 8	9 18·0	9 17·9	N. 5 10—2 22·1				

April 18.—Good definition in the early part of the night, but indifferent towards morning.
No. 6948 was formerly registered Anonymous.

⊙ APRIL 21, 1844.—FACE OF SECTOR EAST—(continued).

Number of B.A.C.	Time by Chronometer.	Micr. for Plumb-line on Dot.	Micr. for Observation of Star.	Micr. for Plumb-line on Dot.	Mean of Micr. for Plumb-line on Dot.	Star's Apparent Zenith Distance.	Barom.	Thermometers.		
								Attd.	Lower.	Out.
	h m s	rev. pts.	rev. pts.	rev. pts.	rev. pts.	° ′ rev. pts.	in.			
Anon.	14 26 4·0	9 0·5	6 2 5	9 0·7	9 0 6	N. 1 20—2 32·1				
4852	14 38 11·0	8 17 1	10 10·0	8 17·0	8 17·05	S. 0 35—1 26·95	30 353	62·4	62 6	55·7
4916	14 50 10·8	8 23·0	4 24·3	8 23·2	8 23·1	N. 0 45—3 32·8				
Anon.	14 57 23·5	9 12·7	8 12·7	9 12·8	9 12·75	N. 1 55—1 0 05				
Anon.	15 1 36 3	9 16·5	5 15·0	9 16·5	9 16·5	N. 1 40—4 1·5				
5032	15 12 11·5	9 16 6	12 12·6	9 16·4	9 16·5	N. 4 20+2 30 1				
5054	15 16 2 2	9 9 2	8 16·3	9 9 4	9 9·3	S. 1 45+0 27·0	30·335	62·0	62 5	55·8
5151	15 32 55·0	9 24·4	10 6·4	9 24·4	9 24·4	N. 4 40+0 16·0				
Anon.	15 38 15 7	10 7·1	10 5 1	10 7 1	10 7·1	N. 2 50—0 2 0				
5227	15 45 3 2	9 11·8	13 6 8	9 12 0	9 11·9	N. 0 45+3 28·9				
5272	15	9 28 8	11 1·8	9 29 0	9 28·9	N. 5 10+1 6·9	30 332	62 0	62 5	56 0
5374	16 5 10·5	9 1·7	10 25 8	9 1·8	9 1·75	N. 4 55—1 24·05				
5435	16 13 34·2	9 2 2	8 11·6	9 2·4	9 2·3	N. 3 25—0 24·7				
Anon.	16 17 53·4	8 2·4	10 13 0	8 2·4	8 2·4	N. 1 5+2 10·6				
5632	16 44 5·8	8 9 4	9 26·3	8 9·2	8 9·3	S. 0 5—1 17·0	30·321	61·5	61·4	55·8
5735	16 58 35 3	8 25·9	12 28·6	8 25·9	8 25·9	0 0+4 2·7	30 317	61·2	61·3	55 8
5817	17 10 52·8	8 23·7	12 25·3	8 23·6	8 23 65	N. 1 25+4 1·65				
5881	17 21 14·7	9 7 8	5 13 4	9 7·9	9 7 85	N. 4 15—3 28 45				
5915	17 27 11·5	8 15 6	12 14·2	8 15·4	8 15·5	S. 3 5—3 32·7				
5960	17 33 47·6	8 27 6	8 11·2		8 27·6	N. 1 50—0 16·4				
5964	17 34 45·2		6 15·8	8 27·6	8 27 6	N. 1 50—2 11 8				
6016	17 42 57·5	8 32 6	13 15·0	8 32·6	8 32·6	N. 2 15+4 16 4	30 292	61 2	61 3	55·4
6074	17 52 55·8	8 29·8	12 29·4	8 29·8	8 29 8	N. 3 40+3 33·6				
6115	17 59 39·5	8 29·3	10 19 0	8 29·4	8 29 35	N. 3 30+1 23 65				
6145	18 3 55·0	8 28·1	11 5·9	8 28·2	8 28·15	N. 3 10+2 11·75				
6186	18 11 13·5	8 15·4	5 6·5	8 15·4	8 15·4	S. 2 50+3 8 9				
6238	18 17 51·5	8 11·7	6 27·0	8 11·7	8 11·7	S. 0 30+1 18·7				
6275	18 23 46·0	8 22 2	4 15·5		8 22·3	N. 0 50—4 6 8				
6285	18 24 49 7		10 17·5	8 22·4	8 22 3	N. 0 50+1 29·2				
6305	18 27 42·7	8 22·3	6 8·5	8 22 3	8 22·3	N. 0 50—2 13·6	30·293	61·2	61·1	55·4
6414	18 46 34·0	8 30 7	11 13·0	8 30·9	8 30·8	N. 3 0+2 16·2			61·2	
6489	18 56 32·6	8 14·7	9 1·7	8 14 5	8 14·6	N. 0 50+0 21·1				
6525	19 1 30 0	8 15 3	6 12·4	8 15·1	8 15·2	N. 5 5—2 2 8				
6639	19 20 55 8	8 18 9	5 26·1	8 18·8	8 18·85	N. 3 55—2 26·75				
Anon.	19	8 19 7	12 30·6	8 19·7	8 19·7	N. 4 5+4 10·9	30·298	61·0	61·4	55·4
6753	19 39 25·3	8 15·0	8 11·7	8 14·9	8 14·95	N. 2 40—0 3·25				
6877	19 58 22 0	8 5·5	11 22·7	8 5 3	8 5·4	N. 1 15+3 17·3				
6948	20 10 0·5	7 28·3	12 21 2	7 28 3	7 28 3	N. 3 25+4 26·9	30 310	61 0	61·2	52 2
7207	20 44 14·3	6 31·3	7 11·2	6 31·1	6 31·2	S. 0 25—0 14·0	30·312	61·0	61 2	52·4
7992	22 52 52·0	7 25·3	6 24·3	7 25·3	7 25·3	N. 3 30—1 1·0	30·312	61·6	65 6	58·6
2293	6 56 17·5	6 29·6	6 20·7	6 29·6	6 29 6	N. 5 10—0 8·9	30·216	64·4	64 8	63·0

☾ APRIL 22, 1844.—FACE OF SECTOR WEST.

4458	13 15 55·2	7 2·5	11 17·3	7 2 4	7 2·45	S. 1 55+4 14·85	30 188	62·0	62 7	51·7
4517	13 27 39·5	6 20·2	6 20·2	6 20·2	6 20·2	N. 5 10+0 0·0				
4548	13 33 44·2	6 20·25	6 24 1	6 20 3	6 20·28	N. 5 10—0 3·82			62·8	
4579	13 40 46 2	6 20·4	5 19 4	6 20 3	6 20·35	N. 1 40+1 0·95	30·183	61·2	62·7	51·0
4623	13 46 46·5	6 19 75	10 25·5	6 19·6	6 19·68	N. 1 45—4 5·82	30 178	61·2		51·6
4686	14 1 36 0	7 20·5	7 28·7	7 20·3	7 20·4	S. 1 40+0 8·3			62·7	
4719	14 9 47·4	7 12 5	11 16·0	7 12·4	7 12·45	N. 5 25—4 3 55				51·8
4784	14 22 50·8	7 12·5	10 1·8	7 12 5	7 12 5	N. 5 10—2 23 3			62·7	
Anon.	14 28 3·5	8 5 4	11 4·9	8 5 4	8 5·4	N. 1 20—2 33·5				
4852	14 38 10·0	9 0·5	7 7·5	9 0·5	9 0·5	S. 0 35—1 27·0				

April 21.—Good definition during the night.

《 APRIL 22, 1844.—FACE OF SECTOR WEST—(continued).

Number of B.A.C.	Time by Chronometer.	Micr. for Plumb-line on Dot.	Micr. for Observation of Star.	Micr. for Plumb-line on Dot.	Mean of Micr. for Plumb-line on Dot.	Star's Apparent Zenith Distance.	Barom.	Attd.	Lower.	Ont.
	h m s	rev. pts.	rev. pts.	rev. pts.	rev. pts.	° ' rev. pts.	in.			
4916	14 50 10·2	9 1·2	12 32·8	9 1·1	9 1·15	N. 0 45—3 31·65				
Anon.	14 57 24·0	9 2·5	10 4·b	9 2·5	9 2·5	N. 1 55—1 2·0			62·8	
Anon.	15 1 34·0	8 32·6	13 1 6	8 32·5	8 32·55	N. 1 40—4 3·05				
5032	15 12 10·7	9 17 2	6 23 7	9 17.1	9 17·15	N. 4 20+2 27·45				
5054	15 16 1 0	9 31 8	10 26·8	9 31 4	9 31·6	S. 1 45+0 29·2	30·166	60·6	62·9	51·2
5151	15 32 53·5	9 28·5	9 13·0	9 26 3	9 28·4	N. 4 40+0 15·4				
Anon.	15 38 14·2	9 30·8	10 1·2	9 31 0	9 30 9	N. 2 50—0 4 3				
5227	15 45 2·0	9 17·3	5 21·4	9 17·2	9 17·25	N. 0 45+3 29·85				
5272	15 51 3·0	8 26·0	7 20·4	8 25·9	8 25·95	N. 5 10+1 5·55				48·3
5374	16 5 9·2	9 18·9	7 25·8	9 13·8	9 13·85	N. 4 55+1 22·05				47·7
5435	16 13 33·2	9 24·8	10 17·3	9 24·9	9 24·85	N. 3 25—0 26·45	30·151	60·2		48·2
Anon.	16 17 53·0	9 26·4	7 16·8	9 26 5	9 26 5	N. 1 5+2 9·65			62·4	
5588	16 37 32·5	10 1·9	14 4·9	10 2 1	10 2·0	N. 2 10—4 2·9				
5632	16 44 4·8	10 14·4	8 1·5	9 14·5	9 14·45	S. 0 5—1 12·95	30·142	59·4		48·4
5735	16 58 34·5	8 31·0	4 32·4	8 30·9	8 30·95	0 0+3 32·55				48·3
5817	17 10 52·0	9 7·0	5 7·3	9 7·0	9 7·0	N. 1 25+3 33·7	30·134	59·4	62·3	48·4
5881	17 21 13·5	8 29·5	12 25·7	8 29·3	8 29·3	N. 1 5—3 30·3				
5915	17 27 10 5	9 12·5	5 16 6	9 12 3	9 12·4	S. 3 5+3 29·8				
5960	17 33 47·2	8 26 5	9 13·1		8 26·45	N. 1 50—0 20·65				
Anon.	17 34 44·5		11 7·1	8 26·4	8 26·45	N. 1 50—2 14·65				
6016	17 42 57·2	8 19·5	4 2·8	8 19·5	8 19·5	N. 2 15+4 16·7	30·133	59·5	62·0	48·0
6074	17	8 10·0	4 12·5	8 10·0	8 10·0	N. 3 40+3 31·5	30·132	59·2	61·9	48·0
6115	17 59 39·2	8 20·3	7 0·5	8 20·3	8 20·3	N. 3 30+1 19·8				
6145	18 3 54·8	8 16·8	6 6·55	8 16·6	8 16·7	N. 3 10+2 10·15				
6186	18 11 11·8	9 1·0	12 13 6	9 1·2	9 1·1	S. 2 50+3 12 5	30·130	59·5'	61·7	47·5
6233	18 17 50·5	9 4·0	10 25 9	9 4·2	9 4·1	S. 0 30+1 21·8				
6275	18 23 45·5	9 4 5	13 12·4		9 4·46	N. 0 50—4 7 92				
6285	18 24 48·8		7 10·0	9 4·4	9 4·48	N. 0 50+1 28 48				
6305	18 27 41·4	9 4·5	11 18·1	9 4·5	9 4 48	N. 0 50—2 13·62	30 130	59·5	61·4	47·2
6414	18 46 32·5	8 22·4	6 9·3	8 22·6	8 22·6	N. 3 0+2 13·2				
6489	18 56 31·5	9 13 0	8 28·15	9 13·0	9 13·0	N. 3 50+0 18·85				
6525	19 1 29·0	9 31·4	12 1·5	9 31·4	9 31·4	N. 5 5—2 4·1	30·131	59·6	61·2	47·8
6753	19 39 24·3	10 6·2	10 10·9	10 6 0	10 6 1	N. 2 40—0 4·8				
7011	20	10 2·1	6 33·5	10 2 1	10 2·1	N. 4 20+3 2·6				
7057	20 25 11 0	10 2·0	12 33·1	10 2·2	10 2·1	N. 4 20—2 31·0	30·135	60·2	59·8	50·4
7992	22 52 51·5	9 24·2	10 28·4	9 24·1	9 24·15	N. 3 30—1 4·25	30·151	61·4	61·2	00·7

δ APRIL 23, 1844.—FACE OF SECTOR EAST.

Number of B.A.C.	Time by Chronometer.	Micr. for Plumb-line on Dot.	Micr. for Observation of Star.	Micr. for Plumb-line on Dot.	Mean of Micr. for Plumb-line on Dot.	Star's Apparent Zenith Distance.	Barom.	Attd.	Lower.	Ont.
1802	5 38 13·2	9 27 6	11 30·6	9 27·8	9 27·7	S. 0 15—2 2·9			64·6	
2293	6 56 20·8	10 18·6	10 7·7	10 18·4	10 18·5	N. 5 10—0 10·8	30·048	64·4	65·0	63·4

♃ APRIL 25, 1844.—FACE OF SECTOR EAST.

Number of B.A.C.	Time by Chronometer.	Micr. for Plumb-line on Dot.	Micr. for Observation of Star.	Micr. for Plumb-line on Dot.	Mean of Micr. for Plumb-line on Dot.	Star's Apparent Zenith Distance.	Barom.	Attd.	Lower.	Ont.
4686	14 1 50·5	8 16·6	8 8·0	8 16·8	8 16·7	S. 1 40+0 8·7	29 971	62·7	63·8	56·8
4719		9 32·7	5 27·8	9 32·7	9 32·7	N. 5 25—4 4·9			63·8	
4784	14 23 5·5	9 21·6	6 29·2	9 21·8	9 21·7	N. 5 10—2 26·5				
Anon.	14 23 16·5	9 27 2	6 26·4	9 27·2	9 27·2	N. 10—2 32·8	29·970	62·4		56·7
4852	14	8 15·3	10 4·0	8 15·3	8 15·3	S. 0 35—1 22·7			63·7	
4916	14 50 52·2	8 20 6	4 19·3	8 20·5	8 20·55	N. 0 45—4 1·25				56·8
Anon.	14 57 38 0	8 6·0	7 2·0	8 6·0	8 6·0	N. 1 55—1 4·0				
Anon.	15 1 50·5	8 30·4	4 27·1	8 30·6	8 30 5	N. 1 40—4 3·4			64·0	
5032	15 12 25·5	9 0·0	11 27·3	8 33·8	8 33·9	N. 4 20+2 27·4	29·974	62·4		56·1

April 22.—Good definition during the first five observations : then the temperature sunk and the definition became very bad, particularly so towards morning.

Nos. 7011 and 7057 were formerly registered Anonymous.

♃ April 25, 1844.—Face of Sector East—(continued).

Number of B.A.C.	Time by Chronometer.	Micr. for Plumb-line on Dot.	Micr. for Observation of Star.	Micr. for Plumb-line on Dot.	Mean of Micr. for Plumb-line. on Dot.	Star's Apparent Zenith Distance.	Barom.	Thermometers.		
								Attd.	Lower.	Out.
	h m s	rev. pts.	rev. pts.	rev. pts.	rev. pts.	° ' rev. pts.	in.			
5054	15 16 16·5	8 16·2	7 19·4	8 16·2	8 16·2	S. 1 45+0 30·8				55·9
5151	15 33 10·5	8 29 7	9 7·2	8 29 5	8 29·6	N. 4 40+0 11·6				55 6
Anon.	15 39 4·0	9 12 3	9 5·8	9 12·5	9 12·4	N. 2 50—0 6 6	29·973	61·6		55·4
5227	15 45 17·2	9 12·8	13 4·4	9 12·8	9 12·6	N. 0 45+3 25·6				
5272	15 51 18·6	9 29·8	10 33·8	9 29·9	9 29·85	N. 5 10+1 3 95			63·8	
5374	16 5 24·2	10 1·0	11 21·5	10 1·0	10 1·0	N. 4 55+1 20·5				
5435	16 15 48·5	9 29·8	9 2·5	9 30·0	9 29·9	N. 3 25—0 27·4			63·7	
Anon.	16 18 8 0	9 28·5	12 1·7	9 28·5	9 28·5	N. 1 5+2 7·2				
5588	16 37 47·2	10 4·0	6 8·2	10 4·0	10 4·0	N. 2 10—4 0·8				
5632	16 44 20·2	9 11·8	10 25·8	9 11·8	9 11·8	S. 0 5—1 14·0	29 970	61·5	63·3	54·7

♀ April 26, 1844.—Face of Sector East.

1802	5 38 14·5	10 15·5	12 19 75	10 15·9	10 15·7	S. 0 15—2 4·05	30·008	64·8		67·8

♃ May 2, 1844.—Face of Sector West.

2293	6 57 0·5	8 0·5	8 11·8	8 0·5	8 0·5	N. 5 10—0 11·3	30·220	64·4	64·2	63·7
4458	13 16 28·2	8 0·5	12 16·5	8 0 5	8 0·5	S. 1 55+4 18·0	30·291	62·8	62·7	55·7
4517	13 26 27·2	8 0·3	8 3·0	8 0·4	8 0 35	N. 5 10—0 2·65				
4548	13 34 31·5	8 0·3	8 6·6	8 0·3	8 0·3	N. 5 10—0 6·3				
4579	13 41 26·2	8 32·8	8 1·3	8 32·7	8 32·75	N. 1 40+0 31·45				
4623	13 47 26·5	8 30·4	13 6·05	8 30·3	8 30·35	N. 1 45—4 9·7			62·7	
4686	14 2 9·0	9 4 7	9 16·55	9 4·6	9 4·65	S. 1 40+0 11·9				
4719	14 10 35·1	8 20·05	12 26·5	8 20·0	8 20·03	N. 5 25—4 6·47	30·285	62·1	62 9	56·4
4784	14 23 38·2	8 22·7	11 15·8	8 22·6	8 22·65	N. 5 10—2 27·15				
Anon.	14 26 43·5	9 12·2	12 13·5	9 12·2	9 12·2	N. 1 20—3 1·3				
4852	14 38 45·9	9 20·2	7 31·0	9 20·2	9 20·2	S. 0 35—1 23·2	30·284	61·8	62·7	56·6
4916	14 50 48 5	9 10·5	13 11·75	9 10·7	9 10·6	N. 0 45—4 1·15				
Anon.	14 58 4·2	9 6 0	10 10·75	9 6·0	9 6·0	N. 1 55—1 4·75				
Anon.	15	8 32·6	13 7·3	8 32·8	8 32·7	N. 1 40—4 8·6				
5092	15 12 56·5	8 21·0	5 30·15	8 20·6	8 20 8	N. 4 20+2 24·65	30·290	62·0	62·3	56·4
5054	15 16 34·0	9 22·1	10 19·9	9 22·3	9 22·2	S. 1 45+0 31·7				
5151	15 33 40·4	9 18 2	9 5·5	9 17·8	9 18·0	N. 4 40+0 12·5	30·292	62·0		56·3
Anon.	15 36 57·2	9 24·0	9 31·2	9 24·0	9 24·0	N. 2 50—0 7·2				
5227	15 45 40·9	9 20·6	5 30·1	9 20·4	9 20·5	N. 0 45+3 24·4				
5272	15 51 51·3	10 1·6	9 1·0	10 1·6	10 1·6	N. 5 10+1 0·6			62·3	
5374	16 5 56·2	9 32·1	8 14·5	9 32·1	9 32·1	N. 4 55+1 17 6				
5435	16 14 17·2	9 23 2	10 19·8	9 23·2	9 23·2	N. 3 25—0 30·6				56·4
Anon.	16 18 32 0	10 9·3	8 2·5	10 9·4	10 9 35	N. 1 5+2 6·85				
5588	16 38 14·2	10 3·1	14 5·6	10 3·5	10 3·3	N. 2 10—4 2·3	30·285	61·8		56·3
5632	16 44 41·8	10 7·2	8 29·6	10 7·0	10 7·1	N. 0 5+1 11·5			62 3	
5735	16 59 11·6	9 24·5	5 28·9	9 24·1	9 24·3	0 0+3 29·4				
5817	17 11 32·3	9 21·0	5 24·8	9 20·6	9 20·8	N. 1 20+0 5·7	30·280	61·4	62·4	54·8
5915	17 27 40·2	10 1·1	6 7·55	10 0·9	10 1·0	S. 3 5—3 27·45				55·1
5960	17 34 28·2	9 5·6	9 28·8			9 5·5	N. 1 50—2 23 3			
5964	17 35 25 7		11 22·5	9 5·4	9 5·5	N. 1 50—2 17·0				
6016	17 43 39·4	8 32·8	4 19·9	8 32·4	8 32 6	N. 2 15+4 12·7				55 0
6074	17 53 40·5	8 33·4	5 3·8	8 33·0	8 33·2	N. 3 40+3 29·4				
6115	18 0 23·5	8 29·3	7 11·2	8 29·2	8 29·25	N. 3 30+1 18·05				
6145	18 4 38·8	8 33·4	6 27·7	8 33·4	8 33 4	N. 3 30+1 5·7				
6186	18 11 43·4	9 11·0	12 26·0	9 10 8	9 10·9	S. 2 50+3 15·1				
6233	18 18 26·9	9 27·3	11 16·8	9 27·4	9 27·35	S. 0 30+1 23·45				

April 26.—As the observed Zenith distances seemed to vary inter se, the plumb-line was removed and all the adjustments examined. The details will be given in the introduction.

♃ May 2, 1844.—Face of Sector West—(continued).

Number of B.A.C.	Time by Chronometer.	Micr. for Plumb-line on Dot.	Micr. for Observation of Star.	Micr. for Plumb-line on Dot.	Mean of Micr. for Plumb-line on Dot.	Star's Apparent Zenith Distance.	Barom.	Thermometers.		
								Attd.	Lower.	Out.
	h m s	rev. pts.	rev. pts.	rev. pts.	rev. pts.	° ' rev. pts.	in.			
6275	18 24 24·5	9 31·1	14 6·1		9 30·75	N. 0 50—4 9·35	30 275	61·5	62·5	54·6
6285	18 25 28·2		8 5·0	9 30·5	9 30·75	N. 0 50+1 25·75				
6305	18	9 30·5	12 13·5	9 30·9	9 30·75	N. 0 50—2 16·75				
6414	18 47 17·0	9 26·0	7 15·45	9 25·8	9 25·9	N. 3 0+2 10·45				
6489	18 57 16·7	9 1·6	8 19·7	9 1·5	9 1·55	N. 3 50+0 15·85				
6525	19 2 16·5	8 14·4	10 22·1	8 14·2	8 14·3	N. 5 5—2 7·8	30 273	61·5	62·3	55·3
6639	19 21 40·5	8 22·0	11 20·4	8 22·4	8 22·2	N. 3 55—2 32·2				
Anon.	19 25	8 23·5	4 15·2	8 23·5	8 23·5	N. 4 5+4 8·3				
6753	19 40 6·6	8 20·7	8 27·3	8 20·5	8 20·6	N. 2 40—0 6 7	30·266	61·5	62·2	55·5
6877	19	8 17·9	5 4·6	8 17·5	8 17·7	N. 1 25+3 13·1			62·2	
7011	20 19 42·2	8 12·5	5 10·4	8 12·7	8 12·6	N. 4 20+3 2·2				
7026	20 21 33·2	8 12·5	5 18·45	8 12·5	8 12·6	N. 4 20+2 26·15				
7057	20 25 58·0	8 12·6	11 11·3	8 12·8	8 12 6	N. 4 20—2 32·7				
Anon.	20 38 21·0	8 5·2	11 25·0	8 5·3	8 5·25	N. 4 0—3 19·75				
7207	20 44 49·2	8 7·9	7 31·2	8 7·9	8 7·9	S. 0 25—0 10·7	30·267	61·5	62·2	57·5
Anon.	20 58 7·5	8 5·6	11 25·5	8 5·9	8 5·7	N. 4 15—3 19 8				
Anon.	21 5 18·2	8 1·1	7 22 2	8 0·7	8 0·9	N. 3 35+0 12·7				
7386	21 13 3·7	8 5·3	4 15·4	8 5·3	8 5·3	N. 1 5+3 23·9			62·2	
7992	22 53 35·2	7 32·5	9 2·6	7 32·7	7 32·6	N. 3 30—1 4·0				

♀ May 3, 1844.—Face of Sector East.

Number of B.A.C.	Time by Chronometer.	Micr. for Plumb-line on Dot.	Micr. for Observation of Star.	Micr. for Plumb-line on Dot.	Mean of Micr. for Plumb-line on Dot.	Star's Apparent Zenith Distance.	Barom.	Thermometers.		
								Attd.	Lower.	Out.
1802	5 38 39·4	8 24·5	10 30·5	8 24·5	8 24·5	S. 0 15—2 6·0	30·251	64·4	64 6	66·4
2233	6 57 12·0	9 10·1	9 1·5	9 10·1	9 10·1	N. 5 10—0 8 6	30·237	64·5	64 6	63·7
4458	13 16 33·5	8 33·1	4 19·45	8 33·1	8 33·1	S. 1 5+4 13·65	30·260	63·4	63 0	59·2
4517	13 26 38·2	9 18·0	9 18·45	9 18·2	9 18·1	N. 5 10+0 0·35				
4548	13 34 43·2	9 18·1	9 15·0	9 18·3	9 18 2	N. 5 10—0 3·2				
4579	13 41 35·3	9 15·3	10 18·95	9 15·4	9 15 35	N. 1 40+1 3 6				58·7
4623	13 47 35·2	9 16·3	5 12·8	9 16·3	9 16·3	N. 1 45—4 3·5				
4686	14 2 15·2	9 7·8	9 0·0	9 7 6	9 7 7	S. 1 40+0 7·7	30 246	62·5	63 0	58·3
4719	14 10 46·5	9 14·8	5 12·1	9 15·0	9 14·9	N. 5 25—4 2 8				
4784	14 23 49·0	9 11·3	6 22·35	9 11·5	9 11·4	N. 5 10—2 23·05				58·6
Anon.	14 28 51·0	9 2·0	6 2 2	9 2·1	9 2·05	N. 1 20—2 33·85				
4652	14 38 52·5	8 18·5	10 9·55	8 18·6	8 18·55	S. 0 35—1 25·0	30·235	62·4	63·0	59 6
4916	14 50 56·0	8 33·6	4 33·4	8 33·5	8 33·55	N. 0 45—4 0·15				
Anon.	14 59 12·5	8 30·2	7 29 4	8 30·2	8 30·2	N. 1 55—1 0 8				59·4
Anon.	15	8 32·7	5 8 8	8 32·5	8 32 6	N. 1 40—3 23·8				
5032	15 13 7·0	8 32 6	11 27·4	8 32·8	8 32·7	N. 4 20+2 28·7	30·232	62·4	62·9	59·4
5054	15 16 39·5	8 16·0	7 21·2	8 16·0	8 16·0	S. 1 45+0 28·8				
5151	15 33 51·3	8 29·0	9 9·9	8 29·0	8 29·0	N. 4 40+0 14·9				
Anon.	15	9 0·8	8 32·6	9 0·8	9 0·8	N. 2 50—0 2·2				59·6
5272	15 52 2·0	10 2·8	11 8·8	10 2·7	10 2·75	N. 5 10+1 6·05				
5374	16 6 7·3	9 26 3	11 15·65	9 26·1	9 26·2	N. 4 55+1 23·45				
5435	16 14 27·4	9 26·2	9 0·1	9 26·2	9 26·2	N. 3 25—0 26·1	30·228	62·4	62·6	59·8
Anon.	16 18 40·8	9 6·3	11 15·3	9 6 3	9 6·3	N. 1 5+2 9 0				
5588	16 38 23·0	10 13·7	6 15·0	10 13·7	10 13·7	N. 2 10—3 32 7				
5632	16 44 49·2	10 3·8	11 19·9	10 3 9	10 3·85	S. 0 5—1 16·05	30·218	62·4	62·0	54·4
5735	16 59 19·0	9 16·3	13 17·7	9 16·7	9 16·5	O 0+4 1·2			61·8	55·4
5817	17 11 40·5	9 18·6	13 19·0	9 18·7	9 18·65	N. 1 25+4 0·35				
5881	17 22 10·6	10 5·4	6 9·45	10 5·4	10 5·4	N. 4 15—3 29·95			61·6	
5916	17 27 45·2	9 32·5	13 33·3	9 32·5	9 32·5	S. 3 5—4 0·8	30·215	61·0		52·3
6016	17 43 48·2	10 20·5	15 2·3	10 20·9	10 20·7	N. 2 15+4 15·6			61·7	50·8
6074	17 53 49·7	10 17·7	14 18·3	10 17·9	10 17·8	N. 3 40+4 0·5				
6115	18 0 33·3	10 8·7	11 32·3	10 8·8	10 8·75	N. 3 30+1 23·55				

May 2.—No. 7026 was formerly registered Anonymous.
    3.—Anon. 15ᵇ.—Bad observation. The star too faint.
    No. 5817.—5 ounces overweight against the Micrometer.
    Bad definition coming on. The temperature descending.

♀ MAY 3, 1844.—FACE OF SECTOR EAST—(continued).

Number of B.A.C.	Time by Chronometer.	Micr. for Plumb-line on Dot.	Micr. for Observation of Star.	Micr. for Plumb-line on Dot.	Mean of Micr. for Plumb-line on Dot.	Star's Apparent Zenith Distance.	Barom.	Attd.	Lower.	Out.
	h m s	rev. pts.	rev. pts.	rev. pts.	rev. pts.	° ' rev. pts.	in.			
6145	18 4 48·0	9 12·7	11 24·6	9 12·2	9 12·45	N. 3 10+2 12·15				
6186	18 11 48·2	8 28·8	5 21·4	8 28·7	8 28·75	S. 2 50+3 7·35				
6233	18 18 33·4	9 7·5	7 22·6	9 7·6	9 7·55	S. 0 30+1 18·95				
6275	18 24 30·5	9 26·2	5 20·6		9 26·1	N. 0 50—4 5·5			62·0	
6285	18 25 35·5		11 22·6	9 26·1	9 26·1	N. 0 50+1 30·5				
6305	18 28 28·2	9 26·0	7 15·0	9 20·1	9 26·1	N. 0 50—2 11·1	30·220	61·0	62·0	48·6
6414	18 47 25·6	9 21·4	12 3·9	9 21·5	9 21·45	N. 3 0+2 16·45				
6489	18 57 26·2	9 15·9	10 2·5	9 16·0	9 15·95	N 3 50+0 20·55	30·216	61·0	61·8	48·5
6525	19 2 26·8	9 12·4	7 11·4	9 12·2	9 12·3	N. 5 5—2 0·9				
6639	19 21 50·2	9 13·7	6 21·6	9 13·6	9 13·65	N. 3 55—2 26·05				
Anon.	19 26 3·5	8 28·1	13 8·1	8 27·9	8 28·0	N. 4 5+4 14·1				
6753	19 40 16·3	8 19·0	8 17·4	8 19·0	8 19·0	N. 2 40—0 1·6	30·217	61·0	61·9	52·0
0048	20 10 54·0	8 12·2	13 2·8	8 12·2	8 12·2	N. 3 25+4 24·6				
7011	20 19 53·0	8 19·8	11 27·8	8 19·8	8 19·82	N. 4 20+3 7·98	30·213	61·0	61·4	50·5
7026	20 21 45·0		11 19·0	8 19·8	8 19·82	N. 4 20+2 33·18				
7057	20 26 8·5	8 19·9	5 26·7	8 19·8	8 19·82	N. 4 20—2 27·12				

♄ MAY 4, 1844.—FACE OF SECTOR WEST.

Number of B.A.C.	Time by Chronometer.	Micr. for Plumb-line on Dot.	Micr. for Observation of Star.	Micr. for Plumb-line on Dot.	Mean of Micr. for Plumb-line on Dot.	Star's Apparent Zenith Distance.	Barom.	Attd.	Lower.	Out.
4458	13 16 35·2	8 27·0	13 12·25	8 27·0	8 27·0	S. 1 55+4 19·25	30·143	63·4	63·3	56·7
4517	13 28 33·2	7 29·45	13 33·0	7 29·4	7 29·43	N. 5 10—0 3·57				
4548	13 34 38·5	7 29·4	8 2·6	7 29·4	7 29·4	N. 5 10—0 7·2				
4579	13 41 33·6	8 21·25	7 23·45	8 21·05	8 21·15	N. 1 40+0 31·7				
4623	13 47 34·3	8 17·9	12 27·5	8 17·7	8 17·8	N. 1 45—4 9·7			63·6	
4686	14 2 16·0	9 7·6	9 21·05	9 7·6	9 7·6	S. 1 40+0 13·45				53·2
4719	14 10 42·5	8 30·0	13 4·1	8 29·8	8 29·9	N. 5 25—4 8·2				
4784	14 23 45·0	9 24·0	12 18·2	9 24·2	9 24·1	N. 5 10—2 28·1			63·0	52·4
Anon.	14 28 50·2	9 29·3	12 32·8	9 29·3	9 29·3	N. 1 20—3 3·5				
4852	14 38 52·2	9 31·7	8 8·6	9 31·7	9 31·7	S. 0 35—1 23·1	30·115	61·2		51·6
4916	14 50 54·2	9 15·2	13 17·4	9 15·2	9 15·2	N. 0 45—4 2·2				
Anon.	14 58 11·0	9 13·4	10 18·9	9 13·5	9 13·45	N. 1 55—1 5·45				
Anon.	15 2 32·7	9 2·9	13 9·3	9 2·9	9 2·9	N. 1 40—4 6·4			63·4	
5032	15 13 3·0	9 3·9	6 14·0	9 3·8	9 3·85	N. 4 20+2 23·85				
5054	15 16 40·5	9 9·0	10 7·55	9 9·0	9 9·0	S. 1 45+0 32·55	30·104	60·6		51·2
5151	15 33 47·5	8 31·3	8 21·6	8 31·2	8 31·25	N. 4 40+0 9·65				
Anon.	15 39 4·6	9 9·8	9 17·95	9 9·9	9 9·85	N. 2 50—0 8·1				
5227	15 45 48·1	10 0·4	6 9·3	10 0·1	10 0·25	N. 0 45+3 24·95			63·3	
5272	15 51 58·0	10 1·8	9 0·1	10 1·75	10 1·78	N. 5 10+1 1·68				
5374	16 6 3·6	9 29·8	8 11·0	9 29·7	9 29·75	N. 4 55+1 18·75				
5435	16	9 26·5	10 21·8	9 26·4	9 26·45	N. 3 25—0 29·35				
Anon.	16	10 1·4	7 28·0	10 1·6	10 1·5	N. 1 5+2 7·5	30·092	60·6		51·8
5586	16 38 21·2	9 22·5	13 23·7	9 22·4	9 22·4	N. 2 10—4 1·25				
5632	16 44 49 2	9 20 3	8 16·2	9 20·0	9 29·15	S. 0 5—1 12·95				
5735	16 59 19·0	9 11·2	5 14·05	9 11·1	9 11·15	0 0+3 31·1				
5817	17 11 39·5	8 27·6	4 29·9	8 27·7	8 27·65	N. 1 25+3 31·75				
5881	17 22 6·5	8 20·0	12 16·4	8 19·8	8 19·9	N. 4 15—3 30·5				
5915	17 27 47·0	8 30·7	5 2·2	8 30·6	8 30·65	S. 3 5—3 28·45				
5960	17 34 35·5	8 9·7	8 32·0		8 9·7	N. 1 50—0 22·3				
5964	17 35 32 5		10 25·4	8 9·7	8 9·7	N. 1 50—2 15·7				
6016	17 43 46·0	8 18·0	4 3·95	8 18·0	8 18·0	N. 2 15+4 14·05	30·074	61·0	61·2	51·0
6074	17 53 47·0	8 17·1	4 19·5	8 16·9	8 17·0	N. 3 40+3 31·5				
6115	18 0 30·2	8 18·0	6 32·4	8 17·8	8 17·9	N. 3 30+1 19·5				
6145	18 4 45·6	8 27·6	6 20·0	8 27·5	8 27·55	N. 3 10+2 7·55				
6186	18 11 50·5	9 0·7	12 14·5	9 0·5	9 0·6	S. 2 50+3 13·9				

May 4.—No. 5374.—Observed at 20 seconds after passing the meridian wire. Definition improving.
No. 6016.—Bad definition.

♄ MAY 4, 1844.—FACE OF SECTOR WEST—(continued).

Number of B.A.C.	Time by Chronometer.	Micr. for Plumb-line on Dot.	Micr. for Observation of Star.	Micr. for Plumb-line on Dot.	Mean of Micr. for Plumb-line on Dot.	Star's Apparent Zenith Distance.	Barom.	Thermometers. Attd.	Lower.	Out.
	h m s	rev. pts.	rev. pts.	rev. pts.	rev. pts.	° ′ rev. pts.	in.			
6233	18 18 34·3	8 33·8	10 23·4	8 34·0	8 33·9	S. 0 30+1 23·5				
6275	18 24 31·0	8 28·6	13 3·6	8 28·6	8 28·6	N. 0 50—4 9·0				
6285	18 25 35·2		7 2·5	8 28·6	8 28·6	N. 0 50+1 26·1				
6305	18 28 28·6	8 28·6	11 10·9	8 28·6	8 28·6	N. 0 50—2 16·3				
6414	18 47 24·0	8 13·7	6 1·3	8 13·9	8 13·8	N. 3 0+2 12·5				
6489	18 57 23·3	8 7·3	7 23·0	8 7·1	8 7·2	N. 3 50+0 18·2				
6525	19 2 23·5	8 7·6	10 14·5	8 7·4	8 7·5	N. 5 5—2 7 0	30·060	60·0	61·3	47·6
6639	19 21 47·3	8 8·6	11 5·1	8 8·6	8 8 6	N. 3 55—2 30·5				
6753	19 40 14·5	7 30·3	8 2·9	7 30·5	7 30·4	N. 2 40—0 6 5				
6877	19 59 9·4	8 4·8	4 23·9	8 4·8	8 4·8	N. 1 25+3 14·9	30·060	60·0	61·3	48·3
6948	20 10 51·2	8 0·7	3 10·55	8 0·5	8 0·6	N. 3 25+4 24·05				
7057	20 26 5·0	7 29·7	10 28·3	7 29·6	7 29·05	N. 4 20—2 32·65				
7207	20 44 52·8	8 32·3	8 19·8	8 32·3	8 32·3	S. 0 25—0 12·5	30·058	60·0	61·2	48·0
7386	21 13 11·8	9 21·2	5 31·6	9 21·6	9 21·4	N. 1 5+3 23·8				

☾ MAY 6, 1844.—FACE OF SECTOR EAST.

Number of B.A.C.	Time by Chronometer.	Micr. for Plumb-line on Dot.	Micr. for Observation of Star.	Micr. for Plumb-line on Dot.	Mean of Micr. for Plumb-line on Dot.	Star's Apparent Zenith Distance.	Barom.	Attd.	Lower.	Out.
4458	13	9 28·0	5 13·4	9 27·6	9 27·8	S. 1 55+4 14·4	30·214		62·6	52·6
4579	13 41 46·5	8 25·1	9 27·9	8 25·3	6 25·2	N. 1 40+1 2·7				
4623	13 47 46·5	8 22·1	4 17·05	8 21·8	8 21·95	N. 1 45—4 4·9				
4686	14 2 27·3	8 18·9	8 12·2	8 18·8	8 18·85	S. 1 40+0 6·65	30·214	61·3	62·3	52·6
4719	14 10 57·4	8 33·6	4 30·0	8 33·4	8 33·5	N. 5 25—4 3·5	30·214	61·3		52·6
4784	14 24 0·5	8 22·6	5 32·9	8 22·4	8 22 5	N. 5 10—2 23·6				
4852	14 39 4·5	8 16·0	10 9·2	8 15·7	8 15·85	S. 0 35—1 27·35				
Anon.	15 2 35·3	7 21·6	3 18·9	7 21·4	7 21·5	N. 1 40—4 2·6			61·3	
5032	15 13 18·5	8 15·6	11 11·1	8 15·4	8 15·5	N. 4 20+2 29·6	30·220	61·2		55·2
5054	15 16 52·2	8 6·4	7 12·6	8 6·4	8 6·4	S. 1 45+0 27·8			61·4	
5151	15 34 3 0	9 6·6	9 22·0	9 6·6	9 6·6	N. 4 40+0 15·4	30·236	60·6	61·4	55·2

♃ MAY 7, 1844.—FACE OF SECTOR WEST.

Number of B.A.C.	Time by Chronometer.	Micr. for Plumb-line on Dot.	Micr. for Observation of Star.	Micr. for Plumb-line on Dot.	Mean of Micr. for Plumb-line on Dot.	Star's Apparent Zenith Distance.	Barom.	Attd.	Lower.	Out.
1802	5 38 49·2	13 22·8	11 18·0	13 23·3	13 23·05	S. 0 15—2 5·05	30·332	62·5	62·2	59·0
4623	13 47 44·5		14 10·3	9 33·7		N. 1 45—4 10·6				
4686	14 2 26·6	9 32·05	10 11·8	9 32·0	9 32·03	S. 1 40+0 13·77	30·400	59·8	62·0	51·6
4719	14 10 52·5	9 1·0	13 10·0	9 0·9	9 0·95	N. 5 25—4 9·05				
4784	14 23 55·7	9 11·5	12 7·0	9 11·7	9 11·6	N. 5 10—2 29·4				
Anon.		9 17·8	12 22·0	9 17·8	9 17·8	N. 1 20—3 4·2	30·397	59·8		51·4
4852	14 39 3·5	9 17·4	7 29·4	9 17·4	9 17·4	S. 0 35—1 22·0			60·6	
4916	14 51 6·0	9 8·0	13 11·0	9 7·9	9 7·9	N. 0 45—4 3·1				51·4
Anon.	14 58 21·6	9 2·5	10 9·8	9 2·8	9 2·65	N. 1 55—1 7·15				
Anon.	15 2 33·6	8 12·6	12 21·1	8 12·8	8 12·7	N. 1 40—4 8·4				
5032	15 13 14·5	8 22·6	6 0·0	8 22·6	8 22·6	N. 4 20+2 22·6				
5054	15 16 51·5	8 33·7	9 33·75	8 33·8	8 33·75	S. 1 45+1 0·0				
7557	21 40 33·0	9 1·9	4 32·1	9 1·9	9 1·9	N. 0 10+4 3·8	30·375	59·2	59·2	52·0
7842	22 27 31·0	9 13·0	4 18·7	9 12·8	9 12·9	N. 0 45+4 28·2	30·386	59·3	59·3	52·0
7992	22 53 53·6	9 1·25	10 4·15	9 .1·2	9 1·23	N. 3 30—1 2·92	30·394	59·2	59·3	54·0

FACE OF SECTOR EAST.

Number of B.A.C.	Time by Chronometer.	Micr. for Plumb-line on Dot.	Micr. for Observation of Star.	Micr. for Plumb-line on Dot.	Mean of Micr. for Plumb-line on Dot.	Star's Apparent Zenith Distance.	Barom.	Attd.	Lower.	Out.
4458	13 16 49·5	10 20·1	6 6·6	10 20·1	10 20·1	S. 1 55+4 13·5	30·406	61·2	60·4	51·4
4517	13 28 52·5	10 32·9	10 33·5	10 33·0	10 32·95	N. 5 10+0 0·55				
4548	13 34 57 2	10 32·9	10 29·8	10 32·9	10 32·9	N. 5 10—0 3·1				
4579	13 41 49·8	10 0·5	11 3·0	10 0·5	10 0·5	N. 1 40+1 2·5			60·3	
5151	15 34 6·0	9 13·3	9 28·3	9 13·3	9 13·3	N. 4 40+0 15·0	30·390	59·5	00·4	51·2

May 6.—Several observations lost from clouds.
Detected a fine spider line attached to the plumb-line and shade.

♂ MAY 7, 1844.—FACE OF SECTOR EAST—(continued).

Number of B.A.C.	Time by Chronometer.	Micr. for Plumb-line on Dot.	Micr. for Observation of Star.	Micr. for Plumb-line on Dot.	Mean of Micr. for Plumb-line on Dot.	Star's Apparent Zenith Distance.	Barom.	Thermometers. Attd.	Lower.	Out.
	b m s	rev. pts.	rev. pts.	rev. pts.	rev. pts.	° ' rev. pts.	in.			
Anon.	15 39 21·5	9 20·2	9 16·55	9 20·1	9 20·15	N. 2 50—0 3·6				
5227	15 46 4 0	9 16·1	13 9·3	9 16 2	9 16·15	N. 0 45+3 27·15				
5272	15 52 17·3	10 3·7	11 10·0	10 3·7	10 3·7	N. 5 10+1 6·3	30·385	59·5	60·4	51·4
5374	16 6 22·5	9 31·3	11 21·7	9 31·4	9 31·35	N. 4 55+1 24·35				51·7
Anon.	16 18 55·8	9 16·3	9 31·8	9 16·2	9 16·25	N. 1 5+0 15·55			59·8	51·8
5388	16 38 38·0	9 25·9	5 27·45	9 26·0	9 25·95	N. 2 10—3 32·5				
5632	16 45 4·6	9 7·3	10 24·4	9 7·3	9 7·3	S. 0 5—1 17·1				
5735	16 59 34·7	9 0·7	13 2·8	9 0·7	9 0·7	0 0+4 2·1	30·378	59·4	59·7	51·3
5817	17 11 56·0	9 0·8	13 1·9	9 0·9	9 0·85	N. 1 23+4 1·05				
5881	17 22 25·0	9 5·3	5 11·5	9 5·4	9 5·35	N. 4 15—3 27·85				50·6
5915	17 28 1·7	8 7·5	12 7·4	8 7·5	8 7·5	S. 3 5—3 33·9				
5900	17 34 52 3	8 29·1	8 11·6		8 29·0	N. 1 50—0 17·4				
5964	17 35 49 8		6 19·0	8 28·9	8 29·0	N. 1 50—2 10·0				
6016	17 44 3·5	8 30·8	13 13·75	8 31·0	8 30·9	N. 2 15+4 16·85	30·370	59·2	59·5	51·3
6074	17 54 5·3	8 27·4	12 29·2	8 27·5	8 27·45	N. 3 40+4 1·75				
6115	18 0 48 5	9 11·5	11 2·0	9 11·4	9 11·45	N. 3 30+1 24 55	30·366	59·0	59·5	51·4
6145	18 5 3·5	8 33·8	11 12·55	8 34·0	8 33·9	N. 3 10+2 12·65				
6186	18 12 4·8	8 20·35	5 12·7	8 20·1	8 20·23	S. 2 50+3 7·53				
6233	18 18 49·5	9 9·3	7 24·3	9 9·5	9 9·4	S. 0 30+1 19·1				
6275	18 24 47·8	9 31·7	5 26·0		9 31·6	N. 0 50—4 5·6				
6285	18 25 51·5		11 27·5	9 31·5	9 31·6	N. 0 50—2 12·5				
6305	18 28 44·5	9 31·6	7 19·9	9 31·6	9 31·6	N. 0 50—2 11·7				
6414	18 47 41·2	10 4·9	12 23·3	10 4·9	10 4·9	N. 3 0+2 18·4	30·374	59·2	59·4	52·3
6525	19 2 42·5	10 5·2	8 4·6	10 5·0	10 5·1	N. 5 5—2 0·5				
6639	19 22 5·5	9 25·9	7 0·2	9 25·5	9 25·7	N. 3 55—2 25·5	30·370	59·2	59·4	51·5
Anon.	19 26 18·0	9 27·5	14 9·2	9 27·7	9 27·6	N. 4 5+4 15·6				
6753	19 40 31·7	9 25·0	9 23·8	9 24·8	9 24·9	N. 2 40—0 1·1				
6877	19 59 25·5	9 2·8	12 22·9	9 2·9	9 2·85	N. 1 25+4 20·05	30·367	59·0	58·8	52·0
6948	20 11 9·2	9 6·9	14 2·1	9 6·8	9 6·85	N. 3 25+4 29·25				
7011	20 20 7·8	9 6·2	12 14·3	9 6·2	9 6·24	N. 4 20+3 8·06				
7026	20 21 59·0		12 6·6	9 6·2	9 6·24	N. 4 20+3 0·36				
7037	20 26 23·0	9 6·4	6 13·9	9 6·2	9 6·24	N. 4 20—2 26·34				
Anon.	20 38 45·2	9 13·2	5 33·8	9 13·1	9 13·15	N. 4 0—3 13·35				
Anon.	20 58 34·5	9 23·5	6 8·1	9 23·5	9 23·5	N. 4 15—3 15·4				
Anon.	21 5 43·6	9 14·0	9 33·15	9 13·9	9 13·95	N. 3 35+0 19·2	30·374	59·2	58·8	52·3
7386	21 13 27·5	9 16·5	13 10·9	9 16·4	9 16·45	N. 1 5+3 28·45				
Anon.	21 17 33·2	9 26·3	13 2·8	9 26·2	9 26·25	N. 4 5+3 10·55				
Anon.	21 30 40·2	9 22·2	6 14·05	*9 22·3	9 22·25	N. 3 35—3 8·2	30·375	59·2	59·2	52·0

♀ MAY 8, 1844. - FACE OF SECTOR WEST.

Number of B.A.C.	Time by Chronometer.	Micr. for Plumb-line on Dot.	Micr. for Observation of Star.	Micr. for Plumb-line on Dot.	Mean of Micr. for Plumb-line on Dot.	Star's Apparent Zenith Distance.	Barom.	Thermometers. Attd.	Lower.	Out.
4458	13 16 50·5	8 25·05	13 12·05	8 25·0	8 25·03	S. 1 55+4 21·02	30·397	60·2	59·7	55·2
4517	13 28 49·5	8 18·5	8 23·8	8 18 3	8 18·4	N. 5 10—0 5·4				54·8
4548	13 34 54·2	8 18 4	8 27·7	8 18·4	8 18·4	N. 5 10—0 9·3				
4579	13 41 49·0	8 24·0	7 27·75	8 24·0	8 24·0	N. 1 40+0 30·25				
4623	13 47 49·0	8 17·5	12 28·4	8 17·7	8 17·6	N. 1 45—4 10·8	30·390	59·6		54·6
4686	14 2 31·0	8 20·0	9 0·0	8 20·2	8 20·1	S. 1 40+0 13·9				
4719	14 10 56·8	7 28·8	12 3·95	7 28·75	7 28·78	N. 5 25—4 9·17			59·7	
4784	14 24 0·0	8 14·5	11 9·7	8 14·7	8 14·6	N. 5 10—2 29·1				
Anon.	14 29 5·2	8 16·3	11 21·45	8 16·1	8 16·2	N. 1 20—3 5·25				53·8
4852	14 39 7·5	9 4·55	7 16·8	9 4·4	9 4·48	S. 0 35—1 21·68				
4916	14 51 9·7	9 5·3	13 9·4	9 5·3	9 5·3	N. 0 45—4 4·1				
Anon.	14 58 26·5	9 3·9	10 10·95	9 3·9	9 3·9	N. 1 55—1 7·05			59·9	53·4
Anon.	15 2 37·7	8 33·4	13 7·05	8 33·3	8 33·35	N. 1 40—4 7·70				

May 7.—Anon. 16ʰ 18ᵐ 55·8 is not the proper star. Telescope mispointed.
Good definition throughout the night.

♀ MAY 8, 1844.—FACE OF SECTOR WEST—(continued).

Number of B.A.C.	Time by Chronometer.	Micr. for Plumb-line on Dot.	Micr. for Observation of Star	Micr. for Plumb-line on Dot.	Mean of Micr. for Plumb-line on Dot.	Star's Apparent Zenith Distance.	Barom.	Thermometers.		
								Attd.	Lower.	Out.
	h m s	rev. pts.	rev. pts.	rev. pts.	rev. pts.	° ′ rev. pts.	in.			
5032	15 13 18·6	9 10·75	6 22·8	9 10·65	9 10·7	N. 4 20+2 21·9	30·391	59·3		53·0
5054	15 16 55·5	9 21·9	10 22·1	9 22·1	9 22·0	S. 1 45+1 0·1			60·0	
5151	15 34 2·5	9 22·0	9 12·75	9 22·2	9 22·1	N. 4 40+0 9·35				53·4
Anon.	15 39 19·2	9 26·0	10 1·3	9 26·0	9 26·0	N. 2 50—0 9·3				
5227	15 46 3·0	9 21·3	5 30·9	9 21·2	9 21·25	N. 0 45+3 24·35				
5272	15 52 13·0	9 19·2	8 18·6	9 18·9	9 19·05	N. 5 10+1 0·45	30·388	59·2		53·6
5374	16 6 18·4	10 0·8	8 18·0	10 0·6	10 0·7	N. 4 55+1 16·7			60·0	
5435	16 14 40·0	9 29·3	10 27·5	9 29·4	9 29·4	N. 3 25—0 32·1				
Anon.	16 18 54·2	9 22·2	7 17·6	9 22·2	9 22·2	N. 1 5+2 4·6				
5588	16 38 36·5	8 33·0	13 2·1	8 32·9	8 32·95	N. 2 10—4 3·15				
5632	16 45 3·8	9 2·5	7 25·9	9 2·3	9 2·4	S. 0 5—1 10·5	30·387	59·2		53·4
5735	16 59 33·6	8 22·5	4 27·2	8 22·4	8 22·45	0 0+3 29·25			60·1	
5817	17 11 54·5	8 27·9	4 31·85	8 27·7	8 27·8	N. 1 25+3 29·95	30·381	59·4		53·7
5881	17 22 21·5	9 1·5	13 0 2	9 1·3	9 1·4	N. 4 15—3 32·8				53·8
5915	17 28 2·0	9 27·3	6 0·7	9 27·4	9 27·35	S. 3 5+3 26·65				
5960	17 34 50·5	9 8·2	9 31·8		9 8·1	N. 1 50—0 23·7				
5964	17		11 25·3	9 8·0	9 8·1	N. 1 50—2 17·2				
6016	17 44 1·2	9 20·0	5 7·5	9 19·8	9 19·9	N. 2 15+4 12·4	30·380	59·0	60·0	54·2
6074	17 54 2·0	9 20·5	5 25·0	9 20·1	9 20·3	N. 3 40+3 29·3				
6115	18 0 45·3	9 12·0	7 28·5	9 11·8	9 11·9	N. 3 30+1 17·4				
6145	18 5 0·2	9 22·1	7 17·2	9 22·1	9 22·1	N. 3 10+2 4·9				
6186	18 12 5·0	9 29·4	13 10·0	9 29·4	9 29·4	S. 2 50+3 14·6	30·375	59·0	60·0	53·8
6233	18 18 48·8	10 16·3	12 5·55	10 16·1	10 16·2	S. 0 30+1 23·35				
6275	18 24 46·8	10 0·8	14 10·9		10 0 8	N. 0 50—4 10·1				
6285	18 25 50·0		8 9·8	10 0·7	10 0·8	N. 0 50+1 25·0				
6305	18 28 43·0	10 0·7	12 18·0	10 0·8	10 0·8	N. 0 50—2 17·2	30·374	59·0	60·0	53·8
6414	18 47 38·6	9 9·1	6 32·0	9 9·1	9 9·1	N. 3 0+2 11·1				
6489	18 57 38·5	9 4·9	8 25·8	9 4·9	9 4·9	N. 3 50+0 15·3				
6525	19 2 38·5	8 24·8	10 31·2	8 25·0	8 24·9	N. 5 5—2 6·3	30·372	59·0	59·8	53·5
6639	19 22 2·2	8 30·3	11 28·7	8 30·4	8 30·35	N. 3 55—2 32·35				
Anon.	19 26 49·5	8 29·3	4 19·8	9 29·3	8 29 3	N. 4 5+4 9·5				
6753	19	8 21·5	8 28·9	8 21·4	8 21·45	N. 2 40—0 7·45	30·368	58·9	59·6	53·6
6877	19 59 24·0	8 22·5	5 7·6	8 22·3	8 22·4	N. 1 25+3 14·8				
6948	20 11 6·0	8 11·1	3 20·7	8 10·7	8 10·9	N. 3 25+4 24·2				
7011	20 20 4·2	8 6·5	5 3·0		8 6·2	N. 4 20+3 3·2				
7026	20 21 54·7	8 6·1	5 11·2	8 6·0	8 6·2	N. 4 20+2 29·0				
7057	20 26 19·8	8 6·1	11 3·95	8 6·3	8 6·2	N. 4 20—2 31·75				
Anon.	20 29	8 9·8	4 21·5	8 9·8	8 9·8	N. 4 5+3 22·3				
Anon.	20 38 43·5	8 4·5	11 25·0	8 4·7	8 4·6	N. 4 0—3 20·4				
7207	20 45 11·5	7 32·3	7 20·25	7 32·3	7 32 3	S. 0 25—0 12·05	30·365	59·0	59·4	53·5
Anon.	20 58 30·0	8 29·5	12 14·5	8 29·5	8 29·5	N. 4 15—3 19·0				
Anon.	21	9 19·0	9 6·9	9 19·0	9 19·0	N. 3 35+0 12·1				
7396	21 13 26·0	9 13·1	5 23·6	9 13·2	9 13·15	N. 1 5+3 23·55				
Anon.	21 17 29·5	9 9·5	6 5·0	9 9·7	9 9·6	N. 5 5+3 4·6	30·360	59·0	59·4	52·8
Anon.	21	9 4·5	12 18·0	9 4·7	9 4·6	N. 3 35—3 13·4				
7557	21 40 36·5	9 1·1	4 32·15	9 0·7	9 0·9	N. 0 10+4 2·75				
7842	22 27 35·2	8 28·2	3 32·8	8 28·0	8 28·1	N. 0 45+4 29·3				
7966	22 48 48·0	9 3·9	10 13·6	9 3·9	9 3·9	N. 0 15—1 9·7				
7992	22 53 57·5	8 14·3	9 16·8	8 14.4	8 14·35	N. 3 30—1 2·45	30·362	59·0	59·5	55·5

♃ MAY 9, 1844.—FACE OF SECTOR EAST.

| 1802 | 5 39 2·5 | 8 29·7 | 11 6·2 | 8 29·6 | 8 29·65 | S. 0 15—2 10·55 | 30·260 | 61·8 | 62·0 | 69·6 |
| 4458 | 13 16 58·0 | 9 21·0 | 5 7·3 | 9 21·0 | 9 21·0 | S. 1 55+4 13·7 | 30·292 | 61·4 | 61·4 | 58·7 |

May 8.—Anon. 19ʰ 26ᵐ 49ˢ Object too faint. Observation uncertain.
Anon. 20ʰ 29ᵐ. Observed at 25 seconds past the middle wire.
The last two Anonymous stars of the 8th were very faint.

♃ MAY 9, 1844.—FACE OF SECTOR EAST—*(continued).*

Number of B.A.C.	Time by Chronometer	Micr. for Plumb-line on Dot.	Micr. for Observation of Star.	Micr. for Plumb-line on Dot.	Mean of Micr. for Plumb-line on Dot.	Star's Apparent Zenith Distance.	Barom.	Thermometers. Attd.	Lower.	Out.
	h m s	rev. pts.	rev. pts.	rev. pts.	rev. pts.	° ′ rev. pts.	In.			
4517	13 29 0·0	9 31·3	9 32·55	9 31·3	9 31·3	N. 5 10+0 1·25				
4548	13 35 5·0	9 31·3	9 28·55	9 31·1	9 31·2	N. 5 10—0 2·65				57·7
4579	13 41 58·0	9 18·5	10 21·5	9 18·5	9 18 5	N. 1 40+1 3·0			61·4	
4623	13	9 0·85	4 29·5	9 1·0	9 0·93	N. 1 45—4 5·43	30·274	60·7		57·8
4680	14 2 38·5	8 27·4	8 20·2	8 27·2	8 27·3	S. 1 40+0 7·1				
4719	14 11 8·0	8 17·5	4 14·5	8 17·4	8 17·45	N. 5 25—4 2·95				
4784	14 24 10·5	8 19·8	5 29·8	8 19·6	8 19·7	N. 5 10—2 23·9	30·272	60·5		57·9
Anon.	14 29 14·0	7 6·1	4 6·75	7 6·3	7 6·2	N. 1 20—2 33·45			61·2	
4852	14 30 15·9	7 30·4	9 22·4	7 30·4	7 30·4	S. 0 35—1 20·0				
4916	14 51 19 0	8 26·8	4 27·35	8 26·9	8 26·85	N. 0 45—3 33·5				57·3
Anon.	14 58 35·3	9 3·5	8 2·55	9 3·4	9 3·45	N. 1 55—1 0·9				
Anon.	15 2 46·7	9 11·7	5 9·0	9 11·3	9 11·5	N. 1 40—4 2·5				
5032	15 13 29·5	9 33·6	12 28·7	9 33·5	9 33·55	N. 4 20+2 29·15			61·4	
5054	15 17 3·5	10 3·8	9 9·7	10 4·0	10 3·9	S. 1 45+0 28·2				56·8
5151	15 34 18·5	10 8·1	10 23·0	10 8·1	10 8·1	N. 4 40+0 14·9				
Anon.	15 39 29·0	9 5·7	9 3·35	9 5·8	9 5·75	N. 2 50—0 2·4				
5227	15 46 11·5	9 22·4	13 16·5	9 22·6	9 22·5	N. 0 45+3 28·0	30·270	60·4	61·2	57·7
5272	15	10 7·0	11 14·0	10 6·5	10 6·75	N. 5 10+1 7·25				
5374	16 6 20·5	0 22·0	11 13·1	9 22·1	9 22·05	N. 4 55+1 25·05				57·7
5435	16 14 49·5	9 15·1	8 23·25	9 15·1	9 15·1	N. 3 25—0 25·85			60·9	
Anon.	16 19 3·0	9 8·3	11 17·45	9 8·3	9 8·3	N. 1 5+2 9·15				
5588	16 38 46·0	9 30·5	5 32·25	9 30·5	9 30·5	N. 2 10—3 32·25				
5632	16 45 12·0	9 22·5	11 6·1	9 22·7	9 22·6	S. 0 5—1 17·5	30·261	60·4		57·7
5735	16 59 42·2	9 12·5	13 15·5	9 12·8	9 12·65	0 0+4 2·85				
5817	17 12 3·2	9 23·5	13 25·25	9 23·6	9 23·55	N. 1 25+4 1·7				
5881	17 22 32·2	10 0·8	6 6·8	10 0·9	10 0·85	N. 4 15—3 28·0				
5915	17 28 9·2	9 18·7	13 18·55	9 18·5	9 18·6	S. 3 5—3 33·95	30·260	60·4		58·7
5960	17 34 59·3	9 27·6	9 10·5		9 27·5	N. 1 50—0 17·0				
5964	17 35 56·5		7 17·2	9 27·4	9 27·5	N. 1 50—2 10·3			60·7	
6016	17 44 10·8	9 33·9	14 17·2	10 0·3	10 0·1	N. 2 15+4 17·1				
6074	17 54 12·5	9 13·0	13 14·75	9 12·8	9 12·9	N. 3 40+4 1·85				
6115	18 0 55·5	9 26·0	11 16·35	9 26·0	9 26·0	N. 3 30+1 24·35	30·262	60·4		58·3
6145	18 5 10·4	9 12·7	11 25·45	9 12·7	9 12·7	N. 3 10+2 12·75	30·262	60·4	60·9	57·4
6186	18 12 12·0	8 20·5	5 12·95	8 20·7	8 20·6	S. 2 50+3 7·65				
6233	18 18 56·5	8 23·1	7 4·65	8 23·2	8 23·15	S. 0 30+1 18·5				
6275	18 24 54·3	9 18·1	5 12·9		9 18·13	N. 0 50—4 5·23				
6285	18 26 58·0		11 15·3	9 18·16	9 18·13	N. 0 50+1 31·17				
6414	18 47 48·5	9 28·2	12 12·3	9 28·0	9 28·1	N. 3 0+2 18·2				
6489	18 57 49·0	10 1·4	10 24·25	10 1·3	10 1·35	N. 3 50+0 22·9				
6525	19	10 8·8	8 9·4	10 9·0	10 8·9	N. 5 5—1 33·5	30·260	60·0	60·6	51·4
6639	19 22 11·8	10 16·65	6 26·4	10 16·6	10 16·63	N. 3 55—3 24·23				
6753	19 40 38·5	9 27·6	9 27·4	9 27·7	9 27·65	N. 2 40—0 0·25				
6877	19 59 32·7	9 10·7	12 30·0	9 10·6	9 10·65	N. 1 25+3 19·35				
6948	20 11 15·8	9 13·2	14 9·0	9 13·6	9 13·4	N. 3 25+4 29·6				
7011	20 20 15·0	9 6·8	12 15·1	9 6·86	9 6·86	N. 4 20+4 8·24				
7026	20 22 5·5		12 6·0	9 7·2	9 6·86	N. 4 20+2 33·14				
7057	20 26 30·5	9 6·9	6 14·6	9 6·6	9 6·86	N. 4 20—2 26·06				
Anon.	20 29 23·0	8 33·0	12 23·9	8 33·1	8 33·05	N. 4 0+3 24·85			60·0	
Anon.	20 38 53·5	9 6·0	5 24·5	9 5·8	9 5·9	N. 4 0—3 15·4				
7207	20	9 22·2	9 3·3	9 22·2	9 22·2	S. 0 25—0 18·9	30·250	59·0	59·8	47·5
Anon.	20 58 41·7	9 12·0	5 31·5	9 11·8	9 11·9	N. 4 15—0 14·4				
Anon.	21 5 50·0	0 7·3	9 26·45	9 7·1	9 7·2	N. 3 35+0 19·25				
7386	21 13 34·8	8 11·7	12 7·0	8 11·8	8 11·75	N. 1 5+3 29·25				
Anon.	21 17 39·5	8 16·3	11 27·8	8 16·3	8 16·3	N. 4 5+3 11·5				
Anon.	21 30 46·0	8 26·3	5 18·55	8 26·5	8 26·4	N. 3 35—3 7·85	30·250	59·2	60·3	48·4

May 9.—No. 6285.—Observed at 29 seconds after passing the meridian wire.
No. 6525.—The lamp going out, and the meridian wire invisible.
Good definition throughout the 9th.

♃ May 9, 1844.—Face of Sector East—(continued).

Number of B. A. C.	Time by Chronometer.	Micr. for Plumb-line on Dot.	Micr. for Observation of Star.	Micr. for Plumb-line on Dot.	Mean of Micr. for Plumb-line on Dot.	Star's Apparent Zenith Distance.	Barom.	Thermometers. Attd.	Lower.	Out.
	h m s	rev. pts.	rev. pts.	rev. pts.	rev. pts.	° ' rev. pts.	in.			
7557	21 40 44·8	8 29·4	13 4·5	8 29·6	8 29·5	N. 0 10+4 9·0				
7857	21 56 59·0	9 11 3	8 5·0	9 11·3	9 11·3	N. 4 45—1 6·3	30·256	59·0	59·6	47·8
7992	22 54 7 5	10 18 0	9 21·9	10 17·8	10 17·9	N. 3 29—0 30·0	30·262	58·7	59·3	46·0

Face of Sector West.

2293	6 57 26·0	8 27·0	9 5·5	8 26·8	8 26·9	N. 5 10—0 12·6	30·255	62·8	62·6	66·4

♀ May 10, 1844.—Face of Sector East.

1802	5	8 6 5	10 16·3	8 6·8	8 6·65	S. 0 15—2 9·65	30·188	62·4	62·4	69·0
2293	6 52 37 0	9 12·1	9 6·3	9 12·3	9 12·2	N. 5 10—0 5·9	30·185	62·8	63·2	66·4

Face of Sector West.

Number of B. A. C.	Time by Chronometer.	Micr. for Plumb-line on Dot.	Micr. for Observation of Star.	Micr. for Plumb-line on Dot.	Mean of Micr. for Plumb-line on Dot.	Star's Apparent Zenith Distance.	Barom.	Attd.	Lower.	Out.
4456	13 11 58·2	10 6·3	14 27·0	10 6·0	10 6·15	S. 1 55+4 20·85				61·3
4517	13 23 56·7	10 0·5	10 4·6	10 0·5	10 0·5	N. 5 10—0 4·1				
4548	13 30 1·3	10 0·5	10 9·25	10 0·4	10 0·45	N. 5 10—0 8·8				61·2
4579	13 36 56·5	9 10·8	8 16·35	9 10 8	9 10·8	N. 1 40+0 28·45				
4623	13 42 57·0	9 25·8	14 3·05	9 26·3	9 26·05	N. 1 45—4 11·0	30·188	58·0	61·2	48·0
4686	13 57 39·0	10 16·8	10 31·4	10 16·8	10 16·8	S. 1 40+0 14·6				
4719	14 6 5·0	10 19·0	14 28·1	10 19·3	10 19·15	N. 5 25—4 8·95				61·0
4784	14 19 7·6	11 18·8	14 12·5	11 18·9	11 18·85	N. 5 10—2 27·65				
Anon.	14 24 13·0	11 5·8	14 10·8	11 6·2	11 6·0	N. 1 20—3 4·8				61·0
4852	14 34 15·7	10 13·4	8 26·7	10 13·5	10 13·45	S. 0 35—1 20·75	30·178	58·2		
4916	14 46 18·2	10 5·6	14 8·95	10 5·7	10 5·65	N. 0 45—4 3·3			60·8	46·4
Anon.	14 53 34·0	9 16·8	10 23·65	9 17·4	9 17·1	N. 1 55—1 6·55				46·3
Anon.	14 57 46·0	9 26·0	14 0·65	9 26·3	9 26·15	N. 1 40—4 8·5				
5032	15 8 26·5	9 15·45	6 26·8	9 15·3	9 15·38	N. 4 20+2 22·68				
5054	15 12 3·8	9 23·8	10 23·55	9 23·8	9 23·8	S. 1 45+0 33·75				45·5
5151	15 29 10·5	9 18·8	9 8·25	9 18·8	9 18·8	N. 4 40+0 10·55				45·4
Anon.	15 34 27·2	9 30·5	10 6·25	9 30·5	9 30·5	N. 2 50—0 9·75				
5227	15 41 11·0	9 27·3	8 2·8	9 27·5	9 27·4	N. 0 45+3 24·6			60·6	
5272	15 47 20·8	9 28·1	8 26·6	9 27·9	9 28·0	N. 5 10+1 1·4				
5331	15 56 30·5	9 30·6	12 10·4		9 30·4	S. 2 25+2 14·0	30·180	58·0	60·6	45·0
Comp.	15		7 14·25	9 30 2	9 30·4	S. 2 25—2 16 15				
5374	16 1 26·0	9 20·0	8 2·0	9 20·0	9 20·0	N. 4 55+1 18·0				
Anon.	16 14 2·8	10 0·9	7 29·7	10 0·8	10 0·85	N. 1 5+2 5·15				
5508	16 21 20·3	10 10·9	11 9·8	10 10·8	10 10·85	S. 0 25+0 32·95				
5588	16 33 45·0	8 33·5	13 3·0	8 33·5	8 33·5	N. 2 10—4 3·5				
5632	16 40 12·0	9 5·7	7 28·8	9 5·5	9 5·6	S. 0 5+1 10·8	30·174	58·4		45·2
5735	16 54 41·5	8 32·8	5 3·2	8 32·4	8 32·6	0 0+3 29·4			60·2	44·7
5817	17 7 2·2	8 24·2	4 27·5	8 24·0	8 24·1	N. 1 25+3 30·6				
5881	17 17 29·5	9 27·4	13 25·75	9 27·4	9 27·4	N. 4 15—3 32·35	30·174	58·2	59·6	44·4
5915	17 23 10·5	10 4·0	6 11·8	10 4·1	10 4·05	S. 3 5—3 26·25				44·2
5960	17 29 58·2	9 29·0	10 19·0	9 29·4	9 29·2	N. 1 50—0 23·8				
6016	17 39 10·2	10 1·6	5 23·0	10 1·4	10 1·5	N. 2 15+4 12·5				
6074	17 49 10·2	10 4·7	6 9·7	10 4·3	10 4·5	N. 3 40+3 28·8				
6115	17	9 21·5	8 2·7	9 21·3	9 21·4	N. 3 30+1 18·7	30·175	58·0	59·7	43·5
6145	18 0 7·7	10 1·6	7 30·9	10 1·6	10 1·6	N. 3 10+2 4·7	30·174	58·0	59·7	43·4
6186	18 7 13·0	10 13·6	13 28·8	10 13·5		S. 0 30+1 23·65				
6233	18 13 57·0	10 7·0	11 30·5	10 6·7	10 6·85	S. 0 30+1 23·65				
6275	18	9 16·1	13 27·7		9 16·1	N. 0 50—4 11·6				
6285	18 20 57·0		7 24·8	9 15·9	9 16·1	N. 0 50+1 25·3				
6305	18 23 50·2	9 16·1	12 0·4	9 16·3	9 16·1	S. 0 50—2 18·3	30·172	58·2	59·7	43·3
6414	18	9 11·8	7 1·2	9 11·6	9 11·7	N. 3 0+2 10·5				

May 10.—No. 1802.—Observed at 16 seconds after passing the meridian wire.
No. 5915.—The seconds of transit doubtful.

♀ MAY 10, 1844.—FACE OF SECTOR WEST—*(continued).*

Number of B. A. C.	Time by Chronometer.	Micr. for Plumb-line on Det	Micr. for Observation of Star.	Micr. for Plumb-line on Dot.	Mean of Micr. for Plumb-line on Dot.	Star's Apparent Zenith Distance.	Barom.	Thermometers.		
								Attd.	Lower.	Out.
	h m s	rev. pts.	rev. pts.	rev. pts.	rev. pts.	o ′ rev. pts.	in.			
6489	18 52 46·0	9 9·4	8 25·6	9 0·3	9 0·35	N. 3 50+0 17·75				
6525	18 57 46·0	8 26·7	10 33·2	8 26·9	8 26·8	N. 5 5—2 6·4	30·168	58·2	59·2	42·5
6753	19 35 37·0	7 6·7	7 13·0	7 6·9	7 6·8	N. 2 40—0 6·2			59·0	
6877	19 54 32·0	8 18·2	5 2·5	8 18·3	8 18·25	N. 1 25+3 15·75	30·167	58·2	58·8	42·0
6948	20 6 14·0	8 16·4	3 26·3	8 16·3	8 16·35	N. 3 25+4 24·05				
7011	20 15 11·5 ⎫	8 27·4	5 23·45	8 27·0	8 27·2	N. 4 20+3 3·75				
7026	20 17 4·0 ⎬		5 29·75	8 27·1	8 27·2	N. 4 20+2 31·45				
7057	20 21 28·0 ⎭	8 27·2	11 24·2	8 27·3	8 27·2	N. 4 20—2 31·0				
Anon.	20 24 20·5		4 17·5	8 5·9		N. 4 5+3 22·4	30·166	58·2	59·0	42·7
Anon.	20 33 50·5	8 16·8	12 0·0	8 16·8	8 16·8	N. 4 0—3 17·2				
7207	20 40 20·5	9 7·5	8 30·5	9 7·7	9 7·6	S. 0 25—0 11·1				
Anon.	20 53 38·5	8 25·5	12 12·2	8 25·5	8 25·5	N. 4 15—3 20·7			59·0	
Anon.	21 0 48·5	8 33·8	8 20·75	8 33·7	8 33·75	N. 3 55+0 13·0				
7386	21 8 34·0	9 11·7	5 21·7	9 12·0	9 11·85	N. 1 5+3 24·15				
Anon.	21 12 37·5		5 20·6	8 26·45		N. 4 5+3 5·85	30·163	58·0	59·1	45·6
Anon.	21 25 45·5	8 9·7	11 22·7	8 9·8	8 9·75	N. 3 35—3 12·95			59·0	
7557	21 35 45·0	8 18·8	4 14·0	8 18·5	8 18·65	N. 0 10+4 4·65	30·160	58·0	59·0	46·9
7657	21 51 56·2	8 31·0	10 7·8	8 31·2	8 31·1	N. 4 45—1 10·7				
7966	22 43 57·0	5 32·0	7 7·2	5 31·6	5 31·8	N. 0 15—1 9·4				
7992	22	6 32·4	8 1·35	6 31·7	6 31·05	N. 3 29—1 4·3	30·168	58·0	58·2	46·0

♄ MAY 11, 1844.—FACE OF SECTOR WEST.

1802	5 34 5·8	8 20·8	6 13·7	8 20·4	8 20·6	S. 0 15—2 6·9	30·140	61·0	61·7	66·0
2293	6 52 33·5	8 19·9	8 30·75	9 20·0	8 19·95	N. 5 10—0 10·8	30·148	61·0	61·6	64·2
Anon.	14 24 16·7	9 18·9	12 22·5	9 18·9	9 18·9	N. 1 20—3 3·6	30·183	61·5		
4852	14 34 19·0	10 1·7	8 14·75	10 1·9	10 1·8	S. 0 35—1 21·05				
4916	14 46 21·5	10 14·7	14 17·7	10 14·8	10 14·75	N. 0 45—4 2·95				
Anon.	14	10 23·3	11 30·1	10 23·0	10 23·15	N. 1 55—1 6·95				
7557	21 35 49·5	11 9·2	7 6·0	11 8·8	11 9·0	N. 0 10+4 3·0				

FACE OF SECTOR EAST.

4458	13 12 5·0	10 21·85	6 7·45	10 21·85	10 21·85	S. 1 55+4 14·4	30·185	61·5		
4517	13 24 8·0	10 23·9	10 23·95	10 23·8	10 23·85	N. 5 10+0 0·1				
4548	13 30 12·5	10 23·9	10 20·95	10 23·9	10 23·9	N. 5 10—0 2·95				
4579	13 36 35·5	9 31·5	10 33·5	9 31·5	9 31·5	N. 1 40+1 2·0				
4623	13 43 5·5	9 14·3	5 8·75	9 14·3	9 14·3	N. 1 45—4 5·55	30·184	61·4		
4686	13 57 46·0	9 5·5	8 31·4	9 5·4	9 5·45	S. 1 40+0 8·05				
5032	15 8 36·8	9 22·7	12 17·25	9 22·7	9 22·7	N. 4 20+2 28·55				
5054	15 12 10·2	9 4·5	8 9·2	9 4·8	9 4·65	S. 1 45+0 29·45				
5151	15	9 25·9	10 7·3	9 26·2	9 26·05	N. 4 40+0 15·25				
Anon.	15 34 36·2	9 27·5	9 23·55	9 27·5	9 27·5	N. 2 50—0 3·95				
5227	15 41 18·5	9 21·5	13 15·05	9 21·6	9 21·55	N. 0 45+3 27·5				
5272	15	9 22·7	10 28·7	9 22·8	9 22·75	N. 5 10+1 5·95				
5331	15 56 37·0	9 0·7	6 24·75	9 0·2	9 0·45	S. 2 25+2 9·7				
5374	16 1 37·5	9 26·3	11 16·6	9 26·5	9 26·4	N. 4 55+1 24·2				
5435	16 9 57·2	9 29·8	9 3·7	9 29·6	9 29·7	N. 3 25—0 26·0				
Anon.	16 14 11·0	9 6·6	11 15·8	9 6·5	9 6·55	N. 1 5+2 9·25				
5508	16 21 27·5	9 3·1	8 8·8	9 2·9	9 3·0	S. 0 25+0 28·2				
5588	16 33 52·5	9 3·4	5 5·9	9 3·4	9 3·4	N. 2 10—3 31·5				
5632	16 40 20·0	9 28·4	11 11·2	9 28·4	9 28·4	S. 0 5—1 16·8				
5735	16 54 49·5	9 22·0	13 23·95	9 21·9	9 21·95	0 0+4 2·0	30·182	61·3		
5817	17 7 11·0	9 29·9	13 30·5	9 29·9	9 29·9	N. 1 25+4 0·6				
5881	17 17 40·0	10 9·3	6 15·0	10 9·2	10 9·25	N. 4 15—3 28·25				

May 10.—The clamp not disturbed during the observations of Nos. 7011, 7026 and 7057.
Remarkably bad definition throughout the 10th.
11.—The plumb-line not adjusted over the upper dot for Nos. 4517, 4548, 4579, 4623 and 4686.
No. 5272.—Observed at 12 seconds after passing the meridian wire.

♄ MAY 11, 1844.—FACE OF SECTOR EAST—(continued.)

Number of B.A.C.	Time by Chronometer.	Micr. for Plumb-line on Dot.	Micr. for Observation of Star.	Micr. for Plumb-line on Dot.	Mean of Micr. for Plumb-line on Dot.	Star's Apparent Zenith Distance.	Barom.	Attd.	Lower.	Out.
	h m s	rev. pts.	rev. pts.	rev. pts.	rev. pts.	° ′ rev. pts.	in.			
5915	17 23 17·0	9 29·4	13 28·95	9 29·3	9 29·35	S. 3 5—3 33·6				
5960	17 30 6·8	9 22·9	9 5·8		9 22·95	N. 1 50—0 17·15				
5964	17 31 8·0		7 11·3	9 23·0	9 22·95	N. 1 50—2 11·65				
6016	17 39 18·5	9 14·0	13 30·2	9 14·1	9 14·05	N. 2 15+4 16·15				
6074	17 49 20·6	9 4·1	13 6·0	9 4·3	9 4·2	N. 3 40+4 1·8				
6115	17 56 3·5	9 22·8	11 12·7	9 22·8	9 22·8	N. 3 30+1 23·9				
6145	17 59 58·2	9 17·0	11 29·6	9 16·9	9 16·95	N. 3 10+2 12·65				
6186	18 7 19·8	9 10·1	6 1·5	9 10·1	9 10·1	S. 2 50+3 8·6				
6233	18 14 4·5	9 14·6	7 29·45	9 14·8	9 14·7	S. 0 30+1 19·25				
6275	18	9 10·5	5 3·3		9 10·45	N. 0 50—4 7·15	30·172	61·0		
6285	18		11 6·5	9 10·4	9 10·45	N. 0 50+1 30·05				
6305	18 24 59·2	9 10·4	6 31·7	9 10·5	9 10·45	N. 0 50—2 12·75				
6414	18 42 56·6	9 10·4	11 27·75	9 10·6	9 10·5	N. 3 0+2 17·25				
6480	18 52 57·0	9 4·0	9 26·5	9 4·0	9 4·0	N. 3 50+0 22·5				
6525	18 57 57·0	9 4·7	7 5·0	9 4·8	9 4·75	N. 5 5—1 33·75	30·164	60·8		
6630	19 17 20·2	9 20·0	6 29·55	9 20·0	9 20·0	N. 3 55—2 24·45				
6753	19 35 46·5	9 7·2	9 5·0	9 7·5	9 7·35	N. 2 40—0 2·35	30·162	60·5		
6877	19 54 41·0	9 22·6	13 7·8	9 22·6	9 22·6	N. 1 25+3 19·2	30·162	60·5		
6948	20 6 24·5	10 7·2	15 2·3	10 7·5	10 7·35	N. 3 25+4 28·95				
7011	20 15 22·8	10 10·8	13 19·7		10 11·03	N. 4 20+3 8·67				
7026	20 17 14·5		13 11·6	10 11·2	10 11·03	N. 4 20+3 0·57				
7057	20 21 38·5	10 11·1	7 19·5	10 11·0	10 11·03	N. 4 20—2 25·53				
Anon.	20 24 30·8		14 4·6	10 9·5		N. 4 5+3 29·1				
Anon.	20 34 1·0	10 26·0	7 13·7	10 26·0	10 26·0	N. 4 0—3 12·3				
7207	20 40 27·4	9 30·6	10 14·4	9 30·8	9 30·7	S. 0 25—0 17·7				
Anon.	20 53 48·8	9 21·4	6 7·15	9 14·8	9 14·85	N. 5 10—3 14·35				
Anon.	21 0 58·5	9 20·0	10 5·8	9 19·7	9 19·85	N. 3 35+0 19·95	30·168	60·3		
7366	21 8 52·7	8 33·2	12 28·3	8 33·5	8 33·35	N. 1 5+3 28·95				
Anon.	21 25 55·5	12 17·5	9 9·7	12 17·5	12 17·5	N. 3 35—3 7 8	30·171	60·2		
7657	21 52 6·8	11 20·8	10 15·15	11 21·0	11 20·9	N. 4 45—1 5·75				
7842	22 22 51·5	12 0·0	16 32·1	11 33·8	11 33·9	N. 0 45+4 32·2	30·179	60·2		
7966	22 44 4·2	10 6·3	9 0·9	10 6·4	10 6·35	N. 0 15—1 5·45				
7992	22 49 15·5	9 28·25	8 32·75	9 28·05	9 28·15	N. 3 29—0 29·4	30·190	60·5		

◊ MAY 13, 1844.—FACE OF SECTOR EAST.

Number of B.A.C.	Time by Chronometer.	Micr. for Plumb-line on Dot.	Micr. for Observation of Star.	Micr. for Plumb-line on Dot.	Mean of Micr. for Plumb-line on Dot.	Star's Apparent Zenith Distance.	Barom.	Attd.	Lower.	Out.
2293	6 52 49·7	10 15·6	10 8·6	10 15·7	10 15·65	N. 5 10—0 7·05	30·268	63·0	63·4	

FACE OF SECTOR WEST.

Number of B.A.C.	Time by Chronometer.	Micr. for Plumb-line on Dot.	Micr. for Observation of Star.	Micr. for Plumb-line on Dot.	Mean of Micr. for Plumb-line on Dot.	Star's Apparent Zenith Distance.	Barom.	Attd.	Lower.	Out.
4458	13 12 8·6	9 18·5	14 4·45	9 18·5	9 18·5	S. 1 55+4 10·95	30·282	62·0	62·4	59·3
4517	13 24 7·8	9 7·4	9 12·2	9 7·4	9 7·4	N. 5 10—0 4·8				
4548	13 30 12·7	9 7·4	9 10·4	9 7·4	9 7·4	N. 5 10—0 9·0				
4579	13 37 7·8	9 29·9	8 33·0	9 29·4	9 29·65	N. 1 40+0 30·65				
4623	13 43 8·0	9 13·9	13 24·3	9 14·0	9 13·95	N. 1 45—4 10·35				
4686	13 57 50·5	9 16·3	9 30·35	9 16·5	9 16·4	S. 1 40+0 13·95				
4719	14 6 16·0	9 10·7	13 19·4	9 10·6	9 10·65	N. 5 25—4 8·75				
4784	14 19 19·2	9 18·2	12 13·0	9 18·8	9 18·5	N. 5 10—2 28·75				
Anon.	14	9 23·6	12 27·8	9 33·8	9 23·7	N. 1 20—3 4·1				
4852	14 34 27·0	9 33·8	8 12·9	9 33·7	9 33·75	S. 3 35—1 21·55	30·270	62·0	62·2	58·2
4916	14	9 23·0	13 26·8	9 23·5	9 23·25	N. 0 45—4 3·55				
Anon.	14 53 45·0	9 22·5	10 28·7	9 22·6	9 22·55	N. 1 55—1 6·15				
Anon.	14 57 57·0	9 14·0	13 20·5	9 14·0	9 14·0	N. 1 44—4 6·5				
5032	15 8 38·5	9 21·9	6 33·2	9 22·0	9 21·95	N. 4 20+2 22·75				
5054	15 12 15·2	10 0·0	10 33·95	10 0·0	10 0·0	S. 1 45+0 33·95				

May 11.—Good definition throughout this night. The image of Fomalhaut superb.
The lower Thermometer in the Telescope room, for comparison with the standard.

☾ May 13, 1844.—FACE OF SECTOR WEST—(continued).

Number of B.A.C.	Time by Chronometer	Micr. for Plumb-line on Dot	Micr. for Observation of Star	Micr. for Plumb-line on Dot	Mean of Micr. for Plumb-line on Dot	Star's Apparent Zenith Distance	Barom.	Thermometers		
								Attd.	Lower	Out.
	h m s	rev. pts.	rev. pts.	rev. pts.	rev. pts.	o ' rev. pts.	in.			
5151	15 29 21·5	0 13·6	9 3·4	0 13·4	0 13·5	N. 4 40+0 10·1				
Anon.	15 34 38·0	9 14·2	9 23·8	9 14·2	9 14·2	N. 2 50—0 9·6				
5227	15 41 22·0	9 31·0	6 6·0	9 30·8	9 30·9	N. 0 45+3 24·9				
5272	15 47 31·5	9 33·6	8 33·0	9 33·6	9 33·6	N. 5 10+1 0·6				
5331	15 57 42·0	10 25·0	13 4·9	10 25·4	10 25·2	S. 2 25+2 13·7				
5374	16 1 37·2	9 25·2	8 7·0	9 25·1	9 25·1	N. 4 55+1 18·1				
5435	16 9 58·2	9 14·1	10 10·9	9 14·3	9 14·2	N. 3 25—0 30·7				
Anon.	16 14 13·5	8 32·0	6 26·6	8 31·9	8 31·95	N. 1 5+2 5·35				
5508	16 21 31·0	8 22·2	9 20·7	8 22·2	8 22·2	S. 0 25+0 32·5				
5588	16 33 55·5	8 21·3	12 23·5	8 21·4	8 21·35	N. 2 10—4 2·15				
5632	16 40 23·2	8 24·3	7 13·5	8 24·35	8 24·35	S. 0 5—1 10·85	30·251	61·5	62·2	58·2
5735	16 54 53·0	8 15·4	4 19·4	8 15·3	8 15·35	0 0+3 29·95				
5817	17 7 13·5	8 10·8	4 13·8	8 10·8	8 10·8	N. 1 25+3 31·0				
5881	17 17 40·5	8 22·3	12 20·55	8 22·3	8 22·3	N. 4 15—3 32·25				
5915	17 23 21·8	9 2·4	5 8·0	9 2·3	9 2·35	S. 3 5—3 24·35				
5960	17 30 9·5	8 20·2	9 8·8		8 20·3	N. 1 50—0 22·5				
5964	17 31 7·0		11 2·0	8 20·4	8 20·3	N. 1 50—2 15·7				
6016	17 39 20·5	8 14·0	3 33·9	8 14·0	8 14·0	N. 2 15+4 14·1				
6074	17 49 1 2	8 9·3	4 13·8	8 9·2	8 9·25	N. 3 40+3 29·45				
6115	17 56 4·5	7 25·7	6 8·3	7 25·6	7 25·65	N. 3 30+1 17·35				
6145	18 0 19·5	7 29·2	5 22·75	7 29·1	7 29·15	N. 3 10+2 6·4				
6186	18 7 24·5	8 13·5	11 28·05	8 13·4	8 13·45	S. 2 50+3 14·6				
6233	18 14 8·2	8 19·2	10 7·5	8 19·2	8 19·2	S. 0 30+1 22·3			62·1	
6275	18 20 6·0	9 7·9	13 16·55		8 8·05	N. 0 50—4 8·5				
6285	18 21 9·0		7 15·5	9 8·2	9 8·05	N. 0 50+1 26·55				
6305	18 24 2·0	9 8·1	11 23·5	9 8·0	9 8·05	N. 0 50—2 15·45				
6414	18	9 13·1	7 1·55	9 13·2	9 13·15	N. 3 0+2 11·6				
6489	18 52 57·5	9 17·0	8 33·6	9 17·3	9 17·15	N. 3 50+0 17·55	30·222	61·2	61·9	59·1
6525	18 57 57·3	10 0·3	12 0·0	10 0·2	10 0·25	N. 5 5—2 5·75				
6639	19	10 1·1	12 31·75	10 1·0	10 1·05	N. 3 55—2 30·7				
Anon.	19	10 2·3	5 26·75	10 2·0	10 2·15	N. 4 5+4 9·4				
6753	19 35 58·2	9 7·0	9 12·1	9 7·0	9 7·0	N. 2 40—0 5·1				
6877	19 54 43·5	9 7·7	5 25·4	9 7·8	9 7·75	N. 1 25+3 10·35				
6948	20 6 25·5	9 6·6	4 15·7	9 6·6	9 6·6	N. 3 25+4 24·9				
7011	20 15 23·0	9 16·3	6 11·2	9 16·2	9 16·12	N. 4 20+3 4·92				
7026	20 17 14·0		6 18·6	9 16·1	9 16·12	N. 4 20+2 31·52				
7057	20 21 39·0	9 16·0	12 11·4	9 16·0	9 16·12	N. 4 20—2 29·28				
Anon.	20 24 31·5	9 21·2	5 31·6	9 21·3	9 21·25	N. 4 5+3 23·65				
Anon.	20 34 1·5	9 28·7	13 11·8	9 28·6	9 28·65	N. 4 0—3 17·15			61·8	
7207	20 40 30·8	9 28·4	9 13·95	9 28·3	9 28·35	S. 0 25—0 14·4	30·215	61·0	61·8	60·0
Anon.	20 53 49·2	9 16·9	13 1·3	9 16·9	9 16·9	N. 4 15—3 18·4				
7386	21 0 59·2	9 23·1	9 7·7	9 23·1	9 23·1	N. 3 35+0 15·4				
7386	21 8 45·5	9 27·8	6 0·3	9 27·3	9 27·3	N. 1 5+3 27·0				
Anon.	21 12 48·2	9 27·1	6 19·8	9 27·2	9 27·15	N. 4 5+3 7·35				
Anon.	21 25 56·0	9 26·5	13 3·3	9 26·4	9 26·45	N. 3 35—3 10·85				
7557	21 35 56·0	9 7·8	5 2·9	9 7·6	9 7·7	N. 0 10+4 4·8				
7657	21 52 7·5	9 5·2	10 15·3	9 5·0	9 5·1	N. 4 45—1 10·2				
Anon.	21 55 58·5	9 5·0	9 10·75	9 5·0	9 5·0	N. 4 45—0 5·75				
7842	22 22 54·0	9 0·8	4 4·8	9 1·0	9 0·9	N. 0 43+4 30·1	30·217	61·1	61·5	61·0
7966	22 44 7·8	8 28·7	10 3·1	8 28·7	8 28·7	N. 0 15—1 8·4				
7992	22 49 17·0	8 26·8	9 28·5	8 27·0	8 26·9	N. 3 30—1 1·6	30·217	61·2	61·6	61·8

May 13.—No. 6639.—Observed at 25 seconds after passing the meridian wire.
A fine observing night.

♂ May 14, 1844.—Face of Sector West.

Number of B.A.C.	Time by Chronometer.	Micr. for Plumb-line on Dot.	Micr. for Observation of Star.	Micr. for Plumb-line on Dot.	Mean of Micr. for Plumb-line on Dot.	Star's Apparent Zenith Distance.	Barom.	Thermometers. Attd.	Lower.	Out.
	h m s	rev. pts.	rev. pts.	rev. pts.	rev. pts.	° ' rev. pts.	in.			
2293	6 52 46·0	10 10·6	10 21·0	10 10·4	10 10·5	N 5 10—0 10·5	30·127	63·6	63·6	65·0

Face of Sector East.

4458	13 12 17·0	9 9·5	4 28·8	9 9·5	9 9·5	S. 1 55+4 14·7	30·110	62·6	63·0	59·4
4517	13 24 20·0	9 31·95	9 31·7	9 31·9	9 31·93	N. 5 10—0 0·23				
4548	13 30 25·0	9 32·0	9 28·3	9 32·0	9 32·0	N. 5 10—0 3·7				
4579	13 37 17·5	9 16·9	10 18·35	9 16·9	9 16·9	N. 1 40+1 1·45	30·105	62·4		58·3
4623	13 43 17·5	9 23·0	5 16·2	9 22·9	9 22·95	N. 1 45—4 6·75				
4680	13 57 57·8	9 12·9	9 4·0	9 12·7	9 12·8	S. 1 40+0 8 8				
4719	14 6 28·0	9 26·4	5 22·2	9 26·4	9 26·4	N. 5 25—4 4·2				
4784	14 19 31·0	9 25·5	7 1·2	9 25·4	9 25·45	N. 5 10—2 24·25				
4852	14 34 35·3	9 1·2	10 25·7	9 1·3	9 1·25	N. 0 35—1 24·45	30·098	62·4	62·7	59·4
4916	14 46 38·3	9 19·9	5 18·75	9 20·1	9 20·0	N. 0 45—4 1·25				
Anon.	14 53 55·2	9 10·0	8 14·45	9 15·9	9 15·95	N. 1 55—1 1·5				
Anon.	14 58 0·6	9 24·3	5 21·4	9 24·2	9 24·25	N. 1 40—4 2·85				
5032	15 8 49·5	9 20·4	12 14·7	9 20·3	9 20·35	N. 4 20+2 28·35				
5054	15 12 22·3	9 25·7	8 30·8	9 25·8	9 25·75	S. 1 45+0 28·95				00·2
5151	15 29 33·5	10 12·3	10 27·0	10 12·2	10 12·25	N. 4 40+0 14·75				59 6
Anon.	15 34 48·5	9 32·4	9 28·35	9 32·5	9 32·45	N. 2 50—0 4·1				59 4
5227	15 41 31·0	10 3·8	13 30·9	10 3·9	10 3·85	N. 0 45+3 27·05	30·087	62·2	62·5	59·0
5272	15 47 44·0	10 27·3	11 33·4	10 27·1	10 27·2	N. 5 10+1 6·2				
5331	15 56 48·8	9 7·75	6 31·8	9 7·75	9 7·75	S. 2 25+2 9·95				
5374	16 1 49·5	9 17·9	11 7·7	9 17·9	9 17·9	N. 4 55+1 23·8				
5435	16	8 31·0	8 5·0	8 31·0	8 31·0	S. 3 25—0 26·0	30·075	61·8		57·7
Anon.	16 14 22·8	8 18·4	10 27·2	8 18·5	8 18·45	N. 1 5+2 8·75				
5508	16 21 39·5	9 5·3	8 10·5	9 5·5	9 5·5	S. 0 25+0 28·0				
5588	16 34 5·5	10 0·8	6 2·0	10 0·9	10 0·85	N. 2 10—3 32·85				
5632	16 40 31·3	9 19·6	11 1·4	9 19·4	9 19·5	S. 0 5—1 15·9				58 3
5735	16 55 1·2	9 21·6	13 22·75	9 21·6	9 21·6	0 0+4 1·15	30·072	61·7		58·0
5817	17 7 22·8	9 18·0	13 17·8	9 17·8	9 17·9	N. 1 25+3 33·9			62·3	
5881	17 17 52·0	9 30·9	6 2·3	9 30·9	9 30·9	N. 4 15—3 28·6				
5915	17 23 28·2	9 25·3	13 23·8	9 25·3	9 25·3	S. 3 5—3 32·5				55·8
5960	17 30 18·5	10 10·3	9 25·9	10 10·2	10 10·25	N. 1 50—0 18·35				
6016	17 39 30·5	10 7·6	14 23·25	10 7·5	10 7·55	N. 2 15+4 15·7	30·064	61·0		55·2
6074	17 49 32·5	9 28·6	13 30·0	9 28·6	9 28·6	N. 3 40+4 1·4				55·2
6115	17 56 15·2	10 6·7	11 30·7	10 6·5	10 6·6	N. 3 30+1 24·1			62·2	55·2
6145	18 0 30·2	9 28·7	12 6·3	9 28·5	9 28·6	N. 3 10+2 11·7				
6186	18 7 31·4	9 13·7	6 4 55	9 13·6	9 13·65	S. 2 50+3 9·1				55·4
6233	18 14 16·2	9 8·1	7 23·2	9 8·1	9 8·1	S. 0 30+1 18·9	30·057	60·6		55·3
6275	18 20 14·5	9 17·3	5 12·5		9 17·23	N. 0 50—4 4·73				
6285	18 21 18·2		11 13 1	9 17·1	9 17·23	N. 0 50+1 29·87				
6305	18	9 17·3	7 6·9	9 17·2	9 17·23	N. 0 50—2 10·33				55·0
6414	18 43 8·2	9 29·1	12 11·6	9 20·3	9 29·2	N. 3 0+2 16·4	30·054	60·5	62·4	55·1
6525	18	9 16·4	7 17·8	9 16·4	9 16·4	N. 5 10—1 32·6				
6639	19 17 32·4	9 14·7	6 23·7	9 14·8	9 14·75	N. 3 55—2 25·05				
Anon.	19 21 44·7	9 0·5	13 21·1	9 6·6	9 6·55	N. 4 5+4 14·55				
6877	19 54 53·0	9 14·0	12 33·0	9 14·0	9 14·0	N. 1 25+3 19·0	30·043	61·0	62·0	57·3
6848	20 6 30·2	9 29·0	14 24·75	9 29·0	9 29·0	N. 4 15—4 29·75				
7011	20 15 34·5	8 31·4	12 6·0	8 31·2	8 31·28	N. 4 20+3 8·72				
7057	20 21 50·5	8 31·3	6 5·7	8 31·2	8 31·28	N. 4 20—2 25·58				
Anon.	20 24 43·2	8 22·4	12 17·0	8 22·2	8 22·3	N. 4 5+3 28·7				
Anon.	20	8 23·9	5 12·75	8 23·7	8 23·8	N. 4 0—3 11·05				
7207	20 40 39·3	8 7·8	8 24·0	8 7·6	8 7·7	S. 0 25—0 16·3				
Anon.	20 54 0·5	8 20·8	5 6·5	8 20·8	8 20·8	N. 4 15—3 14·3				
Anon.	21 1 10·7	8 22·5	9 8·8	8 22·4	8 22·45	N. 3 35+0 20·35				

May 14.—No. 5032.—The seconds of transit doubtful.
No. 6305.—Observed at 30 seconds after passing the meridian wire.
No. 6525.—At 25 seconds after passing the meridian wire.

♂ MAY 14, 1844.—FACE OF SECTOR EAST—(continued).

Number of B.A.C.	Time by Chronometer.	Micr. for Plumb-line on Dot.	Micr. for Observation of Star.	Micr. for Plumb-line on Dot.	Mean of Micr. for Plumb-line on Dot.	Star's Apparent Zenith Distance.	Barom.	Attd.	Lower.	Out.
	h m s	rev. pts.	rev. pts.	rev. pts.	rev. pts.	° ' rev. pts.	in.			
7386	21 8 54·3	9 0·5	12 27·75	9 0·3	0 0·4	N. 1 5+3 27·35				
Anon.	21 13 0·2	8 33·8	12 10·0	8 33·7	8 33·75	N. 4 5+3 10·25	30·048	61·0	61·5	52·2
Anon.	21 26 6·8	9 5·6	5 32·0	9 5·7	9 5·65	N. 3 35—3 7·65				
7557	21 36 4·5	8 20·8	12 27·3	8 20·9	8 20·85	N. 0 10+4 6·45				
7657	21	0 11·6	8 6·1	9 11·6	9 11·6	N. 4 45—1 5·5				
Anon.	21 56 10·0	9 11·7	9 9·5	9 11·5	9 11·6	N. 4 45—0 2·1				
7842	22 23 3·0	8 29·9	13 28·45	8 30·0	8 29·95	N. 0 45+4 32·5				
7902	22 49 27·5	8 19·5	7 23·5	8 19·3	8 19·4	N. 3 30—0 29·9	30·046	60·5	61·3	51·5

☿ MAY 15, 1844.—FACE OF SECTOR EAST.

Number of B.A.C.	Time by Chronometer.	Micr. for Plumb-line on Dot.	Micr. for Observation of Star.	Micr. for Plumb-line on Dot.	Mean of Micr. for Plumb-line on Dot.	Star's Apparent Zenith Distance.	Barom.	Attd.	Lower.	Out.
2293	6 52 57·0	8 19·6	8 13·4	8 19·6	8 19·6	N. 5 10—0 6·2	29·934	64·8	65·0	75·4
Anon.	15 34 52·1	10 20·5	10 17·0	10 20·7	10 20·6	N. 2 50—0 3·6				
5227	15 41 35·0	10 16·7	14 8·8	10 16·65	10 16·65	N. 0 45+3 26·15				
5272	15 47 48·0	11 5·2	12 12·0	11 5·4	11 5·3	N. 5 10+1 6·7				
5331	15 56 52·5	10 30·1	8 19·8	10 29·9	10 30·0	S. 2 25+2 10·2	30·001	64·3		64·2

FACE OF SECTOR WEST.

Number of B.A.C.	Time by Chronometer.	Micr. for Plumb-line on Dot.	Micr. for Observation of Star.	Micr. for Plumb-line on Dot.	Mean of Micr. for Plumb-line on Dot.	Star's Apparent Zenith Distance.	Barom.	Attd.	Lower.	Out.
4458	13 12 16·2	11 18·7	16 6.4	11 18·7	11 18·7	S. 1 55+4 21·7	29·960	64·6	64·3	67·7
4517	13 24 16·5	10 21·2	10 24·7	10 21·0	10 21·1	N. 5 10—0 3·6	29·965	64·6		67·7
4548	13 30 20·7	10 21·1	10 28·5	10 21·0	10 21·05	N. 5 10+0 7·45				
4579	13 37 15·5	9 10·2	8 14·75	9 10·4	9 10·3	N. 1 40+0 29·55				64·6
4623	13 43 15·8	9 11·0	13 22·8	9 11·0	9 11·0	N. 5 10+4 11·8				
4686	13 57 57·5	9 29·3	10 10·7	9 29·1	9 29·2	S. 1 40+0 15·5				
4719	14 6 24·0	9 14·5	13 21·45	9 14·6	9 14·55	N. 5 25—4 6·9	29·959	64·4		67·3
4784	14	8 21·6	11 16·15	8 21·5	8 21·55	N. 5 10—2 28·6				
Anon.	14 24 31·2	8 16·4	11 20·75	8 16·4	8 16·4	N. 2 10—3 4·35				
4852	14	8 26·2	7 5·5	8 26·5	8 26·35	S. 0 35—1 20·85	29·968	64·4		65·4
4916	14 46 36·5	9 2·75	13 7·3	9 2·95	9 2·85	N. 0 45—4 4·45				
Anon.	14 53	9 1·3	10 8·3	9 1·3	9 1·3	N. 1 55—1 7·0				64·8
Anon.	14 58 14·2	9 17·1	13 25·25	9 17·1	9 17·1	N. 1 40—4 8·15				
5032	15 8 45·5	10 8·4	7 19·6	10 8·5	10 8·45	N. 4 20+2 22·85	29·986	64·3		62·6
5054	15 12 22·5	10 20·3	11 21·7	10 20·2	10 20·25	S. 1 45+1 1·45	30·008	64·3		63·4
5435	16 10 8·2	11 18·4	12 14·7	11 18·2	11 18·3	N. 3 25—0 30·4				
Anon.	16 14 21·8	11 25·6	9 19·9	11 25·5	11 25·55	N. 1 5+2 5·65				64·8
5508	16 21 39·2	10 1·1	10 33·8	10 1·1	10 1·1	S. 0 25+0 32·7				
5588	16 34 3·2	9 21·0	13 23·6	9 21·1	9 21·05	N. 2 10—4 2·55				
5632	16 40 30·2	10 8·5	8 30·95	10 8·8	10 8·65	S. 0 5—1 11·7				
5735	16 55 0·3	10 7·5	6 12·25	10 7·8	10 7·65	0 0+3 29·4	30·007	63·8		61·4
5817	17 7 21·0	10 16·8	6 19·9	10 16·6	10 16·7	N. 1 25+3 30·8				
5881	17 17 48·5	10 18·6	14 16·55	10 18·8	10 18·8	N. 4 15—3 31·75				
5915	17	11 23·5	7 29·45	11 23·4	11 23·45	S. 3 5—3 28·0				
5960	17 30 17·0	11 17·1	12 5·6		11 17·05	N. 1 50—0 22·55				
5964	17 31 14·2		13 33·6	11 17·0	11 17·05	N. 1 50—2 16·55				60·5
6016	17 39 28·5	10 14·3	6 0·05	10 14·1	10 14·2	N. 2 15+4 16·45				
6074	17	9 12·5	5 16·45	9 12·3	9 12·4	N. 3 40+3 29·95				
6115	17 56 12·5	9 11·6	7 26·3	9 11·7	9 11·65	N. 3 30+1 19·35	30·015	63·6		60·5
6145	18 0 27·5	9 25·6	7 19·1	9 25·5	9 25·55	N. 3 10+2 6·45				
6186	18 7 31·4	9 31·8	13 13·1	9 31·9	9 31·85	S. 2 50+3 15·25	30·022	63·5		62·0
6233	18 14 15·3	8 28·4	10 17·0	8 28·3	8 28·35	S. 0 30+1 22·65				

May 14.—No. 7657.—Observed at 30 seconds after passing the meridian wire.
Good definition throughout the 14th.
15.—Anon. 14ʰ 53ᵐ. Observed at 10 seconds after passing the meridian wire.
A north-west gale advancing.

♃ MAY 16, 1844.—FACE OF SECTOR WEST.

Number of B.A.C.	Time by Chronometer.	Micr. for Plumb-line on Dot.	Micr. for Observation of Star.	Micr. for Plumb line on Dot.	Mean of Micr. for Plumb-line on Dot.	Star's Apparent Zenith Distance.	Barom.	Thermometers. Attd.	Lower.	Out.
	h m s	rev. pts.	rev. pts.	rev. pts.	rev. pts.	° ' rev. pts.	in.			
1802	5 34 24·5	7 11·4	5 4·7	7 11·2	7 11·3	S. 0 15—2 6·6			64·2	
2293	6 52 52·2	8 2·7	8 13·55	8 2·4	8 2·55	N. 5 10—0 11·0			64·2	
6639	19 17 38·8	9 17·1	12 13·5	9 17·0	9 17·05	N. 3 55—2 30 45	29·939	63·5	63·6	56·8
Anon.	19 21 46·0	9 8·4	4 31·9	9 8·0	9 8·2	N. 4 5+4 10·3				
FACE OF SECTOR EAST.										
4458	13 12 24·0	9 12·2	4 30·6	9 12·2	9 12·2	S. 1 55+4 15·6	30·001	63·4	63·0	55·9
4517	13		9 26·3	9 27·5	9 26·7	9 26·5	N. 5 10+0 1·0			
4548	13 30 32·0	9 26·5	9 22·75	9 26·5	9 26·5	N. 5 10—0 3·75			
4579	13 37 25·2	10 16·1	11 17·55	10 16·0	10 16·05	N. 1 40+1 1·5				56·4
4623	13 43 25·0	10 11·6	6 4·5	10 11·5	10 11·55	N. 1 45—4 7·05	29·985	63·0		55·4
4719	14 6 36·0	10 9·2	6 4·1	10 9·3	10 9·25	N. 5 25—4 5·15			
4852	14 34 42·5	9 20·0	11 9·8	9 19·8	9 19·9	S. 0 35—1 23·9			
4916	14 46 46·0	9 28·9	5 27·5	9 29·0	9 28·95	N. 0 45—4 1·45			
Anon.	14 54 2·5	9 23·8	8 22·0	9 23·9	9 23·85	N. 1 55—1 1·85			
Anon.	14 58 14·0	9 27·0	5 23·6	9 26·8	9 26·9	N. 1 40—4 3·3			64·2
5032	15 8 57·0	10 6·9	13 0·3	10 6·7	10 6·8	N. 4 20+2 27·5			
5054	15 12 29·5	9 26·5	8 30·5	9 26·6	9 26·55	N. 1 45+0 30·05	29·961	62·4		55·5
5151	15 29 41·0	10 5·2	10 20·1	10 5·6	10 5·4	N. 4 40+0 14·7			
Anon.	15 34 56·0	10 18·9	10 14·6	10 19·1	10 19·0	N. 2 50—0 4·4			
5272	15 47 52·0	9 31·5	11 3·8	9 31·8	9 31·65	N. 5 10+1 6·15			
5331	15 56 56·0	9 21·6	7 10·6	9 21·3	9 21·45	S. 2 25+2 10·85			
5374	16 1 57·2	9 20·9	11 11·8	9 21·0	9 20·95	N. 4 55+1 24·85			
5435	16 10 16·3	9 14·5	8 23·0	9 14·6	9 14·55	N. 3 25—0 25·55				57·3
Anon.	16 14 30·3	8 33·8	11 9·8	8 33·9	8 33·85	N. 1 5+2 9·95			63·8
5508	16 21 47·0	9 0·5	8 5·5	9 0·5	9 0·5	S. 0 25+0 28·95			
5588	16 34 13·0	8 31·6	5 0·7	8 31·8	8 31·7	N. 2 10—3 31·0			
5632	16 40 39·0	8 26·8	10 8·6	8 26·8	8 26·8	N. 0 5—1 15·8				57·6
5735	16	8 32·5	13 0·0	8 32·4	8 32·45	0 0+4 1·55	29·943	63·0		63·3
5817	17 7 30·2	9 5·6	13 6·4	9 5·7	9 5·65	N. 1 25+4 0 75			
5881	17 17 59·3	9 7·0	5 13·0	9 6·8	9 6·9	N. 4 15—3 27·9			
5915	17 23 35·5	8 23·0	12 21·5	8 23·0	8 23·0	S. 3 5—3 32·5				62·0
5900	17 30 26·5	8 31 5	8 14·0		8 31·45	N. 1 50—0 17·45			
5904	17 31 24·0		6 20·1	8 31·4	8 31·45	N. 1 50—2 11·35			
6016	17 39 37·8	9 4·1	13 20·65	9 4·3	9 4·2	N. 2 15+4 16·35			
6115	17 56 23·0	9 16·8	11 7·05	9 16·0	9 16·85	N. 3 30+1 24·2	29·936	63·2		60·0
6145	18 0 37·8	9 11·4	11 22·8	9 11·3	9 11·35	N. 3 10+2 11·45			
6186	18 7 38·2	8 25·8	5 16·8	8 25·5	8 25·65	S. 2 50+3 8·85			
6233	18 14 23·4	9 13·5	7 27·85	9 13·5	9 13·5	S. 0 30—1 19·65				58·2
6275	18 20 22·0	9 22·5	5 17·0		9 22·5	N. 0 50—4 5·5			
6285	18 21 25·5		11 18·5	9 22·6	9 22·5	N. 0 50+1 30·0			
6305	18 24 18·4	9 22·4	7 10·0	9 22·5	9 22·5	N. 0 50—2 12·5	29·933	62·7		57·7
6414	18 43 16·0	10 2·7	12 19·85	10 2·9	10 2·8	N. 3 0+2 17·05	29·938	63·5	63·7	57·6
6499	18 53 16·8	9 10·0	10 7·7	9 19·0	9 19·0	N. 3 50+0 22·7			
6523	18 58 17·2	9 24·5	7 25·1	9 24·5	9 24·5	N. 5 5—1 33·4			
6753	19 36 7·0	9 10·5	9 11·9	9 11·7	9 11·6	N. 2 40+0 0·3			
6877	19 55 0·5	9 12·0	12 31·45	9 12·2	9 12·1	N. 1 25+3 19·35			
6948	20	9 18·7	14 16·3	9 18·9	9 13·0	N. 4 20+5 7·88			
7011	20 15 43·0	9 12·8	12 20·8	9 13·0	9 12·92	N. 4 20—2 24·42			
7026	20 17 33·0		12 14·0	9 13·0	9 12·92				
7057	20 21 58·3	9 12·9	6 22·5	9 12·9	9 12·92				
Anon.	20 24 50·5	8 28·3	12 24·2	8 28·3	8 28·3	N. 4 5+3 20·9			
Anon.	20 34 20·5	9 3·9	5 26·3	9 3·6	9 3·75	N. 4 0—3 11·45	29·953	63·5	63·5	62·8
7207	20 40 56·3	8 20·2	9 3·0	8 20·0	8 20·1	S. 0 25—0 16·9			
Anon.	20	9 3·4	5 23·6	9 3·2	9 3·3	N. 4 15—3 13·7			

May 16.—No. 4517.—Observed at 22 seconds after passing the meridian wire ; and No. 6948—at 25 seconds after. The seconds of transit of Anon. 15ʰ 34ᵐ, and of Nos. 5588 and 6753 are doubtful.

♃ MAY 16, 1844.—FACE OF SECTOR EAST—(continued).

Number of B.A.C.	Time by Chronometer.	Micr. for Plumb-line on Dot.	Micr. for Observation of Star.	Micr. for Plumb-line on Dot.	Mean of Micr. for Plumb-line on Dot.	Star's Apparent Zenith Distance.	Barom.	Attd.	Lower.	Out.
	h m s	rev. pts.	rev. pts.	rev. pts.	rev. pts.	° ' rev. pts.	in.			
Anon.	21 1 18·5	9 2·8	9 22·55	9 2·6	9 2·7	N. 3 35+0 19·85				
7386	21 9 2·2	8 24·2	12 19·5	8 24·2	8 24·2	N. 1 5+3 20·3				
Anon.	21 13 8·0	8 30·4	12 8·75	8 30·3	8 30·35	N. 4 5+3 12·4				
Anon.	21 26 15·0	8 18·5	5 11·95	8 18·7	8 18·6	N. 3 35—3 6·65				
7557	21	7 31·7	12 7·95	7 32·0	7 31·85	N. 0 10+4 10·1				
7657	21	7 31·9	6 27·55	7 31·8	7 31·35	N. 4 45—1 4·3				
Anon.	21 56	7 32·9	7 32·9	7 32·8	7 32·85	N. 4 45+0 0·05	29·065	62·5	63·4	55·4
7842	22 23 10·7	7 16·4	12 14·5	7 16·3	7 16·35	N. 0 45+4 32·15				
7966	22 44 23·0	7 16·9	6 11·9	7 17·0	7 16·95	N. 0 15—1 5·05				
7992	22 49 35·3	9 6·5	8 11·2	9 6·7	9 6·6	N. 3 30—0 29·4	29·975	62·0	62·8	56·0

♀ MAY 17, 1844.— FACE OF SECTOR WEST.

Number of B.A.C.	Time by Chronometer.	Micr. for Plumb-line on Dot.	Micr. for Observation of Star.	Micr. for Plumb-line on Dot.	Mean of Micr. for Plumb-line on Dot.	Star's Apparent Zenith Distance.	Barom.	Attd.	Lower.	Out.
2293	6 52 56·5	8 13·2	8 23·7	8 13·3	8 13·25	N. 5 10—0 10·45	29·927	65·3	65·0	68·7
4517	13 24 24·0	7 27·0	7 31·9	7 26·9	7 26·95	N. 5 10—0 4·95	29·915	63·6		56·3
4548	13 30 28·5	7 27·0	8 1·7	7 26·9	7 26·95	N. 5 10—0 8·75				55·6
4579	13 37 23·5	8 21·8	7 25·9	8 21·9	8 21·85	N. 1 40+0 29·95				56·0
4623	13 43 23·5	9 19·5	13 29·95	9 19·4	9 19·45	N. 1 45—4 10·5	29·914	63·2	64·4	56·0
4719	14 6 32·0	8 32·7	13 7·4	8 32·5	8 32·6	N. 5 25—4 8·8				56·2
5054	15 12 29·0	10 0·0	11 1·3	10 0·2	10 0·1	S. 1 45+1 1·2				
5151	15	9 0·6	8 24·0	9 0·5	9 0·55	N. 4 40+0 10·55	29·896	62·5		58·2
Anon.	15 34 53·7	8 23·7	8 32·9	8 23·5	8 23·6	N. 2 50—0 9·3				
5227	15 41 37·2	8 27·1	5 3·25	8 27·0	8 27·05	N. 0 45+3 23·8				
5272	15 47 48·0	8 25·1	7 23·7	8 25·2	8 25·15	N. 5 10+1 1·45				
5331	15 56 56·0	9 3·8	11 19·5	9 3·8	9 3·8	S. 2 25+2 15·7				
Comp.	15 57 36·5		6 22·9	9 3·8	9 3·8	S. 2 25—2 14·9				
5374	16 1 54·5	8 6·8	6 22·3	8 6·7	8 6·75	N. 4 45+1 18·45				
5435	16 10 14·0	8 0·1	8 31·1	7 33·9	8 0·0	N. 3 25—0 31·1	29·883	62·6		60·1
Anon.	16 14 28·8	7 24·5	5 19·8	7 24·5	7 24·5	N. 1 5+2 4·7				
5508	16 21 46·2	7 27·8	8 26·45	7 27·7	7 27·75	S. 0 25+0 32·7				
5588	16 34 10·6	7 16·9	11 19·25	7 17·0	7 16·95	N. 2 10—4 2·3				
5632	16 40 38·0	7 17·3	6 6·45	7 17·1	7 17·2	S. 0 5—1 10·75	29·882	63·4		60·6
5735	16 55 8·0	7 17·6	3 22·0	7 17·0	7 17·6	O 0+3 29·6				
5817	17 7 28·2	7 9·3	3 12·55	7 9·1	7 9·2	N. 1 25+3 30·65				
5881	17 17 56·8	7 13·6	11 11·4	7 13·4	7 13·5	N. 4 15—3 31·9				
6016	17 39 36·0	9 1·3	4 21·0	9 1·3	9 1·3	N. 2 15+4 14·3	29·688	63·8	63·8	63·6
6074	17 49 37·2	9 0·3	5 4·3	9 0·5	9 0·4	N. 3 40+3 30·1				
6115	17 56 20·2	8 28·6	7 9·75	8 28·5	8 28·55	N. 3 30+1 18·9	29·898	63·7		65·3
6145	18 0	8 27·8	6 21·2	8 27·8	8 27·8	N. 3 10+2 6·6				
6186	18 7 39·2	9 4·2	12 18·7	9 4·2	9 4·2	S. 2 50+3 14·5				
6233	18	8 31·5	10 20·0	8 31·7	8 31·6	S. 0 30+1 22·4	29·883	64·0	64·2	65·0
6414	18	9 7·4	6 29·0	9 7·4	9 7·4	N. 3 0+2 12·4				
6489	18 53 13·8	8 19·7	8 2·45	8 19·7	8 19·7	N. 3 50+0 17·25				
6525	18 58 13·5	8 27·8	10 33·6	8 27·8	8 27·8	N. 5 5—2 5·8				

FACE OF SECTOR EAST.

Number of B.A.C.	Time by Chronometer.	Micr. for Plumb-line on Dot.	Micr. for Observation of Star.	Micr. for Plumb-line on Dot.	Mean of Micr. for Plumb-line on Dot.	Star's Apparent Zenith Distance.	Barom.	Attd.	Lower.	Out.
4784	14 19 42·8	10 3·1	7 13·25	10 3·2	10 3·15	N. 5 10—2 23·9				64·4
Anon.	14 24 45·2	9 33·0	6 31·85	9 33·1	9 33·05	N. 1 20—3 1·2				
4916	14 46 50·2	9 32·3	5 30·8	9 32·4	9 32·35	N. 0 45—4 1·55				
Anon.	14 54 6·8	9 29·45	8 26·45	9 29·45	9 29·45	N. 1 55—1 3·0	29·903	62·4		54·9
Anon.	14 58 18·0	10 2·35	5 31·5	10 2·3	10 2·33	N. 1 40—4 4·83				

May 16.—No. 7657 was observed at 15 seconds after passing the meridian wire.
Anon. 21ʰ 56ᵐ.—The observer by accident touched the pulley frame with his elbow.
17.—The sky became overcast after the 6525 observation.

T

(MAY 20, 1844.—FACE OF SECTOR EAST.

Number of B. A.C.	Time by Chronometer.	Micr. for Plumb-line on Dot.	Micr. for Observation of Star.	Micr. for Plumb-line on Dot.	Mean of Micr. for Plumb-line on Dot.	Star's Apparent Zenith Distance.	Barom.	Thermometers.		
								Attd.	Lower.	Out.
	h m s	rev. pts.	rev. pts.	rev. pts.	rev. pts.	o ' rev. pts.	in.			
4517	13 24 42·5	11 21·3	11 21·7	11 21·5	11 21·4	N. 5 10+0 0·3	30·245	61·2	64·2	50·0
4348	13 30 46·8	11 21·4	11 17·7	11 21·3	11 21·35	N. 5 10—0 3·65				
4570	13 37 39·3	11 2·0	12 2·4	11 2·0	11 2·0	N. 1 40+1 0·4				
4623	13 43 45·0	10 17·3	6 10·6	10 17·4	10 17·35	N. 1 45—4 6·75				
4719	14 6 50·5	10 3·7	5 33·5	10 3·5	10 3·6	N. 5 25—4 4·1				
5054	15 12 45·2	9 24·5	8 28·0	9 24·5	9 24·5	S. 1 45+0 30·5	30·242	60·4	63·9	49·4
Anon.	15 35 11·2	9 26·4	9 20·9	9 26·4	9 26·4	N. 2 50—0 5·5				
5227	15 41 53·8	9 3·8	12 29·45	9 4·0	9 3·9	N. 0 45+3 25·55				
5272	15 48 6·5	9 10·8	10 14·9	9 10·8	9 10·8	N. 5 10+1 4·1				
5331	15 57 10·5	10 29·6	8 18·6			10 29·65	S. 2 25+2 11·05				
Comp.	15 57 50·7		13 13·8	10 29·7	10 29·65	S. 2 25—2 18·15				
5374	16 2 11·2	11 13·2	13 1·0	11 13·3	11 13·25	S. 1 45+1 21·75				
5435	16 10 31·5	11 10·3	10 16·05	11 10·0	11 10·15	N. 3 25—0 28·1				
Anon.	16 14 45·0	11 5·0	13 12·75	11 4·9	11 4·95	N. 1 5+2 7·8				
5508	16 22 2·0	10 31·9	10 1·0	10 31·6	10 31·75	S. 0 25+0 30·75			62·6	
5588	16 34 27·5	11 11·7	7 12·4	11 11·5	11 11·6	N. 2 10—3 33·2				
5632	16 40 54·5	10 1·0	11 14·0	10 0·9	10 0·95	S. 0 5—1 13·05	30·230	59·6		48·4
5735	16 55 23·5	10 2·8	14 3·6	10 2·9	10 2·85	0 0+4 0·75				
5817	17 7 45·5	9 20·3	13 19·05	9 20·3	9 20·3	N. 1 25+3 32·75				
5891	17 18 15·0	9 26·5	5 30·8	9 26·5	9 26·5	N. 4 15—3 29·7	30·227	50·4		47·4
6016	17 39 53·5	9 29·1	14 11·0	9 29·5	9 29·3	N. 2 15+4 15·7				
6074	17 49 55·0	9 0·3	13 0·4	9 0·4	9 0·35	N. 3 40+4 0·05				
6115	17	8 31·2	10 20·1	8 31·15	8 31·15	N. 3 30+1 22·95				
6145	18 0 53·0	6 30·6	9 7·5	6 30·6	6 30·6	N. 3 10+2 10·9				
6186	18 7 54·5	6 15·3	3 5·0	6 15·1	6 15·2	S. 2 50+3 10·2				
6233	18 14 39·0	9 13·3	7 26·9	9 13·1	9 13·2	S. 0 30+1 20·3	30·227	59·4		47·7

FACE OF SECTOR WEST.

4784	14 19 46·0	9 18·8	12 13·25	9 18·8	9 18·8	N. 5 10—2 28·45				
Anon.	14 24 51·0	9 22·2	12 27·8	9 22·0	9 22·1	N. 1 20—3 5·7			50·5	
Anon.	14 58	9 33·5	14 7·0	9 33·4	9 33·45	N. 1 40—4 7·55				
6275	18 20 32·5	9 5·3	13 14·1			9 5·3	N. 0 50—4 8·8				
6285	18 21 36·0		7 1·9	9 5·3	9 5·3	N. 0 50+2 3·4				
6305	18 24 29·0	9 5·3	11 20·4	9 5·3	9 5·3	N. 0 50—2 15·1				
6414	18	8 18·5	6 8·1	8 18·6	8 18·55	N. 3 0+2 10·45				
6489	18 53 25·2	8 23·0	8 6·9	8 23·7	8 23·8	N. 3 50+0 16·9				
6525	18 58 25·5	8 15·0	10 22·6	8 15·0	8 15·0	N. 5 5—2 7·6	30·228	59·5	60·8	42·0
6639	19	8 14·0	11 10·7	8 14·1	8 14·05	N. 3 55—2 30·65				
6877	19 55 10·5	7 32·3	4 15·55	7 32·4	7 32·35	N. 1 25+3 16·8				
6948	20 6 53·0	7 21·4	2 30·0	7 21·5	7 21·45	N. 3 25+4 25·45				
7011	20 15	10 4·8	7 3·9	10 4·8	10 4·76	N. 4 20+3 0·86				
7026	20 17 41·7		7 7·45	10 4·7	10 4·76	N. 4 20+2 31·31				
7057	20 22 7·0	10 4·7	13 0·7	10 4·8	10 4·76	N. 4 20—2 29·04				
Anon.	20 24 59·5	9 33·0	6 9·5	9 33·0	9 33·0	N. 4 5+3 23·5				
Anon.	20 34 30·0	10 13·6	13 29·75	10 13·5	10 13·55	N. 4 0—3 16·2				
7207	20 40 58·0	10 19·3	10 4·0	10 19·1	10 19·2	S. 0 25—0 15·2	30·234	50·2	61·2	46·3
Anon.	20 54 17·0	10 1·3	13 18·4	10 1·0	10 1·15	N. 4 15—3 17·25				
Anon.	21 1 27·2	8 32·8	8 17·3	8 32·8	8 32·8	N. 3 35+0 15·5				
7386	21 9 13·0	9 16·0	5 23·85	9 16·1	9 16·05	N. 1 5+3 26·2				
Anon.	21	9 19·7	6 13·3	9 20·0	9 19·85	N. 4 5+3 6·55				
Anon.	21 26 24·0	10 6·6	13 18·6	10 6·5	10 6·55	N. 3 35—3 12·05				
7557	21 36 23·2	8 33·8	4 30·1	8 33·8	8 33·8	N. 0 10+4 3·7				
7657	21 52 35·0	9 4·25	10 13·0	9 4·0	9 4·16	N. 4 45—1 8·84				
Anon.	21 56 26·0	9 4·2	0 9·3	9 4·2	9 4·16	N. 4 45—0 5·14	30·260	50·0	61·0	45·9
7842	22 23 21·2	0 10·5	13 11·1	9 10·5	9 10·5	N. 0 50—4 0·6				

May 20.—The Sector was reversed between 14ʰ 6ᵐ and 14ʰ 19ᵐ
  „ 14 68 „ 15 12 and
  „ 18 14 „ 18 20
But for the Press, all the observations made in one position this day have been arranged for that position in the order of time.
Anon. 14ʰ 58ᵐ.—Observed at 30 seconds after passing the middle wire ; and No. 6639, 25 seconds after.
Bad definition throughout.

☾ MAY 20, 1844.—FACE OF SECTOR WEST—(continued).

Number of B.A.C.	Time by Chronometer.	Micr. for Plumb-line on Dot.	Micr. for Observation of Star.	Micr. for Plumb-line on Dot.	Mean of Micr. for Plumb-line on Dot.	Star's Apparent Zenith Distance.	Barom.	Thermometers. Atid.	Lower.	Out.
	h m s	rev. pts.	rev. pts.	rev. pts.	rev. pts.	° ′ rev. pts.	in.			
7966	22 44 34·0	8 29·1	10 3·4	8 29·3	8 29·2	N. 0 15—1 8·2				
7992	22 49 44·5	9 4·4	10 4·85	9 4·2	9 4·3	N. 3 30—1 0·55	30·262	59·0	61·2	48·0

♂ MAY 21, 1844.—FACE OF SECTOR WEST.

4517	13 24 40·2	13 33 3	14 5·0	13 33·3	13 33·3	N. 5 10—0 5·7	30·302	62·2	63·2	56·0
4543	13 30 44·5	13 33·3	14 8·5	13 33·4	13 33·35	N. 5 10—0 9·15				
4579	13 37 48·5	12 6·5	11 11·6	12 6·3	12 6·4	N. 1 40+0 28·8				
4719	14 6 47·2	10 21·4	14 30·9	10 21·4	10 21·4	N. 5 25—4 9·5			63·2	

FACE OF SECTOR EAST.

4784	14 19 57·5	10 10·0	7 19·2	10 10·0	10 10·0	N. 5 10—2 24·8				
Anon.	14 24 59·5	9 31·1	6 29·8	9 31·0	9 31·05	N. 1 20—3 1·25	30·300	61·6		57·0
4916	14 47 42·0	9 27·0	5 24·5	9 27·1	9 27·05	N. 0 45—4 2·55				
Anon.	14 58 33·3	10 3·7	6 0·45	10 3·9	10 3·8	N. 1 40—4 3·35				55·6
5054	15 12 48·7	9 21·7	8 24·3	9 21·6	9 21·65	S. 1 45+0 31·35				
5151	15 30 0·3	9 20·5	9 33·5	9 20·3	9 20·4	N. 4 40+0 13·1				
Anon.	15 35 15·5	9 15·6	9 9·8	9 15 5	9 15·55	N. 2 50—0 5·75				
5227	15 41 58·0	9 1·9	12 27·75	9 2·0	9 1·95	N. 0 45+3 25·8				
5272	15 48 11·5	8 33·5	10 6·15	8 33·5	8 33·5	N. 5 10+1 6·65				
5331	15 57 15·2	8 4·0	5 27·8	8 3·95	8 3·95	S. 2 25+2 19·75				
Comp.	15 57 55·0		10 23·7	8 3·9	8 3·95	S. 2 25—2 19·75	30·293	61·4		55·0
5374	16 2 16·2	8 15·3	10 4·45	8 15·3	8 15·3	N. 4 55+1 23·15				
5435	16 10 36·2	8 19·2	7 26·65	8 19·1	8 19·15	N. 3 25—0 26·5				
Anon.	16 14 49·3	8 13·9	10 21·5	8 14·0	8 13·95	N. 1 5+2 7·55				
5508.	16 22 5·9	7 31·0	7 1·4	7 30·7	7 30·85	S. 0 25+0 29·45				
5598	16	8 30·3	4 30·1	8 30·0	8 30·15	N. 2 10—4 0·05				

FACE OF SECTOR WEST.

5735	16 55 23·5	8 25·5	4 30·5	8 25·3	8 25·4	0 0+3 28·9				
5817	17 7 44·5	8 25·4	4 29·5	8 25·2	8 25·3	N. 1 25+3 29·8				
5881	17 18 12·0	9 1·0	13 1·05	9 0·9	9 0·95	N. 4 15—4 0·1	30·293	60·8		53·7
6016	17 39 51·5	8 12·0	3 32·5	8 11·9	8 11·95	N. 2 15+4 13·45				
6074	17 49 53·2	8 9·5	4 14·4	8 9·4	8 9·45	N. 3 40+3 29·05				
6115	17 56 36·2	8 3·7	6 21·0	8 3·65	8 3·68	N. 3 30+1 16·68				
6145	18 0 51·5	8 4·8	5 33·0	8 4·6	8 4·7	N. 3 10+2 5·7				
6186	18 8 55·2	8 16·4	11 31·3	8 16·2	8 16·3	S. 2 50+3 15·0	30·289	60·6		53·6
6275	18 20 36·2	7 33·4	12 9·25	7 33·38	7 33·38	N. 0 50—4 9·87				
6285	18 21 40·0		6 7·7	7 33·3	7 33·38	N. 0 50+1 25·08				
6305	18 24 33·5	7 33·5	10 16·1	7 33·3	7 33·38	N. 0 50—2 16·72				

FACE OF SECTOR EAST.

6414	18 43 35·2	8 11·4	10 28·95	8 11·3	8 11·35	N. 3 0+2 17·6			62·7	
6489	18 53 35·5	7 28·5	8 17·8	7 28·5	7 28·5	N. 3 50+0 23·3				
6525	18 58 36·2	7 17·1	5 17·5	7 17·1	7 17·1	N. 5 5—1 33·6	30·288	60·5	62·7	54·0
6639	19 17 59·6	7 21·6	4 30·9	7 21·5	7 21·55	N. 3 55—2 24·65				
Anon.	19 21 11·5	7 4·3	11 18·85	7 4·3	7 4·3	N. 5 5+4 14·55				
6877	19 55 19·7	7 24·8	11 10·3	7 24·6	7 24·7	N. 1 25+3 19·6				
6948	20 7 2·5	8 9·3	13 5·5	8 9·2	8 23·0	N. 3 25+4 30·25				
7011	20 16 1·7	8 23·1	11 31·4	8 23·0	8 23·0	N. 4 20+3 8·0				
7026	20 17 53·2		11 23·35	8 22·9	8 23·0	N. 4 20+3 0·35				
7057	20 22 17·5	8 23·0	5 31·5	8 23·0	8 23·0	N. 4 20—2 25·5				
Anon.	20 25 10·2	8 13·5	12 7·3	8 13·5	8 13·5	N. 4 5+3 27·8				
Anon.	20	8 29·8	5 18·35	8 29·6	8 29·7	N. 4 0—3 11·35				

May 21.—Anon. 15ʰ 35ᵐ.—The seconds doubtful. Also of 6186.
Fair definition, except in the middle of the night.

♂ MAY 21, 1844.—FACE OF SECTOR EAST—(continued.)

Number of B.A.C.	Time by Chronometer.	Micr. for Plumb-line on Dot.	Micr. for Observation of Star.	Micr. for Plumb-line on Dot.	Mean of Micr. for Plumb-line on Dot.	Star's Apparent Zenith Distance.	Barom.	Thermometers.		
								Attd.	Lower.	Out.
	h m s	rev. pts.	rev. pts.	rev. pts.	rev. pts.	° ' rev. pts.	in.			
7207	20 41 5·4	9 9·6	9 27·5	9 9·5	9 9·55	S. 0 25—0 17·95				
Anon.	20		9 27·0	6 14·2	9 26·8	9 26·9	N. 4 15—3 12·7			
Anon.	21 1 37·8	8 17·7	9 4·75	8 17·5	8 17·6	N. 3 35+0 21·15	30·290	60·5	62·7	54·2
7386	21 9 21·4	8 16·8	12 12·7	8 16·8	8 16·8	N. 1 5+3 29·9				
Anon.	21 13 26·7	8 26·5	12 4·8	8 26·6	8 26·55	N. 4 5+3 12·25				
Anon.	21 26 33·8	8 31·0	5 25·1	8 31·2	8 31·1	N. 3 35—3 6 0				
7557	21 36 31·0	6 18·9	12 28·65	8 19·0	8 18·95	N. 0 10+4 9·7				
7657	21 52 46·0	8 27·5	7 22·0	8 27·5	8 27·48	N. 4 45—1 5·48				
Anon.	21 55 37·0	8 27·5	8 27·2	8 27·4	8 27·46	N. 4 45—0 0·28	30·294	60·5	62·2	53·6
7842	22 23 30·2	8 21·3	4 24·35	8 21·3	8 21·3	N. 0 50—3 30·95				
7909	22 33 34·6	8 33·2	10 20·9	8 33·0	8 33·1	N. 3 45+1 21·8				
7966	22 43 43·2	8 14·0	7 9·75	8 14·0	8 14·0	N. 0 15—1 4·25				
7992	22 48 54·4	9 4·4	8 10·35	9 4·3	9 4·35	N. 3 30—0 28·0	30·296	60·2	61·7	57·2

♀ MAY 22, 1844.—FACE OF SECTOR EAST.

Number of B.A.C.	Time by Chronometer.	Micr. for Plumb-line on Dot.	Micr. for Observation of Star.	Micr. for Plumb-line on Dot.	Mean of Micr. for Plumb-line on Dot.	Star's Apparent Zenith Distance.	Barom.	Attd.	Lower.	Out.
2293	6 52 25·2	8 32·5	8 27·8	8 31·8	8 32·15	N. 5 10—0 5·65	30·276	64·2	64·2	67·0
4548	13 29 53.8	10 23·1	10 19·35	10 23·1	10 23·1	N. 5 10—0 3·75	30·280	63·2	63·0	61·5
4579	13 36 47·2	10 5·8	11 6·7	10 5·6	10 5·7	N. 1 40+1 1·0	30·288	63·2		61·5
4623	13 42 46·8	9 3·8	4 30·65	9 3·7	9 3·75	N. 1 45—4 7·1				
4719	14 5 56·8	9 5·5	5 0·95	9 5·4	9 5·45	N. 5 25—4 4·5				61·6
4784	14 19 0·2	8 32·5	6 8·1	8 32·5	8 32·5	N. 5 10—2 24·4				
Anon.	14 24 3·3	8 12·9	5 12·0	8 13·0	8 12·95	N. 1 20—3 0·95	30·280	63·3		62·2
Anon.	14 53 24·3	7 33·1	6 30·8	7 33·2	7 33·15	N. 1 55—1 2·35				
Anon.	14 57 35·8	8 19·2	4 15·0	8 19 0	8 19·1	N. 1 40—4 4·1				

FACE OF SECTOR WEST.

5054	15 11 47·4	8 30·9	9 32·3	8 31·0	8 30·95	S. 1 45+1 1·35				
5151	15 28 55·2	8 11·9	8 2·0	8 11·8	8 11·85	N. 4 40+0 9·85				
Anon.	15 34 12·0	8 5·6	8 15·35	8 5·5	8 5·55	N. 2 50—0 9·8				
5227	15 40 55·2	9 8·9	5 19·85	9 8·8	9 8·85	N. 0 45+3 23·0				
5331	15 55 15·0	10 1·7	12 16·4		10 1·7	S. 2 25+2 14·7				62·4
Comp.	15		7 21·0	10 1·7	10 1·7	S. 2 25—2 14·7				
5374	16 1 11·4	9 26·1	8 9·1	9 26·1	9 26·1	N. 4 5+1 17·0				
5435	16 9 32·1	9 14·5	10 11·7	9 14·5	9 14·5	N. 3 25—0 31·2	30·265	63·0		62·4
Anon.	16 13 47·3	9 18·0	7 13·45	9 18·0	9 18·0	N. 1 5+2 4·55				
5508	16 21 4·8	9 14·8	10 13·95	9 14·7	9 14·75	S. 0 25+0 33·2				
5588	16	9 12·3	13 15·3	9 12·5	9 12·4	N. 2 10—4 2·9				
5632	16 39 56·2		17 12·5	18 23·1		S. 0 5—1 10·6				

FACE OF SECTOR EAST.

5735	16 54 31·0	9 27·5	13 28·0	9 27·5	9 27·5	0 0+4 0·5				
5817	17 6 52·1	9 26·5	13 26·5	9 26·4	9 26·45	N. 1 25+4 0·05				
5915	17 22 57·8	10 5·1	14 3·85	10 5·2	10 5·15	S. 3 5—3 32·7	30·254	63·0		62·4
6016	17 38 59·2	9 32·5	14 14·75	9 32·5	9 32·5	N. 2 15+4 16·25				
6074	17 49 1·2	9 27·6	13 28·3	9 27·4	9 27·5	N. 3 40+4 0·8				
6115	17 55 44·2	9 30·3	11 20·5	9 30·1	9 30·2	N. 3 30+1 24·3				
6145	17 59 59·2	8 31·8	11 9·45	8 31·7	8 31·75	N. 3 10+2 11·7			63·5	
6186	18 7 0·8	8 8·0	4 33·5	8 8·0	8 8·0	S. 2 50+3 8·9				
6233	18 13 45·1	8 28·7	7 10·35	8 28·9	8 28·8	S. 0 30+1 18·45	30·252	63·0		62·5
6275	18 19 43·0	9 2·0	4 30·7		9 1·78	N. 0 50—4 5·08				
6285	18 20 47·0		10 31·6	9 1·8	9 1·78	N. 0 50+1 29·82				
6305	18 23 39·3	9 1·7	6 23·5	9 1·6	9 1·78	N. 0 50—2 12·28				

May 21.—No. 7909 was entered as Anonymous in the observing book.

☿ MAY 22, 1844.—FACE OF SECTOR WEST—(continued).

Number of B.A.C.	Time by Chronometer.	Micr. for Plumb-line on Dot.	Micr. for Observation of Star.	Micr. for Plumb-line on Dot.	Mean of Micr. for Plumb-line on Dot.	Star's Apparent Zenith Distance.	Barom.	Thermometers.		
								Attd.	Lower.	Out.
	h m s	rev. pts.	rev. pts.	rev. pts.	rev. pts.	° ' rev. pts.	In.			
6489	18	8 20·3	8 3·2	8 20·5	8 20·4	N. 3 50+0 17·2	30·247	62·8		62·4
6525	18 57 30·8	8 25·1	10 30·8	8 25·3	8 25·2	N. 5 5—2 5·6				
6639	19 16 54·4	8 19·7	11 16·1	8 20·0	8 19·85	N. 3 55—2 30·25				
Anon.	19 21 6·7	8 25·1	4 15·0	8 25·0	8 25·05	N. 4 5+4 10·05				

FACE OF SECTOR EAST.

6753	19 35 27·2	9 9·4	9 9·5	9 9·3	9 9·35	N. 2 40+0 0·15				

FACE OF SECTOR WEST.

6877	19 54 14·7	9 18·5	6 2·0	9 18·1	9 18·3	N. 1 25+3 16·3				
6948	20	9 15·5	4 23·8	9 15·3	9 15 4	N. 3 25+4 25·6				
7011	20 14 56·6	9 29·5	6 24·3	9 29·5	9 29·44	N. 4 20+3 5·14				
7026	20 16 47·2		6 32·0	9 29·3	9 29·44	N. 4 20+2 31·44				
7057	20 21 12·2	9 29·4	12 24·1	9 29·5	9 29·44	N.4 20—2 28·66				
Anon.	20	9 28·2	6 3·65	9 27·9	9 28·05	N. 4 5+3 24·4				
Anon.	20 33 34·7	9 7·4	12 24·1	9 7·5	9 7·45	N. 4 0—3 16·65				
7207	20 40	9 14·3	9 0·0	9 14·1	9 14·2	S. 0 25—0 14·2	30·233	62·6	63·8	63·0
Anon.	20 53 21·6	9 19·7	13 2·4	9 19·5	9 19·6	N. 4 15—3 16·8				
Anon.	21 0 32·8	9 30·6	9 14·15	9 30·7	9 30·65	N. 3 35+0 16·5				
7386	21 8 17·2	9 33·3	6 6·75	9 33·1	9 33·2	N. 1 5+3 26·45				
Anon.	21	9 21·3	6 13·0	9 21·3	9 21·3	N. 4 5+3 8·3				
Anon.	21 25 29·0	9 12·0	12 22·6	9 12·0	9 12·0	N. 3 35—3 10·6				
7557	21 35 29·2	9 23·0	5 17·0	9 23·0	9 23·0	N. 0 10+4 6·0	30·232	62·6	63·8	62·2
7657	21 51 39·8	9 13·8	10 22·9	9 13·7	9 13·72	N. 4 45—1 9·18				
Anon.	21 55 30·8	9 13·7	9 18·4	9 13·7	9 13·72	N. 4 45—0 4·68				
7842	22 22 26·2	8 30·5	12 31·25	8 30·5	8 30·5	N. 0 50—4 0·75				
7909	22 33 29·0	9 3·2	7 20·2	9 3·4	9 3·3	N. 3 45+1 17·1				
7966	22 43 39·7	8 27·5	10 0·0	8 27·4	8 27·45	N. 0 15—1 6·55	30·235	62·6	63·4	62·6
7992	22 48 49·2	8 25·6	9 25·65	8 25·6	8 25·6	N. 3 30—1 0·05				

♃ MAY 23, 1844.—FACE OF SECTOR EAST.

2293	6	9 16·1	9 11·45	9 15·9	9 16·0	N. 5 10—0 4·55	30·221	68·4		66·8
6186	18 6 56·2	8 20·3	5 11·75	8 20·6	8 20·45	S. 2 50+3 8·7	30·227	63·4	63·2	59·0
6233	18 13 41·6	9 7·8	7 23·5	9 7·5	9 7·65	S. 0 30+1 18·15				
6275	18 19 40·0	9 13·2	5 7·75		9 13·38	N. 0 50—4 5·58				
6285	18 20 43·4		11 10·8	9 13·4	9 13·33	N. 0 50+1 81·47				
6305	18 23 36·2	9 13·4	7 1·2	9 30·3	9 13·33	N. 0 50—2 12·13				
6414	18 42 33·2	9 30·4	12 13·9	9 30·3	9 30·35	N. 3 0+2 17·55				
6480	18	9 28·5	10 18·5	9 28·5	9 28·5	N. 3 50+0 24·0				
6525	18 57 34·2	9 14·8	7 15·45	9 14·9	9 14·85	N. 5 5—1 33·4				
6639	19 16 57·2	9 13·2	12 31·0	9 13·2	9 13·2	N. 3 55—2 24·45				
6753	19 35 23·2	12 31·6	12 31·0	12 31·5	12 31·55	N. 2 40—0 0·55	30·233	63·6	62·9	58·5
6877	19 54 17·5	12 14·5	16 0·4	12 14·5	12 14·5	N. 1 25+3 19·9				
6948	20 6 0·7	10 3·7	15 0·75	10 3·7	10 3·7	N. 3 25+4 31·05				
7011	20 15 0·0	9 21·3	12 31·55	9 21·2	9 21·2	N. 4 20+3 10·35				
7026	20		12 25·75	9 21·2	9 21·2	N. 4 20+3 4·55				
7057	20 21 15·2	9 21·2	6 30·5	9 21·1	9 21·2	N. 4 20—2 24·7				
Anon.	20 24 7·2	9 4·1	13 0·15	9 4·2	9 4·15	N. 4 5+3 30·0				
Anon.	20 33 37·2	9 0·45	5 21·1	9 0·3	9 0·38	N. 4 0—3 13·28				
7207	20 40 4·2	8 33·1	9 17·6	8 33·0	8 33·05	S. 0 25—0 18·55				
Anon.	21	9 19·3	10 7·85	9 19·3	9 19·3	N. 3 35+0 22·55				
7386	21 8 19·2	9 16·6	13 13·7	9 13·7	9 13·65	N. 1 5+3 31·05				
Anon.	21	10 0·7	13 14·6	10 0·7	10 0·7	N. 4 5+8 13·9				

May 22.—The times were noted in terms of the old Molyneux clock in the sector room, instead of Arnold and Dent No. 718 chronometer as hitherto. The column heading need not be altered for this reason.
Good definition throughout the night.
23.—No. 2293.—20 seconds past the meridian wire when bisected.
No. 7026.—The micrometer reading altered one revolution.
Strong southerly wind, and bad definition.

♃ May 23, 1844.—Face of Sector East—(continued).

Number of B.A.C.	Time by Chronometer.	Micr. for Plumb-line on Dot.	Micr. for Observation of Star.	Micr. for Plumb-line on Dot.	Mean of Micr. for Plumb-line on Dot.	Star's Apparent Zenith Distance.	Barom.	Attd.	Lower.	Out.
	h m s	rev. pts.	rev. pts.	rev. pts.	rev. pts.	° ′ rev. pts.	in.			
Anon.	21	9 24·9	6 19·4	9 24·8	9 24·85	N. 3 35—3 5·45	30·225	62·5	62·8	59·0
7557	21 35 28·8	9 7·3	13 17·8	9 7·0	9 7·15	N. 0 10+4 10·65				
7557	21 51 43·0	9 21·3	8 17·0	9 21·1	9 21·15	N. 4 45—1 4·15				
Anon.	21 55 30·0	9 21·2	9 21·3	9 21·0	9 21·15	N. 4 45+0 0·15	30·222	62·4	62·7	59·2
7842	22 22 27·3	9 5·5	5 9·8	9 5·6	9 5·55	N. 0 50—3 29·75				
7909	22 33 30·8	9 5·1	10 27·25	9 5·0	9 5·05	N. 3 45+1 22·2				
7966	22 43 40·2	8 31·4	7 29·3	8 31·3	8 31·35	N. 0 15—1 2·05				
7992	22	9 12·7	8 19·75	9 12·75	9 12·73	N. 3 30—0 26·98	30·230	62·4	62·4	59·1

♀ May 24, 1844.—Face of Sector East.

Number of B.A.C.	Time by Chronometer.	Micr. for Plumb-line on Dot.	Micr. for Observation of Star.	Micr. for Plumb-line on Dot.	Mean of Micr. for Plumb-line on Dot.	Star's Apparent Zenith Distance.	Barom.	Attd.	Lower.	Out.
4517	13	9 30·9	9 29·5	9 30·9	9 30·9	N. 5 10—0 1·4	30·190	63·0	63·0	60·7
4548	13 29 47·0	9 30·9	9 26·25	9 31·0	9 30·95	N. 5 10—0 4·7				
4686	13 57	9 17·8	9 8·65	9 17·5	9 17·65	S. 1 40+0 9·0				
4719	14 5 50·2	9 29·9	5 24·1	9 29·8	9 29·85	N. 5 25—4 5·75				

Face of Sector West.

Number of B.A.C.	Time by Chronometer.	Micr. for Plumb-line on Dot.	Micr. for Observation of Star.	Micr. for Plumb-line on Dot.	Mean of Micr. for Plumb-line on Dot.	Star's Apparent Zenith Distance.	Barom.	Attd.	Lower.	Out.
Anon.	14	9 9·0	12 14·7	9 9·0	9 9·0	N. 1 20—3 5·7	30·182	62·4		60·6
4916	14	9 12·4	13 17·0	9 12·2	9 12·3	N. 0 45—4 4·7				
Anon.	14 58	9 18·5	13 29·5	9 18·4	9 18·45	N. 1 40—4 11·05			63·0	

Face of Sector East.

Number of B.A.C.	Time by Chronometer.	Micr. for Plumb-line on Dot.	Micr. for Observation of Star.	Micr. for Plumb-line on Dot.	Mean of Micr. for Plumb-line on Dot.	Star's Apparent Zenith Distance.	Barom.	Attd.	Lower.	Out.
5054	15 11 45·0	9 17·5	8 20·75	9 17·7	9 17·6	S. 1 45+0 30·85				
Anon.	15	9 27·2	9 22·5	9 27·2	9 27·2	N. 2 50—0 4·7				
5227	15	9 15·1	13 6·4	9 15·1	9 15·1	N. 0 45+3 25·3				
5331	15 55 11·4	9 19·7	7 8·5	9 19·7	9 19·7	S. 2 25+2 11·2	30·180	62·6		60·7
5435	16 9 31·3	9 20·5	8 28·0	9 20·5	9 20·5	N. 3 25—0 26·5				
Anon.	16 13 44·8	9 2·2	11 12·35	9 2·2	9 2·2	N. 1 5+2 10·15				
5508	16 21 1·2	8 25·0	7 28·4	8 24·9	8 24·9	S. 0 25+0 30·55				
5588	16 33 27·2	8 32·0	4 33·0	8 32·1	8 32·05	N. 2 10—3 33·05				
5632	16 39 53·2	8 28·2	10 9·6	8 28·0	8 28·0	S. 0 5—1 15·5	30·170	62·6		60·4

Face of Sector West.

Number of B.A.C.	Time by Chronometer.	Micr. for Plumb-line on Dot.	Micr. for Observation of Star.	Micr. for Plumb-line on Dot.	Mean of Micr. for Plumb-line on Dot.	Star's Apparent Zenith Distance.	Barom.	Attd.	Lower.	Out.
5735	16 54 19·0	8 10·0	4 14·4	8 9·8	8 9·9	0 0+3 29·5				
5817	17 6 39·0	8 18·5	4 22·35	8 18·5	8 18·5	N. 1 25+3 30·15			63·2	
5881	17 17 6·2	8 10·5	12 9·1	8 10·5	8 10·5	N. 4 15—3 32·6				
5915	17 22 47·0	8 25·2	4 32·0	8 24·8	8 24·9	S. 3 5—3 27·0	30·167	62·4		60·4
6016	17 38 45·8	8 10·7	3 30·8	8 10·6	8 10·65	N. 2 15+4 13·85				
6074	17	8 6·1	4 10·7	8 6·0	8 6·05	N. 3 40+3 29·35				
6115	17 55 30·0	7 0·3	6 16·55	7 0·4	7 0·35	N. 3 30+0 17·8				
6145	17	9 29·3	7 23·8	9 29·4	9 29·35	N. 3 10+2 5·55				
6186	18 6 50·0	10 5·9	13 20·0	10 6·0	10 6·0	S. 0 30+3 14·05				
6233	18 13 33·4	10 23·3	12 11·75	10 23·7	10 23·5	S. 0 30+1 22·25				
6275	18 19 30·8	10 12·3	14 20·6		10 12·33	N. 0 50—4 8·27				
6285	18 20 34·8		8 19·9	10 12·2	10 12·33	N. 0 50+1 26·43				
6305	18 23 27·3	10 12·4	12 27·8	10 12·4	10 12·33	N. 0 50—2 15·47				
6414	18 42 23·2	10 9·0	7 31·0	10 8·8	10 8·9	N. 3 0+2 11·9	30·176	62·4		60·4
6489	18 52 23·1	9 19·1	9 1·1	9 19·0	9 19·05	N. 3 50+0 17·95				
6525	18 57 22·2	9 14·9	11 20·05	9 14·8	9 14·85	N. 5 5—2 5·2				
6639	19 16 56·2	9 7·8	12 4·25	9 7·9	9 7·85	N. 3 55+2 30·4				
Anon.	19 21	9 2·0	4 25·5	9 2·0	9 2·0	N. 4 5+4 10·5				
6753	19 35 13·8	8 32·75	9 4·4	8 32·7	8 32·73	N. 2 40—0 5·67				
6877	19 54 8·2	9 3·6	5 21·1	9 3·7	9 3·65	N. 1 25+3 10·55	30·159	64·2	63·0	60·2
6948	20	9 8·0	4 16·6	9 7·9	9 7·95	N. 3 25+4 25·35				

May 24.—The time of 4548 doubtful.
Anon. 14h 58m and 19h 21m bad observations.
Bad definition. Strong south wind.
The times from Molyneux clock No. 159.

♀ MAY 24, 1844.—FACE OF SECTOR WEST—(continued).

Number of B.A.C.	Time by Chronometer.	Micr. for Plumb-line on Dot.	Micr. for Observation of Star.	Micr. for Plumb-line on Dot.	Mean of Micr. for Plumb-line on Dot.	Star's Apparent Zenith Distance.	Barom.	Thermometers.		
								Attd.	Lower.	Out.
	h m s	rev. pts.	rev. pts.	rev. pts.	rev. pts.	° ′ rev. pts.	in.			
7011	20 14 48·2	9 5·3	5 33·0	9 5·1	9 5·08	N. 4 20+3 6·08				
7026	20 16 39·2		6 7·9	9 4·8	9 5·08	N. 4 20+2 31·18				
7057	20 21 4·0	9 5·1	12 0·0	9 5·1	9 5·08	N. 4 20—2 28·92				
Anon.	20	9 6·6	5 15·8	9 6·8	9 6·7	N. 4 5+3 24·9				
Anon.	20	9 9·2	12 25·35	9 9·5	9 9·35	N. 4 0—3 16·0				
7207	20 39 55·3	9 20·0	9 5·25	9 19·9	9 19·95	S. 0 25—0 14·7		63·0		
Anon.	20 53 13·8	9 2·1	12 19·5	9 2·0	9 2·05	N. 4 15—3 17·45				
Anon.	21 0 24·7	9 14·1	8 31·0	9 14·1	9 14·1	N. 3 35+0 17·1				
7386	21 8 9·3	9 20·0	5 26·0	9 20·0	9 20·0	N. 1 5+3 28·0				
Anon.	21	0 12·3	6 4·4	9 12·5	9 12·4	N. 4 5+3 8·0				
7557	21 35 20·4	9 23·4	5 16·7	9 23·0	9 23·2	N. 0 10+4 6·5	30·164	62·4	63·0	59·6
7657	21 51 31·4	8 15·8	9 24·75	8 15·9	8 15·88	N. 4 45—1 8·87				
Anon.	21 55 22·2	8 15·9	8 19·4	8 15·9	8 15·88	N. 4 45—0 3·52				
7842	22 22 18·3	8 15·0	12 14·5	8 15·2	8 15·1	N. 0 50—3 33·4	30·174	62·5	62·9	60·0
7909	22 33 20·2	8 11·5	6 26·8	8 11·6	8 11·55	N. 3 45+1 18·75				
7966	22 43 31·4	8 26·8	9 33·7	8 26·8	8 26·8	N. 0 15—1 6·9				
7992	22 48 40·5	9 7·0	10 5·55	9 7·0	9 7·0	N. 3 30—0 32·55	30·185	62·5	62·8	59·8

♄ MAY 25, 1844.—FACE OF SECTOR EAST.

| 1802 | 5 33 44·0 | 10 5·5 | 12 17·0 | 10 5·8 | 10 5·65 | S. 0 15—2 11·35 | 30·164 | 63·6 | 64·8 | 68·6 |

FACE OF SECTOR WEST.

| 2293 | 6 52 5·1 | 10 33·5 | 11 8·5 | 10 33·5 | 10 33·5 | N. 5 10—0 9·0 | 30·143 | 64·7 | 64·8 | 68·6 |

FACE OF SECTOR EAST.

| 4517 | 13 23 40·3 | 11 19·0 | 11 17·6 | 11 19·0 | 11 19·0 | N. 5 10—0 1·4 | 30·184 | 63·8 | 63·8 | 61·3 |

FACE OF SECTOR WEST.

4686	13 57 14·2	11 5·8	2 22·7	2 7·4		{ S. 1 45—8 17·1 / S. 1 40+0 15·3 }	30·185	63·4		60·8
Anon.	14 23 48·2	9 6·3	12 11·9	9 6·3	9 6·3	N. 1 20—3 5·6			63·8	
Anon.	14 57 21·0	9 29·4	14 4·0	9 29·3	9 29·35	N. 1 40—4 8·65	30·188	63·0		60·2
Anon.	15 34 2·0	9 13·1	9 23·2	9 13·1	9 13·1	N. 2 50—0 10·1	30·182	62·8		60·0
5227	15 40 46·0	9 21·9	5 32·7	9 21·6	9 21·75	N. 0 45+3 23·05				
5331	15 56 6·0	9 24·6	12 5·7		9 24·55	S. 2 25+2 15·15				
Comp.	15 56 45·5		7 10·95	9 24·5	9 24·55	S. 2 25—2 13·6				60·2
5374	16 1 1·2	9 15·3	7 31·65	9 15·5	9 15·4	N. 4 55+1 17·75				60·1
5435	16 9 22·3	9 18·0	10 15·15	9 18·0	9 18·0	N. 3 25—0 31·15	30·180	63·0		
Anon.	16 13 37·0		7 21·3	9 25·6		N. 1 5+2 4·3				
5508	16 20 55·0	9 31·5	10 30·5	9 31·7	9 31·6	S. 0 25+0 32·9				
5588	16 33 19·2	9 4·4	13 7·8	9 4·3	9 4·35	N. 2 10—4 3·45				
5632	16 39 47·1	9 17·5	8 6·45	9 17·2	9 17·35	S. 0 5—1 10·9			63·5	60·5
5735	16	9 23·6	13 23·75	9 23·5	9 23·55	0 0+4 0·2				
5817	17 6 43·0	9 30·75	13 30·8	9 31·0	9 30·88	N. 1 25+3 33·92				61·2
5881	17 17 12·2	9 29·4	6 0·45	9 30·4	9 30·4	N. 4 15—3 29·95	30·184	62·8	63·3	
5915	17 22 49·2	9 3·0	13 0·4	9 2·6	9 2·8	S. 3 5—3 31·6				
6016	17 38 50·3	9 12·1	13 28·45	9 12·3	9 12·2	N. 2 15+4 16·25				
6074	17 48 52·0	9 13·4	13 13·9	9 13·4	9 13·4	N. 3 40+4 0·5				60·7
6115	17 55 35·0	9 19·0	11 8·5	9 19·0	9 19·0	N. 3 30+1 23·5				
6145	17 59 49·8	9 11·5	11 23·4	9 11·5	9 11·5	N. 3 10+2 11·9				60·8
6186	18 6 52·0	8 12·3	5 3·45	8 12·1	8 12·2	S. 2 50+3 8·75				

May 25.—A fair observing night.

♄ MAY 25, 1844.—FACE OF SECTOR EAST—(continued).

Number of B.A.C.	Time by Chronometer.	Micr. for Plumb-line on Dot.	Micr. for Observation of Star.	Micr. for Plumb-line on Dot.	Mean of Micr. for Plumb-line on Dot.	Star's Apparent Zenith Distance.	Barom.	Thermometers. Attd.	Lower.	Out.
	h m s	rev. pts.	rev. pts.	rev. pts.	rev. pts.	° ' rev. pts.	in.			
6233	18 13 36·3	8 21·5	7 1·9	8 21·5		S. 0 30+1 19·6				
6275	18 19 34·2	8 18·8	4 13·0		8 18·8	N. 0 50—4 5·8				
6285	18 20 38·2		10 14·75	8 18·7	8 18·8	N. 0 50+1 29·95				
6305	18 23 31·0	8 18·8	6 6·05	8 18·9	8 18·8	N. 0 50—2 12·75	30·182			61·2
6414	18 42 27·7	8 25·0	11 8·7	8 25·0	8 25·0	N. 3 0+2 17·7				
6489	18 52 28·2	8 23·7	9 12·45	8 23·7	8 23·7	N. 3 50+0 22·75				
6525	18 57 28·1	8 19·2	6 19·8	8 19·4	8 19·3	N. 5 5—1 33·5				
6639	10	8 20·3	5 29·45	8 20·4	8 20·35	N. 3 55—2 24·9	30·188	63·0	63·3	61·3
6753	19 35 17·3	13 25·8	13 24·4	13 25·7	13 25·75	N. 2 40—0 1·35				
6877	19 54 11·7	9 9·8	12 29·7	9 9·8	9 9·8	N. 1 25+3 19·9				
6948	20 5 54·8	9 15·0	14 10·6	9 15·1	9 15·05	N. 3 25+4 29·55				
7011	20 14 53·0	9 5·9	12 16·0	9 5·8	9 5·76	N. 4 20+3 10·24				
7026	20 16 44·2		12 8·5	9 5·7	9 5·76	N. 4 20+3 2·74				
7057	20 21 9·4	9 5·7	6 15·75	9 5·7	9 5·76	N. 4 20—2 24·01				
Anon.	20 24 1·3	8 32·0	12 28·0	8 31·9	8 31·95	N. 4 5+3 30·05				
Anon.	20 33 31·8	9 1·4	5 24·55	9 1·2	9 1·3	N. 4 0—3 10·75				
7207	20 39 58·5	8 24·8	9 8·6	8 24·6	8 24·7	S. 0 25—0 17·9				
Anon.	20 53 18·8	8 20·5	5 16·5	8 29·5	8 29·5	N. 4 15—3 13·0				
Anon.	21 0 29·3	8 23·25	9 11·0	8 23·3	8 23·28	N. 3 35+0 21·72				
7386	21 8 13·2	8 4·5	12 1·4	8 4·5	8 4·5	N. 1 5+3 30·9				
Anon.	21 12 19·0	9 4·6	12 17·75	9 4·6	9 4·6	N. 4 5+3 13·15				
Anon.	21 25 25·7	9 7·0	6 1·3	9 7·0	9 7·0	N. 3 35—3 5·7	30·189	62·6	63·3	60·2
7557	21 35 34·0	9 7·4	13 17·7	9 7·4	9 7·4	N. 0 10+4 10·3				
7657	21 51 37·2	9 30·2	8 26·75	9 30·3	9 30·28	N. 4 45—1 3·53				
Anon.	21 55 28·5	9 30·3	9 31·4	9 30·3	9 30·28	N. 4 45+0 1·12				
7842	22 22 22·3	9 17·8	5 22·5	9 17·5	9 17·65	N. 0 50—3 29·15				
7909	22 33 26·0	9 13·5	11 2·5	9 13·5	9 13·5	N. 3 45+1 23·0				
7966	22 43 35·3	9 4·5	8 2·25	9 4·4	9 4·45	N. 0 15—1 2·2				
7992	22 48 46·2	9 30·5	9 3·5	9 30 3	9 30·4	N. 3 30—0 26·9	30·206	62·5	63·2	61·0

☾ MAY 27, 1844.—FACE OF SECTOR WEST.

Number of B.A.C.	Time by Chronometer.	Micr. for Plumb-line on Dot.	Micr. for Observation of Star.	Micr. for Plumb-line on Dot.	Mean of Micr. for Plumb-line on Dot.	Star's Apparent Zenith Distance.	Barom.	Attd.	Lower.	Out.
1802	5 33 36·2	10 21·2	8 10·55	10 21·0	10 21·1	S. 0 15—2 10·55	30·316	64·0	64·8	66·2

FACE OF SECTOR EAST.

Number of B.A.C.	Time by Chronometer.	Micr. for Plumb-line on Dot.	Micr. for Observation of Star.	Micr. for Plumb-line on Dot.	Mean of Micr. for Plumb-line on Dot.	Star's Apparent Zenith Distance.	Barom.	Attd.	Lower.	Out.
4686	13 57 16·2	10 30·7	10 20·65	10 30·8	10 30·75	S. 1 40+0 10·1	30·356	63·4	63·7	59·5
Anon.	14 23 51·8	11 13·4	8 11·25	11 13·7	11 13·55	N. 1 20—3 2·3	30·350	63·4		59·5
Anon.	14 57 24·2	6 23·15	2 19·3	6 23·8	6 23·22	N. 1 40—4 3·92	30·344	63·2		59·4
Anon.	15 34 6·4	8 33·4	8 28·5	8 33·5	8 33·45	N. 2 50—0 4·95				
5331	15 55 8·3	8 23·5	6 12·1		8 23·45	S. 2 25+2 11·35			63·3	
Comp.			11 7·8	8 23·4	8 23·45	S. 2 25—2 18·35				
5374	16 1 7·0	9 5·6	10 27·95	9 5·8	9 5·7	N. 4 55+1 22·25				60·1
5435	16 9 21·5	8 30·6	8 3·95	8 30·6	8 30·6	N. 3 25—0 26·65				
Anon.	16 13 40·5	8 20·3	10 29·3	8 20·2	8 20·25	N. 1 5+2 9·05				
5508	16 20 57·3	8 32·7	8 2·3	8 32·7	8 32·7	S. 0 25+0 30·4				
5588	16 33 23·0	0 4·3	5 4·95	9 4·5	9 4·4	N. 2 10—3 33·45				
5632	16 39 49·8	8 24·7	10 5·65	8 24·8	8 24·75	S. 0 5—1 14·9	30·338	63·2		59·8

FACE OF SECTOR WEST.

Number of B.A.C.	Time by Chronometer.	Micr. for Plumb-line on Dot.	Micr. for Observation of Star.	Micr. for Plumb-line on Dot.	Mean of Micr. for Plumb-line on Dot.	Star's Apparent Zenith Distance.	Barom.	Attd.	Lower.	Out.
5735	16 54 14·2	8 14·5	4 19·85	8 14·5	8 14·5	0 +3 28·65				
5817	17 6 35·5	8 9·5	4 14·0	8 9·4	8 9·45	N. 1 25+3 29·45				
5881	17 17 2·8	8 28·5	12 27·5	8 28·3	8 28·4	N. 4 15—3 33·1				
5915	17 22 44·6	9 7·0	5 14·3	9 7·0	9 7·0	S. 3 5—3 26·7	30·325	63·4		58·2

May 25.—The seconds of Anon. 21ʰ 12ᵐ uncertain; also of No. 5735 on May 27.
The times by Molyneux clock.

☽ MAY 27, 1844.—FACE OF SECTOR WEST—(continued).

Number of B. A. C.	Time by Chronometer.	Micr. for Plumb-line on Dot.	Micr. for Observation of Star.	Micr. for Plumb-line on Dot.	Mean of Micr. for Plumb-line on Dot.	Star's Apparent Zenith Distance.	Barom.	Thermometers. Attd.	Lower.	Out.
	h m s	rev. pts.	rev. pts.	rev. pts.	rev. pts.	° ′ rev. pts.	in.			
6016	17 38 42·7	8 20·9	4 8·45	8 21·0	8 20·95	N. 2 15+4 12·5				
6074	17	8 24·5	4 29·55	8 24·3	8 24·4	N. 3 40+3 28·85				
6115	17 55 26·2	8 17·5	7 0·0	8 17·5	8 17·5	N. 3 30+1 17·5				
6145	17 59 41·3	7 33·6	5 27·25	7 33·5	7 33·55	N. 3 10+2 6·3				
6186	18 6 47·3	8 14·5	11 29·5	8 14·5	8 14·5	S. 2 50+3 15·0				
6233	18 13 30·4	8 17·0	10 6·25	8 17·0	8 17·0	S. 0 30+1 23·25	30·324	62·8		57·8
6275	18 19 27·1	9 7·4	13 15·9	9 7·3	9 7·3	N. 0 50—4 8·6				
6285	18 20 31·2		7 15·5	9 7·2	9 7·3	N. 0 50+1 25·8				
6305	18 23 23·5	9 7·3	11 24·0	9 7·3	9 7·3	N. 0 50—2 16·7				
6414	18 42 19·3	9 6·5	6 28·75	9 6·5	9 6·5	N. 3 0+2 11·75				
6489	18 52 19·0	9 9·6	8 26·0	9 9·6	9 9·6	N. 3 50+0 17·6	30·320	62·8		58·7
6525	18 57 19·0	8 22·0	10 27·75	8 22·0	8 22·0	N. 5 5—2 5·75				
6639	19	8 29·3	11 25·65	8 29·5	8 29·4	N. 3 55—2 30·25	30·320	63·0		58·4
Anon.	19	8 11·5	4 1·2	8 11·5	8 11·5	N. 4 5+4 10·3				
6753	19 35 9·3	8 22·3	8 28·0	8 22·5	8 22·4	N. 2 40—0 5·6				
6877	19 54 5·1	8 32·3	5 15·85	8 32·0	8 32·15	N. 1 25+3 16·3	30·320	63·0	63·5	
6948	20 6 46·5	8 23·0	5 31·3	8 23·0	8 23·0	N. 3 25+4 25·7				
7011	20 14 45·0	8 25·5	5 20·0	8 25·4	8 25·36	N. 4 20+3 5·36				
7026	20 16 35·5		5 27·45	8 25·3	8 25·36	N. 4 20+2 31·91				
7057	20 21 0·2	8 25·3	11 20·6	8 25·3	8 25·36	N. 4 20—2 29·24				
Anon.	20 23 53·0	8 23·9	4 32·8	8 23·7	8 23·8	N. 4 5+3 25·0				
Anon.	20 33 23·2	8 25·3	12 7·75	8 25·2	8 25·25	N. 4 0—3 16·5	30·313	63·0	63·2	56·3
7207	20	8 26·6	8 12·3	8 26·6	8 26·6	S. 0 25—0 14·3				
Anon.	20 53 10·8	8 29·0	12 12·4	8 29·1	8 29·05	N. 4 15—3 17·35				
Anon.	21 0 20·8	8 31·4	8 14·5	8 31·3	8 31·35	N. 3 35+0 16·85				
7386	21 8 7·0	9 11·8	5 18·45	9 11·5	9 11·65	N. 1 5+3 27·2	30·310	62·6	63·3	54·6
Anon.	21 25 18·2	9 23·8	13 0·9	9 24·0	9 23·9	N. 3 35—3 11·0				
7557	21 35 18·0	10 11·0	6 5·05	10 11·2	10 11·1	N. 0 20+4 6·05				
7657	21 51 27·9	9 21·9	10 31·35	9 22·0	9 21·95	N. 4 45—1 9·4				
Anon.	21 55 19·0	9 22·0	9 25·75	9 21·9	9 21·95	N. 4 45—0 3·8				
7842	22 22 16·0	9 14·3	13 13·3	9 14·5	9 14·4	N. 0 50—3 32·9	30·314	62·5	63·3	53·6
7909	22 33 17·3	9 14·8	7 31·15	9 14·8	9 14·8	N. 4 45—1 17·65				
7966	22 43 29·0	9 19·7	10 25·75	9 19·6	9 19·65	N. 0 15—1 6 1				
7992	22 48 38·0	9 14·9	10 14·5	9 14·9	9 14·9	N. 3 30—0 33·6	30·320	52·8	63·3	52·6

☾ MAY 28, 1844.—FACE OF SECTOR EAST.

| 1802 | 5 33 40·8 | 9 16·6 | 11 28·75 | 9 16·5 | 9 16·55 | S. 0 15—2 12·2 | 30·302 | 64·0 | 63·8 | 63·6 |
| 2293 | 6 52 11·4 | 9 32·1 | 9 27·35 | 9 32·0 | 9 32·05 | N. 5 10—0 4·7 | 30·277 | 64·2 | 64·5 | 64·6 |

FACE OF SECTOR WEST.

4686	13 57 13·0	9 1·8	9 18·0	9 1·6	9 1·7	S. 1 40+0 16·3	30·263	60·0	63·3	49·4
Anon.	14	8 32·2	10 8·45	8 32·5	8 32·35	N. 1 20—3 8·0				
Anon.	15 34 0·1	9 28·6	10 6·05	9 28·8	9 28·7	N. 2 50—0 11·35	30·240	59·6	62·5	47·7
5331	15 56 5·0	9 25·7	12 7·3	9 25·8	9 25·8	S. 2 25+2 15·5				
Comp.	15 56 44·3		7 12·55	9 25·9	9 25·8	S. 2 25—2 13·25				
5374	16 0 50·0	9 24·6	8 7·8	0 24·5	9 24·55	N. 4 55+1 16·55	30·235	60·4		48·7
5435	16 9 20·3	8 31·8	9 30·0	8 32·0	8 31·9	N. 3 25—0 32·1				
Anon.	16 13 36·0	8 31·0	6 25·3	8 31·1	8 31·05	N. 1 5+2 5·75				
5508	16 20 54·0	8 29·4	9 28·95	8 29·2	8 29·3	S. 0 25+0 33·65				
5588	16 33	8 20·0	12 24·0	8 20·3	8 20·15	N. 2 10—4 3·85				
5632	16 39 45·3	8 29·9	7 21·15	8 29·8	8 29·85	S. 0 5—1 8·7	30·234	60·4		47·4

May 27.—Good definition until towards morning.
28.—Remarkably bad definition. Stars below the 6th magnitude will not bear illumination of the wires. For this reason no observations were made after 16ʰ 40ᵐ S.T.
Cleaned the Sector Arch.

x

♉ MAY 29, 1844.—FACE OF SECTOR EAST.

Number of B.A.C.	Time by Chronometer.	Micr. for Plumb-line on Dot.	Micr. for Observation of Star.	Micr. for Plumb-line on Dot.	Mean of Micr. for Plumb-line on Dot.	Star's Apparent Zenith Distance.	Barom.	Thermometers. Attd.	Lower.	Out.
	h m s	rev. pts.	rev. pts.	rev. pts.	rev. pts.	o ' rev. pts.	in.			
4507	13 21 46·3	10 0·5	9 31·8	10 6·6	10 6·55	S. 4 40+0 8·75		62·2		
Anon.	14 23 52·8	8 31·9	5 30·0	8 31·8	8 31·85	N. 1 20—3 1·85	30·233	61·8		58·7
Anon.	14	8 22·3	4 19·0	8 22·1	8 22·2	N. 1 40—4 3·2				
Anon.	15 34 7·8	8 30·5	8 25·0	8 30·0	8 30·25	N. 2 50—0 5·25				
5292	15 49 35·2	9 1·7	7 29·0	9 1·7	9 1·7	S. 4 0+1 6·7	30·230	61·7		58·0
5331	15 56 9·0	9 0·5	6 22·5	6 22·5	9 0·4	S. 2 25+2 11·9				
Comp.	15		11 19·3	9 0·3	9 0·4	S. 2 25—2 18·9				
5374	16 1 8·8	9 2·5	10 24·05	9 2·4	9 2·45	N. 4 55+1 21·6				
5435	16 9 27·3	9 13·7	8 20·7	9 13·5	9 13·6	N. 3 25—0 26·9				
Anon.	16 13 41·2	8 26·5	10 33·9	8 26·4	8 26·45	N. 1 5+2 7·45				
5508	16 20 58·2	8 28·4	7 32·6	8 28·2	8 28·3	S. 0 25+0 29·7				
5588	16 33 24·2	8 31·3	4 31·75	8 30·8	8 31·05	N. 2 10—3 33·3	30·227	61·7		56·7
5735	16	8 11·0	12 12·3	8 11·3	8 11·15	0 0+4 1·15	30·227	61·7	63·4	56·7
5817	17 6 41·0	8 22·2	12 21·9	8 22·3	8 22·25	N. 1 25+3 33·65				55·6
5881	17 17 10·5	8 30·8	5 1·5	9 30·5	9 30·65	N. 4 15—4 29·15				
5915	17 22 47·3	8 2·1	12 0·0	8 2·0	8 2·05	S. 3 5—3 31·95				55·4
6016	17 38 49·8	8 18·0	12 33·75	8 18·1	8 18·05	N. 2 15+4 15·7			63·3	
6074	17 48 51·0	8 18·1	12 18·9	8 18·2	8 18·15	N. 3 40+4 0·75				
6115	17 55 34·0	8 26·3	10 15·75	8 26·0	8 26·15	N. 3 30+1 23·6	30·221	61·4		56·4
6145	17 59 48·6	8 16·5	10 28·3	8 16·3	8 16·4	N. 3 10+2 11·9				
6186	18 6 50·7	8 16·9	5 7·75	8 16·9	8 16·9	S. 3 5—3 9·15				
6233	18 13 35·4	8 6·3	6 20·75	8 6·0	8 6·15	S. 0 30+1 19·4				
6275	18 19 33·2	8 11·0	4 3·95		8 10·63	N. 0 50—4 6·68				
6285	18 20 37·0		10 5·5	8 10·5	8 10·63	N. 0 50+1 28·87				
6305	18 23 29·8	8 10·5	5 31·5	8 10·5	8 10·63	N. 0 50—2 13·13				
6414	18 42 26·7	8 22·1	11 6·4	8 22·3	8 22·2	N. 3 0+2 18·2				
6489	18 52 27·2	8 33·0	9 22·5	8 33·0	8 33·0	N. 3 50+0 23·5	30·225	61·5		59·0
6525	18 57 28·0	9 25·8	7 26·7	9 25·6	9 25·7	N. 5 5—1 33·0				
6639	19 16 50·2	9 24·3	7 0·45	9 24·5	9 24·4	N. 3 55—2 23·95				
Anon.	19 21 3·2	9 24·6	14 6·0	9 24·6	9 24·6	N. 4 5+4 15·4				
6753	19	9 27·8	9 26·8	9 27·9	9 27·85	N. 2 40—0 1·05	30·221	61·5	62·2	58·5
6877	19 54 11·0	8 21·3	12 8·0	8 21·3	8 21·3	N. 1 25+3 20·7	30·217	61·6	62·2	61·3
6948	20 5 54·0	9 18·3	14 15·5	9 18·3	9 18·3	N. 3 25+4 31·2				
7011	20 14 53·2	9 3·0	12 13·7	9 2·8	9 2·94	N. 4 20+3 10·76				
7026	20 16 43·8		12 6·8	9 3·1	9 2·94	N. 4 20+3 3·86				
7057	20 21 9·2	9 3·0	6 12·6	9 2·8	9 2·94	N. 4 20—2 24·34				
Anon.	20 24 1·2	8 21·4	12 17·4	8 21·4	8 21·4	N. 4 5+3 30·0				
7207	20	7 14·75	7 33·7	7 14·9	7 14·83	S. 0 25—0 18·87				
Anon.	20	7 26·5	4 14·7	7 26·4	7 26·45	N. 4 15—3 11·75				
Anon.	21 0 29·0	7 18·5	8 7·25	7 18·4	7 18·45	N. 3 35+0 22·8				
Anon.	21 12 18·0	14 16·0	17 30·3	14 15·9	14 15·9	N. 4 5+3 14·4				
7557	21 35 22·8	10 0·0	14 10·85	10 0·3	10 0·15	N. 0 10+4 10·7	30·213	61·8	62·3	59·2
7657	21 51 36·2	9 16·7	8 13·8	9 16·9	9 16·85	N. 4 45—1 3·05				
Anon.	21 55 27·2	9 17·0	9 18·7	9 16·9	9 16·95	N. 4 45+0 1·85				
7842	22 22 22·3	9 3·0	5 7·7	9 2·8	9 2·9	N. 0 50—3 29·2				
7966	22 43 34·1	11 20·5	10 18·5	11 20·0	11 20·25	N. 0 15—1 1·75				
7992	22 48 45·3	12 9·5	11 17·1	12 9·5	12 9·5	N. 3 30—0 26·4	30·215	61·6	62·3	58·2

♃ MAY 30, 1844.—FACE OF SECTOR WEST.

Number of B.A.C.	Time by Chronometer.	Micr. for Plumb-line on Dot.	Micr. for Observation of Star.	Micr. for Plumb-line on Dot.	Mean of Micr. for Plumb-line on Dot.	Star's Apparent Zenith Distance.	Barom.	Thermometers. Attd.	Lower.	Out.
1878	5 45 5·2	10 21·3	8 22·2	10 21·5	10 21·4	S. 1 55—1 33·2	30·210	63·5	63·5	64·9
2293	6 52 4·0	11 33·4	12 7·4	11 33·4	11 33·4	N. 5 10—0 8·0	30·190	63·6	63·5	64·4
4507	13 21 42·8	9 6·9	9 21·6	9 6·6	9 6·75	S. 4 40+0 14·85	30·234	62·4	62·2	59·7
Anon.	14 23 47·0	10 18·2	13 23·5	10 18·4	10 18·3	N. 1 20—3 5·2	30·234	61·8		58·4

May 29.—Misty to the south. Occasional clouds over the Zenith.

♃ MAY 30, 1844.—FACE OF SECTOR WEST—(continued).

Number of B.A.C.	Time by Chronometer.	Micr. for Plumb-line on Dot.	Micr. for Observation of Star.	Micr. for Plumb-line on Dot.	Mean of Micr. for Plumb-line on Dot.	Star's Apparent Zenith Distance.	Barom.	Attd.	Lower.	Out.
	h m s	rev. pts.	rev. pts.	rev. pts.	rev. pts.	° ′ rev. pts.	In.			
Anon.	14 57 25·2	10 23·7	14 32·2	10 23·8	10 23·75	N. 1 40—4 8·45				
Anon.	15 34 1·7	9 9·9	9 19·65	9 10·0	9 9·95	N. 2 50—0 9·7				
5292	15 49 30·2	9 20·6	10 32·45	9 20·8	9 20·7	S. 4 0+1 11·75				
5331	15 55 4·1	9 3·8	11 19·75		9 3·7	S. 2 25+2 16·05				
Comp.	15 55 43·5		6 23·7	9 3·6	9 3·7	S. 2 25—2 14·0				
5374	16 1 1·2	8 25·7	7 8·15	8 25·9	8 25·8	N. 4 55+1 17·85				
FACE OF SECTOR EAST.										
5435	16	10 7·5	9 15·5	10 7·5	10 7·5	N 3 25—0 26·0				62·4
Anon.	16	9 29·6	12 4·3	9 29·5	9 29·55	N. 1 5+2 8·75				
5508	16	9 7·1	8 11·5	9 7·0	9 7·05	N. 0 25+0 29·55				
5538	16 25 53·8	9 12·8	9 33·8	9 12·6	9 12·7	S. 1 0—0 21·1	30·230	61·4		58·2
5588	16 33 24·5	9 17·3	5 18·75	9 17·0	9 17·15	N. 2 10—3 32·4				
5817	17	9 6·6	13 7·3	9 6·8	9 6·7	N. 1 25—4 0·6	30·240	61·4		57·3
FACE OF SECTOR WEST.										
5881	17 17 4·3	9 10·0	13 9·45	9 10·2	9 10·1	N. 4 15—3 33·35				57·4
5915	17 22 42·8	8 13·5	4 21·2	8 13·5	8 13·5	S. 3 5—3 26·3				
5970	17 31 34·2	8 13·4	0 4·4	8 13·0	8 13·2	S. 5 5—8 8·8				62·0
6074	17 48 45·0	9 10·9	5 16·05	9 10·5	9 10·7	N. 3 40+3 28·65				
6115	17 55 28·0	9 14·5	7 31·5	9 14·3	9 14·4	N. 3 30+1 16·9				57·0
6145	17 59 43·0	9 17·5	7 12·1	9 17·5	9 17·5	N. 3 10+2 5·4				
6186	18 6 46·5	9 31·0	13 12·4	9 31·2	9 31·1	S. 2 50—3 15·3				
6233	18 13 30·4	9 15·0	11 4·4	9 15·0	9 15·0	S. 0 30+1 23·4				56·8
6275	18 19 27·5	9 13·0	13 23·5		9 13·2	N. 0 50—4 10·3				56·8
6285	18 20 31·0		7 21·7	9 13·2	9 13·2	N. 0 50—1 25·5				
6305	18 23 24·0	9 13·3	11 30·25	9 13·3	9 13·2	N. 0 50—2 17·05	30·249	61·5	61·9	56·8
6325	18 57 21·2	8 10·2	10 15·75	8 10·4	8 10·3	N. 5 5—2 5·45				
Anon.	19	8 24·4	4 13·3	8 24·4	8 24·4	N. 4 5+4 11·1	30·249	61·4		56·7
6753	19 35 11·4	8 9·4	8 14·65	8 9·6	8 9·5	N. 1 25+3 16·65				
6877	19 54 6·2	8 10·4	4 27·8	8 10·5	8 10·45	N. 3 25+4 26·15				
6948	20 5 48·3	7 24·8	2 32·5	7 24·5	7 24·65	N. 4 20+3 4·87				
7011	20 14 46·5	8 11·9	5 7·0	8 12·0	8 11·87	N. 4 20+2 32·07				
7026	20 16 37·0	8 12·0	5 13·8	8 11·6	8 11·87	N. 4 20—2 29·63				
7057	20 21 2·0	8 11·7	11 7·5		8 24·75	N. 4 5+3 25·2				
Anon.	20 23 54·4	8 24 7	4 33·55	8 24·8	9 10·6	N. 4 0—3 16·8				
Anon.	20 33 25·0	9 10·5	12 27·4	9 10·7	9 10·6	N. 4 0—3 16·8				
7207	20 39 53·0	9 16·3	9 2·65	9 16·4	9 16·35	S. 0 25—0 13·7	30·246	61·2	62·0	57·1
Anon.	20 53 11·8	9 21·9	13 4·0	9 22·0	9 21·95	N. 4 15—3 16·05				
Anon.	21 0 22·3	8 32·0	8 15·0	8 31·8	8 31·9	N. 3 35+0 16·9				
7386	21 8 7·2	9 11·0	5 17·5	9 11·0	9 11·0	N. 1 5+3 27·5				
Anon.	21 12 3·0	9 24·2	6 15·7	9 24·5	9 24·35	N. 4 5+3 8·65				
Anon.	21 25 19·0	9 13·4	12 23·4	9 13·5	9 13·45	N. 3 35—3 9·95				
7557	21 35 17·0	9 9·5	3 3·2	9 10·1	9 9·8	N. 0 10+4 6·6				
7613	21 44 8·0	10 1·1	8 22·5	10 1·2	10 1·15	S. 4 10—1 12·65				
7657	21 51 30·0	8 20·3	9 28·3	8 20·4	8 20·25	N. 4 45—1 8·05				
Anon.	21 55 21·0	8 20·2	8 23·8	8 20·1	8 20·25	N. 4 45+0 3·55				
7842	22 22 16·1	9 13·7	13 13·3	9 14·1	9 13·9	N. 0 50—3 33·4	30·271	61·0	61·9	55·4

♄ JUNE 1, 1844.— FACE OF SECTOR WEST.

1802	5 33 36·1	10 29·8	8 18·4	10 30·2	10 30·0	S. 0 15—2 11·6	30·204	61·4	61·4	62·2

May 30.—The seconds of No. 7026, and of Anon. 20ʰ 33ᵐ are uncertain.
A very strong South-easter.
Micrometer screw going stiff, was oiled, and the plumb-line shade cleaned after the observations.

♄ JUNE 1, 1844—(continued.)—FACE OF SECTOR EAST.

Number of B.A.C.	Time by Chronometer.	Micr. for Plumb-line on Dot.	Micr. for Observation of Star.	Micr. for Plumb-line on Dot.	Mean of Micr. for Plumb-line on Dot.	Star's Apparent Zenith Distance.	Barom.	Thermometers.		
								Attd.	Lower.	Out.
	h m s	rev. pts.	rev. pts.	rev. pts.	rev. pts.	° ′ rev. pts.	in.			
2293	6 52 14·0	9 23·2	9 19·95	9 23 2	9 23·2	N. 5 10—0 3·25	30·197	62·5	61·5	62·4
4507	13 21 46·8	8 13·4	8 4·2	8 13·4	8 13 4	S. 4 40+0 9·2	30·152	59·1	58·8	50·1
4086	13 57 17·0	9 9·3	8 31·15	9 9·2	9 9·25	S. 1 40+0 12·1				
Anon.	14 10 51·2	9 16·1	11 6·5	9 16·5	9 16·3	S. 3 15—1 24·2				
			FACE OF SECTOR WEST.							
Anon.	14 23 46·5	10 15·5	13 21·5	10 15 3	10 15·4	N. 1 20—3 6·1	30·148	58·8		48·4
Anon.	14 58	10 28·6	6 5·95	10 28·5	10 28·55	N. 1 40—4 22·6	30·141	58·4	58·5	48·4
			FACE OF SECTOR EAST.							
Anon.	15 33	10 28·7	10 23·25	10 28·7	10 28 7	N. 2 50—0 5·45		58·4		
5292	15 49 34·4	10 9·4	9 1·45	10 9·0	10 9·2	S. 4 0+1 7·75				
5331	15 55 8·2	9 9·3	6 30·4		9 9·35	S. 2 25+2 12·95				
Comp.	15 55		11 26·4	9 9·4	9 9·35	S. 2 25—2 17·05				
			FACE OF SECTOR WEST.							
5435	16 9 21·2	10 0·9	10 32·5	10 1·0	10 0·95	N. 3 25—0 31·55		49·4		
5508	16 20 53·2	10 4·7	11 4·45	10 5·1	10 4·9	S. 3 10+0 33·55				
5538	16 25 49·0	9 28·5	9 10·8	9 28·7	9 28·6	S. 1 0—0 17·8				
5588	16 33 18·2	9 25·9	13 29·75	9 26·0	9 25·95	N. 2 10—4 3 8	30·136	58·2	58·0	48·4
			FACE OF SECTOR EAST.							
5881	17	11 11·5	7 17·5	11 11·2	11 11·35	N. 4 15—3 27·85	30·132	58·0		48·8
5970	17 31 27·2	9 21·3	9 3·7	9 21·1	9 21·2	S. 5 0+0 17·5	30·131	58·4	58·0	50·1
6016	17 38 49·4	10 9·4	14 21·6	10 9·0	10 9·2	N. 2 15+4 12·4				
6074	17 48 51·2	9 29·7	13 30·1	9 29·9	9 29·8	N. 3 40+4 0·3				
6145	17 59 49·0	9 31·9	12 9·7	9 32·0	9 31·95	N. 3 10+2 11·75				
6233	18 13 35·2	8 20·2	7 1·45	8 20·0	8 20·1	S. 0 30+1 18·65	30·122	58·4		50·3
6275	18	7 23·8	3 18·85		7 23·75	N. 0 50—4 4·9				
6285	18		9 20·8	7 23·8	7 23·75	N. 0 50+1 31·05				
6305	18 23 30·2	7 23·9	5 12·0	7 23·5	7 23·75	N. 0 50—2 11·75		58·1		
6414	18 42 27·5	9 23·1	12 7·05	9 23·1	9 23 1	N. 3 0+2 17·95				
6525	18 57 28·7	9 18·6	7 19·55	9 18·3	9 18·5	N. 5 5—1 32·9				
6639	19 16 51·2	9 16·2	6 25·75	9 15·6	9 15·9	N. 3 55—2 24·15	30·126	58·8	58·2	53·6
Anon.	19	9 15·8	13 31·4	9 15·7	9 15·75	N. 4 5—4 15·65				
6753	19 35 16·5	9 16·0	9 15·7	9 16 2	9 16·1	N. 2 40—0 0·4				
6877	19 54 11·2	9 11·1	12 31·5	9 11·1	9 11·1	N. 1 25+3 20·4				
6948	20 5 55·0	9 14·75	14 11·7	9 14·5	9 14 63	N. 3 25+4 31·07				
7011	20 14 54·0	9 10·5	12 19·95		9 10·3	N. 4 20+3 9·65				
7026	20 16 44·4	9 10·1	12 13·4	9 10·4	9 10·3	N. 4 20+3 3·1				
7057	20 21 9·2	9 10·2	6 20·5	9 10·3	9 10·3	N. 4 20—2 23·8				
Anon	20 24 1·5	9 29·1	13 24·5	9 28·8	9 28 95	N. 4 5+3 29·55				
Anon.	20 33 35·0	9 26·0	6 15·1	9 26·2	9 26·1	N. 4 0—3 11·0				
7207	20 39 57·4	9 1·8	9 21·35	9 2·0	9 1·9	S. 0 25—0 19·45				
Anon.	20 53 19·8	9 21·7	6 8·45	9 21·2	9 21·45	N. 4 15—3 13 0				
Anon.	21 0 29·5	9 29·4	10 18·5	9 29·5	9 29·45	N. 3 35+0 23 05				
7386	21 8 12·2	9 13·0	13 10·35	9 12·8	9 12·9	N. 1 5+3 31·45				
Anon.	21 12 19·0	10 2·9	13 17·0	10 2·6	10 2·75	N. 4 5+3 14·25				
Anon.	21 25 25·2	9 33·3	6 29·8	9 33·5	9 33·4	N. 3 35—3 3·6				
7557	21 35 22·7	9 16·0	13 28·3	9 16·1	9 16·05	N. 0 10+4 12·25				
7057	21 51 37·3	9 32·3	8 29·55	9 32·0	9 32·23	N. 4 45—1 2·68				
Anon.	21 55 28·0	9 32·1	10 0·4	9 32·5	9 32·23	N. 4 45+0 2·17	30·117	58·5	58·4	53·6
7842	22 22 21·2	9 19·8	5 24·5	9 19·7	9 19·45	N. 0 50—3 28·75				
7909	22 33 25·5	10 5·5	11 29·6	10 4·8	10 5·15	N. 3 45+1 24·45				
7906	22 43 33·9	9 23·0	8 22·0	9 23·3	9 23·15	N 0 15—1 1·15				
7092	22 49 45·2	10 4 7	9 12·5	10 4·2	10 4·45	N. 3 30—0 25·95	30·123	58·5	58·5	53·5

June 1.—Anon. 14ʰ 58ᵐ.—Probably a wrong star bisected.
No. 5881 was observed at 20 seconds after passing the meridian wire.
No. 6016—Hurried.
Before the wind increased, the temperature deceended ; afterwards it rose.
As the Micrometer did not work well, it was this day taken to pieces, when the inside was found to be very dirty. When cleaned the parts seemed to be in good keeping : it was not taken to pieces at the Cape before to-day.

⊙ JUNE 2, 1844.—FACE OF SECTOR WEST.

Number of B.A.C.	Time by Chronometer.	Micr. for Plumb-line on Dot.	Micr. for Observation of Star.	Micr. for Plumb-line on Dot.	Mean of Micr. for Plumb-line on Dot.	Star's Apparent Zenith Distance.	Barom.	Thermometers. Att.	Lower.	Out.
	h m s	rev. pts.	rev. pts.	rev. pts.	rev. pts.	° ' rev. pts.	in.			
4507	13 21 42·7	11 1·8	11 15·75	11 1·8	11 1·8	S. 4 40+0 13·95	30·100	60·0	60·0	58·0
Anon.	14 10	10 4·7	8 19·7	10 4·6	10 4·65	S. 3 15—1 18·95			60·0	
Anon.	14 57 18·2	9 23·2	13 32·75	9 23·6	9 23·4	N. 1 40—4 9·35				
5292	15 49 30·0	10 2·6	11 14·45	10 2·5	10 2·55	S. 4 0+1 11·9				
5331	15 55 3·5	9 5·9	11 21·4		9 5·45	S. 2 25+2 15·95				
Comp.	15		6 24·8	9 5·0	9 5·45	S. 2 25—2 14·63				
5508	16 20 53·0	8 28·9	9 28·55	8 29·3	8 29·1	S. 0 25+0 33·45	30·105	60·0	60·0	56·5

FACE OF SECTOR EAST.

Number of B.A.C.	Time by Chronometer.	Micr. for Plumb-line on Dot.	Micr. for Observation of Star.	Micr. for Plumb-line on Dot.	Mean of Micr. for Plumb-line on Dot.	Star's Apparent Zenith Distance.	Barom.	Att.	Lower.	Out.
5588	16 33 23·5	8 24·1	4 24·1	8 24·4	8 24·25	N. 2 10—4 0·15				

FACE OF SECTOR WEST.

Number of B.A.C.	Time by Chronometer.	Micr. for Plumb-line on Dot.	Micr. for Observation of Star.	Micr. for Plumb-line on Dot.	Mean of Micr. for Plumb-line on Dot.	Star's Apparent Zenith Distance.	Barom.	Att.	Lower.	Out.
5881	17 17 3·0	8 9·6	12 8·45	8 10·4	8 10·0	N. 4 15—3 32·45				
5970	17 31 24 2	8 19·2	9 7·05	8 19·2	8 19·2	S. 5 0+0 21·85				
6016	17 38 42·3	7 28·7	3 16·35	7 28·9	7 28·8	N. 2 15—4 12·45				
6074	17 48 43·4	9 0·1	5 4·75	9 0·1	9 0·1	N. 3 40+3 29·35				
6145	17 59 42·0	9 10·8	7 5·2	9 10·8	9 10·8	N. 3 10+2 5·6				
6233	18 13 29·2	11 0·5	12 24·4	11 0·6	11 0·55	S. 0 30+1 23·85				
6275	18	9 19·5	13 29·25		9 19·52	N. 0 50—4 9·73				
6285	18		7 27·35	9 19·5	9 19·52	N. 0 50+1 26·17				
6305	18	9 19·4	12 1·6	9 19·7	9 19·52	N. 0 50—2 16·08				
6414	18 42 19·2	9 0·3	6 22·4	9 0·3	9 0·3	N. 3 0+2 11·9				
6525	18 57 19·5	9 13·3	11 18·8	9 13·3	9 13·3	N. 5 5—2 5·5				
6639	19 16 42·8	9 19·0	12 15·4	9 19·0	9 19·0	N. 3 55—2 30·4				
Anon.	19 20 55·0	9 23·0	5 16·9	9 23·1	9 23·05	N. 4 5+4 6·15	30·096	59·0	59·2	47·2
6753	19	9 13·5	9 19·25	9 13·3	9 13·4	N. 2 40—0 5·85				
6877	19 54 4·3	9 17·0	6 0·6	9 17·0	9 17·0	N. 1 25+3 10·4	30·095	59·0	58·3	45·0
6948	20 5 47·2	9 21·5	5 29·3	9 21·7	9 21·6	N. 3 25+3 26·3				
7011	20	9 14·7	6 8·8	9 14·8	9 14·74	N. 4 20+3 5·94				
7026	20		6 16·5	9 14·8	9 14·74	N. 4 20+2 32·24				
7057	20 21 0·8	9 14·7	12 10 0	9 14·7	9 14·74	N. 4 20—2 29·26				
Anon.	20 23 53·2	9 18·5	5 28·3	9 18·5	9 18·5	N. 4 5+3 24·2				
Anon.	20 33	9 28·0	13 9·9	9 28·2	9 28·1	N. 4 0—3 15·8				
7207	20 39 52·0	10 1·8	9 23·0	10 1·6	10 1·7	S. 0 25—0 12·7	30·088	57·8	58·3	43·8
7386	21 8 6·2	9 28·0	5 33·45	9 27·6	9 27·8	N. 1 5+3 28·35				
Anon.	21 12 11·0	9 27·6	6 19·45	9 27·5	9 27·55	N. 4 5+3 8·1	30·080	58·6	57·8	45·6
Anon.	21	9 18·4	12 26·8	9 18·4	9 18·4	N. 3 35—3 8·4				
7557	21 35 16·9	9 27·8	5 22·3	9 27·4	9 27·4	N. 0 10+4 5·3				
7613	21 44 8·0	10 12·0	8 33·5	10 12·0	10 12·0	S. 4 10—1 12·5				57·8
7657	21 51 28·8	9 29·5	11 6·55	9 29·6	9 29·53	N. 4 45—1 11·02				
Anon.	21	9 29·4	9 33·8	9 29·6	9 29·53	N. 4 45—0 4·27	30·080	58·4	57·4	44·3
7842	22 22 15·5	10 2·0	14 2·0	10 2·2	10 2·1	N. 0 50—3 33·9				
7909	22 33 18·0	10 3·2	8 18·5	10 2·8	10 3·0	N. 3 45+1 18·5				
7966	22 43 28·2	9 17·6	10 22·65	9 17·6	9 17·6	N. 0 15—1 5·05				
7992	22 48 38·0	9 16·3	10 16·05	9 16·3	9 16·3	N. 3 30—0 33·75	30 084	58·2	58·0	44·5

☾ JUNE 3, 1844.—FACE OF SECTOR EAST.

Number of B.A.C.	Time by Chronometer.	Micr. for Plumb-line on Dot.	Micr. for Observation of Star.	Micr. for Plumb-line on Dot.	Mean of Micr. for Plumb-line on Dot.	Star's Apparent Zenith Distance.	Barom.	Att.	Lower.	Out.
4507	13 21 43·2	8 9·0	7 33·0	8 9·2	8 9·1	S. 4 40+0 10·1	30·008	55·5	58·1	49·4

☿ JUNE 4, 1844.—FACE OF SECTOR EAST.

Number of B.A.C.	Time by Chronometer.	Micr. for Plumb-line on Dot.	Micr. for Observation of Star.	Micr. for Plumb-line on Dot.	Mean of Micr. for Plumb-line on Dot.	Star's Apparent Zenith Distance.	Barom.	Att.	Lower.	Out.
2293	6 52 3·0	9 4·9	9 12·95	9 5·0	9 4·95	N. 5 10—0 8·0	30·181	60·2	60·3	62·3

June 2.—Anon. 14h 10m, observed at 22 seconds after passing the meridian wire.
The observations of Anon. 19h 20m 50s, 20h 33m; Nos. 7011 and 7026 are uncertain because of the images being very faint.
Cold and nearly calm. The small stars will not bear even faint illumination.

♂ JUNE 4, 1844.—FACE OF SECTOR EAST—(continued).

Number of B.A.C.	Time by Chronometer.	Micr. for Plumb-line on Dot.	Micr. for Observation of Star.	Micr. for Plumb-line on Dot.	Mean of Micr. for Plumb-line on Dot.	Star's Apparent Zenith Distance.	Barom.	Thermometers.		
								Attd.	Lower.	Out.
	h m s	rev. pts.	rev. pts.	rev. pts.	rev. pts.	° ' rev. pts.	in.			
7026	20 16		14 0·7	10 30·7	10 30·53	N. 4 20+3 4·17	30·087	57·0	58·2	43·0
7057	20 21	10 30·6	8 6·4	10 30·3	10 30·53	N. 4 20—2 24·13				
Anon.	20 23	11 5·1	15 0·8	11 4·9	11 5·0	N. 4 5+3 29·8				
7207	20 40	8 7·7	8 25·9	8 7·7	8 7·7	S. 0 25—0 18·2				
Anon.	21 0 27·2	9 30·4	10 20·4	9 30·5	9 30·45	N. 3 35+0 23·95				
7386	21 8 10·8	9 22·1	13 19·9	9 21·7	9 21·9	N. 1 5+3 32·0				
Anon.	21 12 16·5	10 3·8	13 19·0	10 3·6	10 3·7	N. 4 5+3 15·3	30·070	57·0	58·2	43·4
7613	21 43 10·0	9 20·5	11 3·3	9 20·6	9 20·55	S. 4 10—1 16·75				
7657	21 51 35·5	10 2·7	9 1·7	10 2·8	10 2·58	N. 4 45—1 0·88				
Anon.	21 55	10 2·8	10 4·6	10 2·0	10 2·58	N. 4 45+0 2·02				
7842	22 22 19·2	9 26·2	9 32·4	9 26·0	9 26·1	N. 0 50—3 27·7	30·068	57·0	58·0	41·8
7909	22 33 24·2	9 27·5	11 18·55	9 27·3	9 27·4	N. 3 45+1 25·15				
7906	22 43 32·2	9 9·4	8 8·8	9 9·2	9 9·3	N. 0 15—1 0·5				
7992	22 48 43·0	9 30·5	9 7·7	9 30·5	9 30·5	N. 3 30—0 22·8	30·067	56·5	57·4	41·0

☿ JUNE 5, 1844.—FACE OF SECTOR EAST.

4507	13 21 43·2	0 4·9	8 30·3	9 4·9	9 4·9	S. 4 40+0 8·6	29·956	58·8	59·3	52·4
Anon.	14	10 17·0	6 14·0	10 17·0	10 17·0	N. 1 40—4 3·0	29·962	58·4		51.2

FACE OF SECTOR WEST.

5292	15 49 28·4	11 9·2	12 23·6	11 9·1	11 9·15	S. 4 0+1 14·45				
5331	15	11 2·0	8 24·45	11 1·0	11 1·5	S. 2 25—2 11·05			59·2	
5508	16	9 0·3	10 0·0	9 0·0	9 0·15	S. 2 25+0 33·85				
5538	16 25 45·8	9 13·6	8 30·4	9 13·5	9 13·55	S. 1 0—0 17·15	29·986	58·5	59·0	50·6

FACE OF SECTOR EAST.

5970	17 31 25·2	9 23·0	9 4·55	9 23·5	9 23·25	S. 5 0+0 18·7	29·980	58·5	58·2	53·0

♂ JUNE 11, 1844.—FACE OF SECTOR EAST.

2293	6 52 8·0	8 28·1	8 26·1	8 28·1	8 28·1	N. 5 10—0 2·0	30·140	58·7	59·0	59·7

☿ JUNE 12, 1844.—FACE OF SECTOR EAST.

6016	17 37 44·2	9 23·5	14 2·95	9 23·1	9 23·3	N. 2 15+4 13·65	30·155	57·2	57·2	52·2
6233	18 13	10 8·9	8 22·75	10 8·5	10 8·7	S. 0 30+1 19·95				52·0
6285	18 20	9 17·0	12 11·5	10 16·7	10 16·87	N. 0 50+1 28·63				
6305	18 23		8 2·65	10 16·9	10 16·87	N. 0 50—2 14·22	30·144	37·6		51·8
6639	19 16 46·0	9 32·1	7 8·8	9 32·0	9 32·05	N. 3 55—2 23·25	30·144	37·6		52·4

☉ JUNE 16, 1844.— FACE OF SECTOR WEST.

2293	6 52 57·8	7 19·3	7 23·35	7 19·4	7 19·35	N. 5 10—0 4·0	30·390	58·8	58·2	54·8
6016	17 39 37·2	7 23·5	3 11·9	7 23·55	7 23·53	N. 2 15+4 11·63	30·496	56·4	56·6	47·0

FACE OF SECTOR EAST.

6074	17 49 44·8	8 25·2	12 25·2	8 25·4	8 25·3	N. 3 40+3 33·9				

FACE OF SECTOR WEST.

6233	18 14 24·8	8 33·4	10 22·95	8 33·3	8 33·35	S. 0 30+1 23·6				56·6

June 4.—Frequently overcast.
Much clouded sky between the 5th and 16th of June: during this interval a long series of measures were taken for Micrometer run.

☉ June 16, 1844.—Face of Sector West—(continued).

Number of B.A.C.	Time by Chronometer.	Micr. for Plumb-line on Dot.	Micr. for Observation of Star.	Micr. for Plumb-line on Dot.	Mean of Micr. for Plumb-line on Dot.	Star's Apparent Zenith Distance.	Barom.	Attd.	Lower.	Out.
	h m s	rev. pts	rev. pts	rev. pts	rev. pts	° ' rev. pts	in.			
6275	18 20 23·0	9 8·9	13 17·6		9 8·7	N. 0 50—4 8·9				
6285	18 21 26·0		7 17·0	9 8·5	9 8·7	N. 0 50+1 25·7				
6414	18 43 15·8	9 8·1	6 30·4	9 7·9	9 8·0	N. 3 0+2 11·6	30·508	56·2	56·2	47·0
			Face of Sector East.							
6525	18 58 22·2	9 28·3	7 28·6	9 28·3	9 28·3	N. 5 5—1 33·7				
			Face of Sector West.							
6639	19 17 37·6	9 10·4	12 6·75	9 10·4	9 10·4	N. 3 55—2 30·35				
Anon.	19 21	9 15·3	5 6·9	9 15·1	9 15·2	N. 4 5+4 8·3				
6753	19 36 4·5	9 13·2	9 18·65	9 13·2	9 13·2	N. 2 40—0 5·45	30·506	56·0	56·2	46·6
6877	19 54 59·5	9 19·6	6 2·25	9 19·6	9 19·6	N. 1 25+3 17·35				
6948	20 6 41·2	9 27·4	5 1·0	9 27·4	9 27·4	N. 3 25+4 26·4				
7011	20 15 39·5	9 33·9	6 27·45	9 33·8	9 33·78	N. 4 20+3 6·33				
7026	20 17 30·0		7 1·05	9 33·5	9 33·78	N. 4 20+2 32·73				
7057	20 21 55·0	9 33·9	12 27·8	9 33·8	9 33·78	N. 4 20—2 28·02				
Anon.	20 24 47·8	10 7·0	6 15·7	10 7·1	10 7·05	N. 4 5+3 25·35				
Anon.	20 34 18·0	10 0·3	13 15·35	10 0·3	10 0·3	N. 4 0—3 15·05				
7207	20	9 24·8	9 7·9	9 24·9	9 24·85	S. 0 25—0 16·95				
Anon.	20	9 33·5	13 13·3	9 33·3	9 33·4	N. 4 15—3 13·9				
Anon.	21 1 15·2	8 17·4	7 32·05	8 17·3	8 17·35	N. 3 35+0 19·3				
7386	21 9 1·5	9 17·3	5 22·3	9 17·1	9 17·2	N. 1 5+3 28·9				
Anon.	21 13 4·8		5 19·05	8 28·6		N. 4 5+3 9·55	30·505	56·0	56·2	46·1
Anon.	21	8 30·4	12 4·4	8 30·3	8 30·35	N. 3 35—3 8·05				
			Face of Sector East.							
1802	5 34 35·6	8 23·2	11 7·55	8 23·1	8 23·15	S. 0 15—2 18·4	30·510	57·7	67·2	55·0
1878	5 46 4·2	8 19·75	10 28·45	8 19·75	8 19·75	S. 1 55—2 8·7				

☾ June 17, 1844.—Face of Sector East.

Number of B.A.C.	Time by Chronometer.	Micr. for Plumb-line on Dot.	Micr. for Observation of Star.	Micr. for Plumb-line on Dot.	Mean of Micr. for Plumb-line on Dot.	Star's Apparent Zenith Distance.	Barom.	Attd.	Lower.	Out.
2293	6 53 6·2	9 6·1	9 5·4	9 6·1	9 6·1	N. 5 10—0 0·7	30·486	58·2	67·6	55·3
6639	19 17 45·2	9 12·0	6 21·15	9 11·9	9 11·95	N. 3 55—2 24·8	30·440	56·0	56·0	50·0
Anon	19 21 57·0	8 15·5	12 29·9	8 15·5	8 15·5	N. 4 5+4 14·4				
6753	19 36 11·5	8 2·5	8 1·9	8 2·5	8 2·5	N. 2 40—0 0·6				
6877	19 55 6 0	8 28·5	12 15·5	8 28·5	8 28·5	N. 1 25+3 21·0				
6948	20 6 48·2	8 28·4	13 26·4	8 28·5	8 28·45	N. 3 25+4 31·95				
7011	20 15 47·0	8 30·4	12 7·95	8 30·5	8 30·46	N. 4 20+3 17·49				
7026	20 17 37·2		11 33·45	8 30·5	8 30·46	N. 4 20+3 2·99				
7057	20 22 2·3	8 30·4	6 8·0	8 30·5	8 30·46	N. 4 20—2 22·46				
Anon.	20 24 54·5	8 23·0	12 19·7	8 23·1	8 23·05	N. 4 5+3 30·65				
Anon.	20 34 25·0	9 11·7	6 2·2	9 11·6	9 11·65	N. 4 0—3 9·45				
7207	20 40 52·4	8 30·3	9 16·0	8 30·1	8 30·2	S. 0 25—0 19·8	30·433	56·0	55·9	50·6
Anon.	20 54 12·8	9 26·1	6 15·0	9 26·1	9 26·1	N. 4 15—3 11·1				
Anon.	21 1 23·2	9 7·1	9 31·0	9 7·1	9 7·1	N. 3 35+0 23·9				
7386	21	8 19·85	12 18·7	8 19·9	8 19·88	N. 1 5+3 32·88				
Anon.	21 13 12·7	9 6·9	12 22·0	9 7·0	9 6·95	N. 4 5+3 15·05				
Anon.	21 26 19·8	9 1·4	5 31·45	9 1·3	9 1·35	N. 3 35—3 3·9				
7557	21	8 30 2	13 9·7	8 30·1	8 30·15	N. 0 10+4 13·55				56·0
			Face of Sector West.							
7613	21 45 3·5	9 8·6	7 26·55	9 8·6	9 8·6	S. 4 10—1 16·05				
7657	21 52 22·5	8 29·4	10 0·75	8 29·2	8 29·33	N. 4 45—1 5·42				
Anon.	21 56 13·2	8 29·4	8 30·1	8 29·3	8 29·33	N. 4 45—0 0·77	30·417	56·0	56·1	50·4

June 16.—No. 1878 transited at about one minute after appt. noon.
17.—No. 7557 was observed at 22 seconds after passing the meridian wire.

☽ June 17, 1844.—Face of Sector West—(continued).

Number of B.A.C.	Time by Chronometer.	Micr. for Plumb-line on Dot.	Micr. for Observation of Star.	Micr. for Plumb-line on Dot.	Mean of Micr. for Plumb-line on Dot.	Star's Apparent Zenith Distance.	Barom.	Thermometers.		
								Attd.	Lower.	Out.
	h m s	rev. pts.	rev. pts.	rev. pts.	rev. pts.	° ′ rev. pts.	in.			
7842	22 23 10·0	9 33·6	13 29·3	9 33·5	9 33·55	N. 0 50—3 29·75	30·414	56·0	56·1	51·0
7909	22 34 12·0	9 16·6	7 28·4	9 16·6	9 16·6	N. 3 45+1 22·2				
7966	22 44 23·2	9 18·1	10 20·3	9 18·1	9 18·1	N. 0 15—1 2·2				
7992	22 49 32·3	9 18·5	10 14·1	9 19·1	9 18·8	N. 3 30—0 29·3	30·414	56·0	56·1	50·7

♂ June 18, 1844.—Face of Sector West.

2293	6 52 57·0	9 10·0	0 15·65	9 9·9	9 9·95	N. 5 10—0 5·7	30·400	58·5	58·5	60·3
6689	19 17 36·2	8 22·5	11 17·8	8 22·6	8 22·55	N. 3 55—2 29·25	30·349	57·5	57·7	56·8
Anon.	19 21 49·0	8 27·1	4 15·0	8 27·1	8 27·1	N 4 5+4 12·1				
6753	19 36 3·7	11 15·8	11 20·0	11 15·6	11 15·7	N. 2 40—0 4·3				

Face of Sector East.

6877	19 55 5·0	10 21·6	14 8·3	10 21·7	10 21·65	N. 1 25+3 20·65				

Face of Sector West.

6948	20	10 1·6	5 9·2	10 1·4	10 1·5	N. 3 25+4 26·3				
7011	20 15 39·0	9 29·6	6 22·25	9 29·5	9 29·52	N. 4 20+3 7·27				
7026	20 17 30·0		6 29·9	9 29·5	9 29·52	N. 4 20+2 33·82				
7057	20 21 54·2	9 29·5	12 22·6	9 29·5	9 29·52	N. 4 20—2 27·08				
Anon.	20		5 5·2	8 30·9		N. 4 5+3 25·7				
Anon.	20	9 26·3	13 5·75	9 26·3	9 26·3	N. 4 0—3 13·45				
7207	20 40 46·1	9 23·9	9 6·8	9 24·0	9 23·95	S. 0 25—0 17·15	30·338	57·0	58·0	56·3
Anon.	21 1 14·5	9 11·9	8 26·6	9 11·6	9 11·75	N. 3 35+0 19·15				
7386	21 9 0·8	9 14·0	5 19·0	9 14·0	9 14·0	N. 1 5+3 29·0				
Anon.	21 13 3·3	9 5·5	5 28·85	9 5·6	9 5·55	N. 4 5+3 10·7	30·328	57·0	58·0	55·9
Anon.	21 26 11·5	8 32·5	12 5·95	8 32·3	8 32·4	N. 3 35—3 7·55				
7557	21 36 11·7	9 9·95	5 0·75	9 10·0	9 9·98	N. 0 10+4 9·23				

Face of Sector East.

7613	21 45 7·3	9 3·6	10 24·75	9 3·5	9 3·55	S. 4 10—1 21·2				
7657	21 52 30·7	9 19·2	8 18·3	9 19·0	9 19·13	N. 4 45—1 0·83				
Anon.	21 56 21·3	9 19·3	9 23·2	9 19·0	9 19·13	N. 4 45+0 4·07				
7842	22 23 16·2	9 7·7	5 15·65	9 7·5	9 7·6	N. 0 50—3 25·95	30·325	57·0	57·6	55·4

Face of Sector West.

7909	22 34 11·8	10 16·5	8 28·9	10 16·3	10 16·4	N. 3 45+1 21·5				
7966	22 44 23·2	10 0·2	11 1·9	10 0·3	10 0·25	N. 0 15—1 1·65				
7992	22 49 32·2	9 7·5	10 2·45	9 7·3	9 7·4	N. 3 30—0 29·05	30·320	57·0	57·6	53·9
1802	5 34 30·2	8 20·6	6 5·1	8 20·4	8 20·5	S. 0 15—2 15·4	30·304	59·4	59·2	63·3
1878	5 45 58·8	8 33·6	6 28·7	8 33·4	8 33·5	N. 1 55—2 4·8				

♂ June 19, 1844.—Face of Sector East.

2293	6 53 4·8	8 28·9	8 29·0	8 28·9	8 28·9	N. 5 10+0 0·1	30·276	59·8	59·3	64·4
Anon.	20 34 24·2	9 21·1	6 12·2	9 21·2	9 21·15	N. 4 0—3 8·95	30·200	57·0	55·2	
Anon.	20 54 12·0	10 5·9	6 28·8	10 6·1	10 6·0	N. 4 15—3 11·2				
7386	21 9 7·2	11 22·5	15 21·9	11 22·3	11 22·4	N. 1 5+3 33·6				
Anon.	21 13 12·2	10 10·4	13 26·1	10 10·4	10 10·4	N. 4 5+3 15·7				
Anon.	21 26 10·2	9 1·1	5 33 05	9 1·0	9 1·05	N. 3 35—3 2·0				

Face of Sector West.

7557	21 36 12·0	9 1·6	4 26·8	9 1·7	9 1·05	N. 0 10+4 8·85				

June 18.—No. 7026.—The seconds doubtful.
The seconds of transit 7842 are doubtful.
Bad definition.

♂ JUNE 19, 1844.—FACE OF SECTOR WEST—(continued).

Number of B.A.C.	Time by Chronometer.	Micr. for Plumb-line on Dot.	Micr. for Observation of Star.	Micr. for Plumb-line on Dot.	Mean of Micr. for Plumb-line on Dot.	Star's Apparent Zenith Distance.	Barom.	Thermometers.		
								Attd.	Lower.	Out.
	h m s	rev. pts.	rev. pts.	rev. pts.	rev. pts.	o ' rev. pts.	in.			
7613	21 45 3·5	10 6·3	8 24·5	10 6·3	10 6·3	S. 4 10—1 15·8				
7657	21 52 22·2	8 14·5	9 19·45	8 14·2	8 14·35	N. 4 45—1 5·1				
Anon.	21 56 13·5	8 14·4	8 14·4	8 14 3	8 14·35	N. 4 45—0 0·05	30·180	56·0	56·8	52·0
7842	22 23 10·0	8 17·7	12 13·35	8 17·7	8 17·7	N. 0 50—3 29·65				

FACE OF SECTOR EAST.

7909	22 34 19·0	8 26 9	10 19·3	8 27·2	8 27·05	N. 3 45+1 26·25				
7966	22 44 29·2	8 14·5	7 16·7	8 14·4	8 14·45	N. 0 15—0 31·75				
7992	22	8 19·5	7 30·5	8 19·1	8 19 3	N. 3 30—0 22·8				
1802	5 34 35·2	7 32·6	10 18·0	7 32·6	7 32·6	S. 0 15—2 19·4	30·220	58·0	58·6	62·0

♃ JUNE 20, 1844.— FACE OF SECTOR WEST.

2293	6 52 56·0	8 10·9	8 15·95	8 10 9	8 10·9	N. 5 10—0 5·05	30·203	59·0	59·4	63·4

FACE OF SECTOR EAST.

6877	19 55 6·0	9 23·4	13 10·0	9 23·6	9 23 5	N. 5 25+3 20·5	30·180	57·5	56·6	
6948	20 6 49·0	9 32·5	14 29·45	9 32·4	0 32·45	D. 3 25+4 31·0				
7011	20 15 47·4	9 9·4	12 21·2	9 9·3		N. 4 20+3 11·9				
7026	20 17 39·2		12 12·2	9 9·4	9 9 3	N. 4 20+3 2·9				
7057	20 22 4·2	9 9·3	6 20·45	9 9·1	9 9·3	N. 4 20—2 22·85				
Anon.	20 24		13 1·0	9 3·7		N. 4 5+3 31·3				
Anon.	20 33	9 6·6	5 30·7	9 6·5	9 6·55	N. 4 0—3 9·85				
7207	20 40 53·2	8 22·0	9 8·8	8 22·0	8 22·0	S. 0 25—0 20·8	30·175	57·0	57·2	48·3

FACE OF SECTOR WEST.

Anon.	21 1 16·5	12 8·7	11 22·3	12 8·6	12 8·65	N. 3 35+0 20·35				
7386	21 9 2·5	11 1·5	7 6·2	11 1·5	11 1·5	N. 1 5+3 29·3				
Anon.	21 13 5·3	8 5·7	4 29·0	8 5·7		N. 4 5+3 10·7				
Anon.	21 26 13·2	11 12·2	14 20·05	11 12·3	11 12·25	N. 3 35—3 7·8				

FACE OF SECTOR EAST.

7557	21 36 18·2	11 14·4	15 28·8	11 14·6	11 14·5	N. 0 10+4 14·3				
7613	21 45 9·3	10 11·4	11 32·45	10 11·3	10 11·35	S. 4 10—1 21·1				
7657	21 52 31·0	9 29·0	8 27·9	9 29·2	9 29·15	N. 4 45—1 1·25				
Anon.	21 56 21·0	9 29·2	9 32·6	9 29·2	9 29·15	N. 4 45+0 3·45	30·180	57·0	57·4	51·5
7842	22 23 17·2	8 27·4	5 2·05	8 27·4	8 27·4	N. 0 50—3 25·35				
7909	22 34 20·2	9 24·7	11 18·6	9 24·5	9 24·6	N. 3 45+1 28·0				
7966	22 44 29·7	9 16·4	8 19·1	9 16·5	9 16·45	N. 0 15—0 31·35	30·177			
7992	22 49 40·2	10 16·8	9 27·9	10 16·6	10 16 7	N. 3 30—0 22·8		57·0	57·3	51·0

♀ JUNE 21, 1844.—FACE OF SECTOR EAST.

2293	6 53 6·2	10 19·8	10 20·7	10 19·4	10 19·6	N. 5 10+0 1·1	30·214	59·0	59·0	61·4
6233	18 14 30·2	9 13·3	7 27·4	9 13·4	9 13·35	S. 0 30+1 19·95	30·250	58·8	58·3	53·4

FACE OF SECTOR WEST.

6285	18		7 18·6	9 9·0	9 9·0	N. 0 50+1 24·4				
6305	18 24 20·8	9 9·0	11 26·45	9 9·0	9 9·0	N. 0 50—2 17·45				
6414	18 43 17·0	8 30·5	6 17·4	8 30·5	8 30·5	N. 3 0+2 13·1	30·275	58·5	58·3	52·1

FACE OF SECTOR EAST.

6639	19 17 47·2	9 31·2	7 6·6	9 31·2	9 31·2	N. 3 55—2 24·6				

z

♀ June 21, 1844.—Face of Sector East—(continued).

Number of B.A.C.	Time by Chronometer.	Micr. for Plumb-line on Dot.	Micr. for Observation of Star.	Micr. for Plumb-line on Dot.	Mean of Micr. for Plumb-line on Dot.	Star's Apparent Zenith Distance.	Barom.	Thermometers.		
								Attd.	Lower.	Out.
	h m s	rev. pts.	rev. pts.	rev. pts.	rev pts.	o ' rev. pts	in.			
6753	19	9 24·0	0 25·2	9 24·4	9 24·2	N. 2 40+0 1·0				

Face of Sector West.

6877	19 55 2·0	9 23·1	6 5·55	9 23·0	9 23·05	N. 1 25+3 17·5	30·276	58·4	58·4	50·9
6948	20	9 7·1	4 15·1	9 7·1	9 7·1	N. 3 25+4 26·0				
7057	20 21 57 5	9 17·9	12 10 85	9 18·1	9 18·0	N. 4 20−2 26·85				
Anon.	20 24	10 14·4	6 22·9	10 14·5	10 14·45	N. 4 5+3 25·55				
Anon	20 34 20·0	9 18·5	12 33·6	9 18·5	9 18·5	N. 4 0−3 15·1				
7207	20 40 50·0	9 21·9	9 4·85	9 21·9	9 21 9	S. 0 25−0 17·05	30·276	58·2	58·8	50·8

♄ June 22, 1844.—Face of Sector East.

6948	20	13 12·4	18 10·4	13 12·5	13 12·45	N. 3 25+4 31·05	30·275	58·0	58·8	53·0
7011	20 15 52·0	9 17·0	12 28·5	9 16·9	9 17·0	N. 4 20+3 11·5				
7026	20		12 23·4	9 17 0	9 17·0	N. 4 20+3 6·4				
7057	20 22 7·7	9 17·0	6 28·4	9 17·1	9 17·0	N. 4 20−2 22·6				
Anon.	20 24	9 15·0	13 11·4	9 15·0	9 15·0	N. 4 5+3 30·4				52·0
Anon.	20 34	9 24·1	6 15·0	9 24·0	9 24·05	N. 4 0−3 9·05				
7207	20 40 58·4	9 3·G	9 23·7	9 3·5	9 3·55	S. 0 25−0 20 15				
Anon.	20	10 1·1	6 24·1	10 1·1	10 1·1	N. 4 15−3 11·0				
Anon.	21 1 28·5	6 32·3	7 22·45	6 32·0	6 32·15	N. 3 35+0 24·3				
7386	21 9 13·6	7 17·6	11 16·9	7 17·8	7 17·7	N. 1 5+3 33·2				
Anon.	21 13 18·4		12 3·7	8 22·7		N. 4 5+3 15·0				
Anon.	21 26 25·8	8 22·4	5 19·9	8 22·3	8 22·35	N. 3 35−3 2·45	30·275	58·0	58·8	55·4

Face of Sector West.

7557	21 36 18·0	9 9·1	5 0·6	9 9·5	9 9·3	N. 0 10+4 8·7				
7613	21 45 9·3	9 14·7	7 32·5	9 14·7	9 14·7	S. 4 40−1 16·2				
7657	21 52 33·8	8 22·6	9 27·9	8 22·8	8 22·8	N. 4 45−1 5·1				
Anon.	21 56 19·6	8 22·9	8 22·8	8 22·9	8 22·8	N. 4 45+0 0·0	30·285	58·0	59·0	55 5
7842	22 23 15 7	8 22·6	12 17·9	8 22·6	8 22·6	N. 0 50−3 29·3				
7909	22 34 18·0	9 1·3	7 13·65	9 1·3	9 1·35	N. 3 45+1 21·65	30·287	58·0	59·0	55·0
7966	22 44 29·0	9 14·2	10 16·4	9 14·3	9 14·25	N. 0 15−1 2 15				
7992	22 49 38·2	9 13·2	10 8·4	9 13·1	9 13·15	N. 3 30−0 29 25	30·290	57·6	59·0	54·8

☾ June 24, 1844.--Face of Sector East.

6285	18	9 27·0	11 22·1		9 26·95	N. 0 50+1 29·15	30·470	50·8	60·0	60·0
6305	18 24 34·2		7 13·75	9 26·9	9 26·95	N. 0 50−2 13·2				

Face of Sector West.

6639	19 17 48·0	9 30·7	12 25·95	9 30·4	9 30·55	N. 3 55−2 29·4				

Face of Sector East.

6753	19 35 21·5	10 8·9	10 9·3	10 8·7	10 8·8	N. 2 40+0 0·5				

Face of Sector West.

6948	20 6 53·0	9 33·3	5 6·45	9 33·3	9 33·3	N. 3 25+4 26·85				
7011	20 15 51·0	9 10·1	6 3·0		9 10·1	N. 4 20+3 7·1				
7026	20 17 41·4		6 11·25	9 10 1	9 10·1	N. 4 20+2 32·85				
Anon.	20 24	9 6·1	5 14·2	9 6·1	9 6·1	N. 4 5+3 25·9				
Anon.	20 34	8 22·3	12 2·0	8 22·3	8 22·3	N. 4 0−3 13·7				
7207	20 40 58·5	8 0·5	7 19·3	8 0·6	8 0·55	S. 0 25−0 15·25				

June 21.—Nos. 6753 and 6948 are bad observations. Clouded after 20ʰ 40ᵐ.

☾ JUNE 24, 1844.—FACE OF SECTOR WEST—(continued).

Number of B.A.C.	Time by Chronometer.	Micr. for Plumb-line on Dot.	Micr. for Observation of Star.	Micr. for Plumb-line on Dot.	Mean of Micr. for Plumb-line on Dot.	Star's Apparent Zenith Distance.	Barom.	Thermometers. Attd.	Lower.	Out.
	h m s	rev. pts.	rev. pts.	rev. pts.	rev. pts.	o ' rev. pts.	in.			
Anon.	20 54 17·0	7 31·7	11 12·0	7 31·7	7 31·7	N. 4 15–3 14·3	30·463	59·7	60·3	59·4
Anon.	21 1 27·2	8 6·7	7 21·45	8 6·7	8 6·7	N. 3 35+0 19 25				
7386	21 9 12·2	8 31·9	5 2·7	8 31·8	8 31·85	N. 1 5+3 20·15				
Anon.	21 13 15·8		4 32·5	8 9·7		N. 4 5+3 11·2				
Anon.	21 26 23·8	9 16·1	12 23·55	9 16·3	9 16·2	N. 3 35–3 7·35				
FACE OF SECTOR EAST.										
7557	21 36 28·3	8 20·5	13 0·45	8 20·6	8 20·55	N. 0 10+4 13·9				
7613	21 45 20·0	8 30·3	10 17·1	8 30·3	8 30·3	S. 4 10–1 20 8				
7657	21 52 40·4	8 14·4	7 12·8	8 14·5	8 14·48	N. 4 45–1 1·63				
Anon.	21 56	8 14·4	8 20·4	8 14·4	8 14·43	N. 4 45+0 5·97	30·455	59·5	60·2	59·2
7842	21 23 27·2	8 5·4	4 14·7	8 5·7	8 5·55	N. 0 50–3 24·85				
7909	22 34 30·3	9 2·6	10 30·5	9 2·6	9 2·7	N. 3 45+1 27·8				
7966	22 44 40·2	8 22·8	7 25·05	8 22·9	8 22·85	N. 0 15–0 31·8	30·438	59·5	60·0	59·4

♂ JUNE 25, 1844.—FACE OF SECTOR EAST.

Number of B.A.C.	Time by Chronometer.	Micr. for Plumb-line on Dot.	Micr. for Observation of Star.	Micr. for Plumb-line on Dot.	Mean of Micr. for Plumb-line on Dot.	Star's Apparent Zenith Distance.	Barom.	Thermometers. Attd.	Lower.	Out.
2293	6 53 9·0	8 20·9	8 24·8	8 21·0	8 20·95	N. 5 10–0 3·85	30·413	62·0	62·0	66·2
6275	18	8 31·9	4 24·8		8 31·9	N. 0 50–4 7·1	30·350	57·5	59·3	51·2
6285	18 21 45·0		10 26·8	8 31·9	8 31·9	N. 0 50+1 28·9				
Anon.	19 21	9 28·6	14 9·8	9 28·8	9 28·7	N. 4 5–4 15·1				
FACE OF SECTOR WEST.										
6753	19 36 17·6	7 31·5	8 1·9	7 31·7	7 31·6	N. 2 40–0 4·3				
FACE OF SECTOR EAST.										
7011	20 15 59·5	8 8·9	11 19·8	8 8·7	8 8·88	N. 4 20+3 10·92				
7026	20 17 51·0	8 8·9	11 12·4	8 9·0	8 8·88	N 4 20+3 3·52				
Anon.	20 24	8 15·1	12 10·45	8 15·1	8 15·1	N. 5 +3 29·35				
Anon.	20 34 38·0	9 4·0	5 27·3	9 4·0	9 4·0	N. 4 0–3 10·7				
7207	20 41 6·2	8 11 3	8 30·95	8 11·3	8 11·3	S. 0 25–0 19·65	30·318	58·2	59·6	49·2
Anon.	20 54	9 15·0	6 4·75	9 15·0	9 15·0	N. 4 15–3 10·25				
Anon.	21 1 35·7	9 5·3	9 29·95	9 5·2	9 5·25	N. 3 35+0 24·7				
7386	21 9 21·0	8 22·4	12 21·0	8 22·3	8 22·35	N. 1 5+3 32·65				
Anon.	21 13 25·2		12 11·55	8 29·5		N. 4 5+3 16·05				
Anon.	21 26 32·7	8 25·3	5 21·6	8 25·2	8 25·25	N. 3 35–3 3·65				
FACE OF SECTOR WEST.										
7613	21 45 17·0	8 14·4	15 30·8	17 11·7		S. 4 5+7 16·4 / S. 4 10–1 14·9				
7657	21 52 37·5	8 9·7	9 15·2	8 9·5	8 9·6	N 4 45–1 5·6				
Anon.	21 56 28·2	8 9·6	8 9·55	8 9·6	8 9·6	N. 4 45+0 0·05				
7909	22 34 26·7	8 16·6	6 28·0	8 16·6	8 16·6	N. 3 45+1 22·6	30·313	58·0	59·4	48·6
7966	22 44 37·8	8 33·2	10 0·15	8 33·2	8 33·2	N. 0 15–1 0·95				
7902	22 49 46·8	9 18·1	10 11·2	9 17·9	9 18·0	N. 3 30–0 27·2	30·310	58·0	59·4	48·8
FACE OF SECTOR EAST.										
1878	5 46 18·2	11 33·6	14 10·4	11 33·7	11 33·65	S. 1 55–2 10·75	30·258	60·2	60·3	65·8

☿ JUNE 26, 1844.—FACE OF SECTOR EAST.

Number of B.A.C.	Time by Chronometer.	Micr. for Plumb-line on Dot.	Micr. for Observation of Star.	Micr. for Plumb-line on Dot.	Mean of Micr. for Plumb-line on Dot.	Star's Apparent Zenith Distance.	Barom.	Thermometers. Attd.	Lower.	Out.
2293	6 53 19·8	11 6·5	11 9·25	11 6·3	11 6·4	N. 5 10+0 2·85	30·209	60·8	61·2	68·3
6753	19 35 27·0	12 10·9	12 10·85	12 10·95	12 10·93	N. 2 40+0 0·02		60·8		

☿ June 26, 1844—(continued.)—Face of Sector West.

Number of B.A.C.	Time by Chronometer.	Micr. for Plumb-line on Dot.	Micr. for Observation of Star.	Micr. for Plumb-line on Dot.	Mean of Micr. for Plumb-line on Dot.	Star's Apparent Zenith Distance.	Barom.	Thermometers. Attd.	Thermometers. Lower.	Thermometers. Out.
	h m s	rev. pts.	rev. pts.	rev. pts.	rev. pts.	o ' rev. pts.	in.			
7011	20 16 54·8	10 5·6	7 0·2		10 5·6	N. 4 20+3 5·4				
7026	20 17 46·0		7 7·8	10 5·6	10 5·6	N. 4 20+2 31·8				
Anon.	20 25 3·6	10 2·7	6 10·3	10 2·9	10 2·8	N. 4 5+3 26·5	30·158	60·8	61·2	61·2
Anon.	20 34 33·5	8 32·0	12 12·0	8 32·0	8 32·0	N. 4 0—3 14·0				
Anon.	20 54 20·8	9 9·4	12 24·05	9 9·3	9 9·35	N. 4 15—3 14·7				
Anon.	21 1 31·4	9 17·0	8 31·5	9 16·9	9 16·95	N. 3 35+0 19·45				
Anon	21 13 20·8	9 27·4	6 16·25	9 27·5	9 27·45	N. 4 5+3 11·2				
Anon.	21 26 28·0	9 20·5	12 28·35	9 20·5	9 20·5	N. 3 35—3 7·85	30·161	61·6	61·4	60·1
7613	21 45 20·5	9 13·7	7 31·8	9 13·9	9 13·8	S. 4 10—1 16·0				
7657	21 52 39 0	8 27·4	9 31·6	8 27·4	8 27·35	N. 4 45—1 4·25				
Anon.	21 56 30·0	8 27·3	8 27·0	8 27·3	8 27·35	N. 4 45+0 0·35				

Face of Sector East.

7842	22 23 32·2	8 9·9	4 19·1	8 9·6	8 9·75	N. 0 50—3 24·65				
7909	22	8 26·5	10 21·0	8 26·3	8 26·4	N. 3 45+1 28·6				
7966	22 44 46·0	8 24·7	7 26·5	8 24·6	8 24·65	N. 0 15—0 32·15				
7992	22 49 55·2	9 13·1	8 25·55	9 13·1	9 13·1	N. 3 30—0 21·55	30·161	61·6	60·4	59·0

♃ June 27, 1844.—Face of Sector West.

5331	15	9 24·9	12 10·2	9 25·0	9 24·95	S. 2 25—2 19·25	30·148	60·4		56·4

♄ June 29, 1844.—Face of Sector East.

7026	20	9 18·8	12 31·2	9 19·0	9 18·9	N. 4 20+3 12·3				
Anon.	20 25 17·2	9 13·3	13 9·95	9 13·1	9 13·2	N. 4 5+3 30·75	30·438	55·2	56·2	42·0
Anon.	20 34 47·2	9 21·0	6 12·0	9 20·8	9 20·9	N. 4 0—3 8·9				
Anon.	20 54	9 15·4	6 6·3	9 15·6	9 15·5	N. 4 15—3 9·2				
Anon.	21 1 44·5	9 6·7	9 30·5	9 6·8	9 6·75	N. 3 35+0 23·75				
7386	21 9 29·4	8 22·4	12 20·45	8 22·8	8 22·6	N. 1 5+3 31·85	30·439	55·0	56·2	41·0
Anon.	21 13 34·2		12 14·9	8 32·1		N. 4 5+3 16·8				
Anon.	21 26 41·3	8 0·7	4 31·55	8 0·4	8 0·55	N. 3 35—3 3·0				
7613	21 45 29·0	8 30·0	10 20·2	8 30·1	8 30·05	S. 4 10—1 23·15				
7657	21 52 53·2	9 9·1	8 9·4	9 9·2	9 9·15	N. 4 45—0 33·75				
Anon.	21 56 43·2	9 9·1	9 11·7	9 9·2	9 9·2	N. 4 45+0 2·55				

Face of Sector West.

7909	22 34 34·8	8 5·2	6 16·5	8 5·3	8 5·25	N. 3 45—1 22·75				

Face of Sector East.

7966	22 44 51·0	8 5·8	7 8·5	8 6·4	8 6·1	N. 0 15—0 31·6				
7992	22 50 1·2	9 0·5	8 13·5	9 0·5	9 0·5	N. 3 30—0 21·0	30·432	55·0	55·8	38·5

☉ June 30, 1844.—Face of Sector West.

Anon.	20 25	7 16·0	3 24·3	7 16·2	7 16·1	N. 4 5+3 25·6	30·326	55·5	54·0	47·2
Anon.	20 34 41·3	10 8·5	13 22·4	10 8·4	10 8·45	N. 4 0—3 13·95				
Anon.	20 54 38·6	9 18·5	12 32·7	9 18·4	9 18·45	N. 4 15—3 14·25				
Anon.	21 1 39·0	9 15·1	8 29·4	9 14·9	9 15·0	N. 3 35+0 19·6				
Anon.	21 18 27·2	9 12·9	6 1·3	9 12·9	9 12·9	N. 4 5+3 11·6				
Anon.	21 26 35·5	9 11·9	12 19·3	9 11·9	9 11·9	N. 3 35—3 7·4				
7613	21 45 25·0	10 11·7	8 29·6	10 12·0	10 11·85	S. 4 10—1 16·25				

June 26.—Good definition.

No. 7909 observed at 20 seconds after passing the meridian wire.

⊙ JUNE 30, 1844.—FACE OF SECTOR WEST—(continued).

Number of B.A.C.	Time by Chronometer.	Micr. for Plumb-line on Dot.	Micr. for Observation of Star.	Micr. for Plumb-line on Dot.	Mean of Micr. for Plumb-line on Dot.	Star's Apparent Zenith Distance.	Barom.	Thermometers.		
								Attd.	Lower.	Out.
	h m s	rev. pts.	rev. pts.	rev. pts.	rev. pts.	° ′ rev. pts.	in.			
7657	21 52 46·2	9 25·6	10 30·4	9 25·8	9 25·75	N. 4 45—1 4·65				
Anon.	21 56 37·0	9 25·8	9 26·4	9 25·8	9 25·75	N. 4 45—0 0·65	30·320	55·2	54·3	45·5

FACE OF SECTOR EAST.

7909	22 34 42·0	10 12·8	12 7·3	10 13·0	10 12·9	N. 3 45+1 28·4				

FACE OF SECTOR WEST.

7992	22 49 56·0	9 19·2	10 13·25	9 19·0	9 19·1	N. 3 30—0 28·15	30·314	55·2	54·3	44·8

UNREDUCED OBSERVATIONS

MADE WITH

BRADLEY'S ZENITH SECTOR

ON

ZWARTKOP STATION, NEAR SIMON'S TOWN:

FROM

JULY TO OCTOBER, 1844.

♃ JULY 25, 1844.—FACE OF SECTOR EAST.

Number of B.A.C.	Time by Chronometer.	Micr. for Plumb-line on Dot.	Micr. for Observation of Star.	Micr. for Plumb-line on Dot.	Mean of Micr. for Plumb-line on Dot.	Star's Apparent Zenith Distance.	Barom.	Attd.	Upper.	Lower.
	h m s	rev. pts.	rev. pts.	rev. pts.	rev. pts.	° ' rev. pts.	in.			
5632	16 45 31·2	11 16·4	17 7·9	11 16·0	11 16·2	N. 0 10+5 25·7				
5735	17 0 2·0		19 13·3	20 3·4		N. 0 20+0 24·1				
5817	17 12 20·3		20 2·15	20 23·6		N. 1 45+0 20·45				
5881	17 23 9·5	9 17·0	10 1·75	9 16·9	9 16·95	N. 4 30+0 18·8				
6016	17 44 41·0		19 27·8	19 30·1		N. 2 35-0 2·3				
6074	17 54 49·0		18 16·2	19 0·2		N. 4 0-0 18·0				
6115	18 1 30·8	9 16·9	6 22·75	9 16·9	9 16·9	N. 3 50-2 28·15				
6186	18 12 18·7	8 21·5	0 21·9	8 21·0	8 21·25	S. 2 30+7 33·35				
6233	18 19 15·2	9 7·5	11 33·0	9 7·6	9 7·55	S. 0 15-2 25·45				
6285	18 26 23·2	9 14·6	15 21·9		9 14·6	N. 1 5+6 7·3				
6305	18 29 16·0		11 13·0	9 14·6	9 14·6	N. 1 5+1 32·4				
6414	18 48 22·0	9 17·0	16 13·9	18 14·2		{ N. 3 15+6 30·9 / N. 3 20-2 0·3				
6489	18 58 26·0	18 2·0	14 9·0	18 2·0	18 2·0	N. 4 10-3 27·0				
6525	19 3 31·5	8 30·4	11 13·6	8 30·2	8 30·3	N. 5 20+2 17·3				
6639	19 22 49·5	9 18·5	11 8·4	9 18·5	9 18·5	N. 4 10+1 23·9				
Anon.	19 27 3·0	18 22·1	18 23·0	18 22·0	18 22·05	N. 4 25+0 1·85				
6877	20 0 1·0	10 22·3	18 24·4	19 20·6		{ N. 1 40+8 2·1 / N. 1 45-0 30·2	28·203	64·0		
6948	20 11 51·2	9 2·5	18 16·7	18 0·2		{ N. 3 40+9 14·2 / N. 3 45-0 16·5				
7011	20 20 54·5	8 33·3	16 25·4			N. 4 35+7 26·1				
7026	20 22 45·0		16 20·1	17 31·6		N. 4 40-1 11·5				
7057	20 27 10·2	17 31·8	10 27·5	8 33·3		{ N. 4 40-7 4·3 / N. 4 35+1 28·2				
Anon.	20 39 31·5	10 0·2	11 7·5	10 0·7	10 0·45	N. 4 15+1 7·05				
7207	20 45 39·5	9 8·2	14 8·0	18 6·2		{ S. 0 10-4 33·8 / S. 0 5+3 32·2				
Anon.	20 58 20·5	11 10·7	12 17·2	11 10·7	11 10·7	N. 4 30+1 6·5				
Anon.	21 6 28·5	11 2·7	16 9·5	20 0·6		{ N. 3 50+5 6·8 / N. 3 55-3 25·1				
7386	21	9 24·7	18 6·7	18 22·4		{ N. 1 20+8 16·0 / N. 1 25-0 15·7				
Anon.	21 18 19·5	18 24·0	17 25·4	18 24·0	18 24·0	N. 4 25-0 32·6				
Anon.	21 31 24·7	9 24·0	11 3·9	9 23·7	9 23·85	N. 3 50+1 13·05				
7557	21 41 7·8	7 27·6	16 20·0	16 25·2		{ N. 0 25+8 26·4 / N. 0 30-0 5·2				
7613	21 49 36·2	11 10·5	17 8·9	20 9·3		{ S. 3 55-5 32·4 / S. 3 50+3 0·4				
7657	21 57 41·5	12 28·9	16 12·3	12 29·0	12 28·95	N. 5 0+3 17·35				
Anon.	22 1 33·0	12 29·1	17 19·0	12 29·5	12 29·3	N. 4 0+4 23·7				
7842	22 28 10·0	10 25·9	11 15·4	10 25·5	10 25·7	N. 1 5+0 23·7				
7909	22 39 25·0	10 11·8	16 27·5	19 10·4		{ N. 4 0+6 15·7 / N. 4 5-2 16·0				
7992	22 54 44·8	10 11·8	14 7·6	10 11·9	10 11·85	N. 3 45+3 29·75				61·0

♀ JULY 26, 1844.—FACE OF SECTOR WEST.

Number	Time	Micr. Plumb	Micr. Star	Micr. Plumb	Mean	Zenith Distance
4852	14 34 30·2	11 8·6	5 5·8	11 8·4	11 8·5	S. 0 20-6 2·7
4916	14 46 33·8	8 31·1	8 18·2	8 30·4	8 30·75	N. 1 0+0 12·55
Anon.	14 53 49·2	8 31·5	5 20·4	8 30·6	8 31·05	N. 2 10+3 10·65
5054	15 12 17·2		6 3·5	9 19·3		S. 1 30-3 15·8
5151	15	9 24·5	4 31·0	9 24·5	9 24·5	N. 4 55+4 27·5
5508	16 21 35·2	12 31·0	8 20·8	12 31·6	12 31·3	S. 0 10-4 10·5

July 25.—Syphon Barometer No. 109 by Buntin, of Paris; its attached Thermometer—centigrade. The equivalents of the scale readings, respectively in English inches and degrees of Far., are printed.
No. 7909 nearly invisible.
The images indicate that the object glass should be drawn out further.
July 26.—Put back the minute hand of the Chronometer 5ᵐ.

♀ July 26, 1844.—Face of Sector West—*(continued)*.

Number of B.A.C.	Time by Chronometer.	Micr. for Plumb-line on Dot.	Micr. for Observation of Star.	Micr. for Plumb-line on Dot.	Mean of Micr. for Plumb-line on Dot.	Star's Apparent Zenith Distance.	Barom.	Thermometers.		
								Attd.	Upper.	Lower.
	h m s	rev. pts.	rev. pts.	rev. pts.	rev. pts.	° ' rev. pts.	in.			
5538	16 26 30·0	12 19·5	7 18·8	12 19·0	12 19·25	S. 0 45—5 0·45				
5588	16	11 26·0	11 13·45	11 26·2	11 26·1	N. 2 25+0 12·65				
5632	16 40 27·8	10 32·2	14 4·1	10 31·6	10 31·9	N. 0 15—3 6·2				
5881	17 17 47·5	10 28·3	10 8·1	10 28·2	10 28·25	N. 4 30+0 20·15				
5915	17 23 27·5		3 17·7	2 25·8		S. 2 45+0 25·9				
6016	17 39 26·2	11 22·4	11 24·6	11 22·3	11 22·35	N. 2 35—0 2·25				
6074	17 49 28·2	11 27·2	12 11·25	11 27·2	11 27·2	N. 4 0—0 18·05				
6115	17 56 11·0	11 22·3	14 17·6	11 22·4	11 22·35	N. 3 50—2 29·25				
6145	18 0 25·5	11 1·0	4 10·8	2 3·4		N. 3 25+6 24·2 N. 3 30—2 7·4				
6186	18 7 28·8	10 32·0	9 31·45	10 32·0	10 32·0	S. 2 35—0 34·55				
6233	18 14 13·2	10 19·7	7 25·45	10 19·5	10 19·6	S. 0 15—2 28·15				
6275	18 20 11·0	9 32·5	9 23·9		9 32·4	N. 1 5+0 8·5				
6285	18 21 15·1		3 22·8		9 32·4	N. 1 5+6 9·6				
6305	18 24 8·0		7 31·55	9 32·3	9 32·4	N. 1 5+2 0·85				
6414	18 43 5·2	9 26·5	2 29·0	9 26·3	9 26·4	N. 3 15+6 31·4				
6489	18 53 4·4	10 8·4	14 3·4	10 8·4	10 8·4	N. 4 10—3 29·0				
6525	18 58 4·6	10 0·8	7 19·0	10 1·0	10 0·9	N. 5 20+2 15·9				
6639	19 17 28·7	10 14·5	8 24·0	10 14·5	10 14·5	N. 4 10+1 24·5				
6948	20 6 32·2	10 27·8	10 12·0	10 27·8	10 27·8	N. 3 45+0 15·8				
7011	20	11 0·9	3 5·7		11 0·5	N. 4 35+7 28·8				
7026	20 17 20·7	11 0·4	3 12·8	11 0·4	11 0·5	N. 4 35+7 21·7				
7057	20 21 47·2		9 5·8	11 0·3	11 0·5	N. 4 35+1 33·7				
Anon.	20 24		2 18·5	2 0·5		N. 4 25—0 18·0				
Anon.	20 34 9·8	11 19·9	10 11·9	11 19·9	11 19·9	N. 4 15+1 8·0				
7207	20 40 37·7	10 6·5	14 4·4	10 6·7	10 6·6	S. 0 5+3 31·8				
Anon.	20 53 58·0	9 32·9	8 26·8	9 32·8	9 32·85	N. 4 30+1 6·05				
Anon.	21 1 7 0	9 7·6	12 33·6	9 7·6	9 7·6	N. 3 55—3 26·0				
7386	21 8 52·2	9 4·4	9 20·1	9 4·4	9 4·4	N. 1 25—0 15·7				
Anon.	21 12 56·6		10 1·7	9 2·9		N. 4 25—0 32·8				
Anon.	21 26 3·7	8 30·1	7 16·2	8 30·0	8 30·05	N. 3 50+1 13·85	28·190	54·1		54·6
7557	21 36 2·8	9 2·4	9 5·8	9 2·3	9 2·6	N. 0 30—0 3·2				
7613	21 44 53·0	9 22·3	12 19·1	9 22·1	9 22·2	S. 3 50+2 30·9				
7657	21 52 15·4	9 9·0	5 25·2	9 9·4	9 9·15	N. 5 0+3 17·95				
Anon.	21 56 5·5	9 9·2	4 25·5	9 9·0	9 9·15	N. 5 0+4 17·65				
7842	22 23 1·2	9 28·3	9 2·1	9 28·2	9 28·25	N. 1 5+0 26·15				
7909	22 34 5·2	9 27·5	12 14·6	9 27·5	9 27·5	N. 4 5—2 21·1				
7966	22 44 14·2	9 18·2	5 31·1	9 18·4	9 18·3	N. 0 30+3 21·2				
7992	22 49 24·5	9 21·7	5 27·2	9 21·8	9 21·75	N. 3 45+3 28·55				

☉ July 28, 1844.—Face of Sector East.

1802	5 34 38·2	9 22·2	17 4·9	9 22·5	9 22·35	0 0+7 16·55	28·288	50·9	51·2	49·0
1878	5 46 6·2	9 31·7	8 6·0	9 31·6	9 31·65	S. 1 35+1 25·65				

☾ July 29, 1844.—Face of Sector East.

5032	15 9 1·0	12 0·7	19 8·7	12 1·2	12 0·95	N. 4 35+7 7·75	28·239	48·0	48·0	48·0
5054	15 12 39·5		14 4·5	10 24·5		S. 1 30—3 17·8				
5151	15 29 46·5	10 24·2	15 20·6	10 24·2	10 24·2	N. 4 55+4 30·4				
Anon.	15 35 2·2	10 12·4	14 22·55	10 12·4	10 12·4	N. 3 5+4 10·15		48·2		48·4
5227	15 41 47·0		18 16·0	19 8·6		N. 0 5—0 24·8				

The upper thermometer scale reads 0° 6 higher than the standard by Jones,—which standard is the lower thermometer.
The micrometer screw touches higher on the mirror plate, when the telescope is clamped on the right hand side of the plumb-line, than when on the left;—as at Heerulogement's Berg and Kamies Berg; indicating that the right hand side of the back arch is rather higher than the left.
July 28.—3 hours before the observations commenced, the object glass was drawn out until the images became sharply defined. This adjustment may perhaps alter the collimation.

❆ July 29, 1844.—Face of Sector East—*(continued).*

Number of B.A.C.	Time by Chronometer.	Micr. for Plumb-line on Dot.	Micr. for Observation of Star.	Micr. for Plumb-line on Dot.	Mean of Micr. for Plumb-line on Dot.	Star's Apparent Zenith Distance.	Barom.	Thermometers.		
								Attd.	Upper.	Lower.
	h m s	rev. pts.	rev. pts.	rev. pts.	rev. pts.	° ′ rev. pts.	in.			
5331	15 56	10 1·8	12 3·85		10 1·4	S. 2 10—2 2·45				
Comp.	15		10 33·4	10 1·0	10 1·4	S. 2 10—6 32·0				
5374	16 2 2·0	19 14·4	16 22·1	19 14·4	19 14·4	N. 5 15—2 26·3				
5435	16 10 22·5	10 0·2	13 23·0	10 0·1	10 0·15	N. 3 40+3 24·85				
5508	16 21 55·4	9 28·8	13 12·6	9 28·8	9 28·8	S. 0 10—3 17·8				
5538	16 26 51·0	9 24·7	14 25·2	9 24·7	9 24·7	S. 0 45—5 0·5				
5588	16 34 20·4	10 8·9	10 25·0	10 9·1	10 9·0	N. 2 25+0 16·0			48·2	48·2
5632	16 40 47·5	8 27·2	5 23·5	8 26·9	8 27·05	N. 0 15—3 3·55	28·205	48·2	48·1	48·1
5735	16 55 17·5	9 7·3	8 23·0	9 7·3	9 7·3	N. 0 20—0 18·3				
5817	17 7 38·3	9 25·7	9 9·3	9 25·9	9 25·8	N. 1 45—0 16·5				
5881	17 18 6·5	9 19·8	10 6·0	9 19·8	9 19·8	N. 4 30+0 20·2				
5915	17 23 47·0	8 23·9	8 2·3	8 24·0	8 24·0	S. 2 45+0 21·65				
5970	17 32 28·5	8 33·0	12 26·3	8 32·8	8 32·9	S. 4 43—3 27·4				
6016	17 39 46·2	9 25·8	9 26·5	9 25·7	9 25·75	N. 2 35+0 0·75				
6074	17 49 47·2	10 17·6	10 2·1	10 17·7	10 17·65	N. 4 0—0 15·55				
6115	17 56 29·8	10 25·3	7 33·0	10 25·4	10 25·35	N. 3 50—2 26·35				
6145	18 0 45·1	11 1·0	8 31·7	11 1·0	11 1·0	N. 3 30—2 3·3				
6186	18 7 50·2	10 15·4	11 19·3	10 15·4	10 15·4	S. 2 35—1 3·9				
6233	18 14 33·2	11 4·5	13 38·9	11 4·5	11 4·5	S. 0 15—2 29·4			47·0	47·0
6285	18 21 34·2	11 17·1	17 28·7	11 17·7	11 17·45	N. 1 5+6 11·25				
6305	18 24 27·4	11 17·5	13 21·0	11 17·5	11 17·45	N. 1 5+2 3·55	28·193	46·4	46·7	46·7
6414	18 43 23·3	10 4·1	8 7·9	10 4·2	10 4·15	N. 3 20—1 30·25				
6489	18 53 24·0	10 8·3	6 17·3	10 8·4	10 8·35	N. 4 10—3 25·05				
6525	18 58 23·8	10 15·2	12 33·5	10 15·4	10 15·3	N. 5 20+2 18·2				
6639	19 17 47·5	10 10·0	12 3·7	10 10·0	10 10·0	N. 4 10+1 27·7				
Anon.	19 22 0·0	9 17·0	9 19·1	9 17·1	9 17·05	N. 2 40+0 2·05				
6753	19 36 14·4	9 22·9	14 8·6	9 23·1	9 23 0	N. 2 55+4 19·6	28·150	45·1	45·6	45·5
6877	19 55 9·2	9 21·0	8 28·3	9 21·0	9 21·0	N. 4 15—0 26·7				
6948	20 6 51·3	9 28·9	10 14·6	9 28·8	9 28·85	N. 3 45+0 19·75				
7011	20 15 49·8	8 26·7	7 25·6		8 26·65	N. 4 40—1 1·05				
7026	20 17 40·8		7 18·5	8 26·6	8 26·65	N. 4 40—1 8·15				
7057	20 22 5·6	8 26·7	1 25·4	8 26·6	8 26·65	N. 4 40—7 1·25				
Anon.	20 24	8 31·4	8 16·3	8 31·5	8 31·45	N. 4 25—0 15·15				
Anon.	20 34 28·2	8 32·7	10 9·4	8 32·9	8 32·8	N. 4 15+1 10·6				
7207	20 40 57·2	8 14·0	4 18·6	8 14·0	8 14·0	S. 0 5+3 29·4	28·129	42·6	43·6	43·3
Anon.	20 54 15·8	9 18·3	10 27·25	9 18·4	9 18·35	N. 4 30+1 8·9				
Anon.	21 1 25·8	9 26·9	6 5·0	9 27·0	9 26·95	N. 3 55—3 21·95				
7386	21 9 12·0	9 16·1	9 2·5	9 16·5	9 16·3	N. 1 25—0 13·8				
Anon.	21 13 15·8	9 23·9	8 27·4	9 23·9	9 23·9	N. 4 25—0 30·5				
Anon.	21 26 23·2	9 29·6	11 13·0	9 29·8	9 29·7	N. 3 50+1 17·3				
7557	21 36 22·5	9 5·0	9 3·0	9 5·0	9 5·0	N. 0 30—0 2·0				
7613	21 45 14·5	9 7·1	6 12·4	9 7·0	9 7·05	S. 3 50+2 26·65				
7657	21 52 34·3	9 33·2	13 19·3	9 33·4	9 33·3	N. 5 0+3 20·0				
Anon.	21 56 25·3	9 33·3	14 23·5	9 33·3	9 33·3	N. 5 0+4 24·2	28·114	41·4	45·2	42·6
7842	22 23 21·7	9 4·5	9 32·8	9 5·2	9 4·85	N. 1 5+0 27·95				
7909	22 34 24·0	9 20·0	7 1·8	9 20·3	9 20·15	N. 4 5—2 18·35				
7966	22 44 34·5	9 12·8	13 0·0	9 12·9	9 12·85	N. 0 30+3 21·15				
7992	22 49	9 29·4	13 28·7	9 29·5	9 29·45	N. 3 45+3 33·25	28·089	40·8	44·5	41·8

Face of Sector West.

1802	5 34 36·0	9 15·5	11 4·3	9 15·5	9 15·5	N.O 5—1 22·8	28·090	50·2	56·2	47·0
1878	5 46 4·0	9 21·5	11 20·7	9 21·3	9 21·4	S. 1 35+1 33·3	28·090	56·3	59·6	53·4
2293	6 53 4·7	8 32·6	4 9·8	8 32·3	8 32·45	N. 5 25+4 22·65	28·111			

July 29.—No. 7992.—Bisected 10 seconds after passing the meridian.

♂ JULY 30, 1844.—FACE OF SECTOR WEST—*(continued)*.

Number of B.A.C.	Time by Chronometer.	Micr. for Plumb-line on Dot.	Micr. for Observation of Star.	Micr. for Plumb-line on Dot.	Mean of Micr. for Plumb-line on Dot.	Star's Apparent Zenith Distance.	Barom.	Thermometers. Attd.	Upper.	Lower.
	h m s	rev. pts.	rev. pts.	rev. pts.	rev. pts.	o ' rev. pts.	in.			
4570	13 37 30·2	8 31·6	12 19·5	8 31·2	8 31·4	N. 2 0−3 22·1	28·111	48·6	49·6	49·7
4623	13 43 30·2	8 31·3	8 29·45	8 31·2	8 31·27	N. 2 0+0 1·8				
4686	13 58 12·0	9 20·5	14 20·4	9 20·8	9 20·65	S. 1 20+4 33·75				
Anon.	14 11 46·5	10 29·3	4 32·1	10 29·6	10 29·45	S. 3 0−5 31·35				
4784	14 19 42·2	8 33·0	7 16·0	8 32·6	8 32·8	N. 5 25+1 16·8				
Anon.	14 24 46·2	9 16·2	8 9·4	9 16·2	9 16·2	N. 1 35+1 6·8	28·109	46·8	48·5	49·0
4916	14 46 56·5	9 16·7	9 11·2	9 16·9	9 16·8	N. 1 0+0 5·6				
Anon.	14 54 7·8	9 20·6	6 16·4	9 20·3	9 20·45	N. 2 10+8 4·05				
Anon.	14 58 19·2	9 20·5	9 18·2	9 20·5	9 20·5	N. 1 55+0 2·3				
5032	15 9 1·0	9 14·8		9 14·2	·9 14·5	N. 4 40−1 31·25				
5054	15 11		7 3·7	10 12·4		S. 1 30−3 8·7	28·110	46·0	47·0	47·2
5151	15 29 45·5	9 33·6	14 11·9	9 33·9	9 33·75	N. 5 0−4 12·15				
Anon.	15 35 1·6	9 32·5	5 31·6	9 32·5	9 32·5	N. 3 5+4 0·9				
5227	15 41 44·3	9 15·4	10 15·2	9 15·8	9 15·6	N. 1 5−0 33·6				
5331	15 57 3·8	9 14·9	7 21·0		9 14·95	S. 2 10−1 27·95				
Comp.	15 57 43·5		2 25·7	9 15·0	9 14·95	S. 2 10−6 23·25				
5435	16 10 22·5	8 24·5	5 11·3	8 24·3	8 24·4	N. 3 40+3 13·1				
5538	16 26 49·4	11 10·5	6 18·5	11 10·6	11 10·55	S. 0 45−4 26·05				
5588	16 34 18·6	8 22·7	8 15·4	8 22·5	8 22·6	N. 2 25+0 7·2				
5632	16 40 46·0	8 32·2	12 9·65	8 32·6	8 32·4	N. 0 15−3 11·25				
5735	16 55 16·2	9 10·8	10 3·7	9 10·7	9 10·75	N. 0 20−0 26·95	28·111	45·3	46·8	46·4
5817	17 7 37·2	9 14·4	10 5·4	9 14·6	9 14·5	N. 1 45−0 24·9				
5881	17 18 5·2	9 8·8	8 30·9	9 8·9	9 8·85	N. 4 30+0 11·95				
5915	17 23 44·5	9 31·2	10 28·1	9 31·3	9 31·25	S. 2 45+0 30·85				
5970	17 32 25·8	10 5·2	6 20·4	10 5·4	10 5·3	S. 4 45−3 18·0				
6016	17 39 44·4	9 16·8	9 25·4		9 16·8	N. 2 25−0 8·6				
6074	17 49 45·8	10 2·3	10 26·8	10 1·4	10 1·65	N. 4 0−0 24·95				
6115	17 56 28·5	8 30·3	11 32·1	8 30·3	8 30·3	N. 5 30−3 1·8				
6145	18 0 43·8	8 29·5	11 9·5	8 29·5	8 29·5	N. 3 30−2 14·0				
6186	18 7 47·5	10 0·9	9 6·0	10 0·8	10 0·85	S. 2 35−0 28·85				
6233	18 14 32·0	10 3·9	7 17·1	10 4·0	10 3·95	S. 0 15−2 20·85				
6275	18 20 29·8	9 25·8	9 24·5	9 26·0	9 25·9	N. 1 5+0 1·4				
6285	18 21 33·5		3 22·7		9 25·9	N. 1 5+6 3·2				
6305	18 24 26·2	9 25·8	7 30·5	9 26·0	9 25·9	N. 1 5+1 29·4	28·111	47·1	46·5	46·2
6414	18 43 22·5	9 24·8	11 31·6	9 24·8	9 24·8	N. 3 20−2 6·8				

☉ AUGUST 4, 1844.—FACE OF SECTOR EAST.

Number of B.A.C.	Time by Chronometer.	Micr. for Plumb-line on Dot.	Micr. for Observation of Star.	Micr. for Plumb-line on Dot.	Mean of Micr. for Plumb-line on Dot.	Star's Apparent Zenith Distance.	Barom.	Thermometers. Attd.	Upper.	Lower.
4686	13 58 39·5	10 21·8	5 30·5	10 21·5	10 21·65	S. 1 20+4 25·15	28·365	48·0	46·5	46·8
Anon.	14 12 15·5	10 14·1	7 22·7	10 14·0	10 14·05	S. 2 55+2 25·35				
4784	14 20 9·5	11 7·0	12 33·5	11 7·0	11 7·0	N. 5 25+1 26·5				
5331	15 57 32·0	11 0·8	13 3·4		11 0·65	S. 2 10−2 2·75				
Comp.	15		17 33·5	11 0·5	11 0·65	S. 2 10−6 32·85				
5435	16	11 17·9	15 4·8	11 17·7	11 17·8	N. 3 40+3 21·0				
5508	16	10 32·3	14 15·4	10 32·2	10 32·25	S. 0 10−3 17·15				
5538	16	10 20·4	15 19·9	10 20·5	10 20·45	S. 0 45−4 33·45				
5588	16	10 16·6	10 32·2	10 16·8	10 16·7	N. 2 25+0 15·5				
5632	16	10 11·5	7 7·8	10 11·3	10 11·4	N. 0 15−3 3·6				
5735	16	10 28·3	10 9·3	10 28·1	10 28·2	N. 0 20−0 18·9				
5817	17	11 11·1	11 27·9	11 11·1	11 11·1	N. 1 45+0 16·8				
5881	17 18 31·8	10 33·6	11 20·0	10 33·4	10 33·5	N. 4 30+0 20·5	28·410	44·4	44·6	44·7
5915	17 24 13·2	9 14·0	8 24·6	9 13·0	9 13·5	S. 2 45+0 22·9				
6016	17	10 25·5	10 26·2	10 25·2	10 25·35	N. 2 35+0 0·85				

July 30.—No. 5054.—Bisected 25 seconds after passing the meridian.
Short intervals of clear sky between July 30 and August 4.
Generally clouded, with occasional heavy rain.

⊙ August 4, 1844.—Face of Sector East—(continued).

Number of B.A.C.	Time by Chronometer.	Micr. for Plumb-line on Det.	Micr. for Observation of Star.	Micr. for Plumb-line on Det.	Mean of Micr. for Plumb-line on Det.	Star's Apparent Zenith Distance.	Barom.	Attd.	Upper.	Lower.
	h m s	rev. pts.	rev. pts.	rev. pts.	rev. pts.	° ′ rev. pts.	in.			
6074	17	11 12·7	10 31·5	11 13·1	11 12·9	N. 4 0—0 15·4				
6115	17	11 5·2	8 12·8	11 5·4	11 5·3	N. 3 50—2 26·5				
6145	18 2 11·0	11 18·3	9 14·2	11 18·3	11 18·3	N. 3 30—2 4·1				
6186	18 8 16·0	8 29·6	9 32·9	8 29·0	8 29·3	S. 2 35—1 3·6				
6233	18 14 58·5	9 19·3	12 13·5	9 19·2	9 19·25	S. 0 15—2 28·25				
6275	18	9 4·8	9 13·8		9 4·65	N. 1 5+0 9 15				
6285	18 22 0·2		15 15·5	9 4·6	9 4·65	N. 1 5+6 10·85				
6305	18 24 53·5	9 4·6	11 7·4	9 4·6	9 4·65	N. 1 5+2 2·75				
6414	18 43 50·2	9 12·7	7 14·2	9 12·3	9 12·5	N. 3 20—1 32·3				
6489	18 53 50·2	9 15·2	5 24·4	9 15·1	9 15·1	N. 4 10—3 24·75				
6325	18 58 50·2	9 2·8	11 21 6	9 3·0	9 2·9	N. 5 20+2 18·7	28·408	43·3	43·6	43·3
6639	19 18 15·2	10 8·0	12 1·2	10 7·9	10 7·95	N. 4 10+1 27·25				
Anon.	19 22	10 18·5	10 18·9	10 18·4	10 18·45	N. 4 25+0 0·45				
6753	19 36 41·3	10 16·9	15 1·5	10 17·2	10 17·05	N. 2 55+4 18·45				
6877	19 55 36·0	10 15·8	9 21·5	10 15·7	10 15·76	N. 1 45—0 28·25				
6948	20 7 18·5	10 12·1	10 30·4	10 12·2	10 12·15	N. 3 45+0 18·25				
7026	20 18 7·7	10 3·8	8 28·2	10 3·9	10 3·88	N. 4 40—1 9·68				
7057	20 22 32·5	10 3·9	3 2·2	10 3·9	10 3·88	N. 4 40—7 1·68				
Anon.	20 24	10 2 9	9 22·0	10 2·9	10 2·0	N. 4 25—0 14·9				
Anon.	20 34 55·5	9 29·6	11 5·6	9 29·6	9 29·6	N. 4 15+1 10 0				
7207	20 41 23·8	9 29·5	5 26·0	9 20·9	9 20·9	S. 0 5+3 28 9	28·410	42·8	43·2	42·8
Anon.	20 54 43·0	10 16·0	11 24·2	10 16·2	10 16·1	N. 4 30+1 8·1				
Anon.	21 2 53·1	11 3 9	7 15·3	11 3·9	11 3 9	N. 3 55—3 22·6				
7286	21 9 39·0	9 10·7	8 29·6	9 10·7	9 10·7	N. 1 25—0 15·1				
Anon.	21 13 42·6		8 31·3	9 28·2		N. 4 25—0 30·9	28·418	43·0	43·2	42·8
Anon.	21 26 50·0	9 24·1	11 7·6	9 24·0	9 24·05	N. 3 50+1 17·55				
7557	21 36 49·6	9 2·6	9 1·4	9 2·4	9 2·5	N. 0 30—0 1·1				
7613	21 45 40·2	9 0·9	6 8·3	9 1·2	9 1·05	S. 3 50+2 26·75				
7657	21 53 2·0	9 24·8	13 10·5	9 24·7	9 24·78	N. 5 0+3 19 72				
Anon.	21 56 53·2	9 24·8	14 15·3	9 24·8	9 24·78	N. 5 0+4 24·52				
7842	22 23 48·6	9 29·2	10 23·7	9 29·3	9 29·25	N. 1 5+0 28·45				
7909	22 34 55·1	10 10·5	7 26·4	10 10·4	10 10·45	N. 4 5—2 18·05				
7966	22 45 1·3	9 24·9	13 13·3	9 24·9	9 24·9	N. 0 30+3 22·4				
7992	22 50 11·3	9 23·5	13 22·3	9 23·7	9 23·6	N. 3 45+3 32·7	28·418	41·9		42·4
1802	5 35 8·8	9 12·0	7 31·4	9 12·0	9 12·0	N. 0 5—1 14·6	28·415	44·2	49·2	45·0
2293	6 53 36·5	9 4·0	14 2·7	9 4·0	9 4·0	N. 5 25+4 32·7	28·438	51·8	57·0	49·6

(August 5, 1844.—Face of Sector West.

Number of B.A.C.	Time by Chronometer.	Micr. for Plumb-line on Det.	Micr. for Observation of Star.	Micr. for Plumb-line on Det.	Mean of Micr. for Plumb-line on Det.	Star's Apparent Zenith Distance.	Barom.	Attd.	Upper.	Lower.
4458	13 12 55·2	11 16·0	11 20·7	11 16·4	11 16·2	S. 1 40+0 4·5	28·380	51·8	58·4	54·6
4686	13 58 30·4	9 12·8	14 10.75	9 13 6	9 13·2	S. 1 20+4 31·55				
Anon.	14 12 11·0	10 6·1	13 5·5	10 6·5	10 6·3	S. 2 55+2 33·2				
4784	14 20 9·7	10 7·7	8 23·7	10 7·3	10 7·5	N. 5 25+1 17·8				
4852	14 35 14·5	10 1·7	13 2·1	10 1·7	10 1·7	S. 0 15+3 0·4				
4916	14 47 17·8	9 18·9	9 11·65	9 18·7	9 18·8	N. 0+0 7·15	28·361	46·4	48·4	49·0
Anon.	14 54 34·5	9 26·9	6 22·8	9 26.9	9 26·9	N. 2 10+3 4·1				
Anon.	14 58 46·4	9 19·3	9 16.7	9 19·3	9 19·3	N. 1 55+0 2·6	28·361	45·3	46·9	47·2
5054	15 13 2·2	9 28·5	6 20·3	9 29·0	9 28·75	S. 1 30—3 8·45				
5151	15 30 13·0	9 29 6	14 7·3	9 29·6	9 29·6	N. 5 0—4 11·7		46·0		46·8
Anon.	15 34	9 26·4	5 25·3	9 26·5	9 26·45	N. 3 5+4 1·15				
5227	15 42 11·2	9 31·6	10 30 9	9 31·9	9 31·75	N. 1 5+0 33·1				
5292	15 50 56·4	9 25·6	6 29·4	9 25·7	9 25·65	S. 3 45—2 30·25				
5331	15 57 29·2	10 19·0	8 25·5	10 19·0	10 19·0	S. 2 10—1 27·5				
Comp.	15 58 9·0		3 29·0	10 19·0	10 19·0	S. 2 10—6 24·0				

Aug. 4.—Anon. 20ʰ 24ᵐ.—Bisected 22 seconds after passing the meridian.

4.—Good definition.

5.—Adjusted the back arch so as to cause the micrometer screw to touch the mirror plate at the same point throughout the range of the sector; but the mean of all equal number of observations, face east and face west, is free from errors of this order.

The upper dot is slightly eccentric with respect to the centre, of which the divided arch is a segment of the circumference; for the right-hand end of the arch is rather further from the dot than the left-hand end.

Attached a new plumb-line. The several adjustments were made before the observations of the 5th.

5.—Anon. 15ʰ 34ᵐ.—Bisected 10 seconds after passing the meridian wire.

(AUGUST 5, 1844.—FACE OF SECTOR WEST—(continued.)

Number of B.A.C.	Time by Chronometer.	Micr. for Plumb-line on Dot.	Micr. for Observation of Star.	Micr. for Plumb-line on Dot.	Mean of Micr. for Plumb-line on Dot.	Star's Apparent Zenith Distance.	Barom.	Thermometers.		
								Attd.	Upper.	Lower.
	h m s	rev. pts.	rev. pts.	rev. pts.	rev. pts.	° ' rev. pts.	in.			
5374	16 2 29·4		13 1·5	9 32·4		N. 5 15—3 3·1			46·0	46·2
5435	16 10 49·5	10 8·9	6 29·0	10 8·7	10 8·8	N. 3 40+3 13·8				
5508	16 22 20·0	9 10·5	6 2·3	9 10·2	9 10·35	S. 0 10—3 8·05				
5538	16 27 14·5	8 19·4	3 26·0	8 19·6	8 19·5	S. 0 45—4 27·5			45·6	45·6
5588	16 34 45·7	8 8·0	8 0·0	8 7·9	8 7·95	N. 2 25+0 7.95				
5632	16 41 12·2	8 27·7	12 4·75	8 27·8	8 27·75	N. 0 15—3 11·0				
5735	16 55 42·2	9 6·9	10 0·1	9 6·8	9 6·85	N. 0 20—0 27·25			45·6	45.6
5817	17 8 3·7	9 14·3	10 6·1	9 14·3	9 14·3	N. 1 45—0 25·8	28·350	44·6		
5881	17 18 32·4	9 0·0	8 31·65	9 8·9	9 8·95	N. 4 30+0 11·3				
5915	17 24 10·3	9 7·9	10 4·95	9 8·0	9 7·95	S. 2 45+0 31·0				
5970	17 32 51·5	9 31·3	6 14·1	9 31·5	9 31·4	S. 4 45—3 17·3				
6016	17	9 23·0	8 32·5	9 22·9	9 22·95	N. 2 35+0 24·45				
6074	17 50 12·8	9 4·8	9 29·7	9 4·8	9 4·8	N. 4 0—0 24·9				
6115	17 56 55·7	9 6·4	12 8·6	9 6·4	9 6·4	N. 3 50—3 2·2				
6145	18 1 10·5	8 21·8	11 2·8	8 21·8	8 21·8	N. 3 30—2 15·0				
6186	18 8 13·9	9 5·7	8 11·7	9 5·8	9 5·75	S. 2 35—0 28·05				
6233	18 14 58·3	9 15·3	10 28·4	9 15·2	9 15·25	S. 0 15—2 20·85			45·2	44·6
6275	18 20	9 4·6	9 3·0		9 4·38	N. 1 5+0 1·38				
6285	18 21 59·6		9 1·5	9 4·3	9 4·38	N. 1 5+6 2·88				
6305	18 24 52·4	9 4·3	7 10·8	9 4·3	·9 4·38	N. 1 5+1 27·58	28·343	44·6	45·0	44·6
6414	18 43 49·5	8 30·9	11 3·6	8 30·5	8 30·7	N. 3 20—2 6·9				
6489	18 53 49·0	8 1·9	12 3·8	8 2·0	8 1·95	N. 4 10—4 1·85				
6525	18 58 48·5	8 6·3	5 31·8	8 6·3	8 6·3	N. 5 20+2 8·5				
6639	19 18 12·8	8 9·9	6 26·3	8 9·8	8 9·85	N. 4 10+1 17·55				
Anon.	19 22 25·5	8 26·0	8 29·8	8 26·0	8 26·0	N. 4 25—0 3·8				
6753	19 36 39·8	9 20·1	5 12·3	9 20·0	9 20·05	N. 2 55+4 7·75				
6877	19 55 34·5	10 2·9	11 5·25	10 3·3	10 3·1	N. 1 45—1 2·15				
6948	20 7 17·5	9 32·0	9 23·6	9 31·7	9 31·85	N. 3 45+0 8·25				
7011	20 16 16·0	10 0·4	11 11·6		10 0·38	N. 4 40—1 11·22				
7026	20 18 17·2		11 18·4	10 0·3	10 0·38	N. 4 40—1 18·02				
7057	20 22 33·0	10 0·4	17 11·2	10 0·4	10 0·38	N. 4 40—7 10·82				
Anon.	20 25 24·0		10 27·25	10 0·5		N. 4 25—0 26·75				
Anon.	20 34 54·0	10 10·5	9 10·3	10 10·5	10 10·5	N. 4 15+1 0·2				
7207	20 41 22·5	10 3·5	14 7·2	10 4·0	10 3·75	S. 0 5+4 3·45				
Anon.	20 54 42·4	9 33·3	8 33·8	9 33·3	9 33·3	N. 4 30+0 33·5				
Anon.	21 1 51·8	10 5·0	14 4·0	10 5·0	10 5·0	N. 3 55—3 33·0	28·316	43·2	48·6	43·5
7386	21 9 37·0	10 10·6	10 33·4	10 10·6	10 10·6	N. 1 25—0 22·8				
Anon.	21 13		11 17·5	10 12·5		N. 4 25—1 5·0				
Anon.	21 26 48·5	10 31·5	9 23·5	10 31·5	10 31·5	N. 3 50+1 8·0			49·4	43·7
7557	21 36 47·5	11 12·5	11 20·9	11 12·5	11 12·5	N. 0 30—0 8·4				
7613	21 45 37·5	12 0·0	5 33·5	12 0·0	12 0·0	S. 3 50+3 2·6				
7657	21 53 0·5	9 9·7	5 33·5	9 9·6	9 9·68	N. 5 0+3 10·18				
Anon.	21 56 51·8	9 9·8	4 28·5	9 9·8	9 9·68	N. 5 0+4 15·18				
7842	22	8 18·2	7 31·6	8 18·2	8 18·2	N. 1 5+0 20·6				
7909	22 34 49·5	9 22·9	12 15·75	9 22·9	9 22·9	N. 4 5—2 26·85				
7966	22 44 59·5	9 6·6	5 26·0	9 6·7	9 6·65	N. 0 30+3 14·65	28·270	43·5		
7992	22 50 9·8	8 31·5	5 9·0	8 31·3	8 31·4	N. 3 45+3 22·4			51·0	43·8
1802	5 35 6·8	9 0·2	10 21·8	9 0·0	9 0·1	N. 0 5—1 21·7	28·253	48·6	55·0	43·6
1878	5 46 34·3	9 16·4	11 14·7	9 16·2	9 16·3	S. 1 35+1 32·4			59·0	47·2
2293	6 53 36·5	9 21·1	13 27·8	9 21·0	9 21·05	N. 5 30—4 6·75	28·277	55·4	63·0	52·6

♂ AUGUST 6, 1844.—FACE OF SECTOR EAST.

Number of B.A.C.	Time by Chronometer.	Micr. for Plumb-line on Dot.	Micr. for Observation of Star.	Micr. for Plumb-line on Dot.	Mean of Micr. for Plumb-line on Dot.	Star's Apparent Zenith Distance.	Barom.	Attd.	Upper.	Lower.
4458	13 13 3·8	9 27·3	9 31·7	9 27·0	9 27·15	S. 1 40—0 4·55	28·230	60·8	68·0	61·2

Aug. 5.—The new plumb-line was broken at 13½ʰ S. T. by a projecting scale of the arch. Filed away the scale and attached another plumb-line.
17ʰ 26ᵐ.—Touched sharply the right-hand pulley-wheel.
No. 6275.—Observed at 30' after passing the meridian.
No. 7057.—The seconds of transit doubtful,
Anon. 21ʰ 13ᵐ.—Observed at 30' after passing the meridian.

♂ August 6, 1844.—Face of Sector East—(continued).

Number of B.A.C.	Time by Chronometer.	Micr. for Plumb-line on Dot.	Micr. for Observation of Star.	Micr. for Plumb-line on Dot.	Mean of Micr. for Plumb-line on Dot.	Star's Apparent Zenith Distance.	Barom.	Thermometers. Attd.	Upper.	Lower.
	h m s	rev. pts.	rev. pts.	rev. pts.	rev. pts.	° ' rev. pts.	in.			
4507	13 23 9·2	9 23·0	13 30·9	9 23·0	9 23·0	S. 4 25—4 7·9			66·0	60·8
4686	13 58 45·4	9 13·2	4 22·3	9 12·0	9 12·6	S. 1 20+4 24·3			64·2	59·0
Anon.	14 12 16·8	8 28·0	6 2·8	8 27·8	8 27·0	S. 2 55+2 25·1			62·5	58·0
4784	14 20 29·7	9 27·0	11 22·3	9 27·2	9 27·1	N. 5 25+1 29·2			60·8	57·0
4852	14 35 24·8	8 33·7	6 8·15	8 33·7	8 33·7	S· 0 15+2 25·55	'		59·8	56·4
4916	14 47 30·2	9 17·0	9 31.9	9 17·2	9 17·1	N. 1 0+0 14·8			58·8	55·5
Anon.	14 54 48·8	9 26·3	13 6·75	9 26·3	9 26·3	N. 2 10+3 14·45			57·2	54·5
Anon.	14 59 0·2	9 30·6	10 10·2	9 30·8	9 30·7	N. 1 55+0 13·5			56·2	53·8
5054	15 13 10·0	9 20·0	13 3·9	9 19·9	9 19·95	S. 1 30—3 17·95			56·2	52·8
5151	15 30 32·0	9 24·6	5 23.75	9 25·0	9 24·8	N. 5 0—4 1·05				
Anon.	15 35 43·4	9 23·3	14 0·7	9 23·1	9 23·2	N. 3 5+4 11·5			57·2	52·0
5227	15 42 23·5	9 22·9	8 33·75	9 22·8	9 22·85	N. 1 5—0 23·1			56·5	51·8
5292	15 50 59·2	9 26·9	12 33·1	9 26·5	9 26·7	S. 3 45—3 6·4			57·6	51·2
5331	15 57 36·2	9 23·1	11 26·8		9 23·25	S. 2 10—2 3·55				
Comp.	15 58		16 21·1	9 23·4	9 23·25	S. 2 10—6 31·85				
5374	16 2 48·5		6 28·1	9 20·05		N. 5 15—2 25 95			56·6	51·0
5435	16 11 6·0	9 19·4	13 8·0	9 19·0	9 19·2	N. 3 40+3 22·8	28·196	48·2	55·5	51·0
5508	16 22 30·0	9 10·6	12 28·7	9 10·7	9 10·65	S. 0 10—3 18·05			55·5	50·2
5538	16 27 24·4	9 7·4	14 7·2	9 7·0	9 7·2	S. 0 45—5 0·0			55·4	50·2
5588	16 34 55·2	9 26·9	10 11·4	9 26·9	9 26·9	N. 2 25+0 18·5				
5632	16 41 22·3	9 22·5	6 21·0	9 22·6	9 22·55	N. 10 5—3 1·55				
5735	16 55 53·0	8 32·6	8 14·8	8 32·9	8 32·75	N. 0 20—0 17·95	28·196	46·8	55·0	49·6
5881	17 18 50·2	9 6·9	9 28·1	9 6·9	9 6·9	N. 3 40+0 21·2			55·0	49·3
5915	17 24 15·3	8 27·6	8 4·9	8 27·6	8 27·6	S. 2 45+0 22·7				
5970	17 32 52·2	9 18·6	13 10·65	9 18·5	9 18·55	S. 4 45—3 26·1				
6016	17 40 26·0	10 15·5	10 17·35	10 15·5	10 15·5	N. 2 35+0 1·85			54·7	48·6
6074	17 50 30·2	10 28·0	10 13·8	10 28·3	10 28·15	N. 4 0—0 14·35	28·182	47·1	54·5	48·5
6115	17 57 13·0	10 30·2	8 4·5	10 30·1	10 30·15	N. 3 50—2 25·65				
6145	18 1 27·2	10 33·0	8 29·75	10 33·0	10 33·0	N. 3 30—2 3·25				
6186	18 8 19·0	9 30.3	11 0·0	9 30·1	9 30·2	S. 2 35—1 3.8				
6233	18 15 7·7	10 2.4	12 31·05	10 2·3	10 2 35	S. 0 15—2 28·7	28·182	46·8	53·0	48·3
6275	18 21 9·0	9 21·6	9 31·7		9 21.55	N. 1 5+0 10·15				
6285	18 22 12·2		15 32·15	9 21·5	9 21·55	N. 1 5+6 10·6				
6305	18 25 5·0	9 21·6	11 24·75	9 21·5	9 21·55	N. 1 5+2 3·2				
6414	18 44 5·2	10 7·0	8 10·3	10 6·9	10 6·95	N. 3 20—1 30·65			54·2	47·8
6489	18 54 6·8	9 32·9	6 8·0	9 33·3	9 33·1	N. 4 10—3 25·1				
6525	18 59 9·4	9 22·0	12 6·0	9 22·0	9 22·0	N. 5 20+2 18·0				
6639	19 18 31·0	9 21·9	11 14·7	9 22·1	9 22·0	N. 4 10+1 26·7				
Anon.	19 22 44·2	9 24·3	9 25·6	9 24·5	9 24·4	N. 4 25+0 1·2				
6753	19 36 55·7	9 31·3	14 14·4	9 31·0	9 31·15	N. 2 55+4 17·25	28·170	46·4	54·4	47·6
6877	19 55 48·5	9 24·3	8 29·75	9 24·35	9 24·35	N. 1 45—0 28·6				
6948	20 7 34·5	10 7·6	10 25·9	10 7·8	10 7·7	N. 3 45+0 18·2			51·5	47·0
7011	20 16 34·5	9 31·0	8 28·9	9 31·1	9 31·1	N. 4 40—1 2·2			50·5	47·0
7026	20 18 25·5		8 23·0	9 31·3	9 31·1	N. 4 40—1 8·1				
7057	20 22 50·2	9 31·1	2 29·5	9 31·0	9 31·1	N. 4 40—7 1·6				
Anon.	20 25 42·7		9 21·55	10 3·0		N. 4 25—0 15·45				
Anon.	20 35 12·2	10 4·6	11 15·0	10 4·8	10 4·7	N. 4 15+1 10·3			51·0	47·2
7207	20 41 32·0	9 20·2	5 24·9	9 20·6	9 20·4	S. 0 5+3 29·5				
Anon.	21 2 19·0	10 3·4	6 15·5	10 3·5	10 3·45	N. 3 55—3 21 95			50·4	47·2
7386	21 9 50·5	9 17·3	9 2·25	9 17·5	9 17·4	N. 1 25—0 15·15				
Anon.	21 14 0·2		8 23·3	9 19·75		N. 4 25—0 30·45	28·152	47·8	50·0	47·5
Anon.	21 27 6·2	9 20·2	11 3·1	9 20·3	9 20·25	N. 3 50+1 16·85				
7557	21 36 59·0	9 0·9	8 32·9	9 0·9	9 0·9	N. 0 30—0 2·0			49·5	47·8
7613	21 45 40·4	8 24·9	5 29·3	8 24·7	8 24·8	S. 3 50+2 29·5				
7657	21 53 20·0	9 19·8	13 5·75	9 20·0	9 19·88	N. 5 0+3 19·87				

Aug. 6.—Good definition until 15ʰ 30ᵐ, and again from 20ʰ S. T.

    Before the commencement of the observations, the sector was adjusted in Azimuth by means of meridianal marks at the distance of 53 yards. The marks require verification. The sector-arch does not swing exactly parallel to the plumb-line.
Calm, with fair definition; foggy next morning.

☌ August 6, 1844.—Face of Sector East—(continued).

Number of B.A.C.	Time by Chronometer.	Micr. for Plumb-line on Dot.	Micr. for Observation of Star.	Micr. for Plumb-line on Dot.	Mean of Micr. for Plumb-line on Dot.	Star's Apparent Zenith Distance.	Barom.	Thermometers.		
								Attd.	Upper.	Lower.
	h m s	rev. pts.	rev. pts.	rev. pts.	rev. pts.	° ' rev. pts.	in.			
Anon.	21 57 11·2	9 19·8	14 10·3	9 19·9	9 19·88	N. 5 0+4 24·42	28·156	47·3	49·0	47·8
7842	22 23 59·0	8 28·6	9 22·0	8 28·7	8 28·65	N. 1 5+0 27·35			51·0	48·4
7909	22 35 7·0	8 26·3	6 9·0	8 26·6	8 26·45	N. 4 5—2 17·45				
7966	22 45 11·0	9 17·0	13 5·0	9 16·9	9 16·95	N. 0 30+3 22·05				
7992	22 50 26·8	9 25.5	13 24·3	9 25·6	9 25·55	N. 3 45+3 32·75	28·158	47·8	50·5	48·4

♅ August 7, 1844.— Face of Sector West.

4548	13 13 1·5	9 25·5	9 32·2	9 25·7	9 25·6	S. 1 40+0 6·6	28·235	55·2	61·8	58·0
4507	13 23	9 15·0	5 16·5	9 15·4	9 15·2	S. 4 25—3 32·7			60·8	57·4
4686	13 58 43·6	9 8·3	14 6·7	9 8·5	9 8·4	S. 1 20+4 32·3			58·4	56·2
Anon.	14 12 15·1	10 0·4	13 0·0	10 0·8	10 0·6	S. 2 55+2 33·4			56·0	55·2
4852	14 35 23·5	8 21·5	11 21·75	8 33·7	8 21·6	S. 0 15+3 0·15			52·5	52·6
4916	14 47 28·2	8 33·7	8 27.5	8 33·7	8 33·7	N. 1 0+0 6·2			51·9	52·1
Anon.	14 54 47·0	9 9·5	6 4·2	9 9·3	9 9·4	N. 2 10+3 5·2				
Anon.	14 58 57·6	10 6·8	10 3·45	10 6·7	10 6·75	N. 1 55+0 3·3				
5054	15 13 9·2	10 22·6	7 14·4	10 22·9	10 22·75	S. 1 30—3 8·35			51·0	51·2
5151	15 30 28·3	10 10·5	14 21·3	10 10·3	10 10·4	N. 5 0—4 10·9				
Anon.	15 35 41·5	10 20·7	6 19·85	10 20·8	10 20·75	N. 3 5+4 0·9				
5227	15 42 21·6	10 19·1	11 18·3	10 19·4	10 19·25	N. 1 5—0 33·05			50·0	50·3
5292	15 50 59·0	11 0·8	8 3·8	11 0·9	11 0·85	S. 3 45—2 31·05				
5331	15 57 34·5	10 27·9	8 33·9		10 27·85	S. 2 10—1 27·95				
Comp.	15 58 14·2		4 4·5	10 27·8	10 27·85	S. 2 10—6 23·35				
5374	16 2 44·2		13 29·75	10 27·6		N. 5 15—3 2·15			49·6	49·4
5435	16 11 2·0	10 31·5	7 18·6	10 31·5	10 31·5	N. 3 40+3 12·9				
5508	16 22 28·4	10 32·0	7 23·75	10 32·2	10 32·1	S. 0 10—3 8·9				
5538	16 27 22·5	11 4·7	6 11·7	11 4·8	11 4·75	S. 0 45—4 27·05				
5588	16 34 57·0	11 7·6	11 0·0	11 7·6	11 7·6	N. 2 25+0 7·6				
5632	16 41 21·0	12 0·7	15 11·6	12 0·9	12 0·8	N. 0 15—3 16·8				
5735	16 55 51·0	10 32·6	11 25·0	10 32·6	10 32·6	N.0 20—0 26·4				
5881	17 18 46·5	9 24·8	9 12·8	9 24·5	9 24·65	N. 4 30+0 11·85				
5915	17 24 14·3	10 19·1	11 16·8	10 19·2	10 19·15	S. 2 45+0 31·65				
5970	17 32 53·2	10 20·6	7 3·0	10 20·7	10 20·65	S. 4 45—3 17·65			49·6	47·5
6016	17 40 23·0	10 0·0	10 9·1	10 0·0	10 0·0	N. 2 35—0 9·1				
6074	17 50 26·2	9 18·5	10 9·75	9 18·3	9 18·4	N. 4 0—0 25·35				
6115	17 57 9·0	9 11·5	12 13·1	9 11·5	9 11·5	N. 3 50—3 1·6				
6145	18 1 23·8	9 26·8	12 7·4	9 26·8	9 26·8	N. 3 30—2 14·6				
6186	18 8 18·2	10 22·8	9 29·4	10 23·0	10 22·9	S. 2 35—0 27·5				
6233	18 15 6·0	9 10·8	6 23·3	9 10·6	9 10·7	S. 0 15—2 21·4				
6275	18 21 5·5	9 30·6	9 30·0		9 30·58	N. 1 5+0 0·58				
6285	18 22 9·2		3 28·0	9 30·5	9 30·58	N. 1 5+6 2·58				
6305	18 25 2·2	9 30·6	8 2·0	9 30·6	9 30·58	N. 1 5+1 28·58	28·241	49·3	49·6	48·7
6414	18 44 2·2	10 7·0	12 15·1	10 7·4	10 7·2	N. 3 20—2 7·9				
6489	18 54 3·5	10 7·4	14 8·8	10 7·5	10 7·45	N. 4 10—4 1·35				
6525	18 59 5·5	10 8·9	7 33·8	10 8·8	10 8·85	N. 5 20+2 9·05				
6639	19 18 27·2	10 3·3	8 19·6	10 3·2	10 3·25	N. 4 10+1 17·65				

♃ August 8, 1844.—Face of Sector East.

4686	13 58 54·0	9 22·3	4 33·5	9 22·8	9 22·55	S. 1 20+4 23·05			55·5	55·0
5538	16 27 33·5	7 6·6	12 7·1	7 6·7	7 6·65	S. 0 45—5 0·45				
5588	16 35 7·6	12 2·9	12 20·5	12 3·0	12 2·95	N. 2 25+0 17·55			49·8	49·8
5632	16 41 32·0	9 1·3	5 32·1	9 1·3	9 1·3	N. 0 15—3 3·2				

Aug. 7.—No. 4507 observed at 25 seconds after passing the meridian.
The sky became clouded at 19ʰ 20ᵐ per chronometer.
Aug. 8.—No. 4686. Bad observation.

♃ August 8, 1844.—Face of Sector East—(continued).

Number of B.A.C.	Time by Chronometer.	Micr. for Plumb-line on Dot.	Micr. for Observation of Star.	Micr. for Plumb-line on Dot.	Mean of Micr. for Plumb-line on Dot.	Star's Apparent Zenith Distance.	Barom.	Thermometers Attd.	Upper.	Lower.
	h m s	rev. pts.	rev. pts.	rev. pts.	rev. pts.	o ′ rev. pts.	in.			
5735	16 56 2·2	9 27·6	9 8·9	9 27·5	9 27·55	N. 0 20—0 18·65				
5817	17 8 25·5	9 22·9	9 6·3	9 22·8	9 22·85	N. 1 45—0 16·55				
5881	17 18 58·8	10 21·6	11 8·35	10 21·4	10 21·5	N. 4 30+0 20·85				
5915	17 24 24·2	9 32·8	9 10·6	9 32·6	9 32·7	S. 2 45+0 22·1		49·0	49·2
5970	17 33 2·1	8 26·9	12 20·55	8 27·0	8 26·95	S. 4 45—3 27·6			
6016	17 40 34·5	9 32·8	10 0·0	9 33·0	9 32·9	N. 2 35+0 1·1	28·282	48·6	49·0	49·0
6074	17 50 36·2	10 22·5	10 7·6	10 22·5	10 22·5	N. 4 0—0 14·9			
6115	17 57 21·3	11 5·5	8 13·2	11 5·5	11 5·5	N. 3 50—2 26·3			
6145	18 1 35·5	11 2·3	8 32·5	11 2·5	11 2·4	N. 3 30—2 3·9		48·8	49·0
6186	18 8 28·2	8 29·4	10 0·3	8 29·0	8 29·2	S. 2 35—1 5·1			
6233	18 15 16·5	8 27·5	11 23·4	8 27·6	8 27·55	S. 0 15—2 29·85			
6275	18 21 17·2	9 27·5	10 2·1		9 27·38	N. 1 5+0 8·72			
6285	18 22 21·4		16 4·6	9 27·4	9 27·38	N. 1 5+6 11·22			
6305	18 25 14·2	9 27·4	11 30·0	9 27·2	9 27·38	N. 1 5+2 2·62			
6414	18 44 14·1	9 21·0	7 22·7	9 21·0	9 21·0	N. 3 20—1 32·3	28·282	47·8	48·8	48·4
6489	18 54 16·2	9 21·5	5 30·35	9 21·7	9 21·6	N. 4 10—3 25·25			
6525	18 59 17·7	10 13·5	12 31·7	10 13·4	10 13·45	N. 5 20+2 18·25		48·2	48·4
6639	19 13 40·0	10 12·0	12 6·2	10 12·1	10 12·05	N. 4 10+1 28·15			
Anon.	19 22 52·4	10 14·6	10 16·5	10 14·5	10 14·55	N. 2 25+0 1·95			
6753	19 37 4·2	10 15·4	14 33·9	10 15·5	10 15·45	N. 2 55+4 18·45			
6877	19 55 57·0	10 21·9	9 28·0	10 22·0	10 21·95	N. 1 45—0 27·95	28·294	50·0	49·0	49·2
2293	6 54 5·7	9 15·7	5 18·8	9 15·9	9 15·8	N. 5 30—3 31·0	28·288	54·1	56·0	54·6

♀ August 9, 1844.—Face of Sector East.

4458	13 13 17·5	6 29·3	6 33·9	6 29·4	6 29·35	S. 1 40—0 4·55		53·4	53·6
4579	13 38 23·5	10 12·3	7 0·55	10 12·5	10 12·4	N. 2 0—3 11·85		53·2	53·4
4686	13 58 58·2	9 29·5	5 6·6	9 29·5	9 29·5	S. 1 20+4 22·9			
4852	14	12 14·5	9 23·7	12 14·4	12 14·45	S. 0 15+2 24·75		51·4	52·0
4916	14 47 42·8	14 8·3	14 23·4	14 8·4	14 8·35	N. 1 0+0 15·05			
Anon.	14 55 2·0	14 20·7	17 33·4	14 20·7	14 20·7	N. 2 10+3 12·7			
5054	15 13 23·8	10 5·3	13 24·1	10 5·4	10 5·35	S. 1 30—3 18·75			
5292	15 51 13·2	7 32·2	11 5·0	7 32·3	7 32·25	S. 4 45—3 6·75			
5331	15 57 49·2		10 25·9	8 23 8		S. 2 10—2 2·1			
Comp.	15 58 30·0		15 21·0	8 23·8		S. 2 10—6 31·2			
5435	16 11 18·6	8 13·5	12 3·1	8 13·5	8 13·5	N. 3 40+3 23·6			

Face of Sector West.

5508	16 22 37·5		5 13·5	8 21·8		S. 0 10—3 8·3			
5588	16 35 6·2	8 20·7	11 13·95	8 21·0	8 20·85	N. 2 25—2 27·1			
5632	16 41 30·0	11 16·2	14 27·7	11 16·5	11 16·35	N. 0 15—3 11·85			
5735	16 56 2·0	11 4·53	11 31·5	11 4·0	11 4·27	N. 0 20—0 27·23			
5915	17 24 25·7	12 3·3	13 0·8	12 3·5	12 3·4	S. 2 45+0 31·4	28·308	49·6	49·8	50·5
5970	17 33 0·5	11 19·0	8 0·95	11 18·9	11 18·95	S. 4 45—3 18·0			
6016	17 40 32·2	10 23·2	10 32·8	10 23·3	10 23·25	N. 2 35—0 9·55			
6074	17 50 36·2	11 11·9	12 3·55	11 11·8	11 11·85	N. 4 0—0 25·7			
6115	17 57 19·0	11 6·2	14 8·5	11 6·3	11 6·25	N. 3 50—3 2·25			
6145	18 1 33·2	11 5·4	13 19·9	11 5·0	11 5·2	N. 3 30—2 14·7			
6186	18 8 26·0	9 8·1	8 14·5	9 8·0	9 8·05	S. 2 35—0 27·55			
6233	18 15 14·8	10 24·2	8 3·8	10 23·8	10 24·0	S. 0 15—2 20·2			
6275	18 21 21·2	10 27·6	10 27·6		10 27·48	N. 1 5—0 0·12			
6285	18 22 19·1		4 26·1	10 27·4	10 27·48	N. 1 5+6 1·38			
6305	18 25 11·7	10 27·5	10 0·3	10 27·4	10 27·48	N. 1 5+1 27·18	28·312	48·4	49·1	40·8
6414	18 44 12·4	9 32·6	12 6·05	9 32·6	9 32·6	N. 3 20—2 7·45			

Aug. 8.—The sky became entirely clouded at 20ʰ per chronometer.
9.—No. 4852. Observed at 25 seconds after passing the meridian.

♀ AUGUST 9, 1844.—FACE OF SECTOR WEST—(continued).

Number of B.A.C.	Time by Chronometer.	Micr. for Plumb-line on Dot.	Micr. for Observation of Star.	Micr. for Plumb-line on Dot.	Mean of Micr. for Plumb-line on Dot.	Star's Apparent Zenith Distance.	Barom.	Thermometers. Attd.	Upper.	Lower.
	h m s	rev. pts.	rev. pts.	rev. pts.	rev. pts.	° ' rev. pts.	in.			
6489	18 54 13·4	10 10·1	14 12·4	10 10·1	10 10.1	N. 4 10—4 2·3				
6525	18 59 15·2	10 1·9	7 28·0	10 2·0	10 1·95	N. 5 20+2 7·95				
Anon.	19 22	11 26·7	12 1·2	11 26·8	11 26·75	N. 4 25—0 8·45			49·0	49·0
6877	19 55 55·0	8 28.5	9 31·4	8 28·5	8 28·5	N. 1 45—1 2·9				
6948	20 7 41·5	9 17·6	9 10·4	9 17·8	9 17·7	N. 3 45+0 7·3				
7011	20 16 42·5	9 14·6	10 25·5		9 14·6	N. 4 40—1 10·9				
7026	20 18 32·5		10 31·1	9 14·6	9 14·6	N. 4 40—1 16·5				
7207	20 41 40·2	11 5·8	15 10·3	11 6·0	11 5·9	S. 0 5+4 4·4	28·306	48·7	49·0	49·0
Anon.	21 2 15·4	8 22·0	12 19·4	8 22·6	8 22·6	N. 3 55—3 30·8				
7386	21 9 56·7	9 6·1	9 28·8	9 6·1	9 6·1	N. 1 25—0 22·7				
Anon.	21 27 13·5	9 9·6	8 1·45	9 8·8	9 9·2	N. 3 50—1 7·75				
7557	21 37 5·8	8 26·0	9 1·6	8 25·9	8 25·95	N. 0 30—0 9·65				
7613	21 45 49·0	9 33·6	13 3·75	9 33·6	9 33·6	S. 3 50+3 4·15				
7667	21 53 25·7	11 1·7	7 26·5	11 1·5	11 1·55	N. 0 5+3 9·05				
Anon.	21 57 16·3	11 1·6	6 21·0	11 1·4	11 1·55	N. 0 5+4 14·55			48·6	48·4
7842	22 24 5·5	9 33·7	9 15·3	9 33·9	9 33· 8	N. 1 5+0 18·5				
7909	22 35 23·3	10 7·1	13 1·1	10 6·8	10 6·95	N. 4 5—2 23·15				
7966	22 45 17·5	10 15·0	7 1·5	10 15·0	10 15·0	N. 0 30+3 13·5				
7992	22 50 32·5	11 10·6	2 22·2	11 10·2	11 10·4	N. 3 45+3 22·2	28·308	48·2	48·5	48·4
1802	5 35 24·2	7 10·3	8 32·65	7 10·3	7 10·3	N. 0 5—1 22·35	28·338	50·2	49·0	49·3
1378	5 46 29·8	9 21·7	11 19·85	9 21·4	9 21·55	S. 1 35+1 32·3				
2293	6 54 1·5	9 8·4	13 15·0	9 8·0	9 8·2	N. 5 30—4 6·8	28·343	52·9	55·0	52·0

♄ AUGUST 10, 1844.—FACE OF SECTOR WEST.

Number of B.A.C.	Time by Chronometer.	Micr. for Plumb-line on Dot.	Micr. for Observation of Star.	Micr. for Plumb-line on Dot.	Mean of Micr. for Plumb-line on Dot.	Star's Apparent Zenith Distance.	Barom.	Attd.	Upper.	Lower.
2293	6 54 7·2	10 14·6	14 21·4	10 14·6	10 14·6	N. 5 30—4 6·8				

☉ AUGUST 11, 1844.—FACE OF SECTOR EAST.

Number of B.A.C.	Time by Chronometer.	Micr. for Plumb-line on Dot.	Micr. for Observation of Star.	Micr. for Plumb-line on Dot.	Mean of Micr. for Plumb-line on Dot.	Star's Apparent Zenith Distance.	Barom.	Attd.	Upper.	Lower.
4686	13 59 7·7	9 26·7	5 2·0	9 26·7	9 26·7	S. 1 20+4 24·7	28·340	66·2	70·0	66·0
4852	14 35 46·2	10 21·1	7 28·3	10 21·1	10 21·1	N. 5 20+2 26·8				
4916	14 47 52 0	12 3·7	12 17·1	12 3·8	12 3·75	N. 1 0+0 13·35			63·1	62·2
Anon.	14 54 10·0	9 29·5	13 9·3	9 29·55	9 29·55	N. 2 10+3 13·75				
5054	15 13 33·0	9 17·7	13 0·8	9 17·7	9 17·7	S. 1 30—3 17·1				
5151	15 30 51·8	10 22·3	6 21·7	10 22·3	10 22·3	N. 5 0—4 0·6			62·5	61·2
Anon.	15 36 4·5	10 7·2	14 17·3	10 7 0	10 7·1	N. 3 5+4 10·2				
5227	15 42	10 13·8	9 23·4	10 13·8	10 13·8	N. 1 5—0 24·4			63·0	61·0
5292	15 51 22·2	10 21·0	13 25·9	10 21·0	10 21·0	S. 3 45—3 4·9				
5331	15 57 58·4	9 21·4	11 23·7		9 21·45	S. 2 10—2 2·25				
Comp.	15 58 38·4		16 18·4	9 21·5	9 21·45	S. 2 10—6 30·95				
5374	16 2 7·5	10 5·0	7 13·0	10 5·0	10 5·0	N. 5 15—2 26·0				
5435	16 11 26·0	10 13·5	14 2·05	10 13·3	10 13·4	N. 3 40+3 22·65				

FACE OF SECTOR WEST.

Number of B.A.C.	Time by Chronometer.	Micr. for Plumb-line on Dot.	Micr. for Observation of Star.	Micr. for Plumb-line on Dot.	Mean of Micr. for Plumb-line on Dot.	Star's Apparent Zenith Distance.	Barom.	Attd.	Upper.	Lower.
5508	16 22 46·5	9 17·9	6 8·1	9 17·7	9 17·8	S. 0 10—3 9·7				
5538	16 27 40·2	9 12·7	4 18·4	9 12·2	9 12·45	S. 0 45—4 28·05				
5588	16 35 14·3	9 21·7	9 13·9	9 21·6	9 21·65	N. 2 25+0 7·75			61·4	60·0
5632	16 41 38·5	10 10·9	13 21·9	10 10·7	10 10·8	N. 0 15—3 11·1				
5735	16 55 58·5	10 30·7	11 23·05	10 30·7	10 30·7	N. 0 20—0 26·35	28·336	59·0	60·0	59·5
5817	17 8 31·5	11 5·8	11 30·7	11 5·8	11 5·8	N. 1 45—0 24·9				
5915	17 24 32·5	11 28·1	12 25·4	11 28·1	11 28·1	S. 2 45—0 31·3				
5970	17 33	11 31·6	8 13·3	11 31·8	11 31·7	S. 4 45—3 18·4			61·0	59·4
6016	17 40 40·5	9 13·6	9 22·25	9 13·7	9 13·65	N. 2 35—0 8·6				

Aug. 9.—Anon. 19ʰ 22ᵐ.—Very faint.
No. 6877.—Detected a spider working a web about the plumb-line shade. Removed the web.
Strong southerly wind. Indifferent definitions.
The seconds of transit of No. 2293 uncertain.
Aug. 11.—No. 5227.—Bisected at 20 seconds after passing the meridian.
No. 5970.—Bisected at 10 seconds after passing the meridian.
Hot air, but fair definition throughout the night.

⊙ AUGÚST 11, 1844.—FACE OF SECTOR WEST—(continued).

Number of B.A.C.	Time by Chronometer.	Micr. for Plumb-line on Dot.	Micr. for Observation of Star.	Micr. for Plumb-line on Dot.	Mean of Micr. for Plumb-line on Dot.	Star's Apparent Zenith Distance.	Barom.	Thermometers. Attd.	Upper.	Lower.
	h m s	rev. pts.	rev. pts.	rev. pts.	rev. pts.	° ′ rev. pts.	in.			
6074	17 50 44·2	8 22·3	9 13·1	8 22·5	8 22·4	N. 4 0—0 25·7			60·2	59·2
6115	17 57 26·2	9 20·5	12 21·7	9 20·7	9 20·6	N. 3 50—3 1·1				
6145	18 1 41·2	9 23·3	12 3·0	9 23·3	9 23·3	N. 3 30—2 13·7				
6186	18 6 35·7	10 16·3	9 21·35	10 16·2	10 16.25	S. 2 35—0 28·9				
0233	18 15 23·9	10 4·0	7 16·1	10 3·9	10 3·95	S. 0 15—2 21·85			60·2	58·7
6275	18 21 23·5	10 7·6	10 5·7		10 7·55	N. 1 5+0 1·85				
6285	18 22 27·2		4 5·0	10 7·4	10 7·55	N. 1 5+6 2·55				
6305	18 25 20·3	10 7·5	8 12·9	10 7·7	10 7·55	N. 1 5+1 28·65				
6414	18 44 19·5	10 18·2	12 25·0	10 18·2	10 18·2	N. 3 20—2 6·8	28·337	57·7	60·4	58·3
6489	18 54 20·6	10 21·8	14 22·9	10 22·2	10 22·0	N. 4 10—4 0·9				
6525	18 59 22·5	10 5·7	7 31·5	10 5·5	10 5·6	N. 5 20+2 8·1				
6639	19 18 45·2	10 33·9	9 15·6	10 33·9	10 33·9	N. 4 10+1 18·3				
Anon.	19 22 57·0	11 10·5	11 18·3	11 10·3	11 10·4	N. 4 25—0 7·9			60·5	58·6
6753	19 37 9·7	11 16·1	7 8·0	11 15·9	11 16·0	N. 2 55+4 8·0				
6877	19 56 3·0	11 16·8	12 20·1	11 18·7	11 18·75	N. 1 45—1 1·35				
0946	20 7 48·3	11 19·0	11 10·4	11 19·0	11 19·0	N. 3 45+0 8·6			60·0	58·0
7011	20 16 48·3	11 31·9	13 6·5	11 31·7	11 31·78	N. 4 40—1 8·72				
7026	20 18 30·0	11 31·5	13 14·9	11 31·8	11 31·78	N. 4 40—1 17·12				
7057	20 23 3·8	11 31·9	19 7·7	11 31·9	11 31·78	N. 4 40—7 9·92				
Anon.	20 25 56·2		12 32·1	12 7·4		N. 4 25—0 24·7				
Anon.	20 35	12 10·5	11 9·4	12 10·5	12 10·5	N. 4 15+1 1·1				
7207	20 41 47·6	11 8·3	15 7·05	11 3·3	11 3·3	S. 0 5+4 3·75				
Anon.	20 55 14·3	10 31·8	9 30·2	10 31·5	10 31·65	N. 4 30+1 1·45				
Anon.	21 2 23·2	10 8·3	14 6·5	10 8·5	10 8·4	N. 3 55—3 32·1				
7386	21 10 5·3	9 20·2	10 8·8	9 20·2	9 20·2	N. 1 25—0 22·6	28·316	58·3	60·0	57·8
Anon.	21 14 19·3		10 14·05	9 8·5		N. 4 25—1 5·55				
Anon.	21 27 20·8	9 8·7	8 0·3	9 8·7	9 8·7	N. 3 50+1 8·4				
7557	21 37 14·3	9 18·2	9 26·45	9 18·0	9 18·1	N. 0 30—0 8·35				
7613	21 45 59·2	10 4·5	13 7·55	10 4·6	10 4·55	S. 3 50+3 3·0				
7657	21 53 33·3	9 1·2	5 23·8	9 1·2	9 1·4	N. 0 5+3 11·4				
7842	22	9 8·5	8 23·1	9 8·5	9 8·5	N. 1 5+0 19·4			60·8	56·4
7909	22 35 21·5	8 31·0	11 23·8	8 31·5	8 31·4	S. 4 5—2 26·4				
7966	22 45 26·3	10 2·8	6 21·7	10 2·8	10 2·8	N. 0 30+3 15·1				
7992	22 50 41·0	10 19·4	6 30·75	10 19·5	10 19·45	N. 3 45+3 22·7	28·316	58·6	61·6	57·5
1802	5 35 33·2	10 10·2	11 30·5	10 10·3	10 10·25	N. 0 5—1 20·25	28·314	63·0	67·0	61·3
1878	5 46 38·2	10 22·9	12 20·0	10 22·9	10 22·9	S. 1 35+1 31·1			67·0	62·8
2293	6 54 9·2	8 18·7	12 25·1	8 18·7	8 18·7	N. 5 30—4 6·4	28·335	68·0	71·0	66·2

☾ AUGUST 12, 1844.—FACE OF SECTOR EAST.

Number of B.A.C.	Time by Chronometer.	Micr. for Plumb-line on Dot.	Micr. for Observation of Star.	Micr. for Plumb-line on Dot.	Mean of Micr. for Plumb-line on Dot.	Star's Apparent Zenith Distance.	Barom.	Thermometers. Attd.	Upper.	Lower.
4458	13 13	9 1·7	9 6·1	9 1·5	9 1·6	S. 1 40—0 4·5	28·283	70·2	76·0	71·4
4686	13 59 12·8	10 16·1	5 24·1	10 16·2	10 16·15	S. 1 20+4 26·05				
Anon.	14 12 45·2	9 33·7	7 8·0	9 33·4	9 33·55	S. 2 55+2 25·55			73·4	70·2
5054	15 13 37·5	10 5·1	13 22·6	10 5·2	10 5·15	S. 1 30—3 17·45			68·0	66·8
5151	15 30 54·0	10 10·4	6 9·2	10 10·3	10 10·35	N. 0 4 1·15			67·5	66·6
Anon.	15 36	10 24·7	15 1·9	10 24·8	10 24·75	N. 3 5+4 11·15			67·5	66·4
5227	15 42 49·2	10 8·9	9 18·7	10 8·8	10 8·85	N. 1 5—0 24·15				
5292	15 51 28·2	10 2·6	13 9·4	10 2·8	10 2·7	S. 3 45—3 6·7			67·5	66·4
5331	15 59 4·0	10 8·6	12 11·6			S. 2 10—2 3·0				
Comp.	15 59 43·3		.17 6·05	10 8·6	10 8·6	S. 2 10—6 31·45				
5374	16 3 11·0		8 2·3	10 28·3		N. 5 5—2 26·0				
5435	16 11 29·3	9 20·7	14 10·9	10 20·6	10 20·65	N. 3 40+3 24·25			67·4	65·6
5508	16 22 56·2	10 10·7	13 28·05	10 10·8	10 10·75	S. 0 10—3 17·9				
5538	16 27 51·2	10 18·6	15 19·05	10 18·7	10 18·65	S. 0 45—5 0·4				

Aug. 12.—No. 4458.—Bisected at 10 seconds after passing the meridian.
Anon. 15ʰ 36ᵐ.—Bisected at 17 seconds after passing the meridian.

☾ AUGUST 12, 1844.—FACE OF SECTOR EAST—(continued).

Number of B.A.C.	Time by Chronometer.	Micr. for Plumb-line on Dot.	Micr. for Observation of Star.	Micr. for Plumb-line on Dot.	Mean of Micr. for Plumb-line on Dot	Star's Apparent Zenith Distance.	Barom.	Thermometers. Attd.	Upper.	Lower.
	h m s	rev. pts.	rev. pts.	rev. pts.	rev. pts.	° ′ rev. pts.	in.			
5588	16 35 25.2	11 2.1	11 18.5	11 1.9	11 2.0	N. 2 25+0 16.5				
5632	16 41 49.0	10 30.1	7 26.75	10 29.9	10 30.0	N. 0 15—3 3.25				
5735	16 56 19.3	10 23.8	10 5.0	10 23.8	10 23.8	N. 0 20—0 18.8				
5817	17 8 42.0	10 31.6	10 14.3	10 31.5	10 31.55	N. 1 45—0 17.25				
5881	17 19 13.9	11 12.9	11 33.4	11 13.0	11 12.95	N. 4 30+0 20.45				
5915	17 24 43.5	10 10.2	9 21.05	10 10.0	10 10.1	S. 2 45+0 23.05				
5970	17 33 22.2	10 4.3	13 31.15	10 4.1	10 4.2	S. 4 45—3 26.95			66.5	64.6
6016	17 40 50.5	10 24.1	10 25.4	10 24.1	10 24.1	N. 2 35+0 1.3				
6074	17 50 53.5	10 30.3	10 15.5	10 30.3	10 30.3	N. 4 0—0 14.8				
6115	17 57 36.2	10 22.4	7 29.4	10 22.4	10 22.4	N. 3 50—2 27.0				
6145	18 1 51.2	10 0.6	7 30.2	10 0.7	10 0.65	N. 3 30—2 4.45				
6186	18 8 46.8	9 7.0	10 10.0	9 6.8	9 6.9	S. 2 35—1 3.1				
6233	18 15 34.2	9 20.7	12 15.0	9 20.6	9 20.65	S. 0 15—2 28.35				
6275	18	9 25.9	10 2.2		9 26.03	N. 1 5+0 10.17				
6285	18 22 37.6		16 2.2	9 26.0	9 26.03	N. 1 5+6 10.17				
6305	18 25 30.5	9 26.1	11 28.9	9 26.1	9 26.03	N. 1 5+2 2.37	28.273	62.2	64.2	63.0
6489	18 54 30.8	10 0.8	6 9.6	10 0.6	10 0.7	N. 4 10—3 25.1				
6525	18 59	11 2.3	10 20.8	11 2.4	11 2.35	N. 5 20+2 18.45				
6639	19 18 54.5	9 31.6	14 33.1	9 31.5	9 31.55	N. 4 10+1 27.85	28.276	63.7	65.0	63.8
6948	20 7 58.2	14 15.2	14 33.0	14 15.0	14 15.1	N. 3 45+0 17.9			65.0	63.2
7011	20 16 57.9	10 33.5	9 32.1	10 33.6	10 33.52	N. 4 40—1 1.42				
7026	20 18 47.4	10 33.4	9 24.3	10 33.5	10 33.52	N. 4 40—1 9.22				
7057	20 23 13.2	10 33.5	3 31.5	10 33.6	10 33.52	N. 4 40—7 2.02				
Anon.	20 26 5.5		10 23.4	11 5.4		N. 4 25—0 16.0				
Anon.	20 35 35.8	11 12.9	12 23.1	11 13.2	11 13.05	N. 4 15+1 10.05				
7207	20 41 58.0	10 32.6	7 2.8	10 32.5	10 32.55	S. 0 5+3 29.75				
Anon.	20 55 23.4	10 26.2	12 0.1	10 26.4	10 26.3	N. 4 30+1 7.8				
Anon.	21 2 32.8	10 17.8	6 28.8	10 17.4	10 17.6	N. 3 55—3 22.8				
7386	21 10 15.2	10 4.9	9 23.9	10 4.9	10 4.9	N. 1 25—0 15.0				
Anon.	21 14 22.8	10 25.6	9 29.6	10 25.8	10 25.7	N. 4 25—0 30.1	28.261	59.4	61.0	61.0
Anon.	21 27 29.6	10 26.5	12 10.1	10 26.5	10 26.5	N. 3 50+1 17.6				
7557	21 37 25.5	10 8.9	10 8.9	10 8.9	10 8.9	N. 0 30—0 1.3				
7613	21 46 10.2	10 13.1	7 18.9	10 13.3	10 13.2	S. 3 50+2 28.3				
7657	21 53 42.7	11 20.1	15 6.5	11 20.0	11 20.18	N. 5 0+3 20.32				
Anon.	21 57 32.2	11 20.2	16 11.0	11 20.4	11 20.18	N. 5 0+4 24.82				
7009	22 35 30.5	10 2.2	7 19.5	10 2.4	10 2.3	N. 4 5—2 16.8				
7966	22 45 37.1	9 30.6	13 18.4	9 30.6	9 30.6	N. 0 30+3 27.0	28.260	57.4	59.8	59.0
7992	22 50 50.5	10 15.4	14 14.2	10 15.4	10 15.4	N. 3 45+3 32.8				
1802	5 35 44.2	9 21.7	8 9.05	9 22.0	9 21.65	N. 0 5—1 12.8	28.274	62.2	64.0	60.8
1878	5 46 47.2	9 25.1	8 1.6	9 25.1	9 25.1	S. 1 35+1 23.5				
2293	6 54 20.5	10 3.3	6 5.55	10 3.1	10 3.2	N. 5 30—3 31.65	28.295	68.4	69.2	65.4

♂ AUGUST 20, 1844.—FACE OF SECTOR WEST.

Number of B.A.C.	Time by Chronometer.	Micr. for Plumb-line on Dot.	Micr. for Observation of Star.	Micr. for Plumb-line on Dot.	Mean of Micr. for Plumb-line on Dot	Star's Apparent Zenith Distance.	Barom.	Attd.	Upper.	Lower.
4458	13	8 5.0	8 6.6	8 5.2	8 5.1	S. 1 40+0 1.5				
4686	13 59 40.2	8 18.6	13 13.6	8 18.6	8 18.6	S. 1 20+4 29.0				
Anon.	14 13 13.7	9 9.7	12 5.6	9 9.65	9 9.65	S. 2 55+2 29.95				
5054	15 14 5.3	9 20.9	6 9.15	9 21.2	9 21.05	S. 1 30—3 11.0				
5151	15 31 20.8	9 11.0	13 20.0	9 11.0	9 11.0	N. 5 0—4 9.0				
5227	15 43 16.2	10 18.5	11 15.6	10 18.5	10 18.5	N. 1 5—0 31.1				
5292	15	9 9.5	6 10.4	9 9.7	9 9.6	S. 3 45—2 33.2				
5374	16	7 6.9	10 7.2	7 6.8	7 6.85	N. 5 15—3 0.35				
5508	16	10 12.1	7 3.2	10 12.4	10 12.25	S. 0 10—3 9.05				
5538	16 28 19.0	10 32.2	6 3.8	10 32.4	10 32.3	S. 0 45—4 28.5				

Aug. 12.—No. 6525.—Bisected at 15 seconds after passing the meridian.

♂ AUGUST 20, 1844—(continued).

At 14 hours mean time, a violent southerly gale forced the tent stays, and drove the tent against the sector. Two guy ropes fortunately held the tent tripod fast, while the arch and micrometer were detached, and the tent cut away,—without any other injury to the instrument than the loss of the plumb-line and bisecting wires. The telescope could not be lowered with safety; it was therefore lashed to the spindle and framework. The gale moderated on the 22nd, when heavy rain commenced. The 23rd was calm, and the 24th and 25th were spent in remounting and adjusting the instrument for observation, in the belief that the storm was over : but the wind became so violent on the 26th and 27th, that prudence required the re-placing of the sector in its packing-case. The weather became fine on the 28th, and the sector was mounted again on the 29th.

☞ The preceding circumstances disconnect the observations made at this Station before the 21st of August, with respect to collimation errors, from those made afterwards.

♃ AUGUST 29, 1844.—FACE OF SECTOR WEST.

Number of B.A.C.	Time by Chronometer.	Micr. for Plumb-line on Dot.	Micr. for Observation of Star.	Micr. for Plumb-line on Dot.	Mean of Micr. for Plumb-line on Dot.	Star's Apparent Zenith Distance.	Barom.	Attd.	Upper.	Lower.
	h m s	rev. pts.	rev. pts.	rev. pts.	rev. pts.	° ' rev. pts.	in.			
2293	6 52 20·2	11 32·9	16 2·6	11 32·7	11 32·8	N. 5 30—4 3·8	28·091	52·0	52·5	49·2

♀ AUGUST 30, 1844.—FACE OF SECTOR WEST.

1802	5 33 58·2	8 27·4	10 10·8	8 27·4	8 27·4	N.0 5—1 17·4	28·129	43·5	43·8	43·2
2293	6 52 26·9	8 29·5	12 32·2	8 29·5	8 29·5	N. 5 30—4 2·7	28·176	48·0	48·0	46·0

♄ AUGUST 31, 1844.—FACE OF SECTOR WEST.

6489	18 52 46·2	9 8·6	13 10·8	9 8·8	9 8·7	N. 4 10—4 2·1	28·180	44·6	45·5	45·2
6639	19 17 10·0	6 19·5	5 2·55	6 19·5	6 19·5	N. 4 10+1 16·05				
Anon.	19 21 22·5	8 23·2	8 30·9	8 23·2	8 23·2	N. 4 25—0 7·7				
6877	19 54 30·5	9 21·6	10 24·3	9 21·5	9 21·55	N. 1 45—1 2·75				
6948	20 6 13·8	9 26·8	9 18·9	9 26·9	9 26·85	N. 3 45+0 7·95				
7011	20 15 12·5	9 13·9	10 26·2		9 13·93	N. 4 40—1 12·27				
7026	20 17 3·5		10 32·8	9 14·0	9 13·93	N. 4 40—1 18·87				
7057	20 21 28·6	9 14·0	16 25·4	9 13·8	9 13·93	N. 4 40—7 11·47				
Anon.	20 24 21·0		9 22·75	8 30·4		N. 4 25—0 26·35				
Anon.	20 33 51·4	9 3·4	8 3·1	9 3·4	9 3·4	N. 4 15+1 0·3				
7207	20 40 17·0	8 12·3	12 16·45	8 12·0	8 12·15	S. 0 5+4 4·3				
Anon.	20 53 39·2	8 19·5	7 19·25	8 19·5	8 19·5	N. 4 30+1 0·25				
Anon.	21 0 49·2	9 7·4	13 6·75	9 7·5	9 7·45	N. 3 55—3 33·3				
7386	21 8 33·0	8 29·6	9 19·9	8 29·7	8 29·65	N. 1 25—0 24·25				
Anon.	21 12 38·5		10 5·7	9 0·7		N. 4 25—1 5·0	28·176	44·2	44·8	44·2
7557	21 35 43·2	8 7·1	8 16·8	8 7·3	8 7·2	N. 4 30—0 9·6				
7613	21 44 30·5	10 14·5	13 17·45	10 14·5	10 14·5	S. 3 50+3 2·95				
7657	21 51 58·8	7 30·8	4 19·7	7 30·8	7 30·73	N. 5 0+3 11·03				
Anon.	21 55 49·7	7 30·6	3 15·3	7 30·7	7 30·73	N. 5 0+4 15·43				
7842	22 22	8 6·5	7 20·2	8 6·5	8 6·5	N. 1 5+0 20·3	28·176	45·0	45·0	45·6

FACE OF SECTOR EAST.

2293	6 52 33·5	8 30·5	4 32·7	8 30·4	8 30·45	N. 5 30—3 31·75	28·156	46·8	48·0	47·0

Aug. 31.—Fair definition when clouds permitted observation.

☉ SEPTEMBER 1, 1844.—FACE OF SECTOR EAST.

Number of D. A. C.	Time by Chronometer.	Micr. for Plumb-line on Det.	Micr. for Observation of Star.	Micr. for Plumb-line on Dot.	Mean of Micr. for Plumb-line on Dot.	Star's Apparent Zenith Distance.	Barom.	Thermometers.		
	h m s	rev. pts.	rev. pts.	rev. pts.	rev. pts.	° ′ rev. pts.	in.	Attd.	Upper.	Lower.
4458	13 11 56·4	8 3·5	8 10·3	8 3·5	8 3·5	S. 1 40—0 6·8	28·180	58·1	57·5	56·0
4686	13 57 37·3	7 32·5	3 10·9	7 32·5	7 32·5	S. 1 20+4 21·6				
5054	15 12 2·5	10 2·1	13 20·5	10 2·1	10 2·1	S. 1 30—3 18·4	28·168	50·0	52·0	51·9
5151	15 29 13·3	9 33·8	5 32·1	9 33·8	9 33·8	N. 5 0—4 1·7				
5292	15 49 55·1	12 3·2	15 8·85	12 3·0	12 3·1	S. 3 45—3 5·75			50·0	50·6
5331	15 56 30·3	10 14·7	12 16·4	10 14·7	10 14·7	S. 2 10—2 1·7				
5374	16 1 29·5	10 32·1	8 3·4	10 32·1	10 32·1	N. 5 15—2 28·7				
5435	16 9 50·2	10 16·2	14 3·4	10 16·1	10 16·15	N. 3 40+3 21·25				
5508	16 21 19·3	10 4·1	13 20·95	10 4·1	10 4·1	S. 0 10—3 16·85				
5538	16 26 15·2	10 7·6	15 6·3	10 7·4	10 7·5	S. 0 45—4 32·8			47·5	48·4
5588	16 33 44·4	10 27·5	11 7·7	10 27·5	10 27·5	N. 2 25+0 14·2				
5632	16 40 12·0	10 9·1	7 3·7	10 9·1	10 9·1	N. 0 15—3 5·4	28·170	46·2	47·3	48·2
6948	20 6 17·2	9 21·5	10 1·0	9 21·2	9 21·35	N. 3 45+0 13·65	28·185	44·4	45·5	45·5

☾ SEPTEMBER 2, 1844.— FACE OF SECTOR WEST.

Number of D. A. C.	Time by Chronometer.	Micr. for Plumb-line on Det.	Micr. for Observation of Star.	Micr. for Plumb-line on Dot.	Mean of Micr. for Plumb-line on Dot.	Star's Apparent Zenith Distance.	Barom.	Attd.	Upper.	Lower.
5054	15 12 6·0	8 29·0	5 15·0	8 29·1	8 29·05	S. 1 30—3 14·05	28·305	49·8	52·0	51·8
5292	15 49 58·5	10 26·7	7 24·45	10 27·1	10 26·9	S. 3 45—3 2·45				

FACE OF SECTOR EAST.

Number of D. A. C.	Time by Chronometer.	Micr. for Plumb-line on Det.	Micr. for Observation of Star.	Micr. for Plumb-line on Dot.	Mean of Micr. for Plumb-line on Dot.	Star's Apparent Zenith Distance.	Barom.	Attd.	Upper.	Lower.
5735	16 54 46·3	8 7·7	7 19·7	8 7·7	8 7·7	N. 0 20—0 22·0	28·304	44·1	45·6	46·4
5817	17 7 7·8	7 27·7	7 7·55	7 27·5	7 27·6	N. 1 45—0 20·05				
5881	17 17 36·2	10 10·5	11 2·8	10 19·4	10 19·45	N. 4 30+0 17·35				
5915	17 23 14·8	9 17·5	8 26·75	9 17·6	9 17·55	S. 2 45+0 24·8				
5970	17 31 56·5	9 7·1	12 31·4	9 7·0	9 7·05	S. 4 45—3 24·35				
6016	17 39 15·2	10 3·3	10 0·9	10 3·1	10 3·2	N. 2 35—0 2·3				
6074	17 49 16·0	10 1·0	9 16·9	10 1·1	10 1·05	N. 4 0—0 18·15				
6115	17 55 59·0	9 29·5	6 33·3	9 29·6	9 29·55	N. 3 50—2 30·25				
6145	18 0 14·0	10 5·8	16 28·9	10 5·7	10 5·75	N. 3 25+6 23·15				
6186	18 7 17·7	10 33·2	11 33·9	10 33·4	10 33·3	S. 2 35—1 0·6				
6233	18 14 1·8	10 12·8	13 3·0	10 12·7	10 12·75	S. 0 15—2 24·25				
6275	18 20 0·7	10 23·4	10 28·3		10 23·38	N. 1 5+0 4·92				
6285	18 21 4·0		16 30·0	10 23·4	10 23·38	N. 1 5+6 6·62				
6305	18 23 57·0	10 23·3	12 21·8	10 23·4	10 23·38	N. 1 5+1 32·42	28·302	42·6	44·5	44·6
6414	18 42	12 10·7	10 9·8	12 10·5	12 10·6	N. 3 20—2 0·8				
6489	18 52 54·4	12 13·1	8 16·4	12 13·2	12 13·15	N. 4 10—3 30·75				
6525	18 57 55·2	13 2·0	15 14·8	13 2·0	13 2·0	N. 5 20+2 12·8				
6639	19 17 18·2	11 5·8	12 28·6	11 5·8	11 5·8	N. 4 10+1 22·8				
Anon.	19 21 30·3	11 14·4	11 9·9	11 14·4	11 14·4	N. 4 25—0 4·5				
6753	·19	10 23·1	14 31·7	10 23·0	10 23·05	N. 2 55+4 8·65				
6877	19 54 39·0	10 28·4	9 30·5	10 28·5	10 28·45	N. 1 45—0 31·95	28·304	42·6	43·5	43·5
6948	20	11 0·6	11 12·8	11 0·6	11 0·6	N. 3 45+0 12·2				
7011	20 15 21·5	10 7·2	9 0·6	10 7·3	10 7·23	N. 4 40—1 6·63				
7026	20 17 12·5	10 7·2	8 26·9	10 7·2	10 7·23	N. 4 40—1 14·33				
7207	20 40 26·4	8 19·7	4 19·3	8 19·6	8 19·65	S. 0 5+4 0 35				
7557	21 35 52·8	9 19·1	9 12·5	9 19·2	9 19·15	N. 0 30—0 6·65	28·290	42·8	44·0	43·2
7613	21 44 43·0	9 14·6	6 14·8	9 14·6	9 14·6	S. 3 50+2 33·8				
7842	22 22 52·2	10 19·8	11 8·8	10 19·7	10 19·75	N. 1 5+0 23·05				
7966	22 44 5·0	10 8·7	13 25·5	10 8·8	10 8·75	N. 0 30+3 16·75				
7992	22 49 14·8	10 31·3	14 24·65	10 31·2	10 31·25	N. 3 45+3 27·4	28·288	42·3	43·5	43·0
1802	5 34 11·1	10 11·4	8 31·8	10 11·4	10 11·4	N. 0 5—1 13·8				
1878	5 45 40·5	10 17·0	8 27·75	10 17·1	10 17·05	S. 1 35+1 23·3	28·250	39·7	40·5	39·6
2293	6 52 43·5	10 7·5	6 9·0	10 7·4	10 7·45	N. 5 30—3 32·45	28·247	44·6	46·6	43 0

Sept. 1.—Clouds intercepted the observations.
2.—No. 6414.—Observed at 20 seconds from the meridian.
No. 6753.—Bad observation.
No. 6948.—Faint. Hazy atmosphere, but good definition.

♂ September 3, 1844.—Face of Sector West.

Number of B.A.C.	Time by Chronometer.	Micr. for Plumb-line on Dot.	Micr. for Observation of Star.	Micr. for Plumb-line on Dot.	Mean of Micr. for Plumb-line on Dot.	Star's Apparent Zenith Distance.	Barom.	Attd.	Upper.	Lower.
	h m s	rev. pts.	rev. pts.	rev. pts.	rev. pts.	° ' rev. pts.	in.			
4458	13 12 35·0	9 10·5	9 7·5	9 10·5	9 10·5	S. 1 40—0 3·0	28·191	61·5	65·2	60·2
5632	16 40 20·2	10 17·4	13 24·75	10 17·2	10 17·3	N. 0 15—3 7·45	28·171	46·0	50·0	50·3
5735	16 54 50·4	10 12·8	11 3·0	10 13·4	10 13·1	N. 0 20—0 23·9			49·2	50·0
5817	17 7 12·0	9 31·8	10 21·05	9 31·8	9 31·8	N. 1 45—0 23·25			48·4	49·3
5881	17 17 41·0	10 9·3	9 29·4	10 9·3	10 9·3	N. 4 30+0 13·9			47·3	48·4
5915	17 23 17·5	11 13·5	12 7·95	11 13·0	11 13·55	S. 2 45+0 28·4			46·6	48·2
5970	17 31 59·0	9 13·7	5 28·1	9 14·0	9 13·85	S. 4 45—3 19·75				
6016	17 39 20·0	8 18·8	8 26·25	8 18·6	8 18·7	N. 2 35—0 7·55			46·2	47·2
6115	17 56	10 5·1	13 4·3	10 5·1	10 5·1	N. 3 50—2 33·2			47·0	47·2

♀ September 4, 1844.—Face of Sector West.

Number of B.A.C.	Time by Chronometer.	Micr. for Plumb-line on Dot.	Micr. for Observation of Star.	Micr. for Plumb-line on Dot.	Mean of Micr. for Plumb-line on Dot.	Star's Apparent Zenith Distance.	Barom.	Attd.	Upper.	Lower.
6753	19 35 52·9	10 6·6	5 31·7	10 6·6	10 6·6	N. 2 55+4 8·9	28·304	43·7	44·8	45·0
6877	19 54 48·0	10 4·3	11 7·35	10 4·4	10 4·35	N. 1 45—1 3·0				
6948	20 6 30·8	11 3·5	10 29·0	11 3·5	11 3·5	N. 3 45+0 8·5			44·6	44·6
7011	20 15 23·2	11 4·3	12 15·15	11 4·3	11 4·3	N. 4 40—1 10·85			44·5	44·5
7026	20 17 20·3		12 22·7	11 4·2	11 4·3	N. 4 40—1 18·4				
7057	20 21 45·3	11 4·3	18 15·0	11 4·4	11 4·3	N. 4 40—7 10·7				
Anon.	20 24 37·5		12 8·7	11 17·0		N. 4 25—0 25·7				
Anon.	20 34 7·7	12 7·5	11 6·6	12 7·5	12 7·5	N. 4 15+1 0·9				
7207	20 40 35·2	10 26·0	14 30·1	10 26·0	10 26·0	S. 0 5+4 4·1				
Anon.	20 53 55·5	11 6·1	10 7·0	11 6·1	11 6·1	N. 3 40+0 33·1			44·3	44·0
Anon.	21 1 5·5	11 6·5	15 6·0	11 6·8	11 6·65	N. 3 55—3 33·35				
7386	21 8 50·6	10 18·7	11 7·8	10 18·9	10 18·8	N. 1 25—0 23·0				
Anon.	21 12 55·2		11 8·7	10 2·0		N. 4 25—1 6·7	28·315	42·8	43·9	43·8
Anon.	21 26 2·5	9 18·3	8 11·25	9 18·3	9 18·3	N. 3 50+1 7·05			43·3	43·6
7557	21 36 0·5	10 0·6	10 10·3	10 0·6	10 0·55	N. 0 30+0 0·75				
7613	21 44 51·0	10 6·7	13 9·75	10 6·9	10 6·8	S. 3 50+3 2·95				
7657	21 52 14·2	9 20·7	6 8·5	9 20·7	9 20·68	N. 5 0+3 12·18	28·325	43·7	44·1	43·8
Anon.	21 56 3·2	9 20·5	5 3·9	9 20·8	9 20·68	N. 5 0+4 16·78			43·2	43·0
7842	22 22 59·5	9 22·2	9 1·0	9 22·1	9 22·1	N. 1 5+0 21·15				
7909	22 34 3·3	9 4·6	11 30·15	9 4·7	9 4·65	N. 4 5—2 25·5				
7966	22 44 12·5	9 9·1	5 26·75	9 9·0	9 9·05	N. 0 30+3 16·3				
7992	22 49 23·5	9 6·5	5 17·2	9 6·5	9 6·5	N. 3 45+3 23·3	28·325	42·6	43·2	42·8
1802	5 34 20·7	10 2·2	11 17·0	10 2·2	10 2·2	N. 0 5—1 14·8	28·297	42·8	43·0	42·4
1878	5 46 4·0	9 14·7	11 6·0	9 14·8	9 14·75	S. 1 35+1 25·25				
2293	6 52 49·8	11 17·3	15 19·0	11 17·3	11 17·3	N. 5 30—4 1·7	28·310	43·5	44·0	43·2

♃ September 5, 1844.—Face of Sector East.

Number of B.A.C.	Time by Chronometer.	Micr. for Plumb-line on Dot.	Micr. for Observation of Star.	Micr. for Plumb-line on Dot.	Mean of Micr. for Plumb-line on Dot.	Star's Apparent Zenith Distance.	Barom.	Attd.	Upper.	Lower.
4458	13 ·	11 30·5	12 2·2	11 30·3	11 30·4	S. 1 40—0 5·8	28·288	55·4	58·0	53·0
4686	13 57 58·	11 28·1	7 6·75	11 28·0	11 28·5	S. 1 20+4 21·75	28·208		56·5	53·6
4852	14	11 8·8	8 17·5	11 8·6	11 8·7	S. 0 15+2 25·2				
5054	15 12 21·5	11 4·8	14 22·7	11 4·6	11 4·7	S. 1 30—3 18·0	28·252	52·5	53·6	52·4
5151	15 29 26·7	10 2·3	5 33·7	10 2·5	10 2·4	N. 5 0—4 2·7			53·0	52·1
5227	15 41 29·5	9 24·0	8 31·3	9 24·2	9 24·1	N. 1 5—0 26·8				
5292	15 50 14·5	10 5·3	13 11·8	10 5·5	10 5·4	S. 3 45—3 6·4			52·0	51·7
5331	16	9 31·0	11 32·6	9 31·6	9 31·6	S. 2 10—2 1·6				
5508	16 21 38·6	9 19·8	13 0·9	9 19·8	9 19·8	S. 0 10—3 15·1			50·8	50·9
5538	16	9 6·4	14 5·7	9 6·3	9 6·45	S. 0 45—4 39·25			50·3	50·4
5632	16 40 30·8	8 25·7	5 20·2	8 25·7	8 25·7	N. 0 15—3 5·5				
5735	16 55 0·2	9 8·7	8 22·0	9 8·8	9 8·75	N. 0 20—0 20·75	28·248	48·4	49·0	50·0
5817	17 7 21·3	8 25·5	8 5·4	8 25·7	8 25·6	N. 1 45—0 20·2				

Sept. 3.—No. 4458.—Leaving the field when observed.
    No. 6115.—Observed at 20 seconds from the meridian.
    Clouded at 18ʰ per chron. Heavy rain towards morning.
    4.—Clouded until 9ʰ m.t.
    No. 1878.—Observed at 16 seconds from the meridian.
    5.—No. 4686.—The seconds uncertain.
    Good definition on the 4th, with strong southerly wind.
    Definition not so good on the 5th.

♃ September 5, 1844.—Face of Sector East—(continued.)

Number of B.A.C.	Time by Chronometer.	Micr. for Plumb-line on Dot.	Micr. for Observation of Star.	Micr. for Plumb-line on Dot.	Mean of Micr. for Plumb-line on Dot.	Star's Apparent Zenith Distance.	Barom.	Thermometers.		
								Attd.	Upper.	Lower.
	h m s	rev. pts.	rev. pts.	rev. pts.	rev. pts.	° ′ rev. pts.	in.			
5881	17 17 48·2	10 6·0	10 24·35	10 6·2	10 6·1	N. 4 30+0 18·25				
5915	17 23 28·5	10 4·0	9 14·0	10 4·3	10 4·15	S. 2 45+0 24·15				
5970	17 32 10·2	10 16·2	14 6·4	10 16·0	10 16·1	S. 4 45—3 24 3		49·3	49·2	
6016	17 39 29·0	10 5·0	10 2·1	10 5·4	10 5·2	N. 2 35—0 3·1				
6074	17 49 29·6	9 33·4	9 14·6	9 33·4	9 33·4	N. 4 0—0 18·8				
6115	17 56 13·4	10 14·1	7 17·7	10 13·9	10 14·0	N. 3 50—2 30·3				
6145	18 0 28·5	10 24·6	8 17·3	10 24·4	10 24·5	N. 3 30—2 7·2		49·1	49·0	
6186	18 7 32·0	9 11·0	10 11·15	9 11·0	9 11·0	S. 2 35—1 0·15				
6233	18 14 15·7	9 26·0	12 17·8	9 26·0	9 26·0	S. 0 15—2 25·8				
6275	18 20 14·2	9 21·2	9 26·5		9 21·43	N. 1 5+0 5·07				
6285	18 21 18·0		15 27·95	9 21·5	9 21·43	N. 1 5+6 6·52				
6305	18 24 11·0	9 21·5	11 19·05	9 21·5	9 21·43	N. 1 5+1 31·0				
6414	18 43 6·5	10 0·8	7 33·0	10 1·1	10 0·95	N. 3 20—2 1·05	28·239	46·8	48·1	48·1
6489	18 53 7·0	10 1·4	6 6·75	10 1·4	10 1·4	N. 4 10—3 28·05				
6525	18 58 7·2	10 33·5	13 13·9	10 33·5	10 33·5	N. 5 20+2 14·4				
6639	19 17 30·8	11 13·4	13 2·85	11 13·4	11 13·4	N. 4 10+1 23·45				
Anon	19 21 43·2	11 13·2	11 9·8	11 13·2	11 13·2	N. 4 25—0 3·4				
6753	19 35 57·5	11 15·5	15 29·5	11 15·5	11 15·5	N. 2 55+4 14·0		48·0	48·0	
6877	19 54 53·0	11 9·6	10 11·2	11 9·4	11 9·5	N 1 45—0 32·3				
6948	20 6 35·3	11 25·5	12 5·0	11 25·5	11 25·5	N. 3 45+0 13·5				
7011	20 15 33·5	11 19·3	10 12·5	11 19·3	11 19·3	N. 4 40—1 6·8				
7026	20 17 24·4	11 19·4	10 4·45	11 19·3	11 19·3	N. 4 40—1 14·85				
7057	20 21 48·8	11 19·3	4 13·0	11 19·2	11 19·3	N. 4 40—7 6·3				
Anon.	20 24 41·8		9 31·8	10 19·4		N. 4 25—0 21·6				
Anon.	20 34 12·2	11 2·5	12 6·6	11 2·5	11 2·5	N. 4 15+1 4·1				
7207	20 40 39·8	9 30·9	5 30·0	9 30·7		S. 0 5+4 0·8				
Anon.	20 54 0·2	11 11·3	12 14·6	11 11·5	11 11·4	N. 4 30+1 3·2				
Anon.	21 1 10·2	10 17·7	6 24·1	10 17·7	10 17·7	N. 3 55—3 27 6				
7386	21 8 55·3	9 1·8	8 16·3	9 2·0	9 1·9	N. 1 25—0 19·6				
Anon.	21 12 59·3		9 7·3	10 8·7		N. 4 25—1 1·4		48·7	47·8	
Anon.	21 26 6·7	10 8·9	11 20·8	10 8·9	10 8·9	N. 3 50+1 11·9				
7557	21 36 5·7	9 31·0	9 31·0	10 3·0	10 3·0	N. 0 30—0 6·0				
7613	21 44 57·0	9 16·3	6 17·4	9 16·3	9 16·3	S. 3 50+2 32·9				
7657	21 52 18·5	9 23·4	13 4·4	9 23·3	9 23·35	N. 5 0+3 15·05	28·201	47·7	49·0	47·5
Anon.	21 56 9·4	9 23·4	14 8·9	9 23·3	9 23·35	N. 5 0+4 19·55				
7842	22 23	9 14·0	10 3·0	9 13·8	9 13·9	N. 1 5+0 23·1				
7909	22 34 7·8	9 28·1	7 5·7	9 27·9	9 28·0	N. 4 5—2 22·3				
7966	22 44 19·0	8 13·9	11 30·75	8 14·0	8 13·95	N. 0 30+3 16·8	28·199	46·4	48·5	47·0
7992	22 49 27·5	8 20·9	12 14·5	8 20·9	8 20·9	N. 3 45+3 27·0	28·125	50·0	52·0	48·8
1802	5 34 25·2	9 27·3	8 14·75	9 27·2	9 27·25	N. 0 5—1 12·5	28·124	50·0	52·2	49·0
1878	5 45 54·4	10 11·9	8 23·55	10 11·7	10 11·8	S. 1 35+1 22·25	28·136	55·4	60·0	53·0
2293	6 52 56·0	13 20·2	9 23·1	13 20·2	13 20·2	N. 5 30—3 31·1				

♀ September 6, 1844.—Face of Sector West.

5817	17 7 26·0	9 29·7	10 19·4	9 29·7	9 29·7	N. 1 45—0 23·7		62·5	62·0	
5915	17 23	9 3·0	9 32·9	9 3·0	9 3·0	S. 2 45+0 29·9	27·971	59·9	62·0	61·8
5970	17	9 27·3	6 7·3	9 27·3	9 27·3	S. 4 45—3 20·0				
6016	17 39 33·5	8 21·1	8 29·55	8 21·5	8 21·3	N. 2 35—0 8·25				
6074	17	10 7·5	10 31·3	10 7·4	10 7·45	N. 4 0—0 23·85		62·6	61·2	
6115	17 56 19·5	11 9·7	14 9·7	11 9·7	11 9·7	N. 3 50—3 0·0				
6145	18 0 34·3	12 30·3	15 10·3	12 30·3	12 30·3	N. 3 30—2 14·0				
6186	18 7 34·0	12 10·4	11 15·0	12 10·2	12 10 3	S. 2 35—0 29·3				
6233	18 14 19·5	9 20·5	6 33·0	9 20·3	9 20·4	S. 0 15—2 21·4				

Sept. 5.—No. 7207. —The seconds of transit doubtful.
No. 7842.—Observed at 15 seconds from the meridian.
6.—No. 5915.—Observed at 20 seconds from the meridian.

♀ SEPTEMBER 6, 1844.—FACE OF SECTOR WEST—(continued).

Number of B.A.C.	Time by Chronometer.	Micr. for Plumb-line on Dot.	Micr. for Observation of Star.	Micr. for Plumb-line on Dot.	Mean of Micr. for Plumb-line on Dot.	Star's Apparent Zenith Distance.	Barom.	Thermometers.		
								Attd.	Upper.	Lower.
	h m s	rev. pts.	rev. pts.	rev. pts.	rev. pts.	o ' rev. pts.	in.			
6275	18 20 18·5	9 28·7	9 26·75		9 28·55	N. 1 5+0 1·8				
6285	18 21 22·0		3 25·7	9 28·5	9 28·55	N. 1 5+6 2·85				
6305	18 24 14·8	9 28·5	8 0·0	9 28·5	9 28·55	N. 1 5+1 28·55	27·967	59·0	62·0	60·4
6414	18 43 12·5	9 19·8	11 25·2	9 19·0	9 19·4	N. 3 20—2 5·8				
6489	18	9 16·5	13 17·3	9 16·5	9 16·5	N. 4 10—4 0·8				
6525	18 58 14·0	10 30·9	8 22·1	10 30·9	10 30·9	N. 5 20+2 8·8			62·0	59·4
6639	19 17	12 3·5	10 20·7	12 3·7	12 3·6	N. 4 10+1 16·9				
Anon.	19 21 49·2	11 17·2	11 25·9	11 17·2	11 17·2	N. 4 25—0 8·7				
6753	19 36 3.3	11 30 1	7 22·2	11 30·1	11 30·1	N. 2 55+4 7·9				
6877	19 54 57 5	10 11·5	11 15·15	10 11·3	10 11·4	N. 1 45—1 3·75				
6948	20 6 41·5	10 14·2	10 7·3	10 14 1	10 14·15	N. 3 45+0 6·85	27·930	59·0	65·0	59·5
7011	20 15 40·2	10 20·1	11 31·5	10 20·0	10 20·1	N. 4 40—1 11·4				
7026	20 17 31·3		12 4·95	10 20·2	10 20·1	N. 4 40—1 18·85				
7057	20 21 56·0	10 20·0	17 32·8	10 20·2	10 20·1	N. 4 40—7 12·7				
Anon.	20 24 48·5		11 14·5	10 22·0		N. 4 25—0 26·5			65·0	59·0
Anon	20 34 18·5	10 21·7	9 22·0	10 21·7	10 21·7	N. 4 15+0 33·7				
7207	20 40 44·0	10 1·0	14 6·1	10 1·0	10 1·0	N. 4 5+4 5·1			66·0	59·0
Anon.	20 54 6·2	9 3·3	8 4·45	9 3·2	9 3·25	N. 4 30+0 32·8	27 920	58·8	66·5	59·0
Anon.	21 1 16·0	9 14·2	13 14·15	9 14·1	9 14·15	N. 3 55—4 0·0				
7386	21	10 9·4	10 33·0	10 9·6	10 9·5	N. 1 25—0 23·5			65·6	58·6
Anon.	21 26 13·0	11 28·5	10 21·6	11 28·6	11 28·55	N. 3 50+1 6·95			65·0	58·4
7557	21 36 10·3	10 17·5	10 26·3	10 17·5	10 17·5	N. 0 30—0 8·8				
7613	21 44 58·0	11 2·7	14 7·55	11 2·7	11 2·7	S. 3 50+3 4·85				
7657	21 52 25·5	10 8·1	6 32·5	10 8·2	10 8·18	N. 5 0+3 9·08				
Anon.	21 56 17·0	10 8·2	5 27·1	10 8·2	10 8·18	N. 5 0+4 15·08			63·6	58·6
7842	22 23 9·8	10 14·4	9 28·8	10 14·5	10 14·45	N. 1 5+0 19·05			63·8	58·5
7966	22	10 17·9	7 3·2	10 18·1	10 18·0	N. 0 30+3 14·8				
7992	22 49 34·3	10 28·7	7 5·9	10 28·7	10 28·7	N. 3 45+3 22·8	27·908	62·6	64·5	59·6
1892	5 34 30 2	10 10·8	11 27·9	10 11·0	10 10·9	N. 0 5—1 17·0	27·941	51·8	52·0	51·0
1878	5 45 57·0	9 24·2	11 17·45	9 24·2	9 24·2	S. 1 35+1 27·25				
2293	6 53 1·2	8 8·4	12 11·25	8 8·4	8 8·4	N. 5 30—4 2·85	27·991	52·0	53·0	51·9

☉ SEPTEMBER 8, 1844.—FACE OF SECTOR WEST.

5227	15 41 42·5	10 3·1	10 31·1	10 3·1	10 3·1	N. 1 5—0 28·0	28·282	58·1	61·5	59·2
5292	15 50 23·2	9 31·8	6 29·75	9 31·6	9 31·7	S. 3 45—3 1·95				
5331	15 56 58·2	9 12·1	7 14·7	9 12·1	9 12·1	S. 2 10—1 31·4			60·7	58·5
5508	16 21 50·5	9 10·5	5 33·25	9 10·5	9 10·5	S. 0 10—3 11·25				
5538	16 26 45·2	9 6·1	4 9·0	9 5·0	9 6·0	S. 0 45—4 31·0				
5632	16 40 43·0	9 3·9	12 12·2	9 4·1	9 4·0	N. 0 15—3 8·2	28·260	53·6	56·5	55·9
5817	17 7 35·2	11 4·5	11 27·8	11 4·7	11 4·6	N. 1 45—0 23·2			54·2	54·5
5881	17 18 5·5	10 5·1	9 24·4	10 4·9	10 5·0	N. 4 30+0 14·6				
5915	17 23 38·6	10 19·1	11 14·0	10 19·0	10 19·05	S. 2 45+0 28·95				
5970	17 32 18·0	9 32·0	6 12·45	9 31·8	9 31·9	S. 4 45—3 19·45				
6016	17 39 33·5	9 10·9	9 19·0	9 11·0	9 10·95	N. 2 35—0 8·05				
6074	17 49 40·0	9 9·5	10 0·2	9 9·5	9 9·5	N. 4 0—0 24·7				
6115	17 56 29·0	9 22·6	12 24·0	9 22·7	9 22·65	N. 3 50—3 1·35				
6145	18 0 44·2	9 19·0	11 33·5	9 19·0	9 19·0	N. 3 30—2 14·5				
6233	18 14 28 6	7 24·8	5 4·1	7 24·8	7 24·8	S. 0 15—2 20·7			51·1	52·0
6275	18 20 27·5	11 3·8	11 2·6		11 4·0	N. 1 5+0 1·4				
6285	18 21 31·2		5 1·7	11 4·0	11 4·0	N. 1 5+6 2·3				
6305	18 24 24·4	11 4·0	9 9·5	11 4·2	11 4·0	N. 1 5+1 28·5	28·252	50·0	51·0	51·4
6414	18 43 22·9	10 2·7	12 9·9	10 2·9·	10 2·8	N. 3 20—2 7·1				
6489	18 53 23·5	9 25·0	13 27·2	9 25·2	9 25·1	N. 4 10—4 2·1				

* Sept. 6.—No. 6639.—Observed at 20 seconds from the meridian.
The sky obscured until 13ʰ 11ᵐ S. T.
High temperature and a difference of about 7° between upper and lower ends of the telescope.
7.—Rain in the afternoon: fog afterwards.

☉ SEPTEMBER 8, 1844.—FACE OF SECTOR WEST—(continued).

Number of B.A.C.	Time by Chronometer.	Micr. for Plumb-line on Dot.	Micr. for Observation of Star.	Micr. for Plumb-line on Dot.	Mean of Micr. for Plumb-line on Dot.	Star's Apparent Zenith Distance.	Barom.	Thermometers. Attd.	Upper.	Lower.
	h m s	rev. pts.	rev. pts.	rev. pts.	rev. pts.	° ' rev. pts.	in.			
6525	18 58 24·5	9 14·7	7 6·4	9 14·5	9 14·6	N. 5 20 +2 8·2				
FACE OF SECTOR EAST.										
6639	19 17 44·2	10 17·7	12 7·0	10 17·9	10 17·8	N. 4 10 +1 23·2				
Anon.	19 21 56·0	9 28·3	9 26·0	9 28·5	9 28·4	N. 4 25 —0 2·4				
6753	19 36 10·8	10 1·0	14 14·5	10 1·2	10 1·1	N. 2 55 +4 13·4	28·252	48·6	49·9	50·0
6877	19 55 6·3	10 0·3	9 2·1	10 0·3	10 0·3	N. 1 45 —0 32·2				
6948	20 6 48·2	9 16·2	9 30·2	9 16·1	9 16·15	N. 3 45 +0 14·05				
7011	20 15 46·5	9 16·4	8 10·3	9 16·4	9 16·45	N. 4 40 —1 6·15				
7026	20 17 37·7	9 16·5	8 2·3	9 16·5	9 16·45	N. 4 40 —1 14·15				
7057	20 22 2·5	9 30·1	11 22·0	9 30·1	9 30·1	N. 4 35 +1 25·9				
Anon.	20 24 55·2		8 7·0	8 28·3		N. 4 25 —0 21·3				
Anon.	20 34 25·2	10 18·2	11 22·65	10 18·2	10 18·2	N. 4 15 +1 4·45	28·237	49·1	50·0	50·1
7207	20 40 54·2	10 10·9	6 10·7	10 11·0	10 10·95	S. 0 5 +4 0·25				
Anon.	20 54 13·1	10 33·4	12 3·2	10 33·5	10 33·45	N. 4 30 +1 3·75				
Anon.	21 1 23·2	11 4·5	7 11·1	11 4·5	11 4·5	N. 3 55 —3 27·4				
7386	21 9 9·0	10 27·0	10 7·5	10 27·0	10 27·0	N. 1 25 —0 19·5				
Anon.	21 13	11 21 3	10 19·5	11 21·5	11 21·4	N. 4 25 —1 1·9				
Anon.	21 26 20·2	11 16·9	12 29·1	11 17·1	11 17·0	N. 3 50 +1 12·1				
7557	21 36 19·6	10 29·7	10 23·5	10 29·8	10 29·75	N. 0 30 —0 6·25			49·8	49·4
7613	21 45 12·0	11 1·3	8 2·3	11 1·2	11 1·25	S. 3 50 +2 32·95				
7657	21 52 31·2	11 1·3	14 17·2	11 1·1	11 1·18	N. 5 0 +3 16·02				
Anon.	21 56 22·5	11 1·1	15 21·6	11 1·2	11 1·18	N. 5 0 +4 0·92				
7842	22 23 18·5	10 7·3	10 31·4	10 7·6	10 7·45	N. 1 5 +0 23·95				
7909	22 34 20·0	10 26·3	8 4·5	10 26·3	10 20·3	N. 4 5 —2 21·8				
7966	22 44 32·0	10 10·2	13 28·0	10 10·4	10 10·3	N. 0 30 +3 17·7				
7992	22 49 41·4	11 2·8	14 30·3	11 2·6	11 2·7	N. 3 45 +3 27·6	28·189	48·0	40·0	48·8
1802	5 34 39·5	10 13·1	9 0·8	10 13·0	10 13·05	N. 0 5 —1 12·25				
1878	5 46 8·6	10 6·8	8 18·3	10 6·6	10 6·7	S. 1 35 +1 22·4	28·087	45·0	46·5	45·0
2293	6 53 9·2	11 17·7	7 20·0	11 17·6	11 17·65	N. 5 30 —3 31·65				

☽ SEPTEMBER 9, 1844.—FACE OF SECTOR WEST.

Number of B.A.C.	Time by Chronometer.	Micr. for Plumb-line on Dot.	Micr. for Observation of Star.	Micr. for Plumb-line on Dot.	Mean of Micr. for Plumb-line on Dot.	Star's Apparent Zenith Distance.	Barom.	Thermometers. Attd.	Upper.	Lower.
4458	13 12 31·0	10 6·5	10 4·1	10 6·5	10 6·5	S. 1 40 —0 2·4	28·058	64·4	68·4	65·4
4686	13 58 12·0	9 31·6	14 23·9	9 31·8	9 31·7	S. 1 20 +4 26·2	28·048	64·4	68·5	64·6
6525	18 58 28·2	10 17·9	8 9·6	10 17·8	10 17·85	N. 5 20 +2 8·25	28·042	49·1	50·1	50·4
Anon.	19 22 2·7	11 18·0	11 27·2	11 18·2	11 18·1	N. 4 25 —0 9·1	28·042	48·2	49·4	49·6
6753	19	11 1·9	6 27·0	11 1·7	11 1·8	N. 2 55 +4 8·8				
6877	19	10 24·7	11 27·9	10 24·8	10 24·75	N. 1 45 —1 3·15				
6948	20 6 55·6	10 10·6	10 3·2	10 10·6	10 10·6	N. 3 45 +0 7·4			50·5	49·6
7011	20 15 55·2	9 15·4	10 27·0	9 15·6	9 15·5	N. 4 40 —1 11·5				
7026	20	9 15·5	10 33·0	9 15·5	9 15·5	N. 4 40 —1 17·5				
7057	20 22 10·5	8 26·0	7 6·9	8 26·2	8 26·1	N. 4 35 +1 19·2				
Anon.	20 34 33·5	10 11·3	9 12·3	10 11·2	10 11·2	N. 4 15 +0 32·9				
7207	20 40 58·0	10 12·2	14 17·75	10 12·1	10 12·15	S. 0 5 +4 5·6				
Anon	20 54 20·8	10 31·4	9 32·5	10 31·4	10 31·4	N. 4 30 +0 32·9				
21 1	21 1 30·5	10 23·8	14 23·6	10 23·8	10 23·8	N. 3 55 —3 33·8				
7386	21 9 14·0	10 1·5	10 25·6	10 1·4	10 1·45	N. 1 25 —0 24·15				
Anon.	21 13 20·4	10 16·9	11 23·95	10 17·0	10 16·95	N. 4 25 —1 7·0	28·028	47·1	48·5	48·8
Anon.	21 26 27·5	10 6·5	9 0·0	10 6·5	10 6·5	N. 3 50 +1 6·5			47·6	48·0
7557	21 36 24·0	10 16·0	10 26·45	10 16·1	10 16·1	N. 0 30 —0 10·35				
7613	21 45 11·2	10 28·4	13 33·4	10 28·5	10 28·45	S. 3 50 +3 4·95				
7657	21 52 40·0	9 29·5	6 21·0	9 29·3	9 29·38	N. 5 0 +3 8·38				
Anon.	21 56 31·0	9 29·3	5 15·7	9 29·4	9 29·38	N. 5 0 +4 13·68				

Sept. 8.—The seconds of transit of Nos. 7909 and 1878 are doubtful. Excellent definition.
9.—No. 6753.—Observed at 20 seconds from the meridian. The zenith frequently clouded.

(SEPTEMBER 9, 1844.—FACE OF SECTOR WEST—(continued).

Number of B.A.C.	Time by Chronometer.	Micr. for Plumb-line on Dot.	Micr. for Observation of Star.	Micr. for Plumb-line on Dot.	Mean of Micr. for Plumb-line on Dot.	Star's Apparent Zenith Distance.	Barom.	Thermometers.		
								Attd.	Upper.	Lower.
	h m s	rev. pts.	rev. pts.	rev. pts.	rev. pts.	o ′ rev. pts.	in.			
7842	22 23 23·7	10 11·0	9 26 6	10 11·0	10 11·0	N. 1 5+0 18·4			46·0	46·5
7909	22 34 28·2	10 1·0	12 29·4	10 1·1	10 1·05	N. 4 5—2 28·35				
7966	22 44 36·5	10 0·4	6 21·3	10 0·6	10 0·5	N. 0 30+3 13·2				
7992	22 49 48·5	9 33·6	6 12·15	9 33·6	9 33·6	N. 3 45+3 21·45	28·026	46·4	46·0	46·5
2293	6 53 16·3	10 6·4	14 9·65	10 6·5	10 6·45	N. 5 30—4 3·2	28·014	49·5	49·0	48·0

There was heavy rain on the 10th and 11th, driven by strong wind, which unfortunately raised the edge of the tent cap, and wet passed into the telescope tube, where the sliding piece of the object glass enters. A dense deposit of vapour upon the inner surface of the object glass was the result. The glass was taken out and wiped on the 12th, and 45 stars were observed that night; but on the morning of the 13th the glass was as densely coated as on the day before. On this occasion, both eye piece and object glass were removed, and a fire was kept up within the tent, until the tube became heated and all moisture effectually driven out.

☞ This occurrence again breaks the continuity of the collimation error, and the observations of the 12th are useless; accordingly they are not printed.

♀ SEPTEMBER 13, 1844.--FACE OF SECTOR WEST.

Number of B.A.C.	Time by Chronometer.	Micr. for Plumb-line on Dot.	Micr. for Observation of Star.	Micr. for Plumb-line on Dot.	Mean of Micr. for Plumb-line on Dot.	Star's Apparent Zenith Distance.	Barom.	Thermometers.		
								Attd.	Upper.	Lower.
	h m s	rev. pts.	rev. pts.	rev. pts.	rev. pts.	o ′ rev. pts.	in.			
4686	13 58 29·6	8 33·2	13 27·7	8 33·0	8 33·1	S. 1 20+4 28·6	28·038	56·5	59·1	58·3

♄ SEPTEMBER 14, 1844.—FACE OF SECTOR WEST.

Number of B.A.C.	Time by Chronometer.	Micr. for Plumb-line on Dot.	Micr. for Observation of Star.	Micr. for Plumb-line on Dot.	Mean of Micr. for Plumb-line on Dot.	Star's Apparent Zenith Distance.	Barom.	Attd.	Upper.	Lower.
4458	13 12 53·0	10 10·6	10 10·0	10 10·3	10 10·45	S. 1 40—0 0·45	28·266	58·6	61·0	57·2
4686	13 58 33·5	10 12·6	15 6·0	10 12·6	10 12·6	S. 1 20+4 27·4	28·252	58·8	60·3	57·5
5054	15 12 59·2	11 16·0	8 3·3	11 16·0	11 16·0	S. 1 30—3 12·7	28·235	55·6	57·2	56·0
5227	15	10 0·4	10 30·2	10 0·4	10 0·4	N. 1 5—0 29·8	28·233	53·6	55·2	54·8
5292	15 50 5·0	10 10·8	7 11·5	10 10·9	10 10·85	S. 3 45—2 33·35				
5508	16	9 33·8	6 24·5	9 33·7	9 33·75	S. 0 10—3 9·25			52·4	52·5
5538	16	9 23·4	4 28·3	9 23·5	9 23·45	S. 0 45—4 29·15	28·214	48·9	51·4	52·0
5632	16 41 9·5	9 26·3	13 3·2	9 26·3	9 26·3	N. 0 15—3 10·9			50·9	51·3
5735	16	9 30·6	10 24·4	9 30·6	9 30·6	N. 0 20—0 27·8				
5881	17 18 32·8	10 1·2	9 24·8	10 1·4	10 1·3	N. 4 30+0 10·5				
5915	17 24 6·5	11 11·4	12 9·8	11 11·6	11 11·5	S. 2 45+0 32·3			48·5	49·2
5970	17 32 44·8	10 25·1	7 8·6	10 25·0	10 25·05	S. 4 45—3 16·45				
6016	17	9 33·5	10 11·0	9 33·7	9 33·6	N. 2 35—0 11·4				
6074	17	12 19·1	13 13·3	12 19·4	12 19·25	S. 4 0—0 28·05			47·2	48·5
6115	17 56 56·3	11 26·4	14 30·6	11 26·4	11 26·4	N. 3 50—3 4·2				
6145	18	10 25·5	13 8·5	10 25·3	10 25·4	N. 3 30—2 17·1			47·2	48·2
6186	18 8 9·5	11 30·4	11 4·95	11 30·0	11 30·2	S. 2 35—0 25·25				

♄ September 14, 1844.—Face of Sector West—(continued).

Number of B.A.C.	Time by Chronometer.	Micr. for Plumb-line on Dot.	Micr. for Observation of Star.	Micr. for Plumb-line on Dot.	Mean of Micr. for Plumb-line on Dot.	Star's Apparent Zenith Distance.	Barom.	Thermometers.		
								Att.	Upper.	Lower.
	h m s	rev. pts.	rev. pts.	rev. pts.	rev. pts.	° ′ rev. pts.	In.			
6233	18 14 56·0	11 20·3	9 3·0	11 20·5	11 20·4	S. 0 15—2 17·4			47·2	47·9
6275	18	10 7·9	10 11·5		10 7·75	N. 1 5—0 3·75				
6285	18		4 9·4	10 7·6	10 7·75	N. 1 5+5 32·35				
6305	18	10 7·7	8 18·0	10 7·8	10 7·75	N. 1 5+1 23·75				
6414	18	9 33·0	12 10·8	9 32·6	9 32·8	N. 3 20—2 12·0	28·187	46·2		47·2
6489	18	9 6·0	13 10·8	9 6·0	9 6·0	N. 4 10—4 4·8				
6525	18	9 6·5	7 2·5	9 6·5	9 6·5	N. 5 20+2 4·0				
6639	19	9 27·0	8 13·1	9 26·6	9 26·8	N. 4 10+1 13·7	28·189	46·2	46·2	47·0
Anon.	19 22	9 28·7	10 4·7	9 28·9	9 28·8	N. 4 25—0 9·9				
6753	19	9 33·5	5 29·3	9 33·5	9 33·5	N. 2 55+4 4·2				
6948	20 7 18·5	10 19·4	10 15·65	10 19·4	10 19·4	N. 3 45+0 3·75	28·189	45·5	46·0	46·6
7011	20 16 17·5	10 25·2	12 6·95	10 25·2	10 25·28	N. 4 40—1 15·67				
7026	20 18 8·2	10 25·4	12 14·95	10 25·3	10 25·28	N. 4 40—1 23·67				
7057	20 22 33·0	10 7·2	8 25·5	10 7·2	10 7·2	N. 4 35+1 15·7				
Anon.	20 25 25·5		10 0·8	9 4·1		N. 4 25—0 30·7				
Anon.	20 34 56·0	9 16·0	8 20·1	9 15·8	9 15·9	N. 4 15+0 29·8				
7207	20 41 20·5	9 13·0	13 22·8	9 13·0	9 13·0	S. 0 5+4 0·8	28·189	44·6	46·0	46·2
Anon.	20 54 43·5	8 31·9	8 4·1	8 31·9	8 31·9	N. 4 30+0 27·8				
Anon.	21 1 53·2	10 11·3	14 15·0	10 11·7	10 11·5	N. 3 55—4 3·5				
7386	21 9 36·5	10 19·5	11 14·0	10 19·6	10 19·55	N. 1 25—0 28·45				
Anon.	21 13 42·5	10 24·4	12 2·4	10 24·5	10 24·45	N. 4 25—1 11·95	28·180	44·1	46·0	45·9
Anon.	21 26 50·5	9 30·6	8 28·0	9 30·8	9 30·7	N. 3 50+1 2·7				
7557	21 36 46·8	10 0·6	10 16·3	10 0·7	10 0·65	N. 0 30—0 15·65				
7613	21 45 33·5	10 32·3	14 8·0	10 32·5	10 32·4	S. 3 50+3 9·6				
7657	21 53 2·8	9 28·8	6 22·8	9 28·7	9 28·73	N. 5 0+3 5·93				
Anon.	21 56 53·5	9 28·6	5 18·4	9 28·8	9 28·73	N. 5 0+4 10·33	28·180	43·0	45·8	45·1
7842	22 23 46·0	9 21·1	9 6·1	9 21·3	9 21·2	N. 1 5+0 15·1				
7909	22 34 51·2	10 14·5	13 12·9	10 14·6	10 14·55	N. 4 5—2 32·35	28·178	43·0	45·0	44·8
7966	22 44 59·0	9 8·8	5 32·5	9 8·6	9 8·7	N. 0 30+3 10·2				
7992	22 50 11·6	9 29·4	6 11·0	9 29·3	9 29·35	N. 3 45+3 18·35	28·178	42·8	45·0	44·8
1802	5 35 7·5	10 13·2	11 32·2	10 13·2	10 13·2	N. 0 5—1 19·0				
1878	5 46 33·8	11 14·7	13 9·55	11 14·6	11 14·65	S. 1 35+1 28·9	28·166	42·5	42·1	41·3

☉ September 15, 1844.—Face of Sector East.

4458	13 12 59·8	10 6·5	10 19·1	10 6·5	10 6·5	S. 1 40—0 12·6	28·308	64·9	67·4	59·1
4686	13 58 41·5	9 9·0	4 26·45	9 9·0	9 9·0	S. 1 20+4 16·55				
4852	14 35 18·3	9 11·5	6 26·9	9 11·5	9 11·5	S. 0 15+2 18·6	28·306	64·0	65·5	59·1
5227	15	8 15·7	7 32·4	8 15·5	8 15·6	N. 1 5—0 17·2				
5331	15	9 19·4	11 27·6	9 19·4	9 19·4	S. 2 10—2 8·2			60·5	57·5
5508	16	9 33·0	13 20·9	9 33·0	9 33·0	S. 0 10—3 21·9				
5632	16 41 15·0	10 10·2	7 9·4	10 10·0	10 10·1	N. 0 15—3 0·7				
5735	16	10 2·4	9 20·1	10 2·6	10 2·5	N. 0 20—0 16·4	28·272	51·6	54·0	54·2
5881	17 18 35·0	9 12·1	9 33·0	9 12·2	9 12·15	N. 4 30+0 20·85				
5915	17 24 14·8	8 14·5	7 27·3	8 14·5	8 14·5	S. 2 45+0 21·2			52·2	53·2
5970	17 32 56·4	10 5·5	14 0·1	10 5·5	10 5·5	S. 4 45—3 26·8			51·7	52·6
6016	17 40 13·2	10 6·4	10 7·8	10 6·4	10 6·4	N. 2 35+0 1·4				
6074	17 50 14·0	10 26·6	10 11·3	10 26·6	10 26·6	N. 4 0—0 15·3				
6115	17 56 57·0	10 21·3	7 29·0	10 21·7	10 21·5	N. 3 50—2 26·5				
6145	18 1 12·3	10 23·2	8 18·8	10 23·4	10 23·3	N. 3 30—2 4·5				
6186	18 8 17·5	9 27·0	10 30·8	9 27·1	9 27·05	S. 2 35—1 3·75				
6233	18	9 18·9	12 13·8	9 18·9	9 18·9	S. 0 15—2 28·9				
6275	18 20 59·5	9 11·4	9 21·7		9 11·68	N. 1 5+0 10·02				
6285	18 22 2·0		15 23·0	9 11·7	9 11·68	N. 1 5+6 11·32				

Sept. 15.—No. 5227.—Bisected when leaving the field.
No. 6186.—The seconds of transit doubtful.
Good definition until 19ʰ 20ᵐ per chronometer.

☉ SEPTEMBER 15, 1844.—FACE OF SECTOR EAST—(continued).

Number of B.A.C.	Time by Chronometer.	Micr. for Plumb-line on Dot.	Micr. for Observation of Star.	Micr. for Plumb-line on Dot.	Mean of Micr. for Plumb-line on Dot.	Star's Apparent Zenith Distance.	Barom.	Attd.	Upper.	Lower.
	h m s	rev. pts.	rev. pts.	rev. pts.	rev. pts.	° ′ rev. pts.	in.			
6305	18 24 55·2	9 11·6	11 15·0	9 12·0	9 11·68	N.1 5+2 3·32			50·1	51·0
6414	18 43 50·7	11 4·8	9 6·7	11 5·0	11 4·9	N.3 20—1 32·2				
6480	18 53 50·5	11 4·8	7 12·7	11 4·8	11 4·8	N.4 10—3 26·1				
6525	18 58 51·0	10 20·1	13 4·1	10 20·1	10 20·1	N.5 20+2 18·0				
6639	19 18 15·0	11 1·3	12 27·0	11 1·7	11 1·5	N.4 10+1 25·5				
Anon.	19 22 26·7	9 23·4	9 24·0	9 23·6	9 23·5	N.4 25+0 0·5	28·273	48·2	49·0	50·0
6753	19 36 41·7	9 19·9	14 3·3	9 19·9	9 19·9	N.2 55+4 17·4				
6877	19 55 37·0	9 13·9	8 18·65	9 13·9	9 13·9	N.1 45—0 29·25				
6948	20 7 19·0	9 15·6	9 32·05	9 15·6	9 15·6	N.3 45+0 16·45				
7011	20 16 17·5	9 16·7	8 12·4	9 17·0	9 16·93	N.4 40—1 4·53				
7026	20 18 8·2	9 16·9	8 5·0	9 17·1	9 16·93	N.4 40—1 11·93				
7057	20 22 33·4	9 28·2	11 23·05	9 28·1	9 28·15	N.4 35+1 28·9				
Anon.	20 25 26·0		9 2·0	9 21·0		N.4 25—0 19·0	28·272	47·5	48·8	49·0
Anon.	20 34 56·2	9 10·3	10 17·9	9 10 2	9 10·25	N.4 15+1 7·65				
7207	20 41 25·5	9 23·5	5 26·75	9 23·6	9 23·55	S.0 5+3 30·8				
Anon.	20 54 43·7	9 29·0	11 1·3	9 29·0	9 29·0	N.4 30+1 6·3				
Anon.	21 1 54·5	9 14·5	5 24·1	9 14·5	9 14·5	N.3 55—3 24·4				
7386	21 9 40·2	8 19·3	8 2·5	8 19·5	8 19·4	N.1 25—0 16·9				
Anon.	21 13 43·5	11 5·0	10 5·95	11 5·2	11 5·1	N.4 25—0 33·15			47·5	48·0
Anon.	21 26 51·1	11 2·9	12 17·4	11 2·8	11 2·85	N.3 50+1 14·55				
7557	21 36 51·3	11 30·6	11 26·95	11 30·6	11 30·6	N.30—0 3·65				
7613	21 45 44·2	11 22·9	8 25·4	11 22·5	11 22·7	S.3 50+2 31·3				
7657	21 53 2·3	10 33·7	14 17·45	10 33·9	10 33·83	N.5 0+3 17·62				
Anon.	21 56 53·3	10 33·9	15 22·3	10 33·8	10 33·83	N.5 0+4 22·47	28·256	46·6	47·1	47·8
7842	22 23 50·2	10 6·5	10 31·9	10 6·5	10 6·5	N.1 5+0 25·4				
7909	22 34 52·2	10 22·4	8 2·1	10 22·5	10 22·45	N.4 5—2 20·35				
7966	22 45 3·2	10 16·6	14 2·45	10 16·5	10 16·55	N.0 30+3 19·9				
7992	22 50 12·2	11 16·5	15 12·25	11 16·4	11 16·4	N.3 45+3 29·8	28·256	46·4	47·0	47·4

FACE OF SECTOR WEST.

2293	6 53 44·0	10 30·2	15 2·0	10 30·0	10 30·1	N.5 30—4 5·9	28·154	46·6	46·0	45·0

☽ SEPTEMBER 16, 1844.—FACE OF SECTOR EAST.

5151	15 30 20·0	12 30·6	8 33·5	12 30·5	12 30·55	N.5 0—3 31·05				

FACE OF SECTOR WEST.

5331	15	10 26·3	8 30·9	10 26·3	10 26·3	S.2 10—1 29·4	28·095	54·5	57·0	56·0

♂ SEPTEMBER 17, 1844.—FACE OF SECTOR WEST.

1802	5 35 21·7	16 21·5	18 7·1	16 21·1	16 21·3	N.0 5—1 19·8				
1878	5 46 47·8	12 14·2	14 10·4	12 14·1	12 14·15	S.1 35+1 30·25	28·172	47·5	46·8	47·6
2293	6 53 54·0	12 23·4	16 29·6	12 23·4	12 23·4	N.5 20—4 6·2	28·182	48·2	48·5	48·0

☿ SEPTEMBER 18, 1844.—FACE OF SECTOR WEST.

4458	13 13 11·5	10 21·0	10 19·4	10 21·0	10 21·0	S.1 40—0 1·6	28·158	60·8	64·0	59·6
4686	13 58 52·5	11 8·0	16 0·5	11 8·0	11 8·0	S.1 20+4 26·5	28·156	61·9	64·5	60·3

FACE OF SECTOR EAST.

5054	15 13 22·7	11 2·2	14 24·35	11 2·4	11 2·3	S.1 30—3 22·05	28·126	60·8	62·8	59·8
5292	15 51 15·5	10 20·1	13 30·6	10 20·1	10 20.1	S.3 45—3 10·5				

Sept. 16 and 17.—Generally enveloped in fog.
18.—No. 5292.—The seconds of transit doubtful.

♀ SEPTEMBER 18, 1844—(continued).—FACE OF SECTOR WEST.

Number of B. A. C.	Time by Chronometer.	Micr. for Plumb-line on Dot.	Micr. for Observation of Star.	Micr. for Plumb-line on Dot.	Mean of Micr. for Plumb-line on Dot.	Star's Apparent Zenith Distance.	Barom.	Attd.	Upper.	Lower.
	h m s	rev. pts.	rev. pts.	rev. pts.	rev. pts.	° ′ rev. pts.	in.			
5538	16 27	12 30·2	8 1·4	12 30·0	12 30·1	S. 0 45—4 28·7			59·2	58·0
5632	16 41 28·5	10 22·9	13 33·5	10 22·9	10 22·9	N. 0 15—3 10·6				
5735	16 56	10 31·4	11 24·2	10 31·2	10 31·3	N. 0 20—0 26·9	28·103	55·4	58·5	57·6
5881	17	9 25·7	9 13·0	9 25·9	9 25·8	N. 4 30+0 12·8				
5915	17 24 26·0	11 9·0	12 7·0	11 9·0	11 9·0	S. 2 45+0 32·0				
5970	17 33 6·0	11 0·3	7 17·7	11 0·7	11 0·5	S. 4 45—3 16·8			55·4	56·0
6016	17	10 11·9	10 21·5	10 11·9	10 11·9	N. 2 35—0 9·6				
6074	17 50 30·2	10 5·1	10 32·4	10 5·0	10 5·05	N. 4 0—0 27·35			54·8	55·2
6115	17 57 13·5	10 24·9	13 28·45	10 24·9	10 24·9	N. 3 50—3 3·55				
6145	18 1 28·5	11 16·1	13 32·5	11 16·1	11 16·1	N. 3 30—2 16·4				
6186	18 8 29·0	11 32·1	11 6·95	11 32·1	11 32·1	S. 2 35—0 25·15			54·5	55·0
6233	18 15 14·5	9 33·8	7 16·0	9 33·6	9 33·7	S. 0 15—2 17·7				
6275	18 21 13·0	9 31·6	9 33·3		9 31·4	N. 1 5—0 1·9				
6285	18 22 17·5	9 31·4	3 31·4	9 31·5	9 31·4	N. 1 5+6 0·0				
6305	18 25 9·5	9 31·3	8 5·0	9 31·2	9 31·4	N. 1 5+1 26·4	28·071	52·5	53·6	54·2
6414	18 44 8·0	13 20·2	15 30·4	13 20·3	13 20·25	N. 3 20—2 10·15				
6489	18 54 8·3	10 16·5	14 22·1	10 16·5	10 16·5	N. 4 10—4 5·6				
6525	18 59 9·0	9 31·1	7 27·2	9 31·1	9 31·1	N. 5 20+2 3·9	28·071	51·8	53·6	54·2
6639	19 18 30·5	9 32·5	8 18·4	9 32·6	9 32·55	N. 4 10+1 14·15				
6877	19 55 51·5	11 1·6	12 9·0	11 2·0	11 1·8	N. 1 45—1 7·2				
6948	20 7 36·5	9 29·8	9 26·4	9 30·0	9 29·9	N. 3 45+0 3·5				
7011	20 16 35·5	8 31·4	10 14·0	8 31·5	8 31·5	N. 4 40—1 16·5				
7026	20 18 26·0	8 31·6	10 21·25	8 31·5	8 31·5	N. 4 40—1 23·75				
7057	20 22 51·0	9 1·9	7 20·6	9 1·9	9 1·9	N. 4 35+1 15·3				
Anon.	20 26 43·3		10 11·5	9 13·9		N. 4 25—0 31·6				
Anon.	20 35 12·5	8 30·5	8 0·7	8 30·5	8 30·5	N. 4 15+0 29·8				
7207	20 41 39·3	8 10·2	12 20·05	8 10·1	8 10·15	S. 0 5+4 9·9				
Anon.	20 55 1·0	9 5·3	8 10·6	9 5·4	9 5·35	N. 4 30+0 28·75	28·042	51·1	52·0	52·0
Anon.	21 2 10·5	8 20·9	12 24·8	8 21·0	8 20·95	N. 3 55—4 3·85				
7386	21 9 55·1	10 0·0	10 29·0	9 33·9	9 33·95	N. 1 25—0 29·05				
Anon.	21 14 0·2	9 19·8	10 31·5	9 20·0	9 19·9	N. 4 25—1 11·6				
Anon.	21 27 7·2	9 13·3	8 11·3	9 13·3	9 13·3	N. 3 50+1 2·0				
7557	21 37 5·5	10 1·5	10 17·9	10 1·5	10 1·5	N. 0 30—0 16·4				
7613	21 45 54·5	10 13·7	13 24·15	10 13·8	10 13·75	S. 3 50+3 10·4				
7657	21 53 19·7	10 2·6	6 30·55	10 2·3	10 2·38	N. 5 0+3 5·83				
Anon.	21 57 10·5	10 2·1	5 27·0	10 2·5	10 2·38	N. 5 0+4 9·38				
7842	22 24 4·5	10 15·6	10 0·9	10 15·6	10 15·6	N. 1 5+0 14·7				
7909	22 35 8·5	10 3·7	13 2·6	10 3·6	10 3·65	N. 4 5—2 32·95	28·014	50·4	51·4	51·4
7966	22 45 17·5	9 19·7	6 11·6	9 19·8	9 19·75	N. 0 30+3 8·15			51·4	51·2
7992	22 50 29·0	10 33·4	7 16·3	10 33·5	10 33·45	N. 3 45+3 17·15	28·013	50·0	51·4	51·2

FACE OF SECTOR EAST.

Number of B. A. C.	Time by Chronometer.	Micr. for Plumb-line on Dot.	Micr. for Observation of Star.	Micr. for Plumb-line on Dot.	Mean of Micr. for Plumb-line on Dot.	Star's Apparent Zenith Distance.	Barom.	Attd.	Upper.	Lower.
1878	5 46 55·5	11 15·4	9 30·45	11 15·5	11 15·45	S. 1 35+1 19·0	27·965	51·6	52·2	48·4
2293	6 53 51·2	10 23·4	6 29·3	10 23·4	10 23·4	N. 5 30—3 28·1	27·974	53·8	52·5	51·5

♃ SEPTEMBER 19, 1844.—FACE OF SECTOR EAST.

Number of B. A. C.	Time by Chronometer.	Micr. for Plumb-line on Dot.	Micr. for Observation of Star.	Micr. for Plumb-line on Dot.	Mean of Micr. for Plumb-line on Dot.	Star's Apparent Zenith Distance.	Barom.	Attd.	Upper.	Lower.
5881	17 18 52·8	12 13·3	13 0·6	12 13·4	12 13·35	N. 4 30+0 21·25			63·0	62·0
5915	17 24 32·5	9 12·3	8 25·7	9 11·9	9 12·1	S. 2 45+0 20·4				
5970	17 33 14·2	9 6·0	13 0·3	9 5·8	9 5·9	S. 4 45—3 28·4	28·026	57·6		
6074	17 50 33·0	11 28·0	11 14·05	11 28·0	11 28·05	N. 4 0—0 14·0				
6115	17 57 16·0	11 23·0	8 31·2	11 23·0	11 23·0	N. 3 50—2 25·8			59·0	59·8
6145	18 1	11 33·3	9 29·0	11 33·2	11 33·25	S. 3 30—2 4·25				
6186	18 8 35·3	10 28·6	11 32·6	10 2 ·7	10 28·65	S. 2 35—1 3·95				

Sept. 18.—Nos. 5538 and 5735.—Observed at 20 seconds from the meridian.
No. 5881.—Leaving the field when bisected.
Indifferent definition this night.
No. 2293.—The seconds of transit doubtful.

♃ September 19, 1844.—Face of Sector East—(continued.)

Number of B.A.C.	Time by Chronometer.	Micr. for Plumb-line on Dot.	Micr. for Observation of Star.	Micr. for Plumb-line on Dot.	Mean of Micr. for Plumb-line on Dot.	Star's Apparent Zenith Distance.	Barom.	Thermometers.		
								Attd.	Upper.	Lower.
	h m s	rev. pts.	rev. pts.	rev. pts.	rev. pts.	° ′ rev. pts.	in.			
6233	18 15 19·5	12 3·7	14 32·75	12 3·8	12 3·75	S. 0 15—2 29·0				
6275	18 21 17·2	11 15·7	11 25·8		11 16·18	N. 1 5+0 9·62				
6285	18 22 21·0		17 27·85	11 15·9	11 16·18	N. 1 5+6 11·47				
6305	18 25 13·8	11 16·4	13 18·85	11 16·7	11 16·19	N. 1 5—2 2·67	28·020	55·2	56·9	58·0
6414	18 44 10·2	11 31·5	10 0·4	11 31·5	11 31·5	N. 3 20—1 31·1				
6489	18 54 10·0	11 23·5	7 31·4	11 23·7	11 23·6	N. 4 10—3 26·2				
6525	18 59 9·5	11 1·7	13 19·3	11 1·5	11 1·6	N. 5 20+2 17·7				
6639	19 18 34·5	10 22·4	12 15·75	10 22·5	10 22·45	N. 4 10+1 27·3				
Anon.	19 22 47·2	10 32·3	10 32·9	10 32·1	10 32·2	N. 4 25+0 0·7				
6877	19 55 56·4	10 24·7	9 30·9	10 24·9	10 24·8	N. 1 45—0 27·9				
6948	20 7 37·8	10 29·8	11 12·6	10 29·8	10 29·8	N. 3 45+0 16·8	28·022	53·2	55·0	55·0
7011	20 16 36·2	10 23·9	9 20·6	10 24·2	10 24·05	N. 4 40—1 3·45				
7026	20 18 27·0	10 24·1	9 13·0	10 24·0	10 24·05	N. 4 40—1 11·05				
7057	20 22 52·3	10 20·5	12 15·0	10 20·5	10 20·5	N. 4 35+1 28·5				
Anon.	20 25 45·0		9 29·45	10 12·3		N. 4 25—0 16·85				
Anon.	20 35	10 33·3	12 6·0	10 33·3	10 33·3	N. 4 15+1 6·7				
7207	20 41 44·4	10 7·7	6 10·5	10 7·8	10 7·75	S. 0 5+3 31·25				
Anon.	20 55 2·5	10 25·3	11 32·0	10 25·5	10 25·4	N. 4 30+1 6·6				
Anon.	21 2 21·5	10 22·3	6 81·8	10 22·3	10 22·3	N. 3 55—3 24·5				
7386	21 9 59·5	9 16·4	8 33·3	9 16·7	9 16·55	N. 1 25—0 17·25				
Anon.	21 14	9 26·6	8 26·6	9 26·6	9 26·6	N. 4 25—1 0·0	28·024	53·4	54·8	54·8

♀ September 20, 1844.—Face of Sector West.

Number of B.A.C.	Time by Chronometer.	Micr. for Plumb-line on Dot.	Micr. for Observation of Star.	Micr. for Plumb-line on Dot.	Mean of Micr. for Plumb-line on Dot.	Star's Apparent Zenith Distance.	Barom.	Attd.	Upper.	Lower.
2293	6 54 5·3	12 12·1	16 17·3	12 12·1	12 12·1	N. 5 30—4 5·2	28·111	48·2	48·0	48·2

♄ September 21, 1844.—Face of Sector East.

Number of B.A.C.	Time by Chronometer.	Micr. for Plumb-line on Dot.	Micr. for Observation of Star.	Micr. for Plumb-line on Dot.	Mean of Micr. for Plumb-line on Dot.	Star's Apparent Zenith Distance.	Barom.	Attd.	Upper.	Lower.
4686	13 59 9·5	10 7·3	5 26·0	10 7·4	10 7·35	S. 1 20+4 15·35	28·134	59·2	64·5	59·3
5632	16 41 43·8	10 28·0	7 26·7	10 28·4	10 28·2	N. 0 15—3 1·5	28·105	53·4	55·2	55·6

Face of Sector West.

Number of B.A.C.	Time by Chronometer.	Micr. for Plumb-line on Dot.	Micr. for Observation of Star.	Micr. for Plumb-line on Dot.	Mean of Micr. for Plumb-line on Dot.	Star's Apparent Zenith Distance.	Barom.	Attd.	Upper.	Lower.
6115	17 57 28·0	12 5·0	15 8·55	12 5·0	12 5·0	N. 3 50—3 3·55				
6145	18	11 24·5	14 7·7	11 24·5	11 24·5	N. 3 30—2 17·2				
6186	18 8 43·5	12 19·5	11 27·25	12 19·5	12 19·5	S. 2 35—0 26·25				
6233	18 15 28·5	11 21·5	9 3·05	11 21·3	11 21·4	S. 0 15—2 18·35				
6275	18 21 26·5	12 0·3	12 1·7		12 0·45	N. 1 5—0 1·25				
6285	18 22 30·5		6 1·0	12 0·5	12 0·45	N. 1 5+5 33·45				
6305	18 25 23·5	12 0·4	10 10·25	12 0·6	12 0·45	N. 3 5+1 24·2	28·111	50·0	52·4	51·8
6414	18 44 21·5	10 29·9	13 5·5	10 30·0	10 29·95	N. 3 20—2 9·55	28·111	49·5	52·0	51·5
6489	18 54 21·5	10 24·5	14 28·5	10 24·0	10 24·45	N. 4 10—4 4·05			51·5	51·3
6639	19 18 45·0	11 14·4	10 0·0	11 14·4	11 14·4	N. 4 10+1 14·4				
6948	20 7 51·0	12 21·5	12 17·9	12 21·6	12 21·55	N. 3 45+0 3·65				
7011	20 16 49·2	12 25·4	14 7·2	12 25·0	12 25·23	N. 4 40—1 15·97				
7026	20 18 39·5		14 14·8	12 25·3	12 25·23	N. 4 40—1 23·57			49·5	49·9
7057	20 23 4·8	12 10·9	10 28·5	12 10·8	12 10·85	N. 4 35+1 16·35				
Anon.	20 25 57·0		11 10·0	10 13·1		N. 4 25—0 30·9			49·4	49·9
Anon.	20 35 27·0	9 33·3	9 4·45	9 33·2	9 33·25	N. 4 15+0 23·8				
7207	20 41 53·0	9 25·7	14 0·85	9 25·6	9 25·65	S. 0 5+4 9·2				
Anon.	21 2	8 32·3	13 3·5	8 32·3		N. 3 55—4 5·2				
7386	21 10 9·0	11 27·8	12 23·25	11 27·9	11 27·85	N. 1 25—0 29·4				
Anon.	21 14 14·0		12 5·8	10 28·5		N. 4 25—1 11·3	28·134	48·2	49·4	49·5
Anon.	21 27 21·2	10 32·0	9 28·9	10 31·7	10 31·85	N. 3 50+1 2·95			49·3	49·3

Sept. 19.—Anon. 21ʰ 2ᵐ.—The seconds of transit doubtful.

♄ SEPTEMBER 21, 1844.—FACE OF SECTOR WEST—*(continued).*

Number of B.A.C.	Time by Chronometer	Micr. for Plumb-line on Dot.	Micr. for Observation of Star.	Micr. for Plumb-line on Dot.	Mean of Micr. for Plumb-line on Dot.	Star's Apparent Zenith Distance.	Barom.	Thermometers		
								Attd.	Upper	Lower
	h m s	rev. pts	rev. pts	rev. pts	rev. pts	° ' rev. pts	in.			
7557	21 37 18·5	9 31·5	10 12·7	9 31·4	9 31·45	N. 0 30—0 15·25				
7613	21 46 9·0	10 30·4	14 6·55	10 30·4	10 30·4	S. 3 50+3 10·15	28·134	47·7	49·0	49·2
7657	21 53 34·0	9 8·5	6 3·1	9 8·1	9 8·23	N. 5 0+3 5·13				
Anon.	21 57 25·5	9 8·3	4 32·4	9 8·0	9 8·23	N. 5 0+4 9·83				

FACE OF SECTOR EAST.

Number of B.A.C.	Time by Chronometer	Micr. for Plumb-line on Dot.	Micr. for Observation of Star.	Micr. for Plumb-line on Dot.	Mean of Micr. for Plumb-line on Dot.	Star's Apparent Zenith Distance.	Barom.	Attd.	Upper	Lower
7909	22 35 20·2	10 17·3	7 30·5	10 17·5	10 17·4	N. 4 5—2 20·9				
7966	22 45 31·4	10 30·5	14 15·9	10 30·5	10 30·5	N. 0 30+3 19·4				
7992	22 50 39·8	12 12·9	16 9·4	12 13·0	12 12·95	N. 3 45+3 30·45	28·142	46·8	47·5	47·7

☽ SEPTEMBER 23, 1844.—FACE OF SECTOR EAST.

Number of B.A.C.	Time by Chronometer	Micr. for Plumb-line on Dot.	Micr. for Observation of Star.	Micr. for Plumb-line on Dot.	Mean of Micr. for Plumb-line on Dot.	Star's Apparent Zenith Distance.	Barom.	Attd.	Upper	Lower
7011	20	12 28·4	11 23·45	12 28·6	12 28·5	N. 4 40—1 5·05	28·028			
7026	20		11 15·2	12 28·5	12 28·5	N. 4 40—1 13·3				
7057	20 23 12·0	10 26·6	12 18·8	10 26·8	10 26·7	N. 4 35+1 26·1				
Anon.	20	11 2·2	10 16·5	11 2·2	11 2·2	N. 4 25—0 19·7				
Anon.	20	11 6·9	12 13·4	11 7·0	11 6·95	N. 4 15+1 6·45				
7207	20 42 1·0	9 33·2	6 0·6	9 33·2	9 33·2	S. 0 5+3 32·6				
Anon.	20 55 19·0	10 28·5	11 33·8	10 28·5	10 28·5	N. 4 30+1 5·3				
Anon.	21 2 32·2	10 32·0	7 6·0	10 32·4	10 32·2	N. 3 55—3 26·2			63·2	62·0
7386	21 10 17·0	10 10·8	9 26·6	10 10·6	10 10·7	N. 1 25—0 18·1				
Anon.	21 14 20·8	11 30·3	10 31·5	11 30·5	11 30·4	N. 4 25—0 32·9				
Anon.	21 27 29·5	12 1·4	13 14·9	12 1·6	12 1·5	N. 3 50+1 13·4				
7557	21 37 29·0	12 0·0	11 28·75	12 0·0	12 0·0	N. 0 30—0 5·25				
7613	21 46 19·5	11 12·5	8 12·75	11 12·1	11 12·3	S. 3 50+2 33·55				
7657	21 53 40·2	11 16·2	14 33·1	11 16·1	11 16·15	N. 5 0+4 20·25	28·024	60·3	62·4	61·0
Anon.	21 57		11 16·1			N. 1 5+0 23·9				
7842	22 24 27·5	10 4·3	10 28·2	10 4·3	10 4·3	N. 4 5—2 21·15				
Anon.	22 35 29·2	9 24·7	7 3·55	9 24·7	9 24·7	N. 4 5—2 21·15				
7966	22 45 41·0	9 24·5	13 7·9	9 24·5	9 24·5	N. 0 30+3 17·4				
7992	22 50 50·0	11 16·1	15 11·1	11 16·1	11 16·1	N. 3 45+3 29·0	28·020	59·2	62·0	60·8
1802	5 35 49·5	12 6·1	10 31·6	12 6·1	12 6·1	N. 0 5—1 8·5	27·981	53·4	55·6	53·8
1878	5 47 18·5	10 30·5	9 12·2	10 30·5	10 30·5	S. 1 35+1 18·3	28·006	53·6	57·0	53·8
2293	6 54 17·3	11 16·0	7 22·9	11 16·0	11 16·0	N. 5 30—3 27·1				

♂ SEPTEMBER 24, 1844.—FACE OF SECTOR EAST.

Number of B.A.C.	Time by Chronometer	Micr. for Plumb-line on Dot.	Micr. for Observation of Star.	Micr. for Plumb-line on Dot.	Mean of Micr. for Plumb-line on Dot.	Star's Apparent Zenith Distance.	Barom.	Attd.	Upper	Lower
4686	13 59 23·0	11 25·7	7 8·6	11 25·7	11 25·7	S. 1 20+4 17·1	28·056	63·1	71·0	63·4

FACE OF SECTOR WEST.

| 5054 | 15 13 45·5 | 11 9·5 | 7 29·3 | 11 9·5 | 11 9·5 | S. 1 30—3 14·2 | | 67·8 | 62·5 | |

☿ SEPTEMBER 25, 1844.—FACE OF SECTOR EAST.

Number of B.A.C.	Time by Chronometer	Micr. for Plumb-line on Dot.	Micr. for Observation of Star.	Micr. for Plumb-line on Dot.	Mean of Micr. for Plumb-line on Dot.	Star's Apparent Zenith Distance.	Barom.	Attd.	Upper	Lower
6115	17 57 44·0	12 15·4	9 23·0	12 15·6	12 15·5	N. 3 50—2 26·5			49·0	50·2
6186	18 8 2·5	11 19·5	12 22·5	11 19·4	11 19·45	S. 2 35—1 3·05				
6233	18 15 47·3	11 10·4	14 4·45	11 10·3	11 10·35	S. 0 15—2 28·1				
6285	18 22 49·2	12 8·4	18 18·0	12 8·4	12 8·43	N. 1 5+6 9·57				
6305	18 25 42·0	12 8·4	14 10·4	12 8·5	12 8·43	N. 1 5+2 1·97	28·280	49·1	48·0	48·9
Anon.	18 44 37·8	13 1·8	11 3·2	13 2·0	13 1·9	N. 3 20—1 32·7				
6639	19 19 3·3	9 4·7	10 31·1	9 4·7	9 4·7	N. 4 10+1 26·4				
Anon.	19 23 15·5	10 8·2	10 8·0	10 8·2	10 8·2	N. 4 25—0 0·2				

Sept. 23.—No. 7011, 7026, and Anon. 21h 57m, faint images.
   Anon. 20h 55m.—The seconds of transit doubtful.
   Clouded until 20 hours per chronometer. Dense fog on the sea.
   Good definitions when the stars were visible.
Sept. 25.—No. 6115.—The seconds of transit doubtful.

♃ SEPTEMBER 25, 1844—(continued).—FACE OF SECTOR WEST.

Number of B.A.C.	Time by Chronometer.	Micr. for Plumb-line on Dot.	Micr. for Observation of Star.	Micr. for Plumb-line on Dot.	Mean of Micr. for Plumb-line on Dot.	Star's Apparent Zenith Distance.	Barom.	Thermometers. Attd.	Upper.	Lower.
	b m s	rev. pts.	rev. pts.	rev. pts.	rev. pts.	° ' rev. pts.	in.			
Anon.	20 55 36·0	10 24·2	9 31·6	10 24·3	10 24·25	N. 4 30+0 26·65	28·323	46·4	47·0	47·5
7386	21 10 24·0	10 5·0	11 1·2	10 5·0	10 5·0	N. 1 25—0 30·2				
Anon.	21 14		11 31·4	10 19·3		N. 4 25—1 12·1				
7657	21 53 54·0	10 16·9	7 12·6	10 16·9	10 16·85	N. 5 0+3 4·25				
Anon.	21 57 45·2	10 16·9	6 8·1	10 16·7	10 16·85	N. 5 0+4 8·75				
7909	22	10 20·4	13 20·85	10 20·5	10 20·45	N. 4 5—3 0·4				
7966	22 45 49·5	10 11·7	7 5·15	10 11·8	10 11·75	N. 0 30+3 6·6				
7992	22 51 2·5	10 31·6	7 15·75	10 31·6	10 31·6	N. 3 45+3 15·85	28·347	46·4	46·5	46·5

♃ SEPTEMBER 26, 1844.—FACE OF SECTOR EAST.

4458	13 13 51·0	10 7·0	10 21·05	10 7·0	10 7·0	S. 1 40—0 14·05			69·8	62·0

FACE OF SECTOR WEST.

4686	13 59 30·5	11 10·5	16 2·3	11 10·6	11 10·55	S. 1 20+4 25·75	28·316	61·7		
4852	14	11 22·6	14 16·95	11 22·6	11 22·6	S. 0 15+2 28·35	28·315	61·0	64·5	60·2

FACE OF SECTOR EAST.

5054	15 13 56·5	11 27·5	15 16·75	11 27·3	11 27·4	S. 1 30—3 23·35	28·298	60·7	63·2	59·4

FACE OF SECTOR WEST.

5227	15 43 4·2	12 27·5	13 22·0	12 27·6	12 27·55	N. 1 5—0 28·45			63·5	60·0
5292	15 51 47·6	13 8·5	10 8·4	13 8·5	13 8·5	S. 3 45—3 0·1				
5331	15 59	11 20·7	9 21·7	11 20·7	11 20·7	S. 2 10—1 33·0				

FACE OF SECTOR EAST.

5508	16 23 12·5	12 33·6	16 22·0	12 33·6	12 33·6	S. 0 10—3 22·4			60·0	58·4

FACE OF SECTOR WEST.

5632	16 42 5·4	11 28·2	15 4·9	11 28·2	11 28·2	N. 0 15—3 10·7				
5881	17 19 24·5	9 25·7	9 14·9	9 25·9	9 25·9	N. 4 30+0 10·9				
5915	17 25 2·5	10 16·8	11 15·0	10 17·0	10 16·9	S. 2 45+0 32·1			57·0	56·5
5970	17 33 43·2	11 12·8	7 28·8	11 12·4	11 12·6	S. 4 45—3 17·8				
6016	17 41 2·0	10 19·9	10 30·6	10 20·1	10 20·0	N. 2 35—0 10·6				
6074	17 51	13 6·4	13 32·0	13 6·0	13 6·2	N. 4 0—0 25·8				

FACE OF SECTOR EAST.

6186	18 9 9·0	14 10·0	15 13·1	14 9·8	14 9·9	S. 2 35—1 3·2				
6414	18 44 42·3	13 11·4	11 12·55	13 11·4	13 11·4	N. 3 20—1 32·85			53·2	53·4
6489	18 54 41·8	12 31·7	9 6·3	12 31·8	12 31·75	N. 4 10—3 25·45				
6525	18 59 41·5	12 20·1	15 2·1	12 20·1	12 20·1	N. 5 20+2 16·0				

FACE OF SECTOR WEST.

6639	19 19 7·0	12 12·3	10 33·3	12 12·3	12 12·3	N. 4 10+1 13·0				
Anon.	19 23 19·8	12 16·5	12 28·9	12 16·6	12 16·55	N. 4 25—0 12·35			51·5	52·0
6753	19 37 33·8	12 5·8	8 2·55	12 5·6	12 5·7	N. 2 55+4 3·15				
6877	19 56 29·0	11 7·9	12 16·4	11 7·9	11 7·9	N. 1 45—1 8·5				
7011	20 17 11·3	10 15·1	11 32·2	10 15·1	10 15·1	N. 4 40—1 17·1				
7026	20 19 2·2	10 15·1	12 5·2	10 15·1	10 15·1	N. 4 40—1 24·1				
7057	20 23 27·0	9 29·2	8 13·5	9 29·4	9 29·3	N. 4 35+1 15·8				
Anon.	20 26 19·5		10 8·4	9 10·5		N. 4 25—0 31·9				
Anon.	20 35 49·0	8 32·9	8 5·3	8 33·3	8 33·1	N. 4 15+0 27·8				
7207	20 42 16·0	11 25·4	16 3·9	11 26·2	11 25·8	S. 0 5+4 12·1				

Sept. 25.—The sky often clouded this night.
26.—Nos. 5331 and 6074.—Observed at 20 seconds from the meridian.
No. 5016.—The seconds of transit doubtful.
Excellent definition from 19h per chronometer.

♃ SEPTEMBER 26, 1844—(continued).—FACE OF SECTOR EAST.

Number of B.A.C.	Time by Chronometer.	Micr. for Plumb-line on Dot.	Micr. for Observation of Star.	Micr. for Plumb-line on Dot.	Mean of Micr. for Plumb-line on Dot.	Star's Apparent Zenith Distance.	Barom.	Attd.	Upper.	Lower.
	h m s	rev. pts.	rev. pts.	rev. pts.	rev. pts.	° ' rev. pts.	in.			
Anon.	20 55 34·5	12 15 2	13 21·0	12 15·4	12 15·3	N. 4 30+1 5·7	28·270	49·0	50·8	50·8
Anon.	21 2 45·0	12 18·6	8 27·9	12 18·7	12 18·65	N. 3 55—3 24·75				
7386	21 10 31·8	12 4·4	11 20·4	12 4·4	12 4·4	N. 1 25—0 18·0				
Anon.	21 14 34·2	12 32·9	11 33·6	12 32·9	12 32·9	N. 4 25—0 33·3				
Anon.	21 27 43·2	11 33·2	13 12·95	11 33·4	11 33·3	N. 3 50+1 13·65				
7557	21 37 43·0	11 23·1	11 17·8	11 23·2	11 23·15	N. 0 30—0 5·35				
7613	21 46 33·5	11 16·9	8 17·8	11 16·6	11 16·75	S. 3 50+2 32·95				
7657	21 53 53·0	11 30·7	15 13·6	11 30·8	11 30·8	N. 5 0+3 16·8				
Anon.	21 57 44·5	11 30·8	16 18·6	11 30·9	11 30·8	N. 5 0+4 21·8				
7842	22 24 41·5	11 18·9	12 9·15	11 18·9	11 18·9	N. 1 5+0 24·25	28·256	47·3	51·0	49·0
7909	22 35 43·2	11 33·8	9 13·1	11 33·8	11 33·8	N. 4 5—2 20·7				
7966	22 45 54·5	11 33·3	15 17·0	11 33·3	11 33·25	N. 0 30+3 17·75				
7992	22 51 3·5	12 20·4	16 14·6	12 20·4	12 20·4	N. 3 45+3 28·2				
1802	5 36 2·5	12 15·1	11 5·8	12 14·9	12 15·0	N. 0 5—1 9·2	28·193	45·3	51·5	45·0
1878	5 47 31·2	11 20·6	10 2·0	11 20·7	11 20·65	S. 1 35+1 18·65				
2293	6 54 31·5	11 33·3	8 6·3	11 33·2	11 33·25	N. 5 30—3 26·95	28·201	46·4	56·5	46·4

♀ SEPTEMBER 27, 1844.—FACE OF SECTOR WEST.

Number of B.A.C.	Time by Chronometer.	Micr. for Plumb-line on Dot.	Micr. for Observation of Star.	Micr. for Plumb-line on Dot.	Mean of Micr. for Plumb-line on Dot.	Star's Apparent Zenith Distance.	Barom.	Attd.	Upper.	Lower.
5054	15 14 2·0	10 21·2	7 7·6	10 21·0	10 21·1	S. 1 30—3 13·5	28·268	73·8	84·0	74·0

FACE OF SECTOR EAST.

Number of B.A.C.	Time by Chronometer.	Micr. for Plumb-line on Dot.	Micr. for Observation of Star.	Micr. for Plumb-line on Dot.	Mean of Micr. for Plumb-line on Dot.	Star's Apparent Zenith Distance.	Barom.	Attd.	Upper.	Lower.
5227	15 43 10·0	11 33·6	11 15·0	11 33·6	11 33·6	N. 1 5—0 18·6				
5292	15 51 55·0	12 0·5	15 13·5	12 0·5	12 0·5	S. 3 45—3 13·0				
5632	16 42 11·0	13 20·9	10 21·05	13 21·1	13 21·0	N. 0 15—2 33·95	28·256	68·5	75·0	69·6
5881	17 19 28·8	12 18·7	13 6·3	12 19·0	12 18·85	N. 4 30+0 21·45				
5915	17 25 8·5	11 17·0	10 29·05	11 16·7	11 16·85	S. 2 45+0 21·8			72·0	68·2
5970	17 33 50·3	11 19·6	15 13·25	11 19·8	11 19·7	N. 4 45—3 27·55				
6016	17 41 9·5	11 19·8	11 19·6	11 19·7	11 19·7	N. 2 35—0 0·1			68·8	66·4
6074	17 51 10·5	11 11·0	10 29·5	11 11·4	11 11·2	N. 4 0—0 15·7				

FACE OF SECTOR WEST.

Number of B.A.C.	Time by Chronometer.	Micr. for Plumb-line on Dot.	Micr. for Observation of Star.	Micr. for Plumb-line on Dot.	Mean of Micr. for Plumb-line on Dot.	Star's Apparent Zenith Distance.	Barom.	Attd.	Upper.	Lower.
6186	18 9 11·2	12 20·0	11 28·2	12 20·0	12 20·0	S. 2 35—0 25·8			66·8	65·3
6233	18 15 55·3	13 0·2	10 16·3	13 0·2	13 0·2	S. 0 15—2 17·9				
6489	18 54 48·0	12 19·6	16 24·65	12 19·7	12 19·75	N. 4 10—4 4·9				
6525	18 59 48·4	12 8·3	10 5·0	12 8·3	12 8·3	N. 5 20+2 3·3			60·0	61·0

FACE OF SECTOR EAST.

Number of B.A.C.	Time by Chronometer.	Micr. for Plumb-line on Dot.	Micr. for Observation of Star.	Micr. for Plumb-line on Dot.	Mean of Micr. for Plumb-line on Dot.	Star's Apparent Zenith Distance.	Barom.	Attd.	Upper.	Lower.
6639	19 19 9·5	13 18·5	15 10·3	13 18·7	13 18·6	N. 4 10+1 25·7				
Anon.	19 23 22·5	13 22·5	13 22·5	13 22·6	13 22·6	N. 4 25—0 0·1				
6753	19 37 37·5	13 2·5	17 19·2	13 2·6	13 2·55	N. 2 55+4 16·65			59·6	60·2
6877	19 56 33·0	11 18·5	10 22·3	11 18·5	11 18·5	N. 1 45—0 30·2			59·5	59·2
6948	20	11 31·1	12 13·3	11 31·1	11 31·1	N. 3 45+0 16·2				
7011	20 17 14·0	10 31·6	9 26·85	10 31·78	10 31·78	N. 4 40—1 4·93				
7026	20 19 4·5	10 31·8	9 19·45	10 31·9	10 31·78	N. 4 40—1 12·33				
7057	20 23 29·5	11 2·5	12 30·5	11 2·3	11 2·4	N. 4 35+1 2·1				
Anon.	20 26 22·5		8 31·7	9 16·5		N. 4 25—0 18·8				
Anon.	20 35 52·5	8 33·1	10 6·0	8 33·4	8 33·25	N. 4 15+1 6·75				
7207	20 42 21·5	10 18·4	6 18·2	10 18·3	10 18·35	S. 0 5+4 0·15				

FACE OF SECTOR WEST.

Number of B.A.C.	Time by Chronometer.	Micr. for Plumb-line on Dot.	Micr. for Observation of Star.	Micr. for Plumb-line on Dot.	Mean of Micr. for Plumb-line on Dot.	Star's Apparent Zenith Distance.	Barom.	Attd.	Upper.	Lower.
Anon.	20 55 42·2	11 7·5	10 14·9	11 7·5	11 7·5	N. 4 30+0 26·6				
Anon.	21 2 51·5	10 4·3	14 10·25	10 4·4	10 4·35	N. 3 55—4 5·9				
7386	21 10 36·5	10 4·4	11 0·4	10 4·2	10 4·3	N. 1 25—0 30·1				

Sept. 27.—No 5054.—The seconds of transit doubtful.
No. 6016.—Faint.
Calm throughout the night. Excellent definition.

♀ SEPTEMBER 27, 1844.—FACE OF SECTOR WEST—*(continued).*

Number of B.A.C.	Time by Chronometer.	Micr. for Plumb-line on Dot.	Micr. for Observation of Star.	Micr. for Plumb-line on Dot.	Mean of Micr. for Plumb-line on Dot.	Star's Apparent Zenith Distance.	Barom.	Thermometers.		
								Attd.	Upper.	Lower.
	h m s	rev. pts.	rev. pts.	rev. pts.	rev. pts.	° ′ rev. pts.	in.			
Anon.	21 14 41·2		11 17·3	10 4·5		N. 4 25—1 12·8				
Anon.	21 27 48·8	10 7·7	9 7·7	10 7·7	10 7·7	N. 3 50+1 0·0	28·215	57·4	59·5	58·2
7557	21 37 46·5	10 19·5	11 1·4	10 19·4	10 19·45	N. 0 30—0 15·95				
7613	21 46 36·5	11 9·8	14 21·5	11 10·0	11 9·9	S. 3 50+3 11·6				
7657	21 54 0·5	10 32·4	7 27·5	10 32·3	10 32·4	N. 5 0+3 4·9				
Anon.	21 57 51·5	10 32·5	6 22·8	10 32·4	10 32·4	N. 5 0+4 9·6				
7842	22 24 45·5	10 23·3	10 10·5	10 23·4	10 23·35	N. 1 5+0 12·85				
7909	22 35 49·8	10 13·8	13 13·5	10 13·7	10 13·75	N. 4 5—2 33·75				
7966	22 45 59·0	10 16·9	7 10·2	10 17·1	10 17·0	N. 0 30+3 6·8				
7992	22 51 10·3	10 10·0	6 27·5	10 10·0	10 10·0	N. 3 45+3 16·5	28·213	55·4	60·0	58·0
2293	6 54 38·5	9 23·4	13 28·0	9 23·2	9 23·3	N. 5 30—4 4·7	28·121	52·5	59·5	51·2

♄ SEPTEMBER 28, 1844.—FACE OF SECTOR WEST.

4458	13 13 58·5	11 7·2	11 5·2	11 7·3	11 7·25	S. 1 40—0 2·05	28·182	84·9	93·5	82·6

FACE OF SECTOR EAST.

4686	13 59 42·0	11 2·6	6 20·1	11 2·4	11 2·5	S. 1 20+4 16·4	28·160	84·9	94·5	82·2
6233	18 16 1·2	10 22·7	13 16·25	10 22·7	10 22·7	S. 0 15—2 27·55	28·103	70·2	73·1	75·0
6489	18 54 50·0	11 9·5	7 16·5	11 9·8	11 9·65	N. 4 10—3 27·15				
6525	18 59 49·5	11 4 7	13 21·4	11 4·9	11 4·8	N. 5 20+2 16·6			71·2	69·6

FACE OF SECTOR WEST.

6630	19 19 16·3	9 17·9	8 3·4	9 17·8	9 17·85	N. 4 10+1 14·45				
Anon.	19 23 28·0	9 12·8	9 22·9	9 12·7	9 12·75	N. 4 25—0 10·15				
6753	19 37 43·0	10 24·5	6 21·5	10 24·5	10 24·5	N. 2 55+4 3·0				
6877	19 56 37·5	9 30·4	11 3·5	9 30·2	9 30·3	N. 1 45—1 7·2				
7057	20 23 35·0	9 12·0	7 30·0	9 12·0	9 12·0	N. 4 35+1 16·0				
Anon.	20 26 27·5	9 4·3	10 0·95	9 4·2	9 4·25	N. 5 20—0 30·7	28·075	64·0	68·0	66·4
Anon.	20 35 57·5	9 3·4	8 9·0	9 3·5	9 3·45	N. 4 15+0 28·45				
7207	20 42 25·2	10 14·5	14 24·8	10 14·7	10 14·6	S. 0 5+4 10·2				

FACE OF SECTOR EAST.

Anon.	20 55 42·3	10 27·2	11 32·8	10 27·4	10 27·3	N. 4 30+1 5·5				
Anon.	21 2 53·2	11 7·0	7 15·15	11 7·2	11 7·1	N. 3 55—3 25·95				
7386	21 10 40·0	11 26·5	11 7·9	11 26·6	11 26·55	N. 1 25—0 18·65				
Anon.	21 14 42·4	12 0·3	10 33·8	12 0·5	12 0·4	N. 4 25—1 0·6				
Anon.	21 27 50·5	11 33·3	13 12·9	11 33·3	11 33·3	N. 3 50+1 13·6		68·4	65·4	
7557	21 37 51·5	12 18·6	12 13·2	12 18·6	12 18·6	N. 0 30—0 5·4				
7613	21 46 43·0	11 20·6	8 20·85	11 20·6	11 20·55	N. 5 0+3 16·95				
7657	21 54 1·5	11 22·6	15 5·5	11 22·6	11 22·55	N. 5 0+3 16·95				
Anon.	21 57 52·3	11 22·5	16 10·0	11 22·5	11 22·55	N. 5 0+4 21·45				
7842	22 24 50·0	11 19·0	12 9·4	11 19·2	11 19·1	N. 1 5+0 24·3	28·058	65·8	68·4	65·6
7909	22 35 51·2	11 22·5	9 16·55	12 3·9	12 3·75	N. 4 5—2 21·2				
7966	22 46 3·8	11 14·5	14 31·75	11 14·3	11 14·4	N. 0 30+3 17·35				
7992	22 51 12·0	11 13·2	15 7·9	11 13·2	11 13·2	N. 3 45+3 28·7				

FACE OF SECTOR WEST.

1802	5 36 11·8	9 22·6	11 8·0	9 22·5	9 22·55	N. 5 30—1 19·45	27·955	65·1	67·2	64·6
1878	5 47 30·0	9 18·7	11 14·8	9 18·7	9 18·7	S. 1 35+1 30·1				

FACE OF SECTOR EAST.

2293	6 54 39·2	7 30·2	4 3·3	7 30·1	7 30·15	N. 5 30—3 26·85	27·903	67·8	70·0	67·6

Sept. 28.—Nos. 6233 and 1878.—The seconds of transit doubtful.

☿ OCTOBER 1, 1844.—FACE OF SECTOR EAST.

Number of B.A.C.	Time by Chronometer.	Micr. for Plumb-line on Dot.	Micr. for Observation of Star.	Micr. for Plumb-line on Dot.	Mean of Micr. for Plumb-line on Dot.	Star's Apparent Zenith Distance.	Barom.	Thermometers.		
								Attd.	Upper.	Lower.
	h m s	rev. pts.	rev. pts.	rev. pts.	rev. pts.	° ′ rev. pts.	in.			
5227	15 43 27·5	12 26·0	12 10·6	12 26·0	12 26·0	N. 1 5—0 15·4				
				FACE OF SECTOR WEST.						
5915	17	10 23·6	11 21·6	10 23·7	10 23·65	S. 2 45+0 31·95	28·146	55·8	59·6	57·8
5070	17 34 4·0	9 15·3	5 31·4	9 14·9	9 15·1	S. 4 45—3 17·7				
6525	18	12 20·3	10 15·9	12 20·5	12 20·4	N. 5 20+2 4·5				
				FACE OF SECTOR EAST.						
6639	19 19 28·5	13 3·3	14 30·0	13 3·5	13 3·4	N. 4 10+1 26·6				
Anon.	19 23	9 25·7	9 25·7	9 25·8	9 25·75	N. 4 25—0 0·05			53·0	53·2
6753	19	11 4·0	15 22·6	11 4·0	11 4·0	N. 2 55+4 18·6				
6877	19 56 51·2	9 24·0	8 28·0	9 24·0	9 24·0	N. 1 45—0 30·0	28·142	51·8	53·0	53·2
7057	20 23 47·0	11 31·0	13 25·5	11 31·1	11 31·05	N. 4 35+1 28·45				
Anon.	20 26 39·2		11 20·7	12 5·4		N. 4 25—0 18·7				
Anon.	20 36 10·0	12 23·8	13 31·0	12 23·8	12 23·8	N. 4 15+1 7·2				
7207	20 42 39·4	11 32·0	7 33·4	11 32·0	11 32·0	S. 0 5+3 32·6				
				FACE OF SECTOR WEST.						
Anon.	20 56 0·0	11 11·9	10 18·4	11 11·9	11 11·9	N. 4 30+0 27·5			51·5	52·0
Anon.	21 3 10·5	12 16·2	16 21·5	12 16·4	12 16·3	N. 3 55—4 5·2				
Anon.	21 14	12 3·8	13 15·2	12 3·7	12 3·75	N. 4 25—1 11·45				
Anon.	21 28 7·0	12 12·2	11 11·35	12 12·2	12 12·2	N. 3 50+1 0·85				
				FACE OF SECTOR EAST.						
7657	21 54 16·0	11 26·9	15 9·6	11 27·3	11 27·1	N. 5 0+3 16·5				
				FACE OF SECTOR WEST.						
7842	22 25 4·0	10 25·7	10 13·0	10 25·8	10 25·75	N. 1 5+0 12·75				
7909	22 36 7·7	11 4·1	14 4·4	11 4·2	11 4·15	N. 4 5—3 0·25				
7966	22 46 16·5	13 3·3	9 30·25	13 3·1	13 3·2	N. 0 30+3 6·95				
7992	22 51 28·5	11 9·9	7 28·15	11 9·6	11 9·75	N. 3 45+3 15·6	28·184	48·2	49·0	50·0
				FACE OF SECTOR EAST.						
1802	5 36 25·5	12 6·4	10 30·5	12 6·4	12 6·4	N. 0 5—1 9·9	28·150	45·9	46·0	45·4
1878	5 47 54·5	12 2·6	10 16·95	12 2·4	12 2·5	S. 1 35+1 19·55				
				FACE OF SECTOR WEST.						
2293	6 54 56·5	11 31·3	16 3·45	11 31·2	11 31·25	N. 5 30—4 6·2	28·162	46·4	46·8	46·2

♀ OCTOBER 2, 1844.—FACE OF SECTOR WEST.

4686	13 59 56·5	12 4·0	16 27·9	12 4·0	12 4·0	S. 1 20+4 23·9	28·184	64·0	68·5	64·4
				FACE OF SECTOR EAST.						
5054	15 14 23·5	11 34·0	15 24·25	11 33·8	11 33·9	S. 1 30—3 24·35	28·160	63·3	65·6	62·0
5292	15 52 18·0	11 7·4	14 19·3	11 7·4	11 7·4	S. 3 45—3 11·9				
5536	16 28 37·5	12 17·6	17 23·0	12 17·6	12 17·6	S. 0 45—5 5·4	28·111	63·0	65·6	61·7
5915	17 25 32·0	10 29·3	10 8·85	10 29·3	10 29·3	S. 2 45—0 20·45				
5970	17 34 13·0	10 6·8	14 2·1	10 6·4	10 6·6	S. 3 45—3 29·5				
				FACE OF SECTOR WEST.						
6233	18 16 18·0	10 8·8	7 23·5	10 8·8	10 8·8	S. 0 15—2 10·3	28·078	55·9	59·0	58·6
Anon.	19 23	12 18·1	12 29·7	12 18·1	12 18·1	N. 4 25—0 11·6			55·4	56·2
6753	19 38 2·8	11 11·5	7 8·1	11 11·5	11 11·5	N. 2 55+4 3·4			55·4	55·9

Oct. 1.—No. 5227.— Very faint.   An uncertain observation.
Some of the early stars could not be seen owing to clouds.
Good definition.

☿ OCTOBER 2, 1844.—FACE OF SECTOR WEST—(continued).

Number of B.A.C.	Time by Chronometer.	Micr. for Plumb-line on Dot.	Micr. for Observation of Star.	Micr. for Plumb-line on Dot.	Mean of Micr. for Plumb-line on Dot.	Star's Apparent Zenith Distance.	Barom.	Thermometer.		
								Attd.	Upper.	Lower.
	h m s	rev. pts.	rev. pts.	rev. pts.	rev. pts.	° ' rev. pts.	in.			
6877	19 56 56·5	10 28·9	12 2·7	10 29·1	10 29·0	N. 1 45—1 7·7			55·0	55·4
7057	20 23 55·5	10 31·4	9 16·1	10 31·3	10 31·35	N. 4 35+1 15·25				
Anon.	20 26 47·5		11 16·95	10 19·5		N. 4 25—0 31·45			54·4	54·6
Anon.	20 36 17·6	10 14·6	9 20·1	10 14·6	10 14·6	N. 4 15+0 28·5				
FACE OF SECTOR EAST.										
Anon.	20 56 3·2	10 33·7	12 4·6	10 33·7	10 33·7	N. 4 30+1 4·9				
Anon.	21 15 2·5	11 4·6	10 4·2	11 4·7	11 4·65	N. 4 25—1 0·45	28·046	52·7	54·0	53·9
Anon.	21 28 10·5	10 19·8	11 32·75	10 19·7	10 19·75	N. 3 50+1 13·0				
Anon.	21 58 13·0	10 18·9	15 5·65	10 18·8	10 18·85	N. 5 0+4 20·8	28·046	51·7	54·0	53·2
FACE OF SECTOR WEST.										
1802	5 36 31·3	10 16·2	12 2·1	10 16·3	10 16·25	N. 0 5—1 19·85				
1878	5 47 57·0	9 31·6	11 27·45	9 31·7	9 31·65	S. 1 35+1 29.8	27·943	53·6	54·5	52·0
FACE OF SECTOR EAST.										
2293	6	9 19·7	5 25·8	9 19·8	9 19·75	N. 5 30—3 27.95	27·955	55·2	55·8	53·0

Oct.—Bad definition in the day-time; better at night.

UNREDUCED OBSERVATIONS

MADE WITH

BRADLEY'S ZENITH SECTOR

ON

CAPE POINT,

FROM

NOVEMBER 1844, TO JANUARY 1845.

♄ NOVEMBER 16; 1844.—FACE OF SECTOR WEST.

Number of B.A.C.	Time by Chronometer.	Micr. for Plumb-line on Dot.	Micr. for Observation of Star.	Micr. for Plumb-line on Dot.	Mean of Micr. for Plumb-line on Dot.	Star's Apparent Zenith Distance.	Barom.	Thermometers.		
								Attd.	Upper.	Lower.
	h m s	rev. pts.	rev. pts.	rev. pts.	rev. pts.	° ′ rev. pts.	in.			
1802	5 33 41·0	12 12·4	18 17·2	12 12·4	12 12·4	N. 0 15—6 4·8	29·457	57·2	57·8	57·5
1878	5 45 8·5	11 12·5	17 27·4	11 12·5	11 12·5	S. 1 25+6 14·9				
2293	6 52 10·0	15 24·4	15 14·5	15 24·3	15 24·35	N. 5 35+0 9·85	29·457	57·0	58·0	57·8
4686	13 57 12·2	12 0·6	12 0·4	12 0·6	12 0·6	S. 1 15—0 0·2	29·473	65·8	69·1	64·5

☉ NOVEMBER 17, 1844.—FACE OF SECTOR EAST.

6233	18 13 37·2	10 4·5	8 19·3	10 4·5	10 4·5	S. 0 5+1 19·2	29·323	69·8	73·8	68·5

♂ NOVEMBER 19, 1844.—FACE OF SECTOR EAST.

7966	22 43 43·2	10 29·6	9 28·0	10 30·0	10 29·8	N. 0 40—1 6·8		60·8	61·0	61·5
7992	22 48 49·3	11 18·0	10 22·8	11 17·8	11 17·9	N. 3 55—0 29·1	29·331			

☿ NOVEMBER 20, 1844.—FACE OF SECTOR EAST.

4686	13 57 34·2	10 9·4	10 12·9	10 9·4	10 9·4	S. 1 15—0 3·5	29·473	60·6	61·6	60·0

♃ NOVEMBER 21, 1844.—FACE OF SECTOR WEST.

7842	22 22 37.5	10 8·0	14 10·6	10 8·0	10 8·0	N. 1 15—4 2·6	29·549	60·8	62·0	61·2
7966	22 43 51·8	10 21·4	11 31·3	10 21·7	10 21·55	N. 0 40—1 9·75				
7992	22 49 3·4	10 24·2	11 26·5	10 24·2	10 24·2	N. 3 55—1 2·3	29·568	58·6	61·0	60·6

FACE OF SECTOR EAST.

1802	5 33	11 11·5	14 7·45	11 11·5	11 11·5	N. 0 10+2 29·95	29·512	56·3	56·9	56·2
1878	5 45 34·0	10 29·6	13 16·0	10 29·8	10 29·7	S. 1 30—2 20·3				
2051	6 14 18·8	11 0·4	13 7·5	11 0·5	11 0·45	N. 4 20+2 7·05	29·407	56·1	56·9	56·0
2246	6 44 3·0	11 6·1	13 12·3	11 6·2	11 6·15	N. 2 0+2 6·15			56·3	56·3
2293	6 52 28·2	11 0·4	11 15·5	11 0·5	11 0·45	N. 1 0+5 15·05			56·3	56·5
2414	7 11 46·2	10 11·0	4 31·3	10 11·2	10 11·1	S. 2 25+5 13·8				
2575	7 30 8·0	10 16·2	14 11·9		10 16·15	S. 3 15—3 29·75	29·470	55·9	56·0	56·3
2580	7 39 51·0		11 19·9	10 16·1	10 16·15	S. 1 15—1 3·75				
2795	8 12 50·7	.9 32·5	10 24·5	9 32·5	9 32·5	S. 1 50—0 20·0		55·6	56·0	
2935	8 34 5·5	10 4·5	11 8·7	10 4·5	10 4·5	S. 0 25—1 4·2				
2964	8 37 22·6		7 7·5	10 2·3		N. 1 45—2 28·8	29·447	55·4	55·6	55·9
4458	13 11	10 10·6	6 11·5	10 11·0	10 10·8	S. 1 30+3 33·3	29·416	62·6	67·0	62·0
4686	13 57 37·8	11 4·0	11 7·5	11 3·9	11 3·95	S. 1 15—0 3·55	29·416	64·4	69·2	64·0

♀ NOVEMBER 22, 1844.—FACE OF SECTOR WEST.

6233	18 13 53·3	12 1·5	13 24·55	12 1·5	12 1·5	S. 0 5+1 23·05	29·386	68·3	72·5	68·4
7842	22 22 44·0	12 27·9	16 30·7	12 27·9	12 27·9	N. 1 15—4 2·8	29·306	64·2	65·6	65·0
7966	22 43 56·5	12 0·5	13 9·9	11 33·8	12 0·15	N. 0 40—1 9·75	29·306	64·2	65·6	65·0
7992	22 49 8·0	12 4·9	13 7·4	12 4·9	12 4·9	N. 3 55—1 2·5	29·304	63·9	65·5	64·7

♄ NOVEMBER 23, 1844.—FACE OF SECTOR EAST.

7842	22 22 48·5	10 17·0	6 16·6	10 17·2	10 17·1	N. 1 15—4 0·5	29·373	64·9	66·9	65·8

The sector is protected at this very exposed Station by a coniform wooden structure, keyed to the rock it stands upon. The weather boarding is covered with canvas.
Nov. 21.—No. 1802.—Bisected when at 20 seconds from the meridian.
No. 4458.—Bisected when at 25 seconds from the meridian.
Clouded sky on the 23rd.

⊙ NOVEMBER 24, 1844.—FACE OF SECTOR EAST.

Number of B.A.C.	Time by Chronometer.	Micr. for Plumb-line on Dot.	Micr. for Observation of Star.	Micr. for Plumb-line on Dot.	Mean of Micr. for Plumb-line on Dot.	Star's Apparent Zenith Distance.	Barom.	Attd.	Upper.	Lower.
	h m s	rev. pts.	rev. pts.	rev. pts.	rev. pts.	° ′ rev. pts.	in.			
7842	22 22 53·2	10 32·4	6 31·7	10 32·4	10 32·4	N. 1 15—4 0·7	29·322	59·5	60·0	60·9
7966	22	11 31·3	10 24·2	11 31·5	11 31·4	N. 0 40—1 7·2	29·321	59·5	60·0	60·9

FACE OF SECTOR WEST.

Number of B.A.C.	Time by Chronometer.	Micr. for Plumb-line on Dot.	Micr. for Observation of Star.	Micr. for Plumb-line on Dot.	Mean of Micr. for Plumb-line on Dot.	Star's Apparent Zenith Distance.	Barom.	Attd.	Upper.	Lower.
1802	5 34 17·5	8 28·5	6 4·9	8 28·5	8 28·5	N. 0 10+2 23·6	29·280	59·1	59·5	59·4
1878	5 45 44·5	11 2·3	8 22·0	11 2·1	11 2·2	S. 1 30—2 14·2				
1922	5 52 16·5	11 14·2	15 1·5	11 13·5	11 13·85	S. 0 55+3 21·65				
1982	6 2 27·2	12 21·4	8 29·95	12 21·1	12 21·25	S. 2 55—3 25·3				
2051	6 14 37·5	11˙10·6	9 10·1	11 10·4	11 10·5	N. 4 20+2 0·4			59·6	59·5
2109	6 22 40·5	11 5·9	7 26·1	11 5·7	11 5·8	N. 1 50+3 13·7				
Com.	6 43	10 33·6	12 24·0		10 33·6	N. 2 0—1 24·4				
2246	6 44 19·5		8 33·5	10 33·6	10 33·6	N.2 0+2 0·1			59·6	59·6
2293	6 52 47·5	10 31·6	10 24·8	10 31·5	10 31·55	N. 5 35+0 6·75	29·260	59·0	59·5	59·6
2458	7 18 14·2	12 15·2	11 4·75	12 15·3	12 15·25	N. 6 20+1 10·5				
2528	7 32 30·5	12 24·1	19 10·2	12 24·1	12 24·08	S. 3 15+6 20·12				
2575	7 39 17·5	12 24·1	9 11·6		12 24·08	S. 3 15—3 12·48				
2580	7 39 58·5		11 26·5	12 24·0	12 24·08	S. 3 15—0 31·58				
2635	7 47 23·5	13 2·1	15 31·7	13 2·2	13 2·15	S. 4 5+2 29·55				
2655	7 51 45·5		10 2·9	11 16·9		N. 4 25+1 14·0				
2710	7 58 21·3	12 17·1	17 22·1	12 17·1	12 17·1	S. 5 10+5 5·0	29·264	59·0	59·6	59·6
2795	8 12 59·3	10 27·9	10 9·4	10 27·9	10 27·9	S. 1 50—0 18·5				
2935	8 34 16·3	11 15·3	10 15·9	11 15·2	11 15·25	S. 0 25—0 33·35	29·264	59·0	59·6	59·8
2964	8 37 37·2		14 8·3	11 7·8		N. 1 45—3 0·5				
3130	9 3 38·0	10 18·7	15 32·75	10 18·6	10 18·65	N. 4 40—5 14·1				
3163	9 9 45·0	10 15·2	9 7·6	10 15·2	10 15·2	S. 3 35—1 7·6				
3257	9 24 49·4	9 32·4	11 30·5	9 32·6	9 32·5	S. 5 25+1 32·0	29·264	59·0	59·8	59·8
3578	10 20	8 21·0	9 29·6	8 20·8	8 20·9	N. 4 5—1 8·7	29·277	60·8	60·6	60·0
4686	13 57	9 28·2	9 27·7	9 28·1	9 28·15	S. 1 15—0 0·45	29·318	64·8	67·8	63·6

❨ NOVEMBER 25, 1844.—FACE OF SECTOR EAST.

Number of B.A.C.	Time by Chronometer.	Micr. for Plumb-line on Dot.	Micr. for Observation of Star.	Micr. for Plumb-line on Dot.	Mean of Micr. for Plumb-line on Dot.	Star's Apparent Zenith Distance.	Barom.	Attd.	Upper.	Lower.
6233	18 14 0·2	11 16·6	9 31·6	11 16·6	11 16·6	S. 0 5+1 19·0			66·6	65·4
1802	5 34 22·0	12 18·1	15 12·5	12 18·1	12 18·1	N. 0 10+2 48·0	29·282	58·5	59·0	58·8
1878	5 45 52·0	12 30·2	15 15·35	12 30·2	12 30·2	S. 1 30—2 19·15				
1922	5 52 24·5	11 20·8	8 2·45	11 20·7	11 20·75	S. 0 55+3 18·3				
1982	6 2 37·0	10 8·8	14 5·8	10 9·2	10 9·0	S. 2 55—3 30·8				
2051	6 14 43·0	10 26·4	12 33·0	10 26·2	10 26·3	N. 4 20+2 6·7			59·5	59·2
2109	6 22 44·0	10 19·0	14 4·5	10 19·1	10 19·05	N. 1 50+3 19·45				
Comp.		11 5·4	9 21·7		11 5·5	N. 2 0—1 17·8				
2246	6		13 11·5	11 5·6	11 5·5	N. 2 0+2 6·0	29·260	58·1	59·6	59·2
2293	6 52 46·8	12 12·0	12 26·1	12 12·0	12 12·0	N. 5 35+0 14·1				
2414	7 12 4·2	10 18·0	14 1·65	10 18·2	10 18·1	S. 2 30—3 17·55				
2458	7 18 13·0	11 9·9	12 28·1	11 10·0	11 9·95	N. 5 20+1 18·15				
2528	7 32 40·2	10 1·7	3 21·25	10 1·6	10 1·65	S. 3 15+6 14·4				
2575	7 39 27·5	10 1·6	13 20·0		10 1·65	S. 3 15—3 18·35				
2580	7 40 8·2		11 4·25	10 1·7	10 1·65	S. 3 15—1 2·6				
2635	7 47 35·5	10 8·1	7 18·7	10 8·3	10 8·2	S. 4 5+2 23·5				
2655	7 51 45·5	10 24·7	12 10·7	10 24·6	10 24·65	N. 4 25+1 20·05				
2710	7 58 35·5	9 18·6	4 21·3	9 18·8	9 18·7	S. 5 10+4 31·4				
2795	8 13 8·0	11 10·7	12 1·1	11 10·6	11 10·65	S. 1 50—0 24·45	29·250	58·3	59·4	59·2
2935	8 34 23·5	10 18·8	11 22·7	10 18·7	10 18·75	S. 0 25—1 3·95				
2964	8 37 40·8		8 25·5	11 21·4		N. 1 45—2 29·9				
3130	9 3 38·5	12 1·4	15 24·7	12 1·5	12 1·45	N. 4 40+3 23·25				
3163	9 9 55·7	11 14·0	12 27·6	11 13·9	11 13·95	S. 3 35—1 13·65				

Nov. 24.—No. 1022.—The arch graduation point 0° 55′ is not well formed.
No. 2935.—Double. The larger observed.
No. 3578.—Observed at 20 seconds past the meridian.
No. 4686.—Observed at 10 seconds past the meridian.
Strong S. E. gale. Pressure 12 pounds on the square foot.

ARC OF THE MERIDIAN.—CAPE OF GOOD HOPE.

☾ NOVEMBER 25, 1844.—FACE OF SECTOR EAST—(continued.)

Number of B.A.C.	Time by Chronometer.	Micr. for Plumb-line on Dot.	Micr. for Observation of Star.	Micr. for Plumb-line on Dot.	Mean of Micr. for Plumb-line on Dot.	Star's Apparent Zenith Distance.	Barom.	Thermometers.		
								Attd.	Upper.	Lower.
	h m s	rev. pts.	rev. pts.	rev. pts.	rev. pts.	° ′ rev. pts.	in.			
3257	9 25 4·2	10 33·4	9 7·75	10 33·7	10 33·55	S. 5 25+1 25·8	29·260	58·6	59·4	59·2
3578	10 20 20·4	11 0·0	9 30·3	11 0·0	11 0·0	N. 4 5—1 3·7	29·270	50·7	60·6	59·6

FACE OF SECTOR WEST.

4458	13 12 11·5	10 1·7	14 5·05	10 1·7	10 1·7	S. 1 30+4 3·35	29·302	64·2	67·5	63·0

♂ NOVEMBER 26, 1844.—FACE OF SECTOR WEST.

5915	17 23 22·5	11 22·3	7 27·05	11 22·0	11 22·15	S. 2 40—3 29·1	29·323	71·1	73·5	70·2
6233	18 14 11·3	11 27·0	13 16·3	11 27·0	11 27·0	S. 0 5+1 23·3	29·312	70·7	73·0	70·5
7842	22 23 1·4	12 3·2	16 7·85	12 3·2	12 3·2	N. 1 15—4 4·05	29·288	68·7	71·0	09·5
7966	22 44 14·7	11 14·0	12 25·65	11 14·0	11 14·0	N. 0 40—1 11·65				
7992	22 49 26·4	11 1·2	12 4·55	11 1·1	11 1·15	N. 3 55—1 3·4	29·288	68·0	70·6	09·0
1802	5 34 26·0	11 16·9	8 27·7	11 16·7	11 16·8	N. 0 10+2 23·1	29·233	61·5	62·5	62·3
1878	5 45 52·0	12 14·7	10 2·0	12 14·8	12 14·75	S. 1 30—2 12·75				
1922	5 52 25·5	12 29·5	16 18·7	12 29·9	12 29·7	S. 0 55+3 23·0			62·2	62·2
1982	6 2 35·2	13 1·4	9 11·35	13 1·4	13 1·4	S. 2 55—3 24·05				
2051	6 14 46·2	12 10·4	10 10·8	12 10·0	12 10·2	N. 4 20+1 38·4				
2109	6 22 50·0	12 21·3	9 8·25	12 21·1	12 21·2	N. 1 50+3 12·95	29·213	61·2	62·0	62·0
2246	6 44 27·5	12 1·5	10 3·3	12 1·5	12 1·5	N. 2 0+1 32·2				
2293	6 52 57·0	11 14·2	11 7·4	11 14·0	11 14·1	N. 5 35+0 6·7				
2414	7 12 2·2	12 13·0	9 2·7	12 13·0	12 13·0	S. 2 30—3 10·3				
2458	7 18 22·8	11 25·1	10 15·4	11 25·0	11 25·3	N. 5 20+1 0·9	29·213	60·8	61·6	61·8
2528	7 32 38·6	11 1·8	17 22·0	11 1·6	11 1·05	S. 3 15+6 20·35				
2575	7 39 25·5	11 1·6	7 23·5		11 1·65	S. 3 15—3 12·15				
2580	7 40 6·5		10 6·0	11 1·6	11 1·65	S. 3 15—0 29·65				
2635	7 47 31·5	11 4·2	14 1·05	11 4·5	11 4·35	S. 4 5+2 30·7				
2655	7 51 54·0		9 27·0	11 6·4		N. 4 25+1 13·4				
2710	7 58 28·5	11 27·4	16 32·75	11 27·5	11 27·45	S. 5 10+5 5·3				
2935	8 34 25·4	9 18·2	9 18·1	9 18·1	9 18·15	S. 0 25—0 32·85	29·213	60·6	61·5	61·4
2964	8 37 46·0		12 16·3	9 15·0		N. 1 45—3 1·3	29·213	60·6	61·4	61·4
3163	9 9 52·5	11 4·3	9 31·25	11 4·3	11 4·3	S. 3 35—1 7·05	29·213	60·6	61·2	61·2
3257	9 24 57·2	10 32·8	12 31·5	10 32·8	10 32·8	S. 5 25+1 32·7	29·213	60·8	61·3	61·2
3926	10 25	10 22·9	8 23·5	10 22·7	10 22·8	N. 3 20+1 33·3	29·229	63·0	66·5	62·5
4458	13 12 15·5	10 19·0	14 22·7	10 19·2	10 19·1	S. 1 30+4 3·6	29·244	65·8	69·6	65·0
4686	13 57 56·2	10 24·0	10 24·95	10 24·0	10 24·0	S. 1 15+0 0·95	29·233	68·0	73·5	66·6

☿ NOVEMBER 27, 1844.—FACE OF SECTOR EAST.

5915	17 23 33·0	14 13·3	18 13·9	14 13·5	14 13·4	S. 2 40—4 0·5	29·256	77·4	81·0	75·5
6233	18 14 17·5	11 8·3	9 22·9	11 8·3	11 8·3	S. 0 5+1 19·4	29·252	78·1	82·0	76·0
7842	22 23 6·0	11 9·9	7 9·45	11 9·8	11 9·85	N. 1 15—4 0·4	29·184	73·4	76·0	73·7
7966	22 44 20·2	11 25·0	10 18·3	11 25·0	11 25·0	N. 0 40—1 6·7				
7992	22 49 26·5	12 22·1	11 25·5	12 22·1	12 22·1	N. 3 55—0 30·6	29·178	72·9	76·0	73·5

♃ NOVEMBER 28, 1844.—FACE OF SECTOR WEST.

7992	22 49 34·5	12 10·4	13 22·4	12 19·3	12 19·35	N. 3 55—1 3·05	29·358	68·1	70·6	69·4

Nov. 26.—Lifted the sector tube to clear the pivot bearing from sand carried up by the wind.
28.—The sky covered. Occasional fogs.

♀ November 29, 1844.—Face of Sector West.

Number of B.A.C.	Time by Chronometer.	Micr. for Plumb-line on Dot.	Micr. for Observation of Star.	Micr. for Plumb-line on Dot.	Mean of Micr. for Plumb-line on Dot.	Star's Apparent Zenith Distance.	Barom.	Thermometers.		
								Attd.	Upper.	Lower.
	h m s	rev. pts.	rev. pts.	rev. pts.	rev. pts.	° ' rev. pts.	in.			
5015	17	11 29·4	7 33·6	11 29·6	11 29·5	S. 2 40—3 29·9	29·251	66·2	66·8	65·9
6233	18	11 25·7	13 15·0	11 25·7	11 25·7	S. 0 5—1 23·3			68·0	66·2

☉ December 1, 1844.—Face of Sector East.

7966	22 44 36·5	9 30·7	8 22·0	9 30·5	9 30·6	N. 0 40—1 8·6	29·459	61·7	63·6	63·0
7092	22 49 43·5	10 9·4	9 12·55	10 9·4	10 9·4	N. 3 55—0 30·85				
1739	5 26 28·5	11 5·3	12 27·5	11 5·1	11 5·2	S. 1 15—1 22·3	29·459	56·7	56·0	56·0
1802	5 34 46·3	12 33·2	15 25·75	12 33·3	12 33·25	N. 0 10—2 26·5			55·6	56·0
1878	5 46 17·0	10 30·8	13 13·7	10 30·8	10 30·8	S. 1 30—2 16·9				
1922	5 52 48·5	10 14·9	6 27·5	10 15·0	10 14·95	S. 0 55—3 21·45				
1982	6 3 1·0	10 25·1	14 20·3	10 25·1	10 25·1	S. 2 55—3 29·2			56·0	56·8
2051	6 15 3·0	12 10·6	14 14·8	12 10·6	12 10·6	N. 4 20+2 4·2				
2109	6 23 9·4	10 0·3	13 18·7	10 0·2	10 0·25	N. 1 50+3 16·45	29·455	55·9	56·2	56·9
2246	6	9 30·8	11 33·8	9 30·8	9 30·8	N. 2 0+2 3·0				
2293	6 53 12·0	9 28·0	10 6·7	9 28·1	9 28·05	N. 5 35+0 12·05				
2414	7 12 28·2	8 27·4	12 9·0	8 27·5	8 27·45	S. 2 30—3 15·55				
2458	7 18 38·3	9 26·6	11 8·8	9 26·8	9 26·7	N. 5 20+1 16·1				
2528	7 33 6·5	10 7·0	3 24·9	10 7·1	10 7·05	S. 3 15+6 16·15	29·442	55·4	56·0	56·5
2575	7 39 53·0	10 7·0	13 23·5		10 7·05	S. 3 15+3 16·45				
2580	7 40 33·2		11 7·85	10 7·1	10 7·05	S. 3 15—1 0·8				
2635	7 48 1·0	10 26·2	8 0·5	10 26·2	10 26·2	S. 4 5+2 25·7				
2655	7	19 29·5	21 14·85	19 29·5	19 29·5	N. 4 25+1 19·35				
2710	7	11 16·3	6 15·9	11 16·3	11 16·3	S. 5 10+5 0·4				
2795	8 13 33·2	10 20·8	11 9·6	10 20·6	10 20·7	S. 1 50—0 22·9	29·436	55·2	55·8	56·3
2935	8 34 49·5	10 8·7	11 10·45	10 8·8	10 8·75	S. 0 25—1 1·7				
2964	8 38 6·2		7 27·6	10 24·8		N. 1 45—2 31·2				
4458	13 12 41·8	11 9·4	7 0·1	11 9·4	11 9·4	S. 1 30+4 0·3	29·461	60·8	62·5	59·5
4686	13 58 21·5	11 10·8	11 22·95	11 19·6	11 19·7	S. 1 15—0 3·25	29·463	62·2	66·2	61·2

☾ December 2, 1844.—Face of Sector East.

5915	17 23 52·0	11 11·6	15 12·05	11 11·7	11 11·65	S. 2 40—4 0·4	29·461	64·8	66·0	64·5
6233	18 14 38·5	12 5·0	10 18·9	12 4·8	12 4·9	S. 0 5+1 20·0			67·2	64·3

Face of Sector West.

7842	22 23 27·2	13 2·9	17 5·4	13 2·9	13 2·9	N. 1 15—4 2·5			68·0	65·3
7966	22 44 40·2	12 31·5	14 7·9	12 31·5	12 31·5	N. 0 40—1 10·4	29·461	64·4	66·5	65·4
7992	22 49 52·3	12 6·2	13 8·7	12 6·3	12 6·25	N. 3 55—1 2·45			66·5	65·4
1739	5	11 16·0	9 31·4	11 16·0	11 16·0	S. 1 15—1 18·6	29·438	57·9	57·6	58·0
1802	5 34 51·2	13 12·7	10 24·65	13 12·7	13 12·7	N. 0 10+2 22·05				
1878	5 46 18·5	12 11·9	9 33·7	12 11·9	12 11·9	S. 1 30—2 12·2				
1922	5 52 51·4	11 24·8	15 14·45	11 24·6	11 24·7	S. 0 55+3 23.75				
1982	6	11 4·8	7 14·8	11 4·8	11 4·8	S. 2 55—3 24·0	29·440	57·9	57·6	58·0
2051	6 15 12·0	8 14·5	6 16·3	8 14·4	8 14·45	N. 4 20+1 32·15				
2109	6 23 15·2	8 23·1	5 10·3	8 22·9	8 23·0	N. 1 50+3 12·7				
2246	6 44 53·0	8 11·4	6 13·0	8 11·0	8 11·2	N. 2 0+1 3·2				
2293	6 53 22·7	9 32·3	9 27·15	9 32·3	9 32·3	N. 5 35+0 5·15	29·434	57·6	57·4	57.7
2414	7 12 28·4	9 27·3	6 18·2	9 27·5	9 27·4	S. 2 30—3 9·2				
2458	7 18 48·5	10 12·5	9 3·3	10 12·4	10 12·45	N. 5 20—1 9·15	29·432	57·3	57·4	57·5
2528	7 33 4·2	19 31·5	17 21·9	19 31·8	19 31·65	S. 3 20—2 9·75				
2575	7 39 53·0	11 0·4	7 23·5		11 0·4	S. 3 15—3 10·9				
2580	7 40 32·5		10 5·0	11 0·4	11 0·4	S. 3 15—0 29·4				

Nov. 29.—Generally clouded or fog bound.
30.—Strong north-west wind with rain.
Dec. 1.—The chronometer times of transit uncertain to a half second, owing to the noise caused by the wind.
Dec. 2.—No. 3130.—The seconds of transit doubtful.
Strong S.E. wind. The chronometer beats inaudible: the seconds of transit depend upon practised counting.
Good definitions.
No. 7842.—Double: the larger observed.

☽ DECEMBER 2, 1844.—FACE OF SECTOR WEST—*(continued).*

Number of B.A.C.	Time by Chronometer.	Mier. for Plumb-line on Dot.	Mier. for Observation of Star.	Micr. for Plumb-line on Dot.	Mean of Micr. for Plumb-line on Dot.	Star's Apparent Zenith Distance.	Barom.	Attd.	Upper.	Lower.
	h m s	rev. pts.	rev. pts.	rev. pts.	rev. pts.	° ′ rev. pts.	in.			
2635	7	11 10·6	14 8·25	11 10·8	11 10·7	S. 4 5+2 31·55				
2655	7 52 20·5		8 30·4	10 8·8		N. 4 25+1 12·4				
2710	7	10 13·9	15 20·4	10 14·1	10 14·0	S. 5 10+5 6·4				
2795	8 13 34·4	10 18·3	10 1·25	10 18·1	10 18·2	S. 1 50—0 16.95			57·4	57·3
2935	8 34 53·5	9 21·4	8 23·6	9 21·4	9 21·4	S. 0 25—0 31·8				
2964	8 38 11·2		12 32·0	9 29·8		N. 1 45—3 2·2				
3130	9 4 12·0	10 7·2	6 25·65	10 7·3	10 7·25	N. 4 35+3 15·6	29·412	56·5	56·7	57·0
3163	9	11 25·2	10 18·5	11 25·2	11 25·2	S. 3 35—1 6·7			56·1	57·0
3257	9 25 23·2	11 0·0	12 33·5	11 0·0	11 0·0	S. 5 25+1 33·5				
3578	10 20 54·5	10 21·0	11 31·3	10 21·0	10 21·0	N. 4 5—1 10·3			57·6	57·0
3926	11 26 13·2	10 31·6	8 32·8	10 31·6	10 31·6	N. 3 20+1 32·8	29·420	57·9	57·5	58·5
4686	13	11 31·5	11 31·0	11 31·6	11 31·55	S. 1 15—0 0·55	29·434	62·5	60·5	61·0

♂ DECEMBER 3, 1844.—FACE OF SECTOR EAST.

Number of B.A.C.	Time by Chronometer.	Mier. for Plumb-line on Dot.	Mier. for Observation of Star.	Micr. for Plumb-line on Dot.	Mean of Micr. for Plumb-line on Dot.	Star's Apparent Zenith Distance.	Barom.	Attd.	Upper.	Lower.
7992	22 49 52·7	10 31·5	10 1·6	10 31·5	10 31·5	N. 3 55—0 29·0	29·398	61·0	62·5	61·3
1739	5	11 2·9	12 25·5	11 2·9	11 2·9	S. 1 15—1 22·6	29·339	57·9	57·8	58·0
1802	5 34 56·8	11 19·9	14 11·5	11 19·7	11 19·8	N. 0 10+2 25·7				
1878	5 46 26·2	10 19·7	13 2·4	10 10·8	10 19·75	S. 1 30—2 16·65				
1922	5 52 57·0	10 12·7	6 25·75	10 12·7	10 12·7	S. 0 55+3 20·95				
1982	6 3 8·5	10 12·0	14 7·7	10 13·0	10 12·95	S. 2 55—3 28·75				
2051	6 15 11·8	10 20·3	12 25.05	10 20·3	10 20·3	N. 4 20+2 4·75				
2109	6 23 18·5	10 15·7	14 0·9	10 16·0	10 15·85	N. 1 50+3 19·05				
2246	6	19 16·7	21 20·1	19 16·9	19 16·8	N. 2 0+2 3·3				
2293	6 53 21·0	11 0·3	11 12·75	11 0·2	11 0·25	N. 5 35+0 12·5	29·327	57·7	58·0	58·2
2414	7 12 38·0	10 20·0	14 1·9	10 20·1	10 20·05	S. 2 30—3 15·85				
2458	7 18 47·0	12 7·9	13 24·75	12 7·9	12 7·9	N. 5 20+1 16·85				
2528	7 33 14·5	11 30·8	14 12·3	11 30·7	11 30·75	S. 3 20—2 15·55				
2575	7 40 1·0	12 19·6	16 1·8		12 19·65	S. 3 15—3 16·15				
2580	7 40 41·0		13 20·5	12 19·7	12 19·65	S. 3 15—1 0·85				
2635	7 48 8·5	12 14·2	9 23·4	12 14·3	12 14·25	S. 4 5+2 24·85				
2655	7 52 20·5		15 3·75	13 19·2		N. 4 25+1 18·55				
2710	7 59 8·5	10 19·9	5 21·3	10 19·7	10 19·8	S. 5 10+4 32·5				
2795	8 13 42·2	10 5·7	10 28·9	10 5·8	10 5·75	S. 1 50—0 23·15				
2935	8 34 57·5	10 11·5	11 13·85	10 12·0	10 11·75	S. 0 25—1 2·1	29·318	57·4	57·8	57·9
2964	8 38 13·5		9 4·7	12 2·1		N. 1 45—2 31·4				
3130	9 4 12·5	11 14·5	15 0·95	11 14·5	11 14·5	N. 4 35+3 20·45				
3163	9 10 28·0	10 22·9	12 0·75	10 22·8	10 22·85	S. 3 35—1 11·9				
3257	9 25 37·0	10 20·8	8 27·3	10 20·6	10 20·7	S. 5 25+1 27·4	29·318	56·1	56·9	57·6
3578	10 20 43·0	10 19·1	9 13·65	10 19·1	10 19·1	N. 4 5—1 5·45			57·5	57·5
4458	13 12 50·0	10 9·1	6 8·2	10 9·0	10 9·05	S. 1 30+4 0·85	29.326	61·5	65·6	60·1
4686	13 58 30·5	10 16·9	10 21·3	10 16·8	10 16·85	S. 1 15—0 4 45			67·4	62·1

♀ DECEMBER 4, 1844.—FACE OF SECTOR WEST.

Number of B.A.C.	Time by Chronometer.	Mier. for Plumb-line on Dot.	Mier. for Observation of Star.	Micr. for Plumb-line on Dot.	Mean of Micr. for Plumb-line on Dot.	Star's Apparent Zenith Distance.	Barom.	Attd.	Upper.	Lower.
5915	17 23 56·5	10 29·5	7 0·4	10 29·5	10 29·5	S. 2 40—3 29·1	29·323	68·4	71·4	67·3
6233	18 14 45·5	10 29·0	12 19·45	10 30·2	10 30·05	S. 0 5+1 23·4			71·2	68·0

FACE OF SECTOR EAST.

Number of B.A.C.	Time by Chronometer.	Mier. for Plumb-line on Dot.	Mier. for Observation of Star.	Micr. for Plumb-line on Dot.	Mean of Micr. for Plumb-line on Dot.	Star's Apparent Zenith Distance.	Barom.	Attd.	Upper.	Lower.
7966	22 44 53·0	12 12·1	11 3·4	12 11·9	12 12·0	N. 0 40—1 8·6	29·237	64·4	65·6	65·0
7992	22 49 56·8	13 5·9	12 9·85	13 5·9	13 5·9	N. 3 55—0 30·05				

Dec. 3.—No. 2580.—The seconds of transit doubtful.
　Very strong wind : chronometer beats inaudible : the registered times uncertain to about one second.

♃ DECEMBER 4, 1844—(continued).—FACE OF SECTOR WEST.

Number of B.A.C.	Time by Chronometer.	Micr. for Plumb-line on Dot.	Micr. for Observation of Star.	Micr. for Plumb-line on Dot.	Mean of Micr. for Plumb-line on Dot.	Star's Apparent Zenith Distance.	Barom.	Attd.	Upper.	Lower.
	b m s	rev. pts.	rev. pts.	rev. pts.	rev. pts.	o ' rev. pts.	in.			
1739	5 26 40·0	10 12·8	8 29·1	10 12·8	10 12·8	S. 1 15—1 17·7	29·201	60·1	60·2	60·2
1802	5 35 0·3	10 24·3	8 3·55	10 24·3	10 24·3	N. 0 10+2 20·75				
1878	5 46 26·5	12 0·8	9 23·3	12 0·5	12 0·65	S. 1 30—2 11·35				
1922	5 52 59·5	12 7·1	15 31·45	12 7·3	12 7·2	S. 0 55+3 24·25				
1982	6 3 0·5	12 9·8	8 20·7	12 9·7	12 9·75	S. 2 55—3 23·05				
2109	6	11 22·2	8 11·0	11 22·2	11 22·2	N. 1 50+3 11·2				
2246	6 45 1·2	11 24·5	9 27·45	11 24·4	11 24·45	N. 2 0+1 31·0				
2293	6 53 31·7	12 19·3	12 14·9	12 19·4	12 19·35	N. 5 35+0 4·45				
2414	7 12 36·5	12 10·7	9 2·6	12 10·7	12 10·7	S. 2 30—3 8·1				
2458	7 18 57·3	12 4·7	10 29·8	12 4·3	12 4·5	N. 5 20+1 8·7				
2528	7	12 19·9	10 10·4	12 20·1	12 20·0	S. 3 20—2 9·6	29·172	59·4	60·2	60·4
2575	7 39 50·7	12 3·1	8 27·0		12 3·05	S. 3 15—3 10·05				
2580	7 40 41·0		11 8·9	12 3·0	12 3·05	S. 3 15—0 28·15				
2635	7 48 5·7	12 1·4	14 33·4	12 1·6	12 1·5	S. 4 5+2 31·9				
2655	7 52 29·0		10 16·75	11 28.0		N. 4 25+1 11·25				
2710	7 50 2·5	13 5·8	18 12·1	13 5·6	13 5·7	S. 5 10+5 6·4				
2795	8 13 43·0	11 30·4	11 13·9	11 30·4	11 30·4	S. 1 50—0 16·5				
2935	8 34 59·5	12 30·3	11 33·4	12 30·4	12 30·35	S. 0 25—0 30·95	29·176	60·1	60·6	60·9
2964	8 38 20·5		15 24·3	12 21·7		N. 1 45—3 2·6				
3130	9 4 21·0	12 31·9	9 17·3	12 31·9	12 31·9	N. 4 35+3 14·6				
3163	9 10 27·5	13 13·8	12 8·0	13 13·0	13 13·65	S. 3 35—1 5·85	29·194	59·7	60·0	60·2
3257	9 25 32·0	11 32·4	13 32·85	11 32·4	11 32·4	S. 5 25+2 0·45				
3578	10	10 10·0	11 20·8	10 10·0	10 10·0	N. 4 5—1 10·8				
4086	13 58 30·5	9 29·5	9 29·25	9 29·3	9 29·3	S. 1 15—0 0·15	29·241	65·5	64·2	69·0

♃ DECEMBER 5, 1844.—FACE OF SECTOR EAST.

Number of B.A.C.	Time by Chronometer.	Micr. for Plumb-line on Dot.	Micr. for Observation of Star.	Micr. for Plumb-line on Dot.	Mean of Micr. for Plumb-line on Dot.	Star's Apparent Zenith Distance.	Barom.	Attd.	Upper.	Lower.
6233	18 14 51·0	11 22·3	10 2·7	11 22·3	11 22·3	S. 0 5+1 19·6	29·292	68·4	70·2	68·1
1739	5 26 47·2	12 21·5	14 8·0	12 21·5	12 21·5	S. 0 10—1 20·5	29·382	61·3	62·2	61·8
1802	5 35 5·0	12 19·1	15 9·9	12 19·1	12 19·1	N. 0 10+2 24·8				
1878	5 46 35·2	11 15·5	13 30·7	11 15·5	11 15·5	S. 1 30—2 15·2				
1922	5 53 6·4	11 4·4	7 15·7	11 4·3	11 4·35	S. 0 55+3 22·65				
1982	6	11 7·7	15 1·15	11 7·7	11 7·7	S. 2 55—3 27·45				
2061	6 15 21·2	11 24·8	13 27·9	11 25·0	11 24·9	N. 4 20+2 3·0				
2109	6 23 27·2	10 12·4	13 28·8	10 12·4	10 12·4	N. 1 50+3 16·4	29·386	61·3	61·5	62·0
2293	6 53 30·2	11 11·9	11 22·6	11 12·0	11 11·95	N. 5 35+0 10·65				
2414	7 12 45·5	10 22·6	14 2·5	10 22·6	10 22·6	S. 2 30—3 13·9				
2458	7 18 56·0	10 27·0	12 8·0	10 27·1	10 27·05	N. 5 20+1 14·95				
2710	7 59 19·2	9 24·0	4 22·75	9 24·0	9 24·0	S. 5 10+5 1·25	29·386	61·5	62·2	62·5
2795	8 13 51·5	9 6·0	9 26·7	9 6·0	9 6·0	S. 1 50—0 0·7				
2935	8 35 6·5	9 4·8	10 4·4	9 4·8	9 4·8	S. 0 25—0 33·6				
2964	8 38 24·0		7 10·8	10 9·7		N. 1 45—2 32·9				
3130	9 4 21·5	10 26·6	14 12·5	10 27·0	10 26·8	N. 4 35+3 19·7				
3163	9 10 38·2	10 23·9	12 1·4	10 23·9	10 23·9	S. 3 35—1 11·5	29·378	60·8	61·0	62·0
3257	9 25 46·5	10 17·2	8 23·9	10 17·0	10 17·1	S. 5 25+1 27·2				
3578	10 21 3·0	13 3·2	11 31·5	13 3·2	13 3·2	N. 4 5—1 5·7			61·5	61·5
3755	10 50 34·0	11 24·8	8 4·0	11 24·8	11 24·8	S. 1 55+3 20·8				
3926	11 26 23·8	12 11·0	14 15·3	12 11·7	12 11·8	N. 3 20+2 3·5	29·378	62·4	62·0	65·2

FACE OF SECTOR WEST.

Number of B.A.C.	Time by Chronometer.	Micr. for Plumb-line on Dot.	Micr. for Observation of Star.	Micr. for Plumb-line on Dot.	Mean of Micr. for Plumb-line on Dot.	Star's Apparent Zenith Distance.	Barom.	Attd.	Upper.	Lower.
4458	13	10 20·7	14 24·4	10 20·8	10 20·75	S. 1 30+4 3·65	29·413	64·0	67·5	63·8

FACE OF SECTOR EAST.

Number of B.A.C.	Time by Chronometer.	Micr. for Plumb-line on Dot.	Micr. for Observation of Star.	Micr. for Plumb-line on Dot.	Mean of Micr. for Plumb-line on Dot.	Star's Apparent Zenith Distance.	Barom.	Attd.	Upper.	Lower.
4086	13 58 39·7	10 8·2	10 11·25	10 8·2	10 8·2	S. 1 15—0 3·05	29·415	64·4	67·6	65·2

Dec. 4.—No. 2655.—The seconds of transit doubtful.
It is to be understood, unless the contrary is stated, that when observations of any of the stars in the working list are omitted, the sky has been covered.
Dec. 5.—Nos. 3578 and 3755.—The seconds of transit doubtful.

132   ARC OF THE MERIDIAN.—CAPE OF GOOD HOPE.

♀ DECEMBER 6, 1844.—FACE OF SECTOR EAST.

Number of D.A.C.	Time by Chronometer.	Micr. for Plumb-line on Dot.	Micr. for Observation of Star.	Micr. for Plumb-line on Dot.	Mean of Micr. for Plumb-line on Dot.	Star's Apparent Zenith Distance.	Barom.	Thermometers.		
								Attd.	Upper.	Lower.
	h m s	rev. pts.	rev. pts.	rev. pts.	rev. pts.	° ′ rev. pts.	In.			
5915	17 24 11·7	10 16·5	14 17·7	10 16·9	10 16·7	S. 2 40—4 1·0	29·434	68·0	70·5	67·6
			FACE OF SECTOR WEST.							
6233	18 14 54·0	9 27·6	11 16·3	9 27·8	9 27·7	S. 0 5+1 22·6			72·0	67·8
			FACE OF SECTOR EAST.							
7842	22 23 44·6	10 0·4	5 32·6	10 0·2	10 0·3	N. 1 15—4 1·7			70·0	67·2
			FACE OF SECTOR WEST.							
7992	22 50 9·5	9 29·8	11 0·05	9 30·0	9 29·9	N. 3 55—1 4·15			71·5	68·5
1739	5 26 47·0	9 26·5	8 9·8	9 26·5	9 26·5	S. 1 15—1 16·7	29·410	61·0	61·8	62·0
1802	5 35 9·0	10 22·8	8 2·9	10 22·7	10 22·75	N. 0 10+2 19·85				
1878	5 46 35·5	11 2·7	8 26·0	11 2·7	11 2·7	S. 1 30—2 10·7				
1922	5 53 7·5	11 1·0	14 26·75	11 1·0	11 1·0	S. 0 55+3 25·75				
1982	6 3 17·5	11 22·1	7 33·5	11 22·2	11 22·15	S. 2 55—3 22·65				
2051	6 15 30·0	10 33·6	9 3·45	10 33·8	10 33·7	N. 4 20+1 30·25				
2109	6 23 32·5	11 6·8	7 29·65	11 6·6	11 6·7	N. 1 50+3 11·05				
2246	6 45 10·2	11 22·6	9 26·0	11 22·5	11 22·55	N. 2 0+1 30·55				
2293	6 53 40·5	10 6·8	10 3·4	10 7·0	10 6·9	N. 5 45+0 3·5	29·410	61·2	62·3	62·0
2414	7 12 45·0	10 29·5	7 22·2	10 29·7	10 29·6	S. 2 30—3 7·4				
2458	7 19 6·0	10 32·7	9 25·0	10 32·3	10 32·5	N. 5 20+1 7·5				
2528	7 33 21·0	11 28·7	9 20·3	11 28·9	11 28·8	S. 3 20—2 8·5				
2575	7 40 8·0	11 17·5	8 8·4		11 17·45	S. 3 15—3 9·05				
2580	7 40 48·8		10 23·7	11 17·4	11 17·45	S. 3 15—0 27·75				
2635	7 48 13·5	10 29·5	13 29·6	10 29·8	10 29·65	S. 4 5+2 33·95				
2655	7 52 37·5		9 9·5	10 20·8		N. 4 25+1 11·3				
2795	8 13 50·5	10 29·4	10 14·0	10 4·4		S. 1 50—0 15·4				
2935	8 35 8·5	10 5·1	9 8·45	10 5·1	10 5·1	S. 0 25—0 30·65				
2964	8 38 29·5		13 3·5	9 33·75		N. 1 45—3 3·75	29·410	60·8	62·2	62·0
3130	9 4 30·2	10 3·0	6 22·95	10 3·1	10 3·05	N. 4 35+3 14·1				
3163	9 10 35·0	10 19·0	9 14·4	10 19·0	10 19·0	S. 3 35—1 4·6				
3257	9 25 39·5	19 27·8	21 28·5	19 27·9	19 27·85	S. 5 5+2 0·65	29·413	60·8	62·0	62·0
3926	·10	10 17·2	8 18·6	10 17·2	10 17·2	N. 3 20+1 32·6				61·8

♄ DECEMBER 7, 1844.— FACE OF SECTOR WEST.

Number of D.A.C.	Time by Chronometer.	Micr. for Plumb-line on Dot.	Micr. for Observation of Star.	Micr. for Plumb-line on Dot.	Mean of Micr. for Plumb-line on Dot.	Star's Apparent Zenith Distance.	Barom.	Thermometers.		
								Attd.	Upper.	Lower.
5915	17	11 12·9	7 16·6	11 12·9	11 12·9	S. 2 40—3 30·3	29·469	68·5	70·6	68·0
			FACE OF SECTOR EAST.							
1730	5	9 32·4	11 20·2	9 32·6	9 32·5	S. 1 15—1 21·7	29·415	60·6	60·8	61·2
1802	5	10 27·3	13 18·55	10 27·4	10 27·35	N. 0 10+2 25·2				
1878	5 46 43·6	11 18·4	13 33·9	11 18·4	11 18·4	S. 1 30—2 15·5				
1922	5 53 16·5	11 26·7	8 5·1	11 26·7	11 26·7	S. 0 55+3 21·6				
1982	6 3 28·8	10 29·6	14 23·5	10 29·7	10 29·7	S. 2 55—3 27·85				
2051	6 15 31·0	10 19·3	12 22·6	10 19·4	10 19·35	N. 4 20+2 3·25				
2109	6 23 36·5	10 13·0	13 30·5	10 13·1	10 13·1	N. 1 50+3 17·45	29·416	60·8	61·5	61·3
2246	6 45 13·5	11 5·1	13 7·3	11 5·1	11 5·1	N. 2 0+2 2·2				
2293	6 53 39·2	11 15·7	11 26·6	11 15·7	11 15·7	N. 5 35+0 10·9				
2414	7 12 55·5	10 23·6	14 3·6	10 23·6	10 23·6	S. 2 30—3 14·0				
2458	7 19 5·0	11 19·0	13 0·0	11 18·9	11 18·95	N. 5 20+1 15·05	29·408	60·3	61·0	61·0
2528	7 33 32·0	10 30·3	13 10·65	10 30·5	10 30·4	S. 3 20—2 14·25				
2575	7 40 19·2	19 28·2	23 9·3		19 28·2	S. 3 15—3 15·1				
2580	7 41 0·2		20 27·4	19 28·2	19 28·2	S. 3 15—0 33·2				
2635	7 48 26·8	13 5·3	10 12·95	13 5·4	13 5·35	S. 4 5+2 26·4				

Dec. 6.—No. 7992.—The time doubtful: image flickering.

♄ DECEMBER 7, 1844.—FACE OF SECTOR EAST—(continued).

Number of B.A.C.	Time by Chronometer.	Micr. for Plumb-line on Dot.	Micr. for Observation of Star.	Micr. for Plumb-line on Dot.	Mean of Micr. for Plumb-line on Dot.	Star's Apparent Zenith Distance.	Barom.	Thermometers. Attd.	Upper.	Lower.
	h m s	rev. pts.	rev. pts.	rev. pts.	rev. pts.	° ' rev. pts.	in.			
2655	7 52 37·5	12 22·7	14 6·0	12 22·0	12 22·8	N. 4 25+1 17·2				
2710	7 59 27·0	12 0·7	15 32·0	12 0·9	12 0·8	S. 5 15—3 31·2				
2795	8 13 59·2	11 14·5	12 2·95	11 14·5	11 14·5	S. 1 50—0 22·45				
2935	8 35 14·5	11 25·1	12 24·9	11 25·1	11 25·1	S. 0 25—0 33·8				
2964	8 38 32·3		9 15·15	12 13·0	12 13·0	N. 1 45—2 31·85				
3257	9 25 55·5	14 22·0	12 28·25	14 22·0	14 22·0	S. 5 25+1 27·75				

⊙ DECEMBER 8, 1844.—FACE OF SECTOR WEST.

Number of B.A.C.	Time by Chronometer.	Micr. for Plumb-line on Dot.	Micr. for Observation of Star.	Micr. for Plumb-line on Dot.	Mean of Micr. for Plumb-line on Dot.	Star's Apparent Zenith Distance.	Barom.	Attd.	Upper.	Lower.
1730	5 26 57·5	8 17·4	7 0·95	8 17·5	8 17·45	S. 1 15—1 16·5	29·294	60·6	60·0	60·2
1802	5 35 18·0	9 2·8	6 16·35	9 2·6	9 2·7	N. 0 10+2 20·35				
1878	5 46 44·5	8 13·1	6 2·7	8 13·1	8 13·1	S. 1 30—2 10·4				
1922	5 53 17·2	8 10·6	12 2·1	8 10·4	8 10·5	S. 0 55+3 25·6				
1982	6 3 27·3	9 12·7	5 24·75	9 12·65	9 12·65	S 2 55—3 21·9	29·294	60·6	60·0	60·2
2051	6 15 38·2	9 17·1	7 20·0	9 17·1	9 17·1	N. 4 20+1 31·1				
2109	6 23 41·2	8 24·9	5 13·6	8 24·8	8 24·85	N. 1 50+3 11·25			59·9	60·0
2246	6 45 19·0	10 14·1	8 17·8	10 14·1	10 14·1	N. 2 0+1 30·3				
2293	6 53 48·8	10 8·8	10 5·05	10 8·7	10 8·75	N. 5 35+0 3·7				
2414	7 12 54·3	11 17·6	8 10·95	11 17·5	11 17·55	S. 2 30—3 6·6				
2528	7 33 30·8	12 1·4	9 27·7	12 1·5	12 1·45	S. 3 20—2 7·75				
2575	7 40 17·5	3 3·8	0 28·75		3 3·8	S. 3 15—3 9·05				
2580	7 40 59·7		2 10·25	3 3·8	3 3·8	S. 3 15—0 27·55				
2635	7 48 24·0	11 29·0	14 28·4	11 29·0	11 29·0	S. 4 5+2 33·4				
2655	7 52 46·2		9 28·95	11 5·6		N. 4 25+1 10·65				
2710	7 59 21·5	11 8·4	7 18·9	11 8·4	11 8·4	S. 5 15—3 23·5				
2795	8 14 0·0	11 17·5	11 1·95	11 17·4	11 17·45	S. 1 50—0 15·5			59·2	59·6
2935	8 35 17·5	10 18·9	9 22·8	10 18·9	10 18·9	S. 0 25—0 30·1				
2964	8 38 38·0		13 24·5	10 21·45		N. 1 45—3 3·05				

FACE OF SECTOR EAST.

3163	9 10 51·2	11 15·5	12 25·9	11 15·5	11 15·5	S. 3 35—1 10·4				
3257	9 25 59·7	10 19·1	8 24·7	10 19·3	10 19·2	S. 5 25+1 28·5				

FACE OF SECTOR WEST.

3578	10 20 20·0	10 28·8	12 6·5	10 28·9	10 28·85	N. 4 5—1 11·65	29·300	59·0	59·4	50·4
3755	10 50 44·4	11 14·2	15 6·1	11 14·4	11 14·3	S. 1 55+3 25·8				

FACE OF SECTOR EAST.

3926	11 26 35·7	11 6·8	13 9·6	11 6·8	11 6·8	N. 3 20+2 2·8	29·310	59·9	63·5	60·2
4015	11 46 20·6	10 32·4	8 8·5	10 32·3	10 32·35	N. 1 20—2 23·85				

FACE OF SECTOR WEST.

4686	13 58 43·2	10 19·4	10 18·95	10 19·4	10 19·4	S. 1 15—0 0·45	29·351	63·0	65·6	62·2

☾ DECEMBER 9, 1844.—FACE OF SECTOR EAST.

5915	17 24 24·5	11 32·4	16 0·4	11 32·0	11 32·2	S. 2 40—4 2·2	29·367	70·9	74·0	69·0
1730	5 27 4·0	11 22·8	13 8·85	11 22·8	11 22·8	S. 1 15—1 20·00	29·341	59·4	59·8	59·9
1802	5 35 23·3	12 0·9	14 25·5	12 1·0	12 0·95	N. 0 10+2 24·55				
1878	5 46 51·2	11 14·0	13 28·8	11 14·0	11 14·0	S. 1 30—2 14·8				
1922	5 53 23·8	10 29·6	7 7·0	10 29·6	10 29·6	S. 0 55+3 22·6				
1982	6 3 34·4	10 14·5	14 7·2	10 14·4	10 14·45	S. 2 55—3 20·75				
2051	6 15 42·5	10 29·1	12 31·95	10 29·2	10 29·15	N. 4 20+2 2·8				

Dec. 7.—Nos. 7842 and 7966 might be observed some days longer but for the thick atmosphere prevailing over this Station. Clouded between 8ʰ 36ᵐ and 9ʰ 25ᵐ chronometer time.

8.—Strong S.E. wind: showers of dust and sand. Good definition.

9.—No. 5915.—The chronometer time uncertain.

☾ DECEMBER 9, 1844.—FACE OF SECTOR EAST—(continued).

Number of B.A.C.	Time by Chronometer.	Micr. for Plumb-line on Dot.	Micr. for Observation of Star.	Micr. for Plumb-line on Dot.	Mean of Micr. for Plumb-line on Dot.	Star's Apparent Zenith Distance.	Barom.	Thermometers. Attd.	Upper.	Lower.
	h m s	rev. pts.	rev. pts.	rev. pts.	rev. pts.	o ' rev. pts.	in.			
2109	6 23 46·2	10 28·0	14 10·8	10 28·2	10 28·1	N. 1 50+3 16·7				
2246	6 45 24·0	10 32·1	12 33·5	10 32·3	10 32·2	N. 2 0+2 1·3				
2293	6 53 52·7	9 21·4	9 31·5	9 21·2	9 21·3	N. 5 35+0 10·2	29·314	59·4	60·0	60·0
2414	7 13 1·5	12 22·2	16 1·8	12 22·0	12 22·1	S. 2 30—3 13·7				
2458	7 19 10·2	12 24·9	14 5·45	12 24·9	12 24·9	N. 5 20+1 14·55				
2528	7 33 38·2	10 18·6	12 32·6	10 18·6	10 18·6	S. 3 20—2 14·0				
2575	7 40 25·5	19 15·7	22 30·3		19 15·8	S. 3 15—3 14·5				
2580	7 41 5·0		20 15·3	19 15·9	19 15·8	S. 3 15—0 33·5				
2635	7 48 31·3	9 17·5	6 24·4	9 17·6	9 17·55	S. 4 5+2 27·15				
2655	7 52 50·7		11 26·7	10 10·5		N. 4 25+1 16·2				
2710	7 59 30·5	10 12·9	14 9·0	10 13·1	10 13·0	S. 5 15—3 30·0				
2795	8 14 6·5	10 12·4	10 33·35	10 12·3	10 12·35	S. 1 50—0 21·0				
2935	8 35 23·5	10 6·9	11 6·9	10 6·9	10 6·9	S. 0 25—1 0·0				
2964	8 38 43·5		7 32·0	10 31·1		N. 1 45—2 33·1	29·304	58·0	59·2	59·2
3130	9 4 43·5	11 10·3	14 30·3	11 10·6	11 10·45	N. 4 35+3 19·85				
3163	9 10 52·0	11 5·8	12 17·3	11 6·0	11 5·9	S. 3 35—1 11·4				
3257	9 25 57·0	11 7·4	9 13·1	11 7·6	11 7·5	S. 5 25+1 28·4	29·304	58·8	59·2	59·4
3755	10 50 51·0	11 26·3	8 5·4	11 26·1	11 26·2	S. 1 55+3 20·8			61·5	59·8
3926	11 26 44·2	12 21·9	14 25·0	12 22·0	12 21·95	N. 3 20+2 3·05	29·318	60·6	62·6	60·0
4015	11	12 13·0	9 23·1	12 13·0	12 13·0	N. 1 20—2 23·9			63·0	60·3
4458	13 14 15·2	10 24·0	6 24·3	10 24·0	10 24·0	S. 1 30+3 33·7	29·327	62·6	67·4	62·2
4686	13 58 55·2	11 5·6	11 9·9	11 5·6	11 5·6	S. 1 15—0 4·3				

♂ DECEMBER 10, 1844.—FACE OF SECTOR WEST.

Number of B.A.C.	Time by Chronometer.	Micr. for Plumb-line on Dot.	Micr. for Observation of Star.	Micr. for Plumb-line on Dot.	Mean of Micr. for Plumb-line on Dot.	Star's Apparent Zenith Distance.	Barom.	Attd.	Upper.	Lower.
6233	18 15 11·7	11 1·4	12 23·8	11 1·6	11 1·5	S. 0 5+1 22·3	29·323	60·7	72·0	68·4
1739	5 27 6·0	11 28·7	10 13·75	11 28·8	11 28·75	S. 1 15—1 15·0	29·128	60·8	61·4	61·2
1802	5 35 26·0	13 5·5	10 21·55	13 5·4	13 5·45	N. 0 10+2 17·9				
1878	5 46 53·0	11 7·4	8 31·7	11 7·4	11 7·4	S. 1 30—2 9·7				
1922	5 53 26·0	9 26·7	13 19·47	9 26·5	9 26·6	S. 0 55+3 23·87				
1982	6 3 35·5	10 27·0	7 7·5	10 27·0	10 27·0	S. 2 55—3 19·5				
2051	6 15 47·0	10 1·0	8 6·25	10 1·0	10 1·0	N. 4 20+1 28·75				
2109	6 23 50·0	9 20·9	6 11·5	9 20·9	9 20·9	N. 1 50+3 9·4				
2246	6 45 28·5	9 33·8	8 4·9	9 33·8	9 33·8	N. 2 0+1 28·9				
2293	6 53 58·5	9 28·9	9 26·5	9 28·7	9 28·8	N. 5 35+0 2·3				
2414	7 13 3·0	10 21·5	7 15·5	10 21·6	10 21·6	S. 2 30—3 6·1			60·5	61·0
2458	7 19 24·0	11 22·5	10 16·4	11 22·5	11 22·5	N. 5 20+1 6·1				
2710	7 59 29·5	13 28·4	10 8·1	13 28·4	13 28·4	S. 5 15—3 20·3	29·117	60·8	60·2	60·6
2795	8 14 8·3	9 33·7	9 20·9	9 33·9	9 33·8	S. 1 50—0 12·9				
2935	8 35 26·0	10 17·8	9 23·9	10 17·8	10 17·8	S. 0 25—0 27·9				
2964	8 38 46·8		14 10·25	11 13·6		N. 1 45—3 5·65				
3130	9 4 48·5	10 32·8	7 21·25	10 32·9	10 32·85	N. 4 35+3 11·6	29·150	60·1	60·2	60·5
3163	9 10 52·0	10 20·0	9 17·25	10 20·0	10 20·0	S. 3 35—1 2·75				

♃ DECEMBER 11, 1844.—FACE OF SECTOR WEST.

Number of B.A.C.	Time by Chronometer.	Micr. for Plumb-line on Dot.	Micr. for Observation of Star.	Micr. for Plumb-line on Dot.	Mean of Micr. for Plumb-line on Dot.	Star's Apparent Zenith Distance.	Barom.	Attd.	Upper.	Lower.
3578	10 20 33·5	11 30·0	13 9·9	11 30·0	11 30·0	N. 4 5—1 13·9	29·455	58·8	59·2	59·2
3755	10 50 57·5	11 11·8	15 5·15	11 11·8	11 11·8	S. 1 55+3 27·25				
3926	11 26 52·5	11 15·2	9 18·8	11 15·3	11 15·25	N. 3 20+1 30·45			50·1	59·6
4458	13 13 20·5	11 27·7	15 31·9	11 27·9	11 27·8	S. 1 30+4 4·1	29·499	61·3	62·2	60·9
4686	13	11 7·2	12 6·7	12 7·2	12 7·2	S. 1 15—0 0·5	29·499	63·1	64·0	61·6

Dec. 9.—No. 3257.—The chronometer time uncertain.
No. 4015.—Close double. The space bisected.
10.—At 7h 33m per chronometer the plumb-line broke. Stretched and attached a new one.
Slight rain in the night. Fair definitions.
11.—No. 4458.—The chronometer time doubtful.

♃ December 12, 1844.—Face of Sector East.

Number of B.A.C.	Time by Chronometer	Micr. for Plumb-line on Dot	Micr. for Observation of Star	Micr. for Plumb-line on Dot	Mean of Micr. for Plumb-line on Dot	Star's Apparent Zenith Distance	Barom.	Attd.	Upper	Lower
	h m s	rev. pts.	rev. pts.	rev. pts.	rev. pts.	° ′ rev. pts.	in.			
7992	22 50 35·1	11 3·5	10 7·3	11 3·5	11 3·5	N. 3 55—0 30·2	29·528	65·7	67·8	66·0
1739	5 27 17·0	9 6·7	10 26·8	9 6·7	9 6·7	S. 1 15—1 20·1	29·469	59·5	59·8	60·0
1802	5 35 30·5	9 27·6	12 18·2	9 27·6	9 27·6	N. 0 10+2 24·6				
1878	5 47 4·4	9 19·9	12 1·2	9 19·8	9 19·85	S. 1 30—2 15·35				
1922	5 53 37·0	10 0·1	6 11·5	10 0·1	10 0·1	S. 0 55+3 22·6				
1982	6 3 48·0	10 3·0	13 30·4	10 3·0	10 3·0	S. 2 55—3 27·4				
2051	6 15 55·5	9 29·9	11 32·7	9 30·0	9 29·95	N. 4 20+2 2·75				
2109	6 23 59·5	9 10·0	12 26·0	9 9·9	9 9·95	N. 1 50+3 16·05	29·467	59·0	59·6	59·8
2246	6 45 37·0	9 20·7	11 22·1	9 20·9	9 20·8	N. 2 0+2 1·3				
2293	6 54 5·5	9 30·1	10 6·9	9 30·2	9 30·15	N. 5 35+0 10·75				
2414	7 13 15·5	9 12·7	12 26·3	9 12·9	9 12·8	S. 2 30—3 13·5				
2458	7 19 31·5	9 23·1	11 3·3	9 23·2	9 23·2	N. 5 20+1 14·1				
2528	7 34 1·5	8 30·1	11 10·1	8 30·3	8 30·2	S. 3 20—2 13·0				
2575	7 40 38·5	17 27·6	21 8·1	17 27·7	17 27·7	S. 3 15—3 14·4				
2580	7 41 19·0		18 26·6	17 27·8	17 27·7	S. 3 15—0 32·9				
2635	7 48 45·2	12 0·0	9 6·7	12 0·0	12 0·0	S. 4 5+2 27·3				
2655	7 54 3·0	11 17·4	12 33·75	11 17·5	11 17·45	N. 4 25+1 16·3				
2710	7 59 44·5	9 6·5	13 2·3	9 6·5	9 6·5	S. 5 15—3 29·8			59·6	59·8
2795	8 14 20·2	10 22·5	11 9·1	10 22·4	10 22·45	S. 1 50—0 20·65				
2935	8 35 37·0	11 16·6	12 16·4	11 16·8	11 16·7	S. 0 25—0 33·7				
2964	8 38 56·0		8 8·4	11 6·9		N. 1 45—2 32·5				
3130	9 4 56·0	10 13·9	13 33·05	10 13·9	10 13·9	N. 4 35+3 19·15	29·412	59·0	59·2	59·6
3163	9 11 5·8	9 22·7	10 33·55	9 22·4	9 22·55	S. 3 35—1 11·0				
3257	9 26 12·2	0 28·0	7 33·5	9 27·0	9 27·05	S. 5 25+1 28·45				
Anon.	9 40		11 16·1	15 1·9		N. 2 25—3 19·8	29·400	58·6	58·8	59·6
3578	10 21 37·2	11 19·5	10 13·3	11 19·5	11 19·5	N. 4 5—1 6·2	29·396	58·8	59·5	59·5
3755	10 51 5·2	10 5·0	6 17·8	10 4·9	10 4·95	S. 1 55+3 21·15			59·6	59·5
3926	11 26 56·2	10 11·8	12 14·8	10 11·9	10 11·85	N. 3 20+2 22·0				
4458	13 13 28·5	14 21·6	10 21·5	14 21·2	14 21·4	S. 1 30+3 33·9	29·400	62·4	66·0	62·0
4686	13 59 9·0	13 4·5	13 8·3	13 4·6	13 4·55	S. 1 15—0 3·75			67·5	63·0

♀ December 13, 1844.—Face of Sector West.

Number of B.A.C.	Time by Chronometer	Micr. for Plumb-line on Dot	Micr. for Observation of Star	Micr. for Plumb-line on Dot	Mean of Micr. for Plumb-line on Dot	Star's Apparent Zenith Distance	Barom.	Attd.	Upper	Lower
5915	17 24 36·0	13 19·4	9 25·2	13 10·5	13 19·45	S. 2 40—3 28·25	29·400	72·0	75·6	70·4
7992	22 50 39·5	10 14·5	11 17·5	10 14·5	10 14·5	N. 3 55—1 3·0	29·291	66·7	69·5	68·0
1739	5 27 19·0	10 21·9	10 21·9	10 21·9	10 21·9	S. 1 15—1 14·0	29·205	63·3	63·2	64·2
1802	5 35 39·0	10 24·3	8 7·25	10 24·4	10 24·35	N. 0 10+2 17·1				
1878	5 47 6·5	11 8·9	1 1·6	11 8·9	11 8·9	S. 1 30—2 7·1				
1922	5 53 39·0	11 9·8	15 4·4	11 9·8	11 9·8	S. 0 55+3 28·6				
1982	6 3 49·5	12 26·2	9 6·9	12 26·1	12 26·1	S. 2 55—3 19·2				
2051	6 16 0·0	12 26·0	10 32·8	12 26·0	12 26·0	N. 4 20+1 27·2				
2109	6 24 3·5	12 24·3	10 1·1	12 24·2	12 24·25	N. 1 50+3 8·15				
2246	6 45 41·2	12 31·8	11 4·1	12 31·8	12 31·8	N. 2 0+1 27·7			64·2	63·8
2293	6 54 11·0	12 4·7	12 3·4	12 4·9	12 4·8	N. 5 35+0 1·4				
2414	7 13 16·5	11 9·2	8 3·75	11 9·2	11 9·2	S. 2 30—3 5·45				
2458	7 19 36·0	9 33·2	8 27·6	9 33·1	9 33·15	N. 5 20+1 5·55				
2528	7 33 52·2	11 7·5	9 1·6	11 7·4	11 7·45	S. 3 20—2 5·85				
2575	7 40 39·5	11 26·2	8 20·4	11 26·3	11 26·3	S. 3 15—3 5·9				
2580	7 41 20·2		1 2·0	11 26·4	11 26·3	S. 3 15—0 24·3				
2635	7 48 45·5	10 18·9	13 20·75	10 18·9	10 18·9	S. 4 5+3 1·85				
2710	7 59 43·0	10 5·3	17 7·9	10 5·4	10 5·4	S. 5 15—3 21·5				
2795	8 14 22·4	9 21·5	9 8·3	9 21·6	9 21·55	S. 1 50—0 13·25	29·142	62·5	63·6	63·2
2935	8 35 39·5	9 6·1	8 12·2	9 6·1	9 6·1	S. 0 25—0 27·9				
2904	8 39 0·2		12 12·5	9 7·0		N. 1 45—3 5·5				

Dec. 12.—No. 2710.—The time doubtful.
Good definitions. Brisk S.E. wind.

♀ December 13, 1844.—Face of Sector West—(continued).

Number of B.A.C.	Time by Chronometer.	Micr. for Plumb-line on Dot.	Micr. for Observation of Star.	Micr. for Plumb-line on Dot.	Mean of Micr. for Plumb-line on Dot.	Star's Apparent Zenith Distance.	Barom.	Thermometers. Attd.	Upper.	Lower.
	h m s	rev. pts.	rev. pts.	rev. pts.	rev. pts.	° ′ rev. pts.	in.			
3130	9 5 1·0	9 10·5	5 33·8	9 10·7	9 10·6	N. 4 35+3 10·8				
3163	9 11 6·7	10 0·1	8 31·95	10 0·2	10 0·15	S. 3 35—1 2·2				
3257	9 26 11·0	8 26·9	10 30·45	8 26·9	8 26·9	S. 5 25+2 3·55				

☉ December 15, 1844.—Face of Sector East.

Number of B.A.C.	Time by Chronometer.	Micr. for Plumb-line on Dot.	Micr. for Observation of Star.	Micr. for Plumb-line on Dot.	Mean of Micr. for Plumb-line on Dot.	Star's Apparent Zenith Distance.	Barom.	Thermometers. Attd.	Upper.	Lower.
1739	5 27 20·5	10 4·1	11 21·75	10 3·8	10 3·95	S. 1 15—1 17·8	29·312	56·3	57·2	57·2
1802	5 35 49·0	9 10·9	11 33·5	9 10·8	9 10·85	N. 0 10+2 22·65				
1878	5 47 16·5	9 12·5	11 25·45	9 12·5	9 12·5	S. 1 30—2 12·95				
1922	5 53 49·5	7 23·5	3 32·3	7 23·5	7 23·5	S. 0 55+3 25·2				
1982	6 3 59·5	9 12·6	13 3·7	9 12·6	9 12·6	S. 2 55—3 25·1				
2051	6 16 8·7	10 13·5	12 14·0	10 13·5	10 13·5	N. 4 20+2 0·5	29·304	56·3	57·0	57·1
2109	6 24 12·3	9 26·1	13 6·5	9 26·2	9 26·15	N. 1 50+3 14·35				
2246	6 45 50·0	9 8·8	11 6·2	9 8·8	9 8·8	N. 2 0+1 31·4				
2293	6 54 19·0	10 3·6	10 11·95	10 3·7	10 3·65	N. 5 35+0 8·3				
2414	7 13 27·2	10 27·9	14 5·4	10 27·9	10 27·9	S. 2 30—3 11·5				
2458	7 19 45·2	11 18·8	12 31·05	11 18·9	11 18·85	N. 5 20+1 12·2				
2580	7 41 31·4	10 32·4	20 30·3	19 32·4	19 32·4	S. 3 15—0 31·9				
2635	7 48 57·0	10 23·0	7 27·3	10 23·0	10 23·0	S. 4 5+2 29·7				
2710	7 59 55·7	10 33·3	14 28·85	10 33·4	10 33·35	S. 5 15+3 29·5	29·290	57·0	57·5	57·2
2795	8 14 32·3	9 28·0	10 13·4	9 28·2	9 28·1	S. 1 50—0 19·3				
4458	13	10 14·2	6 13·7	10 14·2	10 14·2	S. 1 30+4 0·5			59·2	58·6
4086	13 59 21·4	10 9·0	10 12·8	10 9·0	10 9·0	S. 1 15—0 3·8	29·292	59·9	60·7	59·6

☾ December 16, 1844.—Face of Sector East.

Number of B.A.C.	Time by Chronometer.	Micr. for Plumb-line on Dot.	Micr. for Observation of Star.	Micr. for Plumb-line on Dot.	Mean of Micr. for Plumb-line on Dot.	Star's Apparent Zenith Distance.	Barom.	Thermometers. Attd.	Upper.	Lower.
7092	22 50 53.2	11 8·0	10 12·0	11 8·0	11 8·0	N. 3 55—0 30·0	29·233	67·5	69·8	67·5

Face of Sector West.

Number of B.A.C.	Time by Chronometer.	Micr. for Plumb-line on Dot.	Micr. for Observation of Star.	Micr. for Plumb-line on Dot.	Mean of Micr. for Plumb-line on Dot.	Star's Apparent Zenith Distance.	Barom.	Thermometers. Attd.	Upper.	Lower.
1739	5 27 32·0	11 1·0	9 22·5	11 1·0	11 1·0	S. 1 15—1 12·5	29·227	58·1	60·0	59·4
1802	5 35 52·0	10 30·4	8 15·2	10 30·4	10 30·4	N. 0 10+2 15·2				
1878	5 47 19·5	9 25·5	7 19·5	9 25·6	9 25·55	ʀ. 1 30—2 6·05				
1922	5 53 52·2	10 9·5	14 5·2	10 9·3	10 9·4	S. 0 55+3 29·8				
1982	6 4 2·5	11 12·9	7 29·75	11 12·9	11 12·9	S. 2 55—3 17·15				
2051	6 16 12·2	10 19·5	8 27·2	10 19·7	10 19·6	N. 4 20+1 26·4				
2109	6 24 16·0	10 20·0	7 13·8	10 20·0	10 20·0	N. 1 50+3 6·2	29·225	57·7	59·0	59·1
2246	6	9 33·4	8 7·1	9 33·2	9 33·3	N. 2 0+1 26·2				
2293	6 54 23·0	10 10·7	10 9.7	10 10·7	10 10·7	N. 5 35+0 1·0	29·227	57·9	59·2	58·6
2414	7 13 30·2	11 18·8	8 15·4	11 18·4	11 18·6	S. 2 30—3 3·2			59·2	58·8
2710	7 50 58·0	11 14·3	7 27·7	11 14·5	11 14·4	S. 5 15—3 20·7				
2795	8 14 35·5	10 3·8	9 26·4	10 3·9	10 3·85	S. 1 50—0 11·45				
2635	8 35 52·0	10 13·8	9 22·0	10 13·8	10 13·8	S. 0 25—0 25·8				
2964	8 39 12·5		14 4·25	10 31·0		N. 1 45—3 7·25	29·227	58·4	59·5	59·0

♂ December 17, 1844.—Face of Sector West.

Number of B.A.C.	Time by Chronometer.	Micr. for Plumb-line on Dot.	Micr. for Observation of Star.	Micr. for Plumb-line on Dot.	Mean of Micr. for Plumb-line on Dot.	Star's Apparent Zenith Distance.	Barom.	Thermometers. Attd.	Upper.	Lower.
1739	5 27 37·0	10 6·2	8 28·5	10 6.3	10 6·25	S. 1 15—1 11·75	29·554	56·1	57·5	57·0
1802	5 35 56·5	10 24·5	8 9·6	10 24·6	10 24·55	N. 0 10+2 14·95				

Face of Sector East.

Number of B.A.C.	Time by Chronometer.	Micr. for Plumb-line on Dot.	Micr. for Observation of Star.	Micr. for Plumb-line on Dot.	Mean of Micr. for Plumb-line on Dot.	Star's Apparent Zenith Distance.	Barom.	Thermometers. Attd.	Upper.	Lower.
1878	5 47 26·0	12 2·3	14 16·6	12 2·5	12 2·4	S 1 30—2 14·2				
1922	6 53 50·0	11 18·6	7 28·25	11 18·9	11 18·75	S. 0 55+3 24·5				

Dec 13.—Indifferent definitions. Thin fog towards morning.
After the observations were made, the sector was shifted a little in Azimuth (Face West) in the order of reckoning Azimuths, viz: from S. to N. through West.
Dec. 14.—Clouded night. Heavy rain towards morning.
Dec. 16.—Clouded between 7 and 8 hours, chronometer time, and a squall, with heavy rain.

♂ DECEMBER 17, 1844.—FACE OF SECTOR EAST—(continued).

Number of B.A.C.	Time by Chronometer.	Micr. for Plumb-line on Dot.	Micr. for Observation of Star.	Micr. for Plumb-line on Dot.	Mean of Micr. for Plumb-line on Dot.	Star's Apparent Zenith Distance.	Barom.	Thermometer. Attd.	Upper.	Lower.
1982	6 4 9·2	12 6·6	15 31·5	12 6·5	12 6·55	S. 2 55—3 24·95				
2051	6	12 16·0	14 16·5	12 16·1	12 16·05	N. 4 20+2 0·45				
2109	6 24 21·5	10 29·0	14 9·6	10 28·9	10 28·95	N. 1 50+3 14·65	29·554	55·9	56·7	56·3
2246	6 45 50·2	11 24·8	13 23·7	11 24·9	11 24·85	N. 2 0+1 32·85				
2293	6 54 29·0	12 20·2	12 28·35	12 20·2	12 20·2	N. 5 35+0 8·15	29·552	55·4	56·7	56·4
2414	7 13 36·3	10 4·2	13 15·85	10 4·5	10 4·35	S. 2 30—3 11·5				
2458	7	10 11·2	11 23·7	10 11·3	10 11·25	N. 5 20+1 12·45				
2528	7 34 12·7	8 12·9	10 24·8	8 12·8	8 12·85	S. 3 20—2 11·95				
2575	7 40 59·5	17 10·1	10 22·5		17 10·2	S. 3 15—3 12·3				
2580	7 41 40·5		18 7·55	17 10·3	17 10·2	S. 3 15—0 31·35				
2635	7 49 6·6	10 16·1	7 20·6	10 16·2	10 16·15	S. 4 5+2 29·55				
2710	8	11 27·6	15 22·75	11 27·8	11 27·7	S. 5 15—3 29·05				
2705	8 14 42·0	10 13·8	10 32·5	10 13·7	10 13·75	S. 1 50—0 18·75				
2935	8 35 58·8	10 17·0	11 15·2	10 17·0	10 17·0	S· 0 25—0 32·2	29·542	55·2	55·6	55·8
2964	8 39 18·8		7 26·3	10 27·4		N. 1 45—3 1·1				
3130	9 5 18·8	10 27·4	14 11·45	10 27·6	10 27·5	N. 4 35+3 17·95				
3163	9 11 26·5	9 18·0	10 27·05	9 17·9	9 17·95	S. 3 35—1 9·1				
3257	9 26 33·0	8 28·3	6 32·3	8 28·4	8 28·35	S. 5 25+1 30·05	29·542	54·7	55·6	55·6
Anon.	9 40 40·2	8 25·1	5 2·9	8 25·1	8 25·1	N. 2 23—3 22·2				
3578	10 22 0·3	10 24·1	9 17·0	10 24·0	10 24·05	N. 4 5—1 7·05			55·0	55·2

FACE OF SECTOR WEST.

3755	10 51 24·4	9 31·9	13 27·15	9 31·9	9 31·9	S· 1 55+3 29·25	29·542	54·3	55·0	55·3
3926	11 27 17·8	10 1·6	8 6·5	10 1·6	10 1·6	N. 3 20+1 2·9			55·5	55·2
4015	11 48 0·0	10 16·3	13 11·7	10 16·2	10 16·25	N. 1 20—2 29·45			57·0	55·3
4458	13 13 47·5	10 31·0	15 2·9	10 31·0	10 31·0	S. 1 30+4 5·9	29·550	58·1	61·2	57·2

FACE OF SECTOR EAST.

5915	17 25 1·5	11 5·5	15 8·5	11 5·1	11 5·3	S. 2 40—4 3·2	29·585	67·3	72·0	65·5

♂ DECEMBER 18, 1844.—FACE OF SECTOR WEST.

7902	22 51 0·5	10 5·7	11 10·45	10 5·5	10 5·6	N. 3 55—1 4·85	29·540	66·9	69·4	66·4

FACE OF SECTOR EAST.

1739	5 27 43·0	9 21·4	11 5·45	9 21·5	9 21·45	S. 1 15—1 18·0	29·427	59·0	59·8	59·2
1802	5 30 2·8	9 26·0	12 13·8	9 26·0	9 26·0	N. 0 10+2 21·8				

FACE OF SECTOR WEST.

1922	5 54 1·5	10 5·0	14 0·85	10 5·0	10 5·0	S. 0 55+3 29·85	29·422	58·6	59·4	59·5
1982	6 4 10·8	10 23·0	7 5·45	10 23·2	10 23·1	S. 2 55—3 17·65				
2051	6 16 22·0	9 23·4	7 31·0	9 23·3	9 23·35	N. 4 20+1 26·35				
2109	6 24 25·0	9 10·8	6 4·3	9 10·9	9 10·85	N. 1 50+3 6·55			59·5	59·3
2246	6 46 2·5	9 21·8	7 29·1	9 22·0	9 21·9	N. 2 0+1 26·8				
2414	7 13 38·5	9 24·4	6 21·25	9 24·7	9 24·55	S. 2 30—3 3·3				
2458	7 19 58·3	9 14·1	8 10·45	9 13·8	9 13·95	N. 5 20+1 3·5				
2528	7 34 14·5		16 18·5	18 22·5	18 22·5	S. 3 15—3 4·6				
2575	7 41 1·5	9 25·1	6 20·5	9 25·1	9 25·1	S. 3 15—3 4·6				
2580	7 41 42·5		9 25·1		9 25·1	S. 3 15—0 31·?				
2635	7 49 7·5	11 11·0	14 14·9	11 11·0	11 11·0	S. 4 5+3 3·9				
2655	7 53 29·5	11 15·7	10 9·25	11 15·75	11 15·75	N. 4 25+1 0·5				
2710	8 0 5·5	10 17·9	6 32·4	10 17·9	10 17·9	S. 5 15—3 19·5				
2795	8 14 44·0	9 33·2	9 21·9	9 33·0	9 33·1	S. 1 50—0 11·2	29·349	58·3	59·5	59·2
2935	8 36 1·5	10 1·7	9 9·3	10 1·7	10 1·7	S. 0 25—0 26·4				

Dec. 17.—Before commencing the observations, the plumb-line was shortened a little. Calm night. Beautiful definitions.

138   ARC OF THE MERIDIAN.—CAPE OF GOOD HOPE.

♃ DECEMBER 18, 1844.—FACE OF SECTOR WEST—(continued).

Number of B.A.C.	Time by Chronometer.	Micr. for Plumb-line on Dot.	Micr. for Observation of Star.	Micr. for Plumb-line on Dot.	Mean of Micr. for Plumb-line on Dot.	Star's Apparent Zenith Distance.	Barom.	Attd.	Upper.	Lower.
	b m s	rev. pts.	rev. pts.	rev. pts.	rev. pts.	° ' rev. pts.	in.			
2964	8 39 21·5		12 18·4	9 10·9		N. 1 45—3 7·5				
3130	9 5 22·5	9 28·4	6 19·0	9 28·5	9 28·45	N. 4 35+3 9·45				
3163	9 11 29·5	10 6·8	9 5·45	10 6·9	10 6·85	S. 3 35—1 1·4				
3257	9 26 33·0	11 1·4	13 6·75	11 1·4	11 1·4	S. 5 25+2 5·35			59·4	59·4
Anon.	9 40 43·5	9 14·7	13 10·4	9 14·7	9 14·7	N. 2 25—3 20·7	29·310	58·3	59·8	59·4
3403	9 51 24·0	9 29·0	10 24·35	9 29·5	9 29·25	N. 4 0—0 29·1				
Anon.	10 3 30·5	9 29·4	9 13·1	9 29·2	9 29·3	N. 4 0+0 16·2	29·312	57·9	59·4	59·0
3578	10 22 3·8	10 5·0	11 20·75	10 5·0	10 5·0	N. 4 5—1 15·75				
3598	10 24 27·2		7 14·9	11 4·2		N. 4 30+3 23·3			59·0	59·0
3755	10 51 28·5	12 5·6	16 0·75	12 5·8	12 5·7	S. 1 55+3 29·05	29·314	57·7	58·9	58·9
3926	11 27 23·2	12 10·0	10 15·3	12 10·2	12 10·1	N. 3 20+1 28·9	29·316	59·0	59·5	59·0
4458	13 13 52·5	14 16·8	18 22·5	14 17·0	14 16·9	S. 1 30+4 5·6	29·329	62·4	65·2	61·0
4686	13 59 32·5	12 22·6	12 23·05	12 22·6	12 22·6	S. 1 15+0 0·45	29·343	64·2	69·0	62·6
5915	17 25 2·0	13 6·7	9 10·3	13 6·6	13 6·65	S. 2 40—3 30·35	29·351	70·3	76·0	70·4

♄ DECEMBER 19, 1844.—FACE OF SECTOR EAST.

4686	13 59 40·2	11 1·97	11 5·9	11 1·9	11 1·9	S. 1 15—0 4·0	29·337	66·0	69·2	65·6
5915	17 25 9·3	10 33·5	15 4·0	10 33·9	10 33·7	S. 2 40—4 4·3	29·338	71·4	75·0	70·0

♀ DECEMBER 20, 1844.—FACE OF SECTOR EAST.

1739	5 27 52·2	10 22·3	12 5·5	10 22·4	10 22·35	S. 1 15—1 17·15	29·314	62·4	63·4	63·2
1802	5 36 11·8	10 29·4	13 16·5	10 29·5	10 29·45	N. 0 10+2 21·05				
1922	5 54 12·5	10 4·9	6 13·0	10 5·0	10 4·95	S. 0 55+3 25·95				
1982	6 4 22·7	9 28·8	13 18·5	9 28·9	9 28·85	S. 2 55—3 23·65				
2109	6 24 35·2	9 5·2	12 18·0	9 5·4	9 5·3	N. 1 50+3 12·7	29·312	62·1	63·6	62·7
2246	6 46 13·0	8 0·3	9 32·0	8 0·5	8 0·4	N. 2 0+1 31·6	29·300	61·5	63·2	62·6

FACE OF SECTOR WEST.

2414	7 13 47·0	8 25·8	5 23·2	8 25·8	8 25·8	S. 2 30—3 2·6				
2458	7 20 6·7	8 20·0	7 18·4	8 20·0	8 20·0	N. 5 20+1 1·6				

FACE OF SECTOR EAST.

2528	7 34 26·3	10 20·2	12 30·8	10 20·4	10 20·3	S. 3 20—2 10·5	29·300	61·2	62·6	62·2
2575	7 41 23·2	19 18·0	22 28·8		19 18·1	S. 3 15—3 10·7				
2580	7 41 54·5		20 13·5	19 18·2	19 18·1	S. 3 15—0 29·4				
2635	7 49 19·8	13 21·5	10 24·7	13 21·2	13 21·35	S. 4 5+2 30·65				
2655	7 53 39·2	14 5·8	15 18·8	14 5·8	14 5·8	N. 4 25+1 13·0				
2710	8 0 18·5	14 20·1	18 13·25	14 20·2	14 20·15	S. 5 15—3 27·1				

FACE OF SECTOR WEST.

2795	8 14 24·3	14 0·0	13 24·3	14 0·0	14 0·0	S. 1 50—0 9·7	29·264	60·8	62·5	62·0

FACE OF SECTOR EAST.

2964	8 39 31·5		10 13·8	13 15·9		N. 1 45—3 2·1	29·262	60·8	62·5	62·0
3130	9 5 32·5	13 19·8	17 2·0	13 20·0	13 19·9	N. 4 35+3 16·1	29·256	60·8	62·2	61·8
3163	9 11 40·6	13 11·2	14 19·3	13 11·2		S. 3 35—1 8·1				
3257	9 26 46·2	18 15·5	17 18·8	18 15·3	18 15·4	S. 5 25+0 30·6	29·256	60·8	62·2	61·8
Anon.	9 40 54·2	11 20·3	7 31·6	11 21·3	11 20·3	N. 2 25—3 23·2	29·253	60·8	62·3	61·9
3403	9 51 34·2	11 32·4	11 11·05	11 32·5	11 32·45	N. 4 0—0 21·4				
Anon.	10 3 50·5	11 32·4	12 22·1	11 32·4	11 32·4	N. 4 0+0 23·7			62·2	61·8
3578	10 22 14·0	12 19·6	11 11·5	12 20·0	12 19·8	N. 4 5 1 8·3			62·0	61·8

Dec. 18.—No. 5915.—Faint image : difficult.
20.—When reversing at 8h 16m per chronometer, the spindle was found inclined 2"·4.
Anon. 10h 3m.—The seconds of transit uncertain.
A splendid calm night. Excellent definition.

♀ DECEMBER 20, 1844.—FACE OF SECTOR EAST—(*continued*).

Number of B.A.C.	Time by Chronometer.	Micr. for Plumb-line on Dot.	Micr. for Observation of Star.	Micr. for Plumb-line on Dot.	Mean of Micr. for Plumb-line on Dot.	Star's Apparent Zenith Distance.	Barom.	Thermometers.		
								Attd.	Upper.	Lower.
	h m s	rev. pts.	rev. pts.	rev. pts.	rev. pts.	o ′ rev. pts.	in.			
3598	10 24 37·2		17 33·4	14 3·3		N. 4 30+3 30·1				
3755	10 51 40·2	12 19·6	8 31·0	12 19·5	12 19·55	S. 1 55+3 22·55				
3926	11 27 33·2	12 24·4	14 25·9	12 24·5	12 24·45	N. 3 20+2 1·45				
			FACE OF SECTOR WEST.							
4686	13 59 42·2	11 33·1	12 0·7	11 33·0	11 33·05	S. 1 15+0 1·65	29·268	64·2	65·0	63·7

☉ DECEMBER 22, 1844.—FACE OF SECTOR WEST.

2051	6 16 38·5	10 19·6	8 27·65	10 19·6	10 19·6	N. 4 20+1 25·95	29·489	56·1	56·0	56·3
2458	7 20 15·4	11 20·4	10 18·2	11 20·4	11 20·4	N. 5 20+1 2·2			56·2	56·3
2528	7 34 33·2	20 9·7	18 6·95	20 9·8	20 9·75	S. 3 20—2 2·8	29·486	55·4	56·0	56·3
2575	7 41 20·0	11 12·4	8 8·75		11 12·5	S. 3 15—3 3·75				
2580	7 42 1·5		10 23·9	11 12·6	11 12·5	S. 3 15—0 22·0				
2635	7 49 25·8	10 25·0	13 29·4	10 25·0	10 25·0	S. 4 5+3 4·4				
2655	7 53 47·0	9 21·6	8 16·2	9 21·6	9 21·6	N. 4 25+1 5·4				
2710	8 0 23·5	10 7·9	6 23·5	10 7·9	10 7·9	S. 5 15—3 18·4·				
			FACE OF SECTOR EAST.							
2935	8 36 21·0	10 2·4	10 32·0	10 2·2	10 2·3	S. 0 25—0 29·7	29·453	55·3	56·0	56·3
			FACE OF SECTOR WEST.							
3130	9 5 40·2	9 24·0	6 15·55	9 24·0	9 24·0	N. 4 35+3 8·45				
3163	9 11 46·8	10 6·6	9 6·2	10 6·2	10 6·4	S. 3 35—1 0·2				
3257	9 26 51·7	9 33·9	12 5·4	9 33·9	9 33·9	S. 5 25+2 5·5	29·453	55·2	55·6	56·2
Anon.	9 41 1·5	9 12·9	13 7·95	9 12·9	9 12·9	N. 2 25—3 20·05				
3403	9 51 41·5	19 9·0	20 4·4	19 9·1	19 9·05	N. 4 0+0 29·35				
3578	10 22 21·2	10 11·5	11 27·25	10 11·4	10 11·45	N. 4 5—1 15·8	29·443	55·4	55·5	56·1
3598	10		8 8·6	11 31·9		N. 4 30+3 23·3				
3755	10	12 0·3	16 4·0	12 9·4	12 9·35	S. 1 55+3 28·65		55·4	56·0	

♄ DECEMBER 28, 1844.—FACE OF SECTOR EAST.

1739	5 28 28·3	11 20·9	13 1·2	11 21·0	11 20·95	S. 1 15—1 14·25	29·516	64·4		
2458	7 20 44·0	10 33·9	12 7·7	10 33·9	10 33·9	N. 5 20+1 7·8				
2528	7 35 2·6	8 25·4	10 31·8	8 25·4	8 25·4	S. 3 20—2 6·4				
2575	7 41 49·2	17 22·8	20 29·45	17 22·8	17 22·8	S. 3 15—3 6·65				
2635	7 49 56·0	8 33·9	5 33·2	8 33·9	8 33·9	S. 4 5+3 0·7	29·506	60·8	61·0	61·4
2655	7 54 15·5	10 15·4	11 25·2	10 15·4	10 15·4	N. 4 25+1 9·8				
3130	9 6 8·7	10 12·7	13 25·9	10 12·7	10 12·7	N. 4 35+3 13·2	29·506	60·5	61·8	60·8
3163	9 12 16·5	9 15·9	10 20·2	9 15·9	9 15·9	S. 3 35—1 4·3				
3257	9 27 22·3	8 26·3	6 25·3	8 26·4	8 26·35	S. 5 25+2 1·05				
Anon.	9 41 30·2	10 4·5	6 12·55	10 4·5	10 4·5	N. 2 25—3 25·95				
3403	9 52 10·7	9 4·8	8 14·4	9 4·9	9 4·85	N. 4 0—0 24·45	29·504	60·6	61·4	60·8
Anon.	10 4 26·3	9 5·0	9 26·75	9 5·1	9 5·05	N. 4 0+0 21·7				
3578	10 22 50·2	18 3·0	16 25·75	18 2·8	18 2·9	N. 4 5—1 11·15				
3598	10		13 29·7	10 3·1		N. 4 30+3 26·6	29·504	59·7	61·0	60·4
3755	10 52 16·6	8 14·2	4 22·9	8 14·0	8 14·1	S. 1 55+3 25·2	29·501	59·5	60·3	60·4
3926	11 28 9·3	10 2·4	12 1·1	10 2·6	10 2·5	N. 3 20+1 32·6	29·501	59·4	60·2	60·0
4015	11 47 51·2	9 31·8	7 3·55	9 31·6	9 31·7	N. 1 20—2 28·15	29·548	60·6	62·4	61·4
4458	13 14 40·2	9 20·0	5 16·95	9 19·9	9 19·95	S. 1 30+4 3·0	29·559	60·6	62·4	62·6
4686	14 0 20·0	8 18·8	8 21·0	8 18·8	8 18·8	S. 1 15—0 2·2				

Dec. 21.—The sky covered. Rain.

The observer (Mr. Maclear) went to the Royal Observatory on the 23rd, and returned to the Station on the 28th. The 25th and 26th were clouded, and rain fell.

28.—Excellent definitions.

(DECEMBER 30, 1844.—FACE OF SECTOR EAST.

Number of B.A.C.	Time by Chronometer.	Micr. for Plumb-line on Dot.	Micr. for Observation of Star.	Micr. for Plumb-line on Dot.	Mean of Micr. for Plumb-line on Dot.	Star's Apparent Zenith Distance.	Barom.	Therm. Attd.	Therm. Upper.	Therm. Lower.
	h m s	rev. pts.	rev. pts.	rev. pts.	rev. pts.	° ' rev. pts.	in.			
7992	22 51 56·4	11 19·9	10 24·05	11 19·9	11 19·9	N. 3 55—0 29·85	29·487	71·4	74·0	70·5

FACE OF SECTOR WEST.

Number of B.A.C.	Time by Chronometer.	Micr. for Plumb-line on Dot.	Micr. for Observation of Star.	Micr. for Plumb-line on Dot.	Mean of Micr. for Plumb-line on Dot.	Star's Apparent Zenith Distance.	Barom.	Therm. Attd.	Therm. Upper.	Therm. Lower.
1739	5 28 35·2	10 31·5	9 22·6	10 31·4	10 31·45	S. 1 15—1 8·85	29·450	59·7	61·0	61·0
2528	7 35 9·6	18 20·5	16 20·05	18 20·7	18 20·6	S. 3 20—2 0·55	29·406	59·0	59·7	59·5
2575	7 41 56·5	9 23·3	6 22·6		9 23·4	S. 3 15—3 0·8				59·5
2580	7 42 37·5		9 3·8	9 23·5	9 23·4	S. 3 15—0 19·6				
2635	7 50 2·5	9 27·5	13 0·9	9 27·5	9 27·5	S. 4 5+3 7·4				
2655	7 54 23·5	9 25·7	8 22·7	9 25·9	9 25·8	N. 4 25+1 3·1	29·400	59·0	59·6	59·4
3130	9 6 16·5	10 28·2	7 21·75	10 28·2	10 28·2	N. 4 35+3 6·45	29·386	59·1	59·7	59·4
3163	9 12 23·5	10 29·6	9 32·4	10 29·9	10 29·75	S. 3 35—0 31·35				
3257	9 27 20·3	9 18·4	11 26·1	9 18·6	9 18·5	S. 5 25+2 7·6				
Anon.	9 41 38·5	9 0·0	12 32·0	8 33·8	8 33·9	N. 2 25—3 32·1				
3043	9 52 18·5	19 0·0	19 31·6	18 33·9	18 33·95	N. 4 0—0 31·65	29·384	59·0	59·6	59·7
Anon.	10 4 34·2	19 0·0	18 20·75	19 0·0	19 0·0	N. 4 0+0 13·25				
3578	10 22 58·5	10 1·9	11 20·3	10 1·9	10 1·9	N. 4 5—1 18·4				
3598	10 25 21·5		6 33·7	10 20·9		N. 4 30+3 21·2	29·384	50·0	59·7	59·6
3755	10 52 23·6	10 28·1	14 26·0	10 28·3	10 28·2	S. 1 55+3 31·8				
3926	11 28 17·2	10 14·0	8 20·5	10 13·8	10 13·9	N. 3 20+1 27·4	29·384	58·8	59·5	59·6
4015	11 47 58·8	9 25·0	12 23·0	9 25·0	9 25·0	N. 1 20—2 32·0				
4458	13 14 47·2	10 12·0	14 18·75	10 11·9	10 11·95	S. 1 30+4 6·8	29·400	60·7	61·0	60·4
4686	14 0 27·5	11 3·0	11 4·0	11 3·0	11 3·0	S. 1 15+0 1·0	29·408	61·7	62·5	61·2
5632	16 43 0·3	10 31·7	9 13·65	10 31·7	10 31·7	N. 0 20+1 18·05	29·412	60·7	72·2	66·0
5915	17 25 57·5	11 25·2	7 26·15	11 25·1	11 25·15	S. 2 40—3 33·0	29·412	68·1	73·0	67·5

δ DECEMBER 31, 1844.—FACE OF SECTOR WEST.

Number of B.A.C.	Time by Chronometer.	Micr. for Plumb-line on Dot.	Micr. for Observation of Star.	Micr. for Plumb-line on Dot.	Mean of Micr. for Plumb-line on Dot.	Star's Apparent Zenith Distance.	Barom.	Therm. Attd.	Therm. Upper.	Therm. Lower.
1739	5 28 40·0	11 26·8	10 18·15	11 26·8	11 26·8	S. 1 15—1 8·65	29·365	63·7	65·2	64·8

FACE OF SECTOR EAST.

2655	7	11 26·6	13 2·6	11 26·6	11 26·6	N. 4 25+1 10·0	29·345	64·0	65·2	64·2
3130	9 6 22·5	11 0·0	14 13·8	11 0·0	11 0·0	N. 4 35+3 13·8	29·327	63·7	65·1	64·4
3163	9 12 30·5	10 15·4	11 20·3	10 15·4	10 15·4	S. 3 35—1 4·9				

FACE OF SECTOR WEST.

3257	9	11 1·3	13 9·3	11 1·3	11 1·3	S. 5 25+2 8·0				

FACE OF SECTOR EAST.

Anon.	9 41 44·2	9 32·1	6 5·6	9 32·5	9 32·3	N. 2 25—3 26·7				
3403	9 52 24·6	10 24·6	10 0·3	10 24·7	10 24·7	N. 4 0—0 24·4				
Anon.	10 4 40·2	10 24·8	11 11·5	10 24·8	10 24·8	N. 4 0+0 20·7				
3578	10 23 4·2	19 22·7	18 11·9	19 22·7	19 22·7	N. 4 5—1 10·8				
3598	10		17 13·0	13 20·2		N. 4 30+3 26·8	29·312	63·0	65·0	64·0
3755	10 52 30·4	12 11·6	8 20·3	12 11·6	12 11·6	S. 1 55+3 25·3	29·314	62·8	64·5	63·6
4015	11 48 5·7	10 10·8	7 17·2	10 10·8	10 10·8	N. 1 20—2 27·6	29·316	62·6	63·0	62·4
4458	13 14 53·2	10 15·6	6 11·3	10 15·6	10 15·6	S. 1 30+4 4·3	29·316	63·3	66·0	64·5
5632	16 43 7·2	12 4·0	13 26·2	12 4·0	12 4·0	N. 0 20+1 22·2	29·308	67·3	70·4	68·0
5915	17 26 5·0	9 9·1	13 13·2	9 9·1	9 9·1	S 2 40—4 4·1				
6233	18 16 52·5	9 23·9	8 8·2	9 23·7	9 23·8	S. 0 5+1 15·6	29·310	69·3	72·3	68·9

♀ JANUARY 1, 1845.—FACE OF SECTOR WEST.

7992	22 52 4·2	10 11·4	11 14·1	10 11·2	10 11·3	N. 3 55—1 2·8	29·249	71·8	74·2	72·0

Dec. 29.—Rain.
30.—Nearly calm, and beautiful definitions.
31.—The same.
Jan. 1.—The sky generally clouded.

☿ JANUARY 1, 1845.—FACE OF SECTOR WEST — (continued).

Number of B.A.C.	Time by Chronometer.	Micr. for Plumb-line on Dot.	Micr. for Observation of Star.	Micr. for Plumb-line on Dot.	Mean of Micr. for Plumb-line on Dot.	Star's Apparent Zenith Distance	Barom.	Thermometers. Attd.	Upper.	Lower.
	h m s	rev. pts.	rev. pts.	rev. pts.	rev. pts.	° ' rev pts.	in.			
2655	7 54 33·0	11.32·0	10 30·0	11 32·2	11 32·1	N. 4 25+1 2·1	29·288	62·6	63·9	63·2
3130	9	10 3·0	6 31·6	10 3·0	10 3·0	N. 4 35+3 5·4			63·6	63·1
3578	10 23 7·0	14 11·6	15 30·55	14 11·6	14 11·6	N. 4 5—1 18·95				
3598	10 25 30·8		9 13·5	12 32·4		N. 4 30+3 18·9	29·288	62·6	63·6	63·2

♀ JANUARY 3, 1845.— FACE OF SECTOR EAST.

2528	7 35 30·2	11 11·5	13 17·0	11 11·6	11 11·55	S. 2 20—2 5·45	29·489	54·7	55·1	55·3

☉ JANUARY 5, 1845.—FACE OF SECTOR EAST.

2655	7 54 53·0	9 26·5	11 2·0	9 28·5	9 28·5	N. 4 25+1 7·5	29·369	59·5	60·6	60·4
3180	9 6 46·0	9 27·1	13 3·7	9 27·0	9 27·05	N. 4 35+3 10·65	29·367	59·2	60·6	60·4

FACE OF SECTOR WEST.

Anon.	9 42	10 18·8	14 18·3	10 18·9	10 18·85	N. 2 25—3 33·45				
3403	9 52 46·7	21 4·8	22 4·85	21 5·0	21 4·9	N. 4 0—0 33·95				
Anon.	10 5 2·6	21 5·2	20 27·5	21 5·4	21 5·3	N. 4 0+0 11·8				
3578	10 23 25·5	12 7·9	13 27·9	12 8·0	12 7·95	N. 4 5—1 19·95				
3598	10 25 49·0		7 12.1	10 31.1		N. 4 30+3 19·0	29·355	59·0	60·0	59·6
3755	10 52 50·5	9 21·3	13 20·4	9 21·3	9 21·3	S. 1 55+3 33·1			60·3	59·8
3926	11 28 45·5	9 28·5	8 2·8	9 28·5	9 28·5	N. 3 20+1 25·7			60·4	59·5
4015	11 48 26·5	10 30·4	13 30·65	10 30·7	10 30·55	N. 1 20—3 0·1	29·339	58·8	60·0	59·4
4458	13 15 14·0	10 12·9	14 19·55	10 12·9	10 12·9	S. 1 30+4 6·65	29·344	59·9	60·2	59·6
5915	17	11 18·7	7 19·7	11 18·5	11 18·6	S. 2 40—3 32·9	29·371	66·2	70·5	66·0
6233	18	10 22·6	12 7·7	10 22.5	10 22·55	S. 0 5+1 19·15	29·373	67·1	71·6	67·1

♃ JANUARY 9, 1845.—FACE OF SECTOR EAST.

Anon.	9 42 25·2	8 19·5	4 24·2	8 19.8	8 19·65	N. 2 25—3 29·45	29·495	60·8	62·2	61·6
3403	9 53 4·2	10 11·2	9 17·65	10 11·2	10 11·2	N. 4 0—0 27·55				
3578	10 23 44·5	19 8·8	19 8·8	19 8·8	19 8·8	N. 4 5—1 13·9				
3598	10 26 8·2		18 21·9	14 31·65		N. 4 30+3 24·25	29·497	60·6	62·0	61·2
3755	10 53 11·0	9 32.9	6 5·1	9 32·9	9 32·9	S. 1 55+3 27·8				
3926	11 29 4·0	11 32·4	13 29·6	11 32·4	11 32·4	N. 3 20+1 31·2	29·501	60·6	61·8	61·1
4202	12 23 49·2	11 11·9	12 0·2	11 12·0	11 11·95	N. 3 50—0 22·25	29·502	60·6	60·6	60·6
4458	13 15 34·3	9 32·5	5 26·65	9 32·4	9 32·45	S. 1 30+4 3·8	29·504	61·0	61·9	61·0
5632	16 43 48·2	10 22·8	12 9·7	10 22·6	10 22·7	N. 0 20+1 21·0	29·528	67·3	69·4	66·5
5915	17 26 45·4	9 29·4	14 0·9	9 29·4	9 29·4	S. 2 40—4 5·5	29·538	68·0	70·0	67·5
6233	18 17 33·5	9 15·7	8 1·3	9 15·9	9 15·8	S. 0 5+1 14·5			72·0	68·6

♀ JANUARY 10, 1845.—FACE OF SECTOR WEST.

Anon.	9 42 28·0	10 25·2	14 27·95	10 25·0	10 25·1	N. 2 25—4 2·85	29·390	60·8	62·0	61·6
3403	9 53 8·5	19 23·0	20 25·0	19 23·1	19 23·05	N. 4 0—1 1·95				
Anon.	10 5 23·0	19 23·1	19 12·6	19 22·9	19 23·0	N. 4 0+0 10·4				
3598	10 26 11·8		6 33·6	10 17·6		N. 4 30+3 18·0			62·0	61·4
3755	10 53 12·7	10 24·7	14 26·7	11 4·0	10 24·75	S. 1 55+4 1·95	29·363	60·8	62·0	61·4
3926	11 29 7·5	11 4·0	9 15·3	11 4·0	11 4·0	N. 3 20+1 22·7			61·9	61·4
4015	11 48 51·0	9 30·0	12 32·5	9 30·0	9 30·0	N. 1 20—3 2·5			61·6	61·2
4202	12 23 52.0	10 33·7	10 19·1	10 33·7	10 33·7	S. 3 50—0 14·6	29·378	60·8	61·7	61·2

The sky either clouded or rain falling on the 2nd, 3rd, 4th, and part of the 5th.
Jan. 5.—Anon. 9ʰ 42ᵐ.—The line was not adjusted over upper dot. A correction has been applied.
Good definitions. Zenith at times covered.
10.—No. 4015.— The chronometer time doubtful.
Good definitions.

♀ JANUARY 10, 1845.—FACE OF SECTOR WEST—(continued.)

Number of B A.C.	Time by Chronometer	Micr. for Plumb-line on Dot.	Micr. for Observation of Star.	Micr. for Plumb-line on Dot.	Mean of Micr. for Plumb-line on Dot.	Star's Apparent Zenith Distance.	Barom.	Thermometers. Attd.	Upper.	Lower.
	h m s	rev. pts.	rev. pts.	rev. pts.	rev. pts.	o ' rev. pts.	in.			
4458	13 15 37.0	10 22.9	14 32.6	10 23.1	10 23.0	S. 1 30+4 9.6			62.3	61.6
5632	16 43 51.0	11 9.2	9 25.5	11 9.0	11 9.1	N. 0 20+1 17.6	29.308	65.5	70.0	65.0
5915	17 26 46.7	11 7.4	7 7.8	11 7.6	11 7.5	S. 2 40-3 33.7	29.410	67.6	71.2	66.4

♄ JANUARY 11, 1845.—FACE OF SECTOR EAST.

Number of B A.C.	Time by Chronometer	Micr. for Plumb-line on Dot.	Micr. for Observation of Star.	Micr. for Plumb-line on Dot.	Mean of Micr. for Plumb-line on Dot.	Star's Apparent Zenith Distance.	Barom.	Attd.	Upper.	Lower.
7092	22 52 50.5	12 11.5	11 15.7	12 11.3	12 11.4	N. 3 55-0 29.7	29.428	73.9	80.0	73.8
Anon.	9 42 34.7	12 9.8	8 13.95	12 10.2	12 10.0	N. 2 25-3 30.05	29.408	62.8	64.0	63.5
3403	9 53 13.4	10 13.7	9 20.1	10 13.7	10 13.7	N. 4 0-0 27.6				
Anon.	10 5 30.3	10 13.7	10 31.0	10 13.7	10 13.7	N. 4 0+0 17.3			64.0	63.6
3578	10 23 58.5	19 11.3	17 31.4	19 11.4	19 11.35	N. 4 5-1 13.95	29.408	63.0		
3598	10 26 17.2		21 0.2	17 10.3		N. 4 30+3 23.9			63.9	63.5
3755	10 53 21.2	11 6.3	7 11.8	11 6.4	11 6.35	S. 1 55+3 28.55	29.406	62.8	63.9	63.4
3926	11 29 12.5	10 9.2	12 6.5	10 9.2	10 9.2	N. 3 20+1 31.3	29.410	62.6	63.9	63.4
4015	11 48 55.6	9 21.7	6 25.95	9 21.7	9 21.7	N. 1 20-2 29.75	29.411	62.6	63.9	63.4
4202	12 24 0.4	8 29.8	9 18.5	8 29.8	8 29.8	S. 3 50-0 22.7	29.414	62.6	63.6	63.4
4458	13 15 44.3	10 17.8	6 14.5	10 17.9	10 17.85	S. 1 30+4 3.35	29.415	62.8	64.0	63.3
5632	16 43 58.2	11 2.4	12 24.2	11 2.2	11 2.3	N. 0 20+1 21.9	29.438	67.3	71.8	67.0
5915	17 26 55.8	11 11.4	15 15.7	11 11.4	11 11.4	S. 2 40-4 4.3	29.449	68.7	73.6	69.0
6233	18 17 42.7	11 27.2	10 11.8	11 27.2	11 27.2	S. 0 5+1 15.4	29.451	70.7	75.5	70.5

☉ JANUARY 12, 1845.—FACE OF SECTOR WEST.

Number of B A.C.	Time by Chronometer	Micr. for Plumb-line on Dot.	Micr. for Observation of Star.	Micr. for Plumb-line on Dot.	Mean of Micr. for Plumb-line on Dot.	Star's Apparent Zenith Distance.	Barom.	Attd.	Upper.	Lower.
Anon.	9 42 35.3	10 16.2	14 18.0	10 16.2	10 16.2	N. 2 25-4 1.8	29.361	64.6	65.2	65.0
3403	9 53 16.6	19 6.2	20 8.3	19 6.2	19 6.2	N. 4 0-1 2.1				
Anon.	10 5	10 6.2	18 30.7	19 6.4	19 6.3	N. 4 0+0 9.6			65.2	64.9
3598	10 26 20.2	12 0.2	8 17.8	12 0.4	12 0.3	N. 4 30+3 16.5	29.355	64.4	65.2	64.8
3755	10 53 22.8	11 8.8	15 10.45	11 8.9	11 8.85	S. 1 55+4 1.6				
3926	11 29 15.8	10 13.0	8 24.5	10 13.2	10 13.1	N. 3 20+1 22.6	29.342	63.7	64.7	64.3
4015	11 48 57.8	9 10.1	12 12.7	9 10.1	9 10.1	N. 3 20-3 2.6	29.335	63.5	64.2	64.2
4202	12	9 27.1	9 12.5	9 27.1	9 27.1	S. 3 50-0 14.6	29.335	63.5	63.8	63.8
4458	13 15 46.2	9 20.7	13 30.0	9 20.7	9 20.7	S. 1 30+4 9.3	29.335	63.5	64.5	64.1
5632	16 43 59.2	10 18.4	9 1.2	10 18.4	10 18.4	N. 0 20+1 17.2	29.384	68.7	74.6	68.2
5915	17 26 56.2	10 26.7	6 29.3	10 26.7	10 26.7	S. 2 40-3 31.4	29.390	70.5	76.0	70.0
6233	18 17 44.5	10 13.0	11 32.1	10 12.6	10 12.8	S. 0 5+1 19.3	29.402	72.1	76.2	71.2

☿ JANUARY 13, 1845.—FACE OF SECTOR WEST.

Number of B A.C.	Time by Chronometer	Micr. for Plumb-line on Dot.	Micr. for Observation of Star.	Micr. for Plumb-line on Dot.	Mean of Micr. for Plumb-line on Dot.	Star's Apparent Zenith Distance.	Barom.	Attd.	Upper.	Lower.
7092	22 52 57.5	10 7.5	11 9.75	10 7.4	10 7.45	N. 3 55-1 2.3	29.428	73.4	75.8	73.8

♂ JANUARY 14, 1845.—FACE OF SECTOR EAST.

Number of B A.C.	Time by Chronometer	Micr. for Plumb-line on Dot.	Micr. for Observation of Star.	Micr. for Plumb-line on Dot.	Mean of Micr. for Plumb-line on Dot.	Star's Apparent Zenith Distance.	Barom.	Attd.	Upper.	Lower.
3403	9 53 27.2	9 24.5	8 29.4	9 24.5	9 24.5	N. 4 0-0 29.1	29.455	60.4	60.3	60.4
3598	10 26 30.2	9 9.8	12 33.3	9 9.8	9 9.8	N. 4 30+3 23.5	29.457	60.1	60.3	60.2
3755	10 53 34.0	9 17.5	5 22.4	9 17.5	9 17.5	S. 1 55+3 20.4	29.461	60.1	60.4	60.2
3926	11 20 25.8	9 23.0	11 20.0	9 23.0	9 23.0	N. 3 20+1 31.0			60.0	50.8
4015	11	10 4.6	7 9.3	10 4.6	10 4.6	N. 1 20-2 29.3	29.461	59.1	60.1	59.8

☿ JANUARY 15, 1845.—FACE OF SECTOR EAST.

Number of B.A.C.	Time by Chronometer.	Micr. for Plumb-line on Dot.	Micr. for Observation of Star.	Micr. for Plumb-line on Dot.	Mean of Micr. for Plumb-line on Dot.	Star's Apparent Zenith Distance.	Barom.	Thermometers.		
	h m s	rev. pts.	rev. pts.	rev. pts.	rev. pts.	° ′ rev. pts.	in.	Attd.	Upper.	Lower.
7992	22 53 6·2	11 30·1	11 0·7	11 30·1	11 30·1	N. 3 55−0 29·4	29·534	69·6	74·5	70·0
Anon.	9 42 50·7	10 1·1	6 2·7	10 1·1	10 1·1	N. 2 25−3 32·4	29·379	60·8	61·6	61·0
Anon.	10 5 46·5	9 31·8	10 11·9	9 31·8	9 31·8	N. 4 0+0 14·1	29·351	60·6	61·4	61·0
3598	10 26 33·4	9 32·9	13 22·1	9 32·9	9 32·9	N. 4 30+3 23·2			61·2	61·0
3755	10 53 38·5	9 6·1	5 10·5	9 6·1	9 6·1	S. 1 55+3 29·6	29·333	59·9	61·0	60·8
3926	11 29 29·5	9 19·6	11 15·5	9 19·6	9 19·6	N. 3 20+1 29·9				

FACE OF SECTOR WEST.

| 4015 | 11 49 10·3 | 9 6·2 | 12 10·0 | 9 6·2 | 9 6·2 | N. 1 20−3 3·8 | 29·319 | 59·9 | 60·5 | 60·5 |

FACE OF SECTOR EAST.

4202	12 24 17·7	8 33·4	9 20·9	8 33·5	8 33·45	S. 3 50−0 21·45	29·319	59·7	60·4	60·5
5632	16 44 15·2	9 20·8	11 6·5	9 20·6	9 20·7	N. 0 20+1 19·8	29·339	65·1	68·0	64·4
5915	17 27 13·2	9 6·2	13 13·4	9 8·0	9 8·1	S. 2 40−4 5·3				
6233	18 17 0·2	9 22·1	8 7·2	9 22·0	9 22·05	S. 0 5+1 14·85	29·367	72·1	74·0	69·2

♃ JANUARY 16, 1845 —FACE OF SECTOR WEST.

| 5632 | 16 44 16·5 | 10 29·4 | 9 12·2 | 10 29·4 | 10 29·4 | N. 0 20+1 17·2 | 29·311 | 69·6 | 73·5 | 70·9 |

The weather at this station being very uncertain with little prospect of improvement, while pressing matters of more importance than giving to each star an equal number of observations demand attention elsewhere, the sector was in part dismantled in the night of the 17th, and left in charge. On the 21st it was carried over the adjoining hills to an ox wagon, by a party of marines, and on the 23rd it was erected in the centre room of the Royal Observatory.

Jan. 15.—Anon. 10h 5m.—Observation uncertain. Faint image.
16.—Few observations could be made for some days, owing to clouds.

UNREDUCED OBSERVATIONS

MADE WITH

BRADLEY'S ZENITH SECTOR

AT

THE ROYAL OBSERVATORY, NEAR CAPE TOWN:

FROM

JANUARY TO JUNE, 1845.

♀ JANUARY 24, 1845.—FACE OF SECTOR EAST.

Number of B.A.C.	Time by Chronometer.	Micr. for Plumb-line on Dot.	Micr. for Observation of Star.	Micr. for Plumb-line on Dot.	Mean of Micr. for Plumb-line on Dot.	Star's Apparent Zenith Distance.	Barom.	Attd.	Lower.	Out.
	h m s	rev. pts.	rev. pts.	rev. pts.	rev. pts.	° ' rev. pts.	in.			
1739	5 26 0·0	12 23·9	13 27·9	12 23·7	12 23·8	S. 1 40—1 4·1	30·080	67·2	68·0	
1802	5 34 17·2	7 16·2	9 23·4	7 16·0	7 16·1	S. 0 15—2 7·3				
1878	5 45 47·3	10 10·4	12 8·1	10 10·0	10 10·2	S. 1 55—1 31·9				
1922	5 52 19·2	10 14·6	6 10·3	10 14·4	10 14·5	S. 1 20+4 4·2				
1982	6 2 33·4	10 12·8	13 23·95	10 12·8	10 12·8	S. 3 20—3 11·15			68·0	
2109	6 22 37·7	10 19·0	13 18·6	10 18·9	10 18·95	N. 1 25+2 33·65				
2293	6 52 38·6	11 22·2	11 14·3	11 22·2	11 22·2	N. 5 10—0 7·9				
2414	7 12 0·2	9 10·4	12 4·5	9 10·4	9 10·4	S. 2 55—2 28·1			67·5	
2458	7 18 5·2	9 32·1	10 27·8	9 32·1	9 32·1	N. 4 55+0 29·7				
2528	7 32 37·5	9 27·8	11 23·5	9 28·2	9 28·0	S. 3 45—1 29·5				
2575	7 39 25·0	18 26·1	21 21·8		18 26·1	S. 3 40—2 29·7				
2580	7 40 5·8		19 6·0	18 26·1	18 26·1	S. 3 40—0 13·9				
2635	7 47 33·3	10 26·6	7 14·4	10 26·8	10 26·7	S. 4 30+3 12·3				
2655	7 51 37·6	11 7·3	12 6·2	11 7·5	11 7·4	N. 4 0+0 32·8				
2710	7 58 33·6	9 9·0	12 20·7	9 9·0	9 9·0	S. 2 55—2 28·1				
2795	8 13 4·2	9 29·5	9 30·7	9 29·4	9 29·45	S. 2 15—0 1·25	30·073	66·5	67·2	
2935	8 34 18·7	9 22·5	10 3·95	9 22·9	9 22·7	S. 0 50—0 15·25				
2964	8 37 34·7		6 12·6	9 30·1		N. 1 20—3 17·5	30·073	66·5	67·2	

♄ JANUARY 25, 1845.—FACE OF SECTOR WEST.

Number of B.A.C.	Time by Chronometer.	Micr. for Plumb-line on Dot.	Micr. for Observation of Star.	Micr. for Plumb-line on Dot.	Mean of Micr. for Plumb-line on Dot.	Star's Apparent Zenith Distance.	Barom.	Attd.	Lower.	Out.
7992	22 49 4·4	6 14·4	7 16·6	6 14·4	6 14·4	N. 3 30—1 2·2	30·003	69·2	69·4	
1739	5 25 53·2	10 23·9	9 23·1	10 23·8	10 23·85	S. 1 40—1 0·75	30·020	68·8	68·0	
1802	5 34 10·0	10 2·5	7 32·6	10 2·7	10 2·6	S. 0 15—2 4·0				
1878	5	9 16·4	9 16·3	9 16·35		S. 1 55—1 26·85				
1922	5 52 12·0	10 13·9	14 22·0	10 13·9	10 13·9	S. 1 20+4 8·1	30·028	68·5	67·6	
1982	6 2 27·2	11 21·5	8 16·4	11 21·5	11 21·5	S. 3 20—3 5·1				
2051	6 14 21·3	9 27·4	8 13·9	9 27·4	9 27·4	N. 3 55+1 13·5				
2109	6 22 29·5	10 0·6	7 4·9	10 0·7	10 0·65	S. 1 25+2 29·75	30·038	68·0	67·5	
2246	6 44 7·2	10 11·1	8 30·2	10 10·9	10 11·0	N. 1 35+1 14·8				
2293	6 52 29·2	11 7·6	11 20·3	11 7·8	11 7·5	N. 5 10—0 12·8			67·0	
2414	7	11 9·1	8 20·9	11 9·3	11 9·2	S. 2 55—2 22·3				
2458	7 17 55·2	10 7·8	9 15·4	10 7·4	10 7·6	N. 4 55+0 26·2	30·043	67·0	66·8	58·0
2528	7		17 16·9	19 6·7		S. 3 45—1 23·8				
2575	7 39 18·5	10 9·0	7 18·4		10 9·0	S. 3 40—2 24·6				
2580	7 39 59·3		10 0·0	10 9·0	10 9·0	S. 3 40—0 9·0				
2635	7 47 26·2	11 22·9	15 3·9	11 22·7	11 22·8	S. 4 30+3 15·1				
2655	7	11 11·6	10 18·4	11 11·7	11 11·65	N. 4 0+0 27·25				
2710	7 58 27·5	10 4·1	6 33·15	10 4·1	10 4·1	S. 5 40—3 4·95	30·045	67·0	66·6	58·6
2795	8 12 57·0	9 16·5	9 17·9	9 16·5	9 16·5	S. 2 15+0 1·4				
2935	8	9 13·1	9 1·0	9 13·1	9 13·1	S. 0 50—0 12·1				
2964	8 37 26·5		14 17·3	10 30·1		N. 1 20—3 21·2	30·038	67·0	66·3	58·5
5632	16 40 11·7	11 3·1	9 22·3	11 3·1	11 3·1	S. 0 5—1 14·8	30·054	66·5	60·4	64·0
5915	17 23 15·2	11 12·1	7 16·4	11 12·2	11 12·15	S. 3 5—3 29·75	30·062	68·0	66·8	66·4
6233	18 13 56·8	10 33·2	12 20·3	10 33·1	10 33·15	S. 0 30+1 21·15			67·2	

⊙ JANUARY 26, 1845.—FACE OF SECTOR EAST.

Number of B.A.C.	Time by Chronometer.	Micr. for Plumb-line on Dot.	Micr. for Observation of Star.	Micr. for Plumb-line on Dot.	Mean of Micr. for Plumb-line on Dot.	Star's Apparent Zenith Distance.	Barom.	Attd.	Lower.	Out.
5632	16 40 9·4	11 6·0	12 23·9	11 6·0	11 6·0	S. 0 5—1 17·9	30·086	68·2		67·2
5915	17 23 12·2	11 21·0	15 19·8	11 20·8	11 20·9	S. 3 5—3 32·9			67·9	67·8
6233	18 13 54·6	11 19·8	10 1·35	11 19·9	11 19·85	S. 0 30+1 18·5			68·2	70·2

Jan. 24 and 25.—Indifferent definitions.

☾ JANUARY 27, 1845.—FACE OF SECTOR EAST.

Number of B.A.C.	Time by Chronometer.	Micr. for Plumb-line on Dot.	Micr. for Observation of Star.	Micr. for Plumb-line on Dot.	Mean of Micr. for Plumb-line on Dot.	Star's Apparent Zenith Distance.	Barom.	Thermometers. Attd.	Lower.	Out.
	h m s	rev. pts.	rev. pts.	rev. pts.	rev. pts.	° ' rev. pts	in.			
1739	5 25 44·2	11 29·5	12 33·2	11 29·5	11 29·5	S. 1 40—1 3·7	30·018	68·0	67·8	62·2
1802	5 34 1·2	11 14·1	13 21·4	11 14·2	11 14·15	S. 0 15—2 7·25				
1878	5 45 32·2	10 18·4	12 16·25	10 18·5	10 18·45	S. 1 55—1 31·8				
1922	5 52 4·0	9 8·7	5 3·0	9 8·7	9 8·7	S. 1 20+4 5·7				
1982	6 2 17·8	9 27·3	13 2·6	9 27·3	9 27·3	S. 3 20—3 9·3				
2051	6 14 14·0	10 11·9	11 31·45	10 11·9	10 11·9	N. 3 55+1 19·55	30·021	68·0	67·6	62·5
2109	6 22 22·2	10 14·1	13 12·5	10 14·3	10 14·2	N. 1 25+2 32·3				
2246	6 43 59·4	10 11·7	11 29·0	10 11·5	10 11·6	N. 1 35+1 17·4				
2293	6 52 22·5	11 29·8	11 21·2	11 20·8	11 20·8	N. 5 10—0 8·6				
2414	7 11 44·6	11 25·9	14 19·3	11 25·8	11 25·85	S. 2 55—2 27·45	30·005	67·5	67·5	62·4
2458	7 17 48.8	12 13·3	13 9·35	12 13·1	12 13·2	N. 4 55+0 30·15				
2528	7 32 22·6	9 6·3	11 0·95	9 5·9	9 6·1	S. 3 45—1 28·85				
2575	7 39 9·5	18 3·0	20 32·7	18 2·95	18 2·95	S. 3 40—2 29·75				
2580	7 39 50·2		18 15·7	18 2·9	18 2·95	S. 3 40—0 12·75				
2635	7 47 17·8	10 19·8	7 5·5	10 19·6	10 19·7	S. 4 30+3 14·2				
2655	7 51 20·5	10 25·9	11 23·3	10 25·7	10 25·8	N. 4 0+0 31·5				
2710	7 58 18·8	8 26·9	12 1·8	8 26·7	8 26·8	S. 5 40—3 9·0				
2795	8 12 48.5	9 11·7	9 12·0	9 11·7	9 11·7	S. 2 15—0 0·3	30·014	67·4	67·2	62·5
2935	8 34 3·2	9 16·0	9 29·8	9 16·2	9 16·1	S. 0 50—0 13·7				
2964	8 37 19·2		6 16·0	10 0·3		N. 1 20—3 18·3	30·007	67·5	67·1	62·6
5632	16 40 3·7	9 29·1	11 12·4	9 20·0	9 29·05	S. 0 5—1 17·35			67·0	
5915	17 23 6·2	9 15·5	13 16·05	9 15·3	9 15·4	S. 3 5—4 0·65	30·010	67·5	67·2	62·5
6233	18 13 49·3	9 24·2	8 5·6	9 24·3	9 24·25	S. 0 30+1 18·65			67·8	

♂ JANUARY 28, 1845.—FACE OF SECTOR EAST.

Number of B.A.C.	Time by Chronometer.	Micr. for Plumb-line on Dot.	Micr. for Observation of Star.	Micr. for Plumb-line on Dot.	Mean of Micr.	Star's Apparent Zenith Distance.	Barom.	Attd.	Lower.	Out.
7992	22 48 52·0	11 11·6	10 13·0	11 11·6	11 11·6	N. 3 30—0 32·6	29·983	69·5	70·0	79·6

FACE OF SECTOR WEST.

Number of B.A.C.	Time by Chronometer.	Micr. for Plumb-line on Dot.	Micr. for Observation of Star.	Micr. for Plumb-line on Dot.	Mean of Micr.	Star's Apparent Zenith Distance.	Barom.	Attd.	Lower.	Out.
1739	5	10 13·4	9 13·9	10 13·6	10 13·5	S. 1 40—0 33·6	30·033	69·6	69·8	67·0
1802	5 33 54·8	10 10·3	8 7·0	10 10·3	10 10·3	S. 0 15—2 2·7			70·0	
1878	5 45 25·2	10 33·1	9 6·5	10 33·0	10 33·05	S. 1 55—1 26·55				
1922	5 51 57·0	11 4·8	15 14·2	11 4·8	11 4·8	S. 1 20+4 9·4				
1982	6 2 11·8	11 4·6	8 0·0	11 4·8	11 4·7	S. 3 20—3 4·7	30·035	70·0	70·2	66·8
2051	6 14 5·5	10 9·8	8 30·2	10 9·6	10 9·7	N. 3 55+1 13·5				
2109	6 22 14·2	10 12·6	7 18·0	10 12·4	10 12·5	N. 1 25+2 28·5				
2246	6 43 51·5	10 6·4	8 28·5	10 6·4	10 6·4	N. 1 35+1 11·9			70·0	
2293	6 52 13·8	10 22·4	11 1·35	10 22·3	10 22·35	N. 5 10—0 13·0				
2414	7 11 38·5	9 24·3	7 0·4	9 24·5	9 24·4	S. 2 55—2 24·0				
2458	7 17 39·5	9 13·0	8 22·2	9 13·0	9 13·1	N. 4 55+0 24·9	30·035	69·4	69·6	65·2
2528	7 32 16·6	21 19·6	19 29·9	21 19·6	21 19·6	S. 3 45—1 23·7				
2575	7 39 3·5	12 22·0	9 31·2		12 22·05	S. 3 40—2 24·85				
2580	7 39 44·3		12 14·45	12 22·1	12 22·05	S. 3 40—0 7·6				
2635	7 47 11·5	11 33·0	15 17·2	11 33·2	11 33·1	S. 4 30+3 18·1				
2655	7 51 13·2	11 10·5	10 17·6	11 10·3	11 10·4	N. 4 0+0 26·8				
2710	7 58 12·2	11 33·0	8 27·5	11 32·9	11 32·95	S. 5 40—3 5·45				
2795	8 12 41·8	11 20·3	11 22·9	11 20·3	11 20·3	S. 2 15+0 2·6				
2935	8 33 55·6	10 18·1	10 6·6	10 17·9	10 18.0	S. 0 50—0 11·4				
2964	8 37 11·0		13 9·0	9 22·2		N. 1 20—3 20·8	30·030	69·0	69·4	60·5
3130	9 3 5·3	10 16·2	16 17·5	10 16·2	10 16·2	N. 4 15—6 1·3				
3257	9 24 41·0	9 25·6	12 11·0	9 25·6	9 25·6	S. 5 50+2 19·4				
Anon.	9 38 11·7	9 6·8	13 16·4	9 7·0	9 6·9	N. 2 0—4 0·5	30·020	68·5	69·4	62·8
3403	9 49 8·7	9 29·6	11 2·7	9 29·6	9 29·6	N. 3 35—1 7·1				

Jan. 28.—Anon. 9ʰ 38ᵐ.—The seconds of transit doubtful.
Beautiful definitions. Calm.

♀ JANUARY 29, 1845.— FACE OF SECTOR EAST.

Number of B.A.C.	Time by Chronometer.	Micr. for Plumb-line on Dot.	Mier. for Observation of Star.	Micr. for Plumb-line on Dot.	Mean of Mier. for Plumb-line on Dot.	Star's Apparent Zenith Distance.	Barom.	Thermometers.		
								Attd.	Lower.	Out.
	h m s	rev. pts.	rev. pts.	rev. pts.	rev. pts.	° ' rev. pts.	in.			
1739	5 25 35·0	9 17·9	10 20·75	9 17·6	9 17·75	S. 1 40—1 3·0	30·155	67·5	68·0	62·6
1802	5 33 52·2	9 15·5	11 22·1	9 15·4	9 15·45	S. 0 15—2 6·65			67·6	
1878	5 45 22·6	10 1·4	11 32·0	10 1·4	10 1·4	S. 1 55—1 30·6			67·6	
1922	5 51 54·6	9 26·8	5 10·9	9 26·8	9 26·8	S. 1 20+4 6·9				
1982	6 2 9·0	9 12·0	12 19·7	9 12·0	9 12·0	S. 3 20—3 7·7			67·8	
2051	6 14 4·0	10 6·6	11 23·4	10 6·4	10 6·5	N. 3 55+1 16·9			67·6	
2109	6 22 12·2	10 3·9	13 0·25	10 3·7	10 3·8	N. 1 25+2 30·45	30·157	67·5	67·6	62·5
2246	6 43 49·2	10 11·7	11 27·5	10 11·6	10 11·65	N. 1 35+1 15·85				
2293	6 52 12·2	9 29·9	9 20·1	9 29·8	9 29·85	N. 5 10—0 9·75			67·5	
2414	7 11 35·3	8 19·8	11 12·1	8 19·9	8 19·85	S. 2 55—2 26·25				
2458	7 17 38·5	10 11.7	11 6·3	10 11·9	10 11·8	N. 4 55+0 28·5			67·6	
2528	7 32 14·0	20 33·6	22 27·7	20 33·4	20 33·5	S. 3 40—0 12·15				
2575	7 39 0·5	14 24·0	17 17·6		14 24·05	S. 3 40—2 27·55				
2580	7 39 41·5		15 2·2	14 24·1	14 24·05	S. 3 40—0 12·15				
2635	7 47 9·3	10 29·4	7 13·3	10 29·5	10 29·45	S. 4 30+3 16·15				
2655	7 51 11·5	12 2·5	12 33·5	12 2·5	12 2·5	N. 4 0+0 31·0				
2795	8 12 39·5	11 18·8	11 18·0	11 18·8	11 18·8	S. 2 15+0 0·8	30·146	67·0	67·4	62·4
2935	8 33 53·3	10 17·6	10 30·3	10 17·8	10 17·7	S. 0 50—0 12·6				
2964	8 37 7·8		7 3·9	10 23·8		N. 1 20—3 19·9			67·2	
3130	9 3 4·0	10 24·2	13 22·4	10 24·0	10 24·1	N. 4 10+2 32·3			67·2	
3163	9 9 28·5	9 28·6	10 19·3	9 28·6	9 28·6	S. 4 0—0 24·7				
Anon.	9 38 29·7	8 13·7	4 6·65	8 13·8	8 13·75	N. 2 0—4 7·1	30·135	67·0	67·2	61·5
3403	9 49 5·8	9 32·3	8 29·9	9 32·5	9 32·4	N. 1 35—1 2·5				
Anon.	10 1	9 32·3	10 6·4	9 32·4	9 32·35	N. 3 35+0 8·05				
3578	10 19 45·4	10 3·0	8 13·4	10 2·6	10 2·8	N. 3 40—1 23·4				
3598	10 22 8·2		12 31·6	9 16·85		N. 4 5+3 14·75	30·124	66·6	67·0	
3755	10 49 24·5	8 19·4	4 14·9	8 19·6	8 19·6	S. 2 20+4 4·6				
5632	16 39 54·8	8 24·4	10 8·7	8 24·5	8 24·45	S. 0 5—1 18·25	30·130	66·8	66·8	66·2
5015	17 22 57·8	10 15·5	14 16·2	10 15·6	10 15·55	S. 3 5—4 0·65	30·129	66·8	66·8	67·8

♃ JANUARY 30, 1845.—FACE OF SECTOR WEST.

Number of B.A.C.	Time by Chronometer.	Micr. for Plumb-line on Dot.	Mier. for Observation of Star.	Micr. for Plumb-line on Dot.	Mean of Mier. for Plumb-line on Dot.	Star's Apparent Zenith Distance.	Barom.	Attd.	Lower.	Out.
1739	5 25 29·2	11 13·5	10 13·9	11 13·4	11 13·45	S. 1 40—0 33·55	30·058	69·0	68·4	65·1
1802	5 33 46·5	11 18·4	9 13·9	11 18·2	11 18·3	S. 0 15—2 4·4			68·2	
1878	5 45 17·2	11 3·7	9 10·7	11 3·7	11 3·7	S. 1 55—1 27·0				
1922	5 51 48·2	10 33·3	15 8·35	10 33·2	10 33·25	S. 1 20+4 9·1			68·4	
1982	6 2 5·0	11 19·5	8 16·4	11 19·3	11 19·4	S. 3 20—3 3·0				
2051	6 13 56·3	10 30·4	9 16·9	10 30·3	10 30·35	N. 3 55+1 13·45				
2109	6 22 6·0	10 13·6	7 18·55	10 13·5	10 13·55	N. 1 25+2 29·0	30·048	68·5	68·2	64·0
2246	6 43 43·0	10 16·8	9 3·4	10 16·9	10 16·85	N. 1 35+1 13·45			68·2	
2293	6 52 4·8	10 17·5	10 30·25	10 17·3	10 17·4	N. 5 10—0 12·85			68·0	
2414	7 11 30·2	11 32·4	9 10·1	11 32·5	11 32·45	S. 2 55—2 22·35	30·040	68·0	68·0	63·9
2458	7 17 31·3	9 24·9	9 0·3	9 24·9	9 24·9	N. 4 55+0 24·6				
2575	7 38 55·0	11 3·5		11 3·5	11 3·5	S. 3 40—2 23·65			67·8	
2580	7 39 36·0		10 29·7	11 3·5	11 3·5	S. 3 40—0 7·8				
2635	7 47 3·8	11 31·3	15 15·3	11 31·1	11 31·2	N. 4 0+0 18·1				
2655	7 51 4·8	10 18·3	9 25·35	10 18·6	10 18·45	N. 4 0+0 27·1				
2710	7 58 4·2	10 25·4	7 20·95	10 25·35	10 25·35	S. 5 40—3 4·4	30·027	67·6	67·6	63·5
2795	8 12 33·5	10 25·6	10 27·4	10 25·0	10 25·3	S. 2 15+0 2·1				
2935	8 33 47·2	10 19·5	10 8·5	10 19·5	10 19·5	S. 0 50—0 11·0	30·021			
2964	8 37 2·5		14 11·0	10 22·9		N. 1 20—3 22·1		67·6	67·4	63·2
3130	9	10 10·5	7 16·1	10 10·5	10 10·5	N. 4 10+2 23·4				
3163	9 9 23·2	11 13·6	10 26·8	11 13·8	11 13·7	S. 4 0—0 20·0	30·018	67·5	67·3	63·1
Anon.	9 38 23·6	10 32·4	15 7·8	10 32·2	10 32·3	N. 2 0—4 9·5				

Jan. 29.—Brisk south-easter. Fair definitions.
30.—Variable strong southerly wind, and bad images.

♃ JANUARY 30, 1845.—FACE OF SECTOR WEST—(continued).

Number of B. A. C.	Time by Chronometer.	Micr. for Plumb-line on Der.	Micr. for Observation of Star.	Micr. for Plumb-line on Dot.	Mean of Micr. for Plumb-line on Dot.	Star's Apparent Zenith Distance.	Barom.	Thermometers. Attd.	Lower.	Out.
3403	9 40 0·3	11 0·9	12 8·5	11 0·8	11 0·85	N. 3 35—1 7·65				
Anon.	10 1	11 0·9	10 32·0	11 0·9	11 0·9	N. 3 35+0 2·9	29·994	67·3	67·1	63·0
3578	10 19 40·0	10 22·7	12 17·5	10 22·7	10 22·7	N. 3 40—1 28·8				
3598	10 22 2·0		6 27·1	10 3·5		N. 4 5+3 10·4	29·990	67·0	67·1	63·0
5915	17 22 52·5	10 25·0	6 27·75	10 25·0	10 25·0	S. 3 5—3 31·25	30·012	67·8	67·4	71·0

♀ JANUARY 31, 1845.—FACE OF SECTOR WEST.

7992	22 48 37·2	11 2·1	12 2·4	11 2·3	11 2·2	N. 3 30—1 0·2	29·988	72·0	71·1	75·0

FACE OF SECTOR EAST.

1802	5 33 46·0	9 22·6	11 29·0	9 22·7	9 22·65	S. 0 15—2 6·35	29·987	69·2	69·3	65·8
1878	5 45 17·2	10 5·4	12 0·9	10 5·4	10 5·4	S. 1 55—1 29·5			69·3	
1922	5 51 49·0	9 31·1	5 24·4	9 30·9	9 31·0	S. 1 20+4 6·6				
1982	6 2 8·3	10 12·3	13 19·7	10 12·1	10 12·2	S. 3 20—3 7·5			69·4	
2051	6 13 57·0	11 6·3	12 25·0	11 6·3	11 6·3	N. 3 55+1 18·7				
2109	6 22 6·0	10 28·2	13 25·7	10 28·3	10 28·25	N. 1 25+2 31·45				
2246	6 43 44·0	10 24·5	12 6·5	10 24·3	10 24·4	N. 1 35+1 16·1	29·981	69·0	69·4	65·2
2414	7 11 30·2	7 27·8	10 19·35	7 27·9	7 27·85	S. 2 55—2 25·5			69·0	
2458	7	7 28·7	8 23·1	7 28·9	7 28·8	N. 4 55+0 28·3				
2528	7 32 8·0	9 20·5	11 13·7	9 20·3	9 20·4	S. 3 45—1 27·3				
2575	7 38 55·2	18 17·8	21 11·0		18 17·8	S. 3 40—2 27·2				
2580	7 30 36·3		18 30·3	18 17·8	18 17·8	S. 3 40—0 12·5				
2635	7 47 3·2	11 25·9	8 9·7	11 25·9	11 25·9	S. 4 30+3 16·2				
2655	7 51 5·2	10 13·7	11 9·5	10 13·5	10 13·6	N. 4 0+0 29·9				
2710	7 58 5·0	4 30·7	8 5·8	4 30·9	4 30·8	S. 5 40—3 9·0	29·983	69·0	69·0	64·9
2795	8 12 33·5	9 2·0	9 0·5	9 2·0	9 2·0	S. 2 15+0 1·5	29·985	68·8	68·8	64·6
2935	8 33 48·0	9 2·1	9 14·5	9 2·3	9 2·2	S. 0 50—0 12·3				
2964	8 37 3·8		5 23·1	9 9·5		N. 1 20—3 20·4	29·980	68·2	68·6	64·3
3130	9 2 57·8	9 27·5	12 27·3	9 27·4	9 27·45	N. 4 10—2 33·85				
3163	9 9 22·5	8 32·8	9 22·4	8 32·9		S. 4 0—0 23·7	29·973	68·5	67·6	65·0
Anon.	9 38 23·5	10 33·4	6 26·95	10 33·4	10 33·4	N. 2 0—4 6·45				
3403	9 49 0·5	12 0·9	10 30·7	12 0·7	12 0·7	N. 3 35—1 4·1				
Anon.	10 1 16·5	12 0·7	12 7·4	12 0·7	12 0·7	N. 3 35+0 6·7				
3578	10 19 40·0	20 33·2	19 8·8	20 33·2	20 33·2	N. 3 40—1 24·4				
3598	10 22 2·8		23 13·3	19 32·9		N. 4 5+3 14·4			68·3	
3755	10 49 18·8	8 31·9	4 26·6	8 31·9	8 31·9	S. 2 20+4 5·3	29·970	68·5	68·3	64·2

FACE OF SECTOR WEST.

5632	16 39 46·8	9 29·4	8 13·6	9 29·4	9 29·4	S. 0 5—1 15·8	30·007	69·0	68·5	
6233	18 13 31·3	10 2·1	11 21·9	10 1·9	10 2·0	S. 0 30+1 19·9	30·012	69·0	69·2	71·0

♄ FEBRUARY 1, 1845.—FACE OF SECTOR WEST.

7992	22	9 11·1	10 13·0	9 11·1	9 11·1	N. 3 30—1 1·9	30·029	70·8	71·0	74·0
1739	5	10 6·8	9 8·2	10 6·8	10 6·8	S. 1 40—0 32·6	30·060	70·0	68·4	
1802	5 33 40·6	10 26·4	8 25·4	10 26·6	10 26·6	S. 0 15—2 1·1				
1878	5 45 13·5	10 20·9	8 28·8	10 21·1	10 21·0	S. 1 55—1 26·2				
1922	5 51 43·5	11 4·1	15 14·0	11 4·1	11 4·1	S. 1 20+4 9·9				
1982	6 1 58·6	14 3·2	11 0·45	14 3·3	14 3·25	S. 3 20—3 2·8	30·060	69·6	69·3	64·4
2051	6	11 17·0	10 6·0	11 17·3	11 17·3	N. 3 55+1 11·15				
2109	6 22 0·7	10 30·0	8 2·8	10 30·1	10 30·05	N. 1 25+2 27·25				
2246	6 43 37·5	10 30·4	9 18·95	10 30·3	10 30·35	N. 1 35+1 11·4			69·0	
2293	6 51 59·0	11 22·4	12 2·7	11 22·4	11 22·4	N. 5 10—0 14·3	30·049	68·8	69·0	64·3

Jan. 30.—Anon. 10ʰ 1ᵐ.—Very faint.
31.—Indifferent images.
Feb. 1.—Good images. Occasional clouds.

♄ FEBRUARY 1, 1845.—FACE OF SECTOR WEST—(continued).

Number of B.A.C.	Time by Chronometer.	Micr. for Plumb-line on Dot.	Micr. for Observation of Star.	Micr. for Plumb-line on Dot.	Mean of Micr. for Plumb-line on Dot.	Star's Apparent Zenith Distance.	Barom.	Thermometers.		
								Attd.	Lower.	Out.
	h m s	rev. pts.	rev. pts.	rev. pts.	rev. pts.	o ' rev. pts.	in.			
2414	7 11 24·5	12 25·9	10 4·7	12 26·0	12 25·95	S. 2 55—2 21·25				
2458	7 17 25·2	11 1·8	10 12·8	11 1·8	11 1·8	N. 4 55+0 23·0				
2528	7 32 2·0	20 23·7	19 1·7	20 23·6	20 23·65	S. 3 45—1 21·95				
2575	7 38 49·5	11 26·3	9 2·95		11 26·3	S. 3 40—2 23·35				
2580	7 39 30·2		11 18·5	11 26·3	11 26·3	S. 3 40—0 7·8				
2635	7 46 58·0	12 2·1	15 21·8	12 2·3	12 2·2	S. 4 30+3 19·6				
2655	7 50 58·8	11 18·9	10 26·7	11 10·1	11 19·0	N. 4 0+0 26·3				
2795	8 12 27·7	11 14·9	11 17·8	11 14·9	11 14·9	S. 2 15+0 2·9	30·052	69·0	68·9	64·3
2935	8 33 42·0	11 8·7	10 32·6	11 8·8	11 8·75	S. 0 50—0 10·15				
2964	8 36 57·3	11 29·9	15 18·9	11 30·4	11 30·15	N. 1 20—3 22·75				
3130	9	12 24·4	9 30·5	12 24·5	12 24·45	N. 4 10+2 27·95				
3163	9 9 17·2	13 2·1	12 16·1	13 2·0	13 2·05	S. 4 0—0 19·95	30·040	68·5	68·5	64·2
5632	16 39 43·3	11 31·7	10 16·35	11 31·8	11 31·75	S. 0 5—1 15·4	30·095	68·4	68·2	68·2
5915	17	20 32·6	17 2·0	20 32·6	20 32·6	S. 3 5—3 30·6	30·091	68·5	68·3	69·0
6233	18 13 28·2	10 15·0	11 33·45	10 15·2	10 15·1	S. 0 30+1 18·35				

☉ FEBRUARY 2, 1845.—FACE OF SECTOR EAST.

Number of B.A.C.	Time by Chronometer.	Micr. for Plumb-line on Dot.	Micr. for Observation of Star.	Micr. for Plumb-line on Dot.	Mean of Micr. for Plumb-line on Dot.	Star's Apparent Zenith Distance.	Barom.	Attd.	Lower.	Out.
1739	5 25 22·5	10 19·6	11 22·8	10 19·8	10 19·7	S. 1 40—1 3·1	30·107	70·2	70·5	66·4
2051	6 13 50·7	11 1·2	12 19·25	11 1·2	11 1·2	N. 3 55+1 18·05	30·105	70·6	70·6	66·2
2246	6	10 19·5	12 0·9	10 19·5	10 19·5	N. 1 35+1 15·4			70·3	
2293	6 51 59·2	11 9·1	10 33·8	11 9·0	11 9·05	N. 5 10—0 9·25	30·113	70·0	70·2	65·3

FACE OF SECTOR WEST.

2528	7 32 0·2	11 30·0	10 9·8	11 30·0	11 30·0	S. 3 45—1 20·2	30·113	70·0	70·1	65·0

☾ FEBRUARY 3, 1845.—FACE OF SECTOR EAST.

Number of B.A.C.	Time by Chronometer.	Micr. for Plumb-line on Dot.	Micr. for Observation of Star.	Micr. for Plumb-line on Dot.	Mean of Micr. for Plumb-line on Dot.	Star's Apparent Zenith Distance.	Barom.	Attd.	Lower.	Out.
1878	5 45 5·2	11 22·6	13 19·2	11 22·8	11 22·7	S. 1 55—1 30·5	29·926	70·2	70·5	68·6
1922	5 51 37·2	11 19·8	7 13·0	11 19·4	11 19·6	S. 1 20+4 6·6				
1982	6 1 51·5	11 8·3	14 16·6	11 8·3	11 8·3	S. 3 20—3 8·3				
2051	6 13 45·7	11 26·1	13 10·3	11 26·2	11 26·15	N. 3 55+1 18·15				
2109	6 21 55·0	11 14·6	14 11·55	11 14·5	11 14·55	N. 1 25+2 31·0				
2246	6 43 31·2	12 8·8	13 23·8	12 8·6	12 8·7	N. 1 35+1 15·1	29·927	70·0	70·3	68·6
2293	6 51 54·2	12 7·1	11 31·4	12 6·9	12 7·0	N. 0 10—0 9·6				
2414	7 11 18·2	10 33·2	13 24·2	10 33·3	10 33·25	S. 2 55—2 24·95				
2458	7 17 20·2	11 13·7	12 7·95	11 13·7	11 13·7	N. 4 55+0 28·25	29·927	69·8	70·2	67·2
2528	7 31 55·5	10 4·2	11 30·6	10 4·2	10 4·2	S. 3 45—1 26·4				
2575	7 38 43·5	19 1·3	21 28·3	19 1·35	19 1·35	S. 3 40—2 26·95				
2580	7 39 24·0		19 12·25	19 1·4	19 1·35	S. 3 40—0 10·9				
2635	7 46 51·8	9 30·3	6 13·55	9 30·4	9 30·35	N. 3 35+3 16·8				
2655	7 50 53·5	10 20·6	11 16·2	10 20·4	10 20·5	N. 4 0+0 29·7				
2710	7 58 53·5	6 12·5	9 19·4	6 12·5	6 12·5	S. 5 40—3 6·9	29·924	69·4	69·8	66·8
2795	8 12 22·0	7 8·3	7 6·15	7 8·4	7 8·35	S. 2 15+0 2·2				
2935	8 33 36·2	10 24·9	11 3·15	10 25·0	10 24·95	S. 0 50—0 12·2			69·5	
3130	9 2 46·0	12 15·3	15 14·55	12 14·9	12 15·1	N. 4 10+2 33·45				
3163	9 9 11·4	11 23·9	12 12·05	11 23·9	11 23·9	S. 4 0—0 22·75			69·6	
Anon.	9 38 11·6	12 0·5	7 27·5	12 0·5	12 0·5	N. 2 0—4 7·0				
3403	9 48 48·5	12 12·4	11 8·5	12 12·5	12 12·45	N. 3 35—1 3·95	29·911	69·0	69·4	66·9
Anon.	10 1 4·5	12 12·5	12 20·15	12 12·6	12 12·55	N. 3 35+0 7·6				
5632	16 39 36·3	9 29·0	11 13·65	9 29·0	9 29·0	S. 0 5—1 18·65	29·922	68·6	68·6	68·5
5915	17 22 40·5	12 31·0	16 32·4	12 31·2	12 31·1	S. 3 5—4 1·3	29·919	69·0	69·2	70·3
6233	18 13 22·6	11 27·5	10 10·7	11 27·5	11 27·5	S. 0 30+1 16·8				

♂ FEBRUARY 4, 1845.—FACE OF SECTOR WEST.

Number of B.A.C.	Time by Chronometer.	Micr. for Plumb-line on Dot.	Micr. for Observation of Star.	Micr. for Plumb-line on Dot.	Mean of Micr. for Plumb-line on Dot.	Star's Apparent Zenith Distance.	Barom.	Attd.	Lower.	Out.
	h m s	rev. pts.	rev. pts.	rev. pts.	rev. pts.	° ′ rev. pts.	in.			
1878	5	12 1·9	10 10·8	12 2·1	12 2·0	S. 1 55—1 25·2	29·921	69·5	68·4	65·0
1922	5 51 31·3	12 7·1	16 18·8	12 7·3	12 7·2	S. 1 20+4 11·6				
1982	6	12 11·7	9 10·8	12 11·7	12 11·7	S. 3 20—3 0·9				
2051	6	11 12·4	10 1·5	11 12·2	11 12·3	N. 3 55—1 10·8				
2109	6 21 48·8	11 19·9	8 27·6	11 19·0	11 19·9	N. 1 25+2 26·3				
2246	6 43 26·0	11 9·7	9 34·0	11 9·5	11 9·6	N. 1 35+1 9·6			68·8	
2293	6 51 46·8	11 11·0	11 27·45	11 11·0	11 11·0	N. 5 10—0 16·45				
2414	7 11 12·0	11 33·0	9 13·7	11 33·2	11 33·1	S. 2 55—2 19·4				
2458	7 17 13·5	12 0·1	11 18·3	12 0·3	12 6·2	N. 4 55+0 21·9				
2528	7 31 51·5	13 1·5	11 15·1	13 1·6	13 1·55	S. 3 45—1 20·45				
2575	7 38 39·5	12 0·6	9 12·45		12 0·65	S. 3 40—2 22·2				
2580	7		11 29·3	12 0·7	12 0·65	S. 3 40—0 5·35			69·0	
2635	7 46 47·2	12 16·9	12 2·8	12 16·9	12 16·9	S. 4 30+3 19·9				
2655	7 50 48·0	11 20·9	10 31·3	11 21·3	11 21·1	N. 4 0+0 23·8				
2710	7	13 2·4	10 1·3	13 2·5	13 2·5	S. 5 40—3 1·2				
2795	8 12 16·5	13 3·3	13 7·3	13 3·3	13 3·3	S. 2 15+0 4·0	29·910	69·0	69·0	64·2
2935	8 33 30·0	11 14·4	11 6·2	11 14·4	11 14·4	S. 0 50—0 8·2				
2964	8 36 45·0	11 10·3	15 1·4	11 10·5	11 10·4	N. 1 20—3 25·0	29·904	69·0	68·9	64·2
3130	9 2 39·0	10 31·3	8 5·3	10 31·5	10 31·4	N. 4 10+2 26·1				
3163	9. 9 6·3	12 2·4	11 18·7	12 2·5	12 2·45	S. 4 0—0 17·75				
Anon.	9 38 6·0	11 16·0	15 28·9	11 16·0	11 16·0	N. 2 0—4 12·9				
3403	9 48 42·8	11 29·5	13 5·4	11 29·5	11 20·5	N. 3 35—1 9·9				
Anon.	10 0 59·5	11 29·5	11 29·6	11 29·5	11 29·5	N. 3 35—0 0·1			68·6	
3578	10 19 22·2	13 6·1	15 2·7	13 5·9	13 6·0	N. 3 40—1 30·7				
3698	10 22 45·5		9 2·6	12 10·5		N. 4 5+3 7·9			68·6	
3755	10 49 2·1	12 33·5	17 10·3	12 33·5	12 33·5	S. 2 20+4 10·8	29·862	68·0	68·5	64·0

♀ FEBRUARY 14, 1845.—FACE OF SECTOR EAST.

Number of B.A.C.	Time by Chronometer.	Micr. for Plumb-line on Dot.	Micr. for Observation of Star.	Micr. for Plumb-line on Dot.	Mean of Micr. for Plumb-line on Dot.	Star's Apparent Zenith Distance.	Barom.	Attd.	Lower.	Out.
1739	5 25 16·4	8 15·1	9 16·0	8 15·1	8 15·1	S. 0 40—1 0·9	30·090	70·5	70·5	66·8
1802	5 33 33·8	9 4·2	11 7·85	9 4·2	9 4·2	S. 0 15—2 3·65			70·6	
1878	5 45 4·3	9 7·2	11 2·05	9 7·1	9 7·15	S. 1 55—1 28·9				
1922	5 51 36·3	9 21·0	5 12·0	9 21·0	9 21·0	S. 1 20+4 9·0				
1982	6 1 50·0	8 33·0	12 4·6	8 32·9	8 32·95	S. 3 20—3 5·65				
2051	6	9 15·4	10 31·9	9 15·6	9 15·5	N. 3 55+1 16·4				
2109	6 21 54·8	9 10·8	12 4·5	9 10·8	9 10·8	N. 1 25+2 27·7			70·8	
2246	6 43 32·7	11 13·1	12 25·4	11 13 2	11 13·15	N. 1 35+1 12·25				
2293	6 51 55·7	10 32·0	10 20·0	10 32·0	10 32·0	N. 5 10—0 12·0	30·108	70·4	70·9	63·6
2414	7 11 17·6	9 5·1	11 27·7	9 5·0	9 5·05	S. 2 55—2 22·65				
2458	7 17 22·0	8 27·9	9 20·0	8 27·8	8 27·85	N. 4 55+0 26·15			71·0	
2528	7	7 31·4	9 21·3	7 31·4	7 31·4	S. 3 45—1 23·9				
2575	7 38 42·0	16 28·7	19 18·2			S. 3 40—2 23·55				
2580	7 39 22·5		17 3·2	16 28·6	16 28·65	S. 3 40—0 8·55				
2635	7 46 50·3	12 18·0	8 32·75	12 18·0	12 18·0	S. 4 30+3 19·25				
2655	7 50 55·5	11 1·2	11 28·7	11 1·2	11 1·2	N. 4 0+0 27·5				
2710	7 57 51·2	5 29·2	8 33·2	5 29·2	5 29·2	S. 5 40—3 4·0				
2795	8 12 21·5	10 20·8	10 15·1	10 20·7	10 20·75	S. 2 15+0 5·65				
2935	8 33 36·0	10 32·7	11 5·4	10 38·8	10 32·75	S. 0 50—0 6·65				
2964	8 36 52·0		7 1·4	10 26·55		N. 1 20—3 25·15	30·112	69·8	70·7	62·9
3130	9 2 47·3	11 3·1	13 31·9	11 2·9	11 3·0	N. 4 10—2 28·9				
3163	9 9 10·5	10 13·9	10 32·6	10 14·0	10 13·95	S. 4 0—0 18·65	30·110	69·5	70·6	61·7

Feb. 4.—Anon. 10ʰ 0ᵐ 59ˢ.—Faint and uncertain.
14.—Bad images. After the observations, moved the sector a little in Azimuth, contrary to the order of reckoning in Azimuth.

♄ FEBRUARY 15, 1845.—FACE OF SECTOR WEST.

Number of B.A.C.	Time by Chronometer.	Micr. for Plumb-line on Dot.	Micr. for Observation of Star.	Micr. for Plumb-line on Dot.	Mean of Micr. for Plumb-line on Dot.	Star's Apparent Zenith Distance.	Barom.	Thermometers. Attd.	Lower.	Out.
	h m s	rev. pts.	rev. pts.	rev. pts.	rev. pts.	o ' rev. pts.	in.			
1739	5 25 11·0	8 17·0	7 20·3	8 17·0	8 17·0	S. 1 40—0 30·7	30·016	69·6	70·2	68·8
1802	5 33 28·5	8 33·1	6 33 25	8 33·0	8 33·05	S. 0 15—1 33·8				
1878	5 44 58·5	9 20·9	7 31·3	9 20·9	9 20·9	S. 1 55—1 23·6				
1922	5 51 30·5	10 0·3	14 12·3	10 0·1	10 0·2	S. 1 20+4 12·1				
1982	6 1 44·5	10 16·6	7 15·1	10 16·4	10 16·5	S. 3 20—3 1·4				
2109	6 21 48·8	8 32·3	6 8·5	8 32·4	8 32·35	N. 1 25+2 23·85				
2246	6 43 26·5	8 30·0	7 22·6	8 32·0	8 31·0	N. 1 35+1 8·4				
2293	6 51 50·0	9 0·8	9 17·7	9 0·6	9 0·7	N. 5 10—0 17·0	30·037	69·5	70·3	62·6
2414	7 11 11·6	8 8·5	5 23·2	8 8·3	8 8·4	S. 2 55—2 19·2				
2458	7 17 16·0	8 19·3	7 32·15	8 19·2	8 19·25	N. 4 55+0 21·1				
2575	7 38 35·7	12 33·5	10 14·1	12 33·5	12 33·5	N. 3 40—2 19·4				
2580	7 39 16·5		12 29·2	12 33·5	12 33·5	S. 3 40—0 4·3				
2635	7 46 43·0	12 3·0	15 26·2	12 3·0	12 3·0	S. 4 30+3 23·2				
2655	7	9 18·0	8 28·8	9 18·0	9 18·0	N. 4 0+0 23·2				
2710	7 57 44·8	10 3·0	7 3·45	10 2·9	10 2·95	S. 5 40—2 33·5				
2795	8 12 15·0	10 12·8	10 21·0	10 12·7	10 12·75	S. 2 15+0 8·25				
2935	8 33 29·5	10 21·8	10 17·4	10 21·8	10 21·8	S. 0 50—0 4·4				
2964	8 36 45·3		14 21·6	10 27·6		N. 1 20—3 28·0	30·040	59·2	70·3	62·6
3130	9 2 40·0	9 33·5	7 6·6	9 33·5	9 33·5	N. 4 10+2 26·9			70·0	

☉ FEBRUARY 16, 1845.—FACE OF SECTOR EAST.

Number of B.A.C.	Time by Chronometer.	Micr. for Plumb-line on Dot.	Micr. for Observation of Star.	Micr. for Plumb-line on Dot.	Mean of Micr. for Plumb-line on Dot.	Star's Apparent Zenith Distance.	Barom.	Attd.	Lower.	Out.
1739	5 25 7·5	9 30·3	10 30·65	9 30·2	9 30·25	S. 1 40—1 0·4	30·302	68·4	68·3	58·3
1802	5 33 25·5	9 16·8	11 20·4	9 16·7	9 16·75	S. 0 15—2 3·65				
1878	5 44 55·2	9 15·2	11 8·05	9 15·1	9 15·1	S. 1 55—1 27·8	30·307	68·4	68·2	57·8
1922	5 51 27·5	9 16·4	5 6·7	9 16·4	9 16·4	S. 1 20+4 9·7				
1982	6 1 39·5	9 2·7	12 7·6	9 2·8	9 2·8	S. 3 20—3 4·8				
2051	6 13 41·4	9 20·9	11 1·5	9 20·8	9 20·85	N. 3 55+1 14·65				
2100	6 21 48·0	10 11·3	13 4·05	10 11·1	10 11·2	N. 1 25+2 26·85				
2246	6 43 25·6	9 11·0	10 22·3	9 11·2	9 11·1	N. 1 35+1 11·2			67·5	
2293	6 51 51·5	9 33·4	9 19·25	9 33·2	9 33·2	N. 5 10—0 14·05				
2414	7 11 7·4	8 13·5	11 0·5	8 13·5	8 13·5	S. 2 55—2 21·0				
2458	7 17 17·2	8 29·4	9 20·0	8 29·4	8 29·4	N. 4 55+0 24·6	30·311	67·2	67·6	59·0
2528	7	9 18·3	11 6·1	9 18·5	9 18·4	S. 3 45—1 21·7				
2575	7 38 31·0	18 15·7	21 5·3	18 15·7	18 15·7	S. 3 40—2 23·6				
2580	7 39 12·0		18 24·2	18 15·7	18 15·7	S. 3 40—0 8·5				
2635	7 46 38·8	10 18·3	6 31·75	10 18·3	10 18·3	S. 4 30+3 20·55				
2655	7	9 29·7	10 21·4	9 29·8	9 29·75	N. 4 0+0 23·65				
2710	7 57 39·2	5 7·1	8 11·3	5 7·1	5 7·1	S. 5 40—3 4·2	30·317	67·0	67·2	58·9

♂ FEBRUARY 18, 1845.—FACE OF SECTOR WEST.

Number of B.A.C.	Time by Chronometer.	Micr. for Plumb-line on Dot.	Micr. for Observation of Star.	Micr. for Plumb-line on Dot.	Mean of Micr. for Plumb-line on Dot.	Star's Apparent Zenith Distance.	Barom.	Attd.	Lower.	Out.
1739	5 25 2·5		7 9·7	8 6·6		S. 1 40—0 30·9	30·098	69·8	70·5	64·5
1802	5 33 21·0	8 18·3	6 17·0	8 18·3	8 18·3	S. 0 15—2 1·3				
1878	5 44 50·5	10 7·7	8 16·0	10 7·7	10 7·7	S. 1 55—1 24·8				
1922	5 51 22·5	10 6·6	14 18·25	10 6·5	10 6·55	S. 1 20+4 11·7				
1982	6 1 36·2	11 2·9	8 2·1	11 3·0	11 2·95	S. 3 20—3 0·85				
2051	6 13 34·8	9 10·8	7 33·7	9 10·6	9 10·7	N. 1 55+1 11·0				
2100	6 21 41·8	8 0·9	5 0·5	8 0·8	8 0·85	N. 1 25+2 25·35				
2246	6 43 19·3	8 13·0	7 4·25	8 13·0	8 13·0	N. 1 35+1 8·75				
2293	6 51 43·0	8 7·3	8 25·3	8 7·3	8 7·3	N. 5 10—0 18·0				
2458	7 17 9·8	8 26·8	8 6 35	8 26·8	8 26·8	N. 4 55+0 20·45	30·107	69·0	69·5	64·3
2528	7 31 40·0	22 0·6	20 15·85	22 0·8	22 0·7	S. 3 45—1 18·85				

Feb. 15.—Again moved the sector in Azimuth, about 13' in the same direction. Bad images.

16.—After the observations, by means of a small telescope, attached to the spindle so as to command a meridian mark, having a scale of inches and parts of an inch, the sector was moved in Azimuth, contrary to the order of reckoning, 2 inches of the scale. Indifferent images.

18.—Fair definitions.

♂ FEBRUARY 18, 1845.—FACE OF SECTOR WEST—(continued).

Number of B.A.C.	Time by Chronometer.	Micr. for Plumb-line on Dot.	Micr. for Observation of Star.	Micr. for Plumb-line on Dot.	Mean of Micr. for Plumb-line on Dot.	Star's Apparent Zenith Distance.	Barom.	Attd.	Lower.	Out.
	h m s	rev. pts.	rev. pts.	rev. pts.	rev. pts.	° ' rev. pts.	in.			
2575	7 38 38·27	13 3·2	10 17·9		13 3·2	S. 3 40—2 19·3				
2580	7		12 33·55	13 3·2	13 3·2	S. 3 40—0 3·65				
2635	7 46 34·5	13 23·2	17 11·2	13 23·0	13 23·1	S. 4 30+3 22·1				
2655	7 50 43·0	12 31·3	12 9·0	12 31·2	12 31·25	N. 4 0+0 22·25	30·098	69·0	69·3	65·0

♀ FEBRUARY 28, 1845.—FACE OF SECTOR EAST.

Number of B.A.C.	Time by Chronometer.	Micr. for Plumb-line on Dot.	Micr. for Observation of Star.	Micr. for Plumb-line on Dot.	Mean of Micr. for Plumb-line on Dot.	Star's Apparent Zenith Distance.	Barom.	Attd.	Lower.	Out.
1739	5 24 34·8	8 17·2	9 16·2	8 17·3	8 17·25	S. 1 40—0 32·95	30·064	70·0	70·2	64·3
1802	5 32 53·5	9 32·0	11 30·8	9 32·0	9 32·0	S. 0 15—2 1·8				
1878	5 44 22·0	9 17·8	11 9·75	9 17·8	9 17·8	S. 1 55—1 25·95				
1922	5 50 54·8	9 11·1	4 33·4	9 11·2	9 11·15	S. 1 20+4 11·75				
1982	6 1 6·0	9 9·4	12 12·0	9 9·6	9 9·5	S. 3 20—3 2·5				
2051	6 13 11·2	9 32·8	11 11·9	9 32·8	9 32·8	N. 3 55+1 13·1				
2109	6 21 16·2	10 3·2	12 28·9	10 3·4	10 3·3	N. 1 25+2 25·6				
2246	6 42 0·0	10 8·0	11 17·9	10 8·0	10 8·0	N. 1 35+1 9·9				
2293	6 51 21·2	10 27·1	10 10·95	10 27·0	10 27·05	N. 5 10—0 16·1				
2414	7 10 33·3	9 32·0	12 16·45	9 32·0	9 32·0	S. 2 55—2 18·45				
2458	7 16 47·5	9 28·1	10 15·65	9 28·1	9 28·1	S. 4 55+0 21·55	30·064	69·5	69·7	64·0
2575	7 37 57·0	11 3·6	13 23·7		11 3·55	S. 3 40—2 20·15				
2580	7 38 38·0		11 8·1	11 3·5	11 3·55	S. 3 40—0 4·55				
2635	7 46 4·5	11 3·6	7 13·7	11 3·5	11 3·55	S. 4 30+3 23·85				
2655	7 50 19·2	11 26·9	12 15·9	11 26·9	11 26·9	N. 4 0+0 23·0				
2710	7 57 4·2	7 4·1	10 4·9	7 4·0	7 4·05	S. 5 40—3 0·85	30·048	69·4	69·3	63·9
2795	8 11 38·5	10 32·7	10 23·35	10 32·6	10 32·65	S. 2 15+0 9·3				
2935	8 32 55·2	10 31·4	11 1·5	10 31·6	10 31·5	N. 0 50—0 4·0				
2964	8 36 13·2		6 8·0	10 2·6		N. 1 20—3 28·6				
3130	9 2 12·2	10 15·1	13 5·9	10 15·5	10 15·3	N. 4 10+2 24·6				
3163	9 8 25·5	9 14·1	9 29·1	9 14·0	9 14·05	S. 4 0—0 15·05	30·021	68·2	68·4	09·0 65·0
6233	18 12 42;5	9 26·5	8 10·2	9 26·5	9 26·5	S. 0 30+1 16·3				

♄ MARCH 1, 1845.—FACE OF SECTOR EAST.

Number of B.A.C.	Time by Chronometer.	Micr. for Plumb-line on Dot.	Micr. for Observation of Star.	Micr. for Plumb-line on Dot.	Mean of Micr. for Plumb-line on Dot.	Star's Apparent Zenith Distance.	Barom.	Attd.	Lower.	Out.
7992	22 47 50·8	10 3·8	9 10·4	10 4·0	10 3·9	N. 3 30—0 27·5	30·031	69·8	71·2	72·8

FACE OF SECTOR WEST.

Number of B.A.C.	Time by Chronometer.	Micr. for Plumb-line on Dot.	Micr. for Observation of Star.	Micr. for Plumb-line on Dot.	Mean of Micr. for Plumb-line on Dot.	Star's Apparent Zenith Distance.	Barom.	Attd.	Lower.	Out.
1739	5 24 31·4	9 32·7	9 3·9	9 32·5	9 32·6	S. 1 40—0 28·7	30·071	70·2	70·4	65·0
1802	5 32 48·8	8 27·1	6 28·5	8 27·2	8 27·15	S. 0 15—1 32·65				
1878	5 44 19·2	9 15·4	7 26·7	9 15·5	9 15·45	S. 1 55—1 22·75				
1922	5 50 51·0	8 30·7	13 11·5	8 30·7	8 30·7	S. 1 20+4 14·8				
1982	6 1 4·8	9 13·0	6 14·5	9 13·0	9 13·0	S. 3 20—2 32·5				
2109	6 21 10·0	8 23·6	6 0·3	8 23·4	8 23·5	N. 1 25+2 23·2				
2246	6 43 47·3	9 7·2	8 1·9	9 7·2	9 7·2	N. 1 35+1 5·3				
2293	6 51 10·8	9 2·0	9 21·6	9 2·0	9 2·0	N. 5 10—0 19·6				
2414	7 10 31·4	9 21·2	7 6·75	9 21·0	9 21·1	S. 2 55—2 14·35				
2458	7 16 37·5	9 10·5	8 27·0	9 10·3	9 10·4	S. 4 55—0 17·4				
2528	7 31 8·5	10 15·2	6 33·8	10 15·2	10 15·2	S. 3 45—1 15·4				
2575	7 37 55·4	10 9·3	7 27·55		10 9·4	S. 3 40—2 15·85				
2580	7 38 36·5		10 8·6	10 9·5	10 9·4	S. 3 40—0 0·8				70·2
2635	7 46 3·0	9 20·0	13 12·5	9 19·8	9 19·9	S. 4 30+3 26·6				
2655	7 50 10·8	9 18·8	8 32·0	9 19·0	9 18·9	N. 4 0+0 20·0				
2710	7 57 3·5	10 4·4	7 2·5	10 4·1	10 4·25	S. 5 40—3 1·75	30·104	69·8	70·1	60·7
2795	8 11 35·5	9 29·1	10 5·6	9 29·1	9 29·1	S. 2 15+0 10·5				
2935	8 32 50·5	9 17·7	9 16·0	9 17·7	9 17·7	S. 0 50—0 1·7				

Before the observations of March 1 the sector was moved in Azimuth contrary to the order of reckoning in Azimuth.
March 1.—No. 2109.—The seconds of transit doubtful.

♄ MARCH 1, 1845.—FACE OF SECTOR WEST—(continued).

Number of B.A.C.	Time by Chronometer.	Micr. for Plumb-line on Dot.	Micr. for Observation of Star.	Micr. for Plumb-line on Dot.	Mean of Micr. for Plumb-line on Dot.	Star's Apparent Zenith Distance.	Barom.	Thermometers. Attd.	Lower.	Out.
	h m s	rev. pts.	rev. pts.	rev. pts.	rev. pts.	° ′ rev. pts.	in.			
2064	8 36 7·4	9 26·8	13 23·2	9 26·7	9 26·75	N. 1 20—3 30·45		70·0		
3130	9 2 3·8	9 27·5	7 5·35	9 27·5	9 27·5	N. 4 10—2 22·15				
3163	9 8 23·5	10 18·7	10 8·6	10 18·9	10 18·8	S. 4 0—0 10·2	30·104	69·0	70·0	50·6
6233	18 12 38·5	9 31·0	11 15·15	9 31·0	9 31·0	S. 0 30+1 18·15	30·124	69·0	69·0	64·0

☉ MARCH 2, 1845.—FACE OF SECTOR EAST.

Number of B.A.C.	Time by Chronometer.	Micr. for Plumb-line on Dot.	Micr. for Observation of Star.	Micr. for Plumb-line on Dot.	Mean of Micr. for Plumb-line on Dot.	Star's Apparent Zenith Distance.	Barom.	Attd.	Lower.	Out.
1739	5 24 27·5	10 17·8	11 16·3	10 18·0	10 17·9	S. 1 40—0 32·4	30·117	69·1	69·0	62·5
1802	5 32 48·2	10 9·7	12 11·05	10 9·9	10 9·8	S. 0 15—2 1·25				
1878	5 44 15·2	10 15·3	12 7·35	10 15·3	10 15·3	S. 1 55—1 26·05				
1922	5 50 47·8	10 10·7	5 33·3	10 10·7	10 10·7	S. 1 40+4 11·4			68·9	
1982	6 0 57·3	9 13·9	12 16·25	9 13·9	9 13·9	S. 3 20—3 2·35				
2051	6 13 9·5	10 15·4	11 27·75	10 15·4	10 15·4	N. 3 55+1 12·35				
2109	6 21 12·3	9 30·4	12 21·75	9 30·4	9 30·4	N. 1 25+2 25·35				
2246	6 43 50·2	9 17·1	10 27·2	9 17·0	9 17·05	N. 1 35—1 10·15				
2293	6 51 21·0	8 33·0	8 10·5	8 33·0	8 33·0	N. 5 10—0 16·5				
2414	7 10 25·3	8 12·5	10 31·5	8 12·5	8 12·5	S 2 55—2 19·0				
2458	7 16 46·7	8 25·5	9 13·55	8 25·4	8 25·45	N. 4 55+0 22·1	30·145	69·0	68·7	61·1
2528	7	8 14·6	9 33·9	8 14·6	8 14·6	S. 3 45—1 19·3				
2575	7 37 48·2	17 11·8	19 31·5		17 11·9	S. 3 40—2 19·6				
2580	7 38 29·2		17 16·7	17 12·0	17 11·9	S. 3 40—0 4·8				
2635	7 45 54·8	9 2·5	5 12·35	9 2·7	9 2·6	N. 4 30+8 24·25				
2655	7 50 17·5	10 8·0	10 30·75	10 8·0	10 8·0	N. 4 0+0 22·75				
2710	7 56 53·3	5 26·5	8 27·5	5 26·7	5 26·6	S. 5 40—3 0·9				
2795	8 11 31·2	11 3·5	10 28·55	11 3·7	11 3·6	S. 2 15+0 0·05	30·169	68·2	68·2	60·0
2935	8 32 48·7	10 5·3	10 9·0	10 5·3	10 5·3	S. 0 50—0 3·7				
2964	8	10 17·8	6 23·5	10 17·9	10 17·9	S. 1 20—3 28·35				
3130	9 2 10·8	10 24·5	13 14·75	10 24·5	10 24·5	S. 4 10+2 24·25				
3163	9	10 13·9	10 28·75	10 14·8	10 14·35	S. 4 0—0 14·4	30·165	68·0	68·0	59·2
5915	17 21 49·3	11 11·5	15 12·5	11 11·5	11 11·5	S. 3 5—4 1·0	30·222	67·0	66·2	58·8
6233	18 12 37·8	10 12·5	8 29·75	10 12·5	10 12·5	S. 0 30+1 16·75	30·227	66·8	66·3	61·2

☾ MARCH 3, 1845.—FACE OF SECTOR WEST.

Number of B.A.C.	Time by Chronometer.	Micr. for Plumb-line on Dot.	Micr. for Observation of Star.	Micr. for Plumb-line on Dot.	Mean of Micr. for Plumb-line on Dot.	Star's Apparent Zenith Distance.	Barom.	Attd.	Lower.	Out.
1739	5 24 25·5	11 18·8	10 23·05	11 18·8	11 18·8	S. 1 40—0 29·75	30·264	68·0	67·4	61·0
1802	5 32 44·2	10 16·5	8 17·73	10 16·6	10 16·55	S. 0 15—1 32·8				
1878	5 44 13·3	10 3·7	8 15·55	10 3·8	10 3·75	S. 1 55—1 22·2				
1922	5 50 45·8	10 7·7	14 22·2	10 7·8	10 7·75	S. 1 20+4 14·45				
1982	6 0 58·0	10 19·0	7 19·25	10 19·0	10 19·0	S. 1 40+2 33·75				
2051	6 13 0·2	9 3·2	7 29·2	9 3·0	9 3·1	N. 3 55+1 7·9				
2109	6 21 6·5	8 29·3	6 7·25	8 29·4	8 29·35	N. 1 25+2 22·1				
2246	6 43 44·0	8 14·0	7 8·5	8 14·1	8 14·05	N. 1 35+1 5·55				
2293	6 51 9·6	8 33·9	9 20·95	8 33·8	8 33·85	N. 5 10—0 21·1				
2414	7 10 25·3	9 27·2	7 13·1	9 27·2	9 27·2	S. 2 55—2 14·1				
2458	7 16 36·5	9 2·65	8 20·0	9 2·7	9 2·68	N. 4 55+0 16·68				
2528	7 31 2·0	21 3·8	19 24·25	21 4·0	21 3·9	S. 3 45—1 13·65				
2575	7 37 49·5	12 6·0	9 24·5	12 6·1	12 6·1	S. 3 40—2 15·6				
2580	7 38 29·6		12 7·35	12 6·2	12 6·1	S. 3 40+0 1·25				
2635	7 45 56·5	12 31·6	16 24·4	12 31·8	12 31·7	S. 4 30—3 26·7				
2655	7 50 8·3	9 6·0	9 21·4	9 5·8	9 5·9	N. 4 0—0 15·5				
2710	7 56 56·2	10 0·4	7 4·5	10 0·5	10 0·45	S. 5 40—2 20·05				
2795	8 11 30·0	10 1·7	10 14·9	10 1·6	10 1·65	S. 2 15+0 13·25	30·315	67·0	66·8	60·0
2935	8 32 45·5	9 25·4	9 25·0	9 25·4	9 25·4	S. 0 50—0 0·4				

Before the observations of March 2 the sector was moved in Azimuth contrary to the order of reckoning in Azimuth.

March 1.—No. 3163.—The seconds of transit doubtful.

2.—Excellent definitions.

3.—Good definitions.

☾ MARCH 3, 1845.—FACE OF SECTOR WEST—(continued).

Number of B.A C.	Time by Chronometer.	Micr. for Plumb-line on Dot.	Micr. for Observation of Star.	Micr. for Plumb-line on Dot.	Mean of Micr. for Plumb-line on Dot.	Star's Apparent Zenith Distance.	Barom	Thermometers. Attd.	Lower.	Out.
2964	8 36 3·7	9 23·5	13 21·75	0 23·6	0 23·55	N. 1 20—3 32·2				
3130	9	9 30·3	7 10·5	9 30·3	9 30·3	N. 4 10+2 19·8				
3163	9 8 17·0	10 24·0	10 13·25	10 24·0	10 24·0	S. 4 0—0 10·75	30·316	67·0	66·7	56·5
5915	17 22 49·7	11 0·6	7 2·9	11 0·8	11 0·7	S. 3 5—3 31·8	30·314	65·0	64·5	57·5
6233	18 12 34·1	10 19·9	12 4·5	10 19·7	10 19·8	S. 0 30+1 18·7	30·320	65·5	64·8	62·0

♂ MARCH 18, 1845.—FACE OF SECTOR WEST.

Number of B.A C.	Time by Chronometer.	Micr. for Plumb-line on Dot.	Micr. for Observation of Star.	Micr. for Plumb-line on Dot.	Mean of Micr. for Plumb-line on Dot.	Star's Apparent Zenith Distance.	Barom	Thermometers. Attd.	Lower.	Out.
1739	5 25 8·2	10 22·7	9 27·5	10 22·6	10 22·65	S. 1 40—0 29·15	30·003	72·0	73·0	71·0
1802	5 33 27·0	10 13·0	8 13·65	9 12·9	9 12·95	S. 0 15—0 33·3				
1878	5 44 55·0	10 9·6	8 21·6	10 9·5	10 9·55	S. 1 55—1 21·95				
1022	5 51 28·3	9 23·5	14 4·2	9 23·5	9 23·5	S. 1 20+4 14·7				72·5
1982	6 1 40·8	10 30·1	7 32·2	10 30·2	10 30·15	S. 3 20—2 31·95				72·5
2051	6 13 44·2	9 13·3	8 6·9	9 13·3	9 13·3	N. 3 55+1 6·4				
2109	6 21 49·5	8 18·2	5 29·05	8 18·1	8 18·15	N. 1 25+2 22·2				
2246	6 43 27·6	8 18·2	7 14·85	8 18·4	8 18·3	N. 1 35+1 3·45				
2293	6 51 53·5	12 11·4	12 33·0	12 11·8	12 11·6	N. 5 10—0 21·4				72·2
2414	7 11 8·5	10 13·9	8 1·3	10 13·7	10 13·8	S. 2 55—2 12·5				
2458	7 17 20·0	9 18·0	9 2·75	9 17·8	9 17·9	N. 4 55+0 15·15				
2528	7 31 45·2	24 18·1	23 5·6	24 18·1	24 18·1	S. 3 45—1 12·5				
2575	7 38 32·0	15 20·2	13 7·9		15 20·2	S. 3 40—2 12·3				
2580	7 39 13·0		15 23·0	15 20·2	15 20·2	S. 3 40+0 2·8				
2635	7 46 38·8	14 15·2	18 11·1	14 15·0	14 15·1	S. 4 30+3 30·0				
2655	7 50 52·2	11 27·8	11 9·9	11 27·6	11 27·7	N. 4 0+0 17·8				
2710	7 58	12 20·6	9 28·5	12 20·6	12 20·6	S. 5 40—2 26·1				
2795	8 12 13·0	11 19·9	12 1·55	11 19·9	11 19·9	S. 2 15+0 15·65				71·5
2935	8 33 29·0	11 26·0	11 27·0	11 25·9	11 25·9	S. 0 50+0 1·1				
3163	9 8 59·6	12 25·8	12 18·5	12 25·6	12 25·7	S. 4 0—0 7·2	30·017	71·3	71·0	62·2

☉ MARCH 23, 1845.—FACE OF SECTOR EAST.

Number of B.A C.	Time by Chronometer.	Micr. for Plumb-line on Dot.	Micr. for Observation of Star.	Micr. for Plumb-line on Dot.	Mean of Micr. for Plumb-line on Dot.	Star's Apparent Zenith Distance.	Barom	Thermometers. Attd.	Lower.	Out.
1739	5 25 0·5	9 0·8	10 0·2	9 0·6	9 0·7	S. 1 40—0 33·5	29·943	69·6	70·0	66·0
1802	5 33 21·2	9 19·9	11 21·7	9 19·9	9 19·9	S. 0 15—2 1·8				
1878	5 43 48·2	9 19·7	11 11·2	9 19·5	9 19·6	S. 1 55—1 25·6				
1022	5 51 20·6	10 0·5	5 22·4	10 0·3	10 0·4	S. 1 20+4 12·0				
2051	6 13 42·4	11 13·1	12 25·25	11 13·2	11 13·15	N. 3 55+1 12·1				
2109	6 21 45·3	11 11·9	14 2·45	11 11·9	11 11·9	N. 1 25+2 24·55				
2246	6 43 23·5	10 20·6	11 28·85	10 20·6	10 20·6	N. 1 35—1 8·25				
2293	6 52 54·2	11 2·6	10 19·7	11 2·5	11 2·55	N. 5 10—0 16·85	29·960	69·4	69·8	64·2
2528	7 31 34·4	8 24·5	10 8·0	8 24·4	8 24·45	S. 3 45—1 17·55				
2575	7 38 21·5	17 21·0	20 5·1		17 21·0	S. 3 40—2 17·2				
2580	7 39 2·0		17 24·3	17 21·9	17 21·9	S. 3 40—0 2·4				
2635	7 46 27·5	8 27·5	5 1·55	8 27·5	8 27·5	S. 4 30+3 25·95				
2655	7 50 51·0	10 16·2	11 3·4	10 16·2	10 16·2	N. 4 0+0 21·2				
2710	7 57 26·6	5 17·8	8 15·8	5 17·6	5 17·7	S. 5 40—2 32·1				
2795	8 12 4·4	10 3·3	9 24·75	10 3·3	10 3·3	S. 1 20+2 12·55				
2935	8 33 22·2	9 24·1	9 25·35	9 24·0	9 24·05	S. 0 50—0 1·3	29·988	69·0	69·2	63·5
2964	8 36 43·0		5 26·8	9 23·7		N. 1 20—3 30·9				
3130	9 2 44·5	10 13·5	13 1·35	10 13·5	10 13·5	N. 4 10+2 21·85				
3163	9 8 49·5	9 16·3	9 27·1	9 16·1	9 16·2	S. 4 0—0 19·0				
Anon.	9 38 55·2	9 13·4	4 28·4	9 13·4	9 13·4	N. 2 0—4 19·0				
3403	9 48 45·8	9 7·5	7 25·95	9 7·7	9 7·6	N. 3 35—1 15·65	30·007	68·5	68·8	63·5
Anon.	10 1 1·8	9 7·6	9 2·2	9 7·6	9 7·6	N. 3 35+0 5·4				

The observations of 4th March are not printed. A hair was found attached to the plumb-line, near the arch, which explains certain discrepancies.

March 23.—Good definitions.

156   ARC OF THE MERIDIAN.—CAPE OF GOOD HOPE.

☉ MARCH 23, 1845.—FACE OF SECTOR EAST—(continued).

Number of B.A.C.	Time by Chronometer.	Micr. for Plumb-line on Dot.	Micr. for Observation of Star.	Micr. for Plumb-line on Dot.	Mean of Micr. for Plumb-line on Dot.	Star's Apparent Zenith Distance.	Barom.	Thermometers.		
								Attd.	Lower.	Out.
	h m s	rev. pts.	rev. pts.	rev. pts.	rev. pts.	° ′ rev. pts.	in.			
3578	10 19 25·8	9 10·9	7 7·85	9 10·9	0 10·9	N. 3 40—2 3·05				
3755	10 48 50·0	9 7·9	4 22·9	9 7·9	9 7·9	S. 2 20+4 19·0	30·025	68·0	68·4	62·7
7992	22 48 22·2	10 13·1	9 24·0	10 12·9	10 13·0	N. 3 30—0 23·30	30·095	68·8	68·4	67·4

☾ MARCH 24, 1845.—FACE OF SECTOR WEST.

1739	5 24 57·0	9 30·6	9 1·6	9 30·6	9 30·6	S. 1 40—0 29·0	30·049	69·5	69·4	65·5
1802	5 33 16·0	9 18·5	7 20·05	9 18·5	9 18·5	S. 0 15—1 32·45				
2051	6 13 32·0	9 5·2	7 31·45	9 5·1	9 5·15	N. 3 55+1 7·7			69·0	
2246	6 43 16·0	8 33·4	7 29·8	8.33·6	8 33·5	N. 1 35+1 3·7				
2293	6 51 41·8	9 28·0	10 17·0	9 28·1	9 28·05	N. 5 10—0 22·95				
2414	7 10 56·7	10 10·9	7 32·75	10 10·7	10 10·8	S. 2 55—2 12·05				
2528	7 31 33·7	10 10·5	8 32·5	10 10·5	10 10·5	S. 3 45—1 12·0	30·065	68·5	68·7	61·6
2635	7 46 27·2	10 24·0	14 20·1	10 24·0	10 24·0	S. 4 30+3 30·1				
2710	7	11 0·1	8 10·5	11 0·2	11 0·15	S. 5 40—2 23·65				
2795	8 12 0·8	10 1·5	10 17·0	10 1·6	10 1·55	S. 2 15+0 15·45				
2964	8 36 35·8	9 20·2	13 22·5	9 20·3	9 20·25	N. 1 20—4 2·25				
3130	9 2 34·2	9 18·8	7 3·0	9 18·9	9 18·85	N. 4 10+2 15·85			68·1	
3163	9 8 47·6	9 27·7	9 21·8	9 27·9	9 27·8	S. 4 0—0 6·0				
A non.	9 38 57·6	8 15·6	13 5·0	8 15·6	8 15·6	N. 2 0—4 23·4	30·088	67·6	68·0	60·4
3463	9 48 37·1	8 9·5	9 31·5	8 9·5	8 9;5	N. 3 35—1 22·0				
A non.	10 0 53·2	8 9·5	8 20·65	8 9·5	8 9·5	S. 3 35—0 11·15				
3578	10	18 13·0	20 21·3	18 13·0	18 13·0	N. 3 40—2 8·3				
3755	10 48 46·2	11 2·4	15 25·8	11 2·4	11 2·4	S. 2 20+4 23·4	30·090	67·5	68·0	60·2
6233	18 13 6·4	11 22·9	13 7·6	11 23·3	11 23·1	S. 0 30+1 18·5	30·100	67·0	67·0	59·6

♂ MARCH 25, 1845.—FACE OF SECTOR WEST.

2051	6 13 30·3	12 3·8	10 31·65	12 3·6	12 3·7	N. 3 55+1 6·05	30·170	69·4		

FACE OF SECTOR EAST.

2414	7 10 51·6	10 3·0	12 20·3	10 3·0	10 3·0	S. 2 55—2 17·3	30·180	69·0	69·0	65·0
2458	7 17 14·0	10 1·6	10 22·65	10 1·5	10 1·55	N. 4 55+0 21·1	30·190	68·8	69·0	63·0
2528	7 31 27·7	8 23·5	10 7·1	8 23·5	8 23·5	S. 3 45—1 17·6			69·0	
2710	7 57 19·2	5 32·3	8 30·0	5 32·3	5 32·3	S. 5 40—2 31·7				
2795	8 11 58·0	9 27·5	9 15·0	9 27·5	9 27·5	S. 2 15+0 12·5				
2935	8 33 16·0	10 13·8	10 15·35	10 13·7	10 13·75	S. 0 50—0 1·6				
2964	8 36 36·5		6 33·6	10 30·0	10 30·0	N. 1 20—3 30·4				
3130	9 2 38·8	11 17·6	14 4·5	11 17·6	11 17·6	N. 4 10+2 20·9				
3163	9 8 42·3	11 25·3	12 2·0	11 25·3	11 25·3	S. 4 0—0 10·7	30·228	68·0	68·2	61·8
A non.	10 0 56·2	11 20·6	11 14·75	11 20·5	11 20·55	N. 3 35—0 5·8				
3578	10 19 20·2	11 30·7	9 27·4	11 30·9	11 30·8	N. 3 40—2 3·4	30·231	68·4	68·0	62·0
3755	10 48 43·8	10 13·0	5 28·0	10 13·1	10 13·05	S. 2 20+4 19·05			68·0	
5915	17 22 16·8	10 3·1	14 4·7	10 3·3	10 3·2	S. 3 5—1 1·5	30·240	67·0	66·9	60·5
6233	18 13 6·0	10 21·8	9 6·5	10 21·8	10 21·8	S. 0 30+1 15·3	30·252	66·5	66·5	60·0
7992	22 48 16·8	11 31·6	11 9·55	11 31·6	11 31·6	N. 3 30—0 22·05	30·274	68·0	68·0	70·2

♃ MARCH 26, 1845.—FACE OF SECTOR EAST.

1802	5 33 12·2	9 29·1	11 31·0	9 29·1	9 29·1	S. 0 15—2 1·9	30·209	69·6	69·8	66·5
2293	6 51 46·2	12 19·4	12 1·5	12 19·4	12 19·4	N. 5 10—0 17·9				

March 24.—Indifferent definitions.
25.—No. 3163.—The seconds of transit doubtful.

☿ MARCH 26, 1845—(continued).—FACE OF SECTOR WEST.

Number of B.A.C.	Time by Chronometer.	Micr. for Plumb-line on Dot.	Micr. for Observation of Star.	Micr. for Plumb-line on Dot.	Mean of Micr. for Plumb-line on Dot.	Star's Apparent Zenith Distance.	Barom.	Thermometers. Attd.	Lower.	Out.
2935	8	6 16·3	6 19·6	6 16·3	6 16·3	S. 0 50+0 3·3	30·209	68·6	68·6	64·2
2964	8	6 27·1	10 28·9	6 27·3	6 27·2	N. 1 20—4 1·7				
3130	9	9 7·1	6 24·9	9 6·9	9 7·0	N. 4 10+2 16·1				68·1
3163	9	11 16·6	11 10·9	11 16·4	11 16·5	S. 4 0—0 5·6	30·220	68·4		63·0
Anon.	9 38	9 22·5	14 13·4	9 22·7	9 22·6	N. 2 0—4 24·8				
3403	9	9 13·2	11 3·1	9 13·2	9 13·2	N. 3 35—1 23·9				
3578	10	9 12·5	11 21·3	9 12·5	9 12·5	N. 3 40—2 8·8	30·222	68·4	67·8	63·0
3755	10	9 22·0	14 11·5	9 22·0	9 22·0	S. 2 20+4 23·5	30·200	68·5	67·5	62·0
6233	18	9 11·8	10 29·8	9 11·6	9 11·7	S. 0 30+1 18·1	30·163	67·0	67·2	64·2

♃ MARCH 27, 1845.—FACE OF SECTOR EAST.

1739	5 24 48·5	9 4·8	10 4·25	9 4·8	9 4·8	S. 1 40—0 33·45	30·098	70·0	70·5	70·5

FACE OF SECTOR WEST.

2710	7 57 17·0	9 30·9	7 6·6	9 31·0	9 30·95	S. 5 40—2 24·35	30·098	69·8	70·2	68·8

FACE OF SECTOR EAST.

2964	8	10 0·7	6 4·4	10 0·9	10 0·8	N. 1 20—3 30·4				
3130	9 2 33·5	10 16·3	13 3·4	10 16·2	10 16·25	N. 4 10+2 21·15				
3163	9 8 37·0	9 23·0	10 0·0	9 23·2	9 23·1	S. 4 0—0 10·9				
Anon.	9 38	9 25·7	5 6·75	9 25·7	9 25·7	N. 2 0—4 18·95				
3403	9 48 35·0	9 33·9	8 17·15	9 33·8	9 33·85	N. 3 35—1 16·7	30·081	69·6	70·0	67·0
Anon.	10 0 51·8	9 33·8	9 27·7	9 33·8	9 33·8	N. 3 35+0 6·1				
3598	10 21 39·2	8 23·9	11 25·5	8 23·7	8 23·8	N. 4 5+3 1·7				
3755	10 48 38·0	7 25·7	3 5·6	7 25·8	7 25·75	S. 2 20+4 20·15	30·081	69·5	69·6	65·0

FACE OF SECTOR WEST.

5915	17 22 13·2	12 0·4	8 4·35	12 0·4	12 0·4	S. 3 5—3 30·05	30·020	68·5	68·4	63·8
6233	18 12 53·6	11 9·2	12 27·9	11 9·1	11 9·15	S. 0 30+1 18·75	30·020	68·5	68·4	64·3

♀ MARCH 28, 1845.—FACE OF SECTOR WEST.

3163	9	11 13·2	11 8·6	11 13·2	11 13·2	S. 4 0—0 4·6	30·025	72·0	71·8	70·2

♄ MARCH 29, 1845.—FACE OF SECTOR WEST.

3130	9 2 19·1	10 28·5	8 12·95	10 28·5	10 28·5	N. 4 10+2 15·55	29·962	73·7	72·8	65·4
3163	9 8 32·5	11 22·5	11 17·5	11 22·4	11 22·45	S. 4 0—0 4·95				
Anon.	9 37 42·8	10 5·5	14 29·75	10 5·5	10 5·5	N. 2 0—4 24·25				
3403	9 48 22·7	10 17·4	12 5·5	10 17·4	10 17·4	N. 3 35—1 22·1				
Anon.	10 0 38·0	10 17·4	10 29·1	10 17·3	10 17·35	N. 3 35—0 11·75	29·966	73·6	72·6	64·5
3755	10 48 31·0	11 6·2	15 29·9	11 6·0	11 6·1	S. 2 20+3 22·85				
3926	11 24 21·8	9 7·5	8 4·45	9 7·4	9 7·45	N. 2 55+1 3·0				
4015	11 44 5·0	8 33·8	12 22·6	8 33·7	8 33·75	N. 0 55—3 22·85	29·964	72·0	72·2	62·6
4202	12 19 11·5	10 29·4	11 2·0	10 29·4	10 29·4	S. 4 15+0 6·6				72·0
4458	13 10 55·3	10 20·7	15 16·25	10 20·6	10 20·65	S. 1 55+4 29·6				72·0
4686	13 56 35·5	10 18·6	11 6·0	10 18·5	10 18·55	S. 1 40+0 21·45	29·961	71·0	72·0	61·0

March 26.—Anon. 9ʰ 38ᵐ and No. 3403.—Bad images. Strong wind, and general bad definition.

⊙ MARCH 30, 1845.—FACE OF SECTOR WEST.

Number of B.A.C.	Time by Chronometer.	Micr. for Plumb-line on Dot.	Micr. for Observation of Star.	Micr. for Plumb-line on Dot.	Mean of Micr. for Plumb-line on Dot.	Star's Apparent Zenith Distance.	Barom.	Att.	Lower.	Out.
5915	17 22 1·2	12 24·6	8 28·1	12 24·5	12 24·55	S. 3 5—3 30·45	30·169	70·1	61·0	60·5

FACE OF SECTOR EAST.

6233	18 12 46·2	11 26·7	10 12·9	11 26·5	11 26·6	S. 0 30+1 13·7	30·181	70·2	70·4	60·4

♂ APRIL 1, 1845.—FACE OF SECTOR EAST.

Number of B.A.C.	Time by Chronometer.	Micr. for Plumb-line on Dot.	Micr. for Observation of Star.	Micr. for Plumb-line on Dot.	Mean of Micr. for Plumb-line on Dot.	Star's Apparent Zenith Distance.	Barom.	Att.	Lower.	Out.
3130	9 2 14·7	11 8·8	13 28·1	11 8·8	11 8·8	N. 4 10+2 19·3	30·120	72·0	72·2	71·5
3163	9 8 16·6	10 3·5	10 12·6	10 3·7	10 3·6	S. 4 0—0 9·0				
Anon.	9 37 34·5	10 12·0	5 23·6	10 12·0	10 12·0	N. 2 0—4 22·4				
3403	9 48 15·3	10 27·5	9 8·75	10 27·5	10 27·5	N. 3 35—1 18·75				
3755	10 48 17·3	10 12·0	5 23·1	10 12·0	10 12·0	S. 2 20+4 22·9				
4015	11 43 55·8	10 12·1	6 23·25	10 11·9	10 12·0	N. 0 55—3 22·75				

☿ APRIL 2, 1845.—FACE OF SECTOR WEST.

3755	10 48 13·0	10 14·1	15 4·75	10 14·1	10 14·1	S. 2 20+4 24·65	29·948	72·8	72·6	68·4

FACE OF SECTOR EAST.

3926	11 24 9	10 5·0	11 11·0	10 5·2	10 5·1	N. 2 55+1 5·9				
4015	11 43 50·5	10 0·8	6 12·75	10 1·0	10 0·9	N. 0 55—3 22·15				

♀ APRIL 4, 1845.—FACE OF SECTOR WEST.

Number of B.A.C.	Time by Chronometer.	Micr. for Plumb-line on Dot.	Micr. for Observation of Star.	Micr. for Plumb-line on Dot.	Mean of Micr. for Plumb-line on Dot.	Star's Apparent Zenith Distance.	Barom.	Att.	Lower.	Out.
Anon.	9 37	7 28·0	12 19·2	7 28·0	7 28·0	N. 2 0—4 25·2	30·260	68·0	68·0	
3403	9 47 53·2	11 1·2	12 24·75	11 1·3	11 1·25	N. 3 35—1 23·5				
Anon.	10 0 10·0	11 1·3	11 14·95	11 1·3	11 1·3	N. 3 35—0 13·65				
3598	10 20 56·6	10 24·6	7 30·7	10 24·6	10 24·6	N. 4 5+2 27·9	30·263	67·7	68·0	60·8
3755	10 48 2·2	11 4·6	13 29·5	11 4·6	11 4·6	S. 2 20+4 24·9				
3926	11	10 22·4	9 20·9	10 22·4	10 22·4	N. 2 55+1 1·5				
4015	11	11 5·4	14 30·95	11 5·5	11 5·45	N. 0 55—3 25·5				

FACE OF SECTOR EAST.

4202	12 18 40·5	10 32·9	10 28·25	10 32·7	10 32·8	S. 4 15+0 4·55				
4458	13 10 26·3	10 27·5	14 32·1	10 27·4	10 27·45	S. 2 0—4 4·65				
4686	13 56 7·2	10 3·7	9 19·6	10 3·6	10 3·65	S. 1 40+0 18·05	30·241	67·2	68·0	59·0

♄ APRIL 5, 1845.—FACE OF SECTOR EAST.

Number of B.A.C.	Time by Chronometer.	Micr. for Plumb-line on Dot.	Micr. for Observation of Star.	Micr. for Plumb-line on Dot.	Mean of Micr. for Plumb-line on Dot.	Star's Apparent Zenith Distance.	Barom.	Att.	Lower.	Out.
Anon.	9 37 14·0	11 7·5	6 19·65	11 7·5	11 7·5	N. 2 0—4 21·85	30·178	68·5	68·4	
3403	9 47 54·8	10 13·8	8 29·75	10 13·9	10 13·85	N. 3 35—1 18·1				
Anon.	10 0	10 13·8	10 7·5	10 13·8	10 13·8	N. 3 35—0 6·3	30·178	68·4	68·6	60·2
3598	10 20 58·6	10 27·0	13 25·45	10 27·1	10 27·05	N. 4 5+2 32·4				
3755	10 47 57·0	10 14·0	14 23·4	10 14·2	10 14·1	S. 2 25—4 9·3				
3926	11 23 53·5	10 28·6	11 32·6	10 28·7	10 28·65	N. 2 55+1 3·95		08·0		
4202	12 18 35·2	10 8·1	10 3 25	10 8·2	10 8·15	S. 4 15+0 4·9				
4458	13 10 21·7	10 23·3	14 27·75	10 23·5	10 23·4	S. 2 0—4 4·35				
4686	13 56 2·2	10 21·6	10 2·25	10 21·5	10 21·5	S. 1 40+0 19·25	30·161	68·0	67·9	55·6

FACE OF SECTOR WEST.

7992	22 47 23·7	11 7·8	11 33·5	11 8·0	11 7·9	N. 3 30—0 25·6	30·137	67·6	67·3	65·2

March 30.—No. 6233 —The star barely visible through cloud.
April 2.—Generally clouded.
    5.—Good definitions.

⊙ APRIL 6, 1845.—FACE OF SECTOR WEST.

Number of B.A.C.	Time by Chronometer.	Micr. for Plumb-line on Dot.	Micr. for Observation of Star.	Micr. for Plumb-line on Dot.	Mean of Micr. for Plumb-line on Dot.	Star's Apparent Zenith Distance.	Barom.	Thermometers. Attd.	Lower.	Out.
	h m s	rev. pts.	rev. pts.	rev. pts.	rev. pts.	° ′ rev. pts.	in.			
Anon.	9 37 3·5	10 3·5	14 31·45	10 3·7	10 3·6	N. 2 0—4 27·85	30·088	69·0	68·6	59·6
3403	9 47 43·5	9 32·2	11 22·8	9 32·4	9 32·3	N. 3 35—1 24·5				

♂ APRIL 8, 1845.—FACE OF SECTOR WEST.

Number of B.A.C.	Time by Chronometer.	Micr. for Plumb-line on Dot.	Micr. for Observation of Star.	Micr. for Plumb-line on Dot.	Mean of Micr. for Plumb-line on Dot.	Star's Apparent Zenith Distance.	Barom.	Attd.	Lower.	Out.
3403	9 47 32·7	9 33·8	11 24·0	9 33·8	9 33·8	N. 3 35—1 24·2	30·226	67·0	67·5	59·4
Anon.	10 0		10 13·0	10 0·7	10 0·7	N. 3 35—0 12·3				
3598	10	10 31·6	8 4·7	10 31·4	10 31·5	N. 4 5+2 26·8				
3755	10 47 41·4	9 24·0	5 19·0	9 24·0	9 24·0	S. 2 25—4 5·0				
7992	22 46 37·6	9 2·4	9 26·25	9 2·5	9 2·45	N. 3 30—0 23·8	30·400	66·0	66·0	63·0

☿ APRIL 9, 1845.—FACE OF SECTOR EAST.

Number of B.A.C.	Time by Chronometer.	Micr. for Plumb-line on Dot.	Micr. for Observation of Star.	Micr. for Plumb-line on Dot.	Mean of Micr. for Plumb-line on Dot.	Star's Apparent Zenith Distance.	Barom.	Attd.	Lower.	Out.
Anon.	9 37 52·7	10 0·7	5 13·45	10 1·0	10 0·85	N. 2 0—4 21·4	30·363	65·6	65·8	59·5
3403	9 47 33·4	10 12·9	8 27·1	10 12·9	10 12·9	N. 3 35—1 19·8				
Anon.	9 59 48·5	10 12·9	10 3·9	10 12·9	10 12·9	N. 3 35—0 9·0				
3578	10 18 14·0	10 15·3	9 9·4	10 15·3	10 15·3	N. 3 40—2 5·9				
3755	10 47 37·1	9 17·4	13 26·4	9 17·3	9 17·35	S. 2 25—4 9·05	30·362	65·4	65·5	59·4
3926	11 23 32·8	10 6·1	11 10·95	10 6·2	10 6·15	N. 2 55+1 4·8				
4015	11 43 14·3	10 3·1	6 13·65	10 3·2	10 3·15	N. 0 55—3 23·5				
4202	12 18 15·5	9 29·6	9 25·5	9 29·6	9 29·6	S. 4 15+0 4·1				
4458	13 10 1·5	9 26·5	4 32·75	9 26·6	9 26·55	S. 1 55+4 27·8				
4686	13 55 41·7	9 25·4	9 6·25	9 25·5	9 25·45	S. 1 40+0 19·2	30·335	65·0	64·8	58·4
7992	22 47 10·0	10 25·2	10 6·4	10 25·2	10 25·2	N. 3 30—0 18·8	30·248	65·5	65·2	65·4

♃ APRIL 10, 1845.—FACE OF SECTOR WEST.

Number of B.A.C.	Time by Chronometer.	Micr. for Plumb-line on Dot.	Micr. for Observation of Star.	Micr. for Plumb-line on Dot.	Mean of Micr. for Plumb-line on Dot.	Star's Apparent Zenith Distance.	Barom.	Attd.	Lower.	Out.
Anon.	9 36 44·8	9 24·3	14 16·6	9 24·5	9 24·4	N. 2 0—4 26·2	30·120	65·4	65·6	59·4
3403	9 47 24·3	9 14·1	11 5·0	9 14·1	9 14·1	N. 3 35—1 24·9				
Anon.	9 59 40·5	9 14·1	9 28·5	9 13·9	9 14·0	N. 3 35—0 14·5				
3578	10 18 4·0	9 18·3	11 29·6	9 18·4	9 18·35	N. 3 40—2 11·25				
3755	10 47 34·0	9 32·6	5 27·7	9 32·6	9 32·6	S. 2 25—4 4·9	30·113	65·8	65·4	60·3
3926	11 23 24·2	9 25·8	8 26·25	9 25·8	9 25·8	N. 2 55+0 33·55				
4015	11 43 7·2	9 32·1	13 24·0	9 32·1	9 32·1	N. 0 55—3 23·5				
4202	12 18 14·8	9 27·1	10 2·2	9 27·2	9 27·15	S. 4 15+0 9·05				
4458	13 9 58·2	10 3·4	10 3·2	10 3·3	10 3·35	S. 2 0—4 0·15				
4686	13 55 38·5	9 26·2	10 17·4	9 26·3	9 26·25	S. 1 40+0 25·15	30·100	65·0	65·0	57·6
7992	22 47 0·3	9 11·6	10 0·55	9 11·6	9 11·6	N. 3 30—0 22·95	30·041	55·5	55·2	65·8

♀ APRIL 11, 1845.—FACE OF SECTOR EAST.

Number of B.A.C.	Time by Chronometer.	Micr. for Plumb-line on Dot.	Micr. for Observation of Star.	Micr. for Plumb-line on Dot.	Mean of Micr. for Plumb-line on Dot.	Star's Apparent Zenith Distance.	Barom.	Attd.	Lower.	Out.
Anon.	9 37 45·8	9 19·3	4 28·9	9 19·3	9 19·3	N. 2 0—4 24·4	29·940	67·0	66·9	
3403	9 47 27·0	9 16·2	7 29·45	9 16·2	9 16·2	N. 3 35—1 20·75				
Anon.	9 59 43·0	9 16·3	9 6·0	9 16·3	9 16·3	N. 3 35—0 10·3				
3578	10 18 6·9	9 7·0	6 33·65	9 7·2	9 7·1	N. 3 40—2 7·45				
3755	10 47 30·5	8 23·1	12 30·9	8 23·1	8 23·1	S. 2 25—4 7·8	29·933	65·4	66·2	56·8
3926	11 23 25·8	11 0·6	12 4·9	11 0·4	11 0·5	N. 2 55+1 4·4				
4015	11 43 7·5	10 23·1	6 32·8	10 23·1	10 23·1	N. 0 55—3 24·3				
4202	12 18 8·5	10 23·7	10 17·7	10 23·7	10 23·7	S. 4 15+0 0·0				
4458	13 9 54·8	10 1·1	14 4·45	10 0·8	10 0·95	S. 2 0—4 3·5	29·905	64·4	65·8	55·0
4686	13 55 35·2	9 24·6	9 5·35	9 24·7	9 24·65	S. 1 40+0 19·3				

April 6.—Dense fog.
7.—Clouded, or rain falling.
8.—Occasional showers.
9.—No. 4458.—The seconds of transit doubtful.
11.—Anon. 9h 59m.—Very faint: the observation uncertain.

♄ APRIL 12, 1845.—FACE OF SECTOR WEST.

Number of B.A.C.	Time by Chronometer.	Micr. for Plumb-line on Dot.	Micr. for Observation of Star.	Micr. for Plumb-line on Dot.	Mean of Micr. for Plumb-line on Dot.	Star's Apparent Zenith Distance.	Barom.	Thermometers. Attd.	Lower.	Out.
	h m s	rev. pts.	rev. pts.	rev. pts.	rev. pts.	o ′ rev. pts.	in.			
Anon.	9 37 38·2	10 15·6	15 9·1	10 15·6	10 15·6	N. 2 0—4 27·5	30·045	66·0	66·4	59·8
3403	9 47 17·4	10 23·0	12 15·25	10 23·0	10 23·0	N. 3 35—1 26·25				

☉ APRIL 13, 1845.—FACE OF SECTOR WEST.

Anon.	9 59	11 2·3	11 15·4	11 2·3	11 2·3	N. 3 35—0 13·1	30·372	64·6	64·8	54·0
3578	10 17 ·2·0	11 18·3	13 30·0	11 18·1	11 18·2	N. 3 40—2 11·8				
3755	10 47 21·3	11 13·1	7 9·5	11 13·3	11 13·2	S. 2 25—4 3·7				
3926	11 23 12·2	11 3·8	9 4·7	10 3·8	10 3·8	N. 2 55+0 33·1	30·379	64·2		
4202	12 18 1·8	12 20·3	12 31·0	12 20·3	12 20·3	S. 4 15+0 10·7				

☾ APRIL 14, 1845.—FACE OF SECTOR EAST.

Anon.	9 36 33·8	10 25·3	6 1·75	10 25·3	10 25·3	N. 2 0—4 23·55	30·374	63·8	63·6	58·4
3403	9 47 14·8	9 26·7	8 6·6	9 26·7	9 26·7	N. 3 35—1 20·1				
3578	10 17 54·8	9 26·2	7 19·4	9 26·0	9 26·1	N. 3 40—2 6·7				
3755	10 47 17·5	8 26·4	13 0·7	8 26·2	8 26·3	S. 2 25—4 8·4				
3926	11 23 14·0	11 22·4	12 25·45	11 22·4	11 22·4	N. 2 55+1 3·05	30·377	63·6	63·6	58·4

FACE OF SECTOR WEST.

4015	11 42 51·3	11 10·0	15 2·35	11 9·9	11 9·95	N. 0 55—3 26·4				
4202	12 17 57·4	11 0·2	11 10·15	11 0·0	11 0·1	S. 4 15+0 10·05				
4458	13 9 41·7	19 9·5	15 9·9	19 9·6	19 9·55	S. 2 0—3 33·65				
4086	13	11 8·75	12 1·05	11 8·85	11 8·8	S. 1 40+0 26·25	30·362	63·2	63·3	58·4
7992	22 46 44·7	10 17·5	11 5·6	10 17·6	10 17·55	N. 3 30—0 22·05	30·288	63·4	63·2	60·6

♂ APRIL 15, 1845.—FACE OF SECTOR WEST.

Anon.	9 59 21·5	10 14·0	10 27·4	10 14·0	10 14·0	N. 3 35—0 13·4	30·074	64·5	64·8	63·8
3755	10 47 14·6	11 32·8	7 29·75	11 32·9	11 32·85	S. 2 25—4 3·1				
3926	11 23 14·7	10 9·1	9 10·4	10 9·1	10 9·1	N. 2 55+0 32·7	30·063	64·7		63·0
4202	12 17 54·4	10 21·1	10 31·7	10 21·3	10 21·15	S. 4 15+0 10·55				
4458	13 9 38·8	10 4·4	15 4·25	10 4·5	10 4·45	S. 1 55+4 33·8				
4686	13 55 19·5	9 33·6	10 26·0	9 33·7	9 33·65	S. 1 40+0 26·35	30·056	64·5		58·0

♃ APRIL 16, 1845.—FACE OF SECTOR EAST.

3923	11 23 8·5	10 14·0	11 16·6	10 14·0	10 14·0	N. 2 55+1 2·6	30·015	65·4	65·7	61·4
4015	11 42 50·2	10 5·1	6 14·6	10 5·3	10 5·2	N. 0 55—3 24·6				

♄ APRIL 17, 1845.—FACE OF SECTOR WEST.

Anon.	9 59	6 32·4	7 13·3	6 32·6	6 32·5	N. 3 35—0 14·8	30·212	65·6	66·2	57·0
3578	10 17 41·0	10 23·2	12 33·95	10 23·0	10 23·1	N. 3 40—2 10·85				
3926	11 23 0·5	10 22·3	9 23·1	10 22·2	10 22·25	N. 2 55+0 33·15				
4015	11 42 43·7	10 25·5	14 18·4	10 25·5	10 25·5	N. 0 55—3 26·9	30·220	65·6	66·2	55·4
4202	12 17 50·0	11 0·0	11 11·1	10 33·9	10 33·95	S. 4 15+0 11·15		66·0		
4458	13 9 34·5	10 27·0	6 28·5	10 27·1	10 27·05	S. 2 0—3 32·55	30·203	65·0	65·0	57·2
4086	13 55 15·2	10 23·5	11 15·5	10 23·4	10 23·45	S. 1 40+0 26·05				

April 12.—Anon. and 3403.—Seen faintly through cloud.
15.—No. 3926.—The seconds of transit doubtful.
17.—Anon. 9ʰ 59ᵐ.—Uncertain.

♀ APRIL 18, 1845.—FACE OF SECTOR EAST.

Number of B.A.C.	Time by Chronometer.	Micr. for Plumb-line on Dot.	Micr. for Observation of Star.	Micr. for Plumb-line on Dot.	Mean of Micr. for Plumb-line on Dot.	Star's Apparent Zenith Distance.	Barom.	Thermometers.		
								Attd.	Lower.	Out.
Anon.	9 59 19·5	10 23·75	10 14·6	10 23·85	10 23·8	N. 3 35—0 9·2	30·205	66·0	66·2	59·0
3578	10 17 43·4	10 22·3	8 14·5	10 22·2	10 22.25	N. 3 40—2 7·75				
3926	11	10 11·7	11 15·4	10 11·6	10 11·85	N. 2 55+1 3·75	30·218	66·4	66·0	58·2
4015	11 42 44·2	10 5·0	6 14·4	10 5·0	10 5·0	N. 0 55—3 24·6			66·0	
4202	12 17 45·2	10 6·4	9 33·75	10 6·8	10 6·6	S. 4 15+0 6·85				
4458	13 9 31·2	10 9·4	14 11·4	10 9·3	10 9·35	S. 2 0—4 2·05				
4686	13 55 11·7	10 11·0	9 23·3	10 10·8	10 10·9	S. 1 40+0 21·6	30·214	65·0	65·0	54·6

♄ APRIL 19, 1845.—FACE OF SECTOR WEST.

3578	10 17 34·0	10 16·0	12 28·0	10 16·0	10 16·0	N. 3 40—2 12·0	30·211	66·0	66·0	60·5
4015	11 42 37·0	10 1·3	13 28·75	10 1·4	10 1·35	N. 0 55—3 27·4				
4202	12 17 43·5	10 9·6	10 20·5	10 9·4	10 9·5	S. 4 15+0 11·0	30·228	65·8	65·6	60·3
4458	13 9 27·5	10 4·9	6 7·0	10 5·1	10 5·0	S. 2 0—3 32·0				
4686	13 55 8·0	10 12·7	11 5·1	10 12·7	10 12·7	S. 1 40+0 26·4	30·236	65·3	65·1	59·0

☉ APRIL 20, 1845.—FACE OF SECTOR EAST.

3578	10 17 35·5	11 12.0	9 4·4	11 12·0	11 12·0	N. 3 40—2 7·6	30·228	64·8	65·0	58·0
3926	11 22 55·0	10 32·8	12 2·2	10 32·8	10 32·8	N. 2 55—1 3·4	30·241	64·8	64·5	58·2
4202	12 17 38·3	11 13·5	11 5·4	11 13·4	11 13·45	S. 4 15+0 8·05				
4458	13 9 24·2	10 30·5	14 32·3	10 30·5	10 30·5	S. 2 0—4 1·8				
4686	13 55 4·7	11 0·7	10 13·7	11 0·8	11 0·75	S. 1 40+0 21·05	30·218	64·2	64·4	59·0

☾ APRIL 21, 1845.—FACE OF SECTOR WEST.

3578	10 17 26·2	11 22·2	14 0·65	11 22·2	11 22·2	N. 3 40—2 12·45			65·2	
3926	11 22 46·6	11 25·9	10 27·5	11 25·9	11 25·9	N. 2 55+0 32·4				
4015	11 42 29·4	11 19·5	15 13·3	11 19·6	11 19·55	N. 0 55—3 27·55	30·342	63·8	65·2	52·8
4202	12 17 36·5	10 26·0	11 0·7	10 25·8	10 25·9	S. 4 15+0 8·8				
4458	13 9 20·2	10 17·4	6 19·05	10 17·4	10 17·4	S. 2 0—3 32·35				
4686	13 55 1·0	10 15·4	11 7·85	10 15·4	10 15·4	S. 1 40+0 26·45	30·336	62·0	64·0	50·4

FACE OF SECTOR EAST.

7992	22	11 20·9	11 4·95	11 21·1	11 21·0	N. 3 30—0 16·05	30·353	63·6	63·6	63·6

♂ APRIL 22, 1845.—FACE OF SECTOR EAST.

3926	11 22 49·2	11 1·1	12 4·4	11 1·1	11 1·1	N. 2 55+1 3·3			64·7	
4015	11 42 30·9	10 19·7	6 28·0	10 19·7	10 19·7	N. 0 55—3 25·7	30·235	65·0	64·6	59·6
4202	12 17 31·0	10 10·8	10 2·55	10 10·6	10 10·7	S. 4 15+0 8·15			64·6	
4458	13 9 17·5	10 4·4	14 6·6	10 4·5	10 4·45	S. 2 0—4 2·15				
4686	13 54 58·5	10 3·0	9 15·9	10 3·0	10 3·0	S. 1 40+0 21·1	30·218	64·0	64·2	55·6

☿ APRIL 23, 1845.— FACE OF SECTOR WEST.

3578	10 17 20·8	10 4·4	12 16·9	10 4·6	10 4·5	N. 3 40—2 12·4	30·048	65·2	65·4	60·2
3926	11 22 41·2	9 30·3	8 31·35	9 30·3	9 30·3	N. 2 55+0 32·95	30·060	65·1	65·4	56·0
4015	11 42 24·2	9 4·7	12 31·5	9 4·8	9 4·75	N. 0 55—3 26·75				
4202	12 17 31·5	9 33·8	10 11·7	9 33·7	9 33·75	S. 4 15+0 11·95				

ARC OF THE MERIDIAN.—CAPE OF GOOD HOPE.

☿ APRIL 23, 1845.—FACE OF SECTOR WEST—(continued).

Number of B.A.C.	Time by Chronometer.	Micr. for Plumb-line on Dot.	Micr. for Observation of Star.	Micr. for Plumb-line on Dot.	Mean of Micr. for Plumb-line on Dot.	Star's Apparent Zenith Distance.	Barom.	Thermometers.		
								Attd.	Lower.	Out.
	h m s	rev. pts.	rev. pts.	rev. pts.	rev. pts.	° ' rev. pts.	in.			
4458	13 9 15·8	9 18·0	5 20·5	9 18·2	9 18·1	S. 2 0—3 31·6				
4686	13 54 54·0	9 31·6	10 24·7	9 31·5	9 31·55	S. 1 40+0 27·15	30·092	64·4	65·0	54·8

♃ APRIL 24, 1845.—FACE OF SECTOR EAST.

Number of B.A.C.	Time by Chronometer.	Micr. for Plumb-line on Dot.	Micr. for Observation of Star.	Micr. for Plumb-line on Dot.	Mean of Micr. for Plumb-line on Dot.	Star's Apparent Zenith Distance.	Barom.	Attd.	Lower.	Out.
3578	10 17 25·5	10 12·9	8 4·75	10 12·7	10 12·8	N. 3 40—2 8·05	30·255	65·0	65·4	59·6
3926	11 22 45·2	10 26·0	11 28·8	10 25·9	10 25·95	N. 2 55+1 2·85			65·0	
4015	11 42 26·4	10 20·8	6 30·25	10 20·8	10 20·8	N. 0 55—3 24·55				
4202	12 17 27·5	9 30·3	9 21·85	9 30·3	9 30·3	S. 4 15+0 8·45			65·2	
4458	13 9 14·0	10 5·3	14 7·0	10 5·1	10 5·2	S. 2 0—4 1.8			65·0	
4686	13 54 54·6	10 15·3	9 27·1	10 14·9	10 15·1	S. 1 40—0 22·0	30·250	64·8	64·8	60·2

♀ APRIL 25, 1845.—FACE OF SECTOR WEST.

Number of B.A.C.	Time by Chronometer.	Micr. for Plumb-line on Dot.	Micr. for Observation of Star.	Micr. for Plumb-line on Dot.	Mean of Micr. for Plumb-line on Dot.	Star's Apparent Zenith Distance.	Barom.	Attd.	Lower.	Out.
4015	11 42 19·0	10 16·1	14 10·0	10 15·9	10 16·0	N. 0 55—3 28·0	30·205	63·6	63·5	56·0
4202	12 17 26·6	10 26·3	11 4·45	10 26·3	10 26·3	S. 4 15+0 12·15				
4458	13 9 10·5	10 33·0	7 2·8	10 33·1	10 33·05	N. 2 0—3 30·25				
4686	13 54 51·2	10 30·6	11 24·7	10 30·6	10 30·6	S. 1 40+0 28·1	30·219	63·3	63·2	55·4

⊙ APRIL 27, 1845.—FACE OF SECTOR WEST.

Number of B.A.C.	Time by Chronometer.	Micr. for Plumb-line on Dot.	Micr. for Observation of Star.	Micr. for Plumb-line on Dot.	Mean of Micr. for Plumb-line on Dot.	Star's Apparent Zenith Distance.	Barom.	Attd.	Lower.	Out.
3926	11 22 30·0	10 21·5	9 23·45	10 21·6	10 21·55	N. 2 55+0 32·1	30·202	63·6	63·6	59·3

FACE OF SECTOR EAST.

4015	11 42 17·2	10 15·5	6 22·9	10 15·5	10 15·6	N. 0 55—3 26·6	30·195	63·6	63·6	59·3
4202	12 17 19·5	10 19·6	10 10·4	10 19·4	10 19·5	S. 4 15+0 9·1				
4458	13 9 4·6	10 22·0	14 22·6	10 22·0	10 22·0	S. 2 0—4 0·6				
4686	13 54 45·8	10 25·9	10 3·6	10 25·9	10 25·9	S. 1 40+0 22·3	30·166	63·6	63·4	59·1

☿ APRIL 30, 1845.—FACE OF SECTOR WEST.

Number of B.A.C.	Time by Chronometer.	Micr. for Plumb-line on Dot.	Micr. for Observation of Star.	Micr. for Plumb-line on Dot.	Mean of Micr. for Plumb-line on Dot.	Star's Apparent Zenith Distance.	Barom.	Attd.	Lower.	Out.
3598	10 19 20·6	9 23·2	6 31·35	9 23·3	9 23·25	N. 4 5+2 25·9	30·038	64·0	65·0	57·0
3926	11 22 17·5	9 17·0	8 19·35	9 16·8	9 16·9	N. 2 55+0 31·55				
4015	11 42 0·3	9 24·3	13 19·75	9 24·4	9 24·35	N. 0 55—3 29·4				
4202	12 17 7·2	9 33·5	10 12·1	9 33·5	9 33·5	S. 4 15+0 12·6	30·031	63·8	64·3	55·4
4458	13 8 52·0	10 18·4	6 22·0	10 18·5	10 18·45	S. 2 0—3 30·45				
4686	13 54 32·2	10 16·6	11 10·7	10 16·7	10 16·65	S. 1 40+0 28·05				

♀ MAY 2, 1845.—FACE OF SECTOR WEST.

Number of B.A.C.	Time by Chronometer.	Micr. for Plumb-line on Dot.	Micr. for Observation of Star.	Micr. for Plumb-line on Dot.	Mean of Micr. for Plumb-line on Dot.	Star's Apparent Zenith Distance.	Barom.	Attd.	Lower.	Out.
1878	5 46 15·5	10 25·5	8 31·8	10 25·5	10 25·5	S. 1 55—1 27·7	30·200	64·6	65·0	
2293	6 53 14·4	11 4·2	11 22·05	11 4·3	11 4·25	N. 5 10—0 17·8				

FACE OF SECTOR EAST.

3598	10 23 19·5	11 13·6	14 10·4	11 13·7	11 13·65	N 4 5+2 30·75	30·240	63·6	64·2	51·2
4015	11 45 56·2	10 16·9	6 24·2	10 17·1	10 17·0	N. 0 55—3 26·8				
4202	12 20 57·6	10 17·8	10 8·2	10 17·8	10 17·8	S. 4 15+0 9·6				

April 30 — No, 3598. =5th magnitude.
May 2.—The chronometer put forward 4ᵐ.

☉ MAY 4, 1845.—FACE OF SECTOR WEST.

Number of B.A.C.	Time by Chronometer.	Micr. for Plumb-line on Dot.	Micr. for Observation of Star.	Micr. for Plumb-line un Dot.	Mean of Micr. for Plumb-line on Dot.	Star's Apparent Zenith Distance.	Barom.	Thermometers.		
								Attd.	Lower.	Out.
	h m s	rev. pts.	rev. pts.	rev. pts.	rev. pts.	o ′ rev. pts.	in.			
4458	13 12 39·0	11 22·5	15 17·9	11 22·5	11 22·5	S. 2 0—3 29·4	30·096	63·4	63·4	58·4

FACE OF SECTOR EAST.

4686	13 58 19·7	10 9·2	9 19·75	10 9·3	10 9·25	S. 1 40+0 23·5				

☾ MAY 5, 1845.—FACE OF SECTOR EAST.

4458	13 12 36·0	11 0·9	15 0·9	11 0·9	11 0·9	S. 2 0—4 0·0	30·051	63·6	64·0	56·0

♄ JUNE 21, 1845.—FACE OF SECTOR WEST.

5632	16 40 20·0	9 12·1	8 7·9	9 12·1	9 12·1	S. 0 5—1 4·2	30·435	57·5	58·0	50·8
5915	17 23 18·2	9 33·5	6 8·95	9 33·4	9 33·45	S. 3 5—3 24·5				
6233	18 14 5·2	10 8·2	11 29·5	10 8·2	10 8·2	S. 0 30+1 21·3	30·431	57·4	57·7	50·3

☉ JUNE 22, 1845.—FACE OF SECTOR EAST.

5632	16 40 27·2	10 14·9	11 23·4	10 15·0	10 14·95	S. 0 5—1 8·45	30·393	58·8	58·3	51·4
5915	17 23 22·8	10 2·2	13 31·3	10 1·8	10 2·0	S. 3 5—3 29·3				
6233	18 14 12·2	10 6·5	8 23·25	10 6·3	10 6·4	S. 0 30+1 17·15				

☾ JUNE 23, 1845.—FACE OF SECTOR WEST.

5632	16 40 30·2	10 14·4	9 11·25	10 14·4	10 14·4	S. 0 5—1 3·15	30·429	58·5	59·0	55·5
5915	17 23 29·2	11 17·4	7 26·95	11 17·4	11 17·4	S. 3 5—3 25·15				
6233	18 14 15·7	11 3·1	12 23·4	11 3·1	11 3·1	S. 0 30+1 20·3	30·429	57·6	58·4	50·4

☽ JUNE 24, 1845.—FACE OF SECTOR EAST.

5632	16 40 37·8	10 17·0	11 25·7	10 17·0	10 17·0	S. 0 5—1 8·7	30·258	58·8	59·7	58·8
5915	17 23 33·5	10 4·8	14 0·8	10 4·9	10 4·85	S. 3 5—3 29·95				
6233	18 14 23·5	10 15·3	8 32·25	10 15·3	10 15·3	S. 0 30+1 17·05	30·251	58·8	59·7	59·2

☿ JUNE 25, 1845.—FACE OF SECTOR EAST.

5632	16 40 43·5	10 19·8	11 28·65	10 19·8	10 19·8	S. 0 5—1 8·85	30·108	61·0	61·5	62·4

♃ JUNE 26, 1845.—FACE OF SECTOR WEST.

5632	16 40 46·5	10 18·9	9 15·1	10 18·9	10 18·9	S. 0 5—1 3·8	30·265	60·4	60·9	52·4
5915	17 23 45·2	10 32·0	7 8·05	10 32·0	10 32·0	S. 3 5—3 23·95				

♄ JUNE 28, 1845.—FACE OF SECTOR WEST.

5632	16 40 56·8	9 30·0	8 26·0	9 30·0	9 30·0	S. 0 5—1 4·0	30·480	58·4	58·7	45·4
5915	17 23 56·0	10 2·4	6 12·7	10 2·5	10 2·45	S. 3 5—3 23·75	30·495	58·0	58·7	44·0

☾ JUNE 30, 1845.—FACE OF SECTOR EAST.

Number of B.A.C.	Time by Chronometer.	Mier. for Plumb-line on Dot.	Mier. for Observation of Star.	Micr. for Plumb-line on Dot.	Mean of Micr. for Plumb-line on Dot.	Star's Apparent Zenith Distance.	Barom.	Thermometers.		
								Attd.	Lower.	Out.
	h m s	rev. pts.	rev. pts.	rev. pts.	rev. pts.	° ′ rev. pts.	in.			
5915	17 24 6·3	9 33·6	13 29·4	9 33·7	9 33·65	S. 3 5—3 29·75	30·452	58·4	57·8	46·7
6233	18 13 55·0	10 0·4	8 18·2	10 0·4	10 0·4	S. 0 30+1 16·2	30·449	57·2	57·6	44·8

UNREDUCED OBSERVATIONS

MADE WITH

BRADLEY'S ZENITH SECTOR

AT THE NORTHERN EXTREMITY OF THE ARC,

BUSHMAN FLAT, CLANWILLIAM DISTRICT:

IN

JUNE AND JULY, 1847.

♀ June 18, 1847.—Face of Sector East.

Number of B.A.C.	Time by Chronometer.	Micr. for Plumb-line on Dot.	Micr. for Observation of Star.	Micr. for Plumb-line on Dot.	Mean of Micr. for Plumb-line on Dot.	Star's Apparent Zenith Distance.	Barom.	Attd.	Upper.	Lower.
	h m s	rev. pts.	rev. pts.	rev. pts.	rev. pts.	° ′ rev. pts.	in.			
1802	5 40 36·0	10 1·6	9 13·15	10 1·6	10 1·6	S. 4 25+0 22·45	26·410	55·4		54·3
2293	6	10 4·7	6 9·7	10 4·5	10 4·6	N. 1 0—3 28·9				
4517	13 30 36·5	10 12·5	5 17·9	10 12·3	10 12·4	N. 1 0—4 28·5				
4579	13 43 30·5	10 16·6	6 25·4	10 16·6	10 16·55	S. 2 30+3 25·15				
4623	13 49 30·7	10 16·5	10 15·7	10 16·5	10 16·55	S. 2 30+0 0·85	26·485	49·8		50·0
4852	14 40 48·0	10 16·7	7 22·6	10 16·6	10 16·65	S. 4 45+2 28·05				
4891	14 47 52·6	10 16·4	10 3·1	10 16·4	10 16·4	N. 2 25—0 13·3				
4916	14 52 50·6	10 7·8	10 22·55	10 7·6	10 7·7	S. 3 30—0 14·85				
Anon.	15 0 7·2	10 11·0	4 27·1	10 11·2	10 11·1	S. 2 15+5 18·0				
Anon.	15 5	10 2·5	10 21·2	10 2·5	10 2·5	S. 2 35—0 18·7	26·505	50·5		40·8
5032	15 15 4·5	9 23·8	8 6·3	9 23·6	9 23·7	N. 0 10—1 17·4				
5151	15 35 40·3	9 33·8	6 7·55	9 33·6	9 33·7	N. 0 30—3 26·15				
5227	15 47 45·4	6 8·8	5 30·9	6 8·6	6 8·7	S. 3 25+0 11·8				
5272	15 54 1·2	9 27·25	6 27·4	9 26·75	9 27·0	N. 1 0—2 33·6				
5374	16 8 4·0	10 18·7	8 5·1	10 18·5	10 18·6	N. 0 45—2 13·5				
5435	16 16 25·2	10 33·6	6 7·6	10 33·4	10 33·5	S. 0 45+4 25·9				
Anon.	16 20 38·0	10 15·9	8 22·7	10 16·0	10 15·95	S. 3 5+1 27·25				
5498	16 26 38·0	11 8·4	9 6·5	11 8·4	11 8·4	N. 3 40—2 1·9				
5588	16 40 20·6	9 24·1	10 30·7	9 24·1	9 24·1	S. 2 5—1 6·6				
5632	16 46 46·2	9 30·2	7 19·3	9 29·8	9 30·0	S. 4 15+2 10·7				
5735	17 1 16·7	10 7·8	10 20·1	10 7·6	10 7·7	S. 4 10—0 12·4				
5817	17 13 37·8	9 24·4	10 5·2	9 24·4	9 24·4	S. 2 45—0 14·8				
5881	17 24 8·2	10 8·5	11 29·45	10 8·5	10 8·5	0 0+1 20·95				
6016	17 45 45·8	10 4·0	11 10·25	10 3·8	10 3·9	S. 1 55—1 6·33	26·407	48·0		48·1
6074	17 55 48·5	10 26·7	11 19·0	10 26·3	10 26·5	S. 0 30—0 26·5				
6115	18 2 31·6	10 33·6	9 15·3	10 33·8	10 33·5	S. 0 40+1 18·2				
6145	18 6 46·2	11 0·7	10 5·9	11 0·3	11 0·5	S. 1 0+0 28·6				
6233	18 20 31·2	10 29·8	6 9·55	10 29·8	10 29·8	S. 4 40+4 20·05				
Anon.	18 26 29·5	11 21·0	13 14·5	11 21·2	11 21·1	S. 3 25—1 27·4				
6305	18 30 26·0	11 21·1	15 8·2	11 21·1	11 21·1	S. 3 25—3 21·1				
6414	18 49 23·5	11 2·7	10 26·0	11 2·5	11 2·6	S. 1 10—0 10·6				
6489	18 59 25·2	10 14·2	14 26·2	10 14·3	10 14·3	N. 0 50+4 7·7				
6525	19 4 26·2	10 18·4	14 26·2	10 18·6	10 18·5	N. 0 50+4 7·7				
6639	19 23 49·2	9 7·4	12 29·1	9 7·5	9 7·45	S. 0 20—3 21·65				
Anon.	19 28 2·0	9 26·2	11 23·2	9 26·2	9 26·2	S. 0 5—1 31·0				
6753	19 42 14·6	9 4·7	7 23·0	9 4·1	9 4·4	S. 1 30+1 15·4				
6877	20 1 8·2	9 20·0	10 28·0	9 20·0	9 20·0	S. 2 45—1 8·0				
6948	20 12 52·5	9 11·2	11 32·6	9 11·4	9 11·3	S. 0 45—2 21·3				
7011	20 21	9 1·8	10 7·0	9 1·6	9 1·6	N. 0 10+1 5·4				
7026	20 23 41·0		9 33·1	9· 1·4	9 1·6	N. 0 10+0 31·5				
7057	20 28 7·2		4 7·1	9 1·6	9 1·6	N. 0 10—4 28·5				
Anon.	20 31 0·0		11 13·5	9 21·7		S. 0 5—1 25·8				
Anon.	20 40 29·5	9 22·0	13 5·4	9 22·2	9 22·1	S. 0 15—3 17·3				
7207	20 46 54·0	9 28·5	8 11·95	9 28·6	9 28·55	S. 4 35+1 16·6				
Anon.	21 0 16·7	9 21·5	13 7·6	9 21·4	9 21·45	0 0+3 20·15				
Anon.	21 7 27·0	9 19·2	8 7·8	9 19·3	9 19·25	S. 0 35+1 11·45				
7386	21 15 9·8	9 13·5	11 14·4	9 13·5	9 13·5	S. 3 5—2 0·9				
Anon.	21 19 16·5	8 26·8	10 11·2	8 26·0	8 26·85	S. 0 5—1 18·35				
Anon.	21 32 23·2	8 31·5	12 29·4	8 31·4	8 31·45	S. 0 40—3 31·95				
7557	21 42 19·2	9 9·2	11 27·7	9 9·3	9 9·3	S. 4 0—2 18·4				
7657	21 58 35·2	9 27·2	6 31·0	9 27·2	9 27·1	N. 0 35—2 30·1				
Anon.	22 2 26·3	9 27·0	8 2·1	9 27·0	9 27·1	N. 0 35—1 25·0				
7842	22 29 17·4	11 5·0	14 20·2	11 5·0	11 5·0	S. 3 25—3 15·2	26·422	47·7		44·8
7909	22 40 22·6	9 14·9	9 16·25	9 14·8	9 14·85	S. 0 25—0 1·4				
7966	22 50 30·2	9 0·0	15 12·0	9 0·0	9 0·0	S. 4 0—6 12 0				

This station is north-east of, and at a short distance from, a group of stony monticules named t' Korberg.
The distance between the upper dot's centre and dot 5° 30′ on the right hand side of the arch exceeds the distance between it and 5° 40′ on the left hand side by a diameter of the dot hole.

♀ JUNE 18, 1847.—FACE OF SECTOR EAST—(continued).

Number of B.A.C.	Time by Chronometer	Micr. for Plumb-line on Dot.	Micr. for Observation of Star.	Micr. for Plumb-line on Dot.	Mean of Micr. for Plumb-line on Dot.	Star's Apparent Zenith Distance.	Barom.	Thermometers.		
								Attd.	Upper.	Lower.
	b m s	rev. pts.	rev. pts.	rev. pts.	rev. pts.	o ′ rev. pts.	in.			
7992	22 55 42·8	9 17·8	7 3·1	9 17·6	9 17·7	S. 0 40+2 14·6				

♄ JUNE 19, 1847.—FACE OF SECTOR WEST.

| 2293 | 6 59 8·9 | 9 31·5 | 13 9·0 | 9 31·7 | 9 31·6 | N. 1 0—3 11·4 | 26·410 | 55·4 | | 54·3 |

☾ JUNE 21, 1847.—FACE OF SECTOR WEST.

Number of B.A.C.	Time by Chronometer	Micr. for Plumb-line on Dot.	Micr. for Observation of Star.	Micr. for Plumb-line on Dot.	Mean of Micr. for Plumb-line on Dot.	Star's Apparent Zenith Distance.	Barom.	Attd.	Upper.	Lower.
2293	6 59 18·2	10 32·0	14 9·4	10 32·2	10 32·1	N. 1 0—3 11·3	26·706	48·6	51·6	48·0
4517	13 30 40·6	10 3·0	14 15·25	10 3·0	10 2·95	N. 1 0—4 12·3				
4548	13 36 54·6	10 3·0	14 19·05	10 2·8	10 2·95	N. 1 0—4 16·7				
4579	13 43 37·2	10 11·3	13 23·55	10 11·1	10 11·28	S. 2 30+3 12·27				
4623	13 49 38·0	10 11·3	9 32·5	10 11·4	10 11·28	S. 2 30—0 12·28	26·709	37·4	39·2	38·6
4719	14 12 57·8	10 26·8	10 7·55	10 26·6	10 26·7	N. 1 10+0 19·15				
4784	14 26 0·8	10 7·6	8 6·1	10 7·8	10 7·7	N. 0 55+2 1·6				
4891	14 48 9·5	10 3·5	10 1·8	10 3·7	10 3·6	N. 2 25+0 1·8				
4916	14 52 58·2		9 10·5	10 4·0		S. 3 30—0 27·5				
Anon.	15 0 17·2	9 30·8	14 32·55	9 30·4	9 30·6	S. 2 20+5 1·95	26·709	36·5	39·0	37·8
Anon.	15 4 30·0	10 5·8	9 10·4	10 5·6	10 5·7	S. 2 35—0 29·3				
5032	15 15 16·5	9 26·4	10 30·3	9 26·4	9 26·4	N. 0 10—1 3·9				
5151	15 36 2·8	9 33·2	13 11·8	9 33·0	9 33·1	N. 0 30—3 12·7				
Anon.	15 41 14·0	10 13·3	14 12·0	10 13·1	10 13·2	S. 1 20+3 32·8				
5227	15 47 52·0	10 29·1	10 27·5	10 29·5	10 29·3	S. 3 25—0 1·8				
5272	15 54 15·2	10 3·9	12 21·4	10 3·9	10 3·9	N. 1 0—2 17·5				
5374	16 8 19·5	9 20·7	11 17·0	9 20·4	9 20·55	N. 0 45—1 30·45				
5435	16 16 36·2	9 27·6	14 3·5	9 27·8	9 27·7	S. 0 45+4 9·8				
Anon.	16 20 43·0	10 23·6	11 33·3	10 23·4	10 23·5	S. 3 5+1 9·8				
5498	16 26 56·2	10 10·8	11 31·3	10 10·9	10 10·85	N. 3 40—1 20·45				
5588	16 40 29·5	10 18·8	8 30·6	10 19·0	10 18·0	S. 2 5—1 22·3				
5632	16 46 49·6	11 4·1	13 1·9	11 3·9	11 4·0	S. 4 15+1 31·3				
5735	17 1 19·5	9 16·5	8 24·8	9 16·1	9 16·3	S. 4 10—0 25·5				
5817	17 13 45·0	9 10·8	8 15·4	9 11·0	9 10·9	S. 2 45—0 29·5	26·682	35·6	37·2	36·4
6016	17 45 55·0	8 18·8	6 31·6	8 18·6	8 18·6	S. 1 55—1 21·1				
6074	17 56 0·3	10 27·5	9 20·2	10 27·4	10 27·45	S. 0 30—1 7·25				
6115	18 2 43·0	10 22·2	11 25·9	10 22·4	10 22·3	S. 0 40+1 0·6				
6145	18 6 56·8	9 33·0	10 13·4	9 33·0	9 33·0	S. 1 0+0 14·4				
6233	18 20 33·0	9 2·0	14 9·2	10 2·0	10 2·0	S. 4 40+4 7·2				
6285	18 27 39·0		9 12·4	8 21·0		S. 3 20+0 25·4				
6305	18 30 30·0		3 20·8	7 21·5	*	S. 3 25—4 0·7				
6414	18	9 27·4	9 23·5	9 27·4	9 27·4	S. 1 10—0 3·9	26·713	34·2	35·6	35·0
6489	18 59 37·4	9 31·2	11 20·3	9 31·4	9 31·3	S. 0 20+1 23·0				
6639	19 24 1·5	10 13·0	6 10·55	10 13·0	10 13·0	S. 0 20—4 2·45				
Anon.	19 28 15·0	10 30·9	8 19·1	10 30·9	10 30·9	S. 0 5—2 11·8				
6753	19 42 26·0	10 19·8	12 21·5	10 20·0	10 19·9	S. 1 30+2 1·6				
6877	20 1 16·2	10 27·2	9 3·25	10 27·3	10 27·25	S. 2 45—1 24·0				
6946	20 13 3·5	11 2·4	8 0·45	11 2·3	11 2·35	S. 2 45—1 1·9				
7011	20 22 4·5	11 10·5	9 26·6	11 10·3	11 10·36	N. 0 10+1 17·76				
7026	20 23 57·5		9 31·8	11 10·4	11 10·36	N. 0 10+1 12·56				
7057	20 28 19·8	11 10·3	15 24·8	11 10·3	11 10·36	N. 0 10—4 14·44				
Anon.	20 31 12·0	11 3·4	8 31·75	11 3·0	11 3·2	S. 0 5—2 5·45	26·690	33·4	34·5	33·4
Anon.	20 40 42·0	11 6·8	7 9·7	11 6·8	11 6·8	S. 0 15—3 31·1				
7207	20 46 57·0	10 23·4	11 27·1	10 23·8	10 23·6	S. 4 35+1 3·5				
Anon.	21 0 28·5	10 30·2	6 29·8	10 30·2	10 30·2	0 0+4 0·4				

Rainy or foggy weather between the 18th and 21st.

Mr. George Montagu adjusts the upper dot. Mr. Maclear manages below, at the micrometer.

June 21.—Moved the instrument in Azimuth a little, in the order of increasing readings.

Bad definitions.

No. 6414 and Anon. 19h 28m and 21h 0m are too faint.

☾ JUNE 21, 1847.—FACE OF SECTOR WEST—(continued).

Number of B.A.C.	Time by Chronometer.	Micr. for Plumb-line on Dot.	Micr. for Observation of Star.	Micr. for Plumb-line on Dot.	Mean of Micr. for Plumb-line on Dot.	Star's Apparent Zenith Distance.	Barom.	Attd.	Upper.	Lower.
	h m s	rev. pts.	rev. pts.	rev. pts.	rev. pts.	o ' rev. pts.	in.			
Anon.	21 7 38·0	10 26·5	11 21·2	10 26·7	10 26·6	S. 0 35+0 28·6				
7386	21 15 16·0	10 30·3	8 15·75	10 30·2	10 30·25	S. 3 5—2 14·5				
Anon.	21 19 28·5		8 11·0	10 8·3		S. 0 5—1 31·3				
Anon.	21 32 34·0	10 21·3	6 8·6	10 21·5	10 21·4	S 0 40—4 12·8				
7557	21 42 23·0	11 3·5	8 5·75	11 3·7	11 3·6	S. 4 0—2 31·85				
7657	21 58 48·5	10 30·3	13 8·55	10 30·5	10 30·45	N. 0 35—2 12·1				
Anon.	22 2 40·0	10 30·5	12 3·1	10 30·5	10 30·45	N. 0 35—1 6·65				
7842	22 29 23·5	11 16·5	7 20·1	11 16·1	11 16·3	S. 3 25—3 30·2				
7900	22 40 34·6	11 1·5	10 16·0	11 1·7	11 1·6	S. 0 25—0 19·6				
7966	22 50 34·6	10 27·5	12 33·6	10 27·7	10 27·6	S. 3 55+2 6·0				
7092	22 55 54·3	10 27·8	12 25·7	10 27·8	10 27·8	S. 0 40+1 31·9	26·690	32·0	30·8	33·6

♂ JUNE 22, 1847.—FACE OF SECTOR EAST.

Number of B.A.C.	Time by Chronometer.	Micr. for Plumb-line on Dot.	Micr. for Observation of Star.	Micr. for Plumb-line on Dot.	Mean of Micr. for Plumb-line on Dot.	Star's Apparent Zenith Distance.	Barom.	Attd.	Upper.	Lower.
2293	6 59 22·3	12 4·9	8 12·6	12 4·9	12 4·9	N. 1 0—3 26·3	26·731	49·8	49·0	47·8
4517	13 30 50·0	10 13·3	5 18·6	10 13·2	10 13·3	N. 1 0—4 28·7			41·0	40·2
4548	13 36 55·0	10 13·4	5 17·2	10 13·3	10 13·3	N. 1 0—4 30·1				
4579	13 43 51·2	10 17·0	6 25·5	10 17·7	10 17·85	S. 3 30+3 26·35				
4623	13 49 51·2	10 17·9	10 18·0	10 17·9	10 17·85	S. 2 30—0 0·15				
4719	14 12 58·2	10 21·5	10 25·9	10 21·1	10 21·3	N. 1 10+0 4·6	26·743	38·3	40·0	39·0
4784	14 26 1·5	10 15·2	12 1·9	10 15·0	10 15·1	N. 0 55+1 20·8				
Anon.	14 31 8·2	10 28·1	12 6·7	10 28·3	10 28·2	S. 2 55—1 12·5				
4852	14 41 12·0	10 27·0	7 33·5	10 27·4	10 27·2	S. 4 45+2 27·7				
4891	14 48 6·8	11 6·9	10 28·4	11 6·7	11 6·8	N. 2 25—0 12·4				
4916	14 53 14·5	11 13·0	11 28·55	11 28·3	11 13·15	S. 3 30—0 15·4				
Anon.	15 0 30·0	8 16·3	11 32·0	8 16·1	8 16·2	S. 2 20—3 15·8				
Anon.	15 4 41·5	9 1·5	9 17·1	9 1·1	9 1·3	S. 2 35—0 15·8	26·733	37·4	39·0	38·6
5032	15 15 21·4	8 31·0	7 15·2	8 30·8	8 30·9	N. 0 10—1 15·7				
5151	15	8 28·2	5 1·6	8 28·0	8 28·1	N. 0 30—3 26·5				
Anon.	15 41 22·3	9 2·1	4 26·25	9 2·3	9 2·2	S. 1 20+4 9·95				
5227	15 48 7·6	9 19·9	9 8·5	9 19·7	9 19·8	S. 3 25+0 11·3	26·733	37·0	38·5	37·6
5272	15 54 16·0	10 10·4	7 12·8	10 10·2	10 10·3	N. 1 0—2 31·5				
5374	16 8 21·5	10 17·5	8 6·4	10 17·4	10 17·45	N. 0 45—2 11·05				
5435	16 16 43·2	10 17·0	5 27·5	10 17·2	10 17·1	S. 0 45+4 23·6				
Anon.	16 20 50·0	10 32·0	9 11·2	10 32·0	10 32·0	S. 3 5+1 20·8				
5408	16 26 48·8	10 32·6	8 31·5	10 32·3	10 32·45	N. 3 40—2 0·95				
5588	16 40 40·5	10 26·4	11 33·8	10 26·6	10 26·5	S. 2 5—1 7·3				
5632	16 47 9·2	10 24·2	8 13·8	10 24·3	10 24·25	S. 4 15+2 10·85				
5735	17 1 39·5	10 23·4	11 1·5	10 23·4	10 23·4	S. 4 10—0 12·1				
5817	17 13 59·2	10 13·3	10 28·7	10 13·4	10 13·4	S. 2 45—0 15·3	26·725	36·0	37·0	36·5
5881	17 24 25·2	10 13·7	12 2·1	10 14·1	10 13·9	0 0+1 22·2				
6016	17 46 5·5	10 15·6	11 24·5	10 16·0	10 15·8	S. 1 55—1 8·7				
6074	17 56 6·2	11 3·8	11 32·25	11 3·8	11 3·8	S. 0 30—0 28·45				
6115	18 2 49·4	10 22·8	9 7·9	10 22·8	10 22·8	S. 0 40+1 14·9				
6145	18 7 5·0	11 33·8	10 7·1	11 34·0	11 33·9	S. 1 0+1 26·8				
6233	18 20 55·2	9 22·7	5 2·9	9 22·8	9 22·75	S. 4 40+4 19·85				
6285	18 27 55·6	9 28·3	8 25·9	9 28·3	9 28·3	S. 3 20+1 2·5				
6305	18 30 48·4	10 10·5	13 33·4	10 10·6	10 10·55	S. 3 25—3 22·85	26·713	34·9	36·2	35·5
6414	18 40 42·8	10 25·5	16 16·1	10 25·3	10 25·4	S. 1 10+0 9·3				
6480	18 59 43·0	10 28·9	8 28·75	10 28·7	10 28·8	S. 0 20+2 0·05				
6525	19 4 42·2	10 28·8	15 4·5	10 29·0	10 28·8	N. 0 50+4 9·6				
6639	19 24 6·4	10 26·3	14 15·2	10 26·3	10 26·3	S. 0 20—3 22·9				
Anon.	19 28	10 32·6	12 20·4	10 32·4	10 32·5	S. 0 5—1 30·9				
6753	19 42 34·0	11 26·3	9 12·0	11 26·3	11 26·3	S. 1 30+2 14·3				

June 21.—Anon. 21ʰ 32ᵐ is too faint.
22.—No. 1781.—The seconds per chronometer doubtful.

♂ JUNE 22, 1847.—FACE OF SECTOR EAST—(continued).

Number of B.A.C.	Time by Chronometer.	Micr. for Plumb-line on Dot.	Micr. for Observation of Star.	Micr. for Plumb-line on Dot.	Mean of Micr. for Plumb-line on Dot.	Star's Apparent Zenith Distance.	Barom.	Thermometers. Attd.	Upper.	Lower.
	h m s	rev. pts.	rev. pts.	rev. pts.	rev. pts.	° ' rev. pts.	in			
6877	20 1 29·2	10 25·3	12 1·0	10 25·1	10 25·2	S. 2 45—1 9·8	26·700	34·3	35·0	34·8
6948	20 13 10·7	10 4·1	12 26·75	10 4·2	10 4·15	S. 0 45—2 22·6				
7011	20	10 12·9	11 17·2		10 12·78	N. 0 10+1 4·42				
7026	20 23 59·0		11 10·9	10 12·7	10 12·78	N. 0 10+0 32·12				
7057	20 28 24·1	10 12·7	5 18·7	10 12·8	10 12·78	N. 0 10—4 28·08				
Anon.	20 31 16·2	10 11·6	12 4·5	10 12·0	10 11·8	S. 0 5—1 26·7				
Anon.	20 40 46·5	10 15·9	14 0·7	10 16·1	10 16·0	S. 0 15—3 18·7				
7207	20 47 17·5	10 19·3	9 3·6	10 19·1	10 19·2	S. 4 35+1 15·6				
Anon.	21 7 44·2	11 11·5	10 3·1	11 11·7	11 11·6	S. 0 35+1 8·5				
7386	21 15 31·0	11 2·5	13 4·1	11 2·6	11 2·55	S. 3 5—2 1·55				
Anon.	21 19 33·3	11 3·4	12 23·7	11 3·6	11 3·5	S. 0 5—1 20·2				
Anon.	21 32 40·8	10 27·1	14 26·5	10 27·5	10 27·3	S. 0 40—3 33·2				
7557	21 42 41·8	11 1·0	13 19·8	11 1·2	11 1·1	S. 4 0—2 18·7	26·689	33·3	34·0	33·6
7057	21 58 51·4	10 30·0	8 2·3	10 29·8	10 29·9	N. 0 35—2 27·6				
Anon.	22 2 42·4	10 29·8	9 6·5	10 30·0	10 29·9	N. 0 35—1 23·4				
7909	22 40 40·2	11 0·5	11 9·7	11 6·5	11 6·5	S. 0 25—0 3·2	26·693	32·4	33·2	33·2
7966	22 50 53·0	11 14·5	8 31·3	11 14·7	11 14·6	S. 3 55+2 17·3				
7992	22 56 0·2	11 19·0	9 6·5	11 19·0	11 19·0	S. 0 40+2 12·5				
1802	5 40 57·2	12 15·5	11 28·3	12 15·4	12 15·45	S. 4 25+0 21·15	26·693	53·6	52·5	51·0

♀ JUNE 23, 1847.—FACE OF SECTOR WEST.

Number of B.A.C.	Time by Chronometer.	Micr. for Plumb-line on Dot.	Micr. for Observation of Star.	Micr. for Plumb-line on Dot.	Mean of Micr. for Plumb-line on Dot.	Star's Apparent Zenith Distance.	Barom.	Thermometers. Attd.	Upper.	Lower.
2203	6 59 25·2	9 19·6	12 30·5	9 19·6	9 19·6	N. 1 0—3 10·9	26·693	56·8	59·7	54·6
4517	13 30 57·0	9 16·0	13 30·1	9 16·2	9 16·25	N. 1 0—4 13·85				
4548	13 37 0·2	9 16·4	13 33·2	9 16·4	9 16·25	N. 1 0—4 16·95				
4579	13 43 51·4	9 2·2	12 15·1	9 1·8	9 2·1	S. 2 30+3 13·0				
4623	13 49 52·0	9 2·2	8 25·4	9 2·2	9 2·1	S. 2 30—0 10·7	26·654	47·8	49·5	49·0
4719	14 13 4·0	9 25·8	9 8·0	9 25·9	9 25·85	N. 1 10+0 17·85				
4784	14 26 7·5	10 18·8	10 18·8	10 18·8	10 18·8	N. 0 55+2 1·5				
Anon.	14 31 8·0	11 1·0	9 11·6	11 1·0	11 1·0	S. 2 55—1 23·4				
4852	14 41 9·2	9 19·8	12 0·9	9 19·8	9 19·8	S. 4 45+2 15·1				
4891	14 48 13·4	9 12·1	9 11·25	9 12·5	9 12·3	N. 2 25+0 1·05				
4016	14 53 13·5	9 29·1	9 1·7	9 29·1	9 29·1	S. 3 30—0 27·4				
Anon.	15 0 30·5	9 24·8	5 30·3	9 24·9	9 24·85	S. 2 20—3 28·55				
Anon.	15 4 42·0	10 3·8	9 10·4	10 3·6	10 3·7	S. 2 35—0 27·3				
5151	15 36 10·5	10 5·6	13 19·1	10 5·8	10 5·7	N. 0 30—3 13·4				
Anon.	15 41 25·2	10 9·4	14 6·7	10 9·0	10 9·2	S. 1 20+3 31·5				
5227	15 48 6·2	10 8·8	10 8·4	10 9·0	10 8·9	S. 3 25—0 0·5				
5272	15 54 21·2	9 18·2	12 2·3	9 18·4	9 18·3	N. 1 0—2 18·0	26·678	45·1	47·0	46·4
5374	16 8 26·6	9 13·2	11 10·3	9 13·4	9 13·3	N. 0 45—1 13·3				
5435	16 16 46·2	9 2·4	13 12·8	9 2·6	9 2·5	S. 0 45+4 10·3				
Anon.	16 20 58·0	8 31·1	10 5·9	8 31·3	8 31·2	S. 3 5+1 8·7				
5498	16 26 58·0	9 10·9	11 4·9	9 16·8	9 16·65	N. 3 40—1 22·05				
5588	16 40 42·2	8 33·3	7 12·85	8 33·2	8 33·25	S. 2 5—1 20·4				
5632	16 47 6·3	8 8·8	10 7·0	8 9·0	8 8·9	S. 4 15+1 32·1	26·678	44·6	46·5	45·6
5735	17 1 36·5	9 20·5	8 29·4	9 20·5	9 20·5	S. 4 10—0 25·1				
5817	17 13 59·0	9 29·5	9 1·9	9 29·5	9 29·5	S. 2 45—0 27·6				
5881	17 24 30·4	9 12·7	7 13·25	9 13·0	9 12·85	0 0+1 33·6				
0074	17 56 10·0	8 32·8	7 24·9	8 32·8	8 32·8	S. 0 30—1 7·9				
6115	18 2 52·6	9 0·4	10 4·3	9 0·6	9 0·5	S. 0 40+1 3·8				
6145	18 7 7·5	9 6·5	9 6·5	9 6·5	9 6·5	S. 1 0+0 14·5				
6233	18 20 52·0	9 26·2	13 32·4	9 26·0	9 26·1	S. 4 40+4 6·3				
6285	18 27 53·6	10 33·3	10 33·1	10 33·1	10 33·2	S. 3 20+0 26·2				
6305	18 30 47·0		7 6·5	11 6·9		S. 3 25—4 0.4	26·678	44·6	45·6	45·5

June 22.—No. 7011.—Observed at 20 seconds past the meridian.
Fair definitions, but the smaller stars faint.
23.—No. 4579.—The seconds of time doubtful.
Generally good definitions.
Antares appears double.

♀ JUNE 23, 1847 —FACE OF SECTOR WEST—(continued).

Number of B.A.C.	Time by Chronometer.	Micr. for Plumb-line on Dot.	Micr. for Observation of Star.	Micr. for Plumb-line on Dot.	Mean of Micr. for Plumb-line on Dot.	Star's Apparent Zenith Distance.	Barom.	Thermometers. Attd.	Upper.	Lower.
	h m s	rev. pts.	rev. pts.	rev. pts.	rev. pts.	° ′ rev. pts.	in.			
6414	18 49 46·2	11 2·0	10 33·6	11 2·0	11 2·0	S. 1 10—0 2·4				
6489	18 59 46·2	11 2·4	12 26·0	11 2·4	11 2·4	S. 0 20+1 23·6				
6525	19 4 47·0	10 25·4	6 3·0	10 25·5	10 25·45	N. 0 50+4 22·45				
6639	19 24 10·0	10 23·4	6 22·1	10 23·5	10 23·45	S. 0 20—4 1·35				
Anon.	19 28 24·0	10 12·7	8 0·4	10 12·5	10 12·6	S. 0 5—2 12·2	26·085	42·8	45·0	44·0
6753	19 42 35·5	10 30·0	12 31·4	10 30·4	10 30·2	S. 1 30+2 1·2				
6877	20 1 20·2	*11 11·3	9 23·0	11 10·9	11 11·1	S. 2 45—1 22·1				
6948	20 13 13·5	10 17·1	7 13·75	10 17·3	10 17·2	S. 0 45—3 3·45				
7011	20 22 12·5	10 20·0	9 2·9	10 19·9	10 20·0	N. 0 10+1 17·1				
7026	20 24 3·5		9 8·7	10 20·0	10 20·0	N. 0 10+1 11·3				
7057	20 28 28·6	10 20·0	15 1·8	10 20·0	10 20·0	N. 0 10—4 15·8				
Anon.	20 31 21·0	10 4·0	7 33·0	10 3·6	10 3·8	S. 0 5—2 4·8				
Anon.	20 40 50·5	9 26·7	5 29·0	9 26·0	9 26·8	S. 0 15—3 31·8				
7207	20 47 16·0	9 29·5	10 32·6	9 29·5	9 29·5	S. 4 35+1 3·1	26·646	42·4	43·5	42·8
Anon.	21 0 39·4	9 22·7	9 22·9	9 22·9	9 22·8	S. 0 0+3 33·8				
Anon.	21 7 48·6	8 24·8	9 20·25	8 24·9	8 24·85	S. 0 35+0 29·4				
7386	21	8 27·6	6 13·75	8 27·5	8 27·55	S. 0 5—2 13·8				
Anon.	21 19 38·2	8 20·4	6 22·75	8 20·2	8 20·3	S. 0 5—1 31·55				
Anoc.	21 32 45·5	8 18·3	4 4·5	8 17·9	8 18·1	S. 0 40—4 13·6				
7557	21 42 40·5	8 13·6	5 17·25	8 13·7	8 13·65	S. 4 0—2 30·4				
7657	21 58 56·2	8 10·8	10 23·5	8 10·6	8 10·65	S. 3 35—2 12·85				
Anon.	22 2 47·2	8 10·6	9 18·5	8 10·6	8 10·65	N. 0 35—1 7·85				
7842	22 29 39·3	9 20·2	5 25·2	9 20·2	9 20·2	S. 3 25—3 29·0				
7909	22 40 44·5	9 14·0	8 30·4	9 14·4	9 14·2	S. 0 25—0 17·8	26·654	40·6	42·0	41·6
7966	22 50 51·5	8 29·0	11 2·0	8 29·0	8 29·0	S. 3 55+2 7·0				
7992	22 56 4·2	8 24·3	10 22·8	8 24·3	8 24·3	S. 0 40+1 32·5				
1802	5 40 54·8	9 16·9	9 23·35	9 16·7	9 16·8	S. 4 25+0 6·55	26·706	54·1	56·2	52·0

♃ JUNE 24, 1847.—FACE OF SECTOR EAST.

Number of B.A.C.	Time by Chronometer.	Micr. for Plumb-line on Dot.	Micr. for Observation of Star.	Micr. for Plumb-line on Dot.	Mean of Micr. for Plumb-line on Dot.	Star's Apparent Zenith Distance.	Barom.	Attd.	Upper.	Lower.
2293	6 59 30·1	8 25·6	5 2·3	8 25·6	8 25·6	N. 1 0—3 23·3	26·717	57·0	58·0	56·0
4517	13 31 58·8	8 32·3	4 5·5	8 32·5	8 32·4	N. 1 0—4 26·9				
4548	13 37 8·0	8 32·4	4 4·0	8 32·4	8 32·4	N. 1 0—4 28·4				
4579	13 44 0·2	8 2·0	4 12·0	8 2·2	8 2·15	S. 2 30+3 24·15	26·693	44·4	47·0	46·4
4623	13 50 1·0	8 2·2	8 3·3	8 2·2	8 2·15	S. 2 30—0 1·15				
4719	14 13 7·0	9 2·5	9 9·3	9 2·5	9 2·5	N. 1 10+0 6·8				
4784	14 26 10·5	9 5·0	10 26·1	9 5·0	9 5·0	N. 0 55+1 21·1				
Anon.	14 31 18·0	8 19·4	9 31·5	8 19·6	8 19·5	S. 2 55—1 12·0				
4852	14 41 22·0	9 14·0	6 18·9	9 13·8	9 13·9	S. 4 45+2 29·0				
4891	14 48 14·6	9 23·8	9 12·0	9 23·6	9 23·7	N. 2 25—0 11·7				
4916	14 53 24·3	9 10·9	9 28·5	9 10·9	9 10·9	S. 3 30—0 17·6	26·689	41·4	43·5	43·2
Anon.	15 0 39·0	9 13·7	12 29·4	9 13·6	9 13·65	S. 2 20—3 15·75				
Anon.	15 4 51·0	9 3·4	9 20·35	9 3·5	9 3·45	S. 2 35—0 16·9				
5032	15 15 30·2	8 27·6	7 11·7	8 27·6	8 27·6	N. 0 10—1 15·9				
5151	15 36 14·0	8 29·4	5 3·0	8 29·8	8 29·6	N. 0 30—3 26·6				
Anon.	15 41 32·0	8 24·8	4 14·5	8 25·0	8 24·9	S. 1 20+4 10·4				
5227	15 48 17·4	10 1·8	9 24·8	10 1·7	10 1·7	S. 3 25+0 10·9				
5272	15 54 24·6	9 26·5	6 29·1	9 26·5	9 26·5	N. 1 0—2 31·4				
7374	16 8 30·2	10 1·6	7 24·5	10 1·6	10 1·7	N. 0 45—2 11·1				
5435	16 16 52·3	10 30·0	6 6·4	10 30·0	10 30·0	S. 0 45+4 23·6				
Anon.	16 21 8·8	10 9·8	8 23·0	10 9·8	10 9·8	S. 3 5+1 20·8				
5498	16 26 57·3	10 26·4	8 26·6	10 26·0	10 26·2	N. 3 40—1 33·6				
5588	16 40 50·0	10 25·5	11 33·7	10 25·3	10 25·4	S. 2 5—1 8·3	26·680	39·2	40·5	40·5
5632	16 47 19·2	10 3·0	7 27·8	10 3·0	10 3·0	S. 4 15+2 9·2				

June 23.—Nos. 6414, 7207 and Anon. 21ʰ 19ᵐ.—The seconds of time doubtful.
24.—Good definitions.
The sky became covered (fog) at 19ʰ 28ᵐ per chronometer.

♃ JUNE 24, 1847.—FACE OF SECTOR EAST—(continued).

Number of B.A C.	Time by Chronometer.	Micr. for Plumb-line on Dot.	Micr. for Observation of Star.	Micr. for Plumb-line on Dot.	Mean of Micr. for Plumb-line on Dot.	Star's Apparent Zenith Distance.	Barom.	Thermometers.		
								Attd.	Upper.	Lower.
	h m s	rev. pts.	rev. pts.	rev. pts.	rev. pts.	° ′ rev. pts.	in.			
5735	17	9 24·3	10 3·0	9 24·3	9 24·3	S. 4 10—0 12·7				
5817	17 14 8·8	9 9·0	9 25·6	9 9·0	9 9·0	S. 2 45—0 16·6				
5881	17 24 34·0	9 15·0	11 3·0	9 14·6	9 14·8	0 0+1 22·8				
6016	17 46 15·2	9 18·5	10 26·5	9 18·9	9 18·7	S. 1 55—1 7·8				
6074	17 56 15·0	9 25·5	10 19·1	9 25·7	9 25·6	S. 0 30—0 27·5				
6115	18 2 58·5	10 2·7	8 21·3	10 2·9	10 2·8	S. 0 40+1 15·5	26·685	39·6	40·0	40·2
6145	18 7 13·7	9 33·7	9 6·6	9 34·1	9 33·9	S. 1 0+0 27·3				
6233	18 21 5·2	10 6·4	5 20·5	10 6·8	10 6·6	S. 4 40+4 20·1				
6285	18 28 5·2	10 1·5	8 32·8	10 1·4	10 1·45	S. 3 20+1 2·65				
6305	18 30 58·0	10 12·4	14 1·6	10 12·8	10 12·6	S. 3 25—3 23.0				
6414	18 49 52·2	10 8·4	9 33·6	10 8·0	10 8·2	S. 1 10+0 8·6				
6489	18 50 51·6	9 22·3	7 19·75	9 21·7	9 22·0	S. 0 20+2 2·25				
6525	19 4 50·4	9 33·4	14 9·2	9 33·2	9 33·3	N. 0 50+4 9·9				
6639	19 24 15·0	10 8·1	13 30·9	10 7·9	10 8·0	S. 0 20—3 22·9				

♀ JUNE 25, 1847.—FACE OF SECTOR WEST.

Number of B.A C.	Time by Chronometer.	Micr. for Plumb-line on Dot.	Micr. for Observation of Star.	Micr. for Plumb-line on Dot.	Mean of Micr. for Plumb-line on Dot.	Star's Apparent Zenith Distance.	Barom.	Attd.	Upper.	Lower.
4517	13 31 38·0	8 12·0	12 25·25	8 12·3	8 12·18	N 1 0—4 13·07				
4548	13 37 8·8	8 12·1	12 29·25	8 12·3	8 12·18	N. 1 0—4 17·07				
4579	13 44 5·1	8 6·5	11 20·6	8 6·2	8 6·35	S. 2 30+0 14·25				
4923	13 50 1·0	8 6·4	7 29·2	8 6·3	8 6·35	S. 2 30—0 11·15	26·690	44·4	47·0	46·4
4719	14 13 13·0	8 25·5	8 6·45	8 26·1	8 25·8	N. 1 10+0 19·35				
4784	14 26 16·0	8 19·5	6 17·75	8 19·5	8 19·5	N. 0 55+2 1·75				
Anon.	14 31 18·0	8 14·7	6 25·4	8 15·3	8 15·0	S. 2 55—1 23·6				
4852	14 41 17·5	8 6·6	10 24·05	8 7·0	8 6·8	S. 4 45+2 17·25				
4891	14 48 21·8	7 29·5	7 28·35	7 29·6	7 29·55	N. 2 25+0 1·2				
4916	14 53 22·8	8 7·4	7 9·5	8 7·4	8 7·4	S. 3 30—0 24·9	26·600	43·2	45·5	45·0
Anon.	15 0	8 2·0	4 6·9	8 2·0	8 2·0	S. 2 20—3 29·1				
Anon.	15 4 51·0	7 32·1	7 4·6	7 31·9	7 32·0	S. 2 35—0 27·4				
5032	15 15 34·0	9 10·9	10 15·4	9 11·4	9 11·15	N. 0 10—1 4·25				
5151	15 36 19·0	9 14·4	12 27·8	9 14·25	9 14·33	N. 0 30—3 13·47				
Anon.	15 41 33·8	8 20·7	12 17·0	8 20·6	8 20·6	S. 1 20+3 30·4				
5227	15	8 32·0	17 28·3			S. 3 25—8 30·3				
5272	15 54 30·0	9 24·6	12 9·2	9 24·7	9 24·65	N. 1 0—2 18·55	26·600	42·4	43·7	43·9
5374	16 8 35·0	9 26·0	11 23·5	9 25·6	9 25·8	N. 0 45—1 31·7				
5435	16 16 55·0	9 30·7	14 7·6	9 30·5	9 30·6	S. 0 45+4 11·0				
Anon.	16 21 9·5	10 10·2	11 20·7	10 10·2	10 10·2	S. 3 5+1 10·5				
5498	16 27 6·0	9 32·75	11 21·75	9 32·63	9 32·63	N. 3 40—1 23·12				
5588	16 40 52·0	9 8·7	7 23·0	9 8·4	9 8·55	S. 2 5—1 19·55				
5632	16 47 15·0	9 25·0	11 26·4	9 25·1	9 25·1	S. 4 15+2 1·3				
5817	17 14 11·0	8 9·35	7 17·65	8 9·2	8 9·28	S. 2 45—0 25·63				
5881	17 24 37·0	8 4·2	6 6·69	8 4·15	8 4·18	0 0+1 31·49				
6016	17 46 16·0	8 21·0	7 1·0	8 21·0	8 21·0	S. 1 55—1 20·0				
6074	17 56 19·0	8 21·8	7 14·9	8 21·5	8 21·65	S. 0 30—1 6·75				
6115	18 3 1·0	8 26·45	9 30·75	8 26·30	8 26·40	S. 0 40+1 4·35				
6145	18 7 16·5	9 20·85	10 1·15	9 21·0	9 20·93	S. 1 0+0 14·22				
6233	18 21 4·0	10 22·0	14 28·75	10 22·2	10 22·1	S. 4 40+4 6·65				
6285	18 28 5·0	10 23·0	11 13·75	10 22·5	10 22·75	S. 3 20+0 25·0				
6414	18 49 51·0	10 30·4	10 30·45	10 30·4	10 30·40	S. 1 10+0 0·05	26·693	41·0	42·0	41·5
6489	18 59 54·0	11 2·7	12 25·6	11 2·5	11 2·6	S. 0 20+1 23·0				
6639	19 24 30·0	8 26·4	4 24·7	8 26·2	8 26·3	S. 0 20—4 1·6				
6753	19 42 44·0	12 18·9	14 20·5	12 18·7	12 18·8	S. 1 30+2 1·7				
6877	20 1 41·5	13 1·9	11 16·0	13 1·7	13 1·8	S. 2 45—1 19·8	26·693	39·2	40·0	40·8
6948	20 13 23·0	13 26·4	10 26·5	13 20·25	13 26·33	S. 0 45—2 33·83				

June 25.—Anon. 16ʰ 21ᵐ.—The seconds of time doubtful.

♀ JUNE 25, 1847.—FACE OF SECTOR WEST—(continued).

Number of B.A.C.	Time by Chronometer.	Micr. for Plumb-line on Dot.	Micr. for Observation of Star.	Micr. for Plumb-line on Dot.	Mean of Micr. for Plumb-line on Dot.	Star's Apparent Zenith Distance.	Barom.	Thermometers. Attd.	Upper.	Lower.
	h. m. s.	rev. pts.	rev. pts.	rev. pts.	rev. pts.	° ′ rev. pts.	in.			
7011	20 22 21·0	14 11·6	12 28·5	14 11·5	14 11·53	N. 0 10+1 17·03				
7026	20 24 12·0	14 11·6	13 1·6	14 11·5	14 11·53	N. 0 10+1 9·93				
7057	20 28 37·5	14 11·4	18 25·7	14 11·6	14 11·53	N. 0 10—4 14·17				
Anon.	20 31 29·5	11 9·5	9 5·6	11 9·7	11 9·6	S. 0 5—2 4·0				
Anon.	20 40 59·5	11 16·0	7 17·6	11 16·0	11 16·0	S. 0 15—3 32·4				
7207	20 47 23·5	10 9·6	11 13·8	10 9·2	10 9·4	8. 4 35+1 4·4				
Anon.	21 0 55·0	10 0·85	6 0·75	10 0·75	10 0·80	0 0+4 0·05				
Anon.	21 7 55·0	10 29·4	11 23·9	10 29·3	10 29·35	S. 0 35+0 28·55				
7386	21 15 44·0	11 16·3	9 1 25	11 16·2	11 16·25	8. 3 5—2 15·0				
Anon.	21 19 43·0	12 9·0	10 13·0	12 9·2	12 9·1	S. 0 5—1 30·1				
Anon.	21 32 52·0	12 29·45	8 18·65	12 29·5	12 29·48	S. 0 40—4 10·83				
7557	21 42 49·0	13 21·0	10 24·0	13 20·65	13 20·82	S. 4 0—2 30·83	26·689	39·2	40·0	40·0
7657	21 58 4·0	13 23·7	16 3·3	13 24·25	13 24·21	N. 0 35—2 13·09				
Anon.	22 2 55·0	13 24·4	14 32·0	13 24·5	13 24·21	N. 0 35—1 7·79				
7842	22 29 50·0	13 31·5	10 1·5	13 31·5	13 31·5	S. 3 25—3 30·0				
7909	22 40 54·0	14 7·45	13 23·4	14 7·4	14 7·43	S. 0 25—0 18·03				
7992	22 56 13·0	14 25·2	16 22·7	14 25·25	14 25·23	S. 0 40+1 31·47	26·685	39·2	40·0	39·8
1802	5 41 3·2	8 29·3	9 1·1	8 29·3	8 29·3	S. 4 25+0 5·8	26·741	58·1	60·0	55·6

♄ JUNE 26, 1847.—FACE OF SECTOR EAST.

Number of B.A.C.	Time by Chronometer.	Micr. for Plumb-line on Dot.	Micr. for Observation of Star.	Micr. for Plumb-line on Dot.	Mean of Micr. for Plumb-line on Dot.	Star's Apparent Zenith Distance.	Barom.	Attd.	Upper.	Lower.
2293	6 50 38·6	8 26·7	5 2·65	8 26·8	8 26·75	N. 1 0—3 24·1	26·741	60·8	61·5	59·4
4517	13 31 7·0	9 1·6	4 9·0	9 1·4	9 1·5	N. 1 0—4 26·5				
4548	13 37 11·6	9 1·4	4 5·9	9 1·6	9 1·5	N. 1 0—4 29·6	26·705	46·0	47·5	48·2
4579	13 44 10·0	9 27·4	6 2·55	9 27·3	9 27·4	S. 2 30+3 24·85				
4623	13 50 10·0	9 27·5	9 28·55	9 27·4	9 27·4	S. 2 30—0 1·15				
4719	14 13 15·8	10 1·7	10 6·5	10 1·6	10 1·6	N. 1 10+0 4·85				
4784	14 26 19·0	10 9·5	11 30·0	10 9·5	10 9·5	N. 0 55+1 20·5				
Anon.	14 31 27·2	10 1·2	11 13·9	10 1·5	10 1·35	S. 2 55—1 12·55				
4852	14 41 32·2	9 15·0	6 21·1	9 14·9	9 14·95	S. 4 45+2 27·85				
4891	14 48 22·7	9 30·8	9 19·0	9 30·4	9 30·6	N. 2 25+0 11·6				
4916	14 53 34·0	9 27·9	10 10·5	9 27·8	9 27·85	S. 3 30—0 16·65				
Anon.	15 0 48·2	8 19·0	12 1·05	8 19·1	8 19·05	S. 2 20—3 16·0				
Anon.	15 5 0·2	9 11·3	9 27·3	9 11·3	9 11·3	S. 2 35—0 16·0				
5032	15 15 38·0	9 8·2	7 26·45	9 8·4	9 8·3	N. 0 10—1 15·85	26·693	44·2	45·0	46·0
5151	15 33 22·0	9 29·55	6 1·9	9 29·5	9 29·53	N. 0 30—3 27·63				
Anon.	15 41 40·2	9 3·4	4 28·0	9 3·6	9 3·5	S. 1 20+4 9·5				
5227	15 48 26·0	8 25·5	8 14·9	8 25·7	8 25·6	S. 3 25+0 10·7	26·693	44·6	45·2	45·5
5272	15	8 22·0	5 24·4	8 22·0	8 22·0	N. 1 0—2 31·6				
5374	16 8 38·6	8 29·4	6 18·8	8 20·5	8 20·45	N. 0 45—2 10·65				
5435	16 17 1·0	9 11·0	4 20·5	9 11·2	9 11·1	S. 0 45+4 24·6				
Anon.	16 21 18·0	9 18·7	7 30·9	9 18·5	9 18·6	S. 3 5+1 21·7				
5498	16 27 5·2	10 20·2	8 19·35	10 19·3	10 19·35	N. 3 40—2 0·4				
5588	16 40 59·0	10 16·3	11 22·15	10 16·4	10 16·35	S. 2 5—1 5·80				
5632	16 47 29·0	11 1·5	8 25·3	11 1·5	11 1·5	S. 4 15+2 10·2				
5735	17 1 59·0	11 28·35	12 6·9	11 28·4	11 28·38	S. 4 10—0 12·52				
5817	17 14 18·0	11 20·0	12 1·0	11 20·0	11 20·0	S. 2 45—0 15·0				
5881	17 24 43·0	12 8·4	13 29·1	12 8·2	12 8·3	0 0+1 20·8	26·701	42·8	43·0	43·5
6016	17 46 24·0	12 18·2	13 26·45	12 18·0	12 18·1	S. 1 65—1 8·35				
6074	17 56 24·0	12 13·3	13 5·25	12 13·2	12 13·25	S. 0 30—0 26·0				
6115	18 3 8·0	12 26·35	11 9·2	12 26·2	12 26·28	S. 0 40+1 17·08				
6145	18 7 23·0	13 3·7	12 11·5	13 3·6	13 3·6	S. 1 0+0 26·1				
6285	18 28 15·0	13 25·1	13 26·2	13 24·8	13 24·95	S. 3 20+0 1·25				
6305	18 31 13·0	14 8·7	17 31·45	14 7·65	14 8·18	S. 3 25—3 23·27				

June 25.—No. 7207.—The bisection uncertain. Bad lamp light.
Good images. .
Mr. George Montagu made all the observations this night, after the transit of Antares, with seven exceptions.
Antares double.

♄ JUNE 26, 1847.—FACE OF SECTOR EAST—(continued).

Number of B.A.C.	Time by Chronometer.	Micr. for Plumb-line on Dot.	Micr. for Observation of Star.	Micr. for Plumb-line on Dot.	Mean of Micr. for Plumb-line on Dot.	Star's Apparent Zenith Distance.	Barom.	Thermometers.		
								Attd.	Upper.	Lower.
6414	18 50 1.0	15 6.9	14 31.1	15 6.9	15 6.9	S. 1 10+0 9.8	26.701	42.4	43.5	43.0
6489	10 0 1.0	16 3.8	14 0.0	16 3.6	16 3.7	~. 0 20+2 3.7				
6525	19 4 59.0	16 15.0	20 23.3	16 15.2	16 15.1	N. 0 50+4 8.2				
6639	19 24 24.0	17 31.5	21 20.5	17 31.45	17 31.48	S. 0 20-3 23.02				
Anon.	19 28 37.0	19 10.45	21 8.0	19 10.2	19 10.33	S. 0 5-1 31.67				
6753	19 42 52.0	19 33.4	17 18.7	19 33.8	19 33.6	S. 1 30+2 14.9				
6877	20 1 49.0	19 26.1	21 3.4	19 26.0	19 26.05	S. 2 45-1 11.35				
6948	20 13 29.0	20 29.5	23 18.0	20 29.25	20 29.38	S. 0 45-2 22.02				
7011	20 22 25.6	21 23.5	22 27.6	21 23.4	21 23.43	N. 0 10+1 4.17				
7026	20 24 17.0	21 23.4	22 20.0	21 23.4	21 23.43	N. 0 10+0 30.57				
7057	20 28 41.2	21 23.5	16 30.0	21 23.4	21 23.43	N. 0 10-4 27.43				
Anon.	20 31 34.2		15 31.2	14 6.7		S. 0 5-1 24.5				
Anon.	20 41 4.2	11 20.6	15 3.8	11 22.5	11 20.6	S. 0 15-3 17.2				
Anon.	21 0 53.0	11 22.45	15 7.6	11 22.5	11 22.48	0 0+3 19.12	26.701	42.8	43.5	43.0
Anon.	21 8 3.0	12 18.3	15 7.5	12 18.1	12 18.2	S. 0 35+1 10.70				
7386	21 15 50.0	13 2.0	15 3.45	13 2.5	13 2.25	S. 3 5-2 1.20				
Anon.	21 19 51.0	13 10.5	14 31.0	13 10.3	13 10.4	S. 0 5-1 20.6				
Anon.	21 32 59.0	13 28.25	17 29.75	13 28.25	13 28.25	S. 0 40-4 1.50				
7557	21 43 3.0	14 14.8	17 3.0	14 14.8	14 14.8	S. 4 0-2 22.2				
7657	21 58 9.0	14 26.15	11 32.45	14 26.0	14 26.10	N. 0 35-2 27.65				
Anon.	22 3 1.0	14 26.0	18 3.9	14 26.05	14 26.10	N. 0 35-1 22.20				
7842	22 29 59.0	16 4.0	19 24.4	16 4.0	16 4.0	S. 3 25-3 20.4				
7909	22 40 58.0	16 29.8	17 0.5	16 29.5	16 29.65	S. 0 25-0 4.85				
7966	22 51 13.0	17 22.0	15 6.5	17 22.4	17 22.2	S. 3 55+2 15.7				
7992	22 56 19.0	18 17.85	16 7.5	18 17.9	18 17.88	S. 0 40+2 10.38	26.674	42.8	43.0	43.0
1802	5 41 16.4	8 28.8	8 11.4	8 29.2	8 29.0	S. 4 25+0 17.6	26.741	61.7	58.6	66.5

☉ JUNE 27, 1847.—FACE OF SECTOR WEST.

Number of B.A.C.	Time by Chronometer.	Micr. for Plumb-line on Dot.	Micr. for Observation of Star.	Micr. for Plumb-line on Dot.	Mean of Micr. for Plumb-line on Dot.	Star's Apparent Zenith Distance.	Barom.	Attd.	Upper.	Lower.
2293	6 59 42.3	8 15.3	11 26.55	8 15.2	8 15.25	N. 1 0-3 11.3	26.741	64.4	70.0	62.4
4517	13 31 12.6	10 22.4	15 3.05	10 22.5	10 22.45	N. 1 0-4 14.6	26.709	52.2	52.6	53.0
4548	13 37 17.2	10 22.3	15 6.45	10 22.6	10 22.45	N. 1 0-4 18.0				
4579	13 44 10.5	10 2.8	13 16.75	10 3.0	10 2.9	S. 2 30+3 13.85				
4623	13 50 10.8	10 3.0	9 25.5	10 3.2	10 3.1	S. 2 30-0 11.6				
4719	14 13 21.5	9 19.3	9 2.8	9 19.5	9 19.4	N. 1 10+0 16.6				
4784	14 26 24.5	9 11.7	7 12.6	9 11.6	9 11.65	N. 0 55+1 33.05				
Anon.	14 31 28.0	9 16.9	7 27.7	9 16.9	9 16.9	S. 2 55-1 23.2				
4852	14 41 28.0	9 10.5	11 27.9	9 10.7	9 10.6	S. 4 45+2 17.3				
4891	14 48 30.2	9 26.0	9 27.3	9 26.6	9 26.3	N. 2 25-0 1.0				
4916	14 53 33.0	10 32.1	10 5.8	10 32.5	10 32.5	S. 3 30-0 26.7				
Anon.	15 0 49.0	10 8.5	6 14.75	10 8.7	10 8.6	S. 2 20-3 27.85				
Anon.	15 5 1.0	10 3.5	9 12.5	10 3.7	10 3.6	S. 2 35-0 2.1				
5032	15 15 43.2	9 21.7	10 27.9	9 21.9	9 21.8	N. 0 10-1 6.1				
5151	15 36 27.8	9 3.8	12 18.85	9 3.8	9 3.8	N. 0 30-3 15.05				
Anon.	15 41 42.7	8 32.4	12 30.7	8 31.7	8 32.05	S. 1 20+3 32.65				
5227	15 48 25.5	9 24.75	9 23.5	9 24.5	9 24.63	S. 3 25-0 1.13				
5272	15 54 38.5	8 26.4	11 11.5	8 26.6	8 26.5	N. 1 0-2 19.0				
5374	16 8 44.0	8 4.3	10 2.3	8 4.5	8 4.4	N. 0 45-1 31.9				
5435	16 17 3.0	8 1.0	12 11.3	8 0.8	8 0.9	S. 0 45+4 10.4				
Anon.	16 21 17.5		10 20.1	9 14.8		S. 3 5+1 5.3				
5498	16 27 14.6	9 2.5	10 25.0	9 2.3	9 2.4	N. 3 40-1 22.6				
5588	16 41 0.8	8 23.4	7 3.4	8 23.4	8 23.4	S. 2 5-1 20.0				
5632	16 47 26.6	10 7.1	12 5.5	10 8.0	10 7.55	S. 4 15+1 31.95				
5735	17 1 57.0	11 4.7	10 13.2	11 4.8	11 4.75	S. 4 10-0 25.55				

June 26.—Excepting 25, the observations were made this day by Mr. George Montagu.
Very good images, no wind.
No. 1802.—The upper thermometer and the top of the telescope exposed to the sun's rays through the canvas.
27.—Anon. 15ʰ 5ᵐ.—The seconds of transit doubtful.
At 15ʰ 43ᵐ.—Lowered the back angle of top tripod.

ARC OF THE MERIDIAN.—CAPE OF GOOD HOPE.

☉ JUNE 27, 1847.—FACE OF SECTOR WEST—(continued).

Number of B.A.C.	Time by Chronometer.	Micr. for Plumb-line on Dot.	Micr. for Observation of Star.	Micr. for Plumb-line on Dot.	Mean of Micr. for Plumb-line on Dot.	Star's Apparent Zenith Distance.	Barom.	Thermometers.		
								Attd.	Upper.	Lower.
	h m s	rev. pts.	rev. pts.	rev. pts.	rev. pts.	s ′ rev. pts.	in.			
5817	17 14 17·5	10 15·2	9 22·1	10 15·2	10 15·2	S. 2 45—0 27·1				
5881	17 24 47·2	9 17·5	7 18·5	9 17·7	9 17·6	0 0+1 33·1	26·694	46·9	46·8	48·2
6016	17 46 26·0	9 10·6	7 23·9	9 10·6	9 10·6	S. 1 55—1 20·7				
6074	17 56 27·7	8 32·7	7 27·1	8 32·6	8 32·65	S. 0 30—1 5·55				
6115	18 3 10·8	9 11·7	10 16·5	9 11·8	9 11·75	S. 0 40+1 4·75				
6145	18 7 25·8	9 4·0	9 19·4	9 4·1	9 4·05	S. 1 0+0 15·35				
6233	18	9 11·4	13 19·1	9 11·2	9 11·3	S. 4 40+4 7·8				
6305	18 31 7·5	9 17·0	5 17·9	9 17·4	9 17·2	S. 3 25—3 33·3				
6414	18 50 4·0	8 33·8	8 31·4	8 33·8	8 33·8	S. 1 10—0 2·4				
6489	19 0 4·2	9 9·4	11 0·0	9 9·4	9 9·4	S. 0 20+1 24·6				
6525	19 5 4·5	8 23·2	4 1·4	8 23·2	8 23·2	N. 0 50—4 21·8	26·685	44·6	45·2	45·2
6639	19 24 28·0	9 7·9	5 6·7	9 7·0	9 7·9	S. 0 20—4 1·2				
Anon.	19 28 50·0	9 3·9	6 28·5	9 5·1	9 4·5	S. 0 5—2 10·0				
6753	19 42	8 24·5	10 24·4	8 24·3	8 24·4	S. 1 30+2 0·0				
6877	20 1 49·0	9 4·5	7 16·8	9 4·7	9 4·6	S. 2 45—1 21·8				
6948	20 13 31·7	9 2·0	6 0·9	9 2·4	9 2·2	S. 0 45—3 1·3				
7011	20 22 30·2	9 0·5	7 17·5	9 0·7	9 0·07	N. 0 10+1 17·17				
7026	20 24 21·0	9 0·7	7 25·0	9 0·5	9 0·67	N. 0 10+1 9·67				
7057	20 28 46·3	9 0·8	13 16·85	9 0·8	9 0·67	N. 0 10—4 16·18				
Anon.	20 31 38·5	9 1·6	6 30·7	9 1·7	9 1·65	S. 0 5—2 4·95				
Anon.	20 41 8·8	9 22·7	5 26·4	9 22·9	9 22·8	S. 0 15—3 30·4				
7207	20 47 36·5	9 32·6	11 3·4	9 32·7	9 32·65	S. 4 35+1 4·75				
Anon.	21 0 56·2	10 6·3	6 7·5	10 6·4	10 6·35	0 0+3 32·85				
7386	21 15 50·2	10 22·0	8 9·2	10 22·0	10 22·0	S. 3 5—2 12·8				
Anon.	21 19 55·5	10 33·8	9 3·7	10 33·8	10 33·8	S. 0 5—1 30·1				
Anon.	21 33 2·5	11 14·0	7 1·6	11 14·0	11 14·0	S. 0 40—4 12·4				
7557	21 43 0·2	11 3·5	8 6·6	11 3·7	11 3·6	S. 4 0—2 31·0				
7657	21 59 13·8	10 3·3	12 16·4	10 3·3	10 3·25	N. 0 35—2 13·15				
Anon.	22 3 5·0	10 3·1	11 11·0	10 3·3	10 3·25	N. 0 35—1 7·75				
7842	22 29 58·5	10 29·9	7 0·4	10 30·1	10 30·0	S. 3 25—3 29·6				
7909	22 41 2·3	10 25·8	10 9·6	10 25·8	10 25·8	S. 0 25—0 16·2				
7966	22 51 11·5	11 12·5	13 20·6	11 12·7	11 12·6	S. 3 55+2 8·0				
7992	22 56 22·4	11 22·1	13 21·5	11 22·3	11 22·2	S. 0 40—1 33·3	26·678	42·1	42·2	42·6

☾ JUNE 28, 1847.—FACE OF SECTOR EAST.

Number of B.A.C.	Time by Chronometer.	Micr. for Plumb-line on Dot.	Micr. for Observation of Star.	Micr. for Plumb-line on Dot.	Mean of Micr. for Plumb-line on Dot.	Star's Apparent Zenith Distance.	Barom.	Attd.	Upper.	Lower.
4517	13 31 16·0	14 33·5	10 9·3	14 33·8	14 33·65	N. 1 0—4 24·35				
4548	13 37 21·0	14 33·8	10 4·45	15 0·0	14 33·8	N. 1 0—4 29·45				
4623	13 50 20·0	15 5·5	15 8·5	15 5·3	15 5·4	S. 2 30—0 3·1	26·682	50·9	50·5	52·0
4784	14 26 29·7	8 8·2	9 31·0	8 8·2	8 8·2	N. 0 55+1 22·8				
Anon.	14 31 38·0	8 21·5	10 2·1	8 21·5	8 21·5	S. 2 55—1 14·6				
4852	14 41 42·5	10 19·5	7 28·0	10 19·5	10 19·5	S. 4 45+2 25·5				
4891	14 48 32·0	11 12·5	11 0·5	11 12·5	11 12·5	N. 2 25—0 12·0				
4916	14 53 44·0	11 27·8	12 10·5	11 27·3	11 27·55	S. 3 30—0 16·95				
Anon.	15 0 58·0	11 25·5	15 8·0	11 25·5	11 25·5	S. 2 20—3 16·6				
Anon.	15 5 24·0	12 6·6	12 22·5	12 6·6	12 6·6	S. 2 35—0 15·9				
5082	15 15 48·5	12 32·6	11 17·7	12 32·3	12 32·45	N. 0 10—1 14·75	26·682	49·1	50·0	50·5
5151	15 36 32·0	13 24·4	9 33·0	13 24·3	13 24·35	N. 0 30—3 25·35				
Anon.	15 41 50·0	13 19·5	9 9·8	13 19·5	13 19·5	S. 1 20+4 9·6				
5227	15 48 36·4	22 10·0	21 32·5	22 9·2	22 9·6	S. 3 25+0 11·1				
5272	15 54 42·0	23 18·7	20 21·5	23 18·5	23 18·6	N. 1 0—2 31·1				
5374	16 8 48·0	24 6·4	21 30·6	24 6·3	24 6·35	N. 0 45—2 9·75				
5435	16 17 15·0	24 20·0	19 31·0	24 19·8	24 19·9	S. 0 45+4 22·9				
Anon.	16 21 28·0	25 6·0	23 23·4	25 6·0	25 6·0	S. 3 5+1 16·6				

June 27.—At 17ʰ 50ᵐ.—Filled up the plummet cistern with water.
The observations of this night were all made by Mr. Maclear.

(JUNE 28, 1847.—FACE OF SECTOR EAST—(continued).

Number of B.A.C.	Time by Chronometer.	Micr. for Plumb-line on Dot.	Micr. for Observation of Star.	Micr. for Plumb-line on Dot.	Mean of Micr. for Plumb-line on Dot.	Star's Apparent Zenith Distance.	Barom.	Thermometers.		
								Attd.	Upper.	Lower.
	h m s	rev. pts.	rev. pts.	rev. pts.	rev. pts.	° ' rev. pts.	in.			
5498	16 27 24·0	25 27·5	23 28·5	25 27·2	25 27·35	N. 3 40—1 32·85				
5588	16 41 8·0	25 23·5	26 32·4	25 24·0	25 23·75	S. 2 5—1 8 65				
5632	16 47 38·0	26 2·0	23 28·5	26 2·0	26 2·0	S 4 15+2 7·5	26·678	48·2	49·0	49·0
5735	17 2 8·0	26 24·0	27 4·8	26 24·3	26 24·15	S. 4 10—0 14·65				
5817	17 14 27·7	27 7·9	27 25·7	27 7·4	27 7·65	S. 2 45—0 18·05				
5881	17 24 52·3	27 22·0	29 11·0	27 21·5	27 21·75	0 0+1 23 25				
6016	17 46 34·0	27 32·7	29 7·0	27 32·7	27 32·7	S. 1 55—1 8·3				
6074	17 56 34·0	28 13·5	29 7·4	28 13·3	28 13·4	S. 0 30—0 28·0				
6115	18 3 16·8	28 29·3	27 12·5	28 29·0	28 29·15	S. 0 40+1 16·65				
6145	18 7 33·0	29 24·3	28 32·4	29 24·5	29 24·4	S. 1 0+0 26·0				
6233	18 21 25·0	29 20·8	25 2·5	29 20·0	29 20·4	S. 4 40+4 17·9				
6285	18 28 24·6	30 14·0	29 12·9	30 14·4	30 14·2	S. 3 20+1 1·3	26·678	46·4	46·0	47·0
6489	19 0 10·0	15 22·5	13 22·5	15 22·8	15 22·65	S. 0 20+2 0·15				
6525	19 5 9·0	16 12·5	20 22·0	16 12·4	16 12·45	N. 0 50+4 9·55				
6639	19 24 34·0	16 4·9	19 29·4	16 4·6	16 4·75	S. 0 20—3 24·65				
Anon.	19 28 46·0	17 1·5	19 0·0	17 1·5	17 1·5	S. 0 5—1 32·5				
6753	19 43 2·0	17 17·0	15 4·5	17 16·9	17 16·95	S. 1 30+2 12·45				
6877	20 1 58·0	16 32·5	18 11·5	16 32·8	16 32·65	S. 2 45—1 12·85	26·678	45·5	45·0	46·0
6948	20 13 38·0	17 7·1	19 30·6	17 6·9	17 7·0	S. 0 45—2 23·6				
7011	20 22 35·5	17 24·8	18 32·2	17 25·0	17 24·93	N. 0 10+1 7·27				
7026	20 24 26·0	17 25·0	18 26·0	17 25·0	17 24·63	N. 0 10+1 1·07				
7057	20 28 51·0	17 25·0	12 33·5	17 24·8	17 24·93	N. 0 10—4 25·43				
Anon.	20 41 14·0	17 31·5	21 18·0	17 31·1	17 31·3	S. 0 15—3 20·7				
7207	20 47 47·0	18 14·8	16 33·8	18 15·2	18 15·0	S. 4 35+1 15·2				
Anon.	21 1 1·0	18 25·9	22 15·0	18 25·5	18 25·7	0 0+3 23·3				
Anon.	21 8 12·0	18 26·0	17 17·5	18 25·5	18 25·75	S. 0 35+1 8·25				
7386	21 16 0·5	18 27·1	20 29·6	18 27·4	18 27·25	S. 3 5—2 2·35				
Anon.	21 20 0·5	19 0·0	20 20·8	19 0·0	19 0·0	S. 0 5—1 20·8	26·615	43·7	44·5	45·0
Anon.	21 33 9·0	19 5·5	23 5·6	19 5·2	19 .5·35	S. 0 40—4 0·25				
7557	21 43 11·8	19 23·2	22 8·2	19 23·2	19 23·2	S. 4 0—2 19·0				
7657	21 59 18·8	20 10·8	17 18·7	20 10·9	20 10·9	N. 0 35—2 26·2				
Anon.	22 3 9·0	20 10·9	18 24·2	20 11·0	20 10·9	N. 0 35—2 20·7				
7842	22 30 9·0	20 18·0	24 4·3	20 18·4	20 18·2	S. 3 25—3 20·1				
7909	22 41 8·0	20 29·6	21 1·7	20 29·7	20 29·65	S. 0 25—0 5·05				
7966	22 51 22·6	21 10·0	18 28·5	21 9·8	21 9·9	S. 3 55+2 15·4				
7992	22 56 29·0	21 30·5	19 18·9	21 30·3	21 30·4	S. 0 40+2 11·5	26·615	42·8	43·0	43·0

s JUNE 29, 1847.—FACE OF SECTOR WEST.

4517	13	23 17·7	27 32·5	23 17·7	23 17·63	N. 1 0—4 14·87	26·650	50·9	52·0	52·0
4548	13 37 26·0	23 17·7	28 4·2	23 17·4	23 17·63	N. 1 0—4 20·57				
4579	13 44 19·0	14 22·5	18 4·4	14 22·2	14 22·4	S. 2 30+3 16·0				
4623	13 50 19·7	14 22·5	14 13·3	14 22·4	14 22·4	S. 2 30—0 9·1				
4719	14 13 30·0	14 13·9	13 33·2	14 13·6	14 13·75	N. 0 5+1 14·55				
4784	14 26 33·3	14 7·7	12 9·0	14 7·4	14 7·55	N. 0 55+1 32·55				
4852	14 41 38·0	14 11·4	16 30·0	14 11·5	14 11·45	S. 4 45+2 18·55				
4916	14 53 41·2	14 27·2	14 1·40	14 27·5	14 27·55	S. 3 30—0 27·95				
Anon.	15 0 58·0	14 21·5	10 29·0	14 21·4	14 21·45	S. 2 20—3 26·45				
Anon.	15 5 10·5	15 1·7	14 10·0	15 1·5	15 1·5	S. 2 35—0 25·7	26·650	48·2	49·2	49·0
5032	15 15 53·0	15 2·6	16 9·5	15 3·1	15 2·85	N. 0 10—1 6·65				
5151	15 36 37·5	15 0·5	18 16·0	15 0·0	15 0·25	N. 0 30—3 15·70				
Anon.	15 41 52·0	15 17·5	19 16·2	15 17·3	15 17·4	S. 1 20+3 32·8				
5227	15 48 35·5	16 11·6	16 13·2	16 12·0	16 11·8	S. 3 25+0 1·4				
5272	15 54 48·5	15 17·5	18 5·0	15 17·5	15 17·5	N. 1 0—2 21·5				

June 28.—After this date, and including this night, Mr. George Montagu made all the observations at this station. Good definition and calm throughout the night.

♂ JUNE 29, 1847.—FACE OF SECTOR WEST—(continued).

Number of B.A.C.	Time by Chronometer.	Micr. for Plumb-line on Dot.	Micr. for Observation of Star.	Micr. for Plumb-line on Dot.	Mean of Micr. for Plumb-line on Dot.	Star's Apparent Zenith Distance.	Barom.	Thermometers. Attd.	Upper.	Lower.
	h m s	rev. pts.	rev. pts.	rev. pts.	rev. pts.	° ' rev. pts.	in.			
5374	16 8 53·8	15 13·0	17 12·8	15 13·0	15 13·0	N. 0 45—1 33·8				
5435	16 17 13·7	16 16·7	20 28·4	16 16·8	16 16·75	♀. 0 45+4 11·65				
Anon.	16 21 27·0	16 32·8	18 7·1	16 32·5	16 32·65	S. 3 5+1 8·45				
5498	16 27 25·0	16 25·4	18 14·8	16 25·3	16 25·35	N. 3 40—1 23·45				
5588	16 41 10·0	17 15·4	15 30·8	17 15·2	17 15·3	S. 2 5—1 18·5	26·650	46·2	46·5	46·5
5632	16 47 36·0	18 8·8	20 6·7	18 8·1	18 8·45	S. 4 15+1 32·25				
5735	17 2 7·0	18 17·9	17 28·0	18 17·7	18 17·8	S. 4 10—0 23·8				
5817	17 14 28·0	18 19·1	17 27·6	18 18·9	18 19·0	S. 2 45—0 25·4				
5881	17 24 57·2	18 12·6	16 15·0	18 12·8	18 12·7	0 0+1 31·7				
6016	17 46 35·0	19 17·2	17 31·5	19 17·5	19 17·35	S. 1 55—1 19·85				
6074	17 56 37·7	20 11·6	19 7·2	20 12·2	20 11·9	S. 0 30—1 4·7				
6115	18 3 20·5	20 32·3	22 2·8	20 32·5	20 32·4	S. 0 40+1 4·4				
6145	18 7 35·3	21 28·6	22 0·9	21 28·9	21 28·75	S. 1 0+0 15·15				
6233	18 21 21·5	22 29·0	27 7·3	22 29·0	22 29·0	S. 4 40+4 12·3	26·642	44·6	45·0	45·0
6285	18 26 23·0	22 21·4	23 14·2	22 21·5	22 21·45	S. 3 20+0 26·75				
6414	18 50 13·7	22 6·1	22 3·3	22 6·1	22 6·1	S. 1 10—0 2·8				
6480	19 0 14·0	23 21·0	25 14·2	23 21·4	23 21·2	S. 0 20+1 27·0				
6525	19 5 14·5	24 13·5	19 28·6	24 13·8	24 13·65	N. 0 50+4 19·05				
6639	19 24 37·8	18 19·0	11 19·1	18 18·5	18 18·75	S. 0 20—3 33·65				
Anon.	19 28 50·0	14 32·2	12 22·0	14 31·9	14 32·05	S. 0 5—2 10·05				
6753	19 43 4·5	15 0·2	17 1·8	14 33·6	14 33·9	S. 1 30+2 1·9				
6877	20 1 57·5	14 29·5	13 8·8	14 29·0	14 29·25	S. 2 45—1 20·45	26·642	41·9	42·0	42·0
6948	20 13 41·2	15 0·4	11 33·5	15 0·2	15 0·3	S. 0 45—3 0·8				
7011	20 22 40·0	15 14·9	14 0·4	15 15·0	15 15·03	N. 0 10+1 14·63				
7026	20 24 31·0	15 15·0	14 5·8	15 15·1	15 15·03	N. 0 10+1 9·23				
7057	20 28 56·0	15 15·0	19 33·5	15 15·2	15 15·03	N. 0 10—4 18·47				
Anon.	20 31 48·6	15 9·5	13 5·3	15 9·0	15 9·25	S. 0 5—2 3·95				
Anon.	20 41 19·0	15 29·6	11 31·0	15 29·6	15 29·6	S. 0 15—3 32·6				
7207	20 47 44·0	16 3·5	17 10·5	16 4·0	16 3·75	S. 4 35+1 6·75				
Anon.	21 1 6·0	15 12·4	11 15·6	15 12·3	15 12·35	0 0+3 30·75	26·639	41·0	41·5	41·5
Anon.	21 8 15·8	16 0·5	16 31·0	16 0·4	16 0·45	S. 0 35+0 30·55				
Anon.	21 20 5·2	15 24·1	13 29·6	15 24·4	15 24·5	S. 0 5—1 28·65				
Anon.	21 38 12·8	17 0·5	12 25·7	17 1·0	17 0·75	S. 0 40—4 9·05				
7557	21 43 9·8	17 33·5	15 2·8	17 33·5	17 33·5	S. 4 0—2 30·7				
7842	22 30 8·0	19 32·5	16 3·6	19 32·2	19 32·35	S. 3 25—3 28·75				
7900	22 41 11·6	19 20·7	19 4·3	19 20·2	19 20·45	S. 0 25—0 16·15				
7906	22 51 21·0	20 25·8	22 33·5	20 25·3	20 25·55	S. 3 55+2 7·95				
7992	22 56 32·3	22 10·5	24 11·1	22 10·5	22 10·5	S. 0 40+2 0·6	26·630	40·8	40·0	40·8
1802	5 41 25·0	20 13·4	20 17·2	20 12·8	20 13·1	S. 4 25+0 4·1	26·674	56·3	54·2	

♂ JUNE 30, 1847.—FACE OF SECTOR EAST.

Number of B.A.C.	Time by Chronometer.	Micr. for Plumb-line on Dot.	Micr. for Observation of Star.	Micr. for Plumb-line on Dot.	Mean of Micr. for Plumb-line on Dot.	Star's Apparent Zenith Distance.	Barom.	Attd.	Upper.	Lower.
4517	13 31 25·7	8 31·0	4 5·5	8 31·2	8 31·18	N. 1 0—4 25·68				
4548	13 37 30·3	8 31·1	4 2·0	8 31·4	8 31·18	N. 1 0—4 29·18				
4579	13 44 28·7	9 29·9	6 6·0	9 29·5	9 29·62	S. 2 30+3 23·62	26·634	50·9	52·0	
4623	13 50 29·0	9 29·6	9 30·4	9 29·5	9 29·62	S. 2 30—0 0·78				
4710	14 13 34·0	9 24·0	9 30·5	9 23·6	9 23·8	N. 1 10+0 6·7				
4784	14 26 37·6	11 3·2	12 25·25	11 3·2	11 3·2	N. 0 55+1 22·05				
Anon.	14 31 46·2	11 14·4	12 26·25	11 14·7	11 14·55	S. 4 45+2 27·35				
4852	14 41 50·8	12 24·9	9 31·6	12 25·0	12 24·95	S. 4 45+2 27·35				
4916	14 53 52·5	13 33·5	14 16·4	13 33·5	13 33·5	S. 3 30—0 16·9				
Anon.	15 1 7·0	13 31·0	17 13·5	13 31·0	13 31·0	S. 2 20—3 16·5	26·634	49·8	50·0	
Anon.	15 5 19·2	14 5·0	14 20·4	14 4·5	14 4·75	S. 2 35—0 15·65				
5032	15 15 57·3	14 6·8	12 25·7	14 7·0	14 6·9	N. 0 10—1 15·2				

June 29.—Anon. 16ʰ 21ᵐ very faint.
Tolerable definition, and calm throughout the night.

♀ June 30, 1847.—Face of Sector East—(continued).

Number of B.A.C.	Time by Chronometer.	Micr. for Plumb-line on Dot.	Micr. for Observation of Star.	Micr. for Plumb-line on Dot.	Mean of Micr. for Plumb-line on Dot.	Star's Apparent Zenith Distance.	Barom.	Thermometers. Attd.	Upper.	Lower.
	h m s	rev. pts.	rev. pts.	rev. pts.	rev. pts.	° ′ rev. pts.	in.			
5151	15 36 41·4	14 21·4	10 28·9	14 21·6	14 21·5	N. 0 30—3 26·6				
Anon.	15 42 0·5	14 18·4	10 6·6	14 18·7	14 18·55	S. 1 20+4 11·95				
5227	15 48 45·5	16 4·9	15 29·0	16 5·0	16 4·95	S. 3 25+0 9·95				
5272	15 54 51·8	18 1·9	15 3·8	18 1·6	18 1·75	N. 1 0—2 31·95				
5374	16 8 58·0	18 5·6	15 30·0	18 5·7	18 5·65	N. 0 45—2 9·65				
5435	16 17 20·0	18 5·0	13 16·0	18 5·0	18 5·0	S. 0 45+4 23·0				
Anon.	16 21 36·6	18 6·25	16 21·0	18 6·4	18 6·33	S. 3 5+1 19·33				
5498	16 27 24·4	18 29·0	16 29·9	18 28·6	18 28·8	N. 3 40—1 32·9	26·027	47·8	48·0	
5588	16 41 18·5	18 20·8	19 30·7	18 20·7	18 20·75	S. 2 5—1 9·95				
5632	16 47 48·0	18 23·2	16 12·70	18 22·7	18 22·95	S. 4 15+2 10·25				
5735	17 2 18·0	18 24·1	19 3·5	18 24·3	18 24·2	S. 4 10—0 13·3				
5817	17 14 37·0	18 3·5	18 22·4	18 3·5	18 3·5	S. 2 45—0 18·9				
5881	17 25 2·0	18 33·4	20 24·9	18 33·2	18 33·3	0 0+1 25·6				
6016	17 46 43·8	19 21·9	20 33·2	19 21·5	19 21·7	S. 1 55—1 11·5				
6074	17 56 43·5	20 13·5	21 7·6	20 13·2	20 13·35	S. 0 30—0 28·25				
6115	18 3 26·4	20 18·5	19 4·0	20 18·5	20 18·5	S. 0 40+1 14·5				
6145	18 7 42·0	21 11·5	20 10·5	21 11·4	21 11·35	S. 1 0+0 25·85				
6233	18 21 34·5	21 30·5	17 12·0	21 30·0	21 30·25	S. 4 40+4 18·25				
6285	18 28 34·0	21 33 2	20 31·0	21 33·5	21 33·35	S. 3 20+1 1·45				
6305	18 31 27·0	22 17·0	26 6·4	22 16·8	22 16·9	S. 3 25—3 23·5				
6414	18 50 22·0	16 1·8	15 26·4	16 1·4	16 1·6	S. 1 10+0 9·2	26·627	45·5	45·5	
6480	19 0 19·6	16 21·5	14 23·5	16 21·5	16 21·5	S. 0 20+1 32·0				
6525	19 5 18·5	16 13·5	20 25·0	16 13·6	16 13·55	N. 0 50+4 11·45				
6639	19 24 43·3	12 10·5	12 5·5	12 10·2	12 10·35	S. 0 20—3 23·85				
6877	20 2 7·5	10 28·4	12 5·5	10 28·0	10 28·2	S. 2 45—1 11·3	26·627	45·5	45·5	
6948	20 13 47·5	11 9·0	13 31·7	11 8·4	11 8·7	S. 0 45—2 23·0				
7011	20 22 45·0	11 11·5	12 16·4	11 11·3	11 11·35	N. 0 10+1 5·05				
7026	20 24 36·5	11 11·3	12 7·6	11 11·4	11 11·35	N. 0 10+0 30·25				
7057	20 29 1·0	11 11·4	6 17·0	11 11·2	11 11·35	N. 0 10—4 28·35				
Anon.	20 41 24·0	11 8·5	14 27·7	11 8·0	11 8·5	S. 0 15—3 19·45				
7207	20 47 56·8	12 5·7	10 24·2	12 6·0	12 5·85	S. 4 35+1 15·65				
Anon.	21 1 11·0	12 30·5	16 18·4	12 30·0	12 30·25	0 0+3 22·15	26·627	46·0	46·0	
Anon.	21 8 22·0	12 18·7	11 12·0	12 19·0	12 18·85	S. 0 35+1 6·85				
7386	21 16 9·5	12 19·3	14 22·2	12 20·2	12 19·75	S. 3 5—2 2·45				
Anon.	21 20 10·5	14 1·8	15 21·5	14 1·0	14 1·4	S. 0 5—1 20·1				
Anon.	21 33 18·5	14 9·5	18 11·6	14 9·0	14 9·25	S. 0 40—4 2·35				
7557	21 43 21·2	14 17·8	17 5·5	14 17·6	14 17·6	S. 4 0—2 21·9				
7657	21 59 28·0	15 17·5	12 24·5	15 17·2	15 17·35	N. 0 35—2 26·85				
Anon.	22 3 19·0	15 17·2	13 30·8	15 17·2	15 17·2	N. 0 35—1 20·40				
7842	22 30 19·0	15 26·0	19 10·5	15 26·5	15 26·25	S. 3 25—3 18·25				
7909	22 41 17·5	16 12·4	16 18·5	16 12·5	16 12·45	S. 0 25—0 6·05				
7966	22 51 32·0	16 25·1	14 9·2	16 25·5	16 25·3	S. 3 55+2 16·1				
7992	22 56 38·0	17 2·8	14 25·8	17 2·0	17 2·4	S. 0 40+2 10·6	26·591	42·8	42·5	
1802	5 41 37·5	18 16·8	18. 2·8	18 17·3	18 17·05	S. 4 25+0 14·25	26·662	63·0	65·0	

♃ July 1, 1847.—Face of Sector West.

Number of B.A.C.	Time by Chronometer.	Micr. for Plumb-line on Dot.	Micr. for Observation of Star.	Micr. for Plumb-line on Dot.	Mean of Micr. for Plumb-line on Dot.	Star's Apparent Zenith Distance.	Barom.	Thermometers. Attd.	Upper.	Lower.
4517	13 31 31·0	8 31·7	13 15·7	8 32·0	8 32·03	N. 1 0—4 17·67	26·642	51·4	52·0	
4548	13 37 35·0	8 32·0	13 18·2	8 32·4	8 32·03	N. 2 40—20·17				
4579	13 44 27·4	10 1·0	13 18·3	10 1·5	10 1·38	S. 2 30+3 16·92				
4623	13 50 28·0	10 1·5	9 27·25	10 1·5	10 1·38	S. 2 30—0 8·13				
4710	14 13 39·0	11 21·5	11 6·8	11 21·7	11 21·6	N. 1 10+0 14·8				
4784	14 26 42·5	11 31·5	10 1·7	11 31·5	11 31·5	N. 0 55+1 29·8				
Anon.	14 31 44·5	12 27·8	11 8·5	12 27·3	12 27·55	S. 2 55—1 19·05				

June 30.—Good definitions and calm throughout the night.
Nos. 7011, 7026 and 7057.—Very faint.

♃ JULY 1, 1847.—FACE OF SECTOR WEST - (continued).

Number of B.A.C.	Time by Chronometer.	Micr. for Plumb-line on Dot.	Micr. for Observation of Star.	Micr. for Plumb-line on Dot.	Mean of Micr. for Plumb-line on Dot.	Star's Apparent Zenith Distance.	Barom.	Thermometers. Attd.	Upper.	Lower.
	h m s	rev. pts.	rev. pts.	rev. pts.	rev. pts.	° ′ rev. pts.	in.			
4891	14 48 48·2	15 14·5	15 19·2	15 15·0	15 14·75	N. 2 25—0 4·45				
4916	14 53 49·6	16 13·6	17 7·55	16 13·5	16 13·55	S. 3 30+0 28·00				
Anon.	15 1 7·0	16 22·8	12 33·2	16 22·7	16 22·75	S. 2 20—3 23·55				
5032	15 16 1·0	16 32·5	18 7·5	16 33·0	16 32·75	N. 0 10—1 8·75	26·642	50·0	50·5	
5151	15 36 45·5	16 33·0	20 15·7	16 33·0	16 33·0	N. 0 30—3 16·7				
Anon.	15 42 1·0	17 21·5	21 23·0	17 21·2	17 21·35	S. 1 20+4 1·65				
5227	15 48 43·0	18 8·6	18 12·8	18 9·2	18 8·9	S. 3 25+0 3·9				
5272	15 54 56·5	17 30·2	20 18·0	17 30·6	17 30·4	N. 1 0—2 21·6				
5374	16 9 2·0	18 10·4	20 11·5	18 10·5	18 10·45	N. 0 45—2 1·05				
5435	16 17 21·8	19 0·5	23 13·5	19 0·2	19 0·35	S. 0 45+4 13·15				
Anon.	16 21 35·2	19 10·8	20 25·0	19 10·7	19 10·75	S. 3 5+1 14·25	26·642	47·8	49·0	
5498	16 27 32·4	18 22·2	20 13·6	18 23·0	18 22·6	N. 3 40—1 25·0				
5588	16 41 17·8	16 27·25	15 9·5	16 27·20	16 27·23	S. 2 5—1 17·73				
5632	16 47 44·0	17 20·8	19 19·5	17 21·0	17 20·9	S. 4 15+1 32·60				
5817	17 14 36·0	17 11·8	16 21·5	17 12·2	17 12·0	S. 2 45—0 24·5				
5881	17 25 5·0	17 13·7	15 15·8	17 13·8	17 13·75	0 0+1 31·95				
6016	17 46 44·0	17 27·5	16 11·0	17 27·5	17 27·5	S. 1 55—1 16·5				
6074	17 56 46·0	18 4·25	17 0·7	18 4·30	18 4·28	S. 0 30—1 3·58	26·642	46·4	47·0	
6115	18 3 29·0	18 21·7	19 28·25	18 21·8	18 21·75	S. 0 40+1 6·50				
6233	18 21 29·0	19 30·0	24 6·1	19 29·5	19 29·75	S. 4 40+4 10·35				
6285	18 28 31·5	19 33·6	20 29·5	20 0·5	20 0·05	S. 3 20+0 29·45				
6305	18 31 40·5	20 12·0	16 14·5	20 12·4	20 12·0	S. 3 25—3 31·7				
6414	18 50 37·0	20 9·0	20 9·4	20 8·5	20 8·75	S. 1 10+0 0·65				
6489	19 0 22·5	20 12·8	22 5·4	20 12·0	20 12·0	S. 0 20+1 26·5				
6525	19 5 23·0	20 15·25	15 30·7	20 15·0	20 15·13	N. 0 50+4 18·43	26·638	45·9	46·0	
6639	19 24 46·0	20 3·2	16 5·4	20 3·5	20 3·35	S. 0 20—3 31·95				
6877	20 2 6·0	20 11·8	18 25·5	20 11·6	20 11·7	S. 2 45—1 20·2				
6948	20 13 49·7	20 17·5	17 17·0	20 17·0	20 17·25	S 0 45—3 0·25				
7011	20 22 48·2	20 23·6	19 9·5	20 24·2	20 23·9	N. 0 10+1 14·4				
7026	20 24 39·5	20 24·2	19 16·0	20 24·5	20 24·35	N. 0 10+1 8·35				
Anon.	20 31 56·5	20 32·2	18 29·5	20 32·0	20 32·1	S. 0 5—2 2·6				
Anon.	20 41 27·0	19 0·2	15 6·5	19 0·4	19 0·3	S. 0 15—3 27·8	26·638	45·5	45·0	
7207	20 47 53·0	19 13·4	20 21·0	19 13·0	19 13·2	S. 4 35+1 7·8				
Anon.	21 1 14·0	18 32·7	15 2·4	18 33·0	18 32·85	0 0+3 30·45				
Anon.	21 8 24·0	19 5·8	20 4·1	19 6·0	19 5·9	S. 0 35+0 32·2				
7386	21 16 7·5	19 30·5	17 20·5	19 30·8	19 30·65	S. 3 5—2 10·15				
Anon.	21 20 13·5	19 4·8	17 10·8	19 4·85	19 4·85	S. 0 5—1 28·05				
Anon.	21 33 20·5	19 29·6	15 20·6	19 30·3	19 29·95	S. 0 40—4 9·35	26·638	45·0	44·8	
7557	21 43 18·0	21 10·5	18 16·8	21 10·75	21 10·75	S. 4 0—2 27·05				
7842	22 30 18·0	24 15·8	20 21·5	24 16·0	24 15·9	S. 3 25—3 28·4				
7992	22 56 41·0	24 19·5	26 20·0	24 19·7	24 19·6	S. 0 40+2 0·4	26·634	44·1	43·4	
1802	5 41 33·5	25 21·7	25 27·1	25 22·0	25 21·85	S. 4 25+0 5·25	26·737	59·9	60·0	

♀ JULY 2, 1847.—FACE OF SECTOR EAST.

Number of B.A.C.	Time by Chronometer.	Micr. for Plumb-line on Dot.	Micr. for Observation of Star.	Micr. for Plumb-line on Dot.	Mean of Micr. for Plumb-line on Dot.	Star's Apparent Zenith Distance.	Barom.	Thermometers. Attd.	Upper.	Lower.
2293	7 1 5·0	27 4·0	23 17·8	27 4·8	27 4·4	N. 1 0—3 22·6				
4548	13 37 39·0	27 12·9	22 19·0	27 13·0	27 12·95	N. 1 0—4 27·95				
4570	13 44 39·0	28 31·2	25 2·0	28 32·0	28 31·6	S. 2 30+3 29·6				
4923	13 50 38·0	28 33·0	29 2·0	28 33·4	28 33·2	S. 2 30—0 2·8	26·721	50·0	50·0	
4719	14 13 43·0	19 30·6	20 4·5	19 30·6	19 30·6	N. 1 10+0 7·9				
4784	14 26 46·5	21 12·2	23 1·0	21 12·0	21 12·1	N. 0 55+1 22·0				
Anon.	14 31 55·5	21 9·5	22 25·0	21 10·0	21 10·0	S. 1 15—1 15·25				
4852	14 41 59·8	22 20·0	19 28·9	22 20·7	22 20·35	S. 4 45+2 25·45				
4891	14 48 50·2	23 21·0	23 11·3	23 20·8	23 20·9	N. 2 25—0 9·6				

July 1.—No. 5817.—Very faint.
Nos. 6305 and 6414.—Leaving the field.
Indifferent definitions : milky atmosphere.
Much obstruction, and several observations lost from passing clouds.

♀ JULY 2, 1847.—FACE OF SECTOR EAST—(continued).

Number of B.A.C.	Time by Chronometer.	Micr. for Plumb-line on Dot.	Micr. for Observation of Star.	Micr. for Plumb-line on Dot.	Mean of Micr. for Plumb-line on Dot.	Star's Apparent Zenith Distance.	Barom.	Attd.	Upper.	Lower.
	h m s	rev. pts.	rev. pts.	rev. pts.	rev. pts.	° ' rev. pts.	in.			
4016	14 54 1·3	23 21·5	24 7·0	23 21·6	23 21·55	S. 3 30—0 19·45				
Anon.	15 1 16·0	24 0·3	27 27·7	24 9·3	24 9·3	S. 2 20—3 18·4				
Anon.	15 5 28·0	24 3·2	24 20·7	24 3·5	24 3·35	S. 2 35—0 17·35				
5032	15 16 6·5	24 33·0	23 18·0	24 33·2	24 33·1	N. 0 10—1 15·1	26·705	46·0	47·0	
5151	15 36 50·0	26 9·2	22 19·3	26 9·8	26 9·5	N. 0 30—3 24·2				
5227	15 48 54·0	19 16·4	19 7·2	19 16·7	19 16·55	S. 3 25+0 9·35				
5272	15 55 0·5	21 1·4	18 7·4	21 1·8	21 1·6	N. 1 0—2 28·2				
5374	16 9 6·0		14 15·8	16 25·4		N. 0 45—2 10·1				
5435	16 17 29·0	17 8·1	12 19·7	17 8·8	17 8·45	S. 0 45+4 22·75				
Anon.	16 21 46·0	17 20·2	16 1·6	17 20·0	17 20·1	S 3 5+1 18·5				
5498	16 27 33·0	19 21·0	17 23·5	19 21·0	19 21·0	N. 3 40—1 31·5				
5588	16 41 27·0	19 23·4	20 32·3	19 23·2	19 23·3	S. 2 5—1 9·0	26·697	43·0	43·5	
5632	16 47 56·8	20 18·3	18 11·0	20 18·5	20 18·4	S. 4 15+2 7·4				
5735	17 2 27·0		21 29·6	21 13·6		S. 4 10—0 16·0				
5817	17 14 46·5	21 29·4	22 14·0	21 29·5	21 29·45	S. 2 45—0 18·55				
5881	17 25 10·5	22 33·4	24 22·5	22 33·8	22 33·6	0 0+1 22·9				
6016	17 46 52·5	23 20·4	24 30·8	23 20·6	23 20·5	S. 1 55—1 10·3				
6074	17 56 52·0	18 8·55	19 3·0	18 7·9	18 8·23	S. 0 30—0 28·77				
6115	18 3 35·0	18 15·8	17 0·2	18 15·8	18 15·8	N. 0 40+1 15·6				
6145	18 7 50·5	18 21·8	17 30·5	18 21·5	18 21·65	S. 1 0+0 25·15				
6233	18 21 43·0	19 0·5	14 15·4	19 0·2	19 0·35	S. 4 40+4 18·05	26·701	41·0	41·0	
6285	18 28 42·0	17 14·5	16 13·3	17 14·7	17 14·6	S. 3 20+1 1·3				
6305	18 31 35·0	17 27·0	21 16·8	17 26·9	17 26·95	S. 3 25—3 23·65				
6414	18 50 28·7	18 27·5	18 19·0	18 27·45	18 27·45	S. 1 10+0 8·45				
6489	19	18 18·5	16 19·7	18 18·7	18 18·6	S. 0 20+1 32·9				
6525	19 5 26·7	19 27·5	24 4·0	19 27·3	19 27·4	N. 0 50+4 10·6				
6639	19 24 51·5	19 13·8	23 4·9	19 13·6	19 13·7	S. 0 20—3 25·2				
Anon.	19 29 4·0	20 15·4	12 15·0	20 14·8		S. 0 5—2 0·1	26·697	39·9	39·0	
6753	19 43 19·5	20 30·0	18 17·0	20 30·4	20 30·2	S. 1 30+2 13·2				
6877	20 2 15·5	22 7·9	23 19·3	22 7·1	22 7·5	S. 2 45—1 11·8				
6948	20 13 55·8	22 1·5	24 26·3	22 1·5	22 1·5	S. 0 45—2 24·8				
7011	20 22 53·0	25 33·7	27 6·5	26 0·0	25 33·92	N. 0 10+1 8·58				
7057	20 29 9·0	26 0·0	21 8·0	26 0·0	25 33·92	N. 0 10—4 25·92				
Anon.	20 32 2·0		24 15·4	22 17·8		S. 0 5—1 31·6				
Anon.	20 41 31·8	16 19·7	20 4·8	16 19·6	16 19·6	S. 0 15—3 19·2				
7207	20 48 5·0	16 1·5	14 21·0	16 1·5	16 1·5	S. 4 35+1 14·5				
Anon.	21 1 19·0	16 26·0	20 16·0	16 25·7	16 25·85	0 0+3 24·15	26·697	39·6	38·5	
Anon.	21 8 29·3	16 17·0	15 10·0	16 16·7	16 16·85	S. 0 35+1 6·85				
7386	21 16 17·0	16 31·2	18 33·2	16 31·0	16 31·1	S. 3 5—2 2·1				
Anon.	21 20 18·0	16 27·0	18 14·0	16 26·8	16 26·9	S. 0 5+1 21·1				
Anon.	21 33 26·2	17 8·5	21 10·5	17 7·9	17 8·75	S. 0 40—4 1·75				
7557	21 43 28·8	17 0·0	19 22·2	16 33·5	16 33·75	S. 4 0—2 22·45				
7657	21 59 35·5	17 22·5	14 29·5	17 22·0	17 22·02	N. 0 35+2 26·52				
Anon.	22 3 27·0	17 21·9	16 0·3	17 22·0	17 22·02	N. 0 35+1 21·72				
7842	22 30 26·3	17 27·6	21 12·5	17 27·4	17 27·5	S. 3 25—3 19·0				
7009	22 41 25·8	18 16·0	24 3·0	18 16·0	18 16·0	S. 0 25—0 8·0				
7966	22 51 39·6	17 7·4	14 25·3	17 7·2	17 7·3	S. 3 55+2 16·0				
7992	22 56 46·0	18 0·0	15 25·1	18 0·0	18 0·0	S. 0 40+2 8·9	26·693	38·3	37·0	

♄ JULY 3, 1847.—FACE OF SECTOR WEST.

Number of B.A.C.	Time by Chronometer.	Micr. for Plumb-line on Dot.	Micr. for Observation of Star.	Micr. for Plumb-line on Dot.	Mean of Micr. for Plumb-line on Dot.	Star's Apparent Zenith Distance.	Barom.	Attd.	Upper.	Lower.
2293	7 0 10·0	20 8·5	23 18·5	20 8·2	20 8·35	N. 1 0—3 10·15	26·788	59·9	62·0	
4517	13 31 38·5	17 10·9	21 28·2	17 10·7	17 10·83	N. 1 0—4 17·37	26·764	50·0	50·8	
4548	13 37 43·5	17 10·7	21 31·8	17 11·0	17 10·83	N. 1 0—4 20·97				

July 2.—No. 6489.—Leaving the field.
  Anon. 19ʰ 29ᵐ.—Uncertain observation.
  Anon. 20ʰ 32ᵐ.—Hurried observation.
  No. 7207 and Anon. 21ʰ 1ᵐ.—Very faint.
  Good definition and calm throughout the night.

ħ JULY 3, 1847.—FACE OF SECTOR WEST—(continued).

Number of B.A.C.	Time by Chronometer.	Micr. for Plumb-line on Dot.	Micr. for Observation of Star.	Micr. for Plumb-line on Dot.	Mean of Micr. for Plumb-line on Dot.	Star's Apparent Zenith Distance.	Barom.	Thermometers. Attd.	Upper.	Lower.
	b m s	rev. pts.	rev. pts.	rev. pts.	rev. pts.	° ' rev. pts.	In.			
4579	13 44 37·0	18 24·3	22 6·7	18 24·5	18 24·4	S. 2 30+3 16·3				
4623	13 50 37·5	11 9·9	11 1·8	11 10·0	11 9·95	S. 2 30—0 8·15				
4719	14 13 47·5	11 10·4	10 29·8	11 10·8	11 10·6	N. 1 10+0 14·8				
4784	14 26 50·5	11 33·5	10 1·6	11 33·1	11 33·3	N. 1 55+1 31·7				
Anon.	14 31 54·0	12 26·0	11 6·4	12 26·7	12 26·8	S. 2 55—1 20·4				
4852	14 41 55·3	13 17·0	16 4·6	13 16·5	13 16·75	S. 4 45+2 21·85				
4801	14 48 56·0	13 11·3	13 14·8	13 11·4	13 11·35	N. 2 25—0 3·45	26·764	48·2	48·0	
4916	14 54 0·0	14 6·2	13 15·4	14 6·5	14 6·35	S. 3 30—0,24·95				
Anon.	15 1 15·5	14 11·0	10 19·5	14 10·8	14 10·9	S. 2 20—3 25·4				
Anon.	15 5 27·0	14 5·2	13 15·7	14 5·3	14 5·25	S. 2 35—0 23·55				
5032	15 16 8·7	13 31·6	15 5·3	13 31·8	13 31·7	N. 0 10—1 7·6				
5151	15 36 53·5	13 30·2	17 14·3	13 30·0	13 30·1	N. 0 30—3 18·2				
Anon.	15 42 9·0	14 14·4	18 15·2	14 14·8	14 14·6	S. 1 20+4 0·6				
5227	15 48 53·0	14 27·8	14 30·8	14 27·8	14 27·8	S. 3 25+0 3·0				
5272	15 55 5·0	14 32·5	17 21·2	14 33·0	14 32·75	N. 1 0—2 22·45				
5374	16 9 10·3	15 10·7	17 11·7	15 10·5	15 10·6	N. 0 45—2 1·1	26·748	47·8	47·0	
5435	16 17 29·8	15 19·8	20 0·0	15 20·0	15 19·9	S. 0 45+4 14·1				
Anon.	16 21 44·0	15 31·5	17 9·0	15 32·0	15 31·75	S. 3 5+1 11·25				
5493	16 27 40·0	16 6·8	17 32·0	16 6·5	16 6·65	N. 3 40—1 25·35				
5588	16 41 26·0	16 21·8	15 6·5	16 21·8	16 21·8	S. 2 5—1 15·3				
5632	16 47 53·8	17 10·4	19 12·8	17 10·2	17 10·3	S. 4 15+2 2·5				
5735	17 2 23·2	17 16·4	16 30·2	17 16·5	17 16·45	S. 4 10—0 20·25				
5817	17 14 45·0	17 2·6	16 12·8	17 2·5	17 2·55	S. 2 45—0 23·75				
5881	17 25 13·8	16 26·0	14 29·5	16 25·7	16 25·85	0 0+1 30·35				
6016	17 46 52·0	16 28·0	15 11·5	16 27·4	16 27·7	S. 1 55—1 16·20	26·748	44·6	45·0	
6074	17 56 54·0	16 30·2	15 27·2	16 29·8	16 30·0	S. 0 30—1 2·8				
6115	18 3 37·0	16 20·0	17 27·0	16 20·5	16 20·25	S. 0 40+1 6·75				
6145	18 7 51·8	17 4·7	17 22·5	17 5·2	17 4·95	S. 1 0+0 17·55				
6233	18 21 39·0	17 24·4	22 1·4	17 24·0	17 24·2	S. 4 40+4 11·2				
6285	18 28 40·0	17 13·3	18 7·5	17 13·6	17 13·45	S. 3 20+0 28·05				
6305	18	17 17·8	13 21·3	17 17·6	17 17·7	S. 3 25—3 30·4				
6414	18	17 3·8	17 4·9	17 3·8		S. 1 10+0 1·15				
6489	19 0 31·0	16 33·4	18 25·7	16 33·3	16 33·35	S. 0 20+1 23·35				
6525	19 5 31·5	17 8·1	12 21·7	17 7·8	17 7·95	N. 0 50+4 20·25	26·748	42·8	43·0	
6639	19 24	17 20·2	13 20·4	17 20·5	17 20·35	S. 0 20—3 33·95				
6753	19 43 21·0	18 9·6	20 13·9	18 9·4	18 9·5	S. 1 30+2 4·4				
6877	20 2 15·5	18 26·0	17 5·6	18 25·8	18 25·9	S. 2 45—1 20·3				
6948	20 13 58·0	18 44	15 4·5	18 4·7	18 4·55	S. 0 45—3 0·05				
7011	20 22 56·8	17 32·0	16 15·2	17 31·6	17 31·86	N. 0 10+1 16·66	26·745	41·5	41·4	
7026	20 24 47·0	17 31·6	16 23·2	17 32·0	17 31·80	N. 0 10+1 8·66				
7057	20 29 12·0	17 32·0	22 12·5	17 32·0	17 31·86	N. 0 10—1 4·64				
Anon.	20 32 4·5		15 28·8	17 32·5		S. 0 5—2 3·7				
7207	20 48 2·0	14 20·2	15 28·6	14 20·5	14 20·35	S. 4 35+1 8·25				
Anon.	21 1	14 9·9	10 10·4	14 9·9	14 9·0	0 0+3 33·5	26·741	42·4	42·0	
Anon.	21 8 31·8	14 17·8	15 13·7	14 17·0	14 17·4	S. 0 35+0 30·3				
7386	21 16 16·5	14 32·3	12 21·2	14 32·7	14 32·5	S. 3 5—2 11·3				
Anon.	21 20 22·0	14 14·6	12 20·3	14 14·7	14 14·65	S. 0 5—1 28·35				
Anon.	21 33	14 18·9	10 7·0	14 18·6	14 18·75	S. 0 40—4 10·85				
7557	21 49 27·8	14 31·7	12 3·2	14 32·0	14 31·85	S. 4 0—2 28·65				
7657	21 59 40·3	14 29·2	17 10·8	14 29·7	14 29·45	N. 0 35—2 15·35	26·741	42·3	41·8	
7842	22 30 25·0	15 15·3	11 19·8	15 15·4	15 15·35	S. 3 25—3 29·55				
7909	22 41 29·8	15 15·2	14 33·3	15 15·2	15 15·2	S. 3 25—0 15·9				
7966	22 51 38·2	15 32·3	18 8·1	15 32·2	15 32·25	S. 3 55+2 9·85				
7992	22 56 48·2	15 21·6	17 22·0	15 21·4	15 21·5	S. 0 40+2 0·5	26·741	41·4	41·0	
1802	5 41 43·0	16 24·5	16 26·5	16 24·7	16 24·6	S. 4 25+0 1·9	26·791	60·8	59·0	

July 3.—No. 5735.—Wire not well seen.
No. 6305.—Leaving the field.
No. 1802.—Bad definition.
Good definition and calm throughout the night.

☉ JULY 4, 1847.—FACE OF SECTOR EAST.

Number of B.A.C.	Time by Chronometer.	Micr. for Plumb-line on Det.	Micr. for Observation of Star.	Micr. for Plumb-line on Dot.	Mean of Micr. for Plumb-line on Dot.	Star's Apparent Zenith Distance.	Barom.	Atol.	Upper.	Lower.
	h m s	rev. pts.	rev. pts.	rev. pts.	rev. pts.	° ′ rev. pts	in.			
2293	7 0 13·5	17 18·7	13 33·0	17 18·8	17 18·75	N. 1 0—3 19·75	26·792	63·0	64·5	
4517	13 31 43·5	18 1·2	13 12·4	18 1·0	18 1·07	N. 1 0—4 22·87	26·729	50·4	51·0	
4548	13 37 48·3	18 1·0	13 7·2	18 1·1	18 1·07	N. 1 0—4 27·87				
4579	13 44 45·7	18 7·4	14 19·2	18 7·0	18 7·32	S. 2 30+3 22·12				
4623	13 50 46·0	18 7·4	18 10·8	18 7·5	18 7·32	S. 2 30—0 3·48				
4719	14 13 52·0	18 10·4	18 18·0	18 10·7	18 10·55	N. 1 10+0 7·45				
Anon.	14 32 3·0	18 18·2	19 31·5	18 18·5	18 18·35	S. 2 55—1 13·15				
4852	14 42 7·0	18 22·4	15 30·0	18 22·4	18 22·4	S. 4 45+2 26·4				
4891	14 48 50·8	19 28·0	19 17·0	19 27·6	19 27·8	N. 2 23—0 9·9				
4916	14 54 0·2	19 24·1	20 8·9	19 24·4	19 24·25	S. 3 30—0 18·65				
Anon.	15 1 24·0	18 33·4	22 16·8	18 33·2	18 33·3	S. 2 20—3 17·5				
Anon.	15 5 36·0	19 3·2	19 18·5	19 3·3	19 3·25	S. 2 35—0 15·25	26·729	48·0	48·0	
5032	15 16 15·0	19 11·0	17 29·3	19 10·6	19 10·8	N. 0 10—1 15·5				
5151	15 36 50·2	19 17·5	15 26·5	19 17·5	19 17·5	N. 0 30—3 25·0				
Anon.	15 42 17·0	19 3·4	14 28·7	19 3·45	19 3·45	S. 1 20+4 8·75				
5227	15 40 2·3	19 21·1	19 12·6	19 21·1	19 21·1	S. 3 25+0 8·5				
5272	15 55 9·5	20 32·2	18 1·6	20 32·0	20 32·0	N. 1 0—2 30·4				
5374	16 9 15·4	20 17·1	18 6·7	20 16·7	20 16·9	N. 0 45—2 10·2				
5435	16 17 37·3	20 15·1	15 27·0	20 14·8	20 14·95	S. 0 45+4 21·95				
Anon.	16 21 54·0	20 22·5	19 6·6	20 22·7	20 22·6	S. 3 5+1 16·0				
5408	16 27 42·3	20 26·0	18 28·5	20 26·5	20 26·25	N. 3 40—1 31·75	26·717	46·0	45·8	
5588	16 41 35·5	20 11·0	21 19·5	20 10·5	20 10·75	S. 2 5—1 8·75				
5632	16 48 4·7	20 21·0	18 11·7	20 21·5	20 21·25	S. 4 15+2 9·55				
5735	17 2 35·0	20 29·5	21 11·0	20 29·7	20 29·6	S. 4 10—0 15·4				
5817	17 14 54·0	20 10·5	20 29·0	20 10·7	20 10·6	S. 2 45—0 19·0				
5881	17 25 19·7	20 32·0	22 22·4	20 32·0	20 32·0	0 0+1 24·4				
6074	17 56	21 15·7	22 10·4	21 15·8	21 15·75	S. 0 30—0 28·65	26·717	45·1	45·0	
6115	18 3 44·0	21 19·4	20 3·8	21 19·2	21 19·2	S. 0 40+1 15·50				
6145	18 7 50·8	21 17·6	20 26·6	21 17·5	21 17·55	S. 1 0+0 24·05				
6233	18 21 50·8	21 17·5	16 32·0	21 17·0	21 17·25	S. 4 40+4 19·25				
6285	18 28 50·8	22 0·5	20 33·2	22 0·4	22 0·45	S. 3 20+1 1·25				
6305	18 31 44·5	21 29·4	25 19·0	21 29·3	21 29·35	S. 3 25—3 23·65				
6414	18 50 38·0	22 14·4	22 6·5	22 14·5	22 14·45	S. 1 10+0 7·05				
6480	19 0 37·0	22 11·0	20 10·2	22 10·8	22 10·8	S. 0 20+2 0·70	26·717	45·0	45·0	
6525	19 5 36·3	22 22·9	26 33·5	22 22·7	22 22·8	N. 0 50+4 10·70				
6639	19 24 25·1	17 12·5	21 3·3	17 12·5	17 12·5	S. 0 20—3 24·80				
6877	20 2 24·4	18 13·8	19 26·5	18 14·1	18 13·95	S. 2 45—1 12·55				
6948	20 13 14·5	18 23·2	21 12·8	18 22·6	18 22·9	S. 0 45—2 23·90				
7011	20 23 2·8	17 1·4	18 9·5	17 0·5	17 0·93	N. 0 10+1 8·57				
7026	20 24 53·5	17 1·4	18 0·8	17 0·5	17 0·93	N. 0 10—4 33·87				
7057	20 29 19·0	17 1·4	12 11·4	17 0·4	17 0·93	N. 0 10—4 23·53				
Anon.	20 32 11·0	16 29·0	18 23·0	16 29·0	16 29·0	S. 0 5—1 28·0				
7207	20 48 13·7	17 10·3	15 31·4	17 11·0	17 10·65	S. 4 35+1 13·25	26·717	46·4	45·6	
Anon.	21 8 39·0	19 18·5	18 11·3	19 18·3	19 18·4	S. 0 35+1 7·10				
7557	21 43 37·6	23 24·5	26 12·5	23 24·5	23 24·5	S. 4 0—2 22·0	26·717	46·2	45·5	
Anon.	22 3 37·0	19 0·3	17 15·4	19 0·0	19 0·15	N. 0 35—1 18·75				
7842	22 30 35·0	19 6·5	22 27·0	19 7·0	19 6·75	S. 3 25—3 20·25	26·717	45·0	45·0	
7992	22 56 55·6	17 12·5	14 30·6	17 12·3	17 12·4	S. 0 40+2 15·80				

☾ JULY 5, 1847.—FACE OF SECTOR WEST.

Number of B.A.C.	Time by Chronometer.	Micr. for Plumb-line on Det.	Micr. for Observation of Star.	Micr. for Plumb-line on Dot.	Mean of Micr. for Plumb-line on Dot.	Star's Apparent Zenith Distance.	Barom.	Atol.	Upper.	Lower.
4517	13 31 47·4	18 30·5	23 11·9	18 31·0	18 30·77	N. 1 0—4 15·13				
4548	13 37 52·3	18 30·5	23 16·0	18 31·1	18 30·77	N. 1 0—4 19·23				
4579	13 44 46·0	16 23·7	20 4·6	16 23·6	16 23·62	S. 2 30+3 14·98				

July 4.—No. 6074.—Leaving the field.
No. 6305.—Indistinct.
Anon. 22ʰ 3ᵐ.—Faint, and the observation uncertain.
Milky atmosphere; cumuli towards morning. Good definition. Several observations lost.

☽ July 5, 1847.—Face of Sector West—(continued.)

Number of B.A.C.	Time by Chronometer.	Micr. for Plumb-line on Dot.	Micr. for Observation of Star.	Micr. for Plumb-line on Dot.	Mean of Micr. for Plumb-line on Dot.	Star's Apparent Zenith Distance.	Barom.	Thermometers. Attd.	Upper.	Lower
	h m s	rev. pts.	rev. pts.	rev. pts.	rev. pts.	° ′ rev. pts.	in.			
4623	13 50 46·0	16 23·5	16 14·0	16 23·7	16 23·62	S. 2 30—0 9·62	26·662	53·2	54·0	
4719	14 13 56·2	14 3·2	13 21·6	14 3·3	14 3·25	N. 1 10+0 15·65				
4784	14 27 0·0	14 1·2	12 1·5	14 1·1	14 1·15	N. 0 55+1 33·05				
Anon.	14 32 3·0	14 25·2	13 2·5	14 25·3	14 25·25	S. 2 55—1 22·75				
4852	14	14 32·5	17 18·8	14 33·0	14 32·75	S. 4 45+2 20·05				
4891	14 48 59·5	14 19·8	14 21·1	14 19·9	14 19·85	N. 2 25—0 1 25				
Anon.	15 1 24·7	15 3·0	11 11·3	15 3·2	15 3·1	S. 2 20—3 25·8				
Anon.	15 5 36·5	15 27·0	15 1·5	15 27·0	15 27·0	S. 2 35—0 25·5	26·662	50·9	51·0	
5032	15 16 18·6	15 14·8	16 21·8	15 14·8	15 14·8	N. 0 10—1 7·0				
5151	15 37 3·2	16 12·5	19 27·0	16 12·5	16 12·5	N. 0 30—3 15·4				
Anon.	15 42 19·0	17 4·3	21 3·7	17 4·2	17 4·25	S. 1 20+3 33·45				
5227	15 49 1·5	17 17·0	17 19·0	17 17·0	17 17·0	S. 3 25+0 2·0				
5272	15 55 14·0	17 8·3	19 30·0	17 8·7	17 8·5	N. 1 0—2 21·5				
5374	16 9 19·5	16 30·5	18 31·6	16 30·5	16 30·5	N. 0 45—2 1·1	26·662	50·0	49·5	
5435	16 17 39·5	17 9·3	21 23·0	17 9·4	17 9·35	S. 0 45+4 13·65				
Anon.	16 21 53·5	18 16·4	19 32·6	18 16·8	18 16·6	S. 3 5+1 16·0				
5498	16 27 49·5	17 33·8	19 25·0	17 33·5	17 33·65	N. 3 40—1 25·35				
5588	16 41 36·5	18 20·3	17 2·5	18 20·4	18 20·35	S. 2 5—1 17·85				
5632	16 48 3·0	19 17·0	21 10·0	19 16·8	19 16·9	S. 4 15+2 2·1				
5735	17 2 33·0	19 15·3	18 27·5	19 15·0	19 15·15	S. 4 10—0 21·65				
5817	17 14 54·0	19 6·3	18 13·8	19 6·2	19 6·25	S. 2 45+0 26·45	26·662	49·1	48·9	
5881	17 25 23·0	19 5·0	17 8·0	19 5·3	19 5·15	0 0+1 31·15				
6016	17 47 2·0	19 32·5	18 15·1	19 32·45	19 32·45	S. 1 55—1 17·35				
6074	17 57 3·5	20 22·6	19 16·7	20 22·8	20 22·7	S. 0 30—1 6·0				
6115	18 3 46·7	20 22·3	21 27·4	20 22·9	20 22·6	S. 0 40+1 4·8				
6145	18 8 1·5	19 7·6	19 25·1	19 8·1	19 7·85	S. 1 0+0 17·25				
6233	18 21 47·8	19 26·5	24 2·2	19 27·0	19 26·75	S. 4 40+4 9·45				
6285	18 28 50·0	16 31·0	17 24·5	16 30·5	16 30·75	S. 3 20+0 27·75				
6305	18 31 44·0	16 26·5	12 27·4	16 26·8	16 26·65	S. 3 25—3 33·25	26·662	48·0	47·8	
6414	18 50 39·2	16 4·1	17 3·6	16 4·0	16 4·05	S. 1 10—0 2·55				
6489	19 0 39·8	15 14·4	17 3·6	15 15·0	15 14·7	S. 0 20+1 22·9				
6525	19 5 40·0	15 8·0	10 21·1	15 8·4	15 8·2	N. 0 50+4 21·1				
6639	19 24 25·3	14 25·5	10 24·5	14 25·4	14 25·45	S. 0 20—4 0·95	26·650	47·3	47·0	
6753	19 43 29·5	13 33·8	16 2·1	13 33·8	13 33·8	S. 1 30+2 2·3				
6877	20 2 23·8	13 29·3	12 8·5	13 29·0	13 29·15	S. 2 45—1 20·65				
6948	20 14 7·5	13 29·6	10 26·4	13 29·3	13 29·45	S. 0 45—3 3·05				
7011	20 23 6·0	13 26·5	12 9·5	13 26·3	13 26·23	N. 0 10+1 16·73				
7026	20 24 56·7	13 26·3	12 17·4	13 26·1	13 26·23	N. 0 10+1 8·83				
7057	20 29 21·5	13 26·1	18 7·5	13 26·1	13 26·23	N. 0 10—4 15·27				
Anon.	20 32 14·0	13 25·5	11 22·7	13 25·3	13 25·4	S. 0 5—2 2·7				
Anon.	20 41 44·0	13 26·0	9 32·5	13 25·8	13 25·9	S. 0 15—3 27·4				
7207	20 48 10·8	14 10·0	15 16·2	14 10·0	14 10·0	S. 4 35+1 6·2	26·646	47·3	46·8	
Anon.	21 1 31·0	13 29·0	9 32·2	13 28·4	13 28·7	0 0+3 30·5				
Anon.	21 8 41·0	14 18·4	15 14·5	14 18·0	14 18·2	S. 0 35+0 30·3				
7386	21 16 25·7	15 18·5	13 7·0	15 18·8	15 18·65	S. 3 5—2 11·65				
Anon.	21 20 30·5	15 2·0	13 7·4	15 2·0	15 2·0	S. 0 5—1 28·0	26·646	47·3	46·0	
Anon.	21 33 38·0	16 20·0	12 9·0	16 19·4	16 19·7	S. 0 40—4 10·7				
7557	21 43 36·2	16 27·6	13 33·0	16 27·8	16 27·8	S. 4 0—2 28·8				
7657	21 59 49·0	16 14·6	18 28·0	16 14·0	16 14·22	N. 0 35—2 13·78				
Anor.	22 3 40·0	16 14·0	17 24·4	16 14·3	16 14·22	N. 0 35—1 10·18				
7842	22 30 35·0	17 26·3	13 33·0	17 26·8	17 26·55	S. 3 25—3 27·55				
7909	22 41 38·0	17 18·5	17 0·7	17 18·3	17 18·4	S. 2 0—0 17·7				
7066	22 51 47·2	18 13·5	20 21·4	18 13·2	18 13·35	S. 3 55+2 8·05	26·611	46·4	45·5	
7992	22 56 58·3	18 2·3	20 1 0	18 2·4	18 2·35	S. 0 40+1 32·65				
1802	5 41 51·8	21 20·2	21 24·4	21 20·3	21 20·25	S. 4 25+0 4·15	26·602	62·0	61·5	

July 5.—No. 4852.—The wire indistinct, and the observation uncertain.
No. 6305.—Faint, and the observation doubtful.
Good definition, and calm throughout the night.

♂ July 6, 1847.—Face of Sector East.

Number of B.A.C.	Time by Chronometer.	Micr. for Plumb-line on Dot.	Micr. for Observation of Star.	Micr. for Plumb-line on Dot.	Mean of Micr. for Plumb-line on Dot.	Star's Apparent Zenith Distance.	Barom.	Thermometers.		
								Attd.	Upper.	Lower.
	h m s	rev. pts.	rev. pts.	rev. pts.	rev. pts.	° ' rev. pts.	in.			
2293	7	17 31·6	14 12·7	17 31·8	17 31·7	N. 1 0—3 19·0	26·662	65·8	67·8	
4548	13 37 56·5	25 25·7	20 32·4	25 25·6	25 25·65	N. 1 0—4 27·25				
4579	13 44 55·5	17 11·8	13 25·7	17 11·6	17 11·75	S. 2 30+3 20·05				
4623	13 50 55·8	17 11·6	17 17·3	17 12·0	17 11·75	S. 2 30—0 5·55				
4719	14 14 0·8	17 23·0	17 32·5	17 23·0	17 23·0	N. 1 10+0 9·5	26·583	52·7	53·0	
4784	14 27 4·5	18 7·0	19 31·0	18 7·0	18 7·0	N. 0 55+1 24·0				
4852	14 42 18·0	18 30·8	16 5·6	18 30·0	18 30·4	S. 4 45+2 24·8				
4891	14 48 59·8	19 13·2	19 5·3	19 13·5	19 13·35	N. 2 25—0 8·05				
4916	14 54 19·8	19 2·0	19 21·5	19 1·8	19 1·9	S. 3 30—0 19·6	26·575	50·0	50·3	
Anon.	15 1 34·0	19 2·6	22 21·7	19 3·3	19 2·95	S. 2 20—3 18·75				
Anon.	15 5 46·8	18 18·7	18 1·5	18 19·1	18 18·9	S. 2 35+0 17·40				
5032	15 16 24·5	19 1·6	17 22·0	19 1·7	19 1·65	N. 0 10—1 13·65				
5151	15 37 8·0	19 12·0	15 22·5	19 12·0	19 12·0	N. 0 30—3 23·50				
Anon.	15 42 27·5	19 11·0	15 2·3	19 10·9	19 10·95	S. 1 20+4 8·65				
5227	15 49 12·0	19 4·0	18 29·7	19 4·5	19 4·25	S. 3 25+0 8·55				
5272	15 55 17·8	19 25·4	16 31·4	19 26·2	19 25·8	N. 1 0—2 28·40				
5374	16 9 24·3	20 1·4	17 26·4	20 1·4	20 1·4	N. 0 45—2 9·0				
5435	16 17 47·0	20 5·4	15 18·8	20 5·4	20 5·4	S. 0 45+4 20·60				
Anon.	16 21 22·4	20 31·9	19 14·3	20 32·2	20 32·05	S. 3 5+1 17·75				
5498	16 27 50·0	21 7·2	19 12·3	21 7·4	21 7·3	N. 3 40—1 29·0	26·567	47·8	48·0	
5588	16 41 45·0	21 1·3	22 12·3	21 1·0	21 1·15	S. 2 5—1 11·15				
5632	16 48 15·0	21 8·2	19 1·0	21 8·8	21 8·5	S. 4 15+2 7·50				
5735	17 2 45·3	21 19·1	22 1·8	21 19·4	21 19·25	S. 4 10—0 16·55				
5817	17 14 15·4	21 19·8	22 3·7	21 19·8	21 19·8	S. 2 45—0 17·90	26·567	47·8	48·0	
5881	17 25 28·5	20 0·4	21 25·5	20 0·2	20 0·3	0 0+1 25·20				
6016	17 47 10·5	18 30·4	20 8·4	18 30·5	18 30·45	S. 1 55—1 11·05				
6074	17 57 10·0	18 27·5	19 24·9	18 27·3	18 27·4	S. 0 30—0 31·50				
6115	18 3 53·0	19 4·9	17 26·0	19 5·3	19 5·10	S. 0 40+1 13·50				
6145	18 8 8·8	19 13·7	18 24·5	19 14·3	19 14·0	S. 1 0+0 23·50				
6233	18 22 1·0	19 14·5	15 0·2	19 14·8	19 14·65	S. 4 40+4 14·45				
6489	19 0 46·7	17 32·5	16 0·8	17 32·7	17 32·6	S. 0 20+1 31·8	26·567	48·4	48·0	
6877	20 2 35·0	17 21·5	19 3·0	17 21·0	17 21·25	S. 2 45—1 15·75	26·571	48·6	48·6	
7207	20 48 24·0	18 25·3	17 12·3	18 25·0	18 25·15	S. 4 35+1 12·85				
7386	21 16 36·8	16 21·1	18 26·7	16 21·0	16 21·05	S. 3 5—2 5·65				
7557	21 43 48·3	19 30·7	22 22·0	19 31·2	19 30·45	S. 4 0—2 25·55				
7657	21 59 54·7	20 2·7	17 12·0	20 2·4	20 2·55	N. 0 35—2 22·55				
7842	22 30 46·0	19 21·0	23 9·5	19 21·2	19 21·1	S. 3 25—3 22·40	26·548	46·9	47·0	
7002	22 57 5·0	14 19·0	12 13·9	14 19·4	14 19·2	S. 0 40+2 5·30				

♀ July 7, 1847.— Face of Sector West.

Number of B.A.C.	Time by Chronometer.	Micr. for Plumb-line on Dot.	Micr. for Observation of Star.	Micr. for Plumb-line on Dot.	Mean of Micr. for Plumb-line on Dot.	Star's Apparent Zenith Distance.	Barom.	Attd.	Upper.	Lower.
4579	13 44 54·8	14 3·6	17 19·5	14 3·7	14 3·62	S. 2 30+3 15·88	26·508	53·2	54·0	
4623	13 50 55·0	14 3·7	13 29·6	14 3·5	14 3·62	S. 2 30—0 8·02				
4784	14	14 3·3	12 4·6	14 3·9	14 3·6	N. 0 55+1 33·0				
4852	14 42 13·5	14 14·8	17 0·0	14 14·4	14 14·6	S. 4 45+2 19·4				
4891	14 49 14·7	14 5·7	14 8·0	14 5·8	14 5·75	N. 2 25—0 2·25				
5032	15 16 27·6	9 26·9	11 3·2	9 27·3	9 27·1	N. 0 10—1 10·10				
5151	15 37 12·5	9 20·8	13 4·8	9 21·3	9 21·05	N. 0 30—3 17·75				
5227	15 49 11·0	10 20·0	10 24·7	10 20·5	10 20·25	S. 3 25+0 4·45				
5272	15 55 23·3	10 26·2	13 14·4	10 26·5	10 26·35	N. 1 0—2 22·05				
5374	16 9 28·5	11 12·7	13 13·3	11 13·0	11 13·0	N. 0 45—2 0·45				
5498	16 27 59·0	12 3·5	13 28·8	12 4·2	12 3·85	N. 3 40—1 24·95	26·496	48·0	48·0	
5632	16 48 11·8	12 24·0	14 25·0	12 24·25	12 24·25	S. 4 15+2 0·75				
5735	17	12 28·4	12 6·7	12 28·8	12 28·6	S. 4 10—0 21·90				

July 6.—Up to 18h S.T., good definitions, then a haziness partially obscured the sky, and rendered the greater part of the stars invisible, and all so faint as not to admit of good observations being made.

☿ July 7, 1847.—Face of Sector West—(continued).

Number of B.A.C.	Time by Chronometer.	Micr. for Plumb-line on Dot.	Micr. for Observation of Star.	Micr. for Plumb-line on Dot.	Mean of Micr. for Plumb-line on Dot.	Star's Apparent Zenith Distance.	Barom.	Attd.	Upper.	Lower.
	h m s	rev. pts.	rev. pts.	rev. pts.	rev. pts.	o ' rev. pts.	in.			
6115	18 3 55·2	12 16·4	13 22·8	12 16·2	12 16·3	S. 0 40+1 6·50				
6145	18 8 9·5	12 11·2	12 28·8	12 11·2	12 11·2	S. 1 0+0 17·60				
6489	19 0 49·0	1 20·5	17 21·0	15 29·8	15 29·65	S. 0 20+1 26·25				
6630	19 24	15 26·3	11 26·4	15 26·2	15 26·25	S. 0 20−3 33·85				
6877	20 2	15 14·7	13 27·1	15 14·9	15 14·8	S. 2 45−1 21·70	26·481	44·6	44·0	
7386	21 16 35·0	13 12·1	11 0·3	13 12·3	13 12·2	S. 3 5−2 11·90				
Anon.	21 33 47·0	12 21·4	8 10·3	12 21·1	12 21·25	S. 0 40−4 10·95				
7557	21 43 45·0	13 19·8	10 25·4	13 19·7	13 19·75	S. 4 0−2 28·35				
7842	22 30 43·5	13 29·4	10 0·6	13 28·4	13 28·9	S. 3 25−3 28·30	26·457	46·0	46·0	
7992	22 57 7·3	16 2·4	18 2·5	16 2·3	16 2·35	S. 0 40+2 0·15	26·457	44·2	43·0	
1802	5 42 1·0	17 33·5	18 4·0	17 33·5	17 33·5	S. 4 25+0 4·5	26·516	57·2	57·0	

♃ July 8, 1847.—Face of Sector East.

Number of B.A.C.	Time by Chronometer.	Micr. for Plumb-line on Dot.	Micr. for Observation of Star.	Micr. for Plumb-line on Dot.	Mean of Micr. for Plumb-line on Dot.	Star's Apparent Zenith Distance.	Barom.	Attd.	Upper.	Lower.
2293	7 0 32·5	18 5·6	14 21·0	18 5·6	18 5·6	N. 1 0−·3 18·6	26·512	61·0	64·0	
4517	13 31 32·2	15 13·3	10 22·2	15 13·5	15 13·52	N. 1 0−4 25·32				
4548	13 38 6·8	15 30·5	10 19·0	15 13·8	15 13·52	N. 1 0−4 27·62				
4579	13 45 4·5	14 23·9	11 3·2	14 24·8	14 24·57	S. 2 30+3 21·37				
4623	13 50 51·5	14 24·8	14 29·4	14 24·8	14 24·57	S. 2 30−0 4·83	26·496	48·2	40·1	
4710	14 14 10·5	15 12·3	15 21·8	15 12·7	15 12·5	N. 1 10+0 9·30				
4784	14 27 14·0	16 6·3	17 29·4	16 6·7	16 6·5	N. 0 55+1 22·90				
Anon.	14 32 22·0	16 6·7	17 19·2	16 6·8	16 6·75	S. 2 55−1 12·45				
4852	14 42 27·0	16 23·2	13 31·0	16 23·2	16 23·2	S. 4 45+2 26·20				
4891	14 49 17·7	17 21·0	17 13·2	17 21·0	17 21·0	N. 2 25−0 7·80				
Anon.	15 1 43·0	17 23·3	21 7·1	17 22·8	17 23·05	S. 2 20−3 18·05				
Anon.	15 5 56·0	17 24·3	18 8·8	17 24·2	17 24·25	S. 2 35−0 18·55	26·493	45·3	46·0	
5032	15 16 34·0	17 28·8	16 13·6	17 29·4	17 29·1	N. 0 10−1 15·30				
5151	15 37 18·0	17 22·5	13 32·9	17 22·0	17 22·25	N. 0 30−3 23·35				
Anon.	15 42 36·0	17 32·5	13 24·7	17 33·0	17 32·75	S. 1 20+4 8·05				
5227	15 49 21·8	18 6·0	17 31·0	18 5·7	18 5·85	S. 3 25+0 8·85				
5272	15 55 28·4	17 14·5	14 18·7	17 13·9	17 14·2	N. 1 0−2 29·50				
5374	16 9 34·2	18 4·2	15 29·0	18 4·5	18 4·35	N. 0 45−2 9·35	26·493	44·6	45·0	
5435	16 17 56·5	17 31·5	13 10·5	17 31·5	17 31·5	S. 0 45+4 21·0				
Anon.	16 22 13·0	18 5·5	16 22·8	18 5·8	18 5·65	S. 3 5+1 16·85				
5498	16 27 28·1	19 1·0	17 3·6	19 0·6	19 0·8	N. 3 40−1 31·20				
5588	16 41 55·0	19 0·3	20 10·5	19 1·3	19 0·8	S. 2 5−1 9·70				
5632	16 48	19 23·5	17 13·2	19 22·9	19 23·2	S. 4 15+2 10·0				
5735	17 2 55·0	17 30·5	18 10·9	17 30·0	17 30·25	S. 0 10−0 14·65				
5817	17 15 14·0	17 18·9	18 2·2	17 17·9	17 18·4	S. 2 45−0 17·80				
5881	17 25 39·0	17 25·2	19 14·7	17 24·8	17 25·0	S. 0 +1 23·70	26·493	42·4	42·0	
6016	17 47 20·0	17 29·0	19 5·0	17 29·6	17 29·3	S. 1 55−1 9·7				
6074	17 57 20·0	18 10·3	19 5·4	18 9·9	18 10·1	S. 0 30−0 29·3				
6115	18 4 3·2	16 10·2	14 28·8	16 9·8	16 10·0	S. 0 40+1 15·2				
6145	18 8 18·6	16 22·7	15 31·3	16 23·2	16 22·95	S. 1 0+0 25·65				
6233	18 22 11·0	16 16·1	11 31·5	16 16·3	16 16·2	S. 4 40+4 18·70				
6285	18 29 10·3	16 12·6	15 10·7	16 13·2	16 12·9	S. 3 20+1 2·20				
6305	18 32 3·5	16 9·7	19 32·5	16 9·0	16 9·35	S. 3 25−3 23·15	26·485	41·4	41·0	
6414	18 50 57·0	15 28·4	15 21·5	15 29·2	15 28·8	S. 1 10+0 7·30				
6489	19 0 56·0	16 1·2	13 33·7	16 1·4	16 1·3	S. 0 20+2 1·60				
6525	19 5 55·2	16 5·7	20 16·7	16 6·2	16 5·95	N. 0 50+4 10·75				
6639	19 24 20·0	16 0·0	19 24·0	16 0·0	16 0·0	S. 0 20−3 24·0	26·485	41·4	40·8	
6753	19 43 48·0	18 19·7	16 8·5	18 20·0	18 19·85	S. 1 30+2 11·35				
6877	20 2 43·8	18 13·5	19 25·0	18 13·5	18 13·5	S. 2 45−1 11·50				
6948	20 14 24·0	17 16·0	20 7·2	17 15·9	17 15·95	S. 0 45−2 25·25				

July 7.—No. 6639 and 6877.—Leaving the field.
Generally clouded throughout the night. Indifferent observations.
8.—No. 2293.—The seconds of transit uncertain.
No. 5632 and Anon. 21ʰ 20ᵐ.—Leaving the field when observed.
No. 6305.—The plumb-line not adjusted over the upper dot.
Bad definition throughout the night, and the smaller stars exceedingly faint.

♃ JULY 8, 1847.—FACE OF SECTOR EAST—(continued).

Number of B.A.C.	Time by Chronometer.	Micr. for Plumb-line on Dot.	Micr. for Observation of Star.	Micr. for Plumb-line on Dot.	Mean of Micr. for Plumb-line on Dot.	Star's Apparent Zenith Distance.	Barom.	Thermometers.		
								Attd.	Upper.	Lower.
	h m s	rev. pts.	rev. pts.	rev. pts.	rev. pts.	° ' rev. pts.	in.			
7011	20 23 22.0	17 14.5	18 19.5	17 14.0	17 14.15	N. 0 10+1 5.35				
7026	20 25 12.5		18 14.0	17 14.2	17 14.15	N. 0 10+0 33.85				
7057	20 29 37.5	17 14.2	12 24.3	17 13.8	17 14.15	N. 0 10-4 24.20				
Anon.	20 32 30.0	17 1.4	18 27.3	17 0.8	17 1.1	S. 0 5-1 26.20				
7207	20 48 32.0	20 24.8	19 9.5	20 24.8	20 24.8	S. 4 35+1 15.30				
Anon.	21 1 47.0	20 24.0	24 15.3	20 24.5	20 24.25	0 0+3 25.05				
Anon.	21 8 57.5	20 26.2	19 20.3	20 26.2	20 26.2	S. 0 35+1 5.90	26.473	39.6	39.2	
7386	21 16 45.0	20 24.6	22 28.4	20 25.4	20 25.0	S. 3 5-2 3.40				
Anon.	21 20	20 28.2	22 15.4	20 28.2	20 28.2	S. 0 5-1 21.20				
Anon.	21 33 54.2	21 12.2	25 16.1	21 12.2	21 12.2	S. 0 40-4 3.90				
7557	21 43 56.8	21 6.8	23 28.8	21 7.4	21 7.10	S. 4 0-2 21.70				
7657	22 0 4.0	21 24.7	19 1.4	21 24.5	21 24.57	N. 0 35-2 23.17				
Anon.	22 3 54.8	21 24.5	20 6.7	21 24.6	21 24.57	N. 0 35-1 17.87	26.473	40.8	40.0	
7842	22 30 53.6	21 22.5	25 7.5	21 22.7	21 22.6	S. 3 25-3 18.90				
7909	22 41 53.5	22 1.7	22 9.3	22 1.4	22 1.55	S. 0 25-0 7.75				
7966	22 52 7.5	19 12.5	16 30.6	19 12.2	19 12.35	S. 3 55+2 15.75				
7992	22 57 13.8	19 22.0	17 12.3	19 21.6	19 21.8	S. 0 40+2 9.50	26.473	40.8	39.8	

♄ JULY 10, 1847.—FACE OF SECTOR WEST.

Number of B.A.C.	Time by Chronometer.	Micr. for Plumb-line on Dot.	Micr. for Observation of Star.	Micr. for Plumb-line on Dot.	Mean of Micr. for Plumb-line on Dot.	Star's Apparent Zenith Distance.	Barom.	Attd.	Upper.	Lower.
4517	13 32 8.0	11 4.4	15 20.7	11 4.5	11 4.48	N. 1 0-4 16.22				
4548	13 38 15.5	11 4.3	15 24.0	11 4.7	11 4.48	N. 1 0-4 19.52				
4579	13 45 8.0	11 29.8	15 13.7	11 30.0	11 30.08	S. 2 30+3 17.02				
4623	13 51 8.0	11 30.0	11 24.0	11 30.5	11 30.08	S. 2 30-0 6.08				
4719	14 14 18.8	11 21.8	11 6.5	11 21.3	11 21.55	N. 1 10+0 15.05				
4784	14 27 22.0	11 6.8	9 10.0	11 7.3	11 7.05	N. 0 55+1 31.05				
Anon.	14 32 25.0	11 28.3	10 8.8	11 28.8	11 28.55	S. 2 55-1 19.75	26.575	43.7	44.7	
4852	14 42 27.0	11 32.3	14 17.6	11 32.0	11 32.15	S. 4 45+2 19.45				
4891	14 49 27.5	11 17.6	10 20.8	11 17.5	11 17.55	N. 2 25-0 3.25				
4916	14 54 30.8	12 17.6	11 29.0	12 18.0	12 17.8	S. 3 30-0 22.8				
Anon.	15 1 47.0	12 8.5	6 18.0	12 8.15	12 8.15	S. 2 20-3 24.15				
5032	15 16 41.0	10 27.5	12 1.2	10 27.5	10 27.5	N. 0 10-1 7.70	26.575	42.8	43.6	
5151	15 37 25.5	10 24.5	14 7.8	10 24.0	10 24.25	N. 0 30-3 17.55				
Anon.	15 42 40.5	11 4.0	15 4.8	11 3.8	11 3.9	S. 1 20+4 0.90				
5227	15 49 24.0	11 22.5	11 25.8	11 22.8	11 22.65	S. 3 25+0 3.15				
5272	15 55 36.2	10 26.5	13 14.7	10 25.9	10 26.2	N. 1 0-2 22.50				
5374	16 9 42.0	11 21.5	13 22.6	11 21.8	11 21.65	N. 0 45-2 0.95				
5435	16 18 2.0	12 1.6	16 13.5	12 1.0	12 1.3	S. 0 45+4 12.20				
5498	16 28 12.0	11 9.8	13 1.7	11 10.0	11 9.9	N. 3 40-1 25.80	26.575	41.9	42.0	
5588	16 41 58.0	11 17.0	10 2.7	11 17.5	11 17.25	S. 2 5-1 14.55				
5632	16 48 25.5	11 4.2	13 6.0	11 4.0	11 4.1	S. 4 15+2 1.90				
5735	17 2 55.5	10 30.8	10 9.0	10 30.3	10 30.55	N. 4 10-0 21.55				
5817	17 15 16.5	10 5.8	0 14.5	10 5.5	10 5.65	S. 2 45-0 25.15				
5881	17 25 45.5	9 30.4	8 1.3	9 30.0	9 30.2	0 0+1 28.90				
6016	17 47	9 30.0	8 13.0	9 29.4	9 29.7	N. 1 55-1 16.70	26.575	41.4	41.2	
6074	17 57 26.0	9 30.5	8 26.8	9 30.2	9 30.35	S. 0 30-1 3.55				
6115	18 4 9.0	9 32.9	11 6.7	9 32.9	9 32.9	S. 0 40+1 7.80				
6145	18 8 24.0	10 22.1	11 6.6	10 22.1	10 22.1	S. 1 0+0 18.50				
6233	18 22 11.0	10 33.0	15 7.2	10 33.2	10 33.1	S. 4 40+4 8.10				
6285	18 20	11 3.0	11 32.5	11 3.0	11 3.0	S. 3 20+0 29.50				
6305	18 32	10 30.7	7 0.2	10 30.7	10 30.7	S. 3 25-3 30.5	26.575	40.1	40.0	
6414	18 51 2.0	11 2.0	11 3.7	11 2.3	11 2.15	S. 1 10+0 1.55				
6489	19 1 25.0	11 3.5	12 30.0	11 3.7	11 3.6	S. 0 20+1 26.4				
6525	19 6 2.0	11 7.2	6 22.4	11 6.73	11 6.97	N. 0 50+4 18.57				

July 10.—Nos. 6016, 6285, and 6305.—Bisected while leaving the field.
Had definition until 18 hours S.T., when it improved a little. The smaller stars exceedingly faint.

ARC OF THE MERIDIAN.—CAPE OF GOOD HOPE.

♄ JULY 10, 1847.—FACE OF SECTOR WEST – (continued).

Number of B.A.C.	Time by Chronometer.	Micr. for Plumb-line on Dot.	Micr. for Observation of Star.	Micr. for Plumb-line on Dot.	Mean of Micr. for Plumb-line on Dot.	Star's Apparent Zenith Distance.	Barom.	Att.	Upper.	Lower.
6639	19 25 26·0	11 4·5	7 6·2	11 4·0	11 4·25	S. 0 20—3 32·05				
6753	19 43 52·5	10 16·7	12 20·5	10 16·7	10 16·7	S. 1 30+2 3·80				
6877	20 2 47·0	10 19·5	8 33·2	10 19·0	10 19·25	S. 2 45—1 20·05	26·571	39·6	39·0	
6948	20 14 30·0	9 26·0	6 27·3	9 26·6	9 26·3	S. 0 45—2 33·0				
7011	20 23 28·5	11 14·7	9 30·2	11 15·0	11 14·87	N. 0 10+1 18·67				
7026	20 25 19·5	11 15·0	10 8·0	11 15·0	11 14·87	N. 0 10+1 6·87				
7057	20 29 44·5	11 15·0	15 32·6	11 14·5	11 14·87	N. 0 10—4 17·73				
Anon.	20 42 7·0	12 1·0	8 7·0	12 0·4	12 0·7	S. 0 15—3 27·70	26·571	39·6	39·4	
Anon	21 1 54·5	13 19·5	9 22·0	13 19·0	13 19·25	0 0+3 31·25				
Anon.	21 9 4·5	15 25·7	16 23·4	15 25·4	15 25·55	S. 0 35+0 31·85				
7386	21 16 48·8	15 29·5	13 18·2	15 29·5	15 29·5	S. 3 5—2 11·30				
Anon.	21 20 53·5	15 12·2	13 17·1	15 11·6	15 11·9	S. 0 5—1 28·80				
Anon.	21 33	15 12·7	11 4·2	15 13·0	15 12·85	S. 0 40—4 8·65				
7557	21 43 50·0	16 12·2	13 17·5	16 12·5	16 12·35	S. 4 0—2 28·85	26·567	39·9	39·1	
7657	22 0 12·0	15 33·5	18 16·5	16 0·0	16 33·88	N. 0 35—2 16·62				
Anon.	22 4 2·0	16 0·0	17 9·0	16 0·0	16 33·88	N. 0 35—1 9·12				
7842	22 30 57·5	16 7·2	12 13·4	16 7·0	16 7·10	S. 3 25—3 27·70				
7909	22 42 1·0	15 28·8	15 12·5	15 29·0	15 28·9	S. 0 25—0 16·40				
7966	22 52 9·5	16 3·5	18 14·0	16 4·0	16 3·75	S. 3 45+2 10·25				
7992	22 57 21·0	15 19·6	17 19·6	15 19·5	15 19·55	S. 0 40+2 0·05	26·567	39·6	39·0	
1802	5 42 14·6	16 15·0	16 17·2	16 14·7	16 14·85	S. 4 25+0 2·35	26·590	52·0	53·1	

☉ JULY 11, 1847.—FACE OF SECTOR WEST.

Number of B.A.C.	Time by Chronometer.	Micr. for Plumb-line on Dot.	Micr. for Observation of Star.	Micr. for Plumb-line on Dot.	Mean of Micr. for Plumb-line on Dot.	Star's Apparent Zenith Distance.	Barom.	Att.	Upper.	Lower.
4517	13 32 13·5	15 2·4	19 19·0	15 2·3	15 2·48	N. 1 0—4 16·52	26·591	47·3	48·0	
4548	13 38 19·0	15 2·4	19 22·2	15 2·8	15 2·48	N. 1 0—4 19·72				
4579	13 45 14·5	13 22·8	17 4·8	13 23·0	13 22·95	S. 2 30+3 15·85				
4623	13 51 14·5	13 23·0	13 12·2	13 23·0	13 22·95	S. 2 30—0 10·75				
4719	14 14 *23·0	13 9·3	12 28·2	13 9·3	13 9·3	S. 0 45—1 15·10				
4784	14 27 26·5	13 7·8	11 11.4	13 7·5	13 7·65	N. 0 55+1 30·25				
4852	14 42 35·0	12 23·0	15 6·8	12 22·5	12 22·75	S. 4 45+2 18·05				
4891	14 49 31·3	12 8·0	12 9·3	12 7·5	12 7·75	N. 2 25—0 1·55	26·587	45·0	46·2	
4916	14 54 37·5	13 5·6	12 14·7	13 5·6	13 5·6	S. 3 30—0 24·00				
Anon.	15 1 53·0	12 28·3	9 4·4	12 28·6	12 28·45	S. 2 20—3 24·05				
5032	15 16 46·0	11 17·0	12 24·5	11 17·5	11 17·25	N. 0 10—1 7·25				
5151	15 37 30·5	11 8·9	14 26·0	11 9·0	11 8·95	N. 0 30—3 17·05				
Anon.	15 42 47·0	11 5·0	15 8·5	11 5·0	11 5·0	S. 1 20+4 3·50				
5227	15 49 31·0	11 15·5	11 18·5	11 15·5	11 15·45	S. 3 25+0 3·05				
5272	15 55 40·5	11 5·5	13 27·7	11 5·4	11 5·45	N. 1 0—2 22·25	26·583	42·6	43·3	
5374	16 9 46·5	10 27·3	12 28·5	10 28·0	10 27·65	N. 0 45—2 0·85				
5435	16 18 7·0	10 27·8	15 6·8	10 27·3	10 27·55	S. 0 45+4 13·25				
Anon.	16 22 22·5	10 28·9	12 5·5	10 29·3	10 29·1	S. 3 5+1 10·40				
5498	16 28 14·8	10 17·2	12 9·0	10 16·8	10 17·0	N. 3 40—1 26·0				
5588	16 42 4·5	10 8·8	8 26·0	10 8·5	10 8·5	S. 2 5—1 16·65				
5632	16 48 32·5	10 18·0	12 19·5	10 18·5	10 18·25	S. 4 15+2 1·25				
5735	17 3 2·5	10 8·5	9 21·6	10 8·9	10 8·7	S. 4 10—0 21·10				
5817	17 15 23·0	9 23·7	9 1·3	9 23·5	9 23·6	S. 2 45—0 22·30	26·579	40·8	41·0	
5881	17 25 50·0	9 19·0	7 22·4	9 19·0	9 19·0	0 0+1 30·60				
6016	17 47 30·0	11 30·5	10 15·0	11 30·5	11 30·5	S. 1 35—1 15·75				
6074	17 57 31·0	12 6·8	11 4·7	12 6·5	12 6·65	S. 0 30—1 1·95				
6115	18 4	13 32·0	15 5·5	13 31·7	13 31·85	S. 0 40+1 7·65				
6145	18 8 29·5	15 19·7	16 4·0	15 19·0	15 19·35	S. 1 0+0 18·65				

July 10.—Anon. 21ʰ 33ᵐ.—Bisected while leaving the field.
11.—No. 6115.—Bisected while leaving the field.

⊙ July 11, 1847—(*continued*).—Face of Sector East.

Number of B.A.C.	Time by Chronometer.	Micr. for Plumb-line on Dot.	Micr. for Observation of Star.	Micr. for Plumb-line on Dot.	Mean of Micr. for Plumb-line on Dot.	Star's Apparent Zenith Distance.	Barom.	Thermometers.		
								Attd.	Upper.	Lower.
	h m s	rev. pts.	rev. pts.	rev. pts.	rev. pts.	° ′ rev. pts.	in.			
6233	18 22 27·8	15 7·0	10 21·6	15 6·7	15 6·85	S. 4 40+4 19·25	26·579	40·5	40·0	
6285	18 29 26·5	15 17·4	14 14·8	15 17·0	15 17·2	S. 3 20+1 2·40				
6305	18 32 19·0	15 33·2	19 22·0	15 33·8	15 33·5	S. 3 25—3 22·5				
6414	18 51 11·5	16 14·9	16 6·3	16 15·2	16 15·05	S. 1 10+0 8·75				
6489	19 1 9·0	15 29·0	13 30·5	15 29·0	15 29·0	S. 0 20+1 32·50				
6525	19	16 9·4	20 21·1	16 9·0	16 9·2	N. 0 50+4 11·00				
6639	19 25 30·8	16 10·8	20 2·8	16 11·0	16 10·9	S. 0 20—3 25·9				
6753	19 44 1·8	18 2·0	15 24·7	18 2·3	18 2·15	S. 1 30+2 11·45	26·583	39·2	38·5	
6877	20 2 59·0	17 22·7	19 3·2	17 22·3	17 22·5	S. 2 45—1 14·70			"	
6948	20 14 37·5	16 3·9	18 28·8	16 3·2	16 3·55	S. 0 45—2 25·25				
7011	20 23 36·0	16 12·3	17 19·5	16 12·3	16 12·33	N. 0 10+1 7·17				
7026	20 25 25·0	16 12·3	17 13·2	16 12·4	16 12·33	N. 0 10+1 0·87				
7057	20 29 49·6	16 12·4	11 20·7	16 12·3	16 12·33	N. 0 10—4 25·63	26·587	38·8	38·2	
7207	20 48 49·7	17 0·2	15 18·8	16 33·7	16 33·93	S. 4 35+1 15·15				
Anon.	21 2 0·0	16 27·7	20 16·7	16 27·4	16 27·55	0 0+3 23·15				
Anon.	21 9 11·0	16 29·8	15 24·3	16 29·7	16 29·75	S. 0 35+1 5·45				
7386	21 17 1·0	17 2·3	19 5·7	17 2·0	17 2·15	S. 3 5—2 3·55				
Anon.	21 20 59·5		16 20·8	14 33·7		S. 0 5—1 21·10				
Anon.	21 34 3·5	14 24·8	18 28·3	14 25·0	14 24·9	S. 0 40—3 3·40	26·587	37·8	37·1	
7557	21 44 13·5	14 30·0	17 18·2	14 30·0	14 30·0	S. 4 0—2 22·20				
7657	22 0 17·0	13 31·7	11 8·2	13 31·4	13 31·43	N. 0 35—2 23·23				
Anon.	22 4 7·5	13 31·4	12 13·2	13 31·2	13 31·43	N. 0 35—1 18·23				
7842	22 31 10·0	13 27·7	17 16·1	13 28·0	13 27·85	S. 3 25—3 22·25				
7900	22 42 7·0	13 33·5	14 7·7	13 33·0	13 33·25	S. 0 25—0 8·45	26·575	37·4	36·2	
7966	22 52 24·0	13 17·5	11 4·7	13 17·4	13 17·45	S. 3 55+2 12·75				
7992	22 57 28·0	13 18·6	11 8·7	13 18·2	13 18·4	S. 0 40+2 9·70				

July 11.—No. 6305.—The plumb-line not adjusted over the upper dot, before the observation.
    No. 7966.—Doubtful observation.
    Calm throughout the night; heavy dew; fair images.
July 12.—The sector was taken down.

UNREDUCED ·OBSERVATIONS

MADE WITH

BRADLEY'S ZENITH SECTOR

AT

THE ROYAL OBSERVATORY, NEAR CAPE TOWN:

FROM

JUNE TO SEPTEMBER, 1848.

♃ JUNE 1, 1848.—FACE OF SECTOR WEST.

Number of B.A.C.	Time by Chronometer.	Micr. for Plumb-line on Dot.	Micr. for Observation of Star.	Micr. for Plumb-line on Dot.	Mean of Micr. for Plumb-line on Dot.	Star's Apparent Zenith Distance.	Barom.	Thermometers. Attd.	Lower.	Out.
	h m s	rev. pts.	rev. pts.	rev. pts.	rev. pts.	° ′ rev. pts.	in.			
4852	14 35 0·8	9 23·3	9 15·3	9 23·1	9 23·2	S. 0 35—0 7·9	30·321	57·0	57·5	46·8
4916	14 47 3·8	9 31·2	6 12·7	9 31·4	9 31·3	N. 0 40+3 18·6				
Anon.	14 54 19·6	9 9·0	11 23·6	9 9·0	9 9·0	N. 1 55—2 14·6				
5092	15 9 12·3	9 13·5	7 28·0	9 13·3	9 13·4	N. 4 20+1 18·8				
5151	15 29 56·5	10 1·2	10 23·4	10 1·1	10 1·15	N. 4 40—0 22·25	30·329	56·5	57·4	40·2
Anon.	15 35 13·5		10 27·5	9 21·0		N. 2 50—1 6·5				

♀ JUNE 2, 1848.—FACE OF SECTOR WEST.

1802	5 34 47·0		7 4·5	9 26·2		S. 0 15—2 21·7			57·6	
2293	6 53 15·0	10 34·0	11 22·35	10 33·6	10 33·8	N. 5 10—0 22·55	30·317	67·5	57·5	58·7

♄ JUNE 3, 1848.—FACE OF SECTOR WEST.

1802	5 34 52·0	11 30·75	9 10·25	11 30·55	11 30·65	S. 0 15—2 20·4	30·480	59·5	58·2	58·3
2293	6 53 23·0	10 17·4	11 7·0	10 17·0	10 17·2	N. 5 10—0 23·8			58·2	
4517	13 24 53·3	10 16·2	12 13·5	10 16·4	10 10·3	N. 5 10—1 31·2				
4548	13 30 58·3	10 16·5	12 16·85	10 16·3	10 16·4	N. 5 10—2 0·45				
4579	13 37 52·4	11 6·0	12 0·2	11 6·0	11 6·0	N. 1 40—0 28·2			57·2	
4623	13 43 52·6	11 5·9	8 8·4	11 5·7	11 5·8	N. 1 40+2 31·4				
4719	14 7 3·5		8 11·7	11 15·25		N. 5 20+3 3·55				
4784	14	10 31·3	15 7·4	10 31·5	10 31·4	N. 5 10—4 10·0				
Anon.	14 25 10·2	19 29·5	15 15·8	19 29·5	19 29·5	N. 1 15+4 13·7				
4916	14 47 15·2	9 23·0	6 5·4	9 23·0	9 23·0	N. 0 40+3 17·6				
Anon.	14 54 30·7	10 10·7	12 25·5	10 10·6	10 10·65	N. 1 55+2 14·85				
5032	15 9 24·5	10 10·5	8 26·8	10 10·9	10 10·7	N. 4 20+1 17·9	30·506	58·0	58·3	58·4
5151	15 30 9·3	10 31·0	11 21·0	10 31·1	10 31·05	N. 4 40—0 23·95				
Anon.	15 35 25·5	10 27·7	12 0·9	10 27·5	10 27·6	N. 2 50—1 7·3				
5227	15 42 8·5	9 23·8	6 30·1	9 24·0	9 23·9	N. 0 45+2 27·8				
5272	15 48 20·0	10 10·2	10 3·2	10 10·0	10 10·1	N. 5 10+0 6·9			58·4	
5374	16 2 25·5	10 9·5	9 16·0	10 9·4	10 9·45	N. 4 55+0 27·45				
5435	16 10 46·0	10 23·9	12 7·2	10 23·7	10 23·8	N. 3 25—1 17·4				
Anon.	16 14	10 7·5	8 20·75	10 7·4	10 7·45	N. 1 5+1 20·7	30·497	57·8	58·4	58·4
5388	16 34 42·7	9 7·4	13 23·5	9 7·0	9 7·2	N. 2 10—4 16·3				
5632	16 41 9·2	8 31·1	7 33·15	8 31·0	8 31·05	S. 0 5—0 31·9				
5735	16 55 39·8	8 22·8	5 0·2	8 23·2	8 23·0	0 0+3 22·8	30·496	57·8	58·4	58·2

☉ JUNE 4, 1848.—FACE OF SECTOR EAST.

2293	6 53 31·8	8 33·8	7 33·3	8 34·0	8 33·9	N. 5 10—1 0·6	30·448	59·0	59·4	65·0
4517	13 25 2·4	9 1·6	6 25·35	9 2·0	9 1·8	N. 5 10—2 10·45	30·388	57·8	58·2	49·6
4548	13 31 7·5	9 1·9	6 22·9	9 1·9	9 1·9	N. 5 10—2 13·0				
4579	13 38 1·2	9 12·0	8 3·9	9 11·8	9 11·9	N. 1 40—1 8·0				
4623	13 44 0·0	9 11·7	11 29·4	9 11·5	9 11·6	N. 1 40+2 17·8				
4719	14 7 8·2	9 23·8	12 15·0	9 23·6	9 23·7	N. 5 20+2 25·3				
4784	14 20 12·0	9 21·5	4 30·6	9 21·7	9 21·6	N. 5 10—4 25·0				
Anon.	14 25 16·5	9 24·2	13 22·0	9 24·6	9 24·4	N. 1 15+4 31·6				
4852	14 35 19·5	9 22·6	9 16·0	9 22·6	9 22·6	≻. 0 35+0 6·6	30·386	57·8	58·2	40·6
4916	14 47 22·5	9 30·5	13 0·5	9 30·9	9 30·7	N. 0 40+3 3·8				
Anon.	14 54 38·8	9 23·0	6 30·2	9 23·4	9 23·2	N. 1 55—2 27·0				
5092	15 9 32·0	10 10·8	11 16·5	10 10·6	10 10·7	N. 4 20+1 5·8				
5151	15 30 16·5	10 20·0	9 17·3	10 19·8	10 19·9	N. 4 40—1 2·6			58·2	

Two sextant telescopes are fixed to the back of the spindle, (one pointing to the north the other to the south) and command a mark to the south 133 feet distant, in reversed positions. The mark is divided into inches and parts of inches, and one inch = 2′ 12″ in Azimuth.

June 3.—No. 4719.—The observation is uncertain, owing to bad lamp light.

Anon. 16ʰ 14ᵐ.—Hurried.

*.—No. 4784.—The seconds of transit uncertain.

☉ JUNE 4, 1848.—FACE OF SECTOR EAST—(continued).

Number of B.A.C.	Time by Chronometer.	Micr. for Plumb-line on Dot.	Micr. for Observation of Star.	Micr. for Plumb-line on Dot.	Mean of Micr. for Plumb-line on Dot.	Star's Apparent Zenith Distance.	Barom.	Thermometers. Attd.	Lower.	Out.
	h m s	rev. pts.	rev. pts.	rev. pts.	rev. pts.	° ′ rev. pts.	in.			
Anon.	15 35 32·5	10 23·4	9 4·2	10 23·5	10 23·45	N. 2 50—1 19·25				
5227	15 42 15·8	10 25·0	13 3·5	10 24·6	10 24·8	N. 0 45+2 12·7				
5272	15 48 27·0	11 12·7	11 6·8	11 12·5	11 12·6	N. 5 10—0 5·8				
5374	16 2 33·5	8 26·8	9 8·0	8 27·0	8 26·9	N. 4 55+0 15·1				
5435	16 10 53·5	8 8·5	6 12·6	8 8·9	8 8·7	N. 3 25—1 30·1				
5588	16 34 50·0	8 4·1	3 8·5	8 4·2	8 4·15	N. 2 10—4 29·65				
5632	16 41 16·5	8 7·3	8 25·5	8 7·5	8 7·4	S. 0 5—0 18·1	30·363	57·5	57·6	47·4
5735	16 55 46·5	7 33·5	11 8·7	7 33·3	7 33·4	0 0+3 9·3				

☾ JUNE 5, 1848.—FACE OF SECTOR WEST.

4517	13 25 6·0	9 0·9	11 6·4	9 0·9	9 0·9	N. 5 10—1 30·5	30·046	59·6	60·4	63·6
4548	13 31 10·5	9 9·9	11 9·8	9 9·9	9 9·9	N. 5 10—1 33·9				
4579	13 38 4·0	9 19·5	10 14·75	9 19·5	9 19·5	N. 1 40—0 29·25				
4623	13 44 4·0	9 19·5	6 23·0	9 19·5	9 19·5	N. 1 40+2 30·5				
4719	14 7 14·5	10 3·95	7 0·3	10 3·95	10 3·95	N. 5 20+3 3·65		60·4		
Anon.	14 25 20·8	10 17·55	6 6·5	10 17·45	10 17·5	N. 1 15+4 11·0				
4852	14 35 21·6	9 16·3	9 11·0	9 16·7	9 16·5	S. 0 35—0 5·5				
4916	14 47 25·5	9 13·4	5 31·55	9 13·4	9 13·4	N. 0 40+3 15·85		60·4		
Anon.	14 54 42·0	9 5·0	11 21·6	9 4·9	9 4·95	N. 1 55—2 16·65				
5032	15 9 36·2	10 3·5	8 20·3	10 3·5	10 3·5	N. 4 20+1 17·2				
5151	15 30 21·0	10 6·1	10 30·2	10 6·1	10 6·1	N. 4 40—0 24·1				
Anon.	15 35 36·5	9 33·3	11 7·9	9 33·3	9 33·3	N. 2 50—1 8·6				
5227	15 42 18·5	9 26·4	7 0·55	9 26·4	9 26·4	N. 0 45+2 25·85				
5272	15 48 31·5	9 11·8	9 2·5	9 11·5	9 11·65	N. 5 10+0 9·15	30·027	59·5	60·4	62·8

♀ JUNE 16, 1848.—FACE OF SECTOR EAST.

4719	14 8 10·8	11 11·1	14 2·4	11 10·9	11 11·0	N. 5 20+2 25·4	30·228	58·0	58·8	54·3
4784	14 21 17·2	8 25·0	4 1·7	8 25·2	8 25·1	N. 5 10—4 23·4				
Anon.	14 26 21·0		12 30·0	8 30·4		N. 1 15+3 33·6				
4852	14 36 23·5	8 30·0	8 24·3	8 30·4	8 30·2	S. 0 35+0 5·9				
4916	14 48 26·5	9 6·8	12 10·75	9 6·8	9 6·8	N. 0 40+3 3·95				
Anon.	14 55 42·4	10 0·1	7 6·3	10 0·4	10 0·25	N. 1 55—2 27·95				
Anon.	14 59 54·0	10 0·0	13 4·8	10 0·0	10 0·0	N. 1 35+3 4·8	30·234	58·0	58·6	53·5
5151	15 31 20·2	9 23·7	8 21·7	9 23·8	9 23·75	N. 4 40—1 2·05				
Anon.	15 36 35·2	11 1·5	9 17·0	11 1·7	11 1·6	N. 2 50—1 18·6				
5227	15 43 19·4	10 14·0	12 28·6	10 13·8	10 13·9	N. 0 45+2 14·7				
5272	15 49 30·5	11 0·7	10 29·1	11 0·9	11 0·8	N. 5 10—0 5·7				
5374	16 3 30·2	10 6·0	10 21·9	10 6·0	10 6·0	N. 4 55+0 15·9				

♄ JUNE 17, 1848.—FACE OF SECTOR WEST.

4517	13 24 8·5	10 12·4	12 9·75	10 12·2	10 12·3	N. 5 10—1 31·45	30·198	58·4	58·5	55·8
4548	13 30	10 12·3	12 12·2	10 12·4	10 12·35	N. 5 10—1 33·65				
4579	13 37 8·0	9 12·5	10 8·6	9 12·5	9 12·5	N. 1 40—0 30·1				
4623	13 43 8·0	9 12·6	6 16·45	9 12·6	9 12·6	N. 1 40+2 29·15				
4719	14 6 17·5	9 11·1	6 7·7	9 10·7	9 10·9	N. 5 20+3 3·2				
4784	14 19 45·0	9 29·5	14 7·4	9 29·3	9 29·4	N. 5 10—4 12·0				
Anon.	14 24 25·7		5 32·25	10 8·8		N. 1 15+4 10·55				
4852	14 34 26·5	10 13·0	10 7·75	10 13·1	10 13·05	S. 0 35—0 5·3				
4916	14 46 29·7	10 4·3	6 22·7	10 4·5	10 4·4	N. 0 40+3 15·7				

Generally rain or clouded sky from the 6th to the 19th of June.
June 17.—Nos. 4548 and 4784.—Observed at 20 seconds past the meridian.

♄ JUNE 17, 1848.—FACE OF SECTOR WEST—(continued).

Number of B.A.C.	Time by Chronometer.	Micr. for Plumb-line on Dot.	Micr. for Observation of Star.	Micr. for Plumb-line on Dot.	Mean of Micr. for Plumb-line on Dot.	Star's Apparent Zenith Distance.	Barom.	Thermometers.		
								Attd.	Lower.	Out.
	h m s	rev. pts.	rev. pts.	rev. pts.	rev. pts.	° ' rev. pts.	in.	°		
Anon.	14 53 46·5	9 32·2	12 15·5	9 32·0	9 32·1	N. 1 55—2 17·4	30·198	58·0	58·6	56·5
Anon.	14 57·58·5	9 24·2	6 10·2	9 24·4	9 24·3	N. 1 35+3 14·1				
5032	15 8 38·0	10 0·2	8 17·8	9 33·8	10 0·0	N. 4 20+1 16·2				
5151	15 29 24·2	9 15·5	10 5·5	9 15·1	9 15·3	N. 4 40—0 24·2				
Anon.	15 34 40·5	9 14·5	10 23·5	9 14·6	9 14·55	N. 2 50—1 8·95				
5227	15 41 22·0	9 3·6	6 11·9	9 3·9	9 3·75	N. 0 45+2 25·85				
5272	15 47 34·5	9 10·0	9 4·45	9 10·0	9 10·0	N. 5 10+0 5·55				•
5374	16 1 40·5	9 14·6	8 21·75	9 14·6	9 14·6	N. 4 55+0 26·85				
Anon.	16 14 14·5		7 2·55	8 20·3	8 20·3	N. 1 5+1 17·75				
5588	16 33 56·5	8 23·6	13 8·4	8 23·8	8 23·7	N. 2 10—4 18·7				
5632	16 40 24·0	9 26·4	8 30·4	9 26·4	9 26·4	S. 0 5—0 30·0				
5735	16 54 7·0	9 33·9	6 13·4	9 33·9	9 33·9	0 0+3 20·5				
5817	17 7	8 12·6	4 20·4	8 12·6	8 12·6	N. 1 25+3 26·2				
5881	17 17 44·0	9 5·5	13 4·8	9 5·4	9 5·45	N. 4 15—3 33·35				
6016	17 39 23·0	8 32·9	4 14·1	8 32·9	8 32·9	N. 2 15+4 18·8				
6074	17 49 24·4	8 33·0	4 27·0	8 33·0	8 33·0	N. 3 40+4 6·0				
6115	17 56 8·0	9 10·5	7 14·75	9 10·5	9 10·5	N. 3 30+1 29·75				
6145	18 0 23·2	9 16·1	6 29·6	9 16·3	9 16·2	N. 3 10+2 20·6				
6233	18	9 27·7	10 31·65	9 27·8	9 27·75	S. 0 30+1 3·9				
6285	18 21 11·5	9 33·9	7 20·6	9 33·5	9 33·7	N. 0 50+2 13·1				
6305	18 24 4·4	9 33·5	11 27·6	9 33·5	9 33·5	N. 0 50—1 28·1	30·202	58·0	58·4	56·4

⊙ JUNE 18, 1848.—FACE OF SECTOR EAST.

Number of B.A.C.	Time by Chronometer.	Micr. for Plumb-line on Dot.	Micr. for Observation of Star.	Micr. for Plumb-line on Dot.	Mean of Micr. for Plumb-line on Dot.	Star's Apparent Zenith Distance.	Barom.	Attd.	Lower.	Out.
4517	13 24 13·2	9 25·3	7 16·6	9 25·3	9 25·3	N. 5 10—2 8·7	30·204	58·0	58·3	56·0
4548	13 30 20·8	9 25·1	7 13·2	9 25·2	9 25·15	N. 5 10—2 11·95				
4579	13 37 13·2	9 6·0	7 13·2	9 6·2	9 6·2	N. 1 40—1 6·1				
4623	13 43 13·7	9 6·4	11 25·5	9 6·4	9 6·4	N. 1 40+2 19·1				
4784	14 19 20·0	12 4·0	7 11·0	12 1·8	12 2·9	N. 5 10—4 25·0				
Anon.	14 24 31·4		15 0·0	11 1·2		N. 1 15+3 32·8				
4852	14 34 34·2	10 24·8	10 19·05	10 25·0	10 24·9	N. 0 45+0 5·85				
4916	14 46 36·8	10 0·0	13 3·55	9 33·9	9 33·95	N. 0 40+3 3·6				
Anon.	14 53 52·7	7 21·0	4 27·5	7 21·1	7 21·1	N. 1 55—2 27·55				
Anon.	14 58 4·8	7 26·6	10 32·2	7 26·7	7 26·65	N. 1 35+3 5·55				
5032	15 8 46·9	8 23·0	9 28·75	8 23·2	8 23·1	N. 4 20+1 5·65				
5151	15 29 31·2	9 18·0	17 14·1	9 19·0	9 18·5	N. 4 35+7 29·6				
Anon.	15 34 46·0	9 18·1	7 32·75	9 18·1	9 18·1	N. 2 50—1 19·35				
5227	15 41 29·6	9 26·0	12 5·5	9 26·0	9 26·0	N. 0 45+2 13·5				
5272	15 47 41·5	9 30·8	9 25·75	9 31·0	9 30·9	N. 5 10—0 5·15				
5374	16 1 47·5	10 8·7	10 25·1	10 8·9	10 8·8	N. 4 55+0 16·3				
5435	16 10 7·2	10 18·0	8 16·9	10 17·0	10 17·95	N. 3 25—2 1·05				
Anon.	16 14 22·5		11 0·0	9 28·8		N. 1 5+1 5·2				
5588	16 34 4·3	10 10·1	5 14·65	10 10·0	10 10·05	N. 2 10—4 29·4				
5632	16 40 31·5	10 9·6	10 29·75	10 9·3	10 9·45	S. 0 5—0 20·3				
5735	16 55 1·8	9 13·9	12 25·4	9 14·1	9 14·0	0 0+3 11·4				
5817	17 7 22·8	9 14·0	12 28·6	9 14·2	9 14·1	N. 1 25+3 14·5				
5881	17 17 51·1	9 22·1	5 10·9	9 22·1	9 22·1	N. 4 15—4 11·2				
6016	17 39 30·0	9 2·4	4 13·25	9 2·4	9 2·4	N. 2 20—4 23·15				
6074	17 49 31·0	8 31·3	12 27·3	8 31·5	8 31·4	N. 3 40+3 29·9				
6115	17 56 14·2	8 20·6	10 6·9	8 21·0	8 20·8	N. 3 30+1 20·1				
6145	18 0 29·3	9 12·3	11 22·5	9 12·1	9 12·2	N. 4 10+2 10·3				
6233	18 14 17·2	8 31·6	7 15·45	8 31·6	8 31·6	S. 0 30+1 16·15				
6285	18 21 18·8	9 15·5	11 16·2	9 15·7	9 15·6	N. 0 50+2 0·6				
6305	18 24 12·0	9 15·6	7 10·0	9 15·6	9 15·6	N. 0 50—2 5·6	30·205	58·0	58·6	54·4

June 17.—Anon. 16h 14m.—The space between the two stars has always been, and continues to be, bisected.

No. 5817.—Observed at 20 seconds past the meridian.

18.—No. 4517.—The seconds of transit doubtful.

☾ June 19, 1848.—Face of Sector West.

Number of D.A.C.	Time by Chronometer.	Micr. for Plumb-line on Dot.	Micr. for Observation of Star.	Micr. for Plumb-line on Dot.	Mean of Micr. for Plumb-line on Dot.	Star's Apparent Zenith Distance.	Barom.	Thermometers. Attd.	Lower.	Out.
	h m s	rev. pts.	rev. pts.	rev. pts.	rev. pts.	° ' rev. pts.	in.			
1802	5 34 16·8	8 5·4	5 15·85	8 5·7	8 5·55	S. 0 15—2 23·7			58·2	
2203	6 52 48·2	8 15·0	9 1·4	8 14·8	8 14·0	N. 5 10—0 20·5	30·120	58·8	58·8	59·0
4517	13 24 20·0	8 13·8	10 12·3	8 13·8	8 13·8	N. 5 10—1 32·5	30·112	58·5	58·6	51·0
4548	13 30 24·4	8 13·8	10 15·2	8 13·8	8 13·8	N. 5 10—2 1·4				
4579	13 37 18·3	8 8·4	9 5·0	8 8·4	8 8·4	N. 1 40—0 30·6				
4623	13 43 18·4	8 8·4	5 13·55	8 8·5	8 8·45	N. 1 40+2 28·9				
4719	14 6	8 3·0	5 4·4	8 2·9	8 2·95	N. 5 20+2 32·55				
4784	14 19 31·5	10 5·5	14 18·8	10 5·3	10 5·4	N. 5 10—4 13·4				
4852	14 34 36·5	10 6·5	10 2·0	10 6·6	10 6·55	S. 0 35—0 4·55				
4916	14 46 39·8	9 22·2	6 8·0	9 22·3	9 22·25	N. 0 40+3 14·25				
5032	15 8 50·8	10 25·6	9 11·0	10 25·6	10 25·6	N. 4 20+1 14·6				
5151	15 29 35·0	10 27·4	11 20·0	10 27·0	10 27·2	N. 4 40—0 26·8				
Anon.	15 34 50·5	10 9·4	11 21·5	10 9·6	10 9·5	N. 2 50—1 12·0	30·150	58·4	58·6	51·6

♃ June 22, 1848.—Face of Sector West.

Number of D.A.C.	Time by Chronometer.	Micr. for Plumb-line on Dot.	Micr. for Observation of Star.	Micr. for Plumb-line on Dot.	Mean of Micr. for Plumb-line on Dot.	Star's Apparent Zenith Distance.	Barom.	Attd.	Lower.	Out.
4517	13 24 19·0	9 24·1	11 22·3	9 24·0	9 24·05	N. 5 10—1.32·25				
4548	13 30 24·1	9 24·0	11 25·0	9 24·0	9 24·0	N. 5 10—2 1·0				
4579	13 37 17·3	9 2·5	9 32·75	9 2·5	9 2·5	N. 1 40—0 30·25				
4623	13 43 18·0	9 2·5	6 7·4	9 2·5	9 2·5	N. 1 40+2 28·9	30·285	58·0	58·5	50·5
4852	14 34 37·5	10 4·5	9 33·9	10 4·4	10 4·45	S. 0 35—0 4·55				
4916	14 46 40·4	9 30·3	6 15·9	9 30·3	9 30·3	N. 0 40+3 14·4				
Anon.	14 53 56·5	9 25·3	12 10·0	9 25·3	9 25·3	N. 1 55—2 18·7				
5032	15 8 50·0	9 8·8	7 26·85	9 8·6	9 8·7	N. 4 20+1 15·85				
5151	15 29 34·3	9 12·7	10 4·4	9 12·6	9 12·65	N. 4 40—0 25·75				
5227	15 41 33·2	10 16·5	7 25·0	10 16·7	10 16·6	N. 0 45+2 25·6	30·288	58·0	58·3	51·2

♀ June 23, 1848.—Face of Sector East.

Number of D.A.C.	Time by Chronometer.	Micr. for Plumb-line on Dot.	Micr. for Observation of Star.	Micr. for Plumb-line on Dot.	Mean of Micr. for Plumb-line on Dot.	Star's Apparent Zenith Distance.	Barom.	Attd.	Lower.	Out.
4517	13 24 25·2	11 25·8	9 17·7	11 25·8	11 25·8	N. 5 10—2 8·1	30·157	58·0	58·6	52·0
4548	13 30 30·4	11 25·8	9 14·5	11 25·6	11 25·7	N. 5 10—2 11·2				
4579	13 37 24·6	9 21·5	8 17·5	9 21·6	9 21·6	N. 1 40—1 5·0				
4623	13 43 25·2	9 21·7	12 8·75	9 21·5	9 21·6	N. 1 40+2 21·15				
4719	14 6 35·0	9 26·1	12 18·6	9 26·1	9 26·1	N. 5 20+2 26·5				
4784	14 19 38·2	8 29·1	4 6·6	8 29·3	8 29·3	N. 5 10—4 22·6				
Anon.	14 24 42·7	9 14·7	13 13·3	9 14·7	9 14·7	N. 1 15+3 32·6				
4852	14 34 45·5	9 18·0	9 11·5	9 18·0	9 18·0	S. 0 35+0 6·5				
4916	14 46 48·3	9 31·2	13 0·85	9 31·2	9 31·2	N. 0 40+3 3·65				
Anon.	14 54 4·2	10 3·3	7 10·0	10 4·0	10 3·65	N. 1 55—2 27·65				
Anon.	14 58 16·5	9 20·1	12 24·0	9 20·1	9 20·1	N. 1 35+3 3·9				
5032	15 8 57·0	9 30·3	11 2·1	9 30·2	9 30·25	N. 4 20+1 5·85				
5151	15 29 41·3	9 12·8	8 10·4	9 12·6	9 12·7	N. 4 40—1 2·3				
5227	15 41 41·6	9 2·3	11 15·45	9 2·0	9 2·15	N. 0 45+2 13·3				
5272	15 47 53·0	10 9·4	10 4·2	10 9·4	10 9·4	N. 5 10—0 5·2				
5374	16 2 3·2	9 7·3	9 22·7	9 7·3	9 7·3	N. 4 55+0 15·4				
5435	16 10 18·2	9 1·4	7 4·2	9 1·3	9 1·35	N. 3 25—1 31·15				
Anon.	16 14 33·5	9 18·5	10 24·5	9 18·5	9 18·5	N. 1 5+1 6·0				
5588	16 34 15·3	9 33·2	5 3·4	9 33·4	9 33·3	N. 2 10—4 29·9				
5632	16 40 42·4	10 3·3	10 22·7	10 3·0	10 3·15	S. 0 5—0 19·55	30·158	58·0	58·0	50·0
5735	16 55 12·8	10 18·5	13 29·0	10 18·5	10 18·5	0 0+3 5·7				
5817	17 7 33·8	10 3·6	13 18·4	10 3·8	10 3·7	N. 1 25+3 14·7				
5881	17 18 0·5	10 23·0	6 11·3	10 23·2	10 23·1	N. 4 15—4 11·8				
6016	17 39 42·0	9 17·6	4 27·2	9 18·2	9 17·9	N. 2 20—4 24·7				

June 19.—No. 1802.—This observation properly belongs to June 18, 23h 42m m.t.
No. 4719.—Observed at 20 seconds past the meridian.
No. 5151 and Anon. 15h 34m.—The seconds of transit doubtful.
22.—Chronometer inadvertently allowed to "run down." Wound up at 13h S.T.
Thin clouds; small stars invisible: totally overcast at 15h 47m S.T.
23.—Anon. 14h 54m and No. 6016.—Plumb-line apparently touching the arch.

♀ JUNE 23, 1848.—FACE OF SECTOR EAST—(continued).

Number of B.A.C.	Time by Chronometer.	Micr. for Plumb-line on Dot.	Micr. for Observation of Star.	Micr. for Plumb-line on Dot.	Mean of Micr. for Plumb-line on Dot.	Star's Apparent Zenith Distance.	Barom.	Attd.	Lower.	Out.
	h m s	rev. pts.	rev. pts.	rev. pts.	rev. pts.	° ' rev. pts.	in.			
6074	17 49 41·5	9 23·4	13 18·6	9 23·4	9 23·4	N. 3 40+3 29·2				
6115	17 56 24·5	10 4·3	11 23·75	10 4·4	10 4·35	N. 3 30+1 19·4				
6145	18 0 41·0	9 27·5	12 2·0	9 27·1	9 27·3	N. 3 10+2 8·7				
6233	18 14 28·2	9 8·1	7 26·05	9 8·3	9 8·2	S. 0 30+1 16·15				
6285	18 21 30·5	9 24·3	11 24·9	9 24·3	9 24·3	N. 0 50+2 0·6				
6305	18 24 23·3	9 24·3	7 17·95	9 24·3	9 24·3	N. 0 50—2 6·35	30·151	57·2	57·5	51·0

♄ JUNE 24, 1848.—FACE OF SECTOR EAST.

Number of B.A.C.	Time by Chronometer.	Micr. for Plumb-line on Dot.	Micr. for Observation of Star.	Micr. for Plumb-line on Dot.	Mean of Micr. for Plumb-line on Dot.	Star's Apparent Zenith Distance.	Barom.	Attd.	Lower.	Out.
1802	5 34 36·8	12 1·7	14 17·6	12 1·5	12 1·6	S. 0 15—2 16·0				

☉ JUNE 25, 1848.—FACE OF SECTOR EAST.

Number of B.A.C.	Time by Chronometer.	Micr. for Plumb-line on Dot.	Micr. for Observation of Star.	Micr. for Plumb-line on Dot.	Mean of Micr. for Plumb-line on Dot.	Star's Apparent Zenith Distance.	Barom.	Attd.	Lower.	Out.
2293	6 53 6·5	11 27·7	10 32·5	11 27·7	11 27·7	N. 5 10—0 29·2	30·320	58·5	59·2	60·5
4517	13 24 37·2	11 28·5	9 20·55	11 28·5	11 28·5	N. 5 10—2 8·05	30·292	58·4	58·8	56·4
4548	13 30 42·2	11 28·5	9 17·4	11 28·5	11 28·5	N. 5 10—2 11.1				
4579	13 37 36·6	10 18·6	9 12·75	10 18·6	10 18·6	N. 1 40—1 5·85				
4623	13 43 37·5	10 18·5	13 3·95	10 18·4	10 18·45	N. 1 40+2 19·5				
4719	14 6 46·5	10 22·2	13 14·3	10 22·4	10 22·3	N. 5 20+2 26·0				
4784	14 19 49·2	10 21·6	5 31·5	10 21·5	10 21·55	N. 5 10—4 24·05				
Anon.	14 24 53·3	10 5·3	14 5·3	10 5·3	10 5·3	N.1 15+4 0·0				
4852	14 34 56·2	9 30·8	9 24·6	9 30·6	9 30·7	S. 0 35+0 6·1				
4916	14 47 0·0	10 4·0	13 7·6	10 3·6	10 3·8	N. 0 40+3 3·8				
Anon.	14 54 15·6	10 1·4	7 8·3	10 1·6	10 1·5	N. 1 55—2 27·2				
Anon.	14 58 27·8	10 13·4	13 17·8	10 13·5	10 13·45	N. 1 35+3 4·35				
5032	15 9 9·0	10 1·7	11 8·0	10 1·9	10 1·8	N. 4 20+1 6·1				
5151	15 29 53·0	9 22·9	8 20·5	9 23·0	9 22·95	N. 4 40—1 2·45				
Anon.	15 34 9·2	10 0·5	8 15·0	10 0·4	10 0·45	N. 2 50—1 19·45	30·281	58·0	59·0	56·0

☾ JUNE 26, 1848.—FACE OF SECTOR EAST.

Number of B.A.C.	Time by Chronometer.	Micr. for Plumb-line on Dot.	Micr. for Observation of Star.	Micr. for Plumb-line on Dot.	Mean of Micr. for Plumb-line on Dot.	Star's Apparent Zenith Distance.	Barom.	Attd.	Lower.	Out.
2293	6 53 13·2	9 24·8	8 30·2	9 24·8	9 24·8	N. 5 10—0 28·6	30·113	59·0	58·9	64·5
4517	13 24 44·0	9 25·4	7 18·25	9 25·5	9 25·45	N. 5 10—2 7·2	30·120	59·8	59·8	56·0
4548	13 30 48·5	9 25·5	7 14·8	9 25·5	9 25·5	N. 5 10—2 10·7				
4579	13 37 41·6	9 10·0	8 4·05	9 10·2	9 10·1	N. 1 40—1 6·05				
4623	13 43 42·0	9 10·0	11 29·55	9 10·0	9 10·0	N. 1 40+2 19·55				

FACE OF SECTOR WEST.

4719	14 6 49·8	8 30·9	5 28·8	8 30·7	8 30·8	N. 5 20+3 2·0				
4784	14 19 53·2	9 8·3	13 21·4	9 7·7	9 8·0	N. 5 10—4 13·4				
Anon.	14 24 57·0	9 30·6	5 15·8	9 30·4	9 30·5	N. 1 15+4 14·7				
4916	14 47	14 14·0	10 33·5	14 14·0	14 14·0	N. 0 40+3 14·5				
Anon.	14 54 19·0	11 0·9	13 15·9	11 1·0	11 0·95	N. 1 55—2 14·95				

♃ JULY 13, 1848.—FACE OF SECTOR WEST.

Number of B.A.C.	Time by Chronometer.	Micr. for Plumb-line on Dot.	Micr. for Observation of Star.	Micr. for Plumb-line on Dot.	Mean of Micr. for Plumb-line on Dot.	Star's Apparent Zenith Distance.	Barom.	Attd.	Lower.	Out.
4517	13 26 13·7	10 3·0	11 33·6	10 2·4	10 2·7	N. 5 10—1 30·9	30·292	59·0	59·5	56·3
4579	13 39 12·6	10 8·6	11 5·35	10 8·6	10 8·6	N. 1 40—0 30·75	30·292	59·0		56·0
4623	13 45 13·0	10 8·6	7 13·1	10 8·7	10 8·65	N. 1 40+2 29·55			59·4	

June 25.—12ʰ S.T.—Moved the sector in Azimuth 130' contrary to the order of reckoning.
26.—Anon. 14ʰ 24ᵐ and 14ᵗʰ 54ᵐ.—Uncertain observations.
Zenith partially covered: became entirely overcast at 15ʰ per chronometer. Unfavourable weather generally until the 20th of July.

♀ JULY 14, 1848.—FACE OF SECTOR WEST.

Number of B.A.C.	Time by Chronometer.	Micr. for Plumb-line on Dot.	Micr. for Observation of Star.	Micr. for Plumb-line on Dot.	Mean of Micr. for Plumb-line on Dot.	Star's Apparent Zenith Distance.	Barom.	Thermometers. Attd.	Lower.	Out.
		rev. pts.	rev. pts.	rev. pts.	rev. pts.	° ′ rev. pts.	in.			
4548	13 32 24·0	7 23·7	9 25·4	7 23·7	7 23·7	N. 5 10—2 1·7	30·092	59·0	58·8	55·5
4579	13 39 18·5	8 4·0	9 1·45	8 4·0	8 4·0	N. 1 40—0 31·45				
4623	13 45 18·7	8 4·0	5 9·2	8 4·6	8 4·3	N. 1 40+2 29·1	30·100	59·0		55·5
4852	14 36 37·2	12 14·3	12 9·0	12 14·3	12 14·3	S. 0 35—0 4·4	30·101	58·8		55·5
Anon.	14 55 57·2	10 28·8	13 13·8	10 28·8	10 28·8	N. 1 55—2 19·0	30·100	58·8		55·2
Anon.	15 0 9·0	10 25·3	7 11·45	10 25·5	10 25·4	N. 1 35+3 13·95				
5032	15 10 50·2	10 30·6	9 14·25	10 30·6	10 30·6	N. 4 20+1 16·35	30·100	58·8		55·2
5151	15 31	10 24·0	11 15·0	10 24·0	10 24·0	N. 4 40—0 25·0			58·6	

☿ JULY 19, 1848.—FACE OF SECTOR WEST.

Number of B.A.C.	Time by Chronometer.	Micr. for Plumb-line on Dot.	Micr. for Observation of Star.	Micr. for Plumb-line on Dot.	Mean of Micr. for Plumb-line on Dot.	Star's Apparent Zenith Distance.	Barom.	Thermometers. Attd.	Lower.	Out.
1802	5 36 50·8	9 1·6	6 2·4	9 1·8	9 1·7	S. 0 15—2 33·3			57·6	
2293	6 55 21·6	8 14·8	8 26·4	8 15·0	8 14·9	N. 5 10—0 11·5	30·243	57·5	57·6	56·4

♃ JULY 20, 1848.—FACE OF SECTOR WEST.

Number of B.A.C.	Time by Chronometer.	Micr. for Plumb-line on Dot.	Micr. for Observation of Star.	Micr. for Plumb-line on Dot.	Mean of Micr. for Plumb-line on Dot.	Star's Apparent Zenith Distance.	Barom.	Thermometers. Attd.	Lower.	Out.
4517	13 26 52·2	11 5·5	13 1·55	11 5·1	11 5·3	N. 5 10—1 30·25			58·5	
4548	13 32 56·5	11 5·2	13 5·9	11 5·2	11 5·2	N. 5 10—2 0·7				
4579	13 39 50·9	11 10·6	12 7·0	11 10·5	11 10·55	N. 1 40—0 30·45	30·215	59·0		54·1
4623	13 45 51·0	11 10·5	8 15·75	11 10·6	11 10·55	N. 1 40+2 28·8				
4719	14 9 0·8	11 17·4	8 16·4	11 17·4	11 17·4	N. 5 20+3 1·0	30·215	59·0		53·5
4784	14 22 4·5	11 16·8	15 30·45	11 16·7	11 16·75	N. 5 10—4 13·7				
Anon.	14 26 58·2	11 29·8	7 21·1	11 30·0	11 29·9	N. 1 15+4 8·8			58·5	
4852	14 37 9·8	10 16·1	10 16·3	10 16·2	10 16·2	S. 0 35—0 4·2	30·216	50·0		52·0
4916	14 49 13·0	10 9·7	6 30·45	10 10·5	10 10·1	N. 0 40+3 13·65	30·225	59·0		51·0
Anon.	14 56 30·0	10 29·0	13 13·7	10 28·6	10 28·8	N. 1 55—2 18·9				
Anon.	15 0 41·5	10 24·0	7 10·8	10 25·0	10 24·5	N. 1 35+3 13·7	30·221	59·0	58·6	50·5
5032	15 11 23·6	10 19·2	3 9·75	10 19·2	10 19·2	N. 4 20+1 15·45				
5151	15 32 8·2	10 22·0	11 14·6	10 22·0	10 22·0	N. 4 40—0 26·6				
Anon.	15 37 24·0	10 14·7	11 26·6	10 14·5	10 14·6	N. 2 50—1 12·0				
5227	15 44 6·5	10 21·5	7 31·95	10 21·7	10 21·6	N. 0 45+2 23·65	30·235	58·5		49·3
5272	15 50 18·6	11 15·3	11 11·9	11 14·9	11 15·1	N. 5 10+0 3·2				49·3
5374	16	11 22·1	10 31·75	11 22·2	11 22·15	N. 4 55+0 24·4				
5435	16 12 43·7	11 32·1	13 19·3	11 32·0	11 32·05	N. 3 25—1 21·25				49·5
5588	16 36 40·8	10 26·5	15 13·2	10 26·5	10 26·5	N. 2 10—4 20·7	30·239	58·5		49·5
5692	16 43 8·0	10 31·0	10 3·05	10 30·4	10 30·7	S. 0 5—0 27·65	30·239	58·4		49·3
5735	16 57 39·0	11 2·9	7 19·05	11 3·0	11 2·95	0 0+3 17·9	30·240	58·3		48·6
5817	17 9 59·2	10 13·3	6 25·1	10 13·5	10 13·4	N. 1 25+3 22·3	30·240	58·0	58·0	48·0
5881	17 20 26·7	9 23·9	13 26·8	9 24·1	9 24·0	N. 4 15—4 2·8	30·235	58·0		47·6
6016	17 42 6·7	10 12·6	14 27·25	10 12·5	10 12·55	N. 2 20—4 14·7	30·237	58·0		48·4
6074	17 52 8·0	10 11·0	6 7·95	10 11·0	10 11·0	N. 3 40+4 3·05				
6115	17 58 51·2	10 5·3	8 12·6	10 5·1	10 5·2	N. 3 30+1 26·6				
6145	18 3 6·2	10 16·9	7 32·8	10 17·0	10 16·95	N. 3 10+2 18·15				
6233	18 16 53·4	10 16·8	11 25·05	10 16·8	10 16·8	S. 0 30+1 8·25			57·5	
6285	18 23 55·5	10 27·3	8 16·95	10 27·2	10 27·25	N. 0 50+2 10·3				
6305	18 26 48·2	10 27·3	12 24·4	10 27·2	10 27·25	N. 0 50—1 31·15				
6414	18 45 45·0	10 25·5	7 22·25	10 25·6	10 25·55	N. 3 0+3 3·3	30·220	57·3	57·5	47·8
6489	18 55 45·0	10 25·4	11 29·45	10 25·5	10 25·5	N. 3 50+1 9·75	30·215	57·3		47·5
6525	19 0 44·5	10 19·8	11 29·45	10 19·6	10 19·7	N. 5 5—1 9·75				
6639	19 20 8·0	10 17·5	12 10·55	10 17·5	10 17·5	N. 3 55—1 27·05				
Anon.	19 24 20·5	11 1·8	5 20·55	11 1·8	11 1·8	N. 4 5+5 15·25	30·218	57·0		46·6
6753	19 38 35·1	11 11·4	10 8·5	11 11·45	11 11·45	N. 2 40+1 2·95	30·215	57·3		46·2
6948	20 9 12·7	11 4·5	4 28·9	11 4·4	11 4·45	N. 3 25+4 4·55				

July 19.—At 7ʰ per chronometer, shifted the tripod stand so as to place the spindle more central with respect to the roof opening.

20.—At 16ʰ 55ᵐ per chronometer, moved the telescope a little in Azimuth by the upper adjusting screws, in the direction contrary to the order of reckoning.

No. 5632.—The plumb-line apparently touching the arch.

♃ JULY 20, 1848.—FACE OF SECTOR WEST—(continued).

Number of B.A.C.	Time by Chronometer.	Micr. for Plumb-line on Dot.	Micr. for Observation of Star.	Micr. for Plumb-line on Dot.	Mean of Micr. for Plumb-line on Dot.	Star's Apparent Zenith Distance.	Barom.	Thermometers. Attd.	Lower.	Out.
	h m s	rev. pts.	rev. pts.	rev. pts.	rev. pts.	o ′ rev. pts.	in.			
7011	20 18	10 26·5	6 6·0		10 26·6	N. 4 20+4 20·6				
7026	20 20 1·2		6 7·7	10 26·7	10 26·6	N. 4 20+4 18·9	30·210	57·3		46·5
7057	20 24 26·0	10 26·6	11 33·0	10 26·5	10 26·6	N. 4 20−1 6·5				
Anon.	20 27 18·5	10 18·7	5 6·3	10 18·9	10 18·8	N. 4 5+5 12·5				
Anon.	20 36 49·0	10 27·7	12 17·8	10 27·7	10 27·7	N. 4 0−1 24·1				
7207	20 43 17·8	10 33·6	8 26·2	10 33·6	10 33·6	S. 0 25−2 7·4				
Anon.	20 56 37·0	11 16·0	12 33·75	11 15·9	11 15·95	N. 4 15−1 17·8				
Anon.	21 3 46·3	12 3·3	9 21·7	12 3·4	12 3·35	N. 3 35+2 15·65			57·3	
7386	21 11 31·8	12 2·3	6 9·25	12 2·2	12 2·25	N. 1 5+5 27·0				
Anon.	21 15 35·5	12 6·3	6 30·2	12 6·4	12 6·35	N. 4 5+5 10·15				
Anon.	21 28 43·5	12 2·2	13 9·5	12 2·4	12 2·3	N. 3 35−1 7·2				
7557	21 38 42·5	11 33·2	5 22·4	11 32·8	11 33·0	N. 0 10+6 10·6				
7657	21 54 54·2	12 0·6	11 0·0	12 0·8	12 0·7	N. 4 45+1 0·7				
Anon.	21 58 45·5	12 0·6	9 28·3	12 0·7	12 0·65	N. 4 45+2 6·35				
7909	22 36 42·6	12 10·6	8 10·3	12 10·5	12 10·55	N. 3 45+4 0·25	30·170	56·0	57·2	46·5
7966	22 46 53·2	12 9·5	10 31·3	12 9·3	12 9·4	N. 0 15+1 12·1				
7992	22 52 3·2	12 20·2	11 1·85	12 19·9	12 20·05	N. 3 30+1 18·2	30·170	56·0	57·3	48·2

♀ JULY 21, 1848.—FACE OF SECTOR EAST.

Number of B.A.C.	Time by Chronometer.	Micr. for Plumb-line on Dot.	Micr. for Observation of Star.	Micr. for Plumb-line on Dot.	Mean of Micr. for Plumb-line on Dot.	Star's Apparent Zenith Distance.	Barom.	Thermometers. Attd.	Lower.	Out.
1802	5 37 5·2	11 17·0	14 16·25	11 17·0	11 17·0	S. 0 15−2 23·25				
2293	6 55 34·0	12 7·6	11 19·4	12 7·8	12 7·7	N. 5 10−0 22·3				
4517	13 27 0·2	10 32·5	8 26·45	10 32·6	10 32·55	N. 5 10−2 6·1	30·210	58·5	58·0	53·7
4548	13 33 5·3	10 32·6	8 23·0	10 32·8	10 32·7	N. 5 10−2 9·7				
4579	13 39 59·2	11 1·0	9 30·2	11 1·0	11 1·0	N. 1 40−1 4·8				
4623	13	11 1·0	13 21·95	11 0·9	11 0·95	N. 1 40+2 21·0				
4719	14	11 18·5	14 11·0	11 18·1	11 18·3	N. 5 20+2 26·7	30·229	58·5		53·8
4784	14	11 7·7	6 19·8	11 8·1	11 7·9	N. 5 10−4 22·1				
Anon.	14 27	11 3·6	15 4·5	11 3·6	11 3·6	N. 1 15+4 0·9				
4852	14 37 19·1	10 20·0	10 13·4	10 19·8	10 19·9	S. 0 35+0 6·5				
4916	14 49 22·3	11 0·3	14 3·6	11 0·5	11 0·4	N. 0 40+3 3·2				
Anon.	14 56 38·2	11 21·0	8 27·2	11 20·4	11 20·2	N. 1 55−2 27·0				
5032	15 11 31·6	10 15·6	11 21·25	10 15·6	10 15·6	N. 4 20+1 5·65	30·243	58·5	58·5	52·6
5151	15 32 15·8	10 12·6	9 11·05	10 13·0	10 12·8	N. 4 40−1 1·75				
Anon.	15 37	10 3·7	8 15·75	10 3·3	10 3·5	N. 2 50−1 21·75				
5227	15 44 15·2	9 29·0	12 7·6	9 29·0	9 29·0	N. 0 45+2 12·6	30·250	58·0		52·0
5272	15 50 26·3	11 5·2	10 32·75	11 5·2	11 5·2	N. 5 10−0 6·45	30·246	58·0		51·8
5374	16 4 32·2	10 32·2	11 13·7	10 32·2	10 32·2	N. 4 55+0 15·5	30·250	58·0		52·0
5435	16 12 51·8	11 8·2	9 11·2	11 8·4	11 8·3	N. 3 25−1 31·1	30·246	58·0	58·6	51·1
Anon.	16 17 6·8	10 29·7	11 33·4	10 29·7	10 29·7	N. 1 5+1 3·7				
5588	16 36 49·0	10 21·5	5 25·2	10 21·9	10 21·7	N. 2 10−4 30·5				
5632	16 43 16·7	10 24·0	11 8·9	10 24·2	10 24·1	S. 0 5−0 18·8	30·246	57·8		51·3
5735	16 57 47·2	10 20·9	13 29·6	10 20·8	10 20·85	0 0+3 8·75	30·254	57·8		51·0
5817	17 10 7·7	10 10·3	13 23·0	10 10·3	10 10·3	N. 1 25+3 12·7	30·267	58·0		50·6
5881	17 20 34·8	10 26·2	6 13·7	10 26·1	10 26·15	N. 4 15−4 12·45	30·265	58·0	58·4	50·2
6016	17 42 14·6	10 5·4	5 14·0	10 5·8	10 5·6	N. 2 20−4 25·6				
6074	17 52 15·8	10 24·0	14 17·25	10 24·0	10 24·0	N. 3 40+3 27·25	30·268	57·6		49·5
6115	17 58 59·0	11 9·0	12 26·95	11 9·2	11 9·1	N. 3 40+1 17·85	30·268	57·6		49·5
6145	18 3 14·0	11 25·0	14 0·3	11 25·2	11 25·1	N. 3 10+2 9·2			58·2	
6233	18 17 3·0	11 13·8	9 29·3	11 14·0	11 13·9	S. 0 30+1 18·6				
6285	18 24 4·0	11 2·0	13 1·25	11 2·3	11 2·15	N. 0 50+1 33·1				
6305	18 26 56·5	11 2·3	8 28·7	11 2·3	11 2·3	N. 0 50−2 7·6	30·268	58·0		49·4
6414	18 45 54·5	12 22·0	15 15·3	12 22·0	12 22·0	N. 3 0+2 27·3				
6489	18 55 52·5	13 3·5	14 6·7	13 3·5	13 3·5	N. 3 50+1 3·2	30·268	58·0		48·7

July 20.—No. 7011.—Observed at 20 seconds west of the meridian.
21.— No. 4784 and Anon. 14ʰ 27ᵐ.—Observed at 25 seconds west of the meridian.

♀ JULY 21, 1848.—FACE OF SECTOR EAST—(continued).

Number of B.A.C.	Time by Chronometer.	Micr. for Plumb-line on Dot.	Micr. for Observation of Star.	Micr. for Plumb-line on Dot.	Mean of Micr. for Plumb-line on Dot.	Star's Apparent Zenith Distance.	Barom.	Thermometers. Attd.	Lower.	Out.
	h m s	rev. pts.	rev. pts.	rev. pts.	rev. pts.	o ' rev. pts.	in.			
6525	19 0 52·3		10 30·3	12 12·8		N. 5 5−1 16·5				
6639	19 20 16·2	12 21·3	10 18·9	12 21·5	12 21·4	N. 3 55−2 2·5			58·0	
Anon.	19 24 28·5	12 11·8	8 17·6	12 12·0	12 11·9	N. 4 10−3 28·3				
6753	19 38 43·2	12 6·3	12 33·7	12 6·5	12 6·4	N. 2 40+0 27·3	30·281	57·5		47·5
6877	19 57 37·2	10 32·5	15 19·55	10 32·5	10 32·5	N. 1 25+4 21·05	30·286	57·5		47·1
6948	20	11 10·5	8 14·7	11 10·5	11 10·5	N. 3 30−2 29·8				
7011	20 18 18·2	11 9·5	15 24·75	11 9·4	11 9·5	N. 4 20+4 15·25	30·286	57·4		46·7
7026	20 20 9·2	11 9·6	15 17·4	11 9·5	11 9·5	N. 4 20+4 7·9				
7057	20 24 34·2	11 9·4	9 27·55	11 9·6	11 9·5	N. 4 20−1 15·95				
Anon.	20 27 26·8	11 19·0	7 25·0	11 19·0	11 19·0	N. 4 10−3 28·0	30·295	57·5		47·4
7207	20 43 25·8	12 11·5	14 8·4	12 11·5	12 11·5	S. 0 25−1 30·9	30·295	57·5		48·0
7386	21 11 40·2	13 17·2	10 2·2	13 17·2	13 17·2	N. 1 10−3 15·0				
7557	21 38 50·8	12 7·7	9 11·4	12 7·5	12 7·6	N. 0 15−2 30·2				
7066	22 47 1·5	18 25·6	19 26·5	18 25·8	18 25·7	N. 0 15+1 0·8				
7992	22 52 10·8	15 16·3	16 27·0	15 16·1	15 16·2	N. 3 30+1 10·8	30·315	56·2	57·4	48·4

♄ JULY 22, 1848.—FACE OF SECTOR WEST.

Number of B.A.C.	Time by Chronometer.	Micr. for Plumb-line on Dot.	Micr. for Observation of Star.	Micr. for Plumb-line on Dot.	Mean of Micr. for Plumb-line on Dot.	Star's Apparent Zenith Distance.	Barom.	Thermometers. Attd.	Lower.	Out.
4548	13 33 7·7	11 31·5	13 31·5	11 31·7	11 31·6	N. 5 10−1 33·9	30·323	58·3	58·0	56·0
4579	13 40 3·2	11 25·7	12 21·0	11 25·5	11 25·6	N. 1 40−0 29·4				
4623	13 46 3·2	11 25·7	8 30·5	11 26·7	11 26·2	N. 1 40+2 29·7	30·323	58·2	58·0	55·4
4719	14	12 12·1	9 10·5	12 12·5	12 12·3	N. 5 20+3 1·8	30·317	58·5		55·0
4784	14 22 14·8	12 8·2	16 21·3	12 8·0	12 8·1	N. 5 10−4 13·2	30·316	58·3		55·0
Anon.	14 27 20·2	11 32·1	7 22·4	11 32·3	11 32·2	N. 1 15+4 4·8				
4852	14 37 22·5	11 19·0	11 14·65	11 19·0	11 19·0	S. 0 35−0 4·35	30·309	58·5		54·5
4916	14 49 24·6	11 20·4	8 5·75	11 20·0	11 20·2	N. 0 40+3 14·45				
Anon.	14 56 41·0	11 13·0	13 30·95	11 12·8	11 12·9	N. 1 55−2 18·05			57·6	
5032	15 0 53·2	11 5·6	7 26·25	11 6·0	11 5·8	N. 1 35+3 13·55				
5151	15 32 18·0	10 7·5	11 0·45	10 7·9	10 7·7	N. 4 40−0 26·75				
Anon.	15 37 33·0	9 31·4	11 7·45	9 31·4	9 31·4	N. 5 50−1 10·05	30·305	58·0		53·5
5227	15 44 18·7	9 21·5	6 32·7	9 21·3	9 21·4	N. 0 45+2 22·7				
5272	15 50 29·2	9 22·3	9 18·5	9 22·1	9 22·2	N. 5 10+0 3·7	30·305	58·0		53·5
5374	16 4 34·2	9 12·0	8 21·6	9 12·0	9 12·0	N. 4 55+0 24·4				
5435	16 12 55·5	10 5·2	11 26·0	10 5·2	10 5·2	N. 3 25−1 21·7				
Anon.	16 17 10·5	11 7·5	9 26·05	11 7·3	11 7·4	N. 1 5+1 15·35	30·300	58·0		53·8
5588	16 36 52·5	11 25·5	16 12·3	11 25·4	11 25·4	N. 2 10−4 20·9	30·295	58·0		54·0
5632	16 43 20·0	12 14·5	11 20·05	12 14·6	12 14·55	S. 0 5−0 27·9				
5735	16	12 25·1	9 8·0	12 24·9	12 25·0	O 0+3 17·0				
5817	17	11 24·5	8 15·1	11 24·5	11 24·5	N. 1 25+3 23·0				
5881	17 20 38·0	11 15·7	15 18·85	11 15·7	11 15·7	N. 4 15−4 3·15			57·3	
6016	17 42 18·2	10 15·0	14 31·0	10 14·9	10 14·9	N. 2 20−4 16·1				
6074	17 52 19·0	10 24·7	6 22·0	10 24·9	10 24·8	N. 3 40+4 2·8				
6115	17 59 2·0	11 7·6	9 14·6	11 7·6	11 7·6	N. 3 30+1 2·7				
6145	18 3 17·2	11 9·7	8 26·5	11 9·9	11 9·8	N. 3 10+2 17·3				
6233	18 17 0·0	11 15·6	12 23·5	11 15·7	11 15·65	S. 0 30+1 7·85	30·295	57·8		54·5
6285	18 24 7·2	11 15·8	9 6·9	11 15·7	11 15·8	N. 0 50+2 8·0				
6305	18	11 15·8	13 13·05	11 15·8	11 15·8	N. 0 50−1 31·85				
6480	18 55 55·8	9 16·0	8 3·4	9 16·0	9 16·0	N. 3 50+1 12·6				
6525	19 0 56·2	10 5·5	11 14·6	10 5·3	10 5·4	N. 5 5−1 9·2				
6639	19 20 19·4	10 18·4	12 12·9	10 18·6	10 18·5	N. 3 55−1 8·8				
Anon.	19 24 30·5	10 20·8	14 5·0	10 21·0	10 20·9	N. 4 10−3 18·1				
6877	19 57 41·5	11 11·1	6 15·4	11 11·1	11 11·1	N. 1 25+4 29·7				
6948	20 9 22·5	11 25·6	14 12·6	11 25·6	11 25·6	N. 3 30−2 21·0				

July 21.—Generally clouded after 20ʰ 27ᵐ per chronometer.
22.—No. 4719.—Observed at 20 seconds west of the meridian.
No. 5435.—The seconds of transit doubtful.
Opaque atmosphere: small stars invisible.

198

ARC OF THE MERIDIAN.—CAPE OF GOOD HOPE.

♄ JULY 22, 1848.—FACE OF SECTOR WEST—(continued).

Number of B.A.C.	Time by Chronometer.	Micr. for Plumb-line on Dot.	Micr. for Observation of Star.	Micr. for Plumb-line on Dot.	Mean of Micr. for Plumb-line on Dot.	Star's Apparent Zenith Distance.	Barom.	Attd.	Lower.	Out.
	h m s	rev. pts.	rev. pts.	rev. pts.	rev. pts.	° ′ rev. pts.	in.			
Anon.	20 37	12 32·5	14 24·0	12 32·7	12 32·6	N. 4 0—1 25·4				
7207	20 43 29·0	12 32·0	10 25·3	12 33·0	12 32·95	S. 0 25—2 7·65		67·5		
Anon.	20 56 46·5	12 11·5	13 30·9	12 11·5	12 11·5	N. 4 15—1 19·4				
7386	21 11 43·5	11 19·1	14 24·7	11 19·2	11 19·15	N. 1 10—3 5·55				
Anon.	21 15 46·2	11 16·7	15 4·1	11 16·5	11 16·6	N. 4 10—3 21·5				
Anon.	21 28 54·4	10 26·4	11 33·4	10 26·4	10 26·4	N. 3 35—1 7·0				
7557	21 38 54·2	10 17·8	13 3·7	10 18·0	10 17·9	N. 0 15—2 19·8				
7657	21 55 5·5	10 13·2	9 12·9	10 13·0	10 13·1	N. 4 45+1 0·2				
7842	22 25 51·5	9 18·5	2 5·0	9 18·3	9 18·4	N. 0 45+7 13·4				
7909	22 36 54·6	9 32·3	5 32·05	9 32·4	9 32·35	N 3 45+4 0·3				
7966	22 47 4·5	10 31·1	9 19·95	10 31·2	10 31·15	N. 0 15+1 11·2				
7992	22 52 14·2	11 0·3	9 16·15	11 0·7	11 0·5	N. 3 30+1 18·35			57·2	
2293	6 55 37·0	12 14·1	12 25·75	12 14·1	12 14·1	N. 5 10—0 11·65	30·260	56·8	57·4	60·0

⊙ JULY 23, 1848. -FACE OF SECTOR EAST.

Number of B.A.C.	Time by Chronometer.	Micr. for Plumb-line on Dot.	Micr. for Observation of Star.	Micr. for Plumb-line on Dot.	Mean of Micr. for Plumb-line on Dot.	Star's Apparent Zenith Distance.	Barom.	Attd.	Lower.	Out.
4784	14 22 22·8	14 30·3	10 8·0	14 30·3	14 30·3	N. 5 10—4 22·3	30·220	58·6	58·8	55·0
Anon.	14 27 25·4	14 6·4'	18 6·0	14 6·0	14 6·2	N. 1 15+3 33·8				
4852	14	12 10·5	12 5·3	12 10·5	12 10·5	S. 0 35+0 5·2				
4916	14 49 32·6	11 28·8	14 33·35	11 28·8	11 28·8	N. 0 40+3 4·55				
Anon.	14 56 48·6	12 3·1	9 11·4	12 3·3	12 3·2	N. 1 55—2 25·8				
Anon.	15 1 0·5	12 20·4	16 0·0	12 29·4	12 29·4	N. 1 35+3 4·6				
5032	15 11 41·3	12 29·0	14 2·45	12 29·0	12 29·0	N. 4 20+1 7·45				
5151	15 32 25·7	12 21·4	11 19·8	12 21·5	12 21·45	N. 4 40—1 1·65				
Anon.	15 37 42·4	13 3·9	11 18·75	13 3·8	13 3·85	N. 2 50—1 19·1				
5227	15 44 26·4	13 3·5	15 17·25	13 3·2	13 3·35	N. 0 45+2 13·9				
5272	15 50 36·3	13 11·0	13 6·9	13 10·8	13 10·9	N. 5 10—0 4·0	30·222	58·5	58·6	53·1
5374	16 4 42·4	13 0·8	13 16·1	13 0·9	13 0·85	N. 4 55+0 15·25				
5435	16 13 3·5	13 7·5	11 9·55	13 7·5	13 7·5	N. 3 25—1 31·95				
Anon.	16 17		14 15·5	13 9·8		N. 1 5+1 5·7		58·5		
5588	16 37 0·0	12 27·6	7 32·1	12 27·6	12 27·6	N. 2 10—4 20·5				
5632	16 43 27·8	13 0·6	13 19·9	13 0·5	13 0·55	S. 0 5—0 19·35				
5735	16 57 58·2	13 22·9	16 32·0	13 22·7	13 22·8	0 0+3 9·2				
5817	17 10 18·3	13 16·7	16 29·3	13 16·5	13 16·6	N. 1 25+3 12·7		58·3		
5881	17 20 45·5	13 20·5	9 8·95	13 20·4	13 20·45	N. 4 15—4 11·5				
6016	17 42 25·4	12 27·0	8 2·6	12 27·0	12 27·0	N. 2 20—4 24·4				
6074	17 52 26·5	12 5·8	16 0·3	12 5·8	12 5·8	N. 3 40+3 28·5				
6115	17 59 9·5	12 12·5	13 32·0	12 12·3	12 12·4	N. 3 30+1 10·6				
6145	18 3 24·8	12 12·0	14 21·05	12 12·0	12 12·0	N. 3 10+2 9·05	30·228	58·0	58·3	49·5
6233	18 17 14·2	12 15·1	10 31·65	12 15·0	12 15·05	S. 0 30+1 17·4				
6285	18 24 15·0	11 27·5	13 27·5	11 27·9	11 27·6	N. 0 50+1 33·7				
6305	18 27 7·8	11 27·9	9 20·95	11 27·9	11 27·9	N. 0 50—2 6·85				
6414	18 46 3·2	12 2·5	14 31·9	12 2·6	12 2·55	N. 3 0+2 29·35				
6489	18 56 3·5	12 0·9	13 3·9	12 0·7	12 0·8	N. 3 50+1 3·1				
6525	19	12 22·7	11 7·05	12 22·7	12 22·7	N. 5 5—1 15·65				
6639	19 20 27·0	13 12·3	11 11·05	13 12·0	13 12·15	N. 3 55—2 1·1				
Anon.	19 24 30·0	12 10·7	8 20·0	12 10·9	12 10·8	N. 4 10—3 24·8	30·230	57·4	57·9	48·5
6753	19 38 43·8	12 19·8	13 14·5	12 19·8	12 19·8	N. 2 40+0 28·7				
6877	19 57 49·0	12 19·6	17 6·9	12 19·4	12 19·5	N. 1 25+4 21·4				
6948	20 9 30·7	12 7·8	9 11·7	12 7·6	12 7·7	N 3 30—2 30·0	30·230	57·4	57·8	47·0
7011	20 18 20·0	11 10·7	10 26·5	11 11·0	11 10·88	N. 4 20+4 15·62				
7026	20 20 19·0	11 11·0	15 20·2	11 10·9	11 10·88	N. 4 20+4 9·32				
7057	20 24 44·6	11 10·8	9 29·3	11 10·9	11 10·88	N. 4 20—1 15·58				
Anon.	20 27 37·4	12 28·1	8 1·15	12 28·3	12 28·2	N. 4 10—4 27·05				

July 23.—No. 4916.—The seconds of transit doubtful.
Calm: splendid images.
No. 7026.—The seconds of transit doubtful.

⊙ July 23, 1848.—Face of Sector East—(continued).

Number of B. A. C.	Time by Chronometer.	Micr. for Plumb-line on Det.	Micr. for Observation of Star.	Micr. for Plumb-line on Det.	Mean of Micr. for Plumb-line on Det.	Star's Apparent Zenith Distance.	Barom.	Attd.	Lower.	Out.
	h m s	rev. pts.	rev. pts.	rev. pts.	rev. pts.	° ′ rev. pts.	in.			
Anon.	20 37 7·4	11 29·2	9 29·0	11 29·2	11 29·2	N. 4 0—2 0·2				
7207	20 43 37·0	11 2·5	13 0·95	11 2·5	11 2·5	S. 0 25—1 32·45				
Anon.	20 56 55·3	11 5·6	9 11·8	11 6·0	11 5·8	N. 4 15—1 28·0				
Anon.	21 4 5·0	11 24·8	13 30·45	11 24·6	11 24·7	N. 3 35+2 5·75				
7386	21 11 50·0	11 4·0	7 22·6	11 4·0	11 4·0	N. 1 10—3 15·4				
Anon.	21 15 54·0		6 21·75	10 15·9		N. 4 10—3 28·15				
Anon.	21 20 1·5	11 6·8	9 28·3	11 6·8	11 6·8	N. 3 35—1 12·5	30·223	57·0	57·5	46·5
7557	21 39 1·6	11 4·8	8 9·95	11 5·0	11 4·9	N. 0 15—2 28·95				
Anon.	21 59	10 29·7	12 28·1	10 29·7	10 29·7	N. 4 45+1 32·4				
7842	22 25 59·5	11 8·7	9 15·0	11 8·7	11 8·7	N. 0 50—1 27·7	30·230	57·3		45·3
7909	22 37 1·0	12 10·2	16 2·6	12 10·0	12 10·1	N. 3 45+3 26·5				
7966	22 47 12·3	11 13·0	12 15·75	11 12·8	11 12·9	N. 0 15+1 2·85				
7992	22 52 21·5	12 14·0	13 25·6	12 14·0	12 14·0	N. 3 30+1 11·6	30·230	56·5	57·3	46·2

☾ July 24, 1848.—Face of Sector West.

Number of B. A. C.	Time by Chronometer.	Micr. for Plumb-line on Det.	Micr. for Observation of Star.	Micr. for Plumb-line on Det.	Mean of Micr. for Plumb-line on Det.	Star's Apparent Zenith Distance.	Barom.	Attd.	Lower.	Out.
4579	13 40 13·2	11 33·6	12 29·8	11 33·4	11 33·5	N. 1 40—0 30·3	30·297	58·8	58·3	54·8
4623	13 46 14·0	11 33·4	9 33·2	11 33·5	11 33·45	N. 1 40+2 0·25				
4719	14 9 22·5	12 0·9	9 0·0	12 0·9	12 0·9	N. 5 20+3 0·9	30·306	58·8		54·5
4784	14 22 25·2	11 29·1	16 9·35	11 29·0	11 29·05	N. 5 10—4 14·3				
Anon.	14 27 30·7	12 4·2	7 28·7	12 4·2	12 4·2	N. 1 15+4 9·5	30·317	58·5		55·2
4916	14 49 35·8	12 4·6	8 25·0	12 4·7	12 4·65	N. 0 40+3 13·65	30·320	58·4		55·1
Anon.	14 56	12 15·7	14 33·6	12 15·5	12 15·6	N. 1 55—2 18·0				
Anon.	15 1	11 30·5	8 10·4	11 30·7	11 30·6	N. 1 35+3 14·2				
5032	15 11 44·5	11 27·0	10 12·3	11 27·2	11 27·1	N. 4 20+1 14·8	30·321	58·5		55·0
5151	15	11 5·6	11 32·4	11 5·7	11 5·65	N. 4 40—0 26·75	30·324	58·6		55·1
Anon.	15 37 46·0	11 18·7	12 30·5	11 18·7	11 18·7	N. 2 50—1 11·8				
5227	15 44 29·2	11 26·4	9 3·35	11 26·4	11 26·4	N. 0 45+2 23·05				
5272	15 50 39·7	12 31·0	12 28·3	12 31·0	12 31·0	N. 5 10+0 2·7	30·338	58·5		55·0
5374	16 4 45·5	12 18·1	11 28·8	12 18·0	12 18·05	N. 4 55+0 23·25				
5435	16	12 15·9	14 4·5	12 15·8	12 15·85	N. 3 25—1 22·65	30·345	58·5		
Anon.	16 17 21·5		11 3·75	12 16·75		N. 1 5+1 13·0			58·1	54·8
5588	16	13 12·4	18 0·2	13 12·6	13 12·5	N. 2 10—4 21·7				
5632	16 43 30·8	12 10·7	11 17·95	12 10·4	12 10·55	S. 0 5—0 26·6	30·365	58·4		54·0
5735	16 58 1·2	12 13·8	8 30·5	12 13·4	12 13·6	0 0+3 17·1				
5817	17 10 21·5	12 15·4	8 27·4	12 15·6	12 15·5	N. 1 25+3 22·1	30·361	58·5		54·1
5881	17 20 48·6	12 0·1	16 4·3	12 0·1	12 0·1	N. 4 15—4 4·2	30·360	58·5		53·7
6016	17 42 29·0	11 33·7	16 10·45	11 33·8	11 33·75	N. 2 20—4 16·7			57·6	53·6
6074	17 52 30·4	10 24·8	6 23·0	10 25·0	10 24·9	N. 3 40+4 1·9				53·5
6115	17 59 13·4	11 31·6	10 5·6	11 31·8	11 31·7	N. 3 30+1 26·1				
6145	18 3 29·0	12 20·4	10 3·5	12 20·4	12 20·4	N. 3 10+2 16·9	30·349	58·3		53·5
6233	18 17 17·4	12 10·0	13 16·65	12 10·5	12 10·25	N. 2 15+5 8·4				
6285	18 24 18·2	11 22·9	9 14·0	11 23·0	11 22·95	N. 0 50+2 8·95	30·352	58·3		53·8
6305	18 27 11·4	11 22·9	13 21·0	11 22·9	11 22·9	N. 0 50+2 32·1				
6414	18 46 7·0	11 11·5	8 9·0	11 11·7	11 11·6	N. 3 0+3 2·6			57·8	
6489	18 56 7·0	10 21·0	9 8·9	10 20·8	10 20·9	N. 3 50+1 12·0				
6525	19 1 7·0	10 22·6	11 32·1	10 22·6	10 22·6	N 5 5—1 9·5				
6639	19 20 31·0	10 25·0	12 19·5	10 24·9	10 24·9	N. 3 50+1 17·0				
Anon.	19 24 42·5	10 1·3	13 19·4	10 1·4	10 1·35	N. 4 10—3 18·05				
6753	19 38 58·2	9 28·0	8 25·65	9 28·0	9 28·0	N. 2 40+1 2·35				
6877	19 57 52·8	10 10·4	5 14·0	10 10·4	10 10·4	N. 1 25+4 30·4				
7011	20 18 32·8	11 11·5	6 21·0	11 11·5	11 11·5	N. 4 20+4 24·5	30·360	58·0		53·5
7026	20 20 23·3	11 11·7	6 27·9	11 11·5	11 11·6	N. 4 20+4 17·7				
7057	20 24 48·3	11 11·5	12 19·4	11 11·5	11 11·5	N. 4 20—1 7·9	30·355	58·0		53·4

July 24.—No. 4623.—This observation is probably 5 parts of the micrometer in error.

☽ JULY 24, 1848.—FACE OF SECTOR WEST—(continued).

Number of B.A.C.	Time by Chronometer.	Micr. for Plumb-line on Dot.	Micr. for Observation of Star.	Micr. for Plumb-line on Dot.	Mean of Micr. for Plumb-line on Dot.	Star's Apparent Zenith Distance.	Barom.	Attd.	Lower.	Out.
	h m s	rev. pts.	rev. pts.	rev. pts.	rev. pts.	° ′ rev. pts.	in.			
Anon.	20 27 41·0	11 11·3	14 30·0	11 11·4	11 11·35	N. 4 10—3 18·65				
Anon.	20 37 11·4	11 30·0	13 22·7	11 30·0	11 30·0	N. 4 0—1 26·7				
7207	20 43 40·5	11 15·2	9 8·5	11 15·0	11 15·1	S. 0 25—2 6·6				
Anon.	20 56 58·6	10 22·2	12 9·1	10 22·0	10 22·1	N. 4 15—1 21·0				
Anon.	21 4 9·0	10 1·8	7 21·25	10 1·7	10 1·75	N. 3 35+2 14·5	30·355	58·0		52·8
7386	21 11 54·5	10 31·4	14 3·75	10 31·1	10 31·25	N. 1 10—3 6·5	30·355	58·0		53·0
Anon.	21 15		14 6·5	10 18·4		N. 4 10—3 22·1			57·4	
Anon.	21 29 5·1	14 9·8	15 16·9	14 9·4	14 9·6	N. 3 35—1 7·3				
7557	21 39 5·5	13 33·7	16 20·85	13 33·5	13 33·6	N. 0 15—2 21·25	30·350	58·0		53·5
7657	21 55 16·2	13 21·5	12 21·0	13 21·3	13 21·4	N. 4 45+1 0·4	30·350	58·0		53·1
Anon.	21 59 7·3	13 21·3	11 16·0	13 21·3	13 21·3	N. 4 45+2 5·3				
7842	22 26 2·5	11 8·9	12 28·5	11 9·2	11 9·05	N. 0 50—1 19·45	30·346	58·0		53·4
7909	22 37 3·2	11 15·7	7 16·75	11 16·0	11 15·85	N. 3 45+3 33·1			57·2	
7966	22 47 15·8	11 32·8	10 22·5	11 33·2	11 33·0	N. 0 15+1 10·5				
7992	22 52 25·5	12 3·6	15 16·9	12 3·4	12 3·5	N. 3 30+1 18·0	30·350	57·5		53·8
1802	5 37 20·2	12 19·8	9 19·8	12 19·8	12 19·8	S. 0 15—3 0·0	30·405	57·3	57·0	54·2
2293	6 55 48·5	11 29·0	12 7·2	11 29·0	11 29·0	N. 5 10—0 12·2	30·390	58·0	57·4	57·8

♂ JULY 25, 1848.—FACE OF SECTOR EAST.

Number of B.A.C.	Time by Chronometer.	Micr. for Plumb-line on Dot.	Micr. for Observation of Star.	Micr. for Plumb-line on Dot.	Mean of Micr. for Plumb-line on Dot.	Star's Apparent Zenith Distance.	Barom.	Attd.	Lower.	Out.
4623	13 46 20·2	12 33·2	15 21·0	12 33·2	12 33·2	N. 1 40+2 21·6	30·337	58·6		54·0
4719	14 9 28·6	13 12·0	16 6·4	13 12·0	13 12·0	N. 5 20+2 28·4	30·339	58·6		53·5
4784	14 22 33·0	13 27·4	9 6·25	13 27·4	13 27·4	N. 5 10—4 21·15				
Anon.	14 27 37·5	12 22·6	16 23·0	12 22·55	12 22·55	N. 1 15+4 0·45	30·335	58·4		53·0
4852	14 37 40·8	11 25·3	11 19·7	11 25·1	11 25·2	S. 0 35+0 5·5				52·9
4916	14 49 43·5	11 27·0	14 31·95	11 26·9	11 26·95	N. 0 40+3 5·0	30·336	58·6		52·9
Anon.	14 56 59·1	11 19·1	8 27·3	11 19·3	11 19·2	N. 1 55—2 25·9				
Anon.	15 1 11·0	11 22·4	14 28·3	11 22·4	11 22·4	N. 1 35+3 5·9				52·8
5032	15 11 51·6	11 28·0	13 1·3	11 27·9	11 27·95	N. 4 20+1 7·35				52·8
5151	15 32 35·8	12 19·6	11 18·2	12 19·4	12 19·5	N. 4 40—1 1·3				
Anon.	15 37 52·5	12 27·0	11 7·7	12 27·0	12 27·0	N. 2 50—1 19·3	30·338	58·2		53·3
5272	15 50 46·2	13 25·3	13 20·3	13 25·1	13 25·2	N. 5 10—0 4·9				53·2
5374	16 4 52·2	13 19·6	14 1·45	13 1·6		N. 4 55+0 15·85	30·344	58·3		52·8
5435	16	13 7·2	11 10·9	13 7·4	13 7·3	N. 3 25—1 30·4				
Anon.	16 17 28·8		13 1·6			N. 1 5+1 6·0			58·2	52·0
5588	16 37 10·5	11 27·5	6 31·1	11 27·0	11 27·25	N. 2 10—4 30·6				
5632	16 43 38·8	10 21·0	11 5·5			S. 0 5—0 18·0	30·344	58·0		51·9
5735	16 58 8·8	11 8·9	14 18·75	11 8·7	11 8·8	0 0+3 9·95				51·7
5817	17 10 29·2	10 27·1	14 6·4	10 27·3	10 27·2	N. 1 25+3 13·2				51·6
5881	17 20 56·3	10 21·3	6 8·9	10 27·3		N. 4 15—4 12·4	30·341	58·0		51·6
6016	17 42 37·5	10 31·3	6 6·45	10 31·6	10 31·45	N. 2 20—4 25·0	30·340	58·0		51·6
6074	17 52 37·6	11 23·0	15 16·95	11 22·9	11 22·95	N. 3 40+3 28·0				51·7
6115	17 59 20·8	12 27·5	14 12·5	12 27·5	12 27·5	N. 3 30+1 19·0				
6145	18	12 32·2	15 7·95	12 32·3	12 32·3	N. 3 10+2 9·7				52·0
6233	18 17 25·0	12 28·1	11 10·1	12 28·5	12 28·3	S. 0 30+1 18·4	30·340	57·8		51·9
6285	18 24 26·0	13 1·9	15 0·9	13 1·8	13 1·8	N. 0 50+1 33·1				51·8
6305	18 27 18·8	13 1·7	10 27·75	13 1·8	13 1·8	N. 0 50—2 8·05				
6414	18 46 18·0	13 16·7	16 12·7	13 16·7	13 16·7	N. 3 0+2 30·0				
6489	18 56 14·3	13 29·7	14 33·3	13 29·7	13 29·7	N. 3 50+1 3·6				
6525	19	14 3·5	12 21·0	14 3·5	14 3·5	N. 5 5—1 16·5	30·340	58·0	57·8	51·3
6639	19 20 37·3	14 21·4	12 19·4	14 21·4	14 21·4	N. 3 35—2 2·0				
Anon.	19 24 50·0	14 1·6	10 8·5	14 1·4	14 1·5	N. 4 10—3 27·0	30·335	58·0		51·5
6753	19 39 5·0	13 7·0	14 1·65	13 7·0	13 7·0	N. 2 40+0 28·65			57·7	51·5
6877	19 58 0·0	12 10·0	16 31·1	12 10·0	12 10·0	N. 1 25+4 21·1				
7207	20 43 49·0	12 31·9	14 29·0	12 31·7	12 31·8	S. 0 25—1 31·2				

July 24.—Anon. 21ʰ 15ᵐ.—Observation hurried.
 25.—Anon. 15ʰ 1ᵐ.—The seconds of transit doubtful.
 No. 6145.—Observed at ten seconds west of the meridian.
 No. 7207.—The seconds of transit doubtful.
 The sky became overcast at 20 hours per chronometer.

♉ July 26, 1848.—Face of Sector East.

Number of B.A.C.	Time by Chronometer.	Micr. for Plumb-line on Dot.	Micr. for Observation of Star.	Micr. for Plumb-line on Dot.	Mean of Micr. for Plumb-line on Dot.	Star's Apparent Zenith Distance	Barom.	Thermometers.		
								Attd.	Lower.	Out.
	h m s	rev. pts.	rev. pts.	rev. pts.	rev. pts.	° ′ rev pts.	in.			
4548	13 33 32·0	12 0·2	9 25·3	12 0·3	12 0·25	N. 5 10—2 8·95				
4570	13 40 26·6	12 0·9	10 30·75	12 0·7	12 0·8	N. 1 40—1 4·05			55·7	
4623	13 46 27·2	12 0·6	14 22·6	12 0·9	12 0·75	N. 1 40+2 21·85	30·137	59·4		55·5

Face of Sector West.

4719	14	12 17·3	9 15·0	12 17·5	12 17·4	N. 5 20+3 2·4	30·138	59·4	59·0	54·4
4784	14 22 36·0	10 15·2	14 28·7	10 15·2	10 15·2	N. 5 10—4 13·5				54·2
Anon.	14 27 42·0	11 25·0	7 16·0	11 25·2	11 25·1	N. 1 15+4 9·1				54·0
4852	14 37 43·7	11 9·9	11 5·05	11 9·8	11 9·85	S. 0 35—0 4·8				53·6
4916	14 49 46·2	11 5·1	7 25·5	11 5·0	11 5·05	N. 0 40+3 13·55				53·1
Anon.	14 57 2·0	11 11·0	13 30·0	11 11·0	11 11·0	N. 1 55—2 19·0				52·9
Anon.	15 1	11 4·4	7 24·3	11 4·6	11 4·5	N. 1 35+3 14·2				
5032	15 11 55·2	11 27·5	10 13·6	11 27·3	11 27·4	N. 4 20+1 13·8	30·124	59·2		52·4
5151	15 32 41·0	12 11·8	13 5·0	12 11·6	12 11·7	N. 4 40—0 27·3	30·112	59·0		51·6
Anon.	15 37 56·7	12 24·4	14 2·2	12 24·4	12 24·4	N. 2 50—1 11·8				51·5
5227	15 44 41·0	11 21·0	8 31·55	11 21·0	11 21·0	N. 0 45+2 23·45	30·108	59·0		51·5
5272	15 50 50·7	12 1·6	11 31·75	12 1·8	12 1·7	N. 5 10+0 3·9				51·5
5374	16 4 56·0	10 30·0	10 6·9	10 30·0	10 30·0	N. 4 55+0 23·1	30·103	58·8		51·7
5435	16 13 17·5	10 16·7	7 5·75	10 17·0	10 16·85	N. 3 25—1 22·9	30·093	58·8		51·5
Anon.	16 17 31·5		11 16·0	12 31·1		N. 1 5+1 15·1	30·092	59·0		50·7
5588	16 37 13·5	13 33·3	18 21·5	13 33·2	13 33·2	N. 2 10—4 22·3				
5632	16 43 42·0	14 15·0	13 21·85	14 15·3	14 15·15	S. 0 5+0 27·3				50·6
5735	16 58 12·0	13 0·9	9 17·8	13 0·9	13 0·9	N. 0 +3 17·1	30·088	59·0		50·3
5817	17 10 32·1	11 26·6	8 4·8	11 26·6	11 26·6	N. 1 25+3 21·8	30·094	58·8		50·2
5881	17 21 0·0	12 8·7	16 13·0	12 8·5	12 8·6	N. 4 15—4 4·4	30·097	59·0		49·9
6016	17 42 40·0	11 2·0	15 18·9	11 2·0	11 2·0	N. 2 20—4 16·9	30·104	59·0		50·5
6074	17 52 41·0	11 8·6	7 6·9	11 8·8	11 8·7	N. 3 40+4 1·8	30·107	58·6		51·3
6115	17 59 24·0	11 2·5	9 10·95	11 2·5	11 2·5	N. 3 30+1 25·55				
6145	18 3 39·2	10 33·7	8 17·5	11 0·1	10 33·9	N. 3 10+2 16·4	30·107	58·6		51·4
6233	18 17 27·0	10 27·5	12 3·0	10 27·9	10 27·7	S. 0 30+1 9·3				51·4
6285	18 24 29·0	10 19·5	8 10·9	10 19·5	10 19·5	N. 0 50+2 8·6				
6305	18 27 22·0	10 19·5	12 17·3	10 19·7	10 19·6	N. 0 50—1 33·7	30·097	58·5	58·0	51·3
6414	18 46 18·5	11 11·2	8 8·1	11 11·2	11 11·2	N. 3 0+3 3·1	30·095	58·7		51·5
6489	18 56 18·0	11 21·0	10 8·8	11 20·8	11 20·9	N. 3 50+1 12·1				
6525	19	11 21·0	12 32·6	11 21·0	11 21·0	N. 5 5—1 11·6	30·090	58·8		51·0
6639	19	10 32·5	12 26·4	10 32·5	10 32·5	N. 3 55—1 27·9				
Anon	19 24	12 7·5	15 23·2	12 7·5	12 7·5	N. 4 10—3 15·7				
6877	19 58 3·5	11 10·2	6 13·3	11 10·2	11 10·2	N. 1 25+4 30·9				
6948	20 9 45·8	11 20·2	14 8·8	11 20·2	11 20·2	N. 3 30—2 22·6				
7011	20 18 44·0	11 6·0	6 14·5	11 6·0	11 6·0	N. 4 20+4 25·5				
7026	20	11 6·0	6 21·4	11 6·0	11 6·0	N. 4 20+4 18·6				
7057	20 24 59·5	11 6·0	12 17·8	11 5·8	11 5·9	N. 4 20—1 11·9				
Anon.	20 37	10 24·6	12 19·5	10 24·6	10 24·6	N. 4 0—1 28·9				
Anon.	21 4 19·8	11 10·5	8 30·2	11 10·7	11 10·6	N. 3 35+2 14·4	30·075	58·0		49·8
7386	21 12 5·5	11 4·0	14 23·7	11 4·0	11 4·0	N. 1 10—3 6·4	30·074	58·0		49·4
Anon.	21 16 8·5		14 23·7	11 1·9		N. 4 10—3 21·8	30·067	58·0		49·5
Anon.	21 29 16·3	11 6·7	12 14·6	11 6·7	11 6·7	N. 3 35—1 7·9				
7557	21 39 16·5	13 4·7	15 25·5	13 4·9	13 4·8	N. 0 15—2 20·7				
7657	21 55 27·2	13 3·5	12 3·75	13 3·5	13 3·5	N. 4 45+0 33·75	30·057	57·8		49·7
7842	22 26 14·8	10 29·8	12 16·0	10 29·8	10 29·8	N. 0 50—1 20·2			57·6	
7966	22 47 27·0	12 8·4	10 32·75	12 8·5	12 8·45	N. 0 15+1 9·7				
7992	22 52 36·4	12 5·4	10 22·3	12 5·0	12 5·2	N. 3 30+1 16·9	30·046	58·0	57·6	52·4

July 26.—No. 4719. – Observed at 20 seconds west of the meridian.

No. 7026.—Observed at 20 seconds past, and Anon. 20ʰ 37ᵐ, at 22 seconds past meridian.

Several observations missed, owing to clouds.

♀ JULY 28, 1848.—FACE OF SECTOR EAST.

Number of B.A.C.	Time by Chronometer.	Micr. for Plumb-line on Dot.	Micr. for Observation of Star.	Micr. for Plumb-line on Dot.	Mean of Micr. for Plumb-line on Dot.	Star's Apparent Zenith Distance.	Barom.	Attd.	Lower.	Out.
	h m s	rev. pts.	rev. pts.	rev. pts.	rev. pts.	° ' rev. pts.	in.			
1802	5 37 43.2	12 9.0	15 1.6	12 9.0	12 9.0	S. 0 15—2 26.6	30.380	45.0	53.8	50.3
2293	6 56 12.7	13 7.4	12 22.5	13 7.4	13 7.4	N. 5 10—0 18.9	30.395	55.0	54.2	52.0

♄ JULY 29, 1848.—FACE OF SECTOR EAST.

Number of B.A.C.	Time by Chronometer.	Micr. for Plumb-line on Dot.	Micr. for Observation of Star.	Micr. for Plumb-line on Dot.	Mean of Micr. for Plumb-line on Dot.	Star's Apparent Zenith Distance.	Barom.	Attd.	Lower.	Out.
4570	13 40 42.4	12 0.0	10 31.2	12 0.4	12 0.2	N. 1 40—1 3.0			55.0	
4623	13 46 42.4	12 0.4	14 22.7	12 0.4	12 0.4	N. 1 40+2 22.3	30.363	55.7		50.0
4719	14 9 52.2	12 20.5	15 14.5	12 20.5	12 20.5	N. 5 20+2 28.0	30.366	55.8		49.7
Anon.	14 28 0.0	11 14.2	15 14.6	11 14.0	11 14.1	N. 1 15+4 0.5	30.368	55.8	55.1	49.7
4852	14 38 3.1	11 2.2	10 31.3	11 1.8	11 2.0	S. 0 35+0 4.7				49.8
4916	14 50 5.6	11 6.0	14 10.3	11 6.2	11 6.1	N. 0 40+3 4.2	30.371	55.8		49.7
Anon.	14 57 21.7	11 28.4	9 2.3	11 28.4	11 28.4	N. 1 55—2 26.1				
Anon.	15 1 34.0	12 3.8	15 7.75	12 3.4	12 3.6	N. 1 35+3 4.15				49.7
5032	15 12 14.8	12 10.1	13 18.3	12 10.3	12 10.2	N. 4 20+1 8.1	30.376	55.8		49.6
5151	15 32 58.8	12 11.2	11 10.4	12 11.0	12 11.1	N. 4 40—1 0.7				
Anon.	15 38 15.2	12 11.1	10 25.3	12 11.2	12 11.15	N. 2 50—1 19.85	30.378	55.8		49.1
5227	15 44 59.7	12 16.6	14 30.3	12 16.5	12 16.55	N. 0 45+2 13.75				49.2
5272	15 51 8.8	12 30.7	12 26.6	12 30.5	12 30.6	N. 5 10—0 4.0				49.4
5374	16 5 14.2	13 2.0	13 18.5	13 2.0	13 2.0	N. 4 55+0 16.5	30.390	55.6		49.7
5435	16	13 8.4	11 12.25	13 8.3	13 8.35	N. 2 55—1 30.1				
5588	16 37 33.0	12 28.3	7 32.9	12 28.5	12 28.4	N. 2 10—4 29.5				
5632	16 44 0.8	13 12.0	13 31.05	13 12.2	13 12.1	S. 0 5—0 18.95	30.406	55.4		49.8
5735	16 58 31.2	14 2.9	17 13.05	14 2.9	14 2.9	0 0+3 10.15				49.8
5817	17 10 51.2	13 6.8	16 20.1	13 6.8	13 6.8	N. 1 25+3 13.3	30.408	55.4		50.0
5881	17 21 18.5	13 10.0	8 32.6	13 10.0	13 10.0	N. 4 15—1 11.4				50.2
6016	17 42 58.6	12 4.5	7 13.5	12 4.5	12 4.5	N. 2 20—4 25.0	30.410	55.0	55.0	49.7
6074	17 52 59.5	12 8.4	16 3.45	12 8.2	12 8.3	N. 3 40+3 29.15	30.403	54.8		49.4
6115	17 59 32.8	12 2.0	13 22.0	12 2.0	12 2.0	N. 3 80+1 20.0				
6145	18 3 58.4	11 24.0	13 33.0	11 24.2	11 24.1	N. 3 10+2 8.9	30.406	55.0		49.7
6233	18 17 47.0	11 18.6	10 0.1	11 18.5	11 18.55	S. 0 30+1 18.45				49.8
6305	18 27 41.0	11 23.2	9 15.7	11 23.0	11 23.0	N. 0 50—2 7.4	30.403	54.4		50.3
6414	18 40 37.0	12 2.5	14 32.0	12 2.5	12 2.5	N. 3 0+2 29.5				
6489	18 56 36.5	11 2.1	12 7.45	11 2.5	11 2.3	N. 3 50+1 5.15				
6525	19 1 36.0	11 13.7	9 31.8	11 13.8	11 13.8	N. 5 5—1 16.0	30.410	54.5		50.0
6639	19 21 0.0	11 25.2	9 24.6	11 25.0	11 25.1	N. 3 55—2 0.5				
Anon.	19 25 11.0	10 33.6	7 7.7	10 33.7	10 33.65	N. 4 10—3 25.95			54.8	
6753	19 30 27.5	11 5.2	12 1.3	11 5.0	11 5.1	N. 2 40+0 30.2	30.405	54.5		51.0
6877	19 58 22.5	11 6.8	15 28.6	11 6.9	11 6.85	N. 1 25+4 21.75	30.390	54.5		51.1
6948	20 10 3.2	12 0.0	9 5.6	12 0.4	12 0.2	N. 3 30—2 28.6			54.5	
7011	20 19 1.3	12 14.2	16 30.9	12 14.0	12 14.1	N. 4 20+4 16.8				
7026	20	12 14.0	16 23.4	12 14.2	12 14.1	N. 4 20+4 9.3				
7057	20 25 17.2	12 14.2	10 33.3	12 14.2	12 14.2	N. 4 10—3 26.2				
Anon.	20 28 10.2		9 1.8	12 28.0	12 28.0	N. 4 10—3 26.2				
Anon.	20 37 41.0	12 33.0	10 33.0	12 33.0	12 33.0	N. 4 0—2 0.0				
7207	20 44 9.8	12 23.8	14 21.85	12 23.5	12 23.65	S. 0 25—1 32.2	30.400	54.5		50.2
Anon.	20 57 28.2	13 3.7	11 0.7	13 3.6	13 3.65	N. 4 15—1 27.95	30.395	54.6	54.7	49.7
Anon.	21 4 38.3	13 14.2	15 21.5	13 13.8	13 14.0	N. 3 35+2 7.5				
7386	21 12 24.5	13 14.0	10 0.0	13 14.4	13 14.2	N. 1 10—3 14.2				
Anon.	21 16 26.2			10 3.0	13 3.5	N. 4 10—3 26.5				
Anon.	21 20 34.2	12 26.1	11 12.7	12 26.3	12 26.2	N. 3 35—1 13.5	30.372	54.5		50.3
7657	21 55 45.8	13 4.1	13 31.1	13 4.3	13 4.2	N. 4 45+0 26.9	30.380	54.5		50.2
Anon.	21 50 36.8	13 4.2	15 2.2	13 3.8	13 4.0	N. 4 45+1 32.2				
7842	22 26 33.4	11 16.6	9 22.9	11 16.5	11 16.55	N. 0 50—1 27.65	30.378	54.0		50.0
7909	22 37 35.2	11 1.6	14 28.1	11 2.0	11 1.8	N. 3 45+3 26.3				

July 29.—No. 7026.—Observed at 20 seconds from the meridian.
Strong wind on the 29th.

♄ JULY 29, 1848.—FACE OF SECTOR EAST—(continued).

Number of B.A.C.	Time by Chronometer.	Micr. for Plumb-line on Dot.	Micr. for Observation of Star.	Micr. for Plumb-line on Dot.	Mean of Micr. for Plumb-line on Dot.	Star's Apparent Zenith Distance.	Barom.	Thermometers.		
								Attd.	Lower.	Out.
7966	22 47 45·5	10 32·8	12 0·3	10 33·0	10 32·9	N. 0 15+1 1·4		54·0	54·3	50·0
7992	22 52 55·5	11 25·3	13 2·25	11 25·4	11 25·35	N. 3 30+1 10·9	30·390			
1802	5 37 49·4	12 28·3	15 21·7	12 28·5	12 28·4	S. 0 15-2 27·3	30·421	55·0	54·3	54·5
2293	6 56 18·8	12 33·5	12 15·7	12 33·7	12 33·6	N. 5 10-0 17·9	30·441	55·5	54·6	56·6

☉ JULY 30, 1848.—FACE OF SECTOR WEST.

Number of B.A.C.	Time by Chronometer.	Micr. for Plumb-line on Dot.	Micr. for Observation of Star.	Micr. for Plumb-line on Dot.	Mean of Micr. for Plumb-line on Dot.	Star's Apparent Zenith Distance.	Barom.	Attd.	Lower.	Out.
4784	14 22 58·0	10 26·6	15 6·4	10 26·6	10 26·6	N. 5 10-4 13·8	30·412	56·2		52·2
Anon.	14 28		6 27·9	11 2·8		N. 1 15+4 8·9	30·413	56·5		51·5
4852	14 38 6·5	11 10·1	11 6·2	11 10·2	11 10·15	S. 0 35-0 3·95				51·1
Anon.	14 57 24·5	11 32·1	14 17·5	11 32·0	11 32·05	N. 1 55-2 19·45				
Anon.	15 1 36·2	11 30·3	8 17·0	11 30·3	11 30·3	N. 1 35+3 13·3				50·9
5032	15 12 17·3	10 29·7	9 15·5	10 29·6	10 29·65	N. 4 20+1 14·15	30·415	56·4		50·7
5151	15 33 2·0	11 3·1	11 30·15	11 3·0	11 3·05	N. 4 40-0 27·1				
Anon.	15 38 18·5	10 30·7	12 9·4	10 30·5	10 30·6	N. 2 50-1 12·8	30·418	56·4		50·3
5227	15 45 2·5	11 11·3	8 22·3	11 11·5	11 11·4	N. 0 45+2 23·1				50·3
5272	15 51 13·0	12 5·1	12 2·4	12 5·1	12 5·1	N. 5 10+0 2·7	30·420	56·4	55·0	50·3
5374	16 5 18·0	11 32·0	11 8·5	11 32·0	11 32·0	N. 4 55+0 23·5				50·2
5435	16 13 39·2	12 31·7	14 20·3	12 31·6	12 31·65	S. 3 25-1 22·65	30·421	56·4		49·8
Anon.	16 17 54·0	12 32·5	11 18·0	12 32·3	12 32·4	N. 1 5+1 14·4	30·425	56·2		49·8
5588	16 37 36·2	12 17·5	17 5·3	12 17·4	12 17·45	N. 2 10-4 21·85				
5632	16 44 3·5	13 8·9	12 16·0	13 8·9	13 8·9	S. 0 5-0 26·9				49·9
5735	16 58 34·2	12 26·0	9 9·4	12 26·0	12 26·0	N. 4 15-4 2·8	30·430	56·2		49·7
5881	17 21 21·8	12 17·9	16 20·75	12 18·0	12 17·95	N. 4 15-4 2·8	30·429	56·0		49·9
6016	17 43 2·0	12 31·5	17 13·85	12 31·2	12 31·35	N. 2 31·35	30·426	56·0		50·6
6074	17 53 4·0	12 31·7	8 30·05	12 31·7	12 31·7	N. 3 40+4 1 65				50·6
6115	17 59 47·0	12 14·5	10 22·9	12 14·5	12 14·5	N. 2 10-4 21·85				
6145	18 4 2·3	12 0·8	9 18·7	12 1·0	12 0·9	N. 3 10+2 16·2	30·431	55·8		50·2
6233	18 17 50·0	12 20·5	13 30·3	12 20·7	12 20·6	S. 0 30-1 9·7				
6285	18 24 51·2	12 7·3	9 32·0	12 7·1	12 7·2	N. 0 50+2 9·2				49·9
6305	18 27 44·5	12 7·3	14 5·7	12 7·1	12 7·2	N. 0 50-1 32·5	30·428	55·8		49·9
6414	18	11 26·8	8 25·3	11 27·2	11 27·0	N. 3 0+3 1·7	30·434	56·0		50·6
6489	18 56 40·2	11 18·7	10 7·6	11 18·9	11 18·8	N. 3 50+1 11·2				
6525	19 1 9·5	11 2·0	12 12·3	11 1·6	11 1·8	N. 5 5-1 10·5				
6639	19 21 3·2	10 9·1	12 4·0	10 9·1	10 9·1	N. 3 55-1 28·9	30·434	56·0		50·0
Anon.	19 25 15·5	10 31·7	14 16·0	10 31·5	10 31·6	N. 4 10-3 18·4				
6753	19 30 31·0	12 3·6	11 1·5	12 4·0	12 3·8	N. 2 40+1 2·3	30·435	56·0		49·7
6877	19	12 20·0	7 25·0	12 20·0	12 20·0	N. 1 25+4 29·0	30·434	56·1		49·6
6948	20 10	12 11·4	15 0·05	12 11·1	12 11·25	N. 3 30-2 22·8	30·430	56·0		49·4
7011	20 19 5·8	11 29·6	7 4·5	11 29·8	11 29·7	N. 4 20+4 25·2				
7026	20 21 56·2		7 12·1	11 29·8		N. 4 20+4 17·7				
7057	20 25 21·2	11 29·7	13 3·9	11 29·7	11 29·7	N. 4 20-1 8·2				
Anon.	20 28 13·8	11 18·3	15 3·45	11 18·3	11 20·4	N. 4 0-0 19·15	30·430	56·0		48·8
Anon.	20 37 44·0	11 20·7	13 13·25	11 20·4	11 20·55	N. 4 0-1 26·7				
7207	20 44 13·6	10 22·5	8 16·45	10 22·7	10 22·6	S. 0 25-2 6·15	30·430	56·0		48·7
1802	5	11 27·7	8 25·5	11 27·7	11 27·0	N. 0 15-3 2·0	30·425	55·0		48·2

☽ JULY 31, 1848.—FACE OF SECTOR WEST.

Number of B.A.C.	Time by Chronometer.	Micr. for Plumb-line on Dot.	Micr. for Observation of Star.	Micr. for Plumb-line on Dot.	Mean of Micr. for Plumb-line on Dot.	Star's Apparent Zenith Distance.	Barom.	Attd.	Lower.	Out.
1802	5 37 58·0	12 0·2	8 32·0	12 0·6	12 0·4	S. 0 15-3 2·4	30·325	55·0	54·2	48·0
2293	6 56 27·7	11 29·5	12 4·75	11 29·4	11 29·45	N. 5 10-0 9·3			54·5	

July 29.—After the observation of No. 2293, moved the instrument in Azimuth contrary to the order of reckoning.

30.—Anon. 14^h 28^m, observed at 20 seconds, No. 6414, at 26 seconds, and No. 6877, at 20 seconds, past the meridian.

No. 6753.—The seconds of transit doubtful.

Rain began to fall shortly after 21 hours per chronometer.

31.—Put back the chronometer 4^m; also shifted the sector a little, contrarywise, in Azimuth, after the transit of 2293.

ARC OF THE MERIDIAN.—CAPE OF GOOD HOPE.

δ August 1, 1848.—Face of Sector East.

Number of B.A.C.	Time by Chronometer.	Micr. for Plumb-line on Dot.	Micr. for Observation of Star.	Micr. for Plumb-line on Dot.	Mean of Micr. for Plumb-line on Dot.	Star's Apparent Zenith Distance.	Barom.	Thermometers. Attd.	Lower.	Out.
	h. m. s.	rev. pts.	rev. pts.	rev. pts.	rev. pts.	° rev. pts.	in.			
4784	14 19 12·8	12 26·7	8 6·0	12 26·9	12 26·8	N. 5 10−4 20·8	30·225	56·2		51·8
Anon.	14 24 17·0	12 19·0	16 21·1	12 18·6	12 18·8	N. 1 15+4 2·3	30·223	56·5	55·3	50·9
4852	14 34 19·0	11 18·9	11 13·8	11 19·0	11 18·95	S. 0 35+0 5·15				50·5
4916	14 46 22·3	11 8·3	14 12·8	11 8·5	11 8·4	N. 0 40+3 4·4	30·225	56·4		50·0
Anon.	14 53 38·3	12 11·4	9 19·6	12 11·8	12 11·6	N. 1 55−2 26·0				
Anon.	14 57 50·2	12 15·2	15 20·0	12 15·1	12 15·15	N. 1 35+3 4·85	30·225	56·4		49·5
5032	15 8 32·0	12 33·2	14 6·9	12 33·3	12 33·25	N. 4 20+1 7·65				49·3
5151	15 29 16·4	13 1·4	12 0·2	13 1·2	13 1·3	N. 4 40−1 1·1				48·6
Anon.	15	13 10·8	11 24·5	13 10·6	13 10·7	N. 2 50−1 20·2	30·218	55·8		48·5
5227	15 41 16·5	13 0·0	15 13·0	12 33·8	12 33·9	N. 0 45+2 13·1				48·3
5272	15 47 27·2	13 21·5	13 16·9	13 21·4	13 21·45	N. 5 10−0 4·55	20·220	55·8		47·7
5374	16 1 33·0	13 6·5	13 23·0	13 6·9	13 6·7	N. 4 55+0 16·3				46·7
5435	16 9 53·5	12 23·1	10 25·4	12 23·5	12 23·3	N. 3 25−1 31·9	30·220	55·0		46·6
Anon.	16 14 8·5		13 5·7	12 1·0		N. 1 5+1 4·7				
5588	16 33 50·8	12 27·2	7 31·3	12 28·0	12 27·6	N. 2 10−4 30·3				
5632	16	12 5·0	12 23·1	12 5·0	12 5·0	S. 0 5+0 18·1	30·223	55·6		47·1
5735	16 54 47·2	11 25·9	15 1·95	11 25·9	11 25·9	0 0+3 10·05				
5817	17 7 8·3	11 29·2	15 8·4	11 29·4	11 29·3	N. 1 25+3 13·1	30·223	55·6		46·5
5881	17 17 36·4	12 19·3	8 7·0	12 19·5	12 19·4	N. 4 15−4 12·4			53·0	46·7
6016	17 39 16·0	12 29·0	8 3·3	12 29·0	12 29·0	N. 2 20−4 25·7	30·219	55·6		47·0
6074	17 49 17·4	12 23·3	10 18·0	12 23·5	12 23·5	N. 3 40+3 28·5				47·2
6115	17 56 0·2	12 23·7	14 8·2	12 23·5	12 23·6	N. 3 30+1 18·6				47·3
6145	18 0 15·5	11 12·7	13 21·0	11 12·8	11 12·75	N. 3 10+2 8·25	30·213	55·0		47·4
6233	18 14 3·2	11 16·7	9 32·15	11 16·7	11 16·7	N. 0 30+1 18·55				48·0
6285	18 21 4·5	11 33·3	13 33·5	11 33·8	11 33·55	N. 0 50+1 33·95				
6305	18 23 57·5	12 0·0	9 26·3	11 33·8	11 33·9	N. 0 50−2 7·6	30·205	55·5		48·3
6414	18 42 53·5	11 26·1	14 20·9	11 26·3	11 26·2	N. 3 0+2 28·7	30·205	56·0		48·5
6489	18 52 54·5	12 4·9	13 8·9	12 4·9	12 4·9	N. 3 50+1 4·0				
6525	18 57 54·2	11 16·6	9 33·6	11 16·4	11 16·5	N. 5 5−1 16·9	30·200	55·8		49·0
6639	19 17 18·5	11 26·1	9 24·15	11 26·5	11 26·3	N. 3 55−2 2·15				
Anon.	19 21 30·5	11 4·2	7 11·4	11 4·2	11 4·2	N. 4 10−3 26·8	30·190	55·5		49·5
6753	19 35 45·2	11 23·6	12 18·1	11 23·65	11 23·65	N. 2 40+0 28·45	30·190	55·5	54·7	49·5
6877	19 54 30·4	11 4·6	15 25·3	11 4·4	11 4·5	N. 1 25+4 20·8	30·185	55·6		49·6
6948	20 6 22·0	12 11·5	9 16·2	12 11·7	12 11·6	N. 3 30−2 29·4	30·180	55·6		49·6
7011	20 15 20·0	12 16·6	16 33·75	12 16·6	12 16·6	N. 4 30+4 17·15				
7026	20 17 10·8	12 16·7	16 26·7	12 16·4	12 16·6	N. 4 20+4 10·1				
7057	20 21 15·6	12 16·6	11 1·65	12 16·7	12 16·6	N. 4 20−1 14·95				
Anon.	20 24 28·3	12 18·4	8 25·75	12 18·0	12 18·2	N. 4 10−3 26·45				
Anon.	20 33 58·4	13 21·2	11 20·0	13 21·4	13 21·3	N. 4 0−2 0·7				
7207	20 40 26·7	13 6·8	15 4·45	13 6·6	13 6·7	S. 0 25−1 31·75				
Anon.	20 53 46·0	12 22·1	10 26·7	12 22·3	12 22·2	N. 1 35−1 29·5				
Anon.	21 0 56·2	12 21·1	14 27·5	12 21·0	12 21·05	N. 3 35+2 6·45	30·165	55·5		48·5
7386	21 8 42·0	12 27·5	9 12·8	12 27·5	12 27·5	N. 1 10−3 14·7				
Anon.	21 12 45·2		9 3·0	12 33·0		N. 4 10−3 30·0				
Anon.	21 25 52·8	13 0·2	11 18·9	13 0·2	13 0·2	N. 3 35−1 15·3				
7557	21 35 51·5	12 29·5	10 0·2	12 29·5	12 29·5	N. 0 50−2 20·3	30·155	55·5		47·0
7657	21 52 3·2	12 25·3	13 18·5	12 25·5	12 25·4	N. 4 45+0 27·1	30·150	55·0	54·8	47·0
Anon.	21 55 54·3	12 25·5	14 24·0	12 25·5	12 25·5	N. 4 45+1 32·5	30·148	54·5		46·2
7842	22 22 50·0	12 17·1	10 23·0	12 17·5	12 17·3	N. 0 50−1 28·3				
7909	22 33 51·8	13 7·2	16 33·8	13 7·3	13 7·3	N. 3 45+3 26·5				
7966	22 44 2·5	12 33·4	14 1·6	12 33·2	12 33·3	N. 0 15+1 2·3	30·137	54·5		46·5
7992	22 49 12·0	14 0·7	15 12·3	14 0·7	14 0·7	N. 3 30+1 11·6	30·125	54·8	53·0	46·5
1802	5 34 6·0	13 11·5	16 4·6	13 11·4	13 11·45	S. 0 15−2 27·15	30·125	54·8		46·6
2293	6 52 35·5	14 5·6	13 21·5	14 5·8	14 5·7	N. 5 10−0 18·2	30·135	55·5	54·8	52·5

Aug. 1.—No. 5588.—The bisection of the upper dot re-examined and found correct.

♉ AUGUST 2, 1848.—FACE OF SECTOR WEST.

Number of B.A.C.	Time by Chronometer.	Micr. for Plumb-line on Dot.	Micr. for Observation of Star.	Micr. for Plumb-line on Dot.	Mean of Micr. for Plumb-line on Dot.	Star's Apparent Zenith Distance.	Barom.	Thermometers. Attd.	Lower.	Out.
	h m s	rev. pts.	rev. pts.	rev. pts.	rev. pts.	° ′ rev. pts.	in.			
4784	14 19 16·2	13 16·1	17 29·1	13 16·0	13 16·05	N. 5 10—4 13·05	30·100	56·8		53·7
4852	14 34 22·3	12 5·1	12 1·4	12 5·2	12 5·15	S. 0 35—0 3·75	30·108	57·0		53·1
4916	14 46 25·3	12 7·5	8 20·0	12 7·7	12 7·6	N. 0 40+3 12·6	30·111	57·0		52·7
Anon.	14 53 42·0	12 2·6	14 21·5	12 2·4	12 2·5	N. 1 55—2 19·0				
Anon.	14 57 54·0	11 19·7	8 7·8	11 19·9	11 19·8	N. 1 35+3 12·0	30·114	57·2		52·5
5032	15 8 35·0	11 23·5	10 9·4	11 23·6	11 23·55	N. 4 20+1 14·15	30·118	57·2		52·3
5151	15 29 19·5	12 5·7	13 0·3	12 5·8	12 5·75	N. 4 40—0 28·55	30·120	57·0		52·2
Anon.	15 34 36·2	11 25·3	13 4·4	11 25·5	11 25·4	N. 2 50—1 13·0				52·1
5227	15 41 20·0	11 15·9	8 27·35	11 16·1	11 16·0	N. 0 45+2 22·65	30·124	57·0		52·0
5272	15 47 30·2	12 7·7	12 5·7	12 7·9	12 7·8	N. 5 10+0 2·1	30·127	57·0		51·9
5374	16	11 19·4	10 30·1	11 19·0	11 19·2	N. 4 55+0 23·1				51·9
5435	16	11 25·5	13 14·5	11 25·5	11 25·5	N. 3 25—1 23·0	30·128	57·0		52·0
5632	16 40 21·0	11 4·5	10 12·6	11 4·5	11 4·5	S. 0 5+0 25·9	30·129	56·8		52·0
5735	16 54 51·5	11 12·0	7 29·5	11 12·0	11 12·0	0 0+3 16·5	30·131	56·8		52·2
5881	17	11 10·5	15 14·5	11 10·1	11 10·3	N. 4 15—4 4·2	30·135	56·8		51·6
6016	17 39 19·8	11 3·0	15 20·2	11 3·0	11 3·0	N. 2 20—4 17·2	30·133	56·8		51·2
6115	17 56 4·0	11 11·2	9 19·8	11 11·4	11 11·3	N. 3 30+1 25·5			56·8	51·2
6233	18 14 7·2	13 7·0	14 17·8	13 7·0	13 7·0	S. 0 30+1 10·8	30·135	56·6		51·3
6285	18 21 8·2	13 15·9	11 7·9	13 16·1	13 16·0	N. 0 50+2 8·1				
6305	18 24 1·2	13 16·0	15 15·7	13 16·0	13 16·0	N. 0 50—1 33·7	30·134	56·8		50·9
6414	18 42 58·0	13 25·8	10 23·7	13 26·0	13 25·9	N. 3 0+3 2·2	30·160	56·7		50·5
6525	18 57 57·5	11 7·4	12 18·7	11 7·5	11 7·45	N. 5 5—1 11·25	30·140	56·7		50·6
6753	19 35 48·5	13 30·7	12 29·5	13 30·9	13 30·8	N. 2 40+1 1·3	30·137	56·6		50·7
6877	19 54 43·0	12 29·9	8 2·0	12 30·1	12 30·0	N. 1 25+4 28·0	30·135	56·5		50·7

♃ AUGUST 3, 1848.—FACE OF SECTOR EAST.

Number of B.A.C.	Time by Chronometer.	Micr. for Plumb-line on Dot.	Micr. for Observation of Star.	Micr. for Plumb-line on Dot.	Mean of Micr. for Plumb-line on Dot.	Star's Apparent Zenith Distance.	Barom.	Thermometers. Attd.	Lower.	Out.
4784	14 19 23·0	13 2·8	8 15·5	13 2·8	13 2·8	N. 5 10—4 21·3	30·128	57·6	57·2	54·7
Anon.	14 24 27·5		16 5·5			N. 1 15+4 2·5	30·135	57·4		54·0
4852	14 34 30·2	12 23·2	12 18·55	12 23·2	12 23·2	S. 0 35+0 4·65	30·131	57·4		53·6
4916	14 46 33·5	12 30·0	16 1·7	12 30·4	12 30·2	N. 0 40+3 5·9				53·3
Anon.	14 53 49·5	12 33·3	10 7·3	12 33·5	12 33·4	N. 1 55—2 26·1				
Anon.	14 58 1·8	13 1·7	16 7·0	13 1·9	13 1·8	N. 1 35+3 5·2	30·137	57·3		53·3
5032	15 8 43·2	13 13·4	14 21·0	13 13·4	13 13·4	N. 4 20+1 7·6	30·141	57·2		53·0
5151	15 29 27·5	13 9·7	12 9·25	13 9·7	13 9·7	N. 4 40—1 0·45				52·5
Anon.	15 34 44·2	13 12·1	11 27·25	13 12·4	13 12·25	N. 2 50—1 19·0	30·151	57·0		52·6
5227	15 41 27·4	11 31·9	14 12·75	11 32·0	11 31·95	N. 0 45+2 14·8				
5272	15 47 38·5	13 3·9	12 33·8	13 3·7	13 3·8	N. 5 10—0 4·0	30·155	56·8		52·6
5374	16 1 44·0	13 7·3	13 23·6	13 7·5	13 7·4	N. 4 55+0 16·2	30·160	56·7		51·6
5435	16 10 4·7	12 24·6	10 29·1	12 24·6	12 24·6	N. 3 25—1 29·3	30·160	56·7		
Anon.	16 14 18·4		13 23·0	12 17·0		N. 1 5+1 6·0				
5588	16 34 0·8	12 6·7	7 11·9	12 6·9	12 6·8	N. 2 10—4 28·9	30·162	56·6		50·2
5632	16 40 28·2	11 17·2	12 2·4	11 17·4	11 17·3	S. 0 5—0 19·1	30·163	56·6		50·1
5735	16 54 58·5	10 29·3	14 4·6	10 29·1	10 29·2	0 0+3 9·4	30·161	56·6		50·3
5817	17 7 19·2	9 22·3	13 1·8	9 22·5	9 22·4	N. 1 25+3 13·4	30·163	56·6		50·4
5881	17 17 48·5	11 0·25	6 22·6	11 0·55	11 0·4	N. 4 15—4 11·8				50·6
6016	17 39 28·0	10 25·3	6 0·0	10 25·5	10 25·4	N. 2 20—4 25·4	30·166	56·6	56·7	50·7
6074	17 49 29·0	10 20·4	14 15·5	10 20·6	10 20·5	N. 3 40+3 29·0	30·166	56·6		50·7
6115	17 56 12·0	10 26·3	12 11·5	10 26·7	10 26·5	N. 3 30+1 19·0				50·6
6146	18 0 27·2	11 10·2	13 19·05	11 10·3	11 10·25	N. 3 10+2 8·8	30·167	56·6		50·4
6233	18 14 15·0	10 30·6	9 12·5	10 30·8	10 30·6	S. 0 30+1 18·1				
6285	18 21 16·5	11 1·5	13 1·5	11 1·5	11 1·5	N. 0 50+2 0·0	30·168	56·5		50·3
6305	18 24 9·0	11 1·5	8 28·3	11 1·5	11 1·5	N. 0 50—2 7·2				
6414	18 43 6·0	11 22·5	14 17·7	11 22·5	11 22·5	N. 3 0+2 29·2	30·180	56·8		50·4

Aug. 2.—Nos. 4784 and 6753.—The seconds of transit doubtful.
Clouds prevented several observations.

♃ AUGUST 3, 1848.—FACE OF SECTOR EAST—(continued).

Number of B.A.C.	Time by Chronometer.	Micr. for Plumb-line on Dot.	Mier. for Observation of Star.	Mier. for Plumb-line on Dot.	Mean of Micr. for Plumb-line on Dot.	Star's Apparent Zenith Distance.	Barom.	Attd.	Lower.	Out.
	h m s	rev. pts.	rev. pts.	rev. pts.	rev. pts.	° ′ rev. pts.	in.			
6489	18 53 5·2	10 32·6	12 3·2	10 32·5	10 32·55	N. 3 50+1 4·65				
6525	18	11 11·0	9 30·5	11 11·0	11 11·0	N. 5 5—1 14·5	30·187	56·8	56·5	50·3
6639	19 17 29·8	11 6·0	9 4·3	11 6·2	11 6·1	N. 3 55—2 1·8				
Anon.	19 21 42·2	11 10·5	7 10·4	11 10·7	11 10·6	N. 4 10—3 25·2	30·185	56·5		49·6
6753	19 35 56·0	11 14·1	12 9·5	11 14·3	11 14·2	N. 2 40+0 29·3				
6877	19 54 51·0	11 7·1	15 28·55	11 7·5	11 7·3	N. 1 25+4 21·25	30·180	56·5		48·7
6948	20 6 33·5	11 28·0	8 32·6	11 28·3	11 28·15	N. 3 30—2 29·55				
7011	20 15 31·8	12 21·5	17 4·8	12 21·6	12 21·67	N. 4 20+4 17·13				
7026	20 17 22·6	12 21·8	16 32·9	12 21·7	12 21·67	N. 4 20+4 11·23				
7057	20 21 47·8	12 21·0	11 7·5	12 21·8	12 21·67	N. 4 20—1 14·17	30·180	56·2		48·7
Anon.	20 24 40·3	13 24·2	9 32·4	13 24·1	13 24·15	N. 4 10—3 25·75				
Anon.	20 34 11·0	13 2·7	11 4·3	13 2·7	13 2·7	N. 4 0—1 32·4				
7207	20 40 38·0	12 10·6	14 8·8	12 10·4	12 10·5	S. 0 25—1 32·3			56·4	48·4
7386	21 8 53·0	14 9·3	10 29·4	14 9·1	14 9·2	N. 1 10—3 13·8				
Anon.	21 12 57·0		8 31·0	12 28·2		N. 4 10—3 31·2	30·180	56·0		48·7
Anon.	21 26 4·2	11 33·6	10 19·7	11 33·6	11 33·6	N. 3 35—1 13·9				
7557	21 36 3·0	11 18·4	8 24·0	11 18·4	11 18·4	N. 4 20—1 28·4				
7657	21 52 15·2	11 9·0	12 2·6	11 9·8	11 9·85	N. 4 45+0 26·75				
Anon.	21 56	11 9·8	13 8·0	11 9·8	11 9·8	N. 4 45+1 32·2	30·175	56·0	55·8	48·3
1802	5 34 17·8	11 21·2	14 15·1	11 21·1	11 21·15	S. 0 15—2 27·05	30·160	55·7	55·4	51·3
2293	6 52 47·6	12 5·5	11 21·3	12 5·3	12 5·4	N. 5 10—0 18·1	30·150	56·0	55·6	55·0

♀ AUGUST 4, 1848.—FACE OF SECTOR WEST.

Number of B.A.C.	Time by Chronometer.	Micr. for Plumb-line on Dot.	Mier. for Observation of Star.	Mier. for Plumb-line on Dot.	Mean of Micr. for Plumb-line on Dot.	Star's Apparent Zenith Distance.	Barom.	Attd.	Lower.	Out.
4686	13		13 3·4	10 32·7		S. 1 40+2 4·7				
4784	14 19 25·3	9 32·6	14 11·7	9 32·4	9 32·5	N. 5 10—4 13·2	30·070	56·7		53·2
Anon.	14 24 30·3	11 25·6	7 15·0	11 25·6	11 25·65	N. 1 15+4 10·55	30·070	56·8		52·7
4852	14 34 33·5	12 14·6	12 11·0	12 14·7	12 14·65	S. 0 35—0 3·65				
4916	14 46 36·5	12 15·0	9 1·4	12 15·1	12 15·05	N. 0 40+3 13·65	30·074	56·6		52·4
Anon.	14 53 52·0	12 18·6	15 3·0	12 18·4	12 18·5	N. 1 55—2 19·5				
Anon.	14 58 3·7	12 26·8	9 15·7	12 26·7	12 26·75	N. 5 3+3 13·05	30·080	56·8		52·3
5082	15 8 44·5	12 30·9	11 16·2	12 30·9	12 30·9	N. 4 20+1 14·7	30·080	56·8		52·1
5151	15 20 28·3	12 3·5	12 30·4	12 3·3	12 3·35	N. 4 40—0 27·05				
Anon.	15 34 45·2	11 7·7	12 19·3	11 7·7	11 7·7	N. 2 50—1 11·6	30·080	56·6		51·7
5227	15 41 29·7	11 17·5	8 28·2	11 17·1	11 17·3	N. 0 45+2 23·1				
5272	15 47 39·2	11 12·7	11 10·3	11 12·4	11 12·55	N. 5 10+0 2·25	30·090	56·6		51·6
5374	16 1 45·0	11 3·0	10 13·5	11 3·1	11 3·05	N. 4 55+0 23·55	30·091	56·6		51·5
5435	16 10 6·2	11 22·3	13 11·5	11 22·4	11 22·4	N. 3 25—1 23·1				51·3
Anon.	16 14 21·7	12 4·0	10 24·4	12 4·2	12 4·1	N. 1 5+1 13·7				
5588	16 34 3·5	11 30·5	16 18·5	11 30·4	11 30·45	N. 2 10—4 22·05	30·096	56·5		51·3
5632	16 40 31·8	11 20·5	10 28·3	11 20·7	11 20·6	S. 0 5—0 26·3				51·2
5736	16 55 2·0	12 14·5	8 31·6	12 14·9	12 14·7	0 0+3 17·1	30·097	56·5		50·7
5817	17 7 22·4	12 13·8	8 25·6	12 13·9	12 13·85	N. 1 25+3 22·25	30·103	56·4		50·5
5881	17 17 49·4	11 9·5	15 13·2	11 9·1	11 9·3	N. 4 15—4 3·9	30·100	56·3		50·3
5915	17 23 31·2	11 32·0	8 10·2	11 32·0	11 32·0	S. 3 5—3 21·8				
5970	17 32 13·0	11 28·1	3 21·5	11 28·5	11 28·3	S. 5 5—8 6·8				
6016	17 39 29·7	11 14·0	15 31·5	11 14·0	11 14·0	N. 4 20—4 17·5	30·104	56·4		50·3
6074	17 40 30·5	11 16·5	7 15·4	11 16·6	11 16·55	N. 3 40+4 1·15				49·8
6115	17 56 13·5	11 21·8	9 30·85	11 22·2	11 22·0	N. 4 30—1 25·15				
6145	18 0 29·0	11 5·4	8 24·0	11 5·6	11 5·5	N. 3 10+2 15·5				
6186	18 7 34·4	11 2·1	5 9·4	11 2·3	11 2·2	S. 2 5—5 26·8	30·103	56·2		49·5
6233	18 14 18·4	10 20·6	11 30·9	10 20·4	10 20·5	S. 0 30+1 10·4				
6285	18 21 19·0	10 9·2	8 1·4	10 9·6	10 9·4	N. 0 50+2 8·0	30·104	56·2		50·1
6305	18 24 12·0	10 9·6	12 9·0	10 9·3	10 9·45	N. 0 50—1 33·55				

Aug. 3.—No. 6525.—Observed when leaving the field.
Clouds interrupted several observations.
Anon. 21ʰ 56ᵐ.—Very faint: observation uncertain.
4.—No. 4686.—Observed at 15 seconds past the meridian.
Splendid definition until 18 hours chronometer time.

♀ August 4, 1848.—Face of Sector West—(continued).

Number of B.A.C.	Time by Chronometer.	Micr. for Plumb-line on Dot.	Micr. for Observation of Star.	Micr. for Plumb-line on Dot.	Mean of Micr. for Plumb-line on Dot.	Star's Apparent Zenith Distance.	Barom.	Thermometers.		
								Attd.	Lower.	Out.
	h m s	rev. pts.	rev. pts.	rev. pts.	rev. pts.	° ′ rev. pts.	in.			
6414	18 43 7·2	0 13·0	6 10·9	9 13·0	9 13·0	N. 3 0+3 2·1				
6480	18 53 7·2	11 13·1	10 1·3	11 13·0	11 13·05	N. 3 50+1 11·75				
6525	18 58 7·0	11 3·8	12 14·6	11 3·6	11 3·7	N. 5 5—1 10·9	30·095	56·5	56·0	46·6
6639	19 17 30·8	10 22·9	12 17·9	10 23·3	10 23·1	N. 3 55—1 28·8				
Anon.	19 21 44·5	9 23·1	13 5·4	9 23·1	9 23·1	N. 4 10—3 16·3				
6753	19 35 58·2	9 29·8	8 27·0	9 30·0	9 29·9	N. 2 40+1 2·9	30·108	56·0		47·0
6877	19 54 53·2	12 3·0	7 8·7	12 3·0	12 3·0	N. 1 25+4 28·3				
6948	20 6 35·2	12 20·5	15 9·2	12 20·3	12 20·4	N. 3 30—2 22·8	30·110	56·0	55·9	47·5
7011	20 15 33·2	11 30·4	7 6·7	11 30·2	11 30·3	N. 4 20+4 23·6				
7026	20 17 24·7	11 30·2	7 13·8	11 30·3	11 30·3	N. 4 20+4 16·5				
7057	20 21 49·0	11 30·3	13 4·6	11 30·4	11 30·3	N. 4 20—1 8·3				
Anon.	20 24 41·0	9 27·0	13 12·0	9 27·0	9 27·0	N. 4 10—3 19·0				
Anon.	20 34 11·3	10 28·8	12 22·0	10 28·6	10 28·7	N. 4 0—1 27·3	30·116	55·7		47·5
7207	20 40 41·2	11 11·9	9 6·0	11 11·5	11 11·7	S. 0 25—2 5·7				
Anon.	20 53 59·2	11 12·0	12 32·9	11 12·0	11 12·0	N. 4 15—1 20·9	30·123	56·0		47·5
Anon.	21 1 9·0	12 1·8	9 20·75	12 2·0	12 1·9	N. 3 35+2 15·15				
7386	21 8 55·6	12 9·4	15 15·6	12 10·0	12 9·7	N. 1 10—3 5·9	30·123	56·0		47·4
Anon.	21 12 58·2	11 18·5	15 6·5	11 18·5	11 18·5	N. 4 10—3 22·0				
Anon.	21 26 6·3	12 5·5	13 13·0	12 5·6	12 5·55	N. 3 35—1 7·45				
7557	21 36 6·5	12 8·7	14 30·0	12 9·3	12 9·0	N. 0 15—2 21·0	30·123	55·5		46·6
7657	21 52 16·8	13 10·8	12 9·9	13 10·9	13 10·8	N. 4 45+1 0·9	35·121	55·6		46·8
Anon.	21 56 8·0	13 11·0	11 4·3	13 10·8	13 10·9	N. 4 45+2 6·6				
1802	5		9 33·4	13 2·3		S. 0 15—3 2·9	30·125	55·3		48·3
2293	6 52 48·2	11 14·2	11 24·0	11 14·2	11 14·2	N. 5 10—0 9·8	30·120	55·6		51·5

♄ August 5, 1848.—Face of Sector East.

Number of B.A.C.	Time by Chronometer.	Micr. for Plumb-line on Dot.	Micr. for Observation of Star.	Micr. for Plumb-line on Dot.	Mean of Micr. for Plumb-line on Dot.	Star's Apparent Zenith Distance.	Barom.	Thermometers.		
								Attd.	Lower.	Out.
4686	13 58 5·5	11 12·0	8 33·1	11 12·0	11 12·0	S. 1 40+2 12·9	30·096	57·2	57·0	54·4
4852	14 34 42·5	12 22·9	12 17·75	12 22·9	12 22·9	S. 0 35—0 5·15	30·105	57·3		52·2
4916	14	12 20·5	15 25·3	12 20·5	12 20·5	N. 0 40+3 4·8	30·108	57·4		51·6
Anon.	14 54 0·8	14 32·3	12 6·8	14 32·3	14 32·3	N. 1 55—2 25·5	30·112	57·4		51·1
Anon.	14 58 12·7	14 7·2	17 12·9	14 7·4	14 7·3	N. 1 35+3 5·6				
5032	15 8 53·5	14 1·0	15 8·5	14 1·0	14 1·0	N. 4 20+1 7·5				50·6
5151	15 29 38·0	13 30·1	12 29·4	13 30·1	13 30·1	N. 4 40—1 0·7				
Anon.	15 34 54·6	13 28·7	12 9·8	13 28·7	13 28·7	N. 2 50—1 18·9	30·121	56·8		49·7
5227	15 41 38·3	11 24·5	14 4·2	11 24·5	11 24·5	N. 0 45+2 13·7				49·6
5272	15 47 48·8	12 4·5	12 0·7	12 4·7	12 4·6	N. 5 10—0 3·9	30·124	56·8		49·6
5374	16 1 54·4*	10 33·0	11 15·75	10 33·0	10 33·0	N. 4 55+0 16·75			56·9	
5435	16 10 15·0	11 21·9	9 26·0	11 22·1	11 22·0	N. 3 25—1 30·0	30·128	56·8		49·7
5508	16 21 48·0	10 18·2	8 20·65	10 18·0	10 18·1	S. 0 25+1 31·45	30·133	56·7		49·7
5588	16 34 12·2	11 3·0	6 7·0	11 3·2	11 3·1	N. 2 10—4 30·0				40·8
5632	16 40 39·8	10 25·4	11 10·0	10 25·5	10 25·45	N. 3 25+0 18·65	30·141	56·6		49·7
5735	16 55 10·0	11 12·2	14 21·4	11 12·8	11 12·5	0 0+3 8·9	30·148	56·6		49·6
5817	17 7 30·5	11 7·3	14 20·5	11 7·7	11 7·5	N. 1 25+3 13·0	30·149	56·5		49·7
5881	17 17 57·8	11 17·5	7 5·45	11 17·5	11 17·5	N. 4 15—4 12·05				
5915	17 23 39·5	10 20·1	14 1·8	10 20·3	10 20·2	S. 3 5—3 15·6				49·2
5970	17 32 22·2	9 27·0	8 29·0	9 26·6	9 26·8	S. 5 0+0 31·8	30·150	56·3		49·0
6016	17 39 37·4	12 9·8	7 18·6	12 10·0	12 9·9	N. 2 20—4 25·3				48·9
6074	17 40 39·0	12 12·3	16 6·8	12 12·1	12 12·2	N. 3 40+3 28·6				48·9
6115	17 56 22·1	12 18·3	14 3·0	12 18·5	12 18·4	N. 3 30+1 18·6				
6145	18 0 37·2	12 19·5	14 28·4	12 19·5	12 19·5	N. 3 10+2 8·9	30·148	56·2		49·0
6186	18 7 43·0	12 14·5	9 2·95	12 14·5	12 14·5	S. 2 50+8 11·55				49·0
6233	18 14 26·0	12 28·0	11 9·1	12 27·8	12 27·9	S. 0 30+1 18·8				49·1
6285	18 21 27·0	13 8·6	15 8·3	13 8·8	13 8·7	N. 0 50+1 33·6	30·151	56·0		49·2

Aug. 4.—Overcast at 22 hours.

5.—No. 5032.—The seconds of transit doubtful.

♄ AUGUST 5, 1848.—FACE OF SECTOR EAST—(continued).

Number of B.A.C.	Time by Chronometer.	Micr. for Plumb-line on Dot.	Micr. for Observation of Star.	Micr. for Plumb-line on Dot.	Mean of Micr. for Plumb-line on Dot.	Star's Apparent Zenith Distance.	Barom.	Thermometers.		
								Attd.	Lower.	Out.
	h m s	rev. pts.	rev. pts.	rev. pts.	rev. pts.	° ′ rev. pts.	in.			
6305	18 24 19·8	13 8·6	11 0·8	13 8·6	13 8·6	N. 0 50—2 7·8	30·150	56·2		49·2
6414	18 43 15·8	14 4·5	16 33·8	14 4·5	14 4·5	N. 3 0+2 29·3				
6489	18 53 15·4	13 11·2	14 14·9	13 11·1	13 11·15	N. 3 50+1 3·75				
6525	18	13 13·3	11 31·3	13 13·3	13 13·3	N. 5 5—1 16·0	30·155	56·0	56·2	49·2
6639	19 17 39·4	13 13·0	11 11·45	13 13·4	13 13·2	N. 3 45—2 1·75				
Anon.	19 21 51·2	12 23·4	8 32·3	12 23·6	12 23·5	N. 4 10—3 25·2				
6753	19 36 6·3	11 29·9	12 24·45	11 30·0	11 29·95	N. 2 40+0 28·5				
6877	19 55 1·0	11 28·6	16 14·6	11 29·0	11 28·8	N. 1 25+4 19·8	30·160	55·6		46·3
6948	20 6 43·2	11 27·1	8 31·3	11 27·3	11 27·2	N. 3 30—2 29·9				
7011	20 15 41·5	11 24·2	16 6·6	11 24·1	11 24·13	N. 4 20+4 16·47				
7026	20 17 32·5	11 24·1	16 0·7	11 24·1	11 24·13	N. 4 20+4 9·97				
7057	20 21 57·3	11 24·1	10 9·3	11 24·2	11 24·13	N. 4 20—1 14·88	30·165	55·5		45·7
Anon.	20 24 49·8	11 29·9	8 3·45	11 30·2	11 30·05	N. 4 10—3 26·6				
Anon.	20 34 19·8	11 22·8	9 22·15	11 23·0	11 22·9	N. 4 0—2 0·75				
7207	20 40 49·0	11 1·0	12 31·7	11 1·0	11 1·0	S. 0 25—1 30·7	30·169	55·5		44·9
Anon.	20 54 7·2	11 16·4	9 20·1	11 16·4	11 16·4	N. 4 15—1 30·3				
Anon.	21 1 17·3	10 26·9	13 0·5	10 27·1	10 27·0	N. 3 35+2 7·5				44·3
7386	21 9 3·0	10 15·0	7 0·2	10 15·0	10 15·0	N. 1 10—3 14·8	30·175	55·0		44·1
Anon.	21 13		7 2·6	10 33·5		N. 4 10—3 30·9				
7557	21 36 13·5	11 10·1	8 14·1	11 10·1	11 10·1	N. 0 15—2 30·0				
7657	21 52 25·2	11 18·0	12 11·5	11 18·5	11 18·25	N. 4 45+0 27·25	30·181	55·0		43·5
Anon.	21 56 15·8	11 18·5	13 15·2	11 18·5	11 18·5	N. 4 45+1 30·7	30·180	55·0		44·5
7842	22 23 11·8	11 5·5	9 10·5	11 5·3	11 5·4	N. 0 50—1 28·9				
7909	22 34 13·8	10 31·0	14 22·3	10 30·9	10 30·95	N. 3 45+3 25·35				
7966	22 44 24·7	10 25·3	11 27·3	10 25·5	10 25·4	N. 0 15+1 1·9				
7992	22 49 34·3	10 33·0	12 10·5	10 32·8	10 32·9	N. 3 30+1 11·6	30·180	54·7	55·4	44·0
1802	5 34 29·1	10 25·8	13 19·1	10 26·0	10 25·9	S. 0 15—2 27·2	30·140	54·8	54·3	52·5
2293	6 52 57·8	11 33·0	11 15·65	11 33·1	11 33·05	N. 5 10—0 17·4	30·124	55·5		52·5

☾ AUGUST 7, 1848.—FACE OF SECTOR EAST.

1802	5 34 40·4	10 30·2	13 23·9	10 30·2	10 30·2	S. 0 15—2 27·7	30·120	58·0	57·2	56·0
2293	6 53 11·6	13 0·2	12 17·3	13 0·2	13 0·2	N. 5 10—0 16·9			57·5	

♀ AUGUST 11, 1848.—FACE OF SECTOR WEST.

4686	13 58 38·2	11 28·3	13 32·5	11 28·7	11 28·5	S. 1 40+2 4·0	30·117	60·0	60·2	59·0
4852	14 35 13·0	12 26·5	12 19·95	12 26·3	12 26·4	S. 0 35—0 6·45				56·7
4916	14 47 16·2	11 33·8	8 18·55	11 33·6	11 33·7	N. 0 40—3 15·15	30·112	59·8		56·3
Anon.	14 54	12 11·1	14 28·3	12 11·1	12 11·1	N. 1 55—2 17·2				
5032	15 9 23·8	9 12·6	7 31·8	9 12·6	9 12·6	N. 4 20+1 14·8	30·106	59·8		55·7
5151	15 30 8·2	8 19·9	9 12·5	8 19·8	8 19·85	N. 4 40—0 26·65				54·9
Anon.	15 35 24·8	10 2·6	11 14·0	10 2·7	10 2·65	N. 2 50—1 11·35				
5227	15 42 10·5	10 19·3	7 30·2	10 19·5	10 19·4	N. 0 45+2 23·2				
5272	15 48 19·2	10 2·9	9 32·6	10 2·7	10 2·8	N. 5 10+0 4·2	30·100	59·8		54·0
5374	16 2 24·8	10 2·4	9 13·2	10 2·4	10 2·4	N. 4 55+0 23·2				53·4
5435	16 10 46·4	10 2·8	11 24·5	10 3·0	10 2·9	N. 3 25—1 21·6	30·098	59·8		53·3
5508	16 22 20·2	10 22·5	12 9·8	10 22·4	10 22·45	S. 0 25+1 21·35				
5588	16 34 44·0	10 31·6	15 18·6	10 31·7	10 31·65	N. 2 10—4 20·95	30·090	59·8	59·9	53·0
5632	16 41 2·2	10 30·6	10 3·0	10 30·4	10 30·5	S. 0 5—0 27·5				52·8
5735	16 55 42·5	10 29·5	7 13·4	10 29·5	10 29·5	0 0+3 16·1				
5817	17 8 2·6	10 31·3	7 10·3	10 31·3	10 31·3	N. 1 25+3 21·0	30·088	59·6		52·0
5881	17 18 29·3	10 19·8	14 22·5	10 19·5	10 19·5	N. 4 15—4 3·0				51·7

Aug. 5.—Good definition until 19½ hours chronometer time.
Anon. 20ʰ 34ᵐ.—Very difficult.
Anon. 21ʰ 13ᵐ.—Bisected at 20 seconds past the meridian.
7.—After observing No. 2293, moved the spindle in Azimuth in the order of reckoning.
11.—Nos. 5227 and 5632.—The seconds of transit doubtful.

♀ August 11, 1848.—Face of Sector West —(continued).

Number of B.A.C.	Time by Chronometer.	Micr. for Plumb-line on Dot.	Micr. for Observation of Star.	Micr. for Plumb-line on Dot.	Mean of Micr. for Plumb-line on Dot.	Star's Apparent Zenith Distance.	Barom.	Thermometers.		
								Attd.	Lower.	Out.
	h m s	rev. pts.	rev. pts.	rev. pts.	rev. pts.	° ′ rev. pts.	in.			
5015	17 24 12·5	10 27·7	7 5·0	10 27·7	10 27·7	S. 3 5—3 22·7				
5970	17 32 54·4	11 13·0	12 5·05	11 13·0	11 13·0	S. 5 0+0 26·05				51·5
6016	17 40 9·3	10 31·8	15 14·9	10 31·8	10 31·8	N. 2 20—4 17·1	30·088	59·5		51·3
6074	17 50 10·3	11 10·3	7 8·0	11 10·3	11 10·3	N. 3 40+4 2·3				
6115	17 56 53·6	10 22·5	8 31·0	10 22·5	10 22·5	N. 3 30+1 25·5				51·3
6145	18 1 8·8	10 10·0	7 28·45	10 10·1	10 10·05	N. 3 10+2 15·6				
6186	18 8 50·5	10 27·3	13 33·2	10 27·4	10 27·35	S. 2 50+3 5·85	30·076	59·4		51·1
6233	18 14 58·7	10 13·4	11 24·05	10 13·3	10 13·35	S. 0 30+1 10·7				51·1
6285	18 21 59·6	10 7·5	7 33·0	10 7·5	10 7·5	N. 0 50+2 8·5				
6305	18 24 52·3	10 7·5	12 6·0	10 7·5	10 7·5	N. 0 50—1 32·5	30·071	59·0		51·1
6414	18 43 47·5	9 26·6	6 24·3	9 26·5	9 26·55	N. 3 0+3 2·25				
6489	18 53 47·3	10 1·0	8 24·3	10 1·2	10 1·1	N. 3 50+1 10·8				
6525	18 58 46·7	9 12·1	10 22·7	9 11·7	9 11·9	N. 5 5—1 10·8		59·2		
6630	19 18 9·8	9 2·4	10 31·9	9 2·2	9 2·3	N. 3 55—1 29·6				
Anon.	19 22 22·0	9 29·4	13 11·6	9 29·2	9 29·3	N. 4 10—3 16·3	30·065	59·0		52·7
6753	19 36 37·5	9 18·5	8 16·9	9 18·7	9 18·6	N. 2 40+1 1·7	30·050	59·0	59·0	52·9
6877	19 55 33·2	12 2·9	7 9·55	12 2·7	12 2·8	N. 1 25+4 27·25				
6948	20 7 15·0	12 7·4	14 31·65	12 7·6	12 7·5	N. 3 30—2 24·15	30·050	59·0		52·8
7011	20 16 12·0	12 3·0	7 13·4	12 2·6	12 2·55	N. 4 20+4 23·15				
7026	20 18 18·4	12 2·5	7 20·5	12 2·4	12 2·55	N. 4 20+4 16·05				
7057	20 22 29·0	12 2·4	13 10·7	12 2·4	12 2·55	N. 4 20—1 8·15				
Anon.	20 25 20·5	11 28·5	15 14·4	11 28·3	11 28·4	N. 4 10—3 20·0	30·033	58·9		52·5
Anon.	20 34 51·4	11 0·3	12 27·6	11 0·2	11 0·25	N. 4 0—1 26·35				
7207	20 41 22·0	11 4·4	8 33·2	11 4·3	11 4·35	S. 0 25—2 5·15	30·050	58·8		52·7
Anon.	20 54 38·5	10 12·5	12 0·3	10 12·5	10 12·5	N. 4 15—1 21·8	30·043	58·5		52·5
Anon.	21 1 49·2	10 18·4	8 4·8	10 18·8	10 18·6	N. 3 35+2 13·8				
7386	21 9 35·2	10 12·9	13 19·5	10 12·7	10 12·8	N. 1 10—3 6·7				
Anon.	21 13 38·0		13 21·0	9 31·5		N. 4 10—3 23·5	30·048	58·7	58·3	52·5
Anon.	21 26 45·7	9 24·3	10 32·5	9 24·5	9 24·4	N. 3 35—1 8·1				
7557	21 36 45·8	10 15·4	13 2·8	10 15·6	10 15·5	N. 0 15—2 21·3				

♄ August 12, 1848.—Face of Sector East.

4686	13 58 44·2	9 31·1	7 18·5	9 30·9	9 31·0	S. 1 40—2 12·5	30·147	58·8	58·0	55·0
5151	15 30 18·7	13 15·0	12 14·9	13 14·9	13 14·95	N. 4 40—1 0·05				52·3
Anon.	15 35 34·3		10 32·25	12 16·2		N. 2 50—1 17·95				
5227	15 42 18·0	12 17·6	14 31·6	12 17·6	12 17·6	N. 0 45+2 14·0	30·193	58·4		51·9
5272	15 48 29·2	14 2·5	13 33·4	14 2·4	14 2·45	N. 5 10—0 3·05				
5374	16 2 35·2	13 25·5	14 8·6	13 25·5	13 25·5	N. 4 55+0 17·1				50·6
5632	16 41 19·2	12 15·0	12 32·8	12 15·0	12 15·0	S. 0 5—0 17·8				50·4
5735	16 55 40·7	11 27·2	15 3·0	11 27·2	11 27·2	0 0+3 9·8	30·209	58·3		
5881	17 18 38·3	12 13·8	8 2·1	12 14·0	12 13·9	N. 4 15—4 11·8				
5915	17 24 19·0	12 5·2	15 20·7	12 5·0	12 5·1	S. 3 5—3 15·6				

Face of Sector West.

1802	5 35 6·2	13 27·5	10 23·3	13 27·5	13 27·5	N. 0 15—3 4·2	30·435	56·7	56·2	45·3
2293	6 53 35·3	11 15·0	11 22·3	11 15·2	11 15·1	N. 5 10—0 7·2	30·465	56·6	55·7	50·0

☉ August 13, 1848.—Face of Sector West.

4852	14 35 24·5	16 7·7	16 2·65	16 7·9	16 7·8	S. 0 35—0 5·15				
5032	15 9 36·2	13 14·5	11 33·3	13 14·3	13 14·4	N. 4 20+1 15·1	30·436	57·5	57·0	47·6
5151	15 30 20·4	12 32·1	13 25·5	12 32·3	12 32·2	N. 4 40—0 27·3				46·6

Aug. 11.—No. 6186, Anon. 19ʰ 22ᵐ and No. 7011.—The seconds of transit doubtful.
Variable definitions until 21ʰ 36ᵐ chronometer time, when the sky became clouded.
12.—The observer's head touched the eye-piece sharply, after the transit of No. 4686.
No. 5272.—The seconds of transit uncertain.
Overcast at 17½ hours chronometer time.

⊙ August 13, 1848.—Face of Sector West—(continued).

Number of B.A.C.	Time by Chronometer.	Micr. for Plumb-line on Dot.	Micr. for Observation of Star.	Micr. for Plumb-line on Dot.	Mean of Micr. for Plumb-line on Dot.	Star's Apparent Zenith Distance.	Barom.	Thermometers.		
								Attd.	Lower.	Out.
	h m s	rev. pts.	rev. pts.	rev. pts.	rev. pts.	° ′ rev. pts.	in.			
Anon.	15 35 37·2	12 33·4	14 11·1	12 33·6	12 33·5	N. 2 50—1 11·6				
5227	15 42 21·2	11 10·0	8 21·5	11 10·2	11 10·1	N. 0 45+2 22·6				
5272	15 48 30·8	10 8·5	10 5·0	10 8·7	10 8·6	N. 5 10+0 3·6				
5374	16 2 36·5	11 15·2	10 25·3	11 15·2	11 15·2	N. 4 55+0 23·9	30·475	56·6		45·7
5435	16 10 58·1	11 32·4	13 21·0	11 32·4	11 32·4	N. 3 25—1 22·6				45·6
5508	16 22 31·2	12 1·4	13 23·7	12 1·6	12 1·5	S. 0 25+1 22·2	30·467	56·4		45·6
5588	16 34 55·7	12 24·4	17 12·4	12 24·4	12 24·4	N. 2 10—4 22·0				45·6
5632	16 41 23·2	12 28·0	12 2·5	12 28·0	12 28·0	S. 0 5—0 25·5	30·476	56·3		45·7
5735	16 55 53·7	11 29·5	8 14·25	11 29·6	11 29·55	0 0+3 15·3	30·478	56·3	55·6	45·7
5817	17 8 14·2	11 4·5	7 17·2	11 4·5	11 4·5	N. 1 25+3 21·3				45·7
5881	17 18 41·5	11 4·5	15 8·9	11 4·7	11 4·6	N. 4 15—4 4·3				
5915	17 24 2·5	11 6·7	7 19·1	11 6·9	11 6·8	S. 3 5—3 21·7	30·480	55·8		45·3
5970	17 33 4·0	11 4·7	11 30·4	11 4·5	11 4·6	S. 5 0+0 25·8				
6016	17 40 21·3	10 8·7	14 25·9	10 8·5	10 8·6	N. 2 20—4 17·3				
6074	17 50 22·4	9 27·2	5 26·3	9 27·3	9 27·25	N. 3 40+4 0·95	30·480	55·8		45·1
6115	17 57 5·5	10 8·4	8 18·0	10 8·6	10 8·5	N. 3 30+1 24·5				
6145	18 1 20·8	10 14·4	7 33·2	10 14·6	10 14·5	N. 3 10+2 15·3				45·0
6186	18 8 25·8	10 6·5	13 12·9	10 6·7	10 6·6	S. 2 50+3 6·3	30·481	55·7		45·0
6233	18 15 13·8	10 3·1	11 14·5	10 3·3	10 3·3	S. 0 30+1 11·2				
6285	18 22 10·2	9 26·4	7 18·5	9 26·5	9 26·4	N. 0 50+2 7·9	30·484	55·6		45·2
6305	18 25 3·2	9 26·4	11 25·7	9 26·3	9 26·4	N. 0 50—1 33·3				
6414	18 43 59·0	11 3·0	8 1·5	11 3·0	11 3·0	N. 3 0+3 1·5				
6489	18 53 59·0	10 17·5	9 6·3	10 17·55	10 17·55	N. 3 50+1 11·25				
6525	18 58 58·5	10 13·0	11 24·4	10 12·6	10 12·8	N. 5 5—1 11·6				
Anon.	19 22	10 12·3	13 30·2	10 12·1	10 12·2	N. 4 10+3 18·0			54·6	
6753	19 36 50·0	9 33·5	8 31·9	9 33·3	9 33·4	N. 2 40+1 1·5				
6877	19 55 44·5	10 0·5	5 6·8	10 0·1	10 0·3	N. 1 25+4 27·5	30·480	55·7		45·2
6948	20 7 27·4	18 9·5	21 0·2	18 9·5	18 9·5	N. 3 30—2 24·7			54·3	
7011	20 16 25·5	16 3·4	11 14·1	16 3·6	16 3·45	N. 4 20+4 23·35				
7026	20 17 15·5	16 3·5	11 21·4	16 3·3	16 3·45	N. 4 20+4 16·05	30·460	55·5		44·6
7057	20 22 41·2	16 3·4	17 11·9	16 3·5	16 3·45	N. 4 20—1 8·45				
Anon.	20 25 33·5		19 12·4			N. 3 30—3 19·5				
Anon.	20 35 3·2	14 9·2	16 2·0	14 9·4	14 9·3	N. 4 0—1 26·7				
7207	20 41 32·7	14 0·4	11 30·3	14 0·8	14 0·6	S. 0 25—2 4·3	30·470	55·7		44·6
Anon.	20 54 51·2	13 29·4	15 17·4	13 29·0	13 29·2	N. 4 15—1 22·2				
Anon.	21 2 1·2	13 26·8	11 12·0	13 27·0	13 26·9	N. 3 35+2 14·0	30·460	55·5		44·4
7386	21 9 47·2	13 20·3	16 27·25	13 20·3	13 20·3	N. 1 10—3 6·95				
Anon.	21 13 50·2	12 17·5	16 7·5	12 17·5	12 17·5	N. 4 10—3 24·0	30·455	55·0		44·2
Anon.	21 26 58·2	12 18·2	13 25·9	12 18·1	12 18·1	N. 3 35—1 7·8				
7557	21 36 57·7	12 12·7	15 0·3	12 12·9	12 12·8	N. 0 15—2 21·5				
7657	21 53 9·0	12 1·3	11 1·6	12 1·3	12 1·3	N. 4 45+0 33·7				
Anon.	21 56 59·5	12 1·3	9 30·5	12 1·3	12 1·3	N. 4 45+2 4·8	30·448	54·3		44·6
7842	22 23 55·8	12 5·3	13 25·5	12 5·2	12 5·26	N. 0 50—1 20·25	30·440	54·5	54·1	44·5
7909	22 34 57·7	12 17·3	8 19·0	12 17·3	12 17·3	N. 3 45+3 32·3				
7966	22 45 9·5	12 18·0	11 9·3	12 18·0	12 18·0	N. 0 15+1 8·7				
7992	22 50 18·2	14 15·3	12 32·25	14 15·1	14 15·2	N. 3 30+1 16·95	30·437	54·5		44·0
1802	5 35 12·6	14 9·6	11 6·1	14 9·4	14 9·5	S. 0 15—3 3·4	30·375	54·5	53·9	46·5
2293	6 53 41·2	13 10·3	13 18·5	13 10·1	13 10·2	N. 5 10—0 8·3	30·380	55·0	54·0	50·6

℀ August 14, 1848.—Face of Sector East.

4686	13 58 54·0	12 24·8	10 13·2	12 25·0	12 24·9	S. 1 40+2 11·7	30·181	57·6		54·7
4852	14 35 33·0	12 23·8	12 18·8	12 23·6	12 23·7	S. 0 35+0 4·9	30·175	57·4		52·4
5032	15 9 44·8	13 3·4	14 11·5	13 3·4	13 3·4	N. 4 20+1 8·1	30·164	57·0		49·2

Aug. 13.—The stability of the meridian mark suspected.
Bad definitions.

☾ August 14, 1848.—Face of Sector East—(continued).

Number of B.A.C.	Time by Chronometer	Micr. for Plumb-line on Dot	Micr. for Observation of Star	Micr. for Plumb-line on Dot	Mean of Micr. for Plumb-line on Dot	Star's Apparent Zenith Distance	Barom.	Attd.	Lower.	Out.
	h m s	rev. pts.	rev. pts.	rev. pts.	rev. pts.	° ' rev. pts.	in.			
5151	15 30 29·2	13 4·5	12 4·4	13 4·4	13 4·45	N. 4 40—1 0·05				47·7
Anon.	15 35 44·8	12 8·5	10 24·75	12 8·7	12 8·6	N. 2 50—1 17·85				47·6
5227	15 42 29·3	11 26·85	14 6·45	11 26·95	11 26·9	N. 0 45+2 13·55				
5272	15 48 39·7	12 13·4	12 10·0	12 13·4	12 13·4	N. 5 10—0 3·4	30·164	56·8		46·7
5374	16 2 45·2	12 11·2	12 28·7	12 11·1	12 11·15	N. 4 55+0 17·55	30·161	56·6		45·6
5435	16 11 5·8	13 3·0	11 7·2	13 3·1	13 3·05	N. 3 25—1 29·85				45·3
5508	16 22 38·6	12 14·3	10 17·7	12 14·4	12 14·35	S. 0 25+1 30·65	30·158	56·6		45·2
5588	16 35 2·7	12 20·5	7 24·7	12 20·1	12 20·3	N. 2 10—4 29·6				45·2
5632	16 41 30·2	13 3·6	13 22·2	13 3·4	13 3·5	S. 0 5—0 18·7	30·152	56·5		45·2
5735	16 56 1·0	13 12·2	16 21·6	13 12·6	13 12·4	0 0+3 9·2	30·144	56·5	55·8	45·3
5817	17 8 21·5	13 6·2	16 18·3	13 6·3	13 6·25	N. 1 25+3 12·05				
5881	17 18 49·0	13 1·0	8 23·4	13 1·4	13 1·2	N. 4 15—4 11·8				
5915	17 24 30·2	13 4·3	16 19·3	13 4·3	13 4·3	S. 3 5—3 15·0	30·144	56·4		46·4
5970	17 33 12·1	12 30·6	11 32·05	12 30·8	12 30·7	S. 5 0+0 32·05				46·4
6074	17 50 30·2	14 11·6	18 6·3	14 11·4	14 11·5	N. 3 40+3 28·8	30·137	56·4		46·0
6115	17 57 12·8	12 21·2	14 6·9	12 21·4	12 21·3	N. 3 30+1 19·6				45·9
6145	18 1 28·2	12 21·3	14 30·1	12 21·1	12 21·2	N. 3 10+2 8·9				
6186	18 8 33·7	11 9·2	7 31·4	11 9·4	11 9·3	S. 2 50+3 11·9				45·9
6233	18 15 21·3	11 21·4	10 1·95	11 21·4	11 21·4	S. 0 30+1 19·45	30·136	55·6		45·8
0285	18 22 18·0	12 32·4	14 31·4	12 32·4	12 32·4	N. 0 50+1 33·0				
6305	18 25 10·8	12 32·5	10 24·25	12 32·3	12 32·4	N. 0 50—2 8·15	30·129	56·0		45·7
6414	18 44 6·3	13 21·5	16 10·6	13 21·7	13 21·6	N. 3 0+2 29·0	30·128	56·6		45·5
6489	18 54 6·5	13 13·8	14 18·3	13 14·0	13 13·9	N. 3 50+1 4·4				
6525	18 59 7·0	12 30·5	11 14·3	12 30·6	12 30·55	N. 5 5—1 16·25	30·130	56·3		45·5
6639	19 18 31·0	13 0·2	10 32·3	13 0·0	13 0·1	N. 3 55—2 1·8				
Anon.	19 22 43·2	12 22·9	8 31·5	12 23·1	12 23·0	N. 4 10—3 25·5	30·123	56·0		45·0
6753	19 36 58·0	12 7·0	13 0·9	12 7·2	12 7·1	N. 2 40+0 27·8			54·7	
6877	19 55 52·4	12 0·7	16 20·95	12 1·0	12 0·85	N. 1 25+4 20·1	30·120	55·6		44·4
6048	20 7 34·8	12 18·4	9 21·1	12 18·6	12 18·5	N. 3 30—2 31·4				
7026	20	15 6·7	19 16·0	15 6·7	15 6·7	N. 4 20+4 9·3				
7057	20 22 48·8	15 6·7	13 25·1	15 6·7	15 6·7	N. 4 20—1 15·6				
Anon.	20 25 41·5	15 17·5	11 24·2	15 17·5	15 17·5	N. 4 0—1 15·6	30·105	55·5		44·3
Anon.	20 35	15 25·5	13 25·6	15 25·5	15 25·5	N. 4 0—1 33·9				
7207	20 41 40·1	15 0·4	16 30·3	15 0·3	15 0·35	S. 0 25—1 29·95	30·091	55·7		44·0
Anon.	20 54 59·2	13 29·5	12 0·2	13 29·9	13 29·9	N. 4 15—1 29·5				
Anon.	21 2 9·2	13 31·7	16 3·75	13 32·0	13 31·85	N. 3 35+2 5·9				
7386	21 9 54·8	13 14·3	9 32·8	13 13·9	13 14·1	N. 1 10—3 15·3				
Anon.	21 13 58·2		10 13·6	14 10·0		N. 4 10—3 30·4	30·080	55·7	54·6	44·0
Anon.	21 27	13 27·4	12 13·0	13 27·2	13 27·3	N. 4 0—3 14·3				
7657	21 53 16·1	14 13·6	15 6·65	14 13·8	14 13·7	N. 4 45+0 26·95				
Anon.	21 57 6·5	14 13·6	16 11·6	14 13·7	14 13·65	N. 4 45+1 31·95				
7842	22 24 2·7	13 31·9	12 4·0	13 31·7	13 31·8	N. 0 50—1 27·8				
7909	22 35 4·8	13 24·6	17 17·5	13 24·8	13 24·7	N. 3 40+1 30·05				
7966	22 45 15·6	13 23·5	14 25·95	13 23·7	13 23·6	N. 0 15+1 2·35	30·070	54·5	54·1	44·4
7992	22 50 25·3	13 29·8	15 7·8	13 29·8	13 29·8	N. 3 30+1 12·0	30·060	55·0	53·9	46·0
1802	5 35 19·2	12 11·6	15 7·5	12 11·6	12 11·6	N. 2 11·6	30·085	55·0		50·0
2293	6 53 49·6	11 30·4	11 10·0	11 30·4	11 30·4	N. 5 10—0 14·4				

♄ August 19, 1848.—Face of Sector West.

Number of B.A.C.	Time by Chronometer	Micr. for Plumb-line on Dot	Micr. for Observation of Star	Micr. for Plumb-line on Dot	Mean of Micr. for Plumb-line on Dot	Star's Apparent Zenith Distance	Barom.	Attd.	Lower.	Out.
4683	13 59 21·2	13 21·3	15 25·25	13 21·7	13 21·2	S. 1 40+2 4·05	30·313	57·7	57·0	54·7
5151	15	10 21·6	11 13·8	10 21·7	10 21·65	N. 4 40—0 26·15	30·332	57·4		51·7
5227	15 42 55·5	10 20·3	7 31·35	10 20·3	10 20·3	N. 0 45+2 22·95				51·2
5272	15 49 4·2	10 16·3	10 13·1	10 16·3	10 16·3	N. 5 10+0 3·2	30·335	57·4		50·9

Aug. 14.—Indifferent definition.

♄ AUGUST 19, 1848.—FACE OF SECTOR WEST—(continued).

Number of B.A.C.	Time by Chronometer.	Micr. for Plumb-line on Dot.	Micr. for Observation of Star.	Micr. for Plumb-line on Dot.	Mean of Micr. for Plumb-line on Dot.	Star's Apparent Zenith Distance.	Barom.	Attd.	Lower.	Out.
	h m s	rev. pts.	rev. pts.	rev. pts.	rev pts.	° ' rev. pts.	in.			
5374	16 3 10·1	10 16·1	9 26·6	10 15·9	10 16·0	N. 4 55+0 23·4				50·4
5435	16 11 31·2	10 17·4	12 6·1	10 17·6	10 17·5	N. 3 25—1 22·6	30·340	57·3		50·4
5508	16 23 5·0	10 22·4	12 11·5	10 22·5	10 22·45	S. 0 25+1 23·05				50·3
5588	16 35 29·0	10 29·8	15 17·5	10 30·0	10 29·9	N. 2 10—4 21·6	30·347	57·4		50·3
5632	16 41 57·0	10 21·5	9 29·5	10 21·5	10 21·5	S. 0 5—0 26·0				
5735	16 56 27·2	11 19·1	8 2·5	11 18·9	11 19·0	0 0+3 16·5				49·6
5817	17 8 47·5	10 31·6	7 10·6	10 31·5	10 31·55	N. 1 25+3 20·95	30·360	57·0	56·4	48·9
5881	17 19 14·3	11 5·0	15 9·7	11 4·9	11 4·95	N. 4 15—4 4·75				
5915	17 24 57·2	11 20·0	7 33·3	11 20·0	11 20·0	S. 3 5—3 20·7	30·360	56·7		48·6
5970	17 33 39·1	11 25·9	12 17·9	11 25·9	11 25·9	S. 5 0+0 26·0				48·3
6074	17 50 55·4	11 10·0	7 9·5	11 10·1	11 10·05	N. 3 40+4 0·55				
6115	17 57 39·0	10 8·1	8 17·5	10 8·0	10 8·0	S. 3 50+1 24·55				
6145	18 1 54·1	10 4·5	7 23·0	10 4·6	10 4·55	N. 3 10+2 14·65				47·7
6186	18 9 0·2	10 12·2	13 19·8	10 12·0	10 12·1	S. 2 50+3 7·7	30·369	56·4		47·7
6233	18 15 43·7	9 27·1	11 4·4	9 27·1	9 27·1	S. 0 30+1 11·3				
6285	18 22 44·2	8 28·4	6 21·1	8 28·4	8 28·4	N. 0 50+2 7·3				
6305	18 25 37·0	8 28·4	8 28·4	8 28·4	8 28·4	N. 0 50—2 0·0	30·373	56·5		47·4
6414	18	10 22·4	7 21·95	10 22·4	10 22·4	N. 3 0+3 0·45				
6489	18 54 32·0	10 31·2	9 21·5	10 31·2	10 31·2	N. 3 50+1 9·7	30·384	56·5	56·1	47·0
6639	19 18 55·2	10 21·4	12 17·8	10 21·4	10 21·4	N. 3 55—1 30·4				
Anon.	19 23	10 24·0	14 10·3	10 24·0	10 24·0	N. 4 10—3 20·3	30·384	56·5		47·2
6753	19 37 23·0	10 9·9	9 9·3	10 9·7	10 9·8	N. 2 40+1 0·5				47·4
6877	19 56 18·5	10 8·9	5 15·3	10 8·9	10 8·9	N. 1 25+4 27·6	30·388	56·0	55·9	47·0
6948	20 8 0·0	10 30·7	13 21·0	10 30·5	10 30·6	S. 3 30—2 24·4				
7011	20 16 57·8	10 26·5	6 2·8	10 26·1	10 26·3	N. 4 20+4 23·5	30·388	56·4		47·4
7026	20 18 49·0	10 26·0	6 10·0	10 26·0	10 26·0	N. 4 20+4 16·0				
7057	20 23 13·6	10 26·0	12 1·1	10 26·0	10 26·0	N. 4 20—1 9·1	30·388	56·4		47·4
Anon.	20 25	9 26·0	13 12·3	9 26·2	9 26·1	N. 4 10—3 20·2	30·388	56·0	55·6	47·5

☉ AUGUST 20, 1848.—FACE OF SECTOR WEST.

Number of B.A.C.	Time by Chronometer.	Micr. for Plumb-line on Dot.	Micr. for Observation of Star.	Micr. for Plumb-line on Dot.	Mean of Micr. for Plumb-line on Dot.	Star's Apparent Zenith Distance.	Barom.	Attd.	Lower.	Out.
7207	20 42 12·6	10 17·5	8 12·85	10 17·8	10 17·65	S. 0 25—2 4·8	30·385	55·8	55·2	46·2
Anon.	20 55 29·5	10 10·9	11 30·3	10 10·5	10 10·5	N. 4 15—1 19·6				
Anon.	21 2 39·2	10 12·9	7 33·5	10 13·1	10 13·0	N. 3 35+2 13·5				
7386	21 10 25·8	10 17·1	13 24·9	10 17·1	10 17·1	N. 1 10—3 7·8				
Anon.	21 14 28·5	9 30·5	13 19·4	9 30·5	9 30·5	N. 4 10—3 22·0				
Anon.	21 27 36·2	9 9·4	10 17·9	9 9·4	9 9·4	N. 3 35—1 8·5				
7557	21 37 37·0	11 1·0	13 23·5	11 1·0	11 1·0	N. 0 15—2 22·5				
7657	21 53 45·8	10 21·1	9 21·75	10 21·1	10 21·1	N. 4 45+0 33·35				
Anon.	21 57 38·0	10 21·1	8 16·6	10 21·1	10 21·1	N. 4 45+2 4·5				
7842	22 24 34·8	10 25·1	12 12·4	10 25·3	10 25·2	N. 0 50—1 21·2				
7909	22 35 36·2	10 3·4	6 5·1	10 3·3	10 3·35	N. 4 45+3 32·25				
7966	22 45 48·2	11 0·1	9 24·7	11 0·0	11 0·05	N. 0 15+1 9·35				
7992	22 50 56·8	11 25·1	10 7·7	11 24·9	11 25·0	N. 3 30+1 17·3				55·2
1802	5 35 52·2	11 20·9	8 15·9	11 20·9	11 20·9	S. 0 15—3 5·0	30·385	55·5	54·3	51·0
2293	6 54 19·5	11 26·3	11 32·05	11 26·0	11 26·15	N. 5 10—0 5·9	30·395	55·7	54·3	52·7

☾ AUGUST 21, 1848.—FACE OF SECTOR WEST.

Number of B.A.C.	Time by Chronometer.	Micr. for Plumb-line on Dot.	Micr. for Observation of Star.	Micr. for Plumb-line on Dot.	Mean of Micr. for Plumb-line on Dot.	Star's Apparent Zenith Distance.	Barom.	Attd.	Lower.	Out.
2203	6 54 25·2	11 2·0	11 9·6	11 2·2	11 2·1	N. 5 10—0 7·5	30·226	55·5		48·3

Aug. 19.—Anon. 19ʰ 23ᵐ.—Observed at 10 seconds past the meridian. Doubtful observation.

Observation interrupted by occasional clouds, and finally by rain.

20.—Bad definitions.

☿ AUGUST 22, 1848.—FACE OF SECTOR EAST.

Number of B.A.C.	Time by Chronometer.	Micr. for Plumb-line on Dot.	Micr. for Observation of Star.	Micr. for Plumb-line on Dot.	Mean of Micr. for Plumb-line on Dot.	Star's Apparent Zenith Distance.	Barom.	Attd.	Lower.	Out.
	h m s	rev. pts.	rev. pts.	rev. pts.	rev. pts.	° ′ rev. pts.	in.			
5151	15	12 26·4	11 26·5	12 26·2	12 26·3	N. 4 40—0 33·8			58·0	58·2
5227	15 43 13·9	12 30·6	15 10·0	12 31·0	12 30·8	N. 0 45+2 13·2	30·140	57·8		56·7
5272	15	13 18·5	13 16·2	13 18·3	13 18·4	N. 5 10—0 2·2				56·4
5374	16 3 30·2	13 25·5	14 10·3	13 25·5	13 25·5	N. 4 55+0 18·8	30·140	57·8		55·3
5435	16 11 51·0	13 27·0	11 31·4	13 27·0	13 27·0	N. 3 25—1 29·6				54·7
5508	16 23 24·0	13 13·5	11 16·8	13 13·6	13 13·55	S. 0 25—1 30·75				54·2
5588	16 35 48·2	13 12·5	8 16·8	13 12·3	13 12·4	N. 2 10—4 29·6				53·7
5632	16 42 15·6	13 0·1	13 18·4	13 0·1	13 0·1	S. 0 5—0 18·3				53·5
5735	16 56 46·0	13 1·8	16 10·4	13 1·7	13 1·75	O 0+3 8·65	30·148	57·8		53·2
5817	17 9 6·3	13 3·4	16 16·4	13 3·6	13 3·5	N. 1 25+3 12·9				52·8
5881	17 19 28·2	12 29·3	8 17·0	12 29·5	12 29·4	N. 4 15—4 12·4				
5915	17 25 15·5	12 0·0	15 13·9	12 0·0	12 0·0	S. 3 5—3 13·9				52·4
5970	17 33 58·2	11 8·8	10 8·75	11 8·5	11 8·65	S. 5 0+0 33·9	30·154	57·6		52·3
6016	17 41 13·8	11 22·2	6 30·4	11 22·4	11 22·3	N. 2 20—4 25·9				
6074	17 51 14·6	11 16·2	15 10·4	11 16·2	11 16·2	N. 3 40+3 28·2		57·8		52·0
6115	17 57 57·7	11 16·9	13 1·5	11 16·7	11 16·8	N. 3 30+1 18·7				
6145	18 2 13·0	10 14·6	12 22·9	10 14·6	10 14·6	N. 3 10+2 8·3	30·160	57·5		51·7
6186	18 9 19·0	9 21·9	6 8·0	9 21·9	9 21·9	S. 2 50+3 13·9				51·6
6233	18 16 2·0	9 16·6	7 29·7	9 16·7	9 16·65	S. 0 30+1 20·95				
6285	18 23 2·7	11 30·6	13 28·6	11 30·6	11 30·6	N. 0 50+1 32·0				
6305	18 25 56·0	11 30·6	9 21·5	11 30·6	11 30·6	N. 0 50—2 9·1	30·162	57·4		51·3
6414	18 44 51·5	12 20·5	15 14·4	12 20·5	12 20·5	N. 3 0+2 27·9	30·165	57·4		51·0
6489	18 54 51·3	13 9·9	14 12·8	13 9·9	13 9·9	N. 3 50+1 2·9				50·4
6525	18	13 12·3	11 29·4	13 12·4	13 12·4	N. 5 5—1 17·0	30·164	57·3		50·2
6639	19 19 15·7	12 28·2	10 25·6	12 27·0	12 28·05	N. 3 55—2 2·45				
Anon.	19 23 27·5	12 0·4	8 7·2	12 0·8	12 0·8	N. 4 10—3 27·4	30·165	57·0		49·2
6753	19 37 42·7	11 19·5	12 13·4	11 19·5	11 19·5	N. 2 40+0 27·9			56·9	
6877	19 56 37·6	11 18·0	16 2·5	11 18·0	11 18·0	N. 1 25+4 18·5	30·165	57·0		49·0
6048	20 8 19·4	11 24·1	8 26·3	11 24·2	11 24·15	N. 3 30—2 31·85				
7026	20	11 12·5	15 22·4	11 12·8	11 12·5	N. 4 20+4 9·75				
7057	20 23 33·5	11 12·4	9 31·5	11 12·6	11 12·5	N. 4 20—1 15·0	30·160	57·0		49·7
Anon.	20 26 25·8	11 4·3	7 10·0	11 4·4	11 4·35	N. 4 10—3 28·35				
Anon.	20 35 56·0	10 26·9	8 26·1	10 26·5	10 26·7	N. 4 0—2 0·6				
7207	20 42 25·3	10 7·6	12 2·9	10 7·5	10 7·55	S. 0 25—1 29·35	30·157	57·0		49·6
Anon.	20 55 43·8	10 17·1	8 19·95	10 17·4	10 17·25	N. 4 15—1 31·3	30·154	57·0	56·8	48·7
Anon.	21 2 54·3	10 12·0	12 17·3	10 12·1	10 12·05	N. 3 35+2 5·25				
7386	21 10 40·2	11 0·4	7 17·6	11 0·5	11 0·5	N. 1 10—3 16·9				
Anon.	21 14 43·2		7 23·5	11 20·2		N. 4 10—3 30·7	30·150	56·5		47·5
Anon.	21 27 50·2	11 23·0	10 8·8	11 23·2	11 23·1	N. 3 35—1 14·3				
7557	21 37 50·2	11 32·6	8 33·9	11 32·6	11 32·6	N. 0 15—2 32·7	30·150	56·5	56·5	47·0
7657	21 54 1·2	12 5·0	12 30·5	12 5·2	12 5·1	N. 4 45+0 25·4				
Anon.	21 57 52·5	12 5·1	14 1·35	12 5·1	12 5·1	N. 4 45+1 30·25	30·153	56·3		46·5
7842	22 24 48·2	11 8·0	9 11·7	11 8·0	11 8·0	N. 0 50—1 30·3				
7906	22 46 1·0	11 24·0	12 24·5	11 24·1	11 24·05	N. 0 15+1 0·45				
7992	22 51 10·2	12 7·6	13 18·2	12 7·2	12 7·4	N. 3 30+1 10·8	30·143	55·5		45·5
1802	5 36 5·2	12 25·3	15 21·9	12 25·2	12 25·25	S. 0 15—2 30·65	30·140	55·8	54·0	42·5
2203	6 54 34·5	12 17·6	12 3·7	12 17·6	12 17·6	N. 5 10—0 13·9	30·152	55·8	54·2	46·3

☿ AUGUST 23, 1848.—FACE OF SECTOR EAST.

Number of B.A.C.	Time by Chronometer.	Micr. for Plumb-line on Dot.	Micr. for Observation of Star.	Micr. for Plumb-line on Dot.	Mean of Micr. for Plumb-line on Dot.	Star's Apparent Zenith Distance.	Barom.	Attd.	Lower.	Out.
4852	14 36 14·0	11 24·9	11 20·95	11 24·5	11 24·7	S. 0 35+0 3·75	30·145	57·4	57·3	
5032	15 10 35·5	11 22·2	12 30·5	11 22·0	11 22·1	N. 4 20+1 8·4				54·7

Aug. 22.—No. 5272.—Bisected at 25 seconds past the meridian.
No. 5881.—The seconds of transit doubtful.

♀ August 23, 1848—*(continued)*.—Face of Sector West.

Number of B.A.C.	Time by Chronometer.	Micr. for Plumb-line on Dot.	Micr. for Observation of Star.	Micr. for Plumb-line on Dot.	Mean of Micr. for Plumb-line on Dot.	Star's Apparent Zenith Distance.	Barom.	Thermometers. Attd.	Lower.	Out.
	h m s	rev. pts.	rev. pts.	rev. pts.	rev. pts.	° ′ rev. pts.	in.			
5151	15 31 16·0	10 4·8	11 31·4	10 4·8	10 4·8	N. 4 40—0 26·6				54·1
5227	15 43 17·2	10 15·8	7 26·5	10 15·9	10 15·85	N. 0 45+2 23·35				53·7
5272	15 49 26·8	10 31·5	10 29·4	10 31·9	10 31·7	N. 5 10+0 2·3	30·155	57·4		53·5
5374	16 3 32·0	10 12·6	9 23·05	10 12·4	10 12·5	N. 4 55+0 23·45				53·2
5435	16 11 54·5	10 6·6	11 29·4	10 6·6	10 6·6	N. 3 25—1 22·8	30·166	57·3		52·8
5508	16 23 27·4	10 4·4	11 27·55	10 4·4	10 4·4	S. 0 25—1 23·15	30·169	57·3		52·4
5588	16 35 51·5	10 23·2	15 12·6	10 23·2	10 23·2	N. 2 10—4 23·4				51·7
5632	16 42 19·5	10 27·0	10 2·55	10 28·2	10 28·05	S. 0 5—0 25·5				51·4
5735	16 56 49·8	11 4·7	7 23·4	11 4·5	11 4·6	0 0+3 15·2	30·169	57·3		51·5
5817	17 9 10·2	11 6·5	7 20·5	11 6·7	11 6·6	N. 1 25+3 20·1				
5881	17 19 37·0	11 14·2	15 18·4	11 14·0	11 14·1	N. 4 15—4 4·3				
5915	17 25 19·0	11 28·5	8 7·8	11 28·3	11 28·4	S. 3 5—3 20·6				49·8
5970	17	11 33·5	12 26·9	11 33·5	11 33·5	S. 5 0+0 27·4			·	49·3
6016	17 41 17·2	10 16·5	15 0·2	10 16·3	10 16·4	N. 2 20—4 17·8	30·187	56·6		49·1
6074	17 51 18·2	10 12·7	6 11·7	10 12·7	10 12·7	N. 3 40+4 1·0				49·8
6115	17 58 1·0	10 21·5	8 31·5	10 21·5	10 21·5	N. 3 30+1 24·0				
6145	18 2 16·4	10 25·4	8 9·9	10 25·5	10 25·45	N. 3 10+2 15·55	30·195	56·8		50·2
6186	18 9 22·5	11 18·6	14 25·6	11 18·5	11 18·55	S. 2 50+3 7·05				50·0
6233	18 16 6·0	10 29·8	12 8·0	10 29·8	10 29·8	S. 0 30+1 12·2				
6285	18 23 6·3	10 23·3	8 16·5	10 23·1	10 23·2	N. 0 50+2 6·7				
6305	18 25 59·3	10 23·2	12 24·6	10 23·3	10 23·3	N. 0 50—2 1·3	30·204	56·6	56·7	50·0
6414	18 44 54·6	11 10·0	8 9·75	11 10·9	11 10·9	N. 3 0+3 1·15	30·207	56·5		49·5
6489	18 54 54·6	11 3·9	9 28·3	11 3·6	11 3·75	N. 3 50+1 9·45				
6525	18 59 54·2	11 20·2	12 30·8	11 19·8	11 20·0	·N. 5 5—1 10·8	30·208	56·4		49·3
6639	19 19 18·3	12 6·4	14 3·1	12 6·8	12 6·6	N. 3 55—1 30·5				
Anon.	19 23 30·7	13 0·6	16 20·5	13 0·6	13 0·6	N. 4 10—3 19·9	30·210	56·4	56·5	48·8
6753	19 37 46·0	13 10·8	12 11·2	13 10·9	13 10·85	N. 2 40+0 33·05	30·209	56·4		48·5
6877	19 56 41·4	13 3·0	8 9·9	13 3·0	13 3·0	N. 1 25+4 27·1				48·0
6948	20 8 23·0	13 11·3	16 2·2	13 11·3	13 11·3	N. 3 30—2 24·9				
7011	20 17 21·0	12 13·1	7 24·0	12 13·1	12 13·17	N. 4 20+4 23·17				
7026	20 19 12·0	12 13·2	7 31·8	12 13·3	12 13·3	N. 4 20+4 15·37				
7057	20 23 36·8	12 13·1	13 22·0	12 13·2	12 13·17	N. 4 20—1 8·83	30·210	56·5		47·4
Anon.	20 26 29·0	11 14·3	15 0·1	11 14·1	11 14·2	N. 4 10—3 19·9				47·3
Anon.	20 35 59·0	11 12·8	13 6·6	11 12·8	11 12·8	N. 4 0—1 27·8				
7207	20 42 29·2	11 23·2	9 19·4	11 23·3	11 23·25	S. 0 25—2 3·85	30·210	56·5		47·0
Anon.	20 55 46·0	12 0·5	13 21·7	12 0·5	12 0·5	N. 4 15—1 21·2				
Anon.	21 2 57·0	12 5·3	9 25·95	12 5·2	12 5·25	N. 3 45+2 13·3	30·210	56·3		46·7
7386	21 10 43·0	11 11·8	14 20·3	11 11·9	11 11·85	N. 1 10—3 8·45				
Anon.	21 14 45·5	11 23·9	15 11·4	11 23·8	11 23·8	N. 4 10—3 21·9				
Anon.	21 27 53·8	12 5·6	13 14·2	12 5·4	12 5·5	N. 3 35—1 8·7	30·212	56·3		45·8
7557	21 37 54·2	11 18·1	14 7·6	11 18·2	11 18·3	N. 0 15—2 23·45				
7657	21 54 4·2	11 12·4	10 14·0	11 12·3	11 12·35	N. 4 45+0 32·35				
Anon.	21 57 55·5	11 12·4	9 7·0	11 12·3	11 12·35	N. 4 45+2 5·35	30·213	56·3		45·0
7842	22 24 52·4	11 7·5	12 28·5	11 7·6	11 7·55	N. 0 50—1 20·95				
7900	22 35 54·0	11 13·0	7 15·5	11 13·0	11 13·0	N. 3 45+3 31·5	30·210	55·6		44·7
7966	22 46 5·2	11 29·7	10 22·0	11 29·7	11 29·7	N. 0 15+1 7·7				
7992	22 51 14·5	11 31·9	10 16·2	11 31·9	11 31·9	N. 3 30+1 15·7	30·210	55·5	55·4	44·7
1802	5 36 9·5	12 11·5	9 5·3	12 11·3	12 11·4	S. 0 15—3 6·1	30·236	55·0		44·0
2293	6 54 37·0	11 20·4	11 26·4	11 20·4	11 20·4	N. 5 10—0 6·0	30·245	59·5		51·0

♃ August 24, 1848.—Face of Sector East.

6016	17 41 26·0	11 24·3	6 33·2	11 24·3	11 24·3	N. 2 20—4 25·1	30·174	57·7	57·6	55·6
6074	17 51 26·5	12 19·4	16 14·1	12 19·4	12 19·4	N. 3 40+3 28·7				55·8

Aug. 23.—No. 5970.—Bisected at 8 seconds past the meridian. Calm night; indifferent definitions.

♃ AUGUST 24, 1848.—FACE OF SECTOR EAST—(continued).

Number of B.A.C.	Time by Chronometer.	Micr. for Plumb-line on Dct.	Micr. for Observation of Star.	Micr. for Plumb-line on Dot.	Mean of Micr. for Plumb-line on Dot.	Star's Apparent Zenith Distance.	Barom.	Thermometers. Attd.	Lower.	Out.
	h m s	rev. pts.	rev. pts.	rev. pts.	rev. pts.	° ′ rev. pts.	in.			
6115	17 58 9·0	13 10·2	14 30·0	13 10·2	13 10·2	N. 3 30+1 19·8				
6145	18 2 24·0	12 26·2	15 0·8	12 26·0	12 26·1	N. 3 10+2 8·7				
6186	18 0 30·2	12 19·0	9 6·5	12 18·9	12 18·95	S. 2 50+3 12·45	30·176	57·7		55·4
6233	18 16 13·2	12 13·0	10 27·8	12 13·0	12 13·0	S. 0 30+1 19·2				55·4
6285	18 23 14·0	12 18·8	14 18·0	12 18·8	12 18·8	N. 0 50+1 33·2				
6305	18 26 7·5	12 18·7	10 10·45	12 18·0	12 18·8	N. 0 50—2 8·35	30·178	57·6		55·2
6414	18 45 4·0	12 33·0	15 28·8	12 33·0	12 33·0	N. 3 0+2 29·8				55·3
6489	18 55 3·3	12 14·9	13 19·0	12 14·9	12 14·9	N. 3 50+1 4·1				
6525	19 0 3·5	12 13·7	10 30·6	12 13·9	12 13·8	N. 5 5—1 17·2	30·173	57·3		55·3
6753	19 37 54·0	12 10·6	13 5·05	12 10·5	12 10·55	N. 2 40+0 28·5	30·170	57·5	57·2	54·6
6877	19 56 49·0	12 12·8	16 33·1	12 13·0	12 12·9	N. 1 25+4 20·2	30·170	58·0		54·0
7011	20	12 8·4	16 24·4	12 8·5	12 8·45	N. 4 20+4 15·95				
7026	20	12 8·4	16 18·0	12 8·5	12 8·45	N. 4 20+4 9·55				
7057	20 23 45·2	12 8·4	10 27·0	12 8·5	12 8·45	N. 4 20—1 15·45				
7207	20 42 37·0	11 30·6	13 26·8	11 30·5	11 30·55	S. 0 25—1 30·25				
Anon.	20 55 55·3	12 19·5	10 23·5	12 19·4	12 19·45	N. 4 15—1 29·95	30·165	57·6		53·0
Anon.	21 3 6·2	11 32·5	14 5·05	11 32·5	12 32·5	N. 3 35+2 6·55				
7386	21 10 51·2	11 13·7	7 32·0	11 13·8	11 13·75	N. 1 10—3 15·75				
Anon.	21 14 54·1	11 22·1	7 25·8	11 22·1	11 22·1	N. 4 10—3 30·3	30·160	58·0		52·3
Anon.	21 28 2·3	12 8·5	10 27·8	12 8·7	12 8·6	N. 3 35—1 14·8				
7557	21 38 1·8	11 26·5	8 29·95	11 26·6	11 26·55	N. 0 15—2 30·8	30·165	57·7		51·7
7657	21 54 13·3	12 3·6	12 31·3	12 3·6	12 3·6	N. 4 45+0 27·7				
Anon.	21 58 4·4	12 3·0	14 1·9	12 3·6	12 3·6	N. 4 45+1 32·3	30·160	58·0		51·0
7842	22 25 0·0	11 16·5	9 22·05	11 16·7	11 16·6	N. 0 50—1 28·55			57·3	
7909	22 36 2·2	11 25·7	15 17·9	11 25·7	11 25·7	N. 3 45+3 26·2				
7906	22 46 13·0	11 14·0	12 15·8	11 14·2	11 14·1	N. 0 15+1 1·7				
7992	22 51 22·5	12 15·3	13 26·0	12 15·2	12 15·25	N. 3 30+1 10·75	30·160	57·5		49·0
1802	5 36 17·0	12 18·5	15 16·5	12 18·5	12 18·5	S. 0 15—2 32·0	30·205	56·6		48·7
2203	6 54 46·0	13 3·8	12 26·4	13 3·8	13 3·8	N. 5 10—0 11·4			56·2	

♀ AUGUST 25, 1848.—FACE OF SECTOR EAST.

Number of B.A.C.	Time by Chronometer.	Micr. for Plumb-line on Dct.	Micr. for Observation of Star.	Micr. for Plumb-line on Dot.	Mean of Micr. for Plumb-line on Dot.	Star's Apparent Zenith Distance.	Barom.	Thermometers. Attd.	Lower.	Out.
5227	15	11 26·9	14 6·9	11 26·0	11 26·0	N. 0 45+2 14·0			58·6	58·4
5272	15 49 41·2	12 27·0	12 23·4	12 27·0	12 27·0	N. 5 10—0 3·6	30·194	58·6		58·3
5374	16 3 47·0	12 13·4	12 30·4	12 13·4	12 13·4	N. 4 55+0 17·0				57·4
5435	16 12 8·0	12 25·2	10 29·4	12 25·1	12 25·1	N. 3 25—1 29·7	30·203	58·7		57·3
5632	16 42 32·8	12 18·6	13 4·1	12 18·5	12 18·55	S. 0 5—0 19·55				55·6
5817	17 9 23·3	13 15·3	16 29·0	13 15·1	13 15·2	N. 1 25+3 13·8				
5915	17 25 32·5	12 24·3	16 4·4	12 24·1	12 24·2	S. 3 5—3 14·2	30·215	58·7		53·6
5070	17	11 27·6	10 30·2	11 28·0	11 27·8	S. 5 0+0 31·6				53·6
6186	18 9 35·8	11 26·4	8 13·8	11 26·5	11 26·55	S. 2 50+3 12·75				
6233	18 16 19·0	11 32·7	10 13·2	11 32·5	11 32·6	S. 0 30+1 19·4				
6285	18 23 19·5	12 4·1	14 2·6	12 4·0	12 4·05	N. 0 50—2 32·55	30·225	58·4		53·2
6305	18 26 12·7	12 3·9	9 28·9	12 3·9	12 3·9	N. 0 50—2 9·0				53·1

FACE OF SECTOR WEST.

Number of B.A.C.	Time by Chronometer.	Micr. for Plumb-line on Dct.	Micr. for Observation of Star.	Micr. for Plumb-line on Dot.	Mean of Micr. for Plumb-line on Dot.	Star's Apparent Zenith Distance.	Barom.	Thermometers. Attd.	Lower.	Out.
6414	18 45 6·3	12 6·8	9 6·0	12 6·5	12 6·65	N. 3 0+3 0·65	30·230	58·4		52·3
6480	18 55 6·2	12 7·1	10 32·7	12 6·9	12 7·0	N. 3 50+1 8·3				
6525	19 0 5·5	12 19·5	13 31·2	12 19·1	12 19·3	N. 5 5—1 11·0	30·233	58·3		51·7
6639	19 19 30·0	12 6·8	14 3·6	12 7·2	12 7·0	N. 3 55—1 30·6				
6753	19 37 57·2	12 5·0	11 6·4	12 5·2	12 5·1	N. 2 40+0 32·7	30·234	58·3		51·2
6948	20 8 34·5	12 5·6	14 31·6	12 5·8	12 5·7	N. 3 30—2 25·9	30·235	58·5		50·0
7011	20 17 32·2	11 31·7	7 10·05	11 31·9	11 31·8	N. 4 20+4 21·75				
7026	20 19 23·5	11 31·8	7 15·5	11 31·0	11 31·85	N. 4 20+4 16·35				49·7

Aug 24.—Opaque atmosphere.

♀ AUGUST 25, 1848.—FACE OF SECTOR WEST—(continued).

Number of B.A.C.	Time by Chronometer.	Micr. for Plumb-line on Dot.	Micr. for Observation of Star.	Micr. for Plumb-line on Dot.	Mean of Micr. for Plumb-line on Dot.	Star's Apparent Zenith Distance.	Barom.	Attd.	Lower	Out.
	h m s	rev. pts.	rev. pts.	rev. pts.	rev. pts.	o ' rev. pts.	In.			
7057	20 23 48·0	11 31·8	13 7·3	11 31·6	11 31·7	N. 4 20—1 9·6				49·7
Anon.	20 55 57·5	10 1·7	11 23·4	10 1·5	10 1·6	N. 4 15—1 21·8				
Anon.	21 3 9·0	10 6·1	7 28·7	10 5·9	10 6·0	N. 3 35+2 11·3				
7386	21 10 55·5	10 1·5	13 10·5	10 1·3	10 1·4	N. 1 10—3 9·1	30·230	58·0		48·5
Anon.	21 14 57·5	9 13·0	13 3·7	9 13·2	9 13·1	N. 4 10—3 24·6				
Anon.	21 28 5·5	9 13·5	10 22·4	9 13·5	9 13·5	N. 3 35—1 8·9				
7557	21 38 5·4	9 31·5	12 22·2	9 31·3	9 31·4	N. 0 15—2 24·8				
7057	21 54 15·5	10 30·7	9 32·0	10 30·9	10 30·8	N. 4 45+0 32·8				
Anon.	21 58 6·5	10 30·9	8 26·5	10 30·9	10 30·9	N. 4 45+2 4·4	30·220	57·8		48·2
7842	22 25 3·5	10 14·0	12 2·3	10 14·0	10 14·0	N. 0 50—1 22·3				47·7
7909	22 36 5·0	9 25·5	5 27·3	9 25·5	9 25·5	N. 3 45+3 32·2				
7966	22 46 16·5	11 20·7	10 13·0	11 20·9	11 20·8	N. 0 15+1 7·8				
7092	22 51 25·3	11 14·0	9 32·7	11 15·0	11 14·95	N. 3 30+1 16·25	30·220	57·0	57·2	47·8
1802	5 36 20·8	11 11·2	8 5·7	11 11·4	11 11·3	S. 0 15—3 5·6	30·220	56·3	55·1	44·2
2293	6 54 48·2	11 0·7	11 7·2	11 0·3	11 0·5	N. 5 10—0 6·7				

♄ AUGUST 26, 1848.—FACE OF SECTOR WEST.

5735	16 57 7·0	11 1·9	7 21·3	11 2·1	11 2·0	0 0+3 14·7				54·3
5817	17 9 27·0	11 12·8	7 27·0	11 12·7	11 12·75	N. 1 25—3 19·75				54·0
5915	17 25 36·5	12 4·6	8 18·9	12 4·6	12 4·6	S. 3 5—3 19·7	30·174	58·4	57·8	54·0
5970	17 33 18·5	12 15·2	13 10·4	12 15·0	12 15·1	S. 5 0+0 29·3	30·170	58·4		53·9
6186	18 9 39·8	11 26·0	15 0·6	11 26·0	11 26·0	S. 2 50+3 8·6	30·161	58·2		53·6
6233	18 16 22·7	11 7·1	12 20·5	11 7·1	11 7·1	S. 0 30+1 13·4				

FACE OF SECTOR EAST.

6489	18 55 14·5	11 23·3	12 26·75	11 23·3	11 23·3	N. 3 50+1 3·45				
6525	19 0 14·2	11 7·2	9 25·0	11 7·0	11 7·1	N. 5 5—1 16·1	30·168	58·0		53·3
6939	19 19 38·4	11 11·0	9 9·1	11 10·9	11 10·95	S. 3 55—2 1·85			58·0	
6948	20 8 42·8	11 25·8	8 29·3	11 25·0	11 25·7	N. 3 30—2 30·4	30·155	58·0		53·7
7011	20 17 41·0	13 9·8	17 26·8	13 10·0	13 9·9	N. 4 20+4 16·9				
7026	20 19 32·0	13 9·9	17 19·9	13 9·9	13 9·9	N. 4 20+4 10·0				
7057	20 23 57·0	13 9·0	11 28·7	13 9·9	13 9·9	N. 4 20—1 15·2				

FACE OF SECTOR WEST.

7207	20 42 46·0	12 14·3	10 13·0	12 14·5	12 14·4	S. 0 25—2 1·4				

FACE OF SECTOR EAST.

Anon.	20 56 6·7	12 29·1	10 33·3	12 28·9	12 29·0	N. 4 15—1 29·7	30·160	58·0		52·8
Anon.	21 3 17·0	12 20·2	14 27·4	12 20·0	12 20·1	N. 3 35+2 7·3				
7386	21 11 2·5	12 9·1	8 27·4	12 9·2	12 9·15	N. 1 10—3 15·75				
Anon.	21 15 6·2		9 1·0	12 31·0		N. 4 10—3 30·6	30·154	58·0	57·9	51·4
Anon.	21 26 13·6	12 22·5	11 7·8	12 22·5	12 22·5	N. 3 35—1 14·7	30·155	58·0		50·5
7557	21 38 13·2	12 4·5	9 7·95	12 4·9	12 4·7	N. 0 15—2 30·75				50·5
7057	21 54 24·3	12 30·4	13 23·8	12 30·3	12 30·35	N. 4 45+0 27·45				
Anon.	21 58 15·4	12 30·3	14 28·75	12 30·3	12 30·3	N. 4 45+1 32·45				
7842	22 25 11·2	11 29·1	10 0·5	11 29·0	11 29·05	N. 0 50—1 28·55				
7900	22 36 13·1	11 29·7	15 21·8	11 29·5	11 29·6	N. 3 45+3 26·2			57·6	49·8
7966	22 46 24·2	10 30·0	11 31·55	10 30·2	10 30·1	N. 0 15+1 1·45				
7992	22 51 33·5	11 0·9	12 11·0	11 0·8	11 0·85	N. 3 30+1 10·15	30·140	57·5		50·0

Aug. 25.—Good definitions.
26.—Beautiful definitions.

⊙ AUGUST 27, 1848.—FACE OF SECTOR EAST.

Number of B.A.C.	Time by Chronometer.	Micr. for Plumb-line on Dot.	Micr. for Observation of Star.	Micr. for Plumb-line on Dot.	Mean of Micr. for Plumb-line on Dot.	Star's Apparent Zenith Distance.	Barom.	Thermometers. Attd.	Lower.	Out.
5508	16 23 51·8	11 1·9	9 6·2	11 1·9	11 1·0	S. 0 25+1 29·7		58·3		
5735	16 57 14·2	10 31·9	14 7·6	10 32·3	10 32·1	0 0+3 9·5				
5817	17 9 34·5	10 15·0	13 28·4	10 14·6	10 14·8	N. 1 25+3 13·6				
5970	17 34 26·5	9 24·8	8 26·7	9 24·0	9 24·85	S. 5 0+0 32·15				
6186	18 9 47·0	9 22·5	6 10·6	9 22·5	9 22·5	S. 2 50+3 11·9				
6233	18 16 30·0	10 33·6	9 14·7	10 33·5	10 33·55	S. 0 30+1 18·85				
Anon.	21 28 19·5	12 31·8	11 16·3	12 31·8	12 31·8	N. 3 35—1 15·5				
7557	21 38 18·8	12 14·5	9 17·75	12 14·4	12 14·45	N. 0 15—2 30·7				

FACE OF SECTOR WEST.

Number of B.A.C.	Time by Chronometer.	Micr. for Plumb-line on Dot.	Micr. for Observation of Star.	Micr. for Plumb-line on Dot.	Mean of Micr. for Plumb-line on Dot.	Star's Apparent Zenith Distance.	Barom.	Thermometers. Attd.	Lower.	Out.
5632	16 42 41·6	11 11·9	10 20·5	11 12·1	11 12·0	S. 0 5—0 25·5		58·0		48·6
6948	20 8 45·7	10 23·8	13 15·5	10 24·0	10 23·9	N. 3 30—2 25·6	30·192			
7011	20 17 43·5	10 29·4	6 7·5	10 29·4	10 29·4	N. 4 20+4 21·9				
7026	20 19 34·5	10 29·5	6 15·45	10 29·4	10 29·45	N. 4 20+4 14·0				
7057	20 23 59·5	10 29·4	12 5·8	10 29·4	10 29·4	N. 4 20—1 10·4				
Anon.	20 56 9·0	10 19·3	12 9·1	10 19·5	10 19·4	N. 4 15—1 20·7				
Anon.	21 3 20·2	10 14·6	8 2·4	10 14·5	10 14·55	N. 3 35+2 12·15				
7657	21 54 27·5	11 33·0	11 1·2	11 32·9	11 32·95	N. 4 45+0 31·75				
Anon.	21 58 19·0	11 33·0	9 29·0	11 33·0	11 33·0	N. 4 45+2 4·0				
7842	22 25 13·8	11 33·6	13 23·5	11 33·5	11 33·55	N. 0 50—1 23·95		56·8		
7909	22 36 16·2	12 7·5	8 9·6	12 7·5	12 7·5	N. 3 45+3 31·9				
7966	22 46 27·8	13 0·0	11 26·0	13 0·0	13 0·0	N. 0 15+1 8·0				
7992	22 51 37·0	12 21·3	11 5·3	12 21·4	12 21·35	N. 3 30+1 16·05				
1802	5 36 32·0	11 30·6	8 25·0	11 30·6	11 30·6	S. 0 15—3 5·6	30·180	56·5	56·0	52·7
2208	6 54 59·2	11 24·5	11 29·8	11 24·3	11 24·4	N. 5 10—0 5·4	30·205	57·0		56·5

☾ AUGUST 28, 1848. —FACE OF SECTOR EAST.

Number of B.A.C.	Time by Chronometer.	Micr. for Plumb-line on Dot.	Micr. for Observation of Star.	Micr. for Plumb-line on Dot.	Mean of Micr. for Plumb-line on Dot.	Star's Apparent Zenith Distance.	Barom.	Thermometers. Attd.	Lower.	Out.
4686	14 0 14·5	11 23·6	9 14·3	11 23·4	11 23·5	S. 1 40+2 9·2	30·175	59·5		62·8
5632	16 42 49·5	11 7·7	11 26·75	11 7·5	11 7·6	S. 0 5+0 19·15				55·6
5735	16 57 20·1	11 5·4	14 15·4	11 5·5	11 5·45	0 0+3 9·95	30·215	58·8		55·3
5915	17 25 49·8	11 7·0	14 21·75	11 7·2	11 7·1	S. 3 5—3 14·65			59·4	
5970	17 34 32·2	11 2·1	10 3·45	11 2·2	11 2·15	S. 5 0+0 32·7	30·218	58·7		54·4
6186	18 9 53·0	11 1·4	7 22·95	11 1·6	11 1·5	S. 2 50+3 12·55				53·4
6233	18 16 36·0	11 11·3	9 25·55	11 11·2	11 11·25	S. 0 30+1 19·7			59·0	53·3
6948	20 8 53·6	12 11·0	9 14·4	12 10·9	12 10·9	N. 3 30—2 30·5	30·245	58·5		51·0
7011	20 17 52·5	12 13·0	16 29·15	12 13·2	12 13·1	N. 4 20+4 16·05			58·0	
7026	20 19 43·0	12 13·1	16 22·5	12 13·1	12 13·1	N. 4 20+4 9·4				
7057	20 24 7·8	12 13·1	10 31·3	12 13·1	12 13·1	N. 4 20—1 15·8				
Anon.	20 56 18·2	12 3·6	10 7·8	12 3·6	12 3·6	N. 4 15—1 29·9	30·251	58·4		51·3
Anon.	21 3 28·2	11 20·5	13 27·3	11 20·5	11 20·5	N. 3 35+2 6·8			58·2	
Anon.	21 15 17·3	11 3·1	7 6·0	11 3·1	11 3·1	N. 4 10—3 31·1	30·255	58·3		51·5
Anon.	21 28 25·1	11 14·7	0 32·6	11 14·5	11 14·6	N. 3 35—1 16·0				
7557	21 38 24·5	11 11·0	8 14·4	11 11·4	11 11·2	N. 0 15—2 30·8	30·260	58·4	58·2	51·8
7657	21 54 35·8	11 9·8	12 3·0	11 9·8	11 9·8	N. 4 45+0 27·2	30·250	58·0		51·4
Anon.	21 58 58·5	11 9·8	13 7·1	11 9·8	11 9·8	N. 4 45+1 31·3				
7909	22 36 25·2	11 26·6	15 18·9	11 26·6	11 26·6	N. 3 45+3 6·3				
7966	22 46 35·5	11 9·9	12 11·55	11 9·9	11 9·9	N. 0 15+1 1·65			58·0	
7992	22 51 45·2	11 20·9	12 33·0	11 20·7	11 20·8	N. 3 30+1 12·2	30·254	57·9		50·6

♂ AUGUST 29, 1848.—FACE OF SECTOR WEST.

4686	14 0 17·5	11 7·4	13 10·9	11 7·2	11 7·3	S. 1 40+2 3·6	30·264	59·6		62·7

Aug. 27.—Good definitions until 22ʰ chronometer time.
The seconds of transit doubtful of Anon. 20ʰ 56ᵐ and 21ʰ 58ᵐ.
28.—Anon. 21ʰ 58ᵐ.—The seconds of transit doubtful.
Good definitions on the 28th.

♂ AUGUST 29, 1848.—FACE OF SECTOR WEST—(continued).

Number of B.A.C.	Time by Chronometer.	Micr. for Plumb-line on Dot.	Micr. for Observation of Star.	Micr. for Plumb-line on Dot.	Mean of Micr. for Plumb-line on Dot.	Star's Apparent Zenith Distance.	Barom.	Therm. Attd.	Therm. Lower.	Therm. Out.
	h m s	rev. pts.	rev. pts.	rev. pts.	rev. pts.	° ′ rev. pts.	in.			
5508	16 24 1·3	11 5·7	12 29·2	11 5·9	11 5·8	S. 0 25+1 23·4	30·249	59·4	59·1	57·4
5915	17 25 53·2	11 21·5	8 2·6	11 21·4	11 21·45	S. 3 5—3 18·85			58·8	
5970	17 34 35·0	12 4·4	12 33·0	12 4·0	12 4·2	S. 5 0+0 28·8				56·6
6186	18 9 56·5	12 14·0	15 22·95	12 13·9	12 13·95	S. 2 50+3 9·0	30·270	59·0		56·5
6233	18 16 39·7	12 4·8	13 18·4	12 4·6	12 4·7	S. 0 30+1 13·7				56·4
Anon.	20 56 20·2	11 25·0	13 14·8	11 25·0	11 25·0	N. 4 15—1 23·8	30·265	58·6	58·0	54·4
7657	21 54 38·0	12 1·4	11 3·8	11 1·3	11 1·35	N. 4 45+0 31·55	30·257	58·5		53·6
Anon.	21 58 29·3	12 1·2	9 31·6	12 1·4	12 1·3	N. 4 45+2 3·7				
7842	22 25 26·1	12 0·1	13 24·0	12 0·2	12 0·15	N. 0 50—1 23·85			57·6	
7909	22 36 27·5	12 5·4	8 8·0	12 5·4	12 5·4	N. 3 45+3 31·4				
7966	22 46 39·7	12 0·5	10 27·8	12 0·7	12 0·6	N. 0 15+1 6·8				
7992	22 51 48·5	12 23·5	11 8·7	12 23·3	12 23·4	N. 3 30+1 14·7	30·252	58·0		52·5
1802	5 36 44·2	12 16·5	9 10·7	12 16·5	12 16·5	S. 0 15—3 5·8	30·248	57·8	56·6	53·3
2293	6 55 11·8	12 4·2	12 9·5	12 4·0	12 4·1	N. 5 10—0 5·4	30·260	58·0		57·0

♀ AUGUST 30, 1848.—FACE OF SECTOR EAST.

Number of B.A.C.	Time by Chronometer.	Micr. for Plumb-line on Dot.	Micr. for Observation of Star.	Micr. for Plumb-line on Dot.	Mean of Micr. for Plumb-line on Dot.	Star's Apparent Zenith Distance.	Barom.	Therm. Attd.	Therm. Lower.	Therm. Out.
5915	17 26 0·8	11 23·7	15 3·6	11 23·7	11 23·7	S. 3 5—3 13·9			58·8	
5970	17 34 43·5	11 0·1	10 1·0	11 0·0	11 0·05	S. 5 0+0 33·05	30·250	58·8		53·4
6186	18 10 4·0	10 23·9	7 11·0	10 24·1	10 24·0	S. 2 50+3 13·0	30·258	58·7	58·4	53·2
6233	18 16 47·8	11 20·0	9 33·5	11 20·0	11 20·0	S. 0 30+1 20·5				
Anon.	19 24 13·0	12 22·6	8 29·7	12 22·8	12 22·7	N. 4 10—3 27·0				
Anon.	20 27 11·5	12 23·0	8 28·45	12 23·0	12 23·0	N. 4 10—3 28·55	30·275	58·2		53·4
Anon.	20 36 41·8	13 0·8	10 33·5	13 0·9	13 0·85	N. 4 0—2 1·35			58·0	
Anon.	20 56 29·3	13 13·3	11 16·2	13 13·1	13 13·2	N. 4 15—1 31·0				
Anon.	21 3 39·5	13 7·5	15 13·0	13 7·5	13 7·5	N. 3 35+2 5·5	30·282	58·0		53·6
7657	21 54 47·1	13 8·3	13 33·4	13 8·1	13 8·2	N. 4 45+0 25·2				
Anon.	21 58 38·2	13 8·0	15 4·8	13 8·2	13 8·1	N. 4 45+1 30·7			57·8	
7842	22 25 34·3	12 24·9	10 28·5	12 25·0	12 24·95	N. 0 50—1 30·45				
7909	22 36 35·5	12 28·3	16 19·2	12 28·2	12 28·25	N. 3 45+3 24·95				
7992	22 51 56·1	13 18·2	14 28·6	13 18·1	13 18·15	N. 3 30+1 10·45	30·290	58·0	57·8	52·7
1802	5 36 50·2	13 8·1	16 6·45	13 8·2	13 8·15	S. 0 15—2 32·3	30·284	58·0	57·0	55·0
2293	6 55 20·0	13 18·6	13 7·8	13 18·6	13 18·6	N. 5 10—0 10·8	30·288	58·0		57·5

♃ AUGUST 31, 1848.—FACE OF SECTOR WEST.

Number of B.A.C.	Time by Chronometer.	Micr. for Plumb-line on Dot.	Micr. for Observation of Star.	Micr. for Plumb-line on Dot.	Mean of Micr. for Plumb-line on Dot.	Star's Apparent Zenith Distance.	Barom.	Therm. Attd.	Therm. Lower.	Therm. Out.
5915	17 26 5·2	12 33·1	9 13·95	12 33·2	12 33·15	S. 3 5—3 19·2			59·2	57·8
5970	17 34 47·0	13 2·9	13 31·4	13 2·9	13 2·9	S. 5 0+0 28·5	30·220	59·4		57·8
6186	18 10 8·0	12 4·2	14 33·0	11 24·1	11 24·15	S. 2 50+3 8·85				57·5
6233	18 16 51·3	11 14·2	12 27·6	11 14·2	11 14·2	S. 0 30+1 13·4			59·0	57·4
Anon.	19 24 15·5	10 27·3	14 16·0	10 27·2	10 27·25	N. 4 10—3 23·35	30·220	59·2		56·5
Anon.	20 27 14·8	10 27·2	14 15·9	10 27·2	10 27·2	N. 4 10—3 22·7				
Anon.	20 36 45·0	10 24·0	12 20·15	10 24·2	10 24·2	N. 4 0—1 30·05	30·211	58·8	58·8	55·1
Anon.	21 58 41·0	9 33·5	7 29·5	9 33·5	9 33·5	N. 4 45+2 4·0				
7842	22 25 37·8	11 9·8	12 33·2	11 9·9	11 9·85	N. 0 50—1 23·35				
7909	22 36 39·2	11 10·5	7 14·1	11 10·5	11 10·5	N. 3 45+3 30·4				54·4
7992	22 51 59·7	10 26·8	9 11·9	10 26·7	10 26·75	N. 3 30+1 14·85	30·200	58·7	58·2	53·4

FACE OF SECTOR EAST.

Number of B.A.C.	Time by Chronometer.	Micr. for Plumb-line on Dot.	Micr. for Observation of Star.	Micr. for Plumb-line on Dot.	Mean of Micr. for Plumb-line on Dot.	Star's Apparent Zenith Distance.	Barom.	Therm. Attd.	Therm. Lower.	Therm. Out.
5508	16	12 21·0	10 24·05	12 21·0	12 21·0	S. 0 25+1 30·95	30·218	59·6	59·2	58·0
1802	5 36 56·9	12 27·6	15 26·6	12 27·7	12 27·65	S. 0 15—2 32·95	30·164	58·0	57·2	50·5
2293	6 55 26·2	13 20·0	13 8·9	13 20·0	13 20·0	N. 5 10—0 11·1			57·2	

Aug. 29.—Anon. 21ʰ 58ᵐ.—The seconds of transit doubtful.
Good definitions on the 29th and 30th.

♄ September 2, 1848.—Face of Sector East.

Number of B.A C.	Time by Chronometer.	Micr. for Plumb-line on Dot.	Micr. for Observation of Star.	Micr. for Plumb-line on Dot.	Mean of Micr. for Plumb-line on Dot.	Star's Apparent Zenith Distance.	Barom	Thermometers.		
								Att.	Lower.	Out.
	h m s	rev. pts.	rev. pts.	rev. pts.	rev. pts.	° ' rev. pts.	in.			
5015	17		16 32·2	13 18·4		S. 3 5—3 19·8	30·220	60·0	59·8	59·6
5970	17 34 59·5	11 3·2	10 5·6	11 3·4	11 3·6	S. 5 0—0 32·0			59·4	
Anon.	20 36 59·0	13 10·3	11 7·3	13 10·3	13 10·3	N. 4 0—2 3·0	30·214	59·6		58·3
7842	22 25 51·2	12 28·6	10 31·7	12 28·6	12 28·6	N. 0 50—1 30·9				
7909	22 36 53·5	13 18·0	17 9·2	13 18·2	13 18·1	N. 3 45+3 25·1	30·184	59·8	59·4	56·8

END OF THE UNREDUCED SECTOR OBSERVATIONS.

Sept. 2.—No. 5970 and Anon. 20ʰ 36ᵐ.—The seconds of transit doubtful: bad images.

EXAMINATION OF THE RUNS

OF THE

SECTOR MICROMETER

AT

THE SEVERAL LATITUDE STATIONS.

Examination for Run of the Sector Micrometer at Heerelogements Berg.

JUNE 1843.

ARCH TO THE RIGHT.					ARCH TO THE LEFT.				
° '	rev. pts.	rev. pts.	rev. pts.	rev. pts.	° '	rev. pts.	rev. pts.	rev. pts.	rev. pts.
0· 0	5·12·1	8·32·10	6· 0·2	8·31·90	0· 0	15·20·0	8·30·50	15·20·7	8·30·40
5	14·10·2		14·32·1		5	0·23·5		6·24·3	
5	4·18·3	8·31·15	5·28·6	8·31·40	5	15·20·5	8·31·60	14·23·6	8·31·70
10	13·15·45		14·26·0		10	6·22·9		5·25·9	
10	6·25·1	8·32·30	6· 0·0	8·32·20	10	15·27·4	8·31·70	14·11·4	8·31·50
15	15·23·4		14·32·2		15	6·29·7		5·13·9	
15	4·26·2	8·32·10	6· 2·9	8·31·50	15	15·20·6	8·31·90	14· 9·75	8·31·50
20	13·24·3		15· 0·4		20	0·22·7		5·12·25	
20	4·24·5	8·32·50	6·10·9	8·32·00	20	15·27·15	8·31·40	14·18·4	8·31·50
25	13·23·0		15· 8·9		25	6·29·75		5·20·9	
25	5· 4·8	8·31·60	5·30·05	8·31·60	25	15·19·9	8·31·60	14·20·0	8·30·85
30	14· 2·4		14·27·65		30	6·22·3		5·23·15	
30	5·10·6	8·31·70	0· 4·0	8·32·20	30	15·29·1	8·32·60	14·32·8	8·31·50
35	14· 8·3		15· 2·2		35	6·30·5		6· 1·3	
35	5·16·3	8·31·30	5·31·85	8·31·35	35	15·28·8	8·31·30	14·28·4	8·32·10
40	14·13·6		14·29·2		40	6·31·5		5·30·3	
40	5· 9·3	8·31·90	5·30·4	8·32·90	40	16· 3·1	8·31·60	15· 1·0	8·31·30
45	14· 7·2		14·29·3		45	7· 5·5		6· 3·7	
45	5· 5·85	8·30·75	6· 0·95	8·30·75	45	17· 0·4	8·31·60	14·22·5	8·31·80
50	14· 2·6		14·31·7		50	8· 2·8		5·24·7	
50	5· 3·15	8·32·45	4·25·2	8·33·25	50	17· 9·0	8·32·50	15· 1·75	8·31·65
55	14· 1·6		13·24·45		55	8·10·5		6· 4·1	
0·55	6· 7·45	8·31·35	4·24·3	8·30·70	0·55	15·29·95	8·31·95	15· 0·75	8·31·95
1· 0	15· 4·8		13·21·0		1· 0	6·32·0		6· 2·8	
1· 0	5·27·45	8·31·55							
1· 5	14·25·0								
	Mean = 8·31·750		Mean = 8·31·813			Mean = 8·31·688		Mean = 8·31·479	

                                             rev. pts.

Value of the mean 5' of the first degree of the Arch, right and left, = 8·31·6825
But the value for 5' of the first degree, is less than the value for the mean 5' of 5° 30' right and left (see page 226) by . .   ·0979

Value employed for reducing the observations at the Heercloge- } = 8·31·7804
ments Berg Station . . . .

$$1 = \frac{300 \times 34}{303\cdot7804} = 33^{r}\cdot5769$$

$$1 = 0^{r}\cdot987555$$

The above experiments were made on the 1st and 3rd of June.
Temperature on the 1st = 61°.
    "   on the 3rd = 54°.

Examination for the Run of the Sector Micrometer at the Kamies Berg Station.

AUGUST 7, 1843.—TEMPERATURE 59°.

ARCH TO THE RIGHT.

° '	rev. pts		rev. pts	
0· 0	10·26·3	8·32·10	7·12·25	8·31·65
0· 5	19·24·4		16· 9·9	
0· 5	9·19·5	8·31·35	6·16·85	8·31·35
0·10	18·16·85		15·14·2	
0·10	8·15·3	8·32·15	6·10·0	8·32·70
0·15	17·13·45		15· 8·7	
0·15	8·31·2	8·31·95	6·18·25	8·31·65
0·20	17·29·15		15·15·9	
0·20	8· 1·5	8·32·20	6·15·25	8·32·35
0·25	16·33·7		15·13·6	
0·25	6·12·2	8·31·30	6· 2·4	8·31·20
0·30	15· 9·5		14·33·6	
0·30	6·25·4	8·32·30	6· 5·85	8·31·95
0·35	15·23·7		15· 3·8	
0·35	6· 3·5	8·31·15	5·29·35	8·31·65
0·40	15· 0·65		14·27·0	
0·40	5·32·75	8·32·55	5·22·6	8·32·60
0·45	14·31·8		14·21·2	
0·45	6·22·9	8·30·70	5·23·8	8·30·80
0·50	15·19·6		14·20·6	
0·50	6·18·9	8·33·27	5·27·25	8·33·05
0·55	15·18·17		14·26·3	
0·55	5·29·15	8·31·15	5·30·6	8·30·90
1· 0	14·26·3		14·27·5	

Mean = 8·31·8475   Mean = 8·31·8208

8·31·8342

ARCH TO THE LEFT.

° '	rev. pts	
0· 0	14·29·7	8·31·20
0· 5	5·32·5	
0· 5	15·27·3	8·31·85
0·10	6·29·45	
0·10	15·12·4	8·31·45
0·15	6·14·95	
0·15	15· 8·5	8·31·42
0·20	6·11·08	
0·20	15·13·9	8·31·20
0·25	6·16·7	
0·25	15·22·3	8·31·10
0·30	6·25·2	
0·30	15·12·75	8·31·57
0·35	6·15·18	
0·35	15·13·5	8·31·85
0·40	6·15·65	
0·40	15·11·7	8·30·85
0·45	6·14·85	
0·45	15· 9·7	8·31·65
0·50	6·12·05	
0·50	15·15·3	8·31·55
0·55	6·17·75	
0·55	15·11·3	8·31·75
1· 0	6·13·55	

Mean = 8·31·4534

AUGUST 13, 1843.—TEMPERATURE 45°.

ARCH TO THE RIGHT.

° '	rev. pts	
5·30	13·20·3	8·31·95
5·25	4·22·35	
5·25	14· 1·3	8·31·65
5·20	5· 3·65	
5·20	14·21·3	8·32·20
5·15	5·23·1	
5·15	15· 0·9	8·32·40
5·10	6· 2·5	
5·10	15·24·6	8·32·10
5· 5	6·26·5	
5· 5	16· 8·5	8·31·40
5· 0	7·11·1	

Mean = 8·31·95

ARCH TO THE LEFT.

° '	rev. pts	
5·30	6·28·85	8·32·15
5·25	15·27·0	
5·25	6·13·2	8·31·00
5·20	15·10·2	
5·20	6·17·78	8·32·52
5·15	15·16·3	
5·15	5·33·3	8·31·10
5·10	14·30·4	
5·10	5·26·65	8·30·45
5· 5	14·23·1	
5· 5	6·26·2	8·32·30
5· 0	15·24·5	

Mean = 8·31·59

Mean of right and left, = 8·31·77

Value for the mean 5' of the first degree, right and left, . .   = 8·31·6438
But (page 226) this value is less than for the mean 5' of 5° 30' right, and
5° 30' left, or 11 degrees of the arch, by . . . . .   ·0979
Value employed for reducing the observations at the Kamies Berg Station, = 8·31·7417

$$1 = \frac{300 \times 34}{303·7417} = 33''·5812$$

$$1 = 0''·987681$$

Examination for the Run of the Sector Micrometer at the Royal Observatory.

JUNE 5, 1844.—TEMPERATURE 60°.

ARCH TO THE RIGHT.

	0′ to 1°.		1° to 2°.		2° to 3°.	
° ′	rev. pts.	rev. pts.	rev. pts.	rev. pts.	rev. pts.	rev. pts.
0	5·10·9		6·25·4		6· 3·9	
5	14·17·0	8·32·00	15·22·5	8·31·10	15· 2·1	8·32·20
5	6· 1·45		6·29·6		5·27·4	
10	14·32·75	8·31·30	15·28·0	8·32·40	14·25·6	8·32·20
10	5·30·55		7·10·8		5·15·45	
15	14·29·4	8·32·85	16· 8·6	8·31·80	14·13·5	8·32·05
15	5·14·45		6· 7·45		5· 6·25	
20	14·11·85	8·31·40	15· 5·2	8·31·75	14· 3·8	8·31·55
20	6· 9·55		5·23·9		4·20·45	
25	15· 7·6	8·32·05	14·21·6	8·31·70	13·17·8	8·31·35
25	6·20·3		5· 8·55		5· 2·5	
30	15·17·5	8·31·20	14· 5·8	8·31·25	13·33·8	8·31·30
30	7· 0·35		5·15·4		5·22·4	
35	15·32·8	8·32·45	14·12·5	8·31·10	14·20·4	8·32·00
35	7·10·8		5·31·55		5· 8·85	
40	16· 8·0	8·31·20	14·29·6	8·32·05	14· 6·6	8·31·75
40	7· 2·15		5·30·8		4·28·6	
45	16· 0·6	8·32·45	14·20·3	8·32·50	13·26·7	8·32·10
45	6·20·4		5·33·8		5·24·75	
50	15·16·8	8·30·40	14·31·7	8·31·90	14·22·8	8·32·05
50	6·15·25		5·28·6		5·24·95	
55	15·14·1	8·32·85	14·26·3	8·31·70	14·23·1	8·32·15
55	7· 5·55		5· 3·7		5·18·55	
60	16· 2·0	8·31·35	14· 2·0	8·32·30	14·16·4	8·31·85
	Mean =	8·31·7917	Mean =	8·31·7958	Mean =	8·31·8702

JUNE 6, 1844.—TEMPERATURE 59°.

	3° to 4°.		4° to 5°.		5° to 5°·30′.	
0	5·17·7		5·18·05		4·31·05	
5	14·15·0	8·32·20	14·15·8	8·31·75	13·29·4	8·31·45
5	5·11·15		5·30·6		5· 5·85	
10	14· 8·4	8·31·25	14·28·2	8·31·60	14· 3·5	8·31·65
10	5· 3·7		5·17·45		5·28·35	
15	14· 2·6	8·32·00	14·14·8	8·31·35	14·26·5	8·32·15
15	5· 4·2		5· 4·25		6· 3·5	
20	14· 1·7	8·31·50	14· 1·9	8·31·65	15· 1·4	8·31·90
20	5· 7·6		5·33·0		6·18·15	
25	14· 6·3	8·32·70	14·31·5	8·32·50	15·15·2	8·31·05
25	5·12·45		5·22·05		5·27·7	
30	14· 9·4	8·30·95	14·20·0	8·31·95	14·25·6	8·31·90
30	5·20·2		5·32·35			
35	14·18·6	8·32·40	14·29·6	8·31·25		
35	5·11·3		4·33·3			
40	14· 9·5	8·32·20	13·31·7	8·32·40		
40	5·12·45		4·30·15			
45	14·10·4	8·31·05	13·27·0	8·31·75		
45	5·17·5		5·13·7			
50	14·15·2	8·31·70	14·11·4	8·31·70		
50	5·29·0		5· 9·0			
55	14·27·4	8·32·40	14· 6·5	8·31·50		
55	5·19·8		5· 1·9			
60	14·17·7	8·31·90	14· 0·0	8·32·10		
	Mean =	8·32·0042	Mean =	8·31·7917	Mean =	8·31·6833

Examination for the Run of the Séctor Micrometer at the Royal Observatory—*(continued)*.

JUNE 6, 1844.—TEMPERATURE 60°.

ARCH TO THE LEFT.

° '	0° to 1° rev. pts.	rev. pts.	1° to 2° rev. pts.	rev. pts.	2° to 3° rev. pts.	rev. pts.
0· 0 / 5	15·15·8 / 6·18·9	8·30·90	14·26·8 / 5·29·5	8·31·30	14·31·8 / 5·33·3	8·32·50
5 / 10	15·16·55 / 6·18·9	8·31·65	14·30·05 / 5·31·4	8·32·65	14·33·9 / 6· 2·2	8·31·70
10 / 15	15·21·65 / 6·23·8	8·31·85	14·27·55 / 5·29·6	8·31·95	15· 4·53 / 6· 7·8	8·30·75
15 / 20	15·19·45 / 6·21·4	8·32·05	14·26·6 / 5·27·8	8·32·80	15· 6·35 / 6· 7·4	8·32·95
20 / 25	15·18·2 / 6·20·2	8·32·00	14·27·15 / 5·29·3	8·31·85	15· 5·9 / 6· 8·5	8·31·40
25 / 30	15· 5·6 / 6· 8·2	8·31·40	15· 0·09 / 6· 1·8	8·32·28	15· 3·15 / 6· 4·7	8·32·45
30 / 35	15·14·9 / 6·17·5	8·31·40	14·30·7 / 5·33·2	8·31·50	15· 0·3 / 6· 2·6	8·31·70
35 / 40	15· 9·05 / 6·10·75	8·32·30	15· 2·55 / 6· 4·4	8·32·15	14·30·25 / 5·32·3	8·31·95
40 / 45	15·15·05 / 6·18·6	8·30·45	15· 2·0 / 6· 4·2	8·31·80	15· 0·15 / 6· 3·3	8·30·85
45 / 50	15·23·2 / 6·24·4	8·32·80	14·33·05 / 6· 0·4	8·32·65	15· 1·35 / 6· 2·6	8·32·75
50 / 55	15· 4·05 / 6· 6·4	8·31·65	15· 4·85 / 6· 7·7	8·31·15	14·32·15 / 6· 0·5	8·31·65
55 / 60	14·26·9 / 5·28·6	8·32·30	14·33·5 / 6· 2·3	8·31·20	15· 2·15 / 6· 2·9	8·33·25
	Mean = 8·31·7292		Mean = 8·31·9400		Mean = 8·31·9917	

TEMPERATURE 59°.

° '	3° to 4° rev. pts.	rev. pts.	4° to 5° rev. pts.	rev. pts.	5° to 5°30' rev. pts.	rev. pts.
0 / 5	15· 1·85 / 6· 4·4	8·31·45	15· 3·35 / 6· 6·1	8·31·25	15· 7·7 / 6· 9·4	8·32·30
5 / 10	15· 3·45 / 6· 5·5	8·31·95	14·33·0 / 6· 1·7	8·31·30	15·14·4 / 6·18·2	8·30·20
10 / 15	15·10·2 / 6·12·7	8·31·50	14·30·7 / 5·32·8	8·31·90	15· 7·8 / 6·10·5	8·31·30
15 / 20	15·17·65 / 6·19·8	8·31·85	15· 3·3 / 6· 4·4	8·32·90	15· 9·93 / 6·10·9	8·33·03
20 / 25	14·31·25 / 5·32·3	8·32·95	15· 6·15 / 6· 8·4	8·31·75	15· 5·94 / 6· 8·5	8·31·44
25 / 30	15· 4·85 / 6· 7·2	8·31·65	15·15·55 / 6·18·3	8·31·25	15· 5·1 / 6· 6·8	8·32·30
30 / 35	15· 3·9 / 6· 6·0	8·31·90	15·14·45 / 6·17·0	8·31·45		
35 / 40	15· 9·25 / 6·11·5	8·31·75	15·11·25 / 6·13·4	8·31·85		
40 / 45	15· 2·75 / 6· 4·5	8·32·25	15·10·4 / 6·12·5	8·31·90		
45 / 50	14·32·4 / 6· 1·1	8·31·30	15· 7·55 / 6· 9·7	8·31·85		
50 / 55	14·30·05 / 5·30·3	8·33·75	15·13·45 / 6·15·0	8·32·45		
55 / 60	14·32·9 / 6· 1·2	8·31·70	15·14·4 / 6·16·7	8·31·70		
	Mean = 8·32·0000		Mean = 8·31·7958		Mean = 8·31·7617	

3 L

Examination for the Run of the Sector Micrometer at the Royal Observatory—*(continued)*.

Calculation of the value for the mean 5′ of the Arch, from 5° 30′ right to 5° 30′ left.

° ° ′	RIGHT.	LEFT.	MEANS.	DIFFERENCES, from 8·31·8584.
	rev. pts.	*rev. pts.*	*rev. pts.*	*pts.*
0 to 1·0	8·31·7917	8·31·7292	8·31·7605	− 0·0979
1 to 2·0	8·31·7958	8·31·9400	8·31·8679	+ ·0095
2 to 3·0	8·31·8792	8·31·9917	8·31·9354	+ ·0770
3 to 4·0	8·32·0042	8·32·0000	8·32·0021	+ ·1437
4 to 5·0	8·31·7917	8·31·7958	8·31·7938	− ·0646
5 to 5·30	8·31·6833	8·31·7617	8·31·7225	− ·1359
			Mean = 8·31·8584	

rev. pts.

In the determination of the mean (= 8·31·8584), the half degree (5°·0′ to 5°·30′), received the weight $\frac{1}{2}$.

$$1 \overset{rev.}{=} \frac{300 \times 34}{303 \cdot 8584} = 33'\cdot5683$$

$$1 \overset{part.}{=} 0'\cdot987302 \quad l_g \cdot 9.904450$$

Which values for 5′ of the Arch were employed in reducing the observations made at the Royal Observatory, from page 38 to page 93.

Examination for the Run of the Sector Micrometer at Zwartkop Station.

OCTOBER 2 AND 3, 1844.

° ′	ARCH TO THE RIGHT rev. pts.	rev. pts.	rev. pts.	ARCH TO THE LEFT rev. pts.	rev. pts.	rev. pts.	rev. pts.	rev. pts.
0· 0	6· 4·4	15· 2·5	8·32·10	7· 9·2	16· 6·0	8·30·80	5·25·78	14·22·9	8·31·12
5									
5	6·31·6	15·28·8	8·31·20	5·33·05	14·30·7	8·31·65	6·30·9	15·28·4	8·31·50
10									
10	6· 5·0	15· 3·7	8·32·70	6·18·5	15·16·15	8·31·65	7· 0·0	15·31·5	8·31·50
15									
15	6· 0·6	14·32·5	8·31·90	7· 5·5	16· 3·25	8·31·75	6·28·9	15·26·6	8·31·70
20									
20	5·22·5	14·20·4	8·31·90	7·13·15	16·10·8	8·31·65	6·15·9	15·13·4	8·31·50
25									
25	6·18·6	15·15·9	8·31·30	7·29·05	16·25·9	8·30·85	6·33·45	15·30·4	8·30·95
30									
30	6·27·2	15·25·4	8·32·20	7·26·65	16·24·2	8·31·55	6·30·85	15·28·3	8·31·45
35									
35	7·10·65	16· 7·5	8·30·85	7·20·9	16·18·9	8·32·00	7· 1·2	15·33·2	8·32·00
40									
40	6·27·6	15·25·7	8·32·10	7· 6·75	16· 3·7	8·30·95	6·25·5	15·22·7	8·31·20
45									
45	5·20·35	14·17·3	8·30·95	5·22·5	14·20·1	8·31·60	6·33·25	15·30·85	8·31·60
50									
50	5·11·1	14· 9·7	8·32·6	5·28·7	14·26·3	8·31·60	6·23·15	15·20·6	8·31·45
55									
55	5· 3·5	14· 0·9	8·31·4	6· 6·6	15· 4·3	8·31·70	6·20·55	15·18·2	8·31·65
1· 0									
	(a) Mean = 8·31·7667			(c) Mean = 8·31·4792			(d) Mean = 8·31·4683		
4· 0	7· 6·8	16· 4·4	8·31·60	6· 7·65	15· 5·1	8·31·45			
5									
5	7· 7·0	16· 4·0	8·31·00	6·15·2	15·12·6	8·31·40			
10									
10	7·21·25	16·18·95	8·31·70	6·27·3	15·24·0	8·30·70			
15									
15	7·18·9	16·16·4	8·31·50	7·10·0	16· 7·85	8·31·85			
20									
20	7·12·3	16·10·0	8·31·70	7·29·0	16·26·15	8·31·15			
25									
25	7· 6·4	16· 3·9	8·31·50	7·21·5	16·18·6	8·31·10			
30									
30	7·30·7	16·27·55	8·30·85	7·10·0	16· 7·2	8·31·20			
35									
35	7·30·5	16·28·8	8·32·30	7·13·1	16·10·5	8·31·40			
40									
40	8·13·5	17·10·6	8·31·10	7·19·95	16·17·7	8·31·75			
45									
45	7·14·8	16·12·6	8·31·80	8· 7·65	17· 4·65	8·31·00			
50									
50	7· 7·1	16· 4·5	8·31·40	7·13·9	16·11·1	8·31·20			
55									
55	6·29·2	15·27·4	8·32·20	6·29·35	15·27·0	8·31·65			
5· 0									
	(b) Mean = 8·31·5542			(e) Mean = 8·31·3208					

Value of the mean 5′ of the first degree, right and left . . . 8·31·0203

But (page 226) this value is less than for the mean 5′ of 5° 30′, right and left . . . ·0079

Value for the mean 5′ of the 4th degree . . . 8·31·4375

But (page 226) this value is less than for the mean of 5° 30′, right and left . . . ·0646

Value employed in reducing the observations at the Zwartkop Station . . . = 8·31·6102

$$\text{rer. } 1 = \frac{300 \times 34}{303·6102} = 33°·5957$$

$$\text{part. } 1 = = 0°·988109$$

(a) Immediately after sunrise, good clear light. Temperature 56°
(b) In the night by lamp light. Temperature 54°.
(c) In the night by lamp light. Temperature 54°.
(d) In the forenoon, the sun shining. Temperature 60°.
(e) In the night by lamp light. Temperature 53°.

Examination for the Run of the Micrometer at Cape Point Station.

JANUARY 14 AND 15, 1845.

ARCH TO THE LEFT.			ARCH TO THE RIGHT.		ARCH TO THE LEFT.			ACRH TO THE RIGHT	
° '	rev. pts.	rev. pts.	rev. pts.	rev. pts.	° '	rev. pts.	rev. pts.	rev. pts.	rev. pts.
0· 0	16·23·3		7· 7·9		4· 0	7· 2·85		8· 4·5	
5	7·26·05	8·31·25	16· 6·1	8·32·20	5	16· 0·2	8·31·35	17· 1·5	8·31·00
5	16·24·7		7· 5·4		5	7· 0·85		7·18·0	
10	7·26·8	8·31·90	16· 2·7	8·31·30	10	15·32·6	8·31·75	16·14·95	8·30·95
10	16·23·5		7·14·1		10	7· 5·7		6·28·4	
15	7·24·9	8·32·60	16·12·7	8·32·60	15	16· 2·5	8·30·80	15·26·2	8·31·80
15	15·32·1		16· 3·6		15	7· 5·0		6·29·65	
20	6·33·8	8·32·30	7· 5·6	8·32·00	20	16· 3·5	8·32·50	15·27·5	8·31·85
20	15·29·1		16· 1·9		20	7· 7·7		6·25·15	
25	6·31·3	8·31·80	7· 3·8	8·32·10	25	16· 4·9	8·31·20	15·23·5	8·32·35
25	16· 1·4		15·30·1		25	7·25·3		6·30·8	
30	7· 4·0	8·31·40	6·32·5	8·31·60	30	16·22·7	8·31·40	15·28·9	8·32·10
30	15·29·9		16· 6·2		30	7·19·7		7· 2·45	
35	6·32·1	8·31·80	7· 7·95	8·32·25	35	16·17·6	8·31·90	15·33·4	8·30·95
35	16·12·0		16· 4·9		35	6·31·9		7· 5·45	
40	7·13·8	8·32·20	7· 7·45	8·31·45	40	15·30·0	8·32·10	16· 3·95	8·32·50
40	16·12·4		16· 5·5		40	6·31·85		7· 0·95	
45	7·15·6	8·30·80	7· 7·4	8·32·10	45	15·29·8	8·31·95	15·32·4	8·31·45
45	16·12·9		7· 8·4		45	7· 4·6		7· 9·5	
50	7·15·0	8·31·90	16· 5·5	8·31·10	50	16· 2·4	8·31·80	16· 7·4	8·31·90
50	16·16·9		7· 2·8		50	7·10·05		7· 6·4	
55	7·19·6	8·31·30	16· 2·1	8·33·30	55	16· 7·9	8·31·85	16· 3·75	8·31·35
55	16·14·1		7· 7·3		55	7·21·6		6·32·85	
1· 0	7·16·6	8·31·50	16· 4·0	8·30·70	5· 0	16·19·6	8·32·00	15·30·95	8·32·10
	(a) Mean = 8·31·7297		(b) Mean = 8·31·8917			(c) Mean = 8·31·7167		(d) Mean = 8·31·8917	

Value of the mean 5' of the first degree, left and right .   .   .   = 8·31·8105
Value of the mean 5' of the fourth degree, left and right   .   .   = 8·31·7042
But (page 226) the corrections to the mean 5' of 5° 30', right and left, are   ·0079
       and   ·0646

Value employed in reducing the observations at the Cape Point Station   .   = 8·31·5705

$$1 \overset{rev.}{\underset{part.}{=}} \frac{300 \times 34}{303 \cdot 8386} = 33^{r}·5705$$

$$1 = 0^{r}·987366$$

(a) In the afternoon.   Temperature 67°.
(b) Near noon.   Temperature 70°.
(c) In the afternoon.   Temperature 70°.
(d) In the afternoon.   Temperature 70°.

Examination for the Run of the Micrometer at the Royal Observatory.

JUNE 1845.

° '	ARCH TO THE RIGHT		ARCH TO THE LEFT		° '	ARCH TO THE RIGHT		ARCH TO THE LEFT	
	rev. pts	rev. pts	rev. pts	rev. pts		rev. pts	rev. pts	rev. pts	rev. pts
0- 0	5·22·4	8·32·75	5· 1·4	8·31·30	4· 0	5·18·15	8·32·05	5·23·4	8·32·30
5	14·21·15		13·32·7		5	14·16·2		14·21·7	
5	5·19·9	8·31·50	5· 8·0	8·32·00	5	5· 8·3	8·31·70	5·14·8	8·31·80
10	14·17·4		14· 6·0		10	14· 6·0		14·12·6	
10	5·10·9	8·33·00	5·11·0	8·31·70	10	5·33·5	8·32·50	5·17·8	8·31·10
15	14· 9·9		14· 8·7		15	14·32·0		14·14·9	
15	5· 6·15	8·33·05	5·20·4	8·32·70	15	5·11·6	8·32·00	5·16·2	8·33·50
20	14· 5·2		14·19·1		20	14· 9·6		14·15·7	
20	5· 9·4	8·32·50	5·19·4	8·32·00	20	5·17·5	8·32·60	5· 7·25	8·31·65
25	14· 7·9		14·17·4		25	14·16·1		14· 4·9	
25	5·11·75	8·31·85	5·18·3	8·31·30	25	5·12·5	8·32·20	5·11·8	8·32·00
30	14· 9·6		14·15·6		30	14·10·7		14· 9·8	
30	5·11·0	8·32·20	5·17·6	8·32·10	30	5· 1·8	8·31·40	5·10·9	8·32·00
35	14· 9·2		14·15·7		35	13·33.2		14· 8·9	
35	5·12·4	8·31·50	5·23·7	8·32·70	35	5·14·8	8·32·80	5· 9·2	8·32·10
40	14· 9·9		14·22·4		40	14·13·6		14· 7·3	
40	5·12·1	8·32·30	5·19·55	8·31·45	40	5· 9·6	8·31·40	5·10·4	8·32·10
45	14·10·4		14·17·0		45	14· 7·0		14· 8·5	
45	5·11·4	8·31·00	5·10·0	8·32·50	45	5·11·95	8·32·30	5·12·3	8·31·80
50	14· 9·0		14· 8·5		50	14·10·25		14·10·1	
50	5· 5·3	8·33·30	5·10·0	8·31·60	50	5·11·7	8·31·90	5· 7·85	8·32·05
55	14· 4·6		14· 7·6		55	14· 9·0		14· 6·8	
55	5· 9·1	8·31·50	5·13·6	8·32·20	55	5· 5·0	8·32·40	5·12·8	8·32·10
1· 0	14· 6·6		14·11·8		1· 0	14· 4·3		14·10·9	
	Mean = 8·32·2542		Mean = 8·31·9625			Mean = 8·32·1042		Mean = 8·32·1167	

Value of the mean 5' of the first degree, right and left . . . . = 8·32·1084
Value of the mean 5' of the fourth degree, right and left . . = 8·32·1105
But (page 226) the corrections to the mean 5' of 5° 30' right and left, are ·0979
and ·0646

Value employed in reducing the observations at the Royal Observatory,
from page 146 to page 164 . . . . = 8·32·1906

$$1 \text{ rev.} = \frac{300 \times 34}{304 \cdot 1906} = 33''·5317$$

$$1 \text{ part.} = 0''·986226$$

The above measures were taken in Temperature 60°

Examination for the Run of the Sector Micrometer at the Bush'man Flat Station.

JUNE 24 AND JULY 9, 1847.

	ARCH TO THE LEFT.		ARCH TO THE RIGHT.		ARCH TO THE LEFT.		ARCH TO THE RIGHT.	
	rev. pts. / rev. pts.		rev. pts. / rev. pts.		rev. pts. / rev. pts.		rev. pts. / rev. pts.	
0· 0 / 5	16·22·5 / 7·24·75	8·31·75	8· 5·1 / 17· 3·4	8·32·30	17· 2·8 / 8· 5·5	8·31·30	8·18·5 / 17·16·1	8·31·60
5 / 10	16· 3·6 / 7· 6·59	8·31·01	8·17·7 / 17·15·3	8·31·60	17·25·8 / 8·28·2	8·31·00	8·28·35 / 17·26·0	8·31·05
10 / 15	16· 4·75 / 7· 7·3	8·31·45	8· 6·6 / 17· 5·3	8·32·70	17·12·4 / 8·15·4	8·31·00	8·28·25 / 17·27·5	8·33·25
15 / 20	16·28·3 / 7·29·65	8·32·65	8· 0·15 / 16·32·4	8·32·25	17·12·4 / 8·14·35	8·32·05	8· 1·8 / 17· 0·0	8·32·20
20 / 25	17· 8·3 / 8·10·3	8·32·00	8· 9·95 / 17· 8·55	8·32·60	17·10·6 / 8·12·9	8·31·70	7·30·1 / 16·28·1	8·32·00
25 / 30	16·31·9 / 8· 0·9	8·31·00	8·12·7 / 17·10·0	8·31·30	17· 4·7 / 8· 7·75	8·30·95	8· 2·85 / 17· 0·0	8·31·15
30 / 35	16·32·7 / 8· 0·45	8·32·25	8·12·15 / 17·10·0	8·31·85	16·31·8 / 8· 0·2	8·31·60	8·11·8 / 17·10·2	8·32·40
35 / 40	16·10·8 / 7·12·7	8·32·10	8· 9·25 / 17· 6·45	8·31·20	16·25·25 / 7·27·3	8·31·95	8· 5·8 / 17· 3·3	8·31·50
40 / 45	15·33·8 / 7· 2·15	8·31·65	9· 1·7 / 18· 0·0	8·32·30	16·28·1 / 7·30·55	8·31·55	7·28·5 / 16·26·8	8·32·30
45 / 50	16·12·8 / 7·14·9	8·31·90	8·31·7 / 17·29·0	8·31·30	16·28·8 / 7·31·35	8·31·45	7·15·6 / 16·13·0	8·31·40
50 / 55	16·10·0 / 7·12·0	8·32·00	8·31·25 / 17·29·8	8·32·55	16·32·5 / 8· 0·65	8·31·85	6·31·25 / 15·29·5	8·32·25
55 / 1· 0	16·14·0 / 7·16·2	8·31·80	8· 7·6 / 17· 5·0	8·31·40	16·24·6 / 7·27·4	8·31·20	6·20·15 / 15·17·2	8·31·05
	(a) Mean = 8·31·7967		(b) Mean = 8·31·9458		(d) Mean = 8·31·5167		(e) Mean = 8·31·8958	

	ARCH TO THE LEFT.		ARCH TO THE RIGHT.	
4· 0 / 5	17·26·0 / 8·29·05	8·30·95	9·27·5 / 18·25·5	8·32·80
5 / 10	17·27·0 / 8·30·15	8·30·85	9·23·9 / 18·21·3	8·31·40
10 / 15	17·32·0 / 9· 1·4	8·30·60	9·15·4 / 18·13·8	8·32·40
15 / 20	17·22·4 / 8·23·75	8·32·65	9·12·35 / 18· 9·6	8·31·25
20 / 25	17·23·4 / 8·25·65	8·31·75	8·32·45 / 17·31·0	8·32·55
25 / 30	17·17·7 / 8·20·3	8·31·40	9·10·35 / 18· 7·8	8·31·45
30 / 35	17· 5·2 / 8· 7·3	8·31·90	9·13·35 / 18· 9·5	8·30·15
35 / 40	16·28·5 / 7·30·3	8·32·20	9· 0·0 / 17·33·2	8·33·20
40 / 45	16·32·5 / 8· 1·1	8·31·40	9· 2·0 / 17·33·5	8·31·50
45 / 50	16·33·8 / 8· 2·05	8·31·75	9· 2·6 / 18· 0·5	8·31·90
50 / 55	16·21·4 / 7·23·4	8·32·00	9· 4·75 / 18· 2·0	8·31·25
55 / 5· 0	15·24·5 / 6·20·2	8·32·30	9· 7·5 / 18· 6·0	8·32·50
	(c) Mean = 8·31·6458		(f) Mean = 8·31·7958	

Value of the mean 5′ of the first and fourth degrees, to the left = 8·31·6581

Value of the mean 5′ of the first and fourth degrees, to the right = 8·31·8791

Mean or the value employed in reducing the observations at the Bushman Flat Station = 8·31·7661

$$\frac{300 \times 34}{303·7661} = 33'·5785$$

$$\frac{1}{1} = 0·987002$$

(a) Temperature 52°.
(b) „ 53°.
(d) „ 45°.
(e) „ 45°.
(e) „ 46°.
(f) „ 43°.

Examination for the Run of the Sector Micrometer at the Royal Observatory.

JULY AND AUGUST, 1848.

° '	ARCH TO THE LEFT (0° to 1°)			ARCH TO THE RIGHT (0° to 1°)			ARCH TO THE LEFT (1° to 2°)			ARCH TO THE RIGHT (1° to 2°)		
	rev. pts.	rev. pts.		rev. pts.	rev. pts.		rev. pts.	rev. pts.		rev. pts.	rev. pts.	
0· 0 / 5	16· 8·95	7·11·55	8·31·40	7·19·0	16·16·9	8·31·90	7·11·2	16· 9·0	8·31·80	7·21·6	16·19·0	8·31·40
5 / 10	16·10·4	7·12·7	8·31·70	7·26·3	16·23·55	8·31·25	16·27·5	7·28·9	8·32·60	7·14·6	16·12·4	8·31·80
10 / 15	16·12·0	7·14·4	8·31·60	7·11·8	16·10·4	8·32·60	16·28·7	7·31·1	8·31·60	7· 4·4	16· 2·3	8·31·90
15 / 20	16·12·3	7·14·4	8·31·90	7·26·85	16·25·0	8·32·15	16·18·5	7·20·5	8·32·00	7·13·0	16·10·5	8·31·50
20 / 25	16·13·1	7·15·5	8·31·60	7·13·95	16·12·4	8·32·45	16· 9·0	7·11·6	8·31·40	7·11·0	16· 8·6	8·31·60
25 / 30	16· 5·4	7· 8·4	8·31·00	7·11·9	16· 9·0	8·31·10	16·11·7	7·14·2	8·31·50	7·15·8	16·14·0	8·32·20
30 / 35	16·16·5	7·18·95	8·31·55	7·11·55	16·10·0	8·32·45	16·10·0	7·12·8	8·31·20	7·17·5	16·14·6	8·31·10
35 / 40	16·25·8	7·27·7	8·32·10	7· 8·1	16· 5·6	8·31·50	16· 6·2	7· 8·2	8·32·00	7·19·4	16·17·5	8·32·10
40 / 45	16·28·2	7·30·6	8·31·60	7·18·2	16·16·5	8·32·30	16· 2·5	7· 5·35	8·31·15	7·24·0	16·22·3	8·32·30
45 / 50	16·15·9	7·18·15	8·31·75	7·17·95	16·15·3	8·31·35	16· 8·7	7·10·25	8·32·45	7·29·3	16·27·0	8·31·70
50 / 55	16·22·6	7·24·55	8·32·05	7·24·1	16·22·8	8·32·70	16·12·1	7·15·0	8·31·10	7·26·5	16·24·5	8·32·00
55 / 0·60	16·28·4	7·30·0	8·32·40	7·21·5	16·18·9	8·31·40	16·14·8	7·17·5	8·31·30	7·15·05	16·12·8	8·31·75
	Mean =		8·31·7208	Mean =		8·31·9292	Mean =		8·31·6750	Mean =		8.31·7792

° '	ARCH TO THE LEFT (2° to 3°)			ARCH TO THE RIGHT (2° to 3°)			ARCH TO THE LEFT (3° to 4°)			ARCH TO THE RIGHT (3° to 4°)		
	rev. pts.	rev. pts.		rev. pts.	rev. pts.		rev. pts.	rev. pts.		rev. pts.	rev. pts.	
0· 0 / 5	16·31·0	7·32·4	8·32·60	7· 6·7	16· 4·7	8·32·00	16·20·7	7·32·0	8·31·70	7·32·0	16·30·4	8·32·40
5 / 10	16· 7·95	7·10·75	8·31·20	7· 5·4	16· 2·8	8·31·40	16·32·4	7·34·9	8·31·50	7·33·1	16·30·3	8·31·20
10 / 15	16·16·5	7·19·55	8·30·95	7·35·3	16·33·3	8·32·00	16· 5·0	7· 7·25	8·31·75	7· 3·8	16· 2·4	8·32·60
15 / 20	16·19·4	7·20·95	8·32·45	7·28·5	16·26·0	8·31·50	16· 7·3	7· 9·75	8·31·55	7·11·2	16· 8·3	8·31·10
20 / 25	16·22·5	7·25·3	8·31·20	7·18·6	16·16·0	8·31·40	16·15·45	7·17·05	8·32·40	7·16·3	16·14·5	8·32·20
25 / 30	16·29·2	7·30·4	8·32·80	7·19·5	16·16·3	8·30·80	16·26·55	7·29·15	8·31·40	7·30·8	16·28·1	8·31·30
30 / 35	16·16·9	7·19·0	8·31·90	7·10·f	16·15·0	8·32·20	16·28·5	7·30·55	8·31·95	7·25·0	16·23·5	8·32·50
35 / 40	16·18·4	7·21·0	8·31·40	7·18·J	16·16·3	8·31·80	16·28·0	7·30·0	8·32·00	7· 2·8	16· 1·1	8·32·30
40 / 45	16·14·8	7·18·1	8·30·70	7·19·2	16·16·5	8·31·30	16·28·75	7·31·0	8·31·75	7·23·2	16·21·0	8·31·80
45 / 50	16·11·45	7·13·1	8·32·35	7·12·5	16·10·0	8·31·50	16· 0·25	7· 2·85	8·31·40	7·17·5	16·15·3	8·31·80
50 / 55	16· 5·0	7· 8·1	8·30·90	7· 6·6	16· 4·0	8·31·40	16·19·3	7·20·4	8·32·90	7·18·7	16·16·2	8·31·50
55 / ·60	16· 3·5	7· 4·3	8·33·20	7·32·6	16·30·5	8·31·90	16·12·25	7·15·55	8·30·70	7·13·0	16·10·9	8·31·90
	Mean =		8·31·8042	Mean =		8·31·6000	Mean =		8·31·7500	Mean =		8·31·8833

The Temperature during these measures ranged between 55° and 57°.

Examination for the Run of the Sector Micrometer at the Royal Observatory—(continued).

JULY AND AUGUST, 1848.

	ARCH TO THE LEFT.		ARCH TO THE RIGHT.		ARCH TO THE LEFT.		ARCH TO THE RIGHT.	
	4° to 5°.				5° to 5°·30′.			
° ′	rev. pts.	rev. pts.	rev. pts.	rev. pts.	rev. pts.	rev. pts.	rev. pts.	rev. pts.
0· 0	16·17·4 / 7·19·9	8·31·50	7· 7·7 / 16· 5·7	8·32·00	16·16·0 / 7·18·0	8·32·00	7·26·6 / 16·24·5	8·31·90
5	16·13·7 / 7·16·7	8·31·00	7· 7·5 / 16· 5·3	8·31·80	16·11·5 / 7·15·3	8·30·20	7·31·9 / 16·29·5	8·31·60
10	16·31·3 / 7·34·7	8·30·60	7· 7·1 / 16· 5·0	8·31·90	16· 7·1 / 7· 9·5	8·31·60	7·26·9 / 16·25·2	8·32·30
15	16· 0·5 / 7· 2·0	8·32·50	7·18·5 / 10·16·1	8·31·60	16· 1·5 / 7· 3·2	8·32·30	7·23·4 / 16·21·6	8·32·40
20	16·33·8 / 7·36·6	8·31·20	7·17·9 / 16·16·5	8·32·60	16·17·3 / 7·20·25	8·31·05	7·31·1 / 16·28·6	8·31·50
25	16·17·6 / 7·20·3	8·31·30	7·17·75 / 16·15·3	8·31·55	16·20·0 / 7·22·0	8·32·00	7·33·9 / 16·31·6	8·31·70
30	16·12·9 / 7·15·6	8·31·30	7·21·7 / 16·18·5	8·30·80				
35	16·18·3 / 7·20·95	8·31·35	7·23·3 / 16·21·7	8·32·40				
40	16·22·2 / 7·24·45	8·31·75	7·32·1 / 16·29·5	8·31·40				
45	16·22·5 / 7·25·15	8·31·35	7· 2·9 / 16· 0·5	8·31·60				
50	16·26·4 / 7·28·3	8·32·10	7·32·3 / 16·29·75	8·31·45				
55	16·24·1 / 7·26·4	8·31·70	7·35·5 / 16·33·6	8·32·10				
0·60	Mean = 8·31·4708		Mean = 8·31·7667		Mean = 8·31·5250		Mean = 8·31·9000	

Calculation of the value for the mean 5′ of the Arch, from 5° 30′ right to 5° 30′ left.

	LEFT.	RIGHT.	MEANS.
° ° ′	rev. pts.	rev. pts.	rev. pts.
0 to 1· 0	8·31·7208	8·31·9292	8·31·8250
1 to 2· 0	8·31·6750	8·31·7792	·7271
2 to 3· 0	8·31·8042	8·31·6000	·7021
3 to 4· 0	8·31·7500	8·31·8833	·8167
4 to 5· 0	8·31·4708	8·31·7667	·6188
5 to 5·30	8·31·5250	8·31·9000	·7125
			8·31·7356

In the determination of the mean (8·31·7356) the half degree received the weight ½.

$$1 = \frac{300 \times 34}{303·7356} = 33^{r}·58184$$

$$1 = 0^{r}·987701$$

Which values for 5′ of the Arch were employed in reducing the observations made at the Royal Observatory, from page 190 to page 219.

MEAN ZENITH DISTANCES.

COLLECTION OF

ALL THE

RESULTS OF OBSERVATION OF EACH STAR

AT

HEERELOGEMENTS BERG,

AND

DEDUCTION OF MEAN ZENITH DISTANCE, 1843, JANUARY 0.

Note.—The reduction for Azimuthal Error is always to be applied subtractively to the Zenith Distance. The reduction for Curvature of Path is always to be applied subtractively to South Zenith Distance, and additively to North Zenith Distance. The Refraction is always to be applied additively. The Precession, Aberration, and Nutation, have the sign which is proper for reducing the Apparent North Polar Distance of the Star to its mean North Polar Distance, 1843, January 0; and therefore are to be applied with the sign given in the Table when the Star is South of the Zenith, and with the opposite sign when the Star is North of the Zenith.

The numbers included in parentheses in the column " Deduced Mean Zenith Distance, 1843, January 0," are omitted in taking the mean.

Where an asterisk or a positive sign is affixed to a number in the 3rd or 9th columns, the explanation will be found at the bottom of the page.

Mean Zenith Distances of Stars observed at Heerelogements Berg.

FACE OF SECTOR EAST.   FACE OF SECTOR WEST.

Day of Observation 1843.	Apparent Zenith Distance, from Unreduced Observation.	Reduction for Az. Error, and Curv. of Path.	Refraction.	Precession, Aberration, and Nutation.	Deduced Mean Zenith Distance, 1843, Jan. 0; and Mean of Separate Results, uncorrected, for Error of Collimation.	Day of Observation 1843.	Apparent Zenith Distance, from Unreduced Observation.	Reduction for Az. Error, and Curv. of Path.	Refraction.	Precession, Aberration, and Nutation.	Deduced Mean Zenith Distance, 1843, Jan. 0, and Mean of Separate Results, uncorrected of Collimation.
					B.A.C. 1802.						
May 16	2·11·13·47	·01	2·03	- 6·60	2·11· 8·89	May 17	2·11·02·11	·02	2·02	- 6·37	2·11·57·74
18	15·05	·03	2·02	6·13	10·91	19	61·12	·01	2·00	5·90	57·21
20	13·38	·02	2·00	5·66	9·70	23	59·94	·01	2·01	4·93	57·01
22	10·16	·03	2·00	5·18	6·95	26	60·87	·01	1·99	4·18	58·67
24	9·92	·09	2·01	4·68	7·16	28	59·20	·03	1·97	3·67	57·47
31	9·99	* ·12	1·99	- 2·90	8·96	June 1	59·44	·01	1·97	- 2·63	58·77
					2·11· 8·76						2·11·57·81

Error of Collimation . . . = 0· 0·24·52
Resulting Mean Zenith Distance, South = 2·11·33·29

Day	Apparent	Red	Refr	Prec	Deduced	Day	Apparent	Red	Refr	Prec	Deduced
					B.A.C. 2293.						
May 12	3·12·30·95	2·02	2·93	-14·04	3·12·45·90	May 17	3·11·38·71	·02	2·95	-13·28	3·11·54·92
16	29·81	0·01	2·97	13·44	46·21	19	41·27	·01	2·92	12·95	57·13
18	29·42	0·04	2·95	13·11	45·44	21	39·94	·01	2·94	12·61	55·48
20	(23·44)	0·02	2·92	12·78	(39·12)	23	40·93	·02	2·94	12·26	56·11
22	31·29	0·04	2·93	12·43	46·61	25	41·91	·01	2·93	11·90	56·73
24	32·48	0·12	2·94	12·08	47·38	26	42·85	·01	2·90	11·71	57·45
27	31·44	0·18	2·89	11·52	45·67	28	42·46	·03	2·88	11·33	56·64
29	35·11	*0·07	2·89	11·14	(49·07)	30	41·97	·00	2·90	-10·94	55·81
31	32·77	0·09	2·92	10·74	46·34						
June 1	33·44	0·09	2·88	-10·54	46·77						
					3·12·46·29						3·11·56·28

Error of Collimation . . . = 0· 0·25·00
Resulting Mean Zenith Distance, North = 3·12·21·29

Day	Apparent	Red	Refr	Prec	Deduced	Day	Apparent	Red	Refr	Prec	Deduced
					B.A.C. 4458.						
May 12	3·54·46·47	2·68	3·67	-24·00	3·54·23·46	May 15	3·55·36·00	·13	3·74	-24·37	3·55·15·24
16	45·58	0·02	3·73	24·49	24·80	17	37·18	·03	3·72	24·60	16·27
18	45·19	0·05	3·71	24·71	24·14	19	36·74	·01	3·07	24·82	15·58
20	45·78	0·03	3·67	24·93	24·49	21	36·93	·01	3·70	25·03	15·59
22	45·19	0·05	3·68	25·13	23·09	23	37·48	·02	3·68	25·23	15·91
24	46·37	0·02	3·69	25·32	24·72	26	36·93	·01	3·64	25·51	15·05
27	46·17	0·24	3·64	25·59	23·98	28	36·14	·05	3·62	25·68	14·03
29	46·37	0·16	3·63	25·75	24·09	30	37·03	·00	3·65	25·83	14·85
31	47·21	0·12	3·64	25·91	24·82	June 1	37·33	* ·01	3·62	25·90	14·95
June 3	47·36	0·03	3·09	-26·13	24·89	4	37·43	·00	3·64	-26·19	14·88
					3·54·24·31						3·55·15·24

Error of Collimation . . . = 0· 0·25·46
Resulting Mean Zenith Distance, South = 3·54·49·77

No. 1802.—May 31.—Correction for Curvature of Path = - ·057; for Azimuth Error - ·063. Sum = - ·120.
„ 2293.— „ 29.— „ „ „ + ·053; „ „ - ·122. „ = - ·069.
„ 4458.—June 1.— „ „ „ - ·004; „ „ - ·008. „ = - ·012.

Mean Zenith Distances of Stars observed at Heerelogements Berg.

	FACE OF SECTOR EAST.						FACE OF SECTOR WEST.				
Day of Observation 1843.	Apparent Zenith Distance, from Unreduced Observation.	Reduction for Az. Error, and Curr. of Path.	Refraction.	Precession, Aberration, and Nutation.	Deduced Mean Zenith Distance, 1843, Jan. 0; and Mean of Separate Results, uncorrected, for Error of Collimation.	Day of Observation 1843.	Apparent Zenith Distance, from Unreduced Observation.	Reduction for Az. Error, and Curr. of Path.	Refraction.	Precession, Aberration, and Nutation.	Deduced Mean Zenith Distance, 1843, Jan. 0; and Mean of Separate Results, uncorrected, for Error of Collimation.

B.A.C. 4517.

Day	App. Z. D.	Red.	Refr.	Prec.	Deduced	Day	App. Z. D.	Red.	Refr.	Prec.	Deduced
May 16	3·12·44·48	·01	3·05	-22·86	3·13·10·38	May 15	3·11·55·15	·10	3·06	-22·78	3·12·20·89
18	44·33	·04	3·03	23·02	10·34	17	53·71	·02	3·04	22·94	19·67
20	43·54	·02	3·00	23·17	9·69	19	53·82	·01	3·00	23·10	19·91
22	44·43	·04	3·01	23·32	10·72	21	53·91	·01	3·03	23·24	20·17
24	47·14	·01	3·02	23·45	13·60	23	53·52	·02	3·01	23·38	19·89
27	42·16	·18	2·97	23·63	8·58	26	53·27	·01	2·98	23·57	19·81
29	44·53	·12	2·97	23·74	11·12	28	53·47	·03	2·96	23·68	20·08
31	42·75	·09	2·98	23·84	9·48	30	54·16	·00	2·99	23·79	20·94
June 3	43·14	·02	3·02	-23·98	10·12	June 1	53·67	·01	2·96	23·89	20·51
						4	53·62	·00	2·97	-24·02	20·61
					3·13·10·45						3·12·20·25

Error of Collimation . . . = 0· 0·25·10
Resulting Mean Zenith Distance, North = 3·12·45·35

B.A.C. 4548.

Day	App. Z. D.	Red.	Refr.	Prec.	Deduced	Day	App. Z. D.	Red.	Refr.	Prec.	Deduced
May 12	3·12·44·28	2·02	3·00	-22·19	3·13· 7·45	May 15	3·11·52·78	·10	3·06	-22·45	3·12·18·19
16	40·28	0·01	3·05	22·53	5·85	17	50·21	·02	3·04	22·62	15·85
18	40·33	0·04	3·08	22·70	6·02	19	50·51	·01	3·00	22·77	16·27
20	39·94	0·02	3·00	22·65	5·77	21	50·65	·01	3·03	22·92	16·59
22	40·87	0·04	3·01	23·00	6·84	23	49·72	·02	3·01	23·06	15·77
24	41·96	0·01	3·01	23·13	8·09	26	49·86	·01	2·98	23·57	16·09
27	38·46	0·18	2·97	23·32	4·57	28	50·16	·03	2·96	23·37	16·46
29	39·98	0·12	2·97	23·43	6·26	30	50·16	·00	2·99	23·48	16·63
31	39·64	0·00	2·97	23·53	6·05	June 1	49·72	·00	2·96	23·58	16·26
June 3	39·19	0·02	3·02	-23·68	5·87	4	50·51	·00	2·97	-23·72	17·20
					3·13· 6·28						3·12·16·53

Error of Collimation . . . = 0· 0·24·87
Resulting Mean Zenith Distance, North = 3·12·41·40

B.A.C. 4579.

Day	App. Z. D.	Red.	Refr.	Prec.	Deduced	Day	App. Z. D.	Red.	Refr.	Prec.	Deduced
May 12	0·16·40·63	·19	0·27	-22·16	0·16·18·55	May 15	0·17·31·39	·01	0·27	-22·48	0·17· 9·17
16	42·46	·00	·27	22·58	20·15	17	31·84	·00	·27	22·68	9·43
18	42·26	·00	·27	22·78	19·75	19	31·98	·00	·27	22·88	9·37
20	40·83	·10	·27	22·97	18·03	21	32·03	·00	·27	23·06	9·24
22	42·06	·00	·27	23·16	19·17	23	32·92	·00	·27	23·24	9·95
24	40·38	·00	·27	23·32	17·33	26	30·90	·00	·27	23·49	7·68
29	43·84	·01	·26	23·71	20·36	28	31·20	·00	·26	23·64	7·82
31	43·84	·01	·27	23·86	20·24	30	32·03	·00	·27	23·79	8·51
June 3	44·09	·00	·27	-24·05	20·31	June 4	32·87	·00	·26	-24·11	9·02
					0·16·19·32						0·17· 8·91

Error of Collimation . . . = 0· 0·24·79
Resulting Mean Zenith Distance, South = 0·16·44·12

No. 4548.—May 19.—Correction for Curvature of Path + ·004; for Azimuth Error - ·009, = - ·005.
,, June 1.— ,, ,, ,, + ·004; ,, ,, - ·006. = - ·002.
,, 4579.—May 20.— ,, ,, ,, - ·098; ,, ,, - ·200. = - ·100.

Mean Zenith Distances of Stars observed at Heerelogements Berg.

FACE OF SECTOR EAST.						FACE OF SECTOR WEST.					
Day of Observation 1843.	Apparent Zenith Distance, from Unreduced Observation.	Reduction for Ax. Error, and Curv. of Path.	Refraction.	Precession, Aberration, and Nutation.	Deduced Mean Zenith Dist·nce, 1843, Jan. 0; and Mean of Separate Results, uncorrected, for Error of Collimation.	Day of Observation 1843.	Apparent Zenith Distance, from Unreduced Observation	Refraction for Ax. Error, and Curv. of Path.	Refraction.	Precession, Aberration, and Nutation.	Deduced Mean Zenith Distance, 1843, Jan. 0; and Mean of Separate Results, uncorrected, for Error of Collimation.

B.A.C. 4623.

	o ′ ″	″	″	′ ″	o ′ ″		o ′ ″	″	″	′ ″	o ′ ″
May 12	0 14 36·79	·17	0·23	−21·78	0 14 15·07	May 15	0 15 26·62	·01	0·23	−22·10	0 15· 4·74
16	38·13	·00	·23	22·21	16·15	17	27·50	·00	·23	22·31	5·42
18	37·34	·00	·23	22·41	15·16	19	27·25	·00	·23	22·51	4·97
20	37·73	·00	·23	22·60	15·36	21	28·29	·00	·23	22·69	5·83
22	37·88	·00	·23	22·78	15·33	23	28·64	·00	·23	22·87	6·00
24	38·03	·00	·23	22·96	15·30	26	27·65	·00	·23	23·13	4·75
29	38·67	·01	·23	23·35	15·74	28	27·95	·00	·23	23·28	4·90
31	38·62	·01	·23	23·50	15·34	30	27·75	·00	·23	23·43	4·55
June 3	39·41	·00	·23	−23·70	15·94	June 4	28·54	·00	·23	−23·76	5·01
					0 14 15·49						0 15· 5·13

Error of Collimation . . . = 0· 0·24·82
Resulting Mean Zenith Distance, South = 0·14·40·31

B.A.C. 4686.

May 12	3 37 28·68	2·47	3·40	−21·05	3 37· 8·56	May 15	3 38 15·64	·12	3·46	−21·43	3 37 57·55
16	25·62	0·02	3·46	21·55	7·51	17	17·46	·03	3·45	21·68	59·20
18	26·58	0·05	3·44	21·79	8·18	19	16·41	·01	3·40	21·91	57·89
20	27·42	0·03	3·40	22·02	8·77	21	17·59	·01	3·43	22·14	58·87
22	27·57	0·05	3·41	22·25	8·68	23	19·12	·02	3·41	22·36	60·15
24	28·61	0·02	3·42	22·46	9·55	26	16·85	·01	3·37	22·67	57·54
29	28·76	0·15	3·36	22·96	9·01	28	17·64	·04	3·35	22·86	58·09
31	29·69	0·11	3·37	−23·14	9·81	30	18·33	·00	3·39	−23·05	58·67
					3 37· 8 ·76						3 37 58·50

Error of Collimation . . . = 0· 0·24·87
Resulting Mean Zenith Distance, South = 3·37·33·63

B.A.C. 4719.

May 20	3 25 22·42	·02	3·20	−20·65	3 25 46·25	May 17	3 24 35·31	+ ·18	3·24	−20·41	3 24·(59·14)
22	23·60	·04	3·21	20·80	47·57	19	32·50	· ·00	3·20	20·57	56·27
24	24·44	·02	3·21	20·94	48·57	23	32·65	+ ·01	3·21	20·87	56·74
29	22·81	·13	3·16	21·27	47·11	26	33·44	· ·01	3·17	21·08	57·68
31	21·63	·09	3·17	21·39	46·10	28	33·58	· ·04	3·15	21·20	57·89
June 3	21·77	·02	3·22	−21·55	46·52	30	34·08	· ·00	3·18	−21·33	58·59
					3 25 47·02						3 24·57·43

Error of Collimation . . . = 0· 0·24·79
Resulting Mean Zenith Distance, North = 3·25·22·23

No. 4719.—May 17.—Correction for Curvature of Path + ·206; for Azimuth Error − ·025. = + ·181.
  ,, 19.—   ,,   ,,   ,, + ·006;   ,,   ,, − ·009. = − ·003.
  ,, 23.—   ,,   ,,   ,, + ·023;   ,,   ,, − ·017. = + ·006.

Mean Zenith Distances of Stars observed at Heerelogements Berg.

	FACE OF SECTOR EAST.						FACE OF SECTOR WEST.				
Day of Observation 1843.	Apparent Zenith Distance, from Unreduced Observation.	Reduction for Alt. Error, and Curv. of Path.	Refraction.	Precession, Aberration, and Nutation.	Deduced Mean Zenith Distance, 1843, Jan. 0; and Mean of Separate Results, uncorrected, for Error of Collimation.	Day of Observation 1843.	Apparent Zenith Distance, from Unreduced Observation.	Reduction for Alt. Error, and Curv. of Path.	Refraction.	Precession, Aberration, and Nutation.	Deduced Mean Zenith Distance, 1843, Jan. 0; and Mean of Separate Results, uncorrected, for Error of Collimation.

B.A.C. 4784.

May 12	3·11·14·41	2·01	2·98	-19·10	3·11·34·48	May 15	3·10·21·18	·10	3·03	-19·37	3·10·43·48
16	11·15	0·01	3·03	19·45	33·62	17	19·11	·02	3·02	19·54	41·65
20	10·12	0·02	2·97	19·78	32·85	19	21·04	·01	2·98	19·70	43·71
22	10·31	·0·01	2·98	19·94	33·22	21	19·55	·01	3·00	19·86	42·40
29	10·17	0·12	2·94	20·42	33·41	23	18·47	·02	2·99	20·01	41·45
31	10·02	0·09	2·95	20·55	33·43	26	20·44	·01	2·95	20·23	43·61
June 1	10·02	0·09	2·95	20·61	33·49	28	19·85	·03	2·93	20·36	43·11
3	9·33	0·02	2·99	-20·72	33·02	30	19·90	·00	2·96	-20·49	43·35
					3·11·33·44						3·10·42·85

Error of Collimation . . = 0· 0·25·30
Resulting Mean Zenith Distance, North = 3·11· 8·14

Anon. AR. 14·24.

May 18	0·38·60·40	·01	0·02	-19·59	0·38·41·42	May 17	0·39·49·98	·01	0·62	-19·48	0·39·31·11
20	61·78	·00	·61	19·79	42·60	19	50·03	·00	·62	19·69	30·96
22	60·16	·01	·62	19·99	40·78	21	51·06	·00	·62	19·89	31·79
24	60·94	·00	·62	20·17	41·39	23	51·66	* ·03	·62	20·08	32·17
29	59·71	·03	·61	20·61	39·68	26	49·29	·00	·61	20·36	29·54
31	61·59	·02	·61	20·78	41·40	28	51·31	·01	·61	20·53	31·38
June 1	60·99	·02	0·61	-20·86	40·72	30	50·77	·00	0·61	-20·70	30·68
					0·38·41·14						0·39·31·09

Error of Collimation . . = 0· 0·24·98
Resulting Mean Zenith Distance, South = 0·39· 6·12

B.A.C. 4852.

May 12	2·31·22·66	1·70	2·37	-18·19	2·31· 5·14	May 17	2·32·13·81	·02	2·40	-18·78	2·31·57·41
16	21·57	0·01	2·41	18·66	5·31	19	12·93	·01	2·37	19·01	56·28
18	21·33	0·03	2·40	18·89	4·81	21	13·86	·01	2·39	19·23	57·01
20	21·37	0·02	2·37	19·12	4·60	23	15·15	·01	2·38	19·44	58·08
22	21·72	0·03	2·38	19·34	4·73	26	13·02	·01	2·36	19·75	55·62
24	22·95	0·01	2·38	19·55	5·77	28	13·62	·03	2·33	19·95	55·97
27	22·61	0·15	2·35	19·85	4·96	30	14·31	·00	2·36	20·13	56·54
29	23·70	0·10	2·34	20·04	5·90	June 4	15·44	·00	2·34	-20·58	57·20
31	23·50	0·07	2·35	-20·23	5·55						
					2·31· 5·20						2·31·56·76

Error of Collimation . . = 0· 0·25·78
Resulting Mean Zenith Distance, South = 2·31·30·98

No. 4784.—May 22.—Correction for Curvature of Path + ·026; for Azimuth Error - ·037. = ·009.
Anon. 14ʰ 24ᵐ.— „ 23.— „ „ „ - ·025; „ „ - ·003. = ·028.

Mean Zenith Distances of Stars observed at Heerelogements Berg.

	FACE OF SECTOR EAST.						FACE OF SECTOR WEST.				
Day of Observation 1843.	Apparent Zenith Distance, from Unreduced Observation.	Reduction for Az. Error, and Curv. of Path.	Refraction.	Precession, Aberration, and Nutation.	Deduced Mean Zenith Distance, 1843, Jan. 0; and Mean of Separate Results, uncorrected, for Error of Collimation.	Day of Observation 1843.	Apparent Zenith Distance, from Unreduced Observation.	Reduction for Az. Error, and Curv. of Path.	Refraction.	Precession, Aberration, and Nutation.	Deduced Mean Zenith Distance, 1843, Jan. 0; and Mean of Separate Results, uncorrected, for Error of Collimation.

B.A.C. 4801.

Day	° ′ ″	″	″	″	° ′ ″	Day	° ′ ″	″	″	″	° ′ ″
May 12	4 39 57·73	2·90	4·37	-17·43	4 40 (16·63)	May 17	4 39· 8·75	·03	4·43	-17·81	4 39 30·96
16	57·28	0·02	4·44	17·74	19·44	19	7·56	·01	4·37	17·06	29·88
18	57·04	0·06	4·42	17·89	19·29	21	8·60	·01	4·40	18·10	31·09
20	57·68	0·03	4·36	18·03	20·04	23	6·77	·02	4·38	18·23	29·36
22	57·63	0·05	4·39	18·17	20·14	26	7·91	·01	4·34	18·42	30·66
24	58·62	0·02	4·39	18·30	21·29	28	8·10	·05	4·30	18·54	30·89
29	56·79	0·17	4·32	18·60	19·54	30	8·94	·00	4·35	18·65	31·94
31	56·40	0·12	4·33	18·71	19·32	June 4	8·40	·00	4·32	-18·92	31·64
June 3	56·15	0·03	4·38	-18·87	19·37						
					4 40 19·80						4 39 30·80

Error of Collimation . . . = 0· 0·24·50
Resulting Mean Zenith Distance, North = 4·39·55·30

B.A.C. 4916.

Day	° ′ ″	″	″	″	° ′ ″	Day	° ′ ″	″	″	″	° ′ ″
May 18	1 14 36·15	·02	1·18	-17·83	1 14 19·48	May 17	1 15 24·99	·01	1·19	-17·73	1 15· 8·44
20	35·85	·01	1·17	18·04	18·97	19	24·05	·00	1·17	17·94	7·28
22	35·21	·02	1·18	18·13	18·13	21	25·38	·00	1·18	18·14	8·42
24	36·40	·01	1·18	18·44	19·13	23	26·71	·01	1·17	18·34	9·53
27	37·93	·07	1·16	18·72	20·30	26	24·69	·03	1·16	18·63	7·19
29	35·81	·05	1·16	18·90	18·02	28	25·63	·01	1·15	18·81	7·96
31	36·94	·04	1·16	19·08	18·98	30	25·63	·00	1·16	18·99	7·80
June 3	37·34	·01	1·17	-19·33	19·17	June 4	26·76	·00	1·16	-10·42	8·50
					1 14 19·02						1 15· 8·14

Error of Collimation . . . = 0· 0·24·56
Resulting Mean Zenith Distance, South = 1·14·43·58

Anon. AR. 14 53.

Day	° ′ ″	″	″	″	° ′ ″	Day	° ′ ″	″	″	″	° ′ ″
May 18	0· 2·55·67	·00	0·05	-17·10	0· 2·38·56	May 17	0· 3·47·75	·00	0·05	-17·06	0· 3·30·74
20	57·89	·00	·05	40·59	...	19	46·03	·00	·05	17·26	28·82
22	55·57	·00	·05	17·54	38·08	21	47·81	·00	·05	17·45	30·41
24	56·65	·00	·05	17·72	38·98	23	48·05	·00	·05	17·63	31·07
27	58·63	·00	·05	17·99	40·69	26	47·07	·00	·05	17·90	29·22
29	58·33	·00	·05	18·16	40·22	28	48·25	·00	·05	18·07	30·23
31	58·98	·00	·05	18·32	40·71	30	47·17	·00	·05	18·24	28·98
June 3	58·08	·00	·05	-18·55	40·48	June 4	47·41	·00	·05	-18·63	28·83
					0· 2·39·79						0· 3·29·79

Error of Collimation . . . = 0· 0·25·00
Resulting Mean Zenith Distance, South = 0· 3· 4·79

No. 4916.—May 26.—Correction for Curvature of Path - ·025; for Azimuth Error - ·004. = - ·029.

Mean Zenith Distances of Stars observed at Hœrelogements Berg.

FACE OF SECTOR EAST.   **FACE OF SECTOR WEST.**

Anon. AR. 14·58.

Day of Observation 1843.	Apparent Zenith Distance, from Unreduced Observation.	Reduction for Az. Error, and Curv. of Path.	Refraction.	Precession, Aberration, and Nutation.	Deduced Mean Zenith Distance, 1843, Jan. 0; and Mean of Separate Results. uncorrected, for Error of Collimation.
May 18	0 19 41·78	·00	0 32	-16 06	0 10 25·14
20	41·08	·00	·32	17·15	24·85
22	38·08	·00	·31	17·34	21·05
24	39·76	·00	·31	17·51	22·56
27	41·73	·02	·31	17·77	24·25
29	40·45	·01	·31	17·93	22·62
31	40·79	·01	·31	18·09	23·00
June 1	41·43	·01	·31	-18·16	23·57
					0 19 23·41

Day of Observation 1843.	Apparent Zenith Distance, from Unreduced Observation.	Reduction for Az. Error, and Curv. of Path.	Refraction.	Precession, Aberration, and Nutation.	Deduced Mean Zenith Distance, 1843, Jan. 0; and Mean of Separate Results. uncorrected, for Error of Collimation.
May 17	0 20 28·10	·06	0 32	-16·87	0 20 11·49
19	28·04	·00	·31	17·06	11·89
21	29·48	·00	·32	17·24	12·50
23	30·91	·00	·31	17·42	13·80
26	28·79	·00	·31	17·08	11·42
28	30·81	·00	·31	17·85	13·27
30	28·54	·00	·31	-18·01	10·84
					0 20 12·18

Error of Collimation   .   .   .   = 0· 0·24·39
Resulting Mean Zenith Distance, South = 0·10·47·79

B.A.C. 5032.

Day of Observation 1843.	Apparent Zenith Distance, from Unreduced Observation.	Reduction for Az. Error, and Curv. of Path.	Refraction.	Precession, Aberration, and Nutation.	Deduced Mean Zenith Distance, 1843, Jan. 0; and Mean of Separate Results. uncorrected, for Error of Collimation.
May 12	2 24 15·71	1 53	2 25	-15·32	2 24 31·75
16	11·95	0·01	2·28	15·06	29·88
18	10·97	0·03	2·27	15·82	29·03
20	11·36	0·02	2·24	15·99	29·57
24	12·05	0·01	2·25	16·30	30·59
27	10·67	0·14	2·22	16·52	29·27
29	11·56	0·09	2·22	16·65	30·34
31	11·17	0·07	2·22	16·79	30·11
					2 24 30·07

Day of Observation 1843.	Apparent Zenith Distance, from Unreduced Observation.	Reduction for Az. Error, and Curv. of Path.	Refraction.	Precession, Aberration, and Nutation.	Deduced Mean Zenith Distance, 1843, Jan. 0; and Mean of Separate Results. uncorrected, for Error of Collimation.
May 15	2 23 24·27	·07	2 29	-15·58	2 23 42·07
17	22·08	0·02	2·27	15·75	40·08
19	21·59	0·01	2·25	15·91	39·74
21	21·59	0·01	2·26	16·07	39·91
23	21·79	0·01	2·25	16·22	40·25
26	22·28	0·01	2·23	16·44	40·94
28	22·23	0·03	2·21	16·58	40·99
30	23·37	·00	2·23	16·72	42·32
					2 23 40·79

Error of Collimation   .   .   .   = 0· 0·24·64
Resulting Mean Zenith Distance, North = 2·24· 5·43

B.A.C. 5054.

Day of Observation 1843.	Apparent Zenith Distance, from Unreduced Observation.	Reduction for Az. Error, and Curv. of Path.	Refraction.	Precession, Aberration, and Nutation.	Deduced Mean Zenith Distance, 1843, Jan. 0; and Mean of Separate Results. uncorrected, for Error of Collimation.
May 16	3 42 51·14	·02	3 55	-15·39	3 42 39·28
18	52·85	·05	3·53	15·63	40·70
20	51·82	·03	3·48	15·86	39·41
22	54·19	·05	3·51	16·08	41·57
24	55·91	·02	3·50	16·30	43·09
June 3	55·27	·03	3·50	-17·33	41·41
					3 42 40·91

Day of Observation 1843.	Apparent Zenith Distance, from Unreduced Observation.	Reduction for Az. Error, and Curv. of Path.	Refraction.	Precession, Aberration, and Nutation.	Deduced Mean Zenith Distance, 1843, Jan. 0; and Mean of Separate Results. uncorrected, for Error of Collimation.
May 17	3 43 43·72	·03	3 53	-15·51	3 43 31·71
19	41·84	·11	3·49	15·74	20·48
26	41·54	·01	3·47	16·52	28·48
30	43·42	·00	3·47	16·93	29·96
June 1	44·46	·01	3·45	17·14	30·76
4	44·95	·00	3·45	-17·33	30·97
					3 43 30·23

Error of Collimation   .   .   .   = 0· 0·24·66
Resulting Mean Zenith Distance, South = 3·43· 5·57

Anon. 14ʰ 5ᵐ.—May 17.—Correction for Curvature of Path = ·056; for Azimuth Error = ·003. = - ·059.
No. 5054.— „ 19.— „ „ „ - ·105; „ „ - ·011. = - ·114.

Mean Zenith Distances of Stars observed at Heerelogements Berg.

	FACE OF SECTOR EAST.						FACE OF SECTOR WEST.				
Day of Observation 1843.	Apparent Zenith Distance, from Unreduced Observation.	Reduction for Az. Error, and Curv. of Path.	Refraction.	Precession, Aberration, and Nutation.	Deduced Mean Zenith Distance, 1843, Jan. 0; and Mean of Separate Results, uncorrected, for Error of Collimation.	Day of Observation 1843.	Apparent Zenith Distance, from Unreduced Observation.	Reduction for Az. Error, and Curv. of Path.	Refraction.	Precession, Aberration, and Nutation.	Deduced Mean Zenith Distance, 1843, Jan. 0; and Mean of Separate Results, uncorrected, for Error of Collimation.

B.A.C. 5151.

	° ′ ″	″	″	″	° ′ ″		° ′ ″	″	″	″	° ′ ″
May 12	2·42·54·83	1·72	2·54	−13·56	2·43· 9·21	May 17	2·42· 0·61	·02	2·57	−13·95	2·42·17·11
16	50·87	0·01	2·58	13·87	7·31	19	1·30	·01	2·54	14·10	17·93
18	51·72	0·03	2·56	14·02	8·27	21	1·05	·01	2·56	14·25	17·85
20	51·12	0·02	2·54	14·17	7·81	23	1·89	·01	2·54	14·39	18·81
22	51·27	0·03	2·55	14·32	8·11	26	1·30	·01	2·52	14·00	18·41
24	52·72	0·01	2·55	14·46	9·72	28	0·61	·03	2·50	14·73	17·81
27	50·04	0·15	2·52	14·67	7·08	30	1·84	·00	2·53	14·86	19·23
29	50·88	0·10	2·51	14·80	8·09	June 4	0·86	·00	2·51	−15·17	18·54
31	49·94	0·07	2·51	14·03	7·31						
June 3	49·64	0·02	2·54	−15·11	7·27						
					2·43· 8·02						2·42·18·21

Error of Collimation . . . = 0· 0·24·90
Resulting Mean Zenith Distance, North = 2·42·43·12

Anon. AR. 15·34.

May 18	0·52·29·00	·01	0·82	−13·53	0·52·43·34	May 17	0·51·41·60	·01	0·82	−13·45	0·51·55·86
20	29·64	·01	·81	13·70	44·14	19	41·06	·00	·81	13·62	55·49
22	30·53	·01	·82	13·87	45·21	21	30·67	·00	·82	13·79	54·28
24	29·50	·00	·82	14·03	44·44	23	39·58	·00	·81	13·95	54·34
27	28·26	·05	·81	14·26	43·26	26	41·00	·00	·81	14·19	56·60
29	29·20	·03	·80	14·41	44·38	28	40·56	·01	·80	14·34	55·69
31	28·61	·02	·81	14·56	43·96	30	41·05	·00	·81	14·49	56·95
June 3	28·41	·01	·82	−14·78	44·01	June 4	40·01	·00	·81	−14·85	56·57
					0·52·44·10						0·51·55·72

Error of Collimation . . . = 0· 0·24·19
Resulting Mean Zenith Distance, North = 0·52·19·91

B.A.C. 5227.

May 12	1·10·16·29	·78	1·10	−12·30	1·10· 4·31	May 15	1·11· 6·51	·04	1·12	−12·59	1·10·55·00
16	17·38	·01	1·12	12·60	5·80	17	6·71	·01	1·12	12·79	55·03
18	16·44	·02	1·12	12·88	4·66	19	6·41	·00	1·10	12·98	54·53
20	16·74	·01	1·10	13·07	4·76	21	7·60	·00	1·11	13·16	55·55
22	16·54	·01	1·11	13·26	4·38	23	8·24	·01	1·10	13·35	55·98
24	18·22	·01	1·11	13·44	5·88	26	6·91	·00	1·10	13·62	54·39
27	18·37	·07	1·10	13·70	5·70	28	7·70	·01	1·00	13·79	54·99
29	18·22	·05	1·09	13·88	5·38	30	8·73	·00	1·10	13·96	55·87
June 3	19·31	·01	1·11	14·29	6·12	June 4	7·45	·00	1·09	14·37	54·17
					1·10· 5·22						1·10·55·06

Error of Collimation . . . = 0· 0·24·92
Resulting Mean Zenith Distance, South = 1·10·30·14

Mean Zenith Distances of Stars observed at Heerelogements Berg.

FACE OF SECTOR EAST.

Day of Observation 1843.	Apparent Zenith Distance, from Unreduced Observation.	Reduction for Az. Error, and Curv. of Path.	Refraction.	Precession, Aberration, and Nutation.	Deduced Mean Zenith Distance 1843, Jan. 0; and Mean of Separate Results, uncorrected for Error of Collimation.
B.A.C. 5272.					
May 12	3·13·16·80	2·03	3·01	-11·98	3·13·29·76
16	13 74	0·01	3·06	12·26	29·05
18	13·59	0·04	3·04	12·30	28·98
20	14·63	0·02	3·01	12·53	30·15
22	13·99	0·04	3·03	12·66	29·64
24	13·99	0·01	3·02	12·79	29·79
27	13·24	0·18	2·99	12·97	29·02
29	13·84	0·12	2·94	13·09	29·70
June 3	11·91	0·02	3·02	-13·38	28·29
					3·13·29·30

FACE OF SECTOR WEST.

Day of Observation 1843.	Apparent Zenith Distance, from Unreduced Observation.	Reduction for Az. Error, and Curv. of Path.	Refraction.	Precession, Aberration, and Nutation.	Deduced Mean Zenith Distance 1843, Jan. 0; and Mean of Separate Results, uncorrected, for Error of Collimation.
B.A.C. 5272.					
May 15	3·12·25·84	·10	3·07	-12·19	3·12·41·00
17	25·99	·02	3·06	12·33	41·36
19	23·27	·01	3·01	12·46	38·73
21	23·57	·01	3·03	12·60	39·19
23	23·67	·02	3·01	12·72	39·38
26	24·11	·01	3·00	12·91	40·01
28	23·52	·03	2·96	13·03	39·48
30	25·10	·00	3·00	13·15	41·25
June 4	23·77	·00	2·99	-13·43	40·19
					3·12·40·07

Error of Collimation . . . = 0· 0·24·66
Resulting Mean Zenith Distance, North = 3·13· 4·73

B.A.C. 5374. (FACE OF SECTOR EAST)

Day	App. Z. D.	Red.	Refr.	Prec.	Deduced
May 12	2·58·33·69	1·88	2·78	-10·69	2·58·45·28
16	30·38	0·01	2·83	10·93	44·15
18	29·79	0·04	2·81	11·08	43·64
20	31·12	0·02	2·78	11·21	45·00
22	31·27	0·04	2·79	11·34	45·36
24	30·77	0·01	2·79	11·46	45·01
27	29·24	0·17	2·76	11·64	43·47
29	29·39	0·11	2·75	11·75	43·78
June 3	28·45	0·02	2·79	-12·04	43·26
					2·58·44·34

B.A.C. 5374. (FACE OF SECTOR WEST)

Day	App. Z. D.	Red.	Refr.	Prec.	Deduced
May 15	2·57·39·87	·00	2·84	-10·89	2·57·53·51
17	39·67	·02	2·82	11·02	53·49
19	38·58	·01	2·78	11·15	52·50
21	39·83	·01	2·80	11·27	52·89
26	38·83	·01	2·77	11·58	53·17
28	40·26	·03	2·74	11·70	54·67
30	39·77	·00	2·77	11·81	54·35
31	39·77	·00	2·75	11·87	54·39
June 4	38·48	·00	2·76	-12·09	53·33
					2·57·53·59

Error of Collimation . . . = 0· 0·25·37
Resulting Mean Zenith Distance, North = 2·58·18·96

B.A.C. 5435. (FACE OF SECTOR EAST)

Day	App. Z. D.	Red.	Refr.	Prec.	Deduced
May 12	1·27· 9·95	·93	1·35	-0·79	1·27·20·16
16	6·70	·01	1·38	10·15	18·15
20	7·05	·01	1·35	10·35	18·74
22	7·20	·02	1·36	10·49	19·03
24	7·30	·01	1·36	10·63	19·28
27	4·73	·08	1·34	10·83	16·82
29	6·75	·06	1·34	10·96	18·99
June 3	3·99	·01	1·36	-11·27	16·61
					1·27·18·47

B.A.C. 5435. (FACE OF SECTOR WEST)

Day	App. Z. D.	Red.	Refr.	Prec.	Deduced
May 15	1·26·17·62	·04	1·38	-10·00	1·26·29·16
17	17·57	·01	1·37	10·15	29·08
21	17·87	·00	1·36	10·42	29·65
23	15·06	·01	1·35	10·56	26·96
26	16·83	·00	1·35	10·76	28·94
28	18·02	·02	1·33	10·89	30·22
30	17·18	·00	1·35	11·02	29·55
June 4	16·78	·00	1·34	-11·34	29·46
					1·26·29·13

Error of Collimation . . . = 0· 0·24·67
Resulting Mean Zenith Distance, North = 1·26·53·80

Mean Zenith Distances of Stars observed at Heerelogemonts Berg.

	FACE OF SECTOR EAST.						FACE OF SECTOR WEST.				
Day of Observation 1843.	Apparent Zenith Distance, from Unreduced Observation.	Reduction for Az. Error, and Curv. of Path.	Refraction.	Precession, Aberration, and Nutation.	Deduced Mean Zenith Distance 1843, Jan. 0; and Mean of Separate Results, uncorrected for Error of Collimation.	Day of Observation 1843.	Apparent Zenith Distance, from Unreduced Observation.	Reduction for Az. Error, and Curv. of Path.	Refraction.	Precession, Aberration, and Nutation.	Deduced Mean Zenith Distance 1843, Jan. 0; and Mean of Separate Results, uncorrected for Error of Collimation.

Anon. AR. 16·14.

Day E	App. Z.D.	Red.	Refr.	Prec.	Deduced	Day W	App. Z.D.	Red.	Refr.	Prec.	Deduced
May 20	0·51·12·44	·01	0·81	- 9·83	0·51· 3·41	May 17	0·52· 1·91	·01	0·82	- 9·59	0·51·53·13
22	12·59	·01	·81	9·99	3·40	21	1·96	·00	·81	9·91	52·86
24	13·47	·00	·81	10·15	4·13	23	2·35	·00	·81	10·07	53·10
27	12·29	·05	·80	10·39	2·65	26	1·17	·00	·80	10·31	51·66
29	13·92	·03	·80	10·54	4·15	28	0·88	·01	·79	10·46	51·20
31	11·99	·02	0·80	-10·09	2·08	30	1·17	·00	·80	-10·61	51·36
					0·51· 3·30						0·51·52·22

Error of Collimation . . . = 0· 0·24·46
Resulting Mean Zenith Distance, South = 0·51·27·76

B.A.C. 5388.

Day E	App. Z.D.	Red.	Refr.	Prec.	Deduced	Day W	App. Z.D.	Red.	Refr.	Prec.	Deduced
May 18	0·10·17·23	·00	0·16	- 7·76	0·10·25·15	May 19	0· 9·20·48	+ ·10	0·15	- 7·83	0· 9·37·56
20	18·07	·00	·15	7·89	26·71	26	28·74	·00	·16	7·96	36·86
22	19·46	·00	·16	8·03	27·65	28	28·69	·00	·15	8·29	37·13
24	14·02	·00	·16	8·16	(22·34)	30	29·24	·00	·15	8·42	37·81
27	16·04	·01	·15	8·36	25·44	31	28·45	·00	·15	8·55	37·15
29	17·08	·01	·15	8·49	26·31		28·35	·00	·15	- 8·62	37·12
June 3	16·20	·00	0·16	- 8·81	25·17						
					0·10·26·07						0· 9·37·27

Error of Collimation . . . = 0· 0·24·40
Resulting Mean Zenith Distance, North = 0·10· 1·67

B.A.C. 5632.

Day E	App. Z.D.	Red.	Refr.	Prec.	Deduced	Day W	App. Z.D.	Red.	Refr.	Prec.	Deduced
May 12	2· 1·41·82	1·36	1·01	- 6·44	2· 1·35·93	May 15	2· 2·31·64	·07	1·94	- 6·67	2· 2·26·84
16	41·18	0·01	1·94	6·75	36·36	17	31·59	·02	1·93	6·82	26·08
18	40·29	0·03	1·03	6·90	35·29	19	30·41	·01	1·91	6·98	25·33
20	40·24	0·01	1·91	7·05	35·09	21	31·05	·01	1·92	7·13	25·83
22	40·58	0·03	1·02	7·21	35·26	23	31·89	·01	1·01	7·28	26·51
24	40·34	0·01	1·02	7·36	34·80	26	30·75	·01	1·90	7·51	25·13
27	41·47	0·12	1·89	7·59	35·65	28	30·41	·02	1·88	7·66	24·61
29	40·93	0·08	1·89	7·74	35·00	30	33·17	·00	1·90	7·81	27·26
June 3	42·05	0·02	1·91	- 8·11	36·73	June 4	31·10	·00	1·89	- 8·19	24·80
					2· 1·35·58						2· 2·25·89

Error of Collimation . . . = 0· 0·25·16
Resulting Mean Zenith Distance, South = 2· 2· 0·73

No. 5588.—May 19.—Correction for Curvature of Path = + ·098; for Azimuth ·000. = + ·098.

Mean Zenith Distances of Stars observed at Heerelogements Berg.

FACE OF SECTOR EAST. / FACE OF SECTOR WEST.

B.A.C. 5735.

Day of Observation 1843	Apparent Zenith Distance, from Unreduced Observation.	Reduction for Az. Error, and Curv. of Path.	Refraction.	Precession, Aberration, and Nutation.	Deduced Mean Zenith Distance, 1843, Jan. 0; and Mean of Separate Results, uncorrected, for Error of Collimation.	Day of Observation 1843	Apparent Zenith Distance, from Unreduced Observation.	Reduction for Az. Error, and Curv. of Path.	Refraction.	Precession, Aberration, and Nutation.	Deduced Mean Zenith Distance, 1843, Jan. 0; and Mean of Separate Results, uncorrected, for Error of Collimation.
May 12	1·55·17·43	1·29	1·81	− 4·99	1·55·12·96	May 15	1·56· 6·26	·06	1·84	− 5·19	1·56· 2·85
16	17·53	0·01	1·84	5·26	14·10	17	7·45	·02	1·83	5·33	3·93
18	16·20	0·03	1·83	5·40	12·60	19	6·86	·01	1·81	5·47	3·19
20	16·25	0·01	1·81	5·53	12·52	21	6·96	·01	1·82	5·60	3·17
22	15·83	0·02	1·82	5·67	11·93	26	6·46	·01	1·80	5·95	2·30
24	17·18	0·01	1·82	5·81	13·18	28	6·71	·02	1·78	6·09	2·38
31	17·73	0·06	1·79	6·30	13·16	30	7·10	·00	1·80	6·23	2·67
June 3	18·42	0·01	1·81	− 6·50	13·72	June 4	7·25	·00	1·79	− 6·57	2·47
					1·55·13·03						1·56· 2·87

Error of Collimation . . . = 0· 0·24·92
Resulting Mean Zenith Distance, South = 1·55·37·95

B.A.C. 5817.

Day of Observation 1843	Apparent Zenith Distance, from Unreduced Observation.	Reduction for Az. Error, and Curv. of Path.	Refraction.	Precession, Aberration, and Nutation.	Deduced Mean Zenith Distance, 1843, Jan. 0; and Mean of Separate Results, uncorrected, for Error of Collimation.	Day of Observation 1843	Apparent Zenith Distance, from Unreduced Observation.	Reduction for Az. Error, and Curv. of Path.	Refraction.	Precession, Aberration, and Nutation.	Deduced Mean Zenith Distance, 1843, Jan. 0; and Mean of Separate Results, uncorrected, for Error of Collimation.
May 18	0·30·18·07	·01	0·49	− 4·29	0·30·14·26	May 15	0·31· 5·57	·02	0·49	− 4·13	0·31· 1·91
20	17·88	·00	·48	4·39	13·07	17	7·20	·00	·49	4·23	3·46
22	17·43	·01	·48	4·50	13·40	19	6·76	·00	·48	4·34	2·90
24	18·22	·00	·48	4·61	14·09	21	7·06	·00	·48	4·45	3·09
27	18·22	·03	·48	4·78	13·80	26	5·03	·00	·48	4·72	0·79
29	18·17	·02	·48	4·89	13·74	28	6·66	·01	·47	4·83	2·29
31	18·07	·01	·47	5·00	13·53	30	6·81	·00	·48	4·94	2·35
June 3	19·70	·00	·48	− 5·17	15·01	June 1	7·30	·00	·47	5·06	2 71
						4	6·22	·00	0·48	− 5·23	1·47
					0·30·13·99						0·31· 2 33

Error of Collimation . . . = 0· 0·24·17
Resulting Mean Zenith Distance, South = 0·30·38·16

B.A.C. 5881.

Day of Observation 1843	Apparent Zenith Distance, from Unreduced Observation.	Reduction for Az. Error, and Curv. of Path.	Refraction.	Precession, Aberration, and Nutation.	Deduced Mean Zenith Distance, 1843, Jan. 0; and Mean of Separate Results, uncorrected, for Error of Collimation.	Day of Observation 1843	Apparent Zenith Distance, from Unreduced Observation.	Reduction for Az. Error, and Curv. of Path.	Refraction.	Precession, Aberration, and Nutation.	Deduced Mean Zenith Distance, 1843, Jan. 0; and Mean of Separate Results, uncorrected, for Error of Collimation.
May 16	2·15·17·63	·01	2·14	− 3·52	2·15·23·28	May 17	2·14·29·10	·02	2·14	− 3·56	2·14·34·87
18	16·39	·03	2 13	3·59	22·08	19	28·84	·01	2·11	3·62	34·56
20	16·99	·01	2·11	3·65	22·74	21	28·84	·01	2·12	3·69	34·64
22	17·73	·03	2·12	3·72	23·54	26	30·03	·01	2·10	3·86	35·98
24	18·62	·01	2·12	3·79	24·52	28	30·27	·02	2·08	3·93	36·26
27	17·33	·13	2·09	3·89	23·18	30	29·88	·00	2·10	4·00	35·98
29	18·47	·09	2·09	3·96	24·43	31	28·60	·00	2·09	4·03	34·72
June 3	16·15	·02	2·11	− 4·14	22·39	June 4	29·93	·00	2 09	− 4·18	36·20
					2·15·23·27						2·14·35·40

Error of Collimation . . . = 0· 0·23·93
Resulting Mean Zenith Distance, North = 2·14·59·34

Mean Zenith Distances of Stars observed at Heerelogements Berg.

	FACE OF SECTOR EAST.						FACE OF SECTOR WEST.				
Day of Observation 1843.	Apparent Zenith Distance, from Unreduced Observation.	Reduction for Az. Error, and Curv. of Path.	Refraction.	Precession, Aberration, and Nutation.	Deduced Mean Zenith Distance. 1843, Jan. 0; and Mean of Separate Results, uncorrected, for Error of Collimation.	Day of Observation 1843.	Apparent Zenith Distance, from Unreduced Observation.	Reduction for Az. Error, and Curv. of Path.	Refraction.	Precession, Aberration, and Nutation.	Deduced Mean Zenith Distance 1843, Jan. 0; and Mean of Separate Results, uncorrected, for Error of Collimation.
				B.A.C. 5915.							
May 16	5· 0·20·80	·02	4·78	- 1·83	5· 0·23·82	May 17	5· 1·12·09	·04	4·77	- 1·90	5· 1·14·92
18	20·99	·07	4·76	1·96	23·72	19	10·71	·02	4·71	2·03	13·37
20	20·30	·04	4·71	2·10	22·96	21	10·22	* ·12	4·74	2·17	12·67
22	20·84	* ·12	4·73	2·24	23·21	26	10·17	·02	4·69	2·53	12·31
24	21·28	·02	4·73	2·38	23·61	28	10·41	·06	4·64	2·07	12·32
27	20·15	·31	4·67	2·00	21·91	30	13·03	·00	4·08	2·82	14·89
29	21·63	·21	4·67	- 2·74	23·35	31	11·50	·00	4·66	- 2·89	13·27
					5· 0·23·23						5· 1·13·39

Error of Collimation . . = 0· 0·25·08
Resulting Mean Zenith Distance, South = 5· 0·48·31

				B.A.C. 5960.							
May 18	0· 7·51·32	·00	0·13	- 1·98	0· 7·49·47	May 17	0· 8·42·28	·00	0·13	- 1·94	0· 8·40·47
22	51·47	·00	·13	2·13	49·47	21	43·02	·00	·13	2·09	41·06
29	51·01	·01	·13	- 2·42	49·61	26	40·60	·00	·13	2·20	38·44
						28	43·42	·00	·13	2·38	41·17
						30	41·64	·00	0·13	- 2·46	39·31
					0· 7·49·52						0· 8·40·09

Error of Collimation . . = 0· 0·25·29
Resulting Mean Zenith Distance, South = 0· 8·14·80

				B.A.C. 6016.							
May 16	0·19·55·21	·00	0·31	- 1·05	0·19·56·57	May 17	0·19· 6·72	·00	0·31	- 1·08	0·19· 8·11
18	55·46	·00	·31	1·11	56·88	19	5·83	·00	·31	1·14	7·28
20	55·75	·00	·31	1·17	57·23	21	5·24	·00	·31	1·20	6·75
22	56·54	·00	·31	1·23	58·08	26	7·61	·00	·30	1·37	9·28
24	57·43	·00	·31	1·30	59·04	28	6·82	·00	·30	1·44	8·56
27	54·77	·02	·30	1·40	56·45	30	6·67	·00	·30	1·51	8·48
29	55·95	·01	·30	1·47	57·71	31	6·23	·00	·30	1·54	8·07
June 3	54·32	·00	0·31	- 1·65	56·28	June 4	6·97	·00	0·30	- 1·69	8·96
					0·19·57·28						0·19· 8·19

Error of Collimation . . = 0· 0·24·55
Resulting Mean Zenith Distance, North = 0·19·32·73

No. 5915.—May 21.—Correction for Curvature of Path - ·105; for Azimuth Error - ·017. = - ·122.
„ 22 — „ „ „ - ·059; „ „ - ·064. = - ·123.

Mean Zenith Distances of Stars observed at Heerelogements Berg.

FACE OF SECTOR EAST. | FACE OF SECTOR WEST.

Day of Observation 1843.	Apparent Zenith Distance, from Unreduced Observation.	Reduction for At. Error, and Curv. of Path.	Refraction.	Precession, Aberration, and Nutation.	Deduced Mean Zenith Distance, 1843, Jan. 0; and Mean of Separate Results, uncorrected, for Error of Collimation.	Day of Observation 1843.	Apparent Zenith Distance, from Unreduced Observation.	Reduction for At. Error, and Curv. of Path.	Refraction.	Precession, Aberration, and Nutation.	Deduced Mean Zenith Distance, 1843, Jan. 0; and Mean of Separate Results, uncorrected, for Error of Collimation.

B.A.C. 6074.

Day	App. Z.D. E.	Red.	Refr.	Prec.	Ded. Mean E.	Day	App. Z.D. W.	Red.	Refr.	Prec.	Ded. Mean W.
May 16	1·44·39·16	·01	1·66	− 0·32	1·44·41·13	May 17	1·43·40·54	·01	1·65	− 0·33	1·43·51·51
18	38·72	·02	1·65	0·35	40·70	19	48·90	·01	1·63	0·37	50·89
20	38·92	·01	1·63	0·38	40·92	21	49·00	·01	1·64	0·40	51·03
22	39·21	·02	1·64	0·42	41·25	26	40·88	·01	1·62	0·49	51·98
24	41·29	·01	1·64	0·45	43·37	28	50·52	·02	1·61	0·54	52·65
27	38·52	·10	1·61	0·51	40·54	30	50·57	·00	1·62	0·58	52·77
29	40·05	·07	1·62	− 0·56	42·16	31	50·03	·00	1·61	− 0·60	52·24
					1·44·41·44						1·43·51·87

Error of Collimation . . . = 0· 0·24·79
Resulting Mean Zenith Distance, North = 1·44·16·65

B.A.C. 6115.

Day	App. Z.D. E.	Red.	Refr.	Prec.	Ded. Mean E.	Day	App. Z.D. W.	Red.	Refr.	Prec.	Ded. Mean W.
May 16	1·33·20·70	·01	1·48	+ 0·38	1·33·21·70	May 17	1·32·29·42	·01	1·47	+ 0·37	1·32·30·51
18	19·83	·02	1·47	0·36	20·92	19	29·57	·00	1·45	0·34	30·68
20	20·03	·01	1·46	0·33	21·15	21	30·16	·01	1·46	0·32	31·29
22	19·98	·02	1·46	0·30	21·12	23	30·70	·01	1·45	0·29	31·85
24	22·60	·01	1·46	0·27	23·78	26	30·75	·00	1·45	0·24	31·96
27	19·34	·09	1·44	0·22	20·47	28	30·80	·02	1·43	0·20	32·01
29	20·67	·06	1·44	0·18	21·87	30	30·80	·00	1·44	0·16	32·08
June 3	19·64	·01	1·45	+ 0·08	21·00	31	30·31	·00	1·44	+ 0·14	31·61
					1·33·21·51						1·32·31·50

Error of Collimation . . . = 0· 0·25·01
Resulting Mean Zenith Distance, North = 1·32·56·51

B.A.C. 6145.

Day	App. Z.D. E.	Red.	Refr.	Prec.	Ded. Mean E.	Day	App. Z.D. W.	Red.	Refr.	Prec.	Ded. Mean W.
May 16	1·13·40·85	·01	1·16	+ 0·86	1·13·41·14	May 17	1·12·51·96	·01	1·16	+ 0·85	1·12·52·26
18	40·60	·02	1·16	0·84	40·90	19	50·63	·00	1·15	0·83	50·95
20	40·16	·01	1·15	0·49	40·49	21	50·43	·00	1·15	0·80	50·78
22	40·45	·01	1·15	0·79	40·80	23	51·77	·01	1·14	0·77	52·13
24	42·72	·01	1·15	0·76	43·10	26	50·93	·00	1·14	0·73	51·34
27	40·01	·07	1·14	0·71	40·37	28	52·31	·01	1·13	0·69	52·74
29	40·85	·05	1·14	0·67	41·27	30	51·81	·00	1·14	0·65	52·30
June 1	39·32	·03	1·14	0·61	39·82	31	51·82	·00	1·13	0·63	52·32
3	40·80	·01	1·15	+ 0·57	41·37	June 4	52·56	·00	1·14	+ 0·55	53·15
					1·13·41·03						1·12·52·00

Error of Collimation . . . = 0· 0·24·51
Resulting Mean Zenith Distance, North = 1·13·10·51

2 Q

Mean Zenith Distances of Stars observed at Heerelogements Berg.

	FACE OF SECTOR EAST.					FACE OF SECTOR WEST.				
Day of Observation 1843.	Apparent Zenith Distance, from Unreduced Observation.	Reduction for Az. Error, and Curv. of Path.	Refraction.	Precession, Aberration, and Nutation.	Deduced Mean Zenith Distance, 1843, Jan. 0; and Mean of Separate Results, uncorrected, for Error of Collimation.	Day of Observation 1843.	Apparent Zenith Distance, from Unreduced Observation.	Reduction for Az. Error, and Curv. of Path.	Refraction.	Precession, Aberration, and Nutation.	Deduced Mean Zenith Distance, 1843, Jan. 0; and Mean of Separate Results, uncorrected, for Error of Collimation.

B.A.C. 6186.

Day of Obs.	Apparent Z.D.	Red.	Refr.	Prec.	Deduced Mean	Day of Obs.	Apparent Z.D.	Red.	Refr.	Prec.	Deduced Mean
May 16	4·49·28·00	·02	4·61	+2·79	4·49·35·38	May 17	4·50·17·48	·04	4·59	+2·75	4·50·24·78
18	27·46	·07	4·59	2·72	34·70	19	16·99	·02	4·54	2·68	24·19
20	25·44	·03	4·55	2·64	32·60	21	17·63	·02	4·57	2·60	24·78
22	27·21	·06	4·56	2·57	34·28	23	18·86	·03	4·54	2·53	25·90
24	27·11	·02	4·56	2·48	34·13	26	16·49	·02	4·52	2·40	23·39
27	26·97	·30	4·51	2·35	33·53	28	16·69	·06	4·47	2·31	23·41
29	27·56	·20	4·52	2·26	34·14	30	18·52	·00	4·51	2·21	25·24
June 1	28·00	·14	4·50	2·12	34·48	31	17·38	·00	4·49	2·17	24·04
3	28·40	·04	4·55	+2·02	34·93	June 4	17·43	·00	4·50	+1·96	23·89
					4·49·34·24						4·50·24·40

Error of Collimation . . . = 0· 0·25·08
Resulting Mean Zenith Distance, South = 4·49·59·32

B.A.C. 6233.

Day of Obs.	Apparent Z.D.	Red.	Refr.	Prec.	Deduced Mean	Day of Obs.	Apparent Z.D.	Red.	Refr.	Prec.	Deduced Mean
May 16	2·28·30·23	·01	2·37	+2·99	2·28·35·58	May 17	2·29·21·58	·02	2·36	+2·97	2·29·26·89
18	30·48	·03	2·35	2·95	35·75	19	22·08	·01	2·33	2·93	27·33
20	28·36	·02	2·33	2·91	33·58	21	22·52	·01	2·35	2·89	27·75
22	28·75	·03	2·34	2·86	33·92	23	25·09	·01	2·33	2·84	30·25
24	27·91	·01	2·34	2·82	33·06	26	21·44	·01	2·31	2·76	26·50
27	29·98	·15	2·31	2·74	34·88	28	20·40	·03	2·29	2·71	25·37
29	29·05	·10	2·32	2·68	33·95	30	20·65	·00	2·32	2·65	25·62
June 1	29·98	·07	2·31	2·58	34·80	31	21·44	·00	2·30	2·61	26·35
3	30·58	·02	2·33	+2·51	35·40	June 4	19·26	·00	2·31	+2·48	24·05
					2·28·34·55						2·29·26·68

Error of Collimation . . . = 0· 0·26·07
Resulting Mean Zenith Distance, South = 2·29· 0·61

B.A.C. 6275.

Day of Obs.	Apparent Z.D.	Red.	Refr.	Prec.	Deduced Mean	Day of Obs.	Apparent Z.D.	Red.	Refr.	Prec.	Deduced Mean
May 20	1· 9·57·78	·01	1·10	+3·26	1·10· 2·13	May 21	1·10·48·39	·00	1·11	+3·25	1·10·52·75
22	57·86	·01	1·10	3·21	2·21	23	49·48	·01	1·10	3·22	53·79
24	58·32	·01	1·11	3·21	2·63	26	46·32	·00	1·09	3·18	50·59
27	60·00	·07	1·09	3·16	4·18	28	47·50	·01	1·08	3·14	51·71
29	58·12	·05	1·10	3·12	2·29	30	46·86	·00	1·09	3·11	51·06
June 1	58·52	·03	1·09	+3·06	2·64	31	46·32	·00	1·09	3·09	50·50
						June 4	46·32	* ·03	1·09	+2·90	50·37
					1·10· 2·68						1·10·51·54

Error of Collimation . . . = 0· 0·24·43
Resulting Mean Zenith Distance, South = 1·10·27·11

No. 6275.—June 4.—Correction for Curvature of Path - ·025; for Azimuth Error - ·001. = - ·026.

Mean Zenith Distances of Stars observed at Heerelogements Berg.

	FACE OF SECTOR EAST.						FACE OF SECTOR WEST.				
Day of Observation 1843.	Apparent Zenith Distance, from Unreduced Observation.	Reduction for Az. Error, and Curv. of Path.	Refraction.	Precession, Aberration, and Nutation.	Deduced Mean Zenith Distance, 1843, Jan. 0; and Mean of Separate Results, uncorrected, for Error of Collimation.	Day of Observation 1843.	Apparent Zenith Distance, from Unreduced Observation.	Reduction for Az. Error, and Curr. of Path.	Refraction.	Precession, Aberration, and Nutation.	Deduced Mean Zenith Distance, 1843, Jan. 0; and Mean of Separate Results, uncorrected, for Error of Collimation.

B.A.C. 6285.

	° ′ ″	″	″	″	° ′ ″		° ′ ″	″	″	″	° ′ ″
May 16	1· 6·36·02	·00	1·06	+ 3·39	1· 6·40·47	May 17	1· 7·24·85	·01	1·06	+ 3·38	1· 7·29·28
18	35·23	·02	1·06	3·38	39·65	19	23·97	·00	1·05	3·37	28·39
20	35·03	·01	1·05	3·36	39·43	21	24·95	* ·03	1·05	3·35	29·32
22	34·88	·01	1·05	3·34	39·26	23	25·99	·01	1·05	3·32	30·35
24	33·65	·01	1·05	3·31	38·00	26	24·80	·00	1·04	3·28	29·12
27	34·29	·07	1·04	3·27	38·53	28	23·82	·01	1·03	3·25	28·09
29	34·39	·04	1·04	3·23	38·62	30	24·41	·00	1·04	3·21	28·66
June 3	35·67	·01	1·05	+ 3·13	39·84	31	23·87	·00	1·04	+ 3·19	28·10
					1· 6·39·23						1· 7·28·91

Error of Collimation . . = 0· 0·24·84
Resulting Mean Zenith Distance, South = 1· 7· 4·07

B.A.C. 6305.

May 16	1· 8·58·28	·01	1·10	+ 3·68	1· 9· 3·05	May 19	1· 9·47·26	·00	1·08	+ 3·66	1· 9·52·00
18	58·28	·02	1·10	3·03	3·03	21	47·51	·00	1·09	3·65	52·25
20	57·29	·01	1·09	3·66	2·03	23	48·54	·01	1·08	3·63	53·24
22	57·64	·01	1·09	2·36	2·68	26	46·47	·00	1·08	3·59	51·14
24	57·98	·01	1·09	3·62	2·68	28	46·77	·01	1·07	3·56	51·39
27	57·84	·07	1·08	3·58	2·43	30	45·93	·00	1·08	3·53	50·54
29	57·14	·05	1·08	3·55	1·72	31	46·82	·00	1·07	3·51	51·40
June 3	58·48	·01	1·09	+ 3·45	3·01	June 4	46·91	·00	1·07	+ 3·43	51·41
					1· 9· 2·54						1· 9·51·67

Error of Collimation . . = 0· 0·24·57
Resulting Mean Zenith Distance, South = 1· 9·27·11

B.A.C. 6414.

May 20	1· 3·43·02	·01	0·99	+ 5·04	1· 3·38·96	May 19	1· 2·53·00	·00	0·99	+ 5·02	1· 2·48·97
22	42·73	·01	·99	5·07	38·64	21	53·49	1·00	1·00	5·06	49·43
27	42·68	·06	·98	5·13	38·47	26	54·43	·00	0·99	5·12	50·30
29	43·67	·04	·99	5·15	39·47	28	55·52	·01	0·98	5·14	51·35
31	43·71	·03	·98	5·16	39·50	30	54·93	·00	0·98	5·15	50·76
June 3	42·92	·01	0·99	+ 5·17	38·73	June 4	55·57	·00	0·98	+ 5·17	51·38
					1· 3·38·96						1· 2·50·37

Error of Collimation . . = 0· 0·24·30
Resulting Mean Zenith Distance, North = 1· 3·14·66

No. 6285.—May 21.—Correction for Curvature of Path − ·025; for Azimuth Error − ·004. = − ·029.

Mean Zenith Distances of Stars observed at Heerelogements Berg.

	FACE OF SECTOR EAST.						FACE OF SECTOR WEST.				
Day of Observation 1843.	Apparent Zenith Distance, from Unreduced Observation.	Reduction for Az. Error, and Curv. of Path.	Refraction.	Precession, Aberration, and Nutation.	Deduced Mean Zenith Distance, 1843, Jan. 0; and Mean of Separate Results, uncorrected, for Error of Collimation.	Day of Observation 1843.	Apparent Zenith Distance, from Unreduced Observation	Reduction for Az. Error, and Curv. of Path.	Refraction.	Precession, Aberration, and Nutation.	Deduced Mean Zenith Distance, 1843, Jan. 0; and Mean of Separate Results, uncorrected, for Error of Collimation.

B.A.C. 6489.

	° ′ ″	″	″	″	° ′ ″		° ′ ″	″	″	″	° ′ ″
May 16	1·52·40·68	·01	1·78	+ 5·67	1·52·36·78	May 17	1·51·51·15	·01	1·78	+ 5·70	1·51·47·22
18	41·22	·02	1·77	5·73	37·24	19	49·52	·01	1·76	5·76	45·51
20	42·21	·01	1·76	5·79	38·17	21	49·72	·01	1·77	5·82	45·66
22	41·71	·02	1·76	5·85	37·60	26	52·24	·01	1·74	5·94	48·03
24	42·55	·01	1·77	5·89	38·42	28	50·61	·02	1·73	5·98	46·34
27	40·73	·11	1·74	5·96	36·40	30	51·50	·00	1·74	6·01	47·23
29	41·96	·07	1·75	6·00	37·04	June 1	51·20	·00	1·74	6·05	46·89
31	41·47	·05	1·74	+ 6·03	37·13	4	52·58	·00	1·74	+ 6·08	48·24
					1·52·37·42						1·51·46·89

Error of Collimation   .   .   = 0· 0·25·27
Resulting Mean Zenith Distance, North = 1·52·12·16

B.A.C. 6525.

	° ′ ″	″	″	″	° ′ ″		° ′ ″	″	″	″	° ′ ″
May 16	3· 6·11·54	·01	2·95	+ 5·80	3· 6· 8·08	May 17	3· 5·22·22	·02	2·94	+ 5·84	3· 5·19·30
22	11·64	·04	2·92	6·03	8·49	19	21·43	·01	2·91	5·92	18·41
24	14·95	·01	2·92	6·10	11·76	21	22·96	·01	2·93	5·99	19·89
27	11·99	·18	2·89	6·19	8·51	26	23·50	·01	2·89	6·10	20·22
31	12·63	·08	2·88	6·30	9·13	28	23·21	·03	2·86	6·22	19·82
June 3	12·78	·02	2·91	+ 6·37	9·30	30	23·31	·00	2·89	+ 6·27	19·93
					3· 6· 9·31						3· 5·19·60

Error of Collimation   .   .   = 0· 0·24·86
Resulting Mean Zenith Distance, North = 3· 5·44·45

B.A.C. 6639.

	° ′ ″	″	″	″	° ′ ″		° ′ ″	″	″	″	° ′ ″
May 16	1·55·44·54	·01	1·83	+ 7·79	1·55·38·57	May 19	1·54·54·52	·01	1·81	+ 7·94	1·54·48·38
18	45·38	·03	1·82	7·89	39·28	21	55·61	·01	1·82	8·03	49·39
20	46·56	·01	1·81	7·90	40·37	26	56·54	·01	1·79	8·25	50·07
22	46·37	·02	1·81	8·08	40·08	28	57·48	·02	1·78	8·32	50·92
24	48·69	·01	1·81	8·17	42·32	30	55·85	·00	1·79	8·39	49·25
27	45·48	·11	1·79	8·29	38·87	31	56·25	·00	1·78	8·43	49·60
29	45·97	·07	1·80	8·36	39·34	June 1	56·05	·00	1·79	8·46	49·38
June 3	46·02	·01	1·81	+ 8·52	39·30	4	58·12	·00	1·79	+ 8·54	51·37
					1·55·39·77						1·54·49·80

Error of Collimation   .   .   = 0· 0·24·99
Resulting Mean Zenith Distance, North = 1·55·14·78

B.A.C. 7992.

	° ′ ″	″	″	″	° ′ ″		° ′ ″	″	″	″	° ′ ″
May 12	1·31·38·81	- ·98	1·45	+17·93	1·31·21·35	May 25	1·30·48·19	·00	1·43	+20·69	1·30·28·93
18	39·10	+ ·20	1·45	+19·23	21·52	28	49·07	·02	1·41	+21·29	30·07
					1·31·21·44						1·30·29·50

Error of Collimation   .   .   = 0· 0·25·97
Resulting Mean Zenith Distance, North = 1·30·55·47

No. 7992.—May 18.—Correction for Curvature of Path + ·215; for Azimuth Error - ·020. = + ·195.

MEAN ZENITH DISTANCES.

COLLECTION OF

ALL THE

RESULTS OF OBSERVATION OF EACH STAR

AT

THE KAMIES BERG STATION,

AND

DEDUCTION OF MEAN ZENITH DISTANCE, 1843, JANUARY 0.

NOTE.—The reduction for Azimuthal Error is always to be applied subtractively to the Zenith Distance. The reduction for Curvature of Path is always to be applied subtractively to South Zenith Distance, and additively to North Zenith Distance. The Refraction is always to be applied additively. The Precession, Aberration, and Nutation, have the sign which is proper for reducing the Apparent North Polar Distance of the Star to its mean North Polar Distance, 1843, January 0; and therefore are to be applied with the sign given in the Table when the Star is South of the Zenith, and with the opposite sign when the Star is North of the Zenith.

The numbers included in parentheses in the column " Deduced Mean Zenith Distance, 1843, January 0," are omitted in taking the mean.

Where an asterisk or a positive sign is affixed to a number in the 3rd or 9th columns, the explanation will be found at the bottom of the page.

Mean Zenith Distances of Stars observed at Kamies Berg.

FACE OF SECTOR EAST.						FACE OF SECTOR WEST.					
Day of Observation 1843.	Apparent Zenith Distance, from Unreduced Observation.	Reduction for Az. Error, and Curv. of Path.	Refraction.	Precession, Aberration, and Nutation.	Deduced Mean Zenith Distance, 1843, Jan. 0; and Mean of Separate Results, uncorrected, for Error of Collimation	Day of Observation 1843.	Apparent Zenith Distance, from Unreduced Observation.	Reduction for Az. Error, and Curv. of Path.	Refraction.	Precession, Aberration, and Nutation.	Deduced Mean Zenith Distance, 1843, Jan. 0; and Mean of Separate Results, uncorrected, for Error of Collimation

B.A.C. 1802.

July 25	3 47 28·93	·05	3·28	+12·41	3 47 44·57	July 30	3 48 21·08	·05	3·25	+13·59	3 48 37·87
31	27·21	·02	3·22	13·82	44·23	Aug. 1	22·17	·04	3·25	14·05	39·43
Aug. 2	28·04	·04	3·20	14·27	45·47	6	20·89	·02	3·19	15·12	39·18
7	26·61	·00	3·23	15·33	45·17	8	19·65	·02	3·21	15·52	38·36
13	24·14	·02	3·30	+16·47	43·89	12	20·59	·04	3·34	+16·29	40·18
					3 47 44·67						3 48 39·00

Error of Collimation . . = 0· 0·27·17
Resulting Mean Zenith Distance, South = 3· 48·11·84

B.A.C. 2293.

July 25	1 36 12·50	·02	1·38	+ 2·43	1 36 11·43	July 26	1 35 15·90	·20	1·40	+ 2·67	1 35 14·43
27	12·89	·00	1·39	2·90	11·38	28	18·77	·21	1·36	3·13	16·79
29	16·35	·00	1·36	3·36	14·35	30	20·74	·02	1·36	3·59	18·49
31	14·32	·01	1·35	3·82	11·84	Aug. 1	19·21	·01	1·37	4·04	16·53
Aug. 2	14·52	·01	1·34	4·27	11·58	6	19·16	·01	1·34	5·14	15·35
5	14·97	·00	1·34	4·92	11·39	7	19·70	·00	1·35	5·35	15·70
10	17·34	·01	1·41	5·97	12·77	8	20·59	·01	1·35	5·56	16·37
11	17·24	·01	1·40	6·17	12·46	12	20·15	·01	1·39	+ 6·36	15·17
13	17·78	·01	1·38	+ 6·56	12·59						
					1 36 12·20						1 35 16·10

Error of Collimation . . = 0· 0·28·05
Resulting Mean Zenith Distance, North = 1· 35·44·15

B.A.C. 4458.

July 29	5 31 20·25	·01	4·68	-25·27	5 30 59·65	July 26	5 32 16·05	·76	4·73	-25·54	5 31 54·48
31	20·89	·03	4·69	25·08	00·47	Aug. 3	14·57	·07	4·66	24·77	54·39
Aug. 2	19·06	·06	4·69	24·88	59·41	5	14·47	·00	4·08	24·56	54·59
6	19·21	·00	4·62	24·44	59·39	7	13·54	·00	4·64	24·33	53·85
9	19·90	·02	4·65	24·09	60·44	9	13·73	·03	4·61	24·21	54·10
13	16·94	·03	4·74	-23·60	58·05	12	13·73	·06	4·79	-23·73	54·73
					3 30·59·57						5 31·54·36

Error of Collimation . . = 0· 0·27·39
Resulting Mean Zenith Distance, South = 5· 31·26·96

Mean Zenith Distances of Stars observed at Kamies Berg.

FACE OF SECTOR EAST.						FACE OF SECTOR WEST.					
Day of Observation 1843.	Apparent Zenith Distance, from Unreduced Observation.	Reduction for Az. Error, and Curv. of Path.	Refraction.	Precession, Aberration, and Nutation.	Deduced Mean Zenith Distance, 1843, Jan. 0; and Mean of Separate Results, uncorrected, for Error of Collimation.	Day of Observation 1843.	Apparent Zenith Distance, from Unreduced Observation.	Reduction for Az. Error, and Curv. of Path.	Refraction.	Precession, Aberration, and Nutation.	Deduced Mean Zenith Distance, 1843, Jan. 0; and Mean of Separate Results, uncorrected, for Error of Collimation.

B.A.C. 4579.

	o ′ ″	″	″	″	o ′ ′		o ′ ″	″	″	″	o ′ ″
July 29	1·53·14·07	·00	1·60	-23·00	1·52·52·07	July 26	1·54·12·29	·25	1·62	-23·83	1·53·49·83
31	16·69	·01	1·60	23·45	54·83	30	10·22	·02	1·60	23·53	48·27
Aug. 5	15·90	·00	1·60	23·03	54·47	Aug. 3	11·16	·02	1·59	23·21	49·52
6	15·11	·00	1·58	23·75	53·75	7	10·42	·00	1·59	22·84	40·17
12	13·73	·00	1·64	-22·35	53·02	8	10·67	·01	1·58	-22·75	49·49
					1·52·53·63						1·53·49·26

Error of Collimation . . . = 0· 0·27·81
Resulting Mean Zenith Distance, South = 1·53·21·44

B.A.C. 4623.

July 29	1·51· 9·83	·00	1·57	-23·43	1·50·47·97	July 26	1·52· 8·35	·25	1·59	-23·63	1·51·46·06
31	12·30	·01	1·57	23·94	50·58	30	5·20	·02	1·58	23·36	43·49
Aug. 5	10·52	·00	1·57	22·88	49·21	Aug. 1	6·82	·02	1·58	23·20	45·18
6	9·63	·00	1·55	22·79	48·39	3	6·92	·02	1·56	23·05	45·41
12	7·90	·01	1·61	22·22	47·28	7	5·83	·00	1·56	22·70	44·09
13	9·39	·01	1·59	-22·12	48·85	8	4·99	·01	1·55	-22·61	43·92
					1·50·48·71						1·51·44·79

Error of Collimation . . . = 0· 0·28·04
Resulting Mean Zenith Distance, South = 1·51·16·75

B.A.C. 4686.

July 29	5·14· 3·50	·01	4·44	-24·06	5·13·43·87	July 26	5·14·58·91	·72	4·48	-24·24	5·14·38·43
31	3·31	·03	4·44	23·78	43·78	28	59·11	·75	4·52	24·13	38·75
Aug. 2	2·66	·05	4·45	23·80	43·26	30	57·83	·07	4·45	24·00	38·21
5	2·96	·00	4·44	23·58	43·82	Aug. 1	57·33	·05	4·47	23·87	37·88
6	2·37	·00	4·38	23·50	43·25	3	57·53	·07	4·41	23·73	38·14
7	2·66	·01	4·40	23·41	43·64	8	55·95	·02	4·37	23·33	36·97
9	3·41	·02	4·41	23·25	44·55	12	57·88	·05	4·55	-22·97	39·41
13	0·64	·03	4·50	-22·88	42·23						
					5·13·43·55						5·14·38·26

Error of Collimation . . . = 0· 0·27·35
Resulting Mean Zenith Distance, South = 5·14·10·90

Mean Zenith Distances of Stars observed at Kamies Berg.

FACE OF SECTOR EAST.						FACE OF SECTOR WEST.					
Day of Observation 1843.	Apparent Zenith Distance, from Unreduced Observation.	Reduction for Az. Error, and Curr. of Path.	Refraction.	Precession, Aberration, and Nutation.	Deduced Mean Zenith Distance, 1843, Jan. 0; and Mean of Separate Results, uncorrected, for Error of Collimation.	Day of Observation 1843.	Apparent Zenith Distance, from Unreduced Observation.	Reduction for Az. Error, and Curr. of Path.	Refraction.	Precession, Aberration, and Nutation.	Deduced Mean Zenith Distance, 1843, Jan. 0; and Mean of Separate Results, uncorrected, for Error of Collimation.

B.A.C. 4719.

Day	Apparent Z.D.	Az.	Refr.	Prec.	Deduced	Day	Apparent Z.D.	Az.	Refr.	Prec.	Deduced
July 29	1 48 51·36	·00	1·52	-21·36	1·49·14·24	July 20	1·47·54·12	·23	1·54	-21·53	1·48·16·96
31	49·23	·01	1·53	-21·24	11·99	28	54·27	·24	1·55	21·42	17·00
						30	56·09	·02	1·53	21·30	18·90
						Aug. 1	54·17	·02	1·54	-21·18	16·87
					1·49·13·12						1·48·17·43

Error of Collimation . . = 0· 0·27·84
Resulting Mean Zenith Distance, North = 1·48·45·27

B.A.C. 4784.

Day	Apparent Z.D.	Az.	Refr.	Prec.	Deduced	Day	Apparent Z.D.	Az.	Refr.	Prec.	Deduced
July 29	1·34·38·57	·00	1·33	-20·86	1·34·60·76	July 26	1·33·40·59	·20	1·34	-21.01	1·34· 2·74
31	37·04	·01	1·33	20·76	59·12	28	40·59	·21	1·35	20·91	2·64
Aug. 2	37·63	·01	1·33	20·64	59·59	30	42·12	·02	1·33	20·81	4·24
5	36·74	·00	1·33	20·46	58·53	Aug. 1	42·66	·01	1·34	20·70	4·69
6	36·54	·00	1·31	20·40	58·25	3	41·13	·02	1·32	20·59	3·02
7	36·40	·00	1·31	-20·33	59·04	8	41·58	·01	1·31	-20·26	3·14
					1·34·59·05						1·34· 3·41

Error of Collimation . . = 0· 0·27·82
Resulting Mean Zenith Distance, North = 1·34·31·23

Anon. AR. 14 23.

Day	Apparent Z.D.	Az.	Refr.	Prec.	Deduced	Day	Apparent Z.D.	Az.	Refr.	Prec.	Deduced
July 31	2·15·36·35	·01	1·92	-21·82	2·15·16·44	July 26	2·16·32·15	·30	1·93	-22·05	2·16·11·73
Aug. 2	35·95	·02	1·92	-21·72	16·13	28	30·47	·31	1·95	21·96	10·15
						30	30·42	·03	1·92	21·87	10·44
						Aug. 1	28·50	·12	1·93	-21·77	8·54
					2·15·16·29						2·16·10·22

Error of Collimation . . = 0· 0·26·97
Resulting Mean Zenith Distance, South = 2·15·43·25

B.A.C. 4852.

Day	Apparent Z.D.	Az.	Refr.	Prec.	Deduced	Day	Apparent Z.D.	Az.	Refr.	Prec.	Deduced
July 25	4· 7·58·70	·05	3·60	-22·14	4· 7·40·17	July 26	4· 8·54·17	·56	3·53	-22·11	4· 8·35·03
29	56·09	·01	3·50	22·01	38·17	28	54·32	·59	3·57	22·04	35·26
31	58·07	·02	3·51	21·93	30·62	30	54·22	·05	3·51	21·97	35·71
Aug. 2	57·58	·04	3·51	21·84	30·21	Aug. 1	53·08	·04	3·53	21·89	34·08
5	57·63	·00	3·50	21·69	39·44	3	54·22	·05	3·48	21·80	35·85
9	58·61	·02	3·50	21·46	40·63	6	52·98	·02	3·46	21·64	34·78
13	56·29	·02	3·57	-21·20	38·64	8	53·53	·02	3·47	21·52	35·46
						12	53·97	·04	3·60	-21·27	36·26
					4· 7·39·41						4· 8·35·38

Error of Collimation . . = 0· 0·27·98
Resulting Mean Zenith Distance, South = 4· 8· 7·40

Anon. 14h 23m.—Aug. 1.—Correction for Azimuthal Error - ·021 ; for Curvature of Path - ·099. = - 0"·12.

Mean Zenith Distances of Stars observed at Kamies Berg.

FACE OF SECTOR EAST. | FACE OF SECTOR WEST.

Day of Observation 1843.	Apparent Zenith Distance, from Unreduced Observation.	Reduction for Az. Error, and Curv. of Path.	Refraction.	Precession, Aberration, and Nutation.	Deduced Mean Zenith Distance, 1843, Jan. 0; and Mean of Separate Results, uncorrected, for Error of Collimation.	Day of Observation 1843.	Apparent Zenith Distance, from Unreduced Observation.	Reduction for Az. Error, and Curv. of Path.	Refraction.	Precession, Aberration, and Nutation.	Deduced Mean Zenith Distance, 1843, Jan. 0; and Mean of Separate Results, uncorrected, for Error of Collimation.
					B.A.C. 4891.						
July 25	3· 3·24·54	·04	2·65	-19·33	3· 3·46·48	July 26	3· 2·29·77	·38	2·61	-19·30	3· 2·51·30
27	25·03	·00	2·64	19·26	46·93	28	28·39	·40	2·63	19·22	49·84
29	26·66	·01	2·58	19·18	48·41	30	31·20	·04	2·58	19·14	52·88
31	25·63	·01	2·58	19·10	47·30	Aug. 1	30·46	·03	2·60	19·05	52·08
Aug. 2	26·37	·03	2·58	19·01	47·93	3	28·49	·04	2·56	18·96	49·97
5	25·48	·00	2·58	18·86	46·92	6	30·12	·01	2·54	18·81	51·46
9	24·69	·01	2·58	-18·64	45·90	8	29·92	·01	2·55	18·70	51·16
						12	29·48	·03	2·65	-18·40	50·56
					3· 3·47·12						3· 2·51·16

Error of Collimation . . = 0· 0·27·98
Resulting Mean Zenith Distance, North = 3· 3·19·14

Day of Observation 1843.	Apparent Zenith Distance, from Unreduced Observation.	Reduction for Az. Error, and Curv. of Path.	Refraction.	Precession, Aberration, and Nutation.	Deduced Mean Zenith Distance.	Day of Observation 1843.	Apparent Zenith Distance, from Unreduced Observation.	Reduction for Az. Error, and Curv. of Path.	Refraction.	Precession, Aberration, and Nutation.	Deduced Mean Zenith Distance.
					B.A.C. 4916.						
July 25	2·51·10·32	·04	2·49	-20·99	2·50·51·78	July 26	2·52· 8·65	·38	2·45	-20·96	2·51·49·76
27	11·26	·00	2·47	20·94	52·79	28	8·15	·40	2·46	20·91	49·30
29	11·16	·01	2·42	20·88	52·69	30	7·61	·04	2·42	20·85	49·14
31	11·31	·01	2·42	20·82	52·90	Aug. 1	6·62	·03	2·44	20·78	48·25
Aug. 2	10·87	·03	2·42	20·74	52·52	3	7·61	·04	2·40	20·70	49·27
5	10·82	·00	2·42	20·61	52·63	7	7·41	·00	2·40	20·52	49·29
9	11·61	·01	2·42	-20·41	53·61	8	6·96	·01	2·39	-20·47	48·87
					2·50·52·70						2·51·49·13

Error of Collimation . . = 0· 0·28·21
Resulting Mean Zenith Distance, South = 2·51·20·91

Day of Observation 1843.	Apparent Zenith Distance, from Unreduced Observation.	Reduction for Az. Error, and Curv. of Path.	Refraction.	Precession, Aberration, and Nutation.	Deduced Mean Zenith Distance.	Day of Observation 1843.	Apparent Zenith Distance, from Unreduced Observation.	Reduction for Az. Error, and Curv. of Path.	Refraction.	Precession, Aberration, and Nutation.	Deduced Mean Zenith Distance.
					Anon. AR. 14·52.						
July 25	1·39·31·46	·02	1·45	-20·12	1·39·12·77	July 26	1·40·29·23	·22	1·43	-20·10	1·40·10·34
27	32·10	·00	1·44	20·07	13·47	28	28·74	·23	1·43	20·05	9·89
29	31·51	·00	1·41	20·02	12·90	30	28·59	·02	1·41	19·99	9·99
31	31·55	·01	1·42	19·96	13·00	Aug. 1	28·35	·02	1·42	19·93	9·82
Aug. 2	31·75	·02	1·42	19·90	13·25	3	28·40	·02	1·40	19·86	9·92
5	31·80	·00	1·41	19·78	13·43	6	27·80	·01	1·39	19·74	9·44
9	32·49	·01	1·41	19·60	14·29	8	28·20	·01	1·39	19·64	9·94
13	29·28	·01	1·44	-19·38	11·33	12	29·63	·02	1·45	-19·44	11·62
					1·39·13·06						1·40·10·12

Error of Collimation . . = 0· 0·28·53
Resulting Mean Zenith Distance, South = 1·39·41·59

Mean Zenith Distances of Stars observed at Kamies Berg.

FACE OF SECTOR EAST.						FACE OF SECTOR WEST.					
Day of Observation 1843.	Apparent Zenith Distance, from Unreduced Observation.	Reduction for Az. Error, and Curv. of Path.	Refraction.	Precession, Aberration, and Nutation.	Deduced Mean Zenith Distance. 1843, Jan. 0; and Mean of Separate Results, uncorrected, for Error of Collimation.	Day of Observation 1843.	Apparent Zenith Distance, from Unreduced Observation.	Reduction for Az. Error, and Curv. of Path	Refraction.	Precession, Aberration, and Nutation.	Deduced Mean Zenith Distance. 1843, Jan. 0; and Mean of Separate Results, uncorrected, for Error of Collimation.

Anon. AR. 14·57.

Day E	App. Z.D.	Red.	Refr.	Prec.	Deduced	Day W	App. Z.D.	Red.	Refr.	Prec.	Deduced
July 25	1·56·12·89	·03	1·69	-19·93	1·55·54·62	July 26	1·57·11·51	·26	1·67	-19·91	1·56·53·01
27	13·37	·00	1·68	19·89	55·16	30	11·46	·02	1·65	19·81	53·28
29	14·42	·00	1·64	19·84	56·22	Aug. 1	11·02	·02	1·66	19·76	52·90
31	14·47	·01	1·66	19·79	56·33	3	11·36	·02	1·63	19·69	53·28
Aug. 5	14·27	·00	1·64	19·62	56·20	6	10·03	·01	1·62	-19·58	52·06
9	16·05	·01	1·64	-19·45	58·23						
					1·55·56·14						1·56·52·91

Error of Collimation . . = 0· 0·28·38
Resulting Mean Zenith Distance, South = 1·56·24·52

B.A.C. 5032.

Day E	App. Z.D.	Red.	Refr.	Prec.	Deduced	Day W	App. Z.D.	Red.	Refr.	Prec.	Deduced
July 25	0·47·37·38	·01	0·68	-18·29	0·47·56·34	July 26	0·46·41·73	·10	0·67	-18·27	0·47· 0·57
27	36·65	·00	0·68	18·25	55·58	28	42·42	·10	0·68	18·23	1·23
29	37·39	·00	0·67	18·21	56·27	30	42·22	·01	0·67	18·18	1·06
31	36·94	·00	0·67	18·16	55·77	Aug. 1	42·72	·01	0·67	18·13	1·51
Aug. 2	37·04	·01	0·67	18·10	55·80	3	42·18	·01	0·66	18·07	0·90
5	38·67	·00	0·66	18·00	57·33	6	43·06	·00	0·66	17·96	1·68
9	37·04	·00	0·66	17·85	55·55	8	42·37	·00	0·66	17·89	0·92
13	39·21	·00	0·68	-17·66	57·55	12	41·68	·01	0·69	-17·71	0·07
					0·47·56·27						0·47· 0·99

Error of Collimation . . = 0· 0·27·64
Resulting Mean Zenith Distance, North = 0·47·28·63

B.A.C. 5054.

Day E	App. Z.D.	Red.	Refr.	Prec.	Deduced	Day W	App. Z.D.	Red.	Refr.	Prec.	Deduced
July 27	5·19·29·48	* ·03	4·63	-19·97	5·19·14·11	July 26	5·20·25·78	·73	4·58	-19·97	5·20· 9·66
29	28·40	* ·04	4·55	19·95	13·05	28	26·02	·77	4·60	19·96	10·49
31	29·58	·03	4·56	19·93	14·18	30	24·30	·07	4·54	19·94	8·83
Aug. 2	28·94	* ·09	4·54	19·89	13·50	Aug. 1	24·50	·05	4·55	19·91	9·09
5	28·99	·00	4·51	19·82	13·68	3	25·14	·07	4·49	19·87	9·69
7	29·83	·01	4·47	19·76	14·53	6	25·04	·02	4·48	19·80	9·70
9	30·42	·02	4·52	19·70	15·22	8	25·19	·03	4·47	19·73	9·90
13	27·21	·03	4·60	-19·54	12·24	12	24·74	·05	4·66	-19·58	9·77
					5·19·13·81						5·20· 9·61

Error of Collimation . . = 0· 0·27·90
Resulting Mean Zenith Distance, South = 5·19·41·71

No. 5054.—July 27.—Correction for Azimuthal Error ·000; for Curvature of Path - ·030. = - 0"·03.
    ,, 29.—   ,,   ,,   ,, - ·014;   ,,   ,, - ·025. = - 0 ·04.
    Aug. 2.—   ,,   ,,   ,, - ·054;   ,,   ,, - ·037. = - 0 ·09.

Mean Zenith Distances of Stars observed at Kamies Berg.

FACE OF SECTOR EAST.						FACE OF SECTOR WEST.					
Day of Observation 1843.	Apparent Zenith Distance, from Unreduced Observation.	Reduction for Az. Error, and Curr. of Perb.	Refraction.	Precession, Aberration, and Nutation.	Deduced Mean Zenith Distance, 1843, Jan. 0; and Mean of Separate Results, uncorrected, for Error of Collimation.	Day of Observation 1843.	Apparent Zenith Distance, from Unreduced Observation.	Reduction for Az. Error, and Curr. of Perb.	Refraction.	Precession, Aberration, and Nutation.	Deduced Mean Zenith Distance, 1843, Jan. 0; and Mean of Separate Results, uncorrected, for Error of Collimation.

B.A.C. 5151.

July 25	1· 6·16·99	·01	0·95	-16·60	1· 6·34·53	July 26	1· 5·20·25	·14	0·94	-16·59	1· 5·37·64
27	16·10	·00	0·95	16·58	33·63	28	20·74	·15	0·94	16·57	38·10
29	16·04	·00	0·93	16·56	34·13	30	20·84	·01	0·93	16·55	38·31
31	15·21	·01	0·94	16·53	32·67	Aug. 1	20·35	·01	0·93	16·51	37·78
Aug. 2	15·95	·01	0·93	16·49	33·36	3	20·00	·01	0·92	16·47	37·38
5	17·58	·00	0·93	16·43	34·94	6	21·14	·00	0·92	16·40	38·46
9	15·85	·00	0·93	16·31	33·09	8	19·85	·00	0·92	16·34	37·11
13	18·57	·00	0·95	-16·18	35·70	12	19·75	·01	0·96	-16·21	36·91
					1· 6·34·01						1· 5·37·71

Error of Collimation . . = 0· 0·28·15
Resulting Mean Zenith Distance, North = 1· 6· 5·86

Anon. AR. 15·33.

July 25	0·44· 4·84	·01	0·05	-16·74	0·43·48·74	July 26	0·44·00·10	·10	0·64	-16·74	0·44·43·90
27	4·79	·00	0·64	16·74	48·69	28	60·05	·10	0·64	16·74	43·85
29	5·13	·00	0·63	16·73	49·03	30	59·85	·01	0·63	16·72	43·75
31	5·78	·00	0·63	16·71	49·70	Aug. 1	59·85	·01	0·63	16·70	43·77
Aug. 5	4·25	·00	0·63	16·64	48·24	3	60·30	·01	0·62	16·67	44·24
7	4·74	·00	0·62	16·59	48·77	6	59·01	·00	0·62	16·02	43·01
9	5·04	·00	0·63	-16·55	49·12	12	60·35	·01	0·65	-16·46	44·53
					0·43·48·90						0·44·43·86

Error of Collimation . . = 0· 0·27·48
Resulting Mean Zenith Distance, South = 0·44·16·38

B.A.C. 5227.

July 25	2·46·54·77	·04	2·43	-16·81	2·46·40·35	July 26	2·47·51·02	·37	2·40	-16·82	2·47·36·23
27	53·14	·00	2·41	16·82	38·73	28	50·92	·39	2·40	16·83	36·10
29	54·32	·01	2·38	16·83	39·86	30	51·31	·03	2·38	16·83	36·83
31	54·47	·01	2·38	16·83	40·01	Aug. 1	50·57	·02	2·38	16·82	36·11
Aug. 2	54·18	·03	2·37	16·82	39·70	3	50·18	·04	2·35	16·81	35·68
5	53·73	·00	2·36	16·79	39·30	6	50·28	·01	2·34	16·78	35·83
9	54·72	·01	2·37	16·73	40·35	8	50·38	·01	2·35	16·75	35·97
13	51·31	·01	2·42	-16·63	37·09	12	51·02	·03	2·43	-16·66	36·76
					2·46·39·42						2·47·36·19

Error of Collimation . . = 0· 0·28·38
Resulting Mean Zenith Distance, South = 2·47· 7·81

Mean Zenith Distances of Stars observed at Kamies Berg.

FACE OF SECTOR EAST.						FACE OF SECTOR WEST.				
Day of Observation 1843.	Apparent Zenith Distance, from Unreduced Observation.	Reduction for Az. Error, and Curv. of Path.	Refraction.	Precession, Aberration, and Nutation.	Deduced Mean Zenith Distance, 1843, Jan. 0; and Mean of Separate Results, uncorrected, for Error of Collimation.	Day of Observation 1843.	Apparent Zenith Distance, from Unreduced Observation.	Reduction for Az. Error, and Curv. of Path.	Refraction.	Precession, Aberration, and Nutation.	Deduced Mean Zenith Distance, 1843, Jan. 0; and Mean of Separate Results, uncorrected, of Collimation.

B.A.C. 5272.

	° ′ ″	″	″	″	° ′ ″		° ′ ″	″	″	″	° ′ ″
July 25	1·36·39·36	·02	1·40	-14·93	1·36·55·67	July 26	1·35·43·11	·20	1·38	-14·92	1·35·59·21
27	40·55	·00	1·39	14·92	56·86	28	43·90	·21	1·38	14·92	59·99
29	40·40	·00	1·37	14·91	56·68	30	44·54	·02	1·37	14·90	60·79
31	39·76	·01	1·37	14·89	56·01	Aug. 1	43·95	·01	1·37	14·88	60·19
Aug. 2	39·66	·02	1·36	14·87	55·87	3	42·87	·02	1·35	14·86	59·06
5	40·10	·00	1·35	14·83	56·28	6	43·90	·01	1·34	14·81	60·04
9	39·02	·01	1·36	14·75	55·12	8	42·72	·01	1·35	14·77	58·83
13	41·34	·01	1·39	-14·65	57·37	12	43·66	·01	1·40	-14·68	59·73
					1·36·56·23						1·35·59·73

Error of Collimation . . . = 0· 0·28·25
Resulting Mean Zenith Distance, North = 1·36·27·98

B.A.C. 5374.

	° ′ ″	″	″	″	° ′ ″		° ′ ″	″	″	″	° ′ ″
July 25	1·21·55·26	·02	1·18	-13·74	1·22·10·16	July 26	1·20·59·11	·17	1·17	-13·74	1·21·13·85
27	54·91	·00	1·17	13·75	9·83	28	58·92	·18	1·17	13·75	13·66
29	56·25	+·09	1·16	13·75	11·25	30	59·11	·02	1·16	13·75	14·00
31	54·82	·01	1·37	13·75	9·73	Aug. 1	59·11	·01	1·16	13·74	14·00
Aug. 2	54·67	·01	1·16	13·74	9·56	3	58·67	·02	1·14	13·73	13·52
5	55·16	·00	1·15	13·72	10·03	6	59·56	·01	1·14	13·70	14·40
9	54·18	·00	1·15	13·67	9·00	8	59·21	·01	1·14	13·68	14·02
13	56·74	·01	1·18	-13·60	11·51	12	58·32	·01	1·18	-13·62	13·11
					1·22·10·13						1·21·13·82

Error of Collimation . . . = 0· 0·28·16
Resulting Mean Zenith Distance, North = 1·21·41·98

B.A.C. 5435.

	° ′ ″	″	″	″	° ′ ″		° ′ ″	″	″	″	° ′ ″
July 25	0· 9·27·46	·00	0·14	-13·41	0· 9·14·19	July 26	0·10·24·45	·02	0·14	-13·42	0·10·11·15
27	27·95	·00	0·14	13·43	14·66	28	24·94	·02	0·14	13·44	11·62
29	28·25	·00	0·14	13·45	14·94	30	24·89	·00	0·14	13·45	11·58
31	28·49	·00	0·14	13·46	15·17	Aug. 1	24·99	·00	0·14	13·46	11·67
Aug. 2	28·64	·00	0·14	13·47	15·31	3	24·84	·00	0·14	13·47	11·51
5	28·64	·00	0·14	13·47	15·31	6	24·74	·00	0·14	13·47	11·41
9	29·48	·00	0·14	13·45	16·17	8	25·37	·00	0·14	13·46	12·05
13	26·72	·00	0·14	-13·41	13·45	12	25·48	·00	0·14	-13·42	12·20
					0· 9·14·90						0·10·11·65

Error of Collimation . . . = 0· 0·28·37
Resulting Mean Zenith Distance, South = 0· 9·43·27

No. 5374.—July 29.—Correction for Azimuthal Error ·00; for Curvature of Path + ·0″·093.

Mean Zenith Distances of Stars observed at Kamies Berg.

Anon. AR. 16·13.

	FACE OF SECTOR EAST.						FACE OF SECTOR WEST.				
Day of Observation 1843.	Apparent Zenith Distance, from Unreduced Observation.	Reduction for Az. Error, and Curr. of Path.	Refraction.	Precession, Aberration, and Nutation.	Deduced Mean Zenith Distance, 1843, Jan. 0; and Mean of Separate Results, uncorrected, for Error of Collimation.	Day of Observation 1843.	Apparent Zenith Distance, from Unreduced Observation.	Reduction for Az. Error, and Curr. of Path.	Refraction.	Precession, Aberration, and Nutation.	Deduced Mean Zenith Distance, 1843, Jan. 0; and Mean of Separate Results, uncorrected, for Error of Collimation.
July 27	2·27·48·35	·00	2 14	-13·70	2·27·36·70	July 26	2·28·43·22	·33	2·13	-13·68	2·28·31·34
29	46·56	·01	2·11	13·73	34·98	28	45·98	·34	2·13	13·72	34·05
31	47·35	·01	2·13	13·77	35·70	30	43·95	·03	2·11	13·75	32·28
Aug. 2	47·60	·02	2·11	13·79	35·90	Aug. 1	44·05	·02	2·11	13·78	32·36
5	48·39	·00	2·09	13·81	36·67	3	44·05	·08	2·08	13·90	32·30
7	47·26	·00	2·07	13·82	35·51	6	44·54	·01	2·07	13·82	32·78
9	48·64	·01	2·10	13·82	37·11	8	44·74	·01	2·08	13·82	32·99
13	45·43	·01	2 14	-13·81	33·75	12	44·98	·02	2·15	-13·81	33·30
					2·27·35·80						2·28·32·68

Error of Collimation . . . = 0· 0·28·44
Resulting Mean Zenith Distance, South = 2·28· 4·24

B.A.C. 5498.

Day of Observation 1843.	Apparent Zenith Distance, from Unreduced Observation.	Reduction for Az. Error, and Curr. of Path.	Refraction.	Precession, Aberration, and Nutation.	Deduced Mean Zenith Distance.	Day of Observation 1843.	Apparent Zenith Distance, from Unreduced Observation.	Reduction for Az. Error, and Curr. of Path.	Refraction.	Precession, Aberration, and Nutation.	Deduced Mean Zenith Distance.
July 25	4·16·60·70	·05	3·73	-11·15	4·17·15·53	July 26	4·16· 7·16	·53	3·69	-11·15	4·16·21·47
27	61·39	·00	3·71	11·15	16·25	28	6·22	·55	3·66	11·15	20·50
29	61·53	·00	3·65	11·15	16·32	30	6·67	·05	3·65	11·14	21·41
31	59·66	·02	3·69	11·14	14·47	Aug. 1	5·19	·04	3·66	11·14	19·95
Aug. 2	60·40	·04	3·65	11·13	15·14	3	4·94	·05	3·60	11·13	19·62
5	61·09	·00	3·62	11·11	15·82	6	5·29	·02	3·60	11·10	19·97
9	59·56	·01	3·64	11·07	14·26	8	4·79	·02	3·60	11·08	19·45
13	61·88	·02	3·71	-11·01	16·58	12	4·10	·04	3·73	-11·03	18·82
					4·17·15·55						4·16·20·15

Error of Collimation . . . = 0· 0·27·70
Resulting Mean Zenith Distance, North = 4·16·47·85

B.A.C. 5588.

Day of Observation 1843.	Apparent Zenith Distance, from Unreduced Observation.	Reduction for Az. Error, and Curr. of Path.	Refraction.	Precession, Aberration, and Nutation.	Deduced Mean Zenith Distance.	Day of Observation 1843.	Apparent Zenith Distance, from Unreduced Observation.	Reduction for Az. Error, and Curr. of Path.	Refraction.	Precession, Aberration, and Nutation.	Deduced Mean Zenith Distance.
July 25	1·26·16·55	·02	1·26	-11·37	1·26· 6·42	July 26	1·27·12·84	·19	1·24	-11·40	1·27· 2·49
27	17·93	·00	1·25	11·42	7·76	28	13·44	·20	1·25	11·45	3·04
29	17·19	·00	1·23	11·47	6·95	30	13·14	·02	1·23	11·49	2·66
31	17·19	·01	1·25	11·51	6·92	Aug. 1	12·74	·01	1·23	11·53	2·43
Aug. 2	16·64	·01	1·23	11·55	6·31	6	13·14	·01	1·22	11·60	2·85
5	18·17	·00	1·22	11·59	7·80	6	13·39	·01	1·22	11·62	2·98
7	18·22	·00	1·21	11·61	7·82	12	14·33	·01	1·27	-11·65	3·94
9	19·31	·01	1·23	11·63	8·90						
13	16·89	·01	1·25	-11·65	6·48						
					1·26· 7·26						1·27· 2·94

Error of Collimation . . . = 0· 0·27·84
Resulting Mean Zenith Distance, South = 1·26·35·10

2 T

Mean Zenith Distances of Stars observed at Kamies Berg.

FACE OF SECTOR EAST.						FACE OF SECTOR WEST.					
Day of Observation 1843.	Apparent Zenith Distance, from Unreduced Observation.	Reduction for Az. Error, and Curr. of Path.	Refraction.	Precession, Aberration, and Nutation.	Deduced Mean Zenith Distance, 1843, Jan. 0; and Mean of Separate Results, uncorrected. for Error of Collimation.	Day of Observation 1843.	Apparent Zenith Distance, from Unreduced Observation.	Reduction for Az. Error, and Curr. of Path.	Refraction.	Precession, Aberration, and Nutation.	Deduced Mean Zenith Distance, 1843, Jan. 0; and Mean of Separate Results, uncorrected. for Error of Collimation.

B.A.C. 5632.

Day	App. Z.D. (° ′ ″)	Red. (″)	Refr. (″)	Prec. (″)	Deduced (° ′ ″)	Day	App. Z.D. (° ′ ″)	Red. (″)	Refr. (″)	Prec. (″)	Deduced (° ′ ″)
July 25	3 38 16·19	·05	3·18	−11·28	3·38· 8·04	July 26	3 39 13 38	·49	3·15	−11 31	3 39· 4·73
27	17·03	·00	3·16	11·35	8·84	28	14·02	·51	3·15	11·39	5·27
29	16·29	·01	3·14	11·42	8·00	30	15·90	·05	3·11	11·45	7·51
31	17·53	·02	3·14	11·48	9·17	Aug. 1	14·17	·03	3·12	11·51	5·75
Aug. 2	17·68	·04	3·11	11·54	9·21	3	12·69	·20	3·07	11·56	4·00
5	17·48	·00	3·08	11·61	8·95	6	13·43	·02	3·07	11·63	4·85
9	18·02	·01	3·10	11·09	9·42	8	14·57	·02	3·07	11·67	5·95
13	15·70	·02	3·17	−11·74	7·11	12	14·81	·04	3·27	−11·73	6·31
					3·38· 8·59						3·39· 5·55

Error of Collimation . . . = 0· 0·28·48
Resulting Mean Zenith Distance, South = 3·38·37·07

B.A.C. 5735.

Day	App. Z.D. (° ′ ″)	Red. (″)	Refr. (″)	Prec. (″)	Deduced (° ′ ″)	Day	App. Z.D. (° ′ ″)	Red. (″)	Refr. (″)	Prec. (″)	Deduced (° ′ ″)
July 25	3 31 53 09	·05	3·09	− 9·66	3 31·46·47	July 26	3 32 49 93	·47	3·06	− 9·71	3 32·42·81
27	53·24	·00	3·07	9·75	46·56	28	50·03	·50	3·06	9·79	42·80
29	52·20	·01	3·05	9·82	45·42	30	52·10	·04	3·02	9·86	45·22
31	53·93	·02	3·05	9·90	47·06	Aug. 1	50·03	·03	3·02	9·93	43·09
Aug. 2	53·68	·04	3·02	9·97	46·69	3	50·23	·04	2·98	10·00	43·17
5	54·32	·00	2·99	10·06	47·25	6	50·08	·02	2·98	10·09	42·95
9	55·02	·01	3·01	10·17	47·85	8	50·72	·02	2·98	10·14	43 54
13	52·20	·02	3·07	−10·25	45·00	12	50·52	·03	3·10	−10·23	43·36
					3·31·46·54						3·32·43·37

Error of Collimation . . . = 0· 0·28·42
Resulting Mean Zenith Distance, South = 3·32·14·95

B.A.C. 5817.

Day	App. Z.D. (° ′ ″)	Red. (″)	Refr. (″)	Prec. (″)	Deduced (° ′ ″)	Day	App. Z.D. (° ′ ″)	Red. (″)	Refr. (″)	Prec. (″)	Deduced (° ′ ″)
July 25	2 6 51 41	·03	1·85	− 7·99	2 6·45·30	July 26	2 7 48·35	·28	1·83	− 7·97	2 7·41·93
27	52·20	·00	1·84	8·01	46·03	28	48·50	·29	1·83	8·05	41·99
31	52·69	·01	1·83	8·16	46·35	30	49·88	·03	1·81	8·12	43·54
Aug. 2	53·44	·02	1·81	8·23	47·00	Aug. 1	48·70	·02	1·81	8·19	42·30
5	53.46	·00	1·79	8·32	46·93	3	49·04	·03	1·78	8·26	42·53
7	53·14	·00	1·78	8·38	46·54	6	48·35	·01	1·78	8·35	41·77
9	53·98	·01	1·81	8·43	47·35	8	49·59	·01	1·79	8·40	42·97
13	51·61	·01	1·84	− 8·52	44·92	12	49·98	·02	1·86	− 8·50	43·32
					2· 6·46·30						2· 7·42·54

Error of Collimation . . . = 0· 0·28·12
Resulting Mean Zenith Distance, South = 2· 7·14·42

No. 5632.—Aug. 3.—Correction for Azimuthal Error − ·046; for Curvature of Path − ·158. = − 0 ·204.

Mean Zenith Distances of Stars observed at Kamies Berg.

	FACE OF SECTOR EAST.						FACE OF SECTOR WEST.				
Day of Observation 1843.	Apparent Zenith Distance, from Unreduced Observation.	Reduction for Az. Error, and Curv. of Path.	Refraction.	Precession, Aberration, and Nutation.	Deduced Mean Zenith Distance, 1843, Jan. 0; and Mean of Separate Results, uncorrected, for Error of Collimation.	Day of Observation 1843.	Apparent Zenith Distance, from Unreduced Observation.	Reduction for Az. Error, and Curv. of Path.	Refraction.	Precession, Aberration, and Nutation.	Deduced Mean Zenith Distance, 1843, Jan. 0; and Mean of Separate Results, uncorrected, for Error of Collimation.

B.A.C. 5881.

July 25	0 38 42·81	·01	0·56	- 6·09	0 38 49·45	July 26	0 37 47·95	·08	0·55	- 6·12	0 37 54·54
27	43·01	·00	0·55	6·15	. 49·71	28	47·45	·09	0·55	6·18	54·09
29	44·54	·00	0·55	6·21	51·30	30	47·60	·01	0·55	6·24	54·38
31	42·47	·00	0·55	6·27	49·29	Aug. 1	47·31	·01	0·55	6·30	54·15
Aug. 2	42·27	·01	0·54	6·32	49·13	6	47·55	·00	0·54	6·42	54·51
9	42·27	·00	0·54	6·49	49·30	8	46·76	·00	0·54	6·47	53·77
13	43·21	·00	0·55	- 6·56	50·32	12	46·27	·01	0·56	- 6·55	53·37
					0 38 49·79						0 37 54·12

Error of Collimation . . . = 0· 0·27·84
Resulting Mean Zenith Distance, North = 0 38 21·95

B.A.C. 5960.

July 25	1 44 26·86	·02	1·53	- 5·20	1 44 23·17	July 26	1 45 22·72	·23	1·51	- 5·25	1 45 18·75
27	26·57	·00	1·52	5·29	22·80	28	23·75	·24	1·51	5·33	19·69
29	26·42	·00	1·50	5·38	22·54	30	23·01	·02	1·49	5·42	19·06
31	27·50	·01	1·51	5·46	23·54	Aug. 6	22·96	·01	1·47	5·69	18·73
Aug. 2	27·26	·02	1·49	5·54	23·19	7	24·35	·00	1·47	5·73	20·09
5	27·16	·00	1·48	5·66	22·98	8	23·51	·01	1·47	5·76	19·21
9	28·29	·01	1·49	- 5·80	23·97	12	23·75	·02	1·53	- 5·89	19·37
					1 44 23·17						1 45 19·27

Error of Collimation . . . = 0· 0·28·05
Resulting Mean Zenith Distance, South = 1 44 51·22

B.A.C. 5964.

July 25	1 45 28·30	·02	1·54	- 5·09	1 45 24·78	July 26	1 46 24·25	·23	1·52	- 5·14	1 46 20·40
27	27·56	·00	1·53	5·18	23·91	30	24·35	·02	1·51	5·32	20·52
29	27·66	·00	1·52	5·27	23·91	Aug. 3	24·25	·02	1·48	5·48	20·23
31	28·15	·01	1 52	5·36	24·30	6	24·50	·01	1·48	5·59	20·38
Aug. 2	28·40	·02	1·51	5·44	24·45	7	24·99	·00	1·48	5·63	20·64
5	28·49	·00	1·49	5·56	24·42	8	24·65	·01	1·49	5·66	20·47
9	29·14	·01	1·51	- 5·70	24·94	12	25·48	·02	1·55	- 5·80	21·21
					1 45 24·38						1 46 20·58

Error of Collimation . . . = 0· 0·28·10
Resulting Mean Zenith Distance, South = 1 45 52·48

Mean Zenith Distances of Stars observed at Kamies Berg.

FACE OF SECTOR EAST.   FACE OF SECTOR WEST.

B.A.C. 6016.

Day of Observation 1843.	Apparent Zenith Distance, from Unreduced Observation.	Reduction for Az. Error, and Curv. of Path.	Refraction.	Precession, Aberration, and Nutation.	Deduced Mean Zenith Distance, 1843, Jan. 0; and Mean of Separate Results, uncorrected, for Error of Collimation.	Day of Observation 1843.	Apparent Zenith Distance, from Unreduced Observation.	Reduction for Az. Error, and Curv. of Path.	Refraction.	Precession, Aberration, and Nutation.	Deduced Mean Zenith Distance, 1843, Jan. 0; and Mean of Separate Results, uncorrected, for Error of Collimation.
July 25	1 16 38·87	·02	1·12	- 4·02	1 16 35·95	July 26	1 17 35·12	·17	1·11	- 4·07	1 17 31·99
27	39·26	·00	1·12	4·11	36·27	28	35·07	·18	1·11	4·15	31·85
29	38·18	·00	1·11	4·20	35·09	30	34·33	·02	1·10	4 24	31·17
31	39·66	·01	1·11	4·28	36·48	Aug. 1	34·23	·01	1·10	4·32	31·00
Aug. 2	39·06	·01	1·10	4·36	35·79	6	34·72	·01	1·08	4·52	31·27
5	40·69	·00	1·09	4·48	37·30	7	36·05	·00	1·08	4·56	32·57
13	38·23	·01	1·12	- 4·77	34·57	8	35·26	·01	1·08	4·60	31·73
						12	35·51	·01	1·13	- 4·74	31·89
					1·16·35·92						1·17·31·08

Error of Collimation . . . = 0· 0·27·88
Resulting Mean Zenith Distance, South = 1·17· 3·80

B.A.C. 6074.

Day of Observation 1843.	Apparent Zenith Distance, from Unreduced Observation.	Reduction for Az. Error, and Curv. of Path.	Refraction.	Precession, Aberration, and Nutation.	Deduced Mean Zenith Distance, 1843, Jan. 0; and Mean of Separate Results, uncorrected, for Error of Collimation.	Day of Observation 1843.	Apparent Zenith Distance, from Unreduced Observation.	Reduction for Az. Error, and Curv. of Path.	Refraction.	Precession, Aberration, and Nutation.	Deduced Mean Zenith Distance, 1843, Jan. 0; and Mean of Separate Results, uncorrected, for Error of Collimation.
July 25	0· 8· 4·70	·00	0·11	- 2·55	0· 8· 7·36	July 26	0· 7· 8·89	·02	0·11	- 2·59	0· 7·11·57
27	4·40	·00	0·11	2·63	7·14	28	7·36	·02	0·11	2·67	10·12
29	6·13	·00	0·11	2·71	8·95	30	9·29	·00	0·11	2·75	12·15
31	4·30	·00	0·11	2·78	7·19	Aug. 1	8·60	·00	0·11	2·82	11·53
Aug. 2	4·25	·00	0·11	2·86	7·22	6	8·30	·00	0·11	3·01	11·42
5	4·30	·00	0·11	2·97	7·38	7	8·40	·00	0·11	3·05	11·55
9	4·25	·00	0·11	3·11	7·47	8	8·50	·00	0·11	3·07	11·68
11	4·50	·00	0·11	3·18	7·79	12	7·76	·00	0·11	- 3·21	11·08
13	5·73	·00	0·11	- 3·24	9·08						
					0· 8· 7·73						0· 7·11·39

Error of Collimation . . . = 0· 0·28·17
Resulting Mean Zenith Distance, North = 0· 7·39·56

B.A.C. 6115.

Day of Observation 1843.	Apparent Zenith Distance, from Unreduced Observation.	Reduction for Az. Error, and Curv. of Path.	Refraction.	Precession, Aberration, and Nutation.	Deduced Mean Zenith Distance, 1843, Jan. 0; and Mean of Separate Results, uncorrected, for Error of Collimation.	Day of Observation 1843.	Apparent Zenith Distance, from Unreduced Observation.	Reduction for Az. Error, and Curv. of Path.	Refraction.	Precession, Aberration, and Nutation.	Deduced Mean Zenith Distance, 1843, Jan. 0; and Mean of Separate Results, uncorrected, for Error of Collimation.
July 25	0· 3·13·97	·00	0·05	- 1·79	0· 3·12·23	July 26	0· 4·10·71	·01	0·05	- 1·83	0· 4· 8·92
27	14·68	·00	0·05	1·87	12·84	28	11·41	·01	0·05	1·91	9·54
29	12·93	·00	0·05	1·95	11·03	30	11·11	·00	0·05	2·00	9·16
31	14·86	·00	0·05	2·04	12·87	Aug. 1	11·41	·00	0·05	2·08	9·38
Aug. 2	14·56	·00	0·05	2·12	12·49	6	11·21	·00	0·05	2·27	8·99
5	14·81	·00	0·05	2·24	12·62	7	11·41	·00	0·05	2·31	9·15
9	15·45	·00	0·05	2·39	13·11	8	12·29	·00	0·05	2·35	9·99
11	15·16	·00	0·05	2·46	12·75	12	12·25	·00	0·05	- 2·49	9·81
13	13·63	·00	0·05	- 2·53	11·15						
					0· 3·12·34						0· 4· 9·37

Error of Collimation . . . = 0· 0·28·51
Resulting Mean Zenith Distance, South = 0· 3·40·86

Mean Zenith Distances of Stars observed at Kamies Berg.

FACE OF SECTOR EAST.						FACE OF SECTOR WEST.					
Day of Observation 1843.	Apparent Zenith Distance, from Unreduced Observation.	Reduction for A.L. Error, and Curv. of Path.	Refraction.	Precession, Aberration, and Nutation.	Deduced Mean Zenith Distance, 1843, Jan. 0; and Mean of Separate Results, uncorrected, for Error of Collimation.	Day of Observation 1843.	Apparent Zenith Distance, from Unreduced Observation.	Reduction for A.L. Error, and Curv. of Path.	Refraction.	Precession, Aberration, and Nutation.	Deduced Mean Zenith Distance, 1843, Jan. 0; and Mean of Separate Results, uncorrected, for Error of Collimation.

B.A.C. 6145.

July 25	0·22·50·02	·22	0·34	- 1·35	0·22·(48·79)	July 26	0·23·48·44	·05	0·34	- 1·39	0·23·47·34
27	53·48	·00	0·34	1·43	52·39	28	48·09	·05	0·34	1·48	47·80
29	52·64	·00	0·33	1·52	51·45	30	49·03	·00	0·33	1·56	47·80
31	54·27	·00	0·33	1·61	52·99	Aug. 1	48·69	·00	0·33	1·65	47·37
Aug. 2	53·08	·00	0·33	1·69	51·72	3	50·22	·00	0·33	1·74	48·81
5	54·37	·00	0·33	1·82	52·88	6	48·09	·00	0·33	1·80	47·46
9	53·77	·00	0·33	1·98	52·12	8	49·28	·00	0·33	1·94	47·67
13	53·43	·00	0·34	- 2·13	51·64	12	49·58	·00	0·34	- 2·10	47·82
					0·22·52·17						0·23·47·76

Error of Collimation . . = 0· 0·27·79
Resulting Mean Zenith Distance, South = 0·23·19·96

B.A.C. 6233.

July 27	4· 5· 5·88	·00	3·57	- 0·45	4· 5· 9·00	July 26	4· 6· 2·97	·55	3·54	- 0·39	4· 6· 5·57
29	5·09	·01	3·52	0·58	8·02	28	3·36	·58	3·53	0·52	5·79
31	5·63	·02	3·54	0·71	8·44	30	3·26	·05	3·50	0·65	6·06
Aug. 2	6·57	·04	3·50	0·83	9·20	Aug. 1	1·88	·04	3·51	0·77	4·58
5	5·83	·00	3·47	1·02	8·28	3	3·36	·05	3·45	0·90	5·86
7	6·27	·01	3·45	1·14	8·57	6	3·16	·02	3·45	1·08	5·51
9	6·72	·02	3·50	1·26	8·94	8	2·32	·02	3·46	1·20	4·56
11	6·12	·02	3·59	1·38	8·31	12	3·71	·04	3·59	- 1·44	5·82
13	5·48	·02	3·57	- 1·49	7·54						
					4· 5· 8·48						4· 6· 5·47

Error of Collimation . . = 0· 0·28·50
Resulting Mean Zenith Distance, South = 4· 5·36·97

B.A.C. 6275.

July 27	2·46·34·82	·00	2·42	+ 0·52	2·46·37·76	July 26	2·47·29·04	·37	2·41	+ 0·58	2·47·31·66
29	33·37	·01	2·39	+ 0·41	36·16	28	31·12	·39	2·41	+ 0·46	33·60
31	34·59	·01	2·40	+ 0·29	37·27	30	31·08	·03	2·38	+ 0·35	33·78
Aug. 2	35·29	·03	2·38	+ 0·17	37·81	Aug. 1	30·52	·03	2·38	+ 0·23	33·10
5	34·42	·00	2·36	0·00	36·78	3	30·30	·03	2·34	+ 0·11	32·72
11	33·81	·01	2·44	- 0·34	35·90	6	30·39	·01	2·34	- 0·06	32·66
13	33·91	·01	2·43	- 0·44	35·89	8	31·10	·01	2·35	- 0·17	33·27
						12	31·23	·03	2·44	- 0·39	33·25
					2·46·36·80						2·47·33·01

Error of Collimation . . = 0· 0·28·10
Resulting Mean Zenith Distance, South = 2·47· 4·90

No. 6145.—July 25.—Correction for Curvature of Path = - ·0″·22.

Mean Zenith Distances of Stars observed at Kamies Berg.

FACE OF SECTOR EAST.					FACE OF SECTOR WEST.				
Day of Observation 1843.	Apparent Zenith Distance, from Unreduced Observation.	Reduction for Ax. Error, and Curv. of Path.	Refraction.	Precession, Aberration, and Nutation.	Deduced Mean Zenith Distance. 1843, Jan. 0; and Mean of Separate Results, uncorrected for Error of Collimation.	Day of Observation 1843.	Apparent Zenith Distance, from Unreduced Observation.	Reduction for Ax. Error, and Curv. of Path.	Refraction.	Precession, Aberration, and Nutation.	Deduced Mean Zenith Distance. 1843, Jan. 0; and Mean of Separate Results, uncorrected for Error of Collimation.

B.A.C. 6285.

Day of Obs.	Apparent Z.D.	Red.	Refr.	Prec.	Deduced Mean	Day of Obs.	Apparent Z.D.	Red.	Refr.	Prec.	Deduced Mean
July 25	2 43 10·89	·04	2·38	+ 0·78	2 43 14·01	July 26	2 44· 7·45	·36	2·36	+ 0·72	2 44·10 17
27	11·55	·00	2·38	+ 0·66	14·50	28	8·04	·38	2·36	+ 0·61	11·53
29	10·40	·01	2·35	+ 0·55	13·29	30	7·90	·03	2·33	+ 0·49	10·09
31	11·02	·01	2·36	+ 0·43	14·70	Aug. 1	8·44	·18	2·33	+ 0·37	10·96
Aug. 2	12·13	·03	2·33	+ 0·31	14·74	3	7·43	·03	2·29	+ 0·20	9·95
5	11·26	·00	2·31	+ 0·14	13·71	6	7·72	·01	2·29	+ 0·08	10·06
9	12·19	·01	2·33	- 0·08	14·43	8	7·44	·01	2·30	- 0·03	9·70
11	11·34	·01	2·39	- 0·19	13 53	12	8·56	·03	2·39	- 0·25	10·67
13	11·04	·01	2·38	- 0·30	13 11						
					2·43·14·01						2·44·10·47

Error of Collimation . . . = 0· 0·28·23
Resulting Mean Zenith Distance, South = 2·43 42·24

B.A.C. 6305.

Day of Obs.	Apparent Z.D.	Red.	Refr.	Prec.	Deduced Mean	Day of Obs.	Apparent Z.D.	Red.	Refr.	Prec.	Deduced Mean
July 25	2 45 34·30	·04	2·42	+ 1·13	2 45 37·81	July 26	2 46 29·28	·37	2·39	+ 1·07	2 46·32·37
27	34·37	·00	2·41	1·01	37·79	28	30·57	·30	2·39	0·96	33·53
29	32·82	·01	2·38	0·90	36·09	30	30·23	·03	2·37	0·84	33·41
31	34·54	·01	2·39	0·78	37·70	Aug. 1	30·37	·03	2·37	0·72	33·48
Aug. 2	34·94	·03	2·36	0·66	37·93	3	29·85	·03	2·33	0·60	32·75
5	34·27	·00	2·34	0·48	37·09	6	30·44	·01	2·33	0·43	33·19
9	35·11	·01	2·36	0·26	37·72	8	30·55	·01	2·34	0·31	33·19
11	33·76	·01	2·42	0·14	36·31	12	31·38	·03	2·43	+ 0·09	33·87
13	34·55	·01	2·41	+ 0·03	36·98						
					2·45·37·27						2·46·33·22

Error of Collimation . . . = 0· 0·27·97
Resulting Mean Zenith Distance, South = 2·46· 5·24

B.A.C. 6414.

Day of Obs.	Apparent Z.D.	Red.	Refr.	Prec.	Deduced Mean	Day of Obs.	Apparent Z.D.	Red.	Refr.	Prec.	Deduced Mean
July 25	0 32 51·01	·01	0·49	+ 3·80	0 32 55·29	July 26	0 33 45·87	·07	0·48	+ 3·75	0 33 50·08
27	51·11	·00	0·48	3·70	55·29	28	46·12	·08	0·48	3·65	50·17
29	49·13	·00	0·48	3·60	53·21	30	45·82	·01	0·47	3·55	49·83
31	51·95	·00	0·48	3·50	55·93	Aug. 1	45·68	·00	0·48	3·45	49·61
Aug. 2	51·55	·01	0·47	3·40	55·41	3	45·63	·01	0·47	3·35	49·44
5	49·87	·00	0·47	3·25	53·59	6	45·58	·00	0·47	3·19	49·24
11	51·26	·00	0·49	2·94	54·69	8	46·12	·00	0·47	3·09	49·68
13	50·61	·00	0·48	+ 2·84	53·93	12	47·70	·01	0·49	+ 2·89	51·07
					0·32·54·67						0·33·49·88

Error of Collimation . . . = 0· 0·27·61
Resulting Mean Zenith Distance, South = 0· 33·22·28

No. 6285.—Aug. 1.—Correction for Azimuthal Error ·025; for Curvature of Path - ·166. = - 0″·191.

Mean Zenith Distances of Stars observed at Kamies Berg.

	FACE OF SECTOR EAST.						FACE OF SECTOR WEST.				
Day of Observation 1843.	Apparent Zenith Distance, from Unreduced Observation.	Reduction for Az. Error, and Curv. of Path.	Refraction.	Precession, Aberration, and Nutation.	Deduced Mean Zenith Distance. 1843, Jan. 0; and Mean of Separate Results, uncorrected, for Error of Collimation.	Day of Observation 1843.	Apparent Zenith Distance, from Unreduced Observation.	Reduction for Az. Error, and Curv. of Path.	Refraction.	Precession, Aberration, and Nutation.	Deduced Mean Zenith Distance, 1843, Jan. 0; and Mean of Separate Results, uncorrected, for Error of Collimation.

B.A.C. 6489.

	° ′ ″	″	″	″	° ′ ″		° ′ ″	″	″	″	° ′ ″
July 25	0·16· 7·95	·00	0·23	+ 5·11	0·16· 3·07	July 26	0·15·11·26	·03	0·23	+ 5·07	0·15· 6·39
27	7·80	·00	0·23	5·02	3·01	28	8·49	* ·01	0·23	4·98	(3·73)
29	8·84	·00	0·22	4·93	4·13	30	10·96	·00	0·22	4·89	6·29
31	6·96	·00	0·23	4·84	2·35	Aug. 1	11·41	·00	0·22	4·79	6·84
Aug. 2	7·11	·00	0·22	4·75	2·58	3	10·07	·00	0·22	4·70	5·59
5	8·00	·00	0·22	4·00	3·02	6	11·80	·00	0·22	4·55	7·47
9	7·26	·00	0·22	4·40	3·08	8	10·57	·00	0·22	4·45	6·34
11	8·25	·00	0·23	+ 4·31	4·17	12	9·63	·00	0·23	+ 4·26	5·00
					0·16· 3·25						0·15· 6·36

Error of Collimation . . . = 0· 0·28·45
Resulting Mean Zenith Distance, North = 0·15·34·81

B.A.C. 6525.

July 25	1·29·38·91	·02	1·30	+ 5·86	1·29·34·33	July 26	1·28·42·81	·19	1·29	+ 5·82	1·28·38·09
27	38·91	·00	1·29	5·78	34·42	28	42·27	·20	1·28	5·75	37·60
29	40·15	·00	1·28	5·71	35·72	30	43·16	·02	1·27	5·67	38·74
31	39·06	·01	1·28	5·70	34·70	Aug. 1	42·27	·01	1·27	5·59	37·94
Aug. 2	38·96	·01	1·26	5·55	34·66	3	42·96	·02	1·25	5·50	38·69
5	39·36	·00	1·26	5·42	35·20	6	42·66	·01	1·25	5·37	38·53
9	37·48	·01	1·27	5·24	33·50	8	42·61	·01	1·26	5·29	38·57
11	38·77	·01	1·30	+ 5·15	34·91	12	41·08	·01	1·30	+ 5·11	37·26
					1·29·34·68			.			1·28·38·18

Error of Collimation . . . = 0· 0·28·25
Resulting Mean Zenith Distance, North = 1·29·06·43

B.A.C. 6639.

July 25	0·19·12·39	·00	0·27	+ 8·05	0·19· 4·61	July 26	0·18·17·63	·04	0·27	+ 8·01	0·18· 9·85
27	12·59	·00	0·27	7·96	4·90	28	16·79	·04	0·27	7·92	9·10
29	13·43	·00	0·27	7·87	5·83	30	17·23	·00	0·27	7·83	9·67
31	12·39	·00	0·27	7·78	4·88	Aug. 1	17·13	·00	0·27	7·73	9·67
Aug. 2	11·80	·00	0·27	7·68	4·39	3	16·93	·00	0·26	7·63	9·56
5	12·89	·00	0·26	7·53	5·62	6	16·89	·00	0·26	7·48	9·07
9	12·10	·00	0·27	7·33	5·04	8	16·49	·00	0·26	7·38	9·37
11	12·34	·00	0·27	+ 7·22	5·39	12	15·60	·00	0·28	+ 7·17	8·71
					0·19· 5·08						0·18· 9·45

Error of Collimation . . . = 0· 0·27·82
Resulting Mean Zenith Distance, North = 0·18·37·27

No. 6489.—July 28.—Correction for Azimuthal Error = - ·035; for Curvature of Path + ·026. = - 0″·009.

Mean Zenith Distances of Stars observed at Kamies Berg.

Anon. AR. 19·20.

	FACE OF SECTOR EAST.						FACE OF SECTOR WEST.				
Day of Observation 1843.	Apparent Zenith Distance, from Unreduced Observation.	Reduction for Az. Error, and Curv. of Path.	Refraction.	Precession, Aberration, and Nutation.	Deduced Mean Zenith Distance, 1843, Jan. 0; and Mean of Separate Results, uncorrected, for Error of Collimation.	Day of Observation 1843.	Apparent Zenith Distance, from Unreduced Observation.	Reduction for Az. Error, and Curv. of Path.	Refraction.	Precession, Aberration, and Nutation.	Deduced Mean Zenith Distance, 1843, Jan. 0; and Mean of Separate Results, uncorrected, for Collimation.
July 25	0·33·12·93	·01	0·48	+ 8·58	0·33· 4·82	July 26	0·32·18.02	·07	0·47	+ 8·54	0·32· 9·86
27	12·93	·00	0·48	8·50	4·91	28	18·32	·07	0·47	8·46	10·26
29	14·37	·00	0·47	8·41	6·43	30	19·60	·01	0·47	8·37	11·69
31	12·69	·00	0·47	8·32	4·84	Aug. 1	18·86	·00	0·47	8·27	11·06
Aug. 2	11·55	·01	0·47	8·23	3·78	6	17·97	·00	0·46	8·03	10·40
5	12·93	·00	0·46	8·08	5·31	7	19·01	·00	0·46	7·98	11·49
11	13·13	·00	0·48	7·77	5·84	8	17·43	·00	0·46	7·93	9·96
13	12·93	·00	0·48	+ 7·66	5·75	12	16·14	·01	0·48	+ 7·72	8·89
					0·33· 5·21						0·32·10·45

Error of Collimation . . . = 0· 0·27·38
Resulting Mean Zenith Distance, North = 0·32·37·83

B.A.C. 6753.

	FACE OF SECTOR EAST.						FACE OF SECTOR WEST.				
Day of Observation 1843.	Apparent Zenith Distance, from Unreduced Observation.	Reduction for Az. Error, and Curv. of Path.	Refraction.	Precession, Aberration, and Nutation.	Deduced Mean Zenith Distance, 1843, Jan. 0; and Mean of Separate Results, uncorrected, for Error of Collimation.	Day of Observation 1843.	Apparent Zenith Distance, from Unreduced Observation.	Reduction for Az. Error, and Curv. of Path.	Refraction.	Precession, Aberration, and Nutation.	Deduced Mean Zenith Distance, 1843, Jan. 0; and Mean of Separate Results, uncorrected, for Collimation.
July 25	0·54·17·73	·01	0·80	+10·15	0·54·28·67	July 26	0·55·13·63	·12	0·79	+10·10	0·55·24·40
27	18·32	·00	0·79	10·05	29·16	28	13·33	·12	0·79	10·00	24·00
29	16·84	·00	0·78	9·95	27·57	30	12·05	·01	0·78	9·90	22·72
31	19·21	·00	0·79	9·84	29·84	Aug. 3	12·74	·01	0·77	9·68	23·18
Aug. 2	18·62	·01	0·78	9·73	29·12	6	12·44	·00	0·77	9·50	22·71
5	18·71	·00	0·77	9·56	29·04	7	12·54	·00	0·77	9·44	22·75
11	19·06	·00	0·80	9·20	29·06	8	13·33	·00	0·77	9·38	23·48
13	17·78	·00	0·80	+ 9·07	27·65	12	13·48	·01	0·80	+ 9·14	23·41
					0·54·28·76						0·55·23·33

Error of Collimation . . . = 0· 0·27·28
Resulting Mean Zenith Distance, South = 0·54·56·05

B.A.C. 6877.

	FACE OF SECTOR EAST.						FACE OF SECTOR WEST.				
Day of Observation 1843.	Apparent Zenith Distance, from Unreduced Observation.	Reduction for Az. Error, and Curv. of Path.	Refraction.	Precession, Aberration, and Nutation.	Deduced Mean Zenith Distance, 1843, Jan. 0; and Mean of Separate Results, uncorrected, for Error of Collimation.	Day of Observation 1843.	Apparent Zenith Distance, from Unreduced Observation.	Reduction for Az. Error, and Curv. of Path.	Refraction.	Precession, Aberration, and Nutation.	Deduced Mean Zenith Distance, 1843, Jan. 0; and Mean of Separate Results, uncorrected, for Collimation.
July 25	2· 7·17·62	·03	1·86	+12·32	2· 7·31·77	July 26	2· 8·12·84	·28	1·84	+12·26	2· 8·26·66
27	17·43	·00	1·85	12·21	31·49	28	13·48	·30	1·84	12·16	27·18
29	16·04	·00	1·83	12·10	29·97	30	12·74	·03	1·82	12·04	26·57
31	17·72	·01	1·84	11·98	31·53	Aug. 1	12·79	·02	1·82	11·92	26·51
Aug. 2	17·58	·02	1·82	11·86	31·24	6	13·63	·02	1·80	11·80	27·21
5	17·33	·00	1·80	11·67	30·80	6	13·18	·01	1·80	11·61	26·58
11	17·62	·01	1·87	11·27	30·75	8	13·48	·01	1·80	11·47	26·74
13	16·93	·01	1·86	+11·12	29·90	12	13·43	·02	1·87	+11·19	26·47
					2· 7 30·98						2· 8·26·74

Error of Collimation . . . = 0· 0·27·90
Resulting Mean Zenith Distance, South = 2· 7·58·84

Mean Zenith Distances of Stars observed at Kamies Berg.

	FACE OF SECTOR EAST.						FACE OF SECTOR WEST.				
Day of Observation 1843.	Apparent Zenith Distance, from Unreduced Observation.	Reduction for Az. Error, and Curv. of Path.	Refraction.	Precession, Aberration, and Nutation.	Deduced Mean Zenith Distance, 1843, Jan. 0; and Mean of Separate Results, uncorrected, for Error of Collimation.	Day of Observation 1843.	Apparent Zenith Distance, from Unreduced Observation.	Reduction for Az. Error, and Curv. of Path.	Refraction.	Precession, Aberration, and Nutation.	Deduced Mean Zenith Distance, 1843, Jan. 0; and Mean of Separate Results, uncorrected, for Error of Collimation.

B.A.C. 0948.

July 25	0· 6·34·32	·00	0·10	+13·75	0· 6·48·17	July 26	0· 7·30·03	·02	0·10	+13·71	0· 7·43·82
27	34·37	·00	0·10	13·67	48·14	28	31·46	·02	0·10	13·63	45·17
29	32·80	·00	0·10	13·58	46·57	30	30·52	·00	0·10	13·54	44·16
Aug. 2	34·23	·00	0·10	13·40	47·73	Aug. 1	29·73	·00	0·10	13·45	43·28
5	34·18	·00	0·10	13·25	47·53	3	30·18	·00	0·10	13·35	43·63
7	33·78	·00	0·10	13·13	47·01	6	30·38	·00	0·10	13·19	43·67
11	33·78	·00	0·10	12·91	46·79	8	31·07	·00	0·10	13·08	44·25
13	32·89	·00	0·10	+12·78	45·77	12	31·02	·00	0·10	+12·85	43·97
					0· 6·47·21						0· 7·43·99

Error of Collimation . . = 0· 0·28·39
Resulting Mean Zenith Distance, South = 0· 7·15·60

B.A.C. 7011.

Aug. 7	0·47.31·41	·00	0·66	+14·24	0·47·17·83	Aug. 6	0·46·36·99	·00	0·66	+14·29	0·46·23·36
11	31·45	·00	0·69	14·03	18·11	8	37·29	·00	0·66	14·19	23·76
13	32·62	·00	0·68	+13·92	19·38	12	35·13	·01	0·69	+13·98	21·83
					0·47·18·44						0·46·22·98

Error of Collimation . . = 0· 0·27·73
Resulting Mean Zenith Distance, North = 0·46·50·71

B.A.C. 7026.

July 25	0·47·25·03	·01	0·68	+14·97	0·47·10·73	July 26	0·46·29·34	+ ·01	0·68	+14·94	0·46·14·09
27	24·74	·00	0·68	14·91	10·51	28	28·64	- ·11	0·68	14·88	14·33
29	25·44	·00	0·67	14·84	11·27	30	28·89	·01	0·67	14·80	14·75
31	23·86	·00	0·68	14·77	9·77	Aug. 1	29·88	·01	0·67	14·72	15·82
Aug. 2	23·95	·01	0·67	14·69	9·92	3	28·94	·01	0·66	14·64	14·95
5	24·05	·00	0·66	14·55	10·16	6	29·58	·00	0·66	14·50	15·74
7	23·81	·00	0·66	14·45	10·02	8	28·99	·00	0·66	14·40	15·25
11	23·84	·00	0·69	14·24	10·29	12	28 22	·01	0·69	+14·18	14·72
13	24·52	·00	0·68	+14·13	11·07						
					0·47·10·42						0·46·14·96

Error of Collimation . . = 0· 0·27·73
Resulting Mean Zenith Distance, North = 0·46·42·69

No. 7026.—July 26.—Correction for Azimuthal Error - ·101; for Curvature of Path +·113. =+0··01.

3 X

Mean Zenith Distances of Stars observed at Kamies Berg.

FACE OF SECTOR EAST.						FACE OF SECTOR WEST.					
Day of Observation 1843.	Apparent Zenith Distance, from Unreduced Observation.	Reduction for At. Error, and Curr. of Path.	Refraction.	Precession, Aberration, and Nutation.	Deduced Mean Zenith Distance, 1843, Jan. 0; and Mean of Separate Results, uncorrected for Error of Collimation.	Day of Observation 1843.	Apparent Zenith Distance, from Unreduced Observation.	Reduction for At. Error, and Curr. of Path.	Refraction.	Precession, Aberration, and Nutation.	Deduced Mean Zenith Distance, 1843, Jan. 0; and Mean of Separate Results, uncorrected for Error of Collimation.

B.A.C. 7057.

	° ′ ″	″	″	″	° ′ ″		° ′ ″	″	″	″	° ′ ″
July 25	0 44 8·74	·01	0·63	+15·46	0 43 53·90	July 26	0 43 16·19	·09	0·63	+15·43	0 42 61·30
27	10·02	·00	0·63	15·30	55·86	28	14·71	·10	0·63	15·36	59·88
29	10·62	·00	0·63	15·32	55·93	30	15·40	·01	0·62	15·29	60·72
31	9·63	·00	0·63	15·25	55·01	Aug. 1	15·55	·01	0·62	15·21	60·95
Aug. 2	9·23	·01	0·62	15·17	54·67	3	14·91	·01	0·61	15·13	60·38
5	10·12	·00	0·62	15·03	55·71	6	15·35	·00	0·61	14·99	60·97
11	9·57	·00	0·64	14·73	53·48	8	14·91	·00	0·62	14·89	60·64
13	10·14	·00	0·64	+14·61	56·17	12	14·04	·01	0·64	+14·67	60·00
					0 43 55·34						0 43 0·61

Error of Collimation . . . = 0′ 0·27·37
Resulting Mean Zenith Distance, North = 0 43 27·97

Anon. AR. 20·23.

July 31	0 32 50·13	·00	0·47	+15·57	0 32 35·03	July 30	0 31 55·95	·01	0·46	+15·61	0 31 40·79
Aug. 2	49·73	·01	0·46	15·49	34·69	Aug. 1	55·76	·00	0·46	15·53	40·69
5	50·97	·00	0·46	15·35	36·08	3	55·41	·01	0·45	15·45	40·40
7	51·36	·00	0·46	15·25	36·57	6	56·50	·00	0·45	15·30	41·65
11	51·21	·00	0·47	15·04	36·44	8	55·81	·00	0·46	15·20	41·07
13	51·31	·00	0·47	+14·92	36·86	12	53·83	·01	0·47	+14·98	39·31
					0 32 35·98						0 31 40·65

Error of Collimation . . . = 0′ 0·27·66
Resulting Mean Zenith Distance, North = 0 32 8·32

Anon. AR. 20·32.

July 25	0 23 47·90	·00	0·34	+16·80	0 23 31·44	July 26	0 22 54·71	·05	0·34	+16·77	0 22 38·23
27	49·18	·00	0·34	16·74	32·78	28	54·12	·05	0·34	16·70	37·71
29	50·91	·00	0·33	16·67	34·57	30	54·27	·00	0·33	16·63	37·97
31	47·55	·00	0·34	16·59	31·30	Aug. 1	53·08	·00	0·33	16·55	36·86
Aug. 2	48·29	·00	0·33	16·51	32·11	3	53·03	·01	0·33	16·47	36·88
5	49·03	·00	0·33	16·38	32·98	6	53·68	·00	0·33	16·33	37·08
11	49·08	·00	0·34	16·06	33·36	8	53·68	·00	0·33	16·23	37·78
13	48·89	·00	0·34	+15·95	33·28	12	53·77	·01	0·34	+16·00	38·11
					0 23 32·73						0 22 37·65

Error of Collimation . . . = 0′ 0·27·54
Resulting Mean Zenith Distance, North = 0 23 5·19

Mean Zenith Distances of Stars observed at Kamies Berg.

FACE OF SECTOR EAST. / FACE OF SECTOR WEST.

B.A.C. 7207.

Day of Observation 1843.	Apparent Zenith Distance, from Unreduced Observation.	Reduction for Az. Error, and Curv. of Path.	Refraction.	Precession, Aberration, and Nutation.	Deduced Mean Zenith Distance, 1843, Jan. 0; and Mean of Separate Results, uncorrected, for Error of Collimation.	Day of Observation 1843.	Apparent Zenith Distance, from Unreduced Observation.	Reduction for Az. Error, and Curv. of P.th.	Refraction.	Precession, Aberration, and Nutation.	Deduced Mean Zenith Distance, 1843, Jan. 0; and Mean of Separate Results, uncorrected, for Error of Collimation.
July 25	3·59· 2·47	·05	3·48	+17·52	3·59·23·42	July 26	3·59·59·06	·54	3·47	+17·47	4· 0·19·46
27	2·32	·00	3·48	17·41	23·21	28	58·52	·56	3·46	17·36	18·78
29	1·83	·01	3·42	17·30	22·54	30	59·36	·05	3·42	17·24	19·97
31	2·76	·02	3·45	17·17	23·36	Aug. 1	58·27	·04	3·42	17·11	18·76
Aug. 2	3·36	·04	3·41	17·05	23·78	3	59·01	·05	3·37	16·98	19·31
5	3·55	·00	3·38	16·84	23·77	6	58·91	·02	3·37	16·76	19·02
11	2·37	·01	3·51	16·38	22·25	8	59·16	·02	3·38	16·61	19·13
13	2·47	·02	3·48	+16·21	22·14	12	59·95	·04	3·51	+16·30	19·72
					3·59·23·06						4· 0·19·27

Error of Collimation   .   .   . = 0· 0·28·11
Resulting Mean Zenith Distance, South = 3·59·51·16

Anon. AR. 20 52.

Day of Observation 1843.	Apparent Zenith Distance	Reduction	Refraction.	Precession, etc.	Deduced Mean Zenith Distance	Day of Observation 1843.	Apparent Zenith Distance	Reduction	Refraction.	Precession, etc.	Deduced Mean Zenith Distance
July 29	0·38·48·89	·00	0·55	+18·75	0·38·30·60	July 26	0·37·51·90	·08	0·55	+18·83	0·37·33·54
31	46·81	·00	0·55	18·67	28·67	28	51 80	·09	0·55	18·78	33·48
Aug. 2	46·57	·01	0·55	18·62	28·49	30	53·13	·01	0·55	18·72	34·95
5	48·26	·00	0·54	18·49	30·31	Aug. 1	51·96	·01	0·55	18·65	33·85
11	47·11	·00	0·56	18·20	29·47	3	52·04	·01	0·54	18·58	33·99
13	47·31	·00	0·56	+18·09	29·78	6	51·50	·00	0·54	18·45	33·59
						8	51·80	·00	0·54	18·36	33·98
						12	50·22	·01	0·56	+18·15	32·62
					0 38·29·57						0·37·33·75

Error of Collimation   .   .   . = 0· 0·27·91
Resulting Mean Zenith Distance, North = 0· 38· 1·66

Anon. AR. 21· 0

Day of Observation 1843.	Apparent Zenith Distance	Reduction	Refraction.	Precession, etc.	Deduced Mean Zenith Distance	Day of Observation 1843.	Apparent Zenith Distance	Reduction	Refraction.	Precession, etc.	Deduced Mean Zenith Distance
July 27	0· 1· 5·58	+ ·05	0·01	+19·54	0· 0·46·10	July 28	0· 0· 5·04	·00	0·01	+19·51	0· 0·14·46
29	4·74	·00	0·01	19·48	45·27	30	6·27	·00	0·01	19·45	13·17
31	2·42	·00	0·01	19 42	43·01	Aug. 1	5·33	·00	0·01	19·39	14·04
Aug. 2	2·42	·00	0·01	19·34	43·09	6	4·99	·00	0·01	19·17	14·17
5	2·72	·00	0 01	19·21	43·52	7	5·58	·00	0·01	19·12	13·53
11	2·96	·00	0·01	18·91	44·06	8	4·74	·00	0·01	19·07	14·32
13	3·01	·00	0·01	+18·79	44·23	12	3·90	·00	0·01	+18·85	14·94
					0· 0·44·18						0· 0·14·09

Error of Collimation   .   .   . = 0· 0·29·14
Resulting Mean Zenith Distance, North = 0· 0·15·05

Anon. 21ʰ 0ᵐ.—July 27.— Correction for Curvature of Path = + 0″·05. The Zenith Distance of this Star is less than the Error of Collimation: therefore the place on the limb *affected* by the Error of Collimation, and reduced to January 0, 1843, is South for face *West*.

Mean Zenith Distances of Stars observed at Kamies Berg.

	FACE OF SECTOR EAST.						FACE OF SECTOR WEST.				
Day of Observation 1843.	Apparent Zenith Distance, from Unreduced Observation.	Reduction for Az. Error, and Curv. of Path.	Refraction.	Precession, Aberration, and Nutation.	Deduced Mean Zenith Distance, 1843, Jan. 0; and Mean of Separate Results, uncorrected, for Error of Collimation.	Day of Observation 1843.	Apparent Zenith Distance, from Unreduced Observation.	Reduction for Az. Error, and Curv. of Path.	Refraction.	Precession, Aberration, and Nutation.	Deduced Mean Zenith Distance, 1843, Jan. 0; and Mean of Separate Results, uncorrected, for Error of Collimation.

B.A.C. 7386.

	° ′ ″	″	″	″	° ′ ″		° ′ ″	″	″	″	° ′ ″
July 27	2·27· 7·85	·00	2·14	+20·39	2·27·30·38	July 28	2·28· 6·32	·34	2·13	+20·35	2·28·28·46
29	7·55	·01	2·11	20·31	29·96	30	5·03	·03	2·11	20·26	27·37
31	8·54	·01	2·13	20·22	30·88	Aug. 1	6·17	·02	2·11	20·17	28·43
Aug. 2	9·03	·02	2·10	20·12	31·23	3	6·42	·03	2.07	20·07	28·53
5	9·38	·00	2·09	19·96	31·43	6	5·03	·01	2·07	19·90	26·99
11	8·29	·01	2·10	19·57	30·01	8	6·22	·01	2·08	19·77	28·06
13	7·30	·02	2·14	+19·43	28·85	12	7·06	·02	2·16	+19·50	28·70
					2·27·30·39						2·28·28·08

Error of Collimation . . . = 0· 0·28·84
Resulting Mean Zenith Distance, South = 2·27·59·23

Anon. AR. 21·11.

July 29	0·32·35·26	·00	0·46	+20·63	0·32·15·09	July 28	0·31·38·62	·07	0·46	+20·66	0·31·18·35
31	33·83	·00	0·46	20·58	13·71	Aug. 1	39·36	·00	0·46	20·55	19·27
Aug. 2	32·99	·01	0·46	20·52	12·92	3	39·06	·01	0·45	20·49	19·01
5	34·57	·00	0·45	20·41	14·61	6	39·51	·00	0·45	20·37	19·59
11	33·83	·00	0·47	20·14	14·16	11	38·97	·00	0·45	20·28	19·14
13	34·72	·00	0·47	+20·03	15·16	12	37·24	·01	0·47	+20·08	17·62
					0·32·14·28						0·31·18·83

Error of Collimation . . . = 0· 0·27·72
Resulting Mean Zenith Distance, North = 0·31·46·55

Anon. AR. 21·24.

July 27	0· 1· 8·89	·00	0·02	+21·04	0· 1·(30·85)	July 28	0· 2· 3·26	·00	0·02	+21·92	0· 2·25·20
29	4·50	·00	0·02	21·90	26·42	30	2·42	·00	0·02	21·88	24·32
31	5·29	·00	0·02	21·85	27·16	Aug. 1	2·23	·00	0·02	21·82	24·07
Aug. 2	6·08	·00	0·02	21·79	27·89	3	2·77	·00	0·02	21·76	24·55
5	4·74	·00	0·02	21·08	26·44	6	2·72	·00	0·02	21·64	24·38
11	6·08	·00	0·02	21·40	27·50	8	2·07	·00	0·02	21·55	24·24
13	4·20	·00	0·02	+21·29	25·51	12	4·55	·00	0·02	+21·35	25·92
					0· 1·26·82						0· 2·24·07

Error of Collimation . . . = 0· 0·28·92
Resulting Mean Zenith Distance, South = 0· 1·55·74

Mean Zenith Distances of Stars observed at Knmies Berg.

FACE OF SECTOR EAST.						FACE OF SECTOR WEST.					
Day of Observation 1843.	Apparent Zenith Distance, from Unreduced Observation.	Reduction for Az. Error, and Curv. of Path.	Refraction.	Precession, Aberration, and Nutation.	Deduced Mean Zenith Distance, 1843, Jan. 0; and Mean of Separate Results, uncorrected, for Error of Collimation.	Day of Observation 1843.	Apparent Zenith Distance, from Unreduced Observation.	Reduction for Az. Error, and Curv. of Path.	Refraction.	Precession, Aberration, and Nutation.	Deduced Mean Zenith Distance, 1843, Jan. 0; and Mean of Separate Results, uncorrected, for Error of Collimation.

B.A.C. 7557.

	° ′ ″	″	″	″	° ′ ″		° ′ ″	″	″	″	° ′ ″
July 25	3·21·54·76	·27	2·94	+23·13	3·22·20·56	July 26	3·22·53·48	·45	2·93	+23·10	3·23·19·06
27	55·85	·00	2·94	23·06	21·85	28	52·84	·47	2·92	23·03	18·32
29	55·15	·01	2·89	22·99	21·02	30	52·98	·04	2·90	22·96	18·80
31	56·39	·02	2·92	22·91	22·20	Aug. 1	52·14	·03	2·89	22·87	17·87
Aug. 2	56·73	·03	2·89	22·82	22·41	3	53·43	·04	2·95	22·77	19·01
5	56·93	·00	2·86	22·67	22·46	6	52·69	·01	2·85	22·61	18·14
11	56·39	·01	2·96	22·29	21·63	8	52·05	·02	2·85	22·49	17·37
13	55·85	·02	2·93	+22·14	20·90	12	53·82	·03	2·97	+22·21	18·97
					3·22·21·63						3·23·18·44

Error of Collimation . . = 0· 0·28·41
Resulting Mean Zenith Distance, South = 3·22·50·04

B.A.C. 7657.

	° ′ ″	″	″	″	° ′ ″		° ′ ″	″	″	″	° ′ ″
July 25	1·10· 3·51	·01	1·01	+24·12	1· 9·40·39	July 26	1· 9· 8·20	·15	1·01	+24·12	1· 8·44·94
29	3·70	·00	0·99	24·11	40·58	28	7·41	·16	1·00	24·12	44·13
31	3·46	·01	1·00	24·10	40·35	30	8·34	·01	1·00	24·11	45·22
Aug. 2	2·52	·01	0·99	24·07	39·43	Aug. 1	7·60	·01	0·99	24·08	44·50
5	3·85	·00	0·98	24·00	40·83	3	7·06	·01	0·98	24·05	43·98
7	3·51	·00	0·98	23·94	40·55	6	7·85	·00	0·98	23·97	44·86
11	3·95	·00	1·02	23·80	41·17	8	7·36	·01	0·98	23·92	44·41
13	4·05	·01	1·01	+23·72	41·33	12	6·52	·01	1·02	+23·76	43·77
					1· 9·40·58						1· 8·44·48

Error of Collimation . . = 0· 0·28·05
Resulting Mean Zenith Distance, North = 1· 9·12·53

Anon. AR. 21·54.

	° ′ ″	″	″	″	° ′ ″		° ′ ″	″	″	″	° ′ ″
July 25	1·10·43·38	·01	1·02	+24·43	1·10·19·94	July 26	1· 9·45·88	·15	1·02	+24·43	1· 9·22·32
29	41·93	·00	1·00	24·43	18·50	28	44·84	·16	1·01	24·43	21·26
31	41·04	·01	1·01	24·41	17·63	30	46·61	·01	1·01	24·43	23·38
Aug. 2	41·04	·01	1·00	24·39	17·64	Aug. 1	45·68	·01	1·00	24·40	22·27
5	41·38	·00	0·99	24·33	18·04	3	45·14	·01	0·99	24·37	21·75
7	41·48	·00	0·99	24·27	18·20	6	45·58	·00	0·99	24·30	22·27
11	41·58	·00	1·03	24·14	18·47	8	46·07	·01	0·99	24·24	22·81
13	42·47	·01	1·02	+24·05	19·43	12	44·54	·01	1·03	+24·09	21·47
					1·10·18·48						1· 9·22·19

Error of Collimation . . = 0· 0·28·15
Resulting Mean Zenith Distance, North = 1· 9·50·34

No. 7557.—July 25.—Correction for Azimuthal Error = ·044; for Curvature of Path = ·227. = – 0·″27.

Mean Zenith Distances of Stars observed at Kamies Berg.

	FACE OF SECTOR EAST.						FACE OF SECTOR WEST.				
Day of Observation 1843.	Apparent Zenith Distance, from Unreduced Observation.	Reduction for Ax. Error, and Curr. of Path.	Refraction.	Precession, Aberration, and Nutation.	Deduced Mean Zenith Distance. 1843, Jan. 0; and Mean of Separate Results, uncorrected, for Error of Collimation.	Day of Observation 1843.	Apparent Zenith Distance, from Unreduced Observation.	Reduction for Ax. Error, and Curr. of Path.	Refraction.	Precession, Aberration, and Nutation.	Deduced Mean Zenith Distance. 1843, Jan. 0; and Mean of Separate Results, uncorrected, for Error of Collimation.
B.A.C. 7842.											
July 25	2 46 29·98	·04	2 43	+26·93	2 46 59·30	July 26	2 47 27·21	·37	2 42	+26·93	2 47 56·19
27	30·97	·00	2·43	26·92	60·32	28	26·57	·39	2·41	26·91	55·50
29	30·97	·01	2·38	26·90	60·24	30	26·33	·03	2·39	26·88	55·57
31	30·72	·01	2·40	26·87	59·98	Aug. 1	26·72	·03	2·39	26·84	55·92
Aug. 2	31·26	·03	2·38	26·82	60·43	3	27·16	·03	2·35	26·79	56·27
5	34·47	·00	2·36	26·72	(63·55)	6	26·42	·01	2·35	26·68	55·44
11	30·37	·01	2·45	26·45	59·26	8	27·12	·01	2·30	26·60	56·07
13	30·18	·01	2·42	+26·34	58·93	12	28·00	·03	2·45	+26·40	56·82
					2·46.59·78						2·47·55·97

Error of Collimation . . . = 0· 0·28·10
Resulting Mean Zenith Distance, South = 2·47·27·88

B.A.C. 7900.											
July 29	0 11 38 03	·00	0 16	+27·32	0 11 10·87	July 28	0 11 39·51	·03	0 16	+27·32	0 10·12·32
31	37·14	·00	0·16	27·33	9·97	30	42·52	·00	0·16	27·33	15·35
Aug. 2	37·53	·00	0·16	27·33	10·36	Aug. 1	42·17	·00	0·16	27·33	15·00
5	37·98	·00	0·16	27·29	10·85	3	41·38	·00	0·16	27·32	14·22
7	38·13	·00	0·16	27·25	11·04	6	42·03	·00	0·16	27·28	14·91
11	39·11	·00	0·16	27·15	12·12	8	41·19	·00	0·16	27·23	14·12
13	38·27	·00	0·16	+27·07	11·36	12	40·15	·00	0·16	+27·11	13·20
					0·11·10·94						0·10·14·16

Error of Collimation . . . = 0· 0·28·39
Resulting Mean Zenith Distance, North = 0·10·42·55

B.A.C. 7966.											
July 25	3 19 56·84	·04	2 91	+28·44	3 20 28·15	July 26	3 20 54·27	·45	2 91	+28·45	3 21 25·18
29	56·00	·01	2·86	28·44	27·20	28	50·86	·47	2 89	28·45	21·73
31	56·10	·02	2 89	28·42	27·39	30	50·91	·04	2 87	28·43	22·17
Aug. 2	56·25	·03	2·86	28·39	27·47	Aug. 1	51·26	·03	2·87	28·41	22·51
5	56·05	·00	2·83	28·31	27 19	3	51·35	·04	2·82	28·37	23·00
7	56·20	·00	2·83	28·25	27·28	6	51·95	·01	2·82	28·28	23·04
11	55·41	·01	2·94	28·08	26·42	8	51·75	·02	2·83	28·21	22·77
13	55·46	·02	2·90	+27·97	26·31	12	52·89	·03	2·94	+28·02	23·82
					3·20·27·19						3·21·23·03

Error of Collimation . . . = 0· 0·27·92
Resulting Mean Zenith Distance, South = 3·20·55·11

Mean Zenith Distances of Stars observed at Kamies Berg.

	FACE OF SECTOR EAST.						FACE OF SECTOR WEST.				
Day of Observation 1843.	Apparent Zenith Distance, from Unreduced Observation.	Reduction for Az. Error, and Curv. of Path.	Refraction.	Precession, Aberration, and Nutation.	Deduced Mean Zenith Distance, 1843, Jan. 0; and Mean of Separate Results, uncorrected, for Error of Collimation.	Day of Observation 1843.	Apparent Zenith Distance, from Unreduced Observation.	Reduction for Az. Error, and Curv. of Path.	Refraction.	Precession, Aberration, and Nutation.	Deduced Mean Zenith Distance, 1843, Jan. 0; and Mean of Separate Results, uncorrected, for Error of Collimation.
					Fomalhaut B.A.C. 7002.						
July 25	0· 4 47·31	·00	0·07	+28·25	0· 5·15·63	July 26	0· 5 42·96	·00	0·08	+28·27	0· 6·11·31
27	46·37	·00	0·08	23·29	14·74	28	42·47	·00	0·08	28·31	10·86
29	45·68	·00	0·07	28·33	14·08	30	42·82	·00	0·07	28·34	11·23
31	45·68	·00	0·08	28·35	14·11	Aug. 1	42·22	·00	0·07	28·35	10·64
Aug. 2	45·63	·00	0·07	28·36	14·06	3	42·67	·00	0·07	28·35	11·09
5	45·48	·00	0·07	28·33	13·88	6	43·01	·00	0·07	28·32	11·40
11	45·04	·00	0·08	28·21	13·33	8	43·26	·00	0·07	28·29	11·62
13	45·23	·00	0·08	+28·14	13·45	12	43·61	·00	0·08	+28·18	11·87
					0· 5·14·16						0· 6·11·25

Error of Collimation . . . = 0· 0·28·55
Resulting Mean Zenith Distance, South = 0· 5·42·71

MEAN ZENITH DISTANCES.

COLLECTION OF

ALL THE

RESULTS OF OBSERVATION OF EACH STAR

AT

THE ROYAL OBSERVATORY, near CAPE TOWN,

AND

DEDUCTION OF MEAN ZENITH DISTANCE, 1844, JANUARY 0.

NOTE.—The reduction for Azimuthal Error is always to be applied subtractively to the Zenith Distance. The reduction for Curvature of Path is always to be applied subtractively to South Zenith Distance, and additively to North Zenith Distance. The Refraction is always to be applied additively. The Precession, Aberration, and Nutation, have the sign which is proper for reducing the Apparent North Polar Distance of the Star to its mean North Polar Distance, 1844, January 0; and therefore are to be applied with the sign given in the Table when the Star is South of the Zenith, and with the opposite sign when the Star is North of the Zenith.

The numbers included in parentheses in the column " Deduced Mean Zenith Distance, 1844, January 0," are omitted in taking the mean.

Where an asterisk or a positive sign is affixed to a number in the 3rd or 9th columns, the explanation will be found at the bottom of the page.

Mean Zenith Distances of Stars observed at the Royal Observatory.

	FACE OF SECTOR EAST.						FACE OF SECTOR WEST.				
Day of Observation 1843–4.	Apparent Zenith Distance, from Unreduced Observation.	Reduction for Ax. Error, and Curr. of Path.	Refraction.	Precession, Aberration, and Nutation.	Deduced Mean Zenith Distance. 1844, Jan. 0; and Mean of Separate Results, uncorrected, for Error of Collimation.	Day of Observation 1843–4.	Apparent Zenith Distance, from Unreduced Observation.	Reduction for Ax. Error, and Curv. of Path.	Refraction.	Precession, Aberration, and Nutation.	Deduced Mean Zenith Distance. 1844, Jan. 0; and Mean of Separate Results uncorrected, for Error of Collimation.
B.A.C. 1802.											
1843.						1843.					
Nov. 3	0·13·23·19	·00	0 23	+11·85	0·13·35·27	Nov. 1	0·13·23·54	·00	0·23	+12·31	0·13·36·08
13	25·46	·01	·23	9·33	35·01	4	23·34	·00	·23	11·61	35·18
15	25·35	·01	·23	8·79	34·36	10	24·73	·01	·23	10·12	35·07
Dec. 2	29·96	·01	·23	3·82	34·00	14	26·70	·01	·23	9·06	35·98
4	30·94	·01	·23	3·21	34·37	Dec. 1	30·55	·01	·23	4·11	34·88
8	32·52	·02	·23	1·98	34·71	3	31·63	·01	·23	3·51	35·36
12	34·94	·01	·23	0·74	35·00	7	33·41	·01	·23	2·28	35·91
13	37·16	·01	·23	0·43	37·81	11	33·01	·02	·23	+ 1·05	34·87
14	34·40	·02	·23	+ 0·12	34·73	15	35·54	·02	·23	- 0·19	35·56
1844.						1844.					
Jan. 2	39·58	·02	·23	- 5·59	34·20	Jan. 6	41·85	·02	·23	6·71	35·35
4	40·72	·01	·22	6·16	34·77	7	42·40	·02	·23	6·09	35·62
8	41·61	·02	·22	7·26	34·55	9	42·30	·02	·22	7·53	34·97
10	42·45	·02	·22	7·80	34·85	12	43·19	·02	·22	8·33	35·06
11	42·79	·02	·22	8·07	34·92	14	43·24	·03	·23	8·84	34·60
16	45·01	·02	·22	9·35	35·86	15	43·88	·02	·23	9·10	34·99
19	45·01	·02	·22	10·08	35·13	18	44·96	·02	·22	9 84	35·32
21	45·61	·02	·23	10·56	35·26	20	45·41	·02	·22	10·32	35·29
24	45·65	·02	·22	11·24	34·61	22	44·57	·02	·22	10·79	33·98
27	45·95	·02	·23	11·89	34·27	25	47·14	·02	·22	11·46	35·88
29	46·28	·02	·23	12·30	34·19	28	46·59	·02	·23	12·10	34·70
31	47·28	·03	·23	12·70	34·78	30	47·93	·02	·22	12·50	35·03
Feb. 5	47·58	·04	·22	13·63	34·13	Feb. 1	47·33	·02	·22	12·90	34 63
16	50·15	·03	·22	15·31	35·03	2	47·68	·02	·23	13·09	34·80
19	50·49	·03	·23	15·68	35·01	17	50·00	·04	·22	15·46	34·74
April23	50·00	·08	·23	14·05	36·15	21	49·70	·03	·22	15·91	33·98
26	48·86	·03	·22	13·50	35·49	April18	48·72	·03	·22	14·80	34·11
May 3	46·94	·00	·23	12·29	34·88	May 7	47·88	·00	·23	11·49	36·02
9	·42·45	·00	·23	11·08	31·60	11	46 05	·00	·23	10·65	35·63
10	??·35 42·89	·06	·22	10·86	32·19	16	46·35	·00	·23	9·53	37·05
25	41·66	·00	·22	7·35	34·53	27	42·45	·00	·23	6·84	35·84
28	40 82	·00	·23	6·59	34·46	June 1	41·41	·00	·23	5·54	36·10
June 16	34·70	·00	·23	1·13	33·80	18	37·66	·00	0 23	- 0·57	37·32
19	33·71	·00	0 23	- 0·28	33·66						
					0·13·34·68						0·13·35·35

Error of Collimation . . = 0· 0· 0·33
Resulting Mean Zenith Distance, South = 0·13·35·01

B.A.C. 1878.											
1844.						1844.					
June 16	1·53·44·27	·00	1·94	- 2·78	1·53·43·43	May 30	1·53·53·65	·00	1·80	- 7·43	1·53·48·11
25	42·25	·00	1 89	+ 0·09	44·23	June 18	48 12	·01	1·90	- 1·92	48·09
					1·53·43·83						1·53·48·10

Error of Collimation . . = 0· 0· 2·14
Resulting Mean Zenith Distance, South = 1·53·46·97

No. 1802.—May 10.—Correction for Curvature of Path = ·0″·06.

Mean Zenith Distances of Stars observed at the Royal Observatory.

FACE OF SECTOR EAST.

B.A.C. 2293.

Day of Observation 1843-4	Apparent Zenith Distance, from Unreduced Observation	Reduction for Az. Error, and Curv. of Path.	Refraction	Precession, Aberration, and Nutation	Deduced Mean Zenith Distance, 1844, Jan. 0; and Mean of Separate Results, uncorrected, for Error of Collimation
1843.	° ′ ″	″	″	″	° ′ ″
Nov. 3	5·10·21·23	·06	5·13	+12·13	5·10·14·17
13	18·32	·12	5·29	10·01	13·48
15	17·87	·13	5·18	9·54	13·38
Dec. 4	13·03	·21	5·19	4·46	13·55
8	12·44	·47	5·19	3·29	13·87
12	9·63	·26	5·21	2·10	12·48
14	11·55	·32	5·22	1·50	14·95
16	10·37	·32	5·22	+ 0·89	14·38
1844.					
Jan. 2	4·89	·36	5·13	- 4·29	13·95
4	4·20	·26	5·09	4·89	13·92
8	3·31	·33	5·00	6·07	14·14
10	3·01	·42	5·08	6·06	14·33
11	2·57	·40	5·07	6·94	14·18
16	0·54	·43	5·00	8·36	13·56
19	5· 9·59·85	·43	5·10	9·18	13·70
21	60·25	·48	5·15	9·72	14·64
24	57·24	·40	5·10	10·51	12·45
27	57·98	·39	5·14	11·28	14·01
29	57·88	·46	5·18	11·77	14·37
31	56·40	·63	5·14	13·17	13·70
Feb. 5	54·47	·76	5·09	13·41	12·21
17	52·99	·58	5·09	15·85	13·35
19	52·15	·55	5·17	16·20	12·97
April 10	50·87	·61	5·06	19·88	15·20
21	51·21	·74	5·17	19·20	14·93
23	49·34	·75	5·14	19·14	12·87
May 3	51·51	·01	5·17	14·81	14·81
10	54·18	·00	5·13	17·23	16·54
13	53·04	·01	5·18	16·79	15·00
15	53·88	·01	5·00	16·48	15·35
22	54·42	·01	5·14	15·30	14·85
23	55·51	·00	5·13	15·12	15·76
28	55·36	·00	5·17	14·19	14·72
June 1	56·79	·00	5·18	13·39	15·36
4	52·10	·00	5·17	12·77	(10·04)
11	58·03	·00	5·19	11·24	14·46
17	59·31	·00	5·30	9·87	14·48
19	60·10	·00	5·17	9·39	14·66
21	61·09	·00	5·19	8·92	15·20
25	63·80	·01	5·17	7·95	16·91
26	62·81	·00	5·12	- 7·71	15·64
					5·10·14·30

FACE OF SECTOR WEST.

Day of Observation 1843-4	Apparent Zenith Distance, from Unreduced Observation	Reduction for Az. Error, and Curv. of Path.	Refraction	Precession, Aberration, and Nutation	Deduced Mean Zenith Distance, 1844, Jan. 0; and Mean of Separate Results, uncorrected, for Error of Collimation
1843.	° ′ ″	″	″	″	° ′ ″
Nov. 1	5·10·19·55	·09	5·21	+12·50	5·10·12·17
4	18·56	·10	5·16	11·93	11·69
10	17·33	·16	5·25	10·68	11·74
14	16·00	·13	5·27	9·78	11·36
Dec. 7	10·27	·26	5·14	3·50	11·56
11	9·23	·34	5·17	2·40	11·66
15	8·49	·37	5·21	+ 1·19	12·14
1844.					
Jan. 3	2·07	·35	5·11	- 4·59	11·42
6	1·28	·35	5·25	5·48	11·66
7	0·64	·33	5·19	5·78	11·28
9	0·54	·49	5·08	6·37	11·50
12	0·64	·53	5·08	7·23	12·42
14	0·15	·55	5·14	7·80	12·54
15	5· 9 59·65	·53	5·11	8·09	12·31
18	58·08	·53	5·11	8·91	11·57
20	56·69	·53	5·12	9·45	10·73
22	57·93	·35	5·10	9·99	12·67
25	56·54	·34	5·09	10·77	12·06
28	56·10	·45	5·17	11·53	12·35
30	54·72	·39	5·11	12·02	11·46
Feb. 1	55·41	·51	5·19	12·50	12·59
9	54·92	·43	5·17	12·73	12·39
15	51·90	·69	5·15	15·48	11·84
21	51·71	·58	5·07	16·54	12·74
April 9	48·00	·63	5·08	18·91	11·36
11	47·26	·61	5·06	19·84	11·55
May 2	48·84	·02	5·17	18·25	12·24
9	47·56	·02	5·15	17·37	10·06
11	49·34	·03	5·15	17·09	11·55
14	49·63	·03	5·14	16·63	11·37
16	49·14	·01	5·15	16·32	10·60
17	49·68	·00	5·07	16·10	10·91
25	51·11	·03	5·10	14·70	10·94
30	52·10	·00	5·15	13·79	11·04
June 16	56·05	·03	5·29	10·10	11·41
18	54·37	·03	5·23	9·63	9·20
20	55·01	·03	5·17	- 9·16	9·31
					5·10·11·63

Error of Collimation . . . = 0· 0· 1·33

Resulting Mean Zenith Distance, North = 5·10·12·97

Mean Zenith Distances of Stars observed at the Royal Observatory.

	FACE OF SECTOR EAST.						FACE OF SECTOR WEST.				
Day of Observation 1843-4.	Apparent Zenith Distance, from Unreduced Observation.	Reduction for Az. Error, and Curv. of Path.	Refraction.	Precession, Aberration, and Nutation.	Deduced Mean Zenith Distance, 1844, Jan. 0; and Mean of Separate Results, uncorrected, for Error of Collimation.	Day of Observation 1843-4.	Apparent Zenith Distance, from Unreduced Observation.	Reduction for Az. Error, and Curv. of Path.	Refraction.	Precession, Aberration, and Nutation.	Deduced Mean Zenith Distance, 1844, Jan. 0; and Mean of Separate Results, uncorrected, for Error of Collimation.

B.A.C. 4458.

EAST Day	App. Z.D.	Red.	Refr.	Prec.	Deduced	WEST Day	App. Z.D.	Red.	Refr.	Prec.	Deduced
1844.						1843.					
Jan. 7	1·57· 5·00	·14	1·95	+ 3·30	1·57·10·11	Dec. 11	1·57· 2·33	·14	1·93	+ 6·91	1·57·11 03
12	6·87	·17	1·92	2·37	10·99	15	2·28	·15	1·94	6·55	10·62
14	5·54	·17	1·94	+ 1·98	9·29	1844.					
Feb. 12	13·39	·27	1·94	- 4·56	10·50	Jan. 13	5·24	·23	1·94	+ 2·18	9·13
14	14·13	·29	1·96	5·05	10·75	Feb. 5	11·96	·17	1·94	- 2·88	10·85
19	15·96	·23	1·96	6·28	11·41	15	14·92	·29	1·93	5·30	11·26
April 8	25·14	·23	1·95	17·53	9·33	17	14·97	·34	1 93	5·78	10·78
13	26·22	·23	1·96	18·49	9·46	April 11	28·79	·25	1·94	18·11	12·37
21	25·93	·30	1·99	19·93	7·69	14	28·99	·25	1·95	18·68	12·01
May 3	27·75	·01	1·97	21·82	7·89	18	29·18	·30	1·97	19·41	11·44
6	28·49	·00	1·99	22·24	8·24	22	28·94	·31	2·00	20·10	10·53
7	27·61	·00	2·01	22·37	7·25	May 2	32·05	·01	1·99	21·67	12·36
9	27·80	·00	1·97	22·63	7·14	4	33·28	·01	1·97	21·96	13·28
11	28·49	·00	1·96	22·89	7·56	8	35·03	·01	2·00	22·50	14·52
14	28·79	·00	1·96	23·25	7·50	10	34·86	·01	2·01	22·76	14·10
16	29·68	·01	1·97	-23·48	8·16	13	33·97	·01	1·97	23·13	12·80
						15	35·70	·01	1·92	-23 36	14·25
					1·57· 8.95						1·57·11·96

Error of Collimation   . . = 0· 0· 1·50
Resulting Mean Zenith Distance, South = 1·57·10·46

B.A.C. 4507.

EAST Day	App. Z.D.	Red.	Refr.	Prec.	Deduced	WEST Day	App. Z.D.	Red.	Refr.	Prec.	Deduced
1844.						1844.					
May 29	4·40· 8·64	·00	4·71	-24·52	4·30·48·83	May 30	4·40·14·66	·00	4·71	-24·61	4·39·54·76
June 1	9·08	·00	4 78	24·78	49·08	June 2	13·77	·01	4·70	-24·87	53·59
3	9·97	·00	4·78	24·95	49·80						
5	8·49	·00	4·73	-25·10	48·12						
					4·30·48·96						4·39·54·18

Error of Collimation   . . = 0· 0· 2·61
Resulting Mean Zenith Distance, South = 4·39·51·57

B.A.C. 4517.

EAST Day	App. Z.D.	Red.	Refr.	Prec.	Deduced	WEST Day	App. Z.D.	Red.	Refr.	Prec.	Deduced
1844.						1844.					
Feb. 12	5·10·13·58	·65	5·14	- 6·20	5·10·24·27	Feb. 5	5·10·13·33	·42	5·13	- 4·67	5·10·22·71
14	12·34	·70	5·19	6·64	23·47	15	12·39	·69	5·10	6·86	23·66
19	11·06	·55	5·18	7·73	23·42	17	12·09	·83	5·11	7·30	23·67
April 8	4·00	·55	5·17	17·18	25·80	April 11	1·38	·61	5·13	17·64	23·54
13	1·97	·55	5·19	17·94	24·55	14	0·89	·61	5·15	18·09	23·52
21	2·81	·74	5·26	19·05	26·38	18	0·89	·72	5·21	18·65	24·03
May 3	0·35	·01	5·22	20·47	26·03	22	0·00	·74	5·29	19·18	23 72
7	0·54	·01	5·32	20·88	26·73	May 2	5· 9·57·38	·02	5 26	20·36	22·98
9	1·23	·00	5 23	21·07	27·53	4	56·48	·02	5·22	20·58	22 26
11	0·10	·00	5·20	21·25	26·55	8	54·67	·02	5·20	20·98	20·92

Carried forward,

Mean Zenith Distances of Stars observed at the Royal Observatory.

FACE OF SECTOR EAST.　　　　　**FACE OF SECTOR WEST.**

B.A.C. 4517—(continued).

Day of Observation 1843-4.	Apparent Zenith Distance, from Unreduced Observation.	Reduction for Az. Error, and Curv. of Path.	Refraction.	Precession, Aberration, and Nutation.	Deduced Mean Zenith Distance, 1844, Jan. 0; and Mean of Separate Results, uncorrected, for Error of Collimation.	Day of Observation 1843-4.	Apparent Zenith Distance, from Unreduced Observation.	Reduction for Az. Error, and Curv. of Path.	Refraction.	Precession, Aberration, and Nutation.	Deduced Mean Zenith Distance, 1844, Jan. 0; and Mean of Separate Results, uncorrected, for Error of Collimation.
1844.						**1844.**					
May 14	5· 9·59·77	- ·01	5·19	21·51	26·46	May 10	5· 9·55·95	·02	5·32	21·16	22·41
16	60·90	+·10	5·21	21·67	27·97	13	55·26	·03	5·22	21·43	21·88
20	60·30	·00	5·31	21·97	27·58	15	56·45	·01	5·08	21·59	23·11
24	58·62	·00	5·19	22·23	26·04	17	55·11	·00	5·19	21·75	22·05
25	58·62	·00	5·18	-22·29	26·09	21	54·37	·01	5·26	-22·03	21·65
					5·10·25·93						5·10·22·81

Error of Collimation . . . = 0· 0· 1·56
Resulting Mean Zenith Distance, North = 5·10·24·37

B.A.C. 4548.

Day	Apparent Zenith Distance	Red.	Refr.	Prec. &c.	Deduced Mean Z.D.	Day	Apparent Zenith Distance	Red.	Refr.	Prec. &c.	Deduced Mean Z.D.
1844.						**1844.**					
Feb. 12	5·10·11·23	·65	5·14	- 5·05	5·10·21·67	Feb. 5	5·10· 9·80	·42	5·13	- 4·45	5·10·18·96
14	9·63	·70	5·19	6·38	20·50	15	8·44	·70	5·10	6·60	19·44
19	7·90	·55	5·17	7·46	19·98	17	8·74	·83	5·11	7·63	20·05
April 8	0·30	·55	5·17	16·79	21·71	April 11	5· 9·57·24	·61	5·13	17·24	19·00
13	5· 9·58·91	·55	5·18	17·54	21·08	14	57·09	·61	5·15	17·68	19·31
21	60·00	·74	5·26	18·64	23·16	18	57·14	·72	5·21	18·24	19·87
May 3	56·84	·01	5·22	20·07	22·12	22	56·23	·74	5·20	18·77	19·55
7	56·94	·01	5·32	20·47	22·72	May 2	53·78	·02	5·26	19·66	18·98
9	57·38	·00	5·23	20·67	23·28	4	52·89	·02	5·24	20·17	18·28
11	57·09	·00	5·20	20·85	23·14	8	50·82	·02	5·29	20·57	16·66
14	56·35	·01	5·20	21·11	22·65	10	51·31	·02	5·32	20·76	17·37
16	56·30	·01	5·20	21·27	22·76	13	51·11	·03	5·22	21·02	17·32
20	56·40	·00	5·31	21·57	23·28	15	52·64	·01	5·08	21·10	18·90
22	56·30	·01	5·20	21·71	23·20	17	51·36	·00	5·19	21·35	17·90
24	55·36	·00	5·19	-21·83	22·38	21	50·97	·01	5·26	-21·64	17·86
					5·10·22·24						5·10·18·63

Error of Collimation . . . = 0· 0· 1·81
Resulting Mean Zenith Distance, North = 5·10·20·44

B.A.C. 4570.

Day	Apparent Zenith Distance	Red.	Refr.	Prec. &c.	Deduced Mean Z.D.	Day	Apparent Zenith Distance	Red.	Refr.	Prec. &c.	Deduced Mean Z.D.
1844.						**1844.**					
Feb. 12	1·40·49·22	·22	1·66	- 4·57	1·40·55·23	Feb. 5	1·40·40·46	·14	1·66	- 3·06	1·40·54·04
14	49·02	·24	1·68	5·00	55·46	15	47·34	·23	1·65	5·22	53·98
19	48·18	·19	1·68	6·10	55·77	17	47·49	·28	1·65	5·06	54·52
April 8	39·00	·19	1·67	16·04	56·52	April 11	37·91	·21	1·66	16·55	55·91
13	37·42	·18	1·68	16·88	55·80	14	33·67	·21	1·67	17·04	52·17
21	37·62	·25	1·70	18·13	57·20	18	34·31	·24	1·69	17·68	53·44
May 3	37·12	·00	1·69	19·19	58·60	22	34·51	·25	1·71	18·29	54·26
6	36·23	·00	1·71	20·16	58·10	May 2	31·05	·01	1·70	19·66	52·40
7	36·04	·00	1·72	20·28	58·04	6	31·30	·01	1·70	19·92	52·91
9	36·53	·00	1·70	20·51	58·74	8	29·87	·01	1·71	20·39	51·96

Carried forward,

No. 4517.—May 16.—Correction for Azimuthal Error — ·013; for Curvature of Path +·112. = +0″.10.

8 A

Mean Zenith Distances of Stars observed at the Royal Observatory.

	FACE OF SECTOR EAST.						FACE OF SECTOR WEST.				
Day of Observation 1843–4.	Apparent Zenith Distance, from Unreduced Observation.	Reduction for Az. Error, and Curv. of Path.	Refraction.	Precession, Aberration, and Nutation.	Deduced Mean Zenith Distance, 1844, Jan. 0; and Mean of Separate Results, uncorrected, for Error of Collimation.	Day of Observation 1843–4.	Apparent Zenith Distance, from Unreduced Observation.	Reduction for Az. Error, and Curv. of Path.	Refraction.	Precession, Aberration, and Nutation.	Deduced Mean Zenith Distance, 1844, Jan. 0; and Mean of Separate Results, uncorrected, for Error of Collimation.

B.A.C. 4579—(continued).

1844.	° ′ ″	″	″	″	° ′ ″	1844.	° ′ ″	″	″	″	° ′ ″
May 11	1 40 35·54	·00	1·68	20·73	57·95	May 10	1 40 28·09	·01	1·72	20·62	50·42
14	35·00	·00	1·68	21·05	57·73	13	30·26	·01	1·69	20·94	52·88
16	35·05	·00	1·68	21·25	57·98	15	29·17	·00	1·65	21·15	51·97
20	33·96	·00	1·72	21·63	57·31	17	29·57	·00	1·68	21·34	52·59
22	34·56	·00	1·68	-21·80	58·04	21	28·43	·00	1·70	-21·71	51·84
					1·40·57·23						1·40·53·02

Error of Collimation . . . = 0· 0· 2·11
Resulting Mean Zenith Distance, North = 1·40·55·13

B.A.C. 4623.

1844.						1844.					
Feb. 12	1 42 53·38	·22	1·70	4·32	1 42 59·18	Feb. 1	1 42 52·88	·17	1·72	- 2·02	1 42 56·45
14	52·59	·24	1·71	4·75	58·81	5	55·28	·15	1·70	2·85	59·08
19	51·95	·19	1·71	5·82	59·29	15	52·93	·24	1·68	4·96	59·33
April 8	42·86	·19	1·71	15·61	59·99	April 11	42·76	·21	1·70	16·12	60·37
10	40·49	·21	1·65	15·95	57·88	14	40·49	·21	1·70	16·61	58·59
13	41·38	·19	1·71	16·44	59·34	18	39·11	·25	1·72	17·24	57·82
21	41·63	·25	1·74	17·60	60·81	22	39·08	·26	1·75	17·84	59·31
May 3	42·27	·00	1·73	19·34	63·34	May 2	36·15	·01	1·74	19·21	57·09
6	40·89	·00	1·74	19·70	62·33	4	36·15	·01	1·74	19·46	57·34
9	40·36	·00	1·73	20·06	62·15	7	35·26	·01	1·76	19·82	56·83
11	40·25	·00	1·72	20·28	62·25	10	35·06	·01	1·75	19·94	56·74
14	39·06	·00	1·72	20·60	61·38	13	34·86	·01	1·76	20·17	56·78
16	38·76	·00	1·72	20·80	61·28	15	35·51	·01	1·73	20·49	57·72
20	39·06	·00	1·75	21·18	61·99	17	34·07	·00	1·68	20·70	56·45
22	38·72	·00	1·72	-21·36	61·60		35·36	·00	1·71	-20·90	57·97
					1·43· 0·79						1·42·57·90

Error of Collimation . . . = 0· 0· 1·45
Resulting Mean Zenith Distance, North = 1·42·59·34

B.A.C. 4686.

1843.						1843.					
Nov. 2	1 39 47·26	·02	1·62	+ 5·20	1 39 54·06	Oct. 29	1 39 47·26	·03	1·67	+ 4·81	1 39 53·71
3	48·70	·02	1·62	5·29	55·59	31	47·12	·03	1·64	5·01	53·74
8	49·19	·04	1·67	5·70	56·52	Nov. 1	45·39	·03	1·65	5·11	52·12
Dec. 14	45·88	* ·34	1·66	6·12	53·32	5	46·42	·04	1·64	5·46	53·48
1844.						20	46·28	·05	1·67	6·36	54·26
Jan. 1	46·18	·13	1·65	4·55	52·25	Dec. 3	45·34	·07	1·65	6·50	53·42
2	45·24	·13	1·64	4·43	51·18	7	46·97	·09	1·63	6·43	54·92
7	47·66	·12	1·66	3·79	52·99	11	45·44	·12	1·65	6·27	53·24
8	49·44	* 35	1·63	3·65	54·37	15	45·59	·13	1·64	6·07	53·17
11	48·10	·14	1·62	3·22	52·80						

Carried forward,

No. 4686.—Dec. 14.—Correction for Azimuthal Error - ·11; for Curvature of Path - ·23. = - 0"·34.
Jan. 8.—   ,,   ,,   ,, - ·12; ,,   ,, - ·23. = - 0 ·35.
Oct. 29.—The value of the Micrometer reading in the unreduced observations should have been -12·0 instead of -22·9.

Mean Zenith Distances of Stars observed at the Royal Observatory.

FACE OF SECTOR EAST.						FACE OF SECTOR WEST.					
Day of Observation 1843-4.	Apparent Zenith Distance, from Unreduced Observation.	Reduction for Az. Error, and Curv. of Path.	Refraction.	Precession, Aberration, and Nutation.	Deduced Mean Zenith Distance. 1844, Jan. 0; and Mean of Separate Results, uncorrected, for Error of Collimation.	Day of Observation 1843-4.	Apparent Zenith Distance, from Unreduced Observation.	Reduction for Az. Error, and Curv. of Path.	Refraction.	Precession, Aberration, and Nutation.	Deduced Mean Zenith Distance, 1844, Jan. 0; and Mean of Separate Results, uncorrected, for Error of Collimation.
					B.A.C. 4686—(continued).						
1844.	° ′ ″	″	″	″	° ′ ″	1844.	° ′ ″	″	″	″	° ′ ″
Jan. 12	1·39·48·25	·14	1·63	3·07	52·81	Jan. 6	1·39·48·50	·12	1·07	3·92	53·97
14	49·14	·14	1·64	2·77	53·41	13	47·26	·19	1·65	2·92	51·64
18	49·29	·15	1·65	2·12	52·91	16	48·75	·18	1·64	2·45	52·66
25	52·55	·37	1·64	0·91	54·73	19	50·18	·18	1·63	1·95	53·58
27	51·34	·14	1·65	0·54	53·39	26	49·73	·12	1·66	0·73	52·00
29	50·92	·16	1·66	+ 0·17	52·59	28	50·72	·16	1·67	+ 0·36	52·59
Feb. 1	50·08	·22	1·67	- 0·40	51·13	30	51·96	·14	1·66	- 0·02	53·46
12	53·98	·23	1·65	2·60	52·80	Feb. 5	53·29	·15	1·65	1·19	53·60
14	54·67	·25	1·67	3·02	53·07	15	55·81	·24	1·64	3·23	53·98
16	54·87	·20	1·64	3·44	52·87	17	55·56	·29	1·65	3·65	53·27
19	56·50	·19	1·67	4·07	53·91	22	56·55	·25	1·64	4·70	53·24
April 8	1·40· 3·85	·19	1·66	14·14	51·18	April 11	1·40· 6·57	·21	1·65	14·69	53·32
10	5·23	·21	1·61	14·51	52·12	14	8·29	·21	1·66	15·22	54·52
13	7·80	·19	1·67	15·05	54·23	18	9·08	·25	1·67	15·92	54·58
21	6·02	·26	1·69	16·42	51·03	22	8·19	·26	1·67	16·58	53·02
25	8·59	·26	1·67	17·07	52·93	May 2	11·75	·01	1·69	18·13	55·30
May 3	7·60	·01	1·68	18·28	50·99	4	13·28	·01	1·69	18·42	56·54
6	6·57	·00	1·70	18·70	49·57	7	13·59	·01	1·71	18·84	56·45
9	7·01	·00	1·68	19·11	49·58	8	13·72	·01	1·70	18·98	56·43
11	7·95	·00	1·67	19·37	50·25	10	14·41	·01	1·71	19·24	56·87
14	8·69	·00	1·67	19·75	50·61	13	13·77	·01	1·68	19·62	55·82
24	8·89	·00	1·67	20·87	49·69	15	15·30	·00	1·64	19·87	57·07
27	9·97	·00	1·68	21·17	50·48	25	14·84	·01	1·67	20·97	55·53
June 1	11·95	·00	1·71	21·61	52·05	28	16·09	·02	1·71	-21·26	56·52
					1·39·52·47						1·39·54·18

Error of Collimation . . . = 0· 0· 0·86
Resulting Mean Zenith Distance, South = 1·39·53·32

					B.A.C. 4719.						
1844.						1844.					
Feb. 14	5·22·52·88	·73	5·40	- 4·93	5·23· 2·48	Feb. 15	5·22·53·08	·72	5·31	- 5·12	5·23· 2·79
16	52·44	·61	5·30	5·31	2·44	17	53·38	·87	5·33	5·29	3·34
19	52·14	·57	5·30	5·88	2·84	22	52·09	·74	5·30	6·45	3·10
April 8	45·23	·57	5·38	14·34	4·38	April 14	42·07	·64	5·38	15·17	1·98
10	44·34	·63	5·23	14·62	3·56	18	41·87	·76	5·41	15·70	2·22
13	44·00	·57	5·39	15·03	3·85	22	42·22	·77	5·50	16·20	3·15
21	43·45	·77	5·48	16·07	4·23	May 2	39·34	·02	5·47	17·33	2·12
25	40·89	·78	5·41	16·55	2·07	4	37·63	·02	5·47	17·54	0·62
May 3	42·96	·02	5·44	17·44	5·82	7	36·79	·03	5·54	17·84	0·14
6	42·27	·00	5·49	17·74	5·50	9	36·67	·02	5·51	17·93	0·09
9	42·81	·00	5·45	18·03	6·29	10	36·89	·03	5·54	18·12	0·52
14	41·58	·01	5·42	18·47	5·46	13	37·09	·03	5·45	18·39	0·90
16	40·64	·01	5·42	18·64	4·69	15	38·91	·01	5·30	18·56	2·76
20	41·68	·00	5·53	18·95	6·16	17	37·04	·00	5·40	18·72	1·16
											Carried forward,

No. 4686. Jan. 25.—Correction for Azimuthal Error - ·14; for Curvature of Path - ·23. = - 0″·37.

Mean Zenith Distances of Stars observed at the Royal Observatory.

	FACE OF SECTOR EAST.						FACE OF SECTOR WEST.				
Day of Observation 1843–4.	Apparent Zenith Distance, from Unreduced Observation.	Reduction for Az. Error, and Curv. of Path.	Refraction.	Precession, Aberration, and Nutation.	Deduced Mean Zenith Distance. 1844, Jan. 0; and Mean of Separate Results, uncorrected, for Error of Collimation.	Day of Observation 1843–4.	Apparent Zenith Distance, from Unreduced Observation.	Reduction for Az. Error, and Curv. of Path.	Refraction.	Precession, Aberration, and Nutation.	Deduced Mean Zenith Distance. 1844, Jan. 0; and Mean of Separate Results, uncorrected, for Error of Collimation.

B.A.C. 4719—(continued.)

1844.	° ′ ″	″	″	″	° ′ ″	1844.	° ′ ″	″	″	″	° ′ ″
May 22	5·22·41·28	·01	5·41	19·09	5·77	May 21	5·22·36·35	·01	5·46	-19 02	0·82
24	40·05	·00	5·40	-19·23	4·68						
					5·23· 4·39						5·23· 1·71

Error of Collimation . . . = 0· 0· 1·34
Resulting Mean Zenith Distance, North = 5·23· 3·05

Anon. AR. 14ʰ·11ᵐ.

June 1	3·14· 2·54	·00	3·32	-20·74	3·13·45·12	June 2	3·14· 7·72	* ·13	3·25	-20·83	3·13·46·76

Error of Collimation . . . = 0· 0· 0·82
Resulting Mean Zenith Distance, = 3·13·45·94

B.A.C. 4784.

1844.						1844.					
Feb. 12	5· 8·40·82	·65	5·09	- 3·95	5· 8·40·21	Feb. 15	5· 8·40·13	·69	5 06	- 4·49	5· 8·48·99
14	40·03	·70	5·16	4·31	48·80	17	40·82	·83	5·09	4·85	49·93
16	39·40	·58	5·07	48·65	48·65	22	38·05	·71	5·06	5·76	48·16
19	38·35	·55	5·15	5·21	48·16	April 11	30·01	61	5·11	13·77	48·28
April 8	31·74	·55	5·14	13·36	49·60	14	30·25	·61	5·14	14·18	48·96
10	31·54	·60	4·99	13·64	49·57	18	29·07	·72	5·17	14·69	48·21
13	30·80	·55	5·15	14·04	49·44	22	29·86	·74	5·25	15·19	49·56
21	31·04	·74	5·24	15·07	50·61	May 2	26·06	·02	5·23	16·31	47·58
25	26 70	·75	5·17	15·54	(46·66)	4	25·12	·02	5·24	16·52	46·86
May 3	30·11	·01	5·20	16·42	51·72	7	23·84	·02	5·30	16·82	45·94
6	29·56	·00	5·25	16·72	51·53	8	24·13	·02	5·27	16·91	46·29
9	29·27	·00	5·21	17·01	51·40	10	25·56	·02	5·31	17·10	47·95
14	28·92	·01	5·16	17·45	51·52	13	24·48	·03	5·20	17·37	47·02
17	29·27	·01	5·17	17·70	52·13	15	24·63	·01	5·08	17·54	47·24
21	28·38	·01	5·22	18·02	51·61	20	24·77	·01	5·28	-17·94	47·98
22	28·77	·01	5·17	-18·09	52·02						
					5· 8·50·41						5· 8·47·93

Error of Collimation . . . = 0· 0· 1·24
Resulting Mean Zenith Distance, North = 5· 8·49·17

Anon. 14ʰ 11ᵐ.—June 2.—Correction for Azimuthal Error - ·006; for Curvature of Path - ·127. = - 0″·13.
No. 4784.—April 25.—A probable mistake of 5 parts of the Micrometer reading.

Mean Zenith Distances of Stars observed at the Royal Observatory.

FACE OF SECTOR EAST.

Anon. AR. 14·24

Day of Observation 1843–4.	Apparent Zenith Distance, from Unreduced Observation.	Reduction for Az. Error, and Curv. of Path.	Refraction.	Precession, Aberration, and Nutation.	Deduced Mean Zenith Distance, 1844, Jan. 0; and Mean of Separate Results, uncorrected, for Error of Collimation.
1844.					1844.
Feb. 12	1·18·32·13	·17	1·29	- 2·47	1·18·35·72
14	31·74	·19	1·31	2·83	35·09
16	31·29	·15	1·28	3·19	35·61
19	28·38	·15	1·31	3·75	33·29
April 8	21·17	·15	1·30	12·46	34·78
10	20·48	·16	1·27	12·78	34·37
13	20·08	·14	1·30	13·24	35·08
21	21·17	·20	1·33	14·42	36·72
25	20·48	·20	1·31	14·98	36·57
May 3	19·44	·00	1·32	16·02	36·78
9	19·84	·00	1·32	16·74	37·90
17	18·11	·00	1·31	17·61	37·03
21	18·06	·00	1·32	18·01	37·39
22	18·36	·00	1·31	18·10	37·77
27	17·02	·00	1·32	18·55	36·89
29	17·47	·00	1·32	-18·71	37·50
					1·18·36·19

FACE OF SECTOR WEST.

Day of Observation 1843–4.	Apparent Zenith Distance, from Unreduced Observation.	Reduction for Az. Error, and Curv. of Path.	Refraction.	Precession, Aberration, and Nutation.	Deduced Mean Zenith Distance, 1844, Jan. 0; and Mean of Separate Results, uncorrected, for Error of Collimation.
1844.					
April 11	1·18·20·87	·14	1·29	-12·93	1·18·34·95
18	19·99	·19	1·31	13·99	35·10
22	19·79	·20	1·33	14·56	35·48
May 2	18·01	·01	1·32	15·90	35·22
7	15·84	·01	1·33	16·15	33·31
7	15·15	·01	1·34	16·51	32·99
8	14·11	·01	1·34	16·63	32·07
10	14·56	·01	1·35	16·86	32·76
11	15·74	·01	1·31	16·97	34·01
13	15·25	·01	1·32	17·19	33·75
15	15·00	·00	1·29	17·41	33·70
20	13·67	·00	1·34	17·91	32·92
24	13·67	·01	1·31	18·28	33·25
25	13·77	·01	1·31	18·37	33·44
28	11·40	·01	1·34	18·63	31·36
30	14·16	·00	1·32	18·79	34·27
June 1	13·27	·00	1·34	-18·94	33·55
					1·18·33·66

Error of Collimation . . . = 0· 0· 1·27
Resulting Mean Zenith Distance, North = 1·18·34·92

B.A.C. 4852.

FACE OF SECTOR EAST.

Day of Observation 1843–4.	Apparent Zenith Distance, from Unreduced Observation.	Reduction for Az. Error, and Curv. of Path.	Refraction.	Precession, Aberration, and Nutation.	Deduced Mean Zenith Distance, 1844, Jan. 0; and Mean of Separate Results, uncorrected, for Error of Collimation.
1844.					1844.
Feb. 1	0·33·48·32	·07	0·57	+ 0·43	0·33·49·25
12	49·46	·08	·56	- 1·41	48·53
14	49·95	·08	·57	1·76	48·68
16	49·21	·07	·56	2·10	47·60
19	51·48	·06	·57	2·64	49·35
April 8	58·39	·06	·56	11·35	47·54
10	59·28	·07	·55	11·67	48·09
13	59·58	·00	·57	12·16	47·93
17	59·92	·08	·57	12·78	47·63
21	59·82	·09	·58	13·39	46·92
25	64·02	·09	·57	13·08	50·52
May 3	61·75	·00	·57	15·09	47·23
6	59·43	·00	·58	15·48	44·53
9	60·76	·00	·57	15·86	45·47
14	62·29	·00	·57	16·47	46·39
16	62·84	·00	0·57	-16·70	46·71
					0·33·47·65

FACE OF SECTOR WEST.

Day of Observation 1843–4.	Apparent Zenith Distance, from Unreduced Observation.	Reduction for Az. Error, and Curv. of Path.	Refraction.	Precession, Aberration, and Nutation.	Deduced Mean Zenith Distance, 1844, Jan. 0; and Mean of Separate Results, uncorrected, for Error of Collimation.
1844.					
Feb. 15	0·33·48·86	·08	0·56	- 1·93	0·33·47·41
17	48·54	·10	·56	2·28	46·72
22	50·30	·08	·56	3·18	47·60
April 9	58·10	·07	·50	11·51	47·08
14	59·58	·07	·57	12·31	47·77
18	60·52	·00	·57	12·94	48·06
22	50·77	·09	·58	13·54	46·72
May 2	63·53	·00	·57	14·95	49·15
4	63·63	·00	·58	15·22	48·99
7	64·71	·00	·58	15·61	49·68
10	65·03	·00	·58	15·74	49·87
11	65·65	·00	·58	15·99	50·54
13	65·16	·00	·57	16·11	50·11
15	65·85	·00	0·56	-16·59	49·82
					0·33·48·59

Error of Collimation . . . = 0· 0· 0·47
Resulting Mean Zenith Distance, South = 0·33·48·12

Anon. 14ʰ 24ᵐ.—April 11.—Correction for Azimuthal Error - ·162; for Curvature of Path + ·025. = - 0″·14.

3 B

Mean Zenith Distances of Stars observed at the Royal Observatory.

FACE OF SECTOR EAST.						FACE OF SECTOR WEST.				
Day of Observation 1843–4.	Apparent Zenith Distance, from Unreduced Observation.	Reduction for Az. Error, and Curv. of Path.	Refraction.	Precession, Aberration, and Nutation.	Deduced Mean Zenith Distance, 1844, Jan. 0; and Mean of Separate Results, uncorrected, for Error of Collimation.	Day of Observation 1843–4.	Apparent Zenith Distance, from Unreduced Observation.	Reduction for Az. Error, and Curv. of Path.	Refraction.	Precession, Aberration, and Nutation.	Deduced Mean Zenith Distance, 1844, Jan. 0; and Mean of Separate Results, uncorrected for Error of Collimation.

B.A.C. 4916.

Day (East)	App. Z.D.	Red.	Refr.	Prec.	Deduced Mean	Day (West)	App. Z.D.	Red.	Refr.	Prec.	Deduced Mean
1844.						1844.					
Feb. 12	0 42 56·93	·09	0·71	- 1·35	0·42·58·90	Feb. 15	0·42·57·62	·10	0·70	- 1·84	0·42·60·06
14	55·40	·10	·71	1·68	57·69	17	58·71	·12	·71	2·17	61·47
16	55·20	·08	·70	2·00	57·82	22	55·89	·10	·70	3·00	59·49
19	54·07	·08	·71	2·50	57·20	April 9	48·49	·09	·71	10·73	59·84
April 8	48·34	.08	·71	10·58	59·55	14	46·52	·09	·71	11·47	58·61
10	45·48	·09	·70	10·88	56·97	18	46·42	·11	·71	12·05	59·07
13	47·21	·08	·71	11·32	59·16	22	48·05	·11	·73	12·60	61·27
17	45·03	·00	·72	11·90	57·56	May 2	44·59	·00	·72	13·91	59·22
21	46·91	·11	·73	12·46	59·99	4	43·55	·00	·73	14·16	58·44
25	44·49	·11	·71	13·01	58·10	7	42·67	·00	·73	14·52	57·92
May 3	45·58	·00	·72	14·03	60·33	8	41·68	·00	·73	14·04	57·05
9	46·22	·00	·72	14·75	61·69	10	42·47	·00	·73	14·87	58·07
14	44·49	·00	·71	15·31	60·51	11	42·81	·00	·72	14·98	58·51
16	44·20	·00	·72	15·53	60·54	13	42·22	·00	·72	15·20	58·14
17	44·19	·00	·72	15·63	60·54	15	41·33	·00	·70	15·42	57·45
21	43·21	·00	0·72	-16·04	59·97	24	41·09	·00	0·71	-16·33	58·13
					0·42·59·16						0·42·58·92

Error of Collimation   .   .   = 0· 0· 0·12
Resulting Mean Zenith Distance, North = 0·42·59·04

Anon. AR. 14·54.

Day (East)	App. Z.D.	Red.	Refr.	Prec.	Deduced Mean	Day (West)	App. Z.D.	Red.	Refr.	Prec.	Deduced Mean
1844.						1844.					
Feb. 12	1·54·36·62	·25	1·89	- 1·47	1·54·39 73	Feb. 15	1·54·34·48	·27	1·87	- 1·93	1·54·38·01
14	36·55	·27	1·91	1·78	39·07	17	34·73	·32	1·89	2·24	38·54
16	35·91	·22	1·88	2·09	39·66	22	33·24	·27	1·88	3·04	37·89
19	34·83	·21	1·91	2·56	39·09	April 0	26·23	·24	1·89	10·33	38·21
April 8	28·06	·21	1·90	10·19	39·04	14	24·36	·23	1·90	11·02	37·05
10	25·74	23	1·87	10·47	37·85	18	24·56	·28	1·91	11·55	37·74
13	28·06	·21	1·91	10·88	40·64	22	24·46	·28	1·95	12·07	38·20
17	26·53	·25	1·92	11·42	39·62	May 2	21·74	·01	1·93	13·29	36·95
21	26·38	·28	1·94	11·95	39·99	4	21·05	·01	1·94	13·52	36·50
25	22·48	·29	1·01	12·45	36·55	7	19·37	·01	1·96	13·86	35·18
May 3	25·64	·01	1·92	13·41	40·96	8	19·47	·01	1·95	13·96	35·37
0	25·54	·00	1·93	14·07	41·54	10	19·07	·01	1·97	14·18	36·11
14	24·95	·00	1·91	14·59	41·45	11	19·57	·01	1·92	14·29	35·77
16	24·61	·00	1·92	14·79	41·32	13	20·36	·01	1·93	14·49	36·77
17	23·47	·00	1·01	14·89	40·27	15	19·52	+ ·02	1·88	-14·70	36·12
22	24·11	·01	1·91	-15·36	41·37						
					1·54·40·00						1·54·36·96

Error of Collimation   .   .   = 0· 0· 1·52
Resulting Mean Zenith Distance, North = 1·54·38·48

Anon. 14ʰ 54ᵐ.—Correction for Azimuthal Error - ·005; for Curvature of Path + ·025. = + 0″·02.

Mean Zenith Distances of Stars observed at the Royal Observatory.

FACE OF SECTOR EAST. | FACE OF SECTOR WEST.

Anon. AR. 14·58.

Day of Observation 1843–4	Apparent Zenith Distance, from Unreduced Observation.	Reduction for Az. Error, and Curv. of Path.	Refraction.	Precession, Aberration, and Nutation.	Deduced Mean Zenith Distance, 1844, Jan. 0; and Mean of Separate Results, uncorrected, for Error of Collimation.	Day of Observation 1843–4.	Apparent Zenith Distance, from Unreduced Observation.	Reduction for Az. Error, and Curv. of Path.	Refraction.	Precession, Aberration, and Nutation.	Deduced Mean Zenith Distance, 1844, Jan. 0; and Mean of Separate Results, uncorrected, for Error of Collimation.
1844.						**1844.**					
Feb. 16	1·37·52·78	·19	1·61	- 1·61	1·37·56·01	Feb. 17	1·37·50·46	* ·18	1·61	- 1·97	1·37·53·86
19	51·75	·18	1·63	2·28	55·48	April 14	40·49	+ ·02	1·62	10·63	52·76
April 10	42·96	·20	1·60	10·08	54·44	22	42·71	- ·24	1·66	11·68	55·81
13	44·84	·18	1·63	10·49	56·78	May 2	37·23	- ·01	1·65	12·90	51·77
17	44·54	·21	1·64	11·03	57·00	4	30·41	- ·01	1·66	13·13	54·19
21	44·25	·24	1·66	11·55	57·22	7	37·43	- ·01	1·67	13·47	52·56
25	42·37	·25	1·63	12·06	55·81	8	38·12	- ·01	1·67	13·58	53·36
May 6	43·16	·00	1·65	13·35	58·16	10	37·33	- ·01	1·68	13·79	52·79
9	43·26	·00	1·65	13·08	58·59	13	39·31	- ·01	1·64	14·11	55·05
14	42·91	·00	1·63	14·21	58·75	15	37·68	- ·00	1·61	14·31	53·60
16	42·47	·00	1·64	14·41	58·52	20	38·27	+ ·22	1·67	14·80	54·96
17	40·96	·00	1·63	14·51	57·10	24	34·82	- ·01	1·63	15·16	51·60
21	42·42	·00	1·65	14·89	58·96	25	37·18	- ·01	1·63	15·25	54·05
22	41·68	·00	1·63	14·99	58·30	30	37·38	- ·00	1·64	15·67	54·89
27	41·86	·00	1·64	15·43	58·93	June 1	36·59	- ·00	1·67	15·83	54·09
29	42·57	·00	1·64	15·59	59·80	2	36·49	- ·00	1·64	-15·91	54·04
June 5	42·76	·00	1·65	-16·13	60·54						
					1·37·57·67						1·37·53·70

Error of Collimation　.　.　.　= 0· 0· 1·99
Resulting Mean Zenith Distance, North = 1·37·55·68

B.A.C. 5032.

Day	Apparent Z.D.	Red.	Refr.	Prec.	Deduced Mean Z.D.	Day	Apparent Z.D.	Red.	Refr.	Prec.	Deduced Mean Z.D.
1844.						**1844.**					
Feb. 12	4·21·42·93	·55	4·33	- 1·75	4·21·48·46	Feb. 15	4·21·43·97	·59	4·29	- 2·17	4·21·49·84
14	43·08	·60	4·37	2·03	48·88	17	44·39	·71	4·32	2·45	50·45
16	43·94	·50	4·31	2·31	50·06	21	43·57	·49	4·29	3·03	50·40
19	42·29	·47	4·37	2·74	48·99	22	41·28	·60	4·30	3·17	48·15
April 8	37·80	·47	4·35	9·46	51·14	April 9	35·33	·53	4·33	9·58	48·71
10	34·98	·52	4.28	9·70	48·44	11	34·68	·52	4·32	9·82	48·30
13	36·02	·47	4·36	10·05	49·96	14	33·70	·52	4·36	10·17	47·71
17	36·36	·55	4·39	10·51	50·71	18	34·09	·62	4·36	10·62	48·45
21	36·86	·63	4·44	10·96	51·63	22	34·24	·68	4·46	11·06	49·13
25	34·19	·64	4·38	11·38	49·31	May 2	31·48	·02	4·43	12·09	47·98
May 3	35·47	·01	4·39	12·19	52·04	4	30·69	·02	4·45	12·28	47·40
6	36·36	·00	4·43	12·47	53·26	7	29·45	·02	4·49	12·58	46·48
9	35·92	·00	4·42	12·74	53·08	8	28·76	·02	4·47	12·65	45·86
11	35·33	·00	4·40	12·92	52·65	10	29·43	·02	4·50	12·83	46·74
14	35·13	·00	4·37	13·18	52·68	13	29·60	·02	4·41	13·09	47·08
16	34·29	·01	4·39	-13·35	52·02	15	29·70	·01	4·33	-13·26	47·28
					4·21·50·83						4·21·48·12

Error of Collimation　.　.　.　= 0· 0· 1·35
Resulting Mean Zenith Distance, North = 4·21·49·48

Anon. 14ʰ 58ᵐ.—Feb. 17.—Correction for Azimuthal Error - ·274; for Curvature of Path + ·099. = - 0ʳ·18.
April 14.— ,,　　　　　,,　　,, - ·200; ,,　　　,, + ·222. = +0 ·02.
May 20.— ,,　　　　　,,　　,, ·000; ,,　　　,, + ·222. = +0 ·22.
June 1.—It appears that the plumb-line for this observation, bisected point 1° 35′ of the Arch and not 1° 40′ as entered at page 84 of the unreduced observations: the sign of the Micrometer value therefore should be positive.

Mean Zenith Distances of Stars observed at the Royal Observatory.

B.A.C. 5034.

FACE OF SECTOR EAST						FACE OF SECTOR WEST					
Day of Observation 1843-4.	Apparent Zenith Distance, from Unreduced Observation.	Reduction for Az. Error, and Curv. of Path.	Refraction.	Precession, Aberration, and Nutation.	Deduced Mean Zenith Distance, 1844, Jan. 0; and Mean of Separate Results, uncorrected, for Error of Collimation.	Day of Observation 1843-4.	Apparent Zenith Distance, from Unreduced Observation.	Reduction for Az. Error, and Curv. of Path.	Refraction.	Precession, Aberration, and Nutation.	Deduced Mean Zenith Distance, 1844, Jan. 0; and Mean of Separate Results, uncorrected, for Error of Collimation.
1844.	° ′ ″	″	″	″	° ′ ″	1844.	° ′ ″	″	″	″	° ′ ″
Feb. 19	1·45·21·23	·20	1·70	- 0·49	1·45·22·30	Feb. 21	1·45·19·01	·21	1.73	- 0·78	1·45·19·75
April 8	25·92	·20	1·75	7·06	19·51	22	20·73	·26	1.73	0·92	21·28
10	23·97	·22	1·72	8·26	19·21	April 9	27·55	·23	1 74	8·11	20·95
13	27·79	·20	1·76	8·70	20·65	14	29·32	·23	1·75	8·65	21·99
17	27·50	·24	1·77	9·28	19·75	18	28·93	·27	1·76	9·42	21·00
21	26·66	·27	1·79	9·85	18·33	22	28·83	·27	1·79	9·98	20·37
25	30·41	·28	1·77	10·40	21·50	May 2	31·80	·01	1·78	11·33	21·74
May 3	28·43	·01	1·77	11·47	18·72	4	32·14	·01	1·79	11·60	22·32
6	27·45	·00	1·78	11·85	17·38	7	33·57	·01	1·81	11·98	23·39
9	27·84	·00	1·78	12·23	17·39	8	33·67	·01	1·80	12·10	23·36
11	29·08	·00	1·77	12·47	18·38	10	33·32	·01	1·81	12·35	22·77
14	28·58	·00	1·76	12·83	17·51	13	33·52	·01	1·77	12·72	22·56
16	29·67	·00	1·77	13·07	18·37	15	35·00	·00	1 74	12·95	23·79
20	30·11	·00	1·80	13·53	18·38	17	34·75	·00	1·75	13·19	23·31
21	30·05	·00	1·79	13·64	19·10	22	34·90	·00	1·76	-13·75	22·91
24	30·46	·00	1·76	-13·06	18·26						
					1·45·19·05						1·45·22·10

Error of Collimation . . = 0· 0· 1·53
Resulting Mean Zenith Distance, South = 1·45·20·57

B.A.C. 5151.

FACE OF SECTOR EAST						FACE OF SECTOR WEST					
1844.						1844.					
Feb. 16	4·40·21·33	·53	4·61	- 1·58	4·40·26·99	Feb. 15	4·40·22·26	·63	4·60	- 1·46	4·40·27·09
19	19·75	·50	4·68	1·96	25·89	17	23·00	·76	4·63	1·71	28·58
April 8	15·70	·50	4·66	7·88	27·74	21	23·70	·53	4·60	2·21	29·98
13	15·99	·50	4·68	8·41	28·58	22	21·13	·65	4·61	2 33	27·42
17	14·37	·59	4·71	8·82	27·31	April 9	17·23	·57	4·64	7·99	29·29
21	15·80	·67	4·76	9·22	29·11	14	12·64	·50	4·66	8·51	25·25
25	11·45	·68	4·70	9·60	(25·07)	18	12·04	·66	4·68	8·92	25·58
May 3	14·71	·01	4·71	10·32	29·73	22	15·20	·67	4·70	9·31	28·63
6	15·20	·00	4·75	10·58	30·53	May 2	12·34	·02	4·75	10·23	27·30
7	14·81	·00	4·81	10·66	30·28	4	9·53	·02	4·76	10·41	24·68
9	14·71	·00	4·74	10·83	30·28	8	9·23	·02	4·79	10·74	24·74
11	15·06	·00	4·71	10·99	30·76	10	10·42	·02	4·83	10·93	26·14
14	14·56	·00	4·69	11·23	30·48	13	9·97	·03	4·72	11·15	25·81
16	14·51	·01	4·70	11·38	30·59	17	10·42	·00	4·67	11·45	26·54
21	12·93	·01	4·76	11·74	29·42	22	9·72	·01	4·69	-11·81	26·21
27	12·69	·01	4·73	-12·15	29·57						
					4·40·29·15						4·40·26·92

Error of Collimation . . = 0· 0· 1·11
Resulting Mean Zenith Distance, North = 4·40·28·04

No. 5151.—April 25.—This observation is omitted on the supposition that the Micrometer reading is 5 parts in error.

Mean Zenith Distances of Stars observed at the Royal Observatory.

	FACE OF SECTOR EAST.						FACE OF SECTOR WEST.				
Day of Observation 1843–4.	Apparent Zenith Distance, from Unreduced Observation.	Reduction for Az. Error, and Curv. of Path.	Refraction.	Precession, Aberration, and Nutation.	Deduced Mean Zenith Distance, 1844, Jan. 0; and Mean of Separate Results, uncorrected, for Error of Collimation.	Day of Observation 1843–4.	Apparent Zenith Distance, from Unreduced Observation.	Reduction for Az. Error, and Curv. of Path.	Refraction.	Precession, Aberration, and Nutation.	Deduced Mean Zenith Distance, 1844, Jan. 0; and Mean of Separate Results, uncorrected, for Error of Collimation.

Anon. AR. 15·34·44.

Day EAST	App. Z.D.	Red.	Refr.	Prec.	Deduced	Day WEST	App. Z.D.	Red.	Refr.	Prec.	Deduced
1844.	° ′ ″	″	″	″	° ′ ″	1844.	° ′ ″	″	″	″	° ′ ″
April 13	2·49·57·38	·31	2·83	− 7·61	2·50· 7·51	April 9	2·49·53·78	·35	2·81	− 7·16	2·50· 3·40
21	58·03	·42	2·88	8·46	8·95	11	56·25	·35	2·80	7·39	6·09
25	53·48	·42	2·85	8·87	(4·78)	14	54·97	·43	2·82	7·72	5·17
May 3	57·83	·01	2·85	9·66	10·33	18	54·57	·41	2·83	8·15	5·14
7	56·45	·00	2·91	10·04	9·40	22	55·75	·42	2·90	8·57	6·80
9	57·63	·00	2·87	10·22	10·72	May 2	52·89	·01	2·87	9·57	5·32
11	56·10	·00	2·85	10·40	9·35	4	52·00	·01	2·88	9·76	4·63
14	55·95	·00	2·84	10·66	9·45	8	50·82	·01	2·90	10·13	3·84
15	56·45	·00	2·90	10·75	10·00	10	50·37	·01	2·93	10·31	3·60
16	55·66	·01	2·85	10·84	9·34	13	50·52	·02	2·86	10·58	3·94
20	54·57	·00	2·91	11·17	8·65	17	50·82	·00	2·83	10·92	4·57
21	54·32	·01	2·88	11·25	8·44	22	50·32	·01	2·84	11·33	4·48
24	55·36	·00	2·84	11·49	9·69	25	50·03	·01	2·84	11·56	4·42
27	55·11	·00	2·86	11·71	9·08	28	48·79	·03	2·92	11·79	3·47
29	54·82	·00	2·86	11·86	9·54	30	50·42	·00	2·86	−11·93	5·21
June 1	54·62	·00	2·90	−12·08	9·60						
					2·50· 9·38						2·50· 4·67

Error of Collimation . . . = 0· 0· 2·35
Resulting Mean Zenith Distance, North = 2·50· 7·03

B.A.C. 5227.

Day EAST	App. Z.D.	Red.	Refr.	Prec.	Deduced	Day WEST	App. Z.D.	Red.	Refr.	Prec.	Deduced
1844.	° ′ ″	″	″	″	° ′ ″	1844.	° ′ ″	″	″	″	° ′ ″
Feb. 16	0·47·14·87	·09	0·77	+ 0·24	0·47·15·31	Feb. 21	0·47·17·29	·09	0·77	− 0·33	0·47·18·30
19	12·74	·09	·79	− 0·10	13·54	22	15·90	·11	·77	0·45	17·01
April 8	9·88	·09	·78	6·04	16·61	April 9	10·62	·10	·79	6·16	17·47
10	7·96	* ·07	·77	6·28	14·94	11	10·72	·10	·77	6·39	17·78
13	8·94	·09	·79	6·62	16·26	14	9·88	·10	·78	6·74	17·30
17	8·15	·10	·79	7·08	15·92	18	8·30	·12	·79	7·20	16·17
21	9·24	·12	·80	7·53	17·45	22	10·18	·12	·81	7·64	18·51
25	5·98	·12	·79	7·97	14·62	May 2	4·80	·00	·80	8·72	14·32
May 7	7·51	·00	·81	9·24	17·56	4	5·34	·00	·80	8·93	15·07
9	8·35	·00	·79	9·44	18·58	8	4·75	·00	·80	9·34	14·89
11	7·86	·00	·79	9·64	18·29	10	4·99	·00	·81	9·54	15·34
14	7·41	·00	·79	9·93	18·13	13	5·29	·00	·79	9·83	15·91
15	6·52	·00	·78	17·32		17	4·20	·00	·78	10·21	15·19
20	5·93	·00	·81	10·49	17·23	22	3·41	·00	·79	10·67	14·87
21	6·18	·00	·80	10·58	17·56	25	3·46	·00	0·79	−10·94	15·19
24	5·68	·00	0·79	−10·85	17·32						
					0·47·16·67						0·47·16·22

Error of Collimation . . . = 0· 0· 0·22
Resulting Mean Zenith Distance, North = 0·47·16·44

No. 5227.—April 10.—Correction for Azimuthal Error − ·097; for Curvature of Path + ·025. = − 0″·07.

Mean Zenith Distances of Stars observed at the Royal Observatory.

	FACE OF SECTOR EAST.						FACE OF SECTOR WEST.				
Day of Observation 1843–4.	Apparent Zenith Distance, from Unreduced Observation.	Reduction for Ax. Error, and Curv. of Path.	Refraction.	Precession, Aberration, and Nutation.	Deduced Mean Zenith Distance, 1844, Jan. 0; and Mean of Separate Results, uncorrected, for Error of Collimation.	Day of Observation 1843–4.	Apparent Zenith Distance, from Unreduced Observation.	Reduction for Ax. Error, and Curv. of Path.	Refraction.	Precession, Aberration, and Nutation.	Deduced Mean Zenith Distance, 1844, Jan. 0; and Mean of Separate Results, uncorrected, for Error of Collimation.

B.A.C. 5272.

1844.						**1844.**					
Feb. 16	5·10·44·73	·58	5·10	− 1·05	5·10·50·30	Feb. 15	5·10·44·63	·70	5·11	− 0·95	5·10·49·99
April 8	40·97	·55	5·17	6·55	52·14	17	46·40	·84	5·14	1·16	51·86
10	41·22	·61	5·10	6·74	52·45	21	46·21	·58	5·11	1·60	52·34
13	40·68	·55	5·19	7·01	52·33	22	44·92	·71	5·12	1·71	51·04
17	41·17	·66	5·21	7·37	53·09	April 9	38·60	·63	5·20	0·65	49·82
21	40·38	·74	5·27	7·72	52·63	11	38·51	·62	5·12	6·83	49·84
25	37·47	·75	5·22	8·05	49·99	14	37·12	·61	5·17	7·11	48·79
May 3	39·54	·01	5·22	8·09	53·44	18	38·06	·73	5·19	7·46	49·98
7	39·79	·01	5·33	8·99	54·10	22	39·05	·74	5·32	7·80	51·43
9	40·73	·00	5·25	9·14	55·12	May 2	34·16	·02	5·26	8·61	48·01
11	39·44	+ ·03	5·22	9·28	53·97	4	35·23	·02	5·28	8·77	49·26
14	39·69	·01	5·20	9·49	54·37	8	34·01	·02	5·31	9·06	48·36
15	40·18	·01	5·13	9·56	54·86	10	34·95	·02	5·36	9·21	49·50
16	39·04	·01	5·21	9·62	54·46	13	34·16	·03	5·24	9·42	48·79
20	37·62	·00	5·33	9·89	52·84	17	35·00	·00	5·18	− 9·69	49·87
21	40·13	·01	5·28	− 9·95	55·35						
					5·10·53·22						5·10·49·93

Error of Collimation . . . = 0· 0· 1·65
Resulting Mean Zenith Distance, North = 5·10·51·57

B.A.C. 5292.

1844.						**1844.**					
May 29	4· 0·40·18	·00	4·05	−10·51	4· 0·33·72	May 30	4· 0·45·17	·00	4·05	−10·02	4· 0·38·60
June 1	41·22	·00	4·11	−10·84	34·40	June 2	45·32	·01	4·05	10·95	38·41
						5	47·84	·01	4·08	−11·26	40·65
					4· 0·34·10						4· 0·39·22

Error of Collimation . . . = 0· 0· 2·56
Resulting Mean Zenith Distance, South = 4· 0·36·66

B.A.C. 5331.

1844.						**1844.**					
May 11	2·26·16 71	·00	2·46	− 7·83	2·26·11·34	May 10	2·26·20·90	·01	2·52	− 7·72	2·26·15·75
14	16·96	·00	2·44	8·16	11·24	13	20·66	·02	2·46	8·05	15·05
15	17·21	·00	2·41	8·27	11·35	17	22·64	·00	2·42	8·40	16·57
16	17·85	·01	2·45	8·38	11·91	22	21·65	·01	2·44	9·02	15·06
20	18·05	·00	2·51	8·81	11·75	25	22·10	·01	2·45	9·33	15·21
21	17·16	·01	2·48	8·91	10·72	28	22·44	·03	2·51	9·63	15·29
24	18·20	·00	2·44	9·23	11·41	30	22·98	·00	2·46	9·83	15·61
27	18·34	·00	2·46	9·53	11·27	June 2	22·89	·01	2·46	10·13	15·21
29	18·89	·00	2·46	9·74	11·61	27	26·14	·00	2·46	−12·24	16·36
June 1	19·92	·00	2·50	−10·03	12·39						
					2·26·11·50						2·26·15·57

Error of Collimation . . . = 0· 0· 2·03
Resulting Mean Zenith Distance, South = 2·26·13·53

No. 5272.—May 11.—Correction for Curvature of Path = +0"·03.

ARC OF THE MERIDIAN.—CAPE OF GOOD HOPE. 287

Mean Zenith Distances of Stars observed at the Royal Observatory.

FACE OF SECTOR EAST.

Day of Observation 1843-4.	Apparent Zenith Distance, from Unreduced Observation.	Reduction for Az. Error, and Curv. of Path.	Refraction.	Precession, Aberration, and Nutation.	Deduced Mean Zenith Distance, 1844, Jan. 0; and Mean of Separate Results, uncorrected, for Error of Collimation.

FACE OF SECTOR WEST.

Day of Observation 1843-4.	Apparent Zenith Distance, from Unreduced Observation.	Reduction for Az. Error, and Curv. of Path.	Refraction.	Precession, Aberration, and Nutation.	Deduced Mean Zenith Distance, 1844, Jan. 0; and Mean of Separate Results, uncorrected, for Error of Collimation.

Companion of 5331.

East

Day	App. Z.D.	Red.	Refr.	Prec.	Deduced
1844. May 20	2 23 34·94	·00	2 46	- 8·74	2 23 28·66
21	33·36	·01	2 43	8·85	26·93
27	34·75	·00	2 41	9·46	27·70
29	34·20	·00	2 42	9·07	26·05
June 1	36·03	·00	2 45	- 9·96	28·52
					2 23 27·75

West

Day	App. Z.D.	Red.	Refr.	Prec.	Deduced
1844. May 10	2 23 36·92	·01	2·47	- 7·66	2 23 31.72
17	38·15	·00	2·38	8·42	32·11
22	38·35	·01	2·40	8·95	31·79
25	39·44	·01	2·40	9·26	32 57
28	39·78	·03	2 46	9·57	32·64
30	39·04	·00	2·41	9·76	31·09
June 2	38·40	·01	2·47	10·06	30·74
5	41·95	·00	2·43	-10·34	34·04
					2·23·32·16

Error of Collimation . . . = 0· 0· 2·21
Resulting Mean Zenith Distance, South = 2·23·29·96

B.A.C. 5374.

East

Day	App. Z.D.	Red.	Refr.	Prec.	Deduced
1844. April 8	4·55·57·56	·53	4·92	- 5·38	4·56· 7·33
10	56·43	·58	4·86	5·55	6·26
13	57·70	·53	4·94	7·97	7·97
17	57·46	·63	4·96	6·13	7·92
21	57·31	·71	5·02	6·45	8·07
25	53·81	·72	4·97	6·76	(4·82)
May 3	56·72	·01	4·97	7·35	9·03
7	57·61	·00	5·08	7·63	10·32
9	58·30	·00	5·00	7·77	11·07
11	57·46	·00	4·97	7·90	10·33
14	57·07	·01	4·96	8·10	10·12
16	58·10	·01	4·96	8·23	11·28
20	55·04	·00	5·08	8·48	8·60
21	56·43	·01	5·03	8·54	9·99
27	55·54	·00	4·98	8·90	9·42
29	54·89	·00	4·99	- 9·01	8·89
					4·56· 9·11

West

Day	App. Z.D.	Red.	Refr.	Prec.	Deduced
1844. April 9	4·55·56·47	·60	4·95	- 5·47	4·56· 6·29
11	56·18	·59	4·87	5·64	6·10
14	52·43	·59	4·92	5·89	2·65
18	55·08	·70	4·94	6·21	6·13
22	55·34	·71	5·07	6·53	6·23
May 4	50·94	·02	5·01	7·27	3·20
8	52·08	+ ·07	5·02	7·42	4·59
10	50·06	·02	5·06	7·70	2·80
13	51·34	·02	5·11	7·83	4·26
17	51·44	·03	4·99	8·03	4·43
22	51·78	·00	4·91	8·29	4·98
25	50·35	·01	4·95	8·00	3·89
28	51·09	·03	4·96	8·78	4·80
30	50·11	·05	5·08	8·95	4·09
	50·99	·00	4·98	- 9·07	5·04
					4·56· 4·63

Error of Collimation . . . = 0· 0· 2·24
Resulting Mean Zenith Distance, North = 4·56· 6·87

B.A.C. 5435.

East

Day	App. Z.D.	Red.	Refr.	Prec.	Deduced
1844. April 10	3·24·35·42	·41	3·36	- 4·50	3·24·42·87
13	35·61	·37	3·41	4·76	43·41
17	36·11	·44	3·42	5·09	44·18
21	35·61	·50	3·47	5·42	44·00
25	32·95	·51	3·43	5·74	(41·61)

West

Day	App. Z.D.	Red.	Refr.	Prec.	Deduced
1844. April 9	3·24·33·54	·42	3·42	- 4·42	3·24·40·96
11	35·81	·41	3·37	4·59	43·36
14	32·65	·44	3·39	4·84	40·47
18	33·84	·49	3·41	5·17	41·93
22	33·89	·50	3·50	5·50	42·39

Carried forward,

No. 5374.—May 4.—Correction for Azimuthal Error - ·021; for Curvature of Path + ·093. = + L''·07.

Mean Zenith Distances of Stars observed at the Royal Observatory.

FACE OF SECTOR EAST.						FACE OF SECTOR WEST.				
Day of Observation 1843–4.	Apparent Zenith Distance, from Unreduced Observation.	Reduction for Az. Error, and Curv. of Path.	Refraction.	Precession, Aberration, and Nutation.	Deduced Mean Zenith Distance. 1844, Jan. 0; and Mean of Separate Results, uncorrected for Error of Collimation.	Day of Observation 1843–4.	Apparent Zenith Distance, from Unreduced Observation.	Reduction for Az. Error, and Curv. of Path.	Refraction.	Precession, Aberration, and Nutation.	Deduced Mean Zenith Distance. 1844, Jan. 0; and Mean of Separate Results, uncorrected for Error of Collimation.

B.A.C. 5435—(continued.)

1844.						1844.					
May 3	3 24 34·23	·01	3·43	- 6·36	3·24·44·01	May 2	3·24·29·79	·01	3·46	- 6·28	3·24·39·52
9	34·48	·00	3·45	6·80	44·73	4	31·02	·01	3·47	6·43	40·91
11	34·33	·00	3·43	6·95	44·71	8	28·31	·01	3·49	6·73	38·52
14	34·33	·00	3·43	7·16	44·92	13	29·69	·02	3·44	7·09	40·20
16	34·77	·01	3·42	7·30	45·48	15	29·99	·01	3·38	7·23	40·59
20	32·26	·00	3·51	7·58	43·35	17	29·29	·00	3·39	7·37	40·05
21	33·84	·01	3·47	7·65	44·95	22	29·20	·01	3·42	7·71	40·32
24	33·84	·00	3·42	7·85	45·11	25	29·25	·02	3·42	7·91	40·56
27	33·69	·00	3·44	8·04	45·17	28	28·31	·04	3·51	8·10	39·88
29	33·44	·00	3·44	8·17	45·05	June 1	28·85	·01	3·49	- 8·35	40·68
30	34·33	·00	3·44	- 8·23	46·00						
					3·24·44·53						3·24·40·69

Error of Collimation . . = 0· 0· 1·92
Resulting Mean Zenith Distance, North = 3·24·42·61

Anon. AR. 16·14.

1844.						1844.					
April 13	1· 6·17·55	·12	1·10	- 3·85	1· 6·22·38	April 9	1· 6·18·69	·14	1·11	- 3·49	1· 6·23·15
17	17·65	·15	1·11	4·22	22·83	11	22·54	·14	1·09	3·07	(27·16)
21	17·60	·17	1·12	4·58	23·13	14	16·91	·14	1·10	3·95	21·82
25	14·25	·17	1·11	4·93	20·12	18	17·70	·16	1·10	4·31	22·95
May 3	16·02	·00	1·11	5·63	22·76	22	16·66	·17	1·13	4·67	22·29
9	16·17	·00	1·12	6·14	23·43	May 2	13·90	·00	1·12	5·54	20·56
11	16·27	·00	1·11	6·30	23·68	4	14·54	·00	1·12	5·71	21·37
14	15·78	·00	1·11	6·55	23·44	8	11·68	·00	1·13	6·05	18·86
16	16·96	·00	1·11	6·72	24·79	10	12·22	·01	1·14	6·22	19·57
20	14·84	·00	1·13	7·04	23·01	13	12·42	·01	1·11	6·47	19·99
21	14·59	·00	1·12	7·12	22·83	15	12·72	·00	1·09	6·63	20·44
24	17·16	·00	1·11	7·35	25·62	17	11·78	·00	1·10	6·80	19·68
27	16·07	·00	1·11	7·59	24·77	22	11·63	·00	1·11	7·20	19·94
29	14·49	·00	1·12	7·74	23·35	25	11·38	·01	1·11	7·43	19·91
30	15·78	·00	1·11	- 7·82	24·71	28	12·81	·01	1·13	- 7·66	21·59
					1· 6·23·39						1· 6·20·87

Error of Collimation . . = 0· 0· 1·26
Resulting Mean Zenith Distance, North = 1· 6·22·13

B.A.C. 5508.

1844.						1844.					
May 11	0·25·27·84	·00	0·43	- 5·39	0·25·22·88	May 10	0·25·32·53	·00	0·44	- 5·30	0·25·27·67
14	28·53	·00	·43	5·65	23·31	13	32·09	·00	·43	5·56	26·96
16	28·58	·00	·43	5·83	23·18	15	32·29	·00	·42	5·74	26·97
20	30·36	·00	·44	6·17	24·63	17	32·29	·00	·42	5·91	26·80

Carried forward,

Mean Zenith Distances of Stars observed at the Royal Observatory.

	FACE OF SECTOR EAST.						FACE OF SECTOR WEST.				
Day of Observation 1843-4.	Apparent Zenith Distance, from Unreduced Observation.	Reduction for Az. Error, and Curv. of Path.	Refraction.	Precession, Aberration, and Nutation.	Deduced Mean Zenith Distance, 1845, Jan. 0; and Mean of Separate Results, uncorrected, for Error of Collimation.	Day of Observation 1843-4.	Apparent Zenith Distance, from Unreduced Observation	Reduction for Az. Error, and Curv. of Path.	Refraction.	Precession, Aberration, and Nutation.	Deduced Mean Zenith Distance, 1844, Jan. 0; and Mean of Separate Results, uncorrected, for Error of Collimation.

B.A.C. 5508—(continued).

1844.						1844.					
May 21	0·25·29·08	·00	·43	6·26	0·25·23·25	May 22	0·25·32·78	·00	·43	6·34	0·25·26·87
24	30·16	·00	·43	6·51	24·08	25	32·48	·00	·43	6·60	26·31
27	30·01	00	·43	6·77	23·67	28	33·22	·00	·44	6·85	26·81
29	29·32	·00	·43	6·93	22·82	June 1	33·12	·00	·44	7·18	26·88
30	29·18	·00	0·43	- 7·01	22·60	2	33·03	·00	·43	7·26	26·20
						5	33·42	·00	0·43	- 7·50	26·35
					0·25·23·38						0·25·26·73

Error of Collimation . . . = 0· 0· 1·68
Resulting Mean Zenith Distance, South = 0·25·25·06

B.A.C. 5538.

1844.						1844.					
May 30	0·59·39·17	·00	1·00	- 6·46	0·59·33·71	June 1	0·59·42·43	·00	1·02	- 6·62	0·59·36·83
						5	43·07	·00	1·01	6·95	37·13
											0·59·36·98

Error of Collimation . . . = 0· 0· 1·64
Resulting Mean Zenith Distance, South = 0·59·35·35

B.A.C. 5588.

1844.						1844.					
April 13	2· 7·48·39	·23	2·13	- 2·43	2· 7·52·72	April 9	2· 7·46·91	·27	2·13	- 2·15	2· 7·50·92
17	47·50	·28	2·14	2·72	52·08	14	45·23	·26	2·12	2·51	49·60
25	44·94	·32	2·14	3·29	(50·05)	18	45·43	·31	2·13	2·79	50·04
May 3	47·01	·01	2·15	3·85	53·00	22	42·86	·32	2·18	3·08	47·80
7	47·21	·00	2·19	4·12	53·52	May 2	43·46	·01	2·16	3·78	49·39
9	47·45	·00	2·15	4·26	53·86	4	44·49	·01	2·16	3·91	50·55
11	48·19	·00	2·14	4·39	54·72	8	42·62	·01	2·18	4·19	48·98
14	46·86	·00	2·14	4·59	53·59	10	42·27	·01	2·20	4·32	48·78
16	48·09	·01	2·13	4·73	55·54	13	43·00	·01	2·15	4·52	50·26
20	46·52	·00	2·19	4·99	53·70	15	43·21	·01	2·12	4·66	49·98
21	45·68	·01	2·17	5·06	52·90	17	43·46	·00	2·11	4·79	50·36
24	46·66	·00	2·13	5·26	54·05	22	42·86	·01	2·13	5·12	50·10
27	46·27	·00	2·15	5·45	53·87	25	42·32	·01	2·14	5·32	49·77
29	46·42	·00	2·15	5·58	54·15	28	41·92	·02	2·19	5·52	49·61
30	47·31	·00	2·15	5·64	55·10	June 1	41·97	·00	2·18	- 5·77	49·92
June 2	45·58	·01	2·15	- 5·84	53·56						
					2· 7·53·76						2· 7·49·74

Error of Collimation . . . = 0· 0· 2·01
Resulting Mean Zenith Distance, North = 2· 7·51·75

Mean Zenith Distances of Stars observed at the Royal Observatory.

FACE OF SECTOR EAST.

B.A.C. 5632.

Day of Observation 1843-4.	Apparent Zenith Distance, from Unreduced Observation.	Reduction for Az. Error, and Curv. of Path.	Refraction.	Precession, Aberration, and Nutation.	Deduced Mean Zenith Distance, 1844, Jan. 0; and Mean of Separate Results, uncorrected, for Error of Collimation.
1843.	° ′ ″	″	″	″	° ′ ″
Nov. 15	0· 4· 9·25	·00	0·07	+ 0·75	0· 4·10·07
Dec. 2	5·89	·00	·07	2·21	8·17
1844.					
Jan. 1	4·91	·01	·07	3·57	8 54
3	4·42	·00	·07	3·60	8·09
8	6·09	·00	·07	3·64	10·40
12	6·19	·01	·07	3·65	9·00
15	5·80	·01	·07	3·68	9·49
18	5·70	·01	·07	3·60	9·36
25	5·99	·01	·07	3·46	9·51
27	5·04	·01	·07	3·41	8·51
29	5·20	·01	·07	3·35	8·61
Feb. 12	7·08	·01	·07	2·79	9·93
17	8·22	·01	·07	2·53	10·81
19	8·56	·01	·07	+ 2·42	11·04
April 8	9·06	·01	·07	- 0·94	8·18
10	8·76	·01	·07	1·09	7·73
13	10·00	·01	·07	1·32	8·83
17	9·89	·01	·07	1·02	8·33
21	9·65	·01	·07	1·92	7·79
25	12·61	·01	·07	2·23	(10·44)
May 3	10·59	·00	·07	2·84	7·82
7	9·55	·00	·07	3·14	6·48
9	9·15	·00	·07	3·29	5·93
11	9·85	·00	·07	3·45	6·47
14	10·73	·00	·07	3·08	7·12
16	10·83	·00	·07	3·83	7·07
20	13·55	·00	·07	4·13	9·49
24	11·13	·00	·07	4·44	6·76
27	11·72	·00	0·07	- 4·66	7·13
					0 ·4 ·8·48

FACE OF SECTOR WEST.

Day of Observation 1843-4.	Apparent Zenith Distance, from Unreduced Observation.	Reduction for Az. Error, and Curv. of Path.	Refraction.	Precession, Aberration, and Nutation.	Deduced Mean Zenith Distance, 1844, Jan. 0; and Mean of Separate Results, uncorrected, for Error of Collimation.
1843.	° ′ ″	″	″	″	° ′ ″
Dec. 15	0· 4· 6·44	·01	0·07	+ 2·99	0· 4· 9·49
1844.					
Jan. 2	5·30	·01	·07	3·58	8·94
4	6·88	·01	·07	3·61	10·55
9	6·14	·01	·07	3·65	9·85
11	5·80	·01	·07	3·65	9·60
13	5·55	·01	·07	3·64	9·25
16	5·55	·01	·07	3·62	9·23
24	5·95	·00	·07	3·49	9·51
26	6·09	·01	·07	3·44	9·59
28	5·06	·01	·07	3·38	8·50
Feb. 2	6·19	·01	·07	3·21	9·46
14	6·49	·01	·07	2·69	9·24
15	6·49	·01	·07	2·64	9·19
21	6·29	·01	·07	2·31	8·66
22	7·28	·01	·07	+ 2·25	9·59
April 9	11·03	·01	·07	- 1·01	10·08
11	8·17	·01	·07	1·17	7·06
14	13·00	·01	·07	1·39	11·67
18	12·12	·01	·07	1·70	10·48
22	13·65	·01	·07	2·01	11·71
May 2	15·08	·00	·07	2·76	12·39
4	13·65	·00	·07	2·92	10·80
8	16·07	·00	·07	3·22	12·92
10	15·77	·00	·07	3·37	12·47
13	15·72	·00	·07	3·60	12·19
15	14·88	·00	·07	3·75	11·20
17	15·82	·00	·07	3·91	11·98
22	15·97	·00	·07	4·28	11·76
25	15·07	·00	·07	4·51	11·23
28	17·84	·00	0·07	- 4·74	13·17
					0 ·4·10·39

Error of Collimation . . . = 0· 0· 0·95
Resulting Mean Zenith Distance, South = 0· 4· 9·44

B.A.C. 5735.

FACE OF SECTOR EAST.

Day	App. Zenith Dist.	Red.	Refr.	Prec. Ab. Nut.	Deduced Mean Z.D.
1844.					
April 8	0· 2·16·25	·00	0·04	+ 0·19	0· 2·16·10
10	16·94	·00	·04	+ 0·07	16·91
13	14·77	·00	·04	- 0·12	14·93
17	16·94	·00	·04	0·37	17·35
21	16·94	·01	·04	0·63	17·60
May 3	15·46	·00	·04	1·41	16·91
7	16·35	·00	·04	1·08	18·07
9	17·09	·00	·04	1·81	18·94
11	16·25	·00	·04	1·95	18·24

FACE OF SECTOR WEST.

Day	App. Zenith Dist.	Red.	Refr.	Prec. Ab. Nut.	Deduced Mean Z.D.
1844.					
April 9	0· 2·13·83	·00	0·04	+ 0·13	0· 2·13·74
11	14·43	·00	·04	+ 0·01	14·46
14	12·60	·00	·04	- 0·18	12·82
18	12·75	·01	·04	0·44	13·23
22	12·85	·01	·04	0 69	13·57
May 2	9·74	·00	·04	1·48	11·14
4	11·41	·00	·04	1·48	12·93
8	9·59	·00	·04	1·75	11·38
10	9·74	·00	·04	1·88	11·06

Carried forward,

Mean Zenith Distances of Stars observed at the Royal Observatory.

FACE OF SECTOR EAST.						FACE OF SECTOR WEST.					
Day of Observation 1843-4.	Apparent Zenith Distance, from Unreduced Observation.	Reduction for Az. Error, and Curv. of Path.	Refraction.	Precession, Aberration, and Nutation.	Deduced Mean Zenith Distance, 1844, Jan. 0; and Mean of Separate Results, uncorrected, for Error of Collimation.	Day of Observation 1843-4.	Apparent Zenith Distance, from Unreduced Observation.	Reduction for Az. Error, and Curv. of Path.	Refraction.	Precession, Aberration, and Nutation.	Deduced Mean Zenith Distance, 1844, Jan. 0; and Mean of Separate Results, uncorrected, for Error of Collimation.

B.A.C. 5735—(continued).

1844.	° ′ ″	″	″	″	° ′ ″	1844.	° ′ ″	″	″	″	° ′ ″
May 14	0· 2·15·41	·00	·04	2·15	0· 2·17·60	May 13	0· 2·10·28	·00	·04	2·08	0· 2·12·40
16	15·81	·00	·04	2·29	18·14	15	9·74	·00	·04	2·22	12·00
20	15·02	·00	·04	2·56	17·62	17	9·93	·00	·04	2·35	12·32
22	14·77	·00	·04	2·69	17·50	21	9·24	·00	·04	2·63	11·91
25	14·47	·00	·04	2·90	17·41	24	9·83	·00	·04	2·83	12·70
29	15·41	·00	0·04	- 3·18	18·63	27	8·99	·00	0·04	- 3·04	12·07
					0· 2·17·46						0· 2·12·56

Error of Collimation . . . = 0· 0· 2·45
Resulting Mean Zenith Distance, North = 0· 2·15·01

B.A.C. 5817.

1844.						1844.					
April 8	1·27·15·26	·16	1·45	+ 0·74	1·27·15·81	April 9	1·27·15·17	·18	1·46	+ 0·69	1·27·15·76
13	14·38	·16	1·45	0·50	15·17	11	16·25	·18	1·44	0·60	16·91
17	15·17	·19	1·46	0·31	16·13	14	11·81	·18	1·45	0·45	12·63
21	15·91	·22	1·48	+ 0·12	17·05	18	12·70	·21	1·45	0·26	13·68
May 3	14·62	·00	1·48	- 0·48	16·58	22	13·98	·22	1·49	+ 0·07	15·18
7	15·31	·00	1·49	0·08	17·48	May 2	10·33	·01	1·48	- 0·43	12·23
9	15·96	·00	1·47	0·79	18·22	4	12·06	·01	1·48	0·53	14·06
11	14·87	·00	1·46	0·89	17·22	8	10·28	·01	1·40	0 74	12·50
14	14·18	·00	1·46	1·05	16·60	10	10·92	·01	1·50	0·84	13·25
16	15·02	·00	1·44	1·16	17·62	13	11·31	·01	1·47	1·00	13·77
20	13·04	·00	1·50	1·37	15·91	15	11·12	·00	1·45	1·10	13·67
22	14·33	·00	1·46	1·48	17·27	17	10·97	·00	1·44	1·21	13·62
25	14·20	·00	1·46	1·64	17·30	21	10·13	·00	1·44	1·42	13·03
29	13·93	·00	1·47	1·86	17·26	24	10·48	·01	1·46	1·59	13·52
30	14·87	·00	1·47	- 1·92	18·26	27	9·78	·01	1·47	- 1·75	12·90
					1·27·16·93						1·27·13·79

Error of Collimation . . . = 0· 0· 1·57
Resulting Mean Zenith Distance, North = 1·27·15·36

B.A.C. 5881.

1844.						1844.					
April 8	4·12·50·81	·45	4·20	+ 0·68	4·12·53·88	April 9	4·12·50·56	·51	4·23	+ 0·65	4·12·53·63
10	49·87	·50	4·17	0·62	52·92	14	47·90	·50	4·20	0·50	51·10
13	50·46	·45	4·22	0·53	53·70	18	49·71	·60	4·22	0·39	52·94
17	51·20	·54	4·23	0·42	54·47	22	49·38	·61	4·32	+ 0·27	52·82
21	51·20	·61	4·29	+ 0·30	54·58	May 4	49·18	·02	4·20	- 0·09	53·54
May 3	49·72	·01	4 30	- 0·06	54·07	8	46·91	·02	4·31	0·21	51·41
7	51·80	·00	4·34	0·18	56·32	10	47·35	·02	4·36	0·27	51·96
9	51·60	·00	4·26	0·24	56·10	13	47·45	·02	4·26	0·37	52·06
11	51·40	·00	4·25	0·30	55·95	15	47·95	·01	4·20	0·43	52·57

Carried forward,

Mean Zenith Distances of Stars observed at the Royal Observatory.

	FACE OF SECTOR EAST.						FACE OF SECTOR WEST.				
Day of Observation 1843-4.	Apparent Zenith Distance, from Unreduced Observation.	Reduction for Az. Error, and Curr. of Path.	Refraction.	Precession, Aberration, and Nutation.	Deduced Mean Zenith Distance, 1844, Jan. 0; and Mean of Separate Results, uncorrected for Error of Collimation.	Day of Observation 1843-4.	Apparent Zenith Distance, from Unreduced Observation.	Reduction for Az. Error, and Curr. of Path.	Refraction.	Precession, Aberration, and Nutation.	Deduced Mean Zenith Distance, 1844, Jan. 0; and Mean of Separate Results, uncorrected for Error of Collimation.

B.A.C. 5881—(continued).

1844.	° ′ ″	″	″	′ ″	° ′ ″	1844.	° ′ ″	″	″	′ ″	° ′ ″
May 14	4·12·51·06	·00	4·23	0·40	4·12·55·09	May 17	4·12·47·80	·00	4·16	0·49	4·12·52·45
16	51·75	·01	4·17	0·46	56·37	21	45·63	·01	4·30	0·63	50·55
20	49·97	·00	4·35	0·59	54·91	24	47·11	·02	4·23	0·73	52·05
25	49·72	·00	4·22	0·76	54·70	27	46·61	·04	4·27	0·83	51·07
29	50·51	·00	4·28	0·90	55·09	30	46·37	·00	4·26	0·94	51·57
June 1	51·80	+ ·08	4·32	- 1·01	57·21	June 2	47·25	·01	4·25	- 1·04	52·53
					4·12·55·10						4·12·52·19

Error of Collimation . . = 0· 0· 1·46
Resulting Mean Zenith Distance, North = 4·12·53·65

B.A.C. 5915.

1843.	° ′ ″	″	″	′ ″	° ′ ″	1843.	° ′ ″	″	″	′ ″	° ′ ″
Nov. 2	3· 2·57·23	·04	3·00	- 2·27	3· 2·57·92	Nov. 1	3· 2·52·93	·06	3·01	- 2·36	3·2 ·53·52
3	54·81	·04	2·97	- 2·17	55·57	10	53·28	·10	3·02	- 1·48	54·72
15	52·73	* ·11	3·02	- 0·07	54·67	Dec. 3	54·81	* ·37	2·97	+ 0·86	58·27
1844.						11	54·61	·22	2·98	1·02	58·99
Jan. 1	47·40	·24	2·97	+ 3·34	53·47	1844.					
3	46·56	·17	2·95	3·46	52·80	Jan. 2	49·38	·22	2·07	3·40	55·53
8	47·99	·22	2·95	3·74	54·46	4	47·95	·22	2·97	3·52	54·22
12	48·49	·26	2·95	3·94	55·12	9	47·45	·32	2·89	3·80	53·82
13	47·35	·26	2·97	3·99	54·05	11	48·44	·34	2·91	3·89	54·90
15	47·30	·28	2·94	4·08	54·04	18	46·71	·34	2·97	4·20	53·54
19	47·60	·28	2·94	4·23	54·30	24	48·39	·22	2·99	4·39	55·55
25	47·45	·26	2·97	4·42	54·58	25	48·91	·22	3·00	4 45	54·14
27	46·32	·26	2·99	4·47	53·52	28	45·72	·29	3·01	4·49	52·93
29	47·35	·30	3·00	4·52	54·57	30	48·64	·25	2·99	4·54	55·92
Feb. 1	45·70	·41	3·01	4 58	52·88	Feb. 12	45·13	·45	3·00	4·68	52·36
14	47·99	·46	3·04	4·68	55·25	15	46·42	·45	2·93	4·68	53·64
16	47·40	·38	3·00	4·68	54·70	17	47·06	·54	3·00	4·68	54·20
19	47·21	·36	3·04	4·67	54·56	21	46·17	·37	3·00	4·66	53·46
April 8	46·12	·35	3·03	3 35	52·14	22	46·58	·46	3·00	4·65	53·77
10	46·02	·39	3·02	3 26	51·01	April 9	47·60	·41	3·05	3 30	53·54
13	48·44	·36	3·05	3·12	54·25	14	47·45	·40	3·03	3·07	53·15
17	46·56	·42	3·06	2·92	52·12	18	48·88	·47	3·05	2·87	54·33
21	47·01	·48	3·10	2·72	52·35	22	49·87	·48	3·13	2·67	55·19
May 3	44·93	·01	3·11	2·05	50·08	May 2	52·19	·01	3·10	2·10	57·38
7	45·82	·00	3·13	1·80	50·75	4	51·20	·01	3·10	1·90	56·28
9	45·77	·00	3·08	1·68	50·53	8	52·08	·01	3·12	1·74	57·83
11	46·12	·00	3·07	1·55	50·74	10	53·38	·02	3·15	1·61	58·12
14	47·21	·00	3·07	1·35	51·63	13	51·30	·02	3·08	1 42	55·78
16	47·21	·01	3·02	1 22	51·44	15	51·65	·01	3·03	1·28	55·95
22	47·01	·01	3·05	0·80	50·85	24	52·64	·02	3·06	0·66	56·34
25	48·09	·00	3·05	0·59	51·73	27	52·93	·03	3·08	0·45	56·43
29	47·75	·00	3·09	+ 0·30	51·14	30	53·33	·00	3·08	+ 0·23	56·64
					3· 2·53·17						3· 2·55.18

Error of Collimation . . = 0· 0· 1·00
Resulting Mean Zenith Distance, South = 3· 2·54·17

No. 5881.—June 1.—Correction for Azimuthal Error = ·01; for Curvature of Path + ·09. = + 0″·08.
„ 5915.—Nov. 15.— „ „ „ - ·08; „ „ - ·03. = - 0·11.
„ Dec. 3.— „ „ „ - ·13; „ „ - ·24. = - 0·37.

Mean Zenith Distances of Stars observed at the Royal Observatory.

	FACE OF SECTOR EAST.						FACE OF SECTOR WEST.				
Day of Observation 1843-4.	Apparent Zenith Distance, from Unreduced Observation.	Reduction for Az. Error, and Curv. of Path.	Refraction.	Precession, Aberration, and Nutation.	Deduced Mean Zenith Distance, 1844, Jan. 0; and Mean of Separate Results, uncorrected, for Error of Collimation.	Day of Observation 1843-4.	Apparent Zenith Distance, from Unreduced Observation.	Reduction for Az. Error, and Curv. of Path.	Refraction.	Precession, Aberration, and Nutation.	Deduced Mean Zenith Distance, 1844, Jan. 0; and Mean of Separate Results, uncorrected, for Error of Collimation.
					B.A.C. 5900.						
1844.						1844.					
April 10	1 49 40·85	·22	1·81	+ 2·29	1 49 40·15	April 9	1 49 40·55	·23	1·83	+ 2·32	1 49 39·83
13	42·33	·20	1·83	2·21	41·75	14	39·76	·22	1·82	2·19	39·17
17	41·93	·24	1·84	2·10	41·43	18	42·62	·27	1·83	2·08	42·10
21	43·81	·27	1·86	1·99	43·41	22	39·61	·27	1·88	1·97	39·25
May 7	42·82	·00	1·88	1·50	43·20	May 2	37·00	·01	1·86	1·66	37·19
9	43·22	·00	1·85	1·43	43·64	4	37·98	·01	1·86	1·60	38·23
11	43·07	·00	1·85	1·36	43·56	8	36·60	·01	1·87	1·46	37·00
14	41·88	·00	1·85	1·25	42·48	10	36·50	·01	1·89	1·40	36·98
16	42·77	·00	1·82	+ 1·18	43·41	13	37·79	·01	1·85	1·29	38·34
						15	37·74	·00	1·83	+ 1·21	38·36
					1·49·42·56						1·49·38·65

Error of Collimation . . . = 0· 0· 1·96
Resulting Mean Zenith Distance, North = 1·49·40·60

					B.A.C. 5970.						
1844.						1844.					
June 1	5· 0·17·28	·01	5·12	+ 1·25	5· 0·23·64	May 30	5· 0·22·76	·00	5·07	+ 1·41	5· 0·29·24
5	18·46	·00	5·07	+ 0·92	24·45	June 2	21·57	·01	5·10	+ 1·17	27·83
					5· 0·24·04						5· 0·28·53

Error of Collimation . . . = 0· 0· 2·25
Resulting Mean Zenith Distance, South = 5· 0·26·28

					B.A.C. 5964.						
1844.						1844.					
April 17	1·48·39·63	·24	1·82	+ 2·19	1·48·30·02	April 22	1·48·38·40	·27	1·86	+ 2·05	1·48·37·94
21	41·21	·27	1·84	2·08	40·70	May 2	36·08	·01	1·84	1·75	36·16
May 7	42·99	·00	1·86	1·50	43·26	4	37·36	·01	1·84	1·69	37·50
9	42·69	·00	1·83	1·52	43·00	8	35·88	·01	1·85	1·56	36·16
11	41·36	·00	1·83	1·46	41·73	13	37·36	·01	1·83	1·38	37·80
16	41·66	·00	1·80	+ 1·28	42·18	15	36·52	·00	1·81	+ 1·31	37·02
					1·48·41·65						1·48·37·10

Error of Collimation . . . = 0· 0· 2·28
Resulting Mean Zenith Distance, North = 1·48·39·37

					B.A.C. 6016.						
1844.						1844.					
April 13	2·17·30·81	·25	2·29	+ 2·77	2·17·30·08	April 14	2·17·27·70	·28	2·28	+ 2·76	2·17·26·94
17	30·57	·30	2·30	2·71	29·86	18	29·58	·33	2·29	2·69	28·85
21	30·47	·34	2·33	2·63	29·83	22	30·77	·34	2·35	2·61	30·17
											Carried forward,

Mean Zenith Distances of Stars observed at the Royal Observatory.

FACE OF SECTOR EAST.						FACE OF SECTOR WEST.					
Day of Observation 1843–4.	Apparent Zenith Distance, from Unreduced Observation.	Reduction for Az. Error, and Curv. of Path.	Refraction.	Precession, Aberration, and Nutation.	Deduced Mean Zenith Distance, 1844, Jan. 0; and Mean of Separate Results. uncorrected. for Error of Collimation.	Day of Observation 1843–4.	Apparent Zenith Distance, from Unreduced Observation.	Reduction for Az. Error, and Curv. of Path.	Refraction.	Precession, Aberration, and Nutation.	Deduced Mean Zenith Distance, 1844, Jan. 0; and Mean of Separate Results. uncorrected. for Error of Collimation.

B.A.C. 6016—(continued.)

1844.						1844.					
May 3	2 17 29·67	·01	2·34	2·38	2 17 29·63	May 2	2 17 26·82	·01	2·33	2·40	2 17 26·74
7	30·91	·00	2·35	2·28	30·98	4	28·15	·01	2·33	2·36	28·11
9	31·16	·00	2·31	2·23	31·24	8	26·52	·01	2·34	2·26	26·59
11	30·22	·00	2·31	2·18	30·35	10	26·62	·01	2·38	2·21	26·78
14	29·78	·00	2·31	2·10	29·99	13	28·20	·01	2·31	2·13	28·37
16	30·42	·01	2·28	2·04	30·05	15	28·25	·01	2·28	2·07	28·45
20	29·78	·00	2·36	1·92	30·22	17	28·40	·00	2·26	2·01	28·65
22	30·32	·01	2·29	1·85	30·75	21	27·56	·01	2·34	1·89	28·00
25	30·32	·00	2·29	1·76	30·85	24	27·95	·01	2·30	1·79	28·45
29	29·78	·00	2·32	1·62	30·48	27	26·62	·02	2·32	1·69	27·23
June 1	26·52	·01	2·34	1·51	27·34	June 2	26·57	·00	2·33	1·47	27·43
12	27·75	·00	2·33	+ 1·07	29·01	16	25·76	·01	2·38	+ 0·89	27·24
					2·17·30·08						2·17·27·87

Error of Collimation . . = 0· 0· 1·11
Resulting Mean Zenith Distance, North = 2·17·28·98

B.A.C. 6074.

1844.						1844.					
April 10	3 42 12·70	·44	3·09	+ 3·09	3 42 12·86	April 14	3 42 11·22	·45	3·69	+ 3·07	3 42 11·39
13	13·24	·40	3·71	3·08	13·47	18	11·81	·53	3·70	3·06	11·92
17	13·59	·48	3·72	3·06	13·77	22	11·81	·54	3·80	3·03	12·04
21	13·88	·54	3·77	3·04	14·07	May 4	9·74	·01	3·77	2·96	10·54
May 3	14·77	·01	3·79	2·95	15·60	8	11·81	·02	3·77	2·94	12·62
7	16·00	·00	3·81	2·91	16·90	10	9·64	·01	3·79	2·90	10·52
9	16·10	·00	3·74	2·88	16·96	13	9·78	·02	3·74	2·83	10·67
11	16·05	·00	3·74	2·86	16·93	15	10·28	·01	3·70	2·80	11·17
14	15·66	·00	3·74	2·82	16·58	17	10·43	·00	3·65	2·77	11·31
20	14·33	·00	3·82	2·72	15·43	21	9·40	·01	3·78	2·70	10·46
22	15·07	·01	3·71	2·69	16·08	24	9·09	·02	3·72	2·65	10·74
25	14·77	·00	3·71	2·63	15·85	27	9·19	·03	3·75	2·59	10·32
29	15·02	·00	3·75	2 54	16·23	30	8·99	·00	3·75	2·52	10·22
June 1	14·57	·01	3·79	2·47	15·88	June 2	9·69	·01	3·77	+ 2·45	11·00
16	14·18	·00	3·86	+ 2·04	16·00						
					3·42·15·51						3·42·11·00

Error of Collimation . . = 0· 0· 2·25
Resulting Mean Zenith Distance, North = 3·42·13·25

B.A.C. 6115.

1843.						1843.					
Oct. 30	3·30·41·32	·01	3·42	- 1·46	3·30·(46·19)	Nov. 10	3 30 49·87	·11	3·49	- 0·82	3 30 53·57
Nov. 3	48·97	·04	3·46	- 1·24	53·63	1844.					
1844.						April 14	53·71	·42	3·51	+ 3·63	53·17
April 10	55·69	·42	3·50	+ 3·62	55·15	18	53·32	·50	3·51	3·63	52·70

Carried forward,

Mean Zenith Distances of Stars observed at the Royal Observatory.

	FACE OF SECTOR EAST.						FACE OF SECTOR WEST.				
Day of Observation 1843-4.	Apparent Zenith Distance, from Unreduced Observation.	Reduction for Az. Error, and Curv. of Path.	Refraction.	Precession, and Aberration, and Nutation.	Deduced Mean Zenith Distance, 1844, Jan. 0; and Mean of Separate Results, uncorrected, for Error of Collimation.	Day of Observation 1843-4.	Apparent Zenith Distance, from Unreduced Observation.	Reduction for Az. Error, and Curv. of Path.	Refraction.	Precession, and Aberration, and Nutation.	Deduced Mean Zenith Distance, 1844, Jan. 0; and Mean of Separate Results, uncorrected, for Error of Collimation.

B.A.C. 6115—(continued.)

	FACE OF SECTOR EAST.						FACE OF SECTOR WEST.				
1844.	° ′ ″	″	″	″	° ′ ″	1844.	° ′ ″	″	″	″	° ′ ″
April 13	3 30 54 60	·38	3 52	3 63	3 30 54 11	April 22	3 30 53 12	·51	3 61	3 63	3 30 52 59
17	55 54	·45	3 53	3 63	54 99	May 2	51 39	·01	3 58	3 60	51 36
21	56 92	·51	3 57	3 63	56 35	4	52 82	·02	3 58	3 59	52 79
May 3	56 82	·01	3 60	3 60	56 81	8	50 75	·01	3 60	3 56	50 78
7	57 81	·00	3 61	3 57	57 85	10	52 03	·02	3 65	3 55	52 11
9	57 61	·00	3 55	3 60	57 60	13	50 70	·02	3 54	3 52	50 70
11	57 17	·00	3 55	3 54	57 18	15	52 67	·01	3 51	3 50	52 67
14	57 36	·00	3 55	3 51	57 40	17	52 13	·00	3 46	3 47	52 12
16	57 46	·01	3 50	3 49	57 46	21	50 04	·01	3 59	3 42	50 20
20	56 23	·00	3 62	3 43	56 42	24	51 14	·02	3 53	3 37	51 28
22	57 56	·01	3 52	3 40	57 67	27	50 85	·03	3 56	3 32	51 06
25	56 77	·00	3 52	3 35	56 94	30	50 26	·00	3 56	+ 3 26	50 56
29	56 87	·00	3 56	+ 3 28	57 15						
					3 30 56 45						3 30 51 84

Error of Collimation . . = 0· 0· 2·30
Resulting Mean Zenith Distance, North = 3·30·54·15

B.A.C. 6145.

	FACE OF SECTOR EAST.						FACE OF SECTOR WEST.				
1844.						1844.					
April 10	3 11 17 11	·38	3 17	+ 4 02	3 11 15 88	April 14	3 11 14 69	·39	3 18	+ 4 04	3 11 13 44
13	16 57	·35	3 19	4 04	15 87	18	14 09	·46	3 18	4 05	13 36
17	17 01	·41	3 20	4 05	15 75	22	17 16	·47	3 27	4 06	15 90
21	18 74	·47	3 24	4 06	17 45	May 2	12 77	·01	3 25	4 06	11 95
May 3	19 13	·01	3 28	4 05	18 35	4	14 59	·01	3 25	4 05	13 78
7	19 63	·00	3 28	4 04	18 87	8	11 98	·01	3 26	4 03	11 20
9	19 73	·00	3 23	4 02	18 94	10	11 78	·02	3 31	4 02	11 05
11	19 63	·00	3 22	4 01	18 84	13	13 46	·02	3 21	3 99	12 66
14	18 69	·00	3 22	3 98	17 93	15	13 51	·01	3 18	3 97	12 71
16	18 44	·01	3 18	3 96	17 65	17	13 66	·00	3 14	3 95	12 85
20	17 00	·00	3 28	3 92	17 26	21	12 77	·01	3 25	3 90	12 11
22	18 68	·01	3 19	3 89	17 98	24	12 62	·02	3 20	3 86	11 94
25	18 89	·00	3 20	3 81	18 25	27	13 36	·03	3 23	3 81	12 75
29	18 89	·00	3 23	3 77	18 35	30	12 47	·00	3 23	3 75	11 95
June 1	18 74	·01	3 26	+ 3 71	18 28	June 2	12 67	·01	3 24	+ 3 69	12 21
					3 11 17 68						3 11 12 66

Error of Collimation . . = 0· 0· 2·51
Resulting Mean Zenith Distance, North = 3·11·15·17

B.A.C. 6186.

	FACE OF SECTOR EAST.						FACE OF SECTOR WEST.				
1844.						1844.					
April 10	2 51 51 22	·37	2 85	+ 6 49	2 51 60 19	April 9	2 51 54 14	·38	2 87	+ 6 49	2 52 3 12
13	51 62	·33	2 87	6 48	00 64	14	53 64	·37	2 86	6 48	2 61
17	50 88	·40	2 88	6 46	59 82	18	53 25	·44	2 86	6 45	2 12
21	49 50	·45	2 91	6 43	58 39	22	53 05	·45	2 94	6 42	1 96
											Carried forward,

Mean Zenith Distances of Stars observed at the Royal Observatory.

	FACE OF SECTOR EAST.						FACE OF SECTOR WEST.				
Day of Observation 1843–4.	Apparent Zenith Distance, from Unreduced Observation.	Reduction for Az. Error, and Curv. of Path.	Refraction.	Precession, Aberration, and Nutation.	Deduced Mean Zenith Distance, 1844, Jan. 0; and Mean of Separate Results, uncorrected, for Error of Collimation.	Day of Observation 1843–4.	Apparent Zenith Distance, from Unreduced Observation.	Reduction for Az. Error, and Curv. of Path.	Refraction.	Precession, Aberration, and Nutation.	Deduced Mean Zenith Distance, 1844, Jan. 0; and Mean of Separate Results, uncorrected, for Error of Collimation.

B.A.C. 6186—(continued.)

1844.	° ′ ″	″	″	″	° ′ ″	1844.	° ′ ″	″	″	″	° ′ ″
May 3	2·51·47·96	·01	2·94	6·23	2·51·57·12	May 2	2·51·55·62	·01	2·92	6·26	2·52· 4·79
7	48·14	·00	2·94	6·14	57·22	4	54·43	·01	2·92	6·21	3·55
9	48·26	·00	2·90	6·09	57·25	8	55·12	·01	2·93	6·11	4·15
11	49·20	·00	2·89	6·03	58·12	10	55·72	·02	2·97	6·06	4·73
14	49·09	·00	2·89	5·94	58·52	13	55·12	·02	2·88	5·97	3·95
16	49·45	·01	2·85	5·87	58·16	15	55·76	·01	2·85	5 90	4·50
20	50·78	·00	2·95	5·72	59·45	17	55·02	·00	2·82	5·83	3·67
22	49·10	·01	2·87	5·64	57·00	21	55·52	·01	2·92	5·68	4·11
23	49·30	·00	2·89	5·60	57·79	24	54·58	·02	2·87	5·56	2·99
25	49·35	·00	2·87	5·51	57·73	27	55·52	·03	2·90	5·42	3·81
29	49 74	·00	2·00	+ 5·33	57·97	30	55·81	·00	2·90	+ 5 28	3·99
					2·51·58·40						2·52· 3·60

            ° ′ ″
Error of Collimation   .   .   = 0· 0· 2·60
Resulting Mean Zenith Distance, South = 2·52· 1·00

B.A.C. 6233.

1843.	° ′ ″	″	″	″	° ′ ″	1843.	° ′ ″	″	″	″	° ′ ″
Oct. 30	0·30·72·27	·00	0·50	− 2·88	0·30·(69·98)	Dec. 1	0·30·60·42	·02	0·50	+ 0·47	0·30·61·37
Nov. 15	62·79	·01	·51	− 1·77	61·52	3	59·54	·02	·50	0·29	60·31
Dec. 2	60·92	·01	·50	+ 0·38	61·79	9	60·33	·03	·51	0·22	61·03
16	61·46	•· ·14	·50	0·81	62·63	1844.					
1844.						Jan. 2	59·44	·04	·50	2·24	62·14
Jan. 3	58·45	·03	·49	2·31	61·22	9	57·91	·05	·49	2·74	61·09
8	58·85	·04	·50	2·67	61·98	11	56·43	·06	·49	2·88	59·74
15	59·04	·05	·49	3·15	62·63	16	56·18	·06	·50	3·21	59·83
18	57·81	·05	·50	3·34	61·60	22	55·98	·04	·50	3·58	60·02
24	57·31	·04	·50	3·09	61·46	25	55·93	·04	·50	3·75	60·14
26	57·27	·04	·50	3·81	61·54	27	56·82	• ·10	·51	3·86	61·09
29	57·76	·05	·51	3·97	62·19	28	54·65	·05	·51	3·92	59·03
Feb. 1	56·08	·07	·51	4·13	60·65	Feb. 2	56·45	·05	·51	4·18	61·09
12	57·27	·07	·51	4·65	62·36	15	56·18	·07	·50	4·77	61·38
14	56·08	·07	·51	4·73	61·25	17	54·05	·09	·51	4·85	59·92
16	56·82	·06	·51	4·81	62·08	21	53·41	·06	·51	5·01	58·87
19	58·75	·06	·51	4·93	64·13	22	53·78	·08	·51	5·04	59·25
April 10	54·50	·06	·51	6·18	61·13	April 9	54·25	·07	·52	6·17	60·87
13	53·96	·06	·52	6·21	60·63	14	56·52	·07	·51	6·22	63·18
17	53 81	·07	·52	6·24	60·50	18	54·05	·08	·51	6·24	61·32
21	52·28	·08	·52	6·26	58·73	22	53·09	·08	·53	6·26	61·80
May 3	52 28	·00	·53	6·23	59·04	May 2	56·52	·00	·52	6·24	63·28
7	52·43	·00	·53	6·20	59·16	4	56·77	·00	·52	6·23	63·52
9	51·84	·00	·52	6·19	58·54	8	56·62	·00	·53	6·19	63·34
11	52·58	·00	·52	6·15	59·25	10	56·92	·00	·53	6·16	63·61
14	52·23	·00	·52	6·11	58·86	13	55·59	·00	·52	6·12	62·23
16	52·97	·00	·52	6·07	59·56	15	55·93	·00	·51	6·09	62·53
20	53·61	·00	·53	5·99	60·13	17	55·69	·00	·51	6·05	62·25
22	51·79	·00	·52	5·94	58·25	24	55·54	·00	·52	5·89	61·95
											Carried forward,

No. 6233.—Dec. 16.—Correction for Azimuthal Error − ·034; for Curvature of Path − ·102.   = − 0″·14.
      Jan. 27.—   ,,   ,,   ,,   − ·04;   ,,   ,,   − ·06.   = − 0 ·10.

Mean Zenith Distances of Stars observed at the Royal Observatory.

FACE OF SECTOR EAST.						FACE OF SECTOR WEST.					
Day of Observation 1843-4.	Apparent Zenith Distance, from Unreduced Observation.	Reduction for Az. Error, and Curv. of Path.	Refraction.	Precession, Aberration, and Nutation.	Deduced Mean Zenith Distance, 1844, Jan. 0; and Mean of Separate Results, uncorrected, for Error of Collimation.	Day of Observation 1843-4.	Apparent Zenith Distance, from Unreduced Observation	Reduction for Az. Error, and Curv. of Path.	Refraction.	Precession, Aberration, and Nutation.	Deduced Mean Zenith Distance, 1844, Jan. 0; and Mean of Separate Results, uncorrected, for Error of Collimation.

B.A.C. 6233—(continued).

1844.						1844.					
May 23	0·30·51·49	·00	·52	5·92	0·30·57·93	May 27	0·30·56·52	·00	·52	5·81	0·30·62·85
25	52·92	·00	·52	5·86	59·30	30	56·07	·00	·52	5·71	62·90
29	52·72	·00	·52	5·75	58·99	June 2	57·12	·00	·52	5·61	63·25
June 1	51·98	·00	·53	5·65	58·16	16	56·87	·00	0·54	+ 5·03	62·44
12	53·27	·00	·52	5·22	59·01						
21	53·27	·00	0·53	+ 4·78	58·58						
					0·31· 0·45						0·31· 1·49

Error of Collimation . . = 0· 0· 0·52
Resulting Mean Zenith Distance, South = 0·31· 0·97

B.A.C. 6275.

1844.						1844.					
April 13	0·47·37·55	·09	0·80	+ 6·19	0·47·32·07	April 14	0·47·33·28	·10	0·79	+ 6·21	0·47·27·76
17	38·29	·11	·80	6·26	32·72	18	37·53	·12	·79	6·27	31·93
21	39·01	·12	·81	6·31	33·39	22	37·90	·12	·82	6·32	32·28
May 3	40·29	·00	·82	6·41	34·70	May 2	36·49	·00	·81	6·40	30·90
7	40·20	·00	·81	6·41	34·60	4	36·84	·00	·81	6·41	31·24
9	40·56	·00	·80	6·41	34·95	8	35·75	·00	·81	6·41	30·15
11	38·66	·00	·80	6·41	33·05	10	34·27	·00	·82	6·41	28·68
14	41·05	·00	·80	6·39	35·46	13	37·38	·00	·80	6·40	31·73
16	40·29	·00	·79	6·38	34·70	20	37·04	·00	·82	6·34	31·52
22	40·71	·00	·79	6·31	35·19	21	35·98	·00	·81	6·33	30·46
23	40·21	·00	·80	6·30	34·71	24	37·56	·00	·80	6·28	32·08
25	40·00	·00	·79	6·27	34·52	27	37·23	·01	·80	6·23	31·79
29	39·13	·00	·80	6·19	33·74	30	35·55	·00	·80	6·17	30·18
June 1	40·89	·00	·81	6·13	35·57	June 2	36·12	·00	·81	6·10	30·83
25	38·71	·00	0·81	+ 5·29	34·23	16	36·94	·00	0·83	+ 5·66	32·11
					0·47·34·24						0·47·30·91

Error of Collimation . . = 0· 0· 1·67
Resulting Mean Zenith Distance, North = 0·47·32·57

B.A.C. 6285.

1844.						1844.					
April 13	0·50·59·56	·09	0·85	+ 6·25	0·50·54·07	April 14	0·50·60·23	·11	0·85	+ 6·27	0·50·54·70
17	61·09	·11	·85	6·32	55·51	18	60·82	·13	·85	6·33	55·21
21	62·40	·13	·86	6·37	56·76	22	61·69	·13	·87	6·39	56·04
May 3	63·68	·00	·87	6·48	58·07	May 2	58·99	·00	·87	6·48	53·38
7	63·09	·00	·87	6·49	57·47	4	59·34	·00	·87	6·49	53·72
9	64·34	+ ·21	·86	6·50	(58·91)	8	58·25	·00	·87	6·49	52·63
11	63·24	·00	·86	6·49	57·61	10	58·55	·00	·88	6·49	52·94
14	63·06	·00	·86	6·48	57·44	13	59·78	·00	·86	6·49	54·15
16	63·19	·00	·85	6·47	57·57	20	* 60·62	·00	·88	6·43	55·07

Carried forward,

No. 6285.—May 9.—Correction for Curvature of Path = +0″·21.
　„ 20.—An assumed error of 10 divisions of the Micrometer is allowed for.

Mean Zenith Distances of Stars observed at the Royal Observatory.

FACE OF SECTOR EAST.   **FACE OF SECTOR WEST.**

Day of Observation 1843-4.	Apparent Zenith Distance, from Unreduced Observation.	Reduction for Az. Error, and Curv. of Path.	Refraction.	Precession, Aberration, and Nutation.	Deduced Mean Zenith Distance. 1844, Jan. 0; and Mean of Separate Results, uncorrected. for Error of Collimation.	Day of Observation 1843-4.	Apparent Zenith Distance, from Unreduced Observation.	Reduction for Az. Error, and Curv. of Path.	Refraction.	Precession, Aberration, and Nutation.	Deduced Mean Zenith Distance. 1844, Jan. 0; and Mean of Separate Results, uncorrected. for Error of Collimation.

B.A.C. 6285—(continued).

Day (E)	App. Zen. (E)	Red. (E)	Refr. (E)	Prec. (E)	Deduced (E)	Day (W)	App. Zen. (W)	Red. (W)	Refr. (W)	Prec. (W)	Deduced (W)
1844.						1844.					
May 22	0·50·63·01	·00	·85	6·41	0·50·57·45	May 21	0·50·58·92	·00	·87	6·42	0·50·53·37
23	64·64	·00	·86	6·40	59·10	24	59·66	·00	·85	6·38	54·13
25	63·14	·00	·85	6·37	57·62	27	59·04	·01	·86	6·33	53·56
29	62·07	·00	·86	6·30	56·63	30	58·75	·00	·86	6·28	53·33
June 1	64·23	·00	·87	6·23	58·87	June 2	59·41	·00	·86	6·21	54·06
12	61·84	·00	·87	5·92	56·79	16	58·94	·00	·88	5·78	54·04
24	62·35	·00	·86	5·46	57·75	21	57·06	·00	0·87	+ 5·58	52·95
25	62·10	·00	0·87	+ 5·41	57·56						
					0·50·57·27						0·50·53·96

Error of Collimation . . . = 0· 0· 1·66
Resulting Mean Zenith Distance, North = 0·50·55·61

B.A.C. 6305.

Day (E)	App. Zen. (E)	Red. (E)	Refr. (E)	Prec. (E)	Deduced (E)	Day (W)	App. Zen. (W)	Red. (W)	Refr. (W)	Prec. (W)	Deduced (W)
1844.						1844.					
April 10	0·48·35·88	·10	0·81	+ 6·39	0·48·30·20	April 14	0·48·38·35	·10	0·81	+ 6·48	0·48·32·58
13	36·99	·09	·81	6·46	31·25	18	38·55	·12	·81	6·55	32·69
17	38·52	·11	·81	6·53	32·69	22	39·41	·12	·83	6·62	33·50
21	39·24	·12	·82	6·60	33·34	May 2	36·32	·00	·82	6·74	30·40
May 3	41·90	·00	·83	6·70	35·99	4	36·77	·00	·83	6·75	30·85
7	41·31	·00	·83	6·76	35·38	8	35·88	·00	·83	6·76	29·95
11	40·27	·00	·82	6·77	34·32	10	34·79	·00	·84	6·77	28·86
14	42·66	+ ·22	·82	6·76	(36·94)	13	37·61	·00	·82	6·77	31·66
16	40·52	·00	·81	6·76	34·57	20	37·95	·00	·83	6·73	32·05
22	40·74	·00	·81	6·71	34·84	21	36·35	·00	·83	6·72	30·46
23	40·89	·00	·82	6·70	35·01	24	37·59	·00	·83	6·69	31·71
25	40·27	·00	·81	6·67	34·41	27	36·37	·01	·82	6·64	30·54
29	39·90	·00	·82	6·61	34·11	30	36·03	·00	·82	6·59	30·26
June 1	41·26	·00	·83	6·55	35·54	June 2	36·90	·00	·82	6·53	31·28
12	38·82	·00	·83	6·25	33·40	21	35·63	·00	0·83	+ 5·92	30·54
24	39·83	·00	0·82	+ 5·80	34·85						
					0·48·33·99						0·48·31·16

Error of Collimation . . . = 0· 0· 1·42
Resulting Mean Zenith Distance, North = 0·48·32·57

B.A.C. 6414.

Day (E)	App. Zen. (E)	Red. (E)	Refr. (E)	Prec. (E)	Deduced (E)	Day (W)	App. Zen. (W)	Red. (W)	Refr. (W)	Prec. (W)	Deduced (W)
1844.						1844.					
April 10	3· 1·19·48	·30	3·02	+ 6·81	3· 1·15·33	April 9	3· 1·17·21	·37	3·03	+ 6·77	3· 1·13·10
13	21·85	·33	3·03	6·94	17·61	14	18·15	·37	3·02	6·98	13·82
17	21·55	·39	3·04	7·10	17·10	22	20·17	·44	3·10	7·30	15·53
21	23·13	·44	3·07	7·26	18·50	May 2	17·46	·01	3·07	7·65	12·87
May 1	23·38	·01	3·11	7·68	18·80	4	19·48	·01	3·10	7·71	14·80
7	25·31	·00	3·10	7·80	20·61	8	18·10	·01	3·09	7·83	13·35
9	25·11	·00	3·09	7·85	20·35	10	17·51	·01	3·13	7·88	12·75

Carried forward,

No. 6305.—May 14.—Correction for Curvature of Path = + 0'·22.

Mean Zenith Distances of Stars observed at the Royal Observatory.

FACE OF SECTOR EAST.						FACE OF SECTOR WEST.					
Day of Observation 1843–4.	Apparent Zenith Distance, from Unreduced Observation.	Reduction for Az. Error, and Curv. of Path.	Refraction.	Precession, Aberration, and Nutation.	Deduced Mean Zenith Distance, 1844, Jan. 0; and Mean of Separate Results, uncorrected, for Error of Collimation.	Day of Observation 1843–4.	Apparent Zenith Distance, from Unreduced Observation.	Reduction for Az. Error, and Curv. of Path.	Refraction.	Precession, Aberration, and Nutation.	Deduced Mean Zenith Distance, 1844, Jan. 0; and Mean of Separate Results, uncorrected, for Error of Collimation.

B.A.C. 6414—(continued).

1844.						1844.					
May 11	3· 1·24·17	·00	3·05	7·90	3· 1·19·32	May 13	3· 1·18·59	·02	3·04	7·95	3· 1·13·66
14	23·33	·00	3·05	7·97	18 41	17	19·39	·00	2·98	8·03	14·33
16	23·97	·01	3·02	8·01	18·97	20	17·46	·01	3·15	8·09	12·52
21	24·52	·01	3·08	8·10	19·49	24	18·80	·02	3·03	8·14	13·76
23	24·47	·00	3·05	8·12	19·40	27	18·74	·03	3·06	8·16	13·61
25	24·61	·00	3·03	8·15	19·49	June 2	18·99	·01	3·10	8·19	13·79
29	25·11	·00	3·05	8·18	19·98	16	18·59	·02	3·15	8·09	13·63
June 1	24·86	·01	3·09	+ 8·19	19·75	21	20·07	·00	3·09	+ 8·00	15·16
					3· 1·18·87						3· 1·13·78

Error of Collimation . . = 0· 0· 2·55
Resulting Mean Zenith Distance, North = 3· 1·16·33

B.A.C. 6489.

1843.						1843.					
Oct. 30	3· 50·0·81	·01	3·73	- 1·96	3·50·(6·49)	Dec. 3	3·50·11·65	·15	3·75	- 0·46	3·50·15·71
Nov. 2	7·90	·04	3·78	1·87	(13·51)	1844.					
3	7·95	·04	3·75	1·84	(13·50)	April 9	17·28	·47	3·85	+ 7·05	13·61
15	10·27	* ·07	3·81	1·38	15·39	14	15·80	·46	3·84	7·31	11·87
Dec. 2	11·45	·10	3·75	- 0·51	15 61	18	17·57	·55	3·83	7·52	13·33
1844.						22	18·61	·56	3·94	7·72	14·27
April 10	20·14	·46	3·83	+ 7·10	16·41	May 2	15·65	·01	3·90	8·17	11·37
13	19·20	·41	3·85	7·26	15·38	4	17·97	·02	3·93	8·26	13·62
17	19·45	·49	3·86	7·47	15·35	8	15·11	·01	3·93	8·42	10·61
21	20·83	·56	3·90	7·67	16·50	10	17·53	·02	3·99	8·49	13·01
May 2	20·29	·01	3·95	8·22	16·01	13	17·33	·02	3·87	8·60	12·58
9	22·61	·00	3·93	8·45	18 09	17	17·03	·00	3·78	8·72	12·09
11	22·22	·00	3·87	8·53	17·56	20	16·69	·01	4·00	8·81	11·87
16	22·41	·01	3·84	8·69	17·55	22	16·98	·01	3·85	8·86	11·96
21	23·01	·01	3 92	8·83	18·09	24	17·72	·02	3·85	8·90	12·65
23	23·70	·00	3·87	8·88	18·69	27	17·38	·03	3·88	+ 8·96	12·27
25	22·46	·00	3·85	8·92	17·39						
29	23·20	·00	3·87	+ 9·00	18·07						
					3·50·16·86						3·50·12·72

Error of Collimation . . = 0· 0· 2·07
Resulting Mean Zenith Distance, North = 3·50·14·79

B.A.C. 6525.

1844.						1844.					
April 13	5· 3·50·39	·54	5·09	+ 7·13	5· 3·47·81	April 14	5· 3·46·25	·60	5·08	+ 7·19	5· 3·43·54
17	50·84	·64	5·10	7·36	47·94	18	47·83	·71	5·06	7·42	44·76
21	50·10	·73	5·16	7·59	46·94	22	48 81	·73	5·21	7·64	45·65
May 3	51·97	·01	5·21	8·23	48·94	May 2	45·16	·02	5·15	8·18	42·11
7	52·37	·01	5·20	8 42	49·14	4	45·95	·02	5·20	8·28	42·85
											Carried forward,

No. 6489.—Dec. 15.—Correction for Azimuthal Error - ·090; for Curvature of Path + ·020. = - 0"·07.
Note.—The first three observations of No. 6489 are rejected, because no corresponding observations were made near the times with the face West.

Mean Zenith Distances of Stars observed at the Royal Observatory.

	FACE OF SECTOR EAST.						FACE OF SECTOR WEST.				
Day of Observation 1843-4.	Apparent Zenith Distance, from Unreduced Observation.	Reduction for Az. Error, and Curr. of Path.	Refraction.	Precession, Aberration, and Nutation.	Deduced Mean Zenith Distance, 1844, Jan. 0; and Mean of Separate Results, uncorrected, for Error of Collimation.	Day of Observation 1843-4.	Apparent Zenith Distance, from Unreduced Observation.	Reduction for Az. Error, and Curr. of Path.	Refraction.	Precession, Aberration, and Nutation.	Deduced Mean Zenith Distance, 1844, Jan. 0; and Mean of Separate Results, uncor- rected, for Error of Collimation.

					B.A.C. 6525—(continued.)						
1844.						1844.					
May 9	5⌡ 3·53·36	·00	5·19	8·51	5· 3·50·04	May 8	5· 3·46·64	·02	5·19	8·47	5· 3·43·34
11	53·11	·00	5·12	8·60	49·63	10	46·54	·02	5·27	8·56	43·23
14	54·24	+ ·14	5·12	8·73	50·77	13	47·19	·03	5·11	8·69	43·58
16	53·45	·01	5·07	8·81	49·70	17	47·14	·00	5·99	8·85	43·28
21	53·26	·01	5·17	8·99	49·43	20	45·36	·01	5·28	8·96	41·67
23	53·45	·00	5·12	9·06	49·51	22	47·33	·01	5·08	9·03	43·37
25	53·36	·00	5·08	9·12	49·32	24	47·73	·03	5·09	9·09	43·70
29	53·85	·00	5·11	9·23	49·73	27	47·19	·04	5·13	9·18	43·10
June 1	53·95	·01	5·15	9·30	49·79	30	47·48	·00	5·14	9·26	43·36
16	53·16	·00	5·28	+ 9·50	48·94	June 2	47·43	·01	5·21	+ 9·33	43·30
					5· 3·49·18						5· 3·43·39

Error of Collimation . . = 0· 0· 2·89
Resulting Mean Zenith Distance, North = 5· 3·46·28

					B.A.C. 6639.						
1844.						1844.					
April 13	3·53·24·58	·42	3·91	+ 8·60	3·53·19·47	April 14	3 53·23·14	·47	3·89	+ 8·68	3·53·17·88
21	26·45	·57	3·96	9·19	20·65	18	22·35	·55	3·88	8·97	16·71
May 3	27·14	·01	3·97	9·99	21·11	May 2	21·07	·01	3·96	9·92	15·10
7	27·09	·00	4·00	10·23	21·46	4	22·75	·02	3·99	10·05	16·67
9	28·94	·00	3·93	10·35	22·57	8	20·92	·01	3·98	10·29	14·60
11	28·72	·00	3·93	10·46	22·19	13	22·55	+ ·13	3·92	10·57	16·03
14	28·13	·00	3·93	10·62	21·44	16	22·80	·01	3·90	10·72	15·97
21	28·52	·01	3·97	10·95	21·53	20	22·60	+ ·14	4·06	10·91	15·89
23	28·72	+ ·09	3·93	11·04	21·70	22	23·00	·01	3·90	11·00	15·80
25	28·28	·00	3·90	11·12	21·06	24	22·85	·02	3·90	11·08	15·65
29	29·22	·00	3·92	11·26	21·88	27	23·00	·03	3·94	11·19	15·72
June 1	29·02	·01	3·95	11·35	21·61	June 2	22·85	·01	4·00	11·38	15·46
12	29·91	·00	3·96	11·59	22·28	16	22·90	·02	4·06	11·63	15·31
17	28·38	·00	4·02	11·64	20·76	18	23·98	·02	3·06	11·64	16·28
21	28·57	·00	3·98	+11·65	20·90	24	23·83	·01	3·95	+11·64	16·13
					3·53·21·37						3·53·15·95

Error of Collimation . . = 0· 0· 2·71
Resulting Mean Zenith Distance, North = 3·53·18·66

					Anon. AR. 19·21.						
1844.						1844.					
April 17	4· 7·25·93	·53	4·17	+ 9·05	4· 7·20·52	May 2	4· 7·22·47	·02	4·19	+10·14	4· 7·16·50
21	25·04	·60	4·20	9·36	19·28	8	23·66	·02	4·22	10·53	17·33
May 3	28·20	·01	4·21	10·21	22·19	13	23·56	·02	4·16	10·83	16·87
7	27·68	·00	4·24	10·47	21·45	16	24·45	·01	4·14	10·99	17·59

Carried forward,

No. 6525.—May 14.—Correction for Azimuthal Error − ·005; for Curvature of Path + ·144. = + 0″·14.
   „ 6639.— „ 8.— „   „   „   „ ·022; „   „ + ·148. = + 0 ·13.
       „ 20.— „   „   „   „ ·007; „   „ + ·148. = + 0 ·14.
       „ 23.— „   „   „   „ ·000; „   „ + ·093. = + 0 ·09.

Mean Zenith Distances of Stars observed at the Royal Observatory.

FACE OF SECTOR EAST.						FACE OF SECTOR WEST.					
Day of Observation 1843–4.	Apparent Zenith Distance, from Unreduced Observation.	Reduction for Az. Error, and Curv. of Path.	Refraction.	Precession, Aberration, and Nutation.	Deduced Mean Zenith Distance, 1844, Jan. 0; and Mean of Separate Results, uncorrected, for Error of Collimation.	Day of Observation 1843–4.	Apparent Zenith Distance, from Unreduced Observation.	Reduction for Az. Error, and Curv. of Path.	Refraction.	Precession, Aberration, and Nutation.	Deduced Mean Zenith Distance, 1844, Jan. 0; and Mean of Separate Results, uncorrected, for Error of Collimation.

Anon. AR. 10·21—(continued.)

1844.						1844.					
May 14	4· 7·28·64	·00	4·15	10·89	4· 7·21·90	May 22	4· 7·24·20	·01	4·13	11·30	4· 7·17·02
21	28·64	·01	4·21	11·25	21·59	24	24·64	·02	4·14	11·39	17·37
29	29·48	·00	4·16	11·59	22·05	27	24·45	·03	4·18	11·51	17·09
June 1	29·73	·01	4·19	11·70	22·21	30	25·24	·00	4·18	11·63	17·79
17	28·49	·00	4·26	12·04	20·71	June 2	20·35	·01	4·24	11·73	(12·85)
25	29·19	·01	4·24	+12·07	21·35	16	22·47	·02	4·30	12·03	14·72
						18	26·22	·02	4·19	+12·05	18·34
					4· 7·21·33						4· 7·17·06

Error of Collimation . . . = 0· 0· 2·13
Resulting Mean Zenith Distance, North = 4· 7·19·19

B.A.C. 6753.

1844.						1844.					
April 21	2·39·56·79	·39	2·71	+10·65	2·39·48·46	April 14	2·39·52·50	·32	2·67	+10·04	2·39·44·81
May 3	58·42	·01	2·72	11·62	49·51	18	55·06	·38	2·66	10·39	46·95
7	58·91	·00	2·74	11·91	49·74	22	55·20	·39	2·74	10·74	46·87
9	59·75	·00	2·73	12·05	50·43	May 2	53·30	·01	2·71	11·54	44·55
11	57·08	·00	2·69	12·19	48·18	4	53·58	·01	2·73	11·69	44·61
16	60·30	·01	2·67	12·50	50·46	8	52·64	·01	2·73	11·98	43·38
22	60·15	·01	2·67	12·84	49·97	10	53·89	·01	2·77	12·12	41·52
23	59·46	·00	2·69	12·80	49·26	13	54·97	·02	2·68	12·32	45·31
25	58·67	·00	2·67	12·99	48·35	24	54·40	·01	2·67	12·94	44·12
29	58·96	·00	2·60	13·10	48·49	27	54·47	·02	2·70	13·08	44·07
June 1	60·61	·01	2·71	13·28	49·03	30	54·92	·00	2·70	13·20	44·42
17	59·41	·00	2·75	13·05	48·51	June 2	54·22	·01	2·74	13·31	43·64
21	60·99	·00	2·73	13·07	50·05	16	54·02	·01	2·78	13·64	43·75
24	60·49	·01	2·70	13·07	49·51	18	55·75	·01	2·71	13·66	44·79
26	60·02	·00	2·67	13·06	49·03	25	55·75	·01	2·75	+13·67	44·82
					2·39·49·27						2·39·44·71

Error of Collimation . . . = 0· 0· 2·28
Resulting Mean Zenith Distance, North = 2·39·46·99

B.A.C. 6877.

1844.						1844.					
April 17	1·26·55·62	·19	1·46	+11·63	1·26·45·26	April 14	1·26·54·58	·18	1·45	+11·31	1·26·44·54
21	57·70	·22	1·48	12·04	47·01	18	53·94	·21	1·45	11·73	43·45
May 7	60·50	·00	1·49	13·54	48·45	May 2	53·64	·01	1·47	13·10	42·00
9	59·81	·00	1·49	13·70	47·60	4	55·42	·01	1·48	13·28	43·61
11	59·66	·00	1·46	13·87	47·25	8	55·32	·01	1·48	13·62	43·17
14	59·47	·00	1·46	14·10	46·83	10	56·26	·01	1·51	13·79	43·97
16	59·81	·00	1·44	14·24	47·01	13	56·85	·01	1·46	14·02	44·28
21	60·06	·00	1·48	14·58	46·96	20	57·29	·00	1·50	14·52	44·27

Carried forward,

3 G

Mean Zenith Distances of Stars observed at the Royal Observatory.

FACE OF SECTOR EAST. | FACE OF SECTOR WEST.

B.A.C. 6877—(continued.)

Day of Observation 1843-4.	Apparent Zenith Distance, from Unreduced Observation.	Reduction for Az. Error, and Curv. of Path.	Refraction.	Precession, Aberration, and Nutation.	Deduced Mean Zenith Distance, 1844, Jan. 0; and Mean of Separate Results. uncorrected, for Error of Collimation.	Day of Observation 1843-4.	Apparent Zenith Distance, from Unreduced Observation.	Reduction for Az. Error, and Curv. of Path.	Refraction.	Precession, Aberration, and Nutation.	Deduced Mean Zenith Distance, 1844, Jan. 0; and Mean of Separate Results. uncorrected, of Collimation.
1844.						1844.					
May 23	1·26·60·36	·00	1·46	14·71	1·26·47·11	May 22	1·26·56·80	·00	1·45	14·65	1·26·43·60
25	60·36	·00	1·45	14·83	46·98	24	57·05	·01	1·45	14·77	43·72
29	61·15	·00	1·45	15·04	47·56	27	56·80	·01	1·47	14·94	43·32
June 1	60·85	·00	1·47	15·19	47·13	30	57·15	·00	1·47	15·09	43·53
17	61·44	·00	1·50	15·67	47·27	June 2	56·90	·00	1·49	15·23	43·16
18	61·10	·00	1·47	15·68	46·89	16	57·84	·01	1·51	15·65	43·69
20	60·95	·00	1·49	+15·70	46·74	21	57·90	·00	1·49	+15·71	43·77
					1·26·47·07						1·26·43·61

Error of Collimation . . . = 0· 0· 1·73
Resulting Mean Zenith Distance, North = 1·26·45·34

B.A.C. 6948.

Day of Obs.	App. Zenith Dist.	Red.	Refr.	Prec. &c.	Deduced Mean Z.D.	Day of Obs.	App. Zenith Dist.	Red.	Refr.	Prec. &c.	Deduced Mean Z.D.
1844.						1844.					
April 21	3·27·40·84	·51	3·54	+11·89	3·27·31·98	April 18	3·27·38·47	·50	3·46	+11·54	3·27·29·89
May 3	38·57	·01	3·54	13·19	28·91	May 4	38·02	·01	3·54	13·29	28·26
7	43·16	·00	3·55	13·39	33·12	8	38·17	·01	3·54	13·69	28·01
9	43·50	·00	3·57	13·79	33·28	10	38·02	·02	3·60	13·88	27·72
11	42·86	·00	3·50	13·98	32·38	13	38·86	·02	3·48	14·16	28·16
14	43·65	·00	3·48	14·20	32·87	20	39·40	·01	3·58	14·77	28·20
16	45·38	+ ·10	3·43	14·43	34·48	22	39·55	·01	3·46	14·93	28·07
21	44·14	·01	3·53	14·85	32·81	24	39·31	·02	3·47	15·09	27·67
23	44·93	·00	3·49	15·01	33·41	27	39·65	·03	3·51	15·31	27·82
25	43·45	·00	3·47	15·16	31·76	30	40·10	·00	3·50	15·51	28·09
29	45·08	·00	3·47	15·45	33·10	June 2	40·24	·01	3·57	15·71	28·09
June 1	44·95	·01	3·51	15·64	32·81	16	40·34	·02	3·61	16·37	27·56
17	45·82	·00	3·57	16·40	32·99	18	40·24	·02	3·52	16·43	27·31
20	44·88	·00	3·55	16·49	31·04	21	39·95	·00	3·55	16·52	26·98
22	45·82	·00	3·54	+16·54	32·92	24	40·79	·01	3·51	+16·58	27·71
					3·27·32·58						3·27·27·97

Error of Collimation . . . = 0· 0· 2·30
Resulting Mean Zenith Distance, North = 3·27·30·27

B.A.C. 7011.

Day of Obs.	App. Zenith Dist.	Red.	Refr.	Prec. &c.	Deduced Mean Z.D.	Day of Obs.	App. Zenith Dist.	Red.	Refr.	Prec. &c.	Deduced Mean Z.D.
1844.						1844.					
May 3	4·21·48·59	·01	4·47	+13·35	4·21·39·70	April 22	4·21·43·27	·63	4·46	+12·07	4·21·35·03
7	48·67	·00	4·48	13·79	39·36	May 2	42·88	·02	4·42	13·24	34·04
9	48·84	·00	4·50	14·01	39·33	8	43·87	·02	4·47	13·90	34·42
11	49·27	·00	4·41	14·22	39·46	10	44·41	·02	4·54	14·11	34·82
14	49·32	·00	4·39	14·52	39·19	13	45·57	·03	4·39	14·42	35·51
16	48·49	·01	4·33	14·72	38·09	20	41·56	·01	4·51	15·10	30·96
21	48·61	·01	4·40	14·72	37·86	22	45·78	·01	4·37	15·28	34·86
23	50·93	·00	4·40	15·37	39·96	24	46·71	·02	4·38	15·46	35·61
25	50·82	·00	4·38	15·54	39·66	27	46·00	·04	4·43	15·71	34·68

Carried forward,

No. 6948.—May 16.—Correction for Azimuthal Error − ·013; for Curvature of Path + ·112. = +0″·10.

Mean Zenith Distances of Stars observed at the Royal Observatory.

FACE OF SECTOR EAST.   FACE OF SECTOR WEST.

B.A.C. 7011—(continued.)

Day of Observation 1843-4.	Apparent Zenith Distance, from Unreduced Observation.	Reduction for Az. Error, and Curv. of Path.	Refraction.	Precession, Aberration, and Nutation.	Deduced Mean Zenith Distance 1844, Jan. 0; and Mean of Separate Results, uncorrected, for Error of Collimation.	Day of Observation 1843-4.	Apparent Zenith Distance, from Unreduced Observation.	Reduction for Az. Error, and Curv. of Path.	Refraction.	Precession, Aberration, and Nutation.	Deduced Mean Zenith Distance 1844, Jan. 0; and Mean of Separate Results, uncorrected, for Error of Collimation.
1844.	° ′ ″	″	″	″	° ′ ″	1844.	° ′ ″	″	″	″	° ′ ″
May 29	4 21 51·33	·00	4·38	15·87	4 21 39·84	May 30	4 21 45·52	·00	4·42	15·94	4 21 34·00
June 1	50·24	·01	4·43	16·09	38·57	June 2	46·57	·01	4·50	16·16	34·90
17	52·05	·00	4·50	17·02	39·53	16	46·96	·02	4·55	16·97	34·52
20	52·46	·00	4·48	17·13	39·81	18	47·89	·02	4·44	17·06	35·25
22	52·06	·00	4·46	17·20	39·32	24	47·72	·01	4·43	17·26	34·88
25	51·49	·01	4·50	17·29	38·89	26	46·04	·01	4·37	+17·32	33·08
29	52·85	·00	4·58	+17·38	40·05						
					4 21 39·28						4 21 34·44

Error of Collimation . . = 0· 0· 2·42
Resulting Mean Zenith Distance, North = 4 21 36·86

B.A.C. 7026.

Day of Observation 1843-4.	Apparent Zenith Distance, from Unreduced Observation.	Reduction for Az. Error, and Curv. of Path.	Refraction.	Precession, Aberration, and Nutation.	Deduced Mean Zenith Distance 1844, Jan. 0; and Mean of Separate Results, uncorrected, for Error of Collimation.	Day of Observation 1843-4.	Apparent Zenith Distance, from Unreduced Observation.	Reduction for Az. Error, and Curv. of Path.	Refraction.	Precession, Aberration, and Nutation.	Deduced Mean Zenith Distance 1844, Jan. 0; and Mean of Separate Results, uncorrected, for Error of Collimation.
1844.						1844.					
May 3	4 21 39·90	·01	4·47	+13·45	4 21 30·91	May 2	4 21 34·93	·02	4·42	+13·33	4 21 26·00
7	41·08	·00	4·48	13·89	31·63	8	35·77	·02	4·47	14·00	26·22
9	39·86	·00	4·50	14·11	30·25	10	38·19	·02	4·53	14·22	28·48
11	41·27	·00	4·41	14·33	31·35	13	38·26	·03	4·39	14·53	28·09
16	41·77	·01	4·33	14·84	31·25	20	38·05	·01	4·51	15·22	27·33
21	41·05	·01	4·45	15·32	30·17	22	38·18	·01	4·37	15·41	27·13
23	45·20	·00	4·40	15·50	34·10	24	37·92	·02	4·38	15·58	26·70
25	43·41	·00	4·37	15·67	32·11	27	38·64	·04	4·43	15·84	27·19
29	44·52	·00	4·38	16·00	32·90	30	38·80	·00	4·42	16·08	27·14
June 1	43·77	·01	4·43	16·23	31·96	June 2	38·97	·01	4·50	16·30	27·16
4	44·83	·00	4·52	16·44	32·91	16	39·45	·02	4·55	17·13	26·85
17	43·66	·00	4·50	17·17	30·99	18	40·33	·02	4·44	17·22	27·53
20	43·57	·00	4·48	17·30	30·75	24	39·57	·01	4·43	17·43	26·56
22	47·03	·00	4·46	17·36	34·13	26	38·54	·01	4·37	+17·48	25·42
25	44·18	·01	4·50	+17·46	31·21						
					4 21 31·78						4 21 26·99

Error of Collimation . . = 0· 0· 2·40
Resulting Mean Zenith Distance, North = 4 21 29·38

B.A.C. 7057.

Day of Observation 1843-4.	Apparent Zenith Distance, from Unreduced Observation.	Reduction for Az. Error, and Curv. of Path.	Refraction.	Precession, Aberration, and Nutation.	Deduced Mean Zenith Distance 1844, Jan. 0; and Mean of Separate Results, uncorrected, for Error of Collimation.	Day of Observation 1843-4.	Apparent Zenith Distance, from Unreduced Observation.	Reduction for Az. Error, and Curv. of Path.	Refraction.	Precession, Aberration, and Nutation.	Deduced Mean Zenith Distance 1844, Jan. 0; and Mean of Separate Results, uncorrected, for Error of Collimation.
1844.						1844.					
May 3	4 18 26·09	·01	4·41	+13·68	4 18 16·81	April 22	4 18 22·26	·63	4·40	+12·34	4 18 13·69
7	26·86	·00	4·42	14·14	17·14	May 2	20·58	·02	4·36	13·56	11·36
9	26·94	·00	4·45	14·37	17·02	4	20·63	·02	4·41	13·80	11·22
11	27·66	·00	4·36	14·59	17·43	8	21·51	·02	4·41	14·26	11·64
14	27·61	·00	4·33	14·91	17·03	10	22·26	·02	4·48	14·48	12·24
16	28·75	·01	4·27	15·12	17·69	13	23·95	·02	4·33	14·80	13·46
21	27·69	·01	4·39	15·61	16·46	20	23·30	·01	4·45	15·52	12·22
23	28·48	·00	4·35	15·80	17·03	22	24·57	·01	4·31	15·71	13·16

Carried forward,

Mean Zenith Distances of Stars observed at the Royal Observatory.

FACE OF SECTOR EAST.						FACE OF SECTOR WEST.					
Day of Observation 1843-4.	Apparent Zenith Distance, from Unreduced Observation.	Reduction for Az. Error, and Curv. of Path.	Refraction.	Precession, Aberration, and Nutation.	Deduced Mean Zenith Distance 1844, Jan. 0; and Mean of Separate Results, uncorrected, for Error of Collimation.	Day of Observation 1843-4.	Apparent Zenith Distance, from Unreduced Observation.	Reduction for Az. Error, and Curv. of Path.	Refraction.	Precession, Aberration, and Nutation.	Deduced Mean Zenith Distance 1844, Jan. 0; and Mean of Separate Results, uncorrected, for Error of Collimation.

B.A.C. 7057—(continued.)

	° ′ ″	″	″	″	° ′ ″		° ′ ″	″	″	″	° ′ ″
1844.						1844.					
May 25	4 18 29 16	·00	4·32	15 98	4 18 17 50	May 24	4 18 24 31	·02	4·32	15·89	4 18 12 72
29	28·83	·00	4·32	16 33	16·83	27	23·99	·04	4·38	16·16	12·17
June 1	29·36	·01	4·38	16·54	17·17	30	23·61	·00	4·36	16·40	11·57
4	29·04	·00	4·46	16·79	16·71	June 2	23·97	·01	4·46	16·64	11·78
17	30·09	·00	4·45	17·55	17·59	16	25·20	·02	4·49	17·50	12·17
20	30·30	·00	4·43	17·08	17 05	18	26·13	·02	4·38	17·60	12·89
22	30·55	·00	4·40	+17 70	17·19	21	26·35	·01	4·42	+17·72	13·04
					4 18 17 12						4 18 12 36

Error of Collimation . . . = 0· 0· 2·38
Resulting Mean Zenith Distance, North = 4·18·14·74

Anon. AR. 20ʰ·24ᵐ.

	° ′ ″	″	″	″	° ′ ″		° ′ ″	″	″	″	° ′ ″
1844.						1844.					
May 9	4· 7· 5·24	·00	4·25	+14·59	4· 6·54·90	May 8	4· 7· 2·73	+·13	4·22	+14·48	4· 6·52·60
11	9·44	·00	4·17	14·82	58·79	10	2·82	·02	4·28	14·70	52·38
14	9·04	·00	4·14	15 14	58·04	13	4·06	·02	4·14	15·04	53·14
16	10·23	·01	4·08	15·36	58·94	20	3·91	·01	4·26	15·76	52·40
21	8·16	·01	4·20	15 86	56 49	22	4·80	·01	4·12	15·06	52·36
23	10·33	·00	4·16	16·05	58·44	24	5·29	·02	4·13	16·14	53·26
25	10·38	·00	4·14	16·24	58·28	27	5 39	·03	4·19	16·41	53·14
29	10·33	·00	4·13	16·58	57·88	30	5·59	·00	4·17	16·67	53·09
June 1	9·88	·01	4·18	16·83	57·22	June 2	4·00	·01	4·26	16·91	51·94
4	10·13	·00	4·27	17·05	57 35	16	5·74	·02	4·30	17·79	52·23
17	10·97	·00	4·25	17·84	57 38	18	6·08	·02	4·19	17·88	52·37
20	11·61	·00	4·23	17 07	57·87	21	5·93	·01	4·23	18·01	52·14
22	10·72	·00	4·22	18 05	56·89	24	6·28	·01	4·18	18·11	52·34
25	9·60	·01	4·25	18 16	55·78	26	6·87	·01	4·13	18 17	52·82
29	11·07	·00	4·33	+18·25	57·15	30	6 18	·01	4·27	+18·27	52·17
					4 6·57 43						4 6·52·60

Error of Collimation . . . = 0· 0· 2·41
Resulting Mean Zenith Distance, North = 4· 6·55·01

Anon. AR. 20ʰ·34ᵐ.

	° ′ ″	″	″	″	° ′ ″		° ′ ″	″	″	″	° ′ ″
1844.						1844.					
May 7	3·58· 6·11	·00	4·08	+14·88	3·57·55·31	May 2	3 57 50·79	·02	4·02	+14·25	3 57·49·54
9	4·09	·00	4·09	15·12	53 66	8	50·15	·02	4·06	15·00	48·19
11	7·15	·00	4·01	15·36	55·80	10	62 31	·02	4·12	15·25	51·16
14	8·38	·00	3·99	15·71	56·06	13	02·36	·02	3·99	15·60	50·73
16	7·99	·01	3·94	15·94	55 98	20	03·30	·01	4·10	10·37	51·02
21	8·09	·01	4·05	16·48	55·65	22	02·85	·01	3·97	16·58	50·23
23	6·18	·00	4·00	16·68	53 50	24	03·50	·02	3·98	16·78	50·08
											Carried forward,

Anon. 20ʰ 24ᵐ.—May 8.—Correction for Azimuthal Error - ·016; for Curvature of Path + ·146. = +0″·13.

Mean Zenith Distances of Stars observed at the Royal Observatory.

FACE OF SECTOR EAST.

Day of Observation 1843-4.	Apparent Zenith Distance, from Unreduced Observation.	Reduction for Az. Error, and Curv. of Path.	Refraction.	Precession, Aberration, and Nutation.	Deduced Mean Zenith Distance. 1844, Jan. 0; and Mean of Separate Results, uncorrected, for Error of Collimation.

Anon. AR. 20·34—(continued).

1844.	° ′ ″	″	″	″	° ′ ″
May 25	3·58· 8·C8	·00	3·99	16·88	3·57·55·70
June 1	8·43	·01	4·03	17·52	54·93
17	9·96	·00	4·10	18·63	55·43
19	10·46	·00	4·08	18·73	55·81
20	9·57	·00	4·08	18·78	54·87
22	10·36	·00	4·06	18·86	55·56
25	8·73	·01	4·09	18·98	53·83
29	10·51	·00	4·17	+19·10	55·58
					3·57·55·18

FACE OF SECTOR WEST.

Day of Observation 1843-4.	Apparent Zenith Distance, from Unreduced Observation.	Reduction for Az. Error, and Curv. of Path.	Refraction.	Precession, Aberration, and Nutation.	Deduced Mean Zenith Distance. 1844, Jan. 0; and Mean of Separate Results, uncorrected, for Error of Collimation.
1844.	° ′ ″	″	″	″	° ′ ″
May 27	3·57·63·00	·03	4·03	17·07	3·57·49·93
30	62·71	·00	4·02	17·35	49·38
June 2	63·69	·01	4·10	17·61	50·17
16	64·43	·02	4·14	18·58	49·97
18	66·01	·02	4·04	18·68	51·35
21	64·38	·01	4·07	18·82	49·62
24	65·77	·01	4·03	18·94	50·85
26	65·47	01	3·98	19·01	60·43
30	65·52	·01	4·11	+19·12	50·50
					3·57·50·24

Error of Collimation . . . = 0· 0· 2·47
Resulting Mean Zenith Distance, North = 3·57·52·71

B.A.C. 7207.

FACE OF SECTOR EAST.

1844.	° ′ ″	″	″	″	° ′ ″
April21	0·24·46·18	·06	0·42	+14·53	0·24·61·07
May 9	41·34	·00	·42	16·89	58·65
11	42·52	·00	·42	17·13	60·07
14	43·91	·00	·42	17·47	61·80
16	43·31	·00	·41	17·09	61·41
21	42·28	·00	·42	18·20	60·90
23	41·09	·00	·42	18·40	60·51
25	42·33	·00	·41	18·58	61·32
29	41·37	·00	·41	18·92	60·70
June 1	40·80	·00	·42	19·15	60·37
4	42·08	·00	·43	19·37	61·83
17	40·45	·00	·43	20·05	60·93
20	39·46	·00	·42	20·14	60·02
22	40·11	·00	·42	20·20	60·73
25	40·60	·00	0·42	+20·26	61·28
					0·25· 0·77

FACE OF SECTOR WEST.

1844.	° ′ ″	″	″	″	° ′ ″
May 2	0·24·49·44	·00	0·42	+16·02	0·25· 5·88
4	47·66	·00	·42	16·28	4·36
8	48·10	·00	·42	16·78	5·30
10	49·04	·00	·43	17·02	6·49
13	45·78	·00	·41	17·36	3·55
20	44·99	·00	·43	18·10	3·52
22	45·08	·00	·41	18·30	4·69
24	45·49	·00	·41	18·49	4·39
27	45·88	·00	·42	18·75	5·05
30	46·47	·00	·42	19·00	5·89
June 2	47·46	·00	·43	19·23	7·12
16	43·27	·00	·43	20·01	3·71
18	43·07	·00	·42	20·08	3·57
21	43·17	·00	·42	20·17	3·76
24	44·04	·00	0·42	+20·24	5·60
					0·25· 4·86

Error of Collimation . . . = 0· 0· 2·04
Resulting Mean Zenith Distance, South = 0·25· 2·82

Anon. AR. 20 53.

FACE OF SECTOR EAST.

1844.	° ′ ″	″	″	″	° ′ ″
May 7	4·13· 4·09	·00	4·33	+15·67	4·12·52·75
9	5·08	·00	4·35	15·94	53·40
11	5·13	·00	4 27	15·22	53·18
14	5·17	·00	4·28	16·61	52·84
16	5·77	·01	4·18	16·87	53·07

FACE OF SECTOR WEST.

1844.	° ′ ″	″	″	″	° ′ ″
May 2	4·12·50·74	·02	4·27	+14·96	4·12·49·03
8	60·53	·02	4·32	15·81	49·02
10	58·86	·02	4·36	16·08	47·12
13	61·13	·02	4·24	16·48	48·87
20	62·26	·01	4·36	17·37	49·24

Carried forward,

Mean Zenith Distances of Stars observed at the Royal Observatory.

FACE OF SECTOR EAST.

Day of Observation 1843-4.	Apparent Zenith Distance, from Unreduced Observation.	Reduction for Az. Error, and Curv. of Path.	Refraction.	Precession, Aberration, and Nutation.	Deduced Mean Zenith Distance 1844, Jan. 0; and Mean of Separate Results, uncorrected, for Error of Collimation.

FACE OF SECTOR WEST.

Day of Observation 1843-4.	Apparent Zenith Distance, from Unreduced Observation.	Reduction for Az. Error, and Curv. of Path.	Refraction.	Precession, Aberration, and Nutation.	Deduced Mean Zenith Distance 1844, Jan. 0; and Mean of Separate Results, uncorrected, for Error of Collimation.

Anon. AR. 20·53—(continued).

FACE OF SECTOR EAST.

Day of Obs.	App. Zen. Dist.	Reduction	Refraction	Prec., Aber., Nut.	Deduced Mean Z.D.
1844.	° ′ ″	″	″	″	° ′ ″
May 21	4·13· 6·75	·01	4·30	17·50	4·12·53·54
25	6·46	·00	4·24	17·06	52·74
29	7·00	·00	4·23	18·41	53·51
June 1	6·46	·01	4·28	18·72	52·01
17	8·33	·00	4·35	20·07	52·61
19	8·24	·00	4·33	20·20	52·37
22	8·43	·00	4·29	20·37	52·35
25	9·17	·01	4·35	20·53	52·98
29	10·21	·00	4·44	+20·70	53·95
					4·12·52·96

FACE OF SECTOR WEST.

Day of Obs.	App. Zen. Dist.	Reduction	Refraction	Prec., Aber., Nut.	Deduced Mean Z.D.
1844.	° ′ ″	″	″	″	° ′ ″
May 22	4·12·62·71	·01	4·22	17·61	4·12·49·31
24	62·06	·02	4·24	17·85	48·43
27	62·16	·04	4·29	18·19	48·22
30	63·45	·00	4·27	18·51	49·21
June 16	65·57	·02	4·40	20·00	49·95
24	65·17	·01	4·28	20·48	48·90
26	64·78	·01	4·23	20·57	48·43
30	65·22	·01	4·37	+20·74	48·84
					4·12·48·82

Error of Collimation . . . = 0· 0· 2·07
Resulting Mean Zenith Distance, North = 4·12·50·89

Anon. AR. 21·1.

FACE OF SECTOR EAST.

Day of Obs.	App. Zen. Dist.	Reduction	Refraction	Prec., Aber., Nut.	Deduced Mean Z.D.
1844.					
May 7	3·35·18·96	·00	3·68	+16·16	3·35· 6·48
9	19·01	·00	3·70	16·45	6·26
11	19·70	·00	3·63	16·73	6·00
14	20·09	·00	3·64	17·14	6·59
16	19·60	·01	3·56	17·41	5·74
21	20·88	·01	3·66	18·05	6·48
23	22·26	·00	3·62	18·30	7·58
25	21·45	·00	3·60	18·54	6·51
29	22·51	·00	3·61	19·00	7·12
June 1	22·76	·01	3·64	19·32	7·07
4	23·65	·00	3·71	19·62	7·74
17	23·00	·00	3·70	20·71	6·59
22	23·99	·00	3·65	21·03	6·61
25	24·30	·01	3·70	21·19	6·89
29	23·45	·00	3·77	+21·36	5·86
					3·35· 6·08

FACE OF SECTOR WEST.

Day of Obs.	App. Zen. Dist.	Reduction	Refraction	Prec., Aber., Nut.	Deduced Mean Z.D.
1844.					
May 2	3·35·12·54	·01	3·63	+15·42	3·34·00·74
8	11·95	·01	3·68	16·30	59·32
10	12·84	·02	3·70	16·59	59·93
13	15·21	·02	3·61	17·00	61·80
20	15·30	·01	3·71	17·93	61·07
22	16·29	·01	3·59	18·18	61·69
24	16·88	·02	3·60	18·42	62·04
27	16·64	·03	3·66	18·77	61·50
30	16·69	·00	3·63	19·11	61·21
June 16	19·06	·02	3·75	20·64	62·15
18	18·91	·02	3·65	20·78	61·76
20	20·09	·02	3·69	20·91	62·85
24	19·01	·01	3·64	21·14	61·50
26	19·20	·01	3·60	21·24	61·55
30	19·35	·01	3·72	+21·40	61·06
					3·35· 1·39

Error of Collimation . . . = 0· 0· 2·65
Resulting Mean Zenith Distance, North = 3·35· 4·03

B.A.C. 7386.

FACE OF SECTOR EAST.

Day of Obs.	App. Zen. Dist.	Reduction	Refraction	Prec., Aber., Nut.	Deduced Mean Z.D.
1843.					
Oct. 30	1· 6·39·87	·00	1·10	- 2·42	1· 6·(43·39)
1844.					
May 7	1· 7· 8·80	·00	1·15	+17·28	1· 6·52·67
9	9·50	·00	1·15	17·58	53·16
11	9·29	·00	1·13	17·87	52·55

FACE OF SECTOR WEST.

Day of Obs.	App. Zen. Dist.	Reduction	Refraction	Prec., Aber., Nut.	Deduced Mean Z.D.
1844.					
May 2	1· 7· 4·30	·00	1·13	+16·52	1· 6·48·91
4	4·21	·00	1·14	16·83	48·52
8	3·96	·00	1·15	17·43	47·08
10	4·55	·01	1·15	17·72	47·07
13	7·37	·01	1·12	18·15	50·33

Carried forward,

Mean Zenith Distances of Stars observed at the Royal Observatory.

B.A.C. 7386—(continued).

	FACE OF SECTOR EAST.						FACE OF SECTOR WEST.				
Day of Observation 1843–4.	Apparent Zenith Distance, from Unreduced Observation.	Reduction for Az. Error, and Curv. of Path.	Refraction.	Precession, Aberration, and Nutation.	Deduced Mean Zenith Distance, 1844, Jan. 0; and Mean of Separate Results, uncorrected, for Error of Collimation.	Day of Observation 1843–4.	Apparent Zenith Distance, from Unreduced Observation.	Reduction for Az. Error, and Curv. of Path.	Refraction.	Precession, Aberration, and Nutation.	Deduced Mean Zenith Distance, 1844, Jan. 0; and Mean of Separate Results, uncorrected, for Error of Collimation.
1844.	° ′ ″	″	″	″	° ′ ″	1844.	° ′ ″	″	″	″	° ′ ″
May 14	1· 7· 7·71	·00	1·14	18·29	1· 6·50·56	May 20	1· 7· 6·58	·00	1·16	19·08	1· 6·48·66
16	9·64	·00	1·11	18·56	52·19	22	6·82	·00	1·12	19 34	48·60
21	10·23	·00	1·14	19·21	52·16	24	8·35	·01	1·12	19·58	49·88
23	11·36	·00	1·13	19 46	53·03	27	7·56	·01	1·14	19·93	48·76
25	11·22	·00	1·12	19·70	52 64	30	7·80	·00	1·13	20·26	48·73
June 1	11·76	·00	1·13	20·47	52·42	June 2	8·70	·00	1·16	20·58	49·27
4	12·30	·00	1·10	20·77	52·09	16	9·24	·01	1·17	21·75	48 05
17	13·11	00	1·15	21·82	52·44	18	9·34	·01	1·14	21·88	48·59
19	13·78	·00	1·15	21·94	52·09	20	9·04	·01	1·15	22·00	48·78
22	13·49	·00	1·14	22·11	52·52	24	9·49	·00	1·13	+22·20	48·42
25	12·94	·00	1·15	22·25	51·84						
29	12·15	·00	1·18	+22·40	50·03						
					1· 6·52·32						1· 6·48·78

Error of Collimation . . . = 0· 0· 1·77
Resulting Mean Zenith Distance, North = 1· 6·50·55

Anon. AR. 21·12

1844.						1844.					
May 7	4· 6 51·12	·00	4·22	+16·39	4· 6 38·95	May 8	4· 6·45·25	·02	4·22	+16·55	4· 6·32·90
9	52·06	·00	4·24	30 00	30·00	10	46 48	·02	4·25	16·85	33·86
14	50·83	·00	4·18	17·44	37·57	13	47·96	·02	4·14	17·30	34·78
16	52·95	·01	4·08	17·74	39·28	20	47·17	·01	4·25	18·29	33·12
21	52·80	·01	4·20	18·43	38·56	22	48·90	·01	4·12	18·56	34·45
23	54·43	·00	4·15	18·70	39·88	24	48·01	·02	4·13	18·83	33·89
25	53·69	·00	4·13	18·96	38·86	30	49·25	·00	4·17	19 58	33·84
29	54·93	·00	4·14	19·46	39·61	June 2	48 71	·01	4·24	19·93	33·01
June 1	54·78	·01	4·18	19·81	39·14	16	50·14	·02	4·30	21·29	33·13
4	55·81	·00	4·26	20·15	39·02	18	51·27	·02	4·19	21·45	33·09
17	55·57	·00	4·25	21·37	38·45	20	51·27	·03	4·23	21·60	33·87
19	56·21	·00	4·22	21·53	38·90	24	51·77	·01	4 18	21·87	34·07
22	55·52	·00	4·19	21·74	37·97	26	51 77	·01	4·13	21·99	33·90
25	56·55	·01	4·24	21·93	38·85	30	52·16	·01	4·26	+22·20	34·21
29	57·29	·00	4·33	+22·15	39·47						
					4· 6 39·00						4· 6·33·79

Error of Collimation . . . = 0· 0· 2·61
Resulting Mean Zenith Distance, North = 4· 6·36·30

Anon. AR. 21·26.

1844.						1844.					
May 7	3·33·11·20	·00	3·65	+16·98	3·32·57·87	May 8	3·33· 6·06	·01	3·64	+17·14	3·32·52·55
9	11·54	·00	3·66	17·30	57·90	10	6 51	·02	3·66	17·47	52·68
11	11·59	·00	3·59	17·63	57·55	13	8·58	·02	3 57	17·04	54·19

Carried forward.

Mean Zenith Distances of Stars observed at the Royal Observatory.

	FACE OF SECTOR EAST.						FACE OF SECTOR WEST.				
Day of Observation 1843-4.	Apparent Zenith Distance, from Unreduced Observation.	Reduction for Az. Error, and Curv. of Path.	Refraction.	Precession, Aberration, and Nutation.	Deduced Mean Zenith Distance, 18·4, Jan. 0; and Mean of Separate Results, uncorrected, for Error of Collimation.	Day of Observation 1843-4.	Apparent Zenith Distance, from Unreduced Observation.	Reduction for Az. Error, and Curv. of P. h.	Refraction.	Precession, Aberration, and Nutation.	Deduced Mean Zenith Distance, 1844, Jan. 0; and Mean of Separate Results, uncorrected, for Error of Collimation.

Anon. AR. 21·26—(continued).

1844.	o ′ ″	″	″	″	o ′ ″	1844.	o ′ ″	″	″	″	o ′ ″
May 14	3·33·11·74	·00	3·61	18·10	3·32·57·25	May 20	3·33· 7·40	·01	3·68	19·01	3·32·52·00
16	12·73	.01	3·58	18·41	57·80	22	8·83	·01	3·56	19·29	53·09
21	13·37	·01	3·02	19·17	57·83	27	8·43	·03	3·62	19·99	52·03
23	13·91	·00	3·58	19·44	58·05	30	9·47	·00	3·00	20·38	52·69
25	13·17	·00	3·57	19·72	57·52	June 2	11·00	·01	3·66	20·75	53·90
June 1	15·74	·01	3·61	20·03	58·71	16	11·35	·02	3·71	22·23	52·81
17	15·44	·00	3·67	22·3.	56·79	18	11·84	·02	3·02	22·40	53·04
19	17·32	·00	3·63	22·49	58·4.	20	11·59	·02	3·63	22·57	52·03
22	16·87	·00	3·61	22·72	57·76	24	12·04	·01	3·61	22·86	52·78
25	15·09	·01	3·66	22·93	56·41	26	11·54	·01	3·57	22·99	52·11
29	16·33	·00	3·74	+23·17	56·90	30	11·99	·01	3·09	+23·22	52·45
					3·32·57·04						3·32·52·79

Error of Collimation . . . = 0· 0· 2·42
Resulting Mean Zenith Distance, North = 3·32·55·21

B.A.C. 7557.

1843.						1843.					
Oct. 30	0·11·51·47	·00	0·50	- 2·30	0·11·(53·97)	Nov. 4	0·11·58·95	·00	0·20	- 2·66	0·11·61·81
Nov. 3	57·74	·00	·20	2·59	C0·53	1844.					
13	57·05	·01	·21	- 3·16	C0·43	May 7	0·12·18·03	·00	·21	+18·37	59·87
1844.						8	16·99	·00	·21	18·54	58·66
April 13	16·94	·02	·50	+13·94	63·18	10	18·87	·00	·21	18·88	60·20
May 9	23·16	·00	·21	18·71	64·06	11	17·24	·00	·21	19·04	58·41
14	20·65	·00	·21	19·53	61·33	13	19·02	·00	·21	19·37	59·86
16	24·25	·00	·21	19·85	64·61	20	17·93	·00	·21	20·46	57·68
21	23·85	·00	·21	20·61	63·45	22	20·20	·00	·21	20·75	59·66
23	24·79	·00	·21	20·90	64·10	24	20·66	·00	·21	21·04	59·86
25	24·45	·00	·21	21·18	63·48	27	20·25	·00	·21	21·45	59·01
29	24·84	·00	21	21·72	63·33	30	20·79	·00	·21	21·85	59·15
June 1	26·37	·00	·21	22·10	64·48	June 2	19·51	·00	·21	22·22	57·50
17	27·66	·12	·21	23·74	64·25	18	23·39	·00	·21	23·82	59·78
20	28·40	·00	·21	23·97	64·64	19	23·01	·00	·21	23·69	59·33
24	28·00	·00	0·21	+24·23	63·98	22	22·87	·00	0·21	+24·11	58·97
					0·12· 3·54						0·11·59·32

Error of Collimation . . . = 0· 0· 2·11
Resulting Mean Zenith Distance, North = 0·12· 1·43

B.A.C. 7613.

1843.						1843.					
Nov. 15	4· 9·38·97	·11	4·14	- 4·66	4· 9·38·34	Nov. 15	4· 9·39·07	·12	4·19	- 4·61	4· 9·38·53
Dec. 2	39·07	·12	4·10	5·01	38·04	Dec. 3	38·97	·18	4·09	- 5·00	37·88
4	39·07	·19	4·10	- 4·99	37·09						

Carried forward,

No. 7557.—June 17.—Correction for Curvature of Path 4·C·12.
No. 7557.— In taking the m.an, the observations of Novem b.r 3 and 13 are taken as one, to compare with the observation of November 4.

Mean Zenith Distances of Stars observed at the Royal Observatory.

	FACE OF SECTOR EAST.						FACE OF SECTOR WEST.				
Day of Observation 1843-4.	Apparent Zenith Distance, from Unreduced Observation.	Reduction for Az. Error, and Curv. of Path.	Refraction.	Precession, and Aberration, and Nutation.	Deduced Mean Zenith Distance, 1844, Jan. 0; and Mean of Separate Results, uncorrected, for Error of Collimation.	Day of Observation 1843-4.	Apparent Zenith Distance, from Unreduced Observation.	Reduction for Az. Error, and Curv. of Path.	Refraction.	Precession, and Aberration, and Nutation.	Deduced Mean Zenith Distance, 1844, Jan. 0; and Mean of Separate Results, uncorrected, for Error of Collimation.

B.A.C. 7613—(continued).

1844.	° ′ ″	″	′	′	° ′ ″	1844.	° ′ ″	″	′	′	° ′ ″
June 4	4· 9· 9·89	·00	4·30	+24·12	4· 9·38·31	May 30	4· 9·13·94	·00	4·22	+23·52	4· 9·41·68
18	5·50	·00	4·23	25·38	35·11	June 2	14·09	·01	4·29	23·89	42·26
20	5·60	·00	4·24	25·52	35·36	17	10·58	·02	4·29	25·31	40·16
24	5·89	·01	4·22	25·74	35·84	19	10·83	·03	4·24	25·45	40·49
29	3·57	·00	4·37	+25·95	33·89	22	10·44	·01	4·23	25·04	40·30
						25	11·45	·01	4·28	25·79	41·51
						26	10·63	·01	4·17	25·84	40·63
						30	10·39	·01	4·31	+25·98	40·67
					4· 9·36·61						4· 9·40·41

Error of Collimation . . . = 0· 0· 1·90
Resulting Mean Zenith Distance, South = 4· 9·38·51

B.A.C. 7657.

1843.						1843.					
Nov. 3	4·44· 1·16	·05	4·69	− 0·82	4·44· 6·62	Nov. 10	4·44· 0·07	·15	4·76	− 1·32	4·43·66·00
1844.						1844.					
May 9	20·21	·00	4·89	+17·51	7·59	May 10	15·87	·02	4·89	+17·69	63·05
11	20·75	·00	4·80	17·87	7·68	13	16·36	·03	4·76	18·23	62·86
14	21·00	+ ·21	4·82	18·41	7·62	20	17·70	·01	4·91	19·44	63·16
16	22·19	+ ·04	4·77	18·76	8·24	22	17·37	·01	4·75	19·77	62·34
21	21·02	·01	4·84	19·61	6·24	24	17·67	·02	4·76	20·09	62·32
23	22·33	·00	4·78	19·93	7·18	27	17·15	·04	4·83	20·57	61·37
25	22·95	·00	4·76	20·26	7·45	30	18·48	·00	4·82	21·03	62·27
29	23·42	·00	4·78	20·88	7·32	June 2	15·55	·01	4·90	21·47	58·97
June 1	23·79	·01	4·82	21·32	7·28	17	21·08	·02	4·80	23·38	62·57
4	25·56	·00	4·92	21·75	8·73	19	21·40	·03	4·84	23·59	62·62
18	25·61	·00	4·83	23·49	6·95	22	21·40	·01	4·82	23·89	62·32
20	25·20	·00	4·85	23·70	6·35	25	20·00	·01	4·89	24·17	61·61
24	24·82	·01	4·82	24·08	5·55	26	22·24	·01	4·76	24·26	62·73
29	26·68	·00	4·99	+24·50	7·17	30	21·84	·01	4·93	+24·57	62·19
					4·44· 7·20						4·44· 2·43

Error of Collimation . . . = 0· 0· 2·39
Resulting Mean Zenith Distance, North = 4·44· 4·81

Anon. AR. 21 56.

1843.						1843.					
Oct. 30	4·44·30·87	·02	4·68	− 0·42	4·44·(35·95)	Nov. 4	4·44·39·46	·09	4·72	− 0·83	4·44·44·92
Nov. 3	38·97	·05	4·70	− 0·75	44·37	1844.					
1844.						May 13	54·32	·03	4·77	+18·30	40·76
May 14	57·93	·00	4·83	+18·48	44·28	20	54·93	·01	4·92	19·53	40·31
16	60·05	·01	4·78	18·84	45·98	22	55·38	·01	4·76	19·87	40·26
21	59·72	·01	4·85	19·70	44·86	24	56·53	·02	4·78	20·20	41·09

Carried forward,

No. 7657.—June 14.—Correction for Azimuthal Error − ·005; for Curvature of Path + ·213. = + 0″·21.
,, 16.— ,,   ,,   ,, − ·012; ,, ,, + ·052. = + 0·04.

3 T

Mean Zenith Distances of Stars observed at the Royal Observatory.

	FACE OF SECTOR EAST.						FACE OF SECTOR WEST.				
Day of Observation 1843–4.	Apparent Zenith Distance, from Unreduced Observation.	Reduction for Az. Error, and Curv. of Path.	Refraction.	Precession, Aberration, and Nutation.	Deduced Mean Zenith Distance. 1844, Jan. 0; and Mean of Separate Results, uncorrected, for Error of Collimation.	Day of Observation 1843–4.	Apparent Zenith Distance, from Unreduced Observation.	Reduction for Az. Error, and Curv. of Path.	Refraction.	Precession, Aberration, and Nutation.	Deduced Mean Zenith Distance, 1844, Jan. 0; and Mean of Separate Results, uncorrected, for Error of Collimation.

Anon. AR. 21·56—(continued).

1844.						1844.					
May 23	4·44·60·15	·00	4·70	20·04	4·44·44·90	May 27	4·44·56·25	·04	4·85	20·08	4·44·40·38
25	61·11	·00	4·78	20·36	45·53	30	56·50	·00	4·83	21·15	40·18
29	61·83	·00	4·79	21·00	45·62	June 2	55·78	·01	4·91	21·00	30·08
June 1	62·14	·01	4·83	21·45	45·51	17	50·24	·02	4·91	23·56	40·57
4	61·90	·00	4·93	21·89	45·03	19	58·95	·03	4·85	23·77	41·00
18	64·02	·00	4·85	23·66	45·21	22	60·00	·01	4·84	24·08	40·75
20	63·41	·00	4·86	23·88	44·39	25	60·05	·01	4·90	24·37	40·57
24	65·89	·01	4·83	24·27	46·44	26	60·35	·01	4·77	24·45	40·66
29	62·52	·00	5·00	+24·70	42·82	30	59·36	·01	4·94	+24·78	39·51
					4·44·45·00						4·44·40·72

Error of Collimation . . . = 0· 0· 2·14
Resulting Mean Zenith Distance, North = 4·44·42·86

B.A.C. 7842.

1843.						1843.					
Nov. 3	0·47·23·06	·01	0·78	- 1·55	0·47·25·38	Nov. 1	0·47·23·21	·01	0·79	- 1·34	0·47·25·33
15	21·53	·02	·78	- 2·66	24·95	4	24·45	·02	·78	1·66	26·87
1844.						10	23·21	·03	·79	- 2·24	26·21
May 11	46·07	·00	·80	+19·59	27·28	1844.					
14	46·37	·00	·81	20·19	26·99	May 7	42·12	·00	·82	+18·76	24·18
16	46·02	·00	·80	20·58	26·24	8	43·21	·00	·81	18·07	25·05
21	48·74	·00	·81	21·53	28·02	13	44·00	·00	·80	19·09	24·81
23	49·92	·00	·80	21·00	28·82	20	45·13	·00	·82	21·35	24·60
25	50·51	·00	·80	22·26	29·05	22	44·98	·00	·80	21·72	24·06
29	50·46	·00	·80	22·96	28·30	24	46·32	·00	·80	22·08	25·04
June 1	50·91	·00	·81	23·45	28·27	27	46·81	·01	·81	22·61	25·00
4	51·94	·00	·83	23·03	28·84	30	46·32	·00	·81	23·12	24·01
18	53·67	·00	·81	25·83	28·65	June 2	45·82	·00	·82	23·61	23·03
20	54·26	·00	·81	26·06	29·01	17	49·92	·00	·82	25·72	25·02
24	54·76	·00	·81	26·48	29·09	19	50·02	·01	·81	25·95	24·87
26	54·96	·00	0·80	+26·67	29·09	22	50·36	·00	0·81	+26·28	24·89
					0·47·27·87						0·47·24·87

Error of Collimation . . . = 0· 0· 1·50
Resulting Mean Zenith Distance, North = 0·47·26·37

B.A.C. 7909.

1843.						1843.					
Oct. 30	3·45·25·87	·01	3·71	- 0·07	3·45·(20·64)	Nov. 1	3·45·30·36	·07	3·74	- 0·16	3·45·34·19
Nov. 3	32·20	·04	3·72	0·37	36·34	4	30·71	·08	3·74	0·48	34·85
15	31·09	·00	3·74	- 1·55	36·89	10	30·56	·12	3·78	1·09	35·31
1844.						14	30·11	·10	3·79	- 1·46	35·26
May 21	55·09	·01	3·82	+20·66	38·24	1844.					
23	55·49	·00	3·80	21·05	38·24	May 22	50·45	·01	3·77	+20·86	33·35
											Carried forward,

Mean Zenith Distances of Stars observed at the Royal Observatory.

	FACE OF SECTOR EAST.						FACE OF SECTOR WEST.				
Day of Observation 1843–4.	Apparent Zenith Distance, from Unreduced Observation.	Reduction for Az. Error, and Curv. of Path.	Refraction.	Precession, Aberration, and Nutation.	Deduced Mean Zenith Distance, 1844, Jan. 0; and Mean of Separate Results, uncorrected, for Error of Collimation.	Day of Observation 1843–4.	Apparent Zenith Distance, from Unreduced Observation.	Reduction for Az. Error, and Curv. of Path.	Refraction.	Precession, Aberration, and Nutation.	Deduced Mean Zenith Distance, 1844, Jan. 0; and Mean of Separate Results, uncorrected, for Error of Collimation.

B.A.C. 7909—(continued).

1844.						1844.					
May 25	3·45·56·28	·00	3·78	21·43	3·45·38·63	May 24	3·45·52·08	·02	3·78	21·24	3·45·34·60
June 1	57·71	·01	3·82	22·70	38·82	27	51·00	·03	3·85	21·80	33·02
4	58·40	·00	3·91	23·21	39·10	June 2	51·84	·01	3·89	22·68	32·84
19	59·49	·00	3·84	25·47	37·86	17	55·49	·02	3·88	25·21	34·14
20	61·21	·00	3·85	25·00	39·46	18	54·80	·02	3·84	25·34	33·28
24	61·02	·01	3·82	26·09	38·74	22	54·95	·01	3·83	25·85	32·92
26	61·81	+·09	3·79	26·31	39·38	25	55·88	·01	3·88	26·20	33·55
30	61·61	·00	3·91	26·73	38·79	29	56·03	·01	3·98	+26·63	33·37
					3·45·38·37						3·45·33·90

Error of Collimation . . = 0· 0. 2·24
Resulting Mean Zenith Distance, North = 3·45·36·13

B.A.C. 7966.

1843.						1843.					
Oct. 30	0·13·51·53	·00	0·23	- 0·78	0·13·52·54	Oct. 29	0·13·67·87	·00	0·24	- 0·64	0·13·68·75
Nov. 3	58·10	·00	·23	1·27	59·60	Nov. 4	58·14	·00	·23	1·39	59·76
15	56·76	·01	·23	- 2·58	59·56	10	56·32	·01	·23	2·05	58·59
1844.						14	56·71	·01	·24	- 2·48	59·42
May 11	81·05	·00	·24	+19·78	61·51	1844.					
16	81·45	·00	·24	20·85	60·84	May 8	76·85	·00	·24	+19·12	57·97
21	82·24	·00	·24	21·88	60·60	10	77·15	·00	·25	19·56	57·84
23	84·41	·00	·24	22·28	62·37	13	78·14	·00	·24	20·21	58·17
25	84·26	·00	·24	22·07	61·83	20	78·34	·00	·25	21·68	56·91
29	84·70	·00	·24	23·43	61·51	22	79·96	·00	·24	22·08	58·12
June 1	85·30	·00	·24	23·07	61·57	24	79·62	·00	·24	22·48	57·38
4	85·94	·00	·25	24·50	61·69	27	80·42	·00	·25	23·06	57·61
19	88·65	·00	·24	26·75	62·14	June 2	81·45	·00	·24	24·15	57·55
20	89·05	·00	·25	26·68	62·42	17	84·26	·00	·25	26·49	58·02
24	88·60	·00	·24	27·35	61·49	18	84·80	·00	·24	26·62	58·42
26	88·26	·00	·24	27·57	60·03	22	84·31	·00	·24	27·12	57·43
29	88·80	·00	0·25	+27·87	61·18	25	85·49	·00	0·25	·27·47	58·27
					0·14· 0·74						0·13·58·76

Error of Collimation . . = 0· 0· 0·99
Resulting Mean Zenith Distance, North = 0·13·59·75

B.A.C. 7992.

1843.						1843.					
Oct. 30	3·29· 3·53	·01	3·46	- 0·36	3·29· 6·62	Oct. 29	3·29·17·45	·06	3·52	+ 0·48	3·29·20·43
Nov. 3	9·65	·04	3·45	0·13	13·19	Nov. 1	6·73	·06	3·50	+ 0·11	10·06
13	9·25	·08	3·53	1·24	13·94	4	6·14	·07	3·47	- 0·25	9·79
15	9·45	·09	3·47	1·43	14·26	10	7·16	·11	3·52	0·92	11·49
Dec. 2	7·13	·09	3·44	2·76	13·24	14	5·30	·09	3·54	1·34	10·09

Carried forward,

No. 7909.—June 26.—Correction for Curvature of Path + 0'·09.

Mean Zenith Distances of Stars observed at the Royal Observatory.

FACE OF SECTOR EAST.

B.A.C. 7992—(continued).

Day of Observation 1843-4.	Apparent Zenith Distance, from Unreduced Observation.	Reduction for Al. Error, and Curv. of Path.	Refraction.	Precession, Aberration, Nutation.	Deduced Mean Zenith Distance, 1849, Jan. 0; and Mean of Separate Results, uncorrected, for Error of Collimation.
1843.	° ′ ″	″	″	″	° ′ ″
Dec. 4	3·29· 7·57	·14	3 46	2·86	3·29·13·75
12	7·43	·18	3·43	3 19	13·87
13	3·23	·18	3·42	3·22	(9·09)
16	7 03	·22	3·43	3·28	13·52
1844.					
Jan. 10	7·47	·20	3·33	2 83	13·34
13	7·18	·28	3·39	2·66	12·95
16	7·62	·30	3·38	2·46	13·16
19	8·41	·30	3·40	2·24	13·75
24	8·26	·28	3·39	1 82	13·19
25	7·57	·28	3·38	1·73	12·40
27	6·88	·27	3·39	1 53	11·53
31	8·41	·44	3·34	1·12	12·43
Feb. 5	10·78	·49	3·33	- 0·54	13·06
16	11·13	·40	3·34	+ 0·94	13·13
April 10	20·11	·42	3 40	11·06	11·43
13	22·09	·38	3·45	12·34	12·82
17	22·83	·45	3·50	13·26	12·62
21	25·44	·51	3·53	14·18	14·28
May 9	30·38	·00	3 61	18·25	15·74
11	30·97	·00	3·52	18 69	15·80
14	30·48	·00	3·55	19·35	14·08
16	30·97	·01	3·51	19·77	14·70
21	32·36	·01	3·54	20·82	15·07
23	33·36	·00	3·52	21·23	15·65
25	33·44	·00	3·50	21·63	15·31
29	33·94	·00	3·52	22·41	15·05
June 1	34·38	·01	3·54	22·97	14·94
4	37·49	·00	3 62	23·52	17·59
19	37·49	·00	3·56	25·93	15·12
20	37·49	·00	3·57	26·07	14·99
26	38·72	·00	3·51	26·84	15·39
29	39·27	·00	3 69	27·19	15·77
					3·29·13·84

FACE OF SECTOR WEST.

Day of Observation 1843-4.	Apparent Zenith Distance, from Unreduced Observation.	Reduction for Al. Error, and Curv. of Path.	Refraction.	Precession, Aberration, Nutation.	Deduced Mean Zenith Distance, 1844, Jan. 0; and Mean of Separate Results, uncorrected, for Error of Collimation.
1843.	° ′ ″	″	″	″	° ′ ″
Dec. 1	3·29· 4·81	·11	3·44	2·70	3·29·10·84
3	5·40	·14	3·45	2·81	11·52
9	4·51	·18	3·47	3 09	10·89
1844.					
Jan. 5	4·71	·24	3·38	3 06	10·91
7	5·30	·23	3·45	2·98	11·50
9	6·19	·34	3·39	2·88	12·12
12	4·61	·36	3·36	2·72	10·33
14	5·80	·38	3·41	2 60	11·43
18	6·09	·36	3·36	2 32	11·41
20	6·78	·36	3·29	2·16	11·87
26	7 02	·24	3·36	1·63	12·37
30	7·82	·27	3·35	1 23	12·13
Feb. 2	7·87	·30	3·40	- 0·00	11·87
25	10·44	·49	3·33	+ 2·34	10·94
April 14	21·35	·42	3·49	12·57	11·85
22	22·24	·51	3·50	14·41	10·82
May 2	22·48	·01	3·53	16 09	9·31
7	23·55	·02	3·57	17·81	9·29
8	24·01	·01	3·56	18·03	9·53
10	22·10	·02	3 00	18·46	7·29
13	24·85	·02	3·50	19·13	9 20
20	25·89	·01	3 00	20·61	8·67
22	26·38	·01	3·49	21·03	8·83
24	27·86	·02	3·51	21·43	9·92
27	26·83	·03	3·57	22·02	6·35
June 2	26·08	·01	3 00	23·16	7·11
17	31·07	·02	3 60	25·64	9·01
18	31·32	·02	3·56	25·79	9·07
22	31·12	·01	3·55	26·34	8·32
25	33·15	·01	3 60	26·72	10·02
30	32·21	·01	3 63	+27·30	8·53
					3·29·10·48

Error of Collimation . . . . = 0· 0· 1·68
Resulting Mean Zenith Distance, North = 3·29·12·16

B.A.C. 8025.

FACE OF SECTOR EAST.

Day of Observation	Apparent Zenith Distance	Reduction	Refraction	Precession, &c.	Deduced Mean Zenith Distance
1843.					
Nov. 3	1·39·25·00	·02	1 64	- 1·55	1·39·25·07
15	25·39	·04	1·65	- 3·00	24·00
					1·39·24·54

FACE OF SECTOR WEST.

Day of Observation	Apparent Zenith Distance	Reduction	Refraction	Precession, &c.	Deduced Mean Zenith Distance
1843.					
Nov. 4	1·30·26·23	·04	1 65	- 1·69	1·39·26·15
10	26·63	·06	1 67	2·44	25·90
14	27·07	·04	1 68	2·80	25·82
					1·39·25·02

Error of Collimation . . . . = 0· 0· 0·60
Resulting Mean Zenith Distance, South = 1·39·25·23

No. 7992.—Jan. 27.—Correction for Azimuthal Error = - ·71 ; for Curvature of Path + ·006. = - ·27.
     Feb. 5.—   ,,   ,,   ,, - ·522 ;   ,,   ,, + ·035. = - ·49.

Mean Zenith Distances of Stars observed at the Royal Observatory.

	FACE OF SECTOR EAST.						FACE OF SECTOR WEST.				
Day of Observation 1843–4.	Apparent Zenith Distance, from Unreduced Observation.	Reduction for Az. Error, and Curv. of Path.	Refraction.	Precession, Aberration, and Nutation.	Deduced Mean Zenith Distance, 1844, Jan. 0; and Mean of Separate Results, uncorrected, for Error of Collimation.	Day of Observation 1843–4.	Apparent Zenith Distance, from Unreduced Observation.	Reduction for Az. Error, and Curv. of Path.	Refraction.	Precession, Aberration, and Nutation.	Deduced Mean Zenith Distance, 1844, Jan. 0; and Mean of Separate Results, uncorrected, for Error of Collimation.
					B.A.C. 8201.						
1843.	° ′ ″	″	″	″	° ′ ″	1843.	° ′ ″	″	″	″	° ′ ″
Oct. 30	4 44 45·78	·02	4·71	− 0·92	4 44·(49·55)	Nov. 1	4 44 40·01	·09	4·77	− 1·25	4 44 43·44
Nov. 3	39·22	·06	4·71	1·58	42·29	4	41·73	·11	4·73	1·74	44·61
13	40·55	·13	4·80	3·10	42·12	14	42·13	·13	4·83	− 3·23	43·60
15	40·45	·13	4·72	− 3·37	41·67						
					4·44·42·03						4·44·43·88

Error of Collimation . . . $= 0· 0· 0·93$
Resulting Mean Zenith Distance, South $= 4·44·42·96$

MEAN ZENITH DISTANCES.

COLLECTION OF

ALL THE

RESULTS OF OBSERVATION OF EACH STAR

AT

THE ZWARTKOP STATION.

AND

DEDUCTION OF MEAN ZENITH DISTANCE, 1844, JANUARY 0.

NOTE.—The reduction for Azimuthal Error is always to be applied subtractively to the Zenith Distance. The reduction for Curvature of Path is always to be applied subtractively to South Zenith Distance, and additively to North Zenith Distance. The Refraction is always to be applied additively. The Precession, Aberration, and Nutation, have the sign which is proper for reducing the Apparent North Polar Distance of the Star to its mean North Polar Distance, 1844, January 0; and therefore are to be applied with the sign given in the Table when the Star is South of the Zenith, and with the opposite sign when the Star is North of the Zenith.

The numbers included in parentheses in the column " Deduced Mean Zenith Distance, 1844, January 0," are omitted in taking the mean.

Where an asterisk or a positive sign is affixed to a number in the 3rd or 9th columns, the explanation will be found at the bottom of the page.

☞ Owing to stormy weather while at this Station, the Sector had to be twice dismantled and taken to pieces. Consequently the total number of observations are thus separated into three groups, each group having a different error of collimation :—and generally, an unequal number of observations in the reversed positions of the Arch, viz.: Face of Sector East and Face of Sector West.

The groups are divided as follows :—From July 26 to August 20; from August 29 to September 10; from September 13 to October 2.

The mean Zenith distance of each Star has been calculated as follows :—The mean of the observations in each group face East, and the mean of the observations in each group face West, are set down separately; and the weight annexed to each is the least number of observations in either of the corresponding groups.

Then the three means, face East, are respectively multiplied by their weights, and the sums of the products are divided by the sums of the weights. The same course is pursued with the observations, face West.

All observations made on July 25, and not repeated on July 26, are omitted; see note page 97.

The observations on July 25 are very uncertain.

Mean Zenith Distances of Stars observed at the Zwartkop Station.

FACE OF SECTOR EAST. | FACE OF SECTOR WEST.

Day of Observation 1844.	Apparent Zenith Distance, from Unreduced Observation.	Reduction for Ax. Error, and Curv. of Path.	Refraction.	Precession, Aberration, and Nutation.	Deduced Mean Zenith Distance, 1844, Jan. 0; and Mean of Separate Results, uncorrected, for Error of Collimation.	Day of Observation 1844.	Apparent Zenith Distance, from Unreduced Observation.	Reduction for Ax. Error, and Curv. of Path.	Refraction.	Precession, Aberration, and Nutation.	Deduced Mean Zenith Distance, 1844, Jan. 0; and Mean of Separate Results, uncorrected, for Error of Collimation.
				B.A.C. 1802.							
July 28	0· 4·11·52	·00	0·07	+10·20	0· 3·61·39	July 29	0· 4· 3·88	·00	0·07	+10·43	0· 3·53·52
Aug. 4	11·98	·00	·07	11·76	60·29	Aug. 5	4·96	·00	·07	11·96	53·07
12	13·76	·00	·07	13·29	60·54	9	4·32	·00	·07	12·76	51·63
Sept. 2	12·97	·00	·07	16·13	56·91	11	6·40	·00	·07	13·14	53·33
5	14·05	·00	·07	16·35	57·77	30	9·21	·00	·07	15·86	53·42
8	14·30	·00	·07	16·53	57·84	Sept. 4	11·78	·00	·07	16·28	55·57
23	18·01	·00	·07	16·66	61·42	6	9·61	·00	·07	16·42	53·26
26	17·31	·00	·07	16·54	60·84	14	7·63	·00	·07	16·73	50·97
Oct. 1	16·62	·00	·07	+16·22	60·47	17	6·84	·00	·07	16·76	50·15
						28	7·19	·00	·07	16·43	50·83
						Oct. 2	6·78	·00	·07	+16·14	50·71
					0· 3·59·72						0· 3·52·55

Resulting Mean Zenith Distance, North = 0· 3·56·14

Day of Observation 1844.	Apparent Zenith Distance, from Unreduced Observation.	Reduction for Ax. Error, and Curv. of Path.	Refraction.	Precession, Aberration, and Nutation.	Deduced Mean Zenith Distance.	Day of Observation 1844.	Apparent Zenith Distance, from Unreduced Observation.	Reduction for Ax. Error, and Curv. of Path.	Refraction.	Precession, Aberration, and Nutation.	Deduced Mean Zenith Distance.
				B.A.C. 1878.							
July 28	1·35·58·94	·00	1·54	+ 9·04	1·36· 9·52	July 29	1·36· 6·50	·00	1·53	+ 9·28	1·36·17·31
Aug. 12	58·82	·04	1·50	12·28	10·56	Aug. 5	5·61	·00	1·54	10·86	18·01
Sept. 2	58·02	·00	1·57	15·20	13·45	9	5·51	·07	1·54	11·69	18·07
5	55·58	·00	1·53	15·51	12·02	11	4·33	·05	1·50	12·09	17·87
8	55·73	·01	1·54	15·71	12·07	Sept. 4	1·35·58·55	·07	1·56	15·44	15·48
18	52·37	·00	1·52	16·02	9·91	6	1·36· 0·52	·01	1·51	15·58	17·00
23	51·68	·00	1·51	15·96	9·15	14	2·15	·01	1·56	15·97	19·67
26	52·02	·01	1·55	15·86	9·42	17	3·49	·00	1·54	10·02	21·05
Oct. 1	52·91	·01	1·54	+15·58	10·02	28	3·34	·00	1·47	15·77	20·58
						Oct. 2	3·04	·00	1·51	+15·50	20·05
					1·36·10·58						1·36·18·80

Resulting Mean Zenith Distance, South = 1·36·14·69

Day of Observation 1844.	Apparent Zenith Distance, from Unreduced Observation.	Reduction for Ax. Error, and Curv. of Path.	Refraction.	Precession, Aberration, and Nutation.	Deduced Mean Zenith Distance.	Day of Observation 1844.	Apparent Zenith Distance, from Unreduced Observation.	Reduction for Ax. Error, and Curv. of Path.	Refraction.	Precession, Aberration, and Nutation.	Deduced Mean Zenith Distance.
				B.A.C. 2293.							
Aug. 4	5·27·46·69	·01	5·20	+ 1·98	5·27·50·04	July 29	5·27·36·76	·01	5·19	+ 0·60	5·27·41·34
8	48·58	·32	5·21	2·78	50·69	Aug. 5	38·95	·00	5·23	2·15	42·03
12	47·94	·14	5·10	3·59	49·31	9	38·90	·23	5·25	2·99	40·93
31	47·84	·00	5·27	6·68	46·43	10	38·00	·23	5·20	3·19	40·68
Sept. 2	47·15	·00	5·33	6·92	45·56	11	39·29	·16	5·10	3·39	40·64
5	48·48	·01	5·20	7·26	46·41	29	41·86	·03	5·23	6·42	40·64
8	47·94	·02	5·27	7·55	45·64	30	42·95	·03	5·28	6·55	41·65
18	51·45	·01	5·18	8·21	48·41	Sept. 4	43·94	·00	5·34	7·15	42·13
23	52·44	·01	5·17	8·35	49·25	6	42·80	·02	5·18	7·36	40·60
26	52·58	·02	5·28	8·38	49·46	9	42·40	·04	5·23	7·64	40·01
28	52·08	·03	5·02	8·37	49·30	15	39·79	·05	5·28	8·06	36·96

Carried forward,

No. 1878.—Sept. 4.—Correction for Curvature of Path = - 0'·07.

Mean Zenith Distances of Stars observed at the Zwartkop Station.

FACE OF SECTOR EAST.						FACE OF SECTOR WEST.					
Day of Observation 1844.	Apparent Zenith Distance, from Unreduced Observation.	Reduction for Az. Error, and Curv. of Path.	Refraction.	Precession, Aberration, and Nutation.	Deduced Mean Zenith Distance, 1844, Jan. 0; and Mean of Separate Results. uncorrected, for Error of Collimation.	Day of Observation 1844.	Apparent Zenith Distance, from Unreduced Observation.	Reduction for Az. Error, and Curv. of Path.	Refraction	Precession, Aberration, and Nutation.	Deduced Mean Zenith Distance. 1844, Jan. 0; and Mean of Separate Results. uncorrected, for Error of Collimation.
	° ′ ″	″	″	″	° ′ ″		° ′ ″	″	″	″	° ′ ″

B.A.C. 2293—(continued.)

Oct. 2	5·27·51·60	·03	5·16	+ 8·30	5·27·48·43	Sept. 17	5·27·39·49	·01	5·26	8·17	5·27·36·57
						27	40·97	·00	5·21	8·37	37·81
						Oct. 1	39·49	·00	5·27	+ 8·31	36·45
					5·27·48·24						5·27·39·39

Resulting Mean Zenith Distance, North = 5·27·43·82

B.A.C. 4458.

Aug. 6	1·39·55·50	·12	1·56	-23·10	1·39·33·84	Aug. 5	1·40· 4·45	·00	1·59	-23·22	1·39·42·82
9	55·50	·12	1·59	22·74	34·23	7	6·52	·07	1·57	22·98	45·04
12	55·55	·08	1·53	22·36	34·64	20	1·48	·02	1·57	21·27	41·76
Sept. 1	53·28	·00	1·57	19·45	35·40	Sept. 3	2·96	·24	1·56	19·13	45·15
5	54·27	·00	1·59	18·81	37·05	9	2·37	·01	1·54	18·16	45·74
15	47·55	·01	1·57	17·17	31·94	14	0·45	·01	1·57	17·33	44·68
26	46·12	·01	1·56	-15·38	32·29	18	1·58	·00	1·56	16·68	46·46
						28	2·03	·00	1·49	-15·06	48·46
					1·39·34·20						1·39·44·80

Resulting Mean Zenith Distance, South = 1·39·39·50

B.A.C. 4507.

Aug. 6	4·22·37·81	·33	4·11	-23·74	4·22·17·85	Aug. 7	4·22·46·90	* ·35	4·14	-23·63	4·22·27·06

Resulting Mean Zenith Distance, South = 4·22·22·46

B.A.C. 4579.

Aug. 9	1·58· 7·50	·12	1·88	-21·01	1·58·30·27	July 30	1·58·21·19	·00	1·88	-21·93	1·57·37·33

Resulting Mean Zenith Distance, North = 1·58·25·73

B.A.C. 4686.

Aug. 4	1·22·39·23	·00	1·33	-21·81	1·22·18·75	July 30	1·22·47·73	·00	1·32	-22·17	1·22·26·88
6	38·39	·10	1·30	21·64	17·95	Aug. 5	45·56	·00	1·32	21·73	25·15
8	37·16	·09	1·31	21·47	16·91	7	46·30	·05	1·30	21·56	25·99
9	37·01	·09	1·32	21·38	16·86	20	43·04	·02	1·20	20·25	24·06
11	38·79	·07	1·28	21·19	18·81	Sept. 9	40·27	·01	1·27	17·66	23·87
12	40·12	·04	1·27	21·10	20·25	13	42·64	·01	1·29	17·08	26·84
Sept. 1	35·73	·00	1·30	18 76	18·27	14	41·46	·01	1·30	16·93	25·82
5	35·87	·00	1·31	18·22	18·96	18	40·58	·00	1·29	16·34	25·53

Carried forward,

No. 4458.—Aug. 12.—Correction for Azimuthal Error - ·05; for Curvature of Path - ·03. Sum = -0″·08.
Sept. 3 — ,, Curvature of Path = -0″·24.
4507.—Aug. 7.— ,, Azimuthal Error - ·18; for Curvature of Path - ·17. Sum = -0″·35.

Mean Zenith Distances of Stars observed at the Zwartkop Station.

	FACE OF SECTOR EAST.						FACE OF SECTOR WEST.				
Day of Observation 1844.	Apparent Zenith Distance, from Unreduced Observation.	Reduction for Az. Error, and Curr. of Path.	Refraction.	Precession, Aberration, and Nutation.	Deduced Mean Zenith Distance. 1844, Jan. 0; and Mean of Separate Results, uncorrected, for Error of Collimation.	Day of Observation 1844.	Apparent Zenith Distance, from Unreduced Observation.	Reduction for Az. Error, and Curr. of Path.	Refraction.	Precession, Aberration, and Nutation.	Deduced Mean Zenith Distance. 1844, Jan. 0; and Mean of Separate Results, uncorrected, for Error of Collimation.
	° ′ ″	″	″	″	° ′ ″		° ′ ″	″	″	″	° ′ ″

B.A.C. 4686—(continued.)

Sept. 15	1·22·30·74	·01	1·30	16·79	1·22·15·24	Sept. 26	1·22·39·83	·00	1·29	15·16	1·22·25·96
21	29·55	·01	1·29	15·90	14·93	Oct. 2	38·00	·00	1·28	-14·27	25·01
24	31·28	·00	1·28	15·45	17·11						
28	30·59	·01	1·23	-14·85	16·96						
					1 22·17·32						1·22·25·48

Resulting Mean Zenith Distance, South = 1·22·21·40

B.A.C. 4745.

Aug. 4	2·56·32·24	·01	2·85	-21·69	2·56·13·39	July 30	2·56·41·04	·00	2·82	-22·01	2·56·21·85
6	31·99	·22	2·78	21·55	13·00	Aug. 5	40·00	·00	2·82	21·62	21·20
12	32·44	·08	2·71	-21·06	14·01	7	40·19	·12	2·79	-21·47	21·39
					2·56·13·47						2·56·21·48

Resulting Mean Zenith Distance, South = 2·56·17·48

B.A.C. 4784.

Aug. 4	5·25·59·78	·01	5·28	-18·46	5·26·23·51	July 30	5·25·50·20	·01	5·21	-18·76	5·26·14 16
6	5·26· 2·45	·37	5·14	-18·32	26·54	Aug. 5	51·18	·00	5·25	-18·39	14·82
					5·26·24·53						5·26·14 49

Resulting Mean Zenith Distance, North = 5·26·19·51

B.A.C. 4852.

Aug. 6	0·16·32·44	·02	0·26	-19·42	0·16·13·26	Aug. 5	0·16·41·18	·00	0·27	-19·48	0·16·21·97
9	31·65	·18	0·26	19·23	12·50	7	40·94	·01	0·26	19·36	21·83
11	33·67	·01	0·26	19·10	14·82	Sept. 26	35·20	·00	0·26	-14·13	21·33
Sept. 5	32·09	·00	0·26	-16·76	15·59						
					0·16·14·22						0·16·21·71

Resulting Mean Zenith Distance, South = 0·16·17·96

B.A.C. 4916.

Aug. 6	1· 0·14·62	·07	0·95	-18·24	1· 0·33·74	July 30	1· 0· 5·53	·00	0·96	-18·54	1· 0·25·03
9	14·87	·06	·96	18·08	33·85	Aug. 5	7·07	·00	·97	18·29	26·33
11	13·19	·05	·94	-17·96	32·04	7	6·13	·04	·96	-18·19	25·24
					1· 0·33·21						1· 0·25·53

Resulting Mean Zenith Distance, North = 1· 0·29·37

No. 4852.—Aug. 9.—Correction for Azimuthal Error - ·02 ; for Curvature of Path - ·16. = - 0″·18.

Mean Zenith Distances of Stars observed at the Zwartkop Station.

FACE OF SECTOR EAST.						FACE OF SECTOR WEST.					
Day of Observation 1844	Apparent Zenith Distance, from Unreduced Observation.	Reduction for Az. Error, and Curv. of Path.	Refraction.	Precession, Aberration, and Nutation.	Deduced Mean Zenith Distance, 1844, Jan. 0; and Mean of Separate Results, uncorrected, for Error of Collimation.	Day of Observation 1844.	Apparent Zenith Distance, from Unreduced Observation.	Reduction for Az. Error, and Curv. of Path.	Refraction.	Precession, Aberration, and Nutation.	Deduced Mean Zenith Distance, 1844, Jan. 0; and Mean of Separate Results, uncorrected, for Error of Collimation.

Anon. AR. 14 ᵇ 53 ᵐ.

	° ′ ″	″	″	″	° ′ ″		° ′ ″	″	″	″	° ′ ″
Aug. 6	2·11·55·07	·15	2·08	-17·35	2·12·14·35	July 30	2·11·44·79	·00	2·11	-17·62	2·12· 4·52
9	53·34	·13	2·10	17·20	12·51	Aug. 5	44·84	·00	2·13	17·39	4·36
11	54·37	·10	2·06	-17·09	13·42	7	45·93	·08	2·10	-17·30	5·25
					2·12·13·43						2·12· 4·71

Resulting Mean Zenith Distance, North = 2·12· 9·07

Anon. AR. 14 ᵇ 58 ᵐ.

	° ′ ″	″	″	″	° ′ ″		° ′ ″	″	″	″	° ′ ″
Aug. 6	1·55·13·34	·13	1·82	-17·16	1·55·32·19	July 30	1·55· 2·27	·00	1·84	-17·41	1·55·21·52
						Aug. 5	2·57	·00	1·86	17·20	21·63
						7	3·26	·07	1·83	-17·11	22·13
					1·55·32·19						1·55·21·76

Resulting Mean Zenith Distance, North = 1·55·26·98

B.A.C. 5032.

	° ′ ″	″	″	″	° ′ ″		° ′ ″	″	″	″	° ′ ″
July 29	4·39· 2·83	·01	4·48	-15·72	4·39·23·02	July 30	4·38·55·53	·01	4·47	-15·69	4·39·15·68

Resulting Mean Zenith Distance, North = 4·39·19·35

B.A.C. 5054.

	° ′ ″	″	″	″	° ′ ″		° ′ ″	″	″	″	° ′ ″
July 29	1·28· 1·63	·00	1·41	-17·44	1·27·45·60	July 30	1·28·10·62	·16	1·41	-17·43	1·27·54·44
Aug. 6	1·48	·11	1·40	17·26	45·51	Aug. 5	10·86	·00	1·42	17·29	54·99
9	0·69	·09	1·40	17·16	44·84	7	10·96	·06	1·40	17·23	55·07
11	2·32	·07	1·38	17·08	46·55	20	7·45	·02	1·40	16·60	52·23
12	1·96	·04	1·36	17·03	46·25	Sept. 2	5·33	·01	1·40	15·62	51·10
Sept. 1	1·03	·00	1·40	15·72	46·71	14	6·66	·01	1·39	14·44	53·60
5	1·43	·00	1·40	15·35	47·48	24	5·18	·00	1·36	13·30	53·24
18	1·27·57·43	·00	1·37	13·99	44·81	27	5·87	·00	1·34	-12·93	54·28
26	56·14	·01	1·38	13·06	44·45						
Oct. 2	55·15	·01	1·37	-12·31	44·20						
					1·27·45·44						1·27·53·62

Resulting Mean Zenith Distance, South = 1·27·49·53

No. 5054.—July 30.—Correction for Curvature of Path= - 0″·16.

Mean Zenith Distances of Stars observed at the Zwartkop Station.

	FACE OF SECTOR EAST.						FACE OF SECTOR WEST.				
Day of Observation 1844.	Apparent Zenith Distance, from Unreduced Observation.	Reduction for A.L. Error, and Curv. of Path.	Refraction.	Precession, Aberration, and Nutation.	Deduced Mean Zenith Distance, 1844, Jan. 0; and Mean of Separate Results, uncorrected, for Error of Collimation.	Day of Observation 1844.	Apparent Zenith Distance, from Unreduced Observation.	Reduction for A.L. Error, and Curv. of Path.	Refraction.	Precession, Aberration, and Nutation.	Deduced Mean Zenith Distance, 1844, Jan. 0; and Mean of Separate Results, uncorrected, for Error of Collimation.

B.A.C. 5151.

July 29	4 57 44·42	·01	4·78	-13·92	4·58· 3·11	July 30	4 57·33·27	·01	4·77	-13·90	4·57·51·93
Aug. 6	44·58	·34	4·74	13·74	2·72	Aug. 5	34·06	·00	4·82	13·77	52·65
11	45·02	·22	4·68	13·58	3·06	7	34·85	·18	4·75	13·71	53·13
12	44·18	·13	4·61	-13·54	2·20	20	36·73	·07	4·80	-13·18	54·64
					4·58· 2·77						4·57·53·09

Resulting Mean Zenith Distance, North = 4·57·57·93

Anon. AR. 15·34

July 29	3· 7·24·41	·01	3·00	-14·05	3· 7·41·45	July 30	3· 7·15·27	·00	3·00	-14·04	3· 7·32·31
Aug. 6	25·75	·22	2·98	13·92	42·43	Aug. 5	15·52	+ ·02	3·03	13·95	32·52
11	24·46	·14	2·94	-13·79	41·05	7	15·27	·12	2·99	-13·90	32·04
					3· 7·41·64						3· 7·32·29

Resulting Mean Zenith Distance, North = 3· 7·36·97

B.A.C. 5227.

July 29	1· 4·35·50	·00	1·03	-14·11	1· 4·50·64	July 30	1· 4·26·80	·00	1·03	-14·11	1· 4·41·94
Aug. 6	37·18	·08	1·03	14·04	52·17	Aug. 5	27·24	·00	1·04	14·06	42·34
11	35·89	+ ·05	1·01	13·94	50·89	7	27·34	·04	1·03	14·03	42·36
12	36·14	·03	1·00	13·91	51·02	20	29·27	·02	1·02	13·63	43·90
Sept. 1	33·52	·00	1·03	12·72	47·27	Sept. 8	32·33	·01	1·01	12·50	45·83
15	43·01	+ ·22	1·02	11·03	56·18	14	30·55	·01	1·02	12 0z	43·58
27	41·62	·00	0·99	-10·83	53·44	26	31·89	·00	1·01	-10·92	43·82
					1· 4·51·66						1· 4·43·40

Resulting Mean Zenith Distance, North = 1· 4·47·53

B.A.C. 5292.

Aug. 6	3·43 12·89	·28	3·56	-14·83	3·42·61·34	Aug. 5	3·43 22·92	·00	3·61	-14·83	3·43·11·70
9	12·54	·24	3·56	14·81	61·05	7	22·13	·15	3·57	14·83	10·72
11	14·37	·18	3·50	14·79	62·90	20	20·00	·00	3·55	14·58	8·91
12	12·59	·11	3·46	14·78	61·16	Sept. 2	16·79	·03	3·57	13·94	6·39
Sept. 1	13·53	·00	3·56	14·00	63·09	8	17·29	·04	3·51	13·51	7·25
5	12·89	·01	3·56	13·73	62·71	14	19·86	·03	3·53	13·02	10·34
18	8·84	·01	3·49	12·65	59·67	26	19·11	·00	3·51	-11·84	10·78
27	6·37	·00	3·42	11·73	58·06						
Oct. 2	7·45	·03	3·47	-11·17	59·72						
					3·43· 1·28						3·43· 9·44

Resulting Mean Zenith Distance, South = 3·43· 5·36

Anon. 15ʰ 34ᵐ.—Aug. 5.—Correction for Curvature of Path + ·02.   = + 0·02.
No. 5227.—Aug. 11.—Correction for Azimuthal Error — ·05; for Curvature of Path + ·10.   = + 0ʺ·05.
Sept. 15 —   ,,   ,,   ,, — ·01;   ,,   ,,   + ·23.   = + 0 ·22.

Mean Zenith Distances of Stars observed at the Zwartkop Station.

	FACE OF SECTOR EAST.						FACE OF SECTOR WEST.				
Day of Observation 1844.	Apparent Zenith Distance, from Unreduced Observation.	Reduction for Az. Error, and Curv. of Path.	Refraction.	Precession, Aberration, and Nutation.	Deduced Mean Zenith Distance, 1844, Jan. 0; and Mean of Separate Results, uncorrected, for Error of Collimation.	Day of Observation 1844.	Apparent Zenith Distance, from Unreduced Observation.	Reduction for Az. Error, and Curv. of Path.	Refraction.	Precession, Aberration, and Nutation.	Deduced Mean Zenith Distance, 1844, Jan. 0; and Mean of Separate Results, uncorrected, for Error of Collimation.
B.A.C. 5331.											
July 29	2· 8·50·39	·01	2·06	-13·66	2· 8·38·78	July 30	2· 8·58·79	·00	2·07	-13·68	2· 8·47·18
Aug. 4	50·09	·00	2·09	13·72	38·46	Aug. 5	59·23	·00	2·08	13·72	47·59
6	49·30	·16	2·05	13·72	37·47	7	58·79	·08	2·06	13·72	47·05
9	50·73	·01	2·06	13·71	39·07	Sept. 8	55·38	·02	2·03	12·54	44·85
11	50·59	·10	2·02	13·69	38·82	16	57·35	·00	2·02	11·92	47·45
12	49·84	·06	2·00	13·68	38·10	26	53·80	·10	2·02	-11·00	44·72
Sept. 1	51·13	·00	2·05	12·98	40·20						
5	51·23	·00	2·05	12·74	40·54						
15	44·71	·01	2·03	-12·01	34·72						
					2· 8·38·09						2· 8·46·55

Resulting Mean Zenith Distance, South = 2· 8·42·32

	Companion of 5331.										
July 29	2· 6· 6·81	·01	2·02	-13·59	2· 5·55·23	July 29	2· 6·15·45	·00	2·02	-13·60	2· 6· 3·87
Aug. 4	5·97	·00	2·05	13·65	54·37	Aug. 5	14·71	·00	2·04	13·65	3·10
6	6·95	·16	2·01	13·65	55·15	7	15·35	·08	2·02	-13·65	3·64
9	7·60	·01	2·01	13·64	55·96						
11	7·84	·10	1·98	13·62	56·10						
12	7·35	·06	1·95	-13·61	55·63						
					2· 5·55·41						2· 6· 3·54

Resulting Mean Zenith Distance, South = 2· 5·59·47

	B.A.C. 5374.										
July 29	5·13·26·82	·01	5·03	-10·91	5·13·42·75	Aug. 5	5·13·16·15	·00	5·08	-10·87	5·13·32·10
Aug. 4	27·17	·35	5·00	10·86	42·68	20	17·09	·19	5·02	10·84	32·76
11	27·12	·23	4·93	10·77	42·59		18·87	·07	5·05	-10·54	34·39
12	27·12	·13	4·87	-10·75	42·61						
					5·13·42·66						5·13·33·06

Resulting Mean Zenith Distance, North = 5·13·37·87

	B.A.C. 5435.										
July 29	3·42· 5·34	·01	3·56	-10·57	3·42·19·46	July 30	3·41·53·73	·00	3·56	-10·58	3·42· 7·87
Aug. 4	1·54	·01	3·61	10·59	15·73	Aug. 5	54·42	·00	3·59	10·58	8·59
6	3·92	·25	3·54	10·58	17·19		53·54	·14	3·55	-10·57	7·52
9	4·11	·22	3·55	10·56	18·00						
11	3·17	·17	3·48	10·53	17·01						
12	4·75	·10	3·44	-10·52	18·61						
					3·42·17·67						3·42· 7·99

Resulting Mean Zenith Distance, North = 3·42·12·83

No. 5331.—Sept. 26.—Correction for Azimuthal Error - ·00; for Curvature of Path - ·10. = -0·10.

Mean Zenith Distances of Stars observed at the Zwartkop Station.

	FACE OF SECTOR EAST.						FACE OF SECTOR WEST.				
Day of Observation 1844.	Apparent Zenith Distance, from Unreduced Observation.	Reduction for At. Error, and Curv. of Path.	Refraction.	Precession, Aberration, and Nutation.	Deduced Mean Zenith Distance, 1844, Jan. 0; and Mean of Separate Results, uncorrected, for Error of Collimation.	Day of Observation 1844.	Apparent Zenith Distance, from Unreduced Observation	Reduction for At. Error, and Curv. of Path.	Refraction.	Precession, Aberration, and Nutation.	Deduced Mean Zenith Distance, 1844, Jan. 0; and Mean of Separate Results, uncorrected, for Error of Collimation.

B.A.C. 5508.

Day						Day					
July 29	0· 8· 1·63	·00	0·13	-10·55	0· 7·51·21	Aug. 5	0· 8·11·26	·00	0·13	-10·67	0· 7·60·72
Aug. 4	2·27	·00	·13	10·66	51·73	7	10·96	·01	·13	10·69	60·39
6	1·38	·01	·13	10·68	50·82	9	11·01	·01	·13	10·70	60·43
12	1·53	·00	·13	10·71	50·95	11	9·63	·00	·13	10·71	59·05
Sept. 1	2·56	·00	·13	10·32	52·37	20	10·27	·00	·13	10·64	59·76
5	4·29	·00	·13	10·15	54·27	Sept. 8	8 10	·00	·13	10·01	58·22
15	0· 7·57·57	·00	·13	9·61	48·09	14	10·07	·00	·13	- 9·67	60·53
26	57·08	·00	·13	- 8·82	48·39						

| | | | | | 0· 7·51·04 | | | | | | 0· 7·59·84 |

Resulting Mean Zenith Distance, South = 0· 7·55·44

B.A.C. 5538.

Day						Day					
July 29	0·42·11·53	·00	0·68	-10·19	0·41·62·02	July 30	0·42·19·88	·00	0·68	-10·22	0·42·10·34
Aug. 4	12·57	·00	·69	10·33	62·93	Aug. 5	18·44	·00	·68	10·35	8·77
6	12·02	·05	·67	10·36	62·28	7	18·89	·03	·68	10·37	9·17
8	11·58	·04	·68	10·39	61·83	11	17·90	·02	·66	10·41	8·13
12	11·63	·02	·65	10·41	61·85	20	17·46	·01	·67	10·38	7 74
Sept. 1	13·21	·00	·67	10·10	63·78	Sept. 6	14·90	·01	·67	9·81	5·84
5	12·76	·00	·67	9·95	63·48	14	16·81	·01	·67	9·49	7·98
Oct. 2	6·69	·00	·66	- 8 18	59·17	18	17·26	·10	·66	- 9·24	8·58

| | | | | | 0·42· 1·96 | | | | | | 0·42· 8·32 |

Resulting Mean Zenith Distance, South = 0·42· 5·14

B.A.C. 5588.

Day						Day					
July 29	2·25·15·81	·01	2·33	- 8·50	2·25·26·63	July 30	2·25· 7·11	·00	2·33	- 8·52	2·25·17·96
Aug. 4	15·32	·00	2·36	8·60	26·28	Aug. 5	7·86	·00	2·35	8·61	16·82
6	18·28	·17	2·32	8·62	29·05	7	7 51	·09	2·32	8·63	18·37
8	17·34	·15	2·32	8·64	28·15	11	7·66	·08	2·28	- 8·65	18·51
12	16·30	·06	2·25	- 8·65	27·14						

| | | | | | 2·25·27·45 | | | | | | 2·25·18·41 |

Resulting Mean Zenith Distance, North = 2·25·22·93

B.A.C. 5632.

Day						Day					
July 25	0·13·13·37	·10	0·21	- 8·30	0·13·21·78	July 26	0·13·13·09	·00	0·21	- 8·33	0·13·21·63
29	15·71	·00	·21	8·43	24·35	30	8·10	·00	·21	8·46	16·77
Aug. 4	15·66	·00	·21	8·59	24·46	Aug. 5	8·34	·00	·21	8·61	17·16
6	17·68	·02	·21	8·63	26·50	9	8·54	·01	·21	8·65	17·39
8	16·05	·01	·21	8·67	24·92	9	8·00	·01	·21	8·68	16·88
12	16·00	·01	·21	8·72	24·92	11	8·25	·01	·21	8·71	17·16

Carried forward,

No. 5538.—Sept. 18.—Correction for Curvature of Path -0″·10.

Mean Zenith Distances of Stars observed at the Zwartkop Station.

FACE OF SECTOR EAST.						FACE OF SECTOR WEST.					
Day of Observation 1844.	Apparent Zenith Distance, from Unreduced Observation.	Reduction for Az. Error, and Curv. of Path.	Refraction.	Precession, Aberration, and Nutation.	Deduced Mean Zenith Distance, 1844, Jan. 0; and Mean of Separate Results, uncorrected, for Error of Collimation.	Day of Observation 1844.	Apparent Zenith Distance, from Unreduced Observation.	Reduction for Az. Error, and Curv. of Path.	Refraction.	Precession, Aberration, and Nutation.	Deduced Mean Zenith Distance, 1844, Jan. 0; and Mean of Separate Results, uncorrected, for Error of Collimation.

B.A.C. 5632—(continued).

Day	Apparent Z.D.	Red.	Refr.	Prec.	Deduced	Day	Apparent Z.D.	Red.	Refr.	Prec.	Deduced
Sept. 1	0·13·13·88	·00	·21	8·57	0·13·22·66	Sept. 3	0·13·11·85	·00	·21	8·51	0·13·20·57
5	13·78	·00	·21	8 45	22·44	8	11·11	·00	·21	8·35	19·67
15	18·52	·00	·21	8·04	26·77	14	8·44	·00	·21	8·09	16·74
21	17·73	·00	·21	7·71	25·65	18	8·74	·00	·21	7·88	16·83
27	19·26	·00	·20	- 7·32	26·78	26	8·64	·00	·21	- 7·39	16·24
					0·13·24·66						0·13·17·91

Resulting Mean Zenith Distance, North = 0·13·21·29

B.A.C. 5735.

Day	Apparent Z.D.	Red.	Refr.	Prec.	Deduced	Day	Apparent Z.D.	Red.	Refr.	Prec.	Deduced
July 20	0·19·41·92	·00	0·31	- 6·80	0·19·49·03	July 20	0·19·33·37	·00	0·31	- 6·83	0·19·40·51
Aug. 4	41·33	·00	·32	7·00	48·65	Aug. 5	33·07	·00	·32	7·02	40·41
6	42·26	·02	·31	7·05	49·60	9	33·92	·01	·31	7·08	41·30
8	41·57	·02	·31	7·10	48·96	11	33·10	·01	·31	7·12	40·52
12	41·42	·01	·30	7·18	48·89	Sept. 3	33·96	·01	·31	7·16	41·42
Sept. 2	38·26	·00	·32	7·19	45·77	14	36·39	·00	·31	7·17	43·87
5	39·50	·00	·31	7·13	46·94	18	32·53	·00	·31	6·85	39·69
15	43·80	·00	·31	- 6·81	50·92		33·42	+ ·10	·31	- 6·69	40·52
					0·19·48·92						0·19·41·16

Resulting Mean Zenith Distance, North = 0·19·45·04

B.A.C. 5817.

Day	Apparent Z.D.	Red.	Refr.	Prec.	Deduced	Day	Apparent Z.D.	Red.	Refr.	Prec.	Deduced
July 29	1·44·43·70	·00	1·68	- 5·03	1·44·50·41	July 30	1·44·35·40	·00	1·68	- 5·07	1·44·42·15
Aug. 4	43·40	·00	1·70	5·23	50·83	Aug. 5	34·51	·00	1·69	5·26	41·46
8	43·65	·11	1·68	5·34	50·56	11	35·40	·05	1·65	5·41	42·41
12	42·96	·05	1·63	5·43	49·97	Sept. 3	37·03	·00	1·67	5·53	44·23
Sept. 2	40·19	·00	1·69	5·54	47·42	6	36·58	·01	1·62	5·48	43·67
5	40·04	·00	1·67	- 5·50	47·21		37·08	·02	1·66	- 5·45	44·17
					1·44·49·12						1·44·42·81

Resulting Mean Zenith Distance, North = 1·44·45·97

B.A.C. 5981.

Day	Apparent Z.D.	Red.	Refr.	Prec.	Deduced	Day	Apparent Z.D.	Red.	Refr.	Prec.	Deduced
July 29	4·30·19·96	·01	4·34	- 3·14	4·30·27·43	July 30	4·30·11·81	·01	4·34	- 3·16	4·30·19·30
Aug. 4	20·26	·01	4·40	3·30	27·95	Aug. 5	11·17	·00	4·38	3·32	18·87
6	20·95	·31	4·32	3·34	28·30	7	11·71	·16	4·35	3·37	19·27
8	20·60	·26	4·34	3·30	28·07	Sept. 8	13·73	·00	4·33	3·57	21·63
12	20·21	·12	4·20	3·46	27·75		14·43	·04	4·29	3·51	22·19
Sept. 2	17 14	·00	4·37	3·58	25·09	14	10·38	·04	4·31	3·48	18·05
5	18·03	·01	4·33	3·55	25·90	18	12·65	+ ·20	4·25	3·30	20·40

Carried forward,

No. 5735.—Sept. 18.—Correction for Curvature of Path + 0"·10.
,, 5981.— ,, 18.— ,, Azimuthal Error - ·01; for Curvature of Path + ·21. = + 0"·20.

Mean Zenith Distances of Stars observed at the Zwartkop Station.

FACE OF SECTOR EAST.   FACE OF SECTOR WEST.

Day of Observation 1844.	Apparent Zenith Distance, from Unreduced Observation.	Reduction for Az. Error, and Curr. of Path.	Refraction.	Precession, Aberration, and Nutation.	Deduced Mean Zenith Distance, 1844, Jan. 0; and Mean of Separate Results, uncorrected, for Error of Collimation.	Day of Observation 1844.	Apparent Zenith Distance, from Unreduced Observation.	Reduction for Az. Error, and Curr. of Path.	Refraction.	Precession, Aberration, and Nutation.	Deduced Mean Zenith Distance, 1844, Jan. 0; and Mean of Separate Results, uncorrected, for Error of Collimation.

B.A.C. 5881—(continued).

Day	App. Z.D.	Red.	Refr.	Prec.	Deduced	Day	App. Z.D.	Red.	Refr.	Prec.	Deduced
Sept. 15	4 30 20·00	·02	4·29	3·38	4 30 28·25	Sept. 26	4 30 10·77	·00	4·28	- 3·04	4 30 18·09
19	21 00	·01	4·19	3·27	28·45						
27	21·19	·01	4·16	- 3·00	28·34						
					4·30·27·47						4·30·19·73

Resulting Mean Zenith Distance, North = 4·30·23·60

B.A.C. 5915.

Day	App. Z.D.	Red.	Refr.	Prec.	Deduced	Day	App. Z.D.	Red.	Refr.	Prec.	Deduced
July 29	2 45 21·39	·01	2·65	- 4·28	2 45 19·75	July 30	2 45 30·48	·00	2·65	- 4·34	2 45 28·79
Aug. 4	22·63	·00	2·69	4·62	20·70	Aug. 5	30·63	·00	2·68	4·68	28·63
6	22·43	·20	2·65	4·73	20·15	7	31·27	·11	2·66	4·78	29·04
8	21·84	·18	2·65	4·83	19·48	9	31·03	·13	2·65	4·87	28·68
12	22·78	·08	2·57	5·01	20·26	11	30·93	·09	2·60	4·96	28·48
Sept. 2	24·50	·00	2·07	5·51	21·66	Sept. 3	28·06	·00	2·65	5·52	25·19
5	23·86	·00	2·65	5·52	20·99	6	29·54	·12	2·56	5·52	26·46
15	20·05	·02	2·63	5·41	18·15	8	28·60	·03	2·62	5·51	25·68
19	20·16	·01	2·56	5·31	17·40	14	31·92	·03	2·65	5·43	29·11
27	21·54	·00	2·55	5·01	19·08	18	31·62	·00	2·60	5·34	28·88
Oct. 2	20·21	·02	2 58	- 4·76	18·01	26	31·72	·00	2·61	5·06	29·27
						Oct. 1	31·57	·00	2·59	- 4·82	29·34
					2·45·19·60						2·45·28·34

Resulting Mean Zenith Distance, South = 2·45·23·97

B.A.C. 5970.

Day	App. Z.D.	Red.	Refr.	Prec.	Deduced	Day	App. Z.D.	Red.	Refr.	Prec.	Deduced
July 29	4 42 52·14	·01	2·61	- 3·69	4 42 51·05	July 30	4 42 60·54	·01	2·61	- 3·76	4 42 59·38
Aug. 6	53·42	·36	2 61	4·23	51·44	Aug. 5	62·12	·00	2·64	4·17	60·59
8	51·94	·31	2·61	4·35	49·89	7	61·77	·19	2·62	4·29	59·91
12	52·58	·14	2·53	4·57	50·40	9	61·43	·22	2·61	4·41	59·41
Sept. 2	55·15	·00	2·63	5·30	52·48	11	61·03	·19	2·56	4·52	58·88
5	55·20	·01	2·01	5·33	52·47	Sept. 3	59·70	·00	2·61	5·31	57·00
15	50·95	·03	2·59	5·29	48·22	6	59·45	·02	2·52	5·33	56·02
19	51·15	·01	2·52	5·22	48·44	8	59·99	·05	2·59	5·34	57·19
27	51·99	·01	2·51	4·96	49·53	14	62·96	·04	2·61	5·31	60·22
Oct. 2	50·06	·03	2·55	- 4·73	47·85	18	62·61	·01	2·56	5·24	59·92
						26	61·03	·00	2·58	5·00	59·21
						Oct. 1	61·72	·00	2·56	- 4·78	59·50
					4·42·50·18						4·42·59·13

Resulting Mean Zenith Distance, South = 4·42·54·65

No. 5915.—Sept. 6.—Correction for Azimuthal Error - ·01; for Curvature of Path - ·11. = - 0"·12.
„ 5970.—Aug. 11.— „ „ „ - ·16; „ „ - ·03. = - 0 ·19.

Mean Zenith Distances of Stars observed at the Zwartkop Station.

FACE OF SECTOR EAST.

B.A.C. 6016.

Day of Observation 1844.	Apparent Zenith Distance, from Unreduced Observation.	Reduction for Az. Error, and Curv. of Path.	Refraction.	Precession, Aberration, and Nutation.	Deduced Mean Zenith Distance, 1844, Jan. 0; and Mean of Separate Results, uncorrected, for Error of Collimation.
July 25	2·34·57·73	1·19	2·42	- 0·95	2·34·59·91
29	60·74	·01	2 40	1·12	35· 4·34
Aug. 4	60·84	·00	2·52	1·37	4·73
6	61·83	·18	2·48	1·44	5·57
8	61·09	·15	2·48	1·52	4·94
12	61·28	·07	2·41	1·65	5·27
Sept. 2	57·73	·00	2·50	2·09	2·32
5	56·94	·00	2·48	2·11	1·53
15	61·38	·01	2·47	2·08	5·92
27	59·90	·00	2·40	- 1·84	4·14
					2·35· 3·84

FACE OF SECTOR WEST.

B.A.C. 6016.

Day of Observation 1844.	Apparent Zenith Distance, from Unreduced Observation.	Reduction for Az. Error, and Curv. of Path.	Refraction.	Precession, Aberration, and Nutation.	Deduced Mean Zenith Distance, 1844, Jan. 0; and Mean of Separate Results, uncorrected, for Error of Collimation.
July 26	2·34·57·78	·00	2·45	- 0·99	2·34·61·22
30	51·50	·00	2·48	1·16	55·14
Aug. 7	51·01	·10	2·49	1·48	54·88
9	50·56	·11	2·48	1·55	54·48
11	51·50	·08	2·44	1·02	55·48
Sept. 3	52·54	·00	2·48	2·10	57·12
6	51·85	·01	2·39	2·11	56·34
8	52·05	·03	2·47	2·12	58·61
14	48·74	·02	2·48	2·09	53·29
18	50·52	·00	2·43	2·04	54·99
26	49·53	·00	2·45	- 1·87	53·85
					2·34·55·85

Resulting Mean Zenith Distance, North = 2·34·59·84

B.A.C. 6074. (FACE OF SECTOR EAST)

Day of Observation 1844.	Apparent Zenith Distance, from Unreduced Observation.	Reduction for Az. Error, and Curv. of Path.	Refraction.	Precession, Aberration, and Nutation.	Deduced Mean Zenith Distance.
July 25	3·59·42·22	1·82	3·74	+ 0·53	3·59·43·61
29	44·64	·01	3·85	0·37	48·11
Aug. 4	44·78	·01	3·90	0·14	48·53
6	45·82	·27	3·84	+ 0·07	49·32
8	45·28	·24	3 85	0·00	48·80
12	45·38	·10	3·73	- 0·13	49·14
Sept. 2	42·07	·00	3·88	0·60	46·55
5	41·42	·01	3·84	0·63	45·88
15	44·88	·02	3·82	0·64	49·32
19	46·17	·01	3·73	0·61	50·50
27	44·49	·00	3·71	- 0·48	48·08
					3·59·48·05

B.A.C. 6074. (FACE OF SECTOR WEST)

Day of Observation 1844.	Apparent Zenith Distance, from Unreduced Observation.	Reduction for Az. Error, and Curv. of Path.	Refraction.	Precession, Aberration, and Nutation.	Deduced Mean Zenith Distance.
July 26	3·59·42·17	·00	3·79	+ 0·49	3·59·45·47
30	35·35	·00	3·84	0·33	38·86
Aug. 5	35·40	·00	3·89	0·11	39·18
7	34·05	·14	3·85	+ 0·04	38·62
9	34·61	·17	3·84	- 0·03	38·31
11	35·60	·12	3·78	0·10	39·36
Sept. 6	36·44	·01	3·71	0·63	40·77
8	35·60	·04	3·82	0·64	40·02
14	32·29	·03	3·84	0·64	36·74
18	32·98	·01	3·77	0·62	37·36
26	34·51	+ ·08	3·79	- 0·50	38·98
					3·59·39·42

Resulting Mean Zenith Distance, North = 3·59·43·73

B.A.C. 6115. (FACE OF SECTOR EAST)

Day of Observation 1844.	Apparent Zenith Distance, from Unreduced Observation.	Reduction for Az. Error, and Curv. of Path.	Refraction.	Precession, Aberration, and Nutation.	Deduced Mean Zenith Distance.
July 25	3·48·24·99	1·74	3·56	+ 1·28	3·48·25·53
29	26·77	·01	3·67	1·11	29·32
Aug. 4	26·62	·01	3·71	0·87	29·57
6	27·46	·26	3·66	0·79	30·07
8	26·82	·23	3·66	0·72	29·58
12	26·13	·10	3·55	0·58	29·00
Sept. 2	22·92	·00	3·70	+ 0·03	26·59
5	22·87	·01	3·66	- 0·01	26·53
15	26·62	·02	3·64	- 0·07	30·31
19	27·32	·01	3·55	- 0·05	30·91
25	26·62	·01	3·66	+ 0·01	30·26
					3·48·28·86

B.A.C. 6115. (FACE OF SECTOR WEST)

Day of Observation 1844.	Apparent Zenith Distance, from Unreduced Observation.	Reduction for Az. Error, and Curv. of Path.	Refraction.	Precession, Aberration, and Nutation.	Deduced Mean Zenith Distance.
July 26	3·48·23·91	·00	3·61	+ 1·24	3·48·26·28
30	17·43	·00	3·66	1·07	20·02
Aug. 5	17·04	·00	3·70	0·83	19·91
7	17·63	·14	3·67	0·76	20·40
9	16·99	·16	3·66	0·68	19·81
11	18·13	·12	3·60	0·61	21·00
Sept. 3	20·00	+ ·10	3·66	+ 0·02	23·74
6	19·21	·01	3·54	- 0·02	22·76
8	17·88	·04	3·04	0·04	21·52
14	15·06	·03	3·66	0·07	18·76
18	15·71	·01	3·59	0·06	19·35
21	15·71	·00 *	3·61	- 0·04	19·36
					3·48·20·93

Resulting Mean Zenith Distance, North = 3·48·24·90

No. 6074.—Sept. 26.—Correction for Azimuthal Error - ·01 ; for Curvature of Path + ·09. = +0"·08.
„ 6115.— „ 3.— „ „ „ - ·00 ; „ „ + ·10. = + 0 ·10.

Mean Zenith Distances of Stars observed at the Zwartkop Station.

FACE OF SECTOR EAST. / FACE OF SECTOR WEST.

B.A.C. 6145.

Day of Observation 1844.	Apparent Zenith Distance, from Unreduced Observation.	Reduction for Az. Error, and Curr. of Path.	Refraction.	Precession, Aberration, and Nutation.	Deduced Mean Zenith Distance, 1844, Jan. 0; and Mean of Separate Results, uncorrected, for Error of Collimation.	Day of Observation 1844.	Apparent Zenith Distance, from Unreduced Observation.	Reduction for Az. Error, and Curr. of Path.	Refraction.	Precession, Aberration, and Nutation.	Deduced Mean Zenith Distance, 1844, Jan. 0; and Mean of Separate Results, uncorrected, for Error of Collimation.
July 20	3 28 49·55	·01	3·35	+ 1·54	3 28 51·35	July 30	3 28 38·98	·00	3·35	+ 1·50	3 28 40·83
Aug. 4	48·76	·01	3·39	1·28	50·86	Aug. 5	37·99	·00	3·39	1·24	41·14
6	49·60	·25	3·34	1·20	51·49	7	38·38	·13	3·34	1·16	40·43
8	48·96	·22	3·35	1·12	50·97	9	38·28	·16	3·35	1·08	40·39
12	48·41	·10	3·25	0·07	50·59	11	39·27	·11	3·29	1·00	41·45
Sept. 2	44·45	·00	3·38	0·36	47·47	Sept. 6	38·98	·01	3·24	0·30	41·01
5	45·09	·00	3·34	0·31	48·72	8	38·48	·03	3·33	0·27	41·51
15	48·36	·02	3·32	0·23	51·43	14	35·91	·03	3·34	0·23	38·99
10	48·61	·01	3·25	+ 0·23	51·62	18	36·60	·00	3·28	0·23	39·05
						21	35·81	·00	3·30	0·24	38·87
					3·28·50·50						3·28·40·07

Resulting Mean Zenith Distance, North = 3 28 45·59

B.A.C. 6186.

Day of Observation 1844.	Apparent Zenith Distance, from Unreduced Observation.	Reduction for Az. Error, and Curr. of Path.	Refraction.	Precession, Aberration, and Nutation.	Deduced Mean Zenith Distance.	Day of Observation 1844.	Apparent Zenith Distance, from Unreduced Observation.	Reduction for Az. Error, and Curr. of Path.	Refraction.	Precession, Aberration, and Nutation.	Deduced Mean Zenith Distance.
July 25	2 34 28·12	1·27	2·41	+ 1·45	2 34 30·71	July 26	2 34 25·86	·00	2·44	+ 1·37	2 34 29·67
29	22·55	·01	2·48	1·15	26·17	30	31·49	·00	2·48	1·07	35·04
Aug. 4	22·85	·00	2·51	0·72	26·08	Aug. 5	32·28	·00	2 50	0·65	35·43
6	22·05	·19	2·47	0·58	25·51	7	32·83	·10	2·47	0·51	35·71
8	21·37	·16	2·48	0·44	24·13	9	32·78	12	2 48	0·38	35·52
12	23·34	·07	2·41	0·18	25·86	11	31·45	·08	2·43	+ 0·24	34·04
Sept. 2	25·81	·00	2·50	– 0·88	27·43	Sept. 6	31·03	·01	2·39	– 1·01	32 42
5	26·26	·00	2·47	0·98	27·75	14	35·05	·02	2·47	1·17	36·33
15	22·70	01	2·46	1·18	23·97	18	35·15	·00	2·43	1·21	36·37
19	22·50	·01	2·41	1·22	23·68	21	34·06	·00	2·44	1·22	35·28
25	23·39	·01	2·47	1 20	24·65	27	34·51	·00	2·40	– 1·18	35·73
26	23·24	·01	2·45	– 1·19	24·49						
					2·34·25·71						2 34 34 69

Resulting Mean Zenith Distance, South = 2 34 30·20

B.A.C. 6233.

Day of Observation 1844.	Apparent Zenith Distance, from Unreduced Observation.	Reduction for Az. Error, and Curr. of Path.	Refraction.	Precession, Aberration, and Nutation.	Deduced Mean Zenith Distance.	Day of Observation 1844.	Apparent Zenith Distance, from Unreduced Observation.	Reduction for Az. Error, and Curr. of Path.	Refraction.	Precession, Aberration, and Nutation.	Deduced Mean Zenith Distance.
July 20	0 13 23·76	·00	·22	+ 2·44	0 13 26 42	July 30	0 13 32·21	·00	·22	+ 2·38	0 13 34·81
Aug. 4	24·89	·00	·22	2·06	27·17	Aug. 5	32·21	·00	·22	2·00	34·43
6	24·45	·02	·22	1·94	26·50	7	31·66	·01	·22	1·88	33·75
8	23·31	·01	·22	1·82	25·34	9	32·85	·01	·22	1·76	34·82
12	24·81	·01	·21	1·59	26·00	11	31·22	·01	·21	1·64	33·06
Sept. 2	28·85	·00	·22	0·60	29·67	Sept. 6	31·66	·00	·21	0·48	32 35
5	27·32	·00	·22	0·51	28·05	8	32·36	·00	·21	0·42	32·99
15	24·25	·00	·22	0·29	24·76	14	35·62	·00	·22	0·30	36·14
10	24·15	·00	·21	0·24	24·60	18	35·32	·00	·21	0·25	35 78
25	25·04	·00	·22	0·23	25 49	21	34·68	·00	·21	0·23	35·12
28	25·59	·00	·20	+ 0·25	26·04	27	35·12	·00	·21	0·24	35·57
						Oct. 2	33·74	·00	·21	+ 0·29	34·24
					0·13·26·43						0·13·34·34

Resulting Mean Zenith Distance, South = 0 13 30 39

Mean Zenith Distances of Stars observed at the Zwartkop Station.

FACE OF SECTOR EAST. — FACE OF SECTOR WEST.

B.A.C. 0275.

Day of Observation 1844.	Apparent Zenith Distance, from Unreduced Observation.	Reduction for Az. Error, and Curv. of Path.	Refraction.	Precession, Aberration, and Nutation.	Deduced Mean Zenith Distance, 1844, Jan. 0; and Mean of Separate Results, uncorrected, for Error of Collimation.	Day of Observation 1844.	Apparent Zenith Distance, from Unreduced Observation.	Reduction for Az. Error, and Curv. of Path.	Refraction.	Precession, Aberration, and Nutation.	Deduced Mean Zenith Distance, 1844, Jan. 0; and Mean of Separate Results, uncorrected, for Error of Collimation.
Aug. 4	1· 5· 9·04	·00	1·06	+ 3·07	1· 5· 7·03	July 30	1· 4·61·38	·00	1·04	+ 3·36	1· 4·59·06
6	10·03	·08	1·04	2·95	8·04	Aug. 5	61·36	·00	1·06	3·01	59·41
8	8·02	·07	1·04	2·84	6·75	7	60·57	·04	1·04	2·90	58·67
12	10·05	·03	1·01	2·62	8·41	9	59·88	·05	1·04	2·78	58·09
Sept. 2	4·86	·00	1·05	1·66	4·25	11	61·83	·03	1·03	2·67	60·16
5	5·01	·00	1·04	1·56	4·49	Sept. 6	61·78	·00	1·01	1·53	61·26
15	9·96	·01	1·04	1·33	9·60	8	61·38	·01	1·04	1·48	60·93
19	9·51	·00	1·02	+ 1·27	9·26	14	56·30	·01	1·04	1·34	55·99
						18	58·12	·00	1·02	1·28	57·86
						21	58·77	·00	1·03	+ 1·25	58·55
					1· 5· 7·23						1· 4·57·93

Resulting Mean Zenith Distance, North = 1· 5· 2·58

B.A.C. 0285.

Day of Observation 1844.	Apparent Zenith Distance.	Reduction.	Refraction.	Precession &c.	Deduced Mean Zenith Distance.	Day of Observation 1844.	Apparent Zenith Distance.	Reduction.	Refraction.	Precession &c.	Deduced Mean Zenith Distance.
July 25	1· 8·28·79	·54	1·07	+ 3·79	1· 8·25·53	July 26	1· 8·31·06	·00	1·08	+ 3·73	1· 8·28·41
29	32·09	·00	1·10	3·56	30·23	30	24·74	·00	1·10	3·56	22·34
Aug. 5	32·30	·00	1·12	3·21	30·21	Aug. 5	24·42	·00	1·11	3·15	22·38
6	32·05	08	1·10	3·09	29·98	7	24·12	·04	1·10	3·08	22·15
8	32·66	·07	1·10	2·98	30·71	9	22·94	·05	1·10	2·92	21·07
12	31·62	·03	1·07	2·76	29·90	11	24·09	·04	1·08	2·81	22·32
Sept. 2	28·12	·00	1·11	1·79	27·44	Sept. 6	24·30	·00	1·06	1·66	23·79
5	28·02	·00	1·10	1 70	27·42	8	23·85	·01	1·09	1·61	23·32
15	32·76	·01	1·09	1·45	32·39	14	19·94	·01	1·10	1·47	19·56
19	32·91	·00	1·07	1·39	32·59	18	21·57	·00	1 08	1 40	21·25
25	31·03	·00	1·10	+ 1·36	30·77	21	21·03	·00	1·08	+ 1·37	20·74
					1· 8·29·74						1· 8·22·48

Resulting Mean Zenith Distance, North = 1· 8·26·11

B.A.C. 0305.

Day of Observation 1844.	Apparent Zenith Distance.	Reduction.	Refraction.	Precession &c.	Deduced Mean Zenith Distance.	Day of Observation 1844.	Apparent Zenith Distance.	Reduction.	Refraction.	Precession &c.	Deduced Mean Zenith Distance.
July 29	1· 6·10·70	·00	1·06	+ 3·90	1· 6· 7·86	July 30	1· 5·62·64	·00	1·06	+ 3·84	1· 5·59·86
Aug. 4	9·91	·00	1·08	3·54	7·45	Aug. 5	60·85	·00	1·07	3·48	58 44
6	10·35	·08	1·06	3·43	7·90	7	61·83	·04	1·06	3·37	59·48
8	9·78	·07	1·06	3·31	7·46	9	60·45	·05	1·06	3·25	58·21
12	10·03	·03	1·03	3·08	7·95	11	61·90	·03	1·04	3·14	59·77
Sept. 2	5·63	·00	1·07	2·09	4·61	Sept. 6	61·80	·00	1·02	1·95	60·87
5	4·84	·00	1·06	1·90	3·91	8	61·75	·01	1·05	1·89	60·90
15	10·47	·01	1·05	1·72	9·79	14	57·06	·01	1·06	1·74	56·37
19	9·83	·00	1·03	1·66	9·20	18	59·08	·00	1·04	1·67	59·05
25	9·14	·00	1·06	+ 1·61	8·59	21	57·51	·00	1·05	+ 1·64	56·92
					1· 6· 7·47						1· 5·58·99

Resulting Mean Zenith Distance, North = 1· 6· 3·23

Mean Zenith Distances of Stars observed at the Zwartkop Station.

FACE OF SECTOR EAST. — FACE OF SECTOR WEST.

B.A.C. 6414.

Day of Observation 1844.	Apparent Zenith Distance, from Unreduced Observation.	Reduction for Az. Error, and Curv. of Path.	Refraction.	Precession, Aberration, and Nutation.	Deduced Mean Zenith Distance, 1844, Jan. 0; and Mean of Separate Results, uncorrected, for Error of Collimation.	Day of Observation 1844.	Apparent Zenith Distance, from Unreduced Observation.	Reduction for Az. Error, and Curv. of Path.	Refraction.	Precession, Aberration, and Nutation.	Deduced Mean Zenith Distance, 1844, Jan. 0; and Mean of Separate Results, uncorrected for Error of Collimation.
July 25	3 18 52·31	1·52	3·10	+ 6·75	3 18 47·14	July 26	3 18 52·60	·00	3·14	+ 6·70	3 18 49·04
29	56·51	·01	3·19	6·55	53·14	30	46·09	·00	3·19	6·50	42·78
Aug. 4	54·49	·01	3·24	6·24	51·48	Aug. 5	45·99	·00	3·22	6·19	43·02
6	56·12	·23	3·10	6·13	52·95	7	45·00	·12	3·19	6·08	41·99
8	54·49	·20	3·19	6·03	51·45	9	45·45	·14	3·19	5·98	42·52
Sept. 2	52·02	+ ·10	3·22	4·82	50·52	11	46·09	·10	3·14	5·87	43·26
5	51·77	·00	3·19	4·70	50·26	Sept. 6	47·08	·01	3·09	4·66	45·50
15	54·59	·02	3·18	4·37	53·38	8	45·79	·03	3·17	4·59	44·34
19	55·67	·01	3·10	4·27	54·49	14	40·95	·03	3·19	4·40	39·71
25	54·00	·01	3·19	4·16	53·11	18	42·78	·00	3·13	4·29	41·62
26	53·95	·01	3·16	+ 4·14	52·96	21	43·37	·00	3·16	+ 4·23	42·30
					3 18 51·74						3 18 43·23

Resulting Mean Zenith Distance, North = 3 18 47·48

B.A.C. 6489.

Day of Observation 1844.	Apparent Zenith Distance, from Unreduced Observation.	Reduction for Az. Error, and Curv. of Path.	Refraction.	Precession, Aberration, and Nutation.	Deduced Mean Zenith Distance.	Day of Observation 1844.	Apparent Zenith Distance, from Unreduced Observation.	Reduction for Az. Error, and Curv. of Path.	Refraction.	Precession, Aberration, and Nutation.	Deduced Mean Zenith Distance.
July 25	4 7 52·53	1·88	3·87	+ 8·03	4 7 46·49	July 26	4 7 50·56	·00	3·92	+ 7·98	4 7 46·50
29	54·46	·01	3·98	7·84	50·59	Aug. 5	43·79	·00	4·02	7·50	40·31
Aug. 4	54·76	·01	4·04	7·55	51·24	7	44·28	·15	3·97	7·40	40·70
6	54·41	·28	3·97	7·45	50·65	9	43·35	·18	3·98	7·30	39·85
8	54·26	·24	3·98	7·35	50·65	11	44·73	·13	3·91	7·20	41·31
12	54·41	·11	3·86	7 15	51·01	31	43·54	·03	3·99	6·22	41·28
Sept. 2	48·63	·00	4·02	6·14	46·71	Sept. 6	44·83	·01	3·85	5·97	42·70
5	50·90	·01	3·96	6·01	48·86	8	43·54	·04	3·95	5·89	41·56
15	53·42	·02	3·96	5·64	51·72	14	40·87	·03	3·98	5·67	39·15
19	53·32	·01	3·87	5·52	51·66	18	40·08	·01	3·91	5·55	38·43
26	54·07	·02	3·94	5·36	52·63	21	41·61	·00	3·93	5·47	40·07
28	52·39	·03	3·79	+ 5·32	50·83	27	40·77	·00	3·88	+ 5·34	39·31
					4 7 50·27						4 7 40·85

Resulting Mean Zenith Distance, North = 4 7 45·56

B.A.C. 6525.

Day of Observation 1844.	Apparent Zenith Distance, from Unreduced Observation.	Reduction for Az. Error, and Curv. of Path.	Refraction.	Precession, Aberration, and Nutation.	Deduced Mean Zenith Distance.	Day of Observation 1844.	Apparent Zenith Distance, from Unreduced Observation.	Reduction for Az. Error, and Curv. of Path.	Refraction.	Precession, Aberration, and Nutation.	Deduced Mean Zenith Distance.
July 29	5 21 25·18	·01	5·17	+ 8·60	5 21 21·74	Aug. 5	5 21 15·59	·00	5·22	+ 8·30	5 21 12·51
Aug. 4	25·67	·01	5·25	8·34	22·57	7	16·14	·19	5·16	8·21	12·90
6	24·98	·36	5·16	8·25	21·53	9	15·05	·23	5·16	8·12	11·86
8	25·22	·31	5·17	8·17	21·01	11	15·20	·16	5·08	8·03	12·09
12	25·42	·09	5·01	7·98	22·36	Sept. 6	15·89	·02	5·00	6·87	14·00
Sept. 2	19·84	·00	5·21	7·04	18·01	8	15·30	·05	5·13	6·80	13·58
5	21·42	·01	5·17	6·91	19·67	9	15·35	·04	5·11	6·76	13·66
15	24·98	·03	5·15	6·55	23·55	14	11·15	·04	5·17	6·58	9·70
19	24·68	·01	5·02	6·43	23·26	18	11·05	·01	5·07	6·46	9·65
26	23·00	·02	5·11	6·25	21·84	27	10·45	·00	5·03	6·23	9·25
28	23·59	·03	4·92	+ 6·21	22·27	Oct. 1	11·64	·00	5·07	+ 6·18	10·55
					5 21 21·07						5 21 11·60

Resulting Mean Zenith Distance, North = 5 21 16·64

No. 6414.—Sept. 2.—Correction for Curvature of Path + 0"·10.
  „ 6525.—Aug. 12.—Correction for Azimuthal Error - ·14; for Curvature of Path + ·05. = - 0"·09.

Mean Zenith Distances of Stars observed at the Zwartkop Station.

FACE OF SECTOR EAST.　　　　　　FACE OF SECTOR WEST.

B.A.C. 6639.

FACE OF SECTOR EAST.

Day of Observation 1844.	Apparent Zenith Distance, from Unreduced Observation.	Reduction for Az. Error, and Curv. of Path.	Refraction.	Precession, Aberration, and Nutation.	Deduced Mean Zenith Distance, 1844, Jan. 0; and Mean of Separate Results, uncorrected, for Error of Collimation.
July 25	4·10·57·21	1·90	3·92	+10·84	4·10·48·39
29	60·97	·01	4.04	10 66	54·34
Aug. 4	60·77	·01	4·09	10·36	54·49
6	59·98	·29	4·02	10·25	53·46
8	61·41	·25	4·03	10·15	55·04
12	61·11	·11	3·91	9·93	54·98
Sept. 2	56·12	·00	4·08	8·75	51·45
5	56·77	·01	4·03	8·50	52·20
8	56·52	·02	4·02	8·44	52·08
15	58·79	·02	4·02	8·10	54·60
19	60 57	·01	3·94	7·93	56·57
25	59·68	·01	4·03	7·70	56·00
27	58·99	·00	3·93	7·63	55·29
Oct. 1	59·88	·03	3·97	+ 7·51	56·31
					4·10·54·20

FACE OF SECTOR WEST.

Day of Observation 1844.	Apparent Zenith Distance, from Unreduced Observation.	Reduction for Az. Error, and Curv. of Path.	Refraction.	Precession, Aberration, and Nutation.	Deduced Mean Zenith Distance, 1844, Jan. 0; and Mean of Separate Results, uncorrected, for Error of Collimation.
July 26	4·10·57·80	·00	3·97	+10·80	4·10·50·97
Aug. 5	50·94	·00	4·07	10·31	44·70
7	51·04	·15	4·02	10·20	44·71
11	51·08	·13	3·96	9·99	45·52
31	50·34	·08	4·04	8·86	45·49
Sept. 6	50·30	+ ·08	3·89	8·54	45·73
14	47·13	·04	4·03	8·15	42·97
18	47·58	·01	3·96	7·07	43·50
21	47·82	·00	3·98	7·85	43·95
26	46 44	·00	4·00	7·66	42·78
28	47·87	·00	3·85	+ 7·60	44·12
					4·10·44·95

Resulting Mean Zenith Distance, North = 4·10·49·58

Anon. AR. 19·21

FACE OF SECTOR EAST.

Day	Apparent Z.D.	Red.	Refr.	Prec.	Deduced Mean Z.D.
July 29	4·25· 2·03	·01	4·26	+11·17	4·24·55·11
Aug. 4	0·45	·01	4·32	10·88	53·88
6	1·19	·30	4·25	10·78	54·30
8	1·93	·26	4·25	10·07	55·25
Sept. 2	4·24·55·55	·00	4·30	9·27	50·58
5	56 64	·01	4·26	9·11	51·78
8	57·63	·02	4·24	8·95	52·90
15	4·25· 0·49	·02	4·24	8·60	56·11
19	0·69	·01	4·16	8·42	56·42
25	4·24·59·80	·01	4·25	8·18	55·86
27	59·90	·01	4·15	8·11	55·93
Oct. 1	59·95	·03	4·20	7 98	56·14
					4·24·54·36

FACE OF SECTOR WEST.

Day	Apparent Z.D.	Red.	Refr.	Prec.	Deduced Mean Z.D.
Aug. 5	4·24·56·25	·00	4·30	+10·83	4·24·49·72
9	51·65	·19	4·26	10·62	45·10
11	52·19	·13	4·18	10·51	45·73
31	52·39	·03	4·27	9·38	47·25
Sept. 6	51·40	·01	4·11	9·06	46·44
9	51·01	·04	4·21	8·90	46·28
14	50·22	·04	4·26	8·65	45·79
26	47·80	·00	4·23	8·14	43·89
28	49·97	·00	4·07	8·08	45·96
Oct. 2	48·54	·00	4·16	+ 7·95	44·75
					4·24·46·09

Resulting Mean Zenith Distance, North = 4·24·50·23

B.A.C. 6753.

FACE OF SECTOR EAST.

Day	Apparent Z.D.	Red.	Refr.	Prec.	Deduced Mean Z.D.
July 29	2·57·39·75	·01	2·85	+12·62	2·57·23·97
Aug. 4	32·61	·00	2·89	12·28	23·22
6	31·43	·20	2·84	12·16	21·94
8	32·61	·18	2·84	12·03	23·24
Sept. 2	27·87	·00	2·88	10·37	20·38
5	28·22	·00	2·85	10·18	20·89

FACE OF SECTOR WEST.

Day	Apparent Z.D.	Red.	Refr.	Prec.	Deduced Mean Z.D.
Aug. 5	2·57·22·04	·00	2·88	+12·22	2·57·12·70
11	22·29	·09	2·80	11·84	13·16
Sept. 4	23·18	·00	2·87	10·24	15·81
6	22·19	·01	2·75	10·11	14·82
9	23·08	+ ·08	2·82	9·92	16·06
14	18·53	·03	2·85	9·62	11·73

Carried forward,

No. 6639.—Sept. 6.—Correction for Azimuthal Error − ·01; for Curvature of Path + ·09. = + 0´·08.
„ 6753.—Sept. 9.— „ „ „ „ − ·02; „ „ „ + ·10. = + 0 ·08.
Sept. 2.—The Micrometer reading has been increased five divisions.

Mean Zenith Distances of Stars observed at the Zwartkop Station.

	FACE OF SECTOR EAST.						FACE OF SECTOR WEST.				
Day of Observation 1844.	Apparent Zenith Distance, from Unreduced Observation.	Reduction for At. Error, and Curv. of Path.	Refraction.	Precession, Aberration, and Nutation.	Deduced Mean Zenith Distance, 1844, Jan. 0; and Mean of Separate Results, uncorrected, for Error of Collimation.	Day of Observation 1844.	Apparent Zenith Distance, from Unreduced Observation.	Reduction for At. Error, and Curv. of Path.	Refraction.	Precession, Aberration, and Nutation.	Deduced Mean Zenith Distance, 1844, Jan. 0; and Mean of Separate Results, uncorrected, for Error of Collimation.

B.A.C. 6753—(continued.)

	° ′ ″	″	″	″	° ′ ″		° ′ ″	″	″	″	° ′ ″
Sept. 8	2·57·27·62	·01	2·84	9·99	2·57·20·46	Sept. 26	2·57·17·50	·00	2·83	8·98	2·57·11·35
15	31·57	·02	2·84	9·50	24·83	28	17·35	·00	2·72	8·88	11·19
27	30·84	·00	2·78	8·93	24·69	Oct. 2	17·74	·00	2·79	+ 8·72	11·81
Oct. 1	32·76	·02	2·81	+ 8·76	26·79						
					2·57·23·03						2·57·13·39

Resulting Mean Zenith Distance, North = 2·57·18·21

B.A.C. 6877.

July 29	1·44·33·62	·00	1·68	+14·63	1·44·20·67	Aug. 5	1·44·24·28	·00	1·69	+14·18	1·44·11·79
Aug. 4	32·09	·00	1·70	14·25	19·54	9	23·54	·08	1·68	13·91	11·23
6	31·74	·12	1·67	14·12	19·17	11	25·07	·05	1·65	13·76	12·91
8	32·38	·11	1·67	13·98	19·96	31	23·69	·01	1·68	12·22	13·14
Sept. 2	28·43	·00	1·60	12·06	18·06	Sept. 4	23·44	·00	1·69	11·91	13·22
5	28·00	·00	1·68	11·83	17·94	6	22·70	·01	1·62	11·75	12·56
8	28·18	·01	1·67	11·60	18·24	9	23·29	·01	1·66	11·52	13·42
15	31·10	·00	1·67	11·08	21·69	18	19·29	·00	1·64	10·87	10·06
19	32·43	·00	1·64	10·80	23·27	26	18·01	·00	1·66	10·34	9·33
27	30·16	·00	1·64	10·28	21·52	28	19·29	·00	1·61	10·22	10·68
Oct. 1	30·36	·01	1·65	+10·05	21·95	Oct. 2	18·80	·00	1·64	+10·00	10·44
					1·44·20·22						1·44·11·57

Resulting Mean Zenith Distance, North = 1·44·15·90

B.A.C. 6948.

July 29	3·45·19·51	·01	3·63	+16·03	3·45· 7·10	Aug. 5	3·45· 8·15	·00	3 66	+15·07	3·44·56·14
Aug. 4	18·03	·01	3·68	15·73	5·97	9	7·21	·16	3·62	15·44	55·23
6	17·98	·26	3·61	15·62	5·71	11	8·50	·11	3·55	15·32	56·02
12	17·69	·10	3·51	15·26	5·84	31	7·86	·02	3·64	13·92	57·56
Sept. 1	13·48	·00	3·63	13·85	3·27	Sept. 4	8·40	·00	3·65	13·63	58·42
2	12·05	·00	3·66	13·78	1·93	6	6·77	·01	3·49	13·48	56·77
5	13·34	·01	3·62	13·55	3·40	9	7·31	·03	3·58	13·26	57·60
8	13·88	·02	3·60	13·33	4·13	14	3·71	·03	3·62	12·89	54·41
15	16·25	·02	3·61	12·82	7·02	18	3·46	·00	3·56	12·61	54·41
19	16·60	·01	3·54	12·54	7·59	21	3·61	·00	3·59	+12·40	54·80
27	16·01	·00	3·53	+12·01	7·53						
					3·45· 5·33						3·44·56·20

Resulting Mean Zenith Distance, North = 3·45· 0·77

Mean Zenith Distances of Stars observed at the Zwartkop Station.

FACE OF SECTOR EAST.						FACE OF SECTOR WEST.					
Day of Observation 1844.	Apparent Zenith Distance, from Unreduced Observation.	Reduction for Az. Error, and Curv. of Path.	Refraction.	Precession, Aberration, and Nutation.	Deduced Mean Zenith Distance, 1844, Jan. 0; and Mean of Separate Results, uncorrected, for Error of Collimation.	Day of Observation 1844.	Apparent Zenith Distance, from Unreduced Observation.	Reduction for Az. Error, and Curv. of Path.	Refraction.	Precession, Aberration, and Nutation.	Deduced Mean Zenith Distance, 1844, Jan. 0; and Mean of Separate Results, uncorrected, for Error of Collimation.

B.A.C. 7011.

Day	App. Z.D.	Red.	Refr.	Prec.	Deduced	Day	App. Z.D.	Red.	Refr.	Prec.	Deduced
July 29	4 30 25·37	·01	4·51	+17·01	4 39 12·86	Aug. 5	4 39 15·32	·00	4·54	+16·70	4 39 3·16
Aug. 6	24·23	·32	4·49	16·65	11·75	9	15·63	·20	4·49	16·49	3·43
12	25·00	·12	4·36	16·32	12·92	11	17·79	·14	4·41	16·37	5·69
Sept. 2	19·85	·00	4·54	14·90	9·49	31	14·28	·03	4·51	15·04	3·72
5	19·69	·01	4·40	14·68	9·49	Sept. 4	15·68	·00	4·53	14·75	5·46
8	20·33	·02	4·47	14·46	10·32	6	15·14	·02	4·34	14·60	4·86
15	21·93	·02	4·48	13·94	12·45	9	15·04	·04	4·44	14·38	5·06
19	23·00	·01	4·39	13·66	13·72	14	10·92	·04	4·49	14·01	1·36
23	21·41	·01	4·32	13·38	12·34	18	10·10	·01	4·42	13·73	0·78
27	21·53	·01	4·38	+13·11	12·79	21	12·02	·00	4·45	13·51	3·56
						26	9·51	·00	4·46	+13·18	0·79
					4·39·11·81						4·39·3·31

Resulting Mean Zenith Distance, North = 4·39· 7·56

B.A.C. 7026.

Day	App. Z.D.	Red.	Refr.	Prec.	Deduced	Day	App. Z.D.	Red.	Refr.	Prec.	Deduced
July 29	4·39·18·35	·01	4·51	+17·20	4·39· 5·65	Aug. 5	4 39 8·60	·00	4·54	+16·89	4 38 56·25
Aug. 4	16·84	·01	4·56	16·94	4·45	9	10·10	·20	4·49	16·68	57·71
6	18·40	·32	4·48	16·51	5·72	11	9·49	·14	4·41	16·56	57·20
12	17 29	·12	4·36	16·51	5·02	31	7·76	·03	4·51	15·23	57·01
Sept. 2	12·25	·00	4·54	16·05	1·71	Sept. 4	8·22	·00	4·53	14·93	57·62
5	11·73	·01	4·49	14·86	1·35	6	7·78	·02	4·34	14·78	57·32
8	12·42	·02	4·47	14·64	2·23	9	9·11	·04	4·44	14·56	58·95
15	14·62	·02	4·48	14·12	4·96	14	3·02	·04	4·49	14·19	53·28
19	15·49	·01	4·39	13·83	6·04	18	3·18	·01	4·42	13·90	53·69
23	13·26	·01	4·32	13·55	4·02	21	3·12	·00	4·45	13·68	53·89
27	14·22	·01	4·38	+13·27	5·32	26	2·59	·00	4·46	+13·34	53·71
					4·39· 4·13						4·38·55·91

Resulting Mean Zenith Distance, North = 4·39· 0·02

B.A.C. 7057.

Day	App. Z.D.	Red.	Refr.	Prec.	Deduced	Day	App. Z.D.	Red.	Refr.	Prec.	Deduced
July 29	4·35·63·60	·01	4·45	+17·65	4·35·50·39	Aug. 5	4·35·54·14	·00	4·49	+17·34	4·35·41·29
Aug. 4	63·17	·01	4·51	17·39	50·28	11	55·03	·14	4·36	17·01	42·24
6	63·25	·31	4·43	17·28	50·09	31	53·50	·03	4·46	15·66	42·27
12	62·84	·12	4·32	16·95	50·09	Sept. 4	54·27	·00	4·47	15·36	43·38
Sept. 5	58·61	·01	4·43	15·28	47·75	6	52·28	·01	4·29	15·20	41·36
8	59·19	·02	4·41	15·05	48·53	9	52·57	·04	4·39	14·97	41·95
15	62·15	·02	4·43	14·52	52·04	14	49·11	·04	4·44	14·59	38·92
19	61·76	·01	4 34	14·22	51·87	18	48·71	·01	4·37	14·29	38·78
23	59·39	·01	4·27	13·93	49·72	21	49·75	·00	4·40	14·07	40·08
27	61·36	·01	4·33	13·65	52·03	26	49·21	·00	4·40	13·72	39·89
Oct. 1	61·71	·03	4·37	+13·38	52·67	28	49·41	·00	4·25	13·58	40·08
						Oct. 2	48·66	·00	4.34	+13·31	39·69
					4·35·50·56						4·35·40·66

Resulting Mean Zenith Distance, North = 4·35·45·61

Mean Zenith Distances of Stars observed at the Zwartkop Station.

FACE OF SECTOR EAST.   **FACE OF SECTOR WEST.**

Anon. AR. 20·24.

Day of Observation 1844.	Apparent Zenith Distance, from Unreduced Observation.	Reduction for Az. Error, and Curv. of Path.	Refraction.	Precession, Aberration, and Nutation.	Deduced Mean Zenith Distance, 1844, Jan. 0; and Mean of Separate Results, uncorrected for Error of Collimation.	Day of Observation 1844.	Apparent Zenith Distance, from Unreduced Observation.	Reduction for Az. Error, and Curv. of Path.	Refraction.	Precession, Aberration, and Nutation.	Deduced Mean Zenith Distance, 1844, Jan. 0; and Mean of Separate Results, uncorrected for Error of Collimation.
July 29	4·24·45·03	·01	4·27	+17·94	4·24·31·35	Aug. 5	4·24·33·57	·00	4·30	+17·63	4·24·20·24
Aug. 4	45·26	+·10	4·32	17·68	32·02	11	35·60	·13	4·17	17·30	22·34
6	44·73	·30	4·24	17·57	31·10	31	33·96	·03	4·27	15·02	22·28
12	44 19	·11	4·14	17·24	30·98	Sept. 4	34·61	·00	4·29	15·61	23·29
Sept. 5	38·60	·01	4·24	15·53	27·36	6	33·82	·01	4·11	15·45	22·47
8	38·95	·02	4·23	15·30	27·86	14	29·67	·04	4·26	14·83	19·06
15	41·23	·02	4·24	14·75	30·70	18	28·78	·01	4·18	14·52	18·43
19	43·35	·01	4·16	14·44	33·06	21	29·47	·00	4·22	14·29	19·40
23	40·54	·01	4·09	14·14	30·48	26	28·48	00	4·22	13·92	18·78
27	41·42	·01	4·15	13·85	31·71	28	29·67	·00	4·07	13·78	19·96
Oct. 1	41·52	·03	4 19	+13·58	32·10	Oct. 2	28·93	·00	4·16	+13·51	19·58
					4·24.30·67						4·24·20·44

Resulting Mean Zenith Distance, North = 4·24·25·55

Anon. AR. 20·34.

Day of Observation 1844.	Apparent Zenith Distance, from Unreduced Observation.	Reduction for Az. Error, and Curv. of Path.	Refraction.	Precession, Aberration, and Nutation.	Deduced Mean Zenith Distance, 1844, Jan. 0; and Mean of Separate Results, uncorrected for Error of Collimation.	Day of Observation 1844.	Apparent Zenith Distance, from Unreduced Observation.	Reduction for Az. Error, and Curv. of Path.	Refraction.	Precession, Aberration, and Nutation.	Deduced Mean Zenith Distance, 1844, Jan. 0; and Mean of Separate Results, uncorrected for Error of Collimation.
July 29	4·15·44·07	·01	4·12	+18·88	4·15·29·30	Aug. 5	4·15·33·79	·01	4·15	+18·56	4·15·19·37
Aug. 4	43·48	·01	4·17	18·61	29·03	11	34·68	·13	4·03	18·23	20·35
6	43·77	·29	4·10	18·51	29·07	31	33·89	·03	4·13	16·81	21·18
12	43·53	·11	4·00	18·17	29·25	Sept. 4	34·48	·00	4·15	16·40	22·14
Sept. 5	37·65	·01	4·10	16·41	25·33	6	33·30	·01	3·97	16·33	20·93
8	37·99	·02	4·09	16·17	25·89	9	32·51	·03	4·07	16·08	20·47
15	41·16	·02	4·10	15·59	29·65	14	29·45	·04	4·11	15·67	17 85
19	40·22	·01	4·02	14·94	28·97	18	29·45	·01	4·04	15·37	18 13
23	39·97	·01	3·95	14·94	28·97	21	28·46	·00	4·07	15·10	17·43
27	40 27	·00	4·01	14·63	29·65	26	27·47	·00	4·08	14·71	16·84
Oct. 1	40·71	·03	4·06	+14·33	30·41	28	28·11	·00	3·93	14·56	17·48
						Oct. 2	28·16	·00	4·02	+14·26	17·92
					4·15·28·61						4·15·18·90

Resulting Mean Zenith Distance, North = 4·15·23·76

B.A.C. 7207.

Day of Observation 1844.	Apparent Zenith Distance, from Unreduced Observation.	Reduction for Az. Error, and Curv. of Path.	Refraction.	Precession, Aberration, and Nutation.	Deduced Mean Zenith Distance, 1844, Jan. 0; and Mean of Separate Results, uncorrected for Error of Collimation.	Day of Observation 1844.	Apparent Zenith Distance, from Unreduced Observation.	Reduction for Az. Error, and Curv. of Path.	Refraction.	Precession, Aberration, and Nutation.	Deduced Mean Zenith Distance, 1844, Jan. 0; and Mean of Separate Results, uncorrected for Error of Collimation.
July 25	0· 7·12·60	·06	0·11	+19·66	0· 7·32·31	July 26	0· 7·12·21	·00	0·11	+19·60	0· 7·31·92
29	9·84	·00	·12	19·43	29·39	Aug. 5	17·79	·00	·12	18·95	36·86
Aug. 4	9·34	·00	·12	19·02	28·48	9	18·73	·01	·12	18·63	37·47
6	9·94	·01	·12	18·87	28·92	11	18·09	·00	·11	18 47	36·67
12	10·18	·00	·11	18·38	28·07	31	18·63	·00	·12	16·58	35·33
Sept. 2	14·73	·00	·12	16·37	31·22	Sept. 4	18·43	·00	·12	16·17	34·72
5	15·17	·00	·12	16·06	31·35	6	19·42	·00	·11	15·96	35·49
8	14·63	·00	·12	15·75	30·50	9	19·92	·00	·12	15·65	35·69

Carried forward,

Anon. 20ʰ 24ᵐ.—Aug 4.—Correction for Azimuthal Error - ·01; for Curvature of Path + ·11. = +0″·10.

Mean Zenith Distances of Stars observed at the Zwartkop Station.

FACE OF SECTOR EAST.

B.A.C. 7207—(continued).

Day of Observation 1844.	Apparent Zenith Distance, from Unreduced Observation.	Reduction for Az. Error, and Curv. of Path.	Refraction.	Precession, Aberration, and Nutation.	Deduced Mean Zenith Distance, 1844, Jan. 0; and Mean of Separate Results, uncorrected, for Error of Collimation.
Sept. 15	0· 7·11·22	·00	·12	15 04	0· 7·26·38
19	11·67	·00	·11	14·63	26·41
23	13·00	·00	·11	14·24	27·35
27	14·53	·00	·11	13·86	28·50
Oct. 1	13·00	·00	12	+13·50	26·62
					0· 7·28·88

FACE OF SECTOR WEST.

Day of Observation 1844.	Apparent Zenith Distance, from Unreduced Observation.	Reduction for Az. Error, and Curv. of Path.	Refraction.	Precession, Aberration, and Nutation.	Deduced Mean Zenith Distance, 1844, Jan. 0; and Mean of Separate Results, uncorrected, for Error of Collimation.
Sept. 14	0· 7 24·07	·00	·12	15·14	0· 7·39·33
18	24·17	·00	·11	14·73	39·01
21	23·47	·00	·12	14·44	38·03
26	26·34	·00	·12	13·96	40·42
28	24 46	·00	·11	+13·77	38·34
					0· 7·37·00

Resulting Mean Zenith Distance, South = 0· 7·32·94

Anon. AR. 20·53.

Day of Obs. (East)	Apparent Z.D.	Red.	Refr.	Prec. &c.	Deduced Mean Z.D.
July 29	4·30·42·39	·01	4·37	+20·76	4 30·25·99
Aug. 4	41·60	·01	4 42	20·53	25·48
12	41·30	·12	4·24	20·12	25·30
Sept. 5	36·76	·01	4·34	18 33	22·76
8	37·30	·02	4·33	18·07	23·54
15	39·82	·02	4·34	17·45	26·69
19	40·12	·01	4·25	17·10	27·26
23	38·88	·01	4·19	16·74	26·27
26	39·23	·02	4·33	16·48	27·06
28	39·03	·03	4·17	16·31	26·86
Oct. 2	38·44	·03	4·27	+15·97	26·71
					4·30·25·72

Day of Obs. (West)	Apparent Z.D.	Red.	Refr.	Prec. &c.	Deduced Mean Z.D.
Aug. 5	4·30·33·10	·00	4·40	+20·49	4·30·17·01
11	35·03	·14	4·27	20·18	18·98
31	33·84	·03	4·37	18·75	19 43
Sept. 4	32·71	·00	4·40	18·42	18·69
6	32·41	·01	4·20	18 24	18·36
9	32·51	·04	4·31	17·98	18·60
14	27·47	·04	4·36	17·54	14·25
18	28·41	·01	4·28	17·19	15·49
25	26 33	·00	4·36	16·57	14·12
27	26·28	·00	4·26	16·39	14·15
Oct. 1	27·17	·00	4·30	+16·06	15.41
					4·30·16·34

Resulting Mean Zenith Distance, North = 4·30·21·03

Anon. AR. 21· 0

Day of Obs. (East)	Apparent Z.D.	Red.	Refr.	Prec. &c.	Deduced Mean Z.D.
July 29	3·52·57·52	·01	3·76	+21·42	3·52·39·85
Aug. 4	56·86	·01	3·80	21·18	39·49
6	57·52	·27	3·73	21·08	39·90
12	56·68	·10	3·64	20·74	39·48
Sept. 5	51·94	·01	3·73	18·86	36·80
8	52·14	·02	3·72	18·59	37·25
15	55·10	·02	3·74	17·93	40·89
19	55·01	·01	3 66	17·56	41·10
23	53·32	·01	3·61	17·18	39·74
26	54·76	·02	3·72	16·90	41·56
28	53·57	·03	3·59	+16·72	40·41
					3·52·39·68

Day of Obs. (West)	Apparent Z.D.	Red.	Refr.	Prec. &c.	Deduced Mean Z.D.
Aug. 5	3·52·46·61	·00	3·78	+21·13	3·52·29·26
9	48·78	·17	3·74	20·92	31·43
11	47·50	·12	3·67	20·80	30·25
31	46·31	·02	3·76	19·31	30 74
Sept. 4	46·26	·00	3·78	18·95	31·09
6	45·62	·01	3 61	18·77	30·45
9	45·82	·03	3·71	18·49	31·01
14	42·16	·03	3·75	18·03	27·65
18	41·81	·01	3·68	17·65	27·83
21	40·48	·00	3·71	17·36	26·83
27	39·79	·00	3 66	16·81	26·64
Oct. 1	40·48	·00	3 70	+16·45	27·73
					3·52·28·95

Resulting Mean Zenith Distance, North = 3·52·34·32

Mean Zenith Distances of Stars observed at the Zwartkop Station.

	FACE OF SECTOR EAST.						FACE OF SECTOR WEST.				
Day of Observation 1844.	Apparent Zenith Distance, from Unreduced Observation.	Reduction for Az. Error, and Curv. of Path.	Refraction.	Precession, Aberration, and Nutation.	Deduced Mean Zenith Distance, 1844, Jan. 0; and Mean of Separate Results, uncorrected, for Error of Collimation.	Day of Observation 1844.	Apparent Zenith Distance, from Unreduced Observation.	Reduction for Az. Error, and Curv. of Path.	Refraction.	Precession, Aberration, and Nutation.	Deduced Mean Zenith Distance, 1844, Jan. 0; and Mean of Separate Results, uncorrected, for Error of Collimation.
					B.A.C. 7386.						
	° ′ ″	″	″	″	° ′ ″		° ′ ″	″	″	″	° ′ ″
July 29	1·24·46·37	·00	1·36	+22·16	1·24·25·57	Aug. 5	1·24·37·47	·00	1·37	+21·78	1·24·17·06
Aug. 4	45·08	·00	1·38	21·84	24·62	9	37·57	·06	1·36	21·52	17·35
6	45·03	·10	1·35	21·72	24·56	11	37·67	·04	1·33	21·38	17·58
12	45·19	·04	1·32	21·30	25·16	12	36·04	·01	1·37	19·60	17·80
Sept. 5	40·63	·00	1·36	19·09	22·90	Sept. 4	37·27	·00	1·37	19·19	19·45
8	40·73	·01	1·35	18·78	23·29	6	36·78	·00	1·31	18·99	19·10
15	43·30	·01	1·36	18·03	26·62	9	36·14	·01	1·35	18·67	18·81
19	42·96	·00	1·33	17·59	26·70	14	31·89	·01	1·36	18·13	15·11
23	42·12	·00	1·31	17·17	26·26	18	31·30	·00	1·34	17·70	14·94
26	42·22	·01	1·35	16·85	26·71	21	30·95	·00	1·35	17·38	14·92
28	41·57	·01	1·30	+16·64	26·22	25	30·16	·00	1·36	16·06	14·56
						27	30·26	·00	1·33	+16·74	14·85
					1·24·25·36						1·24·16·40

Resulting Mean Zenith Distance, North = 1·24·20·88

Anon. AR. 21ʰ 12ᵐ.

	FACE OF SECTOR EAST.						FACE OF SECTOR WEST.				
July 29	4·24·29·86	·01	4·27	+22·45	4·24·11·67	Aug. 5	4·24·21·47	+ ·09	4·30	+22·21	4·23·63·65
Aug. 4	29·47	·01	4·32	22·23	11·53	11	20·92	·13	4·17	21·91	63·05
6	29·91	·30	4·24	22·16	11·69	31	21·47	·03	4·27	20·46	65·25
12	30·26	·11	4·14	21·85	12·44	Sept. 4	19·79	·00	4·30	20·11	63·98
Sept. 5	25·02	·01	4·24	20·02	9·23	9	19·49	·04	4·21	19·65	64·01
8	24·53	·02	4·23	19·75	8·90	14	14·60	·04	4·26	19·18	59·64
15	27·25	·02	4·25	19·08	12·40	18	14·04	·01	4·18	18·79	60·32
19	26·41	·01	4·16	18·70	11·86	21	15·24	·00	4·22	18·50	60·96
23	27·49	·01	4·10	18·31	13·27	25	14·45	·00	4·26	18·11	60·60
26	27·10	·02	4·23	18·02	13·29	27	13·76	·00	4·16	17·92	60·00
28	25·81	·03	4·08	17·83	12·03	Oct. 1	15·09	·00	4·20	17·54	61·75
Oct. 2	25·96	·03	4·17	+17·45	12·65						
					4·24·11·74						4·24· 1·78

Resulting Mean Zenith Distance, North = 4·24· 6·76

Anon. AR. 21ʰ 25ᵐ.

	FACE OF SECTOR EAST.						FACE OF SECTOR WEST.				
July 25	3·50·46·49	1·76	3·60	+23·66	3·50·24·67	July 26	3·50·47·28	·00	3·65	+23·64	3·50·27·29
29	50·69	0·01	3·73	23·57	30·84	Aug. 5	41·50	·00	3·75	23·33	21·92
Aug. 4	50·94	0·01	3·77	23·37	31·33	9	41·25	·16	3·71	23·14	21·66
6	50·25	0·26	3·70	23·28	30·41	11	41·90	·12	3·64	23·03	22·39
12	50·99	0·10	3·61	22·97	31·53	Sept. 4	40·56	·00	3·64	21·15	23·16
Sept. 5	45·35	0·01	3·70	21·05	27·99	6	40·46	·01	3·59	20·96	23·08
8	45·55	0·02	3·69	20·76	28·46	8	40·02	·03	3·68	20·66	23·01

Carried forward,

Anon. 21ʰ 12ᵐ.—Aug. .—Correction for Curvature of Path + 0·09.

Mean Zenith Distances of Stars observed at the Zwartkop Station.

FACE OF SECTOR EAST.

Day of Observation 1844.	Apparent Zenith Distance, from Unreduced Observation.	Reduction for Az. Error, and Curv. of Path.	Refraction.	Precession, Aberration, and Nutation.	Deduced Mean Zenith Distance, 1844, Jan. 0; and Mean of Separate Results, uncorrected, for Error of Collimation.
			Anon. AR. 21·25—(continued).		
Sept. 15	3 50 47·97	·02	3·71	20 05	3 50 31 61
28	46·84	·01	3·57	19·22	31·18
26	47·08	·02	3·69	18·91	31·84
28	47·03	·03	3·56	18·70	31·86
Oct. 2	46·44	·03	3·64	+18·29	31·76
					3 50 30 34

FACE OF SECTOR WEST.

Day of Observation 1844.	Apparent Zenith Distance, from Unreduced Observation.	Reduction for Az. Error, and Curv. of Path.	Refraction.	Precession, Aberration, and Nutation.	Deduced Mean Zenith Distance, 1844, Jan. 0; and Mean of Separate Results, uncorrected, for Error of Collimation.
Sept. 14	3 50 36 26	·03	3·71	20 15	3 50 19·79
18	35·57	·01	3·65	19·74	19·47
21	36·51	·00	3·68	19·43	20·76
27	33·60	·00	3·63	18·80	18·43
Oct. 1	34·44	·00	3·68	+18·30	19·73
					3 50 21 60

Resulting Mean Zenith Distance, North = 3·50·25·97

B.A.C. 7557.

FACE OF SECTOR EAST.

Day of Observation 1844.	Apparent Zenith Distance, from Unreduced Observation.	Reduction for Az. Error, and Curv. of Path.	Refraction.	Precession, Aberration, and Nutation.	Deduced Mean Zenith Distance.
July 25	0 29 54·86	·24	0 47	+24 69	0 29 30·40
29	58·02	·00	·48	24·54	33·96
Aug. 4	58·91	·00	·49	24·24	35·16
6	58·02	·04	·48	24·12	34·34
12	58·72	·01	·47	23·70	35·48
Sept. 2	53·43	·00	·48	21·69	32·22
5	54·07	·00	·48	21·35	33·20
8	53·83	·00	·48	21·00	33·31
15	56·39	·00	·48	20·16	36·71
23	54·81	·00	·46	19·18	36·09
26	54·71	·00	·48	18·92	36·37
28	54·66	·00	·46	+18·58	36·54
					0 29 34·54

FACE OF SECTOR WEST.

Day of Observation 1844.	Apparent Zenith Distance, from Unreduced Observation.	Reduction for Az. Error, and Curv. of Path.	Refraction.	Precession, Aberration, and Nutation.	Deduced Mean Zenith Distance.
July 26	0 29 56·84	·00	0 47	+24 66	0 29 32·65
Aug. 5	51·70	·00	·48	24·18	28·00
9	50·47	·02	·48	23·92	27·01
11	51·75	·02	·47	23·78	28·42
31	50·52	·00	·48	21·91	29·09
Sept. 4	50·37	·00	·48	21·47	29·38
6	51·31	·00	·46	21·23	30·54
9	49·77	·00	·48	20·88	29·37
14	44·54	·00	·48	20·28	24·74
18	43·80	·00	·47	19·80	24·47
21	44·93	·00	·48	19·43	25·98
27	44·24	·00	·47	+18 70	26·01
					0 29 27·82

Resulting Mean Zenith Distance, North = 0·29·31·18

B.A.C. 7613.

FACE OF SECTOR EAST.

Day of Observation 1844.	Apparent Zenith Distance, from Unreduced Observation.	Reduction for Az. Error, and Curv. of Path.	Refraction.	Precession, Aberration, and Nutation.	Deduced Mean Zenith Distance.
July 25	3 51 41·18	1·94	3·62	+25·71	3 52 8·57
29	35·50	0·01	3·74	25·48	4·71
Aug. 4	33·62	0·01	3·78	25·06	2·45
6	36·34	0·29	3·71	24·00	4·06
12	35 16	0·11	3·63	24·35	3·03
Sept. 2	40·59	0·00	3·76	21·85	6·20
5	39·70	0·01	3·72	21·44	4·85
8	39·75	0·02	3·70	21·02	4 45
15	38·12	0·02	3·72	20 02	1·84
23	40·34	0·01	3·60	18·86	2·79
26	39·75	0·02	3·72	18·44	1·89
28	40·54	0·03	3·57	+18·15	2·23
					3 52 3·91

FACE OF SECTOR WEST.

Day of Observation 1844.	Apparent Zenith Distance, from Unreduced Observation.	Reduction for Az. Error, and Curv. of Path.	Refraction.	Precession, Aberration, and Nutation.	Deduced Mean Zenith Distance.
July 26	3 51 37 72	·00	3·66	+25 66	3 52 7 04
Aug. 5	43·36	·00	3·76	24·98	12·10
9	44·89	·18	3·72	24·63	13·06
11	43·75	·13	3·66	24·44	11·72
31	43·70	·63	3·74	22·11	9·52
Sept. 4	43·70	·00	3·77	21·57	9 04
6	45·58	·01	3 60	21·30	10·47
9	45·68	·03	3·69	20·87	10·21
14	50·27	·04	3·73	20·16	14·12
18	51·06	·01	3·66	19·59	14·30
21	50·82	·00	3·70	19·15	13·67
27	52·25	·00	3·64	+18·29	14·18
					3 52 11·78

Resulting Mean Zenith Distance, South = 3·52·7·85

Mean Zenith Distances of Stars observed at the Zwartkop Station.

	FACE OF SECTOR EAST.						FACE OF SECTOR WEST.				
Day of Observation 1844.	Apparent Zenith Distance, from Unreduced Observation.	Reduction for Az. Error, and Curr. of Path.	Refraction.	Precession, Aberration, and Nutation.	Deduced Mean Zenith Distance, 1844, Jan. 0; and Mean of Separate Results, uncorrected, for Error of Collimation.	Day of Observation 1844.	Apparent Zenith Distance, from Unreduced Observation.	Reduction for Az. Error, and Curr. of Path.	Refraction.	Precession, Aberration, and Nutation.	Deduced Mean Zenith Distance, 1844, Jan. 0; and Mean of Separate Results, uncorrected, for Error of Collimation.

B.A.C. 7657.

Day	App. Z.D.	Red.	Refr.	Prec.	Deduced	Day	App. Z.D.	Red.	Refr.	Prec.	Deduced
July 29	5· 1·60·55	.01	4·88	+25·49	5· 1·39·93	Aug. 5	5· 1·50·85	·00	4·91	+25·35	5· 1·30·41
Aug. 4	60·27	·01	4·94	25·38	39·82	9	49·73	·21	4·86	25·21	29·17
6	60·42	·34	4·84	25·32	39·60	11	52·05	·15	4·77	25·13	31·54
12	60·87	·13	4·74	25·08	40·40	31	51·69	·03	4·87	23·79	32·74
Sept. 5	55·66	·01	4·85	23·33	37·17	Sept. 4	52·82	·00	4·91	23·43	34·30
8	56·02	·02	4·83	23·05	38·38	6	50·35	·02	4·69	23·24	31·78
15	58·20	·03	4·86	22·33	40·70	9	49·07	·04	4·82	22·95	30·90
23	57·54	·01	4·69	21·47	40·75	14	46·65	·04	4·87	22·44	29·04
26	57·39	·02	4·85	21·14	41·08	18	46·55	·01	4·78	22·02	29·30
28	57·54	·08	4·66	20·92	41·25	21	45·86	·00	4·82	21·69	28·99
Oct. 1	57·09	·03	4·82	+20·59	41·29	25	44·99	·00	4·87	21·26	28·60
						27	45·63	·00	4·75	+21·03	29·35
					5· 1·40·04						5· 1·30·13

Resulting Mean Zenith Distance, North = 5· 1·35·09

Anon. AR. 21·55.

Day	App. Z.D.	Red.	Refr.	Prec.	Deduced	Day	App. Z.D.	Red.	Refr.	Prec.	Deduced
July 25	5· 2·37·80	2·27	4·73	+25·77	5· 2·14·49	July 26	5· 2·31·82	·00	4·79	+25·78	5· 2·10·83
29	38·30	0·01	4·89	25·76	17·42	Aug. 5	29·38	·00	4·92	25·63	8·67
Aug. 4	38·61	0·01	4·95	25·65	17·90	9	28·76	·21	4·87	25·49	7·93
6	38·51	0·34	4·85	25·60	17·42	31	29·63	·03	4·88	24·08	10·40
12	38·91	0·13	4·75	25·37	18·16	Sept. 4	30·96	·00	4·92	23·72	12·16
Sept. 5	33·70	0·01	4·86	23·63	14·92	6	29·28	·02	4·70	23·53	10·43
8	34·56	0·02	4·85	23·34	16·05	9	27·90	·04	4·83	23·24	9·45
15	36·59	0·03	4·87	22·62	18·81	14	24·59	·04	4·88	22·73	6·70
23	34·39	0·01	4·70	21·75	17·38	18	23·65	01	4·79	22·30	6·13
26	35·92	0·02	4·86	21·42	19·34	21	24·10	·00	4·83	21·97	6·96
28	35·58	0·03	4·67	21·19	19·03	25	23·03	·00	4·88	21·53	6·38
Oct. 2	34·94	0·03	4·78	+20·75	18·94	27	23·87	·00	4·76	+21·31	7·32
					5· 2·17·57						5· 2· 8·21

Resulting Mean Zenith Distance, North = 5· 2·12·89

B.A.C. 7842.

Day	App. Z.D.	Red.	Refr.	Prec.	Deduced	Day	App. Z.D.	Red.	Refr.	Prec.	Deduced
July 25	1· 5·23·42	·51	1·02	+27·94	1· 4·55·99	July 26	1· 5·25·84	·00	1·03	+27·93	1· 4·58·94
29	27·62	·00	1·06	27·88	60·80	Aug. 5	20·35	·00	1·06	27·68	53·73
Aug. 4	28·11	·00	1·07	27·72	61·46	11	18·28	·05	1·05	27·49	51·79
6	27·03	·08	1·04	27·64	60·35	31	19·17	·03	1·03	27·38	52·79
Sept. 2	22·78	·00	1·06	25·46	58·38	Sept. 4	20·06	·01	1·05	25·68	55·42
5	22·82	+ ·06	1·05	25·11	58·82	6	20·90	·00	1·06	25·23	56·73
8	23·66	·01	1·04	24·76	59·93	9	19·42	·00	1·01	25·00	55·43
15	25·10	·01	1·05	23·87	62·27	9	18·18	·01	1·04	24·63	54·58

Carried forward,

No. 7842.—Sept. 5.—Correction for Curvature of Path + 0″·06.

Mean Zenith Distances of Stars observed at the Zwartkop Station.

FACE OF SECTOR EAST.

Day of Observation 1844.	Apparent Zenith Distance, from Unreduced Observation.	Reduction for Az. Error, and Curv. of Path.	Refraction.	Precession, Aberration, and Nutation.	Deduced Mean Zenith Distance 1844, Jan. 0; and Mean of Separate Results, uncorrected, for Error of Collimation.
			B.A.C. 7842—(continued).		
Sept. 23	1· 5·23·62	·00	1·01	22·78	1· 4·61·85
26	23·96	·00	1·05	22·37	62·64
28	24·01	·01	1·00	+22·09	62·91
					1· 5· 0·49

FACE OF SECTOR WEST.

Day of Observation 1844.	Apparent Zenith Distance, from Unreduced Observation.	Reduction for Az. Error, and Curv. of Path.	Refraction.	Precession, Aberration, and Nutation.	Deduced Mean Zenith Distance 1844, Jan. 0; and Mean of Separate Results, uncorrected, for Error of Collimation.
Sept. 14	1· 5·14·92	·01	1·05	23·99	1· 4·51·97
18	14·53	·00	1·03	23·46	52·10
27	12·70	·00	1·03	22·23	51·50
Oct. 1	12·60	·00	1·04	+21·67	51·97
					1· 4·53·77

Resulting Mean Zenith Distance, North = 1· 4·57·13

B.A.C. 7909.

FACE OF SECTOR EAST.

Day of Observation 1844.	Apparent Zenith Distance, from Unreduced Observation.	Reduction for Az. Error, and Curv. of Path.	Refraction.	Precession, Aberration, and Nutation.	Deduced Mean Zenith Distance 1844, Jan. 0; and Mean of Separate Results, uncorrected, for Error of Collimation.
July 29	4· 3·34·68	·01	3·94	+28·18	4· 3·10·43
Aug. 4	34·97	·01	3·98	28·14	10·80
6	35·57	·28	3·90	28·10	11·09
12	36·21	·11	3·83	27·90	12·03
Sept. 5	30·77	·01	3·91	26·13	8·54
8	31·27	·02	3·90	25·81	9·34
15	32·70	·02	3·92	25·02	11·58
21	32·16	·01	3·90	24·29	11·76
23	31·91	·01	3·78	24·03	11·65
26	32·36	·02	3·91	23·65	12·60
28	31·85	·03	3·75	+23·39	12·18
					4· 3·11·09

FACE OF SECTOR WEST.

Day of Observation 1844.	Apparent Zenith Distance, from Unreduced Observation.	Reduction for Az. Error, and Curv. of Path.	Refraction.	Precession, Aberration, and Nutation.	Deduced Mean Zenith Distance 1844, Jan. 0; and Mean of Separate Results, uncorrected, for Error of Collimation.
Aug. 5	4· 3·26·28	·00	3·95	+28·12	4· 2·62·11
9	24·99	·17	3·92	28·01	60·73
11	26·72	·12	3·85	27·94	62·51
Sept. 4	27·61	·00	3·96	26·23	65·34
9	24·80	·03	3·89	25·70	62·96
14	20·84	·03	3·93	25·14	59·60
18	20·25	·01	3·85	24·66	59·43
25	18·82	·00	3·94	23·78	58·98
27	19·46	·00	3·83	23·52	59·77
Oct. 1	18·97	·00	3·89	+23·00	59·86
					4· 3· 1·13

Resulting Mean Zenith Distance, North = 4· 3· 6·11

B.A.C. 7966.

FACE OF SECTOR EAST.

Day of Observation 1844.	Apparent Zenith Distance, from Unreduced Observation.	Reduction for Az. Error, and Curv. of Path.	Refraction.	Precession, Aberration, and Nutation.	Deduced Mean Zenith Distance 1844, Jan. 0; and Mean of Separate Results, uncorrected, for Error of Collimation.
July 29	0·31·61·69	·00	0·52	+29·16	0·31·33·05
Aug. 4	62·92	·00	·52	29·03	34·41
6	62·58	·04	·51	28·96	34·09
12	62·33	·01	·50	28·67	34·15
Sept. 2	57·34	·00	·52	26·83	31·03
5	57·39	·00	·51	26·47	31·43
8	58·28	·00	·51	26·10	32·69
15	60·45	·00	·51	25·17	35·79
21	59·96	·00	·51	24·32	36·15
23	57·98	·00	·50	24·03	34·45
26	58·33	·00	·51	23·59	35·25
28	57·93	·00	·49	+23·29	35·13
					0·31·33·97

FACE OF SECTOR WEST.

Day of Observation 1844.	Apparent Zenith Distance, from Unreduced Observation.	Reduction for Az. Error, and Curv. of Path.	Refraction.	Precession, Aberration, and Nutation.	Deduced Mean Zenith Distance 1844, Jan. 0; and Mean of Separate Results, uncorrected, for Error of Collimation.
Aug. 5	0·31·55·26	·00	·52	+29·00	0·31·26·78
9	54·13	·02	·51	28·83	25·79
11	55·71	·02	·50	28·73	27·46
Sept. 4	56·89	·0	·52	26·59	30·82
6	55·41	·00	·40	26·35	29·55
9	53·83	·00	·51	25·97	28·37
14	50·87	·00	·51	25·31	26·07
18	48·84	·00	·50	24·75	24·59
25	47·31	·00	·52	23·73	24·10
27	47·51	·00	·50	23·44	24·57
Oct. 1	47·66	·00	·51	+22·84	25·33
					0·31·26·68

Resulting Mean Zenith Distance, North = 0·31·30·32

3 Q

Mean Zenith Distances of Stars observed at the Zwartkop Station.

	FACE OF SECTOR EAST.						FACE OF SECTOR WEST.				
Day of Observation 1844.	Apparent Zenith Distance, from Unreduced Observation.	Reduction for Az. Error, and Curv. of Path.	Refraction.	Precession, Aberration, and Nutation.	Deduced Mean Zenith Distance, 1844, Jan. 0; and Mean of Separate Results, uncorrected, for Error of Collimation.	Day of Observation 1844.	Apparent Zenith Distance, from Unreduced Observation	Reduction for Az. Error, and Curv. of Path.	Refraction.	Precession, and Aberration, and Nutation.	Deduced Mean Zenith Distance, 1844, Jan. 0; and Mean of Separate Results, uncorrected, for Error of Collimation.
	° ′ ″	″	″	″	° ′ ″		° ′ ″	″	″	″	° ′ ″

Fomalhaut B.A.C. 7992.

Day of Observation 1844.	Apparent Zenith Distance	Reduction Az. Error	Refraction	Precession Aberration Nutation	Deduced Mean Zenith Distance	Day of Observation 1844.	Apparent Zenith Distance	Reduction Az. Error	Refraction	Precession Aberration Nutation	Deduced Mean Zenith Distance
July 29	3·47·13·04	+ ·01	3 67	+28·99	3·46·48·33	Aug. 5	3·46·62·92	·00	3·68	+28·96	3·46·37·64
Aug. 4	13·10	− ·01	3·71	28·98	47·82	9	62·72	·16	3·65	28·87	37·34
6	13·15	·26	3·63	28·95	47·57	11	63·22	·12	3·59	28·81	37·88
12	13·20	·10	3·57	28·77	47·90	Sept. 4	63·81	·00	3·70	27·13	40·38
Sept. 2	7·86	·00	3·69	27·32	44·23	6	63·32	·01	3·52	26·92	39·91
5	8·06	·01	3·65	27·02	44·68	9	61·98	·03	3·63	26·59	38·99
8	8·06	·02	3·63	26·71	44·96	14	58·92	·03	3·66	26·01	36·54
15	10·23	·02	3·65	25·89	47·97	18	57·73	·01	3·59	25·52	35·79
21	10·88	·01	3·64	25·13	49·38	25	56·45	·00	3·67	24·61	35·51
23	9·44	·01	3·53	24·87	48·09	27	57·09	·00	3·57	24·33	36·33
26	8·65	·02	3·64	24·47	47·80	Oct. 1	56·20	·00	3·62	+23·79	36·03
28	9·15	·02	3·50	+24·20	48·43						
					3·46·47·21						3·46.37·49

Resulting Mean Zenith Distance, North = 3·46·42·35

MEAN ZENITH DISTANCES.

COLLECTION OF

ALL THE

RESULTS OF OBSERVATION OF EACH STAR

AT

THE CAPE POINT STATION,

AND

DEDUCTION OF MEAN ZENITH DISTANCE, 1844, JANUARY 0.

NOTE.—The reduction for Azimuthal Error is always to be applied subtractively to the Zenith Distance. The reduction for Curvature of Path is always to be applied subtractively to South Zenith Distance, and additively to North Zenith Distance. The Refraction is always to be applied additively. The Precession, Aberration, and Nutation, have the sign which is proper for reducing the Apparent North Polar Distance of the Star to its mean North Polar Distance, 1844, January 0; and therefore are to be applied with the sign given in the Table when the Star is South of the Zenith, and with the opposite sign when the Star is North of the Zenith.

The numbers included in parentheses in the column " Deduced Mean Zenith Distance, 1844, January 0," are omitted in taking the mean.

Where an asterisk or a positive sign is affixed to a number in the 3rd or 9th columns, the explanation will be found at the bottom of the page.

Mean Zenith Distances of Stars observed at the Cape Point Station.

FACE OF SECTOR EAST.   FACE OF SECTOR WEST.

Day of Observation 1844.	Apparent Zenith Distance, from Unreduced Observation.	Reduction for Az. Error, and Curv. of Path.	Refraction.	Precession, Aberration, and Nutation.	Deduced Mean Zenith Distance. 1844, Jan. 0; and Mean of Separate Results, uncorrected, for Error of Collimation.	Day of Observation 1844.	Apparent Zenith Distance, from Unreduced Observation.	Reduction for Az. Error, and Curv. of Path.	Refraction.	Precession, Aberration, and Nutation.	Deduced Mean Zenith Distance, 1844, Jan. 0; and Mean of Separate Results, uncorrected for Error of Collimation.
				B.A.C. 1739.							
Dec. 1	1·14· 4·41	·00	1·22	+ 3·63	1·14· 9·26	Dec. 2	1·14· 8·07	·00	1·22	+ 3·32	1·14·12·61
3	4·12	·03	1·21	3·01	8·31	4	8·96	·00	1·20	2·70	12·86
5	6·19	·03	1·20	2·39	9·75	6	9·94	·01	1·20	2·07	13·20
7	5·01	·03	1·21	1·76	7·95	8	10·14	·00	1·20	1·45	12·79
9	6·64	·00	1·21	1·14	8·99	10	11·62	·01	1·19	+ 0·82	13·62
12	6·59	·00	1·21	+ 0·20	8·00	13	12·61	·00	1·19	- 0·11	13·69
15	8·86	·00	1·21	- 0·73	9·34	16	14·09	·00	1·20	1·04	14·25
18	8·66	·00	1·21	1·66	8·21	17	14·83	·00	1·22	1·35	14·70
20	9·50	·00	1·20	2·27	8·43	30	17·09	·00	1·21	5·26	13·64
28	12·36	·00	1·20	- 4·67	8·89	31	17·89	·00	1·20	- 5·54	13·55
					1·14· 8·71						1·14·13·49

Error of Collimation . . . = 0· 0· 2·39
Resulting Mean Zenith Distance, South = 1·14·11·10

Day of Observation 1844.	Apparent Zenith Distance, from Unreduced Observation.	Reduction for Az. Error, and Curv. of Path.	Refraction.	Precession, Aberration, and Nutation.	Deduced Mean Zenith Distance.	Day of Observation 1844.	Apparent Zenith Distance, from Unreduced Observation.	Reduction for Az. Error, and Curv. of Path.	Refraction.	Precession, Aberration, and Nutation.	Deduced Mean Zenith Distance.
				B.A.C. 1802.							
Nov. 21	0·11·36·71	+ ·10	0·19	+ 6·08	0·11·30·92	Nov. 16	0·11·33·84	·00	0·19	+ 7·50	0·11·26·53
25	35·18	- ·01	·19	4·90	30·46	24	30·44	·00	·19	5·20	25·43
Dec. 1	33·31	·00	·19	3·10	30·40	26	29·95	·00	·19	4·61	25·53
3	32·52	·00	·19	2·49	30·22	Dec. 2	28·91	·00	·19	2·79	26·31
5	31·63	·01	·19	1·87	29·94	4	27·63	·00	·19	2·18	25·64
7	32·02	·00	·19	1·26	30·95	6	26·74	·00	·19	1·56	25·37
9	31·38	·00	·19	+ 0·64	30·93	8	27·23	·00	·19	0·95	26·47
12	31·43	·00	·19	- 0·29	31·91	10	24·82	·00	19	+ 0·33	24·68
15	29·51	·00	·19	1·22	30·92	13	24·02	·00	·19	- 0·60	24·81
18	28·67	·00	·19	2·14	31·00	16	22·15	·00	·19	1·52	23·86
20	27·92	·00	·19	- 2·75	30·86	17	21·90	·00	·19	- 1·83	23·92
					0 11·30·77						0·11·25·32

Error of Collimation . . . = 0· 0. 2·73
Resulting Mean Zenith Distance, North = 0·11·28·05

Day of Observation 1844.	Apparent Zenith Distance, from Unreduced Observation.	Reduction for Az. Error, and Curv. of Path.	Refraction.	Precession, Aberration, and Nutation.	Deduced Mean Zenith Distance.	Day of Observation 1844.	Apparent Zenith Distance, from Unreduced Observation.	Reduction for Az. Error, and Curv. of Path.	Refraction.	Precession, Aberration, and Nutation.	Deduced Mean Zenith Distance.
				B.A.C. 1878.							
Nov. 21	1·28·32·82	·03	1·46	+ 5·52	1·28·39·77	Nov. 16	1·28·36·13	·00	1·45	+ 6·96	1·28·44·54
25	33·96	·04	1·44	4·33	39·69	24	38·84	·00	1·44	4·63	44·91
Dec. 1	36·18	·04	1·46	2·49	40·13	26	40·27	·00	1·43	4·03	45·73
3	36·42	·03	1·45	1·87	39·71	Dec. 2	40·82	·01	1·45	2·18	44·44
5	37·86	·04	1·44	1·24	40·59	4	41·66	·01	1·43	1·55	44·63
7	37·56	·04	1·44	+ 0·61	39·57	6	42·30	·01	1·44	0·92	44·65
9	38·25	·00	1·44	- 0·03	39·66	8	42·59	·00	1·44	+ 0·29	44·32
12	37·71	·00	1·45	0·98	38·18	10	43·29	·01	1·43	- 0·34	44·37
15	40·08	·00	1·45	1·93	39·60	13	45·66	·00	1·42	1·29	45·70
17	38·84	·00	1·46	- 2·56	37·74	16	46·89	·00	1·44	- 2·23	46·08
					1·28·39·45						1·28·44·95

Error of Collimation . . . = 0· 0· 2·75
Resulting Mean Zenith Distance, South = 1·28·42·20

No. 1802 —Nov. 21.—Correction for Curvature of Path + 0″·10.

Mean Zenith Distances of Stars observed at the Cape Point Station.

FACE OF SECTOR EAST. | FACE OF SECTOR WEST.

Day of Observation 1844.	Apparent Zenith Distance, from Unreduced Ob-servation.	Reduction for Az. Error, and Curv. of Path.	Refraction.	Precession, Aberration, and Nutation.	Deduced Mean Zenith Distance, 1844, Jan. 0; and Mean of Separate Results, uncor-rected, for Error of Collimation.	Day of Observation 1844.	Apparent Zenith Distance, from Unreduced Ob-servation.	Reduction for Az. Error, and Curv. of Path.	Refraction.	Precession, Aberration, and Nutation.	Deduced Mean Zenith Distance, 1844, Jan. 0; and Mean of Separate Results, uncor-rected, for Error of Collimation.

B.A.C. 1922.

	° ′ ″	″	″	″	° ′ ″		° ′ ″	″	″	″	° ′ ″
Nov. 25	0·50·58·78	·03	0·93	+ 3·91	0·57· 3·59	Nov. 24	0·57· 2·09	·00	0·93	+ 4·21	0·57· 7·23
Dec. 1	61·89	·00	·94	2·08	4·91	26	3·42	·00	·92	3·61	7·95
3	61·39	·02	·93	1·46	3·76	Dec. 2	4·16	·00	·94	1·77	6·87
5	63·07	·03	·93	0·84	4·81	4	4·65	·00	·92	1·15	6·72
7	62·04	·02	·93	+ 0·21	3·16	6	6·13	·00	·93	+ 0·52	7·58
9	63·02	·00	·93	− 0·43	3·52	8	5·99	·00	·93	− 0·11	6·81
12	63·02	·00	·93	1·37	2·58	10	7·24	·01	·92	0·74	7·41
15	65·59	·00	·93	2·32	4·20	13	8·95	·00	·92	1·69	8·18
17	64·90	·00	·94	2·96	2·88	16	10·13	·00	·93	2·64	8·42
20	66·33	·00	·92	− 3·91	3·34	18	10·18	·00	·93	− 3·28	7·63
					0·57· 3·68						0·57· 7·50

Error of Collimation . . . = 0· 0· 1·91
Resulting Mean Zenith Distance, South = 0·57· 5·59

B.A.C. 1982.

Nov. 25	2·52·48·88	·08	2·81	+ 3·47	2·52·55·08	Nov. 24	2·52·54·31	·00	2·81	+ 3·77	2·52·60·89
Dec. 1	50·46	·00	2·84	1·61	54·91	26	55·54	·01	2·79	3·17	61·49
3	50·90	·00	2·82	0·98	54·64	Dec. 2	55·59	·01	2·83	1·30	59·71
5	52·18	·08	2·81	+ 0·34	55·25	4	56·53	·01	2·80	0·66	59·98
7	51·79	·07	2·81	− 0·30	54·23	6	56·93	·01	2·81	+ 0·02	59·75
9	52·88	·00	2·81	0·05	54·74	8	57·67	·01	2·81	− 0·62	59·85
12	52·23	·00	2·83	1·92	53·14	10	60·04	·02	2·79	1·27	61·54
15	54·51	·00	2·83	2·89	54·45	13	60·33	·01	2·78	2·24	60·86
17	54·65	·00	2·85	3·54	53·96	16	62·36	·00	2·81	3·22	61·95
20	55·04	·00	2·80	− 4·52	54·22	18	61·86	·01	2·83	− 3·87	60·81
					2·52·54·46						2·53· 0·68

Error of Collimation . . . = 0· 0· 3·11
Resulting Mean Zenith Distance, South = 2·52·57·57

B.A.C. 2051.

Nov. 21	4·21·14·10	·09	4·31	+ 3·15	4·21·15·17	Nov. 24	4·20·67·54	·00	4·24	+ 2·33	4·21· 9·45
25	13·76	·11	4·25	2·05	15·85	26	66·55	·01	4·22	1·77	8·99
Dec. 1	11·29	·00	4·30	+ 0·33	15·36	Dec. 2	65·31	·02	4·28	+ 0·04	9·53
3	11·83	·09	4·27	− 0·26	16·27	6	63·44	·02	4·25	− 1·15	8·82
5	10·10	·11	4·24	0·65	15·08	8	64·28	·01	4·24	1·74	10·25
7	10·35	·10	4·25	1·44	15·94	10	61·96	·02	4·21	2·35	8·50
9	9·91	·00	4·25	2·04	16·20	13	60·43	·01	4·20	3·25	7·87
12	9·99	·00	4·27	2·95	17·21	16	59·64	·00	4·24	4·16	8·04
15	7·64	·00	4·27	3·86	15·77	18	59·59	·01	4·27	4·76	8·61
17	7·59	·00	4·31	− 4·46	16·36	22	59·19	·00	4·31	− 5·97	9·47
					4·21·15·91						4·21· 8·95

Error of Collimation . . . = 0· 0· 3·48
Resulting Mean Zenith Distance, North = 4· 2·12·43

3 R

Mean Zenith Distances of Stars observed at the Cape Point Station.

		FACE OF SECTOR EAST.						FACE OF SECTOR WEST.			
Day of Observation 1844.	Apparent Zenith Distance, from Unreduced Observation.	Reduction for Az. Error, and Curv. of Path.	Refraction.	Precession, and Aberration, and Nutation.	Deduced Mean Zenith Distance, 1844, Jan. 0; and Mean of Separate Results, uncorrected, for Error of Collimation.	Day of Observation 1844.	Apparent Zenith Distance, from Unreduced Observation.	Reduction for Az. Error, and Curv. of Path.	Refraction.	Precession, and Aberration, and Nutation.	Deduced Mean Zenith Distance, 1844, Jan. 0; and Mean of Separate Results, uncorrected, for Error of Collimation.

B.A.C. 2109.

Day	Apparent Z.D.	Reduction	Refraction	Precession	Deduced Mean	Day	Apparent Z.D.	Reduction	Refraction	Precession	Deduced Mean
	o ' "	"	"	"	o ' "		o ' "	"	"	"	o ' "
Nov. 25	1·51·59·92	·05	1·82	+ 1·81	1·51·59·88	Nov. 24	1·51·54·24	·00	1·82	+ 2·10	1·51·53·96
Dec. 1	58·93	·00	1·84	+ 0·05	60·72	26	53·50	·01	1·80	+ 1·53	53·76
3	59·52	·04	1·83	- 0·55	61·86	Dec. 2	53·25	·01	1·83	- 0·25	55·32
5	56·90	·05	1·82	1·16	59·83	4	51·77	·01	1·81	0·65	54·42
7	57·94	·04	1·82	1·77	61·49	6	51·62	·01	1·82	1·46	54·89
9	57·20	·00	1·82	2·39	61·41	8	51·82	·00	1·82	2·08	55·72
12	56·56	·00	1·83	3·32	61·71	10	49·99	·01	1·80	2·70	54·48
15	54·88	·00	1·83	4·26	60·97	13	48·76	·01	1·80	3·63	54·18
17	55·18	·00	1·85	4·88	61·91	16	46·83	·00	1·82	4·57	53·22
20	53·25	·00	1·81	- 5·82	60·88	18	47·18	·00	1·83	- 5·20	54·21
					1·52· 1·07						1·51·54·42

Error of Collimation . . . = 0· 0· 3·33
Resulting Mean Zenith Distance, North = 1·51·57·74

B.A.C. 2246.

Day	Apparent Z.D.	Reduction	Refraction	Precession	Deduced Mean	Day	Apparent Z.D.	Reduction	Refraction	Precession	Deduced Mean
Nov. 21	2· 1·13·21	·04	1·99	+ 1·57	2· 1·13·59	Nov. 24	2· 0·67·24	·00	1·97	+ 0·74	2· 1· 8·47
25	13·06	·05	1·97	+ 0·46	14·52	26	65·36	·01	1·95	+ 0·18	7·12
Dec. 1	10·10	·00	1·99	- 1·27	13·36	Dec. 2	65·36	·01	1·98	- 1·57	8·90
3	10·40	·04	1·98	1·87	14·21	4	64·18	·01	1·96	2·17	8·30
7	9·31	·05	1·97	3·08	14·31	6	63·73	·01	1·97	2·78	8·47
9	8·43	·00	1·97	3·70	14·10	8	63·49	·00	1·97	3·39	8·85
12	8·43	·00	1·98	4·69	15·04	10	62·11	·01	1·95	4·01	8·06
15	4·57	·00	1·98	5·58	12·13	13	60·92	·01	1·95	4·95	7·81
17	6·01	·00	2·00	6·21	14·22	16	59·44	·01	1·97	5·89	7·30
20	4·77	·00	1·96	- 7·15	13·68	18	60·03	·00	1·98	- 6·52	8·53
					2· 1·13·94						2· 1· 8·18

Error of Collimation . . . = 0· 0· 2·88
Resulting Mean Zenith Distance, North = 2· 1·11·06

B.A.C. 2293.

Day	Apparent Z.D.	Reduction	Refraction	Precession	Deduced Mean	Day	Apparent Z.D.	Reduction	Refraction	Precession	Deduced Mean
Nov. 21	5·35·14·86	·11	5·53	+ 0·47	5·35·19·81	Nov. 16	5·35· 9·73	·01	5·51	+ 1·73	5·35·13·50
25	13·92	·14	5·46	- 0·59	19·83	24	6·66	·01	5·45	- 0·32	12·42
Dec. 1	12·49	·00	5·52	2·26	20·27	26	6·62	·01	5·42	0·87	12·90
3	12·34	·12	5·48	2·83	20·53	Dec. 2	5·09	·02	5·51	2·54	13·12
5	10·52	·14	5·45	3·41	19·24	4	4·39	·02	5·43	3 12	12·92
7	10·76	·12	5·47	4·00	20·11	6	3·46	·08	5·46	3·70	12·59
9	10·07	·00	5·46	4·59	20·12	8	3·65	·01	5·46	4·29	13·39
12	10·61	·01	5·49	5·49	21·58	10	2·27	·08	5·41	4·89	12·54
15	8·20	·00	5·49	6·39	20·08	13	1·38	·02	5·39	5·79	12·54
17	8·05	·00	5·54	- 7·00	20·59	16	0·99	·00	5·46	- 6·69	13·14
					5·35·20·22						5·35·12·91

Error of Collimation . . . = 0· 0· 3·66
Resulting Mean Zenith Distance, North = 5·35·16·56

Mean Zenith Distances of Stars observed at the Cape Point Station.

FACE OF SECTOR EAST. | FACE OF SECTOR WEST.

B.A.C. 2414.

Day of Observation 1844.	Apparent Zenith Distance, from Unreduced Observation.	Reduction for Az. Error, and Curv. of Path.	Refraction.	Precession, Aberration, and Nutation.	Deduced Mean Zenith Distance, 1844, Jan. 0; and Mean of Separate Results, uncor- rected, for Error of Collimation.	Day of Observation 1844.	Apparent Zenith Distance, from Unreduced Observation.	Reduction for Az. Error, and Curv. of Path.	Refraction.	Precession, Aberration, and Nutation.	Deduced Mean Zenith Distance, 1844, Jan. 0; and Mean of Separate Results, uncor- rected, for Error of Collimation.
Nov. 21	2·28· 1·47	·05	2·44	+ 0·61	2·28· 4·47	Nov. 26	2·28· 9·12	·01	2·39	- 0·79	2·28·10·71
25	1·96	·07	2·41	- 0·50	3·80	Dec. 2	10·21	·01	2·43	2·56	10·07
Dec. 1	3·94	·00	2·44	2·26	4·12	4	11·29	·01	2·39	3·17	10·50
3	3·64	·06	2·42	2·86	3·14	6	11·98	·01	2·41	3·79	10·59
5	5·56	·07	2·40	3·48	4·41	8	12·77	·00	2·41	4·42	10·76
7	5·47	06	2·41	4·10	3·72	10	13·27	·01	2·39	5·06	10·59
9	5·76	·00	2·41	4·74	3·43	13	13·91	·01	2·38	6·03	10·25
12	5·96	·00	2·42	2·67	2·67	16	16·13	·00	2·41	7·01	11·53
15	7·93	·00	2·42	6·68	3·67	18	16·03	·00	2·41	7·67	10·77
17	7·93	·00	2·45	- 7·34	3·04	20	16·72	·00	2·40	- 8·33	10·79
					2·28· 3·65						2·28·10·66

Error of Collimation . . = 0· 0· 3·50
Resulting Mean Zenith Distance, South = 2·28· 7·15

B.A.C. 2458.

Day of Observation 1844.	Apparent Zenith Distance, from Unreduced Observation.	Reduction for Az. Error, and Curv. of Path.	Refraction.	Precession, Aberration, and Nutation.	Deduced Mean Zenith Distance, 1844, Jan. 0; and Mean of Separate Results, uncor- rected, for Error of Collimation.	Day of Observation 1844.	Apparent Zenith Distance, from Unreduced Observation.	Reduction for Az. Error, and Curv. of Path.	Refraction.	Precession, Aberration, and Nutation.	Deduced Mean Zenith Distance, 1844, Jan. 0; and Mean of Separate Results, uncor- rected, for Error of Collimation.
Nov. 25	5·20·51·49	·14	5·22	- 2·16	5·20·58·73	Nov. 24	5·20·43·94	·01	5·22	- 1·90	5·20·51·05
Dec. 1	49·47	·00	5·28	3·80	58·55	26	43·34	·01	5·19	2·43	50·95
3	50·21	·11	5·25	4·37	59·72	Dec. 2	42·60	·02	5·27	4·08	51·93
5	48·33	·14	5·21	4·94	58·34	4	42·16	·02	5·19	4·65	51·98
7	48·43	·12	5·23	5·06	59·06	6	40·98	·03	5·22	5·23	51·40
9	47·94	·00	5·22	6·11	59·27	10	39·59	·03	5·18	6·41	51·15
12	47·49	·01	5·25	7·07	59·74	13	39·05	·02	5·16	7·31	51·50
15	45·61	·00	5·25	7·91	58·77	18	37·03	·01	5·24	8·83	51·09
17	45·86	·00	5·30	8·52	59·68	20	35·15	·00	5·20	9·44	49·79
28	41·27	·00	5·24	-11·91	58·42	22	35·74	·00	5·29	-10·06	51·09
					5·20·59·03						5·20·51·19

Error of Collimation . . = 0· 0· 3·92
Resulting Mean Zenith Distance, North = 5·20·55·11

B.A.C. 2528.

Day of Observation 1844.	Apparent Zenith Distance, from Unreduced Observation.	Reduction for Az. Error, and Curv. of Path.	Refraction.	Precession, Aberration, and Nutation.	Deduced Mean Zenith Distance, 1844, Jan. 0; and Mean of Separate Results, uncor- rected, for Error of Collimation.	Day of Observation 1844.	Apparent Zenith Distance, from Unreduced Observation.	Reduction for Az. Error, and Curv. of Path.	Refraction.	Precession, Aberration, and Nutation.	Deduced Mean Zenith Distance, 1844, Jan. 0; and Mean of Separate Results, uncor- rected, for Error of Collimation.
Nov. 25	3·18·35·64	·09	3·23	- 1·48	3·18·37·30	Nov. 24	3·18·41·29	·00	3·23	- 1·21	3·18·43·31
Dec. 1	37·37	·00	3·27	3·20	37·44	26	41·52	·01	3·21	1·76	42·96
3	37·51	·08	3·24	3·79	36·88	Dec. 2	43·23	·01	3·26	3·50	42·98
7	38·79	·08	3·23	5·02	36·92	4	43·38	·01	3·21	4·10	42·48
9	39·04	·00	3·23	5·65	36·62	6	44·47	·02	3·23	4·71	42·97
12	39·14	·00	3·25	6·61	35·78	13	45·21	·01	3·23	5·33	43·10
17	41·06	·00	3·28	8·24	36·10	18	47·08	·01	3·19	6·93	43·33
20	42·49	·00	3·22	9·24	36·47	22	48·91	·01	3·24	8·58	43·56
28	46·54	·00	3·24	11·93	37·85	30	50·10	·00	3·27	9·91	43·46
1845. Jan. 3	47·48	·00	3·28	-13·94	36·82		52·32	·00	3·24	-12·61	42·95
					3·18·36·82						3·18·43·11

Error of Collimation . . = 0· 0· 3·15
Resulting Mean Zenith Distance, South = 3·18·39·96

Mean Zenith Distances of Stars observed at the Cape Point Station.

	FACE OF SECTOR EAST.						FACE OF SECTOR WEST.				
Day of Observation 1844.	Apparent Zenith Distance, from Unreduced Observation.	Reduction for Az. Error, and Curr. of Path.	Refraction.	Precession, Aberration, and Nutation.	Deduced Mean Zenith Distance, 1844, Jan. 0; and Mean of Separate Results, uncorrected, for Error of Collimation.	Day of Observation 1844.	Apparent Zenith Distance, from Unreduced Observation.	Reduction for Az. Error, and Curr. of Path.	Refraction.	Precession, Aberration, and Nutation.	Deduced Mean Zenith Distance, 1844, Jan. 0; and Mean of Separate Results, uncorrected, for Error of Collimation.

B.A.C. 2575.

	° ′ ″	″	″	″	° ′ ″		° ′ ″	″	″	″	° ′ ″
Nov. 21	3 12 49·92	·07	3·18	− 0·80	3·13· 2·23	Nov. 24	3·13· 6·97	·00	3·14	− 1·58	3·13· 8·53
25	3·13· 1·17	·09	3·14	1 85	2·37	26	7·29	·01	3·12	2·13	8·27
Dec. 1	3·05	·00	3·18	3·55	2 68	Dec. 2	8·53	·01	3·17	3·85	7·84
3	3·34	·08	3·15	4·13	2·28	4	9·37	01	3·12	4·44	8·04
7	4·38	·08	3·14	5·36	2 06	6	10·35	·02	3·14	5·05	8·42
9	4·97	·00	3·14	5·98	2·13	8	10·35	·01	3·14	5·67	7·81
12	5·07	·00	3·15	6 94	1·28	13	13·46	·01	3·10	7·26	9·29
17	7·14	·00	3·19	8·56	1 77	18	14·75	·01	3·15	8·89	9·00
20	8·72	·00	3·12	9·56	2·28	22	15·59	·00	3·18	10·22	8·55
28	12·72	·00	3·15	−12·25	3 62	30	18·50	·00	3·15	−12·92	8·73
					3·13· 2·27						3·13· 8·45

Error of Collimation   .   .   . = 0· 0· 3·09
Resulting Mean Zenith Distance, South = 3·13· 5·36

B.A.C. 2580.

Nov. 21	3·14·22·73	·07	3·20	− 0·83	3·14·25·03	Nov. 24	3·14·28·82	·00	3·16	− 1·62	3·14·30·36
25	23·86	·09	3·16	1·89	25·04	26	30·73	·01	3·14	2·16	31·70
Dec. 1	25·64	·00	3·20	3·58	25·26	Dec. 2	30·97	·01	3 19	3·88	30·27
3	25·59	·08	3·18	4·17	24·52	4	32·21	·01	3·14	4·47	30·87
7	27·22	·08	3·17	5·39	24·92	6	32·60	·02	3·16	5·08	30·66
9	26·93	·00	3·16	6·01	24·08	8	32·80	·01	3·16	5·70	30·25
12	27·52	·00	3·17	6·97	23·72	13	36·01	·01	3·12	7·29	31·83
15	28·50	·00	3·18	7·94	23·74	18	37·19	·01	3·17	8·92	31·43
17	29·05	·00	3·21	8·59	23·67	22	37·69	·00	3·20	10·25	30·64
20	30·07	·00	3·15	− 9·58	24·54	30	40·65	·00	3·18	−12·95	30·88
					3·14·24·45						3·14·30·89

Error of Collimation   .   .   . = 0· 0· 3·22
Resulting Mean Zenith Distance, South = 3·14·27·67

B.A.C. 2635.

Nov. 25	4· 6·30·34	·12	4·01	− 2·12	4· 6·32·11	Nov. 24	4· 6·36·32	·00	4·01	− 1·85	4· 6·38·48
Dec. 1	32·51	·00	4·06	3·81	32·76	26	37·45	·01	3·98	2·39	39·03
3	31·68	·10	4·03	4·39	31·22	Dec. 2	38·29	·02	4·05	4·09	38·23
7	33·21	·10	4·02	5·60	31·53	4	38·64	·02	3·99	4·69	37·92
9	33·95	·00	4·02	6·22	31·75	6	40·66	·02	4·01	5·30	39·35
12	34·09	·00	4·03	7·18	30·94	8	40·12	·01	4·01	5·91	38·21
15	36·46	·00	4·08	8·15	32·34	13	42·54	·01	3·96	7·50	38·99
17	36·32	·00	4·08	8·80	31·60	18	44·56	·01	4 02	9·13	39·44
20	37·40	·00	3·99	9·80	31·59	22	45·05	·00	4·07	10·47	38·65
28	41·40	·00	4·03	−12·50	32·93	30	48·02	·00	4·03	−13·19	38·86
					4· 6·31·88						4· 6·38·72

Error of Collimation   .   .   . = 0· 0· 3·42
Resulting Mean Zenith Distance, South = 4· 6·35·30

B.A.C. 2575.—Nov. 21.—10″ added, as it is evident that an error of 10 divisions of the Micrometer was committed when registering the observation.

Mean Zenith Distances of Stars observed at the Cape Point Station.

FACE OF SECTOR EAST.						FACE OF SECTOR WEST.					
Day of Observation 1844–5.	Apparent Zenith Distance, from Unreduced Observation.	Reduction for Az. Error, and Curv. of Path.	Refraction.	Precession, Aberration, and Nutation.	Deduced Mean Zenith Distance, 1844, Jan. 0; and Mean of Separate Results, uncorrected, for Error of Collimation.	Day of Observation 1844–5.	Apparent Zenith Distance, from Unreduced Observation.	Reduction for Az. Error, and Curv. of Path.	Refraction.	Precession, Aberration, and Nutation.	Deduced Mean Zenith Distance, 1844, Jan. 0; and Mean of Separate Results, uncorrected, for Error of Collimation.

B.A.C. 2655.

Day	App. Z.D.	Red.	Refr.	Prec.	Deduced	Day	App. Z.D.	Red.	Refr.	Prec.	Deduced
1844.	° ′ ″	″	″	″	° ′ ″	1844.	° ′ ″	″	″	″	° ′ ″
Nov. 25	4 25 53·37	·11	4·32	− 3·99	4 26 1·57	Nov. 24	4 25 47·39	·00	4·32	− 3·74	4 25 55·45
Dec. 1	52·68	·00	4·37	5·57	2·62	26	46·80	·01	4·29	4·24	55·32
3	51·89	·10	4·34	6·13	2·26	Dec. 2	45·81	·02	4·36	5·85	56·00
7	50·55	·10	4·33	7·26	2·04	4	44·68	·02	4·30	6·41	55·37
9	49·57	·00	4·33	7·84	1·74	6	44·73	·02	4·32	6·97	56·00
12	49·66	·00	4·34	8·73	− 2·73	8	44·09	·01	4·32	7·55	55·95
20	46·41	·00	4·30	11·17	1·88	18	39·99	·01	4·34	10·55	54·87
28	43·25	·00	4·34	13·67	1·26	22	38·90	·00	4·38	11·79	55·07
31	43·44	·00	4·29	14·61	2·34	30	36·63	·00	4·34	14·30	55·27
1845.						1845.					
Jan. 5	40·98	·00	4·33	−16·16	1·47	Jan. 1	35·64	·00	4·29	−14·90	54·83
					4·26 1·99						4·25·55·41

Error of Collimation . . . = 0· 0· 3·29
Resulting Mean Zenith Distance, North = 4·25·58·70

B.A.C. 2710.

Day	App. Z.D.	Red.	Refr.	Prec.	Deduced	Day	App. Z.D.	Red.	Refr.	Prec.	Deduced
1844.						1844.					
Nov. 25	5 12 45·28	·15	5·09	− 2·48	5 12 47·74	Nov. 24	5 12 52·79	·01	5·09	− 2·21	5 12 55·66
Dec. 1	48·25	·00	5·15	4·13	49·27	26	53·09	·02	5·06	2·74	55·39
3	46·37	·13	5·12	4·71	46·65	Dec. 2	54·17	·02	5·14	4·42	54·87
5	49·09	·15	5·08	5·31	48·71	4	54·17	·02	5·07	5·01	54·21
7	48·48	·13	5·10	5·91	47·54	8	56·09	·01	5·09	6·22	54·95
9	49·67	·00	5·10	6·53	48·24	10	59·25	·03	5·05	6·84	57·43
12	49·87	·01	5·11	7·48	47·49	13	58·00	·02	5·03	7·81	55·26
15	50·16	·00	5·12	8·45	46·83	16	58·85	·00	5·09	8·77	55·17
17	50·61	·00	5·18	9·10	46·69	18	60·04	·01	5·11	9·48	55·71
20	52·53	·00	5·07	−10·10	47·50	22	61·12	·01	5·16	−10·77	55·50
					5·12·47·67						5·12·55·42

Error of Collimation . . . = 0· 0· 3·88
Resulting Mean Zenith Distance, South = 5·12·51·54

B.A.C. 2795.

Day	App. Z.D.	Red.	Refr.	Prec.	Deduced	Day	App. Z.D.	Red.	Refr.	Prec.	Deduced
1844.						1844.					
Nov. 21	1 49 34·33	·04	1·81	− 2·86	1 49 33·24	Nov. 24	1 49 41·73	·00	1·78	− 3·59	1 49 39·92
25	35·86	·05	1·78	3·84	33·75	Dec. 2	43·26	·01	1·80	5·70	39·35
Dec. 1	37·39	·00	1·80	5·43	33·76	4	43·71	·01	1·77	6·27	39·20
3	37·14	·04	1·79	5·98	32·91	6	44·80	·01	1·78	6·85	39·72
5	39·56	·05	1·78	6·55	34·74	8	44·70	·00	1·78	7·43	39·05
7	37·83	·04	1·78	7·14	32·43	10	47·26	·01	1·77	8·03	40·99
9	39·27	·00	1·78	7·73	33·32	13	46·92	·01	1·76	8·95	39·72

Carried forward,

Mean Zenith Distances of Stars observed at the Cape Point Station.

FACE OF SECTOR EAST.						FACE OF SECTOR WEST.					
Day of Observation 1844–5.	Apparent Zenith Distance, from Unreduced Observation.	Reduction for Az. Error, and Curv. of Path.	Refraction.	Precession, Aberration, and Nutation.	Deduced Mean Zenith Distance, 1844, Jan. 0; and Mean of Separate Results, uncorrected, for Error of Collimation.	Day of Observation 1844–5.	Apparent Zenith Distance, from Unreduced Observation.	Reduction for Az. Error, and Curv. of Path.	Refraction.	Precession, Aberration, and Nutation.	Deduced Mean Zenith Distance, 1844, Jan. 0; and Mean of Separate Results, uncorrected, for Error of Collimation.

					B.A.C. 2795—(continued).						
1844.	° ′ ″	″	″	″	° ′ ″	1844.	° ′ ″	″	″	″	° ′ ″
Dec. 12	1·49·39·61	·00	1·79	8·64	1·49·32·76	Dec. 16	1·49·48·70	·00	1·78	9·89	1·49·40·59
15	40·94	·00	1·79	9·57	33·16	18	48·94	·00	1·79	10·53	40·20
17	41·49	·00	1·81	–10·21	33·09	20	50·42	·00	1·77	–11·17	41·02
					1·49·33·32						1·49·39·98

Error of Collimation　　.　　.　= 0· 0· 3·33
Resulting Mean Zenith Distance, South = 1·49·36·65

					B.A.C. 2935.						
1844.						1844.					
Nov. 21	0·24·22·28	·01	0·40	– 4·26	0·24·18·41	Nov. 24	0·24·27·07	·00	0·40	– 4·94	0·24·22·53
25	22·53	·01	·40	5·18	17·74	26	27·57	·00	·40	5·42	22·55
Dec. 1	24·75	·00	·40	6·09	18·46	Dec. 2	28·60	·00	·40	6·95	22·05
3	24·36	·01	·40	7·21	17·54	4	29·44	·00	·40	7·49	22·35
5	26·83	·01	·40	7·76	19·46	6	29·34	·00	·40	8·04	21·70
7	26·63	·01	·40	8·32	18·70	8	30·28	·00	·40	8·60	22·08
9	26·43	·00	·40	8·89	17·94	10	32·45	·00	·40	9·18	23·67
12	26·73	·00	·40	9·77	17·36	13	32·45	·00	·39	10·07	22·77
17	28·21	·00	·40	11·28	17·33	16	34·53	·00	·40	10·98	23·95
22	30·68	·00	·40	–12·85	18·23	18	33·93	·00	·40	–11·59	22·74
					0·24·18·12						0·24·22·64

Error of Collimation　　.　　.　= 0· 0· 2·26
Resulting Mean Zenith Distance, South = 0·24·20·38

					B.A.C. 2964.						
1844.						1844.					
Nov. 21	1·43·24·42	·04	1·70	– 4·91	1·43·30·99	Nov. 24	1·43·18·80	·00	1·68	– 5·59	1·43·26·07
25	23·34	·05	1·68	5·82	30·79	26	18·01	·00	1·67	6·06	25·74
Dec. 1	22·05	·00	1·70	7·30	31·05	Dec. 2	17·12	·01	1·69	7·56	26·36
3	21·86	·04	1·69	7·82	31·33	4	16·72	·01	1·67	8·09	26·47
5	20·38	·05	1·68	8·36	30·37	6	15·59	·00	1·68	8·64	25·91
7	21·41	·04	1·68	8·91	31·96	8	16·28	·00	1·68	9·19	27·15
9	20·16	·00	1·68	9·45	31·31	10	13·71	·01	1·67	9·75	25·12
12	20·77	·00	1·68	10·33	32·78	13	13·86	·01	1·66	10·63	26·14
17	18·20	·00	1·71	11·82	31·73	16	12·13	·00	1·68	11·52	25·33
20	17·22	·00	1·67	–12·73	31·62	18	11·88	·00	1·68	–12·13	25·69
					1·43·31·39						1·43·26·00

Error of Collimation　　.　　.　= 0· 0· 2·70
Resulting Mean Zenith Distance, North = 1·43·28·70

Mean Zenith Distances of Stars observed at the Cape Point Station.

FACE OF SECTOR EAST. | FACE OF SECTOR WEST.

B.A.C. 3130.

Day of Observation 1844-5.	Apparent Zenith Distance, from Unreduced Observation.	Reduction for Az. Error, and Curv. of Path.	Refraction.	Precession, Aberration, and Nutation.	Deduced Mean Zenith Distance, 1844, Jan. 0; and Results, uncorrected, for Error of Collimation.	Day of Observation 1844-5.	Apparent Zenith Distance, from Unreduced Observation.	Reduction for Az. Error, and Curv. of Path.	Refraction.	Precession, Aberration, and Nutation.	Deduced Mean Zenith Distance, 1844, Jan. 0; and Results, uncorrected, for Error of Collimation.
1844.						1844.					
Nov. 25	4 36 63·67	·12	4·51	- 7·75	4·37·15·81	Nov. 24	4 36 58·23	·01	4·50	- 7·53	4·37·10·25
Dec. 3	60·90	·10	4·53	9·61	14 04	Dec. 2	56·11	·02	4·55	9·37	10·01
5	60·16	·12	4·50	10·12	14·66	4	55·13	·02	4·49	9·67	9·47
9	60·31	·00	4·51	11·16	15·98	6	54·63	·02	4·50	10·38	9·49
12	59·02	·00	4·53	11·98	16·13	10	52·16	·02	4·48	11·43	8·05
17	58·43	·00	4·58	13·39	16·40	13	51·37	·01	4·45	12·26	8·07
20	56·61	·00	4·48	14·26	15·35	18	50·04	·01	4·51	13·08	8·22
28	53·74	·00	4·53	16·66	14·93	22	49·05	·00	4·56	14·86	8·47
31	54·34	·00	4·47	17·58	16·39	30	47·08	·00	4·52	17·27	8·87
1845.						1845.					
Jan. 5	51·23	·00	4 51	-19·10	14·84	Jan. 1	46·04	·00	4·48	-17·86	8·38
					4·37·15·54						4·37· 8·93

Error of Collimation . . . = 0· 0· 3·31
Resulting Mean Zenith Distance, North = 4·37·12·24

B.A.C. 3163.

1844.						1844.					
Nov.25	3·34·12·95	·10	3 49	- 6·04	3·34·10·30	Nov. 24	3·34·18·93	·00	3·48	- 5·83	3·34·16·58
Dec. 3	14·68	·08	3·50	7·91	10·19	26	19·47	·01	3·46	6·26	16·66
5	15·08	·10	3·48	8·41	10·05	Dec. 2	19·81	·01	3·52	7·66	15·66
8	16·16	·09	3·49	9·20	10·36	4	20·65	·01	3·47	8·16	15·95
9	15·17	·00	3·49	9·47	9·19	6	21·89	·02	3·48	8 67	16·68
12	15·57	·00	3·50	10·31	8·76	10	23·71	·02	3·46	9·75	17·40
17	17·44	·00	3·54	11·77	9·21	13	24·26	·01	3 44	10·59	17·10
20	18·43	·00	3·47	12·67	9·23	18	25·05	·01	3·49	12·07	16·46
28	22·18	·00	3·50	15·20	10·48	22	26·23	·00	3·53	13·29	16·47
31	21·59	·00	3 46	-16·17	8 88	30	29·05	·00	3·50	-15·85	16·70
					3·34· 9·67						3·34·16·57

Error of Collimation . . . = 0· 0· 3·45
Resulting Mean Zenith Distance, South = 3·34·13·12

B.A.C. 3257.

1844.						1844.					
Nov. 25	5·25·59·04	·16	5·31	- 6·21	5·25·57·98	Nov. 24	5·26· 5·17	·01	5·30	- 6·01	5·26· 4·45
Dec. 3	5·26· 0·62	·13	5·34	7·98	57·85	26	5·86	·02	5·28	6·42	4·70
5	0·43	·16	5·30	8·47	57·10	Dec. 2	6·65	·02	5·36	7·75	4·24
7	0·97	·14	5·32	8·97	57 18	4	7·58	·02	5·29	8·23	4·62
8	1·71	·14	5·31	9·23	57·65	6	7·78	·03	5·31	8·72	4·34
9	1·61	·00	5·31	9·49	57·43	13	10·65	·02	5·25	10·58	5·30
12	1·66	·01	5·33	10·30	56·08	18	12·42	·01	5·32	12·02	5·71

Carried forward,

Mean Zenith Distances of Stars observed at the Cape Point Station.

FACE OF SECTOR EAST.						FACE OF SECTOR WEST.					
Day of Observation 1844-5.	Apparent Zenith Distance, from Unreduced Observation.	Reduction for Az. Error, and Curv. of Path.	Refraction.	Precession, Aberration, and Nutation.	Deduced Mean Zenith Distance. 1844, Jan. 0; and Mean of Separate Results, uncorrected, for Error of Collimation.	Day of Observation 1844-5.	Apparent Zenith Distance, from Unreduced Observation.	Reduction for Az. Error, and Curv. of Path.	Refraction.	Precession, Aberration, and Nutation.	Deduced Mean Zenith Distance. 1844, Jan. 0; and Mean of Separate Results, uncorrected, for Error of Collimation.

B.A.C. 3257—(continued.)

	° ′ ″	″	″	″	° ′ ″		° ′ ″	″	″	″	° ′ ″
1844.						1844.					
Dec. 17	5·26· 3·24	·00	5·40	11·73	5·25·56·91	Dec. 22	5·26·12·57	·01	5·38	13·22	5·26· 4·72
20	3·78	·00	5·28	12·61	56·45	30	14·64	·00	5·33	15·75	4·22
28	8·18	·00	5·34	-15·11	58·41	31	15·04	·00	5·27	-16·08	4·23
					5·25·57·36						5·26· 4·65

Error of Collimation . . = 0· 0· 3·64
Resulting Mean Zenith Distance, South = 5·26· 1·01

Anon. AR. 9·39.

1844.						1844.					
Dec. 12	2·22·59·74	·00	2·33	-12·54	2·23·14·61	Dec. 18	2·22·49·96	·00	2·32	-14·16	2·23· 6·44
17	57·37	·00	2·36	13·86	13 61	22	50·61	·00	2·35	15·29	8·25
20	56·38	·00	2 31	14·72	13·41	30	47·59	·00	2·33	17·66	7·58
28	53·67	·00	2·33	17·05	13·05	1845.					
31	52·93	·00	2·30	17·96	13·19	Jan. 5	46·26	·00	2·33	19·47	8·06
1845.						10	42·90	·00	2·32	21·03	6·25
Jan. 9	50·21	·00	2·33	20·72	13·26	12	43·94	·00	2·30	-21·66	7·90
11	49·02	·00	2·31	21·34	13·27						
15	47·30	·00	2 32	-22·61	12·23						
					2·23·13·33						2·23· 7·41

Error of Collimation . . = 0· 0· 2·96
Resulting Mean Zenith Distance, North = 2·23·10·37

B.A.C. 3403.

1844.						1844.					
Dec. 20	3·59·38·87	·00	3·87	-15·34	3·59·58 08	Dec. 18	3·59·31·27	·01	3·90	-14·79	3·59·49·95
28	35·86	·00	3·91	17·62	57·39	22	31·02	·00	3·94	15·89	50·85
31	35·91	·00	3·86	18·50	58·27	30	28·75	·00	3 91	18·21	50·67
1845.						1845.					
Jan. 9	32·80	·00	3·91	21·19	57·90	Jan. 5	28·48	·00	3·91	19·97	50·36
11	32·75	·00	3·88	21·80	58·43	10	24·51	·01	3·89	21·50	49·89
14	31·27	·00	3·91	-22 73	57·91	12	24·36	·00	3·86	-22·11	50·33
					3·59·58·00						3·59·50·38

Error of Collimation . . = 0· 0· 3·81
Resulting Mean Zenith Distance, North = 3·59·54·19

Mean Zenith Distances of Stars observed at the Cape Point Station.

FACE OF SECTOR EAST. / FACE OF SECTOR WEST.

Anon. AR. 10·2.

Day of Observation 1844-5.	Apparent Zenith Distance, from Unreduced Observation.	Reduction for Az. Error, and Curv. of Path.	Refraction.	Precession, Aberration, and Nutation.	Deduced Mean Zenith Distance, 1844, Jan. 0; and Mean of Separate Results, uncorrected, for Error of Collimation.	Day of Observation 1844-5.	Apparent Zenith Distance, from Unreduced Observation.	Reduction for Az. Error, and Curv. of Path.	Refraction.	Precession, Aberration, and Nutation.	Deduced Mean Zenith Distance, 1844, Jan. 0; and Mean of Separate Results, uncorrected, for Error of Collimation.
1844.						1844.					
Dec. 20	4· 0·23·40	·00	3·89	-15·56	4· 0·42·85	Dec. 18	4· 0·16·00	·01	3·92	-15·03	4· 0·34·94
28	21·43	·00	3·93	17·80	43·16	30	13·08	·00	3·92	18·38	35·38
31	20·44	·00	3·88	18·66	42·98	1845.					
1845.						Jan. 5	11·65	·00	3·92	20·11	35·68
Jan. 11	17·08	·00	3·89	21·93	42·90	10	10·27	·01	3·91	21·62	35 79
15	13·92	·00	3·90	-23·15	40·97	12	9·48	·00	3·88	-22·24	35·60
					4· 0·42·57						4· 0·35·48

Error of Collimation . . . = 0· 0· 3·55
Resulting Mean Zenith Distance, North = 4· 0·39·03

B.A.C. 3578.

Day of Observation 1844-5.	Apparent Zenith Distance	Red.	Refr.	Prec. &c.	Deduced Mean Z.D.	Day of Observation 1844-5.	Apparent Zenith Distance	Red.	Refr.	Prec. &c.	Deduced Mean Z.D.
1844.						1844.					
Nov. 25	4· 4·22·78	·11	3·97	-10·38	4· 4·37 02	Nov. 24	4· 4·17·84	+ ·10	3·97	-10·21	4· 4·32·12
Dec. 3	21·05	·00	3·99	11·87	36·82	Dec. 2	16·26	·01	4·01	11·67	31·93
5	20·80	·11	3·97	12·28	36·94	4	15·77	·01	3·96	12·07	31·79
12	20·31	·00	3·99	13·84	38·14	8	14·93	·01	3·98	12·93	31·83
17	19·47	·00	4·04	15·06	38·57	11	12·71	·02	4·00	13·61	30·30
20	18·23	·00	3·95	15·83	38 01	18	10·88	·01	3·98	15·32	30·17
28	15·42	·00	3·99	17·99	37·40	22	10·83	·00	4·02	16·35	31·20
31	15·77	·00	3·94	18·83	38·54	30	8·26	·00	3·99	18·55	30·80
1845.						1845.					
Jan. 9	13·10	·00	3·99	21·41	38·50	Jan. 1	7·72	·00	3·95	19·08	30·75
11	12·65	·00	3·96	-22·01	38·62	5	6·73	·00	3·98	-20·23	30·94
					4· 4·37·86						4· 4·31·18

Error of Collimation . . . = 0· 0· 3·34
Resulting Mean Zenith Distance, North = 4· 4·34·52

B.A.C. 3598.

Day of Observation 1844-5.	Apparent Zenith Distance	Red.	Refr.	Prec. &c.	Deduced Mean Z.D.	Day of Observation 1844-5.	Apparent Zenith Distance	Red.	Refr.	Prec. &c.	Deduced Mean Z.D.
1844.						1844.					
Dec. 20	4·32·10·43	·00	4·40	-15·98	4·32·30·81	Dec. 18	4·31·63·72	·01	4·44	-15·48	4·32·23·63
28	6·98	·00	4·45	18·13	29·56	22	63·72	·00	4·48	16·50	24·70
31	7·17	·00	4·39	18·97	30·53	30	61·64	·00	4·44	18·69	24·77
1845.						1845.					
Jan. 9	4·66	·00	4·45	21·53	30·64	Jan. 1	59·37	·00	4·40	19·21	22·98
11	4·31	·00	4·41	22·12	30·84	5	59·47	·00	4·44	20·36	24·27
14	3·91	·00	4·45	23·01	31·37	10	58·48	·01	4·42	21·82	24·71
15	3·62	·00	4·42	-23·31	31·35	12	57·00	·00	4·39	-22·42	23·81
					4·32·30·73						4·32·24·12

Error of Collimation . . . = 0· 0· 3·30
Resulting Mean Zenith Distance, North = 4·32·27·43

No. 3578.—Nov. 24.—Correction for Curvature of Path = +0"·10.

Mean Zenith Distances of Stars observed at the Cape Point Station.

B.A.C. 3755.

FACE OF SECTOR EAST.

Day of Observation 1844–5.	Apparent Zenith Distance, from Unreduced Observation.	Reduction for Az. Error, and Curv. of Path.	Refraction.	Precession, Aberration, and Nutation.	Deduced Mean Zenith Distance, 1844, Jan. 0; and Mean of Separate Results, uncorrected, for Error of Collimation.
1844.	° ′ ″	″	″	″	° ′ ″
Dec. 5	1·57· 1·25	·05	1·89	−11·11	1·56·51·98
9	1·25	·00	1·90	11·86	51·29
12	1·59	·00	1·91	12·49	51·01
20	2·96	·00	1·89	14·30	50·57
28	5·59	·00	1·91	16·35	51·15
31	5 69	·00	1·89	17·16	50·42
1845.					
Jan. 9	8·16	·00	1·91	19·69	50·38
11	8·90	·00	1·90	20·29	50·51
14	9·44	·00	1·91	21·19	50·16
15	9·94	·00	1·90	−21·49	50·35
					1·56·50·78

FACE OF SECTOR WEST.

Day of Observation 1844–5.	Apparent Zenith Distance, from Unreduced Observation.	Reduction for Az. Error, and Curv. of Path.	Refraction.	Precession, Aberration, and Nutation.	Deduced Mean Zenith Distance, 1844, Jan. 0; and Mean of Separate Results, uncorrected, for Error of Collimation.
1844.	° ′ ″	″	″	″	° ′ ″
Dec. 8	1·57· 6·19	·00	1·90	−11·67	1·56·56·42
11	7·62	·01	1·92	12·28	57·25
17	9·59	·00	1·94	13·60	57·93
18	9·39	·00	1·91	13·83	57·47
22	9·00	·00	1·93	14·80	56·13
30	12·11	·00	1·91	16·89	57·13
1845.					
Jan. 5	11·42	·00	1·91	18·53	(54·80)
10	16·21	·00	1·90	19·99	58·12
12	15·86	·00	1·89	−20·59	57·16
					1·56·57·20

Error of Collimation . . . = 0· 0· 3·21
Resulting Mean Zenith Distance, South = 1·56·53·99

B.A.C. 3928.

FACE OF SECTOR EAST.

Day of Observation 1844–5.	Apparent Zenith Distance, from Unreduced Observation.	Reduction for Az. Error, and Curv. of Path.	Refraction.	Precession, Aberration, and Nutation.	Deduced Mean Zenith Distance, 1844, Jan. 0; and Mean of Separate Results, uncorrected, for Error of Collimation.
1844.					
Dec. 5	3·21·10·60	·11	3·24	−12·80	3·21·26·53
8	9·91	·09	3·27	13·30	26·39
9	10·15	·00	3·27	13·47	26·89
12	10·05	·00	3·28	14·03	27·36
20	8·57	·00	3·25	15·65	27·47
28	5·76	·00	3·29	17·50	26·55
1845.					
Jan. 9	4·38	·00	3·28	20·51	28·17
11	4·48	·00	3·26	21·04	28·78
14	4·18	·00	3·29	21·86	29·33
15	3·09	·00	3·27	−22·14	28·50
					3·21·27·60

FACE OF SECTOR WEST.

Day of Observation 1844–5.	Apparent Zenith Distance, from Unreduced Observation.	Reduction for Az. Error, and Curv. of Path.	Refraction.	Precession, Aberration, and Nutation.	Deduced Mean Zenith Distance, 1844, Jan. 0; and Mean of Separate Results, uncorrected, for Error of Collimation.
1844.					
Nov. 26	3·20·66·45	·01	3·24	−11·51	3·21·21·19
Dec. 2	65·95	·01	3·29	12·32	21·55
6	65·76	·02	3·27	12·96	21·97
11	63·63	·02	3·29	13·84	20·74
17	62·30	·00	3·30	15·02	20·62
18	62·01	·01	3·28	15·23	20·51
30	60·02	·00	3·28	17·99	21·89
1845.					
Jan. 5	58·94	·00	3·27	19·46	21·67
10	55·98	·01	3·27	20·77	20·01
12	55·88	·00	3·25	−21·32	20·45
					3·21·21·06

Error of Collimation . . . = 0· 0· 3·27
Resulting Mean Zenith Distance, North = 3·21·24·33

B.A.C. 4015.

FACE OF SECTOR EAST.

Day of Observation 1844–5.	Apparent Zenith Distance, from Unreduced Observation.	Reduction for Az. Error, and Curv. of Path.	Refraction.	Precession, Aberration, and Nutation.	Deduced Mean Zenith Distance, 1844, Jan. 0; and Mean of Separate Results, uncorrected, for Error of Collimation.
1844.					
Dec. 8	1·18·29·31	·03	1·27	−12·66	1·18·43·21
9	29·26	·00	1·27	12·81	43·34
28	25 07	·00	1·28	16·51	42·86
31	25·61	·00	1·27	17·21	44·09
1845.					
Jan. 11	23·49	·00	1·27	19·89	44·65
14	23·93	·00	1·28	−20·68	45·89
					1·18·44·01

FACE OF SECTOR WEST.

Day of Observation 1844–5.	Apparent Zenith Distance, from Unreduced Observation.	Reduction for Az. Error, and Curv. of Path.	Refraction.	Precession, Aberration, and Nutation.	Deduced Mean Zenith Distance, 1844, Jan. 0; and Mean of Separate Results, uncorrected, for Error of Collimation.
1844.					
Dec. 17	1·18·23·78	·00	1·30	−14·21	1·18·39·29
30	21·26	·00	1·28	16·97	39·51
1845.					
Jan. 5	19·19	·00	1·28	18·36	38·63
10	16·82	·00	1·27	19·63	37·72
12	16·72	·00	1·26	20·15	38·13
15	15·54	·00	1·27	−20·94	37·75
					1·18·38·54

Error of Collimation . . . = 0· 0· 2·74
Resulting Mean Zenith Distance, North = 1·18·41·27

Mean Zenith Distances of Stars observed at the Cape Point Station.

FACE OF SECTOR EAST.   FACE OF SECTOR WEST.

B.A.C. 4202.

Day of Observation 1844-5	Apparent Zenith Distance, from Unreduced Observation	Reduction for Az. Error, and Curv. of Path.	Refraction.	Precession, and Aberration, and Nutation.	Deduced Mean Zenith Distance, 1844, Jan. 0; and Mean of Separate Results, uncorrected, for Error of Collimation.
1845.					
Jan. 9	3 49 38·03	·00	3 75	-16·53	3 49 25·25
11	37·59	·00	3·72	17·00	24·31
15	38·82	·00	3 73	-17·96	24·59
					3·49·24·72

Day of Observation 1844-5	Apparent Zenith Distance, from Unreduced Observation	Reduction for Az. Error, and Curv. of Path.	Refraction.	Precession, and Aberration, and Nutation.	Deduced Mean Zenith Distance, 1844, Jan. 0; and Mean of Separate Results, uncorrected, for Error of Collimation.
1845.					
Jan. 10	3 49 45·59	·01	3 73	-16·76	3 49 32·55
12	45·59	·00	3 71	-17·24	32·06
					3·49·32·31

Error of Collimation . . . = 0· 0· 3·79
Resulting Mean Zenith Distance, South = 3·49·28·51

B.A.C. 4458.

Day	Apparent Z.D.	Reduction	Refraction.	Prec. &c.	Deduced Mean Z.D.
1844.					
Nov. 21	1 32 13·59	* ·13	1·50	- 9·90	1 32· 5 09
Dec. 1	14·58	·00	1·51	10·11	5·98
3	15·12	·04	1·50	10·20	6·38
9	13·99	·00	1·49	10·56	4·92
12	14·18	·00	1·50	10·82	4·86
15	14·78	·00	1·50	11·10	5·18
28	17·24	·00	1·51	12·72	6·03
31	18·53	·00	1·40	13·17	6·85
1845.					
Jan. 9	18·03	·00	1·51	14·67	4·87
11	17·59	·00	1·50	-15 05	4·04
					1·32· 5·42

Day	Apparent Z.D.	Reduction	Refraction.	Prec. &c.	Deduced Mean Z.D.
1844.					
Nov. 25	1 32 17·59	·00	1·49	- 9 93	1 32· 9·15
26	17·84	·00	1·48	9·95	9·37
Dec. 5	17·89	·01	1·49	10·31	9·06
11	18·33	·01	1·51	10·73	9·10
17	20·11	·00	1·52	11·31	10·32
18	19·81	·00	1·50	11·42	9·89
30	21·00	·00	1·50	13·02	9·48
1845.					
Jan. 5	20·85	·00	1·50	13·95	8·40
10	23·76	·00	1·50	14·86	10·40
12	23·46	·00	1·49	-15·24	9·71
					1·32· 9·49

Error of Collimation . . . = 0· 0· 2·03
Resulting Mean Zenith Distance, South = 1·32· 7·45

B.A.C. 4686.

Day	Apparent Z.D.	Reduction	Refraction.	Prec. &c.	Deduced Mean Z.D.
1844.					
Nov. 20	1 14 56·54	·03	1·22	- 9·13	1 14 48·60
21	56·50	·03	1·21	9·10	48·58
Dec. 1	56·79	·00	1·22	8·98	49·03
3	55·61	·03	1·21	9·01	47·78
5	56·99	·03	1·21	9 04	49·13
9	55·75	·00	1·21	9 15	47·81
12	56·30	·00	1·21	9·29	48·22
15	56·25	·00	1·22	9·45	48·02
19	56·05	·00	1·21	9·72	47·54
28	57·83	·00	1 22	-10·53	48·52
					1·14·48·32

Day	Apparent Z.D.	Reduction	Refraction.	Prec. &c.	Deduced Mean Z.D.
1844.					
Nov. 16	1 14 59·80	·00	1·21	- 9·30	1 14 51·71
24	59·56	* ·04	1·21	9·03	51·70
26	60·94	·00	1·20	8·99	53·15
Dec. 2	59·46	·00	1·22	8·99	51·69
4	59·85	·00	1·19	9·03	52 01
8	59·56	·00	1·21	9 12	51·65
11	59·51	·01	1·22	9·24	51·48
18	60·44	·00	1·21	9 65	52·00
20	61·63	·00	1 21	9·79	53·05
30	60·99	·00	1·22	-10·75	51·46
					1·14·51·99

Error of Collimation . . . = 0· 0· 1·83
Resulting Mean Zenith Distance, South = 1·14·50·16

No. 4458.—Nov. 21.—Correction for Azimuthal Error - ·03 ; for Curvature of Path - ·10. Sum = - 0″·13.
,, 4686.— ,, 24.— ,, ,, ,, ·00 ; ,, ,, - ·04. = - 0 · 04.

Mean Zenith Distances of Stars observed at the Cape Point Station.

FACE OF SECTOR EAST.

B.A.C. 5632.

Day of Observation 1844-5.	Apparent Zenith Distance, from Unreduced Observation.	Reduction for Az. Error, and Curv. of Path.	Refraction.	Precession, and Nutation.	Aberration, and Nutation.	Deduced Mean Zenith Distance, 1844, Jan. 0; and Mean of Separate Results, uncorrected, for Error of Collimation.
1844. Dec. 31	0·20·55·49	·00	0·33		- 0·25	0·20·56·07
1845. Jan. 9	54·30	·00	·34		0·15	54·79
11	55·19	·00	·34		0·15	55·68
15	53·12	·00	·34		- 0·17	53·63
						0·20·55·04

FACE OF SECTOR WEST.

Day of Observation 1844-5.	Apparent Zenith Distance, from Unreduced Observation.	Reduction for Az. Error, and Curv. of Path.	Refraction.	Precession, and Nutation.	Aberration, and Nutation.	Deduced Mean Zenith Distance, 1844, Jan. 0; and Mean of Separate Results, uncorrected, for Error of Collimation.
1844. Dec. 30	0·20·51·39	·00	0·34		- 0·27	0·20·52·00
1845. Jan. 10	50·95	·00	·34		0·15	51·44
12	50·55	·00	·33		0·15	51·03
16	50·55	·00	·33		- 0·18	51·06
						0·20·51·38

Error of Collimation . . . = 0· 0· 1·83
Resulting Mean Zenith Distance, North = 0·20·53·21

B.A.C. 5915.

FACE OF SECTOR EAST.

Day of Observation 1844-5.	Apparent Zenith Distance	Reduction	Refraction.	Precession, and Nutation.	Aberration, and Nutation.	Deduced Mean Zenith Distance
1844. Nov. 27	2·37·45·23	·07	2·48		+ 0·10	2·37·47·83
Dec. 2	45·32	·00	2·55		0·60	48·56
6	44·73	·07	2·53		1·07	48·26
9	43·55	·00	2·52		1·33	47·42
17	42·56	·00	2·56		2·14	47·26
19	41·47	·00	2·52		2·30	46·29
31	41·67	·00	2·52		3·17	47·36
1845. Jan. 9	40·29	·00	2·55		3·68	46·52
11	41·47	·00	2·53		3·78	47·78
15	40·49	·00	2·54		+ 3·95	46·98
						2·37·47·43

FACE OF SECTOR WEST.

Day of Observation 1844-5.	Apparent Zenith Distance	Reduction	Refraction.	Precession, and Nutation.	Aberration, and Nutation.	Deduced Mean Zenith Distance
1844. Nov. 26	2·37·50·56	·01	2·51		+ 0·09	2·37·53·15
29	49·77	·01	2·53		0·30	52·68
Dec. 4	50·56	·01	2·53		0·86	53·96
7	49·38	·01	2·54		1·17	53·08
13	51·29	·01	2·52		1·71	55·51
18	49·32	·01	2·51		2·22	54·04
30	46·71	·00	2·53		3·10	52·34
1845. Jan. 5	46·80	·00	2·54		3·47	52·81
10	46·01	·00	2·54		3·73	52·28
12	48·29	·00	2·52		+ 3·82	54·63
						2·37·53·45

Error of Collimation . . . = 0· 0· 3·01
Resulting Mean Zenith Distance, South = 2·37·50·44

B.A.C. 6233.

FACE OF SECTOR EAST.

Day of Observation 1844-5.	Apparent Zenith Distance	Reduction	Refraction.	Precession, and Nutation.	Aberration, and Nutation.	Deduced Mean Zenith Distance
1844. Nov. 17	0· 5·52·53	·00	0·09		+ 2·65	0· 5·55·27
25	52·33	·00	·09		3·29	55·71
27	52·72	·00	·09		3·46	56·27
Dec. 2	53·32	·00	·10		3·87	57·29
5	52·92	·00	·09		4·13	57·14
31	48·97	·00	·09		6·31	55·37
1845. Jan. 9	47·89	·00	·09		6·95	54·93
11	48·78	·00	·09		7·08	55·95
15	48·23	·00	·09		+ 7·34	55·66
						0· 5·55·95

FACE OF SECTOR WEST.

Day of Observation 1844-5.	Apparent Zenith Distance	Reduction	Refraction.	Precession, and Nutation.	Aberration, and Nutation.	Deduced Mean Zenith Distance
1844. Nov. 22	0· 5·56·33	·00	0·09		+ 3·05	0· 5·59·47
26	56·58	·00	·09		3·37	60·04
29	56·58	·00	·09		3·62	60·29
Dec. 4	56·07	·00	·09		4·05	60·81
6	55·88	·00	·09		4·21	60·18
10	55·59	·00	·09		4·55	60·23
1845. Jan. 5	52·48	·00	·09		6·67	59·24
12	52·03	·00	·09		+ 7·15	59·67
						0· 6· 0·02

Error of Collimation . . . = 0· 0· 2·03
Resulting Mean Zenith Distance, South = 0· 5·57·99

Mean Zenith Distances of Stars observed at the Cape Point Station.

FACE OF SECTOR EAST.

Day of Observation 1844–5.	Apparent Zenith Distance, from Unreduced Observation.	Reduction for Az. Error, and Curr. of Path.	Refraction.	Precession, Aberration, and Nutation.	Deduced Mean Zenith Distance, 1844, Jan. 0; and Mean of Separate Results, uncorrected, for Error of Collimation.
B.A.C. 7842.					
1844. Nov. 23	1·12·45·24	·03	1·17	+15·76	1·12·30·62
24	45·04	·03	1·18	15·70	30·49
27	45·33	·03	1·14	15·54	30·90
Dec. 6	44·05	·03	1·17	+15·23	29·96
					1·12·30·49

FACE OF SECTOR WEST.

Day of Observation 1844–5.	Apparent Zenith Distance, from Unreduced Observation.	Reduction for Az. Error, and Curr. of Path.	Refraction.	Precession, Aberration, and Nutation.	Deduced Mean Zenith Distance, 1844, Jan. 0; and Mean of Separate Results, uncorrected, for Error of Collimation.
B.A.C. 7842.					
1844. Nov. 21	1·12·43·16	·00	1·19	+15·88	1·12·28·47
22	42·96	·00	1·17	15·82	28·31
26	41·14	·00	1·16	15·60	26·70
Dec. 2	43·26	·00	1·17	+15·32	29·11
					1·12·28·15

Error of Collimation   .   .   = 0· 0· 1·17
Resulting Mean Zenith Distance, North = 1·12·29·32

FACE OF SECTOR EAST.

Day of Observation 1844–5.	Apparent Zenith Distance	Red.	Refr.	Prec. &c.	Deduced Mean Zenith Distance.
B.A.C. 7966.					
1844. Nov. 19	0·39·19·72	·01	0·64	+16·44	0·39· 3·91
24	19·32	·01	·64	16·04	3·91
27	19·82	·02	·62	15·83	4·59
Dec. 1	17·94	·00	·64	15·60	2·98
4	17·94	·01	·63	+15·46	3·10
					0·39· 3·70

FACE OF SECTOR WEST.

Day of Observation 1844–5.	Apparent Zenith Distance	Red.	Refr.	Prec. &c.	Deduced Mean Zenith Distance.
B.A.C. 7966.					
1844. Nov. 21	0·39·16·80	·00	0·64	+16·27	0·38·61·17
22	16·80	·00	·63	16·19	61·24
26	14·93	·00	·63	15·90	59·66
Dec. 2	16·16	·00	·64	+15·55	61·25
					0·39· 0·83

Error of Collimation   .   .   = 0· 0· 1·43
Resulting Mean Zenith Distance, North = 0·39· 2·26

FACE OF SECTOR EAST.

Day of Observation 1844–5.	Apparent Zenith Distance	Red.	Refr.	Prec. &c.	Deduced Mean Zenith Distance.
Fomalhaut B.A.C. 7992.					
1844. Nov. 19	3·54·31·27	·08	3·80	+17·64	3·54·17·35
27	29·79	·10	3·70	17·00	16·39
Dec. 1	29·54	·00	3·81	16·74	16·61
3	30·48	·08	3·81	16·62	17·59
4	30·33	·08	3·77	16·57	17·45
12	30·18	·00	3·80	16·25	17·73
16	30·38	·00	3·75	16·15	17·98
30	30·53	·00	3·76	16·18	18·11
1845. Jan. 11	30·67	·00	3·72	16·60	17·79
15	30·97	·00	3·77	+16·84	17·90
					3·54·17·49

FACE OF SECTOR WEST.

Day of Observation 1844–5.	Apparent Zenith Distance	Red.	Refr.	Prec. &c.	Deduced Mean Zenith Distance.
Fomalhaut B.A.C. 7992.					
1844. Nov. 21	3·54·24·16	·00	3·84	+17·46	3·54·10·54
22	23·96	·00	3·78	17·38	10·36
26	23·07	·01	3·74	17·07	9·73
28	23·42	·01	3·75	16·93	10·23
Dec. 2	24·01	·01	3·79	16·68	11·11
6	22·33	·02	3·76	16·48	9·59
13	23·47	·01	3·75	16·22	10·99
18	21·64	·01	3·79	16·12	9·30
1845. Jan. 1	23·67	·00	3·72	16·18	11·21
13	24·16	·00	3·72	+16·72	11·16
					3·54·10·42

Error of Collimation   .   .   = 0· 0· 3·53
Resulting Mean Zenith Distance, North = 3·54·13·96

MEAN ZENITH DISTANCES.

COLLECTION OF

ALL THE

RESULTS OF OBSERVATION OF EACH STAR

AT

THE ROYAL OBSERVATORY, near CAPE TOWN,

AND

DEDUCTION OF MEAN ZENITH DISTANCE, 1845, JANUARY 0.

NOTE.—The reduction for Azimuthal Error is always to be applied subtractively to the Zenith Distance. The reduction for Curvature of Path is always to be applied subtractively to South Zenith Distance, and additively to North Zenith Distance. The Refraction is always to be applied additively. The Precession, Aberration, and Nutation, have the sign which is proper for reducing the Apparent North Polar Distance of the Star to its mean North Polar Distance, 1845, January 0; and therefore are to be applied with the sign given in the Table when the Star is South of the Zenith, and with the opposite sign when the Star is North of the Zenith.

The numbers included in parentheses in the column "Deduced Mean Zenith Distance, 1845, January 0," are omitted in taking the mean.

Where an asterisk or a positive sign is affixed to a number in the 3rd or 9th columns, the explanation will be found at the bottom of the page.

Mean Zenith Distances of Stars observed at the Royal Observatory.

FACE OF SECTOR EAST.   FACE OF SECTOR WEST.

Day of Observation 1845.	Apparent Zenith Distance, from Unreduced Observation.	Reduction for Alt. Error, and Curv. of Path.	Refraction.	Precession, Aberration, and Nutation.	Deduced Mean Zenith Distance, 1845, Jan. 0; and Mean of Separate Results, uncorrected. for Error of Collimation.	Day of Observation 1845.	Apparent Zenith Distance, from Unreduced Observation.	Reduction for Alt. Error, and Curv. of Path.	Refraction.	Precession, Aberration, and Nutation.	Deduced Mean Zenith Distance, 1845, Jan. 0; and Mean of Separate Results, uncorrected. for Error of Collimation.

B.A.C. 1739.

Day	App. Z.D.	Red.	Refr.	Prec./Ab./Nut.	Deduced Mean	Day	App. Z.D.	Red.	Refr.	Prec./Ab./Nut.	Deduced Mean
Jan. 24	1·39·22·42	·10	1·65	−14·65	1·39· 9·32	Jan. 25	1·39·25·73	·15	1·65	−14·87	1·39·12·36
27	22·82	·12	1·65	15·28	9·07	28	26·86	·16	1·63	15·48	12·85
29	23·51	·14	1·65	15·08	9·34	30	26·91	·17	1·64	15·87	12·51
Feb. 2	23·41	·16	1·64	16·43	8·46	Feb. 1	27·85	·18	1·64	16·25	13·06
14	25·58	·11	1·64	18·28	8·83	15	29·72	·11	1·64	18·41	12·84
16	26·07	·04	1·68	18·53	9·18	18	29·53	·07	1·64	18·76	12·34
28	27·50	·01	1·64	19·62	9·51	Mar. 1	31·70	·08	1·64	19·69	13·57
Mar. 2	28·05	·01	1·65	19·74	9·95	3	30·66	·03	1·66	19·80	12·49
23	26·96	·05	1·63	19·88	8·66	18	31·25	·02	1·62	20·02	12·83
27	27·01	·01	1·62	−19·68	8·94	24	31·40	·02	1·64	−19·83	13·19
					1·39· 9·13						1·39·12·80

Error of Collimation . . = 0· 0· 1·84
Resulting Mean Zenith Distance, South = 1·39·10·97

B.A.C. 1802.

Day	App. Z.D.	Red.	Refr.	Prec./Ab./Nut.	Deduced Mean	Day	App. Z.D.	Red.	Refr.	Prec./Ab./Nut.	Deduced Mean
Jan. 24	0·13·45·74	·01	0·23	−14·45	0·13·31·51	Jan. 25	0·13·48·99	·02	0·23	−14·67	0·13·34·53
27	45·79	·02	·23	15·09	30·91	28	50·28	·02	·23	15·30	35·10
29	46·38	·02	·23	15·50	31·09	29	48·60	·02	·23	15·70	33·11
31	46·67	·02	·23	15·89	30·99	Feb. 1	51·85	·02	·23	16·08	35·98
Feb. 14	49·34	·01	·23	18·19	31·37	15	53·14	·01	·23	18·32	35·04
16	49·34	·00	·23	18·44	31·13	18	51·66	·01	·23	18·69	33·19
Mar. 2	51·70	·00	·23	19·77	32·16	Mar. 1	54·27	·01	·23	19·70	34·79
23	51·16	·00	·23	20·09	31·30	18	54·12	·00	·23	19·83	34·52
26	51·06	·00	·23	−19·97	31·32	18	53·63	·00	·23	20·17	33·69
						24	54·47	·00	·23	−20·05	34·65
					0·13·31·35						0·13·34·47

Error of Collimation . . = 0· 0· 1·56
Resulting Mean Zenith Distance, South = 0·13·32·91

B.A.C. 1878.

Day	App. Z.D.	Red.	Refr.	Prec./Ab./Nut.	Deduced Mean	Day	App. Z.D.	Red.	Refr.	Prec./Ab./Nut.	Deduced Mean
Jan. 24	1·53·55·01	·12	1·89	−14·63	1·53·42·15	Jan. 25	1·53·59·99	·18	1·89	−14·85	1·53·46·85
27	55·11	·14	1·89	15·30	41·56	28	60·29	·18	1·87	15·52	46·46
29	56·29	·16	1·90	15·74	42·29	30	59·84	·20	1·88	15·95	45·57
31	57·38	·17	1·87	16·16	42·92	Feb. 1	60·63	·20	1·88	16·36	45·95
Feb. 3	56·39	·18	1·86	16·76	41·31	4	61·62	·21	1·87	16·95	46·33
14	57·97	·12	1·88	18·64	41·09	15	63·19	·12	1·88	18·32	46·16
16	59·05	·04	1·92	18·93	42·00	18	62·01	·08	1·88	19·20	44·61
28	60·88	·01	1·88	20·27	42·48	Mar. 1	64·03	·09	1·88	20·36	45·46
Mar. 2	60·78	·01	1·89	20·43	42·23	3	64·58	·03	1·91	20·52	45·94
23	61·22	·01	1·87	−21·00	42·08	18	64·82	·02	1·85	21·05	45·60
					1·53·42·01	May 2	59·15	·01	1·90	−16·74	44·90
											1·53·45·75

Error of Collimation . . = 0· 0· 1·87
Resulting Mean Zenith Distance, South = 1·53·43·88

Mean Zenith Distances of Stars observed at the Royal Observatory.

FACE OF SECTOR EAST.

Day of Observation 1845.	Apparent Zenith Distance, from Unreduced Observation.	Reduction for Az. Error, and Curv. of Path.	Refraction.	Precession, Aberration, and Nutation.	Deduced Mean Zenith Distance, 1845, Jan. 0; and Mean of Separate Results, uncorrected, for Error of Collimation.
				B.A.C. 1922.	
Jan. 24	1·22·18·27	·09	1·37	-14·53	1·22· 5·02
27	19·75	·10	1·36	15·22	5·79
29	20·93	·12	1·37	15·68	6·52
31	20·63	·13	1·35	16·09	5·76
Feb. 3	20·63	·13	1·34	16·71	5·13
14	23·00	·09	1·36	18·65	5·02
16	23·69	·03	1·39	18·95	6·10
28	25·71	·01	1·36	20·36	6·70
Mar. 2	25·37	·00	1·37	20·53	6·21
23	25·96	·00	1·35	-21·24	6·07
					1·22· 5·89

Error of Collimation . . . = 0· 0· 1·48
Resulting Mean Zenith Distance, South = 1·22· 7·37

Day of Observation 1845.	Apparent Zenith Distance, from Unreduced Observation.	Reduction for Az. Error, and Curv. of Path.	Refraction.	Precession, Aberration, and Nutation.	Deduced Mean Zenith Distance, 1845, Jan. 0; and Mean of Separate Results, uncorrected, for Error of Collimation.
				B.A.C. 1982.	
Jan. 24	3·18· 8·41	·21	3·29	-14·65	3·17·56·84
27	10·23	·25	3·28	15·38	57·86
29	11·81	·29	3·30	15·85	58·97
31	12·01	·31	3·26	16·31	58·65
Feb. 3	11·22	·31	3·24	16·96	57·19
14	13·83	·22	3·26	19·04	57·83
16	14·67	·07	3·34	19·37	58·57
28	16·94	·02	3·28	20·93	59·27
Mar. 2	17·09	·01	3·29	-21·14	59·23
					3·17·58·27

Error of Collimation . . . = 0· 0· 2·18
Resulting Mean Zenith Distance, South = 3·18· 0·45

Day of Observation 1845.	Apparent Zenith Distance, from Unreduced Observation.	Reduction for Az. Error, and Curv. of Path.	Refraction.	Precession, Aberration, and Nutation.	Deduced Mean Zenith Distance, 1845, Jan. 0; and Mean of Separate Results, uncorrected, for Error of Collimation.
				B.A.C. 2051.	
Jan. 27	3·55·52·81	·27	3·91	-14·52	3·56·10·97
29	50·20	·32	3·92	14·97	8·77
31	51·97	·34	3·88	15·40	10·91
Feb. 2	51·33	·35	3·89	15·83	10·70
3	51·43	·35	3·85	16·03	10·96
14	49·71	·24	3·91	18·05	11·43
16	47·98	·08	3·98	18·37	10·25
28	46·45	·02	3·90	19·92	10·25
Mar. 2	45·71	·01	3·92	20·13	9·75
23	45·46	·01	3·89	-21·23	10·57
					3·56·10·46

Error of Collimation . . . = 0· 0· 2·70
Resulting Mean Zenith Distance, North = 3·56· 7·75

FACE OF SECTOR WEST.

Day of Observation 1845.	Apparent Zenith Distance, from Unreduced Observation.	Reduction for Az. Error, and Curv. of Path.	Refraction.	Precession, Aberration, and Nutation.	Deduced Mean Zenith Distance, 1845, Jan. 0; and Mean of Separate Results, uncorrected, for Error of Collimation.
				B.A.C. 1922.	
Jan. 25	1·22·22·11	·13	1·37	-14·76	1·22· 8·59
28	23·40	·13	1·35	15·44	9·18
30	23·10	·14	1·36	15·88	8·44
Feb. 1	23·89	·15	1·36	16·30	8·80
4	25·57	·15	1·35	16·90	9·87
15	26·06	·09	1·36	18·80	8·53
18	25·66	·07	1·36	19·23	7·72
Mar. 1	28·72	·06	1·36	20·45	9·57
3	28·38	·02	1·38	20·61	9·13
18	28·62	·02	1·34	-21·25	8·69
					1·22· 8·85

Day of Observation 1845.	Apparent Zenith Distance, from Unreduced Observation.	Reduction for Az. Error, and Curv. of Path.	Refraction.	Precession, Aberration, and Nutation.	Deduced Mean Zenith Distance, 1845, Jan. 0; and Mean of Separate Results, uncorrected, for Error of Collimation.
				B.A.C. 1982.	
Jan. 25	3·18·14·38	·31	3·29	-14·90	3·18· 2·46
28	14·77	·33	3·26	15·02	2·08
30	16·45	·35	3·28	16·08	3·30
Feb. 1	16·64	·36	3·28	16·53	3·03
4	18·52	·37	3·26	17·17	4·24
15	18·02	·22	3·27	19·21	1·86
18	18·57	·14	3·28	19·68	2·03
Mar. 1	20·88	·15	3·27	21·04	2·96
3	19·65	·06	3·33	21·22	1·70
18	21·43	·04	3·23	-22·05	2·57
					3·18· 2·02

Day of Observation 1845.	Apparent Zenith Distance, from Unreduced Observation.	Reduction for Az. Error, and Curv. of Path.	Refraction.	Precession, Aberration, and Nutation.	Deduced Mean Zenith Distance, 1845, Jan. 0; and Mean of Separate Results, uncorrected, for Error of Collimation.
				B.A.C. 2051.	
Jan. 25	3·55·46·85	·34	3·92	-14·06	3·56· 4·49
28	46·85	·36	3·88	14·75	5·12
30	46·80	·38	3·90	15·19	5·51
Feb. 1	44·53	·40	3·90	15·62	3·65
4	44·18	·41	3·87	16·23	8·87
18	44·38	·15	3·90	18·67	6·80
Mar. 3	41·32	·06	3·98	20·22	5·44
18	39·84	·05	3·84	21·14	4·77
24	41·13	·04	3·89	21·24	6·22
25	39·50	·04	3·91	-21·24	4·61
					3·56· 5·05

Mean Zenith Distances of Stars observed at the Royal Observatory.

FACE OF SECTOR EAST.						FACE OF SECTOR WEST.					
Day of Observation 1845.	Apparent Zenith Distance, from Unreduced Observation.	Reduction for Az. Error, and Curv. of Path.	Refraction.	Precession, Aberration, and Nutation.	Deduced Mean Zenith Distance, 1845, Jan. 0; and Mean of Separate Results, uncorrected, for Error of Collimation.	Day of Observation 1845.	Apparent Zenith Distance, from Unreduced Observation	Reduction for Az. Error, and Curv. of Path.	Refraction.	Precession, Aberration, and Nutation.	Deduced Mean Zenith Distance, 1845, Jan. 0; and Mean of Separate Results, uncorrected, for Error of Collimation.
B.A.C. 2109.											
Jan. 24	1·26·40·25	·09	1·44	-14·01	1·26·55·61	Jan. 25	1·26·30·40	·13	1·44	-14·26	1·26·51·97
27	38·92	·10	1·43	14·75	55·00	28	35·17	·14	1·42	14·99	51·44
29	37·09	·12	1·44	15·22	53·63	30	35·06	·14	1·43	15·46	52·41
31	38·08	·13	1·42	15·69	55·06	Feb. 1	33·94	·15	1·43	15·91	51·13
Feb. 3	37·64	·13	1·41	16·35	55·27	4	33·00	·15	1·42	16·57	50·84
14	34·38	·09	1·43	18·51	54·23	15	30·59	·09	1·43	18·09	50·62
16	33·54	·03	1·46	18·85	53·82	18	32·06	·06	1·43	19·18	52·61
28	32·31	·01	1·43	20·56	54·29	Mar. 1	29·94	·06	1·43	20·67	51·98
Mar. 2	32·06	·01	1·44	20·78	54·27	3	28·86	·02	1·45	20·89	51·18
23	31·28	·00	1·42	-22·09	54·79	18	28·96	·02	1·41	-21·95	52·30
					1·26·54·60						1·26·51·65

Error of Collimation . . . $= 0\cdot\ 0\cdot\ 1\cdot48$
Resulting Mean Zenith Distance, North $= 1\cdot26\cdot53\cdot12$

B.A.C. 2246.											
Jan. 27	1·35·50·69	·11	1·58	-14·54	1·36· 6·70	Jan. 25	1·35·48·13	·14	1·59	-14·03	1·36· 3·61
29	49·16	·13	1·50	15·04	5·60	28	45·27	·15	1·58	14·80	1·50
31	49·41	·14	1·57	15·54	6·38	30	46·80	·16	1·58	15·29	3·51
Feb. 1	48·72	·14	1·58	16·17	6·17	Feb. 1	44·77	·17	1·58	15·78	1·96
3	48·42	·14	1·56	16·25	6·09	4	43·00	·17	1·57	16·48	0·88
14	45·61	·10	1·59	18·69	5·69	15	41·82	·10	1·58	18·78	2·08
16	44·58	·03	1·61	18·97	5·13	18	42·16	·06	1·58	19·33	3·01
28	43·29	·01	1·58	20·80	5·75	Mar. 1	38·76	·07	1·59	21·02	1·30
Mar. 2	43·54	·01	1·60	21·16	6·29	3	39·00	·03	1·60	21·28	1·85
23	41·67	·00	1·58	-22·88	6·13	18	36·93	·02	1·56	22·65	1·12
						24	37·18	·02	1·59	-22·92	1·67
					1·36· 6·00						1·36· 2·05

Error of Collimation . . . $= 0\cdot\ 0\cdot\ 1\cdot98$
Resulting Mean Zenith Distance, North $= 1\cdot36\cdot\ 4\cdot02$

B.A.C. 2293.											
Jan. 24	5· 9·52·21	·30	5·15	-13·44	5·10·10·50	Jan. 25	5· 9·47·38	·44	5·17	-13·70	5·10· 5·91
27	51·52	·35	5·14	14·20	10·51	28	47·18	·47	5·11	14·44	6·26
29	50·39	·41	5·16	14·68	9·82	30	47·33	·50	5·13	14·93	6·89
Feb. 2	50·88	·45	5·12	15·63	11·18	Feb. 1	45·90	·51	5·12	15·40	4·43
3	50·53	·45	5·06	15·85	10·99	4	43·78	·53	5·10	16·08	6·05
14	48·17	·31	5·14	18·14	11·14	15	43·24	·31	5·14	18·33	6·16
16	46·15	·11	5·22	18·51	9·77	18	42·25	·20	5·14	18·86	6·05
28	44·12	·03	5·13	20·41	9·63	Mar. 1	40·67	·22	5·17	20·54	6·16
Mar. 2	43·73	·02	5·17	20·67	9·55	3	39·19	·08	5·20	20·79	5·10

Carried forward,

Mean Zenith Distances of Stars observed at the Royal Observatory.

	FACE OF SECTOR EAST.						FACE OF SECTOR WEST.				
Day of Observation 1845.	Apparent Zenith Distance, from Unreduced Observation.	Reduction for Az. Error, and Curr. of Path.	Refraction.	Precession, Aberration, and Nutation.	Deduced Mean Zenith Distance, 1845, Jan. 0; and Mean of Separate Results, uncorrected, for Error of Collimation.	Day of Observation 1845.	Apparent Zenith Distance, from Unreduced Observation.	Reduction for Az. Error, and Curr. of Path.	Refraction.	Precession, Aberration, and Nutation.	Deduced Mean Zenith Distance, 1845, Jan. 0; and Mean of Separate Results, uncorrected, for Error of Collimation.

B.A.C. 2298—(continued.)

	° ′ ″	″	″	″	° ′ ″		° ′ ″	″	″	″	° ′ ″
Mar. 23	5· 9·43·38	·02	5·11	22·44	5·10·10·91	Mar. 18	5· 9·38·90	·06	5·09	22·18	5·10· 6·11
26	42·35	·03	5·13	-22·54	9·90	24	37·37	·05	5·15	22·48	4·95
						May 2	42·45	·03	5·17	-20·89	(8·48)
					5·10·10·36						5·10· 5·82

Error of Collimation . . . = 0· 0· 2·27
Resulting Mean Zenith Distance, North = 5·10· 8·09

B.A.C. 2414.

Jan. 24	2·53·25·22	·18	2·88	-13·46	2·53·14·46	Jan. 25	2·53·30·94	·27	2·90	-13·75	2·53·19·82
27	25·86	·22	2·87	14·33	14·18	28	29·27	·20	2·86	14·62	17·22
29	27·05	·25	2·89	14·90	14·79	30	30·89	·30	2·87	15·18	18·28
31	27·79	·27	2·85	15·45	14·92	Feb. 1	31·98	·32	2·87	15·73	18·80
Feb. 3	28·33	·28	2·84	16·26	14·63	4	33·80	·32	2·85	16·53	19·80
14	30·60	·19	2·88	18·97	14·32	15	34·00	·19	2·87	19·20	17·48
16	32·23	·06	2·92	19·42	15·07	Mar. 1	38·78	·14	2·89	21·94	19·59
28	34·74	·02	2·87	21·77	15·82	3	39·03	·05	2·91	22·26	19·63
Mar. 2	34·20	·01	2·89	22·10	14·98	18	40·61	·04	2·85	24·14	19·28
25	35·87	·02	2·87	-24·66	14·06	24	41·05	·03	2·88	-24·60	19·30
					2·53·14·78						2·53·18·92

Error of Collimation . . . = 0· 0· 2·07
Resulting Mean Zenith Distance, South = 2·53·16·85

B.A.C. 2458.

Jan. 24	4·55·29·29	·29	4·91	-13·14	4·55·47·05	Jan. 25	4·55·25·84	·42	4·94	-13·41	4·55·43·77
27	29·73	·34	4·90	13·93	48·22	28	24·56	·45	4·88	14·19	43·18
29	28·11	·39	4·92	14·45	47·09	30	24·26	·47	4·89	14·71	43·39
31	27·91	·42	4·87	14·96	47·32	Feb. 1	22·68	·49	4·89	15·21	42·29
Feb. 3	27·86	·43	4·84	15·70	47·97	4	21·60	·50	4·86	15·94	41·90
14	25·79	·29	4·90	18·18	48·58	15	20·81	·30	4·90	18·38	43·79
16	24·26	·10	4·98	18·58	47·72	18	20·17	·19	4·90	18·98	43·86
28	21·25	·03	4·89	20·72	46·83	Mar. 1	17·16	·21	4·93	20·87	42·75
Mar. 2	21·80	·02	4·93	21·02	47·73	3	16·45	·08	4·96	21·10	42·49
25	20·61	·03	4·92	-23·35	49·05	18	14·94	·06	4·86	-22·87	42·61
					4·55·47·76						4·55·43·00

Error of Collimation . . . = 0· 0· 2·38
Resulting Mean Zenith Distance, North = 4·55·45·38

Mean Zenith Distances of Stars observed at the Royal Observatory.

FACE OF SECTOR EAST.						FACE OF SECTOR WEST.					
Day of Observation 1845.	Apparent Zenith Distance, from Unreduced Observation.	Reduction for Az. Error, and Curv. of Path.	Refraction.	Precession, Aberration, and Nutation.	Deduced Mean Zenith Distance, 1845, Jan. 0; and Mean of Separate Results, uncorrected, for Error of Collimation.	Day of Observation 1845.	Apparent Zenith Distance, from Unreduced Observation.	Reduction for Az. Error, and Curv. of Path.	Refraction.	Precession, Aberration, and Nutation.	Deduced Mean Zenith Distance, 1845, Jan. 0; and Mean of Separate Results, uncorrected, for Error of Collimation.

B.A.C. 2528.

	° ′ ″	″	″	″	° ′ ″		° ′ ″	″	″	″	° ′ ″
Jan. 24	3·43·57·38	·24	3·72	-12·93	3·43·47·93	Jan. 25	3·44· 3·00	·35	3·75	-13·24	3·43·53·16
27	58·02	·28	3·71	13·85	47·60	28	3·09	·37	3·70	14·15	52·27
29	58·66	·33	3·73	14·44	47·62	Feb. 1	4·82	·41	3·70	15·32	52·79
31	59·54	·35	3·09	15·03	47·85	2	6·55	·41	3·70	15·60	54·24
Feb. 3	60·43	·36	3·67	15·89	47·85	4	6·30	·42	3·69	16·17	53·40
14	62·90	·25	3·71	18·79	47·57	18	7·88	·16	3·71	19·74	51·69
16	65·07	·08	3·77	19·27	49·49	Mar. 1·	11·28	·18	3·73	22·04	52·79
Mar. 2	67·43	·01	3·74	22·23	48·93	3	13·01	·07	3·77	22·41	54·30
23	69·10	·01	3·09	25·11	47·73	18	14·14	·05	3·68	24·60	53·17
25	69·11	·03	3·73	·25·28	47·53	24	14·63	·04	3·72	-25·20	53·11
					3·43·48·01						3·43·53·09

Error of Collimation . . = 0· 0· 2·54
Resulting Mean Zenith Distance, South = 3·43·50·55

B.A.C. 2575.

Jan. 24	3·38·23·65	·23	3·63	-12·74	3·38·14·31	Jan. 25	3·38·28·68	·35	3·65	-13 05	3·38·18·93
27	23·00	·27	3 62	13·60	13·29	28	28·43	·36	3·60	13·97	17·70
29	25·77	·32	3·64	14·27	14·82	30	29·61	·39	3·61	14·58	18·27
31	26·11	·34	3·00	14·86	14·51	Feb. 1	29·91	·40	3·61	15·15	17·97
Feb. 3	26·36	·35	3·58	15·73	13·86	4	31·04	·41	3·59	16·01	18·21
14	29·71	·24	3·62	18·67	14·42	15	33·80	·24	3·62	18·92	18·26
16	29·60	·08	3·68	19 17	14·09	18	33·90	·15	3·61	19·65	17·71
28	33·06	·02	3·64	21·81	14·84	Mar. 1	37·30	·17	3·64	22·01	18·76
Mar. 2	33·61	·01	3·64	22·19	15·05	3	37·55	·07	3·67	22·38	18·77
23	35·97	·01	3·60	-25·21	14·35	18	40·81	·05	3·59	-24·67	19·68
					3·38·14·35						3·38·18·43

Error of Collimation . . = 0· 0· 2·04
Resulting Mean Zenith Distance, South = 3·38·16·39

B.A.C. 2580.

Jan. 24	3 39·46·29	·23	3·65	-12·72	3·39·36·99	Jan. 25	3·39·51·12	·35	3·67	-13·03	3·39·41·41
27	47·43	·28	3·64	13·64	37·15	28	52·51	·37	3·63	13·95	41·82
29	48·02	·32	3·66	14·25	37·11	30	52·31	·39	3·64	14·54	41·02
31	47·67	·35	3·62	14·84	36·10	Feb. 1	52·31	·40	3·63	15·14	40·40
Feb. 3	49·25	·35	3·60	15·71	36·79	4	54·72	·41	3·62	16·00	41·93
14	51·57	·24	3·64	18·66	36·31	15	55·70	·25	3·64	18·92	40·23
16	51·62	·08	3·70	19·16	36·08	18	56·40	·16	3·63	19·64	40·23
28	55·51	·02	3·61	21·81	37·32	Mar. 2	59·21	·17	3·66	22·00	40·70
Mar. 2	55·27	·01	3·67	22·19	36·74	3	61·23	·07	3·70	22·38	42·48
23	57·63	·01	3·62	-25·22	36·02	18	62·76	·05	3·61	-24·68	41·64
					3·39·36·06						3·39·41·19

Error of Collimation . . = 0· 0· 2·26
Resulting Mean Zenith Distance, South = 3·39·38·92

Mean Zenith Distances of Stars observed at the Royal Observatory.

FACE OF SECTOR EAST.						FACE OF SECTOR WEST.					
Day of Observation 1845.	Apparent Zenith Distance, from Unreduced Observation.	Reduction for Az. Error, and Curv. of Path.	Refraction.	Precession, Aberration, and Nutation.	Deduced Mean Zenith Distance 1845, Jan. 0; and Mean of Separate Results, uncorrected, for Error of Collimation.	Day of Obre.vation 1845.	Apparent Zenith Distance, from Unreduced Observation.	Reduction for Az. Error, and Curv. of Path.	Refraction.	Precession, Aberration, and Nutation.	Deduced Mean Zenith Distance, 1845, Jan. 0; and Mean of Separate Results, uncorrected, for Error of Collimation.

B.A.C. 2635.

Jan. 24	4·31·52·72	·20	4·52	-12·48	4·31·44·47	Jan. 25	4 31·55·40	·44	4·55	-12·80	4·31·46·80
27	54·60	·35	4·51	13·42	45·34	28	58·44	·46	4·49	13·73	48·74
29	56·52	·40	4·53	14·04	46·61	30	58·44	·49	4·50	14·34	48·11
31	56·57	·43	4·48	14·65	45·97	Feb. 1	59·02	·51	4·50	14·95	48·96
Feb. 3	57·16	·44	4·46	15·54	45·64	4	60·22	·52	4·48	15·83	48·35
14	59·58	·30	4·52	18 57	45·23	15	63·47	·31	4·51	18·83	48·84
16	60·86	·10	4·59	19·08	46·27	18	62·39	·20	4·50	19·58	47·11
28	64 12	·03	4·50	21·83	46·76	Mar. 1	66·83	·22	4·54	22·04	49·11
Mar. 2	64·51	·02	4·55	·22·24	46·80	3	66 93	·08	4·58	22·43	49·00
23	66·19	·02	4·50	-25·40	45·21	18	70·18	·06	4·47	24·86	49·73
						24	70·28	·05	4·52	-25·56	49·19
					4·31·45·83						4·31·48·54

Error of Collimation . . . = 0· 0· 1·36
Resulting Mean Zenith Distance, South = 4·31·47·19

B.A.C. 2655.

Jan. 24	4· 0·32·35	·23	4·00	-12·53	4· 0·48·65	Jan. 25	4· 0·26·87	·35	4·02	-12·82	4· 0·43·36
27	31·07	·26	3·98	13·98	48·15	28	26·43	·87	3·96	13·06	43·68
29	30 57	·32	4·00	13·94	48·19	30	26·73	·39	3 98	14·21	44·53
31	29·49	·35	3·96	14·49	47·50	Feb. 1	25·04	·40	3 97	14·76	44·27
Feb. 3	29·29	·35	3·94	15·29	48·17	4	23·47	·41	3·06	15·55	42·57
14	27·12	·24	3·09	18·01	48·88	15	22·88	·25	3 98	18·24	44·85
16	25·30	·08	4·03	18·47	47·74	18	21·94	·16	3·97	19·91	44·06
28	22·08	·02	3·98	20·91	47·55	28	20·61	·17	4·01	21·09	45·54
Mar. 2	22·44	·01	4·02	21·27	47 72	Mar. 1	15·29	·07	4·04	21·44	40·70
23	20·91	·01	3 97	-24·09	48·06	3	17·56	·05	3·95	-23·57	45·03
					4· 0·48·16						4· 0·43·92

Error of Collimation . . . = 0· 0· 2·12
Resulting Mean Zenith Distance, North = 4· 0·46·04

B.A.C. 2710.

Jan. 24	5·38· 7·87	·37	5·63	-12·09	5·38· 1·04	Jan. 25	5·38·14·52	·55	5·06	-12·41	5·38· 7·22
27	10·53	·44	5·61	13·05	2·65	28	14 03	·58	5·60	13·37	5·68
31	10·53	·55	5·58	14·31	1·25	30	15·07	·61	5·61	14·00	6·07
Feb. 3	12·60	·56	5·55	15·23	2·36	Feb. 1	18 22	·65	5·57	15·53	7·61
14	15·46	·38	5·63	18·38	2·33	15	19·90	·39	5·62	18·65	6·48
16	15·26	·13	5·71	18·91	1·93	Mar. 1	22·61	·27	5·65	22·02	5·97
28	18·57	·04	5·60	21·80	2·33	18	23·40	·10	5·70	22·43	6·57
Mar. 2	18·52	·02	5·67	22·23	1·94	24	27·20	·08	5·57	25·06	7·03
23	21·28	·02	5·60	25·71	1·15	27	29·61	·07	5·63	25·83	9·34
25	21·67	·04	5·64	-25·94	1·33		28·92	·06	5·56	-26·16	8·26
					5·38· 1·83						5·38· 7·08

Error of Collimation . . . = 0· 0· 2·63
Resulting Mean Zenith Distance, South = 5· 38· 4·46

B.A.C. 2710.—March 1.—Five divisions of the Micrometer subtracted.—the e.ror which appears to have been committed when reading the register head. The star scarcely comes within the available limits of the Arch.

Mean Zenith Distances of Stars observed at the Royal Observatory.

FACE OF SECTOR EAST.   FACE OF SECTOR WEST.

Day of Observation 1845.	Apparent Zenith Distance, from Unreduced Observation.	Reduction for Ar. Error, and Curr. of Path.	Refraction.	Precession, Aberration, and Nutation.	Deduced Mean Zenith Distance, 1845, Jan. 0; and Mean of Separate Results, uncorrected, for Error of Collimation	Day of Observation 1845.	Apparent Zenith Distance, from Unreduced Observation	Reduction for Ar. Error, and Curr. of Path.	Refraction.	Precession, Aberration, and Nutation.	Deduced Mean Zenith Distance, 1845, Jan. 0; and Mean of Separate Results, uncorrected, for Error of Collimation
					B.A.C. 2795.						
Jan. 24	2·14·58·77	·14	2·24	-11·74	2·14·40·18	Jan. 25	2·15· 1·38	·21	2·25	-12·06	2·14·51·36
27	59·70	·17	2·24	12 69	49 08	28	2·56	·22	2·23	13·00	51·57
29	60·79	·19	2·25	13 31	49·54	30	2 07	·23	2·23	13·62	50·45
31	61 48	·21	2·22	13·92	49·57	Feb. 1	2·86	·24	2·23	14·23	50·62
Feb. 3	62·17	·21	2·21	14·82	49 35	4	3·95	·25	2·22	15·12	50·80
14	65·57	·15	2·24	17·93	49·73	15	8·14	·15	2·24	18·20	52 03
28	69·17	·15	2·23	21 34	49·91	Mar. 1	10·36	·10	2·25	21·56	50·95
Mar. 2	68·93	·01	2·26	21·77	49·41	3	13·07	·04	2·27	21·98	53·32
23	72·38	·01	2·23	25 32	49·28	18	15·44	·03	2·24	24·64	53·01
25	72·33	·02	2·25	-25 56	40·00	24	15·24	·03	2·24	-25·44	52·01
					2·14·49·40						2·14·51·61

Error of Collimation . . = 0· 0· 1·11
Resulting Mean Zenith Distance, South = 2·14·50·51

Day					B.A.C. 2935.	Day					
Jan. 24	0·49·44·96	·05	0·83	-11·12	0·49·34·62	Jan. 25	0·49·48·07	·08	0·83	-11·43	0 49·37·39
27	46·49	·06	·83	12 06	35·20	28	48·76	·08	·82	12·38	37·12
29	47·57	·07	·83	12 60	35·64	30	49 15	·09	·82	13·00	36·88
31	47·87	·07	·82	13·30	35·32	Feb. 1	49·99	·09	·82	13 61	37·11
Feb. 3	47·97	·06	·82	14·21	34·52	4	51·91	·09	·82	14·51	38·13
14	53·44	·06	·83	17·37	36·84	15	55·66	·05	·83	17 64	38 80
28	56·06	·01	·82	20·87	36·00	Mar. 1	58·32	·04	·83	21·11	38·00
Mar. 2	56·35	·00	·83	21·38	35·85	3	59·61	·01	·84	21·55	38·89
23	58·72	·00	·82	25·13	34·41	18	61·09	·01	·83	24·38	37·53
25	58·42	·01	·83	-25·40	33·84	26	63·25	·01	·83	-25·53	38·54
					0·49·35·22						0·49·37·84

Error of Collimation . . = 0· 0· 1·31
Resulting Mean Zenith Distance, South = 0·49·36·53

Day					B.A.C. 29 64.	Day					
Jan. 24	1·17·02·15	·08	1·29	-11·17	1·18·14·53	Jan. 25	1·17·58·50	·12	1·30	-11·48	1·18·11·16
27	61·36	·09	1·29	12·09	14·65	28	58·80	·12	1·29	12·40	12·46
29	59 78	·11	1·30	12·70	13·67	30	57·61	·13	1·29	13·01	11·78
31	59 29	·12	1·28	13·30	13·75	Feb. 1	56·97	·14	1·29	13 61	11·73
Feb. 14	54·60	·08	1·29	17·27	13·08	4	54·75	·14	1·28	14 48	10·37
28	51·20	·01	1·29	20·68	13·16	15	51·70	·08	1·29	17·54	10·54
Mar. 2	51·45	·00	1·30	21·13	13·88	Mar. 1	49·38	·06	1·30	20·91	11·53
23	48·93	·00	1·29	24·81	15·03	3	47·65	·02	1·31	21·33	10·27
25	49·43	·01	1·30	25·07	15·79	24	43·66	·01	1·30	24·95	9·90
27	49 43	·01	1·28	-25·33	16·03	26	44·20	·01	1·29	-25·21	10·69
					1·18·14·36						1·18·11·04

Error of Collimation . . = 0· 0· 1·66
Resulting Mean Zenith Distance, North = 1·18·12·79

Mean Zenith Distances of Stars observed at the Royal Observatory.

FACE OF SECTOR EAST. | FACE OF SECTOR WEST.

B.A.C. 3130.

Day of Observation 1845.	Apparent Zenith Distance, from Unreduced Observation.	Reduction for Ax. Error, and Curv. of Path.	Refraction.	Precession, Aberration, and Nutation.	Deduced Mean Zenith Distance, 1845, Jan. 0; and Mean of Separate Results, uncorrected, for Error of Collimation.	Day of Observation 1845.	Apparent Zenith Distance, from Unreduced Observation.	Reduction for Ax. Error, and Curv. of Path.	Refraction.	Precession, Aberration, and Nutation.	Deduced Mean Zenith Distance, 1845, Jan. 0; and Mean of Separate Results, uncorrected, for Error of Collimation.
Jan. 29	4·11·38·92	·34	4·19	-12·11	4·11·54·88	Jan. 28	4·11·37·53	·41	4·16	-11·81	4·11·53·09
31	40·45	·36	4·14	12·70	56·93	30	35·07	·42	4·16	12·40	51·21
Feb. 3	40·05	·37	4·12	13·57	57·37	Feb. 1	34·63	·43	4·16	12·99	51·35
14	35·57	·25	4·19	16·00	56·11	4	32·80	·18	4·14	13·86	50·62
28	31·32	·03	4·16	20·01	55·46	15	33·59	·07	4·17	16·86	54·55
Mar. 2	30·98	·01	4·21	20·45	55·63	Mar. 1	28·91	·05	4·20	20·24	53·30
23	28·61	·01	4·16	24·25	57·01	3	26·59	·04	4·26	20·67	51·48
25	27·68	·03	4·20	24·53	56·38	24	22·70	·04	4·19	24·39	51·24
27	27·92	·03	4·14	24·80	56·83	26	22·94	·03	4·19	24·07	51·77
April 1	26·10	·06	4·11	-25·39	55·54	29	22·40	·03	4·13	-25·04	51·54
					4·11·56·21						4·11·52·02

Error of Collimation   .   .   = 0· 0· 2·10
Resulting Mean Zenith Distance, North = 4·11·54·11

B.A.C. 3163.

Jan. 29	3·59·35·64	·35	4·00	-11·10	3·59·28·19	Jan. 30	3·59·39·39	·42	3·97	-11·43	3·59·31·51
31	36·63	·38	3·95	11·76	28·44	Feb. 1	40·33	·44	3·96	12·09	31·76
Feb. 3	37·56	·39	3·93	12·73	28·37	4	42·50	·45	3·94	13·05	32·94
14	41·61	·26	3·90	16·15	29·19	Mar. 1	49·94	·19	4·01	20·34	33·42
28	45·16	·03	3·97	20·08	29·02	3	49·40	·07	4·06	20·84	32·55
Mar. 2	45·80	·01	4·02	20·59	29·22	18	52·90	·05	3·97	24·21	32·61
23	49·25	·01	3·96	25·14	28·06	24	54·08	·05	4·00	25·31	32·72
25	49·45	·03	4·01	25·49	27·94	26	54·48	·04	4·00	25·65	32·79
27	49·25	·03	3·95	25·82	27·35	28	55·46	·04	3·92	25·98	33·36
April 1	51·12	·06	3·92	-26·57	28·41	29	55·12	·04	3·94	-26·13	32·89
					3·59·28·42						3·59·32·66

Error of Collimation   .   .   = 0· 0· 2·12
Resulting Mean Zenith Distance, South = 3·59·30·54

Anon. AR. 9·39.

Jan. 29	1·57·38·87	·16	1·96	-10·02	1·57·51·29	Jan. 28	1·57·36·51	·18	1·94	-10·31	1·57·48·58
31	39·51	·17	1·93	11·23	52·50	30	36·51	·20	1·94	10·92	49·17
Feb. 3	38·97	·18	1·92	12·14	52·85	Feb. 4	33·15	·21	1·93	12·44	47·31
Mar. 23	27·14	·01	1·94	23·95	53·02	Mar. 24	22·80	·02	1·96	24·12	48·86
27	27·19	·02	1·93	24·62	53·72	26	21·42	·02	1·95	24·46	47·81
April 1	23·78	·03	1·92	25·37	51·04	April 4	21·02	·01	1·93	24·93	48·80
5	24·33	·02	1·96	25·90	52·17	6	18·41	·01	1·97	25·77	48·75
9	24·77	·01	1·98	26·37	53·11	10	20·04	·02	1·96	26·02	46·38
11	21·81	·01	1·96	26·59	50·35	12	18·76	·01	1·96	26·48	48·46
14	22·65	·02	1·98	-26·88	51·49					-26·69	47·40
					1·57·52·15						1·57·48·15

Error of Collimation   .   .   = 0· 0· 2·00
Resulting Mean Zenith Distance, North = 1·57·50·15

Mean Zenith Distances of Stars observed at the Royal Observatory.

FACE OF SECTOR EAST.   FACE OF SECTOR WEST.

B.A.C. 3403.

Day of Observation 1845.	Apparent Zenith Distance, from Unreduced Observation.	Reduction for Az. Error, and Curr. of Path.	Refraction.	Precession, Aberration, and Nutation.	Deduced Mean Zenith Distance. 1845, Jan. 0; and Mean of Separate Results, uncorrected, for Error of Collimation.	Day of Observation 1845.	Apparent Zenith Distance, from Unreduced Observation.	Reduction for Az. Error, and Curr. of Path.	Refraction.	Precession, Aberration, and Nutation.	Deduced Mean Zenith Distance. 1845, Jan. 0; and Mean of Separate Results, uncorrected, for Error of Collimation.
Jan. 29	3 34 24·00	·29	3 57	-10·44	3 34 37·72	Jan. 28	3 34 19·47	·33	3 54	-10·14	3 34 32·82
31	22 43	·31	3 52	11·04	36·66	30	18·92	·35	3 54	10·74	32·85
Feb. 3	22·57	·32	3 50	11·94	37 09	Feb. 4	16·71	·37	3 52	12·23	32·09
Mar. 23	11·03	·01	3 54	23·55	38·11	Mar. 24	4·77	·04	3 57	23·72	32 02
27	10·00	·03	3 52	24·21	37·70	26	2·90	·03	3 57	24·05	30·49
April 1	7·98	·05	3 50	24·96	36 39	29	4·67	·03	3 52	24·52	32·68
5	8·62	·03	3 58	25·49	37·66	April 4	3·29	·02	3 59	25·37	32·23
9	6·94	·02	3 61	25·97	36·50	6	2·31	·02	3 57	25·62	31·48
11	6·01	·02	3 58	26·19	35·76	8	2·60	·03	3 59	25·86	32·02
14	6·65	·03	3 62	-26·48	36·72	10	1·91	·03	3 58	26·06	31·54
						12	0·58	·02	3 57	-26·29	30·42
					3·34·37·09						3 34·31·88

Error of Collimation . . = 0· 0· 2·61
Resulting Mean Zenith Distance, North = 3 34 34·48

Anon. AR. 10·2.

Day of Observation 1845.	Apparent Zenith Distance, from Unreduced Observation.	Reduction for Az. Error, and Curr. of Path.	Refraction.	Precession, Aberration, and Nutation.	Deduced Mean Zenith Distance.	Day of Observation 1845.	Apparent Zenith Distance, from Unreduced Observation.	Reduction for Az. Error, and Curr. of Path.	Refraction.	Precession, Aberration, and Nutation.	Deduced Mean Zenith Distance.
Jan. 29	3·34·67·94	·29	3·58	- 9·97	3 35·21 20	Jan. 30	3·34·62·86	·35	3·55	-10·26	3 35 16·32
31	66·61	·31	3·54	10·56	20 40	Feb. 4	59·90	·37	3·53	11·76	14·82
Feb. 3	67·50	·01	3·52	11·46	22·47	Mar. 24	49·00	·04	3 58	23·40	15·94
Mar. 23	54·68	·02	3·55	23·23	21·44	29	48·41	·03	3·54	24·23	16·15
25	54·28	·03	3·59	23·58	21 42	April 4	46·54	·02	3·60	25·12	15·24
27	53·98	·05	3·54	23·91	21·38	8	47·87	·03	3·61	25·64	17 09
April 5	53·79	·03	3·50	25·25	22·60	10	45·70	·03	3·59	25·87	15·13
9	51·12	·02	3·62	25·76	20·48	13	47·08	·02	3·66	26·20	16·92
11	49·84	·02	3·59	25·99	19·40	15	46·79	·02	3·56	26·40	16·73
18	50·93	·03	3·61	-26·68	21·19	17	45·41	·01	3·62	-26·59	15·61
					3 35·21·20						3 35·16·00

Error of Collimation . . = 0· 0· 2·60
Resulting Mean Zenith Distance, North = 3 35 18·60

B.A.C. 3578.

Day of Observation 1845.	Apparent Zenith Distance, from Unreduced Observation.	Reduction for Az. Error, and Curr. of Path.	Refraction.	Precession, Aberration, and Nutation.	Deduced Mean Zenith Distance.	Day of Observation 1845.	Apparent Zenith Distance, from Unreduced Observation.	Reduction for Az. Error, and Curr. of Path.	Refraction.	Precession, Aberration, and Nutation.	Deduced Mean Zenith Distance.
Jan. 29	3 38 63·39	·29	3·64	- 9·24	3 39 15·98	Jan. 30	3·38·58·07	·36	3·62	- 9·54	3 39·10·87
31	62·40	·32	3·61	9·84	15·53	Mar. 24	56·19	·38	3·59	11·02	10·42
Mar. 23	49·93	·01	3·62	22·60	16·20	29	44·75	·04	3·65	22·84	11·20
25	49 58	·02	3·65	23·02	16·23	26	44·26	·03	3·64	23·20	11·07
April 9	47·12	·02	3·69	25·33	16·12	April 10	41·84	·03	3 65	25·43	10·91
5	45·59	·02	3·65	25·58	14·80	13	41·30	·02	3·73	25·82	10 83
14	46·33	·03	3·70	25·93	15·93	17	42·24	·01	3·69	26·25	12·17
18	45·29	·02	3·67	26·35	15·29	19	41·10	·02	3·66	26·45	11·19
20	45·44	·01	3·68	26·54	15·65	21	40·66	·03	3·73	26·63	10·99
24	45·00	·02	3·67	-26·87	15·52	23	40·71	·03	3·64	-26·79	11·11
					3·39·15·73						3·39·11·08

Error of Collimation . . = 0· 0· 2·33
Resulting Mean Zenith Distance, North = 3 39 13·40

Mean Zenith Distances of Stars observed at the Royal Observatory.

	FACE OF SECTOR EAST.						FACE OF SECTOR WEST.				
Day of Observation 1845.	Apparent Zenith Distance, from Unreduced Observation.	Reduction for Az. Error, and Curv. of Path.	Refraction.	Precession, Aberration, and Nutation.	Deduced Mean Zenith Distance, 1845, Jan. 0; and Mean of Separate Results, uncorrected, for Error of Collimation.	Day of Observation 1845.	Apparent Zenith Distance, from Unreduced Observation.	Reduction for Az. Error, and Curv. of Path.	Refraction.	Precession, Aberration, and Nutation.	Deduced Mean Zenith Distance, 1845, Jan. 0; and Mean of Separate Results, uncorrected, for Error of Collimation.
	B.A.C. 3598.										
Jan. 29	4 6 55·13	·33	4·11	- 9·23	4· 7· 8·14	Jan. 30	4 6·50·84	·40	4·08	- 9·53	4· 7· 4·05
31	54·79	·35	4·07	9·82	8·33	Feb. 4	48·38	·42	4·05	11·00	3·01
Mar. 27	42·26	·03	4·08	23·31	9·62	April 4	34·57	·02	4·13	24·56	3·24
April 5	39·01	·04	4·13	24·70	7·80	8	33·49	·04	4·14	25·12	2·71
May 2	37·38	·02	4·21	-27·25	8·82	30	32·60	·02	4·13	-27·15	3·86
					4· 7· 8·54						4· 7· 3·37

Error of Collimation . . . = 0· 0· 2·58
Resulting Mean Zenith Distance, North = 4· 7· 5·96

	B.A.C. 3755.										
Jan. 29	2·22·18·66	·20	2·37	- 6·72	2·22·14·11	Feb. 4	2·22·24·78	·26	2·34	- 8·60	2·22·18·26
31	19·35	·22	2·35	7·35	14·13	Mar. 24	37·20	·03	2·38	21·88	17·67
Mar. 23	32·86	·01	2·36	21·67	13·54	26	37·30	·02	2·38	22·32	17·34
25	32·91	·02	2·38	22·10	13·17	29	37·60	·02	2·35	22·95	16·96
27	34·00	·02	2·35	22·53	13·80	April 2	38·44	·01	2·33	23·75	17·01
April 1	36·71	·03	2·33	23·55	15·46	4	38·68	·01	2·39	24·13	16·93
5	36·71	·02	2·38	24·31	14·76	8	40·95	·02	2·39	24·65	18·47
9	36·96	·01	2·40	25·02	14·31	10	41·05	·02	2·38	25·18	18·23
11	38·19	·01	2·38	25·35	15·21	13	42·24	·01	2·43	25·67	18·99
14	37·60	·02	2·41	- 25·82	14·17	15	42·82	·01	2·36	-25·97	19·20
					2·22·14·27						2·22·17·91

Error of Collimation . . . = 0· 0· 1·82
Resulting Mean Zenith Distance, South = 2·22·16·09

	B.A.C. 3928.										
April 2	2·55·39·35	·03	2·87	-21·77	2·56· 3·96	Mar. 29	2·55·36·49	·02	2·89	-21·03	2·55·60·39
5	37·43	·02	2·94	22·29	2·64	April 4	35·01	·01	2·94	22·12	60·06
9	38·27	·02	2·96	22·95	4·16	10	33·09	·03	2·93	23·10	59·09
11	37·87	·02	2·93	23·26	4·04	13	32·64	·02	2·99	23·56	59·17
14	36·54	·02	2·97	23·70	3·19	15	32·25	·01	2·91	23·84	58·99
16	36·10	·02	2·91	23·98	2·97	17	32·69	·01	2·97	24·12	59·77
18	37·23	·02	2·95	24·25	4·41	21	31·95	·02	2·99	24·63	59·55
20	36·88	·01	2·95	24·51	4·33	23	32·50	·02	2·95	24·87	60·30
22	36·79	·02	2·94	24·75	4·46	27	31·66	·02	2·94	25·31	59·89
24	36·34	·02	2·94	-24·98	4·24	30	31·12	·02	2·95	-25·60	59·65
					2·56· 3·84						2·55·59·69

Error of Collimation . . . = 0· 0· 2·08
Resulting Mean Zenith Distance, North = 2·56· 1·77

Mean Zenith Distances of Stars observed at the Royal Observatory.

	FACE OF SECTOR EAST.						FACE OF SECTOR WEST.				
Day of Observation 1845.	Apparent Zenith Distance, from Unreduced Observation.	Reduction for Az. Error, and Curv. of Path.	Refraction.	Precession, Aberration, and Nutation.	Deduced Mean Zenith Distance. 1845, Jan. 0; and Mean of Separate Results, uncorrected, for Error of Collimation.	Day of Observation 1845.	Apparent Zenith Distance, from Unreduced Observation.	Reduction for Az. Error, and Curv. of Path.	Refraction.	Precession, Aberration, and Nutation.	Deduced Mean Zenith Distance. 1845, Jan. 0; and Mean of Separate Results, uncorrected, for Error of Collimation.

B.A.C. 4015.

Day	Apparent Z.D. (° ′ ″)	Red.	Refr. (″)	Prec. (″)	Deduced Mean Z.D. (° ′ ″)	Day	Apparent Z.D. (° ′ ″)	Red.	Refr. (″)	Prec. (″)	Deduced Mean Z.D. (° ′ ″)
April 1	0 52 56·97	·01	0·86	-20·54	0·53 18·36	Mar. 29	0 52 56·87	·01	0·87	-19·95	0·53 17·68
2	57·56	·01	·86	20·74	19 15	April 4	54·26	·00	·89	21·12	16·27
9	56·23	·01	·89	22·03	19·14	14	53·86	·01	·88	22·20	16·98
11	55·44	·01	·88	22·37	18·68	17	53·37	·00	·80	22·86	17·12
16	55·15	·00	·88	23·17	19·20	19	52·88	·00	·89	23·33	17·10
18	55·15	·00	·89	23·47	19·51	21	52·38	·00	·89	23·62	16·89
22	54·06	·01	·89	24·04	18·98	23	52·04	·01	·90	23·91	16·84
24	55·19	·00	·89	24·31	20·39	25	53·02	·01	·80	24·18	18·08
27	53·17	·00	·89	24·69	18·75	30	51·79	·01	·89	24·44	17·11
May 2	52·98	·00	·90	-25·25	19·13		50·41	·01	·89	-25·03	16·32
					0·53·19·13						0·53·17·03

Error of Collimation   .   = 0· 0· 1·05
Resulting Mean Zenith Distance, North = 0·53·18·08

B.A.C. 4202.

Day	Apparent Z.D. (° ′ ″)	Red.	Refr. (″)	Prec. (″)	Deduced Mean Z.D. (° ′ ″)	Day	Apparent Z.D. (° ′ ″)	Red.	Refr. (″)	Prec. (″)	Deduced Mean Z.D. (° ′ ″)
April 4	4 15· 4·49	·04	4·29	-18·79	4·14·49·95	Mar. 29	4 15· 6·51	·04	4·22	-17·43	4·14·53·26
5	4·83	·04	4·30	19·00	50·09	April 10	8·93	·04	4·26	20·05	53·10
9	4·04	·03	4·30	19·85	48·46	13	10·55	·03	4·35	20·65	54·22
11	5·92	·03	4·28	20·26	49·91	14	9·01	·02	4·31	20·85	53·35
18	6·76	·02	4·29	21·60	49·43	15	10·40	·02	4·23	21·04	53·57
20	7·94	·01	4·29	21·96	50·26	17	11·00	·02	4·32	21·42	53·88
22	8·04	·03	4·28	22·31	49·98	19	10·85	·02	4·28	21·79	53·32
24	8·33	·02	4·28	22·65	49·94	21	8·68	·03	4·35	22·14	(50·66)
27	8·97	·02	4·28	23·14	50·09	23	11·79	·03	4·29	22·48	58·57
May 2	9·47	·02	4·35	-23·89	49·91	25	11·98	·03	4·31	22·82	53·44
						30	12·43	·03	4·29	-23·00	53·09
					4·14·49·80						4·14·53·48

Error of Collimation   .   - = 0· 0· 1·84
Resulting Mean Zenith Distance, South = 4·14·51·64

B.A.C. 4458.

Day	Apparent Z.D. (° ′ ″)	Red.	Refr. (″)	Prec. (″)	Deduced Mean Z.D. (° ′ ″)	Day	Apparent Z.D. (° ′ ″)	Red.	Refr. (″)	Prec. (″)	Deduced Mean Z.D. (° ′ ″)
April 4	1 57·41·29	·02	1·98	-14·93	1·57·28·32	Mar. 29	1 57·43·32	·02	1·95	-13·68	1·57·31·57
5	41·58	·02	1·98	15·14	28·40	April 10	45·73	·02	1·97	16·12	31·56
9	41·54	·01	1·99	15·93	27·59	14	46·22	·01	1·99	16·87	31·33
11	42·42	·01	1·97	16·31	28·07	15	47·46	·01	1·97	17·06	32·36
18	43·85	·01	1·99	17·59	28·24	17	47·30	·01	1·98	17·42	31·85
20	44·10	·01	1·98	17·94	28·13	19	47·85	·01	1·98	17·77	32·05
22	43·75	·01	1·97	18·28	27·45	21	47·50	·01	2·02	18·11	31·40
24	44·10	·01	1·97	18·61	27·45	23	48·24	·02	1·98	18·45	31·75
	45·28	·01	1·97	19·09	28·15	25	49·57	·01	1·99	18·78	32·77
May 5	45·87	·01	1·98	-20·27	27·57	30	49·38	·01	1·98	19·55	31·80
						May 4	50·42	·01	1·97	-20·13	32·25
					1·57·27·94						1·57·31·88

Error of Collimation   .   . = 0· 0· 1·97
Resulting Mean Zenith Distance, South = 1·57·29·91

Mean Zenith Distances of Stars observed at the Royal Observatory.

FACE OF SECTOR EAST.

Day of Observation 1845.	Apparent Zenith Distance, from Unreduced Observation.	Reduction for Az. Error, and Curv. of Path.	Refraction.	Precession, Aberration, and Nutation.	Deduced Mean Zenith Distance, 1845, Jan. 0; and Mean of Separate Results, uncorrected, for Error of Collimation.

B.A.C. 4686.

Day of Observation 1845.	Apparent Zenith Distance	Reduction	Refraction	Precession etc.	Deduced Mean
April 4	1·40·17·80	·02	1·68	−11·14	1·40· 8·32
5	18·93	·02	1 69	11·33	9·32
9	18·94	·01	1·69	12·07	8·55
11	19·03	·01	1·68	12·43	8·27
18	21·30	·01	1·70	13·65	9·34
20	20·76	·01	1·68	13·98	8·45
22	20·81	·01	1·69	14·31	8·18
24	21·70	·01	1·68	14·63	8·74
27	21·99	·01	1·68	15·11	8·55
May 4	23·18	·01	1·68	−16·14	8·71
					1·40· 8·64

FACE OF SECTOR WEST.

Day of Observation 1845.	Apparent Zenith Distance	Reduction	Refraction	Precession etc.	Deduced Mean
Mar. 29	1·40·21·15	·01	1·66	− 9·99	1·40·12·81
April 10	24·80	·02	1·68	12·25	14·21
14	25·89	·01	1·69	12·96	14·61
15	25·99	·01	1·68	13·14	14·52
17	25·89	·01	1·69	13·48	13·89
19	26·04	·01	1·68	13·82	13·89
21	26·08	·01	1·72	14·15	13·64
23	26·78	·01	1·69	14·47	13·99
25	27·71	·01	1·69	14·79	14·60
30	27·66	·01	1·69	−15·56	13·78
					1·40·13·99

Error of Collimation . . = 0· 0· 2·68
Resulting Mean Zenith Distance, South = 1·40·11·32

B.A.C. 5632.

Day	East App. Z.D.	Red.	Refr.	Prec.	Deduced Mean	Day	West App. Z.D.	Red.	Refr.	Prec.	Deduced Mean
Jan. 26	0· 4· 8·82	·00	0·07	+ 6·47	0· 4·15·36	Jan. 25	0· 4·11·87	·00	0·07	+ 6·50	0· 4·18·44
27	9·36	·00	·07	6·44	15·87	31	10·89	·00	·07	6·31	17·27
29	8·47	·00	·07	6·38	14·92	Feb. 1	11·28	·00	·07	+ 6·29	17·64
Feb. 3	8·08	·00	·07	+ 6·21	14·36	June 21	22·33	·00	·07	− 3·42	18·98
June 22	18·14	·00	·07	− 3·49	14·72	23	23·36	·00	·07	3·56	19·87
24	17·89	·00	·07	3·62	14·34	26	22·72	·00	·07	3·75	19·04
25	17·74	·00	·07	− 3·69	14·12	28	22·52	·00	·07	− 3·88	18·71
					0· 4·14·81						0· 4·18·56

Error of Collimation . . = 0· 0· 1·88
Resulting Mean Zenith Distance, South = 0· 4·16·69

B.A.C. 5915.

Day	East App. Z.D.	Red.	Refr.	Prec.	Deduced Mean	Day	West App. Z.D.	Red.	Refr.	Prec.	Deduced Mean
Jan. 26	3· 2·46·96	·23	3·00	+ 7·53	3· 2·57·26	Jan. 25	3· 2·50·07	·29	3·01	+ 7·50	3· 2·60·29
27	45·23	·23	3·03	7·55	55·58	30	48·59	·32	2·98	7·61	58·86
29	45·23	·27	3·01	7·59	55·56	Feb. 1	49·23	·33	3·00	7·64	59·54
Feb. 3	44·59	·29	2·97	7·67	54·94	Mar. 3	48·04	·05	3·09	7·56	58·64
Mar. 2	44·89	·01	3·07	7·58	55·53	27	49·77	·03	3·02	6·88	59·64
25	44·40	·02	3·06	6·95	54·39	30	49·38	·03	3·05	6·76	59·16
June 22	50·51	·00	3 13	1·43	55·07	June 21	55·24	·00	3·14	1·50	59·88
24	49·87	·00	3·07	1·26	54·20	23	54·60	·00	3·13	1·34	59·07
30	50·07	·00	3·17	+ 0·78	54·02	26	55·79	·00	3·11	1·10	60·00
						28	55·98	·00	3·19	+ 0·94	60·11
					3· 2·55·17						3· 2·59·52

Error of Collimation . . = 0· 0· 2·17
Resulting Mean Zenith Distance, South = 3· 2·57·35

Mean Zenith Distances of Stars observed at the Royal Observatory.

FACE OF SECTOR EAST.

B.A.C. 6233.

Day of Observation 1845.	Apparent Zenith Distance, from Unreduced Observation.	Reduction for Az. Error, and Curr. of Path.	Refraction.	Precession, Aberration, and Nutation.	Deduced Mean Zenith Distance, 1845, Jan. 0; and Mean of Separate Results, uncorrected for Error of Collimation.
	° ′ ″	″	″	″	° ′ ″
Jan. 26	0·30·51·78	·04	0·50	+ 6·78	0·30·59·02
27	51·92	·04	·51	6·83	59·22
Feb. 3	50·10	·05	·50	7·18	57·73
28	49·61	·00	·51	8·17	58·29
Mar. 2	50·05	·00	·52	8·24	58·81
25	48·62	·00	·52	8·80	57·94
30	47·04	·01	·52	8·89	56·44
June 22	50·44	·00	·53	7·51	58·48
24	50·35	·00	·52	7·30	58·26
30	49·51	·00	·54	+ 7·05	57·10
					0·30·58·13

FACE OF SECTOR WEST.

Day of Observation 1845.	Apparent Zenith Distance, from Unreduced Observation.	Reduction for Az. Error, and Curr. of Path.	Refraction.	Precession, Aberration, and Nutation.	Deduced Mean Zenith Distance, 1845, Jan. 0; and Mean of Separate Results, uncorrected for Error of Collimation.
	° ′ ″	″	″	″	° ′ ″
Jan. 25	0·30·54·39	·05	0·51	+ 6·72	0·30·61·57
31	53·16	·05	·50	7·04	60·65
Feb. 1	51·63	·05	·51	7·09	59·18
Mar. 1	51·43	·02	·51	8·21	60·13
3	51·97	·01	·52	8·27	60·75
24	51·78	·01	·52	8·78	61·07
26	51·38	·00	·51	8·82	60·71
June 21	54·54	·00	·53	7·56	62·63
23	55·55	·00	·53	+ 7·45	63·53
					0·31· 1·16

Error of Collimation . . . = 0· 0· 1·52
Resulting Mean Zenith Distance, South = 0·30·59·64

Fomalhaut B.A.C. 7992.

FACE OF SECTOR EAST.

Day of Observation 1845.	Apparent Zenith Distance, from Unreduced Observation.	Reduction for Az. Error, and Curr. of Path.	Refraction.	Precession, Aberration, and Nutation.	Deduced Mean Zenith Distance, 1845, Jan. 0; and Mean of Separate Results, uncorrected for Error of Collimation.
Jan. 28	3·29·27·85	·24	3·36	− 1·16	3·29·32·13
Mar. 1	32·88	·21	3·40	+ 3·28	32·79
23	37·32	·01	3·45	7·71	33·05
25	38·25	·02	3·45	8·13	33·55
April 9	41·46	·02	3·48	11·41	33·51
21	44·17	·02	3·50	+14·12	33·53
					3·29·33·09

FACE OF SECTOR WEST.

Day of Observation 1845.	Apparent Zenith Distance, from Unreduced Observation.	Reduction for Az. Error, and Curr. of Path.	Refraction.	Precession, Aberration, and Nutation.	Deduced Mean Zenith Distance, 1845, Jan. 0; and Mean of Separate Results, uncorrected for Error of Collimation.
Jan. 25	3·29·24·30	·31	3·41	− 1·46	3·29·28·86
31	26·27	·34	3·39	0·85	30·17
Feb. 1	24·59	·35	3·40	− 0·74	28·38
April 5	34·75	·02	3·47	+10·52	27·68
8	36·53	·03	3·51	11·18	28·83
10	37·37	·03	3·45	11·63	29·16
14	38·25	·02	3·52	+12·54	29·21
					3·29·28·90

Error of Collimation . . . = 0· 0· 2·10
Resulting Mean Zenith Distance, North = 3·29·31·00

MEAN ZENITH DISTANCES.

COLLECTION OF

AI.L THE

RESULTS OF OBSERVATION OF EACH STAR

AT

THE BUSHMAN FLAT STATION,

AND

DEDUCTION OF MEAN ZENITH DISTANCE, 1847, JANUARY 0.

NOTE.—The reduction for Azimuthal Error is always to be applied subtractively to the Zenith Distance. The reduction for Curvature of Path is always to be applied subtractively to South Zenith Distance, and additively to North Zenith Distance. The Refraction is always to be applied additively. The Precession, Aberration, and Nutation, have the sign which is proper for reducing the Apparent North Polar Distance of the Star to its mean North Polar Distance, 1847, January 0; and therefore are to be applied with the sign given in the Table when the Star is South of the Zenith, and with the opposite sign when the Star is North of the Zenith.

The numbers included in parentheses in the column " Deduced Mean Zenith Distance, 1847, January 0," are omitted in taking the mean.

Where an asterisk or a positive sign is affixed to a number in the 3rd or 9th columns, the explanation will be found at the bottom of the page.

Mean Zenith Distances of Stars observed at the Bushman Flat Station.

FACE OF SECTOR EAST.   FACE OF SECTOR WEST.

Day of Observation 1847.	Apparent Zenith Distance, from Unreduced Observation.	Reduction for Az. Error, and Curv. of Path.	Refraction.	Precession, and Aberration, and Nutation.	Deduced Mean Zenith Distance. 1847, Jan. 0; and Mean of Separate Results, uncorrected, for Error of Collimation.	Day of Observation 1847.	Apparent Zenith Distance, from Unreduced Observation.	Reduction for Az. Error, and Curv. of Path.	Refraction.	Precession, and Aberration, and Nutation.	Deduced Mean Zenith Distance. 1847, Jan. 0; and Mean of Separate Results, uncorrected, for Error of Collimation.

B.A.C. 4517.

	° ′ ″	″	″	° ′ ″	° ′ ″		° ′ ″	″	″	° ′ ″	° ′ ″
June 18	0·57·17·54	·01	0·86	−16·24	0·57·34·63	June 21	0·57·33·59	·14	0·89	−16·23	0·57·50·37
22	17·34	·01	·89	16·23	34·45	23	32·01	·01	·87	16·22	49·09
24	19·12	·02	·87	16·22	36·19	25	32·78	·01	·87	16·21	49·85
26	19·52	·03	·87	16·19	36·55	27	31·27	·00	·86	16·17	48·30
28	21·64	·04	86	16·15	38·61	29	31·00	·00	·86	16·13	47·99
30	20·32	·03	·86	16·11	37·26	July 1	28·24	·00	·86	16·09	45·19
July 4	23·30	·02	·87	16·00	40·15	3	28·53	·00	·87	16·03	45·43
8	20·68	·03	·86	−15·84	37·35	5	30·74	·00	·86	15·96	47·56
						10	29·67	·00	·87	15·76	46·30
						11	29·37	·01	·87	−15·71	45·94
					0·57·36·90						0·57·47·62

Error of Collimation . . . = 0· 0· 5·36
Resulting Mean Zenith Distance, North = 0·57·42·26

B.A.C. 4548.

June 22	0·57·15·96	·01	0·89	−15·79	0·57·32·63	June 21	0·57·29·19	·14	0·89	−15·79	0·57·45·73
24	17·64	·02	·87	15·78	34·27	23	28·95	·01	·87	15·79	45·60
26	16·45	·03	·87	15·76	33·05	25	28·83	·01	·87	15·77	45·46
28	16·60	·04	·86	15·73	33·15	27	27·91	·00	·86	15·75	44·52
30	16·87	·03	·86	15·70	33·40	29	25·37	·00	·86	15·72	41·95
July 2	18·08	·03	·87	15·65	34·57	July 1	25·77	·00	·86	15·68	42·31
4	18·16	·02	·87	15·59	34·60	3	24·98	·00	·87	15·62	41·47
6	18·77	·04	·86	15·53	35·12	5	26·70	·00	·86	15·56	43·12
8	18·41	·03	·86	−15·46	34·70	10	26·61	·00	·87	15·38	42·86
						11	26·21	·01	·87	−15·33	42·40
					0·57·33·94						0·57·43·54

Error of Collimation . . . = 0· 0· 4·80
Resulting Mean Zenith Distance, North = 0·57·38·74

B.A.C. 4579.

June 18	2·32· 5·57	·03	2·28	−16·20	2·31·51·62	June 21	2·31·52·85	·37	2·35	−10·25	2·31·38·58
22	6·76	·03	2·35	16·26	52·82	23	53·57	·03	2·30	16·27	39·57
24	4·59	·06	2·31	16·28	50·56	25	54·81	·02	2·31	16·29	40·81
26	5·28	·09	2·31	16·29	51·21	27	54·41	·01	2·28	16·28	40·40
30	4·06	·08	2·29	16·27	50·00	29	56·54	·01	2·28	16·28	42·53
July 2	5·03	·09	2·30	16·25	50·99	July 1	57·45	·01	2·28	16·26	43·46
4	2·58	·06	2·30	16·21	48·61	3	56·83	·00	2·30	16·23	42·00
6	0·54	·11	2·27	16·17	46·53	5	55·53	·00	2·28	16·19	41·62
8	1·84	·09	2·29	−16·12	47·92	7	56·42	·00	2·27	16·15	42·54
						10	58·14	·00	2·32	16·05	44·41
						11	56·39	·01	2·30	−16·02	42·66
					2·31·50·03						2·31·41·77

Error of Collimation . . . = 0· 0· 4·13
Resulting Mean Zenith Distance, South = 2·31·45·90

NOTE.—The observations of B.A.C. 1602 and 2293 are rejected because they are very discordant. The observations were made in the middle of the day, when the upper part of the Sector tent was exposed to strong sunshine.
B.A.C. 4579.—July 2.—The observation corrected for an assumed error of 5 parts of the Micrometer.

Mean Zenith Distances of Stars observed at the Bushman Flat Station.

FACE OF SECTOR EAST. | FACE OF SECTOR WEST.

B.A.C. 4623.

Day of Observation 1847.	Apparent Zenith Distance, from Unreduced Observation.	Reduction for Az. Error, and Curv. of Path.	Refraction.	Precession, Aberration, and Nutation.	Deduced Mean Zenith Distance, 1847, Jan. 0; and Mean of Separate Results, uncorrected, for Error of Collimation.	Day of Observation 1847.	Apparent Zenith Distance, from Unreduced Observation.	Reduction for Az. Error, and Curv. of Path.	Refraction.	Precession, Aberration, and Nutation.	Deduced Mean Zenith Distance, 1847, Jan. 0; and Mean of Separate Results, uncorrected, for Error of Collimation.
June 18	2·29·60·84	·03	2·25	-15·71	2·29·47·35	June 21	2·29·47·38	·36	2·32	-15·77	2·29·33·57
22	59·85	·03	2·32	15·78	46·36	23	40·43	·03	2·27	15·79	35·88
24	58·86	·06	2·28	15 81	45·27	25	48·90	·02	2·28	15·81	35·44
26	58·86	·09	2·27	15·82	45·22	27	48·54	·01	2·25	15·82	34·96
28	56 94	·10	2 25	15·82	43·27	29	51·01	·01	2·25	15·82	37·43
30	59·23	·08	2·25	15 82	45·58	July 1	51·97	·01	2·25	15·81	38·40
July 2	57·23	·09	2 27	15·80	43·61	3	51·95	·00	2·27	15·79	38·43
4	56·56	·06	2·27	15·78	42·99	5	50·50	·00	2·25	15·76	36·99
6	54·52	·10	2·24	15·74	40·92	7	52·08	·00	2·23	15·72	38·59
8	55·23	·09	2·26	-15·00	41·71	10	54·00	·00	2·28	15·64	40·64
						11	49·38	·01	2·27	-15·61	36·03
					2·29·44·23						2·29·36·94

Error of Collimation . . . = 0· 0· 3·64
Resulting Mean Zenith Distance, South = 2·29·40·59

B.A.C. 4719.

Day of Observation 1847.	Apparent Zenith Distance, from Unreduced Observation.	Reduction for Az. Error, and Curv. of Path.	Refraction.	Precession, Aberration, and Nutation.	Deduced Mean Zenith Distance.	Day of Observation 1847.	Apparent Zenith Distance, from Unreduced Observation.	Reduction for Az. Error, and Curv. of Path.	Refraction.	Precession, Aberration, and Nutation.	Deduced Mean Zenith Distance.
June 22	1·10· 4·54	·02	1·08	-12·90	1·10·18·50	June 21	1·10·18·91	·17	1 09	-12·89	1·10·32·72
24	6·72	·03	1·07	12·93	20·69	23	17·63	·01	1 06	12 92	31·60
26	4·79	·04	1·06	12·94	18 75	25	19·11	·01	1·07	12·93	33·10
30	6·62	·04	1·06	12·94	20·58	27	16·39	·00	1·05	12·94	30·38
July 2	7·80	·04	1·06	12·93	21·75	29	14·37	·00	1·05	12·94	28·36
4	7·36	03	1·06	12·91	21·30	July 1	14·62	·00	1·05	12·94	28·61
6	9·38	05	1·05	12·88	23·26	3	14·62	·00	1·07	12·92	28·61
8	9·19	·04	1·06	-12·85	23·06	5	15·46	·00	1·05	12·90	29·41
						10	14·86	·00	1·07	12·80	28·73
						11	14·92	·01	1·07	-12·78	28·76
					1·10·20·99						1·10·30·03

Error of Collimation . . . = 0· 0· 4·52
Resulting Mean Zenith Distance, North = 1·10·25·51

B.A.C. 4784.

Day of Observation 1847.	Apparent Zenith Distance, from Unreduced Observation.	Reduction for Az. Error, and Curv. of Path.	Refraction.	Precession, Aberration, and Nutation.	Deduced Mean Zenith Distance.	Day of Observation 1847.	Apparent Zenith Distance, from Unreduced Observation.	Reduction for Az. Error, and Curv. of Path.	Refraction.	Precession, Aberration, and Nutation.	Deduced Mean Zenith Distance.
June 22	0·55·54·12	·01	0·87	-11·86	0·50· 6·84	June 21	0·56· 8·74	·13	0·87	-11·84	0·56·21·32
24	54·42	·02	·86	11·89	7·15	23	8·64	01	·85	11·88	21·36
26	53·82	·03	·85	11 92	6·56	25	8·89	·01	·85	11·91	21·64
28	56·10	·04	·84	11·93	8·83	27	6·22	·00	·84	11·93	18·99
30	55·35	·03	·84	11·95	8·11	29	5·72	·00	·85	11·94	18·51
July 2	56·19	·03	·85	11·95	8·96	July 1	3·01	·00	·84	11·95	15·80
6	57·28	·04	·84	11·93	10·01	3	4·89	·00	·85	11·94	17·68
8	56·19	·03	·85	-11·91	8 92	5	6·81	·00	·84	11·93	19·58
						7	6·17	·00	·83	11·92	18·92
						10	4·24	·00	·85	11·88	16·97
						11	3·45	·00	·85	-11·86	16 16
					0·56· 8·17						0·56·18 81

Error of Collimation . . . = 0· 0· 5·32
Resulting Mean Zenith Distance, North = 0·56·13·49

Mean Zenith Distances of Stars observed at the Bushman Flat Station.

FACE OF SECTOR EAST.   **FACE OF SECTOR WEST.**

Anon. AR. 14·24.

Day of Observation 1847.	Apparent Zenith Distance, from Unreduced Observation.	Reduction for Ax. Error, and Curr. of Path.	Refraction.	Precession, Aberration, and Nutation.	Deduced Mean Zenith Distance, 1847, Jan. 0; and Mean of Separate Results, uncorrected, for Error of Collimation.	Day of Observation 1847.	Apparent Zenith Distance, from Unreduced Observation.	Reduction for Ax. Error, and Curr. of Path.	Refraction.	Precession, Aberration, and Nutation.	Deduced Mean Zenith Distance, 1847, Jan. 0; and Mean of Separate Results, uncorrected, for Error of Collimation.
June 22	2·54·14·08	·04	2·69	-12·39	2·54· 4·34	June 23	2·54· 3·31	·03	2·63	-12·43	2·53·53·48
24	14·57	·07	2·67	12·46	4·71	25	3·11	·03	2·66	12·49	53·25
26	14·03	·10	2·65	12·52	4·06	27	3·51	·00	2·62	12·54	53·59
28	12·00	·12	2·02	12·56	1·94	July 1	7·61	·01	2·63	12·62	57·61
30	14·87	·10	2·63	12·61	4·79	3	6·28	·00	2·65	12·65	56·28
July 2	11·36	·11	2·64	12·64	1·25	5	3·95	·00	2·62	12·66	53·91
4	13·44	·07	2·65	12·66	3·36	10	6·92	·00	2·65	-12·67	56·90
8	14·13	·10	2·64	-12·68	3·99						
					2·54· 3·56						2·53·55·00

Error of Collimation . . . = 0· 0· 4·28
Resulting Mean Zenith Distance, South = 2·53·59·28

B.A.C. 4852.

Day of Observation 1847.	Apparent Zenith Distance, from Unreduced Observation.	Reduction for Ax. Error, and Curr. of Path.	Refraction.	Precession, Aberration, and Nutation.	Deduced Mean Zenith Distance.	Day of Observation 1847.	Apparent Zenith Distance, from Unreduced Observation.	Reduction for Ax. Error, and Curr. of Path.	Refraction.	Precession, Aberration, and Nutation.	Deduced Mean Zenith Distance.
June 18	4·46·34·86	·06	4·31	-11·69	4·46·27·42	June 23	4·46·22·07	·05	4·34	-11·94	4·46·14·42
22	34·51	·07	4·44	11·90	26·98	25	24·19	·05	4·38	12·03	16·49
24	35·80	·12	4·39	11·99	28·08	27	24·24	·01	4·31	12·10	16·44
26	34·66	·17	4·37	12·07	26·79	29	25·48	·01	4·34	12·17	17·64
28	32·34	·20	4·31	12·14	24·31	July 3	28·74	·00	4·36	12·28	20·82
30	34·17	·16	4·33	12·20	26·14	5	26·96	·00	4·32	12·32	18·96
July 2	32·29	·18	4·35	12·26	24·20	7	26·32	·00	4·28	12·35	18·25
4	33·23	·12	4·36	12·30	25·17	10	26·37	·00	4·37	12·38	18·36
6	31·65	·21	4·32	12·34	23·42	11	24·98	·03	4·36	-12·39	16·92
8	33·03	·17	4·34	-12·37	24·83						
					4·46·25·73						4·46·17·59

Error of Collimation . . . = 0· 0· 4·07
Resulting Mean Zenith Distance, South = 4·46·21·66

B.A.C. 4891.

Day of Observation 1847.	Apparent Zenith Distance, from Unreduced Observation.	Reduction for Ax. Error, and Curr. of Path.	Refraction.	Precession, Aberration, and Nutation.	Deduced Mean Zenith Distance.	Day of Observation 1847.	Apparent Zenith Distance, from Unreduced Observation.	Reduction for Ax. Error, and Curr. of Path.	Refraction.	Precession, Aberration, and Nutation.	Deduced Mean Zenith Distance.
June 18	2·24·46·87	·03	2·17	- 0·45	2·24·58·46	June 21	2·24·61·78	·34	2·25	- 9·52	2·25·13·21
22	47·75	·03	2·24	9·54	59·50	23	61·04	·03	2·19	9·56	12·70
24	48·45	·06	2·22	9·58	60·19	25	61·19	·02	2·21	9·60	12·98
26	48·54	·08	2·21	9·61	60·28	27	59·01	·01	2·18	9·62	10·80
28	48·15	·09	2·18	9·63	59·87	July 1	55·61	·01	2·18	9·66	7·44
July 2	50·52	·08	2·20	9·66	62·30	3	56·59	·00	2·20	9·66	8·45
4	50·22	·06	2·20	9·66	62·02	5	58·77	·00	2·18	9·66	10·61
6	52·05	·10	2·18	9·66	63·79	7	57·78	·00	2·17	9·66	9·61
8	52·30	·08	2 19	- 9·65	64·06	10	56·79	·00	2·21	9·63	8·63
						11	58·47	·01	2·20	- 9·62	10·28
					2·25· 1·16						2·25·10·48

Error of Collimation . . . = 0· 0· 4·66
Resulting Mean Zenith Distance, North = 2·25· 5·82

Mean Zenith Distances of Stars observed at the Bushman Flat Station.

FACE OF SECTOR EAST.						FACE OF SECTOR WEST.					
Day of Observation 1847.	Apparent Zenith Distance, from Unreduced Observation.	Reduction for Az. Error, and Curv. of Path.	Refraction.	Precession, Aberration, and Nutation.	Deduced Mean Zenith Distance. 1847, Jan. 0; and Mean of Separate Results, uncorrected, for Error of Collimation.	Day of Observation 1847.	Apparent Zenith Distance, from Unreduced Observation.	Reduction for Az. Error, and Curv. of Path.	Refraction.	Precession, Aberration, and Nutation.	Deduced Mean Zenith Distance, 1847, Jan. 0; and Mean of Separate Results, uncorrected for Error of Collimation.

B.A.C. 4916.

Day of Observation 1847.	Apparent Z. Dist.	Reduction	Refraction	Prec./Aberr./Nut.	Deduced Mean Z. Dist.	Day of Observation 1847.	Apparent Z. Dist.	Reduction	Refraction	Prec./Aberr./Nut.	Deduced Mean Z. Dist.
June 18	3 29 45·33	·04	3·15	-10·26	3·29·38·18	June 21	3 29 32·84	·52	3·25	-10 41	3·29·25·16
22	44·79	·05	3·25	10·46	37·53	23	32·94	·04	3·19	10·51	25·58
24	42·62	·09	3 21	10·55	35·19	25	35·41	·03	3·20	10·59	27·99
26	43·56	·12	3·19	10·63	36·00	27	33·63	·01	3·17	10·67	26·12
28	43·28	·14	3·16	10·70	35·58	29	34·37	·01	3·17	10·73	26·80
30	43·31	·12	3·16	10·76	35·59	July 1	32·35	·01	3·16	10·80	24·70
July 2	40·79	·13	3·20	10·82	33·04	3	35·36	·00	3·19	10·85	27·70
4	41·58	·08	3·19	10·87	33·82	10	37·48	·00	3·20	10·97	29·71
6	40·64	·15	3·15	-10 91	32·73	11	35·41	·02	3·19	-10·98	27·80
					3·29·35·30						3·29·26·82

Error of Collimation . . . = 0· 0· 4 24
Resulting Mean Zenith Distance, South = 3·29·31·06

Anon. AR. 14·54.

Day of Observation 1847.	Apparent Z. Dist.	Reduction	Refraction	Prec./Aberr./Nut.	Deduced Mean Z. Dist.	Day of Observation 1847.	Apparent Z. Dist.	Reduction	Refraction	Prec./Aberr./Nut.	Deduced Mean Z. Dist.
June 18	2·18· 5·67	·03	2·07	- 9·30	2·17·58·41	June 21	2·17·49·82	·34	2·14	- 9·44	2·17·42·18
22	4·27	·03	2·14	9·49	56·89	23	51·07	·02	2·10	9·53	43·62
24	3·71	·06	2·11	9·58	56·18	25	50·53	·02	2·11	9·62	43·00
26	3·46	·08	2·10	9·66	55·82	27	51·76	·00	2 08	9·69	44·15
28	2·87	·09	2·08	9·73	55·13	29	53·14	·01	2·08	9·76	45·45
30	2·97	·08	2·08	9·78	55·19	July 1	50·01	·01	2·08	9·81	48·27
July 2	1·09	·08	2·10	9·83	53·28	3	54·18	·00	2·10	9·85	46·43
4	1·98	·06	2·09	9·88	54·13	5	53·79	·00	2·08	9·90	45·97
6	0·75	·10	2·07	9·92	52·80	10	55·41	·00	2·10	9·97	47·54
8	1·44	·08	2 09	- 9·95	53 50	11	55 51	·01	2 10	- 9·98	47·62
					2·17·55·13						2·17·45·42

Error of Collimation . . . = 0· 0· 4·86
Resulting Mean Zenith Distance, South = 2·17·50·28

Anon. AR. 14·58.

Day of Observation 1847.	Apparent Z. Dist.	Reduction	Refraction	Prec./Aberr./Nut.	Deduced Mean Z. Dist.	Day of Observation 1847.	Apparent Z. Dist.	Reduction	Refraction	Prec./Aberr./Nut.	Deduced Mean Z. Dist.
June 18	2·34·41·53	·03	2·32	- 8·96	2·34·34·86	June 21	2·34·31·06	·38	2·40	- 9·11	2·34·23·97
22	44·40	·03	2·39	9·15	37·61	23	33·04	·03	2·35	9·20	26·16
24	43·31	·06	2·37	9·25	36·37	25	32·94	·02	2·36	9·29	25·90
26	44·20	·09	2·36	9·32	37·15	27	35·21	·00	2 33	9·36	28·18
28	44·30	·10	2·33	9·40	37 13	29	34·82	·01	2·34	9·43	27·72
30	44·55	·09	2 33	9·47	37·32	July 3	36·74	·00	2·35	9·55	29·54
July 2	42·87	·09	2·36	9·53	35·61	5	34·82	·00	2·33	- 9·60	27·55
4	44·94	·06	2·35	9·58	37·65						
6	42·82	·11	2·33	9·62	35·42						
8	41·68	·07	2 34	- 9·66	34·29						
					2·34·36·34						2·34·27·02

Error of Collimation . . . = 0· 0· 4·66
Resulting Mean Zenith Distance, South = 2·34·31·68

Mean Zenith Distances of Stars observed at the Bushman Flat Station.

FACE OF SECTOR EAST.

Day of Observation 1847.	Apparent Zenith Distance, from Unreduced Observation.	Reduction for Az. Error, and Curv. of Path.	Refraction.	Precession, Aberration, and Nutation.	Deduced Mean Zenith Distance, 1847, Jan. 0; and Mean of Separate Results, uncorrected, for Error of Collimation.
	° ′ ″	″	″	″	° ′ ″
B.A.C. 5032.					
June 18	0· 9· 9·24	·00	0·14	- 7·36	0· 9·16·74
22	10·92	·00	·14	7·52	18·58
24	10·72	·00	·14	7·59	18·45
26	10·77	·01	·14	7·66	18·56
28	11·85	·01	·14	7·72	19 70
30	11·41	·01	·14	7·77	19·31
July 2	11·51	·01	·14	7·81	19·45
4	11·11	·00	·14	7·85	19·10
6	12·94	·01	·14	7·89	20·96
8	11·31	·01	0·14	- 7·92	19·36
					0· 9·19·02

FACE OF SECTOR WEST.

Day of Observation 1847.	Apparent Zenith Distance, from Unreduced Observation.	Reduction for Az. Error, and Curv. of Path.	Refraction.	Precession, Aberration, and Nutation.	Deduced Mean Zenith Distance, 1847, Jan. 0; and Mean of Separate Results, uncorrected, for Error of Collimation.
	° ′ ″	″	″	″	° ′ ″
June 21	0· 9·22·57	·02	0·14	- 7·48	0· 9·30·17
25	22·22	·00	·14	7·63	29·99
27	20·40	·00	·14	7·69	28·23
29	19·85	·00	·14	7·74	27·73
July 1	17·78	·00	·14	7·79	25·71
3	18 92	·00	·14	7·84	26 90
5	19·51	·00	·14	7·87	27·52
7	16·45	·00	·14	7·90	24·49
10	18·82	·00	·14	7·94	26·90
11	19·26	·00	0·14	- 7·94	27·34
					0· 9·27·50

Error of Collimation . . = 0· 0· 4·24
Resulting Mean Zenith Distance, North = 0· 9·23·26

B.A.C. 5151.

FACE OF SECTOR EAST.

Day	Apparent Z.D.	Red.	Refr.	Prec.	Deduced Mean Z.D.
June 18	0·27·53·44	·01	0·42	- 5·27	0·27·59·12
22	53·09	·01	·43	5·44	58·95
24	52·99	·01	·43	5·52	58 93
26	51·98	·02	·43	5·59	57·98
28	54·23	·02	·42	5·65	60·28
30	52·99	·02	·42	5·72	59·11
July 2	55·36	·02	·43	5 77	61·54
4	54·57	·01	·43	5·82	60·81
6	56·06	·02	·42	5·87	62·33
8	56·20	·02	0·42	- 5·91	62·51
					0·28· 0·16

FACE OF SECTOR WEST.

Day	Apparent Z.D.	Red.	Refr.	Prec.	Deduced Mean Z.D.
June 21	0·28· 6·72	·07	0·43	- 5·40	0·28·12·48
23	6·03	·00	·43	5·48	11·94
25	5·06	·00	·43	5·56	11·95
27	4·40	·00	·42	5·62	10·44
29	3·71	·00	·42	5·69	9·82
July 1	2·77	·00	·42	5·75	8·94
3	1·29	·00	·43	5·80	7·52
5	4·06	·00	·42	5·85	10·33
7	1·74	·00	·42	5·89	8·05
10	1·93	·00	·43	5·95	8·31
11	2·43	·00	0·43	- 5·96	8·82
					0·28· 9·87

Error of Collimation . . = 0· 0· 4·86
Resulting Mean Zenith Distance, North = 0·28· 5·01

Anon. AR. 15·35.

FACE OF SECTOR EAST.

Day	Apparent Z.D.	Red.	Refr.	Prec.	Deduced Mean Z.D.
June 22	1·22·24·14	·02	1·28	- 5·26	1·22·20·14
24	24·59	·03	1·26	5·35	20·47
26	23·70	·05	1·25	5·44	19·46
28	23·80	·05	1·24	5·53	19·46
30	26·12	·05	1·25	5·61	21·71
July 4	22·96	·03	1·25	5·75	18·43
6	22·86	·06	1·24	5·82	18·22
8	22·26	·05	1·25	- 5·88	17·58
					1·22·19·43

FACE OF SECTOR WEST.

Day	Apparent Z.D.	Red.	Refr.	Prec.	Deduced Mean Z.D.
June 21	1·22·13·13	·20	1·28	- 5·20	1·22· 9·01
23	11·85	·01	1·25	5·31	7·78
25	10·76	·01	1·26	5·40	6·61
27	12·98	·00	1·24	5·48	8·74
29	13·13	·00	1·24	5·57	8·80
July 1	15·94	·00	1·24	5·65	11·53
3	14·91	·00	1·25	5·72	10·44
5	13·77	·00	1·25	5·79	9·22
10	15·20	·00	1·26	5·93	10·53
11	17·77	·01	1·26	- 5·95	13·07
					1·22· 9·57

Error of Collimation . . = 0· 0· 4·93
Resulting Mean Zenith Distance, South = 1·22·14·50

Mean Zenith Distances of Stars observed at the Bushman Flat Station.

FACE OF SECTOR EAST.　　　　　　　　**FACE OF SECTOR WEST.**

B.A.C. 5227.

Day of Observation 1847.	Apparent Zenith Distance, from Unreduced Observation.	Reduction for Az. Error, and Curv. of Path.	Refraction.	Precession, Aberration, and Nutation.	Deduced Mean Zenith Distance, 1847, Jan. 0; and Mean of Separate Results, uncorrected, for Error of Collimation.	Day of Observation 1847.	Apparent Zenith Distance, from Unreduced Observation.	Reduction for Az. Error, and Curv. of Path.	Refraction.	Precession, Aberration, and Nutation.	Deduced Mean Zenith Distance, 1847, Jan. 0; and Mean of Separate Results, uncorrected, for Error of Collimation.
June 18	3·25·11·65	·04	3·08	− 4·68	3·25·10·01	June 21	3·24·58·22	·51	3·18	− 4·88	3·24·56·01
22	11·16	·05	3·18	4·94	9·35	23	59·51	·04	3·12	5·00	57·59
24	10·77	·09	3·16	5·06	8·78	25	57·73	·03	3·14	5·12	55·72
26	10·57	·12	3·13	5·17	8·41	27	58·88	·01	3·10	5·23	56·74
28	10·96	·14	3·09	5·28	8·63	29	3·25· 1·38	·01	3·10	5·33	59·14
30	9·83	·12	3·11	5·38	7·44	July 1	3·85	·01	3·09	5·44	61·49
July 2	9·23	·13	3·13	5·48	6·75	3	2·96	·00	3·12	5·53	60·55
4	8·39	·10	3·13	5·57	5·85	5	1·98	·00	3·10	5·62	59·46
6	8·44	·15	3·10	5·66	5·73	7	4·40	·00	3·09	5·70	61·79
8	8·74	·12	3·11	− 5·74	5·99	10	3·11	·00	3·13	5·81	60·43
						11	3·01	·02	3·13	− 5·85	60·27
					3·25· 7·69						3·24·59·02

Error of Collimation . . . = 0· 0· 4·34
Resulting Mean Zenith Distance, South = 3·25· 3·36

B.A.C. 5272.

Day of Observation 1847.	Apparent Zenith Distance, from Unreduced Observation.	Reduction for Az. Error, and Curv. of Path.	Refraction.	Precession, Aberration, and Nutation.	Deduced Mean Zenith Distance, 1847, Jan. 0; and Mean of Separate Results, uncorrected, for Error of Collimation.	Day of Observation 1847.	Apparent Zenith Distance, from Unreduced Observation.	Reduction for Az. Error, and Curv. of Path.	Refraction.	Precession, Aberration, and Nutation.	Deduced Mean Zenith Distance, 1847, Jan. 0; and Mean of Separate Results, uncorrected, for Error of Collimation.
June 18	0·58·19·66	·01	0 88	− 3·37	0·58·23·90	June 21	0·58·35·56	·14	0·91	− 3·50	0·58·39·83
22	21·73	·01	·91	3·54	26·17	23	35·07	·01	·89	3·58	39·53
24	21·83	·02	·90	3·60	26·33	25	34·52	·01	·89	3·66	39·06
26	21·64	·03	·89	3·66	26·19	27	34·08	·00	·88	3·73	38·69
28	22·13	·04	·88	3·76	26·73	29	31·61	·00	·88	3·80	36·29
30	21·29	·03	·88	3·83	25·97	July 1	31·51	·00	·88	3·86	36·25
July 2	24·90	·03	·89	3·89	29·74	3	30·07	·00	·80	3·92	35·48
4	22·82	·02	·80	3·95	27·64	5	31·61	·00	·88	3·97	36·46
6	24·80	·04	·88	4·00	29·64	7	31·07	·00	·88	4·02	35·97
8	23·71	·03	0·89	− 4·05	28·62	10	30·02	·00	·89	4·09	35·60
						11	30·87	·01	0·89	− 4·11	35·86
					0·58·27·09						0·58·37·18

Error of Collimation . . . = 0· 0· 5·05
Resulting Mean Zenith Distance, North = 0·58·32·14

B.A.C. 5374.

Day of Observation 1847.	Apparent Zenith Distance, from Unreduced Observation.	Reduction for Az. Error, and Curv. of Path.	Refraction.	Precession, Aberration, and Nutation.	Deduced Mean Zenith Distance, 1847, Jan. 0; and Mean of Separate Results, uncorrected, for Error of Collimation.	Day of Observation 1847.	Apparent Zenith Distance, from Unreduced Observation.	Reduction for Az. Error, and Curv. of Path.	Refraction.	Precession, Aberration, and Nutation.	Deduced Mean Zenith Distance, 1847, Jan. 0; and Mean of Separate Results, uncorrected, for Error of Collimation.
June 18	0·43·39·51	·01	0 66	− 2·00	0·43·42·16	June 21	0·43·56·35	·10	0 68	− 2·13	0·43·59·06
22	41·93	·01	·68	2·17	44·77	23	55·81	·01	·67	2·21	58·68
24	41·88	·02	·67	2·26	44·79	25	55·12	·01	·67	2·30	58·08
26	42·33	·02	·67	2·33	45·31	27	54·92	·00	·66	2·37	57·95
28	43·22	·03	·66	2·41	46·26	29	53·04	·00	·67	2·45	56·16
30	43·31	·02	·66	2·48	46·43	July 1	51·81	·00	·66	2·52	54·99
July 2	42·87	·03	·67	2·55	46·06	3	51·76	·00	·67	2·59	55·02
4	42·77	·02	·67	2·62	46·04	5	51·76	·00	·66	2·65	55·07
6	43·96	·03	·66	2·68	47·27	7	52·40	·00	·66	2·71	55·77
8	43·61	·03	0 66	− 2·74	46·98	10	51·91	·00	·67	2·79	55·37
						11	52·00	·00	0·67	− 2·81	55·48
					0·43·45·61						0·43·56·51

Error of Collimation . . . = 0· 0· 5·45
Resulting Mean Zenith Distance, North = 0·43·51·06

Mean Zenith Distances of Stars observed at the Bushman Flat Station.

	FACE OF SECTOR EAST.						FACE OF SECTOR WEST.				
Day of Observation 1847.	Apparent Zenith Distance, from Unreduced Observation.	Reduction for Az. Error, and Curr. of Path.	Refraction.	Precession, Aberration, and Nutation.	Deduced Mean Zenith Distance, 1847, Jan. 0; and Mean of Separate Results, uncorrected, for Error of Collimation.	Day of Observation 1847.	Apparent Zenith Distance, from Unreduced Observation.	Reduction for Az. Error, and Curr. of Path.	Refraction.	Precession, Aberration, and Nutation.	Deduced Mean Zenith Distance, 1847, Jan. 0; and Mean of Separate Results, uncorrected, for Error of Collimation.

B.A.C. 5435.

June 18	0· 47· 39·89	·01	0·71	− 1·34	0· 47· 39·25	June 21	0· 47· 23·99	·11	0·74	− 1·50	0· 47· 23·12
22	37·62	·01	·74	1·55	36·80	23	24·49	·01	·72	1·60	23·60
24	37·62	·02	·73	1·66	36·07	25	25·18	·01	·73	1·71	24·19
26	38·61	·03	·72	1·75	37·55	27	24·59	·00	·72	1·80	23·51
28	36·93	·03	·72	1·85	35·77	29	25·82	·00	·72	1·89	24·65
30	37·03	·03	·72	1·94	35·78	July 1	27·30	·00	·72	1·98	26·04
July 2	36·78	·03	·73	2·03	35·45	3	28·24	·00	·72	2·07	26·89
4	35·99	·02	·72	2·11	34·58	5	27·79	·00	·72	2·15	26·36
6	34·66	·03	·72	2·19	33·16	10	26·36	·00	·73	2·33	24·76
8	35·05	·03	0·72	− 2·26	33·48	11	27·40	·00	0·73	− 2·37	25·76
					0· 47· 35·85						0· 47· 24·89

Error of Collimation . . . = 0· 0· 5·48
Resulting Mean Zenith Distance, South = 0· 47· 30·37

Anon. AR. 16·14.

June 18	3· 6· 0·49	·04	2·79	− 1·18	3· 5· 62·06	June 21	3· 5· 43·26	·46	2·89	− 1·37	3· 5· 44·32
22	3· 5· 54·12	·04	2·88	1·44	55·52	23	42·17	·03	2·83	1·50	43·47
24	54·12	·08	2·86	1·57	55·33	25	43·95	·03	2·84	1·63	45·13
26	55·01	·11	2·83	1·69	56·04	27	38·81	·01	2·82	1·75	36·87
28	49·97	·13	2·81	1·81	50·84	29	41·92	·01	2·82	1·86	42·87
30	52·67	·11	2·81	1·92	53·45	July 1	47·65	·01	2·81	1·98	48·47
July 2	51·85	·11	2·85	2·03	52·56	3	44·09	·00	2·83	2·09	45·43
4	49·38	·07	2·83	2·14	50·00	5	49·38	·00	2·80	2·19	49·99
6	51·11	·13	2·81	2·24	51·55	11	43·85	·02	2·84	− 2·48	44·19
8	50·22	·11	2·82	− 2·34	50·59						
					3· 5· 53·79						3· 5· 44·86

Error of Collimation . . . = 0· 0· 4·47
Resulting Mean Zenith Distance, South = 3· 5· 49·33

Antares B.A.C. 5498.

June 18	3· 38· 50·97	·04	3·20	+ 0·21	3· 38· 54·01	June 21	3· 39· 6·23	·51	3·40	+ 0·12	3· 39· 9·00
22	51·91	·05	3·40	+ 0·10	55·16	23	4·65	·04	3·34	+ 0·07	7·88
24	53·24	·09	3·37	+ 0·04	56·48	25	3·59	·03	3·35	+ 0·01	6·90
26	52·45	·12	3·34	− 0·01	55·68	27	4·10	·01	3·32	− 0·04	7·45
28	53·08	·14	3·31	0·06	57·21	29	3·26	·01	3·33	0·09	6·67
30	53·93	·12	3·32	0·11	57·24	July 1	1·73	·01	3·32	0·13	5·17
July 2	55·31	·13	3·36	0·16	58·70	3	1·39	·00	3·33	0·18	4·90
4	55·07	·08	3·34	0·20	58·53	5	1·39	·00	3·31	0·22	4·92
6	57·78	·15	3·31	0·24	61·18	7	1·78	·00	3·30	0·26	5·34
8	55·61	·12	3·32	− 0·28	59·09	10	0·94	·00	3·35	0·31	4·60
						11	0·74	·02	3·35	− 0·33	4·40
					3· 38· 57·33						3· 39· 6·11

Error of Collimation . . . = 0· 0· 4·39
Resulting Mean Zenith Distance, North = 3· 39· 1·72

R.A. 16ʰ 14ᵐ.—A faint double star: the observations are very uncertain.

Mean Zenith Distances of Stars observed at the Bushman Flat Station.

FACE OF SECTOR EAST.						FACE OF SECTOR WEST.					
Day of Observation 1847.	Apparent Zenith Distance, from Unreduced Observation.	Reduction for Az. Error, and Curr. of Path.	Refraction.	Precession, Aberration, and Nutation.	Deduced Mean Zenith Distance, 1847, Jan. 0; and Mean of Separate Results, uncorrected, for Error of Collimation.	Day of Observation 1847.	Apparent Zenith Distance, from Unreduced Observation.	Reduction for Az. Error, and Curr. of Path.	Refraction.	Precession, Aberration, and Nutation.	Deduced Mean Zenith Distance, 1847, Jan. 0; and Mean of Separate Results, uncorrected, for Error of Collimation.
					B.A.C. 5588.						
June 18	2· 4·19·90	·02	1·87	+ 1·01	2· 4·22·76	June 21	2· 4· 4·40	·30	1·93	+ 0·82	2· 4· 6·85
22	19·21	·03	1·93	0·76	21·87	23	6·27	·02	1·89	0·71	8·85
24	18·23	·05	1·91	0·65	20·74	25	7·11	·02	1·90	0·59	9·58
26	20·69	·07	1·90	0·53	23·05	27	6·67	·00	1·88	0·48	9·03
28	17·88	·08	1·88	0·42	20·10	29	8·15	·01	1·89	0·37	10·40
30	16·60	·07	1·86	0·31	18·72	July 1	8·91	·01	1·88	0·26	11·04
July 2	17·53	·07	1·90	0·21	19·57	3	11·31	·00	1·89	0·15	13·35
4	17·78	·05	1·89	+ 0·10	19·72	5	8·79	·00	1·87	+ 0·05	10·71
6	15·41	·09	1·88	0·00	17·20	10	12·05	·00	1·90	- 0·19	13·76
8	16·84	·08	1·88	- 0·10	18·54	11	9·98	·01	1·90	- 0·24	11·63
					2· 4·20·23						2· 4·10·52

Error of Collimation . . = 0· 0· 4·85
Resulting Mean Zenith Distance, South = 2· 4·15·37

B.A.C. 5632.

Day	Apparent Zenith Distance	Reduction	Refraction	Precession, &c.	Deduced Mean Z.D.	Day	Apparent Zenith Distance	Reduction	Refraction	Precession, &c.	Deduced Mean Z.D.
June 18	4·16·17·72	·05	3·86	+ 1·49	4·16·23·02	June 21	4·16· 4·49	·64	3·98	+ 1·27	4·16· 9·10
22	17·87	·06	3·99	1·20	23·00	23	5·28	·05	3·91	1·13	10·27
24	16·24	·11	3·95	1·06	21·14	25	8·44	·04	3·92	0·99	13·31
26	17·23	·15	3·93	0·92	21·93	27	5·13	·01	3·89	0·85	9·86
28	14·56	·17	3·88	0·79	19·06	29	5·43	·01	3·90	0·72	10·04
30	17·28	·15	3·88	0·65	21·66	July 1	5·77	·01	3·88	0·58	10·22
July 2	14·47	·16	3·93	0·52	18·76	3	9·63	·00	3·90	0·46	13·99
4	16·59	·10	3·91	0·39	20·79	5	9·23	·00	3·88	0·33	13·44
6	14·56	·19	3·87	0·27	18·51	7	7·90	·00	3·86	0·21	11·97
8	17·03	·37	3·89	+ 0·14	20·69	10	9·03	·00	3·92	+ 0·03	12·98
						11	8·39	·02	3·93	- 0·03	12·27
					4·16·20·86						4·16·11·59

Error of Collimation . . = 0· 0· 4·64
Resulting Mean Zenith Distance, South = 4·16·16·22

B.A.C. 5735.

Day	Apparent Zenith Distance	Reduction	Refraction	Precession, &c.	Deduced Mean Z.D.	Day	Apparent Zenith Distance	Reduction	Refraction	Precession, &c.	Deduced Mean Z.D.
June 18	4· 9·47·75	·05	3·76	+ 3·04	4· 9·54·50	June 21	4· 9·34·82	·02	3·68	+ 2·83	4· 9·40·91
22	48·05	·06	3·89	2·76	54·64	23	35·21	·05	3·81	2·69	41·66
24	47·46	·10	3·85	2·62	53·83	27	34·77	·01	3·79	2·42	40·97
26	47·64	·15	3·83	2·48	53·80	July 3	36·50	·01	3·80	2·28	42·57
28	45·53	·17	3·78	2·35	51·49	5	40·00	·00	3·83	2·01	45·84
30	46·86	·14	3·78	2·21	52·71	7	38·62	·00	3·78	1·88	44·28
July 2	44·20	·15	3·83	2·08	49·96	10	38·37	·00	3·76	1·76	43·89
4	44·79	·10	3·81	1·95	50·45	11	38·72	·00	3·82	1·57	44·11
6	43·66	·18	3·77	1·82	49·07		39·16	·02	3·83	+ 1·51	44·48
8	45·53	·15	3·81	+ 1·69	50·88						
					4· 9·52·13						4· 9·43·19

Error of Collimation . . = 0· 0· 4·47
Resulting Mean Zenith Distance, South = 4· 9·47·66

B.A.C. 5632.—July 8.—Correction for Curvature of Path = - ·21.

4 C

Mean Zenith Distances of Stars observed at the Bushman Flat Station.

FACE OF SECTOR EAST. | FACE OF SECTOR WEST.

B.A.C. 5817.

Day of Observation 1847.	Apparent Zenith Distance, from Unreduced Observation.	Reduction for Az. Error, and Curv. of Path.	Refraction.	Precession, Aberration, and Nutation.	Deduced Mean Zenith Distance. 1847, Jan.0; and Mean of Separate Results, uncorrected, for Error of Collimation.	Day of Observation 1847.	Apparent Zenith Distance, from Unreduced Observation.	Reduction for Az. Error, and Curv. of Path.	Refraction.	Precession, Aberration, and Nutation.	Deduced Mean Zenith Distance. 1847, Jan.0; and Mean of Separate Results, uncorrected, for Error of Collimation.
June 18	2·44·45·38	·03	2·48	+ 4·42	2·44·52·25	June 21	2·44·30·87	·40	2·56	+ 4·23	2·44·37·26
22	44·89	·04	2·56	4·17	51·58	23	32·74	·03	2·51	4·11	39·33
24	43·61	·07	2·54	4·05	50·13	25	34·69	·03	2·52	3·99	41·17
26	45·19	·10	2·52	3·93	51·54	27	33·24	·00	2·50	3·87	39·61
28	43·16	·11	2·49	3 81	49·35	29	34·92	·01	2·50	3·75	41·16
30	41·33	·09	2·49	3·69	47·42	July 1	35 80	·01	2·50	3·63	41·92
July 2	41·68	·10	2·52	3·57	47·67	3	36·55	·00	2·52	3·51	42·58
4	41·24	·07	2·51	3·45	47·13	5	33·88	·00	2·49	3·40	39·77
6	42·32	·12	2·49	3·34	48·03	10	35·16	·00	2·52	3·11	40·79
8	42·42	·10	2·51	+ 3·22	48·05	11	37·98	·01	2·52	+ 3·06	43·55
					2·44·49·32						2·44·40·71

Error of Collimation . . = 0· 0· 4·30
Resulting Mean Zenith Distance, South = 2·44·45·01

B.A.C. 5881.

Day of Observation 1847.	Apparent Zenith Distance, from Unreduced Observation.	Reduction for Az. Error, and Curv. of Path.	Refraction.	Precession, Aberration, and Nutation.	Deduced Mean Zenith Distance.	Day of Observation 1847.	Apparent Zenith Distance, from Unreduced Observation.	Reduction for Az. Error, and Curv. of Path.	Refraction.	Precession, Aberration, and Nutation.	Deduced Mean Zenith Distance.
June 18	0· 0·54·27	·00	0·02	+ 5·60	0· 0·48·69	June 23	0· 1· 6·76	·00	0·02	+ 5·38	0· 0·61·40
22	55·50	·00	·02	5·42	50·10	25	4·68	·00	·02	5·29	59·41
24	56·10	·00	·02	5·33	50·79	27	6·27	·00	·02	5·21	61·08
26	54·12	·00	·02	5·25	48·89	29	4·89	·00	·02	5·12	59·79
28	56·54	·00	·02	5·16	51 40	July 1	5·13	·00	·02	5·03	60·12
30	58·86	·00	·02	5·07	53·81	3	3·55	·00	·02	4·94	58·63
July 2	56·20	·00	·02	4·98	51·24	5	4·34	·00	·02	4·85	59·51
4	57·68	·00	·02	4·90	52·80	10	2·12	·00	·02	4·64	57·50
6	58·47	·00	·02	4·81	53·68	11	3·80	·00	0·02	+ 4·59	59·23
8	56·99	·00	0·02	+ 4·72	52·29						
					0· 0·51·37						0· 0·59·63

Error of Collimation . . = 0· 0· 4·13
Resulting Mean Zenith Distance, North = 0· 0·55·50

B.A.C. 6016.

Day of Observation 1847.	Apparent Zenith Distance, from Unreduced Observation.	Reduction for Az. Error, and Curv. of Path.	Refraction.	Precession, Aberration, and Nutation.	Deduced Mean Zenith Distance.	Day of Observation 1847.	Apparent Zenith Distance, from Unreduced Observation.	Reduction for Az. Error, and Curv. of Path.	Refraction.	Precession, Aberration, and Nutation.	Deduced Mean Zenith Distance.
June 18	1·54·20·15	·02	1·72	+ 7·69	1·54·29·54	June 21	1·54· 5·58	·28	1·77	+ 7·54	1·54·14·61
22	17·83	·03	1·78	7·40	27·07	23	6·67	·02	1·75	7·33	15·73
24	18·72	·05	1·76	7·38	27·81	27	5·98	·00	1·73	7·25	14·94
26	18·18	·07	1·75	7·28	27·14	29	6·82	·01	1·74	7·12	15·87
28	18·22	·08	1·73	7·18	27·05	July 1	10·13	·00	1·73	7·01	18·87
30	15·06	·06	1·73	7·07	23·80	3	10·42	·00	1·75	6·91	19·08
July 2	16·25	·07	1·76	6·96	24·90	5	9·29	·00	1·73	6·80	17·82
6	14·62	·08	1·72	6·75	23·01	10	9·93	·22	1·75	6·53	17·99
8	16·84	·07	1·74	+ 6·64	25·15	11	10·87	·01	1·75	+ 6·47	19 08
					1·54·26·16						1·54·17·09

Error of Collimation . . = 0· 0· 4·54
Resulting Mean Zenith Distance, South = 1·54·21·63

B.A.C. 6016.—July 10.—Correction for Curvature of Path = - 0"·22.

Mean Zenith Distances of Stars observed at the Bushman Flat Station.

FACE OF SECTOR EAST. | **FACE OF SECTOR WEST.**

B.A.C. 6074.

Day of Observation 1847.	Apparent Zenith Distance, from Unreduced Observation.	Reduction for Az. Error, and Curr. of Path.	Refraction.	Precession, Aberration, and Nutation.	Deduced Mean Zenith Distance, 1847, Jan. 0; and Mean of Separate Results, uncorrected, for Error of Collimation.
June 18	0·29·33·63	·01	0·44	+ 8·66	0·29·42·92
22	31·90	·01	·46	8·50	40·85
24	32·84	·01	·45	8·42	41·70
26	34·32	·02	·45	8·33	43·08
28	32·35	·02	·45	8·25	41·03
30	32·10	·02	·45	8·16	40·69
July 2	31·59	·02	·45	8·07	40·09
4	31·71	·22	·45	7·98	39·92
6	28·89	·02	·44	7·89	37·20
8	31·06	·02	0·45	+ 7·80	39·29
					0·29·40·68

Day of Observation 1847.	Apparent Zenith Distance, from Unreduced Observation.	Reduction for Az. Error, and Curr. of Path.	Refraction.	Precession, Aberration, and Nutation.	Deduced Mean Zenith Distance, 1847, Jan. 0; and Mean of Separate Results, uncorrected, for Error of Collimation.
June 21	0·29·19·26	·07	0·46	+ 8·54	0·29·28·19
23	18·62	·01	·45	8·46	27·52
25	19·76	·00	·45	8·38	28·59
27	20·94	·00	·45	8·20	29·68
29	21·78	·00	·45	8·20	30·43
July 1	22·80	·00	·45	8·12	31·46
3	23·66	·00	·45	8·02	32·13
5	20·50	·00	·45	7·94	28·89
10	22·92	·00	·45	7·70	31·07
11	24·50	·00	0·45	+ 7·60	32·61
					0·29·30·06

Error of Collimation . . = 0· 0· 5·31
Resulting Mean Zenith Distance, South = 0·29·35·37

B.A.C. 6115.

Day of Observation 1847.	Apparent Zenith Distance, from Unreduced Observation.	Reduction for Az. Error, and Curr. of Path.	Refraction.	Precession, Aberration, and Nutation.	Deduced Mean Zenith Distance, 1847, Jan. 0; and Mean of Separate Results, uncorrected, for Error of Collimation.
June 18	0·40·51·55	·01	0·61	+ 9·30	0·40·61·45
22	48·29	·01	·63	9·14	58·05
24	48·80	·02	·63	9·06	58·56
26	50·45	·02	·62	8·97	60·02
28	50·02	·03	·62	8·89	59·50
30	47·90	·02	·62	8·80	57·30
July 2	48·99	·02	·63	8·71	58·31
4	48·89	·02	·62	8·62	58·11
6	46·52	·03	·62	8·53	55·64
8	48·59	·02	0·62	+ 8·44	57·63
					0·40·58·46

Day of Observation 1847.	Apparent Zenith Distance, from Unreduced Observation.	Reduction for Az. Error, and Curr. of Path.	Refraction.	Precession, Aberration, and Nutation.	Deduced Mean Zenith Distance, 1847, Jan. 0; and Mean of Separate Results, uncorrected, for Error of Collimation.
June 21	0·40·37·13	·10	0·64	+ 9·18	0·40·46·85
23	37·33	·01	·62	9·10	47·04
25	37·88	·01	·62	9·02	47·52
27	38·27	·00	·62	8·93	47·82
29	37·93	·00	·62	8·85	47·40
July 1	40·00	·00	·62	8·76	49·38
3	40·25	·00	·62	8·67	49·54
5	38·32	·00	·62	8·58	47·52
7	40·00	·00	·62	8·48	49·10
10	41·28	·00	·62	8·34	50·24
11	41·13	·21	0·62	+ 8·29	49·83
					0·40·48·39

Error of Collimation . . = 0· 0· 5·04
Resulting Mean Zenith Distance, South = 0·40·53·42

B.A.C. 6145.

Day of Observation 1847.	Apparent Zenith Distance, from Unreduced Observation.	Reduction for Az. Error, and Curr. of Path.	Refraction.	Precession, Aberration, and Nutation.	Deduced Mean Zenith Distance, 1847, Jan. 0; and Mean of Separate Results, uncorrected, for Error of Collimation.
June 18	1· 0·28·25	·01	0·91	+ 9·70	1· 0·38·85
22	26·47	·01	·94	9·54	36·94
24	26·96	·02	·93	9·46	37·33
26	25·78	·04	·92	9·37	36·03
28	25·68	·04	·92	9·28	35·84
30	25·53	·03	·91	9·20	35·61
July 2	24·84	·04	·93	9·10	34·83
4	24·64	·02	·92	9·01	34·55
6	23·21	·04	·91	8·91	32·99
8	25·33	·04	0·92	+ 8·82	35·03
					1· 0·35·80

Day of Observation 1847.	Apparent Zenith Distance, from Unreduced Observation.	Reduction for Az. Error, and Curr. of Path.	Refraction.	Precession, Aberration, and Nutation.	Deduced Mean Zenith Distance, 1847, Jan. 0; and Mean of Separate Results, uncorrected, for Error of Collimation.
June 21	1· 0·14·22	·15	0·94	+ 9·58	1· 0·24·59
23	14·32	·01	·92	9·50	24·73
25	14·04	·01	·93	9·42	24·38
27	15·16	·00	·91	9·33	25·40
29	14·96	·00	·92	9·24	25·12
July 3	17·33	·00	·92	9·06	27·31
5	17·04	·00	·91	8·96	26·91
7	17·38	·00	·91	8·87	27·16
10	18·27	·00	·92	8·72	27·91
11	18·42	·01	0·93	+ 8·67	28·01
					1· 0·26·15

Error of Collimation . . = 0· 0· 4·82
Resulting Mean Zenith Distance, South = 1· 0·30·98

B.A.C. 6074 —July 4 —Correction for Curvature of Path = (″·21.
,, 6115.— ,, 11.— ,, ,, = -0·21.

Mean Zenith Distances of Stars observed at the Bushman Flat Station.

	FACE OF SECTOR EAST.						FACE OF SECTOR WEST.				
Day of Observation 1847.	Apparent Zenith Distance, from Unreduced Observation.	Reduction for Az. Error, and Curv. of Path.	Refraction.	Precession, and Nutation.	Deduced Mean Zenith Distance, 1847, Jan. 0; and Mean of Separate Results, uncorrected, for Error of Collimation.	Day of Observation 1847.	Apparent Zenith Distance, from Unreduced Observation.	Reduction for Az. Error, and Curv. of Path.	Refraction.	Precession, and Nutation.	Deduced Mean Zenith Distance, 1847, Jan. 0; and Mean of Separate Results, uncorrected, for Error of Collimation.

B.A.C. 6233.

	° ′ ″	″	″	″	° ′ ″		° ′ ″	″	″	″	° ′ ″
June 18	4·42·34·12	·06	4·26	+11·11	4·42·49·43	June 21	4·42·21·43	·71	4·41	+10·94	4·42·36·07
22	33·92	·07	4·41	10·88	49·14	23	20·54	·05	4·31	10·82	35·62
24	34·17	·12	4·36	10·76	49·17	25	20·88	·05	4·35	10·70	35·88
28	31·99	·19	4·30	10·51	46·61	27	22·02	·01	4·31	10·58	36·90
30	32·34	·16	4·30	10·39	46·87	29	26·46	·01	4·31	10·45	41·21
July 2	33·03	·18	4·35	10·25	47·45	July 1	24·54	·01	4·30	10·32	39·15
4	33·33	·12	4·32	10·13	47·66	3	25·38	·00	4·33	10·19	39·90
6	28·58	·21	4·27	9·99	(42·63)	5	23·65	·00	4·28	10·06	37·99
8	32·78	·17	4·32	9·85	46·78	10	22·31	·00	4·34	+ 9·72	36·37
11	33·32	·43	4·34	+ 9·65	46·88						
					4·42·47·78						4·42·37·68

Error of Collimation . . . = 0· 0· 5·05
Resulting Mean Zenith Distance, South = 4·42·42·73

B.A.C. 6285.

	° ′ ″						° ′ ″				
June 22	3·20·36·05	·05	3·12	+11·52	3·20·50·64	June 21	3·20·25·09	·50	3·13	+11·57	3·20·39·29
24	36·20	·08	3·09	11·43	50·64	23	25·88	·04	3·06	11·48	40·38
28	34·86	·13	3·05	11·22	49·00	25	24·09	·03	3·08	11·37	39·11
30	35·01	·11	3·05	11·11	49·06	29	26·42	·01	3·05	11·17	40·63
July 2	34·86	·12	3·09	11·00	48·83	July 1	29·09	·01	3·05	11·06	43·19
4	34·81	·08	3·06	10·89	48·68	4	27·70	·00	3·07	10·94	41·71
8	35·75	·12	3·06	10·65	49·34	5	27·41	·00	3·04	10·83	41·28
11	35·95	·30	3·08	+10·47	49·20	10	29·13	·22	3·08	+10·53	42·52
					3·20·49·42						3·20·41·01

Error of Collimation . . . = 0· 0· 4·21
Resulting Mean Zenith Distance, South = 3·20·45·22

B.A.C. 6305.

	° ′ ″						° ′ ″				
June 18	3·22·58·43	·04	3·06	+11·98	3·23·13·43	June 21	3·22·45·00	·50	3·16	+11·84	3·22·59·50
22	56·70	·05	3·16	11·79	11·60	23	45·29	·04	3·09	11·75	60·09
24	56·55	·09	3·13	11·70	11·29	27	46·38	·01	3·09	11·54	61·00
26	56·28	·12	3·11	11·59	10·86	July 1	47·96	·23	3·08	11·33	62·14
30	56·06	·12	3·09	11·39	10·42	3	49·24	·22	3·12	11·22	63·36
July 2	55·71	·12	3·12	11·27	9·98	5	46·43	·00	3·07	11·10	60·60
4	55·91	·08	3·10	11·16	10·09	10	49·14	·22	3·12	+10·80	62·84
8	56·40	·12	3·10	10·93	10·31						
11	57·04	·31	3·11	+10·74	10·58						
					3·23·10·95						3·23· 1·36

Error of Collimation . . . = 0· 0· 4·80
Resulting Mean Zenith Distance, South = 3·23· 6·16

B.A.C. 6285.—July 10.—Correction for Curvature of Path = - 0″·22.
    „ 6305.— „ 1st, 3rd, and 10th.—Correction for Curvature of Path = - 0·22.

Mean Zenith Distances of Stars observed at the Bushman Flat Station.

FACE OF SECTOR EAST. | **FACE OF SECTOR WEST.**

B.A.C. 6414.

Day of Observation 1847.	Apparent Zenith Distance, from Unreduced Observation.	Reduction for Az. Error, and Curv. of Path.	Refraction.	Precession, Aberration, and Nutation.	Deduced Mean Zenith Distance, 1847, Jan. 0; and Mean of Separate Results, uncorrected, for Error of Collimation.	Day of Observation 1847.	Apparent Zenith Distance, from Unreduced Observation.	Reduction for Az. Error, and Curv. of Path.	Refraction.	Precession, Aberration, and Nutation.	Deduced Mean Zenith Distance, 1847, Jan. 0; and Mean of Separate Results, uncorrected, for Error of Collimation.
June 18	1·10·10·47	·01	1·05	+13·51	1·10·25·02	June 21	1· 9·56·15	·17	1·09	+13·43	1·10·10·50
22	9·19	·02	1·09	13·41	23·67	23	57·63	·01	1·07	13·38	12·07
24	8·49	·03	1·08	13·35	22·89	25	60·05	·01	1·08	13·32	14·44
26	9·68	·04	1·07	13·29	24·00	27	57·63	·00	1·07	13·25	11·95
30	9·09	·04	1·06	13·15	23·26	29	57·24	·00	1·07	13·19	11·30
July 2	8·35	·04	1·08	13·07	22·46	July 1	60·64	·22	1·06	13·11	14·59
4	7·85	·03	1·07	12·99	21·88	3	61·14	·00	1·08	13·04	15·26
8	7·21	·04	1·07	12·83	21·07	5	57·48	·00	1·06	12·96	11·50
11	8·64	·10	1·07	+12·68	22·29	10	61·53	·00	1·08	+12·74	15·35
					1·10·22·95						1·10·13·02

Error of Collimation . . . = 0· 0· 4·97
Resulting Mean Zenith Distance, South = 1·10·17·98

B.A.C. 6489.

Day of Observation 1847.	Apparent Zenith Distance.	Red.	Refr.	Prec.	Deduced Mean Z.D.	Day of Observation 1847.	Apparent Zenith Distance.	Red.	Refr.	Prec.	Deduced Mean Z.D.
June 18	0·21· 8·15	·00	0·32	+14·26	0·21·22·78	June 21	0·20·56·29	·05	0·33	+14·21	0·21·10·78
22	7·21	·00	·33	14·19	21·73	23	56·89	·00	·32	14·17	11·38
24	9·38	·01	·32	14·15	23·84	25	56·29	·00	·32	14·13	10·74
26	10·81	·01	·32	14·11	25·23	27	57·87	·00	·32	14·09	12·28
28	7·31	·01	·32	14·06	21·68	29	60·24	·00	·32	14·03	14·59
30	5·18	·01	·32	14·00	19·49	July 1	59·75	·00	·32	13·98	14·05
July 2	6·07	·03	·32	13·94	20·10	3	59·60	·00	·32	13·91	13·83
4	7·85	·01	·32	13·88	22·04	5	56·20	·00	·32	13·85	10·37
6	4·98	·01	·32	13·82	19·11	7	59·50	·00	·32	13·78	13·60
8	8·74	·01	·32	13·74	22·70	10	59·65	·00	0·32	+13·67	13·64
11	5·08	·03	0·32	+13·63	19·60						
					0·21·21·66						0·21·12·53

Error of Collimation . . . = 0· 0· 4·57
Resulting Mean Zenith Distance, South = 0·21·17·09

B.A.C. 6525.

Day of Observation 1847.	Apparent Zenith Distance.	Red.	Refr.	Prec.	Deduced Mean Z.D.	Day of Observation 1847.	Apparent Zenith Distance.	Red.	Refr.	Prec.	Deduced Mean Z.D.
June 18	0·52·21·92	·01	0·79	+14·54	0·52· 8·16	June 23	0·52·36·49	·01	0·80	+14·50	0·52·22·78
22	23·80	·01	·82	14·51	10·10	27	35·84	·00	·80	14·45	22·19
24	24·09	·02	·81	14·49	10·39	29	33·13	·00	·80	14·41	19·52
26	22·41	·03	·80	14·46	8·72	July 1	32·52	·00	·80	14·37	18·05
28	23·75	·03	·80	14·43	10·09	3	34·31	·00	·81	14·33	20·79
30	25·62	·03	·80	14·39	12·00	5	35·15	·00	·80	14·28	21·67
July 2	24·78	·03	·81	14·35	11·21	10	32·65	·00	0·81	+14·14	19·32
4	24·88	·02	·80	14·30	11·36						
8	24·93	·03	·80	14·20	11·50						
11	26·07	·07	0·81	+14·11	12·70						
					0·52·10·62						0·52·20·75

Error of Collimation . . . = 0· 0· 5·06
Resulting Mean Zenith Distance, North = 0·52·15·68

B.A.C. 6414.—July 1.—Correction for Curvature of Path = -0"·22.
,, 6489.— ,, 2.— ,, ,, = -0·22.

Mean Zenith Distances of Stars observed at the Bushman Flat Station.

B.A.C. 6639.

FACE OF SECTOR EAST.						FACE OF SECTOR WEST.					
Day of Observation 1847.	Apparent Zenith Distance, from Unreduced Observation.	Reduction for Az. Error, and Curv. of Path.	Refraction.	Precession, Aberration, and Nutation.	Deduced Mean Zenith Distance, 1847, Jan. 0; and Mean of Separate Results, uncorrected, for Error of Collimation.	Day of Observation 1847.	Apparent Zenith Distance, from Unreduced Observation	Reduction for Az. Error, and Curv. of Path.	Refraction.	Precession, Aberration, and Nutation.	Deduced Mean Zenith Distance, 1847, Jan. 0; and Mean of Separate Results, uncorrected, for Error of Collimation:
June 18	0·17·57·88	·00	0·27	+16·12	0·18·14·27	June 21	0·17·43·27	·04	0·28	+16·11	0·17 59·62
22	56·65	·01	·28	16·10	13·02	23	44·35	·00	·27	16·10	60·72
24	56·65	·01	·28	16 09	13·01	25	44·11	·00	·27	16·08	60·46
26	56·53	·01	·27	16·06	12·85	27	44·50	·00	·27	16·05	60·62
28	54·92	·01	·27	16·03	11·21	29	46·03	·00	·27	16·02	62·32
30	55·71	·01	·27	16·00	11·97	July 1	47·71	·00	·27	15·98	63·96
July 2	54·38	·01	·28	15·95	10·60	3	45·74	·00	·27	15·93	61·94
4	54·77	·01	·27	15·91	10·94	5	44·75	·00	·27	15·88	60·90
8	55·56	·01	·27	15·80	11·62	7	45·83	·21	·27	15·83	61·72
11	53·69	·03	0·27	+15·70	9·63	10	47·61	·00	0·27	+15·73	63·61
					0·18·11·91						0·18· 1·61

Error of Collimation . . . = 0· 0· 5·15
Resulting Mean Zenith Distance, South = 0·18· 6·76

Anon. AR. 19·22.

Day of Observation 1847.	Apparent Zenith Distance, from Unreduced Observation.	Reduction for Az. Error, and Curv. of Path.	Refraction.	Precession, Aberration, and Nutation.	Deduced Mean Zenith Distance.	Day of Observation 1847.	Apparent Zenith Distance, from Unreduced Observation	Reduction for Az. Error, and Curv. of Path.	Refraction.	Precession, Aberration, and Nutation.	Deduced Mean Zenith Distance.
June 18	0· 3·55·81	·00	0·06	+16·41	0· 4·12·28	June 21	0· 3·41·19	·01	0·06	+16·40	0· 3·57·64
22	55·91	·00	·06	16·40	12·37	23	40·79	·00	·06	16·40	57·25
26	55·14	·00	·06	16·37	11·57	27	42·97	·00	·06	16·36	59·39
28	54·33	·00	·06	16·35	10·74	29	42·92	·00	·06	+16·33	59·31
July 2	52·74	·00	0·06	+16·28	9·08						
					0· 4·11·21						0· 3·58·40

Error of Collimation . . . = 0· 0· 0·41
Resulting Mean Zenith Distance, South = 0· 4· 4·80

B.A.C. 6753.

Day of Observation 1847.	Apparent Zenith Distance, from Unreduced Observation.	Reduction for Az. Error, and Curv. of Path.	Refraction.	Precession, Aberration, and Nutation.	Deduced Mean Zenith Distance.	Day of Observation 1847.	Apparent Zenith Distance, from Unreduced Observation	Reduction for Az. Error, and Curv. of Path.	Refraction.	Precession, Aberration, and Nutation.	Deduced Mean Zenith Distance.
June 18	1·31·22·37	·02	1·38	+17·59	1 31·41·32	June 21	1·31· 8·74	·22	1·43	+17·58	1·31·27·53
22	21·28	·02	1·42	17·58	40·26	23	8·34	·02	1·39	17·58	27 29
26	21 87	·05	1·40	17·55	40·77	25	8·84	·01	1·40	17·56	27·79
28	19·45	·06	1·39	17·52	38·30	27	7·16	·00	1·39	17·54	26·09
July 2	20·19	·06	1·41	17·44	38·96	29	9·03	·00	1·40	17·50	27·93
8	18·37	·05	1·39	17·28	36·99	July 3	11·50	·00	1·40	17·42	30·32
11	18·47	·14	1·40	+17·18	36·91	5	9·43	·00	1·38	17·37	28·18
						10	10·91	·00	1·40	+17·21	29·52
					1·31 39·08						1·31·28·08

Error of Collimation . . . = 0· 0· 5·50
Resulting Mean Zenith Distance, South = 1·31·33·58

B.A.C. 6639.—July 7.—Correction for Curvature of Path= - 0"·21.

Mean Zenith Distances of Stars observed at the Bushman Flat Station.

FACE OF SECTOR EAST. | **FACE OF SECTOR WEST.**

B.A.C. 6877.

Day of Observation 1847.	Apparent Zenith Distance, from Unreduced Observation.	Reduction for Az. Error, and Curv. of Path.	Refraction.	Precession, Aberration, and Nutation.	Deduced Mean Zenith Distance, 1847, Jan. 0; and Mean of Separate Results, uncorrected, for Error of Collimation.	Day of Observation 1847.	Apparent Zenith Distance, from Unreduced Observation.	Reduction for Az. Error, and Curv. of Path.	Refraction.	Precession, Aberration, and Nutation.	Deduced Mean Zenith Distance, 1847, Jan. 0; and Mean of Separate Results, uncorrected, for Error of Collimation.
June 18	2 44 18·52	·03	2 48	+19·02	2 44 39·99	June 21	2 44 2·72	·41	2 57	+19·03	2 44 23·91
22	16·74	·04	2 56	19·03	38·29	23	4·60	·03	2 51	19·03	26·11
26	15·21	·10	2 52	19·01	30·64	25	6 87	·01	2 53	19·02	28·41
28	13·73	·11	2 50	18·98	35·10	27	4·89	·00	2 50	19·00	26·39
30	15·26	·10	2 50	18·96	36·62	29	6·23	·01	2 52	18·97	27·71
July 2	14·77	·10	2 53	18·92	36·12	July 1	6·47	·01	2 50	18·94	27·90
4	14·03	·07	2 50	18·87	35·38	3	6·37	·00	2 53	18·90	27·80
6	10·87	·12	2 48	18·82	32·05	5	6·03	·00	2 49	18·85	27·37
8	15·06	·10	2 50	18·76	36·22	7	4·99	·22	2 49	18·79	26·05
11	11·90	·25	2 52	+18·05	32·82	10	6·62	·00	2 52	+18·09	27·83
					2 44 35·92						2 44 26·95

Error of Collimation . . = 0· 0· 4·49
Resulting Mean Zenith Distance, South = 2·44·31·43

B.A.C. 6948.

Day	App. Z.D.	Red.	Refr.	Prec.	Deduced	Day	App. Z.D.	Red.	Refr.	Prec.	Deduced
June 18	0 43 31·81	·01	0 05	+19·38	0 43 51·83	June 21	0 43 17·39	·11	0 08	+19 44	0 43 37·40
22	30·52	·01	·68	19·46	50·65	23	15·86	·01	·66	19·47	35·98
26	30·50	·03	·67	19·50	50·64	25	19·43	·01	·67	19·50	39·59
28	29·54	·03	·66	19·52	49·69	27	17·98	·00	·66	19·51	38·15
30	30·13	·02	·66	19·52	50·29	29	20·06	·00	·67	19·52	40·25
July 2	28·35	·03	·67	19·52	48·51	July 1	19·02	·00	·66	19·52	39·20
4	29·24	·02	·66	19·51	49·39	3	19·22	·00	·67	19·51	39·40
8	27·91	·03	·66	19·46	48·00	5	16·25	·00	·66	19·50	36·41
11	27·91	·06	0·07	+19·40	47·92	10	20·25	·00	0·67	+19·42	40·34
					0 43 49·66						0 43 38·52

Error of Collimation . . = 0· 0· 5·57
Resulting Mean Zenith Distance, South = 0·43·44·09

B.A.C. 7011.

Day	App. Z.D.	Red.	Refr.	Prec.	Deduced	Day	App. Z.D.	Red.	Refr.	Prec.	Deduced
June 18	0 10 38·91	- ·00	0 16	+19·70	0 10 19·37	June 21	0 10 51·12	·03	0 17	+19·79	0 10 31·47
22	37·94	+ ·09	·17	19·82	18·38	23	50·47	·00	·16	19·85	30·78
26	37·70	- ·01	·17	19·91	17·95	25	50·40	·00	·17	19·89	30·68
28	40·76	·01	·16	19·94	· 20·97	27	50·54	·00	·16	19·93	30·77
30	38·57	·01	·16	19·97	18·75	29	48·03	·00	·17	19·95	28·25
July 2	40·08	·01	·17	19·98	20·26	July 1	47·80	·00	·16	19·97	27·99
4	42·04	·00	·16	19·99	22·21	3	50·03	·00	·17	19·98	30·22
8	38·86	·01	·16	19·98	19·03	5	50·10	·00	·16	19·99	30·27
11	40·86	- ·02	0·17	+19·94	21·07	10	52·02	·00	0·17	+19·96	32·23
					0 10 19·78						0 10 30·30

Error of Collimation . . = 0· 0· 5·26
Resulting Mean Zenith Distance, North = 0·10·25·04

B.A.C. 6877.—July 7.—Correction for Curvature of Path = -0"·22.
 „ 7011.—June 22.— „   „   „ = +0 ·09.

Mean Zenith Distances of Stars observed at the Bushman Flat Station.

	FACE OF SECTOR EAST.						FACE OF SECTOR WEST.				
Day of Observation 1847.	Apparent Zenith Distance, from Unreduced Observation.	Reduction for Az. Error, and Curv. of Path.	Refraction.	Precession, Aberration, and Nutation.	Deduced Mean Zenith Distance, 1847, Jan. 0; and Mean of Separate Results, uncorrected for Error of Collimation.	Day of Observation 1847.	Apparent Zenith Distance, from Unreduced Observation.	Reduction for Az. Error, and Curv. of Path.	Refraction.	Precession, Aberration, and Nutation.	Deduced Mean Zenith Distance, 1847, Jan. 0; and Mean of Separate Results, uncorrected for Error of Collimation.

B.A.C. 7026.

	° ′ ″	″	″	″	° ′ ″		° ′ ″	″	″	″	° ′ ″
June 18	0·10·31·11	·00	0·16	+19·80	0·10·11·47	June 21	0·10·45·98	·02	0·17	+19·89	0·10·26·24
22	31 72	·00	·17	19·92	11·97	23	44·74	·00	·16	19·95	24·95
26	30·19	·01	·16	20·01	10·33	25	43·39	·00	·16	19·99	23·56
28	34·64	·01	·16	20·05	14·74	27	43·13	·00	·16	20 03	23·26
30	29·88	·01	·16	20·08	9·95	29	42·60	·00	·16	20·06	22·79
July 4	33·45	·00	·16	20·10	13·51	July 1	41·83	·00	·16	20·08	21·91
8	33·43	·01	·16	20·09	13·49	3	42·13	·00	·16	20·09	22·20
11	34·44	·02	0·16	+20·06	14·52	5	42·30	·00	·16	20·10	22·36
						10	40·36	·00	0·16	+20·08	20·44
					0·10·12·50						0·10·23·08

Error of Collimation . . . = 0· 0· 5·29
Resulting Mean Zenith Distance, North = 0·10·17·79

B.A.C. 7057.

	° ′ ″	″	″	″	° ′ ″		° ′ ″	″	″	″	° ′ ″
June 18	0· 7·17·54	·00	0·11	+20·03	0· 6·57·62	June 21	0· 7·31·43	·02	0·12	+20·13	0· 7·11·40
22	17·96	·00	·12	20·16	57·92	23	30 08	·00	·11	20·20	9 99
26	18 60	·00	·11	20·20	58·44	25	31·09	·00	·11	20·25	11·55
28	20·58	·00	·11	20·30	60 39	27	29·71	·00	·11	20·29	9·53
30	17·69	·00	·11	20·33	57·47	29	27·45	·00	·11	20·32	7·24
July 2	20·09	·00	·11	20·35	59·85	July 3	31·23	·00	·11	20·36	10·98
4	22·45	·00	·11	20·37	62·19	5	30·61	·00	·11	20·37	10·35
8	21·79	·00	·11	20·37	61·53	10	28·18	·00	0·11	+20·35	7·94
11	20·37	·01	0·11	+20·34	60·13						
					0· 6·59·50						0· 7· 9·87

Error of Collimation . . . = 0· 0· 5·18
Resulting Mean Zenith Distance, North = 0· 7· 4·69

Anon. A.R. 20·24.

	° ′ ″	″	″	″	° ′ ″		° ′ ″	″	″	″	° ′ ″
June 18	0· 3·60·94	·00	0·06	+20·21	0· 4·21·21	June 21	0· 3·47·46	·01	0·06	+20·32	0· 4· 7·83
22	60·05	·00	·06	20·35	20·46	23	48·10	·00	·06	20·39	8·55
26	62·23	·00	·06	20·40	22·75	25	48 89	·00	·06	20·44	9·39
July 2	55·21	·00	·06	20·55	(15·82)	27	47·96	·00	·06	20·48	8·50
4	58·77	·00	·06	20·57	19·40	29	48·94	·00	·06	20·51	9·51
8	60·55	·00	0·06	+20·57	21·18	July 1	50·28	·00	·06	20·54	10·88
						3	49·19	·00	·06	20·56	9·81
						5	50·18	·00	0·06	+20·57	10·81
					0· 4·21·00						0· 4· 9·41

Error of Collimation . . . = 0· 0· 5·80
Resulting Mean Zenith Distance, South = 0· 4·15·21

Mean Zenith Distances of Stars observed at the Bushman Flat Station.

FACE OF SECTOR EAST.						FACE OF SECTOR WEST.					
Day of Observation 1847.	Apparent Zenith Distance, from Unreduced Observation.	Reduction for Az. Error, and Curv. of Path.	Refraction.	Precession, Aberration, and Nutation.	Deduced Mean Zenith Distance, 1847, Jan. 0; and Mean of Separate Results. uncorrected, for Error of Collimation.	Day of Observation 1847.	Apparent Zenith Distance, from Unreduced Observation.	Reduction for Az. Error, and Curv. of Path.	Refraction.	Precession, Aberration, and Nutation.	Deduced Mean Zenith Distance, 1847, Jan. 0; and Mean of Separate Results. uncorrected, for Error of Collimation.

Anon. A.R. 20·34.

Day	App. Z.D.	Red.	Refr.	Prec.	Deduced	Day	App. Z.D.	Red.	Refr.	Prec.	Deduced
June 18	0·12·62·18	·00	0·20	+20·69	0·13·23·07	June 21	0·12·48·55	·03	0·20	+20·81	0·13· 9·53
22	60·80	·00	·20	20·85	21·85	23	47·86	·00	·20	20·89	8·95
26	62·28	·01	·20	20·98	23·45	25	47·27	·00	·20	20·95	8·42
28	58·82	·01	·20	21·02	20·03	27	49·24	·00	·20	21·00	10·44
30	60·16	·01	·20	21·06	21·41	29	47·07	·60	·20	21·04	8·31
July 2	60·30	·01	0·20	+21·09	21·58	July 1	51·81	·00	·20	21·08	13·09
						5	52·20	·00	·20	21·12	13·52
						10	51·91	·00	0·20	+21·13	13·24
					0·13·21·90						0·13·10·69

Error of Collimation . . . = 0· 0· 5·00
Resulting Mean Zenith Distance, South = 0·13·16·29

B.A.C. 7207.

Day	App. Z.D.	Red.	Refr.	Prec.	Deduced	Day	App. Z.D.	Red.	Refr.	Prec.	Deduced
June 18	4·35·49·97	·05	4·16	+21·89	4·36·15·97	June 21	4·35·37·04	·70	4·32	+21·96	4·36· 2·62
22	48·99	·06	4·31	21·98	15·22	23	36·64	·05	4·23	22·00	2·82
28	48·59	·19	4·20	22·04	14·64	25	37·92	·04	4·25	22·02	4·15
30	49·03	·16	4·20	22·05	15·12	27	38·27	·01	4·21	22·04	4·51
July 2	47·90	·17	4·20	22·04	14·03	29	40·25	·01	4·24	22·05	6·53
4	46·66	·11	4·21	22·02	12·78	July 1	41·98	·01	4·20	22·05	7·52
6	46·27	·20	4·16	22·00	12·23	3	41·73	00	4·24	22·03	8·00
8	48·69	·17	4·22	21·96	14·70	5	39·70	·00	4·19	+22·01	5·90
11	48·54	·42	4·25	+21·88	14·25						
					4·36·14·33						4·36· 5·26

Error of Collimation . . . = 0· 0· 4·54
Resulting Mean Zenith Distance, South = 4·36· 9·79

Anon. A.R. 20·54.

Day	App. Z.D.	Red.	Refr.	Prec.	Deduced	Day	App. Z.D.	Red.	Refr.	Prec.	Deduced
June 18	0· 1·60·64	·00	0·03	+21·45	0· 1·39·22	June 21	0· 2·14·71	·00	0·03	+21·61	0· 1·53·13
26	59·70	·00	·03	21·84	37·89	23	14·12	·00	·03	21·72	52·43
28	63·75	·00	·03	21·92	41·86	25	14·36	·00	·03	21·80	52·59
30	62·61	·00	·03	21·99	40·65	27	13·18	·00	·03	21·88	51·33
July 2	64·59	·00	·03	22·04	42·58	29	11·10	·00	·03	21·95	49·18
8	65·48	·00	·03	22·15	43·36	July 1	10·81	·00	·03	22·02	48·82
11	63·60	·00	0·03	+22·17	41·46	3	13·82	·00	·03	22·06	51·79
						5	10·86	·00	·03	22·11	48·78
						10	11 60	·00	0 03	+22·17	49·46
					0· 1·41·00						0· 1·50·83

Error of Collimation . . . = 0· 0· 4·92
Resulting Mean Zenith Distance, North = 0· 1·45·92

Mean Zenith Distances of Stars observed at the Bushman Flat Station.

Anon. A.R. 21·1.

	FACE OF SECTOR EAST.						FACE OF SECTOR WEST.				
Day of Observation 1847.	Apparent Zenith Distance, from Unreduced Observation.	Reduction for Az. Error, and Curv. of Path.	Refraction.	Precession, Aberration, and Nutation.	Deduced Mean Zenith Distance 1847, Jan. 0; and Mean of Separate Results, uncorrected. for Error of Collimation.	Day of Observation 1847.	Apparent Zenith Distance, from Unreduced Observation.	Reduction for Az. Error, and Curv. of Path.	Refraction.	Precession, Aberration, and Nutation.	Deduced Mean Zenith Distance, 1847, Jan. 0; and Mean of Separate Results, uncorrected. for Error of Collimation.
June 18	0·35·44·89	·01	0·54	+21·85	0·36· 7·27	June 21	0·35·28·25	·09	0·56	+22·02	0·35·50·74
22	41·97	·01	·56	22·07	4·59	23	29·04	·01	·54	22·13	51·70
26	44·15	·02	·55	22·20	6·94	25	28·20	·01	·55	22·22	50·96
28	41·73	·02	·54	22·34	4·59	29	30·17	·00	·55	22·37	53·09
30	40·34	·02	·54	22·41	3·27	July 1	31·80	·00	·54	22·44	54·78
July 2	40·34	·02	·55	22·46	3·33	3	29·92	·00	·55	22·49	52·96
4	40·59	·01	·54	22·51	3·63	5	29·92	·00	·54	22·53	52·99
8	39·41	·02	·54	22·58	2·51	10	31·46	·00	0·55	+22·50	54·60
11	38·96	·05	0·55	+22·60	2·06						
					0·36· 4·24						0·35·52·73

Error of Collimation . . . = 0· 0· 5·76
Resulting Mean Zenith Distance, South = 0·35·58·49

B.A.C. 7386.

Day of Observation 1847.	Apparent Zenith Distance, from Unreduced Observation.	Reduction for Az. Error, and Curv. of Path.	Refraction.	Precession, Aberration, and Nutation.	Deduced Mean Zenith Distance 1847, Jan. 0; and Mean of Separate Results, uncorrected. for Error of Collimation.	Day of Observation 1847.	Apparent Zenith Distance, from Unreduced Observation.	Reduction for Az. Error, and Curv. of Path.	Refraction.	Precession, Aberration, and Nutation.	Deduced Mean Zenith Distance, 1847, Jan. 0; and Mean of Separate Results, uncorrected. for Error of Collimation.
June 18	3· 3·51·95	·04	2·78	+22·69	3· 4·17·38	June 21	3· 3·38·52	·46	2·87	+22·84	3· 4· 3·77
22	51·31	·04	2·87	22·89	17·03	23	39·21	·08	2·81	22·93	4·92
26	51·06	·11	2·82	23·05	17·42	25	38·13	·03	2·83	23·01	3·94
28	50·52	·12	2·80	23·11	16·31	29	40·20	·01	2·82	23·08	6·09
30	50·42	·10	2·79	23·17	16·28	July 1	42·82	·01	2·80	23·19	8·80
July 2	50·77	·11	2·84	23·21	16·71	3	41·68	·00	2·82	23·23	7·73
6	47·26	·13	2·77	23·26	13·16	5	41·34	·00	2·79	23·25	7·38
8	49·49	·11	2·81	23·27	15·46	7	41·09	·00	2·78	23·27	7·14
11	49·34	·28	2·84	+23·26	15·16	10	41·68	·00	2·82	+23·27	7·77
					3· 4·16·10						3· 4· 6·39

Error of Collimation . . . = 0· 0· 4·85
Resulting Mean Zenith Distance, South = 3· 4·11·25

Anon. A.R. 21·13.

Day of Observation 1847.	Apparent Zenith Distance, from Unreduced Observation.	Reduction for Az. Error, and Curv. of Path.	Refraction.	Precession, Aberration, and Nutation.	Deduced Mean Zenith Distance 1847, Jan. 0; and Mean of Separate Results, uncorrected. for Error of Collimation.	Day of Observation 1847.	Apparent Zenith Distance, from Unreduced Observation.	Reduction for Az. Error, and Curv. of Path.	Refraction.	Precession, Aberration, and Nutation.	Deduced Mean Zenith Distance, 1847, Jan. 0; and Mean of Separate Results, uncorrected. for Error of Collimation.
June 18	0· 4· 8·30	·00	0·06	+22·10	0· 4·30·46	June 21	0· 3·55·51	·01	0·06	+22·30	0· 4·17·86
22	6·47		·06	22·37	28·90	23	55·26	·00	·06	22·43	17·75
26	6·08		·06	22·59	28·73	25	56·70	·00	·06	22·54	19·30
28	5·88		·06	22·69	28·63	27	56·70	·00	·06	22·64	19·40
30	6·57		·06	22·78	29·41	29	58·13	·00	·06	22·73	20·92
July 2	5·58		·06	22·86	28·50	July 1	59·72	·00	·06	22·82	21·60
8	5·48	·21	·06	23·03	28·36	3	58·42	·00	·06	22·89	21·37
11	5·58	·00	0·06	+23·07	28·71	5	58·18	·00	·06	22·93	21·19
						10	57·98	·00	0·06	+23·06	21·10
					0· 4·28·96						0· 4·20·05

Error of Collimation . . . = 0· 0· 4·45
Resulting Mean Zenith Distance, South = 0· 4·24·51

Anon. A.R. 21ʰ 13ᵐ.—July 6.—Correction for Curvature of Path = - 0″·21.

Mean Zenith Distances of Stars observed at the Bushman Flat Station.

FACE OF SECTOR EAST.   **FACE OF SECTOR WEST.**

Anon. A.R. 21·26.

Day of Observation 1847.	Apparent Zenith Distance, from Unreduced Observation.	Reduction for Az. Error, and Curv. of Path.	Refraction.	Precession, Aberration, and Nutation.	Deduced Mean Zenith Distance, 1847, Jan. 0; and Mean of Separate Results, uncorrected, for Error of Collimation.	Day of Observation 1847.	Apparent Zenith Distance, from Unreduced Observation.	Reduction for Az. Error, and Curv. of Path.	Refraction.	Precession, Aberration, and Nutation.	Deduced Mean Zenith Distance, 1847, Jan. 0; and Mean of Separate Results, uncorrected, for Error of Collimation.
June 18	0·37·47·71	·01	0·57	+22·59	0·38·10·86	June 21	0·37·33·05	·07	0·59	+22·81	0·37·56·38
22	46·48	·01	·59	22·88	9·94	23	32·26	·01	·58	22·95	55·78
26	44·21	·02	·58	23·13	7·90	25	34·99	·01	·58	23·08	58·64
28	45·44	·02	·57	23·24	9·23	27	33·44	·00	·58	23·19	57·21
30	43·37	·02	·57	23·34	7·26	29	36·75	·00	·58	23·29	60·62
July 2	43·96	·02	·58	23·43	7·95	July 1	36·45	·00	·58	23·39	60·41
8	41·84	·02	·58	23·63	6·03	3	34·97	·00	·58	23·47	59·02
11	42·33	·06	0·58	+23·69	6·54	5	35·12	·00	·57	23·54	59·23
						7	34·87	·00	·57	23·60	59·04
						10	37·14 –	·22	0·58	+23·68	61·18
					0·38· 8·21						0·37·58·75

Error of Collimation . . . = 0· 0· 4·73
Resulting Mean Zenith Distance, South = 0·38· 3·48

B.A.C. 7557.

Day of Observation 1847.	Apparent Zenith Distance	Reduction	Refraction.	Precession, etc.	Deduced Mean Zenith Distance	Day of Observation 1847.	Apparent Zenith Distance	Reduction	Refraction.	Precession, etc.	Deduced Mean Zenith Distance
June 18	3·58·34·67	·05	3·61	+23·66	3·58·61·89	June 21	3·58·21·39	·60	3·73	+23·87	3·58·48·39
22	34·38	·06	3·73	23·93	61·98	23	22·82	·04	3·65	23·99	50·42
26	30·92	·14	3·66	24·16	58·(0)	25	22·40	·04	3·68	24·11	50·15
28	34·08	·16	3·63	24·25	61·80	27	22·23	·01	3·66	24·21	50·09
30	31·22	·14	3·63	24·33	59·04	29	22·52	·01	3·66	24·29	50·46
July 2	30·67	·15	3·68	24·40	58·60	July 1	25·24	·01	3·63	24·37	53·23
4	31·12	·10	3·64	24·46	59·12	3	24·55	·00	3·67	24·43	52·65
6	27·61	·17	3·61	24·51	(55·56)	5	24·40	·00	3·62	24·49	52·51
8	31·41	·15	3·64	24·54	59·44	7	24·85	·00	3·60	24·53	52·98
11	30·92	·36	3·08	+24·57	58·81	10	24·35	·00	3·67	+24·56	52·58
					3·58·59·92						3·58·51·35

Error of Collimation . . . = 0· 0· 4·29
Resulting Mean Zenith Distance, South = 3·58·55·63

B.A.C. 7657.

Day of Observation 1847.	Apparent Zenith Distance	Reduction	Refraction.	Precession, etc.	Deduced Mean Zenith Distance	Day of Observation 1847.	Apparent Zenith Distance	Reduction	Refraction.	Precession, etc.	Deduced Mean Zenith Distance
June 18	0·33·23·12	·01	0·51	+22·74	0·33· 0·88	June 21	0·33·40·89	·08	0·52	+23·03	0·33·18·30
22	25·59	·01	·52	23·13	2·97	23	40·15	·01	·51	23·22	17·43
26	25·54	·02	·51	23·47	2·56	25	39·92	·01	52	23·39	17·04
28	26·97	·02	·51	23·62	3·84	27	39·86	·00	·51	23·55	16·82
30	26·33	·02	·51	23·77	3·05	July 3	37·68	·00	·52	23·96	14·24
July 2	26·65	·02	·52	23·90	3·25	5	39·23	·00	·51	24·08	15·66
6	30·57	·02	·51	24·13	6·93	10	36·43	·00	0·52	+24·31	12·64
8	29·96	·02	·51	24·23	6·22						
11	29·90	·05	0·52	+24·35	6·02						
					0·33· 3·97						0·33·16·02

Error of Collimation . . . = 0· 0· 6·03
Resulting Mean Zenith Distance, North = 0·33·9 ·99

Anon. AR. 21ʰ 26ᵐ.—July 10.—Correction for Curvature of Path= -0″·22.

Mean Zenith Distances of Stars observed at the Bushman Flat Station.

	FACE OF SECTOR EAST.						FACE OF SECTOR WEST.				
Day of Observation 1847.	Apparent Zenith Distance, from Unreduced Observation.	Reduction for Ax. Error, and Curv. of Path.	Refraction.	Precession, Aberration, and Nutation.	Deduced Mean Zenith Distance, 1847, Jan. 0; and Mean of Separate Results, uncorrected, for Error of Collimation.	Day of Observation 1847.	Apparent Zenith Distance, from Unreduced Observation.	Reduction for Ax. Error, and Curv. of Path.	Refraction.	Precession, Aberration, and Nutation.	Deduced Mean Zenith Distance, 1847, Jan. 0; and Mean of Separate Results, uncorrected, for Error of Collimation.

Anon. A.R. 21·56.

Day	Apparent Z.D.	Red.	Refr.	Prec.	Deduced Mean	Day	Apparent Z.D.	Red.	Refr.	Prec.	Deduced Mean
June 18	0·34· 1·73	·01	0·52	+22·78	0·33·39·46	June 21	0·34·19·85	·08	0·53	+23·08	0·33·57·22
22	3·31	·01	·53	23·17	40·66	23	16·67	·01	·52	23·27	55·91
26	4·50	·02	·52	23·53	41·47	25	18·73	·01	·53	23·44	55·81
28	5·98	·02	·52	23·60	42·79	27	18·77	·00	·52	23·61	55·68
30	6·28	·02	·52	23·84	42·94	July 5	16·37	·00	·52	24·16	52·73
July 2	4·97	·02	·53	23·97	41·51	10	17·42	·00	0·53	+24·41	53·54
4	7·90	·01	·52	24·10	44·31						
8	8·77	·02	·52	24·32	44·95						
11	8·42	·05	0·53	+24·45	44·45						
					0·33·42·50						0·33·55·15

Error of Collimation . . . = 0· 0· 6·32
Resulting Mean Zenith Distance, North = 0·33·48·83

B.A.C. 7842.

Day	Apparent Z.D.	Red.	Refr.	Prec.	Deduced Mean	Day	Apparent Z.D.	Red.	Refr.	Prec.	Deduced Mean
June 18	3·22·64·25	·04	3·07	+24·02	3·23·31·30	June 21	3·22·49·44	·51	3·17	+24·34	3·23·16·44
26	59·12	·12	3·11	24·82	26·93	23	50·63	·04	3·11	24·54	18·24
28	59·41	·14	3·10	24·98	27·35	25	49·64	·03	3·13	24·73	17·47
July 2	61·24	·12	3·10	25·14	29·36	27	50·03	·01	3·11	24·90	18·03
4	60·50	·13	3·14	25·28	28·79	29	50·87	·01	3·12	25·06	19·04
6	59·27	·08	3·09	25·41	27·69	July 1	51·22	·01	3·10	25·21	19·52
8	57·14	·15	3·07	25·53	25·59	3	50·08	·00	3·13	25·35	18·56
11	60·60	·12	3·10	25·63	29·21	5	52·06	·00	3·08	25·48	20·62
	57·29	·31	3·13	+25·76	25·87	7	51·32	·00	3·06	25·58	19·96
						10	51·91	·00	3·12	+25·72	20·75
					3·23·28·01						3·23·18·86

Error of Collimation . . . = 0· 0· 4·57
Resulting Mean Zenith Distance, South = 3·23·23·44

B.A.C. 7909.

Day	Apparent Z.D.	Red.	Refr.	Prec.	Deduced Mean	Day	Apparent Z.D.	Red.	Refr.	Prec.	Deduced Mean
June 18	0·24·58·62	·00	0·38	+23·13	0·25·22·13	June 21	0·24·40·64	·06	0·39	+23·50	0·25· 4·47
22	56·84	·01	·39	23·62	20·84	23	42·42	·00	·38	23·74	6·54
26	55·21	·01	·38	24·07	19·65	25	42·19	·00	·38	23·96	6·53
28	55·01	·02	·38	24·27	19·64	27	44·00	·00	·38	24·17	8·55
30	54·03	·01	·39	24·47	18·87	29	44·05	·00	·38	24·37	8·80
July 2	52·10	·02	·38	24·65	17·11	July 3	44·30	·00	·38	24·73	9·41
4	52·35	·02	·38	25·11	17·82	5	42·52	·00	·38	24·90	7·80
11	51·66	·06	0·38	+25·30	17·28	10	43·80	·00	0·38	+25·24	9·42
					0·25·19·17						0·25· 7·69

Error of Collimation . . . = 0· 0· 5·74
Resulting Mean Zenith Distance, South = 0·25·13·43

Mean Zenith Distances of Stars observed at the Bushman Flat Station.

FACE OF SECTOR EAST.

Day of Observation 1847.	Apparent Zenith Distance, from Unreduced Observation.	Reduction for Az. Error, and Curv. of Path.	Refraction.	Precession, Aberration, and Nutation.	Deduced Mean Zenith Distance. 1847, Jan. 0; and Mean of Separate Results, uncorrected, for Error of Collimation.

B.A.C. 7906.

FACE OF SECTOR EAST.

Day of Observation 1847.	Apparent Zenith Distance	Red.	Refr.	Prec. Abb. Nut.	Deduced Mean Z.D.
June 18	3 56 20·68	·05	3·57	+24·07	3 56 54·27
22	24·24	·05	3·70	24·56	52·45
26	22·66	·14	3·62	24·99	51·13
28	22·37	·16	3·61	25·19	51·01
30	23·06	·14	3·61	25·37	51·90
July 2	22·96	·15	3·66	25·54	52·01
8	22·71	·15	3·61	25·97	52·14
11	19·75	·36	3·65	+26·14	49·18
					3 56 51·76

FACE OF SECTOR WEST.

Day of Observation 1847.	Apparent Zenith Distance	Red.	Refr.	Prec. Abb. Nut.	Deduced Mean Z.D.
June 21	3 56 13·08	·59	3·70	+24·44	3 56 40·63
23	14·07	·04	3·63	24·67	42·33
27	15·06	·01	3·63	25·09	43·77
29	15·01	·01	3·63	25·28	43·91
July 3	16·89	·00	3·64	25·32	46·15
5	15·11	·00	3·59	25·77	44·47
10	17·28	·00	3·63	+26·08	46·99
					3 56 44·04

Error of Collimation . . . = 0· 0· 3·86
Resulting Mean Zenith Distance, South = 3 56 47·90

Fomalhaut B.A.C. 7992.

FACE OF SECTOR EAST.

Day of Observation 1847.	Apparent Zenith Distance	Red.	Refr.	Prec. Abb. Nut.	Deduced Mean Z.D.
June 18	0 41 21·58	·01	0·62	+23·06	0 41 45·25
22	19·50	·01	·64	23·59	43·72
26	17·41	·02	·63	24·08	42·10
28	18·51	·03	·63	24·31	43·41
30	17·63	·02	·63	24·52	42·76
July 2	15·95	·03	·64	24·72	41·28
4	22·76	·02	·63	24·90	(48·27)
6	12·39	·03	·62	25·08	(38·06)
8	16·54	·02	·63	25·24	42·39
11	16·74	·06	0·64	+25·46	42·78
					0 41 42·96

FACE OF SECTOR WEST.

Day of Observation 1847.	Apparent Zenith Distance	Red.	Refr.	Prec. Abb. Nut.	Deduced Mean Z.D.
June 21	0 41 5·09	·10	0·64	+23·47	0 41 29·09
23	5·68	·01	·63	23·72	30·02
25	4·89	·01	·63	23·97	29·48
27	6·47	·00	·63	24·20	31·30
29	7·75	·00	·63	24·41	32·79
July 1	7·55	·00	·63	24·62	32·80
3	7·65	·00	·63	24·81	33·09
5	5·82	·00	·62	25·00	31·44
7	7·31	·00	·62	25·16	33·09
10	7·21	·00	0·63	+25·39	33·23
					0 41 31·63

Error of Collimation . . . = 0· 0· 5·66
Resulting Mean Zenith Distance, South = 0·41·37·30

MEAN ZENITH DISTANCES.

COLLECTION OF

ALL THE

RESULTS OF OBSERVATION OF EACH STAR

AT

THE ROYAL OBSERVATORY, NEAR CAPE TOWN,

AND

DEDUCTION OF MEAN ZENITH DISTANCE, 1848, JANUARY 0.

NOTE.—The reduction for Azimuthal Error is always to be applied subtractively to the Zenith Distance. The reduction for Curvature of Path is always to be applied subtractively to South Zenith Distance, and additively to North Zenith Distance. The Refraction is always to be applied additively. The Precession, Aberration, and Nutation, have the sign which is proper for reducing the Apparent North Polar Distance of the Star to its mean North Polar Distance, 1848, January 0; and therefore are to be applied with the sign given in the Table when the Star is South of the Zenith, and with the opposite sign when the Star is North of the Zenith.

The numbers included in parentheses in the column " Deduced Mean Zenith Distance, 1848, January 0," are omitted in taking the mean.

Where an asterisk or a positive sign is affixed to a number in the 3rd or 9th columns, the explanation will be found at the bottom of the page.

Mean Zenith Distances of Stars observed at the Royal Observatory.

FACE OF SECTOR EAST.

B.A.C. 1802.

Day of Observation 1848.	Apparent Zenith Distance, from Unreduced Observation.	Reduction for Az. Error, and Curv. of Path.	Refraction.	Precession, Aberration, and Nutation.	Deduced Mean Zenith Distance. 1848, Jan. 0; and Mean of Separate Results, uncorrected, for Error of Collimation.
June 24	0 13 37·03	·00	0·22	− 6·31	0 13 30·94
July 21	29·87	·00	·23	+ 1·28	31·38
28	26·56	·00	·23	3·04	29·83
29	25·87	·00	·23	3·28	29·38
Aug. 1	26·02	·00	·23	3·98	30·23
3	25·23	·00	·23	4·43	29·89
5	25·97	·00	·23	4·87	31·07
7	25·48	·00	·23	5·30	31·01
14	23·30	·00	·23	6·66	30·19
22	22·56	·00	·23	7·97	30·76
24	21·23	·00	·23	8·25	29·71
30	20·93	·00	·23	8·98	30·14
31	20·34	·00	0·23	+ 9·09	29·66
					0·13·30·32

FACE OF SECTOR WEST.

B.A.C. 1802.

Day of Observation 1848.	Apparent Zenith Distance, from Unreduced Observation.	Reduction for Az. Error, and Curv. of Path.	Refraction.	Precession, Aberration, and Nutation.	Deduced Mean Zenith Distance. 1848, Jan. 0; and Mean of Separate Results, uncorrected, for Error of Collimation.
June 2	0 13 31·40	·00	0·22	−12·91	0 13 (18·71)
3	32·09	·00	·23	12·63	(20·29)
18	29·43	·00	·22	− 8·07	21·58
July 19	19·95	·00	·23	+ 0·76	20·94
24	19·26	·00	·23	2·06	21·55
30	17·08	·00	·23	3·52	20·83
31	16·88	·00	·23	3·75	20·86
Aug. 4	16·39	·00	·23	4·65	21·27
12	15·11	·00	·23	6·29	21·63
13	15·90	·00	23	6·48	22·61
20	14·32	·00	·23	7·67	22·22
23	13·23	·00	·23	8·11	21·57
25	13·72	·00	·23	8·38	22·33
27	13·72	·00	·23	8·64	22·59
29	13·53	·00	0·23	+ 8·87	22·63
					0·13·21·74

Error of Collimation . .   = 0· 0· 4·29
Resulting Mean Zenith Distance, South = 0·13·26·03

FACE OF SECTOR EAST.

B.A.C. 2293.

Day of Observation 1848.	Apparent Zenith Distance, from Unreduced Observation.	Reduction for Az. Error, and Curv. of Path.	Refraction.	Precession, Aberration, and Nutation.	Deduced Mean Zenith Distance. 1848, Jan. 0; and Mean of Separate Results, uncorrected, for Error of Collimation.
June 4	5· 9·25·83	·00	5·19	−17·84	5· 0·48·86
25	31·16	·00	5·21	12·92	49·19
26	31·75	·00	5·14	12·57	49·46
July 21	37·97	·01	5·26	5·89	49·11
28	41·33	·00	5·31	4·16	50·80
29	42·32	·01	5·28	3·93	51·52
Aug. 1	42·02	·00	5·26	3·23	50·51
3	42·12	·00	5·24	2·76	50·12
5	42·81	·01	5·26	2·31	50·37
7	43·31	·00	5·22	1·87	50·40
14	45·78	·01	5·28	− 0·40	51·45
22	46·27	·01	5·33	+ 1·09	50·50
24	48·74	·01	5·31	1·43	52·61
30	49·33	·01	5·24	2·34	52·22
31	49·04	·00	5·29	+ 2·48	51·85
					5· 9·50·60

FACE OF SECTOR WEST.

B.A.C. 2293.

Day of Observation 1848.	Apparent Zenith Distance, from Unreduced Observation.	Reduction for Az. Error, and Curv. of Path.	Refraction.	Precession, Aberration, and Nutation.	Deduced Mean Zenith Distance. 1848, Jan. 0; and Mean of Separate Results, uncorrected, for Error of Collimation.
June 2	5· 9·37·73	·00	5·23	−18·28	5· 9·61·24
3	36·49	·00	5·26	18·06	59·81
19	39·75	·00	5·19	14·32	59·26
July 19	48·64	·00	5·24	6·39	60·27
22	48·49	·01	5·21	5·04	59·33
24	47·95	·01	5·25	5·14	58·33
31	50·82	·00	5·34	3·46	59·62
Aug. 4	50·32	·03	5·27	2·53	58·09
12	52·89	·01	5·35	0·80	59·03
13	51·80	·02	5·33	− 0·00	57·71
20	54·17	·06	5·31	+ 0·74	58·68
21	52·59	·06	5·32	0·92	56·93
23	54·07	·03	5·30	1·26	58·08
25	53·38	·04	5·36	1·59	57·11
27	54·67	·03	5·23	1·90	57·97
29	54·67	·02	5·24	+ 2·20	57·69
					5· 9·58·70

Error of Collimation . .   = 0· 0· 4·05
Resulting Mean Zenith Distance, North = 5· 9·54·65

Mean Zenith Distances of Stars observed at the Royal Observatory.

	FACE OF SECTOR EAST.						FACE OF SECTOR WEST.				
Day of Observation 1848.	Apparent Zenith Distance, from Unreduced Observation.	Reduction for Az. Error, and Curv. of Path.	Refraction.	Precession, and Aberration, and Nutation.	Deduced Mean Zenith Distance, 1848, Jan. 0; and Mean of Separate Results, uncorrected, for Error of Collination.	Day of Observation 1848.	Apparent Zenith Distance, from Unreduced Observation.	Reduction for Az. Error, and Curv. of Path.	Refraction.	Precession, and Aberration, and Nutation.	Deduced Mean Zenith Distance, 1848, Jan. 0; and Mean of Separate Results, uncorrected, for Error of Collination.
	° ′ ″	″	″	″	° ′ ″		° ′ ″	″	″	″	° ′ ″

B.A.C. 4517.

June 4	5· 8·42·52	·00	5·32	-13·68	5· 9· 1·52	June 3	5· 8·55·60	·00	5·25	-13·64	5· 9·14·49
18	44·24	·00	5·22	13·94	3·40	5	56·29	·01	5·12	13·72	15·12
23	44·84	·00	5·26	13·92	4·02	17	55·36	·00	5·22	13·93	14·51
25	44·89	·00	5·24	13·90	4·03	19	54·32	·00	5·26	13·94	13·52
26	45·73	·00	5·21	13·88	4·82	22	54·57	·00	5·29	13·93	13·79
July 21	46·81	·01	5·25	-12·78	4·83	July 13	55·90	·00	5·23	13·29	14·42
						20	56·54	·00	5·25	-12·85	14·64
					5· 9· 3·77						5· 9·14·36

Error of Collimation   .   .   . = 0· 0· 5·29
Resulting Mean Zenith Distance, North = 5· 9· 9·06

B.A.C. 4548.

June 4	5· 8·40·00	·00	5·32	-13·21	5· 8·58·53	June 3	5· 8·52·39	·00	5·25	-13·17	5· 9·10·81
18	41·03	·00	5·22	13·50	59·75	5	52·94	- ·01	5·12	13·24	11·29
23	41·77	·00	5·26	13·50	60·53	17	53·18	+ ·09	5·22	13·50	11·99
25	41·87	·00	5·23	13·49	60·59	19	51·45	·00	5·26	13·51	10·22
26	42·27	·00	5·21	13·48	60·96	22	51·85	·00	5·29	13·51	10·65
July 21	43·26	·01	5·25	12·47	60·97	July 14	51·16	·00	5·21	12·89	9·26
26	44·00	·03	5·22	-12·10	61·29	20	52·15	·00	5·25	12·53	9·93
						22	52·94	- ·01	5·25	-12·40	10·58
					5· 9· 0·37						5· 9·10·59

Error of Collimation   .   .   . = 0· 0· 5·11
Resulting Mean Zenith Distance, North = 5· 9· 5·48

B.A.C. 4579.

June 4	1·39·18·52	·00	1·71	-13·42	1·39·33·65	June 3	1·39·32·15	·00	1·69	-13·37	1·39·47·21
18	20·39	·00	1·68	13·94	36·01	5	31·11	·00	1·64	13·47	46·22
23	21·48	·00	1·69	14·01	37·18	17	30·27	·00	1·68	13·92	45·87
25	20·64	·00	1·68	14·02	36·34	19	29·78	·00	1·69	13·96	45·43
26	20·64	·00	1·67	14·03	36·34	22	30·12	·00	1·70	14·00	45·82
July 21	21·68	·00	1·69	13·26	36·63	July 13	29·62	·00	1·68	13·67	44·97
26	22·42	·01	1·68	12·92	37·01	14	28·94	·00	1·67	13·63	44·24
29	23·46	·01	1·71	-12·70	37·86	20	29·93	·00	1·69	13·31	44·93
						22	30·96	·00	1·69	13·19	45·84
						24	30·07	·00	1·69	-13·06	44·82
					1·39·36·38						1·39·45·54

Error of Collimation   .   .   . = 0· 0· 4·58
Resulting Mean Zenith Distance, North = 1·39·40·96

B.A.C. 4548.—June 17.—Correction for Curvature of Path = + 0″·09.

Mean Zenith Distances of Stars observed at the Royal Observatory.

FACE OF SECTOR EAST.   FACE OF SECTOR WEST.

B.A.C. 4623.

Day of Observation 1848.	Apparent Zenith Distance, from Unreduced Observation.	Reduction for Az. Error, and Curv. of Path.	Refraction.	Precession, Aberration, and Nutation.	Deduced Mean Zenith Distance. 1848, Jan.0; and Mean of Separate Results, uncorrected, for Error of Collimation.
June 4	1·41·24·75	·00	1·74	-12·92	1·41·39·41
18	26·00	·00	1·71	13·47	41·21
23	28·05	·00	1·72	13·56	43·33
25	26·42	·00	1·72	13·57	41·71
26	26·47	·00	1·71	13·58	41·76
July 21	27·91	·00	1·72	12·91	42·54
25	28·70	·01	1·73	12·66	43·08
26	28·75	·01	1·71	12·59	43·04
29	29·19	·01	1·75	-12·38	43·31
					1·41·42·15

Day of Observation 1848.	Apparent Zenith Distance, from Unreduced Observation.	Reduction for Az. Error, and Curv. of Path.	Refraction.	Precession, Aberration, and Nutation.	Deduced Mean Zenith Distance. 1848, Jan.0; and Mean of Separate Results, uncorrected, for Error of Collimation.
June 3	1·41·38·18	·00	1·72	-12·86	1·41·52·76
5	37·29	·00	1·68	12·97	51·94
17	35·96	·00	1·71	13·45	51·12
19	35·71	·00	1·72	13·49	50·92
22	35·91	·00	1·74	13·55	51·20
July 13	36·35	·00	1·72	13·29	51·36
14	35·91	·00	1·71	13·25	50·87
20	35·61	·00	1·72	12·96	50·29
22	36·50	·00	1·72	-12·85	51·07
					1·41·51·28

Error of Collimation . . = 0· 0· 4·56
Resulting Mean Zenith Distance, North = 1·41·46·72

B.A.C. 4686.

Day	App. Z.D.	Red.	Refr.	Prec.	Deduced Mean Z.D.
Aug. 5	1·41·19·71	·00	1·71	-12·21	1·41· 9·21
12	19·51	·00	1·71	11·58	9·64
14	18·72	·00	1·71	11·39	9·04
28	16·25	·01	1·68	- 9·79	8·13
					1·41· 9·01

Day	App. Z.D.	Red.	Refr.	Prec.	Deduced Mean Z.D.
Aug. 4	1·41·11·81	·07	1·71	-12·29	1·41· 1·16
11	11·11	·01	1·69	11·68	1·11
19	11·16	·01	1·72	10·86	2·01
29	10·72	·01	1·69	- 9·65	2·75
					1·41· 1·76

Error of Collimation . . = 0· 0· 3·62
Resulting Mean Zenith Distance, South = 1·41· 5·38

B.A.C. 4719.

Day	App. Z.D.	Red.	Refr.	Prec.	Deduced Mean Z.D.
June 4	5·21·32·15	·00	5·54	-10·22	5·21·47·91
16	32·25	·00	5·46	10·65	48·36
23	33·34	·00	5·48	10·77	49·59
25	32·64	·00	5·45	10·78	49·07
July 21	33·54	·01	5·47	10·27	49·27
25	35·21	·03	5·50	10·08	50·76
29	34·82	·02	5·54	- 9·85	50·19
					5·21·49·31

Day	App. Z.D.	Red.	Refr.	Prec.	Deduced Mean Z.D.
June 3	5·21·44·25	·00	5·47	-10·17	5·21·59·89
5	44·35	-·01	5·33	10·26	59·93
17	43·91	·00	5·44	10·67	60·02
19	39·31	+·09	5·48	10·71	55·59
26	42·72	·00	5·42	10·79	58·93
July 20	41·73	·00	5·47	10·32	57·52
25	42·52	+·08	5·47	10·23	58·30
24	41·63	-·01	5·47	10·13	57·22
26	43·12	+·08	5·44	-10·02	58·66
					5·21·58·45

Error of Collimation . . = 0· 0· 4·57
Resulting Mean Zenith Distance, North = 5·21·53·88

B.A.C. 4686.—Aug. 4 —Correction for Curvature of Path = -0"·06.
  „   4719.—June 19.—   „   „   „   = +0 ·09.
  „   „   —July 22.—   „   „   „   = +0 ·09.
  „   „   —   „   26.—   „   „   „   = +0 ·09.

Mean Zenith Distances of Stars observed at the Royal Observatory.

FACE OF SECTOR EAST.						FACE OF SECTOR WEST.					
Day of Observation 1848	Apparent Zenith Distance, from Unreduced Observation.	Reduction for Az. Error, and Curv. of Path.	Refraction.	Precession, Aberration, and Nutation.	Deduced Mean Zenith Distance, 1848, Jan. 0; and Mean of Separate Results, uncorrected, for Error of Collimation.	Day of Observation 1848.	Apparent Zenith Distance, from Unreduced Observation.	Reduction for Az. Error, and Curv. of Path.	Refraction.	Precession, Aberration, and Nutation.	Deduced Mean Zenith Distance, 1848, Jan. 0; and Mean of Separate Results, uncorrected, for Error of Collimation.

B.A.C. 4784.

Day of Obs. E.	Apparent Z.D.	Reduction	Refraction	Prec./Ab./Nut.	Deduced Mean	Day of Obs. W.	Apparent Z.D.	Reduction	Refraction	Prec./Ab./Nut.	Deduced Mean
June 4	5· 7·20·98	·00	5·30	- 9·12	5· 7·35·40	June 3	5· 7·35·80	·00	5·23	- 9·10	5· 7·50·13
16	22·56	·00	5·22	9·63	37·41	17	33·82	+ ·09	5·19	9·66	48·76
18	20·98	·00	5·20	9·68	35·80	19	32·44	·00	5·23	9·71	47·38
23	23·35	·00	5·23	9·79	38·37	26	32·44	·00	5·18	9·83	47·45
25	21·02	·00	5·21	9·82	36·95	July 20	32·14	·00	5·23	9·54	46·91
July 21	23·85	+ ·13	5·23	9·50	38·71	22	32·64	- ·01	5·23	9·46	47·32
23	23·65	- ·01	5·21	9·42	38·27	24	31·55	·01	5·23	9·38	46·15
25	24·78	·03	5·25	9·34	39·34	26	32·34	·01	5·20	9·29	46·82
Aug. 1	25·13	·00	5·26	8·98	39·37	30	32·04	·01	5·28	9·09	46·40
3	24·64	·00	5·20	- 8·86	38·70	Aug. 2	32·78	·00	5·21	8·92	46·91
						4	32·64	- ·03	5·21	- 8·80	46·62
					5· 7·37·84						5· 7·47·35

Error of Collimation . . . = 0· 4·76
Resulting Mean Zenith Distance, North = 5· 7·42·59

Anon. AR. 14·24.

Day of Obs. E.	Apparent Z.D.	Reduction	Refraction	Prec./Ab./Nut.	Deduced Mean	Day of Obs. W.	Apparent Z.D.	Reduction	Refraction	Prec./Ab./Nut.	Deduced Mean
June 4	1·17·11·96	·00	1·33	- 9·38	1·17·22·67	June 3	1·17·27·86	·00	1·31	- 9·31	1·17·38·48
16	13·93	·00	1·31	10·09	25·33	5	25·19	·00	1·28	9·45	35·92
18	13·14	·00	1·30	10 18	24·62	17	24·75	·00	1·30	10·14	36·19
23	12·94	·00	1·31	10·43	24·63	26	28·85	·00	1·30	10·48	(40·63)
25	14·33	·00	1·31	10·44	26·08	July 20	23·02	·00	1·31	10·46	34·79
July 21	15·22	+ ·15	1·31	10·44	27·12	22	24·01	·00	1·31	10·41	35·73
23	14·13	·00	1·31	10·38	25·82	24	23·71	·00	1·31	10·34	35·36
25	14·77	- ·01	1·32	10·38	26·38	26	23·32	·00	1·30	10·27	34·89
29	14·82	·00	1·33	10·14	26·29	30	23·12	+ ·10	1·33	10·09	34·64
Aug. 1	16·60	·00	1·32	9·99	27·91	Aug. 4	24·75	- ·01	1·31	- 9·82	35·87
3	16·80	·00	1·31	- 9·88	27·99						
					1·17·25·89						1·17·35·76

Error of Collimation . . . = 0· 0· 4·93
Resulting Mean Zenith Distance, North = 1·17·30·83

B.A.C. 4852.

Day of Obs. E.	Apparent Z.D.	Reduction	Refraction	Prec./Ab./Nut.	Deduced Mean	Day of Obs. W.	Apparent Z.D.	Reduction	Refraction	Prec./Ab./Nut.	Deduced Mean
June 4	0·35· 6·52	·00	0·60	- 8·74	0·34·58·38	June 1	0·34·52·20	·00	0·60	- 8·48	0·34·44·32
16	5·83	·00	·59	9·59	56·83	5	54·57	·00	·58	8·81	46·34
18	5·78	·00	·59	9·70	56·67	17	54·77	·00	·59	9·65	45·71
23	6 42	·00	·59	9·95	57·06	19	55·51	·00	·59	9·76	46·34
25	6·03	·00	·59	10·04	56·58	22	55·51	·00	·60	9·91	46·20
July 21	6·42	·00	·59	10·33	56·68	July 14	55·65	·00	·59	10·41	45·83
23	5·14	·00	·59	10·29	55·44	20	55·85	·00	·59	10·34	46·10
25	5·43	·00	·60	10·10	55·80	22	55·70	·00	·60	10·31	45·90
29	4·64	·00	·60	10·10	55·14	26	55·26	·00	·59	10·20	45·65

Carried forward,

Mean Zenith Distances of Stars observed at the Royal Observatory.

B.A.C. 4862—(continued).

FACE OF SECTOR EAST.						FACE OF SECTOR WEST.					
Day of Observation 1848.	Apparent Zenith Distance, from Unreduced Observation.	Reduction for Alt. Error, and Curv. of Path.	Refraction.	Precession, Aberration, and Nutation.	Deduced Mean Zenith Distance, 1848, Jan. 0; and Mean of Separate Results, uncorrected, for Error of Collimation.	Day of Observation 1848.	Apparent Zenith Distance, from Unreduced Observation.	Reduction for Alt. Error, and Curv. of Path.	Refraction.	Precession, Aberration, and Nutation.	Deduced Mean Zenith Distance, 1848, Jan. 0; and Mean of Separate Results, uncorrected, for Error of Collimation.
Aug. 1	0·35· 5·09	·00	·60	9·98	0·34·55·71	July 30	0·34·56·10	·00	·60	10·06	0·34·46·64
3	4·59	·00	·59	9·89	55·29	Aug. 2	56·30	·00	·59	9·93	46·96
5	5·09	·00	·59	9·78	55·90	4	56·40	·00	·59	9·83	47·16
14	4·84	·00	·60	9·21	56·23	11	53·63	·00	·59	9·42	44·80
23	3·70	·00	0·59	- 8·47	55·82	13	54·91	·00	0·61	- 9·28	46·24
					0·34·56·25						0·34·40·02

Error of Collimation . . . = 0· 0· 5·12

Resulting Mean Zenith Distance, South = 0·34·51·14

B.A.C. 4916.

FACE OF SECTOR EAST.						FACE OF SECTOR WEST.					
Day	App. Z.D.	Red.	Refr.	Prec./Ab./Nut.	Deduced Mean Z.D.	Day	App. Z.D.	Red.	Refr.	Prec./Ab./Nut.	Deduced Mean Z.D.
June 4	0·41·44·50	·00	0·72	- 7·40	0·41·52·62	June 1	0·41·59·12	·00	0·72	- 7·16	0·42· 7·00
16	44·65	·00	·71	8·22	53·58	3	58·13	·00	·71	7·32	6·16
18	44·30	·00	·71	8·34	53·35	5	56·40	·00	·69	7·48	4·57
22	44·35	·00	·71	8·58	53·64	17	56·25	·00	·71	8·28	5·24
25	44·50	·00	·71	8·67	53·88	19	54·82	·00	·71	8·39	3·92
July 21	43·91	·00	·71	9·03	53·65	22	54·97	·00	·72	8·54	4·23
23	45·24	·00	·71	9·00	54·95	26	55·07	·00	·70	8·71	4·48
25	45·68	·00	·71	8·96	55·35	July 20	54·23	·00	·71	9·04	3·98
29	44·89	·00	·72	8·85	54·46	22	55·02	·00	·71	9·01	4·74
Aug. 1	45·09	·00	·71	8·75	54·55	24	54·23	·00	·71	8·98	3·92
3	46·18	·00	·71	8·67	55·58	26	54·13	·00	·71	8·93	3·77
5	45·49	·00	0·71	- 8·58	54·78	Aug. 2	53·19	·00	·71	8·71	2·61
						4	54·23	·00	·71	8·63	3·57
						11	55·71	·01	0·70	- 8·27	4·67
					0·41·54·20						0·42· 4·49

Error of Collimation . . . = 0· 0· 5·15

Resulting Mean Zenith Distance, North = 0·41·59·34

Anon. A.R. 14·53.

FACE OF SECTOR EAST.						FACE OF SECTOR WEST.					
Day	App. Z.D.	Red.	Refr.	Prec./Ab./Nut.	Deduced Mean Z.D.	Day	App. Z.D.	Red.	Refr.	Prec./Ab./Nut.	Deduced Mean Z.D.
June 4	1·53·26·17	·00	1·95	- 6·54	1·53·34·66	June 1	1·53·38·42	·01	1·96	- 6·31	1·53·46·68
16	25·23	·00	1·93	7·31	34·47	3	38·17	·00	1·93	6·46	46·56
18	25·63	·00	1·92	7·41	34·96	5	36·39	·00	1·88	6·61	44·88
23	25·53	·00	1·93	7·65	35·11	17	35·65	·00	1·91	7·36	44·92
25	25·97	·00	1·92	7·73	35·62	22	34·37	·00	1·94	7·60	43·91
July 21	26·17	·00	1·93	8·09	36·19	26	38·07	·00	1·91	7·77	(47·75)
23	27·35	·01	1·92	8·07	37·33	July 14	34·07	·00	1·91	8·13	44·11
25	27·26	·01	1·93	8·03	37·21	20	34·17	·00	1·94	8·10	44·21
	27·06	·01	1·93	7·94	36·94	22	35·01	·00	1·93	8·08	45·02
Aug. 1	27·16	·00	1·94	7·85	36·95	24	35·06	·01	1·93	8·05	45·03
3	27·06	·00	1·92	- 7·78	36·76	26	34·07	·00	1·92	- 8·01	44·00

Carried forward,

Mean Zenith Distances of Stars observed at the Royal Observatory.

FACE OF SECTOR EAST						FACE OF SECTOR WEST					
Day of Observation 1848.	Apparent Zenith Distance, from Unreduced Observation.	Reduction for Az. Error, and Curv. of Path.	Refraction.	Precession, Aberration, and Nutation.	Deduced Mean Zenith Distance, 1848, Jan. 0; and Mean of Separate Results, uncorrected, for Error of Collimation.	Day of Observation 1848.	Apparent Zenith Distance, from Unreduced Observation.	Reduction for Az. Error, and Curv. of Path.	Refraction.	Precession, Aberration, and Nutation.	Deduced Mean Zenith Distance, 1848, Jan. 0; and Mean of Separate Results, uncorrected, for Error of Collimation.

Anon. A.R. 14·53—(continued).

Day	Apparent Z.D.	Red.	Refr.	Prec.	Deduced Mean	Day	Apparent Z.D.	Red.	Refr.	Prec.	Deduced Mean
Aug. 5	1·53·27·65	·01	1·93	− 7·70	1·53·37·27	July 30	1·53·33·63	·00	1·95	7·91	1·53·43·49
						Aug. 2	34·07	·00	1·92	7·81	43·80
						4	34·56	·01	1·92	7·74	44·21
						11	35·85	·02	1·91	− 7·41	45·15
					1·53·36·12						1·53·44·71

Error of Collimation . . = 0· 0· 4·29
Resulting Mean Zenith Distance, North = 1·53·40·42

Anon. A.R. 14·57.

Day	Apparent Z.D.	Red.	Refr.	Prec.	Deduced Mean	Day	Apparent Z.D.	Red.	Refr.	Prec.	Deduced Mean
June 16	1·36·45·49	·00	1·64	− 6·98	1·36·54·11	June 17	1·36·54·67	·00	1·63	− 7·04	1·37· 3·34
18	46·23	·00	1·63	7·09	54·95	July 14	54·52	·00	1·63	7·87	4·02
23	44·60	·00	1·64	7·33	53·57	20	54·28	·00	1·65	7·87	3·80
25	45·04	·00	1·64	7·43	54·11	22	54·13	·00	1·65	7·85	3·63
July 23	45·29	·00	1·64	7·84	54·77	24	54·77	·00	1·64	7·83	4·24
25	46·57	·01	1·65	7·81	56·02	26	54·77	·00	1·64	7·80	4·21
29	44·84	·01	1·66	7·73	54·22	30	53·88	·00	1·66	7·70	3·24
Aug. 1	45·54	·00	1·66	7·65	54·85	Aug. 2	52·60	·00	1·64	7·62	1·86
3	45·88	·00	1·64	7·59	55·11		53·64	·01	1·64	− 7·55	2·82
5	46·28	·00	1·64	− 7·51	55·43						
					1·36·54·71						1·37· 3·46

Error of Collimation . . = 0· 0· 4·37
Resulting Mean Zenith Distance, North = 1·36·59·09

B.A.C. 5032.

Day	Apparent Z.D.	Red.	Refr.	Prec.	Deduced Mean	Day	Apparent Z.D.	Red.	Refr.	Prec.	Deduced Mean
June 4	4·20·39·31	·00	4·49	− 4·83	4·20·48·63	June 1	4·20·52·15	·01	4·51	− 4·64	4·20·61·29
18	39·16	·00	4·41	5·57	49·14	3	51·26	·00	4·43	4·76	60·45
23	39·36	·00	4·45	5·77	49·58	5	50·57	·01	4·32	4·89	59·77
25	39·61	·00	4·42	5·84	49·87	17	49·58	·00	4·40	5·52	59·50
July 21	39·16	·00	4·45	6·17	49·78	19	48·00	·00	4·44	5·61	58·05
23	40·94	·01	4·43	6·15	51·51	22	49·24	·00	4·46	5·73	59·43
25	40·84	·01	4·45	6·12	51·40	July 14	49·73	·00	4·40	6·19	60·32
Aug. 1	41·58	·01	4·49	6·05	52·11	20	48·84	·00	4·45	6·18	59·47
3	41·14	·01	4·47	5·98	51·59	22	48·09	·01	4·44	6·16	59·28
5	41·09	·00	4·43	5·92	51·44	24	48·20	·01	4·43	6·14	58·76
14	40·99	·01	4·44	5·85	51·27	26	47·21	·00	4·42	6·11	57·74
23	41·58	·01	4·46	5·48	51·51	30	47·56	·01	4·49	6·02	58·06
	41·88	·02	4·41	− 4·97	51·24	Aug. 2	47·56	·00	4·43	5·95	57·94
						4	48·10	·02	4·42	5·88	58·38
						11	48·20	·04	4·39	5·61	58·16
						13	48·50	·02	4·52	− 5·52	58·52
					4·20·50·70						4·20·59·07

Error of Collimation . . = 0· 0· 4·19
Resulting Mean Zenith Distance, North = 4·20·54·88

Mean Zenith Distances of Stars observed at the Royal Observatory.

B.A.C. 5151.

FACE OF SECTOR EAST.

Day of Observation 1848.	Apparent Zenith Distance, from Unreduced Observation.	Reduction for Az. Error, and Curv. of Path.	Refraction.	Precession, Aberration, and Nutation.	Deduced Mean Zenith Distance, 1848, Jan. 0; and Mean of Separate Results, uncorrected, for Error of Collimation.
June 4	4·39·23·85	·00	4·81	− 2·87	4·39·31·53
16	24·39	·00	4·75	3·52	32·66
18	24·31	·00	4·72	3·62	32·65
23	24·15	·00	4·77	3·83	32·75
25	24 00	·00	4·74	3·91	32·65
July 21	24·69	·01	4·77	4·42	33·87
23	24·79	·01	4·75	4·42	33·95
25	25·13	·03	4·77	4·41	34·28
29	25·73	·01	4·81	4·38	34·91
Aug. 1	25·33	·00	4·80	4·34	34·47
3	25·97	·00	4·74	4·31	35·02
5	25·73	·01	4·77	4·26	34·75
12	26·37	·00	4·76	4·07	35·20
14	26·38	·01	4·79	4·00	35·16
22	26·62	·02	4·69	− 3·66	34·95
					4·39·33·92

FACE OF SECTOR WEST.

Day of Observation 1848.	Apparent Zenith Distance, from Unreduced Observation.	Reduction for Az. Error, and Curv. of Path.	Refraction.	Precession, Aberration, and Nutation.	Deduced Mean Zenith Distance, 1848, Jan. 0; and Mean of Separate Results, uncorrected, for Error of Collimation.
June 1	4·39·38·02	·01	4·83	− 2·68	4·39·45·52
3	36·35	·00	4·75	2·80	43·90
5	36·20	·01	4·64	2·93	43·76
17	36·10	·00	4·72	3·57	44·39
19	33·53	·00	4·76	3·66	41·95
22	34·57	·00	4·78	3·79	43·14
July 14	35·31	·00	4·71	4·38	44·40
20	33·73	·00	4·79	4·42	42·94
22	33·58	·01	4·76	4·42	42·75
24	33·58	·01	4·75	4·42	42·74
26	33·04	·00	4·75	4·41	42·20
30	33·23	·01	4·81	4·37	42·40
Aug. 2	31·80	·00	4·75	4·32	40·87
4	33·28	·02	4·75	4·29	42·30
11	33·68	·04	4·72	4·10	42·46
13	33·04	·02	4·85	4·03	41·90
19	34·17	·03	4·78	3·79	42·71
23	33·73	·03	4·73	− 3·61	42·04
					4·39·42·91

Error of Collimation . . . = 0· 0· 4·50
Resulting Mean Zenith Distance, North = 4·39·38·42

Anon. A.R. 15·34.

FACE OF SECTOR EAST.

Day of Observation 1848.	Apparent Zenith Distance, from Unreduced Observation.	Reduction for Az. Error, and Curv. of Path.	Refraction.	Precession, Aberration, and Nutation.	Deduced Mean Zenith Distance, 1848, Jan. 0; and Mean of Separate Results, uncorrected, for Error of Collimation.
June 4	2·49· 7·41	·00	2·92	− 2·54	2·49·12·87
16	8·05	·00	2·87	3·32	14·24
18	7·31	·00	2·86	3·44	13·61
25	7·21	·00	2·86	3·80	13·87
July 21	4·94	·00	2·88	4·55	12·37
23	7·55	·01	2·87	4·56	14·97
25	7·36	·01	2·89	4·57	14·81
29	6·81	·01	2·91	4·57	14·27
Aug. 1	6·47	·00	2·90	4·54	13·91
3	7·05	·00	2·87	4·52	15·04
5	7·75	·01	2·88	4·49	15·11
12	8·69	·00	2·88	4·33	15·90
14	8·79	·00	2·90	− 4·27	15·96
					2·49·14·38

FACE OF SECTOR WEST.

Day of Observation 1848.	Apparent Zenith Distance, from Unreduced Observation	Reduction for Az. Error, and Curv. of Path.	Refraction.	Precession, Aberration, and Nutation.	Deduced Mean Zenith Distance, 1848, Jan. 0; and Mean of Separate Results, uncorrected, for Error of Collimation.
June 1	2·49·20·00	01	2·92	− 2·33	2·49·25·24
3	19·21	·00	2·87	2·47	24·55
5	17·92	·01	2·80	2 61	23·32
17	17·58	·00	2·85	3·38	23·81
19	14·57	·00	2·88	3·49	20 94
July 20	14·57	·00	2·90	4·53	22·00
22	16·05	·01	2·88	4·55	23·47
24	14·76	·01	2·87	4·56	22·18
26	14·76	·00	2·87	4·57	22·20
30	13·78	·01	2·91	4·56	21·24
Aug. 2	13·58	·00	2·87	4·53	20·98
4	14·96	·01	2·87	4·51	22·33
11	15·21	·02	2·85	4·36	22·40
13	14·96	·01	2·93	− 4·30	22·18
					2·49·22·63

Error of Collimation . . . = 0· 0· 4·13
Resulting Mean Zenith Distance, North = 2·49·18·51

Mean Zenith Distances of Stars observed at the Royal Observatory.

	FACE OF SECTOR EAST.						FACE OF SECTOR WEST.				
Day of Observation 1848.	Apparent Zenith Distance, from Unreduced Observation.	Reduction for Az. Error, and Curv. of Path.	Refraction.	Precession, Aberration, and Nutation.	Deduced Mean Zenith Distance. 1848, Jan. 0; and Mean of Separate Results, uncorrected. for Error of Collimation.	Day of Observation 1848.	Apparent Zenith Distance, from Unreduced Observation.	Reduction for Az. Error, and Curv. of Path.	Refraction.	Precession, Aberration, and Nutation.	Deduced Mean Zenith Distance, 1848, Jan. 0; and Mean of Separate Results, uncorrected, for Error of Collimation.

B.A.C. 5227.

	° ′ ″	″	″	″	° ′ ″		° ′ ″	″	″	″	° ′ ″
June 4	0·46·19·71	·00	0·80	− 2·08	0·46·22·50	June 3	0·46·34·62	·00	0·79	− 2·00	0·46·37·41
16	21·08	·00	·79	3·00	25·47	5	32·70	·00	·77	2·16	35·63
18	20·50	·00	·78	3·14	24·42	17	32·70	·00	·78	3·07	36·55
23	20·30	·00	·79	3·46	24·55	22	32·45	·00	·79	3·40	36·64
July 21	19·61	·00	·79	4·60	25·00	July 20	30·52	·00	·79	4·58	35·89
23	20·89	·00	·70	4·63	26·31	22	29·58	·00	·79	4·62	34·99
29	20·75	·00	·80	4·69	26·24	24	29·93	·00	·79	4·65	35·37
Aug. 1	20·10	·00	·80	4·69	25·59	26	30·33	·00	·79	4·67	35·79
3	21·78	·00	·79	4·68	27·25	30	29·98	·00	·80	4·69	35·47
5	20·70	·00	·79	4·67	26·16	Aug. 2	29·54	·00	·79	4·69	35·02
12	20·99	·00	·79	4·56	26·34	4	29·98	·00	·79	4·68	35·45
14	20·55	·00	·80	4·51	25·86	11	30·08	·01	·78	4·58	35·43
22	20·20	·00	·78	4·24	25·22	13	29·49	·00	·80	4·54	34·83
25	20·90	·00	0·78	− 4·11	25·88	19	29·83	·01	·79	4·36	34·97
						23	30·23	·01	0·79	− 4·20	35·21

0·46·25·49				0·46·35·04

Error of Collimation . . . = 0· 0· 5·08
Resulting Mean Zenith Distance, North = 0·46·30·57

B.A.C. 5272.

June 4	5· 9·54·27	− ·00	5·36	− 1·14	5·10· 0·77	June 3	5·10· 6·82	·00	5·27	− 1·08	5·10·13·17
16	54·37	·00	5·27	1·77	1·41	5	9·04	·01	5·14	1·19	15·36
18	54·91	·00	5·24	1·86	2·01	17	5·48	·00	5·24	1·81	12·53
23	54·86	·00	5·30	2·03	2·24	July 20	3·16	·00	5·32	2·76	11·24
July 21	53·63	·01	5·29	2·77	1·68	22	3·65	·01	5·28	2·78	11·70
23	56·05	·01	5·27	2·79	4·10	24	2·67	·01	5·27	2·79	10·72
25	55·16	·03	5·30	2·79	3·22	26	3·90	·00	5·27	2·79	11·96
29	56·05	·02	5·34	2·79	4·16	30	2·67	·01	5·34	2·79	10·79
Aug. 1	55·51	·00	5·33	2·78	3·62	Aug. 2	2·07	·00	5·27	2·77	10·11
3	56·05	·00	5·27	2·76	4·08	4	2·22	·03	5·27	2·75	10·21
5	56·15	·01	5·29	2·74	4·17	11	4·15	·04	5·24	2·63	11·98
12	56·99	·00	5·28	2·61	4·88	13	3·56	·02	5·40	2·58	11·52
14	56·64	− ·01	5·33	2·56	4·52	19	3·16	·03	5·32	2·41	10·86
22	57·83	+ ·12	5·23	2·30	5·48	23	2·27	·03	5·26	− 2·26	9·76
25	56·44	− ·02	5·22	− 2·18	3·82						

5·10· 3·34				5·10·11·57

Error of Collimation . . . = 0· 0· 4·11
Resulting Mean Zenith Distance, North = 5·10· 7·45

B.A.C. 5272.—Aug. 22.—Correction for Curvature of Path = +0″·14.

Mean Zenith Distances of Stars observed at the Royal Observatory.

FACE OF SECTOR EAST.

B.A.C. 5374.

Day of Observation 1849.	Apparent Zenith Distance, from Unreduced Observation.	Reduction for Az. Error, and Curv. of Path.	Refraction.	Precession, Aberration, and Nutation.	Deduced Mean Zenith Distance, 1849, Jan. 0; and Mean of Separate Results, uncorrected, for Error of Collimation.
June 4	4 55 14·91	·00	5·10	+ 0·15	4 55 19·86
16	15·71	·00	5·02	- 0·50	21·23
18	16·10	·00	5·01	0·60	21·71
23	15·21	·00	5·04	0·82	21·07
July 21	15·31	·01	5·04	1·66	22·00
23	15·06	·01	5·02	1·69	21·76
25	15·66	·03	5·04	1·71	22·38
29	16·30	·02	5·09	1·74	23·11
Aug. 1	16·10	·00	5·09	1·74	22·93
3	16·00	·00	5·03	1·74	22·77
5	16·54	·01	5·04	1·73	23·30
12	16·89	·00	5·03	1·66	23·58
14	17·33	·01	5·09	1·63	24·04
22	18·57	·02	4·99	1·43	24·97
25	16·79	·02	4·98	- 1·34	23·09
					4·55·22·52

FACE OF SECTOR WEST.

B.A.C. 5374.

Day of Observation 1849.	Apparent Zenith Distance, from Unreduced Observation.	Reduction for Az. Error, and Curv. of Path.	Refraction.	Precession, Aberration, and Nutation.	Deduced Mean Zenith Distance, 1849, Jan. 0; and Mean of Separate Results, uncorrected, for Error of Collimation.
June 3	4 55 27·11	·00	5·02	+ 0·21	4 55 31·92
17	26·52	·00	4·99	- 0·54	32·05
July 20	24·10	·00	5·06	1·64	30·80
22	24·10	·01	5·03	1·67	30·79
24	22·96	·01	5·02	1·70	29·67
26	22·82	·00	5·02	1·72	29·56
30	23·21	·01	5·09	1·73	30·02
Aug. 2	22·82	·00	5·02	1·74	29·58
4	22·77	·03	5·02	1·74	29·50
11	22·92	·04	5·00	1·67	29·55
13	23·61	·02	5·14	1·64	30·37
19	23·11	·03	5·07	1·52	29·67
23	23·16	·03	5·01	- 1·41	29·55
					4·55·30·23

Error of Collimation . . . = 0· 0· 3 86
Resulting Mean Zenith Distance, North = 4·55·26·38

FACE OF SECTOR EAST.

B.A.C. 5435.

Day of Observation 1849.	Apparent Zenith Distance, from Unreduced Observation.	Reduction for Az. Error, and Curv. of Path.	Refraction.	Precession, Aberration, and Nutation.	Deduced Mean Zenith Distance, 1849, Jan. 0; and Mean of Separate Results, uncorrected, for Error of Collimation.
June 4	3 23 56·69	·00	3·52	+ 0·84	3 23 59·37
18	51·80	·00	3·46	- 0·03	(55·29)
23	55·65	·00	3·48	0·29	(59·42)
July 21	55·70	·00	3·48	1·38	60·56
23	54·86	·01	3·47	1·42	59·74
25	56·39	·02	3·49	1·46	61·32
29	56·69	·01	3·51	1·52	61·71
Aug. 1	54·91	·00	3·51	1·55	59·97
3	57·28	·00	3·47	1·56	62·31
5	56·79	·01	3·48	1·57	61·83
14	56·94	·01	3·51	1·53	61·97
22	57·18	·01	3·45	1·39	62·01
25	57·08	·01	3·44	- 1·32	61·83
					3·24· 1·00

FACE OF SECTOR WEST.

B.A.C. 5435.

Day of Observation 1849.	Apparent Zenith Distance, from Unreduced Observation.	Reduction for Az. Error, and Curv. of Path.	Refraction.	Precession, Aberration, and Nutation.	Deduced Mean Zenith Distance, 1849, Jan. 0; and Mean of Separate Results, uncorrected, for Error of Collimation.
June 3	3 24 9·23	·00	3·46	+ 0·91	3 24 11·78
July 20	5·43	·00	3·49	- 1·35	10·27
22	4·99	·01	3·47	1·40	9·85
24	4·05	·01	3·47	1·44	8·95
26	3·80	·00	3·46	1·47	8·73
30	4·05	·01	3·51	1·53	9·08
Aug. 2	3·70	·00	3·46	1·56	8·72
4	3·60	·02	3·46	1·57	8·61
11	5·08	·03	3·45	1·56	10·06
13	4·10	·01	3·55	1·54	9·18
19	4·10	·02	3·50	1·46	9·04
23	3·90	·02	3·46	- 1·37	8·71
					3·24· 9·42

Error of Collimation . . . = 0· 0· 4·21
Resulting Mean Zenith Distance, North = 3·24· 5·21

Mean Zenith Distances of Stars observed at the Royal Observatory.

FACE OF SECTOR EAST.

Day of Observation 1848.	Apparent Zenith Distance, from Unreduced Observation.	Reduction for Az. Error, and Curv. of Path.	Refraction.	Precession, Aberration, and Nutation.	Deduced Mean Zenith Distance, 1848, Jan. 0; and Mean of Separate Results, uncorrected, for Error of Collimation.

Anon. A.R. 16·14.

Day	App. ZD	Red.	Refr.	Prec.	Deduced
June 18	1· 5·38·72	·00	1·11	+ 0·10	1· 5·39·73
23	39·51	·00	1·12	- 0·23	40·86
July 21	37·24	·00	1·12	1·64	40·00
23	39·21	·00	1·12	1·70	42·03
25	39·51	·01	1·12	1·76	42·38
Aug. 1	38·22	·00	1·13	1·91	41·26
3	39·51	·00	1·12	- 1·94	42·57
					1· 5·41·26

FACE OF SECTOR WEST.

Day of Observation 1848.	Apparent Zenith Distance, from Unreduced Observation.	Reduction for Az. Error, and Curv. of Path.	Refraction.	Precession, Aberration, and Nutation.	Deduced Mean Zenith Distance, 1848, Jan. 0; and Mean of Separate Results, uncorrected, for Error of Collimation.
June 3	1· 5·54·03	·00	1·12	+ 1·22	1· 5(53·93)
17	51·11	·00	1·11	+ 0·17	52·05
July 22	48·74	·00	1·12	- 1·67	51·53
24	46·42	·00	1·12	1·73	49·27
26	48·50	·00	1·12	1·79	51·41
30	47·81	·00	1·13	1·88	50·82
Aug. 4	47·11	·01	1·11	- 1·96	50·17
					1· 5·50·88

Error of Collimation . . . = 0· 0· 4·81
Resulting Mean Zenith Distance, North = 1· 5·46·07

B.A.C. 5508.

Day (East)	App. ZD	Red.	Refr.	Prec.	Deduced	Day (West)	App. ZD	Red.	Refr.	Prec.	Deduced
Aug. 5	0·26· 4·65	·00	0·44	- 1·85	0·26· 3·24	Aug. 11	0·25·54·67	·00	0·44	- 1·93	0·25·53·18
14	3·86	·00	·45	1·94	2·37	13	55·51	·00	·45	1·94	54·02
22	3·95	·00	·44	1·90	2·49	19	56·35	·00	·45	1·93	54·87
27	2·92	·00	·45	1·56	2·56	23	56·45	·00	·44	1·89	55·00
31	4·15	·00	0·44	- 1·71	2·88	29	56·69	·00	0·44	- 1·77	55·36
					0·26· 2·51						0·25·54·49

Error of Collimation . . . = 0· 0· 4·01
Resulting Mean Zenith Distance, South = 0·25·58·50

B.A.C. 5588.

Day (East)	App. ZD	Red.	Refr.	Prec.	Deduced	Day (West)	App. ZD	Red.	Refr.	Prec.	Deduced
June 4	2· 7·16·39	·00	2·20	+ 3·04	2· 7·15·55	June 3	2· 7·29·57	·00	2·16	+ 3·11	2· 7·28·62
18	16·63	·00	2·16	2·11	16·68	17	27·20	·00	2·15	2·18	27·17
23	16·14	·00	2·17	1·81	16·50	July 20	25·23	·00	2·18	0·44	26·97
July 21	15·55	·00	2·18	0·40	17·33	22	25·03	·00	2·16	0·36	26·83
23	16·54	·01	2·16	0·33	18·36	24	24·24	·01	2·17	0·29	26·11
25	15·45	·01	2·18	0·26	17·36	26	23·65	·00	2·16	0·23	25·58
29	16·54	·01	2·19	0·14	18·58	30	24·09	·00	2·19	+ 0·11	26·17
Aug. 1	15·75	·00	2·19	0·06	17·88	Aug. 4	23·89	·01	2·16	- 0·01	26·05
3	17·13	·00	2·17	+ 0·02	19·28	11	24·98	·02	2·15	0·11	27·22
5	16·04	·01	2·17	- 0·02	18·22	13	23·94	·01	2·21	0·12	26·26
14	16·44	·00	2·19	0·13	18·76	19	24·34	·01	2·18	0·14	26·65
22	16·44	·01	2 16	- 0·12	18·71	23	22·56	·01	2·17	- 0·11	24·83
					2· 7·17·77						2· 7·26·54

Error of Collimation . . . = 0· 0· 4·39
Resulting Mean Zenith Distance, North = 2· 7·22·15

Mean Zenith Distances of Stars observed at the Royal Observatory.

	FACE OF SECTOR EAST.						FACE OF SECTOR WEST.				
Day of Observation 1848.	Apparent Zenith Distance, from Unreduced Observation.	Reduction for Az. Error, and Curv. of Path.	Refraction.	Precession, Aberration, and Nutation.	Deduced Mean Zenith Distance. 1848, Jan. 0; and Mean of Separate Results, uncorrected, for Error of Collimation	Day of Observation 1848.	Apparent Zenith Distance, from Unreduced Observation.	Reduction for Az. Error, and Curv. of Path.	Refraction.	Precession, Aberration, and Nutation.	Deduced Mean Zenith Distance. 1848, Jan. 0; and Mean of Separate Results, uncorrected, for Error of Collimation

B.A.C. 5632.

June 4	0· 4·42·12	·00	0·08	+ 3·63	0· 4·45·83	June 3	0· 4·28·49	·00	0·08	+ 3·71	0· 4·32·28
18	39·95	·00	·08	2·54	42·57	17	30·37	·00	·08	2·61	33·06
23	40·09	·00	·06	2·16	42·93	July 20	32·69	·00	·08	0·47	33·24
July 21	41·43	·00	·08	0·42	41·93	22	32·44	·00	·08	0·37	32·89
23	40·89	·00	·08	0·39	41·30	24	33·73	·00	·08	0·28	34·09
25	41·73	·00	·08	0·24	42·05	26	33·04	·00	·08	0·19	33·31
29	41·28	·00	·08	+ 0·07	41·43	30	33·43	00	·08	+ 0·04	33·55
Aug. 1	42·12	·00	·08	- 0·04	42·16	Aug. 2	34·42	·00	·08	- 0·07	34·48
3	41·14	·00	·08	0·10	41·12	4	34·02	·00	·06	0·13	33·97
5	41·58	·00	·08	0·16	41·50	11	32·84	·00	·08	0·30	32·02
12	42·42	·00	·08	0·32	42·18	13	34·81	·00	·08	0·33	34·56
14	41·53	·00	·08	0·35	41·26	19	34·32	·00	·08	0·40	34·00
22	41·93	·00	·08	0·40	41·61	23	34·81	·00	·08	0·40	34·49
25	40·69	·00	·08	0·39	40·38	27	34·81	·00	0·08	- 0·38	34·51
28	41·09	·00	0·08	- 0·37	40·80						
					0· 4·41·94						0· 4·33·64

Error of Collimation . . = 0· 0· 4·15
Resulting Mean Zenith Distance, South = 0· 4·37·79

B.A.C. 5735.

June 4	0· 1·49·93	·00	0·03	+ 5·01	0· 1·44·95	June 3	0· 1·63·27	·00	0·03	+ 5·08	0· 1·58·22
18	52·01	·00	·03	3·95	48·09	17	60·99	·00	·03	4·03	56·99
23	51·12	·00	·03	3·59	47·56	July 20	58·53	·00	·03	1·84	56·72
July 21	49·39	·00	·08	1·78	47·64	22	57·54	·00	·03	1·73	55·84
23	49·83	·00	·03	1·68	48·18	24	57·64	·00	·03	1·03	56·04
25	50·57	·00	·03	1·58	49·02	26	57 64	·00	·03	1·53	56·14
29	50·77	·00	·03	1·39	49·41	30	57·14	·00	·03	1·35	55·82
Aug. 1	50·67	·00	·03	1·26	49·44	Aug. 2	57·04	·00	·03	1·22	55·85
3	50·03	·00	·03	1·18	48·88	4	57·64	·00	·03	1·15	56·52
5	49·54	·00	·03	1·11	48·46	11	56·45	·00	·03	0·92	55·56
12	50·43	·00	·03	0·90	49·56	13	55·86	·00	·03	0·87	55·02
14	49·83	·00	·03	0·85	49·01	19	57·04	·00	·03	0·76	56·31
22	49·29	·00	·03	0·73	48·59	23	55·76	·00	·03	0·72	55·07
27	50·13	·00	·03	0·70	49·46	26	55·27	·00	0·03	+ 0·70	54·60
28	50·57	·00	0·03	+ 0·70	49·90						
					0· 1·48·54						0· 1·56 05

Error of Collimation . . = 0· 0· 3·75
Resulting Mean Zenith Distance, North = 0· 1·52·30

B.A.C. 5817.

June 18	1·26·55·07	·00	1·47	+ 5·22	1·26·51·32	June 17	1·27· 6·62	+ ·10	1·47	+ 5·29	1·26·62·90
23	55·27	·00	1·48	4·90	51·85	July 20	2·77	- ·00	1·49	3·30	60·96
July 21	53·29	·00	1·49	3·25	51·53	22	3·46	·00	1·48	3·20	61·74
23	53·29	·00	1·49	3·15	51·63	24	2·57	·00	1·48	3·10	60·95

Carried forward,

B.A.C. 5817.—June 17.—Correction for Curvature of Path = + 0″·10.

Mean Zenith Distances of Stars observed at the Royal Observatory.

FACE OF SECTOR EAST. · FACE OF SECTOR WEST.

Day of Observation 1848	Apparent Zenith Distance, from Unreduced Observation.	Reduction for Az. Error, and Curv. of Path.	Refraction.	Precession, Aberration, and Nutation.	Deduced Mean Zenith Distance, 1848, Jan. 0; and Mean of Separate Results, uncorrected, for Error of Collimation.	Day of Observation 1848.	Apparent Zenith Distance, from Unreduced Observation.	Reduction for Az. Error, and Curv. of Path.	Refraction.	Precession, Aberration, and Nutation.	Deduced Mean Zenith Distance, 1848, Jan. 0; and Mean of Separate Results, uncorrected, for Error of Collimation.

B.A.C. 5817—(continued.)

Day	App. Z.D.	Red.	Refr.	Prec.	Mean	Day	App. Z.D.	Red.	Refr.	Prec.	Mean
July 25	1·26·53·78	·01	1·49	3·05	1·26·52·21	July 26	1·27· 2·28	·00	1·48	3·00	1·26·60·76
29	53·88	·00	1·50	2·87	52·51	Aug. 4	2·72	·01	1·48	2·62	61·57
Aug. 1	53·68	·00	1·49	2·74	52·43	11	1·49	·01	1·47	2·38	60·57
3	53·98	·00	1·48	2·66	52·80	13	1·78	·01	1·51	2·33	60·95
5	53·59	·00	1·48	2·58	52·49	19	1·44	·01	1·50	2·19	60·74
14	52·65	·00	1·50	2·30	51·85	23	0·60	·01	1·48	2·13	59·94
22	53·49	·01	1·48	2·14	52·62	26	0·25	·01	1·47	+ 2·09	59·62
25	54·38	·01	1·48	2·10	53·75						
27	54·18	·01	1·49	+ 2·09	53·57						

1·26·52·37   1·27· 0·97

Error of Collimation . . . = 0· 0· 4·30
Resulting Mean Zenith Distance, North = 1·26·56·67

B.A.C. 5881.

Day	App. Z.D.	Red.	Refr.	Prec.	Mean	Day	App. Z.D.	Red.	Refr.	Prec.	Mean
June 18	4·12·34·61	·00	4·28	+ 6·31	4·12·32·58	June 17	4·12·46·32	·00	4·26	+ 6·36	4·12·44·22
23	34·02	·00	4·31	6·08	32·25	July 20	42·91	·00	4·24	4·85	42·30
July 21	33·38	·01	4·32	4·80	32·89	22	42·56	·01	4·30	4·76	42·09
23	34·31	·01	4·33	4·72	33·91	24	41·52	·01	4·31	4·68	41·14
25	33·43	·02	4·32	4·64	33·09	26	41·83	·00	4·30	4·60	41·03
29	34·41	·01	4·35	4·49	34·26	30	42·91	·01	4·35	4·45	42·80
Aug. 1	33·43	·00	4·35	4·36	33·40	Aug. 2	41·52	·00	4·30	4·35	41·47
3	34·02	·00	4·31	4·31	34·02	4	41·82	·02	4·30	4·28	41·82
5	33·77	·01	4·32	4·25	33·83	11	42·71	·04	4·29	4·08	42·88
12	34·02	·00	4·32	4·05	34·29	13	41·43	·01	4·40	4·03	41·79
14	34·02	·01	4·34	4·00	34·35	19	40·98	·03	4·35	3·90	41·40
22	33·43	·02	4·29	+ 3 8˙	33·85	23	41·43	·03	4·32	+ 3·88	41·89

4·12·33·56   4·12·42·07

Error of Collimation . . . = 0· 0· 4·25
Resulting Mean Zenith Distance, North = 4·12·37·81

B.A.C. 5915.

Day	App. Z.D.	Red.	Refr.	Prec.	Mean	Day	App. Z.D.	Red.	Refr.	Prec.	Mean
Aug. 5	3· 3· 3·85	·01	3·13	+ 2·74	3· 3· 9·71	Aug. 4	3· 2·57·72	·02	3·11	+ 2·81	3· 3· 3·62
12	3·85	·00	3·12	2·36	9·33	11	56·83	·03	3·11	2·41	2·32
14	4·44	·01	3·14	2·26	9·83	13	57·82	·01	3·18	2·31	3·30
22	5·53	·01	3·11	1·93	10·56	19	58·81	·02	3·15	2·04	3·98
25	5·23	·01	3·11	1·84	10·17	23	58·91	·02	3·13	1·90	3·92
28	4·79	·01	3·10	1·76	9·64	26	59·80	·02	3·10	1·81	4·69
30	5·53	·01	3·11	1·72	10·35	29	60·64	·01	3·09	1·74	5·46
Sept. 2	5·62	·01	3·07	+ 1·67	10·35	31	60·29	·02	3·08	+ 1·70	5·05

3· 3· 9·99   3· 3· 4·04

Error of Collimation . . . = 0· 0· 2·98
Resulting Mean Zenith Distance, South = 3· 3· 7·02

Mean Zenith Distances of Stars observed at the Royal Observatory.

FACE OF SECTOR EAST.

Day of Observation 1848.	Apparent Zenith Distance, from Unreduced Observation.	Reduction for Az. Error, and Curr. of Path.	Refraction.	Precession, Aberration, and Nutation.	Deduced Mean Zenith Distance, 1848, Jan. 0; and Mean of Separate Results, uncorrected, for Error of Collimation.
					B.A.C. 5970.
	° ′ ″	″	″	″	° ′ ″
Aug. 5	5· 0·31·41	·02	5·14	+ 4·73	5· 0·41·26
14	31·66	·01	5·17	4·35	41·17
22	33·48	·02	5·11	4·10	42·67
25	31·21	·02	5·11	4·02	40·32
27	31·76	·02	5·15	3·97	40·86
28	32·30	·02	5·10	3·95	41·33
30	32·64	·02	5·12	3·92	41·66
Sept. 2	31·61	·01	5·05	+ 3·87	40·52
					5· 0·41·22

Error of Collimation . . = 0· 0· 2·57
Resulting Mean Zenith Distance, South = 5· 0·38·65

Day of Observation 1848.	Apparent Zenith Distance, from Unreduced Observation.	Reduction for Az. Error, and Curr. of Path.	Refraction.	Precession, Aberration, and Nutation.	Deduced Mean Zenith Distance, 1848, Jan. 0; and Mean of Separate Results, uncorrected, for Error of Collimation.
					B.A.C. 6016.
June 18	2·17·22·81	·00	2·33	+ 8·18	2·17·16·96
23	21·28	·00	2·34	7·91	15·71
July 21	20·39	·00	2·35	6·39	16·41
23	21·57	·01	2·35	6·22	17·09
25	20·98	·01	2·35	6·11	17·21
29	20·98	·01	2·36	5·90	17·43
Aug. 1	20·29	·00	2·36	5·75	16·90
3	20·59	·00	2·34	5·65	17·28
5	20·68	·01	2·35	5·56	17·46
22	20·09	·01	2·33	4·89	17·52
24	20·88	·00	2·32	+ 4·82	18·38
					2·17·17·18

Error of Collimation . . = 0· 0· 4·32
Resulting Mean Zenith Distance, North = 2·17·21·50

Day of Observation 1848.	Apparent Zenith Distance, from Unreduced Observation.	Reduction for Az. Error, and Curr. of Path.	Refraction.	Precession, Aberration, and Nutation.	Deduced Mean Zenith Distance, 1848, Jan. 0; and Mean of Separate Results, uncorrected, for Error of Collimation.
					B.A.C. 6074.
June 18	3·42·10·28	·00	3·77	+ 9·06	3·42· 4·99
23	9·59	·00	3·78	8·84	4·53
July 21	7·66	·01	3·80	7·48	3·97
23	8·90	·01	3·80	7·38	5·31
25	8·40	·02	3·80	7·28	4·90
29	9·54	·01	3·82	7·09	6·26
Aug. 1	8·90	·00	3·82	6·95	5·77
3	9·39	·00	3·79	6·86	6·32
5	8·99	·01	3·80	6·76	6·02
14	9·19	·01	3·82	6·38	6·62
22	8·60	·01	3·77	6·10	6·26
24	9·09	·01	3·75	+ 6·03	6·80
					3·42· 5·65

Error of Collimation . . = 0· 0· 3·74
Resulting Mean Zenith Distance, North = 3·42· 0·39

FACE OF SECTOR WEST.

Day of Observation 1848.	Apparent Zenith Distance, from Unreduced Observation.	Reduction for Az. Error, and Curr. of Path.	Refraction.	Precession, Aberration, and Nutation.	Deduced Mean Zenith Distance, 1848, Jan. 0; and Mean of Separate Results, uncorrected, for Error of Collimation.
					B.A.C. 5970.
	° ′ ″	″	″	″	° ′ ″
Aug. 4	5· 0·24·66	·03	5·12	+ 4·77	5· 0·34·52
11	25·73	·05	5·11	4·47	35·26
13	25·48	·02	5·23	4·39	35·08
19	25·68	·04	5·18	4·18	35·00
23	27·06	·05	5·14	4·07	36·22
26	28·94	·04	5·10	3·99	37·99
29	28·45	·02	5·09	3·93	37·45
31	28·15	·03	5·07	+ 3·90	37·09
					5· 0·36·08

Day of Observation 1848.	Apparent Zenith Distance, from Unreduced Observation.	Reduction for Az. Error, and Curr. of Path.	Refraction.	Precession, Aberration, and Nutation.	Deduced Mean Zenith Distance, 1848, Jan. 0; and Mean of Separate Results, uncorrected, for Error of Collimation.
					B.A.C. 6016.
June 17	2·17·32·90	·00	2·32	+ 8·23	2·17·26·99
July 20	31·15	·00	2·36	6·39	27·12
22	29·77	·00	2·34	6·28	25·83
24	29·18	·01	2·34	6·17	25·34
26	28·98	·00	2·34	6·06	25·26
30	29·38	·01	2·36	5·85	25·88
Aug. 2	28·68	·00	2·33	5·70	25·31
4	28·39	·01	2·34	5·60	25·12
11	28·78	·02	2·33	5·29	25·80
13	28·59	·01	2·39	5·21	25·76
23	28·09	·01	2·35	+ 4·85	25·58
					2·17·25·82

Day of Observation 1848.	Apparent Zenith Distance, from Unreduced Observation.	Reduction for Az. Error, and Curr. of Path.	Refraction.	Precession, Aberration, and Nutation.	Deduced Mean Zenith Distance, 1848, Jan. 0; and Mean of Separate Results, uncorrected, for Error of Collimation.
					B.A.C. 6074.
June 17	3·42·20·25	·00	3·75	+ 9·10	3·42·14·90
July 20	17·34	·00	3·82	7·53	13·63
22	17·09	·01	3·78	7·43	13·43
24	16·20	·01	3·79	7·33	12·65
26	16·11	·00	3·78	7·24	12·65
30	15·96	·01	3·82	7·04	12·73
Aug. 4	15·46	·02	3·78	6·81	12·41
11	16·00	·03	3·77	6·51	13·83
13	15·27	·01	3·87	6·42	12·71
19	14·87	·03	3·84	6·20	12·48
23	15·32	·02	3·80	+ 6·06	13·04
					3·42·13·13

B.A.C. 5970.—Aug. 23.—Correction for Curvature of Path = - 0″·02.

Mean Zenith Distances of Stars observed at the Royal Observatory.

FACE OF SECTOR EAST.

FACE OF SECTOR WEST.

B.A.C. 6115.

Day of Observation 1848.	Apparent Zenith Distance, from Unreduced Observation.	Reduction for Az. Error, and Curv. of Path.	Refraction.	Precession, Aberration, and Nutation.	Deduced Mean Zenith Distance, 1848, Jan. 0; and Mean of Separate Results, uncorrected, for Error of Collimation.	Day of Observation 1848.	Apparent Zenith Distance, from Unreduced Observation.	Reduction for Az. Error, and Curv. of Path.	Refraction.	Precession, Aberration, and Nutation.	Deduced Mean Zenith Distance, 1848, Jan. 0; and Mean of Separate Results, uncorrected, for Error of Collimation.
June 18	3 30 53·44	·00	3·57	+ 9·63	3 30 47·38	June 17	3 30 62·97	·00	3·56	+ 9·67	3 30 56·86
23	52·74	·00	3·59	9·41	46·92	July 20	59·86	·00	3·62	8·09	55·39
July 21	51·21	·00	3·61	8·03	46·79	22	60·25	·01	3·59	7·98	55·85
23	52·94	·01	3·61	7·93	48·61	24	59·36	·01	3·60	7·88	55·07
25	52·35	·02	3·61	7·83	48·11	26	58·82	·00	3·59	7·78	54·63
29	53·34	·01	3·63	7·62	49·34	30	58·87	·01	3·63	7·57	54·92
Aug. 1	51·95	·00	3·63	7·48	48·10	Aug. 2	58·77	·00	3·59	7·43	54·93
3	52·35	·00	3·60	7·38	48·57	4	58·42	·02	3·59	7·33	54·66
5	51·95	·01	3·60	7·28	48·26	11	58·77	·03	3·58	7·00	55·32
14	52·94	·01	3·62	6·87	49·68	13	57·78	·01	3·67	6·91	54·53
22	52·05	·01	3·59	6·56	49·07	19	57·83	·02	3·64	6·67	54·78
24	53·14	·01	3·56	+ 6·48	50·21	23	57·29	·02	3·61	+ 6·52	54·36
					3 30 48·42						3 30 55·11

Error of Collimation . . . = 0· 0· 3·84
Resulting Mean Zenith Distance, North = 3 30 51·76

B.A.C. 6145.

Day of Observation 1848.	Apparent Zenith Distance, from Unreduced Observation.	Reduction for Az. Error, and Curv. of Path.	Refraction.	Precession, Aberration, and Nutation.	Deduced Mean Zenith Distance, 1848, Jan. 0; and Mean of Separate Results, uncorrected, for Error of Collimation.	Day of Observation 1848.	Apparent Zenith Distance, from Unreduced Observation.	Reduction for Az. Error, and Curv. of Path.	Refraction.	Precession, Aberration, and Nutation.	Deduced Mean Zenith Distance, 1848, Jan. 0; and Mean of Separate Results, uncorrected, for Error of Collimation.
June 18	3 11 17·34	·00	3·24	+ 9·99	3 11 10·59	June 17	3 11 27·51	·00	3·23	+10·03	3 11 20·71
23	15·76	·00	3·26	9·77	9·25	July 20	25·09	·00	3·28	8·40	19·97
July 21	16·25	·00	3·27	8·35	11·17	22	24·25	·01	3·25	8·29	19·20
23	16·10	·01	3·27	8·25	11·12	24	23·86	·01	3·26	8·18	18·93
25	16·75	·00	3·27	8·13	11·89	26	23·36	·00	3·25	8·08	18·53
29	15·96	·01	3·29	7·92	11·32	30	23·16	·01	3·29	7·87	18·57
Aug. 1	15·31	·00	3·29	7·76	10·84	Aug. 4	22·47	·02	3·26	7·61	18·10
3	15·86	·00	3·28	7·66	11·46	11	22·57	·03	3·25	7·25	18·54
5	15·96	·01	3·27	7·56	11·66	13	22·28	·01	3·33	7·17	18·43
14	15·96	·01	3·29	7·12	12·12	19	21·63	·02	3·30	6·90	18·01
22	15·36	·01	3·25	6·78	11·82	23	22·62	·02	3·27	+ 6·74	19·13
24	15·76	·01	3·23	+ 6·71	12·27						
					3 11 11·20						3 11 18·92

Error of Collimation . . . = 0· 0· 3·81
Resulting Mean Zenith Distance, North = 3 11 15·11

B.A.C. 6186.

Day of Observation 1848.	Apparent Zenith Distance, from Unreduced Observation.	Reduction for Az. Error, and Curv. of Path.	Refraction.	Precession, Aberration, and Nutation.	Deduced Mean Zenith Distance, 1848, Jan. 0; and Mean of Separate Results, uncorrected, for Error of Collimation.	Day of Observation 1848.	Apparent Zenith Distance, from Unreduced Observation.	Reduction for Az. Error, and Curv. of Path.	Refraction.	Precession, Aberration, and Nutation.	Deduced Mean Zenith Distance, 1848, Jan. 0; and Mean of Separate Results, uncorrected, for Error of Collimation.
Aug. 5	2 51 52·15	·01	2·94	+ 6·73	2 52 1·81	Aug. 4	2 51 45·62	·02	2·92	+ 6·81	2 51 55·33
14	52·50	·00	2·95	6·06	1·51	11	46·52	·03	2·92	6·27	55·68
22	54·47	·01	2·92	5·53	2·91	13	46·97	·01	2·90	6·13	56·08
24	53·04	·00	2·90	5·41	1·35	19	48·35	·02	2·97	5·72	57·02
25	53·34	·01	2·92	5·35	1·60	23	47·71	·02	2·94	5·47	56·10
27	52·50	·01	2·94	5·24	0·67	26	49·24	·02	2·91	5·29	57·42
28	53·14	·01	2·92	5·19	1·24	29	49·64	·01	2·90	5·14	57·67
30	53·59	·01	2·92	+ 5·08	1·58	31	49·49	·02	2·89	+ 5·04	57·40
					2 52 1·58						2 51 56·59

Error of Collimation . . . = 0· 0· 2·50
Resulting Mean Zenith Distance, South = 2 51 59·09

B.A.C. 6145.—July 25.—Correction for Curvature of Path = + 0″·02.

Mean Zenith Distances of Stars observed at the Royal Observatory.

FACE OF SECTOR EAST.						FACE OF SECTOR WEST.					
Day of Observation 1848.	Apparent Zenith Distance, from Unreduced Observation.	Reduction for Az. Error, and Curv. of Path.	Refraction.	Precession, Aberration, and Nutation.	Deduced Mean Zenith Distance, 1848, Jan. 0; and Mean of Separate Results, uncorrected, for Error of Collimation.	Day of Observation 1848.	Apparent Zenith Distance, from Unreduced Observation.	Reduction for Az. Error, and Curv. of Path.	Refraction.	Precession, Aberration, and Nutation.	Deduced Mean Zenith Distance, 1848, Jan. 0; and Mean of Separate Results, uncorrected, for Error of Collimation.

B.A.C. 6233.

	° ′ ″	″	″	″	° ′ ″		° ′ ″	″	″	″	° ′ ″
June 18	0 30 49 53	·00	0 52	+11 24	0 30 61 29	June 17	0 30 37 43	·00	0 52	+11 30	0 30 49 25
23	49 53	·00	·52	10 94	60 99	July 20	41 73	·00	·53	9 04	51 30
July 21	51 95	·00	·53	8 96	61 44	22	41 34	·00	·52	8 89	50 75
23	50 77	·00	·53	8 81	60 11	24	41 88	·00	·52	8 74	51 14
25	51 76	·00	·53	8 67	60 96	26	42 77	·00	·52	8 59	51 88
29	51 81	·00	·53	8 37	60 71	30	43 16	·00	·53	8 30	51 99
Aug. 1	51 90	·00	·53	8 15	60 58	Aug. 2	44 25	·00	·52	8 08	52 85
3	51 46	·00	·53	8 01	60 00	4	43 85	·00	·52	7 93	52 30
5	52 15	·00	·53	7 86	60 54	11	44 15	·00	·52	7 45	52 12
14	52 79	·00	·53	7 25	60 57	13	44 64	·00	·54	7 31	52 49
22	54 27	·00	·52	6 76	61 55	19	44 74	·00	·53	6 93	52 20
24	52 55	·00	·52	6 64	59 71	23	45 63	·00	·53	6 70	52 86
25	52 74	·00	·52	6 59	59 85	26	46 82	·00	·52	6 53	53 87
27	52 20	·00	·53	6 48	59 21	29	47 11	·00	·52	6 38	54 01
28	53 04	·00	·52	6 43	59 99	31	47 82	·00	0 52	+ 6 29	54 63
30	53 83	00	0 52	+ 6 33	60 68						
					0 31 0 51						0 30 52 24

Error of Collimation . . . = 0 0 4 13
Resulting Mean Zenith Distance, South = 0 30 56 38

B.A.C. 6285.

June 18	0 51 7 76	·00	0 87	+11 78	0 50 56 85	June 17	0 51 20 10	·00	0 86	+11 83	0 51 9 13
23	7 76	·00	·87	11 52	57 11	July 20	17 34	·00	·88	9 86	8 36
July 21	6 28	·00	·88	9 79	57 37	22	15 95	·00	·87	9 72	7 10
23	6 87	·00	·88	9 65	58 10	24	16 00	·00	·87	9 58	7 29
25	6 28	·01	·87	9 52	57 62	26	15 66	·00	·87	9 45	7 06
Aug. 1	7 11	·00	·88	9 04	58 95	30	16 25	·00	·88	9 17	7 96
3	7 16	·00	·87	8 90	59 13	Aug. 2	15 16	·00	·87	8 97	7 06
5	6 77	·00	·87	8 77	58 87	4	15 07	·00	·87	8 83	7 11
14	6 18	·00	·88	8 18	58 88	11	15 56	·01	·87	8 37	8 05
22	5 19	·00	·87	7 70	58 36	13	14 97	·00	·89	8 24	7 62
24	6 37	·00	·86	7 59	59 04	19	14 37	·01	·88	7 88	7 36
25	5 73	·00	0 87	+ 7 54	59 06	23	13 78	·01	0 87	+ 7 65	6 99
					0 50 58 33						0 51 7 59

Error of Collimation . . . = 0 0 4 63
Resulting Mean Zenith Distance, North = 0 51 2 96

B.A.C. 6305.

June 18	0 48 47 31	·00	0 83	+12 01	0 48 36 13	June 17	0 48 58 66	·00	0 82	+12 06	0 48 47 42
23	46 56	·00	·83	11 77	35 62	July 20	55 65	·00	·84	10 10	46 39
July 21	45 33	·00	·84	10 03	36 14	22	54 96	·00	·83	9 97	45 82
23	46 07	·00	·84	9 90	37 01	24	54 71	·00	·83	9 83	45 71
25	44 89	·00	·83	9 76	35 96	26	55 11	·00	·83	9 69	46 25

Carried forward,

Mean Zenith Distances of Stars observed at the Royal Observatory.

B.A.C. 6305—(continued).

FACE OF SECTOR EAST						FACE OF SECTOR WEST					
Day of Observation 1848.	Apparent Zenith Distance, from Unreduced Observation.	Reduction for Az. Error, and Curv. of Path.	Refraction.	Precession, Aberration, and Nutation.	Deduced Mean Zenith Distance, 1848, Jan. 0; and Mean of Separate Results, uncorrected, for Error of Collimation.	Day of Observation 1848.	Apparent Zenith Distance, from Unreduced Observation.	Reduction for Az. Error, and Curv. of Path.	Refraction.	Precession, Aberration, and Nutation.	Deduced Mean Zenith Distance, 1848, Jan. 0; and Mean of Separate Results, uncorrected, for Error of Collimation.
July 29	0·48·45·53	·00	·84	9·48	0·48·36·89	July 30	0·48·54·32	·00	·84	9·41	0·48·45·75
Aug. 1	45·83	·00	·84	9·28	36·89	Aug. 2	53·13	·00	·83	9·21	44·75
3	45·72	·00	·83	9·14	37·41	4	53·28	·00	·83	9·07	45·04
5	45·13	·00	·83	9·00	36·96	11	54·32	·01	·83	8·60	46·54
14	44·79	·00	·84	8·41	37·22	13	53·53	·00	·85	8·47	45·91
22	43·85	·00	·83	7·92	36·76	19	52·84	·01	·84	8·09	45·58
24	44·59	·00	·82	7·80	37·61	23	51·55	·01	0·83	+ 7·86	44·51
25	43·95	·00	0·83	+ 7·75	37·03						
					0·48·36·74						0·48·45·81

Error of Collimation . . . = 0· 0· 4·53
Resulting Mean Zenith Distance, North = 0·48·41·27

B.A.C. 6414.

FACE OF SECTOR EAST						FACE OF SECTOR WEST					
Day of Observation	Apparent Zenith Distance	Reduction for Az. Error, etc.	Refraction	Precession, etc.	Deduced Mean	Day of Observation	Apparent Zenith Distance	Reduction for Az. Error, etc.	Refraction	Precession, etc.	Deduced Mean
July 21	3· 1·34·13	·00	3·11	+11·92	3· 1·25·32	July 20	3· 1·44·01	- ·00	3·12	+11·98	3· 1·35·15
23	36·15	·01	3·11	11·81	27·44	24	43·31	·01	3·10	11·75	34·65
25	36·80	·02	3·11	11·09	28·20	26	43·81	- ·00	3·08	11·63	35·26
29	36·30	·01	3·12	11·45	27·96	30	42·43	+ ·15	3·12	11·39	34·31
Aug. 1	35·51	·00	3·11	11·27	27·35	Aug. 2	42·92	- ·00	3·09	11·21	34·80
3	36·00	·00	3·10	11·15	27·95	4	42·82	·02	3·11	11·09	34·82
5	36·10	·01	3·10	11·02	28·17	11	42·97	·02	3·08	10·65	35·38
14	35·81	·00	3·12	10·97	28·46	13	42·23	·01	3·16	10·53	34·85
22	34·72	·01	3·09	9·99	27·81	19	41·19	·02	3·14	10·16	34·15
24	36·60	·00	3·07	+ 9·87	29·80	23	41·88	·02	3·10	9·93	35·03
						25	41·39	- ·02	3·09	+ 9·81	34·65
					3· 1·27·85						3· 1·34·82

Error of Collimation . . . = 0· 0· 3·49
Resulting Mean Zenith Distance, North = 3· 1·31·33

B.A.C. 6489.

FACE OF SECTOR EAST						FACE OF SECTOR WEST					
Day of Observation	Apparent Zenith Distance	Reduction for Az. Error, etc.	Refraction	Precession, etc.	Deduced Mean	Day of Observation	Apparent Zenith Distance	Reduction for Az. Error, etc.	Refraction	Precession, etc.	Deduced Mean
July 21	3·50·36·74	·01	3·96	+12·82	3·50·27·87	July 20	3·50·45·93	·00	3·97	+12·87	3·50·37·03
23	36·64	·01	3·96	12·71	27·88	22	46·03	·01	3·92	12·77	37·17
25	37·14	·02	3·95	12·61	28·46	24	45·43	·01	3·93	12·66	36·69
29	38·67	·01	3·97	12·38	30·25	26	45·53	·00	3·92	12·55	36·90
Aug. 1	37·53	·00	3·95	12·21	29·27	30	44·64	·01	3·97	12·32	36·28
3	38·18	·00	3·94	12·09	30·03	Aug. 4	45·19	·02	3·96	12·03	37·10
5	37·29	·01	3·94	11·97	29·25	11	44·25	·03	3·92	11·61	36·53
14	37·93	·01	3·97	11·43	30·46	13	44·69	·01	4·02	11·49	37·21
22	36·45	·01	3·93	10·95	29·42	19	43·16	·03	3·99	11·13	35·99
24	37·63	·01	3·90	10·83	30·69	23	42·92	·02	3·95	10·89	35·96
26	36·99	·01	3·91	+10·71	30·18	25	41·78	·03	3·93	+10·77	34·91
					3·50·29·43						3·50·36·53

Error of Collimation . . . = 0· 0· 3·55
Resulting Mean Zenith Distance, North = 3·50·32·98

B.A.C 6414—July 30.—Correction for Curvature of Path = + 0″·16.

Mean Zenith Distances of Stars observed at the Royal Observatory.

FACE OF SECTOR EAST.						FACE OF SECTOR WEST.					
Day of Observation 1848.	Apparent Zenith Distance, from Unreduced Observation.	Reduction for Az. Error, and Curr. of Path.	Refraction.	Precession, Aberration, and Nutation.	Deduced Mean Zenith Distance. 1848, Jan. 0; and Mean of Separate Results, uncorrected. for Error of Collimation.	Day of Observation 1848.	Apparent Zenith Distance, from Unreduced Observation.	Reduction for Az. Error, and Curr. of Path.	Refraction.	Precession, Aberration, and Nutation.	Deduced Mean Zenith Distance, 1848, Jan. 0; and Mean of Separate Results, uncorrected, for Error of Collimation.

B.A.C. 6525.

Day	Z.D.	Red.	Refr.	Prec.	Deduced	Day	Z.D.	Red.	Refr.	Prec.	Deduced
July 21	5· 4·10·12	·01	5·23	+13·33	5· 4· 2·01	July 20	5· 4·16·79	·00	5·24	+13·38	5· 4· 8·65
23	10·96	·01	5·22	13·24	2·93	22	17·33	·01	5·18	13·29	9·21
25	10·12	·03	5·21	13·15	2·15	24	17·04	·01	5·19	13·19	9·03
29	10·61	·02	5·23	12·95	2·87	26	14·96	·00	5·17	13·10	7·03
Aug. 1	9·73	·00	5·21	12·79	2·15	30	16·05	·01	5·24	12·90	8·38
3	12·10	·00	5·20	12·69	(4·61)	Aug. 2	15·31	·00	5·19	12·74	7·76
5	10·61	·01	5·21	12·58	3·23	4	15·65	·03	5·22	12·63	8·21
14	10·37	·01	5·24	12·08	3·52	11	15·75	·04	5·17	12·25	8·63
22	9·63	·02	5·19	11·63	3·17	13	14·96	·02	5·30	12·14	8·10
24	9·43	·01	5·15	11·52	3·05	23	15·75	·03	5·22	11·57	9·37
26	10·52	·02	5·16	+11·41	4·25	25	14·67	·04	5·19	+11·46	8·36
					5· 4· 2·93						5· 4· 8·43

Error of Collimation . . = 0· 0· 2·75
Resulting Mean Zenith Distance, North = 5· 4· 5·68

B.A.C. 6639.

Day	Z.D.	Red.	Refr.	Prec.	Deduced	Day	Z.D.	Red.	Refr.	Prec.	Deduced
July 21	3 53·50·37	·00	4·03	+14·69	3·53·39·71	July 20	3·53·59·70	·00	4·02	+14·74	3·53·48·98
23	51·75	·01	4·01	14·58	41·17	22	58·37	·01	3·98	14·64	47·70
25	50·86	·02	4·00	14·48	40·36	24	58·17	·01	3·99	14·53	47·62
29	52·34	·01	4·02	14·25	42·10	26	58·86	·00	3·97	14·42	48·41
Aug. 1	50·71	·00	4·00	14·08	40·63	30	57·87	·01	4·03	14·20	47·69
3	51·06	·00	4·00	13·96	41·10	Aug. 4	57·97	·02	4·01	13·90	48·06
5	51·11	·01	4·02	13·83	41·29	11	57·18	·03	3·96	13·45	47·66
14	51·06	·01	4·02	13·25	41·82	19	56·39	·03	4·04	12·92	47·48
22	50·42	·02	4·00	12·72	41·68	23	56·29	·02	4·01	12·65	47·63
26	51·01	·01	3·96	+12·45	42·51	25	56·20	·03	3·99	+12·32	47·64
					3·53·41·24						3·53·47·89

Error of Collimation . . = 0· 0· 3·33
Resulting Mean Zenith Distance, North = 3·53·44·56

Anon. A.R. 19·21.

Day	Z.D.	Red.	Refr.	Prec.	Deduced	Day	Z.D.	Red.	Refr.	Prec.	Deduced
July 21	4· 7·51·30	·01	4·27	+15·02	4· 7·40·54	July 20	4· 8· 2·97	·00	4·26	+15·07	4· 7·52·16
23	54·76	·01	4·25	14·92	44·08	22	1·38	·01	4·22	14·97	50·62
25	52·59	·02	4·24	14·82	41·99	24	1·43	·01	4·23	14·87	50·78
29	53·62	·01	4·26	14·60	43·27	26	3·75	·00	4·21	14·76	53·20
Aug. 1	52·78	·00	4·24	14·43	42·59	30	1·08	·01	4·27	14·54	50·80
3	54·36	·00	4·24	14·31	44·29	Aug. 4	3·16	·02	4·25	14·25	53·14
5	54·36	·01	4·26	14·19	44·42	11	3·16	·03	4·19	13·81	53·51
14	54·07	·01	4·27	13·61	44·72	13	1·48	·01	4·32	13·58	52·11
22	52·19	02	4·24	13·08	43·33	19	4· 7·59·20	·01	4·29	13·28	50·20
30	52·59	·01	4·22	+12·54	44·26	23	59·00	·03	4·25	13·01	50·81
						31	56·19	·02	4·19	+12·47	47·89
					4· 7·43·35						4· 7·51·38

Error of Collimation . . = 0· 0· 4·02
Resulting Mean Zenith Distance, North = 4· 7·47·37

Anon. A.R. 19ʰ 21ᵐ.—Aug. 19.—Correction for Curvature of Path = + 0″·02.

Mean Zenith Distances of Stars observed at the Royal Observatory.

FACE OF SECTOR EAST.						FACE OF SECTOR WEST.					
Day of Observation 1846.	Apparent Zenith Distance, from Unreduced Observation.	Reduction for Az. Error, and Curv. of Path.	Refraction.	Precession, Aberration, and Nutation.	Deduced Mean Zenith Distance, 1846, Jan. 0; and Mean of Separate Results, uncorrected, for Error of Collimation.	Day of Observation 1846.	Apparent Zenith Distance, from Unreduced Observation.	Reduction for Az. Error, and Curv. of Path.	Refraction.	Precession, Aberration, and Nutation.	Deduced Mean Zenith Distance, 1846, Jan. 0; and Mean of Separate Results, uncorrected, for Error of Collimation.

B.A.C. 6753.

	° ′ ″	″	″	″	° ′ ″		° ′ ″	″	″	″	° ′ ″
July 21	2 40 26·96	·00	2·76	+15·95	2 40 13·77	July 20	2 40 36·50	·00	2·76	+16·00	2 40 23·26
23	28·35	·01	2·75	15·84	15·25	24	35·90	·01	2·74	15·78	22·85
25	28·30	·02	2·74	15·72	15·30	30	35·85	·01	2·77	15·41	23·20
29	29·83	·01	2·76	15·47	17·11	Aug. 2	34·87	·00	2·73	15·21	22·39
Aug. 1	28·10	·00	2·74	15·28	15·56	4	36·45	·01	2·75	15·07	24·12
3	28·94	·00	2·74	15·14	16·54	11	35·26	·02	2·71	14·57	23·38
5	28·15	·01	2·76	15·00	15·90	13	35·06	·01	2·79	14·42	23·42
14	27·46	·01	2·76	14·35	15·86	19	34·08	·02	2·77	13·96	22·87
22	27·56	·01	2·74	13·73	16·56	23	33·24	·02	2·75	13·65	22·32
24	28·15	·01	2·72	+13·57	17·29	25	32·30	·02	2·74	+13·50	21·52
					2 40 15·91						2 40 22·93

Error of Collimation . . . $= 0·\ 0·\ 3·51$
Resulting Mean Zenith Distance, North $= 2·40·19·42$

B.A.C. 6877.

	° ′ ″	″	″	″	° ′ ″		° ′ ″	″	″	″	° ′ ″
July 21	1 27 35·12	·00	1·51	+17·22	1 27 10·41	July 22	1 27 43·66	·00	1·49	+17·16	1 27 27·99
23	35·46	·00	1·51	17·10	19·87	24	44·35	·00	1·49	17·04	28·80
25	35·17	·01	1·50	16·98	19·68	26	44·85	·00	1·49	16·91	29·43
29	35·81	·00	1·50	16·71	20·60	30	42·97	+ ·10	1·51	16·64	27·94
Aug. 1	34·87	·00	1·50	16·50	19·87	Aug. 2	41·98	·00	1·49	16·42	27·05
3	35·32	·00	1·50	16·35	20·47	4	42·28	·01	1·50	16·27	27·50
5	33·88	·00	1·51	16·19	19·20	11	41·24	·01	1·48	15·71	27·00
14	34·18	·00	1·51	15·46	20·23	13	41·49	·01	1·52	15·55	27·45
22	32·60	·01	1·50	14·77	19·32	19	41·59	·01	1·51	15·03	28·06
24	34·28	·00	1·48	+14·59	21·17	23	41·09	·01	1·50	+14·68	27·90
					1 27 19·98						1 27 27·91

Error of Collimation . . . $= 0·\ 0·\ 3·97$
Resulting Mean Zenith Distance, North $= 1·27·23·95$

B.A.C. 6948.

	° ′ ″	″	″	″	° ′ ″		° ′ ″	″	″	″	° ′ ″
July 21	3 28 23·40	·00	3·59	+18·02	3 28 8·97	July 20	3 28 30·92	·00	3·59	+18·07	3 28 16·44
23	23·21	·01	3·59	17·93	8·86	22	32·10	·01	3·54	17·98	17·65
29	24·59	·01	3·58	17·62	10·54	26	30·52	·00	3·55	17·78	16·29
Aug. 1	23·80	·00	3·56	17·45	9·91	30	30·32	·01	3·59	17·56	16·34
3	23·65	·00	3·57	17·32	9·90	Aug. 4	30·32	·02	3·57	17·26	16·61
5	23·30	·01	3·58	17·19	9·68	11	28·98	·03	3·52	16·78	15·69
14	21·82	·01	3·59	16·56	8·84	13	28·44	·01	3·63	16·63	15·43
22	21·38	·01	3·56	15·93	9·00	19	28·74	·02	3·60	16·17	16·15
26	22·81	·01	3·53	15·60	10·73	23	28·24	·02	3·57	15·85	15·94
28	22·71	·01	3·56	+15·43	10·83	25	27·25	·03	3·57	15·69	15·10
						27	27·55	·02	3·57	+15·52	15·58
					3 28 9·73						3 28 16·11

Error of Collimation . . . $= 0;\ 0·\ 3·19$
Resulting Mean Zenith Distance, North $= 3·28·12·92$

B.A.C. 6877.—July 30.—Correction for Curvature of Path $= +0″·10$.

4 L

Mean Zenith Distances of Stars observed at the Royal Observatory.

FACE OF SECTOR EAST.						FACE OF SECTOR WEST.					
Day of Observation 1848.	Apparent Zenith Distance, from Unreduced Observation.	Reduction for Az. Error, and Curr. of Path.	Refraction.	Precession, Aberration, and Nutation.	Deduced Mean Zenith Distance, 1848, Jan. 0; and Mean of Separate Results, uncorrected, for Error of Collimation.	Day of Observation 1848.	Apparent Zenith Distance, from Unreduced Observation.	Reduction for Az. Error, and Curr. of Path.	Refraction.	Precession, Aberration, and Nutation.	Deduced Mean Zenith Distance, 1848, Jan. 0; and Mean of Separate Results, uncorrected, for Error of Collimation.

B.A.C. 7011.

Day of Obs.	Apparent Z.D.	Red.	Refr.	Prec. &c.	Deduced Mean	Day of Obs.	Apparent Z.D.	Red.	Refr.	Prec. &c.	Deduced Mean
July 21	4·22·29·39	·01	4·52	+18·57	4·22·15 33	July 20	4·22·34·67	·00	4·52	+18·61	4·22·(20·58)
23	29·76	·01	4·52	18·49	15·78	24	38·53	·01	4·48	18·46	24·54
29	30·92	·01	4·52	18 23	17·20	26	39·51	·00	4·47	18·37	25·61
Aug. 1	31·27	·00	4·49	18·07	17·09	30	39·22	·01	4·53	18·18	25·56
3	31·25	·00	4·50	17 96	17·79	Aug. 4	37·64	·02	4·50	17·90	24·22
5	30·60	·01	4·52	17·84	17·27	11	37·19	·04	4·44	17·46	24·13
24	30·08	·01	4·45	16·49	18·03	13	·37·39	·02	4·58	17·32	24·63
26	31·02	·02	4·45	16·34	19·11	19	37·54	·03	4·54	16·88	25·17
28	30·18	·02	4·48	+16·17	18·47	23	37·21	·03	4·52	16·57	25·13
						25	35·81	·03	4·50	16·41	23·87
						27	35·96	·02	4·50	+16·25	24·19
					4·22·17·41						4·22·24·71

Error of Collimation . . . = 0· 0· 3·65
Resulting Mean Zenith Distance, North = 4·22·21·06

B.A.C. 7026.

Day of Obs.	Apparent Z.D.	Red.	Refr.	Prec. &c.	Deduced Mean	Day of Obs.	Apparent Z.D.	Red.	Refr.	Prec. &c.	Deduced Mean
July 21	4·22·22·13	- ·01	4·52	+18·68	4·22· 7·96	July 20	4·22·33·00	·00	4·52	+18·71	4·22·18·81
23	23·53	·01	4·52	18·61	9·43	24	31·81	- ·01	4·48	18·56	17·72
29	23·51	+ ·08	4·51	18·34	9·76	26	32·70	+ ·09	4·47	18·48	18·78
Aug. 1	24·30	·00	4·49	18·19	10·60	30	31·81	· 01	4·53	18·29	18·04
3	25·42	·00	4·50	18·07	11·85	Aug. 4	30·62	·02	4·50	18·02	17·08
5	24·17	- ·01	4·52	17·90	10·72	11	30·18	·04	4·44	17·57	17·01
14	23·51	·01	4·52	17·36	10·66	13	30·18	·02	4·58	17·43	17·31
22	23·96	·02	4·49	16·76	11·67	19	30·13	·03	4·54	16·99	17·65
24	23·76	·01	4·45	16·61	11·59	23	29·51	·03	4·51	16·08	17·31
26	24·20	·02	4·45	16·45	12·18	25	30·48	·03	4·49	16·53	18·41
28	23·61	·02	4·48	+16·28	11·79	27	28·16	·02	4·50	+16·37	16·27
					4·22·10·75						4·22·17·67

Error of Collimation . . . = 0· 0· 3·46
Resulting Mean Zenith Distance, North = 4·22·14·21

B.A.C. 7057.

Day of Obs.	Apparent Z.D.	Red.	Refr.	Prec. &c.	Deduced Mean	Day of Obs.	Apparent Z.D.	Red.	Refr.	Prec. &c.	Deduced Mean
July 21	4·19·10·66	·01	4·47	+18 93	4·18·56·19	July 20	4·19·20·00	·00	4·46	+18·97	4·19· 5·49
23	11·03	·01	4·46	18·86	56·62	24	18·02	·01	4·42	18·82	4·21
29	11·70	·01	4·46	18·60	57·55	26	14·66	·00	4·42	18·74	(0·34)
Aug. 1	11·65	·00	4·44	18·44	57·65	30	18·32	·01	4·47	18·55	4·23
3	12·42	·00	4·44	18·34	58·52	Aug. 4	18·22	·02	4·44	18·28	4·36
5	11·77	·01	4·47	18·22	58·01	11	18·37	·04	4·39	17·83	4·89
14	11·01	·01	4·47	17·62	57·85	13	18·07	·02	4·52	17·69	4·88
22	11·60	·02	4·43	17·02	58·99	19	17·43	·03	4·48	17·43	4·63
24	11·16	·01	4·39	16·86	58·68	23	17·70	·03	4·46	16·94	5·19
26	11·41	·02	4·40	16·09	59·10	25	16·94	·03	4·44	16·78	4·57
28	10·81	·02	4·43	+16·53	58·69	27	16·15	·02	4·44	+16·61	3·96
					4·18·57·99						4·19· 4·64

Error of Collimation . . . = 0· 0· 3·33
Resulting Mean Zenith Distance, North = 4·19· 1·31

B.A.C. 7026.—July 26,—Correction for Curvature of Path = + 0″·09.
    "   "   —   " 29.—   "   "   "   = +0 ·09.

Mean Zenith Distances of Stars observed at the Royal Observatory.

FACE OF SECTOR EAST.   **FACE OF SECTOR WEST.**

Day of Observation 1848	Apparent Zenith Distance, from Unreduced Observation.	Reduction for Az. Error, and Curr. of Path.	Refraction.	Precession, Aberration, and Nutation.	Deduced Mean Zenith Distance, 1848, Jan. 0; and Mean of Separate Results, uncorrected, for Error of Collimation.	Day of Observation 1848.	Apparent Zenith Distance, from Unreduced Observation.	Reduction for Az. Error, and Curr. of Path.	Refraction.	Precession, Aberration, and Nutation.	Deduced Mean Zenith Distance, 1848, Jan. 0; and Mean of Separate Results, uncorrected, for Error of Collimation.
					Anon. A.R. 20·24.						
July 21	4· 7·51·60	·01	4·27	+19·11	4· 7·36·75	July 20	4· 7·60·26	·00	4·27	+19·14	4· 7·45·30
23	52·54	·01	4·27	19·03	37·77	24	60·83	·01	4·23	18·99	46·06
29	53·38	·01	4·26	18·77	38·86	30	60·34	·01	4·28	18·72	45·80
Aug. 1	53·13	·00	4·24	18·61	38·76	Aug. 4	60·49	·02	4·25	18·44	46·28
3	53·82	·00	4·25	18·50	39·57	11	59·50	·03	4·19	17·90	45·67
5	52·98	·01	4·27	18·38	38·86	13	60·00	·01	4·32	17·85	46·46
14	52·29	·01	4·27	17·78	38·77	19	59·30	·03	4·28	17·40	46·15
22	51·25	·02	4·24	17·16	38·31	23	59·60	·03	4·26	17·08	46·75
30	51·06	·01	4·22	+16·50	38·77	31	56·83	·02	4·19	+16·41	44·59
					4· 7·38·49						4· 7·45·92

Error of Collimation . . = 0· 0· 3·71
Resulting Mean Zenith Distance, North = 4· 7·42·20

Day of Observation 1848	Apparent Zenith Distance	Reduction	Refraction	Precession, Aberration, and Nutation	Deduced Mean	Day of Observation 1848	Apparent Zenith Distance	Reduction	Refraction	Precession, Aberration, and Nutation	Deduced Mean
					Anon. A.R. 20·33.						
July 23	3·58·52·64	·01	4·11	+19·56	3·58·37·18	July 20	3·58·62·62	·00	4·11	+19·66	3·58·47·07
29	52·84	·01	4·11	19·30	37·64	22	61·33	·01	4·06	19·59	45·79
Aug. 1	52·15	·00	4·09	19·15	37·00	24	61·05	·01	4·08	19·52	45·60
3	54·42	·00	4·09	19·04	39·47	26	57·87	+·11	4·07	19·44	42·61
5	52·10	·01	4·12	18·92	37·29	30	60·05	·01	4·12	19·25	44·91
14	52·94	·01	4·12	18·32	38·73	Aug. 4	59·45	·02	4·09	18·98	44·54
22	52·25	·02	4·08	17·69	38·62	11	60·39	·03	4·04	18·53	45·87
30	51·50	·01	4·07	17·00	38·56	13	60·05	·01	4·16	18·39	45·81
Sept. 2	49·87	·01	4·02	+16·73	37·15	23	58·06	·03	4·11	17·60	45·44
						31	56·74	·02	4·05	+16·91	43·86
					3·58·37·97						3·58·45·15

Error of Collimation . . = 0· 0· 3·59
Resulting Mean Zenith Distance, North = 3·58·41·56

Day of Observation 1848	Apparent Zenith Distance	Reduction	Refraction	Precession, Aberration, and Nutation	Deduced Mean	Day of Observation 1848	Apparent Zenith Distance	Reduction	Refraction	Precession, Aberration, and Nutation	Deduced Mean
					B.A.C. 7207.						
July 21	0·23·55·90	·00	0·41	+20·09	0·24·16·40	July 20	0·23·45·53	·00	0·41	+20·15	0·24· 6·09
23	54·37	·00	·41	19·98	14·76	22	45·28	·00	·41	20·03	5·72
25	55·60	·00	·41	19·85	15·86	24	46·32	·00	·41	19·91	6·64
29	54·61	·00	·41	19·58	14·60	30	46·76	·00	·41	19·50	6·67
Aug. 1	55·06	·00	·41	19·36	14·83	Aug. 4	47·21	·00	·41	19·11	6·73
3	54·52	·00	·41	19·20	14·13	11	47·74	·00	·40	18·49	6·63
5	56·10	·00	·41	19·03	15·54	13	48·50	·00	·42	18·30	7·31
14	56·84	·00	·41	18·21	15·46	20	48·10	·01	·41	17·60	6·10
22	57·43	·00	·41	17·30	15·23	23	49·09	·00	·41	17·28	6·78
24	56·54	·00	·41	+17·18	14·13	26	51·45	·00	·40	+16·06	8·81
					0·24·15·09						0·24· 6·75

Error of Collimation . . = 0· 0· 4·17
Resulting Mean Zenith Distance, South = 0·24·10·92

Anon. A.R. 20ʰ 33ᵐ.—July 26.—Correction for Curvature of Path= + 0ʳ·11.

Mean Zenith Distances of Stars observed at the Royal Observatory.

FACE OF SECTOR EAST.

Anon. A.R. 20·53.

Day of Observation 1848.	Apparent Zenith Distance, from Unreduced Observation.	Reduction for Az. Error, and Curv. of Path.	Refraction.	Precession, Aberration, and Nutation.	Deduced Mean Zenith Distance, 1848, Jan. 0; and Mean of Separate Results, uncorrected, for Error of Collimation.
July 23	4·13·58·76	·01	4·37	+20·56	4·13·42·56
29	58·81	·01	4·37	20·35	42·82
Aug. 1	57·28	·00	4·36	20·21	41·43
5	56·49	·01	4·39	20·00	40·67
14	57·28	·01	4·38	19·43	42·22
22	55·50	·02	4·35	18·81	41·02
24	56·84	·01	4·31	18·64	42·50
26	57·08	·01	4·31	18·47	42·91
28	56·89	·01	4·34	18·29	42·93
30	55·80	·01	4·32	+18·11	42·00
					4·13·42·13

Error of Collimation . . = 0· 0· 4·14
Resulting Mean Zenith Distance, North = 4·13·46·26

FACE OF SECTOR WEST.

Anon. A.R. 20·53.

Day of Observation 1848.	Apparent Zenith Distance, from Unreduced Observation.	Reduction for Az. Error, and Curv. of Path.	Refraction.	Precession, Aberration, and Nutation.	Deduced Mean Zenith Distance, 1848, Jan. 0; and Mean of Separate Results, uncorrected, for Error of Collimation.
July 20	4·14·8·84	·00	4·37	+20·64	4·13·52·57
22	7·26	·01	4·32	20·59	50·98
24	5·68	·01	4·34	20·53	49·48
Aug. 4	5·78	·02	4·35	20·06	50·05
11	4·89	·03	4·30	19·04	49·52
13	4·49	·01	4·43	19·50	49·41
20	7·06	·05	4·40	18·97	52·44
23	5·48	·03	4·37	18·72	51·10
25	4·89	·03	4·36	18·35	50·87
27	3·01	·02	4·35	18·38	48·96
29	2·91	·02	4·32	+18·20	49·01
					4·13·50·40

Anon. AR. 21·0. (EAST)

Day of Observation 1848.	Apparent Zenith Distance	Reduction	Refraction	Precession, &c.	Deduced Mean Zenith Distance
July 23	3·36·12·84	·01	3·72	+20·92	3·35·55·63
29	14·57	·01	3·72	20·70	57·58
Aug. 1	13·54	·00	3·71	20·56	56·69
5	14·57	·01	3·74	20·34	57·96
14	12·99	·01	3·72	19·74	56·96
22	12·35	·01	3·70	19·10	56·94
24	13·63	·01	3·67	18·92	58·37
26	14·37	·01	3·67	18·74	59·29
28	13·88	·01	3·69	18·56	59·00
30	12·60	·01	3·68	+18·36	57·91
					3·35·57·63

Error of Collimation . . = 0· 0· 3·48
Resulting Mean Zenith Distance, North = 3·36· 1·12

Anon. AR. 21·0. (WEST)

Day of Observation 1848.	Apparent Zenith Distance	Reduction	Refraction	Precession, &c.	Deduced Mean Zenith Distance
July 20	3·36·22·62	·00	3·72	+21·00	3·36·5·34
24	21·49	·01	3·69	20·89	4·28
26	21·39	·00	3·68	20·82	4·25
Aug. 4	22·13	·02	3·70	20·40	5·41
11	20·79	·03	3·66	19·96	4·46
13	20·99	·01	3·77	19·81	4·94
20	20·50	·04	3·75	19·27	4·94
23	20·30	·02	3·72	19·01	4·99
25	18·33	·03	3·71	18·83	3·18
27	19·16	·02	3·70	+18·65	4·19
					3·36·4·60

B.A.C. 7386. (EAST)

Day of Observation 1848.	Apparent Zenith Distance	Reduction	Refraction	Precession, &c.	Deduced Mean Zenith Distance
July 21	1· 8· 4·44	·00	1·17	+21·48	1· 7·44·13
23	4·01	·00	1·17	21·40	43·81
29	5·23	·00	1·17	21·11	45·29
Aug. 1	4·74	·00	1·17	20·93	44·98
3	5·62	·00	1·17	20·81	45·98
5	4·64	·00	1·18	20·07	45·15
14	4·14	·00	1·17	19·95	45·36
22	2·56	·00	1·17	19·20	44·53
24	3·70	·00	1·17	18·99	45·87
26	3·70	·00	1·16	+18·79	46·07
					1· 7·45·12

Error of Collimation . . = 0· 0· 4·09
Resulting Mean Zenith Distance, North = 1· 7·49·21

B.A.C. 7386. (WEST)

Day of Observation 1848.	Apparent Zenith Distance	Reduction	Refraction	Precession, &c.	Deduced Mean Zenith Distance
July 20	1· 8 14·58	·00	1·17	+21·51	1· 7·54·24
22	13·77	·00	1·16	21·44	53·49
24	12·84	·00	1·16	21·36	52·64
26	12·93	·00	1·16	21·27	52·82
Aug. 4	13·43	·01	1·17	20·74	53·85
11	12·64	·01	1·15	20·21	53·57
13	12·39	·00	1·19	20·04	53·54
20	11·65	·01	1·18	19·39	53·33
23	10·91	·01	1·17	19·09	52·98
25	10·27	·01	1·17	+18·89	52·54
					1· 7·53·30

Mean Zenith Distances of Stars observed at the Royal Observatory.

FACE OF SECTOR EAST. / FACE OF SECTOR WEST.

Anon. A.R. 21ʰ 12ᵐ.

Day of Observation 1848.	Apparent Zenith Distance, from Unreduced Observation.	Reduction for Az. Error, and Curv. of Path.	Refraction.	Precession, and Aberration, and Nutation.	Deduced Mean Zenith Distance, 1848, Jan. 0; and Mean of Separate Results, uncorrected, for Error of Collimation.	Day of Observation 1848.	Apparent Zenith Distance, from Unreduced Observation.	Reduction for Az. Error, and Curv. of Path.	Refraction.	Precession, and Aberration, and Nutation.	Deduced Mean Zenith Distance, 1848, Jan. 0; and Mean of Separate Results, uncorrected, for Error of Collimation.
July 23	4· 7·51·45	·01	4·27	+21·41	4· 7·34·30	July 20	4· 7·57·93	·00	4·27	+21·47	4· 7·40·73
29	49·13	·01	4·26	21·23	32·15	22	58·02	·01	4·21	21·43	40·79
Aug. 1	49·62	·00	4·25	21·11	32·76	24	57·43	·01	4·23	21·39	40·26
3	48·44	·00	4·25	21·02	31·67	26	57·72	·00	4·22	21·33	40·61
5	48·74	+·08	4·28	20·92	32·18	Aug. 4	57·52	·02	4·25	20·97	40·78
14	49·23	·01	4·27	20·36	33·13	11	56·04	·03	4·19	20·57	39·63
22	48·93	·02	4·25	19·74	33·42	13	55·55	·01	4·32	20·43	39·43
24	49·33	·01	4·21	19·57	33·96	20	56·64	·05	4·30	19·91	40·98
26	49·03	·01	4·22	19·40	33·84	23	57·62	·03	4·27	19·65	42·21
28	48·54	·01	4·23	+19·21	33·55	25	54·96	·02	4·25	+19·48	39·71
					4· 7·33·10						4· 7·40·51

Error of Collimation . . . = 0· 0· 3·71
Resulting Mean Zenith Distance, North = 4· 7·36·80

Anon. A.R. 21ʰ 25ᵐ.

Day of Observation 1848.	Apparent Zenith Distance	Reduction	Refraction	Precession, &c.	Deduced Mean Zenith Distance	Day of Observation 1848.	Apparent Zenith Distance	Reduction	Refraction	Precession, &c.	Deduced Mean Zenith Distance
July 23	3·34·14·07	·01	3·69	+21·97	3·33·55·78	July 20	3·34·19·31	·00	3·69	+22·02	3·34· 0·98
29	13·08	·01	3·68	21·83	54·95	22	19·51	·01	3·64	21·99	1·15
Aug. 1	11·31	·00	3·67	21·68	53·30	24	19·21	·01	3·66	21·95	0·91
3	12·69	·00	3·67	21·60	54·76	26	18·62	·00	3·65	21·90	0·87
14	12·29	·01	3·69	20·93	55·04	Aug. 4	19·06	·02	3·67	21·55	1·16
22	12·29	·01	3·67	20·29	55·06	11	18·42	·03	3·62	21·14	0·87
24	11·80	·01	3·65	20·11	55·33	13	18·71	·01	3·73	21·00	1·43
26	11·90	·01	3·65	19·93	55·61	20	18·02	·05	3·71	20·46	1·22
27	11·11	·01	3·67	19·84	54·93	23	17·83	·03	3·70	20·20	1·30
28	10·62	·01	3·66	+19·74	54·53	25	17·63	·03	3·67	+20·03	1·24
					3·33·54·99						3·34· 1·06

Error of Collimation . . . = 0· 0· 3·04
Resulting Mean Zenith Distance, North = 3·33·58·03

B.A.C. 7557.

Day of Observation 1848.	Apparent Zenith Distance	Reduction	Refraction	Precession, &c.	Deduced Mean Zenith Distance	Day of Observation 1848.	Apparent Zenith Distance	Reduction	Refraction	Precession, &c.	Deduced Mean Zenith Distance
July 21	0·13·23·01	·00	0·23	+22·68	0·13· 0·56	July 20	0·13·31·96	·00	0·23	+22·70	0·13· 9·49
23	24·24	·00	·23	22·61	1·86	22	33·28	·00	·23	22·65	10·86
Aug. 1	23·90	·00	·23	22·20	1·93	24	31·85	·00	·23	22·58	9·50
3	24·79	·00	·23	22·07	2·95	26	32·39	·00	·23	22·50	10·12
5	23·21	·00	·23	21·94	1·50	Aug. 4	32·10	·00	·23	22·01	10·32
22	20·54	·00	·23	20·45	0·32	11	31·80	·00	·23	21·48	10·55
24	22·61	·00	·23	20·23	2·61	13	31·60	·00	·23	21·31	10·52
26	22·46	·00	·23	20·01	2·68	20	30·61	·00	·23	20·65	10·19
27	22·51	·00	·23	19·90	2·84	23	29·68	·00	·23	20·34	9·57
28	22·42	·00	·23	+19·79	2·86	25	28·34	·00	·23	+20·13	8·44
					0·13· 2·01						0·13· 9·96

Error of Collimation . . . = 0· 0· 3·97
Resulting Mean Zenith Distance, North = 0·13· 5·98

Anon. A.R. 21ʰ 12ᵐ.—Aug. 5.—Correction for Curvature of Path= +0″·09.

4 M

Mean Zenith Distances of Stars observed at the Royal Observatory.

FACE OF SECTOR EAST.

Day of Observation 1848.	Apparent Zenith Distance, from Unreduced Observation.	Reduction for At. Error, and Curv. of Path.	Refraction.	Precession, Aberration, and Nutation.	Deduced Mean Zenith Distance, 1848, Jan. 0; and Mean of Separate Results, uncorrected, for Error of Collimation.

B.A.C. 7657.

FACE OF SECTOR EAST.

Day	App. Z.D.	Red.	Refr.	Prec.	Deduced
July 29	4·45·26·57	·02	4·91	+22·65	4·45· 8·81
Aug. 1	26·77	·00	4·91	22·58	9·10
3	26·42	·00	4·89	22·52	8·79
5	26·92	·01	4·94	22·44	9·41
14	26·02	·01	4·92	22·00	9·53
22	25·09	·02	4·91	21·44	8·54
24	27·36	·01	4·86	21·28	10·93
26	27·11	·02	4·87	21·11	10·85
28	26·87	·02	4·88	20·93	10·80
30	24·89	·01	4·86	+20·75	8·99
					4·45· 9·58

FACE OF SECTOR WEST.

Day	App. Z.D.	Red.	Refr.	Prec.	Deduced
July 20	4·45·34·27	·00	4·91	+22·70	4·45·16·48
22	33·78	·01	4·86	22·71	15·92
24	33·98	·01	4·88	22·70	16·15
26	33·34	·00	4·87	22·69	15·52
Aug. 4	34·47	·02	4·90	22·48	16·87
13	33·20	·02	4·98	22·06	16·19
20	32·94	·06	4·95	21·59	16·24
23	31·95	·03	4·93	21·36	15·49
25	32·40	·04	4·90	21·20	16·06
27	31·36	·02	4·89	21·02	15·21
29	31·16	·02	4·85	+20·84	15·15
					4·45·15·93

Error of Collimation . . = 0· 0· 3·18
Resulting Mean Zenith Distance, North = 4·45·12·76

Anon. AR. 21·55.

FACE OF SECTOR EAST.

Day	App. Z.D.	Red.	Refr.	Prec.	Deduced
July 23	4·46· 5·58	·01	4·93	+22·81	4·45·47·69
29	5·39	·02	4·92	22·75	47·54
Aug. 1	5·68	·00	4·92	22·09	47·91
3	5·39	·00	4·90	22·63	47·66
5	3·90	·01	4·95	22·56	46·28
14	5·14	·01	4·93	22·13	47·93
22	3·46	·02	4·92	21·57	46·79
24	5·49	·01	4·87	21·42	48·93
26	5·03	·02	4·88	21·25	49·24
28	4·50	·02	4·89	21·07	48·30
30	3·90	·01	4·87	+20·89	47·87
					4·45·47·83

FACE OF SECTOR WEST.

Day	App. Z.D.	Red.	Refr.	Prec.	Deduced
July 20	4·46·13·44	·00	4·92	+22·79	4·45·55·57
24	12·40	·01	4·89	22·80	54·48
Aug. 1	13·68	·02	4·91	22·60	55·97
26	11·91	·02	4·99	22·19	54·09
20	11·61	·06	4·96	21·73	54·78
23	12·40	·03	4·94	21·50	55·81
25	11·51	·04	4·91	21·33	55·05
27	11·12	·02	4·90	21·16	54·84
29	10·82	·02	4·86	20·98	54·68
31	11·11	·03	4·85	+20·79	55·14
					4·45·55·10

Error of Collimation . . = 0· 0· 3·64
Resulting Mean Zenith Distance, North = 4·45·51·47

B.A.C. 7842.

FACE OF SECTOR EAST.

Day	App. Z.D.	Red.	Refr.	Prec.	Deduced
July 23	0·48·59·06	·00	0·84	+23·92	0·48·35·98
29	59·11	·00	·84	23·82	36·13
Aug. 1	58·47	·00	·84	23·73	35·58
5	57·87	·00	·85	23·55	35·17
14	58·96	·00	·84	23·00	36·80
22	56·49	·00	·84	22·31	35·02

FACE OF SECTOR WEST.

Day	App. Z.D.	Red.	Refr.	Prec.	Deduced
July 22	0·49· 8·31	·00	0·83	+23·92	0·48·45·22
24	7·21	·00	·84	23·91	44·14
26	6·47	·00	·83	23·88	43·42
Aug. 13	6·42	·00	·85	23·07	44·20
20	5·48	·01	·85	22·50	43·82
23	5·73	·01	·85	22·21	44·36

Carried forward,

Mean Zenith Distances of Stars observed at the Royal Observatory.

FACE OF SECTOR EAST.   FACE OF SECTOR WEST.

B.A.C. 7842—(continued).

Day of Observation 1848.	Apparent Zenith Distance, from Unreduced Observation.	Reduction for Az. Error, and Curv. of Path.	Refraction.	Precession, and Aberration, and Nutation.	Deduced Mean Zenith Distance, 1848, Jan. 0; and Mean of Separate Results, uncorrected, for Error of Collimation.	Day of Observation 1848.	Apparent Zenith Distance, from Unreduced Observation.	Reduction for Az. Error, and Curv. of Path.	Refraction.	Precession, and Aberration, and Nutation.	Deduced Mean Zenith Distance, 1848, Jan. 0; and Mean of Separate Results, uncorrected, for Error of Collimation.
Aug. 24	0 48 58·22	·00	·83	22·11	0 48 36·94	Aug. 25	0 49 4·39	·01	·84	22·01	0 48 43·21
26	58 22	·00	·84	21·91	37·15	27	2·76	·00	·84	21·80	41·80
30	56·34	·00	·84	21·47	35·71	29	2·86	·00	·83	21·58	42·11
Sept. 2	55·90	·00	·83	+21·12	35·61	31	3·30	·00	·83	+21·35	42·84
					0 48 36·01						0 48 43·51

Error of Collimation . . . = 0· 0· 3·75
Resulting Mean Zenith Distance, North = 0·48·39·76

B.A.C. 7909.

Day	Apparent Z.D.	Red.	Refr.	Prec.	Deduced Mean	Day	Apparent Z.D.	Red.	Refr.	Prec.	Deduced Mean
July 23	3 47 6·92	·01	3·92	+23·67	3 46 47·16	July 20	3 47 14·57	·00	3·90	+23·61	3 46 54·86
29	6·72	·01	3·90	23·69	46·92	22	14·62	·01	3·86	23·65	54·82
Aug. 1	6·92	·00	3·90	23·66	47·16	Aug. 13	13·44	·01	3·88	23·68	53·63
5	5·78	·00	3·92	23·58	46·12	20	12·65	·01	3·96	23·26	53·34
14	7·22	·01	3·91	23·21	47·01	20	12·60	·05	3·94	22·82	53·67
24	6·62	·01	3·88	22·51	47·98	23	11·86	·02	3·92	22·59	53·17
26	6·62	·01	3·87	22·35	48·13	25	12·55	·03	3·90	22·43	53·99
28	6·72	·01	3·88	22·16	48·43	27	12·25	·02	3·89	22·26	53·86
30	5·39	·01	3·87	21·97	47·28	29	11·76	·02	3·87	22·07	53·54
Sept. 2	5·54	·01	3·83	+21·67	47·69	31	10·77	·02	3·85	+21·87	52·73
					3 46 47·48						3 46 53·76

Error of Collimation . . . = 0· 0· 3·14
Resulting Mean Zenith Distance, North = 3·46·50·62

B.A.C. 7966.

Day	Apparent Z.D.	Red.	Refr.	Prec.	Deduced Mean	Day	Apparent Z.D.	Red.	Refr.	Prec.	Deduced Mean
July 21	0 15 34·37	·00	0·27	+24·32	0 15 10·32	July 20	0 15 45·53	·00	0·27	+24·31	0 15 21·49
23	36·40	·00	·27	24·33	12·34	22	44·64	·00	·27	24·33	20·58
29	34·97	·00	·27	24·29	10·95	24	43·95	·00	·27	24·34	19·88
Aug. 1	35·85	·00	·27	24·22	11·90	26	43·16	·00	·27	24·33	19·09
5	35·46	·00	·27	24·08	11·65	Aug. 13	42·18	·00	·27	23·64	18·81
14	35·90	·00	·27	23·57	12·60	20	42·82	·00	·27	23·09	20·00
22	34·03	·00	·27	22·91	11·39	23	41·19	·00	·27	22·81	18·65
24	35·26	·00	·27	22·71	12·82	25	41·29	·00	·27	22·61	18·95
26	35·01	·00	·27	22·51	12·77	27	41·48	·00	·27	22·40	19·35
28	35·21	·00	·27	+22·29	13·19	29	40·30	·00	·27	+22·18	18·39
					0 15 11·99						0 15 19·52

Error of Collimation . . . = 0· 0· 3·76
Resulting Mean Zenith Distance, North = 3·15·15·76

Mean Zenith Distances of Stars observed at the Royal Observatory.

	FACE OF SECTOR EAST.						FACE OF SECTOR WEST.				
Day of Observation 1848.	Apparent Zenith Distance, from Unreduced Observation.	Reduction for Az. Error, and Curv. of Path.	Refraction.	Precession, Aberration, and Nutation.	Deduced Mean Zenith Distance, 1848, Jan. 0; and Mean of Separate Results, uncorrected, for Error of Collimation.	Day of Observation 1848.	Apparent Zenith Distance, from Unreduced Observation.	Reduction for Az. Error, and Curv. of Path.	Refraction.	Precession, Aberration, and Nutation.	Deduced Mean Zenith Distance, 1848, Jan. 0; and Mean of Separate Results, uncorrected, for Error of Collimation.
					Fomalhaut B.A.C. 7992.						
	° ′ ″	″	″	″	° ′ ″		° ′ ″	″	″	″	° ′ ″
July 21	3 30 44·25	·00	3·63	+23·81	3 30 24·07	July 20	3 30 51·56	·00	3·61	+23·78	3 30 31·39
23	45·04	·01	·63	23·86	24·80	22	51·71	·01	3·58	23·84	31·44
29	44·35	·01	·62	23·93	24·03	24	51·36	·01	3·60	23·88	31·07
Aug. 1	45·04	·00	·62	23·92	24·74	26	50·27	·01	3·57	23·91	29·92
5	45·04	·01	·64	23·80	24·91	Aug. 13	50·32	·01	3·67	23·57	30·41
14	45·43	·01	·63	23·52	25·53	20	50·67	·04	3·65	23·16	31·12
22	44·25	·01	·62	23·01	24·85	23	49·09	·02	3·64	22·94	29·77
24	44·20	·01	·60	22·86	24·93	25	49·63	·03	3·62	22·78	30·44
26	43·61	·01	·59	22·09	24·50	27	49·43	·02	3·61	22·60	30·42
28	45·63	·01	·60	22·52	26·70	29	48·10	·01	3·59	22·42	29·26
30	43·90	·01	·59	+22·33	25·15	31	48·25	·02	3·58	+22·23	29·58
					3 30 24·92						3 30 30·44

Error of Collimation .   . = 0· 0· 2·76
Resulting Mean Zenith Distance, North = 3 30 27·68

ABSTRACT

OF THE

RESULTING MEAN ZENITH DISTANCES,

AND

CALCULATION OF THE AMPLITUDES OF THE SECTOR STATIONS.

Abstract of the Resulting Mean Zenith Distances.

HEERENLOGEMENT'S BERG.

No. of Star in B.A.C. or approximate R.A.	E	W	Z.D. North or South	Mean Zenith Distance, 1843, January 0.
1802	6	6	S	2·11·33·29
2293	8	8	N	3·12·21·29
4458	10	10	S	3·54·49·77
4517	9	10	N	3·12·45·35
4548	10	10	N	3·12·41·40
4579	9	9	S	0·16·44·12
4623	9	9	S	0·14·40·31
4686	8	8	S	3·37·33·63
4719	6	5	N	3·25·22·23
4784	8	8	N	3·11·8·14
R.A.	7	7	S	0·39·6·12
4852	9	8	S	2·31·30·98
4891	8	8	N	4·39·55·30
4916	8	8	S	1·14·43·58
R.A.	8	8	S	0·3·4·79
R.A.	8	7	S	0·19·47·79
5032	8	8	N	2·24·5·43
5054	6	6	S	3·43·5·57
5151	10	8	N	2·42·43·12
R.A.	8	8	N	0·52·19·91
5227	9	8	S	1·10·30·14
5272	9	9	N	3·13·4·73
5374	9	9	S	2·58·18·96
5435	8	8	N	1·26·53·80
R.A.	6	6	S	0·51·27·76
5588	6	6	N	0·10·1·67
5632	9	9	S	2·2·0·73
5735	8	8	S	1·55·37·95
5817	8	9	S	0·30·38·16
5881	8	8	N	2·14·59·34
5915	7	7	S	5·0·48·31
5930	3	5	S	0·8·14·80
6016	8	8	N	0·19·32·73
6074	7	7	N	1·44·16·65
6115	8	8	N	1·32·56·51
6145	9	9	N	1·13·16·51
6186	9	9	S	4·49·59·32
6233	9	9	S	2·29·0·61
6275	6	7	S	1·10·27·11
6285	8	8	S	1·7·4·07
6305	8	8	S	1·9·27·11
6414	6	6	N	1·3·14·66
6489	8	8	N	1·52·12·16
6525	6	6	N	3·5·44·45
6639	8	8	N	1·55·14·78
7992	2	2	N	1·30·55·47

KAMIES-SECTOR BERG.

No. of Star	E	W	N/S	Mean Zenith Distance
1802	5	5	S	3·48·11·84
2293	9	8	N	1·35·44·15
4458	6	6	S	5·31·26·96
4579	5	5	S	1·53·21·44
4623	6	6	S	1·51·16·75
4686	8	7	S	5·14·10·90
4719	2	4	N	1·48·45·27
4784	6	6	N	1·34·31·23

KAMIES-SECTOR BERG—continued.

No. of Star in B.A.C. or approximate R.A.	E	W	Z.D. North or South	Mean Zenith Distance, 1843, January 0.
4852	2	4	S	2·15·43·25
4891	7	8	S	4·8·7·40
4916	7	8	N	3·3·19·14
R.A.	7	7	S	2·51·20·91
5032	8	8	S	1·39·41·59
R.A.	6	5	S	1·56·24·52
5054	8	8	N	0·47·28·63
5151	8	8	S	5·19·41·71
5227	8	8	N	1·6·5·86
5272	7	7	S	0·44·16·38
5374	8	8	S	2·47·7·81
5435	8	8	N	1·36·27·98
R.A.	8	8	S	1·21·41·98
5498	8	8	S	0·9·43·27
5508	8	8	N	2·28·4·24
5588	8	8	N	4·10·47·85
5632	9	7	S	1·26·35·10
5735	8	8	S	3·32·14·95
5817	8	8	S	0·7·14·42
5881	7	7	N	0·38·21·95
5960	7	7	S	1·44·51·22
5964	7	7	S	1·45·52·48
6016	7	8	S	1·17·3·80
6074	9	8	N	0·7·39·56
6115	9	8	S	0·3·40·86
6145	7	8	S	4·5·36·97
6233	7	8	S	2·47·4·90
6285	9	8	S	2·43·42·24
6305	9	8	S	0·33·22·28
6414	8	8	S	0·15·34·81
6489	8	7	N	1·29·06·43
6525	8	8	N	0·18·37·27
6639	8	8	N	0·32·37·83
6753	8	8	S	0·54·56·05
6877	8	8	S	0·7·58·84
6948	8	8	S	0·7·15·60
7011	3	3	N	0·46·50·71
7026	9	8	N	0·46·42·69
7057	8	8	N	0·43·27·97
R.A.	6	6	N	0·32·8·32
R.A.	6	6	N	0·23·5·19
7207	8	8	N	3·50·51·16
R.A.	6	8	N	0·38·1·66
R.A.				
7396	7	7	S	2·27·59·23
R.A.	6	7	N	0·31·46·55
7557	8	8	S	3·22·50·04
7657	8	8	N	1·9·12·53
R.A.	8	8	N	1·9·50·34
7842	7	8	S	2·47·27·88
7909	7	7	N	0·10·42·55
7966	8	8	S	3·20·55·11
7992	8	8	S	0·5·42·71

ZWART KOP.

No. of Star in B.A.C. or approximate R.A.	E	W	Z.D. North or South	Mean Zenith Distance, 1844, January 0.
1802	9	11	N	0·3·56·14
1878	9	10	S	1·36·14·69
2293	12	14	N	5·27·43·82
4458	7	8	S	1·39·39·50
4507	1	1	S	4·22·22·46
4579	1	1	N	1·58·25·73
4686	12	10	S	1·22·21·40
4745	3	3	S	2·56·17·48
4784	2	2	N	5·26·19·51
4852	4	3	S	0·16·17·96
4916	3	3	N	1·0·29·37
R.A.	3	3	N	2·12·9·07
R.A.	1	3	N	1·55·26·98
5032	1	1	N	4·39·19·35
5054	10	8	S	1·27·49·53
5151	4	4	N	4·57·57·93
R.A.	3	3	N	3·7·36·97
5227	3	3	N	1·4·47·53
5292	9	7	S	3·43·5·36
5331	9	6	S	2·8·42·32
R.A.	6	3	S	2·5·59·47
5374	4	3	N	5·13·37·87
5485	6	3	N	3·42·12·83
5508	8	7	S	0·7·55·44
5538	8	8	S	0·42·5·14
5588	5	4	N	2·23·22·93
5632	11	11	N	0·13·21·29
5735	8	8	N	1·44·45·97
5817	6	6	N	4·30·23·60
5881	10	8	N	4·30·23·60
5915	11	12	S	2·45·23·97
5970	10	12	S	4·42·54·65
6016	10	11	N	2·34·59·84
6074	11	11	N	3·59·43·73
6115	11	12	N	3·48·24·90
6145	9	10	N	3·28·45·59
6186	12	11	S	2·34·30·20
6233	11	12	S	0·13·30·39
6275	8	10	N	1·5·2·58
6305	10	10	N	1·8·26·11
6414	11	11	N	1·6·3·23
6489	12	12	N	3·18·47·48
6525	11	11	N	4·7·45·56
6639	14	11	N	5·21·16·64
6753	12	10	N	4·10·49·58
6877	10	9	N	4·24·50·23
6948	11	10	N	2·57·18·21
7011	10	11	N	1·44·15·90
7026	11	11	N	3·45·0·77
7057	11	11	N	4·39·7·56
R.A.	11	11	N	4·39·0·02
R.A.	11	11	N	4·35·45·61
7207	13	13	S	4·24·25·55
R.A.	11	11	N	4·15·23·76
R.A.	11	12	N	0·7·32·94
R.A.	11	11	N	4·30·21·03
R.A.	11	12	N	3·52·34·32

Abstract of the Resulting Mean Zenith Distances.

Zwart Kop—continued.

No. of Star in B.A.C. or approximate R.A.	No. of Observations; Face of Sector E	W	North or South	Mean Zenith Distance, 1844, January 0.
7386	11	12	N	1·24·20·88
B.A. h m 8712	12	11	N	4·24· 6·76
B.A. h m 8725	12	12	N	3·50·25·97
7557	12	12	N	0·29·31·18
x7613	12	12	S	3·52· 7 85
7067	11	12	N	5· 1·35 09
B.A. h m 8166	12	12	N	5· 2·12·89
7842	11	12	N	1·4 ·57·13
7909	11	10	N	4· 3· 6·11
7966	12	11	N	0·31·30·32
x7992	12	11	N	3·46·42·35

Cape Point.

1739	10	10	S	1·14·11·10
y1802	11	11	N	0·11·28·05
√1878	10	10	S	1·28·42 20
1922	10	10	S	0·57· 5·59
1982	10	10	S	2·52·57·57
y2051	10	10	N	4·21·12·43
⌐2109	10	10	N	1·51·57·74
2246	10	10	N	2· 1·11·06
y2293	10	10	N	5·35·16·56
y2414	10	10	S	2·28· 7·15
y2458	10	10	S	5·20·55·11
2528	10	10	S	3·18·39·96
2575	10	10	S	3·13· 5·36
2580	10	10	S	3·14·27·67
2635	10	10	N	4· 6·35·30
2655	10	10	N	4·25·58·70
y2710	10	10	S	5·12·51·54
2795	10	10	S	1·49·36·65
2935	10	10	S	0·24·20·38
2964	10	10	N	1·43·28·70
3130	10	10	N	4·37·12·24
3163	10	10	N	3·34·13·12
3257	10	10	S	5·26· 1·01
R.A. h m	8	6	N	2·23·10·37
3403	6	6	N	3·59·54 19

Cape Point—continued.

No. of Star in B.A.C. or approximate R.A.	No. of Observations; Face of Sector E	W	Z.D.	Mean Zenith Distance, 1844, January 0.
B.A. h m	5	5	N	4· 0·39·03
3578	10	10	N	4· 4·31·52
3598	7	7	N	4·32·27·43
3755	10	8	S	1·56·53·99
3928	10	10	N	3·21·24 33
4015	6	6	N	1·18·41·27
4202	3	2	S	3·49·28·51
x4456	10	10	S	1·32· 7·45
y4686	10	10	S	1·14·50·16
y5632	4	4	N	0·20·53·21
x5915	10	10	S	2·37·50·44
x6233	9	8	S	0· 5·57·99
7842	4	4	N	1·12·29·32
7966	5	4	N	0·39· 2·26
y7992	10	10	N	3 54·13·06

North-Sector Station, Bushman Flat.

1847, Jan. 0.

4517	8	10	N	0 57·42 26
4548	9	10	N	0·57·38·74
4579	9	11	S	2·31·45·90
4623	10	11	S	2·29·40·59
4719	8	10	N	1·10 25 51
4784	8	11	N	4·46·21 66
B.A. h m 4852	10	9	S	2·53·59·28
4891	9	10	N	2 25· 5·82
4916	9	10	N	3·29·31·06
5032	10	7	S	2·34 31·68
5082	10	10	N	2·56·13·49
5151	10	11	N	0·28· 5·01
B.A. h m 5227	8	10	S	1 22 14·50
5227	10	11	S	3·25· 3·36
5272	10	11	S	0·58·32·14
5374	10	11	N	0·43·51·06
5435	10	10	S	0·47 30·37

North Sector Station, Bushman Flat—continued.

No. of Star in B.A.C. or approximate R.A.	No. of Observations; Face of Sector E	W	North or South	Mean Zenith Distance, 1847, January 0.
R.A. h m 1·13	10	9	S	3· 5·49·33
5498	10	11	N	3·39· 1·72
5588	10	10	S	2· 4·15·37
y5632	10	11	S	4·16·16·22
5735	10	9	S	4· 9·47·66
5817	10	10	S	2 44·45·01
5861	10	9	N	0· 0·55·50
6016	9	9	S	1·54·21·63
6074	10	10	S	0·29·35 37
6115	10	11	S	0·40·53·42
6145	10	10	S	1· 0·30·98
x6233	9	9	S	4·42·42·73
6285	8	8	S	3·20·45·22
6305	9	7	S	3·23· 6·16
6414	9	9	S	1 10·17·98
6489	11	10	S	0·21 17·09
6525	10	7	N	0·52 15·68
6639	10	10	S	0·18· 6·76
R.A. h m 16·21	5	4	S	0· 4· 4·80
6753	7	8	S	1·31·33·58
6877	10	10	S	2·44·31·43
6948	9	9	S	0·43·44·09
7011	9	9	N	0·10·25·04
7026	8	9	N	0·10·17·79
7057	9	8	N	0· 7· 4·69
R.A. h m	5	8	S	0· 4·15·21
B.A. h m	6	8	S	0·13·16 29
7207	9	8	S	4·36· 9·79
7207	7	9	N	0· 1·45·92
7386	9	8	S	0·35 58 49
7386	9	9	S	3· 4·11·25
R.A. h m	9	9	S	0· 4·24·51
R.A. h m	8	10	S	0·38· 3·48
7557	9	10	S	3·58·55·63
7657	9	7	N	0·33· 9·99
R.A. h m	9	6	N	0·33·48·83
7842	9	10	S	3·23 23·44
7909	8	8	S	0·25·13·43
7966	8	7	S	3 56·47·90
x7992	10	8	S	0 41·37·30

Abstract of Resulting Mean Zenith Distances of Stars observed at the Royal Observatory.

No. of Star in B.A.C. or approximate R.A.	No. of Observations Pace of Sector E	W	Year of Observation.	North South	Mean Zenith Distance, Jan. 0, of each year.
1739	10	10	1845	S	1·39·10·97
1802 {	33	32	1844	S	0·13·35·01
	10	10	1845	S	0·13·32·91
	13	13	1848	S	0·13·26·03
1878 {	2	2	1844	S	1·53·45·97
	10	11	1845	S	1·53·43·88
1922	10	10	1845	S	1·22· 7·37
1982	9	10	1845	S	3·18· 0·45
2051	10	10	1845	N	3·56· 7·75
2109	10	10	1845	N	1·26·53·12
2246	10	11	1845	N	1·36· 4·02
2293 {	40	38	1844	N	5·10·12·97
	11	11	1845	N	5·10· 8·09
	15	16	1848	N	5· 9·54·65
2414	10	10	1845	S	2·53·16·85
2458	10	10	1845	S	4·55·45·38
2528	10	10	1845	S	3·43·50·55
2575	10	10	1845	S	3·38·16·99
2580	10	10	1845	S	3·39·38·92
2635	10	11	1845	S	4·31·47·19
2655	10	10	1845	N	4· 0·46·04
2710	10	10	1845		5 38· 4 46
2795	10	10	1845	S	2·14·50·51
2935	10	10	1845	S	0·49·36·53
2964	10	10	1845	N	1·18·12·79
3130	10	10	1845	N	4·11·54·11
3163	10	10	1845	S	3·59·30·54
R.A.	10	10	1845	N	1·57·50·15
3403	10	11	1845	N	3·34·34·48
R.A.	10	10	1845	N	3·35·18·60
3578	10	10	1845	N	3·39·13·40
3598	5	5	1845	N	4· 7· 5·96
3755	10	10	1845	S	2·22·16·09

No. of Star approximate R.A.	No. of Observations Pace of Sector E	W	Year of Observation.	North South	Mean Zenith Distance, Jan. 0, of each year.
3928	10	10	1845	N	2 56· 1·77
4015	10	10	1845	N	0 53·18·08
4202	10	10	1845	S	4·14·51·64
4458 {	16	16	1844	S	1·57·10·46
	10	11	1845	S	1·57·29·91
4507	4	2	1844	S	4 39·51·57
4517 {	15	15	1844	N	5·10·24·37
	6	7	1848	N	5· 9· 9·06
4548 {	15	15	1844	N	5·10·20·44
	7	8	1848	N	5·9· 5·48
4579 {	15	15	1844	N	1·40·55·13
	8	10	1848	N	1·39·40·96
4623 {	15	15	1844	N	1·42·59·34
	9	9	1848	N	1·41·46·72
4686 {	33	33	1844	S	1·39·53·32
	10	10	1845	S	1·40·11·32
	4	4	1848	S	1·41· 5·38
4719 {	16	15	1844	N	5·23· 3·05
	7	9	1848	N	5·21·53·88
4745	1	1	1844	S	3·13·45·94
4784 {	15	15	1844	N	5· 8·49·17
	10	11	1848		5· 7·42·59
4852 {	16	17	1844	N	1·18·34·92
	11	9	1848	N	1·17·30·83
	16	15	1844	S	0·33·48·12
	14	14	1848	S	0·34·51·14
4916 {	16	16	1844	N	0·42·59·04
	12	14	1848	N	0·41·59·34
	16	15	1844	N	1·54·38·48
	12	14	1848	N	1·53·40·42
R.A. {	17	16	1844	N	1·37·55·68
	10	9	1848	N	1·36·59·09
5032 {	16	16	1844	N	4·21·49·48
	13	16	1848	N	4·20·54·88
5054	16	15	1844	S	1·45·20·57
5151 {	15	15	1844	N	4·40·28·04
	15	18	1848	N	4·39·38·42
R.A. {	15	15	1844	N	2·50· 7·03
	13	14	1848	N	2·49·18·51

No. of Star in B.A.C. or approximate R.A.	No. of Observations Pace of Sector E	W	Year of Observation.	North South	Mean Zenith Distance, Jan. 0, of each year.
5227 {	16	15	1844	N	0·47·16·44
	14	15	1848	N	0·46·30·57
5272 {	16	15	1844	N	5 10·51·57
	15	14	1848	N	5·10· 7·45
5292	2	3	1844	S	4· 0 36·66
5331	10	9	1844	S	2·26·13·53
R.A.	5	8	1844	S	2 23·29·96
5374 {	15	15	1844	N	4·56· 6·87
	15	13	1848	N	4·55·26·38
5435 {	15	15	1844	N	3·24·42·61
	12	12	1848	N	3·24· 5·21
	15	14	1844		1· 6 22·13
	7	6	1848	N	1· 5·46·07
5508 {	9	10	1844	S	0·25·25·06
	5	5	1848	S	0·25 58·50
5538	1	2	1844	S	0·59·35·35
5588 {	15	15	1844	N	2· 7·51·75
	12	12	1848	N	2· 7·22·15
5632 {	28	30	1844	S	0· 4· 9·44
	7	7	1845	S	0· 4·16·69
	15	14	1848	S	0· 4·37·79
5735 {	15	15	1844	N	0· 2·15·01
	15	14	1848		0· 1·52·30
5817 {	15	15	1844	N	1·27·15·36
	13	11	1848	N	1·26·56·67
5881 {	15	15	1844	N	4·12·53·65
	12	12	1848	N	4·12·37·81
5915 {	31	31	1844	N	3· 2·54·17
	9	10	1845	S	3· 2·57·35
	8	8	1848	S	3· 3· 7·02
5960	9	10	1844	N	1·49·40·60
5964	6	6	1844	N	1·48·39·37
5970 {	2	2	1844	S	5· 0·26·28
	8	8	1848	S	5· 0·36·60
6016 {	15	15	1844	N	2·17·28·98
	11	11	1846	N	2·17·21·50
6074 {	15	15	1844	N	3·42·13·25
	12	11	1848	N	3·42· 9·39
6115 {	15	15	1844	N	3·30·54·15
	12	12	1848	N	3·30·51·76

Abstract of Resulting Mean Zenith Distances of Stars observed at the Royal Observatory.

No. of Star in B.A.C. or approximate R.A.	No. of Observations Face of Sector E	No. of Observations Face of Sector W	Year of Observation	N./S. North or South	Mean Zenith Distance, Jan. 0, of each year
6145	15	15	1844	N	3·11·15·17
	12	11	1848	N	3·11·15·11
6186	15	15	1844	S	2·52· 1·00
	8	8	1848	S	2·51·59·09
6233	33	32	1844	S	0·31· 0·97
	10	10	1845	S	0·30·59·64
	16	15	1848	S	0·30·56·38
6275	15	15	1844	N	0·47·32·57
6285	16	16	1844	N	0·50·55·61
	12	12	1848	N	0·51· 2·96
6305	15	15	1844	N	0·48·32·57
	13	12	1848	N	0·48·41·27
6414	15	15	1844	N	3· 1·16·33
	10	11	1848	N	3· 1·31·33
6489	14	15	1844	N	3·50·14·79
	11	11	1848	N	3·50·32·98
6525	15	15	1844	N	5· 3·46·28
	10	11	1848	N	5· 4· 5·68
6639	15	15	1844	N	3·53·18·66
	10	10	1848	N	3·53·44·56
B.A. 1941	10	10	1844	N	4· 7·19·19
	10	11	1848	N	4· 7·47·37
6753	15	15	1844	N	2·39·46·99
	10	10	1848	N	2 40·19·42
6877	15	15	1844	N	1·26·45·34
	10	10	1848	N	1·27·23·95
6948	15	15	1844	N	3·27·30·27
	10	11	1848	N	3·28·12·92
7011	16	15	1844	N	4·21·36·86
	9	10	1848	N	4·22·21·06
7026	15	14	1844	N	4·21·29·38
	11	11	1848	N	4·22·14·21
7057	15	15	1844	N	4·18·14·74
	11	10	1848	N	4·19· 1·31
B.A. 7371	15	15	1844	N	4· 6·55·01
	9	9	1848	N	4· 7·42·20
B.A. 7523	15	16	1844	N	3·57·52·71
	9	10	1848	N	3·58·41·56
7207	15	15	1844	S	0·25· 2·82
	10	10	1848	S	0·24·10·92
B.A. 7913	14	13	1844	N	4·12·50·89
	10	11	1848	N	4·13·46·26
B.A. 816	15	15	1844	N	3·35· 4·03
	10	10	1848	N	3·36· 1·12
7386	15	15	1844	N	1· 6 50·55
	10	10	1848	N	1· 7·49·21
B.A. 11 19	15	14	1844	N	4· 6·36·39
	10	10	1848	N	4· 7·36·80
B.A. 71 45	14	14	1844	N	3·32·55·21
	10	10	1848	N	3 33·58·03
7557	14	15	1844	N	0·12· 1·43
	10	10	1848	N	0·13· 5·98
7613	8	10	1844	S	4· 9 38·51
7657	15	15	1844	N	4·44· 4·81
	10	11	1848	N	4·45·12·76
B.A. 81 30	13	14	1844	N	4·44·42·86
	11	10	1848	N	4·45·51·47
7842	15	15	1844	N	0·47·26·37
	10	10	1848	N	0·48 39·76
7909	12	13	1844	N	3·45·36·13
	10	10	1848	N	3·46·50·62
7966	16	16	1844	N	0·13·59·75
	10	10	1848	N	0·15·15·76
7992	36	36	1844	N	3·29·12·16
	6	7	1845	N	3·29·31·00
	11	11	1848	N	3·30·27·68

THE following Table contains the Annual Precessions in N.P.D. of Stars observed with the Zenith Sector for the years 1844, 1845, and 1848; also the Annual Precessions for the epochs of the several Catalogues with which the N.P.D.'s deduced from these observations have been compared in order to determine the annual proper motions. The Precessions are computed with PETERS' Constants.

No. in B.A.C. or approximate R.A.	LACAILLE, 1750.		PIAZZI, 1800.		BRISBANE, 1825.		JOHNSON, 1830.		HENDERSON, 1833.	MACLEAR, 1834.	ANNUAL PRECESSIONS FOR THE SECTOR OBSERVATIONS.		
	No.	Ann. Precess	No.	Ann. Precess	No.	Ann. Precess	No.	Ann. Precess	Ann. Precess	Ann. Precess	1844.	1845.	1848.
1739		...	v. 140	- 3·128	970	- 3·055	124	- 3·036			- 2·993	- 2·9895	...
1802	90	- 2·566	196	2·409	1010	2·333	133	2·314	- 2·305	- 2·302	2·270	2·267	- 2·258
1878	97	- 1·560	267	1·407	1063	1·333	140	1·314	- 1·305	...	1·2715	1·268	- 1·259
1922		...	297	- 0·836	1097	...	143	- 0·742		...	- 0·699	- 0·696	...
1982		...	vi. 9	+ 0·058	1145	...	146	+ 0·149		...	+ 0·191	+ 0·194	...
2051	102	+ 0·939	8i	1·105	1207	+ 1·188	149	1·206	+ 1·216	...	1·253	1·256	...
2109		...	136	1·815	1247	...	153	1·911		...	1·956	1·9595	...
2246		...	259	3·688	1371	...	158	3·784		...	3·828	3·832	...
2293	112	4·241	304	4·407	1419	4·490	164	4·508	4·517	...	4·554	4·557	+ 4·567
2414	118	5·893	vii. 68	6·038	1536	6·109	175	6·127	6·135	...	6·168	6·171	...
2458	120	6·384	104	0·546	1591	6·628	177	6·644	6·653	...	6·689	6·692	...
2528		...		...		...		...		...	7·858	7·861	...
2575		...									8·399	8·402	...
2580		...	214	8·330	1735	8·395	181	8·413		...	8·452	8·455	...
2635		...	254	8·917	1801	...	186	8·999		...	9·038	9·040	...
2655		...	277	9·239	1825	...		...		...	9·374	9·377	...
2710	129	9·636	306	9·768	1876	9·831	189	9·848		✕	9·884	9·887	...
2795		...	viii. 47	10·858	1968	...	195	10·939		...	10·976	10·979	...
2935		...	145	12·369	2127	...	201	12·449		...	12·486	12·4885	...
2964		...	162	12·595	2160	...	204	12·675		...	12·712	12·715	...
3130		...	ix. 7	14·276	2352	...		...		...	14·387	14·3895	...
3163		...	40	14·656	2407	...		...		14·733	14·756	14·759	...
B.A.											16·363	16·365	...
3403		...		...		...		...		...	16·886	16·888	...
B.A.											17·440	17·442	...
3578		...	x. 82	18·107	3011	18·147	240	18·156		...	18·179	18·180	...
3598		...	91	18·196	3032	...		...		...	18·266	18·268	...
3755		...	199	19·063	3293	19·091		...		...	19·114	19·115	...
3928	176	19·772	xi. 103	19·8025	3641	19·817	263	19·820		...	19·828	19·8285	...
4015		...	172	20·0045	3811	20·010	267	20·011		...	20·014	20·014	...
4202		...	xii. 92	20·000	4068	19·969		...		...	19·980	19·979	...
4458	212	19·223	xiii. 53	19·148	4417	19·110	301	19·101	19·097	...	19·079	19·078	...
4507		...	99	18·866	4496	18·8215	304	18·812		...	18·786	18·784	...
4517		...	112	18·8075	4519	18·764		...		...	18·729	18·727	18·722
4548		...	146	18·616	4571	...		...		...	18·532	18·530	18·524
4579		...	178	18·384	4619	18·333	306	18·322		...	18·293	18·291	18·2845
4623	220	18·277	216	18·169	4682	18·115	310	18·103		...	18·071	18·069	18·062
4686	226	17·7135	293	17·589	4766	17·527	317	17·513		17·505	17·477	17·474	17·467
4719		...		...		...		...		...	17·101	17·098	17·090
4745		...	xiv. 40	16·992	4863	...		...		...	16·864	16·861	16·853
4784		...	82	16·6065	4925	...		...		...	16·477	16·474	16·465
B.A.											16·221	16·218	16·209
4852		...	150	15·836	5129	15·755	339	15·736		...	15·689	15·686	15·676
4916		...	204	15·166	5115	15·081		...		...	15·011	15·008	14·997
B.A.											14·581	14·577	14·567
B.A.											14·327	14·323	14·312
5032		...	xv. 22	13·828	5266	13·730	356	13·711		...	13·656	13·652	13·640
5054		...	34	13·607	5293	...	360	13·483		...	13·424	13·421	13·409
5151		...	123	12·460	5406	...	367	12·333		...	12·273	12·269	12·256
B.A.											11·906	11·901	11·888
5227		...	174	11·629	5499	11·517	370	11·492		...	11·428	11·424	11·410
5272	264	+11·400	207	11·177	5538	...	377	11·041	+11·023	...	10·977	10·973	10·959
5292		...	217	11·0055	5554	10·887	380	10·859		...	10·791	10·786	10·772
5331		...	248	10·519	5591	10·4005	384	+10·372		...	10·303	10·298	10·283
B.A.											10·252	10·248	10·233
5374		...	280	+10·133	5629	+10·347		...		...	+ 9·926	+ 9·921	+ 9·907

Annual Precessions in N.P.D.—continued.

No. in B A.C. or approximate R.A.	LACAILLE, 1750. No.	Ann. Proces	PIAZZI, 1800. No.	Ann. Proces	BRISBANE, 1825. No.	Ann. Proces	JOHNSON, 1830. No.	Ann. Proces	HENDERSON, 1833. Ann. Proces	MACLEAR, 1834. Ann. Proces	ANNUAL PRECESSIONS FOR THE SECTOR OBSERVATIONS. 1844.	1845.	1848.
5435	...	...	XVI. 36	+ 9·501	5685	...	...	...	...	...	+ 9·285	+ 9·280	+ 9·266
B.A. 16ʰ13ᵐ	...	...	...	...	...	...	...	...	...	...	8·955	8·951	8·396
5508	...	...	92	8·609	5747	+ 8·484	405	+ 8·454	...	...	8·381	8·376	8·360
5538	...	...	111	8·220	5767	8·091	408	8·062	...	...	7·988	7·983	7·967
5588	...	...	...	...	...	...	...	...	...	...	7·381	7·376	7·361
5632	282	7·352	184	7·038	5851	6·960	415	6·9285	6·913	...	6·854	6·849	6·833
5735	...	...	268	5·891	5950	5·758	422	5·726	...	...	5·649	5·643	5·627
5817	...	...	XVII. 23	4·8475	...	...	...	...	...	...	4·604	4·598	4·582
5881	...	...	86	3·984	...	...	435	3·784	...	...	3·707	3·701	3·685
5915	299	3·771	121	3·480	6116	3·338	439	3·304	3·287	...	3·222	3·216	3·198
5900	...	...	102	2·879	6156	...	...	...	...	...	2·630	2·624	...
5964	...	...	167	2·796	6163	...	...	...	...	...	2·549	2·543	...
5970	304	3·033	174	2·734	6169	+ 2·588	444	2·554	✕.	...	2·470	2·464	2·446
6016	...	...	227	2·080	...	...	...	...	...	...	1·833	1·826	1·809
6074	...	...	294	1·203	...	...	450	1·0345	...	...	0·956	0·950	0·9335
6115	312	+ 0·896	343	0·6155	...	...	457	+ 0·447	...	+ 1·012	+ 0·368	+ 0·363	+ 0·346
6145	...	...	367	+ 0·245	...	...	...	...	...	...	- 0·004	- 0·009	- 0·026
6186	315	- 0·063	XVIII. 17	- 0·359	6360	- 0·503	461	- 0·536	...	- 0·559	0·619	0·625	0·642
6233	317	0·664	46	0·943	6391	1·098	464	1·127	- 1·145	1·151	1·209	1·214	1·232
6275	...	...	72	1·478	...	...	...	...	...	...	1·730	1·735	...
6285	...	...	79	1·509	...	...	...	...	...	1·765	1·822	1·828	1·845
6305	...	...	96	1·8215	...	...	...	...	...	2·018	2·073	2·078	2·0955
6414	...	...	...	...	...	...	...	...	...	...	3·713	3·719	3·736
6489	328	4·059	257	4·3315	...	...	481	4·494	...	...	4·570	4·576	4·592
6525	...	...	293	4·761	...	...	...	...	...	...	4·9955	5·001	5·017
6639	...	...	XIX. 102	6·389	...	...	...	...	...	...	6·619	6·624	6·640
B.A. 19ʰ21ᵐ	...	...	...	...	...	...	...	...	...	...	6·965	6·970	6·986
6753	...	...	237	7·8965	...	...	...	...	...	8·069	8·119	8·124	8·139
6877	...	...	366	9·388	...	...	500	9·535	...	...	9·603	9·608	9·623
6948	...	...	...	...	...	...	...	...	...	...	10·490	10·495	10·509
7011	...	...	...	...	...	...	...	...	...	...	11·152	11·150	11·169
7026	...	...	...	...	...	...	...	...	...	...	11·286	11·290	11·304
7057	...	...	...	...	...	...	...	...	...	...	11·603	11·607	11·620
B.A.	...	...	...	...	...	...	...	...	...	...	11·807	11·812	11·825
B.A.	...	...	...	...	...	...	...	...	...	...	12·469	12·473	12·486
7207	...	...	XX. 307	12·722	...	...	524	12·848	...	...	12·907	12·911	12·924
B.A.	...	...	...	...	...	...	...	...	...	...	13·778	13·782	13·793
B.A.	...	...	477	14·065	...	...	...	...	...	...	14·227	14·231	14·242
7386	...	...	XXI. 46	14·538	...	...	530	14·647	...	...	14·697	14·700	14·711
B.A.	...	...	...	...	...	...	...	...	...	...	14·937	14·940	14·951
B.A.	...	...	...	...	...	...	...	...	...	...	15·678	15·682	15·691
7557	...	...	250	16·073	7074	16·149	541	16·165	...	16·177	16·208	16·211	16·220
7613	378	16·371	308	16·521	7094	16·504	544	16·610	·▲·	...	16·651	16·654	16·663
7657	...	...	351	16·887	7112	16·952	...	...	...	...	17·003	17·005	17·0135
B.A.	...	...	...	...	...	...	...	...	...	...	17·179	17·182	17·190
7842	...	...	XXII. 123	18·185	7176	18·2335	564	18·246	...	18·254	18·274	18·276	18·282
7909	...	...	187	18·574	...	...	...	...	...	...	18·651	18·653	18·658
7966	...	...	234	18·892	...	...	572	18·938	...	...	18·960	18·961	18·966
7992	389	-18·966	253	-19·040	7225	-19·075	575	-19·083	-19·087	-19·089	-19·103	-19·104	-19·108

Investigation of the Proper Motions in N.P.D.

In order to determine, as far as practicable, the proper motions in N.P.D. of the Stars observed with the Zenith Sector, the places deduced from the observations made at the Observatory have been compared with the positions given in the following catalogues :—

1. La Caille's Catalogue of 398 principal Stars for 1750, inserted by Mr. Baily in Vol. V of the Memoirs of the Royal Astronomical Society.

2. Piazzi's Catalogue for 1800.

3. Brisbane's Paramatta Catalogue for 1825.

4. Johnson's St. Helena Catalogue for 1830.

5. Henderson's Declinations of the principal fixed Stars for 1833. Inserted in Vol. X of the Royal Astronomical Society's Memoirs.

6. Cape Observations, Vol. I, 1834.

In a subsequent investigation it will be shown that the latitude of La Caille's Observatory in Cape Town, derived from the latitude of the Royal Observatory, by the application of the amplitude of the two stations as observed with Bradley's Sector, is very nearly 2″ greater than the value used by La Caille in the reduction of his observations. It will be necessary, therefore, to increase the declinations observed by La Caille in Cape Town by this quantity before comparing them with the recent determinations. This correction has been made accordingly.

The Catalogues of Piazzi, Brisbane, and Johnson have been taken without alteration; but Henderson's declinations and the Cape observations have been diminished 0″·05, in order to allow for the difference in the adopted latitudes.

The proper motion (m) of a star is found by means of the following formula :—

$$m = \frac{\Delta - \Delta'}{t} - \Pi.$$

where Δ is the N.P.D. for 1845, Δ' that of the Catalogue, t the interval in years between the epoch of the Catalogue and 1845, and Π the mean of the annual precessions for these two periods.

The results—which are arranged in the following table—exhibit in many cases considerable discordances; but, perhaps, on the whole they are not greater than might have been anticipated, if we take into consideration, in addition to the usual sources of error, the low altitude of the Stars as observed by Piazzi, and the comparatively short interval of time elapsed between the recent observations and the epochs of the three later Catalogues.

The values deduced from the comparisons with La Caille are undoubtedly entitled to great confidence; and they have been, accordingly, exclusively adopted in every instance. But some uncertainty still attaches to the other assumed proper motions. It is not probable, however, that the more correct values to be assigned hereafter will materially affect the results, or alter to any sensible amount the amplitudes finally deduced from the observations with the Sector.

In the table of proper motions a column is introduced containing the values derived from the Sector Observations alone in an interval of about four years.

Annual Proper Motions in N.P.D. of Stars observed with Bradley's Zenith Sector.

CATALOGUE AND EPOCH.

No. of Star in B.A.C. or approximate R.A.	LACAILLE, 1750.		PIAZZI, 1800.		BRISBANE, 1825.		JOHNSON, 1830.		HENDERSON, 1833.		MACLEAR, 1834.		Four years observation with the Zen. Sect.	Adopted Annual Proper Motion.
	Annual Proper Motion	No. of Observ.	Annual Proper Motion	No. of Observ.	Annual Proper Motion	No. of Observ.	Annual Proper Motion	No. of Observ.	Annual Proper Motion	No. of Observ.	Annual Proper Motion	No. of Observ.		
1739	...		+0·063	8	-0·075	11	-0·002	6	...		...		...	...
1802	+0·025	19	+0·014	30	+0·039	70	-0·004	30	-0·049	141	+0·015	40	+0·02	+0·025
1878	-0·418	19	-0·368	8	-0·447	17	-0·340	8	-0·556	10	...		...	-0·42
1922	...		-0·044	8	...		-0·123	8	...		...		...	...
1982	...		-0·034	8	...		-0·028	8	...		...		...	...
2051	+0·003	10	-0·038	10	+0·130	5	+0·152	36	+0·110	10	...		...	0·00
2109	...		-0·052	9	...		+0·050	5	...		...		...	...
2246	...		+0·011	17	...		+0·037	7	...		...		...	...
2293	-0·019	12	+0·064	17	+0·004	27	+0·100	47	+0·043	20	...		+0·02	-0·02
2414	+0·015	9	-0·031	6	-0·052	19	-0·039	36	-0·074	10	...		...	+0·015
2458	-0·019	9	+0·044	17	-0·099	17	+0·093	47	+0·110	10	...		...	-0·02
2580	...		-0·057	8	-0·024	5	-0·139	6	...		...		...	...
2635	...		+0·007	11	...		-0·187	5	...		...		...	...
2655	...		+0·029	6	...		...		...		...		...	...
2710	-0·010	7	-0·031	13	-0·126	26	-0·191	24	...		...		...	-0·01
2795	...		-0·070	12	...		-0·138	6	...		...		...	...
2935	...		-0·013	6	...		-0·054	8	...		...		...	...
2964	...		-0·028	8	...		-0·074	9	...		...		...	...
3130	...		+0·047	6	...		...		...		...		...	...
3163	...		-0·158	9	...		...		...		-0·161	7	...	-0·16
3578	...		+0·025	8	+0·031	8	+0·119	21	...		...		...	...
3598	...		+0·056	5	...		...		...		...		...	...
3755	...		+0·151	7	+0·037	6	...		...		...		...	...
3928	+0·057	10	+0·026	9	+0·138	5	+0·084	15	...		...		...	+0·06
4015	...		+0·016	24	-0·101	9	+0·022	6	...		...		...	...
4202	...		+0·206	8	+0·023	4	...		...		...		...	...
4458	+0·068	24	+0·107	9	+0·002	26	+0·072	6	-0·083	10	...		...	+0·07
4507	...		+0·021	9	-0·075	19	-0·194	5	...		...		...	...
4517	...		+0·091	9	+0·136	4	...		...		...		+0·10	+0·10
4548	...		+0·126	9	...		...		...		...		+0·20	+0·15
4579	...		+0·186	16	+0·256	9	+0·217	7	...		...		+0·24	+0·22
4623	+0·022	6	+0·104	8	-0·114	10	+0·184	6	...		...		+0·08	+0·02
4686	+0·503	11	+0·544	34	+0·530	27	+0·401	9	+0·391	12	...		+0·48	+0·50
4784	...		+0·097	23	...		...		...		...		+0·16	+0·13
4852	...		+0·248	10	+0·299	10	+0·122	5	...		...		+0·07	+0·20
4916	...		+0·058	10	-0·132	12	...		...		...		-0·08	0·00
5032	...		+0·056	11	+0·040	4	+0·219	10	...		...		0·00	0·06
5054	...		+0·046	9	...		-0·013	7	...		...		...	...
5151	...		+0·127	14	...		+0·101	6	...		...		+0·13	+0·13
5227	...		+0·074	6	-0·014	6	+0·077	5	...		...		+0·04	+0·05
5272	+0·056	8	+0·079	8	...		+0·163	5	...		+0·106	4	+0·06	+0·06
5292	...		+0·118	12	-0·049	15	+0·020	7	...		...		...	...
5331	...		+0·037	8	-0·057	8	-0·046	8	...		...		...	...
R.A. 16h 43m	...		+0·051	7	-0·006	5	...		...		...		...	...
5374	...		+0·175	9	...		...		...		...		+0·19	+0·18
5435	...		+0·030	6	...		...		...		...		+0·07	+0·05
5508	...		+0·039	17	-0·033	9	-0·033	5	...		...		-0·01	0·00
5538	...		+0·068	6	+0·100	0	-0·073	7	...		...		...	...
5592	+0·251	18	+0·291	17	+0·270	12	+0·197	9	+0·181	34	...		+0·22	+0·25
5735	...		+0·030	6	-0·115	4	-0·011	10	...		...		+0·04	0·00
5817	...		+0·100	9	...		...		...		...		+0·08	+0·10
5881	...		+0·174	15	...		+0·281	12	...		...		+0·25	+0·22
5915	-0·014	12	+0·074	15	+0·042	18	-0·055	6	-0·097	12	...		0·00	-0·01
5960	...		+0·062	10	...		...		...		...		...	...
5964	...		+0·050	10	...		...		...		...		...	...
5970	-0·054	6	+0·034	14	+0·018	17	-0·211	6	...		...		...	-0·05
6016	...		+0·078	12	...		...		...		...		+0·05	+0·07
6074	...		+0·075	17	...		+0·176	7	...		+0·124	8	+0·02	+0·10

D

Annual Proper Motions in N.P.D.—continued.

No. of Star in B.A.C. or approximate R.A.	LACAILLE, 1750.		PIAZZI, 1800.		BRISBANE, 1825.		JOHNSON, 1830.		HENDERSON, 1833.		MACLEAR, 1834.		Four years observation with the Zen. Sect.	Adopted Annual Proper Motion.
	Annual Proper Motion.	No. of Obervts.	Annual Proper Motion.	No. of Obervts.	Annual Proper Motion.	No. of Obervts.	Annual Proper Motion.	No. of Obervts.	Annual Proper Motion.	No. of Obervts.	Annual Proper Motion.	No. of Obervts.		
6115	+0·179	9	+0·269	12	...		+0·264	7	...		...		+0·23	+0·18
6145	...		+0·105	20	...		...		...		...		+0·03	+0·10
6186	+0·139	9	+0·247	11	+0·233	21	+0·006	7	...		+0.169	7	+0·14	+0·14
6233	+0·151	16	+0·245	15	+0·264	4	+0·014	9	+0·072	96	+0·129	19	+0·07	+0·15
6275	...		+0·061	15	...		...		...		...		...	+0·06
6285	...		+0·167	9	...		...		...		+0·027	7	0·00	+0·10
6305	...		+0·083	8	...		...		...		-0·063	2	-0·09	0·00
6489	-0·009	8	+0·061	16	...		+0·116	13	...		...		+0·03	-0·01
6525	...		+0·082	7	...		...		...		...		+0·14	+0·10
6639	...		+0·138	13	...		...		...		...		+0·15	+0·15
6753	...		+0·096	11	...		...		...		+0·044	4	+0·02	+0·05
6877	...		+0·060	7	...		-0·068	5	...		...		-0·04	0·00
7207	...		+0·066	7	...		-0·039	5	...		...		-0·06	0·00
B.A. m^{h}c^{m}	...		+0·063	4	...		...		...		...		-0·04	0 00
7386	...		+0·178	6	...		-0·033	5	...		...		+0·04	+0·10
7557	...		+0·139	9	-0·031	7	-0·053	7	...		-0·084	2	+0·07	+0·10
7613	+0·038	15	+0·097	7	+0·043	8	-0·162	8	...		...		...	+0·04
7657	...		+0·093	13	-0·023	4	...		...		...		+0·02	+0·05
7842	...		+0·048	9	-0·036	6	-0·080	7	...		-0·070	5	-0·07	-0·04
7909	...		+0·059	5	...		...		...		...		+0·03	+0·05
7966	...		+0·087	13	...		+0·016	9	...		...		-0·04	+0·05
7992	+0·179	19	+0·201	74	+0·226	146	+0·182	58	+0·185	39	+0·191	48	+0·20	+0·18

THE following Table, which is derived from the Abstract on pp. 420 and 421, contains the Mean Zenith Distances of Stars observed at the Royal Observatory, with Bradley's Zenith Sector, reduced to the same epoch,—viz., 1845, January 0, and corrected for assumed proper motion. The number in the 4th column, expressing the weight of the result for each year of observation, is obtained from the expression $\dfrac{E.W}{E+W}$, where E and W denote respectively the number of observations with the face of the Sector East or West.

When a star has been observed at two separate periods, and the results have been corrected for proper motion, the mean zenith distance, contained in column 8, has been obtained by combining these values according to their respective weights; but where no correction for proper motion has been made, the arithmetic mean, without reference to the weights, has been adopted.

The weight in column 9 annexed to a mean result is, in the former case, the sum of the separate values; in the latter, it is taken $= \dfrac{4\,ab}{a+b}$, a and b being the weights for each year.

No. of Star in B.A.C. or approximate R.A.	Mean Year of Observation.	Mean Z.D. reduced to 1845·0, by precession alone.	WEIGHT.	Adopted Annual Proper Motion.	Correction to 1845·0 for P.M.	Mean Z.D. 1845·0, corrected for Proper Motion.	GENERAL MEAN.	WEIGHT.
1739	1845·15	S 1·39·10·97	5·0	...	...		S 1·39·10·97	5·0
1802 {	1844·15	S 0·13·32·74	16·25	+0·025	+0·021	S 0·13·32·761 }	S 0·13·32·78	27·75
	1845·15	32·91	5·0	,,	-0·004	32·906		
	1848·54	32·82	6·5		-0·088	32·732		
1878 {	1844·44	S 1·53·44·70	1·0	-0·42	-0·235	S 1·53·44·465 }	S 1·53·44·04	6·24
	1845·20	43·88	5·24	,,	+0·084	43·964		
1922	1845·14	S 1·22·7·37	5·0	...	...		S 1·22·7·37	5·0
1982	1845·14	S 3·18·0·45	4·74	...	...		S 3·18·0·45	4·74
2051	1845·15	N 3·56·7·75	5·0	0·00	0·00	N 3·56·7·75	N 3·56·7·75	5·0
2109	1845·14	N 1·26·53·12	5·0	...	...		N 1·26·53·12	5·0
2246	1845·15	N 1·36·4·02	5·24	...	...		N 1·36·4·02	5·24
2293 {	1844·16	N 5·10·8·42	19·49	-0·02	+0·017	N 5·10·8·437 }	N 5·10·8·34	32·73
	1845·15	8·09	6·5	,,	-0·003	8·087		
	1848·54	8·34	7·74		-0·071	8·269		
2414	1845·15	S 2·53·16·85	5·0	+0·015	0·00	S 2·53·16·85	S 2·53·16·85	5·0
2458	1845·15	N 4·55·45·38	5·0	-0·02	0·00	N 4·55·45·38	N 4·55·45·38	5·0
2528	1845·15	S 3·43·50·55	5·0	...	...		S 3·43·50·55	5·0
2575	1845·14	S 3·38·16·39	5·0	...	...		S 3·38·16·39	5·0
2580	1845·14	S 3·39·38·92	5·0	...	...		S 3·39·38·92	5·0
2635	1845·14	S 4·31·47·19	5·24	...	...		S 4·31·47·19	5·24
2655	1845·14	N 4·0·46·04	5·0	...	...		N 4·0·46·04	5·0
2710	1845·15	S 5·38·4·46	5·0	-0·01	0·00	S 5·38·4·46	S 5·38·4·46	5·0
2795	1845·15	S 2·14·50·51	5·0	...	...		S 2·14·50·51	5·0
2935	1845·15	S 0·49·36·53	5·0	...	...		S 0·49·36·53	5·0
2964	1845·15	N 1·18·12·79	5·0	...	...		N 1·18·12·79	5·0
3130	1845·16	N 4·11·54·11	5·0	...	...		N 4·11·54·11	5·0
3163	1845·16	S 3·59·30·54	5·0	-0·16	+0·03	S 3·59·30·57	S 3·59·30·57	5·0
B.A. r° w	1845·18	N 1·57·50·15	5·0	...	...		N 1·57·50·15	5·0
3403	1845·18	N 3·34·34·48	5·24	...	...		N 3·34·34·48	5·24
B.A. r° w	1845·18	N 3·35·18·60	5·0	...	...		N 3·35·18·60	5·0
3578	1845·19	N 3·39·13·40	5·0	...	...		N 3·39·13·40	5·0
3596	1845·20	N 4·7·5·96	2·5	...	...		N 4·7·5·96	2·5
3755	1845·18	S 2·22·16·09	5·0	...	...		S 2·22·16·09	5·0
3928	1845·28	N 2·56·1·77	5·0	+0·06	+0·017	N 2·56·1·79	N 2·56·1·79	5·0
4015	1845·28	N 0·53·18·08	5·0	...	...		N 0·53·18·08	5·0
4202	1845·28	S 4·14·51·64	5·0	...	...		S 4·14·51·64	5·0
4458 {	1844·16	S 1·57·29·54	8·0	+0·07	+0·059	S 1·57·29·599 }	S 1·57·29·71	13·24
	1845·29	29·91	5·24	,,	-0·020	29·890		
4507	1844·41	S 4·40·10·36	1·33	...	...		S 4·40·10·36	1·33
4517 {	1844·24	N 5·10·5·64	7·5	+0·10	-0·076	N 5·10·5·564 }	N 5·10·5·57	10·73
	1848·48	5·23	3·23	,,	+0·348	5·578		
4548 {	1844·24	N 5·10·1·91	7·5	+0·15	-0·114	N 5·10·1·796 }	N 5·10·1·73	11·23
	1848·49	1·03	3·73	,,	+0·522	1·582		

Mean Zenith Distances of Stars observed at the Royal Observatory, with Bradley's Zenith Sector, reduced to 1845·0—*continued.*

No. of Star in B.A.C. or approxi- mate R.A.	Mean Year of Observation	Mean Z.D. reduced to 1845·0, by precession alone.	WEIGHT.	Adopted Annual Pro- per Motion.	Correction to 1845·0 for P.M.	Mean Z.D. 1845·0, corrected for Proper Motion.	GENERAL MEAN.	WEIGHT.
4579 {	1844·24	N 1·40·36·84	7·5	+0·22	−0·168	N 1·40·36·672 }	N 1·40·36·64	11·94
	1848·50	35·82	4·44	„	+0·771	36·591 }		
4623 {	1844·24	N 1·42·41·27	7·5	+0·02	−0·015	N 1·42·41·255 }	N 1·42·41·15	12·0
	1848·50	40·91	4·5	„	+0·070	40·980 }		
4686 {	1844·12	S 1·40·10·80	16·5	−0·50	+0·440	S 1·40·11·240 }	S 1·40·11·22	23·5
	1845·29	11·32	5·0	„	−0·145	11·175 }		
	1848·62	12·97	2·0	„	−1·610	11·160 }		
4719 {	1844·26	N 5·22·45·95	7·74	...	...	....	N 5·22·45·56	10·44
	1848·50	45·16	3·94	...	...			
4745	1844·41	S 3·14· 2·80	0·5	...	...	....	S 3·14· 2·80	0·5
4784 {	1844·25	N 5· 8·32·69	7·5	+0·13	−0·097	N 5· 8·32·593 }	N 5· 8·32·54	12·74
	1848·50	32·00	5·24	„	+0·454	32·454 }		
B.A.14ʰ94ᵐ {	1844·26	N 1·18·18·69	8·24	...	...	....	N 1·18·19·09	12·36
	1848·50	19·48	4·05	...	...			
4852 {	1844·23	S 0·34· 3·81	7·74	+0·20	+0·154	S 0·34· 3·964 }	S 0·34· 3·69	14·74
	1849·53	4·10	7·0	„	−0·706	3·304 }		
4918 {	1844·25	N 0·42·44·03	8·0	0·00	0·00	N 0·42·44·03 }	N 0·42·44·17	14·46
	1848·51	44·35	6·46	„	0·00	44·35 }		
B.A.14ʰ94ᵐ {	1844·25	N 1·54·23·00	7·74	...	...	....	N 1·54·24·01	14·08
	1848·51	24·12	6·46	...	...			
B.A.14ʰ49ᵐ {	1844·28	N 1·37·41·86	8·24	...	...	....	N 1·37·41·70	12·03
	1848·53	42·03	4·74	...	...			
5032 {	1844·24	N 4·21·35·82	8·0	+0·06	−0·045	N 4·21·35·775 }	N 4·21·35·89	15·17
	1848·53	35·81	7·17	„	+0·213	36·023 }		
5054	1844·26	S 1·45·33·99	7·74	...	...	...	S 1·45·33·99	7·74
5151 {	1844·26	N 4·40·15·77	7·5	+0·13	−0·096	N 4·40·15·674 }	N 4·40·15·67	15·68
	1848·53	15·20	8·18	„	+0·460	15·680 }		
B.A.12ʰ94ᵐ {	1844·34	N 2·49·55·13	7·5	...	...	....	N 2·49·54·65	14·20
	1848·51	54·17	6·74	...	...			
5227 {	1844·26	N 0·47· 5·01	7·74	+0·05	−0·037	N 0·47· 4·973 }	N 0·47· 4·98	14·98
	1848·53	4·82	7·24	„	+0·177	4·997 }		
5272 {	1844·25	N 5·10·40·59	7·74	+0·06	−0·045	N 5·10·40·545 }	N 5·10·40·55	14·98
	1848·53	40·35	7·24	„	+0·211	40·561 }		
5292	1844·41	S 4· 0·47·45	1·2	...	...	....	S 4· 0·47·45	1·2
5331	1844·42	S 2·26·23·83	4·74	...	...	....	S 2·26·23·83	4·74
B.A.13ʰ90ᵐ	1844·39	S 2·23·40·21	3·08	...	...	....	S 2·23·40·21	3·08
5374 {	1844·34	N 4·55·56·94	7·5	+0·18	−0·118	N 4·55·56·822 }	N 4·55·56·79	14·46
	1848·53	56·12	6·96	„	+0·037	56·757 }		
5435 {	1844·34	N 3·24·33·33	7·5	+0·05	−0·033	N 3·24·33·297 }	N 3·24·33·26	13·5
	1848·53	33·03	6·0	„	+0·177	33·207 }		
B.A.14ʰ13ᵐ {	1844·34	N 1· 6·13·17	7·24	...	...	....	N 1· 6·13·04	8·94
	1848·50	12·90	3·23	...	...			
5508 {	1844·39	S 0·25·33·44	4·74	0·00	0·00	S 0·25·33·44 }	S 0·25·33·43	7·24
	1848·63	33·40	2·5	„	0·00	33·40 }		
5538	1844·42	S 0·59·43·34	0·67	...	...	....	S 0·59·43·34	0·67
5586 {	1844·34	N 2· 7·44·37	7·5	...	...	....	N 2· 7·44·31	13·33
	1848·53	44·25	6·0	...	...			
5632 {	1844·14	S 0· 4·16·29	14·75	+0·25	+0·215	S 0· 4·16·505 }	S 0· 4·16·49	25·49
	1845·28	16·09	3·5	„	−0·070	16·620 }		
	1848·54	17·27	7·24	„	−0·885	16·385 }		
5735 {	1844·34	N 0· 2· 9·36	7·5	0·00	0·00	N 0· 2· 9·36 }	N 0· 2· 9·29	14·74
	1848·54	9·21	7·24	„	0·00	9·21 }		
5817 {	1844·34	N 1·27·10·76	7·5	+0·10	−0·008	N 1·27·10·094 }	N 1·27·10·74	13·46
	1848·55	10·44	5·96	„	+0·355	10·795 }		
5861 {	1844·34	N 4·12·49·94	7·5	+0·22	−0·145	N 4·12·49·795 }	N 4·12·49·74	13·5
	1848·55	48·89	6·0	„	+0·780	49·670 }		
5915 {	1844·12	S 3· 2·57·39	15·5	−0·01	−0·009	S 3· 2·57·381 }	S 3· 2·57·38	24·24
	1845·28	57·35	4·74	„	+0·003	57·353 }		
	1848·63	57·40	4·0	„	+0·036	57·436 }		

Mean Zenith Distances of Stars observed at the Royal Observatory, with Bradley's Zenith Sector, reduced to 1845·0—*continued.*

No. of Star in B.A.C. or approximate R.A.	Mean Year of Observation.	Mean Z.D. reduced to 1845·0, by precession alone.	WEIGHT.	Adopted Annual Proper Motion	Correction to 1845·0 for P.M.	Mean Z.D. 1845·0, corrected for Proper Motion.	GENERAL MEAN.	WEIGHT.
5960	1844·32	N 1·49·37·97	4·74	...	...	....	N 1·49·37·97	4·74
5964	1844·33	N 1·48·36·82	3·0	...	...	....	N 1·48·36·82	3·00
5970	1844·42	S 5· 0·28·75	1·0	-0·05	-0·029	8 5· 0·28·721		
	1848·63	29·23	4·0	"	+0·181	29·411	S 5· 0·29·27	5·0
6016	1844·37	N 2·17·27·15	7·5	+0·07	-0·044	N 2·17·27·106		
	1848·35	26·95	5·5	"	+0·248	27·198	N 2·17·27·14	13·0
6074	1844·36	N 3·42·12·29	7·5	+0·10	-0·064	N 3·42·12·226		
	1848·55	12·22	5·74	"	+0·355	12·575	N 3·42·12·38	13·24
6115	1844·34	N 3·30·53·78	7·5	+0·18	-0·118	N 3·30·53·662		
	1848·55	52·82	6·0	"	+0·639	53·459	N 3·30·53·57	13·5
6145	1844·34	N 3·11·15·17	7·5	+0·10	-0·066	N 3·11·15·104		
	1848·55	15·06	5·74	"	+0·355	15·415	N 3·11·15·24	13·24
6186	1844·34	S 2·52· 0·38	7·5	+0·14	+0·092	S 2·52· 0·472		
	1848·63	0·99	4·0	"	-0·508	0·482	S 2·52· 0·48	11·5
6233	1844·17	S 0·30·59·76	16·25	+0·15	+0·124	8 0·30·59·884		
	1845·28	59·64	5·0	"	-0·042	59·598		
	1848·56	60·05	7·74	"	-0·534	59·516	S 0·30·59·74	28·99
6275	1844·38	N 0·47·34·30	7·5	+0·06	-0·040	N 0·47·34·260	N 0·47·34·26	7·5
6285	1844·38	N 0·50·57·43	8·0	+0·10	-0·062	N 0·50·57·368		
	1848·55	57·45	6·0	"	+0·355	57·805	N 0·50·57·56	14·0
6305	1844·37	N 0·48·34·64	7·5	0·00	0·00	N 0·48·34·64		
	1848·55	35·01	6·24	"	0·00	35·01	N 0·48·34·81	13·74
6414	1844·37	N 3· 1·20·05	7·5	"	...	....		
	1848·60	20·14	5·24	...	...		N 3· 1·20·10	12·34
6489	1844·27	N 3·50·19·36	7·24	-0·01	+0·007	N 3·50·19·367		
	1848·60	19·23	5·5	"	-0·036	19·194	N 3·50·19·29	12·74
6525	1844·37	N 5· 3·51·27	7·5	+0·10	-0·063	N 5· 3·51·207		
	1848·60	50·66	5·24	"	+0·360	51·020	N 5· 3·51·13	12·74
6639	1844·38	N 3·53·25·28	7·5	+0·15	-0·093	N 3·53·25·187		
	1848·60	24·66	5·0	"	+0·540	25·200	N 3·53·25·19	12·5
B.A.C.17ʰ11ᵐ	1844·38	N 4· 7·26·16	5·0	...	...	....		
	1848·61	26·42	5·24	...	...		N 4· 7·26·29	10·23
6753	1844·38	N 2·39·55·11	7·5	+0·05	-0·031	N 2·39·55·079		
	1848·60	55·03	5·0	"	+0·180	55·210	N 2·39·55·13	12·5
6877	1844·38	N 1·26·54·94	7·5	0·00	0·00	N 1·26·54·94		
	1848·60	55·10	5·0	"	0·00	55·10	N 1·26·55·00	12·5
6948	1844·38	N 3·27·40·76	7·5	...	...	....		
	1848·60	41·42	5·24	...	...		N 3·27·41·09	12·34
7011	1844·40	N 4·21·48·01	7·74	...	...	....		
	1848·60	47·58	4·74	...	...		N 4·21·47·80	11·76
7026	1844·41	N 4·21·40·66	7·24	...	...	....		
	1848·60	40·32	5·5	...	...		N 4·21·40·49	12·5
7057	1844·39	N 4·18·26·34	7·5	...	...	....		
	1848·60	26·47	5·24	...	...		N 4·18·26·41	12·34
B.A.C.m	1844·42	N 4· 7· 6·83	7·5	...	...	....		
	1848·61	6·72	4·5	...	...		N 4· 7· 6·78	11·25
B.A.C.m	1844·41	N 3·58· 5·16	7·74	...	...	....		
	1848·61	4·11	4·0	...	...		N 3·58· 4·65	11·76
7207	1844·39	S 0·24·49·91	7·5	0·00	0·00	S 0·24·49·91		
	1848·60	49·67	"	0·00	49·67		S 0·24·49·81	12·5
B.A.C.m	1844·41	N 4·13· 4·67	6·74	...	...	....		
	1848·60	4·89	5·24	...	...		N 4·13· 4·78	11·79
B.A.C.bₒ m	1844·41	N 3·35·18·26	7·5	0·00	0·00	N 3·35·18·26		
	1848·60	18·41	5·0	"	0·00	18·41	N 3·35·18·32	12·5
7386	1844·41	N 1· 7· 5·25	7·5	+0·10	-0·059	N 1· 7· 5·191		
	1848·60	5·10	5·0	"	+0·360	5·460	N 1· 7· 5·30	12·5
B.A.C.m	1844·42	N 4· 6·51·33	7·24	...	...	....		
	1848·60	51·95	5·0	...	...		N 4· 6·51·64	11·83

E

Mean Zenith Distances of Stars observed at the Royal Observatory, with Bradley's Zenith Sector, reduced to 1845·0—*continued*.

No. of Star in B.A.C. or approximate R.A.	Mean Year of Observation.	Mean Z.D. reduced to 1845·0, by precession alone.	WEIGHT.	Adopted Annual Proper Motion.	Correction to 1845·0 for P.M.	Mean Z.D. 1845·0, corrected for Proper Motion.	GENERAL MEAN.	WEIGHT.
		° ′ ″	″	″	″	° ′ ″	° ′ ″	
B.A.31ʰ 52ᵐ {	1844·42	N 3·33·10·89	7·0	...	...	....	N 3·33·10·93	11·67
	1848·60	10·96	5·0	...	...	....		
7557 {	1844·15	N 0·12·17·64	7·24	+0·10	–0·085	N 0·12·17·555 }	N 0·12·17·61	12·24
	1848·60	17·33	5·0	„	+0·360	17·690 }		
7613	1844·17	S 4· 9·21·86	4·44	+0·04	+0·030	S 4· 9·21·89	S 4· 9·21·89	4·44
7657 {	1844·17	N 4·44·21·81	7·5	+0·05	–0·042	N 4·44·21·768 }	N 4·44·21·83	12·74
	1848·60	21·74	5·24	„	+0·180	21·920 }		
B.A.31ʰ 56ᵐ {	1844·17	N 4·44·60·04	6·74	...	...	....	N 4·44·59·97	11·79
	1848·61	59·91	5·24	...	...	....		
7842 {	1844·16	N 0·47·44·64	7·5	–0·04	+0·034	N 0·47·44·674 }	N 0·47·44·72	12·5
	1848·61	44·93	5·0	„	–0·144	44·786 }		
7909 {	1844·16	N 3·45·54·78	6·24	+0·05	–0·042	N 3·45·54·738 }	N 3·45·54·78	11·24
	1848·61	54·66	5·0	„	+0·180	54·840 }		
7966 {	1844·16	N 0·14·18·71	8·0	+0·05	–0·042	N 0·14·18·668 }	N 0·14·18·81	13·0
	1848·60	18·87	5·0	„	+0·180	19·050 }		
7992 {	1844·16	N 3·29·31·26	18·0	+0·18	–0·151	N 3.29·31·109 }	N 3·29·31·08	26·73
	1845·18	31·00	3·23	„	+0·032	31·032 }		
	1848·61	30·36	5·5	„	+0·650	31·010 }		

CALCULATION OF THE AMPLITUDES.

In the determination of the Amplitudes of the Celestial Arcs, each Station has been referred independently to the Royal Observatory.

The tables which follow, exhibit the details of the calculation.

Column 3 contains the Mean Zenith Distance of each Star derived from the Abstracts at pp. 418, 419 and reduced to 1845·0 by precession alone.

Column 4 gives the weight of each result $= \dfrac{EW}{E+W}$ (E being the number of observations with the face of the Sector East, W the number with the face West).

Column 6 contains the correction for proper motion due to the interval between 1845 and the year of observation.

Columns 8 and 9 are obtained directly from the table at pp. 427—430: but in reference to this it must be noted, that in all cases where a star has been observed at the Royal Observatory in the years 1844 and 1848, and no proper motion has been assigned to it, the observations at the Heerenlogement's Berg, Kamies Berg, Zwart Kop, and Cape Point Stations, which were made between the years 1843 and 1845, have all been compared with the Observatory observations of the earlier year only; but those made at the North-End Bushman Flat Station in 1847 have been compared with the mean of the results for both epochs, obtained as explained in the remarks at p. 427.

Column 11 gives the weight of the amplitude furnished by each star, $= \dfrac{ab}{a+b}$ (a and b being the separate weights at the two stations.)

Royal Observatory to Heerenlogement's Berg Sector Station.

No. of Star in B.A.C. or approxi-mate R.A.	Year of Obser-vation.	Mean Z.D., 1845, Jan. 0, uncorrected for Proper Motion.	Weight.	Annual Proper Motion.	Correc-tion for Proper Motion.	Mean Year of Obser-vation.	Mean Z.D., 1845, Jan. 0.	Weight.	Amplitude.	Weight.	Seconds of Amplitude, minus 58″, multiplied by Weight.
	1840.	° ′ ″		″	′	1840.	° ′ ″		1° 57′·		
1802	+3·39	S 2·11·28·75	3·00	+0·025	+0·04	+5·95	S 0·13·32·78	27·75	56·01	2·71	2·7371
2293	3·39	N 3·12·12·18	4·00	−0·02	+0·03	5·95	N 5·10· 8·34	32·73	56·13	3·57	4·0341
4458	3·39	S 3·55·27·93	5·00	+0·07	+0·11	4·73	S 1·57·29·71	13·24	58·33	3·63	12·0979
4517	3·39	N 3·12· 7·90	4·74	+0·10	−0·16	6·36	N 5·10· 5·57	10·73	57·83	3·29	9·3107
4548	3·39	N 3·12· 4·34	5·00	+0·15	−0·24	6·37	N 5·10· 1·73	11·23	57·63	3·46	9·0998
4579	3·39	S 0·17·20·70	4·50	+0·22	+0·35	6·37	N 1·40·36·64	11·94	57·69	3·27	8·7963
4623	3·39	S 0·15·16·45	4·50	+0·02	+0·03	6·37	N 1·42·41·15	12·0	57·63	3·27	8·6001
4686	3·39	S 3·38· 8·58	4·00	+0·50	+0·80	6·01	S 1·40·11·22	23·5	58·16	3·42	10·8072
4719	3·40	N 3·24·48·03	2·73			4·26	N 5·42·45·95	7·74	57·92	2·02	5·8984
4784	3·39	N 3·10·35·19	4·00	+0·13	−0·21	6·38	N 5· 8·32·54	12·74	57·56	3·04	7·7824
B.A.14ʰ·94ᵐ	3·39	S 0·39·38·59	3·50			4·26	N 1·18·18·69	8·24	57·28	2·46	5·6088
4852	3·39	S 2·32· 2·35	4·23	+0·20	+0·32	6·38	S 0·34· 3·69	14·74	58·98	3·29	13·0942
4916	3·40	S 1·15·13·00	4·00	0·00	0·00	6·39	N 0·42·44·17	14·46	57·77	3·13	8·6701
B.A.14ʰ·54ᵐ	3·40	S 0· 3·33·94	4·00			4·25	N 1·54·23·90	7·74	57·84	2·64	7·4976
B.A.14ʰ·57ᵐ	3·39	S 0·20·16·43	3·73			4·28	N 1·37·41·36	8·24	57·79	2·57	7·1703
5032	3·39	N 2·23·38·12	4·00	+0·06	−0·10	6·38	N 4·21·35·89	15·17	57·87	3·17	9·0979
5054	3·40	S 3·43·32·42	3·00			4·26	S 1·45·33·99	7·74	58·43	2·16	7·4088
5151	3·39	N 2·42·18·58	4·44	+0·13	−0·21	6·40	N 4·40·15·67	15·68	57·30	3·46	7·9580
B.A.15ʰ·54ᵐ	3·40	N 0·51·56·11	4·00			4·34	N 2·49·55·13	7·5	59·02	2·61	10·4922
5227	3·39	S 1·10·52·99	4·50	+0·05	+0·08	6·40	N 0·47· 4·98	14·98	58·05	3·46	10·5530
5272	3·39	N 3·12·42·78	4·50	+0·06	−0·10	6·39	N 5·10·40·55	14·98	57·87	3·46	9·9302
5374	3·39	N 2·57·59·11	4·50	+0·18	−0·29	6·44	N 4·55·56·79	14·46	57·97	3·43	10·1871
5435	3·39	N 1·26·35·23	4·00	+0·05	−0·08	6·44	N 3·24·33·26	13·50	58·11	3·09	9·6099
B.A.15ʰ·16ᵐ	3·39	S 0·51·45·67	3·00			4·34	N 1· 6·13·17	7·24	58·84	2·12	8·1408
5588	3·39	N 0· 9·46·91	3·00			4·34	N 2· 7·44·37	7·5	57·46	2·14	5·2644
5632	3·39	S 2· 2·14·44	4·50	+0·25	+0·40	5·99	N 0· 4·16·49	25·49	58·35	3·82	12·7970
5735	3·39	S 1·55·49·25	4·00	0·00	0·00	6·44	N 0· 2· 9·29	14·74	58·54	3·15	11·1510
5817	3·39	S 0·30·47·37	4·23	+0·10	+0·16	6·45	N 1·27·10·74	13·46	53·27	3·22	10·5294
5881	3·40	N 2·14·51·93	4·00	+0·22	−0·35	6·45	N 4·12·49·74	13·5	58·16	3·09	9·7644
5915	3·39	S 5· 0·54·75	3·50	−0·01	−0·02	6·01	S 3· 2·57·36	24·24	57·35	3·06	7·1910
5960	3·39	S 0· 8·20·06	1·875			4·32	N 1·49·37·97	4·74	58·03	1·34	4·0602
6016	3·40	N 0·19·29·07	4·00	+0·07	·0·11	6·46	N 2·17·27·14	13·0	58·18	3·06	9·7308
6074	3·39	N 1·44·14·74	3·50	+0·10	−0·16	6·46	N 3·42·12·38	13·24	57·80	2·77	7·7560
6115	3·39	N 1·32·55·77	4·00	+0·18	−0·29	6·45	N 3·30·53·57	13·5	58·09	3·09	9·5481
6145	3·40	N 1·13·16·52	4·50	+0·10	−0·16	6·44	N 3·11·15·24	13·24	58·88	3·36	13·0368
6186	3·40	S 4·49·58·08	4·50	+0·14	+0·22	6·49	S 2·52· 0·48	11·5	57·82	3·23	9·1086
6233	3·40	S 2·28·58·19	4·50	+0·15	+0·24	6·00	S 0·30·59·74	28·99	58·69	3·90	14·3910
6275	3·40	S 1·10·23·65	3·23	+0·06	+0·10	4·38	N 0·47·34·26	7·5	58·01	2·26	6·8026
6285	3·39	S 1· 7· 0·43	4·00	+0·15	+0·24	6·47	N 0·50·57·56	14·0	57·55	3·11	9·7965
6305	3·39	S 1· 9·22·96	4·00	0·00	0·00	6·46	N 0·48·34·81	13·74	57·77	3·10	8·5870
6414	3·40	N 1· 3·22·09	3·00			4·37	N 3· 1·20·05	7·74	57·96	2·14	6·3344
6489	3·40	N 1·52·21·30	4·00	−0·01	+0·02	6·44	N 3·50·19·29	12·74	57·97	3·04	9·0288
6525	3·39	N 3· 5·54·45	3·00	+0·10	−0·16	6·49	N 5· 3·51·13	12·74	56·84	2·43	4·4712
6639	3·40	N 1·55·28·02	4·00	+0·15	−0·24	6·49	N 3·53·25·19	12·5	57·41	3·03	7·3023
7992	3·38	N 1·31·33·67	1·00	+0·18	−0·29	5·98	N 3·29·31·08	26·73	57·70	0·96	2·5920
									Sums.	132·03	383·8164

Mean Amplitude = 1·57·57·907

Royal Observatory to Kamies Berg Sector Station.

No. of Star in B.A.C. or approxi-mate R.A.	KAMIES BERG.					ROYAL OBSERVATORY.			Amplitude.	Weight.	Seconds of Amplitude, minus 33″, multiplied by Weight.
	Year of Obser-vation.	Mean Z.D., 1845, Jan. 0, uncorrected for Proper Motion.	Weight.	Annual Proper Motion	Correc-tion for Proper Motion.	Mean Year of Obser-vation.	Mean Z.D., 1845, Jan. 0.	Weight.			
	1840.	° ′ ″		″	″	1840.	° ′ ″		3° 34′.		
1802	+3·59	S 3·48· 7·30	2·50	+0·025	+0 03	+5·95	S 0·13·32·78	27·75	34·55	2·29	3·5495
2293	3·59	N 1·35·35·04	4·23	-0·02	+0·03	5·95	N 5·10· 8·34	32·73	33·27	3·75	1·0125
4458	3·59	S 5·32· 5·12	3·00	+0 07	+0·10	4·73	S 1·57·29·71	13·24	35·51	2·45	6·1495
4579	3·59	S 1·53·58·02	2·50	+0·22	+0·31	6·37	N 1·40·36·64	11·94	34·97	2·07	4·0779
4623	3·59	S 1 51·52·89	3·00	+0·02	+0·08	6·37	N 1·42·41·15	12·0	34·07	2·40	2·5680
4686	3·59	S 5·14·45·85	3·73	+0·50	+0·70	6·01	N 1·40·11·22	23·5	35·33	3·22	7·5026
4719	3·57	N 1·48·11·07	1·33	..	..	4·26	N 5·22·45·95	7·74	34·88	1·13	2·1244
4784	3·58	N 1·33·58·28	3·00	+0·13	-0·18	6·38	N 5· 8·32·54	12·74	34·44	2·43	3·4992
B.A.14	3·57	S 2·16·15·72	1·33	..	..	4·26	N 1·18·18·69	8·24	34·41	1·15	1·6215
4852	3·59	S 4· 8·39·77	3·73	+0·20	+0·28	6·38	S 0·34· 3·69	14·74	35·36	2·98	7·0328
4916	3·58	S 2·51·50·93	3·50	0·00	0 00	6·38	N 0·42·44·17	14·46	35·10	2·82	5·9220
	3·59	S 1·40·10·74	4·00	..	..	4·25	N 1·54·23·90	7·74	34·64	2·64	4·3296
	3·58	S 1·56·53·16	2·73	..	..	4·28	N 1·37·41·36	8·24	34·52	2·05	3·1160
5032	3·59	N 0·47· 1·32	4·00	+0·06	-0·08	6·38	N 4·21·35·89	15·17	34·65	3·17	5·2305
5054	3·59	S 5·20· 8·50	4·00	..	..	4·26	S 1·45·33·99	7·74	34·57	2·64	4·1448
5151	3 59	N 1· 5·41·32	4·00	+0·13	-0·18	6·40	N 4·40·15·67	15·68	34·53	3·19	4·8807
	3·59	S 0·44·40·18	3·50	..	..	4·34	N 2·49·55·13	7·5	35·31	2·39	5·5209
5227	3·59	S 2·47·30·66	4·00	+0·05	+0·07	6·40	N 0·47· 4·98	14·98	35·71	3·16	5·5636
5272	3·59	N 1·36· 6·03	4·00	+0·06	-0·08	6·39	N 5·10·40·55	14·98	34·60	3·16	5·0560
5374	3·59	N 1·21·22·13	4·00	+0·18	-0·25	6·44	N 4·55·56·79	14·46	34·91	3·13	5·9783
5435	3·59	S 0·10· 1·84	4·00	+0·05	+0·07	6·44	N 3·24·33·26	13·5	35·17	3·09	6·7053
	3·59	S 2·28·22·15	4·00	..	..	4·34	N 1· 6·13·17	7·24	35·32	2·58	5·9856
5586	3 59	S 1·26·49·86	3·94	..	..	4·34	N 2· 7·44·37	7·5	34·23	2·58	3·1734
5632	3·59	S 3·38·50·78	4·00	+0·25	+0·35	5·99	S 0· 4·16·49	25·49	34·64	3·46	5·6744
5735	3·59	S 3·32·26·25	4·00	0·00	0·00	6·44	N 0· 2· 9·29	14·74	35·54	3·15	8·0010
5817	3·59	S 2· 7·23·63	4·00	+0·10	+0·14	6·45	N 1·27·10·74	13·46	34·51	3·08	4·6508
5881	3·59	N 0·36·14·54	3 50	+0·22	-0·31	6·45	N 4·12·49·74	13·5	35·51	2·78	6·9778
5930	3·58	S 1·44·56·48	3·50	..	..	4·32	N 1·49·37·97	4·74	34·45	2·01	2·9145
5964	3·59	S 1·45·57·59	3·50	..	..	4·33	N 1·48·36·82	3·00	34·41	1·62	2·2842
6016	3·59	S 1 17· 7·46	3·73	+0·07	+0·10	6·46	N 2·17·27·14	13·0	34·70	2·90	4·9300
6074	3·59	N 0· 7·37·65	4·23	+0·10	-0·14	6·46	N 3·42·12·38	13·24	34·87	3·21	6·0027
6115	3·59	S 0· 3·41·60	4·23	+0·18	+0·24	6·45	N 3·30·53·57	18·5	35·41	3 22	7·7602
6145	3·59	S 0·23·19·95	3·73	+0·10	+0·14	6·44	N 3·11·15·24	13·24	35·33	2·91	6·7603
6233	3·59	S 4· 5·34·55	4·23	+0·15	+0·20	6·00	S 0·30·59·74	28 99	35·78	3·69	7·4169
6275	3·59	S 2·47· 1·44	3·73	+0·06	+0·08	4·38	N 0·47·34·26	7·5	35·78	2·49	6·9222
6285	3 59	S 2·43 38·60	4·23	+0 10	+0·14	6·47	N 0·50·57·56	14·0	36·30	3·25	10·7250
6305	3 59	S 2·46· 1·09	4·23	0·00	0·00	6·46	N 0·48·34·81	13·74	35·90	3·23	9·3870
6414	3·59	S 0·33·14·85	4·00	..	..	4·37	N 3· 1·20·05	7·5	34·90	2·61	4·9590
6489	3·59	N 0·15·43·95	3·50	-0·01	+0·01	6·44	N 3·50·19·29	12·74	35·38	2·89	6·7337
6525	3·59	N 1·29·16·43	4·00	+0·10	-0·14	6·49	N 5· 3·51·13	12·74	34·84	3·04	5·5936
6639	3·59	N 0·18·50·51	4·00	+0·15	-0·21	6·49	N 3·53·25·19	12·5	34·69	3·03	5·7267
	3·59	N 0·32·51·77	4·00	..	..	4·38	N 4· 7·26·16	5·0	34·39	2·22	3·0858
6753	3·59	S 0·54·39·81	4·00	+0·05	+0·07	6 49	N 2·39·55·13	12·5	35·01	3·03	6·0903
6877	3·59	S 2· 7·39·63	4·00	0·00	0·00	6·49	N 1·26·55·00	12·5	34·63	3·03	4·9389
6948	3·59	S 0· 6·54·62	4·00	..	..	4·38	N 3·27·40·76	7·5	35·38	2·61	6·2118
7011	3·59	N 0·47·13·01	1·50	..	..	4·40	N 4·21·48·01	7·74	35·06	1·26	2·5200
7026	3·59	N 0·47· 5·26	4·23	..	..	4 41	N 4·21·40·66	7·24	35·40	2·67	6·4080
7057	3·59	N 0·43·51·17	4·00	..	..	4·39	N 4·18·26·34	7·5	35·17	2·61	5·6637
	3·59	N 0·32·31·95	3 00	..	..	4·42	N 4· 7· 6·63	7·5	34·88	2·14	4·0232
	3·59	N 0·23·30·13	4·00	..	..	4·41	N 3·58· 5·18	7·74	35·03	2·64	5·4120
7207	3·59	S 3·59·25·35	4·00	0·00	0·00	6·49	S 0·24·49·81	12·5	35·54	3·03	7·6962
	3·59	N 0·38·29·22	3·43	..	..	4·41	N 4·13· 4·67	6·74	35·45	2·37	5·5615
	3·59	N 0· 0·43·51	3·50	0·00	0·00	6·51	N 3·35·18·32	12·5	34·81	2·73	4·9413
7386	3·59	S 2·27·29·84	3·50	+0·10	+0·14	6·51	N 1· 7· 5·30	12·5	35·28	2·73	6·2244
	3·59	N 0·32·16·43	3·00	..	..	4·42	N 4· 5·31·99	7·24	35·40	2·12	4·0280
	3·59	S 0· 1·24·38	3·23	..	..	4·42	N 3·33·10·89	7·0	35·27	2·21	5·0167
7557	3·59	S 3·24·17·63	4·00	+0·10	+0·14	4 15	N 0·12·17·61	12·24	35·38	3·01	7·1638

Royal Observatory to Kamies Berg Sector Station—*continued.*

Star's No. B.A.C. or approximate R.A.	KAMIES BERG.					ROYAL OBSERVATORY.			Amplitude.	Weight.	Seconds of Amplitude, minus 33", multiplied by Weight.
	Year of Observation.	Mean Z.D., 1845, Jan. 0, uncorrected for Proper Motion.	Weight.	Annual Proper Motion.	Correction for Proper Motion.	Mean Year of Observation.	Mean Z.D., 1845, Jan. 0.	Weight.			
	1840.	° ′ ″		′	″	1840.	° ′ ″		3° 34′.		
7657	+3·59	N 1· 9·46·53	4·00	+0·05	-0·07	+6·38	N 4·44·21·83	12·74	35·37	3·04	7·2048
ʙ.ᴀ.ᴄ.ʰ ᵐ	3·59	N 1·10·24·70	4·00	..		4·17	N 4·45· 0·04	6·74	35·34	2·51	5·8734
7842	3·59	S 2·46·51·34	3·73	-0·04	-0·06	6·38	N 0·47·44·72	12·50	36·00	2·87	8 6100
7909	3·59	N 0·11·19·85	3·50	+0·05	-0·07	6·38	N 3·45·54·78	11·24	35·00	2·67	5·3400
7966	3·59	S 3·20·17·19	4·00	+0·05	+0·07	6·38	N 0·14·18·81	13·00	36·07	3·06	9·3942
-7992	3 59	S 0· 5· 4·51	4·00	+0·18	+0·25	5·98	N 3·29·31·08	26·73	35·84	3·48	9·8832
								Sums.	170·98		352·4558

Mean Amplitude = 3° 34′ 35″·061.

Royal Observatory to Zwart Kop Sector Station.

	ZWART KOP.					ROYAL OBSERVATORY.					Seconds of Amplitude, minus 33′, multiplied by Weight.
	1840.	° ′ ″		″	″	1840.	° ′ ″		0° 17′.		
-1802	+4·66	N 0· 3·58·41	4·95	+0·025	-0·01	+5·95	S 0·13·32·78	27·75	31·18	4·20	13·3560
-1978	4·66	S 1·36·13·42	4·74	-0·42	-0·14	4·82	S 1·53·44·04	6·24	30·76	2·69	7·4244
-2293	4·66	N 5·27·39·27	6·46	-0·02	+0·01	5·95	N 5·10· 8·34	32·73	30·94	5·39	15·8466
-4458	4·67	S 1·39·58·58	3·73	+0·07	+0·02	4·73	N 1·57·29·71	13·24	31·11	2·91	9·0501
4507	4·60	S 4·22·41·24	0·50	..		4·41	S 4·40·10·36	1·33	29·12	0·36	0·4032
4579	4·60	N 1·58· 7·44	0·50	+0·22	-0·09	6·37	N 1·40·36·64	11·94	30·71	0·48	1·3008
-4686	4·66	S 1·22·38·88	5·45	+0·50	+0·17	6·01	S 1·40·11·22	23·50	32·17	4·42	18·4314
4745	4·59	S 2·56·34·34	1·50	..		4·41	S 3·14· 2·80	0·50	28·46	0·37	0·1702
4784	4·58	N 5·26· 3·03	1·00	+0·18	-0·05	6·38	N 5. 8·32·54	12·74	30·44	0·93	2·2692
4852	4·66	S 0·16·33·65	1·71	+0·20	+0·07	6·38	S 0·34· 3·69	14·74	29·97	1·53	3·0141
4916	4·59	N 1· 0·14·36	1·50	0·00	+0·00	6·38	N 0·42·44·17	14·46	30·19	1·36	2·9784
ʙ.ᴀ.ᴄ.ʰ ᵐ	4·59	N 2·11·54·49	1·50	..		4·25	N 1·54·23·90	7·74	30·59	1·26	2·2634
ʙ.ᴀ.ᴄ.ʰ ᵐ	4·59	N 1·55·12·66	0·75	..		4·28	N 1·37·41·36	8·24	31·30	0·69	2·2770
5032	4·59	N 4·39· 5·69	0·50	+0·06	-0·02	6·38	N 4·21·35·89	15·17	29·78	0·48	0·8544
5054	4·66	S 1·28· 2·95	4·44	..		4·26	S 1·45·33·99	7·74	31·04	2·82	8·5728
5151	4·60	N 4·57·45·66	2·00	+0·13	-0·05	6·40	N 4·40·15·67	15·68	29·94	1·77	3·4338
ʙ.ᴀ.ᴄ.ʰ ᵐ	4·59	N 3· 7·25·07	1·50	..		4·34	N 2·49·55·13	7·50	29·94	1·25	2·4250
5227	4·65	N 1· 4·36·10	3·50	+0·05	-0·02	6·40	N 0·47·15·98	14·98	31·10	2·34	8·8040
5292	4·67	S 3·43·16·15	3·94	..		4·41	S 4· 0·47·45	1·20	31·30	0·92	3·0360
5331	4·65	S 2· 8·52·62	3·60	..		4·42	S 2·26·23·83	4·74	31·21	2·05	6·5805
ʙ.ᴀ.ᴄ.ʰ ᵐ	4·59	S 2· 6· 9·72	2·00	..		4·39	S 2·23·40·21	3·08	30·49	1·21	3·0129
5374	4·60	N 5·13·27·94	1·71	+0·18	-0·07	6·44	N 4·55·56·79	14·46	31·08	1·53	4·7124
5435	4·59	N 3·42· 3·55	2·00	+0·05	-0·02	6·44	N 3·24·33·26	13·50	30·27	1·74	3·9498
5508	4·65	S 0· 8· 3·82	3·73	0·00	0·00	6·51	S 0·25·33·43	7·24	29·61	2·46	8·9606
5538	4·66	S 0·42·13·13	4·00	..		4·42	S 0·59·43·34	0·67	30·21	0·57	1·2597
5588	4·59	N 2·25·15·55	2·22	..		4·34	N 2· 7·44·37	7·50	31·18	1·71	5·4378
-5632	4·65	N 0·13·14·44	5·50	+0·25	-0·09	5·99	S 0· 4·16·49	25·49	30·84	4·52	12·8368
5735	4·64	N 0·19·39·39	4·00	0·00	0·00	6·44	N 0· 2· 9·29	14·74	30·10	3·15	6 6150
5817	4·63	N 1·44·41·37	3·00	+0·10	-0·04	6·45	N 1·27·10·74	13·46	30·59	2·45	6·3455
5881	4·65	N 4·30·19·89	4·44	+0·22	-0·08	6·45	N 4·12·49·74	18·50	30·07	3·34	6·9138
-5915	4·66	S 2·45·27·19	5·74	-0·01	0·00	6·01	S 3· 2·57·38	24·24	30·19	4·64	10·1616
-5970	4·66	S 4·42·57·12	5·45	-0·05	-0·02	6·53	S 5· 0·29·27	5·00	32·17	3·74	10·8837
6016	4·65	N 2·34·58·01	5·24	+0·07	-0·02	6·46	N 2·17·27·14	13·00	30·85	3·74	10·6590
6074	4·65	N 3·59·42·77	5·50	+0·10	-0·02	6·46	N 3·24·33·26	13·24	30·35	3·89	12·6175
6115	4·65	N 3·48·24·53	5·74	+0·18	-0·06	6·45	N 3·30·53·57	13·50	30·90	4·03	11·6870
6145	4·65	N 3·28·45·59	5·74	+0·10	-0·04	6·44	N 3·11·15·24	13·24	30·31	3·49	8·0619
6186	4·65	S 2·34·29·58	5·74	+0·14	+0·05	6·49	S 2·52· 0·48	11·50	30·85	3·83	10·9155

Royal Observatory to Zwart Kop Sector Station—*continued.*

		ZWART KOP.					ROYAL OBSERVATORY.					Seconds of Amplitude, minus 28″, multiplied by Weight.
Star's No. B.A.C. or approximate B.A.	Year of Observation.	Mean Z.D., 1845, Jan. 0, uncorrected for Proper Motion.	Weight.	Annual Proper Motion.	Correction for Proper Motion.	Mean Year of Observation.	Mean Z.D., 1845, Jan. 0.	Weight.	Amplitude.	Weight.	
	1840.	° ′ ″		″	″	1840.	° ′ ″		0° 17′.		
6233	+4·66	S 0·13·29·18	5·74	+0·15	+0·05	+6·00	S 0·30·59·74	28·99	30·51	4·79	12·0229
6275	4·65	N 1· 5· 4·31	4·44	+0·06	-0·02	4·38	N 0·47·34·26	7·50	30·03	2·79	5·6637
6285	4·65	N 1· 8·27·93	5·50	+0·10	-0·04	6·47	N 0·50·57·56	14·00	30·33	3·95	9·2035
6305	4·65	N 1· 6· 5·30	5·00	0·00	0·00	6·46	N 0·48·34·81	13·74	30·49	3·67	9·1583
6414	4·65	N 3·18·51·20	5·50	..	..	4·37	N 3· 1·20·05	7·50	31·15	3·17	9·9855
6489	4·65	N 4· 7·50·13	6·00	-0·01	0·00	6·44	N 3·50·19·29	12·74	30·84	4·08	11·5872
6525	4·66	N 5·21·21·63	5·50	+0·10	-0·04	6·49	N 5· 3·51·13	12·74	30·46	3·84	9·4464
6639	4·65	N 4·10·56·20	6·16	+0·15	-0·05	6·49	N 3·53·25·19	12·50	30·96	4·13	12·2248
B.A.19ʰ·21ᵐ	4·65	N 4·24·57·20	5·45	..	..	4·38	N 4· 7·26·16	5·00	31·04	2·61	7·9344
6753	4·66	N 2·57·26·33	4·74	+0·05	-0·02	6·49	N 2·39·55·13	12·50	31·18	3·44	10·9392
6877	4·66	N 1·44·25·50	5·50	0·00	0·00	6·49	N 1·26·55·00	12·50	30·50	3·82	9·5500
6948	4·65	N 3·45·11·26	5·24	..	..	4·38	N 3·27·40·76	7·50	30·50	3·08	7·7000
7011	4·65	N 4·39·18·71	5·24	..	..	4·40	N 4·21·48·01	7·74	30·70	3·13	8·4510
7026	4·65	N 4·39·11·30	5·50	..	..	4·41	N 4·21·40·66	7·24	30·64	3·13	8·2632
7057	4·66	N 4·35·57·21	5·74	..	..	4·39	N 4·18·26·34	7·50	30·87	3·25	9·3275
B.A.Nº·24ᵐ	4·66	N 4·24·37·37	5·50	..	..	4·42	N 4· 7· 6·83	7·50	30·54	3·17	8·0518
B.A.20ʰ·23ᵐ	4·66	N 4·15·36·23	5·74	..	..	4·41	N 3·58· 5·18	7·74	31·05	3·30	10·0650
7207	4·65	S 0· 7·20·03	6·50	0·00	0·00	6·49	S 0·24·49·81	12·50	29·78	4·28	7·6184
B.A.20ʰ·29ᵐ	4·66	N 4·30·34·81	5·50	..	..	4·41	N 4·13· 4·67	6·74	30·14	3·03	6·4842
B.A.1ʰ·0ᵐ	4·65	N 3·52·48·55	5·74	0·00	0·00	6·51	N 3·35·18·32	12·50	30·23	3·93	8·7639
7386	4·65	N 1·24·35·58	5·74	+0·10	-0·04	6·51	N 1· 7· 5·30	12·50	30·24	3·93	8·8032
B.A.21ʰ·19ᵐ	4·66	N 4·24·21·70	5·74	..	..	4·42	N 4· 6·51·33	7·24	30·37	3·20	7·5840
B.A.21ʰ·23ᵐ	4·66	N 3·50·41·65	6·00	..	..	4·42	N 3·33·10·89	7·00	30·76	3·23	8·9148
7557	4·65	N 0·29·47·39	6·00	+0·10	-0·04	6·49	N 0·12·17·61	12·24	29·74	4·03	7·0122
7613	4·65	S 3·51·51·20	6·00	+0·04	+0·01	4·17	S 4· 9·21·89	4·44	30·68	2·55	6·8340
7657	4·66	N 5· 1·52·09	5·74	+0·05	-0·02	6·38	N 4·44·21·83	12·74	30·24	3·96	8·8704
B.A.21ʰ·34ᵐ	4·66	N 5· 2·30·07	6·00	..	..	4·17	N 4·45· 0·04	6·74	30·03	3·17	6·4351
7842	4·65	N 1· 5·15·40	5·74	-0·04	+0·01	6·38	N 0·47·44·72	11·50	29·93	3·93	10·5717
7909	4·66	N 4· 3·24·76	5·24	+0·05	-0·02	6·38	N 3·45·54·78	11·24	29·98	3·57	6·9972
7966	4·66	N 0·31·49·28	5·74	+0·05	-0·02	6·38	N 0·14·18·81	13·00	30·45	3·98	9·7510
7992	4·66	N 3·47· 1·45	5·74	+0·18	-0·06	5·98	N 3·29·31·08	26·73	30·31	4·73	10·9263
								Sums.	198·50	515·1666	

Mean Amplitude = δ·17·30·505.

Royal Observatory to Cape Point Sector Station.

		CAPE POINT.					ROYAL OBSERVATORY.			Seconds of Amplitude multiplied by Weight.
	1840.	° ′ ″		″	″	1840.	° ′ ″		0° 25′.	
1739	+4·96	S 1·14· 8·17	5·00	..	..	+5·15	S 1·39·10·97	5·00	2·86	2·50	7·1500
1802	4·92	N 0·11·30·32	5·00	+0·025	..	5·15	N 0·13·32·78	27·75	3·10	4·59	14·2290
1876	4·92	S 1·28·40·93	5·00	-0·42	-0·03	4·82	S 1·53·44·04	6·24	3·14	2·78	8·7292
1922	4·93	S 0·57· 4·89	5·00	..	..	5·14	S 1·22· 7·37	5·00	2·48	2·50	6·2000
1982	4·93	S 2·52·57·76	5·00	..	..	5·14	S 3·18· 0·45	4·74	2·69	2·43	6·5367
2051	4·93	N 4·21·11·18	5·00	0·00	0·00	5·15	N 3·56· 7·75	5·00	3·43	2·50	8·5750
2109	4·93	N 1·51·55·78	5·00	..	..	5·14	N 1·26·53·12	5·00	2·66	2·50	6·6500
2246	4·93	N 2· 1· 7·23	5·00	..	..	5·15	N 1·36· 4·02	5·24	3·21	2·56	8·2176
2293	4·92	N 5·35·12·01	5·00	-0·02	0·00	5·95	N 5·10· 8·34	32·73	2·67	4·34	15·9278
2414	4·93	S 2·28·13·32	5·00	+0·015	0·00	5·15	S 2·53·16·85	5·00	3·53	2·50	8·8250
2459	4·94	N 5·20·48·42	5·00	-0·02	0·00	5·15	N 4·55·45·38	5·00	3·04	2·50	7·6000
2528	4·95	S 3·18·47·82	5·00	..	..	5·15	S 3·43·50·55	5·00	2·73	2·50	6·8250

Royal Observatory to Cape Point Sector Station—*continued.*

No. of Star in B.A.C. or approximate R.A.	CAPE POINT.					ROYAL OBSERVATORY.					Seconds of Amplitude, multiplied by Weight.
	Year of Observation.	Mean Z.D., 1845, Jan. 0, uncorrected for Proper Motion.	Weight.	Annual Proper Motion.	Correction for Proper Motion.	Mean Year of Observation.	Mean Z.D., 1845, Jan. 0.	Weight.	Amplitude.	Weight.	
	1840.	° ′ ″		″	″	1840.	° ′ ″		0° 25′.		
2575	+4·94	S 3·13·13·76	5·00	..	..	+5·14	S 3·38·16·39	5·00	2·63	2·50	6·5750
2580	4·94	S 3·14·36·12	5·00	..	..	5·14	S 3·39·38·92	5·00	2·80	2·50	7·0000
2635	4·94	S 4· 6·44·34	5·00	..	..	5·14	S 4·31·47·19	5·24	2·85	2·56	7·2960
2655	4·95	N 4·25·49·33	5·00	..	..	5·14	N 4· 0·46·04	5·00	3·29	2·50	8·2250
-2710	4·93	S 5·13· 1·42	5·00	-0·01	0·00	5·15	S 5·38· 4·46	5·00	3·04	2·50	7·6000
2795	4·93	S 1·49·47·63	5·00	..	..	5·15	S 2·14·50·51	5·00	2·88	2·50	7·2000
2935	4·93	S 0·24·32·87	5·00	..	..	5·15	S 0·49·36·53	5·00	3·66	2·50	9·1500
2964	4·93	N 1·43·15·99	5·00	..	..	5·15	N 1·18·12·79	5·00	3·20	2·50	8·0000
3130	4·95	N 4·36·57·85	5·00	..	..	5·16	N 4·11·54·11	5·00	3·74	2·50	9·3500
3163	4·95	S 3·34·27·88	5·00	-0·16	0·00	5·16	S 3·59·30·57	5·00	2·69	2·50	6·7250
R.A.9ʰ39ᵐ	4·99	N 2·22·53·99	3·43	..	..	5·18	N 1·57·50·15	5·00	2·84	2·03	7·7952
3403	5·00	N 3·59·37·31	3·00	..	..	5·18	N 3·34·34·48	5·24	2·83	1·91	5·4053
R.A.9ʰ3ᵐ	5·00	N 4· 0·21·59	2·50	..	..	5·18	N 3·35·18·60	5·00	2·99	1·67	4·9933
3578	4·96	N 4· 4·16·34	5·00	..	..	5·19	N 3·39·13·40	5·00	2·94	2·50	7·3500
3598	5·00	N 4·32· 9·17	3·50	..	..	5·20	N 4· 7· 5·96	2·50	3·21	1·46	4·6866
3755	4·98	S 1·57·13·10	4·44	..	..	5·18	S 2·22·16·09	5·00	2·99	2·35	7·0265
3928	4·97	N 3·21· 4·50	5·00	+0·06	0·00	5·28	N 2·56· 1·79	5·00	2·71	2·50	6·7750
4015	5·00	N 1·18·21·26	3·00	..	..	5·28	N 0·53·18·08	5·00	3·18	1·88	5·9784
4202	5·03	S 3·49·48·49	1·20	..	..	5·28	S 4·14·51·64	5·00	3·15	0·97	3·0555
-4458	4·96	S 1·32·26·53	5·00	+0·07	0·00	4·73	S 1·57·29·71	13·24	3·18	3·63	11·5434
-4686	4·93	S 1·15· 7·64	5·00	+0·50	+0·04	6·01	S 1·40·11·22	23·50	3·54	4·12	14·5848
-5632	5·02	N 0·20·46·36	2·00	+0·25	0·00	5·99	S 0· 4·16·49	25·49	2·85	1·85	5·2725
-5915	4·97	S 2·37·53·66	5·00	-0·01	0·00	6·01	S 3· 2·57·38	24·24	3·72	4·15	15·4380
-6233	4·96	S 0· 5·56·78	4·23	+0·15	0·00	6·00	S 0·30·59·74	28·99	2·96	3·69	10·9224
7842	4·91	N 1·12·47·59	2·00	-0·04	0·00	6·38	N 0·47·44·72	12·50	2·87	1·72	4·9364
7966	4·91	N 0·39·21·22	2·22	+0·05	0·00	6·38	N 0·14·18·81	13·00	2·91	1·90	4·5790
-7992	4·96	N 3·54·33·06	5·00	+0·18	0·00	5·98	N 3·29·31·08	26·73	1·98	4·21	8·3358
								Sums .	101·80		311·2644

Mean Amplitude = 0·25·3·058

Royal Observatory to North Sector Station, Bushman Flat.

	NORTH SECTOR STATION.					ROYAL OBSERVATORY.					Seconds of Amplitude, minus 44°, multiplied by Weight.
	1840.	° ′ ″		″	″	1840.	° ′ ″		4° 11′.		
4517	+7·49	N 0·58·19·71	4·44	+0·10	+0·25	+0·37	N 5·10· 5·57	10·73	45·61	3·14	5·0554
4548	7·49	N 0·58·15·79	4·74	+0·15	+0·37	6·37	N 5·10· 1·73	11·23	45·57	3·33	5·2281
4579	7·49	S 2·31· 9·33	4·95	+0·22	-0·55	6·37	N 1·40·36·64	11·94	45·42	3·50	4·9700
4623	7·49	S 2·29· 4·46	5·24	+0·02	-0·05	6·37	N 5·22·45·56	12·00	45·56	3·65	5·6940
4719	7·49	N 1·10·59·70	4·44	..	..	6·38	N 5·22·45·56	10·44	45·86	3·12	5·8032
4784	7·49	N 0·56·46·43	4·63	+0·13	+0·32	6·38	N 5· 8·32·54	12·74	45·79	3·40	6·0860
R.A..ʰ..ᵐ	7·49	S 2·53·26·83	3·73	..	..	6·38	N 1·18·19·09	12·36	45·92	2·87	5·5104
4852	7·49	S 4·45·50·30	4·74	+0·20	-0·50	6·38	S 4·39·53·19	14·46	46·11	3·59	7·5749
4916	7·49	S 3·29· 1·05	4·50	0·00	0·00	6·38	N 0·42·44·17	14·46	45·22	3·43	4·1846
R.A..ʰ..ᵐ	7·49	S 2·17·21·14	5·00	..	..	6·38	N 1·54·24·01	14·08	45·15	3·69	4·2435
R.A..ʰ..ᵐ	7·49	S 2·34· 3·05	4·12	..	..	6·40	N 1·37·41·70	12·03	44·75	3·07	2·3925
5032	7·49	N 0· 9·50·55	5·00	+0·06	+0·15	6·38	N 4·21·35·89	15·17	45·19	3·76	4·4744
5151	7·49	N 0·28·29·54	5·24	+0·13	+0·32	6·40	N 4·40·15·67	15·68	45·81	3·93	7·1133
R.A..ʰ..ᵐ	7·49	S 1·21·50·72	4·44	..	..	6·42	N 2·49·54·65	14·20	45·37	3·38	4·6306
5227	7·49	S 3·24·40·52	5·24	+0·05	-0·12	6·40	N 0·47· 4·98	14·98	45·38	3·88	5·3544
5272	7·49	N 0·58·54·08	5·24	+0·06	+0·15	6·39	N 5·10·40·55	14·98	46·32	3·88	9·0016

Royal Observatory to North Sector Station, Bushman Flat—*continued.*

No. of Star in B.A.C. or approxi- mate R.A.	Year of Obser- vation.	Mean Z.D., 1845, Jan. 0, uncorrected for Proper Motion.	Weight.	Annual Proper Motion.	Correc- tion for Proper Motion.	Mean Year of Obser- vation.	Mean Z.D., 1845, Jan. 0.	Weight.	Amplitude.	Weight.	Seconds of Amplitude, minus 44″, multiplied by Weight.
									4° 11′.		
	1840.	° ′ ″		″	″	1840.	° ′ ″				
5374	+7·49	N 0·44·10·89	5·24	+0·18	+0·45	+6·44	N 4·55·56·79	14·46	45·45	3·85	5·5825
5435	7·49	S 0·47·11·82	5·00	+0·05	−0·12	6·44	N 3·24·33·26	13·50	44·96	3·65	3·5040
R.A.14ʰ·12ᵐ	7·49	S 3· 5·31·44	4·47	..	..	6·42	N 1· 6·13·04	8·94	44·48	3·10	1·4880
5588	7·49	S 2· 4· 0·63	5·00	..	..	6·44	N 2· 7·44·31	13·33	44·94	3·64	3·4216
5632	7·49	S 4·16· 2·53	5·24	+0·25	−0·62	5·99	S 0· 4·16·49	25·49	45·42	4·35	6·1770
5735	7·49	S 4· 9·36·39	4·74	0·00	0·00	6·44	N 0· 2· 9·29	14·74	45·68	3·59	6·0312
5817	7·49	S 2·44·35·83	5·00	+0·10	−0·25	6·45	N 1·27·10·74	13·46	46·32	3·65	8·4680
5881	7·49	N 0· 1· 2·89	4·74	+0·22	+0·55	6·45	N 4·12·49·74	13·50	46·30	3·51	8·0730
6016	7·49	S 1·54·17·99	4·50	+0·07	−0·17	6·46	N 2·17·27·14	13·00	44·96	3·34	3·2064
6074	7·49	S 0·29·33·48	5·00	+0·10	−0·25	6·46	N 3·42·12·38	13·24	45·61	3·63	5·8443
6115	7·49	S 0·40·52·71	5·24	+0·18	−0·45	6·45	N 3·30·53·57	13·50	45·83	3·78	6·9174
6145	7·49	S 1· 0·31·01	5·00	+0·10	−0·25	6·44	N 3·11·15·24	13·24	46·00	3·63	7·2600
6233	7·49	S 4·42·45·17	4·50	+0·15	−0·37	6·00	S 0·30·59·74	28·99	45·06	3·90	4·1340
6285	7·49	S 3·20·48·89	4·00	+0·10	−0·25	6·47	N 0·50·57·56	14·00	46·20	3·11	6·8420
6305	7·49	S 3·23·10·33	3·94	0·00	0·00	6·46	N 0·48·34·81	13·74	45·14	3·06	3·4884
6414	7·49	S 1·10·25·43	4·50	..	..	6·49	N 3· 1·20·10	12·34	45·53	3·30	5·0490
6489	7·49	S 0·21·26·25	5·24	−0·01	+0·02	6·44	N 3·50·19·29	12·74	45·58	3·71	5·7876
6525	7·49	N 0·52· 5·67	4·12	+0·10	+0·25	6·49	N 5· 3·51·13	12·74	45·21	3·11	3·7631
6639	7·49	S 0·18·20·02	5·00	+0·15	−0·37	6·49	N 3·53·25·19	13·50	44·84	2·87	2·9988
R.A.16ʰ·34ᵐ	7·49	S 0· 4·18·76	2·22	..	..	6·50	N 4· 7·28·29	10·23	45·05	1·82	1·9110
6753	7·49	S 1·31·49·84	3·73	+0·05	−0·12	6·49	N 2·39·55·13	12·50	44·85	2·87	2·4395
6877	7·49	S 2·44·50·65	5·00	0·00	0·00	6·49	N 1·26·55·00	12·50	45·65	3·57	5·8905
6948	7·49	S 0·44· 5·09	4·50	..	..	6·49	N 3·27·41·09	12·34	46·18	3·30	7·1940
7011	7·49	N 0·10· 2·72	4·50	..	..	6·50	N 4·21·47·80	11·76	45·08	3·25	3·5100
7026	7·49	N 0· 9·55·20	4·23	..	..	6·50	N 4·21·40·49	12·50	45·29	3·16	4·0764
7057	7·49	N 0· 6·41·47	4·23	..	..	6·50	N 4· 7· 6·78	12·34	44·94	2·96	2·9610
R.A.17ʰ·34ᵐ	7·49	S 0· 4·38·86	3·08	..	..	6·51	N 4· 7· 6·78	11·25	45·64	2·42	3·9688
R.A.17ʰ·37ᵐ	7·49	S 0·13·41·25	3·43	..	..	6·51	N 3·58· 4·65	11·76	45·90	2·66	5·0540
7207	7·49	S 4·36·35·62	4·23	0·00	0·00	6·49	S 0·24·49·81	12·50	45·81	3·16	5·7196
R.A.17ʰ·50ᵐ	7·49	N 0· 1·18·34	3·94	..	..	6·51	N 4·13· 4·78	11·79	46·44	2·95	7·1980
R.A.17ʰ·50ᵐ	7·49	S 0·36·26·96	4·23	0·00	0·00	6·51	N 3·35·18·32	12·50	45·28	3·16	4·0448
7386	7·49	S 3· 4·40·66	4·50	+0·10	−0·25	6·51	N 1· 7· 5·30	12·50	45·71	3·31	6·6601
R.A.18ʰ·19ᵐ	7·49	S 0· 4·54·40	4·23	..	..	6·51	N 4· 6·51·64	11·83	46·04	3·12	6·3648
R.A.18ʰ·21ᵐ	7·49	S 0·38·34·85	4·44	..	..	6·51	N 3·33·10·93	11·67	45·78	3·22	5·7316
7557	7·49	S 3·59·28·06	4·74	+0·10	−0·25	6·38	N 0·12·17·61	12·24	45·42	3·42	4·8564
7657	7·49	S 0·32·35·98	3·94	+0·05	+0·12	6·38	N 4·44·21·83	12·74	45·73	3·01	5·2073
R.A.19ʰ·5ᵐ	7·49	N 0·33·14·46	3·60	..	..	6·39	N 4·44·59·97	11·79	45·51	2·75	4·1525
7842	7·49	S 3·23·59·99	4·74	−0·04	+0·10	6·38	N 0·47·44·72	12·50	44·81	3·44	2·7864
7909	7·49	S 0·25·50·74	4·00	+0·05	−0·12	6·38	N 3·45·54·78	11·24	45·40	2·95	4·1300
7966	7·49	S 3·57·25·82	3·73	+0·05	−0·12	6·38	N 0·14·18·81	13·00	44·51	2·90	1·4790
7992	7·49	S 0·42·15·51	4·44	+0·18	−0·45	5·98	N 3·29·31·08	26·73	46·14	3·81	8·1534
									Sums .	190·50	287·7523

Mean Amplitude = 4° 11′ 45″·511.

Abstract of the Resulting Astronomical Amplitudes of the Sector Stations, and Reduction of the Amplitudes to the Theodolite Station Points.

ARC.	Astronomical Amplitudes of the Sector Station Points.	Reduction to the Theodolite Station Points.	Reference. Vol. 1.	Astronomical Amplitudes of the Theodolite Station Points.	No. of Stars observed.
	° ′ ″	″	page.	° ′ ″	
Royal Observatory to North End...........	N 4·11·45·511	....	...	N 4·11·45·511	57
„ „ Kamies-Sector Berg...	N 3·34·85·061	-0·917	572	N 3·34·84·144	63
„ „ Heerenlogement's Berg	N 1·57·57·907	-3·737	572	N 1·57·54·170	45
„ „ Zwart Kop..........	S 0·17·30·595	-1·680	573	S 0·17·28·915	68
„ „ Cape Point...........	S 0 25· 3·058	∴...	...	S 0·25· 3·058	39

Determination of the Amplitude of the Arc, Royal Observatory to Rogge Bay Guard House, Cape Town.

No. of Star in A.S.C.	No. of Star in B.A.C.	Annual Precession in N.P.D. for 1841·5.	CAPE TOWN.			ROYAL OBSERVATORY.		Amplitude uncorrected for Proper Motion.	Annual Proper Motion.	Correction for 6·5 years.	Amplitude	Weight.	Seconds of Amplitude minus 46', multiplied by Weight.
			Year of Observation.	Mean Z.D., reduced to 1845·0, by precession alone.	Weight.	Mean Z.D., 1845·0.	Weight.						
								0° 0'			0° 0'		
699	1802	- 2·276	1838·5	S 0·14·21·18	3·73	S 0·13·32·78	27·75	48·40	+0·025	+0·16	48·56*	3·29	8·4224
732	1878	- 1·279	,,	S 1·54·35·18	3·43	S 1·53·44·04	6·24	51·14	-0·42	-2·74	48·40*	2·21	5·3040
791	2051	+ 1·245	,,	N 3·55·19·75	2·55	N 3·56· 7·75	5·00	48·00	0·00	0·00	48·00*	1·69	3·3800
848	2246	3·820	,,	N 1·35·15·54	1·43	N 1·36· 4·02	5·24	48·48	..	..	48·48	1·12	2·7776
869	2293	4·546	,,	N 5· 9·20·33	4·28	N 5·10· 8·34	32·73	48·01	-0·02	-0·13	47·88*	3·78	7·1064
903	2414	6·161	,,	S 2·54· 5·29	3·50	S 2·53 16·85	5·00	48·44	+0·015	+0·10	48·54*	2·06	5·2324
915	2458	6·681	,,	N 4·54·57·97	3·50	N 4·55·45·38	5·00	47·41	-0·02	-0·13	47·28*	2·06	2·6368
957	2580	8·445	,,	S 3·40·27·54	2·73	S 3·39·38·92	5·00	48·62	..	..	48·62	1·77	4·6374
1015	2795	10·970	,,	S 2·15·40·82	0·67	S 2·14·50·51	5·00	50·31	..	..	50·31	0·59	2·6429
1061	2935	12·479	,,	S 0·50·25·14	2·92	S 0·49·36·53	5·00	48·61	..	..	48·61	1·84	4·8024
1070	2964	12·706	,,	N 1·17·23·75	0·67	N 1·18·12·79	5·00	49·04	..	..	49·04	0·59	1·7986
1115	3190	14·381	,,	N 4·11· 7·39	1·00	N 4·11·54·11	5·00	46·72	..	..	46·72	0·83	0·5976
1243	3578	18·175	,,	N 3·38·25·06	4·12	N 3·39·13·40	5·00	48·34	..	..	48·34	2·26	5·2684
1299	3755	19·113	,,	S 2·23· 3·65	4·24	S 2·22·16·09	5·00	47·56	..	..	47·56	2·29	3·5724
1356	3928	19·827	,,	N 2·55·13·82	5·74	N 2·56· 1·79	5·00	47·97	+0·06	+0·39	48·36*	2·67	6·3012
1378	4015	20·013	,,	N 0·52·29·28	5·65	N 0·53·18·08	5·00	48·80	..	..	48·80	2·65	7·4200
1433	4202	19·981	,,	S 4·15·40·01	4·95	S 4·14·51·64	5·00	48·37	..	..	48·37	2·49	5·9013
1527	4458	19·084	,,	S 1·58 18·07	4·44	S 1·57·29·71	13·24	48·36	+0·07	+0·46	48·82*	3·33	9·3906
1562	4579	18·298	,,	N 1·39·48·91	5·50	N 1·40·36·64	11·94	47·73	+0·22	+1·43	49·16	3·77	11·9132
1579	4623	18·077	,,	N 1·42·52·97	6·24	N 1·42·41·15	12·00	48·19	+0·02	+0·13	48·31*	4·11	9·4941
1604	4686	17·484	,,	S 1·40·56·13	6·24	S 1·40·11·22	23·50	44·91	+0·50	+3·25	48·16*	4·93	10·6488
1661	4852	15·698	,,	S 0·34·51·12	5·74	S 0·34· 3·69	14·74	47·43	+0·20	+1·30	48·73	4·13	11·2749
1774	5151	12·283	,,	N 4·99·27·48	5·50	N 4·40·15·67	15·68	48·19	+0·13	+0·84	49·03	4·07	12·3321
1797	5227	11·439	,,	N 0·46·16·94	5·24	N 0·47· 4·98	14·98	48·04	+0·05	+0·33	48·37	3·88	9·1956
1835	5331	10·315	,,	S 2·27·12·18	5·24	S 2·26·23·83	4·74	48·35	..	..	48·35	2·49	5·8515
1866	5435	9·298	,,	N 3·23·44·43	4·63	N 3·24·33·26	13·50	48·83	+0·05	+0·33	49·16	3·45	10·9020
1889	5508	8·394	,,	S 0·26·21·85	4·95	S 0·25·33·43	7·24	48·42	0·00	0·00	48·42	2·94	7·1148
1915	5632	6·868	,,	S 0· 5· 3·38	5·96	S 0· 4·16·49	25·49	46·84	+0·25	+1·62	48·46*	4·83	11·8818
1947	5755	5·662	,,	N 0· 1·20·76	4·44	N 0· 2· 9·29	14·74	48·53	0·00	0·00	48·53	3·41	8·6273
1969	5817	4·618	,,	N 1·26·22·63	5·14	N 1·27·10·74	13·46	48·11	+0·10	+0·65	48·76	3·72	10·2672
2007	5915	3·236	,,	S 3· 3·45·54	5·14	S 3· 2·57·36	24·24	48·16	-0·01	-0·07	48·09*	4·24	8·8616
2079	6115	+ 0·383	,,	N 3·30· 6·40	5·14	N 3·30·53·57	13·50	47·17	+0·18	+1·17	48·34*	3·72	8·7048
2101	6186	- 0·604	,,	S 2·52·47·91	5·14	S 2·52· 0·48	11·50	47·43	+0·14	+0·91	48·34*	3·55	8·3070
2110	6233	1·194	,,	S 0·37·47·71	5·14	S 0·30·59·74	28·99	47·99	+0·15	+0·97	48·94*	4·37	12·8478
2741	7992	-19·099	,,	N 3·28·43·77	1·71	N 3·29·31·08	26·73	47·31	+0·18	+1·17	48·48*	1·61	3·9928

Taking the mean of the whole, we have by 35 stars, the Amplitude .... = 0̊· 0· 48·475

Omitting the results uncorrected for proper motion, we obtain from 24 stars .... = 0· 0· 48·495

If we include those stars only whose proper motions have been determined by comparisons with
La Caille, and are distinguished by an asterisk in col. 12, the Amplitude is found by 16 stars = 0· 0· 48·336

The Zenith Distances observed in Cape Town are derived from the results given at pp. 106 and 107 of part II. The weight

assigned to each star = $\dfrac{EW}{E+W}$, E and W being the number of observations with the face of the Sector East or West.

The Zenith Distances observed at the Royal Observatory are abstracted from the general table of results, pp. 427—430.

With the amplitude last determined, we obtain the latitude of the Rogge Bay Guard House, and thence the latitude
of La Caille's Observatory, as follows:—

Latitude of the Royal Observatory .... 33·56· 3·20

Amplitude .... 0· 0·48·34

Latitude of the Guard House... 33·55·14·86

Reduction of the Guard House to La Caille's Observatory, see part II, page 111. 0·45

Latitude of La Caille's Observatory.. 33·55·15·31

The value adopted by La Caille in the reduction of his Observations (see Memoirs
Royal Ast. Society, vol. v., p. 105) is............................... 33 55·13·3

Difference.......... 2·01

Mean Right Ascensions and Mean North Polar Distances for 1845, January 0, of Stars observed with Bradley's Zenith Sector.

No. of Star in A.S.C.	No. of Star in B.A.C.	Star's Name	Mean R.A.	Annual Precession	Mean N.P.D.	Annual Precession	Proper Motion in N.P.D.
			h m s	s	° ′ ″	″	″
072	1739	ε Columbæ	5·25·42·77	+2·125	125·35·14·17	- 2·990	
-699	1802	α Columbæ...✓	5·34· 2·36	2·169	124· 9·35·98	2·267	+0·025
-732	1878	β Columbæ	5·45·29·90	2·107	125·49·47·24	1·268	-0·42
746	1922	γ Columbæ	5·52· 2·51	2·124	125·18·10·57	- 0·896	
767	1982	θ Columbæ	6· 2·12·78	2·054	127·14· 3·65	+ 0·194	
-791	2051	ζ Canis Majoris	6·14·21·89	2·300	119·59·55·45	1·256	0·00
810	2109	Canis Majoris	6·22·25·43	2·223	122·29·10·08	1·960	
848	2240	κ Canis Majoris	6·44· 3·15	2·240	122·19·59·18	3·832	
-869	2293	ε Canis Majoris	6·52·32·08	2·356	118·45·54·86	4·557	-0·02
-901	2414	π Argûs	7·11·40·07	2·118	126·49·20·05	6·171	+0·015
-915	2458	η Canis Majoris	7·17·57·87	2·372	119· 0·17·82	6·692	-0·02
	2528	Puppis	7·32·16·24	2·121	127·39·53·75	7·861	
	2575	Puppis	7·39· 3·05	2 137	127·34·19·59	8·402	
957	2580	c Puppis	7·39·43·96	2·137	127·35·42·12	8·455	
969	2635	b Puppis	7·47· 9·47	2·122	128·27·50·39	9·040	
977	2655	Puppis	7·51·29·42	2·390	119·55·17·16	9·377	
-990	2710	ζ Argûs	7·58· 8·19	2·110	129·34· 7·66	9·887	-0·01
1015	2795	q Puppis	8·12·45·02	2·252	126·10·53·71	10·979	
1061	2935	b Mali	8·34· 2·15	2·345	124·45·39·73	12·489	
1070	2964	a Mali	8·37·21·92	2·409	122·37·50·41	12·715	
1115	3130	e Mali	9· 3·22·38	2·539	119·44· 9·09	14·390	
1129	3163	l Velorum	9· 9·30·25	2·365	127·55·33·77	14·759	-0·16
		Antliæ	9·38·43·64	2·588	121·58·13·05	16·365	
	3403	Antliæ	9·49·24·16	2·648	120·21·28·72	16·888	
		Antliæ	10· 1·40·10	2·685	120·20·44·60	17·442	
1243	3578	α Antliæ	10·20· 3·77	2·741	120·16·49·80	18·180	
1251	3598	δ Antliæ	10·22·27·49	2·755	119·48·57·24	18·268	
1299	3755	Antliæ	10·49·30·25	2·774	126·18·19·29	19·115	
1356	3928	Hydræ	11·25·23·04	2·950	121· 0· 1·41	19·829	+0·06
1378	4015	Hydræ	11·45· 5·37	3·014	123· 2·45·12	20·014	
1433	4202	Centauri	12·20· 8·91	3·163	128·10·54·84	19·979	
-1527	4458	ι Centauri	13·11·54·13	3·369	125·53·32·91	19·078	+0·07
	4507	Centauri	13·22· 4·61	3·445	128·36·13·56	18·784	
1544	4517	Hydræ	13·23·55·55	3·333	118·45·57·63	18·727	+0·10
1553	4548	Hydræ	13·30· 0·33	3·352	118·46· 1·47	18·530	+0·15
1562	4579	i Centauri	13·36·53·72	3·417	122·15·26·56	18·291	+0·22
1579	4623	k Centauri	13·42·53·79	3·436	122·13·22·05	18·009	+0·02
-1604	4686	θ Centauri	13·57·34·85	3·541	125·36·14·42	17·474	+0·50
	4719	Hydræ	14· 6· 3·67	3·451	118·33·17·64	17·098	
	4745	Ψ Centauri	14·11· 9·32	3·620	127·10· 6·00	16·861	
1637	4784	52 Hydræ	14·19· 6·60	3·490	118·47·30·66	16·474	+0·13
		Centauri	14·24· 9·77	3·575	122·37·44·11	16·218	
1661	4852	Centauri	14·34·11·68	3·643	124·30· 6·89	15·686	+0 20
	4916	Centauri	14·46·14·92	3·651	123·13·19·03	15·007	0·00
		Lupi	14·53·31·13	3·646	122· 1·39·19	14·577	
		Lupi	14·57·42·76	3·664	122·18·21·50	14·323	
1731	5032	2 Lupi	15· 8·24·90	3·626	119·34·27·31	13·652	+0·06
1738	5054	φ' Lupi	15·11·59·18	3·785	125·41·37·19	13·421	
1774	5151	40 Libræ	15·29· 8·95	3·663	119·15·47·53	12·209	+0·13
		Lupi	15·34·24·59	3 721	121· 6· 8·55	11·901	
1797	5227	χ Lupi	15·41· 7·42	3·788	123· 8·58·22	11·424	+0·05
1816	5272	ρ Scorpii	15·47·19·58	3 685	118·45·22·65	10·973	+0·06
1821	5292	η Lupi	15·49·51·95	3·950	127·56·50·65	10·786	
1835	5331	θ Lupi	15·56·25·75	3 916	126·22·27·03	10·298	
		Lupi	15·57· 5·✓6	3·917	126·19·43·41	10·248	
1848	5374	Scorpii	16· 1·24·94	3·715	119· 0· 6·41	9·921	+0·18
1866	5435	Scorpii	16· 9·45·11	3·770	120·31·29·94	9·280	+0·05
		Scorpii	16·13·58·87	3·843	122·49·50·16	8·951	
1889	5508	Scorpii	16·21·15·88	+3·901	124·21·36·63	+ 8·376	0·00

Mean Right Ascensions and Mean North Polar Distances for 1845, January 0, of Stars observed with Bradley's Zenith Sector—continued.

No. of Star in A.S.C.	No. of Star in B.A.C.	Star's Name.	Mean R.A.	Annual Precession.	Mean N.P.D.	Annual Precession.	Proper Motion in N.P.D.
			h m s	s	° ′ ″	″	″
	5538	Scorpii	16·26·11·12	+3·927	124·55·46·54	7·983	
	5588	Scorpii	16·33·41·29	3·842	121·48·18·89	7·376	
1915	5632	ε Scorpii	16·40· 7·94	3·918	124· 0·19·69	6·849	+0.25
1947	5735	Scorpii	16·54·37·99	3·933	123·53·53·91	5·643	0·00
1969	5817	Scorpii	17· 6·58·91	3·899	122·28·52·46	4·598	+0·10
1994	5881	d Ophiuchi	17·17·27·74	3·821	119·43·13·46	3·701	+0·22
2007	5915	λ Scorpii	17·23· 5·28	4·065	126·59· 0·58	3·216	-0·01
2024	5960	Scorpii	17·29·55·35	3·902	122· 6·25·23	3·624	
	5964	Scorpii	17·30·52·63	3·903	122· 7·26·38	2·543	
	5970	κ Scorpii	17·31·46·05	4·143	128·56·32·47	2·464	-0·05
2042	6016	Sagittarii	17·39· 6·60	3·891	121·38·36·06	1·826	+0·07
2052	6074	Sagittarii	17·49· 8·16	3·849	120·13·50·82	0·950	+0·10
2079	6115	γ² Sagittarii	17·55·51·10	3·856	120·25· 9·63	+0·363	+0·18
2088	6145	Sagittarii	18· 0· 6·17	3·866	120·44·47·96	-0·009	+0·10
2101	6186	η Sagittarii	18· 7· 8·17	4·070	126·48· 3·68	0·625	+0·14
-2110	6233	ε Sagittarii	18·13·53·00	3·966	124·27· 2·94	1·214	+0·15
	6275	Sagittarii	18·19·50·85	3·940	123· 8·28·94	1·735	+0·06
2126	6285	Sagittarii	18·20·54·68	3·938	123· 5· 5·64	1·828	+0·10
2135	6305	Sagittarii	18·23·47·55	3·938	123· 7·28·39	2·078	0·00
	6414	Sagittarii	18·42·44·47	3·857	120·54·43·10	3·719	
2196	6489	ζ Sagittarii	18·52·44·73	3·825	120· 5·43·91	4·576	-0·01
2212	6525	Sagittarii	18·57·45·08	3·784	118·52·12·07	5·001	+0·10
2261	6639	Sagittarii	19·17· 8·34	3·800	120· 2·38·01	6·624	+0·15
		Sagittarii	19·21·20·56	3·788	119·48·36·91	6·970	
2312	6753	Sagittarii	19·35·34·77	3·813	121·16· 8·07	8·124	+0·05
2355	6877	Sagittarii	19·54·29·21	3·818	122·29· 8·20	8·608	0·00
	6948	Sagittarii	20· 6·12·23	3·741	120·28·22·11	10·495	
	7011	Capricorni	20·15·10·79	3·701	119·34·15·40	11·156	
	7026	Capricorni	20·17· 1·57	3·697	119·34·22·71	11·290	
	7057	Capricorni	20·21·26·57	3·691	119·37·36·79	11·607	
		Capricorni	20·24·18·98	3·689	119·48·56·42	11·812	
		Capricorni	20·33·49·19	3·674	119·57·58·55	12·473	
2454	7207	α Microscopii	20·40·16·31	3·770	124·20·53·01	12·911	0·00
		Microscopii	20·53·36·80	3·624	119·42·58·42	13·782	
		Piscis Australis	21· 0·46·73	3·621	120·20·44·88	14·231	0·00
2518	7386	4 Piscis Australis	21· 8·31·46	3·657	122·48·57·90	14·700	+0·10
		Piscis Australis	21·12·36·19	3·581	119·49·11·56	14·940	
		Piscis Australis	21·25·43·69	3·559	120·22·52·27	15·682	
2577	7557	ι Piscis Australis	21·35·41·99	3·596	123·43·45·59	16·211	+0·10
-2598	7613	γ Gruis	21·44·31·52	3·655	128· 5·25·09	16·654	+0·04
2608	7657	η Piscis Australis	21·51·55·13	3·467	119·11·41·37	17·005	+0·05
		Piscis Australis	21·55·46·12	3·456	119·11· 3·23	17·182	
2689	7842	β Piscis Australis	22·22·40·86	3·430	123· 8·18·48	18·276	-0·04
	7909	19 Piscis Australis	22·33·44·08	3·356	120·10· 8·42	18·653	+0·05
2728	7966	γ Piscis Australis	22·43·53·61	3·361	123·41·44·39	18·961	+0·05
-2741	7999	Fomalhaut	22 49· 4·22	+3·310	120·26·32·12	-19·104	+0·18

The North Polar Distances are deduced from the Zenith Distances observed with the Sector, and given in the general table at pp. 427—430.

VOL. II.

ERRATA ET ADDENDA.

While the observations at the several Sector Stations were in progress, all observed stars not found in the Royal Astronomical Society's Catalogue were termed "anonymous," or abbreviated "anon." Of these the following were found afterwards in the British Association Catalogue, Nos. 4719, 4745, 4916, 5538, 5588, 5964, 6275, 6414, 6948, 7011, 7026, 7057, 7909, 7966, which numbers were substituted when calculating the Mean Zenith Distances.

The "field-book" journal of the sector observations pages 1—219, was printed before the calculation of the Mean Zenith Distances. By the latter operation the following errors in recording, and of the press, were discovered.

PAGE		FOR	READ
2	May 15, No. 4784	Chronr. 14·18·53·5	14·19·3·5
13	May 30, No. 5272	Chron. 15·47·53·5	15·47·53·5
14	May 31, No. 5681	Chron. 17·18·42·0	17·18·4·4
42	Dec. 16, No. 2293	Chron. 6· 6·55·0	6·54·55·0
43	Jan. 4, No. 2293	Chron. 6· 5·58·5	6·55·58·5
43	Jan. 9, No. 7992	S. 3·30	N. 3·30
46	Feb. 12, No. 4548	rev. 11·17·75	10·17·75
"	" "	rev. + 1·11·37	+0·11·37
49	Feb. 16, No. 4686	Chronr. 13·53·20·5	13·58·20·5
50	Feb. 17, No. 4686	S. 1°·41′	S. 1°·40′.
51	Apr. 8, No. 3632	3632	5632
57	Apr. 21, No. 5735	Baz. 32·317	30·317
58	Apr. 22, No. 5915	N. 3°·5′	S. 3°·5′.
80	May 27, No. 5331	Chron. 15·55·8·3	15·56·8·3
84	June 1, anon	N. 1°·40′...	N. 1·35
"	" "	rev. — 4·22·6	+4·22·6
96	July 25, No. 6948	N. 3·45 — 0·16·5	N. 3·45+0·16·5
99	July 30, top	Continued	Omit
103	Aug. 7, No. 4548	No. 4548...	4458
126	Nov. 21, No. 2575	rev. 3·29·75	3·19·75
134	Dec. 9, No. 4458	Chron. 13·14·15·2	13·13·15·2
155	March 18, No. 1802	rev. 9·12·9	10·12·9
"	" "	rev. 9·12·95	10·12·95
"	" "	— 0·33·3...	— 1·33·3
166	June 18, No. 6016	— 1·6·33	— 1·6·35
179	July 2, anon	rev. + 1·21·1	— 1·21·1
"	" anon	rev. + 1·21·72	— 1·21·72
185	July 10, No. 6016	N. 1·55	S. 1·55
192	June 17, No. 5735	Chron. 16·54·7·0	16·54·54·7
228	Jan. 14, "Value employed in reducing the &c."	rev. 8·31·5705	8·31·6386
317	No. 4579	App. Z.D. 1·58·21·19	1·57·57·38
		Mean Z.D. 1·57·37·33	1·58·21·19
341	No. 2651	Mean Z.D. 4·2·12·43	4·21·12·43
404	No. 5970	Collim. 0·0·2·57...	0·0·2·54
	The corrections for precession ab^n. &c., have been computed for 5964 instead of 4970.	Z.D. 5·0·38·65	5·0·36·60 The numbers given in the column "read," are correct.
412	Anon A.R. 20·53	18°35	18°55
	Aug. 25	50·87	50·67
	Face West	Z.D. 4·13·50·40	4·13·50·38
		Col. 00·4·14	0·0·4·13
415	No. 7966. Resulting Z.D. North	3·15·15·76	0·15·15·76
	No. 3928 has been printed No. 3926 in the unreduced observations made at Cape Point and		the Royal Observatory Stations.